TWELFTH EDITION

Sociology

A Down-to-Earth Approach

James M. Henslin
Southern Illinois University, Edwardsville

PEARSON

Boston Columbus Indianapolis New York San Francisco Upper Saddle River
Amsterdam Cape Town Dubai London Madrid Milan Munich Paris Montréal Toronto
Delhi Mexico City São Paulo Sydney Hong Kong Seoul Singapore Taipei Tokyo

To my fellow sociologists,

who do such creative research on social life and who communicate the sociological imagination to generations of students. With my sincere admiration and appreciation,

Jim Henslin

Editor in Chief: Dickson Musslewhite
Publisher: Charlyce Jones Owen
Editorial Assistant: Maureen Diana
Director of Marketing: Brandy Dawson
Senior Marketing Manager: Maureen Prado Roberts
Development Editor: Dusty Friedman
Program Manager: LeeAnn Doherty
Project Manager: Marianne Peters-Riordan
Manufacturing Buyer: Diane Peirano
Creative Director: Blair Brown
Art Director: Kathryn Foot
Cover Illustration: Kenneth Batelman
Digital Media Director: Brian Hyland
Digital Media Editor: Alison Lorber
Media Project Manager: Nikhil Bramahavar
Full-Service Project Management: Lindsay Bethoney
Composition: PreMediaGlobal USA, Inc.
Printer/Binder: R.R.Donnelley & Sons
Cover Printer: Lehigh-Phoenix Color
Text Font: 10/12 Galliard Std-Roman

Credits and acknowledgments borrowed from other sources and reproduced, with permission, in this textbook appear on the appropriate page within text [or on page CR-1].

Library of Congress Control Number: 2013948984

10 9 8 7 6 5 4 3

Student Version:
ISBN 10: 0-205-99164-5
ISBN 13: 978-0-205-99164-8

Books A La Carte
ISBN 10: 0-205-99189-0
ISBN 13: 978-0-205-99189-1

PEARSON

Brief Contents

Contents

Chapter 3 Socialization 61

Chapter 4 Social Structure and Social Interaction 93

THROUGH THE AUTHOR'S LENS

Vienna: Social Structure and Social Interaction in a Vibrant City

One of the most difficult sociological concepts to grasp is *social structure*. The concreteness of the photos helps capture this concept, changing it from abstract to part of everyday life. Students have no problem understanding *social interaction*, of course, and in this photo essay they can see how social structure provides the contours for social interaction. (pages 106–107)

THROUGH THE AUTHOR'S LENS

When a Tornado Strikes: Social Organization Following a Natural Disaster

As I was watching television on March 20, 2003, I heard a report that a tornado had hit Camilla, Georgia. "Like a big lawn mower," the report said, it had cut a path of destruction through this little town. In its fury, the tornado had left behind six dead and about 200 injured. (pages 119–120)

Chapter 5 How Sociologists Do Research 124

Part II Social Groups and Social Control

Chapter 6 Societies to Social Networks 144

Chapter 7 Bureaucracy and Formal Organizations 170

Chapter 8 Deviance and Social Control 193

Part III Social Inequality

Chapter 9 Global Stratification 225

THROUGH THE AUTHOR'S LENS

The Dump People: Working and Living and Playing in the City Dump of Phnom Penh, Cambodia

I went to Phnom Penh, the capital of Cambodia, to inspect orphanages, to see how well the children were being cared for. While there, I was told about people who live in the city dump. *Live there?* I could hardly believe my ears. I knew that people made their living by picking scraps from the city dump, but I didn't know they actually lived among the garbage. This I had to see for myself. (pages 248–249)

Chapter 10 Social Class in the United States 256

Chapter 11 Sex and Gender 287

THROUGH THE AUTHOR'S LENS

Work and Gender: Women at Work in India

Traveling through India was both a pleasure and an eye-opening experience. The country is incredibly diverse, the people friendly, and the land culturally rich. For this photo essay, wherever I went—whether city, village, or countryside—I took photos of women at work. (pages 298–299)

Chapter 13 The Elderly 358

Part IV Social Institutions

Chapter 14 The Economy 387

THROUGH THE AUTHOR'S LENS

Small Town USA
Stuggling to Survive

All across the nation, small towns are struggling to survive. Parents and town officials are concerned because so few young adults remain in their home town. There is little to keep them there, and when they graduate from high school, most move to the city. With young people leaving and old ones dying, the small towns are shriveling. I took most of these photos in the South. (pages 404–405)

Chapter 15 Politics 420

Chapter 16 Marriage and Family 450

Chapter 17 Education 486

Chapter 18 Religion 512

THROUGH THE AUTHOR'S LENS

Holy Week in Spain

Taking these photos of Holy Week being observed in Spain—in Malaga, a capital city, and Almuñecar, a small town in Granada—was both enjoyable and a challenge. The rituals here, like those of religious groups everywhere, are designed to evoke memories, create awe, inspire reverence, and stimulate social solidarity. (pages 522–523)

Chapter 19 Medicine and Health 545

Part V Social Change

Chapter 20 Population and Urbanization 578

THROUGH THE AUTHOR'S LENS

A Walk Through El Tiro in Medellin, Colombia

One of the most significant changes in our time is the global rush of poor, rural people to the cities of the Least Industrialized Nations. Some of these settlements are dangerous. I was fortunate to be escorted by an insider through this section of Medellin, Colombia. (pages 596–597)

Chapter 21 Collective Behavior and Social Movements 613

Chapter 22 Social Change and the Environment 638

Special Features

Down-to-Earth Sociology

Cultural Diversity in the United States

Cultural Diversity around the World

Mass Media in Social Life

THINKING CRITICALLY

Sociology and the New Technology

Guide to Social Maps

To the Student ... from the Author

WELCOME TO SOCIOLOGY! I've loved sociology since I was in my teens, and I hope you enjoy it, too. Sociology is fascinating because it is about human behavior, and many of us find that it holds the key to understanding social life.

If you like to watch people and try to figure out why they do what they do, you will like sociology. Sociology pries open the doors of society so you can see what goes on behind them. *Sociology: A Down-to-Earth Approach* stresses how profoundly our society and the groups to which we belong influence us. Social class, for example, sets us on a particular path in life. For some, the path leads to more education, more interesting jobs, higher income, and better health, but for others, it leads to dropping out of school, dead-end jobs, poverty, and even a higher risk of illness and disease. These paths are so significant that they affect our chances of making it to our first birthday, as well as of getting in trouble with the police. They even influence our satisfaction in marriage, the number of children we will have—and whether or not we will read this book in the first place.

When I took my first course in sociology, I was "hooked." Seeing how marvelously my life had been affected by these larger social influences opened my eyes to a new world, one that has been fascinating to explore. I hope that you will have this experience, too.

From how people become homeless to how they become presidents, from why people commit suicide to why women are discriminated against in every society around the world—all are part of sociology. This breadth, in fact, is what makes sociology so intriguing. We can place the sociological lens on broad features of society, such as social class, gender, and race–ethnicity, and then immediately turn our focus on the smaller, more intimate level. If we look at two people interacting—whether quarreling or kissing—we see how these broad features of society are playing out in their lives.

We aren't born with instincts. Nor do we come into this world with preconceived notions of what life should be like. At birth, we have no concepts of race–ethnicity, gender, age, or social class. We have no idea, for example, that people "ought" to act in certain ways because they are male or female. Yet we all learn such things as we grow up in our society. Uncovering the "hows" and the "whys" of this process is also part of what makes sociology so fascinating.

One of sociology's many pleasures is that as we study life in groups (which can be taken as a definition of sociology), whether those groups are in some far-off part of the world or in some nearby corner of our own society, we gain new insights into who we are and how we got that way. As we see how *their* customs affect *them*, the effects of our own society on us become more visible.

This book, then, can be part of an intellectual adventure: It can lead you to a new way of looking at your social world—and in the process, help you to better understand both society and yourself.

I wish you the very best in college—and in your career afterward. It is my sincere desire that *Sociology: A Down-to-Earth Approach* will contribute to that success.

James M. Henslin
Department of Sociology
Southern Illinois University, Edwardsville

P.S. I enjoy communicating with students, so feel free to comment on your experiences with this text. You can write me at henslin@aol.com

To the Instructor … from the Author

REMEMBER WHEN YOU FIRST GOT "HOOKED" on sociology, how the windows of perception opened as you began to see life-in-society through the sociological perspective? For most of us, this was an eye-opening experience. This text is designed to open those windows onto social life, so students can see clearly the vital effects of group membership on their lives. Although few students will get into what Peter Berger calls "the passion of sociology," we at least can provide them the opportunity.

To study sociology is to embark on a fascinating process of discovery. We can compare sociology to a huge jigsaw puzzle. Only gradually do we see how the pieces fit together. As we begin to see the interconnections, our perspective changes as we shift our eyes from the many small, disjointed pieces to the whole that is being formed. Of all the endeavors we could have entered, we chose sociology because of the ways in which it joins the "pieces" of society together and the challenges it poses to "ordinary" thinking. It is our privilege to share with students this process of awareness and discovery called the sociological perspective.

As instructors of sociology, we have set ambitious goals for ourselves: to teach both social structure and social interaction and to introduce students to the sociological literature—both the classic theorists and contemporary research. As we accomplish this, we would also like to enliven the classroom, encourage critical thinking, and stimulate our students' sociological imagination. Although formidable, these goals *are* attainable. This book is designed to help you reach them. Based on many years of frontline (classroom) experience, its subtitle, *A Down-to-Earth Approach*, was not proposed lightly. My goal is to share the fascination of sociology with students and in doing so to make your teaching more rewarding.

Over the years, I have found the introductory course especially enjoyable. It is singularly satisfying to see students' faces light up as they begin to see how separate pieces of their world fit together. It is a pleasure to watch them gain insight into how their social experiences give shape to even their innermost desires. This is precisely what this text is designed to do: to stimulate your students' sociological imagination so they can better perceive how the "pieces" of society fit together—and what this means for their own lives.

Filled with examples from around the world as well as from our own society, this text helps to make today's multicultural, global society come alive for students. From learning how the international elite carve up global markets to studying the intimacy of friendship and marriage, students can see how sociology is the key to explaining contemporary life—and their own place in it.

In short, this text is designed to make your teaching easier. There simply is no justification for students to have to wade through cumbersome approaches to sociology. I am firmly convinced that the introduction to sociology should be enjoyable and that the introductory textbook can be an essential tool in sharing the discovery of sociology with students.

The Organization of This Text

The text is laid out in five parts. Part I focuses on the sociological perspective, which is introduced in the first chapter. We then look at how culture influences us (Chapter 2), examine socialization (Chapter 3), and compare macrosociology and microsociology (Chapter 4). After this, we look at how sociologists do research (Chapter 5). Placing research methods in the fifth chapter does not follow the usual sequence, but doing so allows students to first become immersed in the captivating findings of sociology—then, after their interest is awakened, they learn how sociologists gather their data. Students respond very well to this approach, but if you prefer the more traditional order, simply teach this chapter as the second chapter. No content will be affected.

Part II, which focuses on groups and social control, adds to the students' understanding of how far-reaching society's influence is—how group membership penetrates even our thinking, attitudes, and orientations to life. We first examine the different types of groups that have such profound influences on us and then look at the fascinating area of group dynamics (Chapter 6). We then examine the impact of bureaucracy and formal organizations (Chapter 7). After this, we focus on how groups "keep us in line" and sanction those who violate their norms (Chapter 8).

In Part III, we turn our focus on social inequality, examining how it pervades society and how it has an impact on our own lives. Because social stratification is so significant, I have written two chapters on this topic. The first (Chapter 9), with its global focus, presents an overview of the principles of stratification. The second (Chapter 10), with its emphasis on social class, focuses on stratification in the United States. After establishing this broader context of social stratification, we examine gender, the most global of the inequalities (Chapter 11). Then we focus on inequalities of race–ethnicity (Chapter 12) and those of age (Chapter 13).

Part IV helps students become more aware of how social institutions encompass their lives. We first look at the economy, the social institution that has become dominant in U.S. society (Chapter 14) and then at politics, our second overarching social institution (Chapter 15). We then place the focus on marriage and family (Chapter 16) and education (Chapter 17). After this, we look at the significance of religion (Chapter 18) and, finally, that of medicine (Chapter 19). One of the emphases in this part of the book is how our social institutions are changing and how their changes, in turn, have an impact on our own lives.

With its focus on broad social change, Part V provides an appropriate conclusion for the book. Here we examine why our world is changing so rapidly, as well as catch a glimpse of what is yet to come. We first analyze trends in population and urbanization, those sweeping forces that affect our lives so significantly but that ordinarily remain below our level of awareness (Chapter 20). Our focus on collective behavior and social movements (Chapter 21) and social change and the environment (Chapter 22) takes us to the "cutting edge" of the vital changes that engulf us all.

Themes and Features

Six central themes run throughout this text: down-to-earth sociology, globalization, cultural diversity, critical thinking, the new technology, and the influence of the mass media on our lives. For each of these themes, except globalization, which is incorporated throughout the text, I have written a series of boxes. These boxed features are one of my favorite components of the book. They are especially useful for introducing the controversial topics that make sociology such a lively activity.

Let's look at these six themes.

Down-to-Earth Sociology

As many years of teaching have shown me, textbooks are all too often written to appeal to the adopters of texts rather than to the students who will learn from them. In writing this book, my central concern has been to present sociology in a way that not only facilitates understanding but also shares its excitement. During the course of writing other texts, I often have been told that my explanations and writing style are "down-to-earth," or accessible and inviting to students—so much so that I chose this phrase as the book's subtitle. The term is also featured in my introductory reader, *Down-to-Earth Sociology: Introductory Readings*, now in its 15th edition (New York: Free Press, 2014).

This first theme is highlighted by a series of boxed features that explore sociological processes that underlie everyday life. The topics that we review in these **Down-to-Earth Sociology** boxes are highly diverse. Here are some of them.

- the experiences of W. E. B. Du Bois in studying U.S. race relations (Chapter 1)
- what applied sociologists do (Chapter 1)
- how gossip and ridicule enforce adolescent norms (Chapter 3)
- how football can help us understand social structure (Chapter 4)
- beauty and success (Chapter 4)
- fraudulent social research (Chapter 5)
- the McDonaldization of society (Chapter 7)
- serial killers (Chapter 8)
- the lifestyles of the super-rich (Chapter 10)
- the American dream and actual social mobility (Chapter 10)
- how to get a higher salary by applying sociology (Chapter 11)
- living in the dorm: contact theory (Chapter 12)
- sex in nursing homes (Chapter 13)
- women navigating male-dominated corporations (Chapter 14)
- the life of child soldiers (Chapter 15)
- the health benefits of marriage (Chapter 16)
- home schooling (Chapter 17)
- terrorism in the name of God (Chapter 18)
- the international black market in human body parts (Chapter 19)
- biofoods (Chapter 20)
- mass hysteria (Chapter 21)

This first theme is actually a hallmark of the text, as my goal is to make sociology "down to earth." To help students grasp the fascination of sociology, I continuously stress sociology's relevance to their lives. To reinforce this theme, I avoid unnecessary jargon and use concise explanations and clear and simple (but not reductive) language. I also use student-relevant examples to illustrate key concepts, and I base several of the chapters' opening vignettes on my own experiences in exploring social life. That this goal of sharing sociology's fascination is being reached is evident from the many comments I receive from instructors and students alike that the text helps make sociology "come alive."

Globalization

In the second theme, globalization, we explore the impact of global issues on our lives and on the lives of people around the world. All of us are feeling the effects of an increasingly powerful and encompassing global economy, one that intertwines the fates of nations. The globalization of capitalism influences the kinds of skills and knowledge we need and the types of work available to us—and whether work is available at all. Globalization also underlies the costs of the goods and services we consume and whether our country is at war or peace—or in some uncharted middle ground between the two, some sort of perpetual war against unseen, sinister, and ever-threatening enemies lurking throughout the world. In addition to the strong emphasis on global issues that runs throughout this text, I have written a separate chapter on global stratification (Chapter 9). I also feature global issues in the chapters on social institutions and the final chapters on social change: population, urbanization, social movements, and the environment.

In addition to this global focus that runs throughout the text, the next theme, cultural diversity, also has a strong global emphasis.

Cultural Diversity around the World and in the United States

The third theme, cultural diversity, has two primary emphases. The first is cultural diversity around the world. Gaining an understanding of how social life is "done" in other parts of the world often challenges our taken-for-granted assumptions about social life. At times, when we learn about other cultures, we gain an appreciation for the life of other peoples; at other times, we may be shocked or even disgusted at some aspect of another group's way of life (such as female circumcision) and come away with a renewed appreciation of our own customs.

To highlight this first subtheme, I have written a series of boxes called **Cultural Diversity around the World**. Among the topics with this subtheme are

- food customs that shock people from different cultures (Chapter 2)
- dancing with the dead (Chapter 2)
- where virgins become men (Chapter 3)
- human sexuality in Mexico and Kenya (Chapter 8)
- how blaming the rape victim protects India's caste system (Chapter 9)
- female circumcision (Chapter 11)
- the life of child workers (Chapter 14)
- China's new capitalism (Chapter 14)
- the globalization of capitalism (Chapter 14)
- love and arranged marriage in India (Chapter 16)
- female infanticide in China and India (Chapter 20)
- the destruction of the rain forests and indigenous peoples of Brazil (Chapter 22)

In the second subtheme, **Cultural Diversity in the United States**, we examine groups that make up the fascinating array of people who form the U.S. population. The boxes I have written with this subtheme review such topics as

- the controversy over the use of Spanish or English (Chapter 2)
- the terms that people choose to refer to their own race–ethnicity (Chapter 2)
- how the Amish resist social change (Chapter 4)
- how our social networks produce social inequality (Chapter 6)
- the upward social mobility of African Americans (Chapter 10)
- our shifting racial–ethnic mix (Chapter 12)
- the author's travels with a Mexican who transports undocumented workers to the U.S. border (Chapter 12)
- Pentecostalism among Latino immigrants (Chapter 18)
- human heads, animal sacrifices, and religious freedom (Chapter 18)

Seeing that there are so many ways of "doing" social life can remove some of our cultural smugness, making us more aware of how arbitrary our own customs are—and how our taken-for-granted ways of thinking are rooted in culture. The stimulating contexts of these contrasts can help students develop their sociological imagination. They encourage students to see connections among key sociological concepts such as culture, socialization, norms, race–ethnicity, gender, and social class. As your students' sociological imagination grows, they can attain a new perspective on their experiences in their own corners of life—and a better understanding of the social structure of U.S. society.

Critical Thinking

In our fourth theme, critical thinking, we focus on controversial social issues, inviting students to examine various sides of those issues. In these sections, titled **Thinking Critically**, I present objective, fair portrayals of positions and do not take a side—although occasionally I do play the "devil's advocate" in the questions that close each of the topics. Like the boxed features, these sections can enliven your classroom with a vibrant exchange of ideas. Among the social issues addressed are

- whether we are prisoners of our genes (Chapter 2)
- whether rapists are sick (Chapter 5)
- our tendency to conform to evil authority, as uncovered by the Milgram experiments (Chapter 6)
- how labeling keeps some people down and helps others move up (Chapter 8)
- how vigilantes fill in when the state breaks down (Chapter 8)
- the three-strikes-and-you're-out laws (Chapter 8)
- bounties paid to kill homeless children in Brazil (Chapter 9)
- the welfare debate (Chapter 10)
- emerging masculinities and femininities (Chapter 11)
- whether it is desirable to live as long as Methuselah (Chapter 13)
- targeted killings (Chapter 15)
- distance learning (Chapter 17)
- medically assisted suicide (Chapter 19)
- abortion as a social movement (Chapter 21)
- cyberwar and cyber defense (Chapter 22)

These *Thinking Critically* sections are based on controversial social issues that either affect the student's own life or focus on topics that have intrinsic interest for students. Because of their controversial nature, these sections stimulate both critical thinking and lively class discussions. These sections also provide provocative topics for in-class debates and small discussion groups, effective ways to enliven a class and present sociological ideas. In the Instructor's Manual, I describe the nuts and bolts of using small groups in the classroom, a highly effective way of engaging students in sociological topics.

Sociology and the New Technology

The fifth theme, sociology and the new technology, explores an aspect of social life that has come to be central in our lives. We welcome these new technological tools, since they help us to be more efficient at performing our daily tasks, from making a living to communicating with others—whether those people are nearby or on the other side of the globe. The significance of our new technology, however, extends far beyond the tools and the ease and efficiency they bring to our lives. The new technology is better envisioned as a social revolution that will leave few aspects of our lives untouched. Its effects are so profound that it even changes the ways we view life.

This theme is introduced in Chapter 2, where technology is defined and presented as a major aspect of culture. The impact of technology is then discussed throughout the text. Examples include how technology is related to cultural change (Chapter 2), the control of workers (Chapter 7), the maintenance of global stratification (Chapter 9), social class (Chapter 10), and social inequality in early human history (Chapter 14). We also look at the impact of technology on dating (Chapter 16), family life (Chapter 16), education (Chapter 17), religion (Chapter 18), medicine (Chapter 19), and war (Chapter 22). The final chapter (Chapter 22), "Social Change and the Environment," concludes the book with a focus on the effects of technology.

To highlight this theme, I have written a series of boxes called **Sociology and the New Technology.** In these boxes, we explore how technology affects our lives as it changes society. We examine how technology

- blurs the distinction between reality and fantasy (Chapter 6)
- might make social networking the dominant form of social organization (Chapter 7)
- is used to avoid work ("cyberloafing") (Chapter 7)
- is being used to organize family life (Chapter 16)
- is changing the way people find mates (Chapter 16)
- is leading to designer babies (Chapter 16)
- leads to the dilemma of how to ration medical care (Chapter 19)
- has created controversy about rationing medical care (Chapter 19)
- is changing how war is waged (Chapter 22)

The Mass Media and Social Life

In the sixth theme, we stress how the mass media affect our behavior and permeate our thinking. We consider how the media penetrate our consciousness to such an extent that they even influence how we perceive our own bodies. As your students consider this theme, they may begin to grasp how the mass media shape their attitudes. If so, they will come to view the mass media in a different light, which should further stimulate their sociological imagination.

To make this theme more prominent for students, I have written a series of boxed features called **Mass Media in Social Life**. Among these are

- the presentation of gender in computer games (Chapter 3)
- the worship of thinness—and how this affects our body images (Chapter 4)
- the slowly changing status of women in Iran (Chapter 11)
- the propaganda and profits of war (Chapter 15)
- God on the Net (Chapter 18)

What's New in This Edition?

Because sociology is about social life and we live in a changing global society, an introductory sociology text must reflect the national and global changes that engulf us, as well as represent the new sociological research. I have written fifteen new boxes for this edition of *Sociology: A Down-to-Earth Approach*. This edition also has hundreds of new references and more than 300 new instructional photos. I have either selected or taken each of the photos, which are tied directly into the content of the text. I have designed it so that the photos and their captions are part of the students' learning experience.

I won't bother listing the numerous changes that run throughout the text. Instead, on the two pages that follow this note (xxxii–xxxiii), I have listed just the topics, boxed features, and tables and figures that are new in this edition. This gives you the best idea of how extensively this edition is revised.

Visual Presentations of Sociology

Showing Changes over Time

In presenting social data, many of the figures and tables show how data change over time. This feature allows students to see trends in social life and to make predictions on how these trends might continue—and even affect their own lives. Examples include

- Figure 1.6 *U.S. Marriage, U.S. Divorce* (Chapter 1);
- Figure 3.2 *Transitional Adulthood: A New Stage in Life* (Chapter 3);
- Figure 8.2 *How Much Is Enough? The Explosion in the Number of Prisoners* (Chapter 8);
- Figure 10.3 *The More Things Change, the More They Stay the Same: Dividing the Nation's Income* (Chapter 10);
- Figure 16.2 *In Two-Paycheck Marriages, How Do Husbands and Wives Divide Their Responsibilities?* (Chapter 16);
- Figure 16.5 *The Number of Children Americans Think Are Ideal* (Chapter 16);
- Figure 16.9 *The Decline of Two-Parent Families* (Chapter 16);
- Figure 16.13 *Cohabitation in the United States* (Chapter 16);
- Figure 17.1 *Educational Achievement in the United States* (Chapter 17); and
- Figure 20.10 *How the World Is Urbanizing* (Chapter 20).

Through the Author's Lens Using this format, students are able to look over my shoulder as I experience other cultures or explore aspects of this one. These eight photo essays should expand your students' sociological imagination and open their minds to other ways of doing social life, as well as stimulate thought-provoking class discussion.

Vienna: Social Structure and Social Interaction in a Vibrant City appears in Chapter 4. The photos I took in this city illustrate how social structure surrounds us, setting the scene for our interactions, limiting and directing them.

When a Tornado Strikes: Social Organization Following a Natural Disaster When a tornado hit a small town just hours from where I lived, I photographed the aftermath of the disaster. The police let me in to view the neighborhood where the tornado had struck, destroying homes and killing several people. I was impressed by how quickly people were putting their lives back together, the topic of this photo essay (Chapter 4).

Community in the City, in Chapter 6, is also from Vienna. This sequence of four photos focuses on strangers who are helping a man who has just fallen. This event casts doubt on the results of Darley and Latane's laboratory experiments. This short sequence was serendipitous in my research. One of my favorite photos is the last in the series, which portrays the cop coming toward me to question why I was taking photos of the accident. It fits the sequence perfectly.

The Dump People of Phnom Penh, Cambodia Among the culture shocks I experienced in Cambodia was not to discover that people scavenge at Phnom Penh's huge city dump—this I knew about—but that they also live there. With the aid of an interpreter, I was able to interview these people, as well as photograph them as they went about their everyday lives. An entire community lives in the city dump, complete with restaurants amidst the smoke and piles of garbage. This photo essay reveals not just these people's activities but also their social organization (Chapter 9).

Work and Gender: Women at Work in India As I traveled in India, I took photos of women at work in public places. The more I traveled in this country and the more photos I took, the more insight I gained into gender relations. Despite the general dominance of men in India, women's worlds are far from limited to family and home. Women are found at work throughout the society. What is even more remarkable is how vastly different "women's work" is in India than it is in the United States. This, too, is an intellectually provocative photo essay (Chapter 11).

Small Town USA: Struggling to Survive To take the photos for this essay, I went off the beaten path. On a road trip from California to Florida, instead of following the interstates, I followed those "little black lines" on the map. They took me to out-of-the-way places that the national transportation system has bypassed. Many of these little towns are putting on a valiant face as they struggle to survive, but, as the photos show, the struggle is apparent, and, in some cases, so are the scars (Chapter 14).

Holy Week in Spain, in Chapter 18, features processions in two cities in Spain: Malaga, a provincial capital, and Almuñecar, a smaller city in Granada. The Roman Catholic heritage of Spain runs so deeply that the *La Asunción de María* (The Assumption of Mary) is a national holiday, with the banks and post offices closed. City streets carry such names as (translated) Conception, Piety, Humility, Calvary, Crucifixion, and The Blessed Virgin. In large and small towns throughout Spain, elaborate processions during Holy Week feature *tronos* that depict the biblical account of Jesus' suffering, death, and resurrection. I was allowed to photograph the preparations for one of the processions, so this essay also includes "behind-the-scenes" photos.

During the processions, the participants walk slowly for one or two minutes; then, because of the weight of the *tronos*, they rest for one or two minutes. This process repeats for about six hours. As you will see, some of the most interesting activities occur during the rest periods.

A Walk Through El Tiro in Medellin, Colombia One of the most significant social changes in the world is taking place in the Least Industrialized Nations. In the search for a better life, people are abandoning rural areas. Fleeing poverty, they are flocking to the cities, only to be greeted with more poverty. Some of these settlements of the new urban poor are dangerous. I was fortunate to be escorted by an insider through a section of Medellin, Colombia, that is controlled by gangs (Chapter 20).

Other Photo Essays To help students better understand subcultures, I have retained the photo essay on standards of beauty in Chapter 2. I have also kept the photo essay in Chapter 12 on ethnic work, as it helps students see that ethnicity doesn't "just happen." Because these photo essays consist of photos taken by others, they are not a part of the series, *Through the Author's Lens*. I think you will appreciate the understanding these two photo essays can give your students.

Photo Collages Because sociology lends itself so well to photographic illustrations, this text also includes photo collages. In Chapter 1, the photo collage, in the shape of a wheel, features some of the many women who became sociologists in earlier generations, women who have largely gone unacknowledged as sociologists. In Chapter 2, students can catch a glimpse of the fascinating variety that goes into the cultural relativity of beauty. The collage in Chapter 6 illustrates categories, aggregates, and primary and secondary groups, concepts that students sometimes wrestle to distinguish. The photo collage in Chapter 11 lets students see how differently gender is portrayed in different cultures.

Other Photos by the Author Sprinkled throughout the text are photos that I took in Austria, Cambodia, India, Latvia, Spain, and the United States. These photos illustrate sociological principles and topics better than photos available from commercial sources. As an example, while in the United States, I received a report about a feral child who had been discovered living with monkeys and who had been taken to an orphanage in Cambodia. The possibility of photographing and interviewing that child was one of the reasons that I went to Cambodia. That particular photo is on page 64. Another of my favorites is on page 195.

Other Special Pedagogical Features

In addition to chapter summaries and reviews, key terms, and a comprehensive glossary, I have included several special features to aid students in learning sociology. **In Sum** sections help students review important points within the chapter before going on to new materials. I have also developed a series of **Social Maps**, which illustrate how social conditions vary by geography. All the maps in this text are original.

Learning Objectives I have written learning objectives for each chapter. These learning objectives are presented in a list at the beginning of the chapter, at the point where the specific material is presented, and again in the chapter's Summary and Review. These learning objectives provide a guiding "road map" for your students.

Chapter-Opening Vignettes Each chapter opens with a vignette that features a down-to-earth illustration of a major aspect of the chapter's content. Three of these vignettes are new to this edition (Chapters 5, 7, and 22). Several of them are based on my research with the homeless, the time I spent with them on the streets and slept in their shelters (Chapters 1, 10, and 19). Others recount my travels in Africa (Chapters 2 and 11) and Mexico (Chapters 16 and 20). I also share my experiences when I spent a night with street people at DuPont Circle in Washington, D.C. (Chapter 4). For other vignettes, I use current and historical events (Chapters 5, 7, 9, 12, 17, 18, 21, and 22), composite accounts (Chapter 14), classical studies in the social sciences (Chapters 3, 8, and 13), and even scenes from novels (Chapters 6 and 15). Many students have told their instructors that they find these vignettes compelling, that they stimulate interest in the chapter.

Thinking Critically about the Chapters I close each chapter with critical thinking questions. Each question focuses on a major feature of the chapter, asking students to reflect on and consider some issue. Many of the questions ask the students to apply sociological findings and principles to their own lives.

On Sources Sociological data are found in a wide variety of sources, and this text reflects that variety. Cited throughout this text are standard journals such as the *American Journal of Sociology*, *Social Problems*, *American Sociological Review*, and *Journal of Marriage and Family*, as well as more esoteric journals such as the *Bulletin of the History of Medicine*, *Chronobiology International*, and *Western Journal of Black Studies*. I have also drawn heavily from standard news sources, especially the *New York Times* and the *Wall Street Journal*, as well as more unusual sources such as *El País*. In addition, I cite unpublished research and theoretical papers by sociologists.

Acknowledgments

The gratifying response to this text's earlier editions indicates that my efforts at making sociology down to earth have succeeded. The years that have gone into writing this text are a culmination of the many years that preceded its writing—from graduate school to that equally demanding endeavor known as classroom teaching. No text, of course, comes solely from its author. Although I am responsible for the final words on the printed page, I have received excellent feedback from instructors who have taught from the first eleven editions. I am especially grateful to

Reviewers of the First through Eleventh Editions

Francis O. Adeola, *University of New Orleans*
Brian W. Agnitsch, *Marshalltown Community College*
Sandra L. Albrecht, *The University of Kansas*
Christina Alexander, *Linfield College*
Richard Alman, *Sierra College*
Gabriel C. Alvarez, *Duquesne University*
Kenneth Ambrose, *Marshall University*
Alberto Arroyo, *Baldwin–Wallace College*
Karren Baird-Olsen, *Kansas State University*
Rafael Balderrama, *University of Texas—Pan American*
Linda Barbera-Stein, *The University of Illinois*
Brenda Blackburn, *California State University—Fullerton*
Ronnie J. Booxbaum, *Greenfield Community College*
Cecil D. Bradfield, *James Madison University*
Karen Bradley, *Central Missouri State University*
Francis Brouer, *Worcester State College*
Valerie S. Brown, *Cuyahoga Community College*
Sandi Brunette-Hill, *Carrol College*
Richard Brunk, *Francis Marion University*
Karen Bullock, *Salem State College*
Allison R. Camelot, *California State University—Fullerton*
Paul Ciccantell, *Kansas State University*
John K. Cochran, *The University of Oklahoma*
James M. Cook, *Duke University*
Joan Cook-Zimmern, *College of Saint Mary*
Larry Curiel, *Cypress College*
Russell L. Curtis, *University of Houston*
John Darling, *University of Pittsburgh—Johnstown*
Ray Darville, *Stephen F. Austin State University*
Jim David, *Butler County Community College*
Nanette J. Davis, *Portland State University*
Vincent Davis, *Mt. Hood Community College*
Lynda Dodgen, *North Harris Community College*
Terry Dougherty, *Portland State University*
Marlese Durr, *Wright State University*
Helen R. Ebaugh, *University of Houston*
Obi N. Ebbe, *State University of New York—Brockport*
Cy Edwards, Chair, *Cypress Community College*
John Ehle, *Northern Virginia Community College*
Morten Ender, *U.S. Military Academy*
Rebecca Susan Fahrlander, *Bellevue University*
Louis J. Finkle, *Horry-Georgetown Technical College*
Nicole T. Flynn, *University of South Alabama*
Lorna E. Forster, *Clinton Community College*
David O. Friedrichs, *University of Scranton*
Bruce Friesen, *Kent State University—Stark*
Lada Gibson-Shreve, *Stark State College*
Norman Goodman, *State University of New York—Stony Brook*
Rosalind Gottfried, *San Joaquin Delta College*
G. Kathleen Grant, *The University of Findlay*
Bill Grisby, *University of Northern Colorado*
Ramon Guerra, *University of Texas—Pan American*
Remi Hajjar, *U.S. Military Academy*
Donald W. Hastings, *The University of Tennessee—Knoxville*
Lillian O. Holloman, *Prince George's Community College*
Michael Hoover, *Missouri Western State College*
Howard R. Housen, *Broward Community College*
James H. Huber, *Bloomsburg University*
Erwin Hummel, *Portland State University*
Charles E. Hurst, *The College of Wooster*
Nita Jackson, *Butler County Community College*
Jennifer A. Johnson, *Germanna Community College*
Kathleen R. Johnson, *Keene State College*
Tammy Jolley, *University of Arkansas Community College at Batesville*
David Jones, *Plymouth State College*
Arunas Juska, *East Carolina University*
Ali Kamali, *Missouri Western State College*
Irwin Kantor, *Middlesex County College*
Mark Kassop, *Bergen Community College*

Myles Kelleher, *Bucks County Community College*
Mary E. Kelly, *Central Missouri State University*
Alice Abel Kemp, *University of New Orleans*
Diana Kendall, *Austin Community College*
Gary Kiger, *Utah State University*
Gene W. Kilpatrick, *University of Maine—Presque Isle*
Jerome R. Koch, *Texas Tech University*
Joseph A. Kotarba, *University of Houston*
Michele Lee Kozimor-King, *Pennsylvania State University*
Darina Lepadatu, *Kennesaw State University*
Abraham Levine, *El Camino Community College*
Diane Levy, *The University of North Carolina—Wilmington*
Stephen Mabry, *Cedar Valley College*
David Maines, *Oakland University*
Ron Matson, *Wichita State University*
Armaund L. Mauss, *Washington State University*
Evelyn Mercer, *Southwest Baptist University*
Robert Meyer, *Arkansas State University*
Michael V. Miller, *University of Texas—San Antonio*
John Mitrano, *Central Connecticut State University*
W. Lawrence Neuman, *University of Wisconsin—Whitewater*
Charles Norman, *Indiana State University*
Patricia H. O'Brien, *Elgin Community College*
Robert Ostrow, *Wayne State*
Laura O'Toole, *University of Delaware*
Mike K. Pate, *Western Oklahoma State College*
Lawrence Peck, *Erie Community College*
Ruth Pigott, *University of Nebraska—Kearney*
Phil Piket, *Joliet Junior College*
Trevor Pinch, *Cornell University*
Daniel Polak, *Hudson Valley Community College*
James Pond, *Butler Community College*
Deedy Ramo, *Del Mar College*
Adrian Rapp, *North Harris Community College*
Ray Rich, *Community College of Southern Nevada*
Barbara Richardson, *Eastern Michigan University*
Salvador Rivera, *State University of New York—Cobleskill*
Howard Robboy, *Trenton State College*
Paulina X. Ruf, *University of Tampa*
Michael Samano, *Portland Community College*
Michael L. Sanow, *Community College of Baltimore County*
Mary C. Sengstock, *Wayne State University*
Walt Shirley, *Sinclair Community College*
Marc Silver, *Hofstra University*
Roberto E. Socas, *Essex County College*
Susan Sprecher, *Illinois State University*
Mariella Rose Squire, *University of Maine at Fort Kent*
Rachel Stehle, *Cuyahoga Community College*
Marios Stephanides, *University of Tampa*
Randolph G. Ston, *Oakland Community College*
Vickie Holland Taylor, *Danville Community College*
Maria Jose Tenuto, *College of Lake County*
Gary Tiederman, *Oregon State University*
Kathleen Tiemann, *University of North Dakota*
Judy Turchetta, *Johnson & Wales University*
Stephen L. Vassar, *Minnesota State University—Mankato*
William J. Wattendorf, *Adirondack Community College*
Jay Weinstein, *Eastern Michigan University*
Larry Weiss, *University of Alaska*
Douglas White, *Henry Ford Community College*
Stephen R. Wilson, *Temple University*
Anthony T. Woart, *Middlesex Community College*
Stuart Wright, *Lamar University*
Mary Lou Wylie, *James Madison University*
Diane Kholos Wysocki, *University of Nebraska—Kearney*
Stacey G. H. Yap, *Plymouth State College*
William Yoels, *University of Alabama Birmingham*

I couldn't ask for a more outstanding team than the one that I have the pleasure to work with at Allyn and Bacon. I want to thank Charlyce Jones-Owen, who joined the team for this 12th edition, for coordinating the many tasks that were necessary to produce this new edition; Dusty Friedman, always a pleasure to work with, for attending to what seemed to be an infinite number of details—and for her constant encouragement; Jenn Albanese, who once again provided excellent research, tracking down both standard and esoteric items that made an impact on the book; Diane Elliott, who thought along with me as she did the copy editing; and Kate Cebik, for her creativity in photo research—and for her willingness to "keep on looking."

I do appreciate this team. It is difficult to heap too much praise on such fine, capable, and creative people. Often going "beyond the call of duty" as we faced nonstop deadlines, their untiring efforts coalesced with mine to produce this text. Students, whom we constantly kept in mind as we prepared this edition, are the beneficiaries of this intricate teamwork.

Since this text is based on the contributions of many, I would count it a privilege if you would share with me your teaching experiences with this book, including suggestions for improving the text. Both positive and negative comments are welcome. This is one way that I continue to learn.

I wish you the very best in your teaching. It is my sincere desire that *Sociology: A Down-to-Earth Approach* contributes to your classroom success.

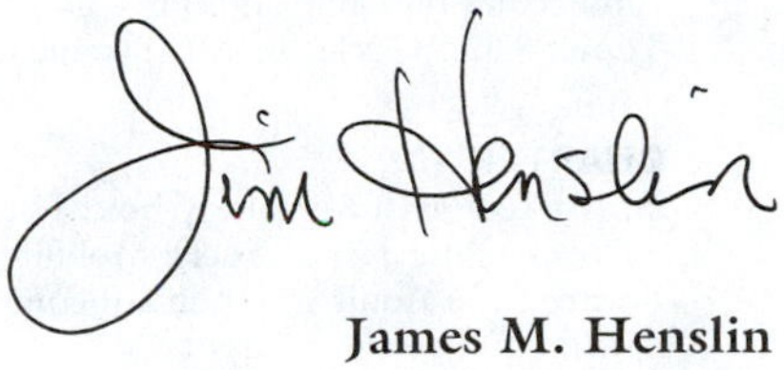

James M. Henslin
Professor Emeritus
Department of Sociology
Southern Illinois University, Edwardsville

I welcome your correspondence. You can reach me at henslin@aol.com

WHAT'S NEW IN THE 12TH EDITION?

CHAPTER 1

Topic: The divorce rate of couples who cohabit before marriage is about the same as those who did not cohabit.

CHAPTER 2

Cultural Diversity around the World box: Dancing with the Dead

CHAPTER 3

Down-to-Earth Sociology box: Gossip and Ridicule to Enforce Adolescent Norms

Topic: Gender messages from homosexual parents

Topic: Babies might have an inborn sense of fairness, indicating that, like language, morality is a capacity hardwired in the brain

Topic: Sociologists are doing research on how the individual's sense of identity is related to morality, guilt, and shame

Topic: Average number of commercials Americans are exposed to has jumped to 200,000 a year

CHAPTER 4

Topic: The U.S. Army is trying to apply body language to alert soldiers to danger when interacting with civilians in a military zone

Topic: Students give higher ratings to better-looking teachers

Topic: To become slender, some women inject themselves daily with hCG, a hormone that comes from the urine of pregnant women

CHAPTER 5

New chapter opening vignette

Topic: Researchers used Facebook to identify the race–ethnicity of friendships of college students

Topic: Malls track patrons through their Smartphones so stores can send them targeted ads

Topic: Face-recognition cameras at kiosks classify people by age and sex and post targeted ads

Topic: Bionic mannequins analyze customers' age, sex, and race–ethnicity

CHAPTER 6

Topic: Classic laboratory findings on group size and helping are compared with the real world

Topic: Research on millions confirms Milgram's 6 degrees of separation

Topic: Network analysis is being used to reduce gang violence

CHAPTER 7

New chapter opening vignette

Sociology and the New Technology box: Social Networking as the New Contender: A Cautious Prediction

Topic: Of U.S. workers, 47% are women and 31% are minorities

Topic: The medical reform law requires lactation rooms for mothers returning to work

CHAPTER 8

Thinking Critically section: The Saints and the Roughnecks: Labeling in Everyday Life

Thinking Critically section: Vigilantes: When the State Breaks Down

Topic: The number of U.S prisoners has begun to drop

Topic: Participant observation of youth gangs confirms research that ideas of masculinity encourage violence, including homicide

Topic: *Diversion* as a way to avoid labeling youthful offenders as delinquent

Topic: The *angry anarchist* added to Merton's typology of responses to goals and means

Topic: Citigroup fined over a *half billion dollars* for selling fraudulent subprime mortgages

Topic: California is releasing some prisoners whose third crime under the three-strikes law was not violent

Topic: The elimination of lead in gasoline could be the main cause for the drop in crime

Topic: To keep crime statistics low, the police don't record some crimes

CHAPTER 9

Cultural Diversity around the World box: Rape: Blaming the Victim and Protecting the Caste System

Topic: Under apartheid, South Africa's beaches had four separate sections: for whites, Africans, Asians, and "mixed races"

Topic: India's caste system is slowly being replaced by a social class system

Topic: Poet in Qatar sentenced to life in prison for writing a poem critical of the royal family

Topic: Chinese leaders block Internet access to Facebook and Twitter

Topic: The Picosecond laser scanner can read molecules on a human body

Topic: Silent Circle, an unbreakable encryption app

CHAPTER 10

Down-to-Earth Sociology box: The American Dream: Research on Social Mobility

Figure 10.6 Adult Children's Income Compared with That of Their Parents

Topic: Preschools that cost $37,000 a year have waiting lists

Topic: Microsoft co-founder Paul Allen's 414-foot yacht has two helicopters, a swimming pool, and a submarine

Topic: The top fifth of the U.S. population receives 50.2% of the nation's income

Topic: Status inconsistent men are twice as likely to have heart attacks as status consistent men; status inconsistent women do not have more heart attacks

Topic: Most of the poor now live in the suburbs

Topic: With poverty increasing, 21 million U.S. children are poor

CHAPTER 11

Down-to-Earth Sociology box: Applying Sociology: How to Get a Higher Salary

Topic: Women in jobs that give them authority and men in nurturing occupations reaffirm their gender at home

Topic: A "tough femininity" that incorporates masculine violence is emerging among female juvenile delinquents

Topic: Both males and females who are given a single dose of testosterone seek higher status and show less regard for the feelings of others

Topic: Dominance behavior, such as winning a game, produces higher levels of testosterone

Topic: Health workers have developed a strategy to get entire villages to renounce female circumcision

Topic: A movement to end male circumcision

Topic: With our economic crisis, children's poverty is higher now than it was in 1967—and in all the years in between

CHAPTER 12

Topic: Predatory lending increased monthly payments for home mortgages, causing many African Americans to lose their homes when the economic crisis hit

Topic: Countrywide fined $335 million for predatory lending

Topic: The United Auburn tribe's casino in California nets $30,000 *a month* for each tribal member

Topic: In 2012, Mazie Hirono became the first Asian American woman to be elected to the U.S. Senate

Topic: U.S. Supreme Court upheld the states' right to check the immigration status of anyone they stop or arrest

Topic: President Obama signed an Executive Order allowing work permits to unauthorized immigrants who meet certain qualifications

CHAPTER 13

Down-to-Earth Sociology box: What Do You Think about the Red Sock? Sex in Nursing Homes

CHAPTER 14

Figure 14.4 The Globalization of Capitalism: U.S. Workers Who Work for Foreign-Owned Businesses

Topic: China's new capitalism has lifted *a half billion people* out of poverty

CHAPTER 15

Thinking Critically section: Targeted Killings

Down-to-Earth Sociology box: The Revolving Door of Power

Mass Media in Social Life box: The Propaganda and Profits of War

Down-to-Earth Sociology box: The Rape of Nanking: A Report on Dehumanization

Topic: The transfer of authority in Cuba as an example of Weber's routinization of charisma

Topic: The communist rulers of China, sensitive to online communications, change course if they sense strong sentiment in some direction

Topic: Super PACS that raise unlimited cash for individual candidates

CHAPTER 16

Down-to-Earth Sociology box: Health Benefits of Marriage: Living Longer

Down-to-Earth Sociology box: Family Structure: Single Moms and Married Moms

Sociology and the New Technology box: "How Should We Handle Family Disagreements?" Use Your App

Figure 16.4 Marriage and Length of Life

Topic: New Bianchi research on the gendered division of family labor

Topic: Single women who give birth are taking longer to get married

Topic: About one-fourth (23 percent) of U.S. children are born to cohabiting parents

Topic: On average, the children of cohabiting parents aren't as healthy as the children of married parents

Topic: Men who marry live longer than men who remain single or are divorced

Topic: Men who cohabit live longer than men who remain single or are divorced

Topic: Some "day care centers" are open round-the-clock

Topic: Marriages between Asian Americans and whites and African American women and white men have lower divorce rates than the national average

Topic: Gender equality in the initiation of marital violence indicates the need to direct anti-violence socialization to both females and males
Topic: New research on 13,000 cases of sibling incest
Topic: Online dating sites are so specialized that one targets "green singles" and another targets women who like men with mustaches

CHAPTER 17
Down-to-Earth Sociology box: How I Became a Fairy: Education and the Perpetuation of Social Inequality
Topic: National sample of students, kindergarten through fifth grade, shows teachers bias against boys
Topic: *juku* (cram schools) in Japan
Topic: In Russia, officials have begun to check the content of history books for their degree of patriotism
Topic: Most Washington, D.C., high school graduates operate at the fifth grade level

CHAPTER 18
Topic: The Pope has begun to tweet, sending messages in 145 characters or less

CHAPTER 19
Topic: U.S. health researchers infected Guatemalans with syphilis to study the effectiveness of penicillin
Topic: Drug-resistant tuberculosis
Topic: CRK (carbapenem resistant Klebsiella) struck the medical center at the National Institutes of Health
Topic: Workplace care as a means to reduce medical costs
Topic: Congress exempted itself from medical reform

CHAPTER 20
Down-to-Earth Sociology box: BioFoods: What's in *Your* Future?
Figure 20.11 How the World Is Urbanizing
Topic: Europe's oldest town, going back 6,500 years, discovered in Bulgaria
Topic: To encourage births, one Russian city is giving its citizens a day off work to make love and awarding prizes to women who give birth on Russia day
Topic: Indian officials say that female infanticide, which has led to India having an extra 37 million men, is a major cause of sexual harassment and rape

CHAPTER 21
Tourette's Syndrome at a school in New York as a case of mass hysteria
Minecraft as a fad
Multiple realities and social movements

CHAPTER 22
New chapter opening vignette
Thinking Critically section: The Island Nations: "Come See Us While We Are Still Here"
Topic: Car and truck engines that burn natural gas will become common
Topic: The U.S. Cyber Command coordinates cyber warfare with the National Security Agency
Topic: The *Stuxnet worm* and the disruption of Iran's nuclear program
Topic: China has accused the United States of tens of thousands of cyberattacks against its military websites
Topic: Both Russia and the United States still claim the *right of first strike*, the right to strike the other with nuclear weapons even though the other has not launched any
Topic: To protect its interests in Africa, the U.S. government has formed AFRICOM, a rapid-response military force
Topic: The nuclear catastrophe at Fukushima, Japan

A Note from the Publisher on the Supplements

Instructor Supplements

Unless otherwise noted, instructor supplements are available at no charge to adopters—in electronic formats through the Instructor's Resource Center (www.pearsonhighered.com/irc).

Instructor's Manual and Test bank

For each chapter in the text, the Instructor's Manual provides a list of key changes to the new edition, chapter summaries and outlines, learning objectives, key terms and people, discussion topics, classroom activities, recommended films and Web sites, and additional references. The Instructor's Manual also includes sample syllabi and a section by Jim Henslin on using small, in-class discussion groups.

Test bank

The Test Bank contains approximately 125 questions per chapter in multiple-choice, true/false, short answer, essay, and matching formats. There is also a set of questions based on the text's figures, tables, and maps. The questions are correlated to the in-text learning objectives for each chapter.

MyTest Computerized Test Bank

The printed Test Bank is also available online through Pearson's computerized testing system, MyTest. The user-friendly interface allows you to view, edit, and add questions, transfer questions to tests, and print tests in a variety of fonts. Search and sort features allow you to locate questions quickly and to arrange them in whatever order you prefer. The Test Bank can be accessed anywhere with a free MyTest user account. There is no need to download a program or file to your computer.

PowerPoint Presentation Slides

Lecture PowerPoint Presentations are available for this edition. The lecture slides outline each chapter of the text, while the line art slides provide the charts, graphs, and maps found in the text. PowerPoint software is not required as PowerPoint viewer is included.

MySocLab™

MySocLab is a learning and assessment tool that enables instructors to assess student performance and adapt course content—without investing additional time or resources. MySocLab is designed with instructor flexibility in mind—you decide the extent of integration into your course—from independent self-assessment to total course management. The lab is accompanied by an instructor's manual featuring easy-to-read media grids, activities, sample syllabi, and tips for integrating technology into your course.

New features in MySocLab include:

- Social Explorer—the premier interactive demographics Web site.
- MySocLibrary—with over 100 classic and contemporary primary source readings.
- The Core Concepts in Sociology videos—streaming videos presented in documentary style on core sociological concepts.
- The Social Lens—a sociology blog updated weekly with topics ranging from politics to pop culture.
- Chapter Audio—streaming audio of the entire text.

About the Author

JIM HENSLIN was born in Minnesota, graduated from high school and junior college in California and from college in Indiana. Awarded scholarships, he earned his master's and doctorate degrees in sociology at Washington University in St. Louis, Missouri. After this, he won a postdoctoral fellowship from the National Institute of Mental Health and spent a year studying how people adjust to the suicide of a family member. His primary interests in sociology are the sociology of everyday life, deviance, and international relations. Among his many books are *Down-to-Earth Sociology: Introductory Readings* (Free Press), now in its 15th edition, and *Social Problems* (Pearson), now in its 11th edition. He has also published widely in sociology journals, including *Social Problems* and *American Journal of Sociology.*

While a graduate student, Jim taught at the University of Missouri at St. Louis. After completing his doctorate, he joined the faculty at Southern Illinois University, Edwardsville, where he is Professor Emeritus of Sociology. He says, "I've always found the introductory course enjoyable to teach. I love to see students' faces light up when they first glimpse the sociological perspective and begin to see how society has become an essential part of how they view the world."

Jim enjoys reading and fishing, and he also does a bit of kayaking and weight lifting. His two favorite activities are writing and traveling. He especially enjoys visiting and living in other cultures, since this brings him face to face with behaviors and ways of thinking that challenge his perspectives and "make sociological principles come alive." A special pleasure has been the preparation of "Through the Author's Lens," the series of photo essays that appear in this text.

Jim moved to Latvia, an Eastern European country formerly dominated by the Soviet Union, where he had the experience of becoming an immigrant. There he observed firsthand how people struggle to adjust to capitalism. While there, he interviewed aged political prisoners who had survived the Soviet gulag. He then moved to Spain, where he was able to observe how people adjust to a declining economy and the immigration of people from contrasting cultures. (Of course, for this he didn't need to leave the United States.) To better round out his cultural experiences, Jim is making plans for travel to South Korea and again to India, and later to South America, where he expects to do more photo essays to reflect their fascinating cultures. He is grateful to be able to live in such exciting social, technological, and geopolitical times—and to have access to portable broadband Internet while he pursues his sociological imagination.

The author at work—sometimes getting a little too close to "the action" preparing the "Through the Author's Lens" photo essay on pages 510–511.

Photo by Anita Henslin

CHAPTER 1

The Sociological Perspective

Listen to Chapter 1 on MySocLab

Learning Objectives

After you have read this chapter, you should be able to:

1.1 Explain why both history and biography are essential for the sociological perspective. (p. 2)

1.2 Know the focus of each social science. (p. 4)

1.3 Trace the origins of sociology, from tradition to Max Weber. (p. 7)

1.4 Summarize the opposing arguments in the debate about values in sociological research. (p. 12)

1.5 State what *Verstehen* is and why it is valuable. (p. 13)

1.6 Trace the development of sociology in North America and explain the tension between objective analysis and social reform. (p. 15)

1.7 Explain the basic ideas of symbolic interactionism, functional analysis, and conflict theory. (p. 22)

1.8 Explain how research versus reform and globalization are likely to influence sociology. (p. 29)

I quickly scanned the room filled with 100 or so bunks. *I was relieved to see that an upper bunk was still open. I grabbed it, figuring that attacks are more difficult in an upper bunk. Even from the glow of the faded red-and-white exit sign, its faint light barely illuminating this bunk, I could see that the sheet was filthy. Resigned to another night of fitful sleep, I reluctantly crawled into bed.*

I kept my clothes on.

The next morning, I joined the long line of disheveled men leaning against the chain-link fence. Their faces were as downcast as their clothes were dirty. Not a glimmer of hope among them.

No one spoke as the line slowly inched forward.

When my turn came, I was handed a cup of coffee, a white plastic spoon, and a bowl of semiliquid that I couldn't identify. It didn't look like any food I had seen before. Nor did it taste like anything I had ever eaten.

My stomach fought the foul taste, every spoonful a battle. But I was determined. "I will experience what they experience," I kept telling myself. My stomach reluctantly gave in and accepted its morning nourishment.

> "The room was strangely silent. Hundreds of men were eating, each immersed in his own private hell, . . ."

The room was strangely silent. Hundreds of men were eating, each one immersed in his own private hell, his mind awash with disappointment, remorse, bitterness.

As I stared at the Styrofoam cup that held my coffee, grateful for at least this small pleasure, I noticed what looked like teeth marks. I shrugged off the thought, telling myself that my long weeks as a sociological observer of the homeless were finally getting to me. "It must be some sort of crease from handling," I concluded.

I joined the silent ranks of men turning in their bowls and cups. When I saw the man behind the counter swishing out Styrofoam cups in a washtub of murky water, I began to feel sick to my stomach. I knew then that the jagged marks on my cup really had come from another person's mouth.

How much longer did this research have to last? I felt a deep longing to return to my family—to a welcome world of clean sheets, healthy food, and "normal" conversations.

The Sociological Perspective

1.1 Explain why both history and biography are essential for the sociological perspective.

Read on MySocLab
Document: Peter L. Berger, Invitation to Sociology

Why were these men so silent? Why did they receive such despicable treatment? What was I doing in that homeless shelter? After all, I hold a respectable, professional position, and I have a home and family.

You are in for an exciting and eye-opening experience. Sociology offers a fascinating view of social life. The *sociological perspective* (or imagination) opens a window onto unfamiliar worlds—and offers a fresh look at familiar ones. In this text, you will find yourself in the midst of Nazis in Germany and warriors in South America. Sociology is broad, and your journey will even take you to a group that lives in a city dump. (If you want to jump ahead, you can see the photos I took of the people who live—and work and play—in a dump in Cambodia on pages 248–249.) You will also find yourself looking at your own world in a different light. As you view other worlds—or your own—the sociological perspective enables you to gain a new perception of social life. In fact, this is what many find appealing about sociology.

The sociological perspective has been a motivating force in my own life. Ever since I took an introductory course in sociology as a freshman in college, I have been enchanted by the perspective that sociology offers. I have enjoyed both observing other groups and questioning my own assumptions about life. I sincerely hope the same happens to you.

Seeing the Broader Social Context

The **sociological perspective** stresses the social contexts in which people live. It examines how these contexts influence people's lives. At the center of the sociological perspective is the question of how groups influence people, especially how people are influenced by their **society**—a group of people who share a culture and a territory.

To find out why people do what they do, sociologists look at **social location**, the corners in life that people occupy because of their place in a society. Sociologists look at how jobs, income, education, gender, race–ethnicity, and age affect people's ideas and behavior. Consider, for example, how being identified with a group called *females* or with a group called *males* when you were growing up has shaped *your* ideas of who you are. Growing up as a female or a male has influenced not only how you feel about yourself but also your ideas of what you should attain in life and how you relate to others. Even your gestures and the way you laugh come from your identifying with one of these groups.

Sociologist C. Wright Mills (1959) put it this way: "The sociological imagination [perspective] enables us to grasp the connection between history and biography." By *history*, Mills meant that each society is located in a broad stream of events. This gives each society specific characteristics—such as its ideas about what roles are proper for men and women. By *biography*, Mills referred to your experiences within a specific historical setting, which gives you your orientations to life. In short, you don't do what they do because you inherited some internal mechanism, such as instincts. Rather, *external* influences—your experiences—become part of your thinking and motivation. In short, the society in which you grow up, and your particular location in that society, lie at the center of what you do and how you think.

Consider a newborn baby. As you know, if we were to take the baby away from its U.S. parents and place it with the Yanomamö Indians in the jungles of South America, his or her first words would not be in English. You also know that the child would not think like an American. The child would not grow up wanting credit cards, for example, or designer clothes, a car, a cell phone, an iPod, and video games. He or she would take his or her place in Yanomamö society—perhaps as a food gatherer, a hunter, or a warrior—and would not even know about the world left behind at birth. And, whether male or female, the child would grow up assuming that it is natural to want many children, not debating whether to have one, two, or three children.

People around the globe take their own views of the world for granted. Something inside us Americans tells us that hamburgers are delicious, small families desirable, and designer clothing attractive. Yet something inside some of the Sinai desert Arab tribes tells them that warm, fresh camel's blood makes a fine drink and that everyone should have a large family and wear flowing robes (Murray 1935; McCabe and Ellis 1990). That "something" certainly isn't an instinct. As sociologist Peter Berger (1963/2014) phrased it, that something is *society within us.*

Although obvious, this point frequently eludes us. We often think and talk about people as though their behavior were caused by their sex ("men are like that"), their race ("they are like that"), or some other factor transmitted by their genes. The sociological perspective helps us escape from this cramped, personal view by exposing the broader social context that underlies human behavior. It helps us see the links between what people do and the social settings that shape their behavior.

If you have been thinking along with me—and I hope you have—you should be thinking about how *your* social groups have shaped *your* ideas and desires. Over and over in this text, you will see that the way you look at the world is the result of your exposure to specific human groups. I think you will enjoy the process of self-discovery that sociology offers.

The Global Context—and the Local

As is evident to all of us—from the labels on our clothing that say Hong Kong, Brunei, or Macau to the many other imported products that have become part of our daily lives—our world has become a global village. How life has changed! Our predecessors

Watch on **MySocLab**
Video: What is Sociology? The Basics

Explore on **MySocLab**
Activity: The Development of American Society

sociological perspective understanding human behavior by placing it within its broader social context

society people who share a culture and a territory

social location the group memberships that people have because of their location in history and society lived on isolated farms and in small towns. They grew their own food and made their own clothing, buying only sugar, coffee, and a few other items that they couldn't produce. Beyond the borders of their communities lay a world they perceived only dimly.

And how slow communications used to be! In December 1814, the United States and Great Britain signed a peace treaty to end the War of 1812. Yet two weeks *later*, their armies fought a major battle at New Orleans. Neither the American nor the British forces there had heard that the war was over (Volti 1995).

Now we can grab our cell phone or use the Internet to communicate instantly with people anywhere on the planet. News flashes from around the world are part of our everyday life. At the same time that we are engulfed in instantaneous global communications, we also continue to occupy our own little corners of life. Like those of our predecessors, our worlds, too, are marked by differences in family background, religion, job, age, gender, race–ethnicity, and social class. In these smaller corners of life, we continue to learn distinctive ways of viewing the world.

Watch on **MySocLab**
Video: Sociology in Focus

One of the beautiful—and fascinating—aspects of sociology is that it enables us to look at both parts of our current reality: being part of a global network *and* having unique experiences in our smaller corners of life. This text reflects both of these worlds, each so vital in understanding who we are.

1.2 Know the focus of each social science.

Sociology and the Other Sciences

Watch on **MySocLab**
Video: Sociology: Thinking Like a Sociologist

Just as humans today have an intense desire to unravel the mysteries around them, so did people in ancient times. Their explanations were not based only on observations, however, but were mixed with magic and superstition.

To satisfy their basic curiosity about the world, humans gradually developed **science**, systematic methods for studying the social and natural worlds and the knowledge obtained by those methods. *Sociology*, the study of society and human behavior, is one of these sciences.

A useful way of comparing these sciences—and of gaining a better understanding of sociology's place—is to divide them into the natural and the social sciences.

The Natural Sciences

The **natural sciences** are the intellectual and academic disciplines that are designed to explain and predict the events in our natural environment. The natural sciences are divided into specialized fields of research according to subject matter, such as biology, geology, chemistry, and physics. These are further subdivided into even more highly specialized areas. Biology is divided into botany and zoology; geology into mineralogy and geomorphology; chemistry into its organic and inorganic branches; and physics into biophysics and quantum mechanics. Each area of investigation examines a particular "slice" of nature.

science the application of systematic methods to obtain knowledge and the knowledge obtained by those methods

natural sciences the intellectual and academic disciplines designed to comprehend, explain, and predict events in our natural environments

social sciences the intellectual and academic disciplines designed to understand the social world objectively by means of controlled and repeated observations

The Social Sciences

People have also developed the **social sciences**, which examine human relationships. Just as the natural sciences attempt to objectively understand the world of nature, the social sciences attempt to objectively understand the social world. Just as the world of nature contains ordered (or lawful) relationships that are not obvious but must be discovered through controlled observations, so the ordered relationships of the human or social world are not obvious and must be revealed by means of repeated observations.

Like the natural sciences, the social sciences are divided into specialized fields based on their subject matter. These divisions—anthropology, economics, political science, psychology, and sociology—are, like the natural sciences, subdivided further into specialized fields. Anthropology includes cultural and physical anthropology; economics has macro (large-scale) and micro (small-scale) specialties; political science has theoretical and applied branches; psychology may be clinical or experimental; and sociology has its quantitative and qualitative branches. Since our focus is sociology, let's contrast sociology with each of the other social sciences.

Anthropology. Anthropology, which traditionally focuses on tribal peoples, is closely related to sociology. The chief goal of anthropologists is to understand *culture*, a people's total way of life. Culture includes a group's (1) *artifacts*, such as its tools, art, and weapons; (2) *structure*, the patterns that determine how its members interact with one another (such as positions of leadership); (3) *ideas and values*, the ways the group's beliefs affect its members' lives; and (4) *forms of communication*, especially language.

Students working on their doctorates in anthropology used to spend a period of time living with a tribal group. In their reports, they emphasized the group's family (kin) relationships. As there are no "undiscovered" groups left in the world, this focus on tribal groups has given way to the study of groups in agricultural settings and, increasingly, in industrialized society (Welker et al. 2011). When they study the same groups that sociologists do, anthropologists place more emphasis on artifacts, authority (hierarchy), and language, especially kinship terms.

Economics. Economics concentrates on a single social institution. Economists study the production and distribution of the material goods and services of a society. They want to know what goods are being produced, what they cost, and how those goods are distributed. Economists also are interested in the choices that determine production and consumption; for example, they study what motivates people to buy one item instead of another.

Political Science. Political science focuses on politics and government. Political scientists examine how governments are formed, how they operate, and how they are related to the other institutions of society. Political scientists are especially interested in how people attain ruling positions, how they maintain those positions, and the consequences of their actions for the people they govern.

Psychology. The focus of psychology is on processes that occur *within* the individual, inside what they call the "skin-bound organism." Experimental psychologists do research on intelligence, emotions, perception, memory, even sleep and dreams. Some study how personality is formed and the causes and treatment of mental illness. Clinical psychologists work as therapists, helping people resolve personal problems, such as recovering from abuse or addiction to drugs. Others work as counselors in school and work settings, where they give personality tests, intelligence tests, and vocational aptitude tests.

Sociology. Sociology overlaps these other social sciences. Like anthropologists, sociologists also study culture; they, too, do research on group structure and belief systems, as well as on how people communicate with one another. Like economists, sociologists do research on how a society's goods and services are distributed, especially how that distribution results in inequality. Like political scientists, sociologists study how people govern one another, especially how those in power affect people's lives. And like psychologists, sociologists also study how people adjust to the difficulties of life.

With such similarities, what distinguishes sociology from the other social sciences? Unlike anthropologists, sociologists focus primarily on industrialized and postindustrialized societies. Unlike economists and political scientists, sociologists do not concentrate on a single social institution. And unlike psychologists, sociologists stress factors *external* to the individual to determine what influences people and how they adjust to life. These differences might not be entirely clear, so let's go to the Down-to-Earth Sociology box on the next page and, in an updated ancient tale, consider how members of different disciplines might perceive the same subject matter.

Down-to-Earth Sociology

An Updated Version of the Old Elephant Story

It is said that in the recent past, five wise men and women, all blindfolded, were led to an elephant and asked to explain what they "saw." The first, an anthropologist, tenderly touching the trunk and the tusks, broke into a large grin and said, "This is really primitive. I feel very comfortable here. Concentrate on these."

The second, an economist, feeling the mouth, said, "This is what counts. What goes in here is distributed throughout the body. Concentrate your research on what goes in here and how it is distributed."

The third, a political scientist, feeling the gigantic ears, announced, "This is the power center. What goes in here controls the entire beast. Concentrate your studies here."

The fourth, a psychologist, stroking the top of the elephant's head, smiled contentedly and said, "This is the only thing that counts. All feeling and thinking take place inside here. To understand this beast, we'll study this part."

Then came the sociologist (of course!), who, after feeling the entire body, said, "You can't understand the beast by concentrating on only one part. Each is but part of the whole. The trunk and tusks, the mouth, the ears, the head—all are important. But so are the parts of the beast that you haven't mentioned. We must remove our blindfolds so we can see the larger picture. We have to see how everything works together to form the entire animal."

Pausing for emphasis, the sociologist added, "And we also need to understand how this creature interacts with similar creatures. How does its life in groups influence its behavior?"

I wish I could conclude this tale by saying that the anthropologist, the economist, the political scientist, and the psychologist were dazzled on hearing the wisdom of the sociologist, and, amidst gasps of wonderment, they tore off their blindfolds, joined together, and began to examine the entire animal. But, alas and alack! On hearing this sage advice, the specialists stubbornly bound their blindfolds even tighter so they could concentrate all the more on their particular part. And if you listened very, very carefully, you could even hear them mutter, "Don't touch the tusks." "Stay away from the mouth—that's my area." "Take your hands off the ears." "The top of the head is mine—stay away from it."

The traditional version of the blind men and the elephant does not include social scientists. This photo was taken in Amber Fort, Rajasthan, India.

The Goals of Science

The first goal of each science is to *explain* why something happens. The second goal is to make **generalizations**, that is, to go beyond the individual case and make statements that apply to a broader group or situation. For example, a sociologist wants to explain not only why Mary went to college or became an armed robber but also why people with her characteristics are more likely than others to go to college or to become armed robbers. To achieve generalizations, sociologists look for *patterns*, recurring characteristics or events. The third scientific goal is to *predict*, to specify in the light of current knowledge what will happen in the future.

To attain these goals, scientists do not rely on magic, superstition, or common beliefs; instead, they do systematic research. They explain exactly how they did their research so it can be reviewed by others. Secrecy, biases, and "trying to prove the way you want something to be" go against the grain of science.

Sociologists and other scientists also move beyond **common sense**—the prevailing ideas in a society, the things that "everyone knows" are true. "Everyone" can be as misguided today as everyone was when common sense dictated that the world was flat or that no human could ever walk on the moon. As sociologists do their research, their findings may confirm or contradict commonsense notions about social life.

Do you want to test your own common sense? Take the little Down-to-Earth Sociology quiz on the next page.

generalization a statement that goes beyond the individual case and is applied to a broader group or situation

common sense those things that "everyone knows" are true

Down-to-Earth **Sociology**

Enjoying a Sociology Quiz—Testing Your Common Sense

Some findings of sociology support commonsense understandings of social life, and others contradict them. Can you tell the difference? To enjoy this quiz, complete *all* the questions before turning the page to check your answers.

1. **True/False** More U.S. students are killed in school shootings now than ten or fifteen years ago.
2. **True/False** The earnings of U.S. women have just about caught up with those of U.S. men.
3. **True/False** With life so rushed and more women working for wages, today's parents spend less time with their children than parents of previous generations did.
4. **True/False** It is more dangerous to walk near topless bars than fast-food restaurants.
5. **True/False** Most rapists are mentally ill.
6. **True/False** A large percentage of terrorists are mentally ill.
7. **True/False** Most people on welfare are lazy and looking for a handout. They could work if they wanted to.
8. **True/False** Compared with women, men make more eye contact in face-to-face conversations.
9. **True/False** As measured by their divorce rate, couples who live together before marriage are usually more satisfied with their marriages than couples who did not live together before marriage.

The Risks of Being a Sociologist

Sometimes the explorations of sociologists take them into nooks and crannies that people would prefer remain unexplored. For example, a sociologist might study how muggers choose their victims or how people make decisions to cheat on their spouses. Since sociologists are intrigued with understanding social life, they don't stop doing research because people disapprove of it or feel uncomfortable about it. Sociologists consider all realms of human life legitimate avenues to explore, and they research both the respectable and the downright disreputable.

When sociologists do research on organizations, they sometimes face pressure to keep things secret. Every group, it seems, nourishes some ideal image that it presents to others. Because sociologists are interested in knowing what is *really* going on, they peer behind the scenes to get past those sugar-coated images (Berger 1963, 2014). An objective report can threaten a group's image, leading to pressure and conflict—all part of the adventure, and risk, of being a sociologist.

Origins of Sociology

1.3 Trace the origins of sociology, from tradition to Max Weber.

Watch on **MySocLab**
Video: Sociology: The Big Picture

Tradition Versus Science

So when did sociology begin? Even ancient peoples tried to figure out how social life works. They, too, asked questions about why war exists, why some people become more powerful than others, and why some are rich but others are poor. However, they often based their answers on superstition, myth, even the positions of the stars. They did not *test* their assumptions.

Science, in contrast, requires theories that can be tested by research. Measured by this standard, sociology emerged about the middle of the 1800s, when social observers began to use scientific methods to test their ideas. Three main events set the stage for the challenge to tradition and the emergence of sociology.

The first was the social upheaval of the Industrial Revolution. As agriculture gave way to factory production, masses of people moved to cities in search of work. The city's greeting was harsh: miserable pay, long hours, and dangerous work. To help their family survive, even children worked in these miserable conditions, some of them chained to machines to keep them from running away. With their ties to the land broken and their world turned upside down, no longer could people count on tradition to provide the answers to the difficult questions of life.

Upsetting the entire social order, the French Revolution removed the past as a sure guide to the present. This stimulated Auguste Comte to analyze how societies change. Shown here is a battle at the Hotel de Ville in Paris in 1830.

scientific method the use of objective, systematic observations to test theories

The second was the social upheaval of political revolution. The American and French revolutions swept away the existing social orders—and with them the answers they had provided. Before this period, tradition had ruled. The reply to questions of "why" was "We do this because it has always been done this way." A new social order challenges traditional answers, stimulates original thinking, and brings new ideas. The ideas that emerged during this period challenged tradition even further. Especially powerful was the new idea that each person possesses inalienable rights. This idea caught fire to such an extent that people were willing to die for it, forcing many traditional Western monarchies to give way to more democratic forms of government.

The third was the imperialism (empire building) of the time. The Europeans had conquered so many countries that their new colonies stretched across the world, from Asia and Africa to North and South America. This exposed them to radically different ways of life, and they began to ask why cultures differ.

The industrial revolution, political revolution, and imperialism, then, led to a questioning of traditional answers. At this same time, **the scientific method**—using objective, systematic observations to test theories—was being tried in chemistry and physics. This uncovered many secrets that had been concealed in nature. With traditional answers failing, the next step was to apply the scientific method to questions about social life. The result was the birth of sociology.

Let's take a quick overview of some of the main people in this development.

Down-to-Earth Sociology

Testing Your Common Sense—Answers to the Sociology Quiz

1. **False.** More students were shot to death at U.S. schools in the early 1990s than now (National School Safety Center 2013). See page 508.
2. **False.** Over the years, the wage gap has narrowed, but only slightly. On average, full-time working women earn about 72 percent of what full-time working men earn. This low figure is actually an improvement over earlier years. See Figures 11.7 and 11.8 on pages 311–312.
3. **False.** Today's parents actually spend more time with their children (Bianchi 2010). To see how this could be, see Figure 16.2 on page 457.
4. **False.** The crime rate outside fast-food restaurants is considerably higher. The likely reason is that topless bars hire private security and parking lot attendants (Linz et al. 2004).
5. **False.** Sociologists compared the psychological profiles of prisoners convicted of rape and prisoners convicted of other crimes. Their profiles were similar. Like robbery, rape is learned behavior. See pages 141–142.
6. **False.** Extensive testing of Islamic terrorists shows that they actually tend to score more "normal" on psychological tests than most "normal" people do. As a group, they are in better mental health than the rest of the population (Sageman 2008b:64). See page 444.
7. **False.** Most people on welfare are children, young mothers with few skills, or are elderly, sick, mentally challenged, or physically handicapped. Less than 2 percent fit the stereotype of an able-bodied man. See page 278.
8. **False.** Women make considerably more eye contact (Henley et al. 1985).
9. **False.** Until recently, the divorce rate of couples who cohabited before marriage was higher than those who did not cohabit. Now the divorce rate seems to be about the same (Manning and Cohen 2011). Neither divorce rate indicates that the couples who previously cohabited are more satisfied with their marriages.

Auguste Comte and Positivism

Auguste Comte (1798–1857) suggested that we apply the scientific method to the social world, a process known as **positivism**. With the bloody upheavals of the French Revolution fresh in his mind—and he knew that the crowds had cheered at the public execution of the king and queen of France—Comte started to wonder what holds society together. He asked why we have social order instead of anarchy or chaos. And when society becomes set on a particular course, what causes it to change?

Auguste Comte (1798–1857), who is credited as the founder of sociology, began to analyze the bases of the social order. Although he stressed that the scientific method should be applied to the study of society, he did not apply it himself.

These were pressing questions, and Comte decided that the scientific method held the key to answering them. Just as the scientific method had revealed the law of gravity, so, too, it would uncover the laws that underlie society. Comte called this new science **sociology**—"the study of society" (from the Greek *logos*, "study of," and the Latin *socius*, "companion," or "being with others"). The purpose of this new science, he said, would not only be to discover social principles but also to apply them to social reform. Comte developed a grandiose view: Sociologists would reform society, making it a better place to live.

Applying the scientific method to social life meant something quite different to Comte than it does to sociologists today. To Comte, it meant a kind of "armchair philosophy"—drawing conclusions from informal observations of social life. Comte did not do what we today call research, and his conclusions have been abandoned. But because he proposed that we observe and classify human activities to uncover society's fundamental laws and coined the term *sociology* to describe this process, Comte often is credited with being the founder of sociology.

Herbert Spencer and Social Darwinism

Herbert Spencer (1820–1903), who grew up in England, is sometimes called the second founder of sociology. Spencer disagreed sharply with Comte. He said that sociologists should *not* guide social reform. If they did, he said, it would interfere with a natural process that improves societies. Societies are evolving from a lower form ("barbarian") to higher ("civilized") forms. As generations pass, a society's most capable and intelligent members ("the fittest") survive, while the less capable die out. These fittest members produce a more advanced society—unless misguided do-gooders get in the way and help the less fit (the lower classes) survive.

Herbert Spencer (1820–1903), sometimes called the second founder of sociology, coined the term "survival of the fittest." Spencer thought that helping the poor was wrong, that this merely helped the "less fit" survive.

Spencer called this principle *the survival of the fittest.* Although Spencer coined this phrase, it usually is credited to his contemporary, Charles Darwin. Where Spencer proposed that societies evolve over time as the fittest people adapt to their environment, Darwin applied this idea to organisms. Because Darwin is better known, Spencer's idea is called *social Darwinism.* History is fickle, and if fame had gone the other way, we might be speaking of "biological Spencerism."

Spencer's idea that it was wrong to help the poor offended many. Some wealthy businessmen of the time, however, liked the concept of the survival of the fittest: They saw themselves as "the fittest"—and therefore superior. I'm sure that Spencer's views also helped some of them avoid feeling guilty for living like royalty while people around them went hungry.

Like Comte, Spencer did armchair philosophy instead of conducting scientific research. His ideas about society became popular, and he was sought after as a speaker in both England and the United States. Eventually, social Darwinism was discredited, and few today remember Spencer.

The next sociologist, in contrast, has a name that is recognized around the world.

positivism the application of the scientific approach to the social world

sociology the scientific study of society and human behavior

class conflict Marx's term for the struggle between capitalists and workers

bourgeoisie Marx's term for capitalists, those who own the means of production

proletariat Marx's term for the exploited class, the mass of workers who do not own the means of production

social integration the degree to which members of a group or a society feel united by shared values and other social bonds; also known as social cohesion

Karl Marx and Class Conflict

Karl Marx (1818–1883) not only influenced sociology but also left his mark on world history. Marx's influence has been so great that even the *Wall Street Journal*, that staunch advocate of capitalism, has called him one of the three greatest modern thinkers (the other two being Sigmund Freud and Albert Einstein).

Like Comte, Marx thought that people should try to change society. His proposal for change was radical: revolution. This got him thrown out of Germany, and he settled in England. Marx believed that the engine of human history is **class conflict**. Society is made up of two social classes, he said, and they are natural enemies: the **bourgeoisie** (boo-shwa-ZEE) (the *capitalists*, those who own the means of production—the money, land, factories, and machines) and the **proletariat** (the exploited workers, who do not own the means of production). Eventually, the workers will unite and break their chains of bondage. The workers' revolution will be bloody, but it will usher in a classless society, one free of exploitation. People will work according to their abilities and receive goods and services according to their needs (Marx and Engels 1848/1967).

Karl Marx (1818–1883) believed that the roots of human misery lay in class conflict, the exploitation of workers by those who own the means of production. Social change, in the form of the workers overthrowing the capitalists was inevitable from Marx's perspective. Although Marx did not consider himself a sociologist, his ideas have influenced many sociologists, particularly conflict theorists.

Marxism is not the same as communism. Although Marx proposed revolution as the way for workers to gain control of society, he did not develop the political system called *communism*. This is a later application of his ideas. Marx himself felt disgusted when he heard debates about his insights into social life. After listening to some of the positions attributed to him, he shook his head and said, "I am not a Marxist" (Dobriner 1969:222; Gitlin 1997:89).

Unlike Comte and Spencer, Marx did not think of himself as a sociologist—and with his reputation for communism and revolution, many sociologists wish that no one else did either. Marx spent years studying in the library of the British Museum in London, where he wrote widely on history, philosophy, economics, and political science. Because of his insights into the relationship between the social classes, Marx is generally recognized as a significant early sociologist. He introduced *conflict theory*, one of today's major perspectives in sociology. Later, we will examine this perspective in detail.

Emile Durkheim and Social Integration

Until the time of Emile Durkheim (1858–1917), sociology was viewed as part of history and economics. Durkheim, who grew up in France, wanted to change this, and his major professional goal was to get sociology recognized as a separate academic discipline (Coser 1977). He achieved this goal in 1887 when the University of Bordeaux awarded him the world's first academic appointment in sociology.

Durkheim's second goal was to show how social forces affect people's behavior. To accomplish this, he conducted rigorous research. Comparing the suicide rates of several European countries, Durkheim (1897/1966) found that each country has a different suicide rate—and that these rates remain about the same year after year. He also found that different groups within a country have different suicide rates and that these, too, remain stable from year to year. Males are more likely than females to kill themselves, Protestants more likely than Catholics or Jews, and the unmarried more likely than the married. From these observations, Durkheim concluded that suicide is not what it appears—simply a matter of individuals here and there deciding to take their lives for personal reasons. Instead, *social factors underlie suicide*, which is why a group's rate remains fairly constant year after year.

The French sociologist Emile Durkheim (1858–1917) contributed many important concepts to sociology. His comparison of the suicide rates of several countries revealed an underlying social factor: People are more likely to commit suicide if their ties to others in their communities are weak. Durkheim's identification of the key role of social integration in social life remains central to sociology today.

In his search for the key social factors in suicide, Durkheim identified **social integration**, the degree to which people are tied to their social groups: He found that people who have weaker social ties are more likely to commit suicide. This, he said, explains why Protestants, males, and the unmarried have higher suicide rates. This is how it works: Protestantism encourages greater freedom of thought and action; males are more independent than females; and the unmarried lack the ties and responsibilities that come with marriage. In other words, members of these groups have fewer of the social bonds that keep people from committing suicide. In Durkheim's term, they have less social integration.

Although strong social ties help protect people from suicide, Durkheim noted that in some instances, strong bonds encourage suicide. An example is people who, torn apart by grief, kill themselves after the death of a spouse. Their own feelings are so integrated with those of their spouses that they prefer death rather than life without the one who gave it meaning.

Durkheim believed that modern societies produce feelings of isolation, much of which comes from the division of labor. In contrast, members of traditional societies, who work alongside family and neighbors and participate in similar activities, experience a high degree of social integration. The photo below shows nomads in Mongolia as they shear cashmere off their goats.

Despite the many years that have passed since Durkheim did his research, the principle he uncovered still applies: People who are less socially integrated have higher rates of suicide. Even today, more than a century later, those same groups that Durkheim identified—Protestants, males, and the unmarried—are more likely to kill themselves.

Read on **MySocLab**
Document: Emile Durkheim, The Division of Labor

It is important for you to understand the principle that was central in Durkheim's research: *Human behavior cannot be understood only in terms of the individual; we must always examine the social forces that affect people's lives.* Suicide, for example, appears to be such an intensely individual act that psychologists should study it, not sociologists. As Durkheim stressed, however, if we look at human behavior only in reference to the individual, we miss its *social* basis.

Applying Durkheim. Did you know that 29,000 whites and 2,000 African Americans will commit suicide this year? Of course not. And you probably are wondering if anyone can know something like this before it happens. Sociologists can. How? Sociologists look at **patterns of behavior**, recurring characteristics or events.

The patterns of suicide let us be even more specific. Look at Figure 1.1 on the next page. There you can see the methods by which African Americans and whites commit suicide. These patterns are so consistent that we can predict with high certainty that of the 29,000 whites, about 15,500 will use guns to kill themselves, and that of the 2,000 African Americans, 60 to 70 will jump to their deaths.

These patterns—both the numbers and the way people take their lives—recur year after year. This indicates something far beyond the individuals who kill themselves. They reflect conditions in society, such as the popularity and accessibility of guns. They also reflect conditions that we don't understand. I am hoping that one day, this textbook will pique a student's interest enough to investigate these patterns.

Max Weber and the Protestant Ethic

Max Weber (Mahx VAY-ber) (1864–1920), a German sociologist and a contemporary of Durkheim, also held professorships in the new academic discipline of sociology. Like Durkheim and Marx, Weber is one of the most influential of all sociologists, and you will

patterns of behavior recurring behaviors or events

value free the view that a sociologist's personal values or beliefs should not influence social research

values the standards by which people define what is desirable or undesirable, good or bad, beautiful or ugly

objectivity value neutrality in research

FIGURE 1.1 How Americans Commit Suicide

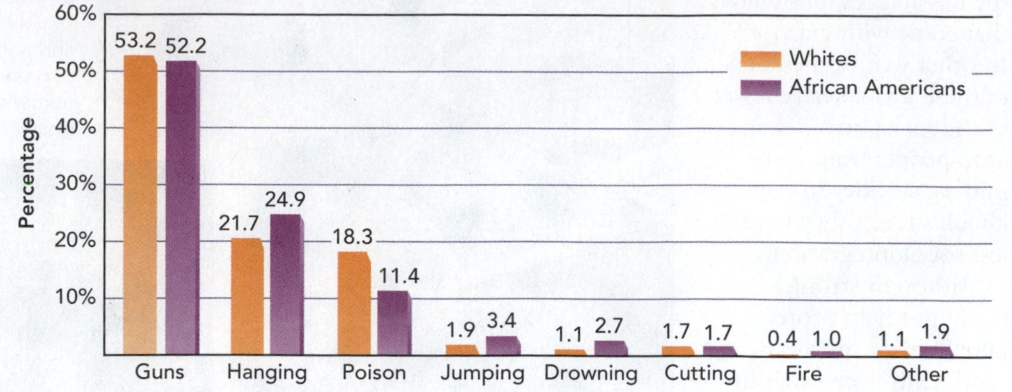

Note: These totals are the mean of years 2001–2010. ("Mean" is explained in Table 5.2 on page 129.)

Source: By the author. Based on Centers for Disease Control and Prevention 2012 and earlier years.

Max Weber (1864–1920) was another early sociologist who left a profound impression on sociology. He used cross-cultural and historical materials to trace the causes of social change and to determine how social groups affect people's orientations to life.

come across his writings and theories in later chapters. For now, let's consider an issue Weber raised that remains controversial today.

Religion and the Origin of Capitalism. Weber disagreed with Marx's claim that economics is the central force in social change. That role, he said, belongs to religion. Weber (1904/1958) theorized that the Roman Catholic belief system encouraged followers to hold on to their traditional ways of life, while the Protestant belief system encouraged its members to embrace change. Roman Catholics were taught that because they were Church members, they were on the road to heaven, but Protestants, those of the Calvinist tradition, were told that they wouldn't know if they were saved until Judgment Day. Uncomfortable with this, the Calvinists began to look for a "sign" that they were in God's will. They found this "sign" in financial success, which they took as a blessing that indicated that God was on their side. To bring about this "sign" and receive spiritual comfort, they began to live frugal lives, saving their money and investing it in order to make even more. This, said Weber, brought about the birth of capitalism.

Weber called this self-denying approach to life the *Protestant ethic*. He termed the desire to invest capital in order to make more money the *spirit of capitalism*. To test his theory, Weber compared the extent of capitalism in Roman Catholic and Protestant countries. In line with his theory, he found that capitalism was more likely to flourish in Protestant countries. Weber's conclusion that religion was the key factor in the rise of capitalism was controversial when he made it, and it continues to be debated today (Kalberg 2011). We'll explore these ideas in more detail in Chapter 7.

Read on **MySocLab**
Document: Max Weber, Asceticism and the Spirit of Capitalism

1.4 Summarize the opposing arguments in the debate about values in sociological research.

Values in Sociological Research

Weber raised another issue that remains controversial among sociologists. He said that sociology should be **value free**. By this, he meant that a sociologist's **values**—beliefs about what is good or desirable in life and the way the world ought to be—should not affect his or her research. Weber wanted **objectivity**, value neutrality, to be the hallmark of social research. If values influence research, he said, sociological findings will be biased.

That bias has no place in research is not a matter of debate. All sociologists agree that no one should distort data to make them fit preconceived ideas or personal values. It is equally clear, however, that because we sociologists—like everyone else—are members of a particular society at a given point in history, we, too, are infused with values of all sorts. Our values do play a role in our research. For example, values are part of the reason that one sociologist chooses to do research on how poverty affects life chances while another turns a sociological eye on violence against women.

Because values can lead to unintended distortions in research, sociologists stress the need of **replication**, repeating a study in order to compare the new results with the original findings. If an individual's values have distorted research findings, replication by other sociologists should uncover the bias and correct it.

Despite this consensus, however, values remain a hotly debated topic in sociology (Burawoy 2007; Simonds 2013). As summarized in Figure 1.2, the disagreement centers on the proper purposes and uses of sociology. Regarding its *purpose*, some sociologists take the position that their goal should be simply to advance understanding of social life. Sociologists should gather data on any topic that interests them and then use the best theory available to interpret their findings. Others are convinced that sociologists have the moral responsibility of investigating the social arrangements that harm people—the causes of poverty, crime, racism, war, and other forms of human exploitation.

There is also disagreement over the *uses* of sociology. Those who say that sociology's purpose is to understand human behavior take the position that the knowledge gained by social research belongs to both the scientific community and the world. It can be used by anyone for any purpose. In contrast, those who say that sociologists should focus on harmful social conditions take the position that the purpose of their research should be to alleviate human suffering and improve society. Some also say that sociologists should spearhead social reform.

FIGURE 1.2 The Debate over Values in Sociological Research

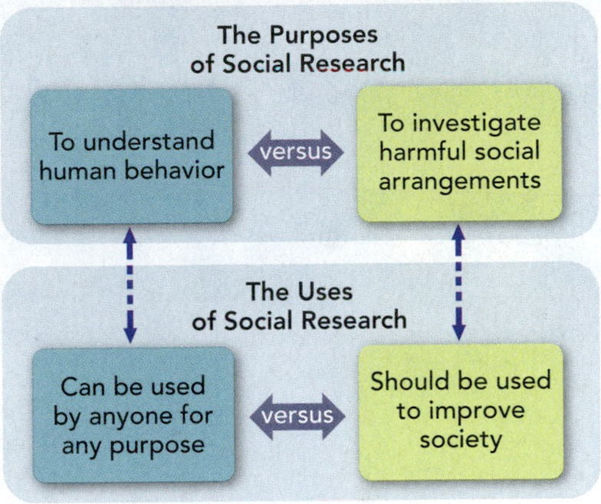
The Purposes of Social Research
To understand human behavior
versus
To investigate harmful social arrangements
The Uses of Social Research
Can be used by anyone for any purpose
versus
Should be used to improve society

Source: By the author.

Although few sociologists take such one-sided views and this debate is more complicated than the argument summarized here, this sketch does identify its major issues. Here is how sociologist John Galliher (1991) expressed today's majority position:

> *Some argue that social scientists, unlike politicians and religious leaders, should merely attempt to describe and explain the events of the world but should never make value judgments based on those observations. Yet a value-free and nonjudgmental social science has no place in a world that has experienced the Holocaust, in a world having had slavery, in a world with the ever-present threat of rape and other sexual assault, in a world with frequent, unpunished crimes in high places, including the production of products known by their manufacturers to cause death and injury as has been true of asbestos products and continues to be true of the cigarette industry, and in a world dying from environmental pollution by these same large multinational corporations.*

Verstehen and Social Facts

1.5 State what *Verstehen* is and why it is valuable.

Weber and *Verstehen*

Max Weber also stressed that to understand human behavior, we should use ***Verstehen*** (vare-shtay-in) (a German word meaning "to understand"). Perhaps a better translation of this term is "to grasp by insight." By emphasizing *Verstehen*, Weber meant that the best interpreter of human behavior is someone who "has been there," someone who can understand the feelings and motivations of the people being studied. In short, we must pay attention to what are called **subjective meanings**—how people interpret their situation in life, how they view what they are doing and what is happening to them.

To better understand this term, let's return to the homeless in our opening vignette. As in the photo on the next page, why were the men so silent? Why were they so unlike the noisy, sometimes boisterous college students who swarm dorms and cafeterias?

replication the repetition of a study in order to test its findings

Verstehen a German word used by Weber that is perhaps best understood as "to have insight into someone's situation"

subjective meanings the meanings that people give their own behavior

Perhaps from this photo taken in Athens, Greece, you can see why silence is common in homeless shelters. An optimistic view of life and exciting things to talk about are not part of the homeless.

Verstehen can help explain this. When I interviewed men in the shelters (and, in other settings, homeless women), they revealed their despair. Because you know—at least on some level—what the human emotion of despair is, you can do *Verstehen*; that is, you can apply your knowledge of despair to understand their situation. You know that people in despair feel a sense of hopelessness. The future looks bleak, hardly worth plodding toward. Consequently, why is it worth talking about? Who wants to hear another hard-luck story?

By applying *Verstehen*—your understanding of what it means to be human and to face some situation in life—you gain insight into other people's behavior. In this case, you can understand these men's silence, their lack of communication in the homeless shelter.

Durkheim and Social Facts

In contrast to Weber's emphasis on *Verstehen* and subjective meanings, Durkheim stressed what he called **social facts**. By this term, he meant a group's recurring patterns of behavior. Examples of social facts in the United States include June being the most popular month for weddings and suicide rates being higher among the elderly. You probably knew both of these social facts, but did you know this one? More births occur on Tuesdays than on any other day of the week (Martin et al. 2011:Table 1-3).

Durkheim said that we must use social facts to interpret social facts. In other words, each pattern reflects some condition of society. People all over the country don't just coincidentally decide to do similar things, whether that is to get married or to commit suicide. If this were the case, in some years, middle-aged people would be the most likely to kill themselves, in other years, young people, and so on. *Patterns that hold true year after year indicate that as thousands and even millions of people make their individual decisions, they are responding to conditions in their society.* It is the job of the sociologist, then, to uncover social facts and to explain them through other social facts. To see how this works, let's look at how the social facts I mentioned—weddings, suicide, and births—are explained by other social facts.

How Social Facts and *Verstehen* Fit Together

Social facts and *Verstehen* go hand in hand. As a member of U.S. society, you know how June weddings are related to the end of the school year and how this month, now locked in tradition, common sentiment, and advertising, carries its own momentum. As for suicide among the elderly (see Chapter 13), you probably already have a sense of the greater despair that many older Americans feel.

But do you know why more Americans are born on Tuesday than on any other day of the week? You would expect Tuesday to be no more common than any other day, and that is how it used to be. But no longer (Martin et al. 2011). To understand this change, we need to combine social facts and *Verstehen*. Four social facts are relevant: First, technology has made the hospital a dominating force in the U.S. medical system. Second, medical technology has made births by cesarean section safer. Third, as discussed in Chapter 19 (page 552), doctors have replaced midwives in the delivery of babies. Fourth, medicine in the United States is a business, with profit a major goal. These four social facts have coalesced to make an operation that used to be a last resort for emergencies now so routine that one-third (33 percent) of all U.S. babies are now delivered in this manner (*Statistical Abstract* 2013:Table 90).

If we add *Verstehen* to these social facts, we gain insight that goes far beyond the cold statistics. Let's try it. You know that most American mothers-to-be prefer to give birth in a hospital. You can also understand how influential physicians can be at such an emotionally charged and vulnerable moment and how alternatives can appear so slim. Finally, you can also understand that physicians would schedule births for a time that is most convenient for them, which happens to be Tuesdays. (Mondays are filled with

social facts Durkheim's term for a group's patterns of behavior appointments, as well as sniffles and fevers from the weekend, and a Tuesday delivery provides enough time to take care of the new mother and child to best assure free weekends.) Combine *Verstehen* with social facts and you have the answer.

Sociology in North America

1.6 Trace the development of sociology in North America and explain the tension between objective analysis and social reform.

Transplanted to U.S. soil, sociology first took root at the University of Kansas in 1890, at the University of Chicago in 1892, and at Atlanta University (then an all-black school) in 1897. From there, sociology spread rapidly throughout North America, jumping from 4 instructors offering courses in 1880 to 225 instructors and 59 sociology departments just twenty years later (Lengermann and Niebrugge 2007).

Some universities were slow to adopt sociology. Not until 1922 did McGill University establish Canada's first department of sociology. Harvard University did not open its sociology department until 1930, and it took until 1946 for the University of California at Berkeley to do so.

The University of Chicago initially dominated North American sociology. Albion Small (1854–1926), who founded this department, also launched *The American Journal of Sociology* and was its editor from 1895 to 1925. Members of this sociology faculty whose ideas continue to influence today's sociologists include Robert Park (1864–1944), Ernest Burgess (1886–1966), and George Herbert Mead (1863–1931). Mead developed the symbolic interactionist perspective, which we will examine later.

Sexism at the Time: Women in Early Sociology

As you may have noticed, all the sociologists we have discussed are men. In the 1800s, sex roles were rigid, with women assigned the roles of wife and mother. In the classic German phrase, women were expected to devote themselves to the four K's: *Kirche, Küche, Kinder, und Kleider* (the four C's in English: church, cooking, children, and clothes). Trying to break out of this mold meant risking severe disapproval.

Few people, male or female, attained any education beyond basic reading and writing and a little math. Higher education, for the rare few who received it, was reserved primarily for men. Of the handful of women who did pursue higher education, some became prominent in early sociology. Marion Talbot, for example, was an associate editor of the *American Journal of Sociology* for thirty years, from its founding in 1895 to 1925. The influence of some early female sociologists went far beyond sociology. Grace Abbott became chief of the U.S. government's Children's Bureau, and Frances Perkins was the first woman to hold a cabinet position, serving twelve years as Secretary of Labor under President Franklin Roosevelt. The photo wheel on the next page portrays some of these early sociologists.

Most early female sociologists viewed sociology as a path to social reform. They focused on ways to improve society, such as how to stop lynching, integrate immigrants into society, and improve the conditions of workers. As sociology developed in North America, a debate arose about the proper purpose of sociology. Should it be to reform society or to do objective research on society? Those who held the university positions won the debate. They feared that advocating for social causes would jeopardize the reputation of sociology—and their own university positions. It was these men who wrote the history of sociology. Distancing themselves from the social reformers, they ignored the early female sociologists (Lengermann and Niebrugge 2007). Now that women have regained their voice in sociology—and have begun to rewrite its history—early female sociologists are again, as here, being acknowledged.

Harriet Martineau (1802–1876) provides an excellent example of how the contributions of early female sociologists were ignored. Although Martineau was from England, she is included here because she did extensive analyses of U.S. social customs.

Read on **MySocLab**
Document: Harriet Martineau, Society in America

FIGURE 1.3 The Forgotten Sociologists

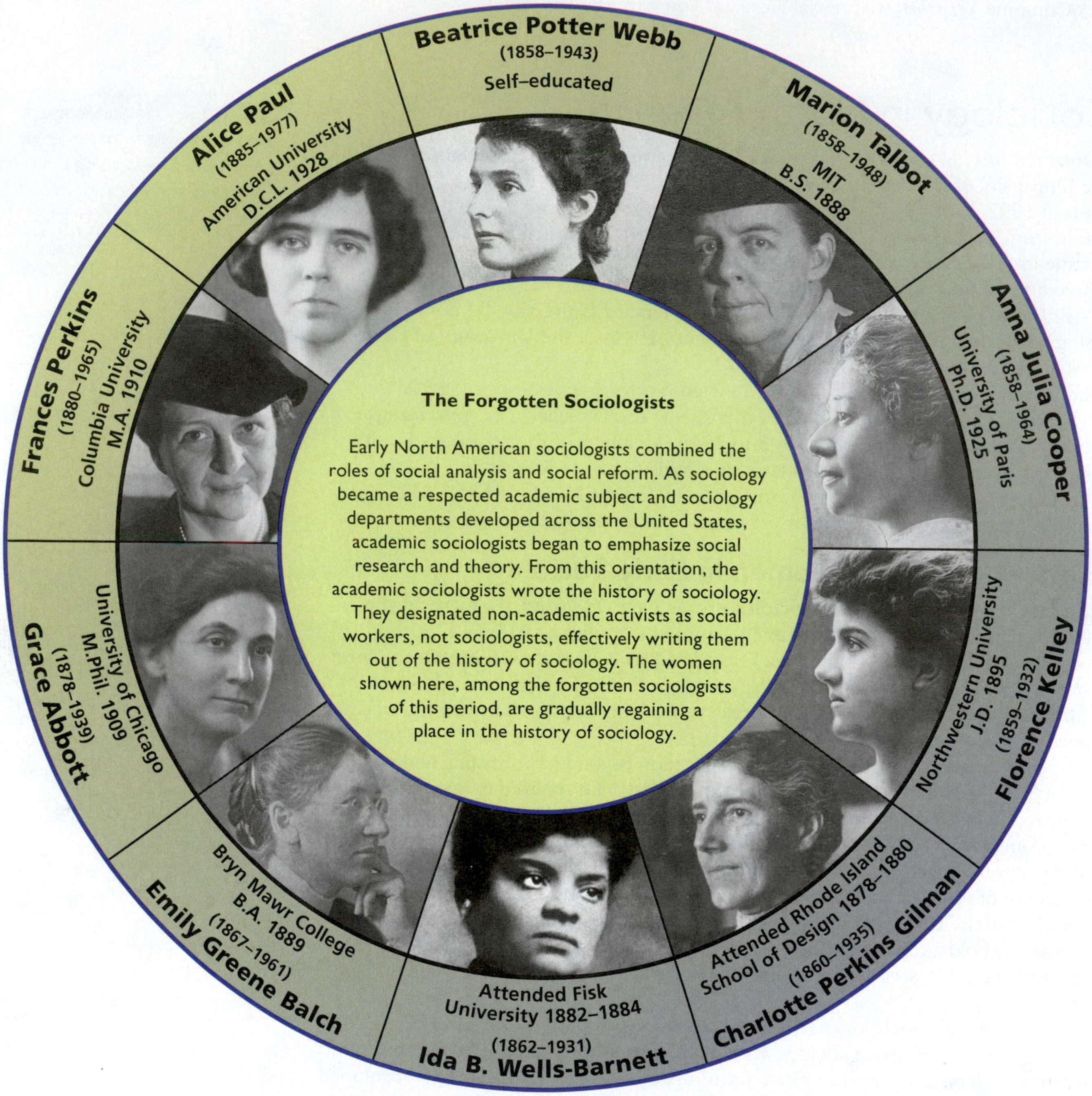

Beatrice Potter Webb
(1858–1943)
Self-educated
Marion Talbot
(1858–1948)
MIT
B.S. 1888
Anna Julia Cooper
(1858–1964)
University of Paris
Ph.D. 1925
Florence Kelley
(1859–1932)
J.D. 1895
Northwestern University
Charlotte Perkins Gilman
(1860–1935)
Attended Rhode Island
School of Design 1878–1880
Ida B. Wells-Barnett
(1862–1931)
Attended Fisk
University 1882–1884
Emily Greene Balch
(1867–1961)
B.A. 1889
Bryn Mawr College
Grace Abbott
(1878–1939)
M.Phil. 1909
University of Chicago
Frances Perkins
(1880–1965)
Columbia University
M.A. 1910
Alice Paul
(1885–1977)
American University
D.C.L. 1928
The Forgotten Sociologists
Early North American sociologists combined the roles of social analysis and social reform. As sociology became a respected academic subject and sociology departments developed across the United States, academic sociologists began to emphasize social research and theory. From this orientation, the academic sociologists wrote the history of sociology. They designated non-academic activists as social workers, not sociologists, effectively writing them out of the history of sociology. The women shown here, among the forgotten sociologists of this period, are gradually regaining a place in the history of sociology.

Source: Photo wheel copyright 2014 © James M. Henslin.

Sexism was so pervasive that when Martineau first began to analyze social life, she would hide her writing beneath her sewing when visitors arrived; writing was "masculine" and sewing "feminine" (Gilman 1911/1971:88). Despite her extensive and acclaimed research on social life in both Great Britain and the United States, until recently Martineau was known primarily for translating Comte's ideas into English. The Down-to-Earth Sociology box on the next page features Martineau's research on the United States.

Down-to-Earth **Sociology**

Harriet Martineau and U.S. Customs: Listening to an Early Feminist

The breadth of Martineau's research is striking. In 1834, two or three decades before Durkheim and Weber were born, Martineau began a two-year study of U.S. customs. Traveling by foot, horseback, stagecoach, and steamboat, she visited twenty of the then twenty-four states. She observed and interviewed Americans, from those who lived in poverty to Andrew Jackson, then the President of the United States, with whom she had dinner (Lengermann and Niebrugge 2007). She spoke with both slaveholders and abolitionists. She also visited prisons and attended sessions of the U.S. Supreme Court. To summarize her research, in 1837 she published Society in America, *from which these excerpts are taken.*

Concerning women not being allowed to vote

One of the fundamental principles announced in the Declaration of Independence is that governments derive their just powers from the consent of the governed. How can the political condition of women be reconciled with this?

Governments in the United States have power to tax women who hold property . . . to fine, imprison, and execute them for certain offences. Whence do these governments derive their powers? They are not "just," as they are not derived from the consent of the women thus governed. . . .

The democratic principle condemns all this as wrong; and requires the equal political representation of all rational beings. Children, idiots, and criminals . . . are the only fair exceptions. . . .

Concerning the education of women

The intellect of woman is confined by an unjustifiable restriction. . . . As women have none of the objects in life for which an enlarged education is considered requisite, the education is not given. . . . [S]ome things [are] taught which . . . serve to fill up time . . . to improve conversation, and to make women something like companions to their husbands, and able to teach their children somewhat. . . . There is rarely or never a . . . promotion of clear intellectual activity. . . . [A]s long as women are excluded from the objects for which men are trained . . . intellectual activity is dangerous: or, as the phrase is, unfit. Accordingly marriage is the only object left open to woman.

Interested in social reform, Harriet Martineau (1802–1876) turned to sociology, where she discovered the writing of Comte. She became an advocate for the abolition of slavery, traveled widely, and wrote extensive analyses of social life.

Concerning sex and slavery, and relations between white women and men in the South

[White American women] are all married young . . . and there is ever present an unfortunate servile class of their own sex [female slaves] to serve the purposes of licentiousness [as sexual objects for white slaveholders]. . . . [When most] men carry secrets which their wives must be the last to know . . . there is an end to all wholesome confidence and sympathy, and woman sinks to be the ornament of her husband's house, the domestic manager of his establishment, instead of being his all-sufficient friend. . . . I have seen, with heart-sorrow, the kind politeness, the gallantry, so insufficient to the loving heart, with which the wives of the south are treated by their husbands. . . . I know the tone of conversation which is adopted towards women; different in its topics and its style from that which any man would dream of offering to any other man. I have heard the boast of chivalrous consideration in which women are held throughout their woman's paradise; and seen something of the anguish of crushed pride, of the conflict of bitter feelings with which such boasts have been listened to by those whose aspirations teach them the hollowness of the system. . . .

For Your Consideration

➔ How do you think relations between men and women have changed since Martineau did her research?

Racism at the Time: W. E. B. Du Bois

W(illiam) E(dward) B(urghardt) Du Bois (1868–1963) spent his lifetime studying relations between African Americans and whites. Like many early North American sociologists, Du Bois combined the role of academic sociologist with that of social reformer.

Not only was sexism assumed to be normal during this early period of sociology but so was racism. This made life difficult for African American professionals such as W. E. B. Du Bois (1868–1963). After earning a bachelor's degree from Fisk University, Du Bois became the first African American to earn a doctorate at Harvard. He then studied at the University of Berlin, where he attended lectures by Max Weber. After teaching Greek and Latin at Wilberforce University, Du Bois moved to Atlanta

University in 1897 to teach sociology and do research. He remained there for most of his career (Du Bois 1935/1992).

The Down-to-Earth Sociology box on the next page features Du Bois' description of race relations when he was in college.

It is difficult to grasp how racist society was at this time. As Du Bois passed a butcher shop in Georgia one day, he saw the fingers of a lynching victim displayed in the window (Aptheker 1990). When Du Bois went to national meetings of the American Sociological Society, restaurants and hotels would not allow him to eat or room with the white sociologists. How times have changed. Not only would today's sociologists boycott such establishments but also they would refuse to hold meetings in that state. At that time, however, racism, like sexism, prevailed throughout society, rendering it mostly invisible to white sociologists. Du Bois eventually became such an outspoken critic of racism that the U.S. State Department, fearing he would criticize the United States abroad, refused to issue him a passport (Du Bois 1968).

Each year between 1896 and 1914, Du Bois published a book on relations between African Americans and whites. Not content to collect and interpret objective data, Du Bois, along with Jane Addams and others from Hull-House (see the next section), was one of the founders of the National Association for the Advancement of Colored People (NAACP) (Deegan 1988). Continuing to battle racism both as a sociologist and as a journalist, Du Bois eventually embraced revolutionary Marxism. At age 93, dismayed that so little improvement had been made in race relations, he moved to Ghana, where he was buried (Stark 1989).

Until recently, Du Bois' work was neglected by sociologists. As a personal example, during my entire graduate program at Washington University, the faculty never mentioned him. Today, however, sociologists are rediscovering Du Bois, reading and discussing his research. Of his almost 2,000 writings, *The Philadelphia Negro* (1899/1967) stands out. In this analysis, Du Bois pointed out that some successful African Americans were breaking their ties with other African Americans and "passing as white." This, he said, weakened the African American community by depriving it of their influence.

Jane Addams: Sociologist and Social Reformer

Of the many early sociologists who combined the role of sociologist with that of social reformer, none was as successful as Jane Addams (1860–1935), who was a member of the American Sociological Society from its founding in 1905. Like Harriet Martineau, Addams, too, came from a background of wealth and privilege. She attended the Women's Medical College of Philadelphia but dropped out because of illness (Addams 1910/1981). On a trip to Europe, Addams saw the work being done to help London's poor. The memory wouldn't leave her, she said, and she decided to work for social justice.

Jane Addams (1860–1935) a recipient of the Nobel Prize for Peace, worked on behalf of poor immigrants. With Ellen G. Starr, she founded Hull-House, a center to help immigrants in Chicago. She was also a leader in women's rights (women's suffrage), as well as the peace movement of World War I.

In 1889, Addams co-founded Hull-House with Ellen Gates Starr. Located in Chicago's notorious slums, Hull-House was open to people who needed refuge—to immigrants, the sick, the aged, the poor. Sociologists from the nearby University of Chicago were frequent visitors at Hull-House. With her piercing insights into the exploitaton of workers and how rural immigrants adjusted to city life, Addams strove to bridge the gap between the powerful and the powerless. She co-founded the American Civil Liberties Union and campaigned for the eight-hour workday and for laws against child labor. She wrote books on poverty, democracy, and peace. Addams' writings and efforts at social reform were so outstanding that in 1931, she was a co-winner of the Nobel Prize for Peace. She and Emily Greene Balch are the only sociologists to have won this coveted award.

Down-to-Earth **Sociology**

W. E. B. Du Bois: The Souls of Black Folk

Du Bois wrote more like an accomplished novelist than a sociologist. The following excerpts are from pages 66–68 of *The Souls of Black Folk* (1903). In this book, Du Bois analyzes changes that occurred in the social and economic conditions of African Americans during the thirty years following the Civil War.

For two summers, while he was a student at Fisk, Du Bois taught in a segregated school in a little log cabin that he said was "way back in the hills" of rural Tennessee. These excerpts help us understand conditions at that time.

It was a hot morning late in July when the school opened. I trembled when I heard the patter of little feet down the dusty road, and saw the growing row of dark solemn faces and bright eager eyes facing me. . . . There they sat, nearly thirty of them, on the rough benches, their faces shading from a pale cream to deep brown, the little feet bare and swinging, the eyes full of expectation, with here and there a twinkle of mischief, and the hands grasping Webster's blue-black spelling-book. I loved my school, and the fine faith the children had in the wisdom of their teacher was truly marvelous. We read and spelled together, wrote a little, picked flowers, sang, and listened to stories of the world beyond the hill. . . .

On Friday nights I often went home with some of the children,—sometimes to Doc Burke's farm. He was a great, loud, thin Black, ever working, and trying to buy these seventy-five acres of hill and dale where he lived; but people said that he would surely fail and the "white folks would get it all." His wife was a magnificent Amazon, with saffron face and shiny hair, uncorseted and barefooted, and the children were strong and barefooted. They lived in a one-and-a-half-room cabin in the hollow of the farm near the spring. . . .

Often, to keep the peace, I must go where life was less lovely; for instance, 'Tildy's mother was incorrigibly dirty, Reuben's larder was limited seriously, and herds of untamed insects wandered over the Eddingses' beds. Best of all I loved to go to Josie's, and sit on the porch, eating peaches, while the mother bustled and talked: how Josie had bought the sewing-machine; how Josie worked at service in winter, but that four dollars a month was "mighty little" wages; how Josie longed to go away to school, but that it "looked like" they never could get far enough ahead to let her; how the crops failed and the well was yet unfinished; and, finally, how mean some of the white folks were.

In the 1800s, most people were poor, and formal education beyond the first several grades was a luxury. This photo depicts the conditions of the people Du Bois worked with.

For two summers I lived in this little world. . . . I have called my tiny community a world, and so its isolation made it; and yet there was among us but a half-awakened common consciousness, sprung from common joy and grief, at burial, birth, or wedding; from common hardship in poverty, poor land, and low wages, and, above all, from the sight of the Veil that hung between us and Opportunity. All this caused us to think some thoughts together; but these, when ripe for speech, were spoken in various languages. Those whose eyes twenty-five and more years had seen "the glory of the coming of the Lord," saw in every present hindrance or help a dark fatalism bound to bring all things right in His own good time. The mass of those to whom slavery was a dim recollection of childhood found the world a puzzling thing: it asked little of them, and they answered with little, and yet it ridiculed their offering. Such a paradox they could not understand, and therefore sank into listless indifference, or shiftlessness, or reckless bravado.*

*"The Veil" is shorthand for the Veil of Race, referring to how race colors all human relations. Du Bois' hope, as he put it, was that "sometime, somewhere, men will judge men by their souls and not by their skins" (p. 261).

Talcott Parsons and C. Wright Mills: Theory Versus Reform

Like Du Bois and Addams, many early North American sociologists saw society, or parts of it, as corrupt and in need of reform. During the 1920s and 1930s, for example, Robert Park and Ernest Burgess (1921) not only studied crime, drug addiction, juvenile delinquency, and prostitution but also offered suggestions for how to alleviate these social problems. But by the 1940s, the emphasis shifted from social reform to social theory. A major sociologist of this period, Talcott Parsons (1902–1979), developed abstract models of society that influenced a generation of sociologists. His models of how the parts of society work together harmoniously did nothing to stimulate social activism.

C. Wright Mills (1916–1962) was a controversial figure in sociology because of his analysis of the role of the power elite in U.S. society. Today, his analysis is taken for granted by many sociologists and members of the public.

Another sociologist, C. Wright Mills (1916–1962), deplored such theoretical abstractions. Trying to push the pendulum the other way, he urged sociologists to get back to social reform. In his writings, he warned that the nation faced an imminent threat to freedom—the coalescing of interests of a *power elite*, the top leaders of business, politics, and the military. Shortly after Mills' death came the turbulent late 1960s and the 1970s. This precedent-shaking era sparked interest in social activism, making Mills' ideas popular among a new generation of sociologists.

The Continuing Tension: Basic, Applied, and Public Sociology

Basic Sociology. As we have seen, two contradictory aims—analyzing society versus working toward its reform—have run through North American sociology since its founding. This tension is still with us. As we saw in Figure 1.2 on page 13, some sociologists see their proper role as doing **basic** (or **pure**) **sociology**, analyzing some aspect of society with no goal other than gaining knowledge. Others reply, "Knowledge for what?" They argue that gaining knowledge through research is not enough, that sociologists need to use their expertise to help reform society, especially to help bring justice and better conditions to the poor and oppressed.

Applied Sociology. As Figure 1.4 shows, one attempt to go beyond basic sociology is **applied sociology**, using sociology to solve problems. Applied sociology goes back to the roots of sociology: As you have seen, sociologists founded the NAACP. Today's applied sociologists lack the broad vision that the early sociologists had of reforming society, but their application of sociology is wide-ranging. Some work for business firms to solve problems in the workplace, while others investigate social problems such as pornography, rape, pollution, or the spread of AIDS. Sociology is even being applied to find ways to disrupt terrorist groups (Sageman 2008a) and to improve technology for the mentally ill (Kelly and Farahbakhsh 2013). To see some of the variety of work that applied sociologists do, look at the Down-to-Earth Sociology box on the next page.

Public Sociology. To encourage sociologists to apply sociology, the American Sociological Association (ASA) is promoting a middle ground between research and reform called **public sociology**. By this term, the ASA refers to harnessing the sociological perspective for the benefit of the public. Of special interest to the ASA is getting politicians and policy makers to apply the sociological understanding of how society works as they develop social policy (American Sociological Association 2004). Public sociology would incorporate both items 3 and 4 of Figure 1.4.

The lines between basic, applied, and public sociology are not always firm. In the Cultural Diversity box on page 22, you can see how basic sociology can morph into public sociology.

basic (or **pure**) **sociology** sociological research for the purpose of making discoveries about life in human groups, not for making changes in those groups

applied sociology the use of sociology to solve problems—from the micro level of classroom interaction and family relationships to the macro level of crime and pollution

public sociology applying sociology for the public good; especially the use of the sociological perspective (how things are related to one another) to guide politicians and policy makers

FIGURE 1.4 Comparing Basic and Applied Sociology

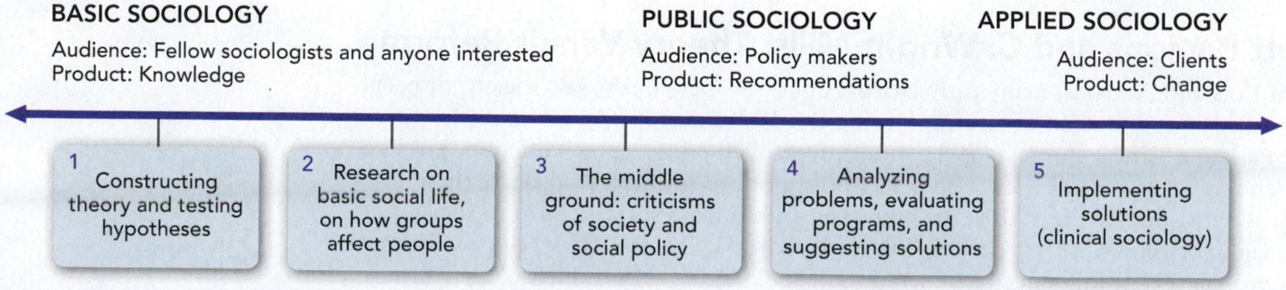

Source: By the author. Based on DeMartini 1982, plus events since then.

Down-to-Earth Sociology

Careers in Sociology: What Applied Sociologists Do

Most sociologists teach in colleges and universities, where they share sociological knowledge with students, as your instructor is doing with you in this course. Applied sociologists, in contrast, work in a wide variety of areas—from counseling children to studying how diseases are transmitted. To give you an idea of this variety, let's look over the shoulders of five applied sociologists.

Leslie Green, who does marketing research at Vanderveer Group in Philadelphia, Pennsylvania, earned her bachelor's degree in sociology at Shippensburg University. She helps to develop strategies to get doctors to prescribe particular drugs. She sets up the meetings, locates moderators for the discussion groups, and arranges payments to the physicians who participate in the research. "My training in sociology," she says, "helps me in 'people skills.' It helps me to understand the needs of different groups, and to interact with them."

How can Dora the Explorer be an example of applied sociology? The text explains the reason.

Stanley Capela, whose master's degree is from Fordham University, works as an applied sociologist at HeartShare Human Services in New York City. He evaluates how children's programs—such as ones that focus on housing, AIDS, group homes, and preschool education—actually work, compared with how they are supposed to work. He spots problems and suggests solutions. One of his assignments was to find out why it was taking so long to get children adopted, even though there was a long list of eager adoptive parents. Capela pinpointed how the paperwork got bogged down as it was routed through the system and suggested ways to improve the flow of paperwork.

Laurie Banks, who received her master's degree in sociology from Fordham University, analyzes statistics for the New York City Health Department. As she examined death certificates, she noticed that a Polish neighborhood had a high rate of stomach cancer. She alerted the Centers for Disease Control and Prevention, whose researchers conducted interviews in the neighborhood. CDC traced the cause of the cancer to eating large amounts of sausage. In another case, Banks compared birth certificates with school records. She found that lack of prenatal care and problems at birth—low birth weight and birth complications—were linked to low reading skills and behavior problems in school.

Daniel Knapp, who earned a doctorate from the University of Oregon, applied sociology by going to the city dump. Moved by the idea that urban wastes could be recycled and reused, he first tested this idea by scavenging in a small way—at the city dump in Berkeley, California. After starting a company called Urban Ore, Knapp (2005) did research on how to recycle urban waste and worked to change waste disposal laws. As a founder of the recycling movement in the United States, Knapp's application of sociology continues to influence us all.

Clara Rodriguez, who earned her doctorate at the University of Washington, also illustrates how wide-ranging applied sociology is. Rodriguez is the sociological consultant for *Dora the Explorer*. She advises on the social implications of what the viewers will see on this program. This ranges from advice about Dora as a role model for girls to what aspects of Latino culture to present and even to colors, music, and Spanish phrases (Havrilla 2010).

From just these few examples, you can catch a glimpse of the variety of work that applied sociologists do. Some work for corporations, others are employed by government and private agencies, and some run their own businesses. You can also see that you don't need a doctorate in order to work as an applied sociologist.

Social Reform Is Risky. As some sociologists have found, often to their displeasure, promoting social reform is risky. This is especially the case if they work with oppressed people to demand social change. What someone wants to "reform" is inevitably something that someone else wants to keep just the way it is. Those who resist change can be formidable opponents—and well connected politically. For their efforts, some sociologists have been fired. In a couple of cases, entire departments of sociology have been taken over by their university administrators for "taking sociology to the streets," siding with the poor and showing them how to use the law to improve their lives.

With roots that go back a century or more, this contemporary debate about the purpose and use of sociology is likely to continue for another generation. At this point, let's consider how theory fits into sociology.

Cultural Diversity in the United States

Unanticipated Public Sociology: Studying Job Discrimination

Basic sociology—research aimed at learning more about some behavior—can turn into public sociology. Here is what happened to Devah Pager (2003). When Pager was a graduate student at the University of Wisconsin in Madison, she did volunteer work at a homeless shelter. When some of the men told her how hard it was to find work if they had been in prison, she wondered if the men were exaggerating. Pager decided to find out what difference a prison record makes in getting a job. She sent pairs of college men to apply for 350 entry-level jobs in Milwaukee. One team was African American, and one was white. Pager prepared identical résumés for the teams, but with one difference: On each team, one of the men said he had served eighteen months in prison for possession of cocaine.

FIGURE 1.5 Call-Back Rates by Race–Ethnicity and Criminal Record

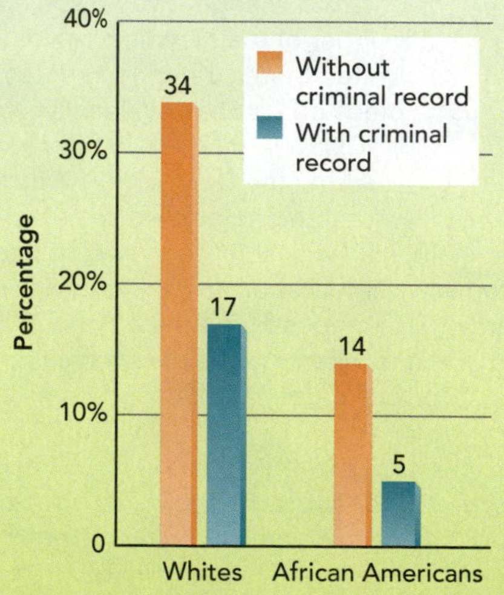

Source: Courtesy of Devah Pager.

Figure 1.5 shows the difference that the prison record made. Men without a prison record were two or three times more likely to be called back.

But Pager came up with another significant finding. Look at the difference that race–ethnicity made. White men with a prison record were more likely to be offered a job than African American men who had a clean record!

Sociological research often remains in obscure journals, read by only a few specialists. But Pager's findings got around, turning basic research into public sociology. Someone told President George W. Bush about the research, and he announced in his State of the Union speech that he wanted Congress to fund a $300 million program to provide mentoring and other support to help former prisoners get jobs (Kroeger 2004).

And it isn't just Wisconsin. When Pager repeated her research in New York City, she found similar results (Pager et al. 2009).

As you can see, sometimes only a thin line separates basic and public sociology.

For Your Consideration

➔ What findings would you expect if women had been included in this study?

1.7 Explain the basic ideas of symbolic interactionism, functional analysis, and conflict theory.

theory a general statement about how some parts of the world fit together and how they work; an explanation of how two or more facts are related to one another

Theoretical Perspectives in Sociology

Facts never interpret themselves. To make sense out of life, we use our common sense. That is, to understand our experiences (our "facts"), we place them into a framework of more-or-less related ideas. Sociologists do this, too, but they place their observations into a conceptual framework called a theory. A **theory** is a general statement about how some parts of the world fit together and how they work. It is an explanation of how two or more "facts" are related to one another.

Sociologists use three major theories: symbolic interactionism, functional analysis, and conflict theory. Each theory is like a lens through which we can view social life. Let's first examine the main elements of each theory and then apply each to the U.S. divorce rate to see why it is so high. As we do this, you will see how each theory, or perspective, provides a distinct interpretation of social life.

Watch on **MySocLab**
Video: George Ritzer: Importance of Sociological Theory

Symbolic Interactionism

The central idea of **symbolic interactionism** is that *symbols*—things to which we attach meaning—are the key to understanding how we view the world and communicate with one another. Two major sociologists who developed this perspective are George Herbert Mead (1863–1931) and Charles Horton Cooley (1864–1929). Let's look at the main elements of this theory.

George Herbert Mead (1863–1931) is one of the founders of symbolic interactionism, a major theoretical perspective in sociology. He taught at the University of Chicago, where his lectures were popular. Although he wrote little, after his death students compiled his lectures into an influential book, *Mind, Self, and Society.*

Symbols in Everyday Life. Without symbols, our social life would be no more sophisticated than that of animals. For example, without symbols, we would have no aunts or uncles, employers or teachers—or even brothers and sisters. I know that this sounds strange, but it is symbols that define our relationships. There would still be reproduction, of course, but no symbols to tell us how we are related to whom. We would not know to whom we owe respect and obligations, or from whom we can expect privileges—two elements that lie at the essence of human relationships.

I know it is vague to say that symbols tell you how you are related to others and how you should act toward them, so let's make this less abstract:

Read on **MySocLab**
Document: Herbert Blumer, The Nature of Symbolic Interactionism

> *Suppose that you have fallen head over heels in love. Finally, after what seems forever, it is the night before your wedding. As you are contemplating tomorrow's bliss, your mother comes to you in tears. Sobbing, she tells you that she had a child before she married your father, a child that she gave up for adoption. Breaking down, she says that she has just discovered that the person you are going to marry is this child.*

You can see how the symbol will change overnight—and your behavior, too! The symbols "boyfriend" and "brother"—or "girlfriend" and "sister"—are certainly different, and, as you know, each symbol requires rather different behavior.

Not only do relationships depend on symbols but so does society itself. Without symbols, we could not coordinate our actions with those of others. We could not make plans for a future day, time, and place. Unable to specify times, materials, sizes, or goals, we could not build bridges and highways. Without symbols, we would have no movies or musical instruments, no hospitals, no government, no religion. The class you are taking could not exist—nor could this book. On the positive side, there would be no war.

In Sum: Symbolic interactionists analyze how social life depends on the ways we define ourselves and others. They study face-to-face interaction, examining how people make sense out of life and their place in it.

Applying Symbolic Interactionism. Look at Figure 1.6 on the next page, which shows U.S. marriages and divorces over time. Let's see how symbolic interactionists would use changing symbols to explain this figure. For background, you should understand that marriage used to be a *lifelong commitment.* A hundred years ago (and less), getting divorced was viewed as immoral, a flagrant disregard for public opinion, and the abandonment of adult responsibilities. Let's see what changed.

The meaning of marriage: Historically in the West, marriage was based on obligation and duty. By the 1930s, young people were coming to view marriage in a different way, a change that was reported by sociologists of the time. In 1933, William Ogburn observed that people were placing more emphasis on the personality of their potential mates. Then in 1945, Ernest Burgess and Harvey Locke reported that people were expecting more affection, understanding, and compatibility from marriage. As feelings became more important in marriage, duty and obligation became less important. Eventually, marriage came to be viewed as an arrangement that was based mostly on feelings—on attraction and intimacy. Marriage then became an arrangement that could be broken when feelings changed.

symbolic interactionism a theoretical perspective in which society is viewed as composed of symbols that people use to establish meaning, develop their views of the world, and communicate with one another

FIGURE 1.6 U.S. Marriage, U.S. Divorce

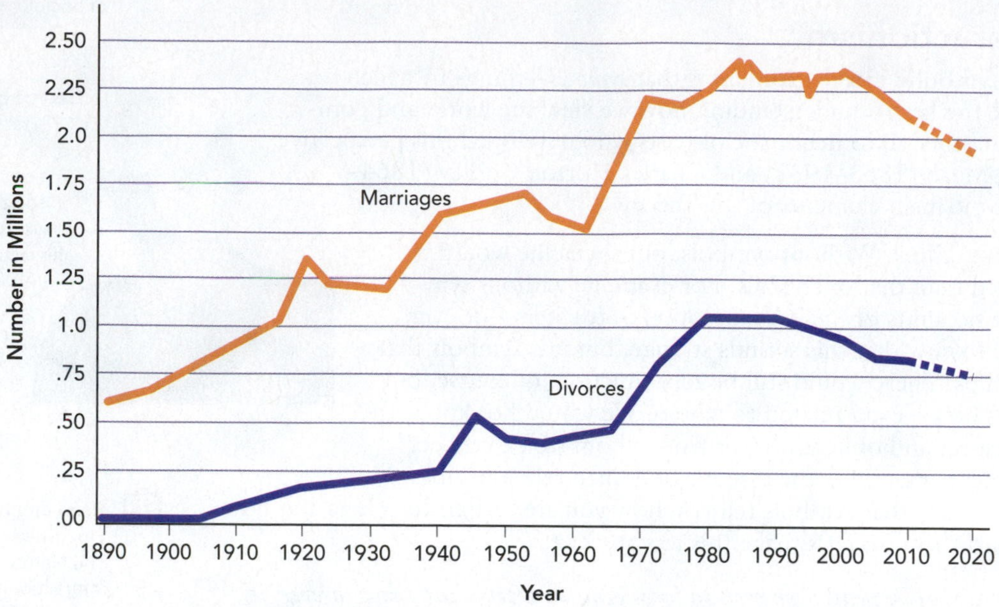

Source: By the author. Based on *Statistical Abstract of the United States* 1998:Table 92 and 2013:Tables 81, 134; earlier editions for earlier years. The broken lines indicate the author's estimates.

The meaning of divorce: As divorce became more common, its meaning also changed. Rather than being a symbol of failure, divorce came to indicate freedom and new beginnings. Removing the stigma from divorce shattered a strong barrier that had prevented husbands and wives from breaking up.

The meaning of parenthood: Parents used to have little responsibility for their children beyond providing food, clothing, shelter, and moral guidance. And they needed to do this for only a short time, because children began to contribute to the support of the family early in life. Among some people, parenthood is still like this. In Colombia, for example, children of the poor often are expected to support themselves by the age of 8 or 10. In industrial societies, however, we assume that children are vulnerable beings who must depend on their parents for financial and emotional support for many years—often until they are well into their 20s. In some cases, this is now being extended to the age of 30. The greater responsibilities that we assign to parenthood place heavier burdens on today's couples and, with them, more strain on marriage.

The meaning of love: And we can't overlook the love symbol. As surprising as it may sound, to have love as the main reason for marriage weakens marriage. In some depth of our being, we expect "true love" to deliver constant emotional highs. This expectation sets people up for crushed hopes, as dissatisfactions in marriage are inevitable. When they come, spouses tend to blame one another for failing to deliver the illusive satisfaction.

In Sum: Symbolic interactionists look at how changing ideas (or symbols) of marriage, divorce, parenthood, and love put pressure on married couples. No single change is *the* cause of our divorce rate. Taken together, however, these changes provide a strong push toward marriages breaking up.

functional analysis a theoretical framework in which society is viewed as composed of various parts, each with a function that, when fulfilled, contributes to society's equilibrium; also *known as functionalism* and *structural functionalism*

Functional Analysis

The central idea of **functional analysis** is that society is a whole unit, made up of interrelated parts that work together. Functional analysis (also known as *functionalism* and *structural functionalism*) is rooted in the origins of sociology. Auguste Comte and

Herbert Spencer viewed society as a kind of living organism, similar to an animal's body. Just as a person or animal has organs that function together, they wrote, so does society. And like an organism, if society is to function smoothly, its parts must work together in harmony.

Emile Durkheim also viewed society as being composed of many parts, each with its own function. He said that when all the parts of society fulfill their functions, society is in a "normal" state. If they do not fulfill their functions, society is in an "abnormal" or "pathological" state. To understand society, then, functionalists say that we need to look at both *structure* (how the parts of a society fit together to make the whole) and *function* (what each part does, how it contributes to society).

Robert Merton and Functionalism. Robert Merton (1910–2003) dismissed the comparison of society to a living organism, but he did maintain the essence of functionalism—the image of society as a whole unit composed of parts that work together. Merton used the term *functions* to refer to the beneficial consequences of people's actions: Functions help keep a group (society, social system) in balance. In contrast, *dysfunctions* are the harmful consequences of people's actions. They undermine a system's equilibrium.

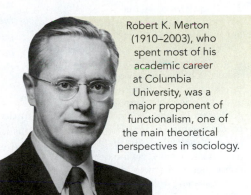

Robert K. Merton (1910–2003), who spent most of his academic career at Columbia University, was a major proponent of functionalism, one of the main theoretical perspectives in sociology.

Functions can be either manifest or latent. If an action is *intended* to help some part of a system, it is a *manifest function*. For example, suppose that government officials become concerned that women are having so few children. Congress offers a $10,000 bonus for every child born to a married couple. The intention, or manifest function, of the bonus is to increase childbearing within the family unit. Merton pointed out that people's actions can also have *latent functions*; that is, they can have *unintended* consequences that help a system adjust. Let's suppose that the bonus works. As the birth rate jumps, so does the sale of diapers and baby furniture. Because the benefits to these businesses were not the intended consequences, they are latent functions of the bonus.

Of course, human actions can also hurt a system. Because such consequences usually are unintended, Merton called them *latent dysfunctions*. Let's assume that the government has failed to specify a "stopping point" with regard to its bonus system. To collect more bonuses, some people keep on having children. The more children they have, however, the more they need the next bonus to survive. Large families become common, and poverty increases. As welfare and taxes jump, the nation erupts in protest. Because these results were not intended and because they harmed the social system, they would be latent dysfunctions of the bonus program.

In Sum: From the perspective of functional analysis, society is a functioning unit, with each part related to the whole. Whenever we examine a smaller part, we need to look for its functions and dysfunctions to see how it is related to the larger unit. This basic approach can be applied to any social group, whether an entire society, a college, or even a group as small as a family.

Applying Functional Analysis. Now let's apply functional analysis to the U.S. divorce rate. Functionalists stress that industrialization and urbanization undermined the traditional functions of the family. For example, before industrialization, the family formed an economic team. On the farm, where most people lived, each family member had jobs or "chores" to do. The wife was in charge not only of household tasks but also of raising small animals, such as chickens, milking cows, collecting eggs, and churning butter. She also did the cooking, baking, canning, sewing, darning, washing, and cleaning. The daughters helped her. The husband was responsible for caring for large animals, such as horses and cattle, for planting and harvesting, and for maintaining buildings and tools. The sons helped him.

This certainly doesn't sound like life today! But what does it have to do with divorce? Simply put, there wasn't much divorce because the husband and wife formed an economic unit in which each depended on the other for survival. There weren't many alternatives.

Other functions also bound family members to one another: educating the children, teaching them religion, providing home-based recreation, and caring for the sick and elderly. All these were functions of the family, certainly quite different from today's situation. To further see how sharply family functions have changed, look at this example from the 1800s:

When Phil became sick, he was nursed by Ann, his wife. She cooked for him, fed him, changed the bed linens, bathed him, read to him from the Bible, and gave him his medicine. (She did this in addition to doing the housework and taking care of their six children.) Phil was also surrounded by the children, who shouldered some of his chores while he was sick. When Phil died, the male neighbors and relatives made the casket while Ann, her mother, and female friends washed and dressed the body. Phil was then "laid out" in the front parlor (the formal living room), where friends, neighbors, and relatives paid their last respects. From there, friends moved his body to the church for the final message and then to the grave they themselves had dug.

In Sum: When the family loses functions, it becomes more fragile, making an increase in divorce inevitable. These changes in economic production illustrate how the family has lost functions. When making a living was a cooperative, home-based effort, husbands and wives depended on one another for their interlocking contributions to a mutual endeavor. With their individual paychecks, today's husbands and wives increasingly function as separate components in an impersonal, multinational, and even global system. The fewer functions that family members share, the fewer are their "ties that bind"—and these ties are what help husbands and wives get through the problems they inevitably experience.

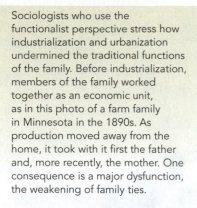

Sociologists who use the functionalist perspective stress how industrialization and urbanization undermined the traditional functions of the family. Before industrialization, members of the family worked together as an economic unit, as in this photo of a farm family in Minnesota in the 1890s. As production moved away from the home, it took with it first the father and, more recently, the mother. One consequence is a major dysfunction, the weakening of family ties.

Conflict Theory

Conflict theory provides a third perspective on social life. Unlike the functionalists, who view society as a harmonious whole, with its parts working together, conflict theorists stress that society is composed of groups that compete with one another for scarce resources. The surface might show cooperation, but scratch that surface and you will find a struggle for power.

Karl Marx and Conflict Theory. Karl Marx, the founder of conflict theory, witnessed the Industrial Revolution that transformed Europe. He saw that peasants who had left the land to work in cities earned barely enough to eat. Things were so bad that the average worker died at age 30, the average wealthy person at age 50 (Edgerton 1992:87). Shocked by this suffering and exploitation, Marx began to analyze society and history. As he did so, he developed **conflict theory**. He concluded that the key to human history is *class conflict*. In each society, some small group controls the means of production and exploits those who are not in control. In industrialized societies, the struggle is between the *bourgeoisie*, the small group of capitalists who own the means to produce wealth, and the *proletariat*, the mass of workers who are exploited by the bourgeoisie. The capitalists control the legal and political system: If the workers rebel, the capitalists call on the power of the state to subdue them.

When Marx made his observations, capitalism was in its infancy and workers were at the mercy of their employers. There was none of what many workers take for granted today—minimum wages, eight-hour days, coffee breaks, five-day work weeks, paid vacations and holidays, medical benefits, sick leave, unemployment compensation, Social Security, and, for union workers, the right to strike. Marx's analysis reminds us that these benefits came not from generous hearts but from workers forcing concessions by their employers.

Conflict Theory Today. Many sociologists extend conflict theory beyond the relationship of capitalists and workers. They examine how opposing interests run through every layer of society—whether in a small group, an organization, a community, or an entire society. For example, when teachers, parents, or the police try to enforce conformity, this creates resentment and resistance. It is the same when a teenager tries to "change the rules" to gain more independence. Throughout society, then, there is a constant struggle to determine who has authority or influence and how far that dominance goes (Turner 1978; Piven 2008; Manza and McCarthy 2011).

Sociologist Lewis Coser (1913–2003) pointed out that conflict is most likely to develop among people who are in close relationships. These people have worked out ways to distribute power and privilege, responsibilities and rewards. Any change in this arrangement can lead to hurt feelings, resentment, and conflict. Even in intimate relationships, then, people are in a constant balancing act, with conflict lying uneasily just beneath the surface.

Feminists and Conflict Theory. Just as Marx examined conflict between capitalists and workers, many feminists analyze conflict between men and women. Their primary focus is the historical, contemporary, and global inequalities of men and women—and how the traditional dominance by men can be overcome to bring about equality of the sexes. Feminists are not united by the conflict perspective, however. They tackle a variety of topics and use whatever theory applies. (Feminism is discussed in Chapter 11.)

Applying Conflict Theory. To explain why the U.S. divorce rate is high, conflict theorists focus on how men's and women's relationships have changed. For millennia, men dominated women, and women had few alternatives other than to accept that dominance. As industrialization transformed the world, it brought women the ability to meet their basic survival needs without depending on a man. This new ability gave them the power to refuse to bear burdens that earlier generations accepted as inevitable. The

conflict theory a theoretical framework in which society is viewed as composed of groups that are competing for scarce resources result is that today's women are likely to dissolve a marriage that becomes intolerable—or even just unsatisfactory.

In Sum: The dominance of men over women was once considered natural and right. As women gained education and earnings, however, they first questioned and then rejected this assumption. As wives strove for more power and grew less inclined to put up with relationships that they defined as unfair, the divorce rate increased. From the conflict perspective, then, our high divorce rate does not mean that marriage has weakened but, rather, that women are making headway in their historical struggle with men.

Putting the Theoretical Perspectives Together

Which of these theoretical perspectives is *the* right one? As you have seen, each is a lens that produces a contrasting picture of divorce. The pictures that emerge are quite different from the commonsense understanding that two people are simply "incompatible." Because each theory focuses on different features of social life, each provides a distinct interpretation. Consequently, we need to use all three theoretical lenses to analyze human behavior. By combining the contributions of each, we gain a more comprehensive picture of social life.

macro-level analysis an examination of large-scale patterns of society; such as how Wall Street and the political establishment are interrelated

micro-level analysis an examination of small-scale patterns of society; such as how the members of a group interact

social interaction one person's actions influencing someone else; usually refers to what people do when they are in one another's presence, but also includes communications at a distance

Levels of Analysis: Macro and Micro

A major difference between these three theoretical perspectives is their level of analysis. Functionalists and conflict theorists focus on the **macro level**; that is, they examine large-scale patterns of society. In contrast, symbolic interactionists usually focus on the **micro level**, on **social interaction**—what people do when they are in one another's presence. These levels are summarized in Table 1.1.

To make this distinction between micro and macro levels clearer, let's return to the example of the homeless, with which we opened this chapter. To study homeless people, symbolic interactionists would focus on the micro level. They would analyze what homeless people do when they are in shelters and on the streets. They would

TABLE 1.1 Three Theoretical Perspectives in Sociology

Theoretical Perspective	Usual Level of Analysis	Focus of Analysis	Key Terms	Applying the Perspective to the U.S. Divorce Rate
Symbolic Interactionism	Microsociological: examines small-scale patterns of social interaction	Face-to-face interaction, how people use symbols to create social life	Symbols Interaction Meanings Definitions	Industrialization and urbanization changed marital roles and led to a redefinition of love, marriage, children, and divorce.
Functional Analysis (also called functionalism and structural functionalism)	Macrosociological: examines large-scale patterns of society	Relationships among the parts of society; how these parts are functional (have beneficial consequences) or dysfunctional (have negative consequences)	Structure Functions (manifest and latent) Dysfunctions Equilibrium	As social change erodes the traditional functions of the family, family ties weaken, and the divorce rate increases.
Conflict Theory	Macrosociological: examines large-scale patterns of society	The struggle for scarce resources by groups in a society; how the elites use their power to control the weaker groups	Inequality Power Conflict Competition Exploitation	When men control economic life, the divorce rate is low because women find few alternatives to a bad marriage. The high divorce rate reflects a shift in the balance of power between men and women.

Source: By the author.

also analyze their communications, both their talk and their **nonverbal interaction** (gestures, use of space, and so on). The observations I made at the beginning of this chapter about the silence in the homeless shelter, for example, would be of interest to symbolic interactionists.

This micro level would not interest functionalists and conflict theorists. They would focus instead on the macro level, how changes in some parts of society increase homelessness. Functionalists might stress that jobs have dried up—how there is less need for unskilled labor and that millions of jobs have been transferred to workers overseas. Or they might focus on changes in the family, that families are smaller and divorce more common. This means that many people who can't find work end up on the streets because they don't have others to fall back on. For their part, conflict theorists would stress the struggle between social classes. They would be interested in how the decisions of international elites affect not only global production and trade but also the local job market, unemployment, and homelessness.

Read on **MySocLab**
Document: Joel M. Charon, What Does It Mean to Be Human? Human Nature, Society, and Culture

Trends Shaping the Future of Sociology

1.8 Explain how research versus reform and globalization are likely to influence sociology.

Two major trends indicate changing directions in sociology. Let's look again at the relationship of sociology to social reform, and then at globalization.

Sociology's Tension: Research Versus Reform

Three Stages in Sociology. As you have seen, a tension between social reform and social analysis runs through the history of sociology. To better understand this tension, we can divide sociology into three time periods (Lazarsfeld and Reitz 1989). During the *first* phase, which lasted until the 1920s, the primary purpose of sociological research was to improve society. During the *second* phase, from the 1920s until World War II, the concern switched to developing abstract knowledge. We are now in a *third* phase, which began around the end of World War II, in which sociologists seek ways to apply their research findings. Many sociology departments offer courses in applied sociology, with some offering internships in applied sociology at both the graduate and undergraduate levels.

Diversity of Orientations. I want to stress that sociology is filled with diverse opinions. (From my observations, I would say that when two sociologists meet, they will express three firmly held, contradictory opinions on the same topic.) In any event, to divide sociology into three separate phases overlooks as much as it reveals. During the first phase, for example, some leading sociologists campaigned against helping the poor, saying that their deaths were good for the progress of society (Stokes 2009). Similarly, during the second phase, many sociologists who wanted to reform society chafed at knowledge being the goal of research. And today, many sociologists want the emphasis to remain on basic sociology. Some say that applied sociology is not "real" sociology; it is just social work or psychology masquerading as sociology. As you can see, sociologists do not move in lockstep toward a single goal.

Each particular period, however, does have basic emphases, and this division of sociology into three phases pinpoints major trends. The tension that has run through sociology—between gaining knowledge and applying knowledge—will continue. During this current phase, the pendulum is swinging toward applying sociological knowledge.

Globalization

A second major trend, globalization, is also leaving its mark on sociology. **Globalization** is the breaking down of national boundaries because of advances in communications, trade, and travel. Because the United States dominates sociology and we U.S. sociologists tend to concentrate on events and relationships that occur in our own country, most

nonverbal interaction communication without words through gestures, use of space, silence, and so on

globalization the growing interconnections among nations due to the expansion of capitalism

globalization of capitalism capitalism (investing to make profits within a rational system) becoming the globe's dominant economic system

of our findings are based on research in the United States. Globalization is destined to broaden our horizons, directing us to a greater consideration of global issues. This, in turn, is likely to motivate us to try more vigorously to identify universal principles.

Application of Globalization to This Text. You are living at a great historical moment, something that doesn't make life easy. You are personally experiencing globalization, one of the most significant events in all of world history. This process is shaping your life, your hopes, and your future—sometimes even twisting them. As globalization shrinks the globe, that is, as people around the world become more interconnected within the same global village, your welfare is increasingly tied to that of people in other nations. From time to time in the following pages, you will also explore how the **globalization of capitalism**—capitalism becoming the world's dominant economic system—is having profound effects on your life. You will also confront the developing *new world order*, which, if it can shave off its rough edges, also appears destined to play a significant role in your future.

To help broaden your horizons, in the following chapters you will visit many cultures around the world, looking at what life is like for the people who live in those cultures. Seeing how *their* society affects their behavior and orientations to life should help you understand how *your* society influences what you do and how you feel about life. This, of course, takes you to one of the main goals of this book.

I wish you a fascinating sociological journey, one with new insights around every corner.

MySocLab

Study and Review on MySocLab

CHAPTER 1 Summary and Review

The Sociological Perspective

1.1 Explain why both history and biography are essential for the sociological perspective.

What is the sociological perspective?

The **sociological perspective** stresses that people's social experiences—the groups to which they belong and their experiences within those groups—underlie their behavior. C. Wright Mills referred to this as the intersection of biography (the individual) and history (broad social factors that influence the individual). Pp. 2–4.

Sociology and the Other Sciences

1.2 Know the focus of each social science.

What is science, and where does sociology fit in?

Science is the application of systematic methods to obtain knowledge and the knowledge obtained by those methods. The sciences are divided into the **natural sciences,** which seek to explain and predict events in the natural environment, and the **social sciences,** which seek to understand the social world objectively by means of controlled and repeated observations. **Sociology** is the scientific study of society and human behavior. Pp. 4–7.

Origins of Sociology

1.3 Trace the origins of sociology, from tradition to Max Weber.

When did sociology first appear as a separate discipline?

Sociology emerged as a separate discipline in the mid-1800s in western Europe, during the onset of the Industrial Revolution. Industrialization affected all aspects of human existence—where people lived, the nature of their work, their relationships, and how they viewed life. Early sociologists who focused on these social changes include Auguste Comte, Herbert Spencer, Karl Marx, Emile Durkheim, Max Weber, Harriet Martineau, and W. E. B. Du Bois. Pp. 7–12.

Values in Sociological Research

1.4 Summarize the opposing arguments in the debate about values in sociological research.

Should the purpose of sociological research be only to advance human understanding or also to reform society?

Sociologists agree that research should be objective, that is, the researcher's **values** and beliefs should not influence conclusions. But sociologists do not agree on the uses and purposes of sociological research. Some say that its purpose should be only to advance understanding of human behavior; others say that its goal should be to reform harmful social arrangements. Pp. 12–13.

Verstehen and Social Facts

1.5 State what *Verstehen* is and why it is valuable.

How do sociologists use *Verstehen* and social facts to study human behavior?

According to Weber, to understand why people act as they do, sociologists must try to put themselves in their shoes. He used the German verb ***Verstehen,*** "to grasp by insight," to describe this essentially subjective approach. Although not denying the importance of *Verstehen,* Emile Durkheim emphasized the importance of uncovering **social facts,** the patterns of society that influence how people behave. Contemporary sociologists use both approaches to understand human behavior. Pp. 13–15.

Sociology in North America

1.6 Trace the development of sociology in North America and explain the tension between objective analysis and social reform.

When were the first academic departments of sociology established in the United States?

The earliest departments of sociology were established in the late 1800s at the universities of Kansas, Chicago, and Atlanta. P. 15.

What was the position of women and minorities in early sociology?

Sociology developed during a historical period of deep sexism and racism, and the contributions of women and minorities were largely ignored. The few women, such as Harriet Martineau, and minorities, such as W. E. B. Du Bois, who received the education necessary to become sociologists felt the sting of discrimination. Pp. 15–20.

What are the differences between basic (or pure) sociology, applied sociology, and public sociology?

Basic (or **pure**) **sociology** is sociological research whose purpose is to make discoveries. **Applied sociology** is sociology used to solve problems. **Public sociology** is using sociology to benefit the public, or large numbers of people. Pp. 20–22.

Theoretical Perspectives in Sociology

1.7 Explain the basic ideas of symbolic interactionism, functional analysis, and conflict theory.

What is a theory?

A **theory** is a general statement about how facts are related to one another. A theory provides a conceptual framework for interpreting facts. P. 22.

What are sociology's major theoretical perspectives?

Sociologists use three primary theoretical frameworks to interpret social life. **Symbolic interactionists** examine how people use symbols to develop and share their views of the world. Symbolic interactionists usually focus on the **micro level**—on small-scale, face-to-face interaction. **Functionalists,** in contrast, focus on the **macro level**—on large-scale patterns of society. They stress that a social system is made up of interrelated parts. When working properly, each part fulfills a function that contributes to the system's stability. **Conflict theorists** also focus on large-scale patterns of society. They stress that society is composed of competing groups that struggle for scarce resources.

With each perspective focusing on different features of social life and each providing a unique interpretation, no single theory is adequate. The combined insights of all three perspectives yield a more comprehensive picture of social life. Pp. 23–29.

Trends Shaping the Future of Sociology

1.8 Explain how research versus reform and globalization are likely to influence sociology.

What trends are likely to have an impact on sociology?

Sociology has gone through three phases: The first was an emphasis on reforming society; the second had its focus on basic sociology; the third, today's phase, is taking us closer to our roots of applying sociology to social change. Public sociology is the most recent example of this change. A second major trend, **globalization**, is likely to broaden sociological horizons, refocusing research and theory away from its concentration on U.S. society. Pp. 29–30.

Thinking Critically about Chapter 1

1. Do you think that sociologists should try to reform society or to study it dispassionately?
2. Of the three theoretical perspectives, which one would you prefer to use if you were a sociologist? Why?
3. Considering the macro- and micro-level approaches in sociology, which one do you think better explains social life? Why?

CHAPTER 2

Culture

Listen to Chapter 2 on MySocLab

Learning Objectives

After you have read this chapter, you should be able to:

2.1 Explain what culture is, how culture provides orientations to life, and what practicing cultural relativism means. (p. 34)

2.2 Know the components of symbolic culture: gestures, language, values, norms, sanctions, folkways, mores, and taboos; also explain the Sapir-Whorf hypothesis. (p. 41)

2.3 Distinguish between subcultures and countercultures. (p. 47)

2.4 Discuss the major U.S. values and explain value clusters, value contradictions, value clashes, how values are lenses of perception, and ideal versus real culture. (p. 51)

2.5 Take a position on the issue of the existence of cultural universals and contrast sociobiology with sociology. (p. 54)

2.6 Explain how technology changes culture and what cultural lag and cultural leveling are. (p. 56)

When I first arrived in Morocco, *I found the sights that greeted me exotic—not unlike the scenes in* Casablanca *or* Raiders of the Lost Ark. *The men, women, and even the children really did wear those white robes that reach down to their feet. What was especially striking was that the women were almost totally covered. Despite the heat, they wore not only full-length gowns but also head coverings that reached down over their foreheads with veils that covered their faces from the nose down. You could see nothing but their eyes—and every eye seemed the same shade of brown.*

And how short everyone was! The Arab women looked to be, on average, 5 feet, and the men only about 3 or 4 inches taller. As the only blue-eyed, blond, 6-foot-plus person around, and the only one who was wearing jeans and a pullover shirt, in a world of white-robed short people I stood out like a creature from another planet. Everyone stared. No matter where I went, they stared. Wherever I looked, I saw people watching me intently. Even staring back had no effect. It was so different from home, where, if you caught someone staring at you, that person would look embarrassed and immediately glance away.

And lines? The concept apparently didn't even exist. Buying a ticket for a bus or train meant pushing and shoving toward the ticket man (always a man—no women were visible in any public position), who took the money from whichever outstretched hand he decided on.

> "Everyone stared. No matter where I went, they stared."

And germs? That notion didn't seem to exist here either. Flies swarmed over the food in the restaurants and the unwrapped loaves of bread in the stores. Shopkeepers would considerately shoo off the flies before handing me a loaf. They also offered home delivery. I watched a bread vendor deliver a loaf to a woman who was standing on a second-floor balcony. She first threw her money to the bread vendor, and he then threw the unwrapped bread up to her. Unfortunately, his throw was off. The bread bounced off the wrought-iron balcony railing and landed in the street, which was filled with people, wandering dogs, and the ever-present urinating and defecating donkeys. The vendor simply picked up the unwrapped loaf and threw it again. This certainly wasn't his day: He missed again. But he made it on his third attempt. The woman smiled as she turned back into her apartment, apparently to prepare the noon meal for her family.

What Is Culture?

2.1 Explain what culture is, how culture provides orientations to life, and what practicing cultural relativism means.

Watch on MySocLab Video: Culture: The Basics

culture the language, beliefs, values, norms, behaviors, and even material objects that characterize a group and are passed from one generation to the next

What is culture? The concept is sometimes easier to grasp by description than by definition. For example, suppose you meet a young woman from India who has just arrived in the United States. That her culture is different from yours is immediately evident. You first see it in her clothing, jewelry, makeup, and hairstyle. Next, you hear it in her speech. It then becomes apparent by her gestures. Later, you might hear her express unfamiliar beliefs about relationships or what is valuable in life. All of these characteristics are indicative of **culture**—the language, beliefs, values, norms, behaviors, and even material objects that are passed from one generation to the next.

In northern Africa, I was surrounded by a culture quite different from mine. It was evident in everything I saw and heard. The **material culture**—such things as jewelry, art, buildings, weapons, machines, and even eating utensils, hairstyles, and clothing—provided a sharp contrast to what I was used to seeing. There is nothing inherently "natural" about material culture. That is, it is no more natural (or unnatural) to wear gowns on the street than it is to wear jeans.

I also found myself immersed in an unfamiliar **nonmaterial culture**, that is, a group's ways of thinking (its beliefs, values, and other assumptions about the world) and doing (its common *patterns of behavior*, including language, gestures, and other forms of interaction). North African assumptions that it is acceptable to stare at others in public and to push people aside to buy tickets are examples of nonmaterial culture. So are U.S. assumptions that it is wrong to do either of these things. Like material culture, neither custom is "right." People simply become comfortable with the customs they learn during childhood, and—as happened to me in northern Africa—uncomfortable when their basic assumptions about life are challenged.

Culture and Taken-for-Granted Orientations to Life

To develop a sociological imagination, it is essential to understand how culture affects people's lives. If we meet someone from a different culture, the encounter may make us aware of culture's pervasive influence on all aspects of a person's life. Attaining the same level of awareness regarding our own culture, however, is quite another matter. We usually take *our* speech, *our* gestures, *our* beliefs, and *our* customs for granted. We assume that they are "normal" or "natural," and we almost always follow them without question. As anthropologist Ralph Linton (1936) said, "The last thing a fish would ever notice would be water." So also with people: Except in unusual circumstances, most characteristics of our own culture remain imperceptible to us.

Yet culture's significance is profound; it touches almost every aspect of who and what we are. We came into this life without a language; without values and morality; with no ideas about religion, war, money, love, use of space, and so on. We possessed none of these fundamental orientations that are so essential in determining the type of people we become. Yet by this point in our lives, we all have acquired them—and take them for granted. Sociologists call this *culture within us.* These learned and shared ways of believing and of doing (another definition of culture) penetrate our being at an early age and quickly become part of our taken-for-granted assumptions about what normal behavior is. *Culture becomes the lens through which we perceive and evaluate what is going on around us.* Seldom do we question these assumptions. Like water to a fish, the lens through which we view life remains largely beyond our perception.

The rare instances in which these assumptions are challenged, however, can be upsetting. Although as a sociologist I should be able to look at my own culture "from the outside," my trip to Africa quickly revealed how fully I had internalized my own culture. My upbringing in Western culture had given me assumptions about aspects of social life that had become rooted deeply in my being—what are "appropriate" eye contact, hygiene, and the use of space. But in this part of Africa these assumptions were useless in helping me navigate everyday life. No longer could I count on people to stare only surreptitiously, to take precautions against invisible microbes, or to stand in line in an orderly fashion, one behind the other.

As you can tell from the opening vignette, I found these unfamiliar behaviors unsettling—they violated my basic expectations of "the way people *ought* to be"—and I did not even realize how firmly I held these expectations until they were challenged so abruptly. When my nonmaterial culture failed me—when it no longer enabled me to make sense out of the world—I experienced a disorientation known as **culture shock**. In the case of buying tickets, the fact that I was several inches taller than most Moroccans and thus able to outreach others helped me to adjust partially to their different ways of doing things. But I never did get used to the idea that pushing ahead of others was "right," and I always felt guilty when I used my size to receive preferential treatment.

Culture shock is a two-way street, of course. You can imagine what culture shock people from a tribal society would experience if they were thrust into the United States. This actually happened, as the Cultural Diversity box on the next page describes.

material culture the material objects that distinguish a group of people, such as their art, buildings, weapons, utensils, machines, hairstyles, clothing, and jewelry

nonmaterial culture a group's ways of thinking (including its beliefs, values, and other assumptions about the world) and doing (its common patterns of behavior, including language and other forms of interaction); also called *symbolic culture*

culture shock the disorientation that people experience when they come in contact with a fundamentally different culture and can no longer depend on their taken-for-granted assumptions about life

Watch on **MySocLab**
Video: The Big Picture: Culture

Watch on **MySocLab**
Video: Lynette Spillman, Sociologists and Culture

What a tremendous photo for sociologists! Seldom are we treated to such cultural contrasts. Can you see how the cultures of these women have given them not only different orientations concerning the presentation of their bodies but also of gender relations?

Cultural Diversity **in the United States**

Culture Shock: The Arrival of the Hmong

Imagine that you were a member of a small tribal group in the mountains of Laos. Village life and the clan were all you knew. There were no schools, and you learned everything you needed to know from your relatives. U.S. agents recruited the men of your village to fight communists, and they gained a reputation as fierce fighters. When the U.S. forces were defeated in Vietnam, your people were moved to the United States so they wouldn't be killed in reprisal.

Here is what happened. Keep in mind that you had never seen a television or a newspaper and that you had never gone to school. Your entire world had been the village.

They put you in a big house with wings. It flew.

They gave you strange food on a tray. The Sani-Wipes were hard to chew.

After the trip, you were placed in a house. This was an adventure. You had never seen locks before, as no one locked up anything in the village. Most of the village homes didn't even have doors, much less locks.

You found the bathroom perplexing. At first, you tried to wash rice in the bowl of water, which seemed to be provided for this purpose. But when you pressed the handle, the water and rice disappeared. After you learned what the toilet was for, you found it difficult not to slip off the little white round thing when you stood on it. In the village, you didn't need a toilet seat when you squatted in a field to defecate.

When you threw water on the electric stove to put out the burner, it sparked and smoked. You became afraid to use the stove because it might explode.

And no one liked it when you tried to plant a vegetable garden in the park.

Your new world was so different that, to help you adjust, the settlement agency told you (Fadiman 1997):

1. To send mail, you must use stamps.
2. The door of the refrigerator must be shut.
3. Do not stand or squat on the toilet since it may break.
4. Always ask before picking your neighbor's flowers, fruit, or vegetables.
5. In colder areas you must wear shoes, socks, and appropriate outerwear. Otherwise, you may become ill.
6. Always use a handkerchief or a tissue to blow your nose in public places or inside a public building.
7. Picking your nose or ears in public is frowned upon in the United States.
8. Never urinate in the street. This creates a smell that is offensive to Americans. They also believe that it causes disease.

Children make a fast adjustment to a new culture, although, as with these Hmong children in elementary school in St. Paul, Minnesota, they are caught between the old and the new.

To help the Hmong assimilate, U.S. officials dispersed them across the nation. This, they felt, would help them to adjust to the dominant culture and prevent a Hmong subculture from developing. The dispersal brought feelings of isolation to the clan- and village-based Hmong. As soon as they had a chance, the Hmong moved from these towns scattered across the country to live in areas with other Hmong, the major one being in California's Central Valley. Here they renewed village relationships and helped one another adjust to the society they had never desired to join.

For Your Consideration

➔ Do you think you would have reacted differently if you had been a displaced Hmong? Why did the Hmong need one another more than their U.S. neighbors to adjust to their new life? What cultural shock do you think a U.S.-born 19-year-old Hmong would experience if his or her parents decided to return to Laos?

ethnocentrism the use of one's own culture as a yardstick for judging the ways of other individuals or societies, generally leading to a negative evaluation of their values, norms, and behaviors

An important consequence of culture within us is **ethnocentrism**, a tendency to use our own group's ways of doing things as a yardstick for judging others. All of us learn that the ways of our own group are good, right, and even superior to other ways of life. As sociologist William Sumner (1906), who developed this concept, said, "One's own group is the center of everything, and all others are scaled and rated with reference to it." Ethnocentrism has both positive and negative consequences. On the positive side, it creates in-group loyalties. On the negative side, ethnocentrism can lead to discrimination against people whose ways differ from ours.

The many ways in which culture affects our lives fascinate sociologists. In this chapter, we'll examine how profoundly culture influences everything we are and whatever we do. This will serve as a basis from which you can start to analyze your own assumptions of reality. I should give you a warning at this point: You might develop a changed perspective on social life and your role in it. If so, life will never look the same.

cultural relativism not judging a culture but trying to understand it on its own terms

In Sum: To avoid losing track of the ideas under discussion, let's pause for a moment to summarize and, in some instances, clarify the principles we have covered.

Explore on **MySocLab**
Activity: The Asian Population in the United States: A Diversity of Cultures

1. There is nothing "natural" about material culture. Arabs wear gowns on the street and feel that it is natural to do so. Americans do the same with jeans.
2. There is nothing "natural" about nonmaterial culture. It is just as arbitrary to stand in line as to push and shove.
3. Culture penetrates deeply into our thinking, becoming a taken-for-granted lens through which we see the world and obtain our perception of reality.
4. Culture provides implicit instructions that tell us what we ought to do and how we ought to think. It establishes a fundamental basis for our decision making.
5. Culture also provides a "moral imperative"; that is, the culture that we internalize becomes the "right" way of doing things. (I, for example, believed deeply that it was wrong to push and shove to get ahead of others.)
6. Coming into contact with a radically different culture challenges our basic assumptions about life. (I experienced culture shock when I discovered that my deeply ingrained cultural ideas about hygiene and the use of personal space no longer applied.)
7. Although the particulars of culture differ from one group of people to another, culture itself is universal. That is, all people have culture, for a society cannot exist without developing shared, learned ways of dealing with the challenges of life.
8. All people are ethnocentric, which has both positive and negative consequences.

For an example of how culture shapes our ideas and behavior, consider how some people dance with the dead. You can read about this in the Cultural Diversity around the World box on the next page.

Practicing Cultural Relativism

To counter our tendency to use our own culture as the standard by which we judge other cultures, we can practice **cultural relativism**; that is, we can try to understand a culture on its own terms. This means looking at how the elements of a culture fit together, without judging those elements as inferior or superior to our own way of life.

With our own culture embedded so deeply within us, practicing cultural relativism is difficult to do. It is likely that the Malagasy custom of dancing with the dead seemed both strange and wrong to you. It is similar with stabbing bulls to death in front of joyful crowds that shout "Olé!" Most U.S. citizens have strong feelings that it is wrong to do this. If we practice cultural relativism, however, we will view both dancing with the dead and bullfighting from the perspective of the cultures in which they take place. It will be *their* history, *their* folklore, *their* ideas of bravery, sex roles, and mortality that we will use to understand their behavior.

You may still regard dancing with the dead as strange and bullfighting as wrong, of course, particularly if your culture, which is deeply ingrained in you, has no history of dancing with the dead or of bullfighting. We all possess culturally specific ideas about how to show respect to the dead. We also possess culturally specific ideas

Many Americans perceive bullfighting as a cruel activity that should be illegal everywhere. To most Spaniards, bullfighting is a sport that pits matador and bull in a unifying image of power, courage, and glory. Cultural relativism requires that we suspend our own perspectives in order to grasp the perspectives of others, something easier described than attained.

Cultural Diversity **around the World**

Dancing with the Dead

At last the time had come. The family had so looked forward to this day. They would finally be able to take their parents and uncle out of the family crypt and dance with them.

The celebration isn't cheap, and it had taken several years to save enough money for it. After all, if the dead saw them in old clothing, they would think that they weren't prospering. And the dead needed new shrouds, too.

And a band had to be hired—a good one so the dead could enjoy their favorite music.

And friends and relatives had to be invited to the celebration—and fed a meal with meat.

The family members entered the crypt with respect. Carefully removing the dead, they tenderly ran their fingers across the skulls, remembering old times. After sharing the latest family news with the dead, they dressed the dead in their new shrouds. As the band played cheerful tunes, they danced with the dead. The dancing was joyful, as the family members took turns twirling the dead to the fast, musical rhythms

Everyone was happy, including the dead, who would be put back in their crypt, not to dance again for another four to seven years.

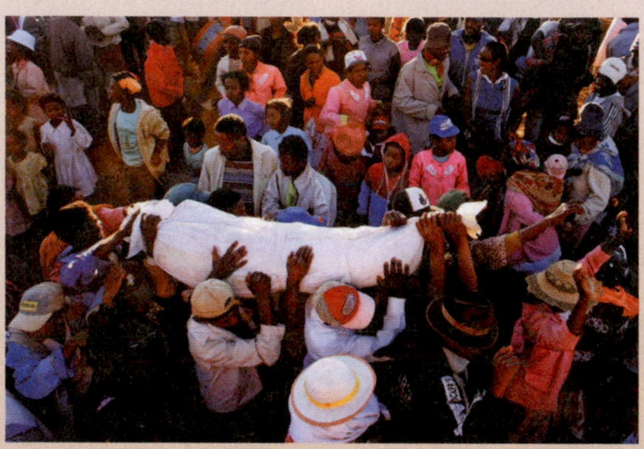

In this photo, taken in Madagascar, the body, exhumed and wrapped in a new shroud, is being paraded among other celebrants of Famadihana.

This celebration, which occurs in Madagascar, an island nation off the west coast of Africa, is called *famadihana* (fa-ma-dee-an). Its origin is lost in history, but the dancing is part of what the living owe the dead. "After all," say the Malagasy, "We owe everything to the dead. If our ancestors hadn't lived and taken care of us, we wouldn't be here."

Like many people around the world, the traditional Malagasy believe that only a fine line separates the living from the dead. And like many people around the world, they believe that this line is so fine that the dead communicate with the living in dreams. The primary distinction is probably the *famadihana*, a custom that seems to be unique to Madagascar.

In a few years, the living will join the dead. And a few years after that, these newly dead will join the living in this dance. The celebration of life and death continues.

For Your Consideration

➔ How does the *famadihana* differ from your culture's customs regarding the dead? Why does the *famadihana* seem strange to Americans and so ordinary to the traditional Malagasy? How has your culture shaped your ideas about death, the dead, and the living?

Sources: Based on Bearak 2010; Consulate General of Madagascar in Cape Town 2012.

about how to treat animals, ideas that have evolved slowly and match other elements of our culture. In some areas of the United States, cock fighting, dog fighting, and bear–dog fighting were once common. Only as the culture changed were they gradually eliminated.

Cultural relativism is an attempt to refocus our lens of perception so we can appreciate other ways of life rather than simply asserting, "Our way is right." Although none of us can be entirely successful at practicing cultural relativism, look at the photos on page 40 and try to appreciate the cultural differences they illustrate about standards of beauty. I think you will enjoy the Cultural Diversity box on the next page, too, but my best guess is that you will evaluate these "strange" foods through the lens of your own culture.

Although cultural relativism helps us avoid cultural smugness, this view has come under attack. In a provocative book, *Sick Societies* (Edgerton 1992), anthropologist Robert Edgerton suggests that we develop a scale for evaluating cultures on their "quality of life,"

Cultural Diversity around the World

You Are What You Eat? An Exploration in Cultural Relativity

Here is a chance to test your ethnocentrism and ability to practice cultural relativity. You probably know that the French like to eat snails and that in some Asian cultures, chubby dogs and cats are considered a delicacy ("Ah, lightly browned with a little doggy sauce!"). You might also know that in some cultures, the bull's penis and testicles are prized foods (Jakab 2012). But did you know that cod sperm is a delicacy in Japan (Halpern 2011)? That flies, scorpions, crickets, and beetles are on the menu of restaurants in parts of Thailand (Gampbell 2006)? That on the Italian island of Sardinia, *casu marzi*, a cheese filled with live maggots, is popular (Herz 2012)?

Marston Bates (1967), a zoologist, noted this ethnocentric reaction to food:

> *I remember once, in the llanos of Colombia, sharing a dish of toasted ants at a remote farmhouse. . . . My host and I fell into conversation about the general question of what people eat or do not eat, and I remarked that in my country people eat the legs of frogs.*
>
> *The very thought of this filled my ant-eating friends with horror; it was as though I had mentioned some repulsive sex habit.*

What some consider food, even delicacies, can turn the stomachs of others. These roasted grub worms were for sale in Bangkok, Thailand.

Then there is the experience of a friend, Dusty Friedman, who told me:

> *When traveling in Sudan, I ate some interesting things that I wouldn't likely eat now that I'm back in our society. Raw baby camel's liver with chopped herbs was a delicacy. So was camel's milk cheese patties that had been cured in dry camel's dung.*

You might be able to see yourself eating frog legs and toasted ants, beetles, even flies. (Or maybe not.) Perhaps you could even stomach cod sperm and raw camel liver, maybe even dogs and cats, but here's another test of your ethnocentrism and cultural relativity. Maxine Kingston (1975), an English professor whose parents grew up in China, wrote:

> *"Do you know what people in [the Nantou region of] China eat when they have the money?" my mother began. "They buy into a monkey feast. The eaters sit around a thick wood table with a hole in the middle. Boys bring in the monkey at the end of a pole. Its neck is in a collar at the end of the pole, and it is screaming. Its hands are tied behind it. They clamp the monkey into the table; the whole table fits like another collar around its neck. Using a surgeon's saw, the cooks cut a clean line in a circle at the top of its head. To loosen the bone, they tap with a tiny hammer and wedge here and there with a silver pick. Then an old woman reaches out her hand to the monkey's face and up to its scalp, where she tufts some hairs and lifts off the lid of the skull. The eaters spoon out the brains."*

For Your Consideration

➔ What is your opinion about eating toasted ants? Beetles? Flies? Fried frog legs? Cod sperm? Maggot cheese? About eating puppies and kittens? About eating brains scooped out of a living monkey?

➔ If you were reared in U.S. society, more than likely you think that eating frog legs is okay; eating ants or beetles is disgusting; and eating flies, cod sperm, maggot cheese, dogs, cats, and monkey brains is downright repugnant. How would you apply the concepts of ethnocentrism and cultural relativism to your perceptions of these customs?

much as we do for U.S. cities. He also asks why we should consider cultures that practice female circumcision, gang rape, or wife beating, or cultures that sell little girls into prostitution, as morally equivalent to those that do not. Cultural values that result in exploitation, he says, are inferior to those that enhance people's lives.

Standards of Beauty

Standards of beauty vary so greatly from one culture to another that what one group finds attractive, another may not. Yet, in its *ethnocentrism*, each group thinks that its standards are the best— that the appearance reflects what beauty "really" is.

As indicated by these photos, around the world men and women aspire to their group's norms of physical attractiveness. To make themselves appealing to others, they try to make their appearance reflect those standards.

Ecuador

New Guinea

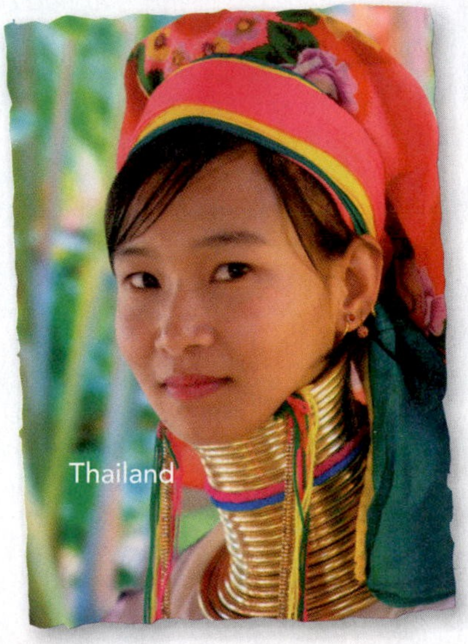

Thailand

China

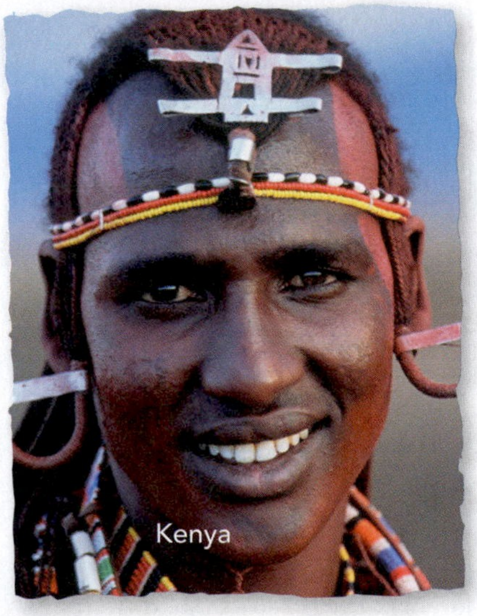

Kenya

Angola

Tibet

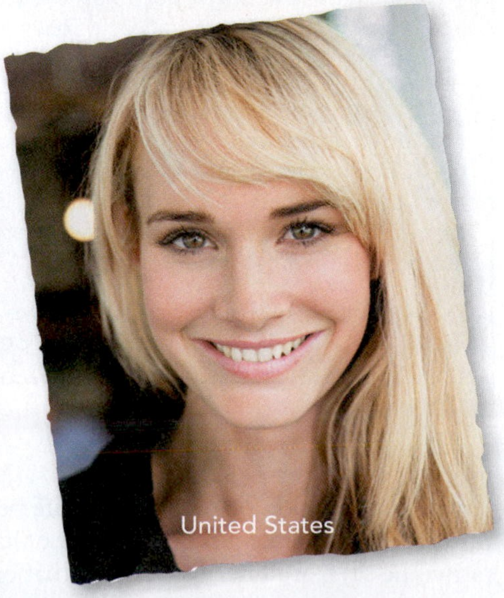

United States

Edgerton's sharp questions and incisive examples bring us to a topic that comes up repeatedly in this text: the disagreements that arise among scholars as they confront contrasting views of reality. It is such questioning of assumptions that keeps sociology interesting.

Components of Symbolic Culture

2.2 Know the components of symbolic culture: gestures, language, values, norms, sanctions, folkways, mores, and taboos; also explain the Sapir-Whorf hypothesis.

Sociologists often refer to nonmaterial culture as **symbolic culture**, because it consists of the symbols that people use. A **symbol** is something to which people attach meaning and that they use to communicate with one another. Symbols include gestures, language, values, norms, sanctions, folkways, and mores. Let's look at each of these components of symbolic culture.

Gestures

Gestures, movements of the body to communicate with others, are shorthand ways to convey messages without using words. Although people in every culture of the world use gestures, a gesture's meaning may change completely from one culture to another. North Americans, for example, communicate a succinct message by raising the middle finger in a short, upward stabbing motion. I wish to stress "North Americans," because this gesture does not convey the same message in most parts of the world.

Watch on **MySocLab**
Video: Culture: Thinking Like a Sociologist

I had internalized this finger gesture to such an extent that I thought everyone knew what it meant, but in Mexico I was surprised to find that it is not universal. When I was comparing gestures with friends in Mexico, this gesture drew a blank look. After I explained its meaning, they laughed and said they would show me their rudest gesture. They placed one hand under an armpit, brought their other hand to the opposite shoulder, and moved their upper arm up and down. To me, they simply looked as if they were imitating a monkey, but to my Mexican hosts the gesture meant "Your mother is a whore"—the worst possible insult in their culture.

Some gestures are so closely associated with emotional messages that the gestures themselves summon up emotions. For example, my introduction to Mexican gestures took place at a dinner table. It was evident that my husband-and-wife hosts were trying to hide their embarrassment at using their culture's obscene gesture at their dinner table. And I felt the same way—not about *their* gesture, of course, which meant nothing to me—but about the one I was teaching them.

Misunderstanding and Offense. Gestures not only facilitate communication but also, because they differ around the world, can lead to misunderstanding, embarrassment, or worse. One time in Mexico, for example, I raised my hand to a certain height to indicate how tall a child was. My hosts began to laugh. It turned out that Mexicans use three hand gestures to indicate height: one for people, a second for animals, and yet another for plants. They were amused because I had used the plant gesture to indicate the child's height. (See Figure 2.1 on the next page.)

To get along in another culture, then, it is important to learn the gestures of that culture. If you don't, you will fail to achieve the simplicity of communication that gestures allow. You may also overlook or misunderstand much of what is happening, run the risk of appearing foolish, and possibly offend people. In some cultures, for example, you would provoke deep offense if you were to offer food or a gift with your left hand, because the left hand is reserved for dirty tasks, such as wiping after going to the toilet. Left-handed Americans visiting Arabs, please note!

Suppose for a moment that you are visiting southern Italy. After eating one of the best meals in your life, you are so pleased that when you catch the waiter's eye, you smile broadly and use the standard U.S. "A-OK" gesture of putting your thumb and forefinger together

symbolic culture another term for nonmaterial culture

symbol something to which people attach meaning and then use to communicate with one another

gestures the ways in which people use their bodies to communicate with one another

FIGURE 2.1 Gestures to Indicate Height, Southern Mexico

Source: By the author.

and making a large "O." The waiter looks horrified, and you are struck speechless when the manager angrily asks you to leave. What have you done? Nothing on purpose, of course, but in that culture this gesture refers to a lower part of the human body that is not mentioned in polite company. (Ekman et al. 1984)

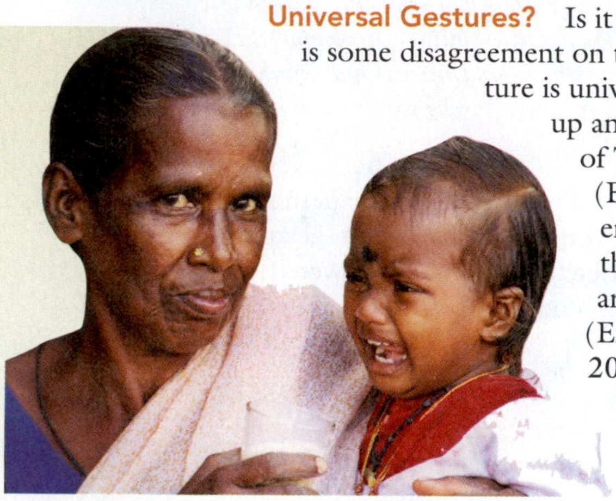

Although most gestures are learned, and therefore vary from culture to culture, some gestures that represent fundamental emotions such as sadness, anger, and fear appear to be inborn. This crying child whom I photographed in India differs little from a crying child in China—or the United States or anywhere else on the globe. In a few years, however, this child will demonstrate a variety of gestures highly specific to his Hindu culture.

Universal Gestures? Is it really true that there are no universal gestures? There is some disagreement on this point. Some anthropologists claim that no gesture is universal. They point out that even nodding the head up and down to indicate "yes" is not universal. In an area of Turkey, nodding the head up and down means "no" (Ekman et al. 1984). However, ethologists, researchers who study the biological bases of behavior, claim that expressions of anger, pouting, fear, and sadness are built into our biological makeup and are universal (Eibl-Eibesfeldt 1970:404; Horwitz and Wakefield 2007). They point out that even infants who are born blind and deaf, who have had no chance to learn these gestures, express themselves in the same way.

Although this matter is not yet settled, we can note that gestures tend to vary remarkably around the world.

Language

The primary way in which people communicate with one another is through **language**—symbols that can be combined in an infinite number of ways for the purpose of communicating abstract thought. Each word is actually a symbol, a sound to which we have attached some particular meaning. Although all human groups have language, there is nothing universal about the meanings given to particular sounds. Like gestures, in different cultures the same sound may mean something entirely different—or may have no meaning at all. In German, for example, *gift* means "poison," so if you give a box of chocolates to a non-English-speaking German and say, "Gift, eat,". . . .

language a system of symbols that can be combined in an infinite number of ways and can represent not only objects but also abstract thought

Because *language allows culture to exist*, its significance for human life is difficult to overstate. Consider the following effects of language.

Language Allows Human Experience to Be Cumulative. By means of language, we pass ideas, knowledge, and even attitudes on to the next generation. This allows others to build on experiences in which they may never directly participate. As a result, humans are able to modify their behavior in light of what earlier generations have learned. This takes us to the central sociological significance of language: *Language allows culture to develop by freeing people to move beyond their immediate experiences.*

Without language, human culture would be little more advanced than that of the lower primates. If we communicated by grunts and gestures, we would be limited to a short time span—to events now taking place, those that have just taken place, or those that will take place immediately—a sort of slightly extended present. You can grunt and gesture, for example, that you are thirsty or hungry, but in the absence of language how could you share ideas concerning past or future events? There would be little or no way to communicate to others what event you had in mind, much less the greater complexities that humans communicate—ideas and feelings about events.

Language Provides a Social or Shared Past. Without language, we would have few memories, since we associate experiences with words and then use those words to recall the experience. In the absence of language, how would we communicate the few memories we had to others? By attaching words to an event, however, and then using those words to recall it, we are able to discuss the event. This is highly significant: Our talking is far more than "just talk." As we talk about past events, we develop shared understandings about what those events mean. In short, through talk, people develop a shared past.

Language Provides a Social or Shared Future. Language also extends our time horizons forward. Because language enables us to agree on times, dates, and places, it allows us to plan activities with one another. Think about it for a moment. Without language, how could you ever plan future events? How could you possibly communicate goals, times, and plans? Whatever planning could exist would be limited to rudimentary communications, perhaps to an agreement to meet at a certain place when the sun is in a certain position. But think of the difficulty, perhaps the impossibility, of conveying just a slight change in this simple arrangement, such as "I can't make it tomorrow, but my neighbor can take my place, if that's all right with you."

Language Allows Shared Perspectives. Our ability to speak, then, provides us with a social (or shared) past and future. This is vital for humanity. It is a watershed that distinguishes us from animals. But speech does much more than this. When we talk with one another, we are exchanging ideas about events; that is, we are sharing perspectives. Our words are the embodiment of our experiences, distilled into a readily exchangeable form, one that is mutually understandable to people who have learned that language. *Talking about events allows us to arrive at the shared understandings that form the basis of social life.*

Not sharing a language while living alongside one another, however, invites miscommunication and suspicion. This risk, which comes with a diverse society, is discussed in the Cultural Diversity box on the next page.

Language Allows Shared, Goal-Directed Behavior. Common understandings enable us to establish a *purpose* for getting together. Let's suppose you want to go on a picnic. You use speech not only to plan the picnic but also to decide on reasons for having the picnic—which may be anything from "because it's a nice day and it shouldn't be wasted studying" to "because it's my birthday." Language permits you to blend individual activities into an integrated sequence. In other words, as you talk, you decide when and where you will go; who will drive; who will bring the hamburgers, the potato chips, the soda; where and when you will meet. Only because of language can you participate in such a common yet complex event as a picnic—or build roads and bridges or attend college classes.

In Sum: The sociological significance of language is that it takes us beyond the world of apes and allows culture to develop. Language frees us from the present, actually giving us a social past and a social future. That is, language gives us the capacity to share understandings about the past and to develop shared perceptions about the future. Language

Cultural Diversity **in the United States**

Miami—Continuing Controversy over Language

Immigration from Cuba and other Spanish-speaking countries has been so vast that most residents of Miami are Latinos. Half of Miami's 400,000 residents have trouble speaking English. *Sixty percent* of Miamians speak English at home. Controversy erupted when a debate among the candidates for mayor of Miami was held only in Spanish. Many English-only speakers say that not being able to speak Spanish is a handicap to getting work. "They should learn Spanish," some reply. As Pedro Falcon, an immigrant from Nicaragua, said, "Miami is the capital of Latin America. The population speaks Spanish."

This pinpoints the problem, as the English-speakers see it: Miami, they stress, is in the United States, not in Latin America.

Controversy over immigrants and language isn't new. The millions of Germans who moved to the United States in the 1800s brought their language with them. Not only did they hold religious services in German but they also opened schools where the students were taught in German; published German-language newspapers; and spoke German at home, in the stores, and in the taverns.

Mural on Calle Ocho in Miami

Some of their English-speaking neighbors didn't like this one bit. "Why don't those Germans assimilate?" they wondered. "Just whose side would they fight on if we had a war?"

This question was answered with the participation of German Americans in two world wars. It was even a general descended from German immigrants (Eisenhower) who led the armed forces that defeated Hitler.

What happened to all this German language? The first generation of immigrants spoke German almost exclusively. The second generation assimilated, speaking English at home, but also speaking German when visiting their parents. For the most part, the third generation knew German only as "that language" that their grandparents spoke.

The same thing is happening with the Latino immigrants, but at a slower pace. Spanish is being kept alive longer because Mexico borders the United States, and there is constant traffic between the countries. The continuing migration from Mexico and other Spanish-speaking countries also feeds the language.

If Germany bordered the United States, there would still be a lot of German spoken here.

Sources: Based on Kent and Lalasz 2007; Salomon 2008; Costantini 2011; Nelson 2013.

For Your Consideration

➔ Do you think that Miami points to the future of the United States? Like the grandchildren of the European immigrants who lost the ability to speak their grandparent's native language, when do you think the grandchildren of Mexican and South American immigrants will be unable to speak Spanish?

also allows us to establish underlying purposes for our activities. In short, *language is the basis of culture*.

Language and Perception: The Sapir-Whorf Hypothesis

In the 1930s, two anthropologists, Edward Sapir and Benjamin Whorf, were intrigued when they noticed that the Hopi Indians of the southwestern United States had no words to distinguish the past, the present, and the future. English, in contrast—as well as French, Spanish, Swahili, and other languages—carefully distinguishes these three time frames. From this observation, Sapir and Whorf began to think that words might be more than labels that people attach to things. Eventually, they concluded that *language has embedded within it ways of looking at the world.* In other words, language not only expresses our thoughts and perceptions, but language also *shapes* the way we think and perceive (Sapir 1949; Whorf 1956).

The **Sapir-Whorf hypothesis** challenges common sense: It indicates that rather than objects and events forcing themselves onto our consciousness, it is our language that determines our consciousness, and hence our perception of objects and events. Sociologist Eviatar Zerubavel (1991) points out that his native language, Hebrew, does not have separate words for jam and jelly. Both go by the same term, and only when Zerubavel learned English could he "see" this difference, which is "obvious" to native English speakers. Similarly, if you learn to classify students as Jocks, Goths, Stoners, Skaters, Band Geeks, and Preps, you will perceive students in entirely different ways from someone who does not know these classifications.

When I lived in Spain, I was struck by the relevance of the Sapir-Whorf hypothesis. As a native English speaker, I had learned that the term *dried fruits* refers to apricots, apples, and so on. In Spain, I found that *frutos secos* refers not only to such objects but also to things like almonds, walnuts, and pecans. My English makes me see fruits and nuts as quite separate types of objects. This seems "natural" to me, while combining them into one unit seems "natural" to Spanish speakers. If I had learned Spanish first, my perception of these objects would be different.

Although Sapir and Whorf's observation that the Hopi do not have tenses was wrong (Edgerton 1992:27), they did stumble onto a major truth about social life. Learning a language means not only learning words but also acquiring the perceptions embedded in that language. In other words, language both reflects and shapes our cultural experiences (Boroditsky 2010). The racial–ethnic terms that our culture provides, for example, influence how we see both ourselves and others, a point that is discussed in the Cultural Diversity box on the next page.

Sapir-Whorf hypothesis Edward Sapir and Benjamin Whorf's hypothesis that language creates ways of thinking and perceiving

values the standards by which people define what is desirable or undesirable, good or bad, beautiful or ugly

norms expectations of "right" behavior

sanctions either expressions of approval given to people for upholding norms or expressions of disapproval for violating them

positive sanction a reward or positive reaction for following norms, ranging from a smile to a material reward

negative sanction an expression of disapproval for breaking a norm, ranging from a mild, informal reaction such as a frown to a formal reaction such as a prize or a prison sentence

Values, Norms, and Sanctions

To learn a culture is to learn people's **values**, their ideas of what is desirable in life. When we uncover people's values, we learn a great deal about them, since values are the standards by which people define what is good and bad, beautiful and ugly. Values underlie our preferences, guide our choices, and indicate what we hold worthwhile in life.

Every group develops expectations concerning the "right" way to reflect its values. Sociologists use the term **norms** to describe those expectations (or rules of behavior) that develop out of a group's values. The term **sanctions** refers to the reactions people receive for following or breaking norms. A **positive sanction** expresses approval for following a norm, and a **negative sanction** reflects disapproval for breaking a norm. Positive sanctions can be material, such as a prize, a trophy, or money, but in everyday life they usually consist of hugs, smiles, a pat on the back, or even handshakes and "high fives." Negative sanctions can also be material—being fined in court is one example—but negative sanctions, too, are more likely to be symbolic: harsh words, or gestures such as frowns, stares, clenched jaws, or raised fists. Getting a raise at work is a positive sanction, indicating that you have followed the norms clustering around work values. Getting fired, in contrast, is a negative sanction, indicating that you have violated these norms. The North American finger gesture discussed earlier is, of course, a negative sanction.

Because people can find norms stifling, some cultures relieve the pressure through *moral holidays*, specified times when people are allowed to break norms. Moral holidays such as Mardi Gras often center on getting rowdy. Some

Many societies relax their norms during specified occasions. At these times, known as moral holidays, behavior that is ordinarily not permitted is allowed. This photo was taken at Mardis Gras in New Orleans. When a moral holiday is over, the usual enforcement of rules follows.

Cultural Diversity in the United States

Race and Language: Searching for Self-Labels

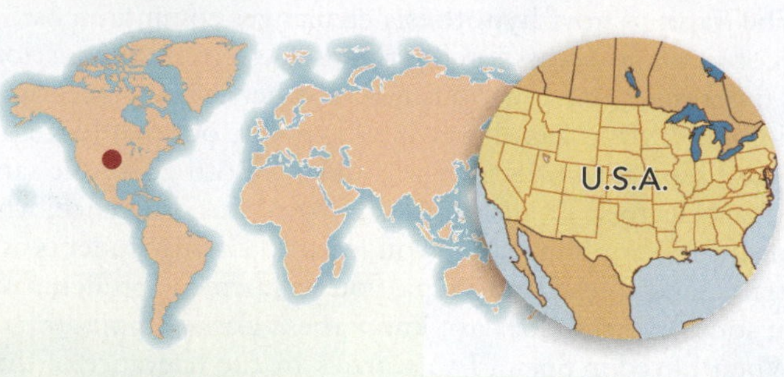

The groups that dominate society often determine the names that are used to refer to racial–ethnic groups. If those names become associated with oppression, they take on negative meanings. For example, the terms *Negro* and *colored people* came to be associated with submissiveness and low status. To overcome these meanings, those referred to by these terms began to identify themselves as *black* or *African American*. They infused these new terms with respect—a basic source of self-esteem that they felt the old terms denied them.

In a twist, African Americans—and to a lesser extent Latinos, Asian Americans, and Native Americans—have changed the rejected term *colored people* to *people of color*. Those who embrace this modified term are imbuing it with meanings that offer an identity of respect. The term also has political meanings. It implies bonds that cross racial–ethnic lines, mutual ties, and a sense of identity rooted in historical oppression.

The ethnic terms we choose—or which are given to us—are major self-identifiers. They indicate both membership in some particular group and a separation from other groups.

There is *always* disagreement about racial–ethnic terms, and *colored people* is no exception. Although most rejected the term, some found in it a sense of respect and claimed it for themselves. The acronym NAACP, for example, stands for the National Association for the Advancement of Colored People. The new term, *people of color*, arouses similar feelings. Some individuals whom this term would include point out that this new label still makes color the primary identifier of people. They stress that humans transcend race–ethnicity, that what we have in common as human beings goes much deeper than what you see on the surface. They stress that we should avoid terms that focus on differences in the pigmentation of our skin.

The language of self-reference in a society that is so conscious of skin color is an ongoing issue. As long as our society continues to emphasize such superficial differences, the search for adequate terms is not likely to ever be "finished." In this quest for terms that strike the right chord, the term *people of color* may become a historical footnote. If it does, it will be replaced by another term that indicates changing self-identifications within a changing culture.

For Your Consideration

➔ What terms do you use to refer to your race–ethnicity? What "bad" terms do you know that others have used to refer to your race–ethnicity? What is the difference in meaning between the terms you use and the "bad" terms? Where does that meaning come from?

activities for which people would otherwise be arrested are permitted—and expected—including public drunkenness and some nudity. The norms are never completely dropped, however—just loosened a bit. Go too far, and the police step in.

Some societies have *moral holiday places*, locations where norms are expected to be broken. The red-light district of a city is one example. There, prostitutes are allowed to work the streets, bothered only when political pressure builds to "clean up" the area. If these same prostitutes attempt to solicit customers in adjacent areas, however, they are promptly arrested. Each year, the hometown of the team that wins the Super Bowl becomes a moral holiday place—for one night.

One of the more interesting examples is "Party Cove" at Lake of the Ozarks in Missouri, a fairly straitlaced area of the country.

During the summer, hundreds of boaters—those operating everything from cabin cruisers to jet skis—moor their vessels together in a highly publicized cove, where many get drunk, take off their clothes, and dance on the boats. In one of the more humorous incidents, boaters complained that a nude woman was riding a jet ski outside of the cove. The water patrol investigated but refused to arrest the woman because she was within the law—she had sprayed shaving cream on certain parts of her body. The Missouri Water Patrol has even given a green light to Party Cove, announcing in the local newspaper that officers will not enter this cove, supposedly because "there is so much traffic that they might not be able to get out in time to handle an emergency elsewhere."

Folkways, Mores, and Taboos

Norms that are not strictly enforced are called **folkways**. We expect people to follow folkways, but we are likely to shrug our shoulders and not make a big deal about it if they don't. If someone insists on passing you on the right side of the sidewalk, for example, you are unlikely to take corrective action, although if the sidewalk is crowded and you must move out of the way, you might give the person a dirty look.

Other norms, however, are taken much more seriously. We think of them as essential to our core values, and we insist on conformity. These are called **mores** (MORE-rays). A person who steals, rapes, or kills has violated some of society's most important mores. As sociologist Ian Robertson (1987:62) put it,

> *A man who walks down a street wearing nothing on the upper half of his body is violating a folkway; a man who walks down the street wearing nothing on the lower half of his body is violating one of our most important mores, the requirement that people cover their genitals and buttocks in public.*

You can see, then, that one group's folkways can be another group's mores: A man walking down the street with the upper half of his body uncovered is deviating from a folkway, but a woman doing the same thing is violating the mores. In addition, the folkways and mores of a subculture (discussed in the next section) may be the opposite of mainstream culture. For example, to walk down the sidewalk in a nudist camp with the entire body uncovered would conform to that subculture's folkways.

A **taboo** refers to a norm so strongly ingrained that even the thought of its violation is greeted with revulsion. Eating human flesh and parents having sex with their children are examples of such behaviors. When someone breaks a taboo, the individual is usually judged unfit to live in the same society as others. The sanctions are severe and may include prison, banishment, or death.

Read on **MySocLab**
Document: Horace Miner, Body Ritual Among the Nacirema

The violation of *mores* is a serious matter. In this case, it is serious enough that security at an international rugby match in Edinburgh, Scotland, has swung into action. The rugby fan, who has painted his face in his country's colors, seems to be in the process of reclaiming the norm of covering up.

Many Cultural Worlds

2.3 Distinguish between subcultures and countercultures.

Subcultures

Before beginning this section, get an introduction to subcultures by looking at the photo essay on the next two pages.

Groups of people who occupy some small corner in life, such as an occupation, tend to develop specialized ways of communicating with one another. To outsiders, their talk, even if it is in English, can sound like a foreign language. Here is one of my favorite quotations by a politician:

> *There are things we know that we know. There are known unknowns; that is to say, there are things that we now know we don't know. But there are also unknown unknowns; there are things we do not know we don't know. (Donald Rumsfeld, quoted in Dickey and Barry 2006:38)*

Whatever Rumsfeld, the former secretary of defense under George W. Bush, meant by his statement probably will remain a known unknown. (Or would it be an unknown unknown?)

folkways norms that are not strictly enforced

mores norms that are strictly enforced because they are thought essential to core values or the well-being of the group

taboo a norm so strong that it brings extreme sanctions, even revulsion, if violated

Looking at Subcultures

Subcultures can form around any interest or activity. Each subculture has its own values and norms that its members share, giving them a common identity. Each also has special terms that pinpoint the group's corner of life and that its members use to communicate with one another. Some of us belong to several subcultures.

As you can see from these photos, most subcultures are compatible with the values and norms of the mainstream culture. They represent specialized interests around which its members have chosen to build tiny worlds. Some subcultures, however, conflict with the mainstream culture. Sociologists give the name *countercultures* to subcultures whose values (such as those of outlaw motorcyclists) or activities and goals (such as those of terrorists) are opposed to the mainstream culture. Countercultures, however, are exceptional, and few of us belong to them.

Each subculture provides its members with values and distinctive ways of viewing the world. What values and perceptions do you think are common among body builders?

Membership in this subculture is not easily awarded. Not only must high-steel ironworkers prove that they are able to work at great heights but also that they fit into the group socially. Newcomers are tested by members of the group, and they must demonstrate that they can take joking without offense.

Specialized values and interests are two of the characteristics that mark subcultures. What values and interests distinguish the modeling subculture?

The subculture that centers around tattooing previously existed on the fringes of society, with seamen and circus folk its main participants. It now has entered mainstream society, but not to this extreme.

With their specialized language and activities, surfers are highly recognized as members of a subculture. This surfer is "in the tube."

The truck driver subculture, centering on their occupational activities and interests, is also broken into smaller subcultures that reflect their experiences of race–ethnicity.

Why would anyone decorate herself like this? Among the many reasons, one is to show solidarity (appreciation, shared interest) with the subculture that centers on comic book characters.

Even subcultures can have subcultures. The rodeo subculture is a subculture of "western" subculture. The values that unite its members are reflected in their speech, clothing, and specialized activities, such as the one shown here.

subculture the values and related behaviors of a group that distinguish its members from the larger culture; a world within a world

counterculture a group whose values, beliefs, norms, and related behaviors place its members in opposition to the broader culture

We have a similar problem in sociology. Try to figure out what this means:

> *These narratives challenge the "blaming the victim" approach, which has been dominant in the public discourse. The first and oldest is the well-known liberal narrative, here termed the structure/context counter-narrative. The other two counter-narratives—the agency/resistance counter-narrative and voice/action counter-narrative—are built on the analysis of the structure/context counter-narrative.* (Krumer-Nevo and Benjamin 2010:694)

As much as possible, I will spare you from such "insider" talk.

Sociologists and politicians form a **subculture**, *a world within the larger world of the dominant culture.* Subcultures are not limited to occupations; they include any corner in life in which people's experiences lead them to have distinctive ways of looking at the world. Even if we cannot understand the quotation from Donald Rumsfeld, it makes us aware that politicians don't view life in quite the same way most of us do.

U.S. society contains *thousands* of subcultures. Some are as broad as the way of life we associate with teenagers, others as narrow as those we associate with bodybuilders—or with politicians. Some U.S. ethnic groups also form subcultures: Their values, norms, and foods set them apart. So might their religion, music, language, and clothing. Even sociologists form a subculture. As you are learning, they also use a unique language in their efforts to understand the world.

Countercultures

Look what a different world this person is living in:

> *If everyone applying for welfare had to supply a doctor's certificate of sterilization, if everyone who had committed a felony were sterilized, if anyone who had mental illness to any degree were sterilized—then our economy could easily take care of these people for the rest of their lives, giving them a decent living standard—but getting them out of the way. That way there would be no children abused, no surplus population, and, after a while, no pollution. . . .*
>
> *When the . . . present world system collapses, it'll be good people like you who will be shooting people in the streets to feed their families.* (Zellner 1995:58, 65)

Welcome to the world of the Aryan supremacist survivalists, where the message is much clearer than that of politicians—and much more disturbing.

The values and norms of most subcultures blend in with mainstream society. In some cases, however, as with the survivalists quoted above, some of the group's values and norms place it at odds with the dominant culture. Sociologists use the term **counterculture** to refer to such groups. To better see this distinction, consider motorcycle enthusiasts and motorcycle gangs. Motorcycle enthusiasts—who emphasize personal freedom and speed *and* affirm cultural values of success through work or education—are members of a subculture. In contrast, the Hells Angels, Pagans, and Bandidos not only stress freedom and speed but also value dirtiness and contempt toward women, work, and education. This makes them a counterculture.

Why are members of the Hells Angels part of a counterculture and not a subculture?

An assault on core values is always met with resistance. To affirm their own values, members of the mainstream culture may ridicule, isolate, or even attack members of the counterculture. The Mormons, for example, were driven out of several states before they finally settled in Utah, which was at that time a wilderness. Even there, the federal government would not let them practice *polygyny* (one man having more than one wife), and Utah's statehood was made conditional on its acceptance of monogamy (Anderson 1942/1966; Williams 2007).

Values in U.S. Society

2.4 Discuss the major U.S. values and explain value clusters, value contradictions, value clashes, how values are lenses of perception, and ideal versus real culture.

An Overview of U.S. Values

As you know, the United States is a **pluralistic society**, made up of many different groups. The United States has numerous religious and racial–ethnic groups, as well as countless interest groups that focus on activities as divergent as hunting deer or collecting Barbie dolls. Within this huge diversity, sociologists have tried to identify the country's **core values**, those that are shared by most of the groups that make up U.S. society. Here are ten core values that sociologist Robin Williams (1965) identified:

Read on **MySocLab**
Document: Edward E. Telles, Mexican Americans and Immigrant Incorporation

1. *Achievement and success.* Americans praise personal achievement, especially outdoing others. This value includes getting ahead at work and school and attaining wealth, power, and prestige.
2. *Individualism.* Americans cherish the ideal that an individual can rise from the bottom of society to its very top. If someone fails to "get ahead," Americans generally find fault with that individual rather than with the social system for placing roadblocks in his or her path.
3. *Hard work.* Americans expect people to work hard to achieve financial success and material comfort.
4. *Efficiency and practicality.* Americans award high marks for getting things done efficiently. Even in everyday life, Americans consider it important to do things fast, and they seek ways to increase efficiency.
5. *Science and technology.* Americans have a passion for applied science, for using science to control nature—to tame rivers and harness winds—and to develop new technology, from iPads to the self-driving cars now being tested.
6. *Material comfort.* Americans expect a high level of material comfort. This includes not only plentiful food, fashionable clothing, and ample housing but also good medical care, late-model cars, and recreational playthings—from smartphones to motor homes.
7. *Freedom.* This core value pervades U.S. life. It underscored the American Revolution, and Americans pride themselves on their personal freedom.
8. *Democracy.* By this term, Americans refer to majority rule, to the right of everyone to express an opinion, and to representative government.
9. *Equality.* It is impossible to understand Americans without being aware of the central role that the value of equality plays in their lives. Equality of opportunity (part of the ideal culture discussed later) has significantly influenced U.S. history and continues to mark relations between the groups that make up U.S. society.
10. *Group superiority.* Although it contradicts the values of freedom, democracy, and equality, Americans regard some groups more highly than others and have done so throughout their history. The denial of the vote to women, the slaughter of Native Americans, and the enslavement of Africans are a few examples of how the groups considered superior have denied equality and freedom to others.

In an earlier publication, I updated Williams' analysis by adding these three values.

1. *Education.* Americans are expected to go as far in school as their abilities and finances allow. Over the years, the definition of an "adequate" education has changed, and today a college education is considered an appropriate goal for most Americans. Those who have an opportunity for higher education and do not take it are sometimes viewed as doing something "wrong"—not merely as making a bad choice, but as somehow being involved in an immoral act.

pluralistic society a society made up of many different groups

core values the values that are central to a group, those around which it builds a common identity

2. *Religiosity.* There is a feeling that "every true American ought to be religious." This does not mean that everyone is expected to join a church, synagogue, or mosque but that everyone ought to acknowledge a belief in a Supreme Being and follow some set of matching precepts. This value is so pervasive that Americans stamp "In God We Trust" on their money and declare in their national pledge of allegiance that they are "one nation under God."
3. *Romantic love.* Americans feel that the only proper basis for marriage is romantic love. Songs, literature, mass media, and folk beliefs all stress this value. Americans grow misty-eyed at the theme that "love conquers all."

Value Clusters

As you can see, values are not independent units; some cluster together to form a larger whole. In the **value cluster** that surrounds success, for example, we find education, hard work, material comfort, and individualism bound up together. Americans are expected to go far in school, to work hard afterward, and then to attain a high level of material comfort, which, in turn, demonstrates success. Success is attributed to the individual's efforts; lack of success is blamed on his or her faults.

Value Contradictions

You probably were surprised to see group superiority on the list of dominant American values. This is an example of what I mentioned in Chapter 1, how sociology upsets people and creates resistance. Few people want to bring something like this into the open. It violates today's *ideal culture*, a concept we will discuss shortly. But this is what sociologists do—they look beyond the façade to penetrate what is really going on. And when you look at our history, there is no doubt that group superiority has been a dominant value. It still is, but values change, and this one is diminishing.

Value contradictions, then, are part of culture. Not all values come wrapped in neat, pretty packages, and you can see how group superiority contradicts freedom, democracy, and equality. There simply cannot be full expression of freedom, democracy, and equality along with racism and sexism. Something has to give. One way in which Americans in the past sidestepped this contradiction was to say that freedom, democracy, and equality applied only to some groups. The contradiction was bound to surface over time, however, and so it did with the Civil War and the women's liberation movement. *It is precisely at the point of value contradictions, then, that one can see a major force for social change in a society.*

An Emerging Value Cluster

A value cluster of four interrelated core values—leisure, self-fulfillment, physical fitness, and youthfulness—is emerging in the United States. So is a fifth core value—concern for the environment.

1. *Leisure.* The emergence of leisure as a value is reflected in a huge recreation industry—from computer games, boats, vacation homes, and spa retreats to sports arenas, home theaters, adventure vacations, and luxury cruises.
2. *Self-fulfillment.* This value is reflected in the "human potential" movement, which emphasizes becoming "all you can be," and in magazine articles, books, and talk shows that focus on "self-help," "relating," and "personal development."
3. *Physical fitness.* Physical fitness is not a new U.S. value, but the greater emphasis on it is moving it into this emerging cluster. You can see this trend in the publicity given to nutrition, organic foods, weight, and diet; the joggers, cyclists, and backpackers; the marathons; and the countless health clubs and physical fitness centers.

value cluster values that together form a larger whole

value contradiction values that contradict one another; to follow the one means to come into conflict with the other

Physical fitness is part of an emerging value cluster.

4. *Youthfulness*. Valuing youth and disparaging old age are also not new, but some analysts note a sense of urgency in today's emphasis on youthfulness. They attribute this to the huge number of aging baby boomers, who, aghast at the physical changes that accompany their advancing years, are attempting to deny or at least postpone their biological fate. Some physicians are even claiming that aging is not a normal life event but a disease (Nieuwenhuis-Mark 2011).
5. *Concern for the environment*. During most of U.S. history, the environment was viewed as something to be exploited—a wilderness to be settled, forests to be cleared for farmland and lumber, rivers and lakes to be fished, and animals to be hunted. One result was the near extinction of the bison and the extinction in 1914 of the passenger pigeon, a species of bird previously so numerous that its annual migration would darken the skies for days. With their pollution laws and lists of endangered species, today's Americans have developed an apparently long-term concern for the environment.

In Sum: Values don't "just happen." They are related to conditions of society. This emerging value cluster is a response to fundamental changes in U.S. culture. Earlier generations of Americans were focused on forging a nation and fighting for economic survival. But today, millions of Americans are freed from long hours of work, and millions retire from work at an age when they anticipate decades of life ahead of them. This new value cluster centers on helping people maintain their health and vigor during their younger years and enabling them to enjoy their years of retirement.

Only when an economy produces adequate surpluses can a society afford these emerging values. To produce both longer lives and retirement, for example, takes a certain stage of economic development. Concern for the environment is another remarkable example. People act on environmental concerns only *after* they have met their basic needs. The world's poor nations have a difficult time "affording" this value at this point in their development (MacLennan 2012).

When Values Clash

Challenges in core values are met with strong resistance by the people who hold them dear. They see change as a threat to their way of life, an undermining of both their present and their future. Efforts to change gender roles, for example, arouse intense controversy, as do same-sex marriages. Alarmed at such onslaughts against their values, traditionalists fiercely defend the family relationships and gender roles they grew up with. Some use the term *culture wars* to refer to the clash in values between traditionalists and those advocating change, but the term is highly exaggerated. Compared with the violence directed against the Mormons, today's culture clashes are but mild disagreements.

Values as Distorting Lenses

Values and their supporting beliefs are lenses through which we see the world. The views that these lenses provide are often of what life *ought* to be like, not what it is. For example, Americans value individualism so highly that they tend to see almost everyone as free and equal in pursuing the goal of success. This value blinds them to the significance of the circumstances that keep people from achieving success. The dire consequences of family poverty, parents' low education, and dead-end jobs tend to drop from sight. Instead, Americans see the unsuccessful as not taking advantage of opportunities, or as

Values, both those held by individuals and those that represent a nation or people, can undergo deep shifts. It is difficult for many of us to grasp the pride with which earlier Americans destroyed trees that took thousands of years to grow, are located only on one tiny speck of the globe, and that we today consider part of the nation's and world's heritage. But this is a value statement, representing current views. The pride expressed on these woodcutters' faces represents another set of values entirely.

having some inherent laziness or dull minds. And they "know" they are right, because the mass media dangle before their eyes enticing stories of individuals who have succeeded despite the greatest of handicaps.

"Ideal" Versus "Real" Culture

Many of the norms that surround cultural values are followed only partially. Differences always exist between a group's ideals and what its members actually do. Consequently, sociologists use the term **ideal culture** to refer to the values, norms, and goals that a group considers ideal, worth aiming for. Success, for example, is part of ideal culture. Americans glorify academic progress, hard work, and the display of material goods as signs of individual achievement. What people actually do, however, usually falls short of the cultural ideal. Compared with their abilities, for example, most people don't work as hard as they could or go as far as they could in school. Sociologists call the norms and values that people actually follow **real culture.**

2.5 Take a position on the issue of the existence of cultural universals and contrast sociobiology with sociology.

ideal culture a people's ideal values and norms; the goals held out for them

real culture the norms and values that people actually follow; as opposed to *ideal culture*

cultural universal a value, norm, or other cultural trait that is found in every group

Cultural Universals

With the amazing variety of human cultures around the world, are there any **cultural universals**—values, norms, or other cultural traits that are found everywhere?

To answer this question, anthropologist George Murdock (1945) combed through the data that anthropologists had gathered on hundreds of groups around the world. He compared their customs concerning courtship, marriage, funerals, games, laws, music, myths, incest taboos, and even toilet training. He found that these activities are present in all cultures, but *the specific customs differ from one group to another*. There is no universal form of the family, no universal way of toilet training children, nor a universal music. And as you noticed in the box on dancing with the dead, there is no universal way of disposing of the deceased.

Incest is another remarkable example. Groups don't even agree on what incest is. The Mundugumors of New Guinea extend the incest taboo so far that for each man, seven of every eight women are ineligible marriage partners (Mead 1935/1950). Other groups go in the opposite direction and allow some men to marry their own daughters (La Barre 1954). Some groups even *require* that brothers and sisters marry one another, although only in certain circumstances (Beals and Hoijer 1965). The Burundi of Africa even insist that a son have sex with his mother—but only to remove a certain curse (Albert 1963). Such sexual relations, so surprising to us, are limited to special people (royalty) or to extraordinary situations (such as the night before a dangerous lion hunt). No society permits generalized incest for its members.

In Sum: Although there are universal human activities (singing, playing games, storytelling, preparing food, marrying, child rearing, disposing of the dead, and so on), there is no universal way of doing any of them. Humans have no biological imperative that results in one particular form of behavior throughout the world. As indicated in the following Thinking Critically section, although a few sociologists take the position that genes significantly influence human behavior, almost all sociologists reject this view.

Watch on **MySocLab**
Video: The Role of Humor

THINKING CRITICALLY

Are We Prisoners of Our Genes? Sociobiology and Human Behavior

A controversial view of human behavior, called **sociobiology** (also known as neo-Darwinism and evolutionary psychology), provides a sharp contrast to the perspective of this chapter, that the key to human behavior is culture. Sociobiologists (evolutionary psychologists, evolutionary anthropologists) believe that because of natural selection, biology is a basic cause of human behavior.

Unlike this beautiful ant, we humans are not controlled by instincts. Sociobiologists, though, are exploring the extent to which genes influence our behavior.

Charles Darwin (1859), who, as we saw in Chapter 1, adopted Spencer's idea of *natural selection*, pointed out that the genes of a species—the units that contain an individual's traits—are not distributed evenly among a population. The characteristics that some members inherit make it easier for them to survive their environment, increasing the likelihood that they will pass their genetic traits to the next generation. Over thousands of generations, the genetic traits that aid survival become common in a species, while those that do not aid survival become less common or even disappear. Natural selection explains not only the physical characteristics of animals but also their behavior, since over countless generations, instincts emerged.

Edward Wilson (1975), an insect specialist, set off an uproar when he claimed that human behavior, like the behavior of cats, rats, bats, and gnats, has been bred into *Homo sapiens* through evolutionary principles. Wilson went on to claim that competition and cooperation, envy and altruism—even religion, slavery, genocide, and war and peace—can be explained by sociobiology. He provocatively added that because human behavior

sociobiology a framework of thought in which human behavior is considered to be the result of natural selection and biological factors: a fundamental cause of human behavior

technology in its narrow sense, tools; its broader sense includes the skills or procedures necessary to make and use those tools

new technology the emerging technologies of an era that have a significant impact on social life

can be explained in terms of genetic programming, sociobiology will eventually absorb sociology, as well as anthropology and psychology.

Obviously, sociologists disagree with Wilson. It is not that sociologists deny that biology is important in human behavior—at least in the sense that it takes a highly developed brain to develop human culture and abstract thought and that there would be no speech if humans had no tongue or larynx. That to stay alive we must eat and keep from freezing certainly motivates some of our behavior. Biology is so significant that it could even underlie the origin of gender inequality. This is one of the theories we discuss in Chapter 11, pages 295–296.

Some sociologists are developing what they call *genetics-informed sociology*, which places an emphasis on the influence of genes on human behavior. They are coming up with interesting findings. For example, people with the gene DRD2 are more likely than people without this gene to abuse alcohol ("The Interaction of Genes . . ." 2012). Similarly, males who have the gene 9R/9R average fewer sexual partners than people without this gene. The 9R/9R individuals are also less likely to binge drink and more likely to wear seat belts (Guo et al. 2008).

With these findings, where is the social? Simply put, the genes don't determine people's behavior. Rather, their influence is modified by social experiences. On the obvious level, Arabs with the gene DRD2 who live in a society where alcohol is difficult to find are less likely to abuse alcohol than are Americans with this gene who hang around bars. Similarly, subcultures that encourage or discourage sexual behavior override the 9R/9R gene. To their surprise, researchers have even found that social experiences can change a person's genes (Ledger 2009).

In Sum: To say that genes have an influence on human behavior is a far cry from saying that genetics determines human behavior, that we act as we do because of genetics. On the contrary, pigs act like pigs and spiders act like spiders because instincts control their behavior. We humans, in contrast, possess a self and engage in abstract thought. We develop purposes and goals and discuss the reasons that we do things. Unlike pigs and spiders, we are immersed in a world of symbols that we use to consider, reflect, and make reasoned choices. Because we humans are not prisoners of our genes, we have developed fascinatingly diverse ways of life around the world—which we will be exploring in this text. ■

2.6 Explain how technology changes culture and what cultural lag and cultural leveling are.

Technology in the Global Village

The New Technology

The gestures, language, values, folkways, and mores that we have discussed—all are part of symbolic (nonmaterial) culture. Culture, as you recall, also has a material aspect: a group's *things*, from its houses to its toys. Central to a group's material culture is its technology. In its simplest sense, **technology** can be equated with tools. In a broader sense, technology also includes the skills or procedures necessary to make and use those tools.

We can use the term **new technology** to refer to an emerging technology that has a significant impact on social life. Although people develop minor technologies all the time, most are only slight modifications of existing technologies. Occasionally, however, they develop a technology that makes a major impact on human life. It is primarily to these innovations that the term *new technology* refers. Five hundred years ago, the new technology was the printing press. For us, the new technology consists of the microchip, computers, satellites, and the Internet.

Language is the basis of human culture around the world. The past decade has seen major developments in communication—the ease and speed with which we can talk to people across the globe. This development is destined to have vital effects on culture. This photo of teens texting was taken in a village in Ethiopia.

The sociological significance of technology goes far beyond the tool itself. *Technology sets the framework for a group's nonmaterial culture.* It is obvious that if a group's technology changes, so do the ways people do things. But the effects of technology go far beyond this. Technology also influences how people think and how they relate to one another. An example is gender relations. Through the centuries and throughout the world, it has been the custom (nonmaterial culture) for men to dominate women. Today's global communications (material culture) make this custom more difficult to maintain. For example, when Arab women watch Western television, they observe an unfamiliar freedom in gender relations. As these women use e-mail and cell phones to talk about what they have seen, they both convey and create discontent, as well as feelings of sisterhood. These communications motivate some of them to agitate for social change. (If you want to jump ahead and read about an incipient women's movement in an Arab country, go to page 295.)

In today's world, the long-accepted idea that it is proper to withhold rights on the basis of someone's sex can no longer be sustained. What usually lies beyond our awareness in this revolutionary change is the role of the new technology, which joins the world's nations into a global communications network.

LITERATURE
BOOK
DAVE CARPENTER
"JUST THINK OF IT AS IF YOU'RE READING A LONG TEXT-MESSAGE."

Technological advances are now so rapid that there can be cultural gaps between generations.

Cultural Lag and Cultural Change

Three or four generations ago, sociologist William Ogburn (1922/1950) coined the term **cultural lag**. By this, Ogburn meant that not all parts of a culture change at the same pace. When one part of a culture changes, other parts lag behind.

cultural lag Ogburn's term for human behavior lagging behind technological innovations

Ogburn pointed out that *a group's material culture usually changes first, with the nonmaterial culture lagging behind.* This leaves the nonmaterial (or symbolic) culture playing a game of catch-up. For example, when we get sick, we can type our symptoms into a computer and get an instant diagnosis and recommended course of treatment. In some tests, computer programs outperform physicians. Yet our customs have not caught up with our technology, and we continue to visit the doctor's office.

Sometimes nonmaterial culture never does catch up. We can rigorously hold onto some outmoded form—one that once was needed but that long ago was bypassed by technology. Have you ever wondered why our "school year" is nine months long, and why we take summers off? For most of us, this is "just the way it is," and we have never questioned it. But there is more to this custom than meets the eye. In the late 1800s, when universal schooling came about, the school year matched the technology of the time. Most parents were farmers, and for survival they needed their children's help at the crucial times of planting and harvesting. Today, generations later, when few people farm and there is no need for the "school year" to be so short, we still live with this cultural lag.

Technology and Cultural Leveling

For most of human history, communication was limited and travel was slow. Consequently, in their smaller groups living in relative isolation, people developed highly distinctive ways of life as they responded to the particular situations they faced. The unique characteristics they developed that distinguished one culture from another tended to change little over time. The Tasmanians, who live on a remote island off the coast of Australia, provide an extreme example. For thousands of years, they had no contact with other people. They were so isolated that they did not even know how to make clothing or fire (Edgerton 1992).

cultural diffusion the spread of cultural traits from one group to another; includes both material and nonmaterial cultural traits

Except in such rare instances as this, humans have always had *some* contact with other groups. During these contacts, people learned from one another, adopting things they found desirable. In this process, called **cultural diffusion**, groups are most open to

cultural leveling the process by which cultures become similar to one another; refers especially to the process by which Western culture is being exported and diffused into other nations

changes in their technology or material culture. They usually are eager, for example, to adopt superior weapons and tools. In remote jungles in South America, one can find metal cooking pots, steel axes, and even bits of clothing spun in mills in South Carolina. Although the direction of cultural diffusion today is primarily from the West to other parts of the world, cultural diffusion is not a one-way street—as bagels, woks, hammocks, and sushi in the United States attest.

With today's trade, travel, and communications, cultural diffusion is occurring rapidly. Daily, we use products from around the world. Jet planes have made it possible to journey around the globe in a matter of hours. In the not-so-distant past, a trip from the United States to Africa was so unusual that only a few adventurous people made it, so few that newspapers would herald their feat. Today, hundreds of thousands make the trip each year.

The changes in communication are no less vast. Communication used to be limited to face-to-face speech, written messages that were passed from hand to hand, and visual signals such as smoke or light reflected from mirrors. Despite newspapers and even the telegraph, people in some parts of the United States did not hear that the Civil War had ended until weeks and even months after it was over. Today's electronic communications transmit messages across the globe in seconds, and we learn almost instantaneously what is happening on the other side of the world. During the Iraq War, reporters traveled with U.S. soldiers, and for the first time in history, the public was able to view live videos of battles as they took place. When Navy Seals executed Osama bin Laden under President Obama's orders, Obama and Hillary Clinton watched the helicopter land in bin Laden's compound, listened to reports of the killing, and watched the Seals leave (Schmidle 2011).

Travel and communication bridge time and space to such an extent that there is almost no "other side of the world" anymore. One result is **cultural leveling**, a process in which cultures become more and more similar to one another. The globalization of capitalism brings with it both technology and Western culture. Japan, for example, has adopted not only capitalism but also Western forms of dress and music, transforming it into a blend of Western and Eastern cultures.

Cultural leveling is occurring rapidly, with some strange twists. These men from an Amazon tribe, who have just come back from a week hunting in the jungle, are wearing traditional headdress and using traditional weapons, but you can easily spot something else that is jarringly out of place.

Cultural leveling is apparent to any international traveler. The golden arches of McDonald's welcome visitors to Tokyo, Paris, London, Madrid, Moscow, Hong Kong, and Beijing. When I visited a jungle village in India—no electricity, no running water, and so remote that the only entrance was by a footpath—I saw a young man sporting a cap with the Nike emblem.

Although the bridging of geography, time, and culture by electronic signals and the adoption of Western icons do not in and of themselves mark the end of traditional cultures, the inevitable result is some degree of *cultural leveling*. We are producing a blander, less distinctive way of life—U.S. culture with French, Japanese, and Brazilian accents, so to speak. Although the "cultural accent" remains, something vital is lost forever.

MySocLab — Study and Review on MySocLab

CHAPTER 2 Summary and Review

What Is Culture?

2.1 Explain what culture is, how culture provides orientations to life, and what practicing cultural relativism means.

How do sociologists understand culture?

All human groups possess **culture**—language, beliefs, values, norms, and material objects that they pass from one generation to the next. **Material culture** consists of objects such as art, buildings, clothing, weapons, and tools. **Nonmaterial** (or **symbolic**) **culture** is a group's ways of thinking and its patterns of behavior. **Ideal culture** is a group's ideal values, norms, and goals. **Real culture** is people's actual behavior, which often falls short of their cultural ideals. Pp. 34–35.

What are cultural relativism and ethnocentrism?

People are **ethnocentric**; that is, they use their own culture as a yardstick for judging the ways of others. In contrast, those who embrace **cultural relativism** try to understand other cultures on those cultures' own terms. Pp. 35–41.

Components of Symbolic Culture

2.2 Know the components of symbolic culture: gestures, language, values, norms, sanctions, folkways, mores, and taboos; also explain the Sapir-Whorf hypothesis.

What are the components of nonmaterial culture?

The central component of nonmaterial culture is **symbols**, anything to which people attach meaning and that they use to communicate with others. Universally, the symbols of nonmaterial culture are **gestures**, **language**, **values**, **norms**, **sanctions**, **folkways**, and **mores.** Pp. 41–42.

Why is language so significant to culture?

Language allows human experience to be goal-directed, co-operative, and cumulative. It also lets humans move beyond the present and share a past, a future, and other common perspectives. According to the **Sapir-Whorf hypothesis**, language even shapes our thoughts and perceptions. Pp. 42–45.

How do values, norms, sanctions, folkways, and mores reflect culture?

All groups have **values**, standards by which they define what is desirable or undesirable, and **norms**, rules or expectations about behavior. Groups use **positive sanctions** to show approval of those who follow their norms and **negative sanctions** to show disapproval of those who violate them. Norms that are not strictly enforced are called **folkways**, while **mores** are norms to which groups demand conformity because they reflect core values. Pp. 45–47.

Many Cultural Worlds

2.3 Distinguish between subcultures and countercultures.

How do subcultures and countercultures differ?

A **subculture** is a group whose values and related behaviors distinguish its members from the general culture. A **counterculture** holds some values that stand in opposition to those of the dominant culture. Pp. 47–51.

Values in U.S. Society

2.4 Discuss the major U.S. values and explain value clusters, value contradictions, value clashes, how values are lenses of perception, and ideal versus real culture.

What are some core U.S. values?

Although the United States is a **pluralistic society**, made up of many groups, each with its own set of values, certain values dominate. These are called its **core values**. Core values do not change without opposition. Some values cluster together to form a larger whole called **value clusters**. **Value contradictions** (such as equality versus sexism and racism) indicate areas of tension, which are likely points of social change. Leisure, self-fulfillment, physical fitness, youthfulness, and concern for the environment form an emerging value cluster. Pp. 51–54.

Cultural Universals

2.5 Take a position on the issue of the existence of cultural universals and contrast sociobiology with sociology.

Do cultural universals exist?

Cultural universal refers to a value, norm, or other cultural trait that is found in all cultures. Although all human groups have customs concerning cooking, childbirth, funerals, and so on, because these customs differ from one culture to another, there are no cultural universals. Pp. 54–56.

Technology in the Global Village

2.6 Explain how technology changes culture and what cultural lag and cultural leveling are.

How is technology changing culture?

William Ogburn coined the term **cultural lag** to describe how a group's nonmaterial culture lags behind its changing technology. With today's technological advances in trade, travel, and communications, **cultural diffusion** is occurring rapidly. This leads to **cultural leveling**, groups becoming similar as they adopt items from other cultures. Much of the richness of the world's diverse cultures is being lost in the process. Pp. 56–59.

Thinking Critically about Chapter 2

1. Do you favor ethnocentrism or cultural relativism? Explain your position.
2. Do you think that the language change in Miami, Florida (discussed on page 44), indicates the future of the United States? Why or why not?
3. Are you a member of any subcultures? Which one(s)? Why do you think that your group is a subculture and not a counterculture? What is your group's relationship to the mainstream culture?

CHAPTER 3

Socialization

Listen to Chapter 3 on MySocLab

Learning Objectives

After you have read this chapter, you should be able to:

3.1 Explain how feral, isolated, and institutionalized children help us understand that "society makes us human." (p. 62)

3.2 Use the ideas and research of Cooley (looking-glass self), Mead (role taking), and Piaget (reasoning) to explain socialization into the self and mind. (p. 67)

3.3 Explain how the development of personality and morality and socialization into emotions are part of how "society makes us human." (p. 70)

3.4 Discuss how gender messages from the family, peers, and the mass media teach us society's gender map. (p. 74)

3.5 Explain why the family, the neighborhood, religion, day care, school, peer groups, and the workplace are called agents of socialization. (p. 79)

3.6 Explain what total institutions are and how they resocialize people. (p. 84)

3.7 Identify major divisions of the life course and discuss the sociological significance of the life course. (p. 86)

3.8 Understand why we are not prisoners of socialization. (p. 90)

The old man was horrified when he found out. *Life never had been good since his daughter lost her hearing when she was just 2 years old. She couldn't even talk—just fluttered her hands around trying to tell him things.*

Over the years, he had gotten used to this. But now . . . he shuddered at the thought of her being pregnant. No one would be willing to marry her; he knew that. And the neighbors, their tongues would never stop wagging. Everywhere he went, he could hear people talking behind his back.

If only his wife were still alive, maybe she could come up with something. What should he do? He couldn't just kick his daughter out into the street.

After the baby was born, the old man tried to shake his feelings, but they wouldn't let loose. Isabelle was a pretty name, but every time he looked at the baby he felt sick to his stomach.

He hated doing it, but there was no way out. His daughter and her baby would have to live in the attic.

> "Her behavior toward strangers, especially men, was almost that of a wild animal, manifesting much fear and hostility."

Unfortunately, this is a true story. Isabelle was discovered in Ohio in 1938 when she was about 6½ years old, living in a dark room with her deaf-mute mother. Isabelle couldn't talk, but she did use gestures to communicate with her mother. An inadequate diet and lack of sunshine had given Isabelle a disease called rickets.

> *[Her legs] were so bowed that as she stood erect the soles of her shoes came nearly flat together, and she got about with a skittering gait. Her behavior toward strangers, especially men, was almost that of a wild animal, manifesting much fear and hostility. In lieu of speech she made only a strange croaking sound. (Davis 1940/2014:156–157)*

When the newspapers reported this case, sociologist Kingsley Davis decided to find out what had happened to Isabelle after her discovery. We'll come back to that later, but first let's use the case of Isabelle to gain insight into human nature.

Society Makes Us Human

"What do you mean, society makes us human?" is probably what you are asking. "That sounds ridiculous. I was born a human." The meaning of this statement will become more apparent as we get into the chapter. Let's start by considering what is human about human nature. How much of a person's characteristics comes from "nature" (heredity) and how much from "nurture" (the **social environment**, contact with others)? Experts are trying to answer the nature–nurture question by studying identical twins who were separated at birth and were reared in different environments, such as those discussed in the Down-to-Earth Sociology box on the next page.

Another way is to examine children who have had little human contact. Let's consider such children.

3.1 Explain how feral, isolated, and institutionalized children help us understand that "society makes us human."

Feral Children

> *The naked child was found in the forest, walking on all fours, eating grass and lapping water from the river. When he saw a small animal, he pounced on it. Growling, he ripped at it with his teeth. Tearing chunks from the body, he chewed them ravenously.*

This is an apt description of reports that have come in over the centuries. Supposedly, these **feral** (wild) **children** could not speak; they bit, scratched, growled, and walked on

Down-to-Earth Sociology

Heredity or Environment? The Case of Jack and Oskar, Identical Twins

Identical twins are almost identical in their genetic makeup. They are the result of one fertilized egg dividing to produce two embryos. (Some differences can occur as genetic codes are copied.) If heredity determines personality—or attitudes, temperament, skills, and intelligence—then identical twins should be identical, or almost so, not only in their looks but also in these characteristics.

The fascinating case of Jack and Oskar helps us unravel this mystery. From their experience, we can see the far-reaching effects of the environment—how social experiences override biology.

Jack Yufe and Oskar Stohr are identical twins. Born in 1932 to a Roman Catholic mother and a Jewish father, they were separated as babies after their parents divorced. Jack was reared in Trinidad by his father. There, he learned loyalty to Jews and hatred of Hitler and the Nazis. After the war, Jack and his father moved to Israel. When he was 17, Jack joined a kibbutz and later served in the Israeli army.

Oskar's upbringing was a mirror image of Jack's. Oskar was reared in Czechoslovakia by his mother's mother, who was a strict Catholic. When Oskar was a toddler, Hitler annexed this area of Czechoslovakia, and Oskar learned to love Hitler and to hate Jews. He joined the Hitler Youth. Like the Boy Scouts, this organization was designed to instill healthy living, love of the outdoors, friendships, and patriotism—but this one added loyalty to Hitler and hatred for Jews.

In 1954, the two brothers met. It was a short meeting, and Jack had been warned not to tell Oskar that they were Jews. Twenty-five years later, in 1979, when they were 47 years old, social scientists at the University of Minnesota brought them together again. These researchers figured that because Jack and Oskar had the same genes, any differences they showed would have to be the result of their environment—their different social experiences.

Not only did Jack and Oskar hold different attitudes toward the war, Hitler, and Jews, but their basic orientations to life were also different. In their politics, Jack was liberal, while Oskar was more conservative. Jack was a workaholic, while Oskar enjoyed leisure. And, as you can predict, Jack was proud of being a Jew. Oskar, who by this time knew that he was a Jew, wouldn't even mention it.

That would seem to settle the matter. But there were other things. As children, Jack and Oskar had both excelled at sports but had difficulty with math. They also had the same rate of speech, and both liked sweet liqueur and spicy foods. Strangely, each flushed the toilet both before and after using it, and they each enjoyed startling people by sneezing in crowded elevators.

The relative influence of heredity and the environment in human behavior has fascinated and plagued researchers. Twins intrigue researchers, especially those twins who were separated at birth.

For Your Consideration

➤ Heredity or environment? How much influence does each have? The question is far from settled, but at this point it seems fair to conclude that the *limits* of certain physical and mental abilities are established by heredity (such as ability at sports and aptitude for mathematics), while attitudes are the result of the environment. Basic temperament, though, seems to be inherited. Although the answer is still fuzzy, we can put it this way: For some parts of life, the blueprint is drawn by heredity; but even here the environment can redraw those lines. For other parts, the individual is a blank slate, and it is up to the environment to determine what is written on that slate.

Sources: Based on Begley 1979; Chen 1979; Wright 1995; Segal and Hershberger 2005; Ledger 2009; Johnson et al. 2009; Segal 2011.

all fours. They drank by lapping water, ate grass, tore eagerly at raw meat, and showed insensitivity to pain and cold.

social environment the entire human environment, including interaction with others

Why am I even mentioning stories that sound so exaggerated? Consider what happened in 1798. In that year, such a child was found in the forests of Aveyron, France. "The wild boy of Aveyron," as he became known, would have been written off as another folk myth, except that French scientists took the child to a laboratory and studied him. Like the feral children in the earlier informal reports, this child gave no indication of feeling the cold. Most startling, though, when he saw a small animal, the boy would growl, pounce on it, and devour it uncooked. Even today, the scientists' detailed reports make fascinating reading (Itard 1962).

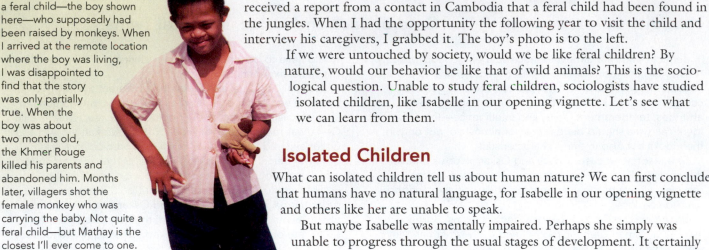

One of the reasons I went to Cambodia was to interview a feral child—the boy shown here—who supposedly had been raised by monkeys. When I arrived at the remote location where the boy was living, I was disappointed to find that the story was only partially true. When the boy was about two months old, the Khmer Rouge killed his parents and abandoned him. Months later, villagers shot the female monkey who was carrying the baby. Not quite a feral child—but Mathay is the closest I'll ever come to one.

Ever since I read Itard's account of this boy, I've been fascinated by the seemingly fantastic possibility that animals could rear human children. In 2002, I received a report from a contact in Cambodia that a feral child had been found in the jungles. When I had the opportunity the following year to visit the child and interview his caregivers, I grabbed it. The boy's photo is to the left.

If we were untouched by society, would we be like feral children? By nature, would our behavior be like that of wild animals? This is the sociological question. Unable to study feral children, sociologists have studied isolated children, like Isabelle in our opening vignette. Let's see what we can learn from them.

Isolated Children

What can isolated children tell us about human nature? We can first conclude that humans have no natural language, for Isabelle in our opening vignette and others like her are unable to speak.

But maybe Isabelle was mentally impaired. Perhaps she simply was unable to progress through the usual stages of development. It certainly looked that way—she scored practically zero on her first intelligence test. But after a few months of language training, Isabelle was able to speak in short sentences. In just a year, she could write a few words, do simple addition, and retell stories after hearing them. Seven months later, she had a vocabulary of almost 2,000 words. In just two years, Isabelle reached the intellectual level that is normal for her age. She then went on to school, where she was "bright, cheerful, energetic . . . and participated in all school activities as normally as other children" (Davis 1940/2014).

Read on MySocLab
Document: Kingslely Davis, Final Note on a Case of Extreme Isolation

As discussed in the previous chapter, language is the key to human development. Without language, people have no mechanism for developing thought and communicating their experiences. Unlike animals, humans have no instincts that take the place of language. If an individual lacks language, he or she lives in a world of internal silence, without shared ideas, lacking connections to others.

Without language, there can be no culture—no shared way of life—and culture is the key to what people become. Each of us possesses a biological heritage, but this heritage does not determine specific behaviors, attitudes, or values. It is our culture that superimposes the specifics of what we become onto our biological heritage.

Institutionalized Children

Other than language, what else is required for a child to develop into what we consider a healthy, balanced, intelligent human being? We find part of the answer in an intriguing experiment.

The Skeels/Dye Experiment. Back in the 1930s, orphanages were common because parents were more likely than now to die before their children were grown. Children reared in orphanages tended to have low IQs. "Common sense" (which we noted in Chapter 1 is unreliable) made it seem obvious that their low intelligence was because of poor brains ("They're just born that way"). But two psychologists, H. M. Skeels and H. B. Dye (1939), began to suspect a social cause.

Skeels (1966) provided this account of a "good" orphanage in Iowa, one where he and Dye were consultants:

> *Until about six months, they were cared for in the infant nursery. The babies were kept in standard hospital cribs that often had protective sheeting on the sides, thus effectively limiting visual stimulation; no toys or other objects were hung in the infants' line of vision. Human interactions were limited to busy nurses who, with the speed born of practice and necessity, changed diapers or bedding, bathed and medicated the infants, and fed them efficiently with propped bottles.*

Perhaps, thought Skeels and Dye, the problem was the absence of stimulating social interaction, not the children's brains. To test their controversial idea, they selected thirteen infants who were so slow mentally that no one wanted to adopt them. They placed them in an institution for mentally retarded women. They assigned each infant, then about 19 months old, to a separate ward of women who ranged in mental age from 5 to 12 and in chronological age from 18 to 50. The women were pleased. They enjoyed taking care of the infants' physical needs—diapering, feeding, and so on. And they also loved to play with the children. They cuddled them and showered them with attention. They even competed to see which ward would have "its baby" walking or talking first. In each ward, one woman became particularly attached to the child and figuratively adopted him or her:

> *As a consequence, an intense one-to-one adult–child relationship developed, which was supplemented by the less intense but frequent interactions with the other adults in the environment. Each child had some one person with whom he [or she] was identified and who was particularly interested in him [or her] and his [or her] achievements. (Skeels 1966)*

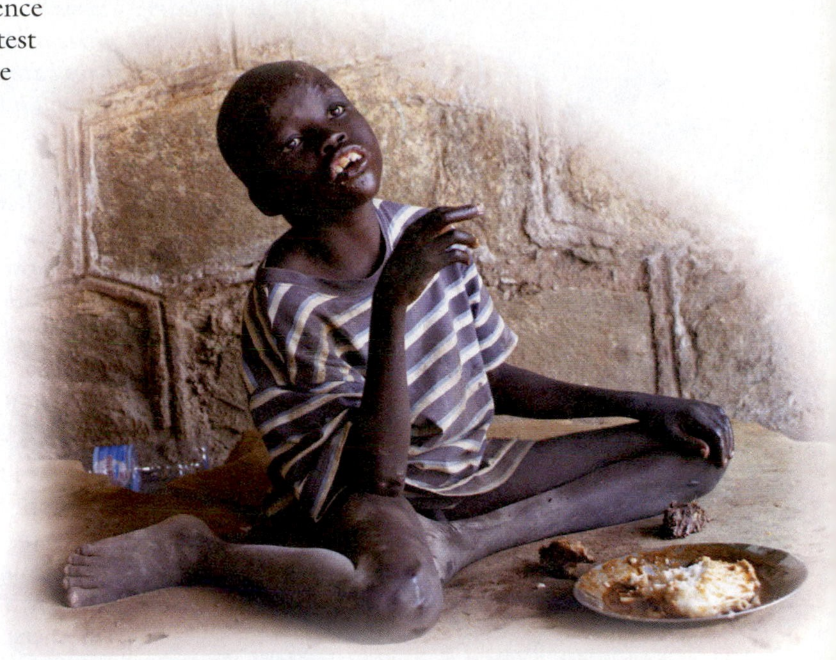

A child in an orphanage in Juba, Sudan. The treatment of this child is likely to affect his ability to reason and to function as an adult.

The researchers left a control group of twelve infants at the orphanage. These infants received the usual care. They also had low IQs, but they were considered somewhat higher in intelligence than the thirteen in the experimental group. Two and a half years later, Skeels and Dye tested all the children's intelligence. Their findings are startling: Those who were cared for by the women in the institution gained an average of 28 IQ points while those who remained in the orphanage lost 30 points.

What happened after these children were grown? Did these initial differences matter? Twenty-one years later, Skeels and Dye did a follow-up study. The twelve in the control group, those who had remained in the orphanage, averaged less than a third-grade education. Four still lived in state institutions, and the others held low-level jobs. Only two had married. The thirteen in the experimental group, those cared for by the institutionalized women, had an average education of twelve grades (about normal for that period). Five had completed one or more years of college. One had even gone to graduate school. Eleven had married. All thirteen were self-supporting or were homemakers (Skeels 1966). Apparently, "high intelligence" depends on early, close relations with other humans.

Orphanage Research in India. The Skeels/Dye findings have been confirmed by research in India, where some orphanages are like those that Skeels and Dye studied—dismal places where unattended children lie in bed all day. When researchers added stimulating play and interaction to the children's activities, not only did the children's motor skills improve, but so did their IQs (Taneja et al. 2002).

The longer that children lack stimulating interaction, though, the more difficulty they have intellectually (Meese 2005). From another heart-wrenching case, that of Genie, you can see how important timing is in the development of "human" characteristics.

Timing and Human Development. Genie, a child in California, was discovered when she was 13 years old. She had been locked in a small room and tied to a potty chair since she was 20 months old:

> *Apparently, Genie's father (70 years old when Genie was discovered in 1970) hated children. He probably had caused the death of two of Genie's siblings. Her 50-year-old mother was partially blind and frightened of her husband. Genie could not speak, did not know how to chew, was unable to stand upright, and could not straighten her hands and legs. On intelligence tests, she scored at the level of a 1-year-old. After intensive training,*

Genie learned to walk and to put garbled, three-word sentences together. Genie's language remained primitive as she grew up. She would take anyone's property if it appealed to her, and she went to the bathroom wherever she wanted. At the age of 21, she was sent to a home for adults who cannot live alone. (Pines 1981)

In Sum: From Genie's pathetic story and from the research on institutionalized children, we can conclude that the basic human traits of intelligence and the ability to establish close bonds with others depend on early interaction with other humans. In addition, there seems to be a period prior to age 13 in which children must learn language and experience human bonding if they are to develop normal intelligence and the ability to be sociable and follow social norms.

Deprived Animals

Like humans, monkeys need interaction to thrive. Those raised in isolation are unable to interact with other monkeys. In this photograph, we see one of the monkeys described in the text. Purposefully frightened by the experimenter, the monkey has taken refuge in the soft terrycloth draped over an artificial "mother."

Finally, let's consider animals that have been deprived of normal interaction. In a series of experiments with rhesus monkeys, psychologists Harry and Margaret Harlow demonstrated the importance of early learning. The Harlows (1962) raised baby monkeys in isolation. As shown in the photo to the left, they gave each monkey two artificial mothers. One "mother" was only a wire frame with a wooden head, but it did have a nipple from which the baby could nurse. The frame of the other "mother," which had no bottle, was covered with soft terrycloth. To obtain food, the baby monkeys nursed at the wire frame.

When the Harlows (1965) frightened the baby monkeys with a mechanical bear or dog, the babies did not run to the wire frame "mother." Instead, they would cling pathetically to their terrycloth "mother." The Harlows concluded that infant–mother bonding is not the result of feeding but, rather, of what they termed "intimate physical contact." To most of us, this phrase means cuddling.

The monkeys raised in isolation could not adjust to monkey life. Placed with other monkeys when they were grown, they didn't know how to participate in "monkey interaction"—to play and to engage in pretend fights—and the other monkeys rejected them. Despite their futile attempts, they didn't even know how to have sexual intercourse. The experimenters designed a special device that allowed some females to become pregnant. Their isolation, however, made them "ineffective, inadequate, and brutal mothers." They "struck their babies, kicked them, or crushed the babies against the cage floor."

In one of their many experiments, the Harlows isolated baby monkeys for different lengths of time and then put them in with the other monkeys. Monkeys that had been isolated for shorter periods (about three months) were able to adjust to normal monkey life. They learned to play and engage in pretend fights. Those isolated for six months or more, however, couldn't make the adjustment, and the other monkeys rejected them. In other words, the longer the period of isolation, the more difficult its effects are to overcome. In addition, there seems to be a critical learning stage: If this stage is missed, it may be impossible to compensate for what has been lost. This may have been the case with Genie.

Because humans are not monkeys, we must be careful about extrapolating from animal studies to human behavior. The Harlow experiments, however, support what we know about children who are reared in isolation.

In Sum: Society Makes Us Human Babies do not develop "naturally" into social adults. If children are reared in isolation, their bodies grow, but they become little more than big animals. Without the concepts that language provides, they can't grasp relationships between people (the "connections" we call brother, sister, parent, friend, teacher, and so on). And without warm, friendly interactions, they can't bond with others. They don't become "friendly" or cooperate with others. In short, it is through human contact that people learn to be members of the human community. This process by which we learn the ways of society (or of particular groups), called **socialization**, is what sociologists have in mind when they say, "Society makes us human."

To add to our understanding of how society makes us human, let's look at how we develop our self-concept, our ability to "take the role of others," and our ability to reason.

Socialization into the Self and Mind

3.2 Use the ideas and research of Cooley (looking-glass self), Mead (role taking), and Piaget (reasoning) to explain socialization into the self and mind.

When you were born, you had no ideas. You didn't know that you were a son or daughter. You didn't even know that you were a he or she. How did you develop a **self**, your image of who you are? And how did you develop your ability to reason? Let's find out.

Cooley and the Looking-Glass Self

About a hundred years ago, Charles Horton Cooley (1864–1929), a symbolic interactionist who taught at the University of Michigan, concluded that producing a self is an essential part of how *society* makes us human. He said that *our sense of self develops from interaction with others.* To describe the process by which this unique aspect of "humanness" develops, Cooley (1902) coined the term **looking-glass self**. He summarized this idea in the following couplet:

Each to each a looking-glass
Reflects the other that doth pass.

Watch on **MySocLab**
Video: Socialization: The Basics

Read on **MySocLab**
Document: Charles Horton Cooley, The Looking-Glass Self

The looking-glass self contains three elements:

1. *We imagine how we appear to those around us.* For example, we may think that others perceive us as witty or dull.
2. *We interpret others' reactions.* We come to conclusions about how others evaluate us. Do they like us for being witty? Do they dislike us for being dull?
3. *We develop a self-concept.* How we interpret others' reactions to us frames our feelings and ideas about ourselves. A favorable reflection in this *social mirror* leads to a positive self-concept; a negative reflection leads to a negative self-concept.

Watch on **MySocLab**
Video: Melissa Milkie, The Looking Glass Self

Note that the development of the self does *not* depend on accurate evaluations. Even if we grossly misinterpret how others think about us, those misjudgments become part of our self-concept. Note also that *although the self-concept begins in childhood, its development is an ongoing, lifelong process.* During our everyday lives, we monitor how others react to us. As we do so, we continually modify the self. The self, then, is never a finished product—it is always in process, even into our old age.

Mead and Role Taking

Another symbolic interactionist, George Herbert Mead (1863–1931), who taught at the University of Chicago, pointed out how important play is in developing a self. As we play with others, we learn to **take the role of the other**. That is, we learn to put ourselves in someone else's shoes—to understand how someone else feels and thinks and to anticipate how that person will act.

This doesn't happen overnight. We develop this ability over a period of years (Mead 1934; Denzin 2007). Psychologist John Flavel (1968) asked 8- and 14-year-olds to explain a board game to children who were blindfolded and also to others who were not. The 14-year-olds gave more detailed instructions to those who were blindfolded, but the 8-year-olds gave the same instructions to everyone. The younger children could not yet take the role of the other, while the older children could.

socialization the process by which people learn the characteristics of their group—the knowledge, skills, attitudes, values, norms, and actions thought appropriate for them

self the unique human capacity of being able to see ourselves "from the outside"; the views we internalize of how others see us

looking-glass self a term coined by Charles Horton Cooley to refer to the process by which our self develops through internalizing others' reactions to us

taking the role of the other putting yourself in someone else's shoes; understanding how someone else feels and thinks, so you anticipate how that person will act

Mead analyzed *taking the role of the other* as an essential part of learning to be a full-fledged member of society. At first, we are able to take the role only of *significant others*, as this child is doing. Later we develop the capacity to take the role of the *generalized other*, which is essential not only for cooperation but also for the control of antisocial desires.

As we develop this ability, at first we can take only the roles of **significant others**, individuals who significantly influence our lives, such as parents or siblings. By assuming their roles during play, such as dressing up in our parents' clothing, we cultivate the ability to put ourselves in the place of significant others.

As our self gradually develops, we internalize the expectations of more and more people. Our ability to take the role of others eventually extends to being able to take the role of "the group as a whole." Mead used the term **generalized other** to refer to our perception of how people in general think of us.

Taking the role of others is essential if we are to become cooperative members of human groups—whether they are family, friends, or co-workers. This ability allows us to modify our behavior by anticipating how others will react—something Genie never learned.

As Figure 3.1 illustrates, we go through three stages as we learn to take the role of the other:

1. *Imitation.* Under the age of 3, we can only mimic others. We do not yet have a sense of self separate from others, and we can only imitate people's gestures and words. (This stage is actually not role taking, but it prepares us for it.)
2. *Play.* During the second stage, from the ages of about 3 to 6, we pretend to take the roles of specific people. We might pretend that we are a firefighter, a wrestler, a nurse, Supergirl, Spider-Man, a princess, and so on. We like costumes at this stage and enjoy dressing up in our parents' clothing or tying a towel around our neck to "become" Superman or Wonder Woman.
3. *Team Games.* This third stage, organized play, or team games, begins roughly when we enter school. The significance for the self is that to play these games, we must be able to take multiple roles. Baseball was one of Mead's favorite examples. To play baseball, each player must be able to take the role of any other player. It isn't enough that players know their own role; they also must be able to anticipate what everyone else on the field will do when the ball is hit or thrown.

FIGURE 3.1

How We Learn to Take the Role of the Other: Mead's Three Stages

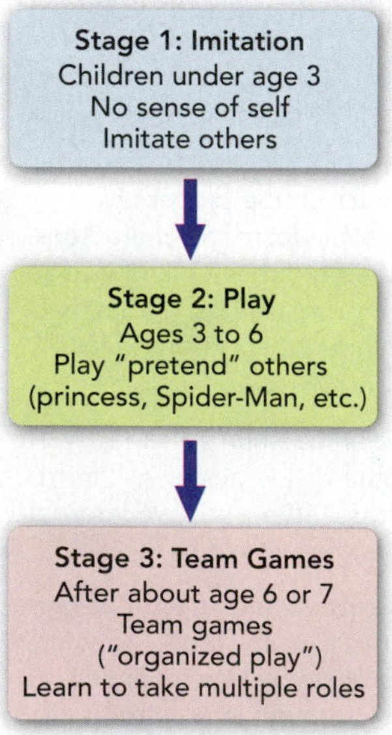

Source: By the author.

Mead also said that the self has two parts, the "I" and the "me." The "I" is *the self as subject*, the active, spontaneous, creative part of the self. In contrast, the "me" is *the self as object*. It is made up of attitudes we internalize from our interactions with others. Mead chose these pronouns because in English, "I" is the active agent, as in "I shoved him," while "me" is the object of action, as in "He shoved me." Mead stressed that we are not passive in the socialization process. We are not like robots, with programmed software shoved into us. Rather, our "I" actively evaluates the reactions of others and organizes them into a unified whole. Mead added that the "I" even monitors the "me," fine-tuning our ideas and attitudes to help us better meet what others expect of us.

In Sum: In studying these details, be careful not to miss the main point, which some find startling: *Both our self and our mind are social products.* Mead stressed that we cannot think without symbols. But where do these symbols come from? Only from society, which gives us our symbols by giving us language. If society did not provide the symbols, we would not be able to think and so would not possess a self-concept or that entity we call the mind. The self and mind, then, like language, are products of society.

significant other an individual who significantly influences someone else

Piaget and the Development of Reasoning

The development of the mind—specifically, how we learn to reason—was studied in detail by Jean Piaget (1896–1980). This Swiss psychologist noticed that when young children take intelligence tests, they often give similar wrong answers. This set him to thinking that the children might be using some consistent, but incorrect, reasoning. It might even indicate that children go through some natural process as they learn how to reason.

To help his students understand the term *generalized other*, Mead used baseball as an illustration. Why are team sports and organized games excellent examples to use in explaining this concept?

Stimulated by this intriguing possibility, Piaget set up a laboratory where he could give children of different ages problems to solve (Piaget 1950, 1954; Flavel et al. 2002). After years of testing, Piaget concluded that children go through a natural process as they develop their ability to reason. This process has four stages. (If you mentally substitute "reasoning" or "reasoning skills" for the term *operational* as you review these stages, Piaget's findings will be easier to understand.)

generalized other the norms, values, attitudes, and expectations of people "in general"; the child's ability to take the role of the generalized other is a significant step in the development of a self

1. **The sensorimotor stage** (from birth to about age 2). During this stage, our understanding is limited to direct contact—sucking, touching, listening, looking. We aren't able to "think." During the first part of this stage, we do not even know that our bodies are separate from the environment. Indeed, we have yet to discover that we have toes. Neither can we recognize cause and effect. That is, we do not know that our actions cause something to happen.
2. **The preoperational stage** (from about age 2 to age 7). During this stage, we *develop the ability to use symbols*. However, we do not yet understand common concepts such as size, speed, or causation. Although we are learning to count, we do not really understand what numbers mean.
3. **The concrete operational stage** (from about age 7 to age 12). Although our reasoning abilities are more developed, they remain *concrete*. We can now understand numbers, size, causation, and speed, and we are able to take the role of the other. We can even play team games. Unless we have concrete examples, however, we are unable to talk about concepts such as truth, honesty, or justice. We can explain why Jane's answer was a lie, but we cannot describe what truth itself is.

Jean Piaget in his office.

4. **The formal operational stage** (after the age of about 12). We now are capable of abstract thinking. We can talk about concepts, come to conclusions based on general principles, and use rules to solve abstract problems. During this stage, we are likely to become young philosophers (Kagan 1984). If we were shown a photo of a slave during our concrete operational stage, we might have said, "That's wrong!" Now at the formal operational stage we are likely to add, "If our country was founded on equality, how could anyone own slaves?"

id Freud's term for our inborn basic drives

ego Freud's term for a balancing force between the id and the demands of society

superego Freud's term for the conscience; the internalized norms and values of our social groups

Global Aspects of the Self and Reasoning

Cooley's conclusions about the looking-glass self appear to be true for everyone around the world. So do Mead's conclusions about role taking and the mind and self as social products, although researchers are finding that the self may develop earlier than Mead indicated. Piaget's theory is also being refined (Burman 2013). Although children everywhere begin with the concrete and move to the abstract, researchers have found that the stages are not as distinct as Piaget concluded. The ages at which individuals enter the stages also differ from one person to another (Flavel et al. 2002). Even during the sensorimotor stage, for example, children show early signs of reasoning, which may indicate an innate ability that is wired into the brain.

Interestingly, some people seem to get stuck in the concreteness of the third stage and never reach the fourth stage of abstract thinking (Kohlberg and Gilligan 1971; Suizzo 2000). College, for example, nurtures the fourth stage, and people with this experience apparently have more ability for abstract thought. Social experiences, then, can modify these stages.

3.3 Explain how the development of personality and morality and socialization into emotions are part of how "society makes us human."

Learning Personality, Morality, and Emotions

Our personality, emotions, and internal control are also vital aspects of who we are. Let's look at how we learn these essential aspects of our being.

Watch on **MySocLab** **Video:** Socialization: The Big Picture

Freud and the Development of Personality

As the mind and the self develop, so does the personality. Sigmund Freud (1856–1939) developed a theory of the origin of personality that had a major impact on Western thought. Freud, a physician in Vienna in the early 1900s, founded *psychoanalysis*, a technique for treating emotional problems through long-term exploration of the subconscious mind. Let's look at his theory.

Freud believed that personality consists of three elements. Each child is born with the first element, an **id**, Freud's term for inborn drives that cause us to seek self-gratification. The id of the newborn is evident in its cries of hunger or pain. The pleasure-seeking id operates throughout life. It demands the immediate fulfillment of basic needs: food, safety, attention, sex, and so on.

The id's drive for immediate gratification, however, runs into a roadblock: primarily the needs of other people, especially those of the parents. To adapt to these constraints, a second component of the personality emerges, which Freud called the ego. The **ego** is the balancing force between the id and the demands of society that suppress it. The ego also serves to balance the id and the **superego**, the third component of the personality, more commonly called the *conscience.*

The superego represents *culture within us*, the norms and values we internalize from our social groups. As the *moral* component of the personality, the superego provokes feelings of guilt or shame when we break social rules, or pride and self-satisfaction when we follow them.

According to Freud, when the id gets out of hand, we follow our desires for pleasure and break society's norms. When the superego gets out of hand, we become overly rigid in following those norms and end up wearing a straitjacket of rules that can make our lives miserable. The ego, the balancing force, tries to prevent either the superego or the id from dominating. In the emotionally healthy individual, the ego succeeds

Shown here is Sigmund Freud in 1931 as he poses for a sculptor in Vienna, Austria. Although Freud was one of the most influential theorists of the twentieth century, most of his ideas have been discarded.

in balancing these conflicting demands of the id and the superego. In the maladjusted individual, the ego fails to control the conflict between the id and the superego. Either the id or the superego dominates this person, leading to internal confusion and problem behaviors.

Sociological Evaluation. Sociologists appreciate Freud's emphasis on socialization—his assertion that the social group into which we are born transmits norms and values that restrain our biological drives. Sociologists, however, object to the view that inborn and subconscious motivations are the primary reasons for human behavior. *This denies the central principle of sociology:* that factors such as social class (income, education, and occupation) and people's roles in groups underlie their behavior (Epstein 1988; Bush and Simmons 1990).

Feminist sociologists have been especially critical of Freud. Although what I just summarized applies to both females and males, Freud assumed that "male" is "normal." He even referred to females as inferior, castrated males (Chodorow 1990; Gerhard 2000). It is obvious that sociologists need to continue to research how we develop personality.

Kohlberg and the Development of Morality

If you have observed young children, you know that they want immediate gratification and show little or no concern for others. ("Mine!" a 2-year-old will shout, as she grabs a toy from another child.) Yet, at a later age, this same child will be considerate of others and try to be fair in her play. How does this change happen?

Kohlberg's Theory. Psychologist Lawrence Kohlberg (1975, 1984, 1986; Reed 2008) concluded that we go through a sequence of stages as we develop morality. Building on Piaget's work, he found that children start in the *amoral stage* I just described. For them, there is no right or wrong, just personal needs to be satisfied. From about ages 7 to 10, children are in what Kohlberg called a *preconventional stage.* They have learned rules, and they follow them to stay out of trouble. They view right and wrong as what pleases or displeases their parents, friends, and teachers. Their concern is to get rewards and to avoid punishment. At about age 10, they enter the *conventional stage.* During this period, morality means following the norms and values they have learned. This is followed by a *postconventional stage* in which individuals reflect on abstract principles of right and wrong and judge people's behavior according to these principles.

Criticisms of Kohlberg. Carol Gilligan, another psychologist, was one of the first to criticize Kohlberg. She noticed that Kohlberg had studied only boys. When she interviewed men and women, she concluded that women are more likely to evaluate morality in terms of personal relationships—how an act affects others and the harm it might bring to loved ones. Other researchers followed up, finding that both men and women use personal relationships and abstract principles when they make moral judgments (Wark and Krebs 1996).

To test Kohlberg's theory, researchers checked how it applies in different cultures. They found that the preconventional and conventional stages apply around the world. Most societies, though, do not have the postconventional stage of universal reasoning. This stage appears to be mostly a Western concept (Jensen 2009). Apparently, there is no universal, abstract way of figuring what is moral. Instead, different cultures have their own ways to determine morality, and each teaches its members to use its norms in deciding what is moral.

Research with Babies. Researchers have developed ingenious experiments to see if babies have a morality (Bloom 2010; Hamlin and Wynn 2011). In one experiment, they showed babies a puppet that helps another puppet and one that interferes with that puppet. They found that babies—even under 1 year of age—prefer the "good" puppet and want the "bad" puppet punished. From these experiments, some draw the intriguing conclusion that we are born with a basic morality and a desire to punish those who break our moral codes. Others suggest that the experiments are flawed (Scarf et al. 2012). More research should eventually settle the question.

The Cultural Relativity of Morality. If babies do have an inborn sense of fairness, it indicates that, like language, morality is a "capacity hardwired" in the brain. Just as society lays a particular language onto the child's linguistic capacity, so society lays its particular ideas of what is moral onto the child's moral capacity. As languages differ around the world, so do moralities. When people violate whatever morality they have learned, it arouses the emotions of guilt and shame. Sociologists are studying how people's sense of identity is connected to morality and these emotions (Stets and Carter 2012).

Let's turn to how we learn emotions, another essential element of who we are as humans.

Socialization into Emotions

Sociologists have found that our emotions are not simply the results of our biology (Hochschild 2008; Stets 2012). Like the mind, our emotions also depend on socialization. This may sound strange. Don't all people get angry? Doesn't everyone cry? Don't we all feel guilt, shame, sadness, happiness, fear? What has socialization to do with our emotions?

Global Emotions. At first, it may look as though socialization is not relevant to our emotions, that we simply express universal feelings. The research of Paul Ekman, a psychologist, seems to support this idea. After studying emotions in several countries, Ekman (1980) found that everyone experiences six basic emotions: anger, disgust, fear, happiness, sadness, and surprise. Ekman also found that people show the same facial expressions when they feel these emotions. A person from Peru, for example, can tell from just the look on an American's face that she is angry, disgusted, or fearful, and she can tell from the Peruvian's face that he is happy, sad, or surprised. Because we all show the same facial expressions when we experience these six emotions, Ekman concluded that they are hardwired into our biology.

A study of facial expressions at the Paralympics supports this observation (Matsumoto and Willingham 2009). Upon learning if they had won or lost, people who were blind from birth showed the same facial expressions as those of sighted people, something they could not have learned.

Expressing Emotions: Following "Feeling Rules." What, then, does sociology have to do with emotions? If we have universal facial expressions to express our emotions, then this is biology, something that Darwin noted back in the 1800s (Horwitz and Wakefield 2007:41). Facial expressions, however, are only one way by which we show our feelings. We also use our bodies, voices, and gestures.

> *Jane and Sushana have been best friends since high school. They were hardly ever apart until Sushana married and moved to another state a year ago. Jane has been waiting eagerly at the arrival gate for Sushana's flight, which has been delayed. When Sushana exits, she and Jane hug one another, giving out squeals of glee" and even jumping a bit.*

What emotions are these people expressing? Are these emotions global? Is their way of expressing them universal?

If you couldn't tell from their names that these were women, you could tell from their behavior. To express delight, U.S. women are allowed to give "out squeals of glee" in public places and to jump as they hug. In contrast, in the same circumstances, U.S. men are expected to shake hands or to give a brief hug. If they gave "squeals of glee," they would be violating fundamental "gender rules."

Not only do we have "gender rules" for expressing emotions, but we also have "feeling rules" based on culture, social class, relationships, and settings. Consider *culture*. Two close Japanese friends who meet after a long separation don't shake hands or hug—they bow. Two Arab men will kiss. *Social class* is so significant that it, too, cuts across other lines, even gender. Upon seeing a friend after a long absence, upper-class women and men are likely to be more reserved in expressing their delight than are lower-class women and men. *Relationships* also make a big difference. We express our feelings more openly if we are with close friends, more guardedly if we are at a staff meeting with the corporate CEO. The *setting*, then, is also important, with different settings having different "rules" about emotions. As you know, the emotions you can express at a rock concert differ considerably from those you express in a classroom. If you think about your childhood, you will realize that a good part of your early socialization centered on learning your culture's feeling rules.

What We Feel

Joan, a U.S. woman who had been married for seven years, had no children. When she finally gave birth and the doctor handed her a healthy girl, she was almost overcome with joy. Tafadzwa, in Zimbabwe, had been married for seven years and had no children. When the doctor handed her a healthy girl, she was almost overcome with sadness.

You can easily understand why the U.S. woman felt happy, but why did the woman in Zimbabwe feel sad? The effects of socialization on our emotions go much deeper than guiding how, where, and when we express our feelings. Socialization also affects *what* we feel (Clark 1997). In Zimbabwe culture, to not give birth to a male child lowers a woman's social status and is even considered a good reason for her husband to divorce her (Horwitz and Wakefield 2007:43).

Research Needed. Ekman identified only six emotions as universal in facial expression, but I suspect that there are more. Around the world, the emotions of confusion, despair, disgust, helplessness, and shock are also likely to produce similar facial expressions. To find out, we need cross-cultural research. We also need more research into how culture guides people in how they express their feelings, even in what they feel—and how these might differ by age, gender, social class, and race–ethnicity.

Society within Us: The Self and Emotions as Social Control

Much of our socialization is intended to turn us into conforming members of society. Socialization into the self and emotions is essential in this process, for *both the self and our emotions mold our behavior.* Although we like to think that we are "free," consider for a moment some of the factors that influence how you act: the expectations of your friends and parents; of neighbors and teachers; classroom norms and college rules; city, state, and federal laws. For example, if in a moment of intense frustration, or out of a devilish desire to shock people, you wanted to tear off your clothes and run naked down the street, what would stop you?

The answer is your socialization—*society within you*. Your experiences in society have resulted in a self that thinks along certain lines and feels particular emotions. This helps to keep you in line. Thoughts such as "Would I get kicked out of school?" and "What would my friends (parents) think if they found out?" represent an awareness of the self in relationship to others. So does the desire to avoid feelings of shame and embarrassment.

gender the behaviors and attitudes that a society considers proper for its males and females; masculinity or femininity

gender socialization learning society's "gender map," the paths in life set out for us because we are male or female

Your *social mirror*, then—the result of your being socialized into a self and emotions—sets up effective internal controls over your behavior. In fact, socialization into self and emotions is so effective that some people feel embarrassed just thinking about running naked in public!

In Sum: Socialization is essential for our development as human beings. From our interaction with others, we learn how to think, reason, and feel. The net result is the shaping of our behavior—including our thinking and emotions—according to cultural standards. This is what sociologists mean when they refer to *society within us*.

And remember how we began this chapter—that society makes us human? Socialization into emotions is part of this process.

3.4 Discuss how gender messages from the family, peers, and the mass media teach us society's gender map.

Socialization into Gender

Socialization into gender is also part of the way that society turns us into certain types of people—and sets up heavy controls over us. Let's get a glimpse of how this happens.

Learning the Gender Map

Watch on **MySocLab** **Video:** Florence Denmark, Gender vs. Sex

For a child, society is unexplored territory. A major signpost on society's map is **gender**, the attitudes and behaviors that are expected of us because we are a male or a female. In learning the *gender map* (called **gender socialization**), we are nudged into different lanes in life—into contrasting attitudes and behaviors. We take direction so well that, as adults, most of us act, think, and even feel according to our culture's guidelines regarding what is appropriate for our sex.

The significance of gender is emphasized throughout this book, and we focus on gender in Chapter 11. For now, though, let's briefly consider some of the *gender messages* that we get from our family and the mass media.

Gender Messages in the Family

Parents. Our parents are the first to introduce us to the gender map. Sometimes they do this consciously, perhaps by bringing into play pink and blue, colors that have no meaning in themselves but that are now associated with gender. Our parents' own gender orientations are embedded so firmly that they do most of their gender teaching without being aware of what they are doing.

This is illustrated in a classic study by psychologists Susan Goldberg and Michael Lewis (1969), whose results have been confirmed by other researchers (Connors 1996; Clearfield and Nelson 2006; Best 2010).

Goldberg and Lewis asked mothers to bring their 6-month-old infants into their laboratory, supposedly to observe the infants' development. Covertly, however, they also observed the mothers. They found that the mothers kept their daughters closer to them. They also touched their daughters more and spoke to them more frequently than they did to their sons. By the time the children were 13 months old, the girls stayed closer to their mothers during play, and they returned to their mothers sooner and more often than the boys did.

Then Goldberg and Lewis did a little experiment. They set up a barrier to separate the children from their mothers, who were holding toys. The girls were more likely to cry and motion for help; the boys, to try to climb over the barrier.

Goldberg and Lewis concluded that the mothers had subconsciously rewarded their daughters for being passive and dependent, their sons for being active and independent.

It is in the family that we first learn how to do gender, how to match our ideas, attitudes, and behaviors to those expected of us because of our sex. This photo is from Papua New Guinea.

Toys and Play. Our family's gender lessons are thorough. On the basis of our sex, our parents give us different kinds of toys.

Frank and Ernest

The *gender roles* that we learn during childhood become part of our basic orientations to life. Although we refine these roles as we grow older, they remain built around the framework established during childhood.

Boys are more likely to get guns and "action figures" that destroy enemies. Girls are more likely to be given dolls and jewelry. Some parents try to choose "gender neutral" toys, but kids know what is popular, and they feel left out if they don't have what the other kids have. The significance of toys in gender socialization can be summarized this way: Most parents would be upset if someone gave their son Barbie dolls.

Explore on **MySocLab**
Activity: Single Parent Households

We also learn gender through play. Parents subtly "signal" to their sons that it is okay for them to participate in more rough-and-tumble play. In general, parents expect their sons to get dirtier and to be more defiant, their daughters to be daintier and more compliant (Gilman 1911/1971; Nordberg 2010). And in large part, parents get what they expect.

Our experiences in socialization lie at the heart of the sociological explanation of male–female differences. For a fascinating account of how socialization can trump biology, read the Cultural Diversity box on the next page.

Gay and Lesbian Parents. Do the gender messages that homosexual parents give their children differ from those of heterosexual parents? The initial findings indicate that there are differences. In their play, the children of lesbian couples and gay male couples show less gender stereotyping. That is, the boys show more behaviors that are traditionally considered feminine, and the girls more behaviors that are traditionally considered masculine (Goldberg et al. 2012). This research is in its infancy, though, and this particular study is limited. It was based not on observation of the children but on reports from the parents, which can be quite biased.

If these initial findings hold up, an area of research will be how the parents give their gender messages. It is likely that these parents show less stereotypical masculine and feminine behaviors and are more tolerant of their children's behavior that does not conform to traditional ideas of masculinity and femininity.

Gender Messages from Peers

Sociologists stress how this sorting process into gender that begins in the family is reinforced as children are exposed to other aspects of society. Of those other influences, one of the most powerful is the **peer group**, individuals of roughly the same age who are linked by common interests. Examples of peer groups are friends, classmates, and "the kids in the neighborhood."

As you grew up, you saw girls and boys teach one another what it means to be female or male. You might not have recognized what was happening, however, so let's eavesdrop on a conversation between two eighth-grade girls studied by sociologist Donna Eder (2007).

CINDY: The only thing that makes her look anything is all the makeup . . .
PENNY: She had a picture, and she's standing like this. (Poses with one hand on her hip and one by her head)
CINDY: Her face is probably this skinny, but it looks that big 'cause of all the makeup she has on it.
PENNY: She's ugly, ugly, ugly.

peer group a group of individuals, often of roughly the same age, who are linked by common interests and orientations

Cultural Diversity around the World

When Women Become Men: The Sworn Virgins

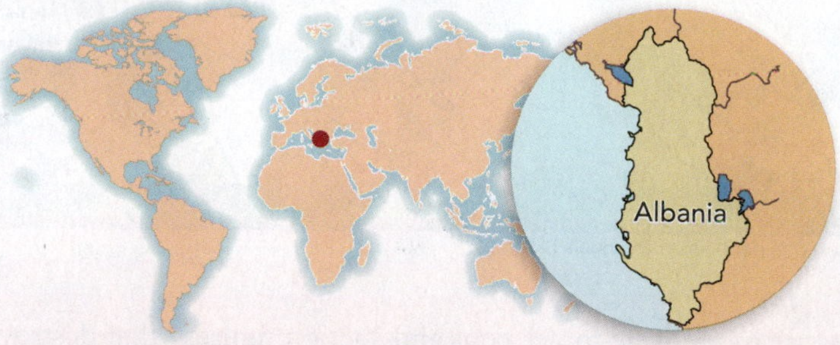

"I will become a man," said Pashe. "I will do it."

The decision was final. Taking a pair of scissors, she soon had her long, black curls lying at her feet. She took off her dress—never to wear one again in her life—and put on her father's baggy trousers. She armed herself with her father's rifle. She would need it.

Going before the village elders, she swore to never marry, to never have children, and to never have sex.

Pashe had become a sworn virgin—and a man.

There was no turning back. The penalty for violating the oath was death.

In northern Albania, where Pashe Keqi lives, and in parts of Bosnia and Serbia, some women become men. They are neither transsexuals nor lesbians. Nor do they have a sex-change operation, something which is unknown in those parts.

This custom, which goes back centuries, is a practical matter, a way to protect and support the family. In these traditional societies, women stay home and take care of the children and household. They can go hardly anywhere except to the market and mosque. Women depend on men for survival.

And when there is no man? This is the problem.

Pashe's father was killed in a blood feud. In these traditional groups, when the family patriarch (male head) dies and there are no male heirs, how are the women to survive? In the fifteenth century, people in this area hit upon a solution: One of the women gives an oath of lifelong virginity and takes over the man's role. She then becomes a social he—she wears male clothing, carries a gun, owns property, and moves freely throughout the society.

She drinks in the tavern with the men. She sits with the men at weddings. She prays with the men at the mosque. When a man wants to marry a girl of the family, she is the one who approves or disapproves of the suitor.

In short, the woman really becomes a man. Actually, a social man, sociologists would add. Her biology does not change, but her gender does. Pashe had become the man of the house, a status she occupied her entire life.

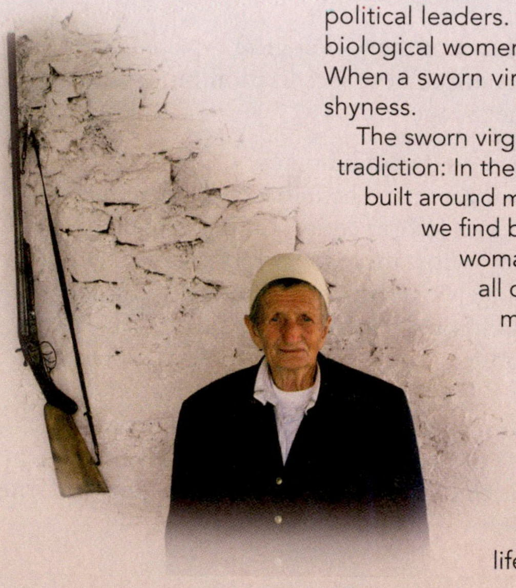

Sokol (Zhire) Zmajli, aged 80, changed her name from Zhire to the male name Sokol when she was young. She heads the family household consisting of her nephew, his wife, their sons, and their wives.

Taking this position at the age of 11—Pashe is in her 70s now—also made her responsible for avenging her father's murder. But when his killer was released from prison, her 15-year-old nephew (she is his uncle) rushed in and did the deed instead.

Sworn virgins walk like men, they talk like men, and they hunt with the men. They also take up manly occupations. They become shepherds, security guards, truck drivers, and political leaders. Those around them know that they are biological women, but in all ways they treat them as men. When a sworn virgin talks to women, the women recoil in shyness.

The sworn virgins of Albania are a fascinating cultural contradiction: In the midst of a highly traditional group, one built around male superiority that severely limits women, we find both the belief and practice that a biological woman can do the work of a man and function in all of a man's social roles. The sole exception is marriage.

Under communist rule until 1985, with travel restricted by law and custom, mountainous northern Albania had been cut off from the rest of the world. Now there is a democratic government, and the region is connected to the world by better roads, telephones, and even television. As modern life trickles into these villages, few women want to become men. "Why should we?" they ask. "Now we have freedom. We can go to the city and work and support our families."

For Your Consideration

➔ How do the sworn virgins of Albania help to explain what gender is? Apply functionalism: How was the custom and practice of sworn virgins functional for this society? Apply symbolic interactionism: How do symbols underlie and maintain a woman's shift to becoming a man in this society? Apply conflict theory: How do power relations between men and women underlie this practice?

Sources: Based on Zumbrun 2007; Bilefsky 2008; Young and Twigg 2009.

Do you see how these girls were giving gender lessons? They were reinforcing images of appearance and behavior that they thought were appropriate for females.

It isn't only girls who reinforce cultural expectations of gender. Boys do the same thing. Sociologist Melissa Milkie (1994), who studied junior high school boys, found that much of their talk centered on movies and TV programs. Of the many images they saw, the boys would single out those associated with sex and violence. They would amuse one another by repeating lines, acting out parts, and joking and laughing at what they had seen.

If you know boys in their early teens, you've probably seen a lot of behavior like this. You may have been amused, or even have shaken your head in disapproval. But did you peer beneath the surface? Milkie did. What is really going on? The boys, she concluded, were using media images to develop their identity as males. They had gotten the message: "Real" males are obsessed with sex and violence. Not to joke and laugh about murder and promiscuous sex would have marked a boy as a "weenie" or a "nerd," labels to be avoided at all costs.

Gender Messages in the Mass Media

As you can see with the boys Milkie studied, a major guide to the gender map is the **mass media**, forms of communication that are directed to large audiences. Let's look further at how media images help teach us **gender**, the behaviors and attitudes considered appropriate for our sex.

Watch on **MySocLab**
Video: Socialization in Focus: Socialization

Television, Movies, and Cartoons. If you've watched youngsters while they are watching children's videos or television, you've probably noticed how engrossed they are. They can hardly lift their eyes from "the action" when you try to get their attention. What are children learning through these powerful media that transmit ideas through words and moving images? One major lesson is that males are more important than females, as male characters outnumber female characters two to one (S. Smith et al. 2012a).

In children's cartoons, females used to be portrayed as less brave and more dependent. Reflecting women's changing position in society, more dominant, aggressive females are now being featured. Kim Possible divides her time between cheerleading practice and saving the world from evil. With tongue in cheek, the Powerpuff Girls are touted as "the most elite kindergarten crime-fighting force ever assembled." This changed gender portrayal is especially evident in the violent females who play lead characters in action movies, from the assassin in *Kill Bill* to *Katnis Everdeen*, whose athletic, archery, and fighting skills are nothing short of amazing.

A key part of gender is body image, and the mass media are effective in teaching us what we "should" look like. While girls are presented as more powerful than they used to be, they have to be skinny and gorgeous and wear the latest fashions. Such messages present a dilemma for girls: Continuously thrust before them is a model that is almost impossible to replicate in real life.

Video Games. The movement, color, virtual dangers, unexpected dilemmas, and ability to control the action make video games highly appealing. High school and college students find them a seductive way of escaping from the demands of life. The first members of the "Nintendo Generation," now in their 30s, are still playing video games—with babies on their laps.

Sociologists have begun to study how video games portray the sexes, but we know little about their influence on the players' ideas of gender. The message of male dominance continues, as females are even more underrepresented in video games than on television: 90 percent of the main characters are male (Williams et al. 2009). Some video games, though, reflect cutting-edge changes in sex roles, the topic of the Mass Media in Social Life box on the next page.

mass media forms of communication, such as radio, newspapers, and television that are directed to mass audiences

Mass Media in Social Life

Lara Croft, Tomb Raider: Changing Images of Women in the Mass Media

With digital advances, video games have crossed the line from games to something that more closely resembles interactive movies. Costing several million dollars to produce and market, some video games introduce new songs by major rock groups (Levine 2008). One game (*Grand Theft Auto 4*) cost $100 million ("Top 10 . . ." 2010). Sociologically, what is significant is the *content* of video games. They expose gamers not only to action but also to ideas and images. Just as in other forms of the mass media, the gender images of video games communicate powerful messages.

Lara Croft, an adventure-seeking archeologist and star of *Tomb Raider* and its many sequels, is the essence of this new gender image. Lara is smart, strong, and able to utterly vanquish foes. With both guns blazing, Lara breaks stereotypical gender roles and dominates what previously was the domain of men. She was the first female protagonist in a field of muscle-rippling, gun-toting macho caricatures (Taylor 1999).

Yet the old remains powerfully encapsulated in the new. As the photo here makes evident, Lara is a fantasy girl for young men of the digital generation. No matter her foe, no matter her predicament, Lara oozes sex. Her form-fitting outfits, which flatter her voluptuous figure, reflect the mental images of the men who created this digital character.

The mass media not only reflect gender stereotypes but they also play a role in changing them. Sometimes they do both simultaneously. The image of the "new" Lara Croft not only reflect women's changing role in society, but also, by exaggerating the change, it molds new stereotypes.

These men decided to give Lara a makeover, and in 2013 they presented a "more vulnerable and realistic" Lara (Parker 2012). The new Lara, shown here, doesn't seem more vulnerable. Her weapon is huge, she is outstandingly accurate, and she kills a lot of men. She is more realistic in the sense that the new graphics make her look almost human, but she still manages to ooze sex whenever she moves. My best guess is that her creators have not had a mental makeover.

For Your Consideration

A sociologist who reviewed this text said, "It seems that for women to be defined as equal, we have to become symbolic males—warriors with breasts." Why is gender change mostly one-way—females adopting traditional male characteristics? These two questions should help: Who is moving into the traditional territory of the other? Do people prefer to imitate power or weakness?

Advertising. From an early age, you have been bombarded with stereotypical images of gender. If you are average, you are exposed to a blistering 200,000 commercials a year (Kacen 2011). In commercials geared toward children, boys are more likely to be shown as competing in outdoor settings, while girls are more likely to be portrayed as cooperating in indoor settings. Action figures are pitched to boys, and dolls to girls (Kahlenberg and Hein 2010).

As adults, we are still peppered with ads. Although their purpose is to sell products—from booze and bras to cigarettes and cell phones—these ads continue our gender lessons. The stereotypical images—from cowboys who roam the wide-open spaces to scantily clad women whose physical assets couldn't possibly be real—become part of our own images of the sexes. So does advertising's occasional attention-grabbing stereotype-breaking images.

In Sum: "Male" and "female" are powerful symbols. When we learn that different behaviors and attitudes are expected of us because we are a girl or a boy, we learn to interpret the world in terms of gender. Whether overt and exaggerated or subtle and below our awareness, the mass media continue the gender lessons begun at home and reinforced by our peers. Gender serves as a primary basis for **social inequality**—giving privileges and obligations to one group of people while denying them to another, something we will analyze in following chapters.

social inequality a social condition in which privileges and obligations are given to some but denied to others

agents of socialization people or groups that affect our self concept, attitudes, behaviors, or other orientations toward life

Agents of Socialization

Individuals and groups that influence our orientations to life—our self-concept, emotions, attitudes, and behavior—are called **agents of socialization**. We have already considered how three of these agents—the family, our peers, and the mass media—influence our ideas of gender. Now we'll look more closely at how agents of socialization prepare us in ways other than gender to take our place in society. We will consider the family, then the neighborhood, religion, day care, school and peers, and the workplace.

3.5 Explain why the family, the neighborhood, religion, day care, school, peer groups, and the workplace are called agents of socialization.

The Family

As you know, the first group to have a major impact on who you become is your family. Your experiences in the family are so intense that they last a lifetime. These experiences establish your initial motivations, values, and beliefs. In your family, you receive your basic sense of self, ideas about who you are and what you deserve out of life. It is here that you began to think of yourself as strong or weak, smart or dumb, good-looking or ugly—or more likely, somewhere in between.

Not all families are the same, of course. Let's look at the difference that social class makes in how families socialize their children.

Watch on **MySocLab**
Video: Socialization: Thinking Like a Sociologist

Read on **MySocLab**
Document: D. Terri Heath, Parents' Socialization of Children

Social Class and Type of Work. Sociologist Melvin Kohn (1959, 1963, 1977, 2006) found that the main concern of working-class parents is that their children stay out of trouble. To keep them in line, they tend to use physical punishment. Middle-class parents, in contrast, focus more on developing their children's curiosity, self-expression, and self-control. They are more likely to reason with their children than to punish them physically.

Why should there be such differences? Kohn wondered. As a sociologist, he knew that the reason was life experiences of some sort, and he found the answer in the world of work. Blue-collar workers are usually told exactly what to do. Since they expect their children's lives to be like theirs, they stress obedience. The work of middle-class parents, in contrast, requires more initiative, and they socialize their children into the qualities they find valuable.

This photo captures an extreme form of family socialization. The father seems to be more emotionally involved in the goal—and in more pain—than his daughter, as he pushes her toward the finish line in the Teen Tours of America Kid's Triathlon.

Kohn was still puzzled. Some working-class parents act more like middle-class parents, and vice versa. As Kohn probed further, the pieces fell into place. The key turned out to be the parents' types of jobs. Middle-class office workers are supervised closely, and Kohn found that they follow the working-class pattern of child rearing, emphasizing conformity. And some blue-collar workers, such as those who do home repairs, have a good deal of freedom. These workers follow the middle-class model in rearing their children (Pearlin and Kohn 1966; Kohn and Schooler 1969).

Social Class and Play. Working-class and middle-class parents also have different ideas of how children develop, ideas that have fascinating consequences for children's play (Lareau 2002; Bodovski and Farkas 2008). Working-class parents see their children as being like wildflowers—they develop naturally. Since the child's development will take care of itself, good parenting primarily means providing food, shelter, and comfort. These parents set limits on their children's play ("Don't go near the railroad tracks") and let them play as they wish. To middle-class parents, in contrast, children are like tender houseplants—they need a lot of guidance to develop correctly. These parents want their children's play to accomplish something. They may want them to play baseball, for example, not for the enjoyment of the sport but to help them learn how to be team players.

Read on **MySocLab**
Document: Ferdinand Tonnies, Gemeinschaft and Gesellschaft

The Neighborhood

As all parents know, some neighborhoods are better than others for children. Parents try to move to the better neighborhoods—if they can afford them. Their common-sense evaluations are borne out by sociological research. Children from poor neighborhoods are more likely to get in trouble with the law, to become pregnant, to drop out of school, and even to have worse mental health (Levanthal and Brooks-Gunn 2000; Wheaton and Clarke 2003; DeLuca and Dayton 2009; Clarke et al. 2013).

Sociologists have found that parenting is easier in the more affluent neighborhoods. Among the major advantages these parents have are less crime, stronger ties among the neighbors, more support groups, and being able to rely more on one another in times of need (Byrnes and Miller 2012). There are also fewer families in transition, so the adults are more likely to know the local children and their parents. This better equips them to help keep the children safe and out of trouble.

Religion

How important is religion in your life? Most Americans belong to a local congregation, but what if you are among the 16 percent who do not identify with a religion (Newport 2010)? We would miss the point if we were to assume that religion influences only people who are "religious." Religion plays a powerful role even for people who wouldn't be caught dead near a church, synagogue, or mosque. How? Religious ideas so pervade U.S. society that they provide the foundation of morality for both the religious and the nonreligious.

For many Americans, the influence of religion is more direct. This is especially true for the two of every five Americans who report that during a typical week they attend a religious service (Gallup Poll 2010). On the obvious level, through their participation in religious services, they learn doctrines, values, and morality, but the effects of religion on their lives go far beyond this. As they learn beliefs about the hereafter, for example, they also learn what kinds of clothing, speech, and manners are appropriate for formal occasions. Life in congregations also provides them a sense of identity, a feeling of belonging. Religious participation also helps to integrate immigrants into their new society, offers an avenue of social mobility for the poor, provides social contacts for jobs, and, for African Americans, has been a powerful influence in social change.

Read on **MySocLab**
Document: Dan Clawson, et al. Caring for Our Young: Child Care in Europe and the United States

Day Care

It is rare for social science research to make national news, but occasionally it does. This is what happened when researchers published their findings on 1,200 kindergarten children they had studied since they were a month old. They observed the children multiple times both at home and at day care. They also videotaped the children's interactions with their mothers (National Institute of Child Health and Human Development 1999; Guensburg 2001). What caught the media's attention? Children who spend more time in day care have weaker bonds with their mothers and are less affectionate toward them. They are also less cooperative with others and more likely to fight and to be "mean." By the time they get to kindergarten, they are more likely to talk back to teachers and to disrupt the classroom. This holds true regardless of the quality of the day care, the family's social class, or whether the child is a girl or a boy (Belsky 2006). On the positive side, the children scored higher on language tests.

Are we producing a generation of "smart but mean" children? This is not an unreasonable question, since the study was well designed and an even larger study of children in England has come up with similar findings (Belsky 2006). Some point out that the differences between children who spend a lot of time in day care and those who spend less time are slight. Others stress that with 5 million children in day care (*Statistical Abstract* 2013:Table 589), slight differences can be significant for society.

The researchers continued to test these children as they went through school, and the surprise is how these initial effects of day care have continued. At age 15, the children who had lower-quality care and those who spent more time in child care did slightly worse academically and had slightly more behavioral problems than the children who had higher-quality care or who spent less time in child care (Vandell et al. 2010).

manifest functions the intended beneficial consequences of people's actions

latent functions unintended beneficial consequences of people's actions

The School

Part of the **manifest function**, or *intended* purpose, of formal education is to teach knowledge and skills, such as reading, writing, and arithmetic. Schools also have **latent functions**, *unintended consequences* that help the social system. Let's look at this less obvious aspect of education. At home, children learn attitudes and values that match their family's situation in life. At school, they learn a broader perspective that helps prepare them to take a role in the world beyond the family. At home, a child may have been the almost exclusive focus of doting parents, but in school, the child learns *universality*—that the same rules apply to everyone, regardless of who their parents are or how special they may be at home. The Cultural Diversity box on the next page explores how these new values and ways of looking at the world sometimes even replace those the child learns at home.

Sociologists have also identified a *hidden curriculum* in our schools. This term refers to values that, although not taught explicitly, are part of a school's "cultural message." For example, the stories and examples that are used to teach math and English may bring with them lessons in patriotism, democracy, justice, and honesty. There is also a *corridor curriculum*, what students teach one another outside the classroom. Unfortunately, the corridor curriculum seems to emphasize racism, sexism, illicit ways to make money, and coolness (Hemmings 1999). You can determine for yourself how each of these is functional and dysfunctional.

Conflict theorists point out that social class separates children into different educational worlds. Children born to wealthy parents go to private schools, where they learn skills and values that match their higher position. Children born to middle-class parents go to public schools, where they learn that good jobs, even the professions, beckon, while children from blue-collar families learn that not many of "their kind" will become professionals or leaders. This is one of the many reasons that children from blue-collar families are less likely to take college prep courses or to go to college. In short, our schools reflect and reinforce our social class divisions. We will return to this topic in Chapter 17.

Schools are a primary agent of socialization. One of their functions is to teach children the attitudes and skills they are thought to need as adults.

Peer Groups

As a child's experiences with agents of socialization broaden, the influence of the family decreases. Entry into school marks only one of many steps in this transfer of allegiance. One of the most significant aspects of education is that it exposes children to peer groups that help children resist the efforts of parents and schools to socialize them.

When sociologists Patricia and Peter Adler (1998) observed children at two elementary schools in Colorado, they saw how children separate themselves by sex and develop separate gender worlds. The norms that made boys popular were athletic ability, coolness, and toughness. For girls, popularity came from family background, physical appearance (clothing and use of makeup), and the ability to attract popular boys. In this children's subculture, academic achievement pulled in opposite directions: High grades lowered the popularity of boys, but for girls, good grades increased their standing among peers.

You know from your own experience how compelling peer groups are. It is almost impossible to go against a peer group, whose cardinal rule seems to be "conformity or rejection." Anyone who doesn't do what the others want becomes an "outsider,"

Cultural Diversity in the United States

Immigrants and Their Children: Caught between Two Worlds

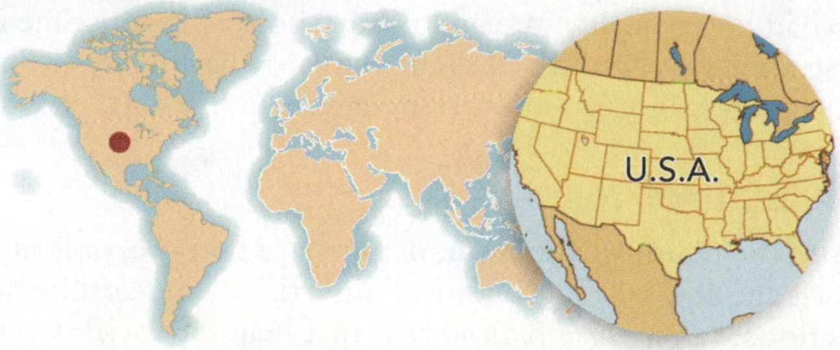

It is a struggle to adapt to a new culture, to learn behaviors and ways of thinking that are at odds with ones already learned. This exposure to two worlds can lead to inner turmoil. One way to handle the conflict is to cut ties with your first culture. Doing so, however, can create a sense of loss, one that is perhaps recognized only later in life.

Richard Rodriguez, a literature professor and essayist, was born to working-class Mexican immigrants. Wanting their son to be successful in their adopted land, his parents named him Richard instead of Ricardo. Although his English–Spanish hybrid name indicates his parents' aspirations for their son, it was also an omen of the conflict that Richard would experience.

Like other children of Mexican immigrants, Richard first spoke Spanish—a rich mother tongue that introduced him to the world. Until the age of 5, when he began school, Richard knew only fifty words in English. He describes what happened when he began school:

> *The change came gradually but early. When I was beginning grade school, I noted to myself the fact that the classroom environment was so different in its styles and assumptions from my own family environment that survival would essentially entail a choice between both worlds. When I became a student, I was literally "remade"; neither I nor my teachers considered anything I had known before as relevant. I had to forget most of what my culture had provided, because to remember it was a disadvantage. The past and its cultural values became detachable, like a piece of clothing grown heavy on a warm day and finally put away.*

As happened to millions of immigrants before him, whose parents spoke German, Polish, Italian, and so on, learning English eroded family and class ties and ate away at his ethnic roots. For Rodriguez, language and education were not simply devices that eased the transition to the dominant culture. They also slashed at the roots that had given him life.

To face conflicting cultures is to confront a fork in the road. Some turn one way and withdraw from the new culture—a clue that helps to explain why so many Latinos drop out of U.S. schools. Others turn the other way. Cutting ties with their family and cultural roots, they embrace the new culture.

Rodriguez took the second road. He excelled in his new language—so much, in fact, that he graduated from Stanford University and then became a graduate student in English at the University of California at Berkeley. He was even awarded a Fulbright fellowship to study English Renaissance literature at the University of London.

But the past shadowed Rodriguez. Prospective employers were impressed with his knowledge of Renaissance literature. At job interviews, however, they would skip over the Renaissance training and ask him if he would teach the Mexican novel and be an adviser to Latino students. Rodriguez was also haunted by the image of his grandmother, the warmth of the culture he had left behind, and the language and ways of thinking to which he had become a stranger.

Richard Rodriguez represents millions of immigrants—not just those of Latino origin but those from other cultures, too—who want to integrate into U.S. culture yet not betray their past. Fearing loss of their roots, they are caught between two cultures, each beckoning, each offering rich rewards.

Sources: Based on Richard Rodriguez 1975, 1982, 1990, 1991, 1995.

For Your Consideration

➔ I saw this conflict firsthand with my father, who did not learn English until after the seventh grade (his last in school). He left German behind, eventually coming to the point that he could no longer speak it, but broken English and awkward expressions remained for a lifetime. Then, too, there were the lingering emotional connections to old ways, as well as the haughtiness and slights of more assimilated Americans. He longed for security by grasping the past, its ways of thinking and feeling, but at the same time he wanted to succeed in the everyday reality of the new culture. Have you seen similar conflicts?

a "nonmember," an "outcast." For preteens and teens just learning their way around in the world, it is not surprising that the peer group rules. As you know, peer groups can be vicious in enforcing their norms, the focus of the Down-to-Earth Sociology box below.

As a result, the standards of our peer groups tend to dominate our lives. If your peers, for example, listen to rap, Nortec, death metal, rock and roll, country, or gospel, it is almost inevitable that you also prefer that kind of music. In high school, if your friends take math courses, you probably do, too (Crosnoe et al. 2008). It is the same for clothing styles and dating standards. Peer influences also extend to behaviors that violate social norms. If your peers are college-bound and upwardly striving, this is most likely what you will be; but if they use drugs, cheat, and steal, you are likely to do so, too.

Down-to-Earth **Sociology**

Gossip and Ridicule to Enforce Adolescent Norms

Adolescence is not known as the turbulent years for nothing. During this period of our lives, the security of a self-identity rooted in parental relations and family life is being ripped from us as we attempt to piece together a strong sense of individual identity. This sense of who we are apart from our parents and siblings does not come easily. At this stage of life, we simply don't know who we are yet, and seldom do we have a good sense of whom we will become. The process of developing a sense of self by evaluating the reflections we receive from others is not new, but its severity at this point of life grows acute. Here is what sociologist Donna Eder said about her research on adolescent girls.

I became concerned while reading studies on adolescent girls. Many of these studies reported a drop in girls' self-esteem and self-image when they entered junior high school. I hired both female and male assistants to observe lunchtime interaction along with me as I wanted to study both girls and boys from different social class backgrounds. We also attended after-school sports events and cheerleading practices. All of us took field notes after we left the setting and tape-recorded lunchtime conversations.

Some of the things we observed were painful to watch. Through our recordings of gossip and ridicule, we learned a lot about what might make girls so insecure. For one thing, much of the gossip involved negative comments on other girls' appearances as well as their "stuck up" behavior. The only time that anyone disagreed with someone's negative evaluation was if they did so early on, right after the remark was made. Once even one other person agreed with it, no one seemed willing to challenge the "group" view. So in order to participate in the gossip, you pretty much needed to join in with the negative comments or else be sure to speak up quickly.

When we studied teasing, we also saw the power of a response to shape the meaning of an exchange. One day during volleyball practice, a girl said that another girl was showing off her new bra through her white tee-shirt. The girl responded by saying, "If I want to show off my bra, I'll do it like this," lifting her shirt up. By responding playfully, she disarmed the insulter, and her teammates all joined in on the laughter.

In this large middle school, status hierarchies were based on appearance, social class, and intelligence. Those at the bottom of the status rankings were isolates, eating lunch by themselves or with other low status students. As isolates, they were frequent targets of ridicule from students trying to build themselves up by putting others down. Both boys and girls picked on the isolates, most of whom lacked the skills to turn the exchanges into playful ones.

Gossip and ridicule increase the status insecurity of this time of life.

For Your Consideration

➔ What was school like for you at this age? Did you observe anything like this? Why do you think peer groups at this stage in life are so critical, even vicious? Why do peer groups, at all stages of life, produce isolates?

Source: Redacted from Eder 2014.

The Workplace

Another agent of socialization that comes into play somewhat later in life is the workplace. Those initial jobs that we take in high school and college are much more than just a way to earn a few dollars. From the people we rub shoulders with at work, we learn not only a set of skills but also perspectives on the world.

Most of us eventually become committed to some particular type of work, often after trying out many jobs. This may involve **anticipatory socialization**, learning to play a role before entering it. Anticipatory socialization is a sort of mental rehearsal for some future activity. We may talk to people who work in a particular career, read novels about that type of work, or take a summer internship in that field. Such activities allow us to become aware of what would be expected of us. Sometimes this helps people avoid committing themselves to an empty career, as with some of my students who tried student teaching, found that they couldn't stand it, and then moved on to other fields more to their liking.

An intriguing aspect of work as a socializing agent is that the more you participate in a line of work, the more this work becomes part of your self-concept. Eventually, you come to think of yourself so much in terms of the job that if someone asks you to describe yourself, you are likely to include the job in your self-description. You might say, "I'm a teacher," "I'm a nurse," or "I'm a sociologist."

Resocialization

3.6 Explain what total institutions are and how they resocialize people.

What does a woman who has just become a nun have in common with a man who has just divorced? The answer is that they both are undergoing **resocialization**; that is, they are learning new norms, values, attitudes, and behaviors to match their new situation in life. In its most common form, resocialization occurs each time we learn something contrary to our previous experiences. A new boss who insists on a different way of doing things is resocializing you. Most resocialization is mild—only a slight modification of things we have already learned.

Resocialization can also be intense. People who join Alcoholics Anonymous (AA), for example, are surrounded by reformed drinkers who affirm the destructive consequences of excessive drinking. Some students experience an intense period of resocialization when they leave high school and start college—especially during those initially scary days before they find companions, start to fit in, and feel comfortable. The experiences of people who join a cult or begin psychotherapy are even more profound: They learn views that conflict with their earlier socialization. If these ideas "take," not only does the individual's behavior change but he or she also learns a fundamentally different way of looking at life.

Total Institutions

Relatively few of us experience the powerful agent of socialization that sociologist Erving Goffman (1961) called the **total institution**. He coined this term to refer to a place in which people are cut off from the rest of society and where they come under almost total control of the officials who are in charge. Boot camps, prisons, concentration camps, convents, some religious cults, and some military schools, such as West Point, are total institutions.

A person entering a total institution is greeted with a **degradation ceremony** (Garfinkel 1956), an attempt to remake the self by stripping away the individual's current identity and stamping a new one in its place. This unwelcome greeting may involve fingerprinting, photographing, or shaving the head. Newcomers may be ordered to strip, undergo an examination (often in a humiliating, semipublic setting), and then put on a uniform that designates their new status. Officials also take away the individual's *personal identity kit*, items such as jewelry, hairstyles, clothing, and other body decorations used to express individuality.

Total institutions are isolated from the public. The bars, walls, gates, and guards not only keep the inmates in but also keep outsiders out. Staff members supervise the

anticipatory socialization the process of learning in advance an anticipated future role or status

resocialization the process of learning new norms, values, attitudes, and behaviors

total institution a place that is almost totally controlled by those who run it, in which people are cut off from the rest of society and the society is mostly cut off from them

degradation ceremony a term coined by Harold Garfinkel to refer to a ritual whose goal is to remake someone's self by stripping away that individual's self-identity and stamping a new identity in its place day-to-day lives of the residents. Eating, sleeping, showering, recreation—all are standardized. Inmates learn that their previous statuses—student, worker, spouse, parent—mean nothing. The only thing that counts is their current status.

No one leaves a total institution unscathed: The experience brands an indelible mark on the individual's self and colors the way he or she sees the world. Boot camp, as described in the Down-to-Earth Sociology box below, is brutal but swift. Prison, in contrast, is brutal and prolonged. Neither recruit nor prisoner, however, has difficulty in knowing that the institution has had profound effects on attitudes and orientations to life.

Down-to-Earth Sociology

Boot Camp as a Total Institution

The bus arrives at Parris Island, South Carolina, at 3 A.M. The early hour is no accident. The recruits are groggy, confused. Up to a few hours ago, the young men were ordinary civilians. Now, as a sergeant sneeringly calls them "maggots," their heads are buzzed (25 seconds per recruit), and they are quickly thrust into the harsh world of Marine boot camp.

Buzzing the boys' hair is just the first step in stripping away their identity so that the Marines can stamp a new one in its place. The uniform serves the same purpose. There is a ban on using the first person "I." Even a simple request must be made in precise Marine style or it will not be acknowledged. ("Sir, Recruit Jones requests permission to make a head call, Sir.")

Every intense moment of the next eleven weeks reminds the recruits, men and women, that they are joining a subculture of self-discipline. Here, pleasure is suspect and sacrifice is good. As they learn the Marine way of talking, walking, and thinking, they are denied the diversions they once took for granted: television, cigarettes, cars, candy, soft drinks, video games, music, alcohol, drugs, and sex.

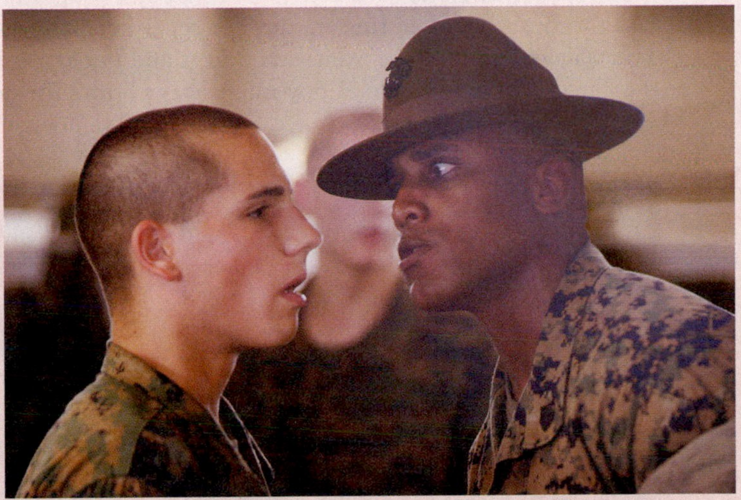
A recruit with a drill instructor.

Lessons are taught with fierce intensity. When Sergeant Carey checks brass belt buckles, Recruit Robert Shelton nervously blurts, "I don't have one." Sergeant Carey's face grows red as his neck cords bulge. "I?" he says, his face just inches from the recruit. With spittle flying from his mouth, he screams, "'I' is gone!"

"Nobody's an individual" is the lesson that is driven home again and again. "You are a team, a Marine. Not a civilian. Not black or white, not Hispanic or Indian or some hyphenated American—but a Marine. You will live like a Marine, fight like a Marine, and, if necessary, die like a Marine."

Each day begins before dawn with close-order formations. The rest of the day is filled with training in hand-to-hand combat, marching, running, calisthenics, Marine history, and—always—following orders.

"An M-16 can blow someone's head off at 500 meters," Sergeant Norman says. "That's beautiful, isn't it?"

"Yes, sir!" shout the platoon's fifty-nine voices.

"Pick your nose!" Simultaneously fifty-nine index fingers shoot into nostrils.

The pressure to conform is intense. Those who are sent packing for insubordination or suicidal tendencies are mocked in cadence during drills. ("Hope you like the sights you see/ Parris Island casualty.") As lights go out at 9 P.M., the exhausted recruits perform the day's last task: The entire platoon, in unison, chants the virtues of the Marines.

Recruits are constantly scrutinized. Subpar performance is not accepted, whether a dirty rifle or a loose thread on a uniform. The underperformer is shouted at, derided, humiliated. The group suffers for the individual. If one recruit is slow, the entire platoon is punished.

The system works.

One of the new Marines (until graduation, they are recruits, not Marines) says, "I feel like I've joined a new society or religion."

He has.

For Your Consideration

➔ Of what significance is the recruits' degradation ceremony? Why are recruits not allowed video games, cigarettes, or calls home? Why are the Marines so unfair as to punish an entire platoon for the failure of an individual? Use concepts in this chapter to explain why the system works.

Sources: Based on Garfinkel 1956; Goffman 1961; Ricks 1995; Dyer 2007.

3.7 Identify major divisions of the life course and discuss the sociological significance of the life course.

Socialization through the Life Course

You are at a particular stage in your life now, and college is a good part of it. You know that you have more stages ahead as you go through life. These stages, from birth to death, are called the **life course** (Elder 1975, 1999). The sociological significance of the life course is twofold. First, as you pass through a stage, it affects your behavior and orientations. You simply don't think about life in the same way when you are 35, are married, and have a baby and a mortgage as you do when you are 18 or 20, single, and in college. (Actually, you don't even see life the same way as a freshman and as a senior.) Second, your life course differs by social location. Your social class, race–ethnicity, and gender, for example, map out distinctive worlds of experience.

This means that the typical life course differs for males and females, the rich and the poor, and so on. To emphasize this major sociological point, in the sketch that follows, I will stress the *historical* setting of people's lives. Because of your particular social location, your own life course may differ from this sketch, which is a composite of stages that others have suggested (Levinson 1978; Carr et al. 1995; Quadagno 2010).

Watch on MySocLab **Video:** Socialization on the Job

Childhood (from birth to about age 12)

Consider how remarkably different your childhood would have been if you had grown up in Europe a few hundred years ago. Historian Philippe Ariès (1965) noticed that in European paintings from about A.D. 1000 to 1800, children were always dressed in adult clothing. If they were not depicted stiffly posed, as in a family portrait, they were shown doing adult activities.

From this, Ariès drew a conclusion that sparked a debate among historians. He said that Europeans of this era did not regard childhood as a special time of life. They viewed children as miniature adults and put them to work at an early age. At the age of 7, for example, a boy might leave home for good to learn to be a jeweler

life course the stages of our life as we go from birth to death

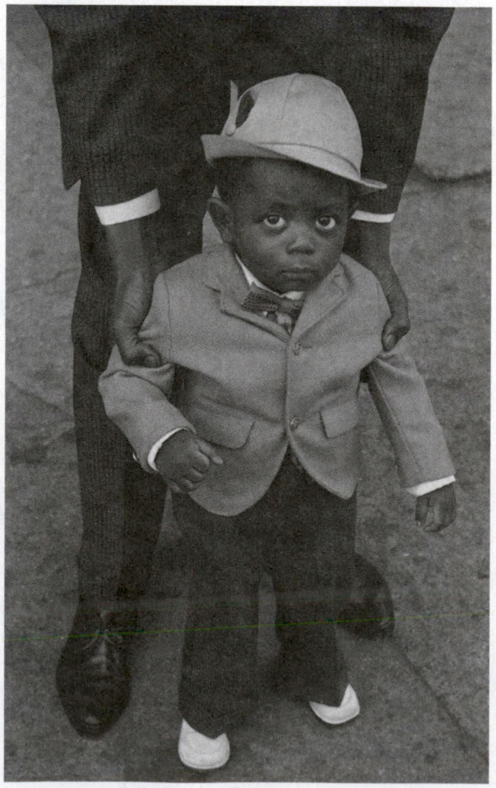

From paintings, such as this one of Sir Walter Raleigh from 1602, some historians conclude that Europeans once viewed children as miniature adults who assumed adult roles early in life. From the 1959 photo taken in Harlem, New York, you can see why this conclusion is now being challenged, if not ridiculed.

or a stonecutter. A girl, in contrast, stayed home until she married, but by the age of 7, she assumed her share of the household tasks. Historians do not deny that these were the customs of that time, but some say that Ariès' conclusion is ridiculous, that other evidence indicates that these people viewed childhood as a special time of life (Orme 2002).

Until about 1900, having children work like adults was common around the world. Even today, children in the Least Industrialized Nations work in many occupations—from blacksmiths to waiters. As tourists are shocked to discover, children in these nations also work as street peddlers, hawking everything from shoelaces to chewing gum.

Child rearing, too, used to be remarkably different. Three hundred years ago, parents and teachers considered it their *moral* duty to *terrorize* children. To keep children from "going bad," they would frighten them with bedtime stories of death and hellfire, lock them in dark closets, and force them to witness events like this:

> *A common moral lesson involved taking children to visit the gibbet [an upraised post on which executed bodies were left hanging], where they were forced to inspect the rotting corpses as an example of what happens to bad children when they grow up. Whole classes were taken out of school to witness hangings, and parents would often whip their children afterwards to make them remember what they had seen. (DeMause 1975)*

Industrialization transformed the way we perceive children. When children had the leisure to go to school and postpone taking on adult roles, parents and officials came to think of them as tender and innocent, as needing more care, comfort, and protection. Such attitudes of dependency grew, and today we view children as needing gentle guidance if they are to develop emotionally, intellectually, morally, even physically. We take our view for granted—after all, it is only "common sense." Yet, as you can see, our view is not "natural." It is, instead, rooted in society—in geography, history, and economic development.

In Sum: Childhood is more than biology. Everyone's childhood occurs at some point in history and is embedded in specific social locations, especially social class and gender. *These social factors are as vital as our biology, for they determine what our childhood will be like.* Although a child's *biological* characteristics (such as being small and dependent) are universal, the child's *social* experiences (the kind of life the child lives) are not. Because of this, sociologists say that childhood varies from culture to culture.

In many societies, manhood is not bestowed upon males simply because they reach a certain age. Manhood, rather, signifies a standing in the community that must be achieved. Shown here is an initiation ceremony in Indonesia, where boys, to lay claim to the status of manhood, must jump over this barrier.

Adolescence (ages 13–17)

It might seem strange to you, but adolescence is a *social invention*, not a "natural" age division. In earlier centuries, people simply moved from childhood to young adulthood, with no stopover in between. The Industrial Revolution allowed adolescence to be invented. It brought such an abundance of material surpluses that for the first time in history people in their teens were not needed as workers. At the same time, education became more important for achieving success. As these two forces in industrialized societies converged, they created a gap between childhood and adulthood. The term *adolescence* was coined to indicate this new stage in life (Hall 1904), one that has become renowned for uncertainty, rebellion, and inner turmoil.

To mark the passage of children into adulthood, tribal societies hold *initiation rites.* This grounds the self-identity, showing these young people how they fit in the society. In the industrialized world, however, adolescents must "find" themselves. They grapple with the dilemma of "I am neither a child nor an adult. Who am I?" As they attempt to carve out an identity that is distinct from both the "younger" world being left behind and the "older"

FIGURE 3.2 Transitional Adulthood: A New Stage in the Life Course

Who has completed the transition?

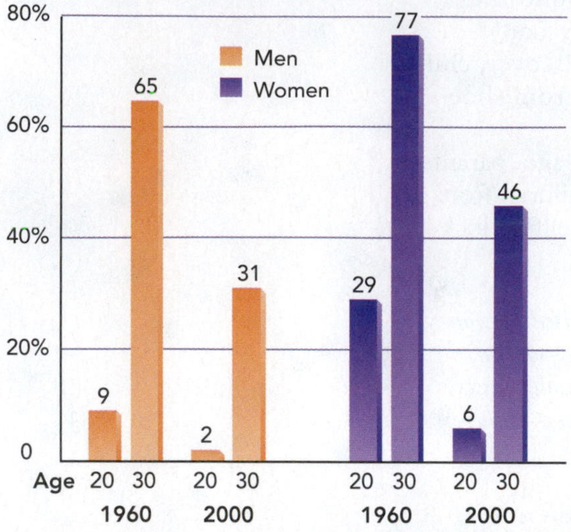

The bars show the percentage who have completed the transition to adulthood, as measured by leaving home, finishing school, getting married, having a child, and being financially independent.

Source: Furstenberg et al. 2004.

world that still lingers out of reach, adolescents develop their own subcultures, with distinctive clothing, hairstyles, language, gestures, and music. We usually fail to realize that contemporary society, not biology, created this period of inner turmoil that we call *adolescence*.

Transitional Adulthood (ages 18–29)

If society invented adolescence, can it also invent other periods of life? As Figure 3.2 illustrates, this is actually happening now. Postindustrial societies are adding another period of extended youth to the life course, which sociologists call **transitional adulthood** (also known as *adultolescence*).

After high school, millions of young adults postpone adult responsibilities by going to college. They are mostly freed from the control of their parents, yet they don't have to support themselves. After college, many live at home, so they can live cheaply while they establish themselves in a career—and, of course, continue to "find themselves." During this time, people are "neither psychological adolescents nor sociological adults" (Keniston 1971). At some point during this period of extended youth, young adults ease into adult responsibilities. They take full-time jobs, become serious about a career, engage in courtship rituals, get married—and go into debt.

The Middle Years (ages 30–65)

The Early Middle Years (ages 30–49). During their early middle years, most people are more sure of themselves and of their goals in life. As with any point in the life course, however, the self can receive severe jolts. Common upheavals during this period are divorce and losing jobs. It may take years for the self to stabilize after such ruptures.

The early middle years pose a special challenge for many U.S. women, who have been given the message, especially by the media, that they can "have it all." They can be superworkers, superwives, and supermoms—all rolled into one superwoman. Reality, however, hits them in the face: too little time, too many demands, even too little sleep. Something has to give, and attempts to resolve this dilemma are anything but easy.

The Later Middle Years (ages 50–62 or so). During the later middle years, health issues and mortality begin to loom large as people feel their bodies change, especially if they watch their parents become frail, fall ill, and die. The consequence is a fundamental reorientation in thinking—*from time since birth to time left to live* (Neugarten 1976). With this changed orientation, people attempt to evaluate the past and come to terms with what lies ahead. They compare what they have accomplished with what they had hoped to achieve. Many people also find themselves caring not only for their own children but also for their aging parents. Because of this double burden, which is often crushing, people in the later middle years are sometimes called the "sandwich generation."

In contrast, many people experience few of these stresses and find late middle age to be the most comfortable period of their lives. They enjoy job security or secure marriages and a standard of living higher than ever before. They live in a bigger house (one that may even be paid for), drive newer cars, and take longer and more exotic vacations. The children are grown, the self is firmly planted, and fewer upheavals are likely to occur.

As they anticipate the next stage of life, however, most people do not like what they see.

transitional adulthood a term that refers to a period following high school when young adults have not yet taken on the responsibilities ordinarily associated with adulthood; also called *adultolescence*

The Older Years (about age 63 on)

The Transitional Older Years (ages 63–74). In agricultural societies, when most people died early, old age was thought to begin at around age 40. As industrialization brought improved nutrition, medicine, and public health, allowing more people to live longer, the beginning of "old age" gradually receded. Today, people who enjoy good health don't think of their 60s as old age but as an extension of their middle years. This change is so recent that a *new stage of life* seems to be evolving, the period between retirement (averaging about 63) and old age—which people are increasingly coming to see as beginning around age 75 ("Schwab Study" 2008). We can call this stage the **transitional older years**. Increasingly during this stage of the life course, people are more aware of death and feel that "time is closing in" on them.

Researchers who are focusing on this transitional stage of life have found that social isolation harms both the body and brain, that people who are more integrated into social networks stay mentally sharper (Ertel et al. 2008). With improved health, two-thirds of the men and two-fifths of the women between their late 60s and age 75 continue to be sexually active (Lindau et al. 2007). Not only are people in this stage of life having more sex but they also are enjoying it more (Beckman et al. 2008).

Because we have a self and can reason abstractly, we can contemplate death. In our early years, we regard death as a vague notion, a remote possibility. As people see their parents and friends die and observe their own bodies no longer functioning as before, however, the thought of death becomes less abstract. Increasingly during this stage in the life course, people feel that "time is closing in" on them.

This January 1937 photo from Sneedville, Tennessee, shows Eunice Johns, age 9, and her husband, Charlie Johns, age 22. The groom gave his wife a doll as a wedding gift. The new husband and wife planned to build a cabin, and, as Charlie Johns phrased it, "go to housekeepin'." This couple illustrates the cultural relativity of life stages, which we sometimes mistake as fixed. It also is interesting from a symbolic interactionist perspective—that of changing definitions.

The marriage lasted. The couple had 7 children, 5 boys and 2 girls. Charlie died in 1997 at age 83, and Eunice in 2006 at age 78. The two were buried in the Johns Family Cemetery.

The Later Older Years (age 75 or so on). As with the preceding periods of life, except the first one, there is no precise beginning point to this last stage. For some, the 75th birthday may mark entry into this period of life. For others, that marker may be the 80th or even the 85th birthday. For most, this stage is marked by growing frailty and illness. For all who reach this stage, it is ended by death. For some, the physical decline is slow, and a rare few manage to see their 100th birthday mentally alert and in good physical health.

Applying the Sociological Perspective to the Life Course

In Chapter 1, you learned about the sociological perspective, especially how your *social location* is vitally important for what you experience in life. Your social location, such as your social class, gender, and race–ethnicity, is also highly significant for your life course. If you are poor, for example, you likely will feel older sooner than most wealthy people, for whom life is less harsh. Individual factors—such as your health or marrying early or entering college late—can also throw your life course "out of sequence."

As you learned, the sociological perspective stresses not just social location but also the broad streams of history. These, too drastically affect your life course. As sociologist C. Wright Mills (1959) would say, if employers are beating a path to your door, or failing to do so, you will be more inclined to marry, to buy a house, and to start a family—or to postpone these life course events.

This takes us to the sociological significance of the life course. Our life course does not merely reflect biology, things that occur naturally to all of us as we add years to our lives. Rather, *social* factors influence our life course. Since you live in a period of rapid social change, you can expect changes that will send your life course in unexpected directions.

transitional older years an emerging stage of the life course between retirement and when people are considered old; about age 63 to 74

3.8 Understand why we are not prisoners of socialization.

Are We Prisoners of Socialization?

From our discussion of socialization, you might conclude that sociologists think of people as robots: The socialization goes in, and the behavior comes out. People cannot help what they do, think, or feel, as everything is a result of their exposure to socializing agents.

Sociologists do *not* think of people in this way. Although socialization is powerful, and affects all of us profoundly, we have a self. Established in childhood and continually modified by later experience, our self is dynamic. Our self is not a sponge that passively absorbs influences from the environment, but, rather, it is a vigorous, essential part of our being that allows us to act on our environment.

Precisely because people are not robots, individual behavior is hard to predict. The countless reactions of others merge in each of us. As the self develops, we each internalize or "put together" these innumerable reactions, which become the basis for how we reason, react to others, and make choices in life. The result is a unique whole called the *individual.*

Rather than being passive sponges in this process, *each of us is actively involved in the construction of the self.* Our experiences in the family and other groups during childhood lay down our basic orientations to life, but we are not doomed to keep these orientations if we do not like them. We can purposely expose ourselves to other groups and ideas. Those experiences, in turn, have their own effects on our self. In short, we influence our socialization as we make choices. We can change even the self within the limitations of the framework laid down by our social locations. And that self—along with the options available within society—is the key to our behavior.

feral children children assumed to have been raised by animals, in the wilderness, isolated from humans

MySocLab — Study and Review on MySocLab

CHAPTER 3 Summary and Review

Society Makes Us Human

3.1 Explain how feral, isolated, and institutionalized children help us understand that "society makes us human."

How much of our human characteristics come from "nature" (heredity) and how much from "nurture" (the social environment)?

Observations of isolated, institutionalized, and **feral children** help to answer the nature–nurture question, as do experiments with monkeys that were raised in isolation. Language and intimate social interaction—aspects of "nurture"—are essential to the development of what we consider to be human characteristics. Pp. 62–67.

Socialization into the Self and Mind

3.2 Use the ideas and research of Cooley (looking-glass self), Mead (role taking), and Piaget (reasoning) to explain socialization into the self and mind.

How do we acquire a self?

Humans are born with the *capacity* to develop a **self**, but the self must be socially constructed; that is, its contents depend on social interaction. According to Charles Horton Cooley's concept of the **looking-glass self**, our self develops as we internalize others' reactions to us. George Herbert Mead identified the ability to **take the role of the other** as essential to the development of the self. Mead concluded that even the mind is a social product. Pp. 67–68.

How do children develop reasoning skills?

Jean Piaget identified four stages that children go through as they develop the ability to reason: (1) *sensorimotor*, in which understanding is limited to sensory stimuli such as touch and sight; (2) *preoperational*, the ability to use symbols; (3) *concrete operational*, in which reasoning ability is more complex but not yet capable of complex abstractions; and (4) *formal operational*, or abstract thinking. Pp. 68–70.

Learning Personality, Morality, and Emotions

3.3 Explain how the development of personality and morality and socialization into emotions are part of how "society makes us human."

How do sociologists evaluate Freud's psychoanalytic theory of personality development?

Sigmund Freud viewed personality development as the result of our **id** (inborn, self-centered desires) clashing with the demands of society. The **ego** develops to balance the id and the **superego**, the conscience. Sociologists, in contrast, do not examine inborn or subconscious motivations but, instead, consider how *social* factors—social class, gender, religion, education, and so forth—underlie personality. Pp. 70–71.

How do people develop morality?

That even babies exhibit a sense of morality seems to indicate that a basic morality could be inborn. Lawrence Kohlberg identified four stages children go through as they learn morality: amoral, preconventional, conventional, and postconventional. As they make moral decisions, both men and women use personal relationships and abstract principles. The answer to "What is moral?" differs from society to society. Pp. 71–72.

How does socialization influence emotions?

Socialization influences not only *how we express our emotions* but also *what emotions we feel*. Socialization into emotions is one of the means by which society produces conformity. Pp. 72–74.

Socialization into Gender

3.4 Discuss how gender messages from the family, peers, and the mass media teach us society's gender map.

How does gender socialization affect our sense of self?

Gender socialization—sorting males and females into different roles—is a primary way that groups control human behavior. Children receive messages about **gender** even in infancy. A society's ideals of sex-linked behaviors are reinforced by its social institutions. Pp. 74–79.

Agents of Socialization

3.5 Explain why the family, the neighborhood, religion, day care, school, peer groups, and the workplace are called agents of socialization.

What are the main agents of socialization?

The **agents of socialization** include the family, neighborhood, religion, day care, school, **peer groups**, the **mass media**, and the workplace. Each has its particular influences in socializing us into becoming full-fledged members of society. Pp. 79–84.

Resocialization

3.6 Explain what total institutions are and how they resocialize people.

What is resocialization?

Resocialization is the process of learning new norms, values, attitudes, and behavior. Most resocialization is voluntary, but some, as with the resocialization of residents of **total institutions**, is involuntary. Pp. 84–85.

Socialization through the Life Course

3.7 Identify major divisions of the life course and discuss the sociological significance of the life course.

Does socialization end when we enter adulthood?

Socialization occurs throughout the life course. In industrialized societies, the **life course** can be divided into childhood, adolescence, young adulthood, the middle years, and the older years. The West is adding two new stages, **transitional adulthood** and **transitional older years**. Using the sociological perspective, we can see how both the streams of history and social location—geography, gender, race–ethnicity, social class—influence the life course. Pp. 86–89.

Are We Prisoners of Socialization?

Although socialization is powerful, we are not merely the sum of our socialization experiences. Just as socialization influences our behavior, so we act on our environment and influence even our self-concept. Pp. 89–90.

Thinking Critically about Chapter 3

1. What two agents of socialization have influenced you the most? Can you pinpoint their influence on your attitudes, beliefs, values, or other orientations to life?
2. Summarize your views of the "proper" relationships of women and men. What in your socialization has led you to have these views?
3. How does the text's summary of the life course compare with your experiences? Use the sociological perspective to explain both the similarities and the differences.

CHAPTER 4

Social Structure and Social Interaction

Listen to Chapter 4 on MySocLab

Learning Objectives

After you have read this chapter, you should be able to:

4.1 Distinguish between macrosociology and microsociology.

4.2 Explain the significance of social structure and its components: culture, social class, social status, roles, groups, and social institutions; compare the functionalist and conflict perspectives on social structure; and explain what holds society together.

4.3 Discuss what symbolic interactionists study and explain dramaturgy, ethnomethodology, and the social construction of reality.

4.4 Explain why we need both macrosociology and microsociology to understand social life.

My curiosity had gotten the better of me. *When the sociology convention was over, I climbed aboard the first city bus that came along. I didn't know where the bus was going, and I didn't know where I would spend the night.*

This was my first visit to Washington, D.C., so everything was unfamiliar to me. I had no destination, no plans, not even a map. I carried no billfold, just a driver's license shoved into my jeans for emergency identification, some pocket change, and a $10 bill tucked into my sock. My goal was simple: If I saw something interesting, I would get off the bus and check it out.

As we passed row after row of apartment buildings and stores, I could see myself riding buses the entire night. Then something caught my eye. Nothing spectacular—just groups of people clustered around a large circular area where several streets intersected.

I got off the bus and made my way to what turned out to be Dupont Circle. I took a seat on a sidewalk bench. As the scene came into focus, I noticed several streetcorner men drinking and joking with one another. One of the men broke from his companions and sat down next to me. As we talked, I mostly listened.

As night fell, the men said that they wanted to get another bottle of wine. I contributed. They counted their money and asked if I wanted to go with them. As we left the circle, the three men began to cut through an alley. "Oh, no," I thought. "This isn't what I had in mind."

> "Suddenly one of the men jumped up, smashed the empty bottle against the sidewalk, and …"

I had but a split second to make a decision. I held back half a step so that none of the three was behind me. As we walked, they passed around the remnants of their bottle. When my turn came, I didn't know what to do. I shuddered to think about the diseases lurking within that bottle. In the semidarkness I faked it, letting only my thumb and forefinger touch my lips and nothing enter my mouth.

When we returned to Dupont Circle, we sat on the benches, and the men passed around their new bottle of Thunderbird. I couldn't fake it in the light, so I passed, pointing at my stomach to indicate that I was having digestive problems.

Suddenly one of the men jumped up, smashed the emptied bottle against the sidewalk, and thrust the jagged neck outward in a menacing gesture. He glared straight ahead at another bench, where he had spotted someone with whom he had some sort of unfinished business. As the other men told him to cool it, I moved slightly to one side of the group—ready to flee, just in case.

4.1 Distinguish between macrosociology and microsociology.

Levels of Sociological Analysis

On this sociological adventure, I almost got in over my head. Fortunately, it turned out all right. The man's "enemy" didn't look our way, the man put the broken bottle next to the bench "in case he needed it," and my intriguing introduction to a life that up until then I had only read about continued until dawn.

Sociologists Elliot Liebow (1967/1999), Mitchell Duneier (1999), and Elijah Anderson (1978, 1990, 1990/2006) have written fascinating accounts about men like my companions from that evening. Although streetcorner men may appear to be disorganized—simply coming and going as they please and doing whatever feels good at the moment—sociologists have analyzed how, like us, these men are influenced by the norms and beliefs of our society. This will become more apparent as we examine the two levels of analysis that sociologists use.

macrosociology analysis of social life that focuses on broad features of society, such as social class and the relationships of groups to one another; usually used by functionalists and conflict theorists

microsociology analysis of social life that focuses on social interaction; typically used by symbolic interactionists

Macrosociology and Microsociology

The first level, **macrosociology**, focuses on broad features of society. Conflict theorists and functionalists use this approach to analyze such things as social class and how groups are related to one another. If they were to analyze streetcorner men, for example, they would stress that these men are located at the bottom of the U.S. social class system. Their low status means that many opportunities are closed to them: The men have few job skills, little education, hardly anything to offer an employer. As "able-bodied" men, however, they are not eligible for welfare—even for a two-year limit—so they hustle to survive. As a consequence, they spend their lives on the streets.

In the second level, **microsociology**, the focus is on **social interaction**, what people do when they come together. Sociologists who use this approach are likely to analyze the men's rules, or "codes," for getting along; their survival strategies ("hustles"); how they divide up money, wine, or whatever other resources they have; their relationships with girlfriends, family, and friends; where they spend their time and what they do there; their language; their pecking order; and so on. Microsociology is the primary focus of symbolic interactionists.

Sociologists use both macro and micro levels of analysis to study social life. Those who use macrosociology to analyze the homeless (or any human behavior) focus on broad aspects of society, such as the economy and social classes. Sociologists who use the microsociological approach analyze how people interact with one another. This photo illustrates social structure (the disparities between power and powerlessness are amply evident). It also illustrates the micro level (the isolation of this man).

Because each approach has a different focus, macrosociology and microsociology yield distinctive perspectives; both are needed to gain a fuller understanding of social life. We cannot adequately understand streetcorner men, for example, without using macrosociology. It is essential that we place the men within the broad context of how groups in U.S. society are related to one another: As is true for ourselves, the social class of these men helps to shape their attitudes and behavior. Nor can we adequately understand these men without microsociology: Their everyday situations also form a significant part of their lives—as they do for all of us.

Let's look in more detail at how these two approaches in sociology work together to help us understand social life. As we examine them more closely, you may find yourself feeling more comfortable with one approach than the other. This is what happens with sociologists. For reasons that include personal background and professional training, sociologists find themselves more comfortable with one approach and tend to use it in their research. Both approaches, however, are necessary to understand life in society.

The Macrosociological Perspective: Social Structure

4.2 Explain the significance of social structure and its components: culture, social class, social status, roles, groups, and social institutions; compare the functionalist and conflict perspectives on social structure; and explain what holds society together.

Why did the street people in our opening vignette act as they did, staying up all night drinking wine, prepared to use a lethal weapon? Why don't *we* act like this? Social structure helps us answer such questions.

The Sociological Significance of Social Structure

To better understand human behavior, we need to understand *social structure*, the framework of society that was already laid out before you were born. **Social structure** refers to the typical patterns of a group, such as the usual relationships between men and women or students and teachers. *The sociological significance of social structure is that it guides our behavior.*

social interaction what people do when they are in one another's presence; includes communications at a distance

Because this term may seem vague, let's consider how you experience social structure in your own life. As I write this, I do not know your race–ethnicity. I do not know your religion. I do not know whether you are young or old, tall or short, male

Watch on **MySocLab**
Video: Social Interaction

social structure the framework of society that surrounds us; consists of the ways that people and groups are related to one another; this framework gives direction to and sets limits on our behavior

social class large numbers of people who have similar amounts of income and education and who work at jobs that are roughly comparable in prestige

status the position that someone occupies in a social group (also called social status)

or female. I do not know whether you were reared on a farm, in the suburbs, or in the inner city. I do not know whether you went to a public high school or to an exclusive prep school. But I do know that you are in college. And this, alone, tells me a great deal about you.

From this one piece of information, I can assume that the social structure of your college is now shaping what you do. For example, let's suppose that today you felt euphoric over some great news. I can be fairly certain (not absolutely, mind you, but relatively confident) that when you entered the classroom, social structure overrode your mood. That is, instead of shouting at the top of your lungs and joyously throwing this book into the air, you entered the classroom in a fairly subdued manner and took your seat.

The same social structure influences your instructor, even if he or she, on the one hand, is facing a divorce or has a child dying of cancer or, on the other, has just been awarded a promotion or a million-dollar grant. Your instructor may feel like either retreating into seclusion or celebrating wildly, but most likely he or she will conduct class in the usual manner. In short, social structure tends to override our personal feelings and desires.

And how about street people? Just as social structure influences you and your instructor, so it also establishes limits for them. They, too, find themselves in a specific location in the U.S. social structure—although it is quite different from yours or your instructor's. Consequently, they are affected in different ways. Nothing about their social location leads them to take notes or to lecture. *Their behaviors, however, are as logical an outcome of where they find themselves in the social structure as are your own.* In their position in the social structure, it is just as "natural" to drink wine all night as it is for you to stay up studying all night for a crucial examination. It is just as "natural" for them to break off the neck of a wine bottle and glare at an enemy as it is for you to nod and say, "Excuse me," when you enter a crowded classroom late and have to claim a desk on which someone has already placed books. To better understand social structure, read the Down-to-Earth Sociology box on the next page.

Social class and social status are significant factors in social life. Fundamental to what we become, they affect our orientations to life. Can you see how this photo illustrates this point?

In Sum: People learn their behaviors and attitudes because of their location in the social structure (whether those are privileged, deprived, or in between), and they act accordingly. This is as true of street people as it is of us. *The differences in our behavior and attitudes are not because of biology (race–ethnicity, sex, or any other supposed genetic factors), but to our location in the social structure.* Switch places with street people and watch your behaviors and attitudes change!

Because social structure is so vital for us—affecting who we are and what we are like—let's look more closely at its major components: culture, social class, social status, roles, groups, and social institutions.

Culture

In Chapter 2, we considered culture's far-reaching effects on our lives. At this point, let's simply summarize its main impact. Sociologists use the term *culture* to refer to a group's language, beliefs, values, behaviors, and even gestures. Culture also includes the material objects that a group uses. Culture is the broadest framework that determines what kind of people we become. If we are reared in Chinese, Arab, or U.S. culture, we will grow up to be like most Chinese, Arabs, or Americans. On the outside, we will look and act like them, and on the inside, we will think and feel like them.

Social Class

To understand people, we must examine the social locations that they hold in life. Especially significant is *social class*, which is based on income, education, and occupational prestige. Large numbers of people who have similar amounts of income and education and who work at jobs that are roughly comparable in prestige make up a **social class**. It is hard to overemphasize this aspect of social structure, because our social class influences not only our behaviors but also our ideas and attitudes.

We have this in common, then, with the street people described in this chapter's opening vignette: We both are influenced by our location in the social class structure. Theirs may be a considerably less privileged position, but it has no less influence on their lives. Social class is so significant that we shall spend an entire chapter (Chapter 10) on this topic.

Social Status

When you hear the word *status*, you are likely to think of prestige. These two words are wedded together in people's minds. As you saw in the box on football, however, sociologists use **status** in a different way—to refer to the *position* that someone occupies. That position may carry a great deal of prestige, as in the case of a judge or an astronaut, or it may bring little prestige, as in the case of a convenience store clerk or a waitress at the

Down-to-Earth Sociology

College Football as Social Structure

To gain a better idea of what *social structure* is, let's use the example of college football (Dobriner 1969). You probably know the various positions on the team: center, guards, tackles, ends, quarterback, running backs, and the like. Each is a *status*; that is, each is a social position. For each of the statuses shown in Figure 4.1, there is a *role*; that is, each of these positions has certain expectations attached to it. The center is expected to snap the ball, the quarterback to pass it, the guards to block, the tackles to tackle or block, the ends to receive passes, and so on. Those role expectations guide each player's actions; that is, the players try to do what their particular role requires.

Let's suppose that football is your favorite sport and you never miss a home game at your college. Let's also suppose that you graduate, get a great job, and move across the country. Five years later, you return to your campus for a nostalgic visit. The climax of your visit is the biggest football game of the season. When you get to the game, you might be surprised to see a different coach, but you are not surprised that each playing position is occupied by people you don't know: All the players you knew have graduated, and their places have been filled by others.

This scenario mirrors *social structure*, the framework around which a group exists. In football, this framework consists of the coaching staff and the eleven playing positions. The game does not depend on any particular individual but, rather, on *social statuses*, the positions that the individuals occupy. When someone leaves a position, the game can go on because someone else takes over that position or status and plays the role. The game will continue even though not a single individual remains from one period of time to the next. Notre Dame's football team endures today even though Knute Rockne, the Gipper, and his teammates are long dead.

Even though you may not play football, you do live your life within a clearly established social structure. The statuses that you occupy and the roles you play were already in place before you were born. You take your particular positions in life, others do the same, and society goes about its business. Although the specifics change with time, the game—whether of life or of football—goes on.

FIGURE 4.1 Team Positions (Statuses) in Football

Source: By the author.

For Your Consideration

➔ How does social structure influence your life? To answer this question, you can begin by analyzing your social statuses.

local truck stop. The status may also be looked down on, as in the case of a streetcorner man, an ex-convict, or a thief.

Like other aspects of social structure, statuses are part of our basic framework of living in society. The example I gave of students and teachers who come to class and do what others expect of them despite their particular circumstances and moods illustrates how statuses affect our actions—and those of the people around us. Our statuses—whether daughter or son, teacher or student—*provides guidelines for how we are to act and feel.* Like other aspects of social structure, statuses set limits on what we can and cannot do. Because social statuses are an essential part of the social structure, all human groups have them.

Status Sets. All of us occupy several positions at the same time. You may simultaneously be a son or daughter, a worker, a date, and a student. Sociologists use the term **status set** to refer to all the statuses or positions that you occupy. Obviously your status set changes as your particular statuses change. For example, if you graduate from college, take a full-time job, get married, buy a home, and have children, your status set changes to include the positions of worker, spouse, homeowner, and parent.

Ascribed and Achieved Statuses. An **ascribed status** is involuntary. You do not ask for it, nor can you choose it. At birth, you inherit ascribed statuses such as your race–ethnicity, sex, and the social class of your parents, as well as your statuses as female or male, daughter or son, niece or nephew. Others, such as teenager and senior citizen, are related to the life course we discussed in Chapter 3. They are given to you later in life.

Achieved statuses, in contrast, are voluntary. These you earn or accomplish. As a result of your efforts, you become a student, a friend, a spouse, or a lawyer. Or, for lack of effort (or for efforts that others fail to appreciate), you become a school dropout, a former friend, an ex-spouse, or a debarred lawyer. As you can see, achieved statuses can be either positive or negative; both college president and bank robber are achieved statuses.

Status Symbols. People who are pleased with their social status often want others to recognize their position. To elicit this recognition, they use **status symbols**, signs that identify a status. For example, people wear wedding rings to announce their marital status; uniforms, guns, and badges to proclaim that they are police officers (and, not so subtly, to let you know that their status gives them authority over you); and "backward" collars to declare that they are Lutheran ministers or Roman Catholic or Episcopal priests.

Because some social statuses are negative, so are their status symbols. The scarlet letter in Nathaniel Hawthorne's book by the same title is one example. Another is the CONVICTED DUI (Driving Under the Influence) bumper sticker that some U.S. courts require convicted drunk drivers to display if they want to avoid a jail sentence.

All of us use status symbols. We use them to announce our statuses to others and to help smooth our interactions in everyday life. Can you identify your own status symbols and what they communicate? For example, how does your clothing announce your statuses of sex, age, and college student?

Master Statuses. A **master status** cuts across your other statuses. Some master statuses are ascribed. One example is your sex. Whatever you do, people perceive you as a male or as a female. If you are working your way through college by flipping burgers, people see you not only as a burger flipper and a student but also as a *male* or *female* burger flipper and a *male* or *female* college student. Other ascribed master statuses are race–ethnicity and age.

Some master statuses are achieved. If you become very, very wealthy (and it doesn't matter whether your wealth comes from a successful invention, a hit song, or from winning the lottery—it is still *achieved* as far as sociologists are concerned), your wealth is likely to become a master status. For example, people might say, "She is a very rich burger flipper"—or, more likely, "She's very rich, and she used to flip burgers!"

Similarly, people who become disfigured find, to their dismay, that their condition becomes a master status. For example, a person whose face is scarred from severe burns

status set all the statuses or positions that an individual occupies

ascribed status a position an individual either inherits at birth or receives involuntarily later in life

achieved statuses positions that are earned, accomplished, or involve at least some effort or activity on the individual's part

status symbols indicators of a status, especially items in that display prestige

master status a status that cuts across the other statuses that an individual occupies

Master statuses are those that overshadow our other statuses. Shown here is Stephen Hawking, who is severely disabled by Lou Gehrig's disease. For some, his master status is that of a person with disabilities. Because Hawking is one of the greatest physicists who has ever lived, however, his outstanding achievements have given him another master status, that of a world-class physicist in the ranking of Einstein.

will be viewed through this unwelcome master status regardless of their occupation or accomplishments. In the same way, people who are confined to wheelchairs can attest to how their wheelchair overrides all their other statuses and influences others' perceptions of everything they do.

Status Inconsistency. Our statuses usually fit together fairly well, but some people have a mismatch among their statuses. This is known as **status inconsistency** (or discrepancy). A 14-year-old college student is an example. So is a 40-year-old married woman who is dating a 19-year-old college sophomore.

These examples reveal an essential aspect of social statuses: Like other components of social structure, our statuses come with built-in *norms* (that is, expectations) that guide our behavior. When statuses mesh well, as they usually do, we know what to expect of people. This helps social interaction to unfold smoothly. Status inconsistency, however, upsets our expectations. In the preceding examples, how are you supposed to act? Are you supposed to treat the 14-year-old as you would a young teenager, or as you would your college classmate? Do you react to the married woman as you would to the mother of your friend, or as you would to a classmate's date?

Roles

All the world's a stage
And all the men and women merely players.
They have their exits and their entrances;
And one man in his time plays many parts ...

(William Shakespeare, As You Like It, *Act II, Scene 7)*

Like Shakespeare, sociologists see roles as essential to social life. When you were born, **roles**—the behaviors, obligations, and privileges attached to a status—were already set up for you. Society was waiting with outstretched arms to teach you how it expected you to act as a boy or a girl. And whether you were born poor, rich, or somewhere in between, that, too, attached certain behaviors, obligations, and privileges to your statuses.

Watch on **MySocLab**
Video: Social Structure and Social Roles

The difference between role and status is that you *occupy* a status, but you *play* a role (Linton 1936). For example, being a son or daughter is your status, but your expectations of receiving food and shelter from your parents—as well as their expectations that you show respect to them—are part of your role. Or, again, your status is student, but your role is to attend class, take notes, do homework, and take tests.

Roles are like fences. They allow us a certain amount of freedom, but for most of us that freedom doesn't go very far. Suppose that a woman decides that she is not going to wear dresses—or a man that he will not wear suits and ties—regardless of what anyone says. In most situations, they'll stick to their decision. When a formal occasion comes along, however, such as a family wedding or a funeral, they are likely to cave in to norms that they find overwhelming. Almost all of us follow the guidelines for what is "appropriate" for our roles. Few of us are bothered by such constraints. Our socialization is so thorough that we usually *want* to do what our roles indicate is appropriate.

The sociological significance of roles is that they lay out what is expected of people. As individuals throughout society perform their roles, those many roles mesh together to form this thing called *society.* As Shakespeare put it, people's roles provide "their exits and their entrances" on the stage of life. In short, roles are remarkably effective at keeping people in line—telling them when they should "enter" and when they should "exit," as well as what to do in between.

status inconsistency ranking high on some dimensions of social status and low on others; also called *status discrepancy*

role the behaviors, obligations, and privileges attached to a status

group people who interact with one another and who believe that what they have in common is significant; also called a *social group*

social institution the organized, usual, or standard ways by which society meets its basic needs

Explore on **MySocLab**
Activity: Congregational Membership, Primary Groups, and Secondary Groups

Groups

A **group** consists of people who interact with one another and who feel that the values, interests, and norms they have in common are important. The groups to which we belong—just like social class, statuses, and roles—are powerful forces in our lives. By belonging to a group, we assume an obligation to affirm the group's values, interests, and norms. To remain a member in good standing, we need to show that we share those characteristics. This means that *when we belong to a group, we yield to others the right to judge our behavior*—even though we don't like it!

Although this principle holds true for all groups, some groups wield influence over only small segments of our behavior. For example, if you belong to a stamp collectors' club, the group's influence may center on your display of knowledge about stamps and perhaps your fairness in trading them. Other groups, in contrast, such as the family, control many aspects of our behavior. When parents say to their 15-year-old daughter, "As long as you are living under our roof, you had better be home by midnight," they show an expectation that their daughter, as a member of the family, will conform to their ideas about many aspects of life, including their views on curfew. They are saying that as long as the daughter wants to remain a member of the family in good standing, her behavior must conform to their expectations.

In Chapters 6 and 7, we will examine groups in detail. For now, let's look at the next component of social structure, social institutions.

Social Institutions

At first glance, the term *social institution* may seem cold and abstract—with little relevance to your life. In fact, however, **social institutions**—the standard or usual ways that a society meets its basic needs—vitally affect your life. They not only shape your behavior, but they even color your thoughts. How can this be?

The first step in understanding how this can be is to look at Figure 4.2 on the next page. Look at what social institutions are: the family, religion, education, the economy, medicine, politics, law, science, the military, and the mass media. *By weaving the fabric of society, social institutions set the context for your behavior and orientations to life. If your social institutions were different, your orientations to life would be different.*

Social institutions are so significant that an entire part of this book, Part IV, focuses on them.

Comparing Functionalist and Conflict Perspectives

The functionalist and conflict perspectives give us quite different views of social institutions. Let's compare their views.

The Functionalist Perspective. Because the first priority of human groups is to survive, all societies establish customary ways to meet their basic needs. As a result, no society is without social institutions. In tribal societies, some social institutions are less visible because the group meets its basic needs in more informal ways. A society may be too small to have people specialize in education, for example, but it will have established ways of teaching skills and ideas to the young. It may be too small to have a military, but it will have some mechanism of self-defense.

What are society's basic needs? Functionalists identify five *functional requisites* (basic needs) that each society must meet if it is to survive (Aberle et al. 1950; Mack and Bradford 1979).

1. *Replacing members.* Obviously, if a society does not replace its members, it cannot continue to exist. With reproduction fundamental to a society's existence, and the need to protect infants and children universal, all groups have developed some version of the family. The family gives the newcomer to society a sense of belonging by providing a *lineage*, an account of how he or she is related to others. The family also functions to control people's sex drive and to maintain orderly reproduction.

FIGURE 4.2 Social Institutions in Industrial and Postindustrial Societies

Social Institution	Basic Needs	Some Groups or Organizations	Some Statuses	Some Values	Some Norms
Family	Regulate reproduction, socialize and protect children	Relatives, kinship groups	Daughter, son, father, mother, brother, sister, aunt, uncle, grandparent	Sexual fidelity, providing for your family, keeping a clean house, respect for parents	Have only as many children as; you can afford, be faithful to your spouse
Religion	Concerns about life after death, the meaning of suffering and loss; desire to connect with the Creator	Congregation, synagogue, mosque, denomination, charity, clergy associations	Priest, minister, rabbi, imam, worshipper, teacher, disciple, missionary, prophet, convert	Honoring God and the holy texts such as the Tora, the Bible, and the Qur'an	Attend worship services, contribute money, follow the teachings
Education	Transmit knowledge and skills across generations	School, college, student senate, sports team, PTA, teachers' union	Teacher, student, dean, principal, football player, cheerleader	Academic honesty, good grades, being "cool"	Do homework, prepare lectures, don't snitch on classmates
Economy	Produce and distribute goods and services	Credit unions, banks, credit card companies, buying clubs	Worker, boss, buyer, seller, creditor, debtor, advertiser	Making money, paying bills on time, producing efficiently	Maximize profits, "the customer is always right," work hard
Medicine	Heal the sick and injured, care for the dying	AMA, hospitals, pharmacies, HMOs, insurance companies	Doctor, nurse, patient, pharmacist, medical insurer	Hippocratic oath, staying in good health, following doctor's orders	Don't exploit patients, give best medical care available
Politics	Allocate power, determine authority, prevent chaos	Political party, congress, parliament, monarchy	President, senator, lobbyist, voter, candidate, spin doctor	Majority rule, the right to vote as a privilege and a sacred trust	Be informed about candidates, vote
Law	Maintain social order, enforce norms	Police, courts, prisons	Judge, police officer, lawyer, defendant, prison guard	Trial by one's peers, innocence until proven guilty	Give true testi-mony, follow the rules of evidence
Science	Master the environment	Local, state, regional, national, and international associations	Scientist, researcher, technician, administrator, journal editor	Unbiased research, open dissemination of research findings, originality	Follow scientific method, be objective, disclose findings, don't plagiarize
Military	Provide protection from enemies, enforce national interests	Army, navy, air force, marines, coast guard, national guard	Soldier, recruit, enlisted person, officer, veteran, prisoner, spy	Willingness to die for one's country, obedience unto death	Follow orders, be ready to go to war, sacrifice for your buddies
Mass Media	Disseminate information, report events, mold public opinion	TV networks, radio stations, publishers, association of bloggers	Journalist, newscaster, author, editor, publisher, blogger	Timeliness, accuracy, freedom of the press	Be accurate, fair, timely, and profitable

Source: By the author.

2. *Socializing new members.* Each baby must be taught what it means to be a member of the group into which it is born. To accomplish this, each human group develops devices to ensure that its newcomers learn the group's basic expectations. As the primary "bearer of culture," the family is essential to this process, but other social institutions, such as religion and education, also help meet this basic need.

Functionalist theorists have identified *functional requisites* for the survival of society. One, providing a sense of purpose, is often met through religious groups. To most people, snake handling, as in this church service in Kingston, Georgia, is nonsensical. From a functional perspective, however, it makes a great deal of sense. Can you identify its sociological meanings?

3. *Producing and distributing goods and services.* Every society must produce and distribute basic resources, from food and clothing to shelter and education. Consequently, every society establishes an *economic* institution, a means of producing goods and services along with routine ways of distributing them.
4. *Preserving order.* Societies face two threats of disorder: one internal, the potential for chaos, and the other external, the possibility of attack. To protect themselves from internal threat, they develop ways to police themselves, ranging from informal means such as gossip to formal means such as armed groups. To defend themselves against external conquest, they develop a means of defense, some form of the military.
5. *Providing a sense of purpose.* Every society must get people to yield self-interest in favor of the needs of the group. To convince people to sacrifice personal gains, societies instill a sense of purpose. Human groups develop many ways to implant such beliefs, but a primary one is religion, which attempts to answer questions about ultimate meaning. Actually, all of a society's institutions are involved in meeting this functional requisite; the family provides one set of answers about the sense of purpose, the school another, and so on.

The Conflict Perspective. Although conflict theorists agree that social institutions were designed originally to meet basic survival needs, they do not view social institutions as working harmoniously for the common good. On the contrary, conflict theorists stress that powerful groups control our social institutions, manipulating them in order to maintain their own privileged position of wealth and power (Useem 1984; Domhoff 1999a, 1999b, 2006, 2007).

Conflict theorists point out that a fairly small group of people has garnered the lion's share of our nation's wealth. Members of this elite group sit on the boards of our major corporations and our most prestigious universities. They make strategic campaign contributions to influence (or control) our lawmakers, and it is they who are behind the nation's major decisions: to go to war or to refrain from war; to increase or to decrease taxes; to raise or to lower interest rates; and to pass laws that favor or impede moving capital, technology, and jobs out of the country.

Feminist sociologists (both women and men) have used conflict theory to gain a better understanding of how social institutions affect gender relations. Their basic insight is that gender is also an element of social structure, not simply a characteristic of individuals. In other words, throughout the world, social institutions divide males and females into separate groups, each with unequal access to society's resources.

In Sum: Functionalists view social institutions as working together to meet universal human needs, but conflict theorists regard social institutions as having a single primary purpose—to preserve the social order. For them, this means safeguarding the wealthy and powerful in their positions of privilege.

Changes in Social Structure

Our social structure is not static. It continuously evolves as it responds to changing values, to new technology, and to contact with cultures around the world. These changes have vital effects on our lives, sometimes in dramatic ways. Globalization is one of the best examples. As our economy adjusts to this fundamental change, we find our lives marked by uncertainty as jobs disappear and new requirements are placed on the careers we are striving for. Sometimes it seems that we have to stay at a running pace just to keep up with the changes.

In short, the corner in life that we occupy, though small and seemingly private, is not closed off. Rather, as our social structure changes, it pushes and pulls and stretches us in different directions.

What Holds Society Together?

Not only are we in the midst of social change so extensive that it threatens to rip our society apart but our society also has antagonistic groups that would love to get at one another's throats. In the midst of all this, how does society manage to hold together? Sociologists have proposed two answers. Let's examine them, starting with a bit of history.

social integration the degree to which members of a group or a society are united by shared values and other social bonds; also known as *social cohesion*

Mechanical and Organic Solidarity. Sociologist Emile Durkheim (1893/1933) was interested in how societies manage to create **social integration**—their members united by shared values and other social bonds. He found the answer in what he called **mechanical solidarity**. By this term, Durkheim meant that people who perform similar tasks develop a shared way of viewing life. Think of a farming community in which everyone is involved in growing crops—planting, cultivating, and harvesting. Because they have so much in common, they share similar views about life. Societies with mechanical solidarity tolerate little diversity in behavior, thinking, or attitudes; their unity depends on sharing similar views.

As societies get larger, they develop different kinds of work, a specialized **division of labor**. Some people mine gold, others turn it into jewelry, and still others sell it. This disperses people into different interest groups where they develop different ideas about life. No longer do they depend on one another to have similar ideas and behaviors. Rather, they depend on one another to do specific work, with each person contributing to the group.

Durkheim called this new form of solidarity **organic solidarity**. To see why he used this term, think about your body. The organs of your body need one another. Your lungs depend on your heart to pump your blood, and your heart depends on your lungs to oxygenate your blood. To move from the physical to the social, think about how you need your teacher to guide you through this course and how your teacher needs students in order to have a job. You and your teacher are *like two organs in the same body.* (The "body" in this case is the college.) Like the heart and lungs, although you perform different tasks, you need one another.

The change to organic solidarity changed the basis for social integration. In centuries past, you would have had views similar to your neighbors because you lived in the same village, farmed together, and had relatives in common. To catch a glimpse of why, look at the photo above. But no longer does social integration require this. Like organs in a body, our separate activities contribute to the welfare of the group. The change from mechanical to organic solidarity allows our society to tolerate a wide diversity of orientations to life and still manage to work as a whole.

Durkheim used the term *mechanical solidarity* to refer to the shared consciousness that develops among people who perform similar tasks. Can you see from this photo why this term applies so well to small farming groups, why they share such similar views about life? This photo was taken in Virginia.

Gemeinschaft and Gesellschaft. Ferdinand Tönnies (1887/1988) also analyzed this fundamental shift in relationships. He used the term ***Gemeinschaft*** (Guh-MINE-shoft), or "intimate community," to describe village life, the type of society in which everyone knows everyone else. He noted that in the society that was emerging, short-term relationships, individual accomplishments, and self-interest were replacing the personal ties, kinship connections, and lifelong friendships that marked village life. Tönnies called this new type of society ***Gesellschaft*** (Guh-ZELL-shoft), or "impersonal association." He did not mean that we no longer have intimate ties to family and friends but, rather, that our lives no longer center on them. Few of us take jobs in a family business, for example, and

mechanical solidarity Durkheim's term for the unity (a shared consciousness) that people feel as a result of performing the same or similar tasks

division of labor the splitting of a group's or a society's tasks into specialties

organic solidarity Durkheim's term for the interdependence that results from the division of labor; as part of the same unit, we all depend on others to fulfill their jobs

The warm, more intimate relationships of *Gemeinschaft* society are apparent in the photo taken at this weekly market in Myanmar. The more impersonal relationships of *Gesellschaft* society are evident in this Internet cafe in Seattle, where customers are ignoring one another.

Gemeinschaft a type of society in which life is intimate; a community in which everyone knows everyone else and people share a sense of togetherness

Gesellschaft a type of society that is dominated by impersonal relationships, individual accomplishments, and self-interest

contracts replace handshakes. Much of our time is spent with strangers and short-term acquaintances.

How Relevant Are These Concepts Today? I know that *Gemeinschaft*, *Gesellschaft*, and *mechanical* and *organic solidarity* are strange terms and that Durkheim's and Tönnies' observations must seem like a dead issue. The concern these sociologists expressed, however—that their world was changing from a community in which people were united by close ties and shared ideas and feelings to an anonymous association built around impersonal, short-term contacts—is still very real. In large part, this same concern explains the rise of Islamic fundamentalism (Volti 1995). Islamic leaders fear that Western values will uproot their traditional culture, that cold rationality will replace the warm, informal, personal relationships among families and clans. They fear, rightly so, that this will also change their views on life and morality. Although the terms may sound strange, even obscure, you can see that the ideas remain a vital part of today's world.

In Sum: Whether the terms are *Gemeinschaft* and *Gesellschaft* or *mechanical solidarity* and *organic solidarity*, they indicate that as societies change, so do people's orientations to life. *The sociological point is that social structure sets the context for what we do, feel, and think, and ultimately, then, for the kind of people we become.* As you read the Cultural Diversity box on the next page, which describes one of the few remaining *Gemeinschaft* societies in the United States, think of how fundamentally different your life would be if you had been reared in an Amish family.

4.3 Discuss what symbolic interactionists study and explain dramaturgy, ethnomethodology, and the social construction of reality.

The Microsociological Perspective: Social Interaction in Everyday Life

As you have seen, macrosociologists focus on the broad features of society. Microsociologists, in contrast, examine narrower slices of social life. Their primary focus is *face-to-face interaction*—what people do when they are in one another's presence. Before you study the main features of social interaction, look at the photo essay on the next two pages. See if you can identify both social structure and social interaction in each of the photos.

Cultural Diversity in the United States

The Amish: *Gemeinschaft* Community in a *Gesellschaft* Society

One of the best examples of a *Gemeinschaft* community in the United States is the Old Order Amish, followers of a group that broke away from the Swiss-German Mennonite church in the 1600s and settled in Pennsylvania around 1727. Most of today's 225,000 Old Order Amish live in just three states—Pennsylvania, Ohio, and Indiana.

Because Amish farmers use horses instead of tractors, most of their farms are 100 acres or less. To the ten million tourists who pass through Lancaster County each year, the rolling green pastures, white farmhouses, simple barns, horse-drawn buggies, and clotheslines hung with somber-colored garments convey a sense of innocence reminiscent of another era. Although just 65 miles from Philadelphia, "Amish country" is a world away.

The differences are striking: the horses and buggies from so long ago, the language (a dialect of German known as Pennsylvania Dutch), and the plain clothing—often black, no belt, whose style has remained unchanged for almost 300 years. Beyond these externals is a value system that binds the Amish together, with religion and discipline the glue that maintains their way of life.

Amish life is based on separation from the world—an idea taken from Christ's Sermon on the Mount—and obedience to the church's teachings and leaders. This rejection of worldly concerns, writes sociologist Donald Kraybill (2002), "provides the foundation of such Amish values as humility, faithfulness, thrift, tradition, communal goals, joy of work, a slow-paced life, and trust in divine providence." The Amish believe that violence is bad, even personal self-defense, and they register as conscientious objectors during times of war. They pay no Social Security, and they receive no government benefits.

To maintain their separation from the world, Amish children attend schools that are run by the Amish, and they attend only until the age of 13. (In 1972, the Supreme Court ruled that Amish parents have the right to take their children out of school after the eighth grade.) To go to school beyond the eighth grade would expose the children to values that would drive a wedge between the children and their community.

The *Gemeinschaft* of village life that has been largely lost to industrialization remains a vibrant part of Amish life. The Amish make their decisions in weekly meetings, where, by consensus, they follow a set of rules, or *Ordnung*, to guide their behavior. Brotherly love and the welfare of the community are paramount values. In times of birth, sickness, and death, neighbors pitch in with the chores. The family is also vital for Amish life. Nearly all Amish marry, and divorce is forbidden. The major events of Amish life take place in the home, including weddings, births, funerals, and church services. In these ways, they maintain the bonds of intimate community.

Because they cannot resist all change, the Amish try to adapt in ways that will least disrupt their core values. Urban sprawl poses a special threat, since it has driven up the price of farmland. Unable to afford farms, about half of Amish men now work at jobs other than farming. The men go to great lengths to avoid leaving the home. Most work in farm-related businesses or operate woodcraft shops, but some have taken jobs in factories. With intimate, or *Gemeinschaft,* society essential to the Amish way of life, concerns have grown about how the men who work for non-Amish businesses are being exposed to the outside world. Some are using modern technology such as cell phones and computers at work. During the economic crisis, some who were laid off from their jobs even accepted unemployment checks—violating the fundamental principle of taking no help from the government.

Despite the threats posed by a materialistic and secular culture, the Amish are managing to retain their way of life. Perhaps the most poignant illustration of how greatly the Amish differ from the dominant culture is this: When in 2006 a non-Amish man shot several Amish girls and himself at a one-room school, the Amish community raised funds not only for the families of the dead children but also for the family of the killer.

Sources: Aeppel 1996; Kephart and Zellner 2001; Kraybill 2002; Johnson-Weiner 2007; Scolforo 2008; Buckley 2011.

For Your Consideration

→ If you had been reared in an Amish family, how would your ideas, attitudes, and behaviors be different? What do you like and dislike about Amish life? Why?

THROUGH THE AUTHOR'S LENS

Vienna: Social Structure and Social Interaction

We live our lives within social structure. Just as a road is to a car, providing limits to where it can go, so social structure limits our behavior. Social structure—our culture, social class, statuses, roles, group memberships, and social institutions—points us in particular directions in life. Most of this direction-giving is beyond our awareness. But it is highly effective, giving shape to our social interactions, as well as to what we expect from life.

These photos that I took in Vienna, Austria, make visible some of social structure's limiting, shaping, and direction-giving. Most of the social structure that affects our lives is not physical, as with streets and buildings, but social, as with norms, belief systems, obligations, and the goals held out for us because of our ascribed statuses. In these photos, you should be able to see how social interaction takes form within social structure.

Vienna provides a mixture of the old and the new. Stephan's Dom (Cathedral) dates back to 1230, the carousel to now.

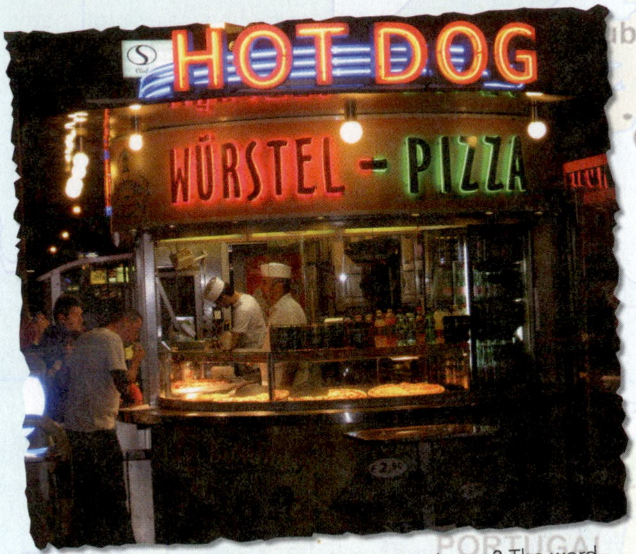

And what would Vienna be without its wieners? The word wiener actually comes from the name Vienna, which is Wien in German. Wiener means "from Vienna."

The main square in Vienna, Stephan Platz, provides a place to have a cup of coffee, read the newspaper, enjoy the architecture, or just watch the hustle and bustle of the city.

Part of the pull of the city is its offering of rich culture. I took this photo at one of the many operas held in Vienna each night.

In the appealing street cafes of Vienna, social structure and social interaction are especially evident. Can you see both in this photo?

The city offers something for everyone, including unusual places for people to rest and to talk and to flirt with one another.

And what would Vienna be without its world-famous beers? The city's entrepreneurs make sure that the beer is within easy reach.

To be able to hang out with friends, not doing much, but doing it in the midst of stimulating sounds and sights—this is the vibrant city.

Symbolic Interaction

Symbolic interactionists are especially interested in how people view things and how this, in turn, affects their behavior and orientations to life. Of the many areas of social life that symbolic interactionists study, let's look at just a few aspects of social interaction—stereotypes, personal space, eye contact, smiling, and body language.

Stereotypes in Everyday Life. You are familiar with how important first impressions are, how they set the tone for interaction. You also know that when you first meet someone, you notice certain features of the individual, especially the person's sex, race–ethnicity, age, height, body shape, and clothing. But did you know that this sets off a circular, self-feeding reaction? Your assumptions about these characteristics—many of which you don't even know you have—shape not only your first impressions but also how you act toward that person. This, in turn, influences how that person acts toward you, which then affects how you react, and so on. Most of this self-feeding cycle occurs without your being aware of it.

In the Down-to-Earth Sociology box on the next page, let's look at how beauty or people's attractiveness sets off this reciprocal reaction.

Personal Space. We all surround ourselves with a "personal bubble" that we go to great lengths to protect. We open the bubble to intimates—to our friends, children, and parents—but we're careful to keep most people out of this space. In a crowded hallway between classes, we might walk with our books clasped in front of us (a strategy often chosen by females). When we stand in line, we make certain there is enough space so that we don't touch the person in front of us and aren't touched by the person behind us.

At times, we extend our personal space. In the library, for example, you might place your coat on the chair next to you—claiming that space for yourself even though you aren't using it. If you want to really extend your space, you might even spread books in front of the other chairs, keeping the whole table to yourself by giving the impression that others have just stepped away.

The amount of space that people prefer varies from one culture to another. South Americans, for example, like to be closer when they talk to others than do people reared in the United States. Anthropologist Edward Hall (1959; Hall and Hall 2014) recounts a conversation with a man from South America who had attended one of his lectures.

> *He came to the front of the class at the end of the lecture. . . . We started out facing each other, and as he talked I became dimly aware that he was standing a little too close and that I was beginning to back up. Fortunately I was able to suppress my first impulse and*

How people use space as they interact is studied by sociologists who have a microsociological focus. What do you seen in common in these two photos?

Down-to-Earth **Sociology**

Beauty May Be Only Skin Deep, But Its Effects Go On Forever: Stereotypes in Everyday Life

Mark Snyder, a psychologist, wondered whether **stereotypes**—our assumptions of what people are like—might be self-fulfilling. He came up with an ingenious way to test this idea. Snyder (1993) gave college men a Polaroid snapshot of a woman (supposedly taken just moments before) and told each man that he would be introduced to her after they talked on the telephone. Actually, the photographs—showing either a pretty or a homely woman—had been prepared before the experiment began. The photo was *not* of the woman the men would talk to.

Stereotypes came into play immediately. As Snyder gave each man the photograph, he asked him what he thought the woman would be like. The men who saw the photograph of the attractive woman said that they expected to meet a poised, humorous, outgoing woman. The men who had been given a photo of the unattractive woman described her as awkward, serious, and unsociable.

The men's stereotypes influenced the way they spoke to the women on the telephone, who did *not* know about the photographs. The men who had seen the photograph of a pretty woman were warm, friendly, and humorous. This, in turn, affected the women they spoke to: They responded in a warm, friendly, outgoing manner. And the men who had seen the photograph of a homely woman? On the phone, they were cold, reserved, and humorless, and the women they spoke to became cool, reserved, and humorless. Keep in mind that the women did not know that their looks had been evaluated. Keep in mind, too, that the photos that the men saw were not of these women. In short, stereotypes tend to produce behaviors that match the stereotype. Figure 4.3 illustrates this principle.

Beauty might be only skin deep, but it has real consequences. Higher earnings are one result. Bosses are more willing to hire people whom they perceive as good-looking, others are more willing to interact with them, and the good-looking bring in more clients. The result is serious money. On average, the more attractive earn between 10 and 15 percent more than plain folks, about $200,000 over a lifetime (Judge et al. 2009; Hamermesh 2011).

One more thing: Teacher evaluations follow the same pattern. Students give higher ratings to their better-looking teachers (Ponzo and Scoppa 2012).

FIGURE 4.3 How Self-Fulfilling Stereotypes Work

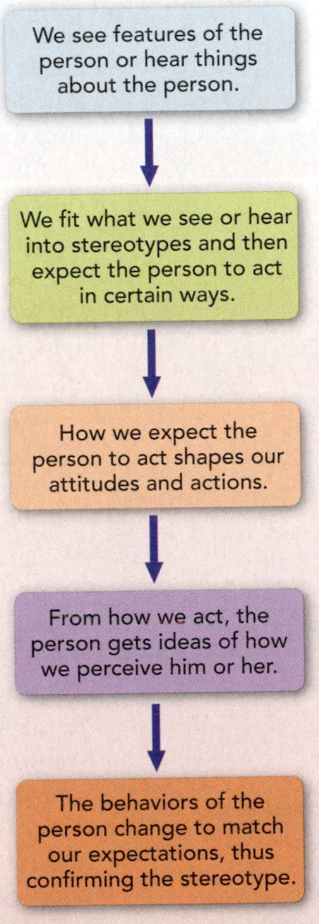
We see features of the person or hear things about the person.
We fit what we see or hear into stereotypes and then expect the person to act in certain ways.
How we expect the person to act shapes our attitudes and actions.
From how we act, the person gets ideas of how we perceive him or her.
The behaviors of the person change to match our expectations, thus confirming the stereotype.

Source: By the author.

Based on the experiments summarized here, how do you think women would modify their interactions if they were to meet these two men? And if men were to meet these two men, would they modify their interactions in the same way?

For Your Consideration

➤ In our research, we have barely tapped the surface of how stereotypes influence how we react to one another. Instead of beauty, consider body type, gender, and race–ethnicity. How do you think they affect those who do the stereotyping and those who are stereotyped?

stereotype assumptions of what people are like, whether true or false

body language the ways in which people use their bodies to give messages to others

remain stationary because there was nothing to communicate aggression in his behavior except the conversational distance. . . .

By experimenting I was able to observe that as I moved away slightly, there was an associated shift in the pattern of interaction. He had more trouble expressing himself. If I shifted to where I felt comfortable (about twenty-one inches), he looked somewhat puzzled and hurt, almost as though he were saying, "Why is he acting that way? Here I am doing everything I can to talk to him in a friendly manner and he suddenly withdraws. Have I done anything wrong? Said something I shouldn't?" Having ascertained that distance had a direct effect on his conversation, I stood my ground, letting him set the distance.

As you can see, despite Hall's extensive knowledge of other cultures, he still felt uncomfortable in this conversation. He first interpreted the invasion of his personal space as possible aggression, since people get close (and jut out their chins and chests) when they are hostile. But when he realized that this was not the case, Hall resisted his impulse to move.

After Hall analyzed situations like this, he observed that North Americans use four different "distance zones."

1. *Intimate distance.* This is the zone that the South American had unwittingly invaded. It extends to about 18 inches from our bodies. We reserve this space for comforting, protecting, hugging, intimate touching, and lovemaking.
2. *Personal distance.* This zone extends from 18 inches to 4 feet. We reserve it for friends and acquaintances and ordinary conversations. This is the zone in which Hall would have preferred speaking with the South American.
3. *Social distance.* This zone, extending from about 4 to 12 feet, marks impersonal or formal relationships. We use this zone for such things as job interviews.
4. *Public distance.* This zone, extending beyond 12 feet, marks even more formal relationships. It is used to separate dignitaries and public speakers from the general public.

Eye Contact. One way that we protect our personal bubble is by controlling eye contact. Letting someone gaze into our eyes—unless the person is an eye doctor—can be taken as a sign that we are attracted to that person, even as an invitation to intimacy. Wanting to become "the friendliest store in town," a chain of supermarkets in Illinois ordered its checkout clerks to make direct eye contact with each customer. Female clerks complained that male customers were taking their eye contact the wrong way, as an invitation to intimacy. Management said they were exaggerating. The clerks' reply was, "We know the kind of looks we're getting back from men," and they refused to continue making direct eye contact with them.

Eye contact is a fascinating aspect of everyday life. We use fleeting eye contact for most of our interactions, such as those with clerks or people we pass in the hall between classes. Just as we reserve our close personal space for intimates, so, too, we reserve soft, lingering eye contact for them.

Smiling. In the United States, we take it for granted that clerks will smile as they wait on us. But it isn't this way in all cultures. Apparently, Germans aren't used to smiling clerks, and when Wal-Mart expanded into Germany, it brought its American ways with it. The company ordered its German clerks to smile at their customers. They did—and the customers complained. The German customers interpreted the smiles as flirting (Samor et al. 2006).

Body Language. While we are still little children, we learn to interpret **body language**, the ways people use their bodies to give messages to others. This skill in interpreting facial expressions, posture, and gestures is essential for getting through everyday life. Without it—as is the case for people with Asperger's syndrome—we wouldn't know how to react to others. It would even be difficult to know whether someone was serious or joking.

Applied Body Language. Our common and essential skill of interpreting body language has become a tool for both business and government. In some hotels, clerks are taught how to "read" the body language of arriving guests (head sunk into the shoulders, a springy step) to know how to greet them (Petersen 2012). "Reading" body language has also become a tool in the fight against terrorism. Because many of our body messages lie beneath our consciousness, airport personnel and interrogators are being trained to look for telltale facial signs—from a quick downturn of the mouth to rapid blinking—that might indicate nervousness or lying (Davis et al. 2002). The U.S. army is also trying to determine how to apply body language to alert soldiers to danger when interacting with civilians in a military zone (Yager et al. 2009).

These applications are an interesting twist for an area of sociology that had been entirely theoretical. Let's now turn to dramaturgy, a special area of symbolic interactionism.

dramaturgy an approach, pioneered by Erving Goffman, in which social life is analyzed in terms of drama or the stage; also called *dramaturgical analysis*

impression management people's efforts to control the impressions that others receive of them

front stage place where people give performances

back stages places where people rest from their performances, discuss their presentations, and plan future performances

role performance the ways in which someone performs a role; showing a particular "style" or "personality"

Dramaturgy: The Presentation of Self in Everyday Life

It was their big day, two years in the making. Jennifer Mackey wore a white wedding gown adorned with an 11-foot train and 24,000 seed pearls that she and her mother had sewn onto the dress. Next to her at the altar in Lexington, Kentucky, stood her intended, Jeffrey Degler, in black tie. They said their vows, then turned to gaze for a moment at the four hundred guests.

That's when groomsman Daniel Mackey collapsed. As the shocked organist struggled to play Mendelssohn's "Wedding March," Mr. Mackey's unconscious body was dragged away, his feet striking—loudly—every step of the altar stairs.

"I couldn't believe he would die at my wedding," the bride said. (Hughes 1990)

Sociologist Erving Goffman (1922–1982) added a new twist to microsociology when he recast the theatrical term **dramaturgy** into a sociological term. Goffman (1959/1999) used the term to mean that social life is like a drama or a stage play: Birth ushers us onto the stage of everyday life, and our socialization consists of learning to perform on that stage. The self that we studied in the previous chapter lies at the center of our performances. We have ideas about how we want others to think of us, and we use our roles in everyday life to communicate these ideas. Goffman called our efforts to manage the impressions that others receive of us **impression management**.

Read on **MySocLab**
Document: Erving Goffman, The Presentation of Self in Everyday Life

Stages. Everyday life, said Goffman, involves playing our assigned roles. We have **front stages** on which to perform them, as did Jennifer and Jeffrey. (By the way, Daniel Mackey didn't really die—he had just fainted.) But we don't have to look at weddings to find front stages. Everyday life is filled with them. Where your teacher lectures is a front stage. And if you wait until your parents are in a good mood to tell them some bad news, you are using a front stage. In fact, you spend most of your time on front stages: A front stage is wherever you deliver your lines. We also have **back stages**, places where we can retreat and let our hair down. When you close the bathroom or bedroom door for privacy, for example, you are entering a back stage.

In *dramaturgy*, a specialty within sociology, social life is viewed as similar to the theater. In our everyday lives, we all are actors. Like those in the cast of The Big Bang Theory, we, too, perform roles, use props, and deliver lines to fellow actors—who, in turn, do the same.

The same setting can serve as both a back and a front stage. For example, when you get into your car and look over your hair in the mirror or check your makeup, you are using the car as a back stage. But when you wave at friends or if you give that familiar gesture to someone who has just cut in front of you in traffic, you are using your car as a front stage.

Role Performance, Conflict, and Strain. As discussed earlier, everyday life brings many statuses. We may be a student, a shopper, a worker, and a date, as well as a daughter or a son. Although the roles attached to these statuses lay down the basic outline for our performances, they also allow a great deal of flexibility. The particular interpretation that you give a role, your "style," is known as **role performance**. Consider how you play your role as a son or daughter. Perhaps you play the role of ideal daughter or son—being respectful, coming home at the hours your parents set,

FIGURE 4.4 Role Strain and Role Conflict

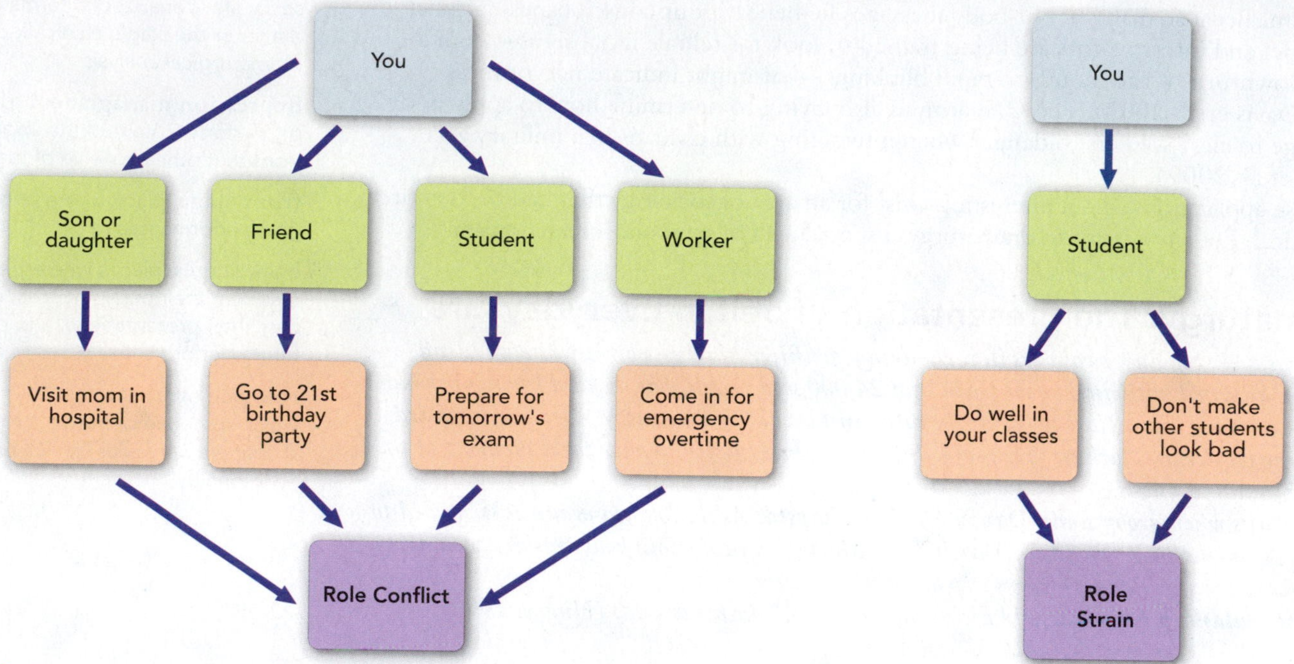

Source: By the author.

and happily running errands. Or this description may not even come close to your particular role performance.

Ordinarily, our statuses are separated sufficiently that we find little conflict between our role performances. Occasionally, however, what is expected of us in one status (our role) is incompatible with what is expected of us in another status. This problem, known as **role conflict**, is illustrated in Figure 4.4, in which family, friendship, student, and work roles come crashing together. Usually, however, we manage to avoid role conflict by segregating our statuses, although doing so can require an intense juggling act.

Sometimes the *same* status contains incompatible roles, a conflict known as **role strain**. Suppose that you are exceptionally well prepared for a particular class assignment. Although the instructor asks an unusually difficult question, you find yourself knowing the answer when no one else does. If you want to raise your hand, yet don't want to make your fellow students look bad, you will experience role strain. As illustrated in Figure 4.4, the difference between role conflict and role strain is that role conflict is conflict *between* roles, while role strain is conflict *within* a role.

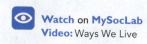

Watch on **MySocLab**
Video: Ways We Live

role conflict conflicts that someone feels *between* roles because the expectations are at odds with one another

role strain conflicts that someone feels within a role

sign-vehicle the term used by Goffman to refer to how people use social setting, appearance, and manner to communicate information about the self

Sign-Vehicles. To communicate information about the self, we use three types of **sign-vehicles**: the social setting, our appearance, and our manner. The *social setting* is the place where the action unfolds. This is where the curtain goes up on your performance, where you find yourself on stage playing parts and delivering lines. A social setting might be an office, dorm, living room, classroom, church, or bar. It is wherever you interact with others. The social setting includes *scenery*, the furnishings you use to communicate messages, such as desks, blackboards, scoreboards, couches, and so on.

The second sign-vehicle is *appearance*, or how you look when you play your roles. On the most obvious level is your choice of hairstyle to communicate messages about yourself. (You might be proclaiming "I'm wild and sexy" or "I'm serious and professional" and, quite certainly, "I'm masculine" or "I'm feminine"). Your appearance also includes props, which are like scenery except that they decorate your body rather than the setting. Your most obvious prop is your costume, ordinarily called clothing. You switch costumes as you play your roles, wearing different costumes for attending class, swimming, jogging or working out at the gym, and dating.

Your appearance lets others know what to expect from you and how they should react. Think of the messages that props communicate. Some people use clothing to say they are college students, others to say they are older adults. Some use clothing to let you know they are clergy, others to give the message that they are prostitutes. In the same way, people choose models of cars, brands of liquor, and the hottest cell phone to convey messages about the self.

The body itself is a sign-vehicle. Its shape proclaims messages about the self. The meanings that are attached to various shapes change over time, but, as explored in the Mass Media box on the next page, thinness currently screams desirability.

The third sign-vehicle is *manner*, the attitudes you show as you play your roles. You use manner to communicate information about your feelings and moods. When you show that you are angry or indifferent, serious or in good humor, you are indicating what others can expect of you as you play your roles.

Teamwork. Being a good role player brings positive responses from others, something we all covet. To accomplish this, we use **teamwork**—two or more people working together to help a performance come off as planned. If you laugh at your boss's jokes, even though you don't find them funny, you are doing teamwork to help your boss give a good performance.

If a performance doesn't come off quite right, the team might try to save it by using **face-saving behavior**.

> *Suppose your teacher is about to make an important point. Suppose also that her lecturing has been outstanding and the class is hanging on every word. Just as she pauses for emphasis, her stomach lets out a loud growl. She might then use a face-saving technique by remarking, "I was so busy preparing for class that I didn't get breakfast this morning."*

It is more likely, however, that both the teacher and class will simply ignore the sound, giving the impression that no one heard a thing—a face-saving technique called *studied nonobservance*. This allows the teacher to make the point or, as Goffman would say, it allows the performance to go on.

Becoming the Roles We Play.

> *Have you ever noticed how some clothing simply doesn't "feel" right for certain occasions? Have you ever changed your mind about something you were wearing and decided to change your clothing? Or maybe you just switched shirts or added a necklace?*

What you were doing was fine-tuning the impressions you wanted to make. Ordinarily, we are not this aware that we're working on impressions, but sometimes we are, especially those "first impressions"—the first day in college, a job interview, visiting the parents of our loved one for the first time, and so on. Usually we are so used to the roles we play in everyday life that we tend to think we are "just doing" things, not that we are actors on a stage who manage impressions. Yet every time we dress for school, or for any other activity, we are preparing for impression management.

A fascinating characteristic of roles is that *we tend to become the roles we play*. That is, roles become incorporated into our self-concept, especially roles for which we prepare long and hard and that become part of our everyday lives. Helen Ebaugh (1988) experienced this firsthand when she quit being a nun to become a sociologist. With her own heightened awareness of *role exit*, she interviewed people who had left marriages, police work, the military, medicine, and religious vocations. Just as she had experienced, the role had become intertwined so extensively with the individual's self-concept that leaving it threatened the person's identity. The question these people struggled with was "Who am I, now that I am not a nun (or wife, police officer, colonel, physician, and so on)?"

teamwork the collaboration of two or more people to manage impressions jointly

face-saving behavior techniques used to salvage a performance (interaction) that is going sour

Mass Media in **Social Life**

"Nothing Tastes as Good as Thin Feels": Body Images and the Mass Media

When you stand before a mirror, do you like what you see? Do you watch your weight or work out? Where did you get your ideas about what you should look like?

"Your body isn't good enough!" Daily, you are bombarded with this message. The way to improve your body, of course, is to buy the advertised products: diet programs, hair extensions, "uplifting" bras, butt reducers, and exercise equipment. Muscular hulks on TV show off machines that magically produce "six-pack abs" and incredible biceps—in just a few minutes a day. Female celebrities go through tough workouts without even breaking into a sweat. Members of the opposite sex will flock to you if you purchase that wonder-working workout machine.

We try to shrug off such messages, knowing that they are designed to sell products, but the messages penetrate our thinking and feelings. They help to shape the ideal images we hold of how we "ought" to look. Those models so attractively clothed and coiffed as they walk down the runway, could they be any thinner? For women, the message is clear: You can't be thin enough. The men's message is also clear: You can't be muscular enough. Everybody loves a hulk.

The message is powerful. With impossibly shaped models for Victoria's Secret and skinny models showing off the latest fashions in *Vogue* and *Seventeen*, half of U.S. adolescent girls feel fat and count calories (Grabe et al. 2008). Sixty percent of girls think that the secret to popularity is being thin (Zaslow 2009). Some teens even call the plastic surgeon. Anxious lest their child trail behind in her race for popularity, some parents pay $5,000 just to give their daughters a flatter tummy (Gross 1998). And the mothers? To remain or become slender, some inject themselves daily with hCG, a hormone that comes from the urine of pregnant women (Hartocollis 2011).

Cruise the Internet, and you will find "thinspiration" videos on YouTube that feature emaciated girls proudly displaying their skeletal frames. You will also find "pro-ana" (pro-anorexic) sites where eating disorders are promoted as a lifestyle choice (Zaslow 2009). The title of this box, "Nothing Tastes as Good as Thin Feels," is taken from one of these sites.

And attractiveness does pay off in cold cash. "Good-looking" men and women earn the most, "average-looking" men and women earn average amounts, and the "plain" and the "ugly" earn the least (Hamermesh 2011). Then there is that fascinating cash "bonus" available to "attractive" women: Even if they are bubble-heads, they attract and marry higher-earning men (Kanazawa and Kovar 2004).

More popularity *and* more money? Maybe you can't be thin enough after all. Maybe those exercise machines are a good investment. If only we could catch up with the Japanese, who have developed a soap that "sucks the fat right out of your pores" (Marshall 1995). You can practically hear the jingle now.

For Your Consideration

➔ What images do you have of your body? How do cultural expectations of "ideal" bodies underlie your images? Can you recall any advertisements or television programs that have influenced your body image?

➔ Most advertising that focuses on weight is directed at women. Women are more likely than men to be dissatisfied with their bodies and to have eating disorders (Honeycutt 1995; Austin et al. 2009). Of all cosmetic surgery, 90 percent is performed on women (American Society for Aesthetic Plastic Surgery 2012). Do you think that the targeting of women in advertising creates these attitudes and behaviors? Or do you think that these attitudes and behaviors would exist even if there were no such ads? Why?

➔ To counteract the emphasis on being skinny, some clothing companies are featuring "plus-size" models. What do you think of this?

All of us contrast the reality we see when we look in the mirror with our culture's ideal body types. The thinness craze, discussed in this box, encourages some people to extremes, as with Nicole Richie. It also makes it difficult for larger people to have positive self-images. Overcoming this difficulty, Rebel Wilson is in the forefront of promoting an alternative image.

A statement made by a former minister illustrates how roles become part of the person. Notice how a role can linger even after the individual is no longer playing that role:

> *After I left the ministry, I felt like a fish out of water. Wearing that backward collar had become a part of me. It was especially strange on Sunday mornings when I'd listen to someone else give the sermon. I knew that I should be up there preaching. I felt as though I had left God.*

Applying Impression Management. I can just hear someone say, "Impression management is interesting, but is it really important?" It certainly is. Impression management can even make a vital difference in your career. To be promoted, you must be perceived as someone who *should* be promoted. You must appear dominant. For men, giving this impression is less of a problem because stereotypes join masculinity and dominance at the hip. For women, though, stereotypes separate femininity and dominance.

How can a woman appear dominant? She could swagger, curse, and tell dirty jokes. This would get her noticed—but it is not likely to put her on the path to promotion. Career counselors do advise women to tone down the femininity, but in a rather different way. Female executives, they say, should avoid showing a lot of skin and use makeup that doesn't have to be reapplied during the day. During business meetings, they should place their hands on the table, not in their laps. And they should not carry a purse, but stash it inside a briefcase (Needham 2006; Brinkley 2008; Agins 2009; Agno and McEwen 2011).

Phil blows his interview before even sitting down.

Both individuals and organizations do impression management, trying to communicate messages about the self (or organization) that best meets their goals. At times, these efforts fail.

A common saying is that much success in the work world depends not on what you know but on who you know. This is true, but let's add the sociological twist: Much success in the work world depends not on what you know, but on your ability to give the impression that you know what you should know.

Ethnomethodology: Uncovering Background Assumptions

Certainly one of the strangest words in sociology is *ethnomethodology*. To better understand this term, consider the word's three basic components. *Ethno* means "folk" or "people"; *method* means how people do something; *ology* means "the study of." Putting them together, then, *ethno–method–ology* means "the study of how people do things." What things? **Ethnomethodology** is the study of how people use commonsense understandings to make sense of life.

> *Let's suppose that during a routine office visit, your doctor remarks that your hair is rather long, then takes out a pair of scissors and starts to give you a haircut. You would feel strange about this, because your doctor would be violating* ***background assumptions****—your ideas about the way life is and the way things ought to work. These assumptions, which lie at the root of everyday life, are so deeply embedded in our consciousness that we are seldom aware of them, and most of us fulfill them unquestioningly. Thus, your doctor does not offer you a haircut, even if he or she is good at cutting hair and you need one!*

The founder of ethnomethodology, sociologist Harold Garfinkel, had his students do little exercises to uncover background assumptions. Garfinkel (1967, 2002) asked his students to act as though they did not understand the basic rules of social life. Some of his students tried to bargain with supermarket clerks; others would inch close to people and stare directly at them. They were met with surprise,

ethnomethodology the study of how people use background assumptions to make sense out of life

background assumption a deeply embedded, common understanding of how the world operates and of how people ought to act

All of us have *background assumptions,* deeply ingrained assumptions of how the world operates. What different background assumptions do you think are operating here? If the annual "No Pants! Subway Ride" gains popularity, will background assumptions for this day change?

bewilderment, even indignation and anger. In one exercise, Garfinkel asked students to act as though they were boarders in their own homes. They addressed their parents as "Mr." and "Mrs.," asked permission to use the bathroom, sat stiffly, were courteous, and spoke only when spoken to. As you can imagine, the other family members didn't know what to make of their behavior:

> *They vigorously sought to make the strange actions intelligible and to restore the situation to normal appearances. Reports (by the students) were filled with accounts of astonishment, bewilderment, shock, anxiety, embarrassment, and anger, and with charges by various family members that the student was mean, inconsiderate, selfish, nasty, or impolite. Family members demanded explanations: What's the matter? What's gotten into you? . . . Are you sick? . . . Are you out of your mind or are you just stupid?* (Garfinkel 1967)

In another exercise, Garfinkel asked students to take words and phrases literally. When one student asked his girlfriend what she meant when she said that she had a flat tire, she said:

> *What do you mean, "What do you mean?" A flat tire is a flat tire. That is what I meant. Nothing special. What a crazy question!*

Another conversation went like this:

ACQUAINTANCE: How are you?

STUDENT: How am I in regard to what? My health, my finances, my schoolwork, my peace of mind, my ... ?

ACQUAINTANCE: (red in the face): Look! I was just trying to be polite. Frankly, I don't give a damn how you are.

Students can be highly creative when they are asked to break background assumptions. The young children of one of my students were surprised one morning when they came down for breakfast to find a sheet spread on the living room floor. On it were dishes, silverware, lit candles—and bowls of ice cream. They, too, wondered what was going on, but they dug eagerly into the ice cream before their mother could change her mind.

This is a risky assignment to give students, because breaking some background assumptions can make people suspicious. When a colleague of mine gave this assignment, a couple of his students began to wash dollar bills in a laundromat. By the time they put the bills in the dryer, the police had arrived.

In Sum: Ethnomethodologists explore *background assumptions*, the taken-for-granted ideas about the world that underlie our behavior. Most of these assumptions, or basic rules of social life, are unstated. We learn them as we learn our culture, and it is risky to violate them. Deeply embedded in our minds, they give us basic directions for living everyday life.

The Social Construction of Reality

On a visit to Morocco, in northern Africa, I decided to buy a watermelon. When I indicated to the street vendor that the knife he was going to use to cut the watermelon was dirty (encrusted with filth would be more apt), he was very obliging. He immediately bent down and began to swish the knife in a puddle on the street. I shuddered as I looked at the passing burros that were urinating and defecating as they went by. Quickly, I indicated by gesture that I preferred my melon uncut after all.

"If people define situations as real, they are real in their consequences," said sociologists W. I. and Dorothy S. Thomas in what has become known as *the definition of the situation*, or the **Thomas theorem.** For that vendor of watermelons, germs did not exist. For me, they did. And each of us acted according to our definition of the situation. My perception and behavior did not come from the fact that germs are real but, rather, from *my having grown up in a society that teaches that germs are real.* Microbes, of course, *objectively* exist, and whether or not germs are part of our thought world makes no difference as to whether we are infected by them. Our behavior, however, does not depend on the *objective* existence of something but, rather, on our *subjective interpretation*, on what sociologists call our *definition of reality.* In other words, it is not the reality of microbes that impresses itself on us, but society that impresses the reality of microbes on us.

Thomas theorem William I. and Dorothy S. Thomas' classic formulation of the definition of the situation: "If people define situations as real, they are real in their consequences"

social construction of reality the use of background assumptions and life experiences to define what is real

Let's consider another example. Do you remember the identical twins, Oskar and Jack, who grew up so differently? As discussed on page 63, Oskar was reared in Germany and learned to love Hitler, while Jack was reared in Trinidad and learned to hate Hitler. As you can see, what Hitler meant to Oskar and Jack (and what he means to us) depends not on Hitler's acts but, rather, on how we view his acts—that is, on our definition of the situation.

Sociologists call this the **social construction of reality**. From the social groups to which we belong (the *social* part of this process), we learn ways of looking at life. We learn ways to view Hitler and Osama bin Laden (they're good, they're evil), germs (they exist, they don't exist), and *just about everything else in life.* In short, through our interaction with others, we *construct reality*; that is, we learn ways of interpreting our experiences in life.

Read on **MySocLab**
Document: The Social Construction of Reality

The *social construction of reality* is sometimes difficult to grasp. We sometimes think that meanings are external to us, that they originate "out there" somewhere, rather than in our social group. To better understand the social construction of reality, let's consider pelvic examinations.

Gynecological Examinations. When I interviewed a gynecological nurse who had been present at about 14,000 vaginal examinations, I analyzed *how doctors construct social reality in order to define the examination as nonsexual* (Henslin and Biggs 1971/2014). It became apparent that the pelvic examination unfolds much as a stage play does. I will use "he" to refer to the physician because only male physicians were part of this study. Perhaps the results would be different with female gynecologists.

> Scene 1 (the patient as person) *In this scene, the doctor maintains eye contact with his patient, calls her by name, and discusses her problems in a professional manner. If he decides that a vaginal examination is necessary, he tells a nurse, "Pelvic in room 1." By this statement, he is announcing that a major change will occur in the next scene.*

> Scene 2 (from person to pelvic) *This scene is the depersonalizing stage. In line with the doctor's announcement, the patient begins the transition from a "person" to a "pelvic." The doctor leaves the room, and a female nurse enters to help the patient make the transition. The nurse prepares the "props" for the coming examination and answers any questions the woman might have.*

What occurs at this point is essential for the social construction of reality, for *the doctor's absence removes even the suggestion of sexuality.* To undress in front of him could suggest either a striptease or intimacy, thus undermining the reality that the team is so carefully defining: that of nonsexuality.

The patient, too, wants to remove any hint of sexuality, and during this scene, she may express concern about what to do with her panties. Some mutter to the nurse, "I don't want him to see these." Most women solve the problem by either slipping their panties under their other clothes or placing them in their purse.

> Scene 3 (the person as pelvic) *This scene opens when the doctor enters the room. Before him is a woman lying on a table, her feet in stirrups, her knees tightly together, and her*

body covered by a drape sheet. The doctor seats himself on a low stool before the woman and says, "Let your knees fall apart" (rather than the sexually loaded "Spread your legs"), and begins the examination.

The drape sheet is crucial in this process of desexualization, for it *dissociates the pelvic area from the person*: Leaning forward and with the drape sheet above his head, the physician can see only the vagina, not the patient's face. Thus dissociated from the individual, the vagina is transformed dramaturgically into an object of analysis. If the doctor examines the patient's breasts, he also dissociates them from her person by examining them one at a time, with a towel covering the unexamined breast. Like the vagina, each breast becomes an isolated item dissociated from the person.

In this third scene, the patient cooperates in being an object, becoming, for all practical purposes, a pelvis to be examined. She withdraws eye contact from the doctor and usually from the nurse, is likely to stare at a wall or at the ceiling, and avoids initiating conversation.

Scene 4 (from pelvic to person) *In this scene, the patient is "repersonalized." The doctor has left the examining room; the patient dresses and fixes her hair and makeup. Her reemergence as a person is indicated by such statements to the nurse as "My dress isn't too wrinkled, is it?" showing a need for reassurance that the metamorphosis from "pelvic" back to "person" has been completed satisfactorily.*

Scene 5 (the patient as person) *In this final scene, sometimes with the doctor seated at a desk, the patient is once again treated as a person rather than as an object. The doctor makes eye contact with her and addresses her by name. She, too, makes eye contact with the doctor, and the usual middle-class interaction patterns are followed. She has been fully restored.*

In Sum: For an outsider to our culture, the custom of women going to male strangers for a vaginal examination might seem bizarre. But not to us. We learn that pelvic examinations are nonsexual. To sustain this definition requires teamwork—doctors, nurses, and the patient working together to *socially construct reality*.

It is not just pelvic examinations or our views of germs that make up our definitions of reality. Rather, *our behavior depends on how we define reality*. Our definitions (our constructions of reality) provide the basis for what we do and how we view life. To understand human behavior, then, we must know how people define reality.

4.4 Explain why we need both macrosociology and microsociology to understand social life.

The Need for Both Macrosociology and Microsociology

As noted earlier, we need both macrosociology and microsociology. Without one or the other, our understanding of social life would be vastly incomplete. The photo essay on the next two pages should help to make clear why we need *both* perspectives.

To illustrate this point, consider two groups of high school boys studied by sociologist William Chambliss (1973/2014). Both groups attended Hanibal High School. In one group were eight middle-class boys who came from "good" families and were perceived by the community as "going somewhere." Chambliss calls this group the "Saints." In the other group were six lower-class boys who were seen as headed down a dead-end road. Chambliss calls this group the "Roughnecks."

Boys in both groups skipped school, got drunk, got in fights, and vandalized property. The Saints were actually truant more often and involved in more vandalism, but the Saints had a good reputation. The Roughnecks, in contrast, were seen by teachers, the police, and the general community as no good and headed for trouble.

THROUGH THE AUTHOR'S LENS

When a Tornado Strikes: Social Organization Following a Natural Disaster

As I was watching television on March 20, 2003, I heard a report that a tornado had hit Camilla, Georgia. "Like a big lawn mower," the report said, it had cut a path of destruction through this little town. In its fury, the tornado had left behind six dead and about 200 injured.

From sociological studies of natural disasters, I knew that immediately after the initial shock the survivors of natural disasters work together to try to restore order to their disrupted lives. I wanted to see this restructuring process firsthand. The next morning, I took off for Georgia.

These photos, taken the day after the tornado struck, tell the story of people in the midst of trying to put their lives back together. I was impressed at how little time people spent commiserating about their misfortune and how quickly they took practical steps to restore their lives.

As you look at these photos, try to determine why you need both microsociology and macrosociology to understand what occurs after a natural disaster.

For children, family photos are not as important as toys. This girl has managed to salvage a favorite toy, which will help anchor her to her previous life.

Personal relationships are essential in putting lives together. Consequently, reminders of these relationships are one of the main possessions that people attempt to salvage. This young man, having just recovered the family photo album, is eagerly reviewing the photos.

After making sure that their loved ones are safe, one of the next steps people take is to recover their possessions. The cooperation that emerges among people, as documented in the sociological literature on natural disasters, is illustrated here.

In addition to the inquiring sociologist, television teams also were interviewing survivors and photographing the damage. This was the second time in just three years that a tornado had hit this neighborhood.

Formal organizations also help the survivors of natural disasters recover. In this neighborhood, I saw representatives of insurance companies, the police, the fire department, and an electrical co-op. The Salvation Army brought meals to the neighborhood.

No building or social institution escapes a tornado as it follows its path of destruction. Just the night before, members of this church had held evening worship service. After the tornado, someone mounted a U.S. flag on top of the cross, symbolic of the church members' patriotism and religiosity—and of their enduring hope.

Like electricity and gas, communications need to be restored as soon as possible.

The owners of this house invited me inside to see what the tornado had done to their home. In what had been her dining room, this woman is trying to salvage whatever she can from the rubble. She and her family survived by taking refuge in the bathroom. They had been there only five seconds, she said, when the tornado struck.

The boys' reputations set them on separate paths. Seven of the eight Saints went on to graduate from college. Three studied for advanced degrees: One finished law school and became active in state politics, one finished medical school, and one went on to earn a Ph.D. The four other college graduates entered managerial or executive training programs with large firms. After his parents divorced, one Saint failed to graduate from high school on time and had to repeat his senior year. Although this boy tried to go to college by attending night school, he never finished. He was unemployed the last time Chambliss saw him.

In contrast, two of the Roughnecks dropped out of high school. They were later convicted of separate murders and sent to prison. Of the four boys who graduated from high school, two had done exceptionally well in sports and were awarded athletic scholarships to college. They both graduated from college and became high school coaches. Of the two others who completed high school, one became a small-time gambler and the other disappeared "up north," where he was last reported to be driving a truck.

To understand what happened to the Saints and the Roughnecks, we need to grasp *both* social structure and social interaction. Using *macrosociology*, we can place these boys within the larger framework of the U.S. social class system. This reveals how opportunities open or close to people depending on their social class and how people learn different goals as they grow up in different groups. We can then use *microsociology* to follow their everyday lives. We can see how the Saints manipulated their "good" reputations to skip classes and how their access to automobiles allowed them to protect their reputations by spreading their troublemaking around different communities. In contrast, the Roughnecks, who did not have cars, were highly visible. Their lawbreaking, which was limited to a small area, readily came to the attention of the community. Microsociology also reveals how their reputations opened doors of opportunity to the first group of boys while closing them to the other.

Read on **MySocLab**
Document: Through a Sociological Lens: Social Structure and Family Violence

It is clear that we need both kinds of sociology, and both are stressed in the following chapters.

MySocLab — **Study** and **Review** on **MySocLab**

CHAPTER 4 Summary and Review

Levels of Sociological Analysis

4.1 Distinguish between macrosociology and microsociology.

What two levels of analysis do sociologists use?

Sociologists use macrosociological and microsociological levels of analysis. In **macrosociology**, the focus is placed on large-scale features of social life, while in **microsociology**, the focus is on **social interaction**. Functionalists and conflict theorists tend to use a macrosociological approach, while symbolic interactionists are likely to use a microsociological approach. Pp. 94–95.

The Macrosociological Perspective: Social Structure

4.2 Explain the significance of social structure and its components: culture, social class, social status, roles, groups, and social institutions; compare the functionalist and conflict perspectives on social structure; and explain what holds society together.

How does social structure influence our behavior?

The term **social structure** refers to the social envelope that surrounds us and establishes limits on our behavior. Social structure consists of culture, social class, social statuses, roles, groups, and social institutions. Our location in the social structure underlies our perceptions, attitudes, and behaviors. Culture lays the broadest framework, while **social class** divides people according to income, education, and occupational prestige. Each of us receives **ascribed statuses** at birth; later we add **achieved statuses**. Our statuses guide our roles, put boundaries around our behavior, and give us orientations to life. These are further influenced by the **groups** to which we belong, and our experiences with social institutions. These components of society work together to help maintain social order. Pp. 95–100.

What are social institutions?

Social institutions are the standard ways that a society develops to meet its basic needs. As summarized in Figure 4.2 (page 101), industrial and postindustrial societies have ten social institutions—the family, religion, education, economy, medicine, politics, law, science, the military, and the mass media. From the functionalist perspective, social institutions meet universal group needs, or *functional requisites.* Conflict theorists stress how the elites of society use social institutions to maintain their privileged positions. Pp. 95–102.

What holds society together?

According to Emile Durkheim, in agricultural societies, people are united by **mechanical solidarity** (having similar views and feelings). With industrialization comes **organic solidarity** (people depend on one another to do their more specialized jobs). Ferdinand Tönnies pointed out that the informal means of control in ***Gemeinschaft*** (small, intimate) societies are replaced by formal mechanisms in ***Gesellschaft*** (larger, more impersonal) societies. Pp. 103–104.

The Microsociological Perspective: Social Interaction in Everyday Life

4.3 Discuss what symbolic interactionists study and explain dramaturgy, ethnomethodology, and the social construction of reality.

What is the focus of symbolic interactionism?

In contrast to functionalists and conflict theorists, who as macrosociologists focus on the "big picture," symbolic interactionists tend to be microsociologists and focus on face-to-face social interaction. Symbolic interactionists analyze how people define their worlds, and how their definitions, in turn, influence their behavior. P. 104.

How do stereotypes affect social interaction?

Stereotypes are assumptions of what people are like. When we first meet people, we classify them according to our perceptions of their visible characteristics. Our ideas about these characteristics guide our reactions to them. Our behavior, in turn, can influence them to behave in ways that reinforce our stereotypes. Pp. 108, 110–111.

Do all human groups share a similar sense of personal space?

In examining how people use physical space, symbolic interactionists stress that we have a "personal bubble" that we carefully protect. People from different cultures use "personal bubbles" of varying sizes, so the answer to the question is no. Americans typically use four different "distance zones": intimate, personal, social, and public. Pp. 108, 110.

What is body language?

Body language is using our bodies to give messages. We do this through facial expressions, posture, smiling, and eye contact. Interpreting body language is becoming a tool in business and in the fight against terrorism. P. 110.

What is dramaturgy?

Erving Goffman developed **dramaturgy** (or dramaturgical analysis), in which everyday life is analyzed in terms of the stage. At the core of this analysis is **impression management**, our attempts to control the impressions we make on others. For this, we use the **sign-vehicles** of setting, appearance, and manner. Our **role performances** on the **front stages** of life often call for **teamwork** and **face-saving behavior**. They sometimes are hampered by **role conflict** or **role strain**. Pp. 111–115.

What is ethnomethodology?

Ethnomethodology is the study of how people make sense of everyday life. Ethnomethodologists try to uncover **background assumptions**, the basic ideas about the way life is that guide our behavior. Pp. 115–116.

What is the social construction of reality?

The phrase **social construction of reality** refers to how we construct our views of the world, which, in turn, underlie our actions. Pp. 116–118.

The Need for Both Macrosociology and Microsociology

4.4 Explain why we need both macrosociology and microsociology to understand social life.

Why are both levels of analysis necessary?

Because macrosociology and microsociology focus on different aspects of the human experience, each is necessary for us to understand social life. Pp. 118–121.

Thinking Critically about Chapter 4

1. The major components of social structure are culture, social class, social status, roles, groups, and social institutions. Use social structure to explain why Native Americans have such a low rate of college graduation. (See Table 12.3 on page 344.)
2. Dramaturgy is a form of microsociology. Use dramaturgy to analyze a situation with which you are intimately familiar (such as interaction with your family or friends or at work or in one of your college classes).
3. To illustrate why we need both macrosociology and microsociology to understand social life, analyze the situation of a student getting kicked out of college.

How Sociologists Do Research

5 CHAPTER

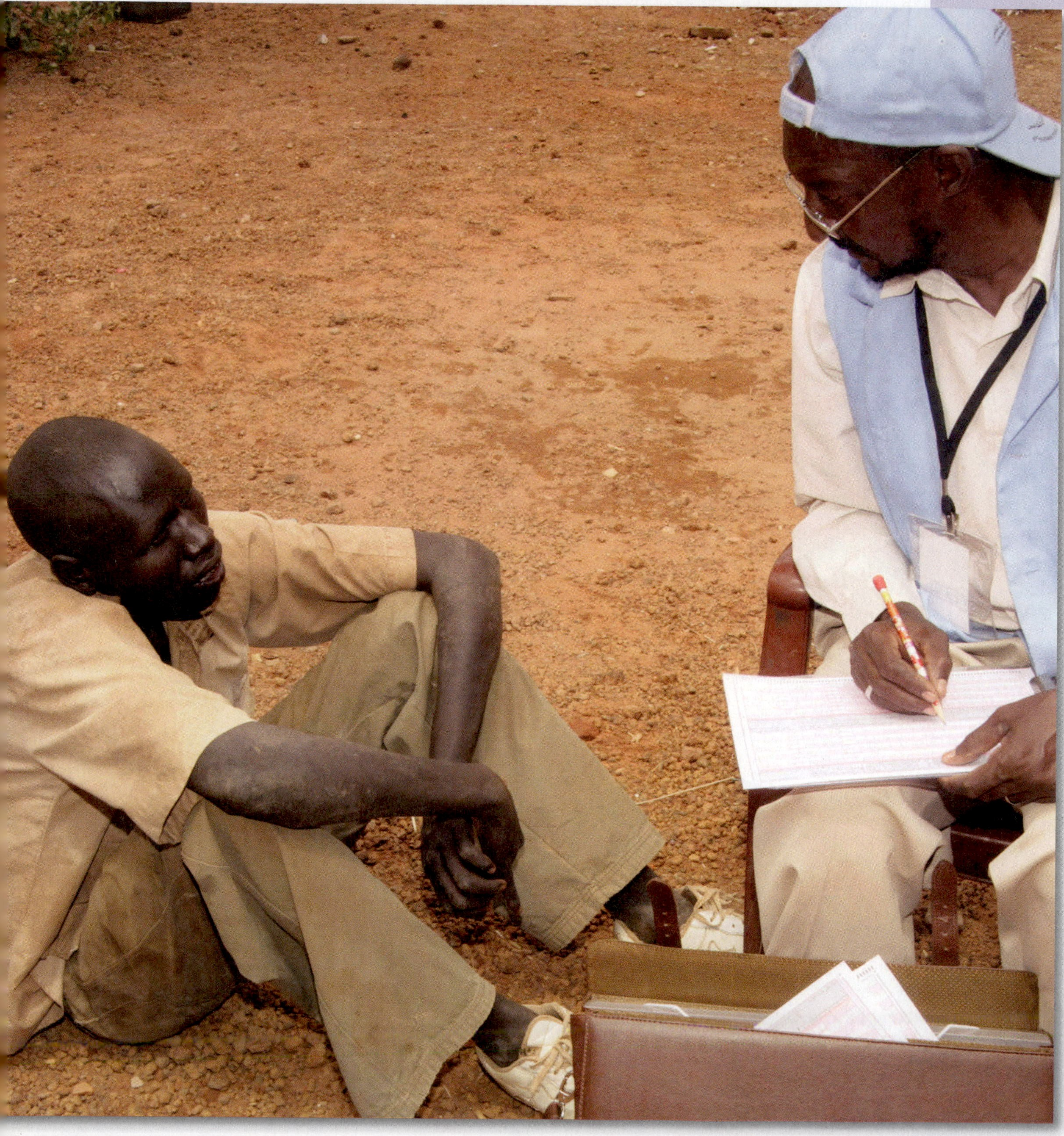

Raymond Sheehan, a 49-year-old New York *retired crime scene investigator, had just gotten out of the shower. He was standing before the mirror shaving when Barbara Sheehan, his 47-year-old wife, used two handguns to pump eleven bullets into him. When the police arrived, they found Raymond's blood-splattered body lying on the bathroom floor. The water in the sink was still running.*

"He was an evil man," the wife testified at her murder trial. Clutching her heart and sobbing, she said, "He was going to kill me. I could see it in his face. I saw his eyes and I saw the gun."

"Did he have a holster in his underpants?" asked the incredulous prosecuting attorney. "You're a manipulative liar. You simply hated him, and you killed him."

The couple's 21-year-old son testified how he was going to college out of state because he feared that being around his father would drive him to suicide. He told the jury that when he was 10 years old, he had seen his mother on the kitchen floor, in just a bra, hot pasta sauce thrown onto her body.

"Did he have a holster in his underpants?"

The couple's 25-year-old daughter told the jury that her father was so explosive he would punch her mother when they got stuck in traffic.

The wife recounted perverse sex acts that her husband had forced on her.

"You profited from his cold-blooded murder," the prosecutor thundered. "Your children shared with you the $660,000 they collected on his life insurance."

Barbara Sheehan broke down when she was asked to hold the gun and reenact how she had shot her husband. The judge let her use a pointed finger instead.

Victim or executioner?

The jury was deadlocked for two days. On the third day, the jurors brought in a verdict. Barbara Sheehan, they concluded, was not guilty of murder. She was guilty, though, of illegal gun possession. The judge declared Barbara not guilty of murder and sentenced her to five years in prison on the gun charge.

Based on Bilefsky 2011a, 2011b, 2011c, 2011d; Dwyer 2011.

Learning Objectives

After you have read this chapter, you should be able to:

5.1 State what topics are valid for sociologists to study. (p. 125)

5.2 Explain why common sense can't replace sociological research. (p. 125)

5.3 Know the 8 steps of the research model. (p. 126)

5.4 Know the main elements of the 7 research methods: surveys, participant observation, case studies, secondary analysis, analysis of documents, experiments, and unobtrusive measures; state why sociological research can lead to controversy. (p. 129)

5.5 Explain how gender is significant in sociological research. (p. 139)

5.6 Explain why it is vital for sociologists to protect the people they study; discuss the two cases that are presented. (p. 139)

5.7 Explain how research and theory work together in sociology. (p. 141)

What Is a Valid Sociological Topic?

5.1 State what topics are valid for sociologists to study.

Sociologists do research on just about every area of human behavior. On the macro level, they study such broad matters as race relations (Korgen 2010), the military (Caforio 2006), and the global economic crisis (Guthrie and Slocum 2010). On the micro level, they study such individualistic matters as pelvic examinations (Henslin and Biggs 1971/2014), how people interact on street corners (W. H. Whyte 1989; W. F. Whyte 2001), and even shyness (Scott 2006). Sociologists study nuns and prostitutes, cops and criminals, as well as all kinds of people in between. In fact, no human behavior is ineligible for sociological scrutiny—whether that behavior is routine or unusual, respectable or repulsive, pleasing or disgusting.

What happened to Barbara and Raymond, then, is also a valid topic of sociological research. But exactly *how* would you research spouse abuse? As we look at how sociologists do research, we shall try to answer this question.

Common Sense and the Need for Sociological Research

5.2 Explain why common sense can't replace sociological research.

First, why do we need sociological research? Why can't we simply depend on common sense, on "what everyone knows"? As noted in Chapter 1 (pages 6–8), commonsense ideas may or may not be true. Common sense, for example, tells us that spouse abuse has a significant impact on the lives of the people who are abused.

Watch on **MySocLab**
Video: Sociological Theory and Research: The Big Concept

Although this particular idea is accurate, we need research to test commonsense ideas, because not all such ideas are true. After all, common sense also tells us that if a woman is abused, she will pack up and leave her husband. Research, however, shows that the reality of abuse is much more complicated than this. Some women do leave right away, some even after the first incident of abuse. For a variety of reasons, however, some women suffer abuse for years. A main reason is that they feel trapped and don't perceive any viable alternatives.

Read on **MySocLab**
Document: Association Is Not Causation

This brings us to the need for sociological research: We may want to know why some women put up with abuse, while others don't. Or we may want to know something entirely different, such as why some people abuse the people they say they love.

In order to answer a question, we need to move beyond guesswork and common sense. We want to *know* what is really going on. Let's look at how sociologists do their research.

5.3 Know the 8 steps of the research model.

A Research Model

As shown in Figure 5.1, scientific research follows eight basic steps. This is an ideal model, however, and in the real world of research, some of these steps may run together. Some may even be omitted.

hypothesis a statement of how variables are expected to be related to one another, often according to predictions from a theory

variable a factor thought to be significant for human behavior, which can vary (or change) from one case to another

1. Selecting a Topic

The first step is to select a topic. What do you want to know more about? Many sociologists simply follow their curiosity, their drive to learn more about social life. They become interested in a particular topic and they pursue it, as I did in studying the homeless. Some sociologists choose a topic because funding is available, others because they want to help people better understand a social problem—and perhaps to help solve it. Let's use spouse abuse as our example.

FIGURE 5.1 The Research Model

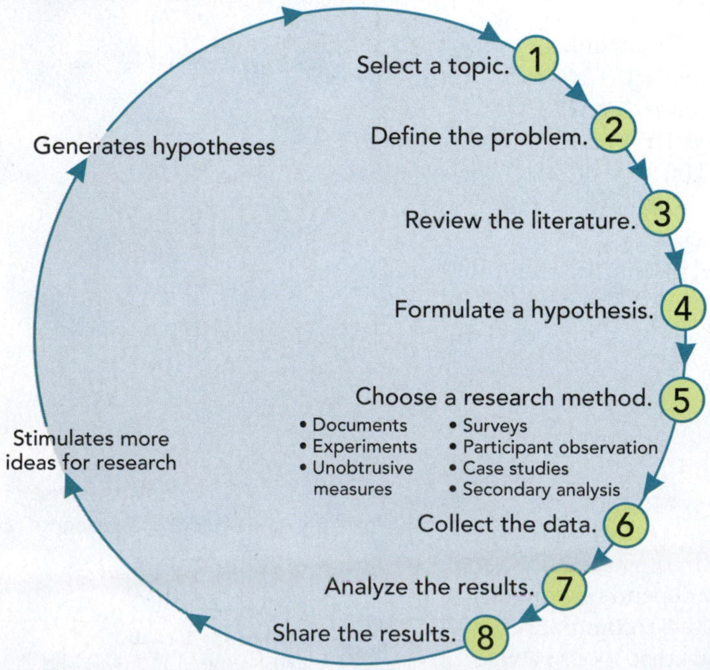
Select a topic. 1
Define the problem. 2
Review the literature. 3
Formulate a hypothesis. 4
Choose a research method. 5
• Documents
• Experiments
• Unobtrusive measures
• Surveys
• Participant observation
• Case studies
• Secondary analysis
Collect the data. 6
Analyze the results. 7
Share the results. 8
Stimulates more ideas for research
Generates hypotheses

Source: Adapted from Figure 2.2 of Schaefer 1989.

2. Defining the Problem

The second step is to define the problem, to specify what you want to learn about the topic. My interest in the homeless grew until I wanted to learn about homelessness across the nation. Ordinarily, sociologists' interests are much more focused than this; they examine some specific aspect of a topic, such as how homeless people survive on the streets. In the case of spouse abuse, sociologists may want to know whether violent and nonviolent husbands have different work experiences. Or they may want to learn what can be done to reduce spouse abuse.

3. Reviewing the Literature

You must read what has been published on your topic. This helps you to narrow the problem, identify areas that are already known, and learn what areas need to be researched. Reviewing the literature may also help you to pinpoint the questions that you will ask. You might even find out that what you are interested in learning has been answered already. You don't want to waste your time rediscovering what is already known.

4. Formulating a Hypothesis

The fourth step is to formulate a **hypothesis**, a statement of what you expect to find according to predictions from a theory. A hypothesis predicts a relationship between or among **variables**, factors that change, or vary, from one person or situation to another. For example, the statement "Men who are more socially isolated are likelier to abuse their wives than men who are more socially integrated" is a hypothesis.

Your hypothesis will need **operational definitions**—that is, precise ways to measure the variables. In this example, you would need operational definitions for three variables: social isolation, social integration, and spouse abuse.

Because sociologists find all human behavior to be valid research topics, their research ranges from the macro level of the globalization of capitalism to the micro level of social interaction. Shown here are competitors in *The Redneck Games* in East Dublin, Georgia, as they take belly flops into a mud pit. Sociologists would study the leadership of the organization, relationship of visitors to townspeople, and the activities and interaction of the participants.

5. Choosing a Research Method

You then need to decide how you are going to collect your data. Sociologists use seven basic **research methods** (or **research designs**), which are outlined in the next section. You will want to choose the research method that will best answer your particular questions.

6. Collecting the Data

When you gather your data, you have to take care to assure their **validity**; that is, your operational definitions must measure what they are intended to measure. In this case, you must be certain that you really are measuring social isolation, social integration, and spouse abuse—and not something else. Spouse abuse, for example, seems to be obvious. Yet what some people consider abusive is not regarded as abuse by others. Which definition will you choose? In other words, you must state your operational definitions so precisely that no one has any question about what you are measuring.

You must also be sure that your data are reliable. **Reliability** means that if other researchers use your operational definitions, their findings will be consistent with yours. If your operational definitions are sloppy, husbands who have committed the same act of violence might be included in some research but excluded from other studies. You would end up with erratic results. If you show a 10 percent rate of spouse abuse, for example, but another researcher using the same operational definitions determines it to be 30 percent, the research is unreliable.

7. Analyzing the Results

You will have been trained in a variety of techniques to analyze your data—from those that apply to observations of people in small settings to the analysis of large-scale surveys. If a hypothesis has been part of your research, now is when you will test it. (Some research, especially participant observation and case studies, has no hypothesis. You may know so little about the setting you are going to research that you cannot even specify the variables in advance.)

If statistical techniques apply to your research, you are likely to use a program such as MicroCase and SPSS (Statistical Package for the Social Sciences). Some software, such as the Methodologist's Toolchest, provides advice about collecting data and even about ethical issues.

8. Sharing the Results

To wrap up your research, you will write a report to share your findings with the scientific community. You will review how you did your research and specify your operational definitions. You will also compare your findings with published reports on the topic and analyze how they support or disagree with theories that others have applied.

When research is published, usually in a scientific journal or a book, it "belongs" to the scientific community. Your findings will be available for *replication*; that is, others can repeat your study to see if they come up with similar results. As Table 5.1 on the next page illustrates, sociologists often summarize their findings in tables. As finding is added to finding, scientific knowledge builds.

Watch on **MySocLab**
Video: Sociology in Focus: Sociological Theory and Research

operational definition the way in which a researcher measures a variable

research method (or research design) one of seven procedures that sociologists use to collect data: surveys, participant observation, case studies, secondary analysis, documents, experiments, and unobtrusive measures

validity the extent to which an operational definition measures what it is intended to measure

reliability the extent to which research produces consistent or dependable results

TABLE 5.1 How to Read a Table

Tables summarize information. Because sociological findings are often presented in tables, it is important to understand how to read them. Tables contain six elements: title, headnote, headings, columns, rows, and source. When you understand how these elements fit together, you know how to read a table.

1. The *title* states the topic. It is located at the top of the table. What is the title of this table? Please determine your answer before looking at the correct answer at the bottom of this page.

2. The *headnote* is not always included in a table. When it is present, it is located just below the title. Its purpose is to give more detailed information about how the data were collected or how data are presented in the table. What are the first eight words of the headnote for this table?

3. The *headings* tell what kind of information is contained in the table. There are three headings in this table. What are they? In the second heading, what does $n = 25$ mean?

Comparing Violent and Nonviolent Husbands

Based on interviews with 150 husbands and wives in a Midwestern city who were getting a divorce.

Husband's Achievement and Job Satisfaction	Violent Husbands ($n = 25$)	Nonviolent Husbands ($n = 125$)
He started but failed to complete high school or college.	44%	27%
He is very dissatisfied with his job.	44%	18%
His income is a source of constant conflict.	84%	24%
He has less education than his wife.	56%	14%
His job has less prestige than his father-in-law's.	37%	28%

Source: Modification of Table 1 in O'Brien 1975.

4. The *columns* present information arranged vertically. What is the fourth number in the second column and the second number in the third column?

5. The *rows* present information arranged horizontally. In the fourth row, which husbands are more likely to have less education than their wives?

6. The *source* of a table, usually listed at the bottom, provides information on where the data in the table originated. Often, as in this instance, the information is specific enough for you to consult the original source. What is the source for this table?

Some tables are much more complicated than this one, but all follow the same basic pattern. To apply these concepts to a table with more information, see page 344.

ANSWERS

1. Comparing Violent and Nonviolent Husbands
2. Based on interviews with 150 husbands and wives
3. Husband's Achievement and Job Satisfaction, Violent Husbands, Nonviolent Husbands. The n is an abbreviation for number, and $n = 25$ means that 25 violent husbands were in the sample.
4. 56%, 18%
5. Violent Husbands
6. A 1975 article by O'Brien (listed in the References section of this text).

Let's look in greater detail at the fifth step to see what research methods sociologists use.

5.4 Know the main elements of the 7 research methods: surveys, participant observation, case studies, secondary analysis, analysis of documents, experiments, and unobtrusive measures; state why sociological research can lead to controversy.

Research Methods (Designs)

As we review the seven research methods (or *research designs*) that sociologists use, we will continue our example of spouse abuse. As you will see, the method you choose will depend on the questions you want to answer. So that you can have a yardstick for comparing the results of your research, you will want to know what "average" is in your research findings. Table 5.2 summarizes the three ways that sociologists measure average.

Surveys

Let's suppose that you want to know how many wives are abused each year. Some husbands also are abused, of course, but let's assume that you are going to focus on wives. An appropriate method for this purpose would be the **survey**, in which you would ask individuals a series of questions. Before you begin your research, however, you must deal with practical matters that face all researchers. Let's look at these issues.

Selecting a Sample. Ideally, you might want to learn about all wives in the world, but obviously you don't have enough resources to do this. You will have to narrow your **population**, the target group that you are going to study.

Let's assume that your resources (money, assistants, time) allow you to investigate spouse abuse only among the students on your campus. Let's also assume that your college enrollment is large, so you won't be able to survey all the married women who are enrolled. Now you must select a **sample**, individuals from among your target population. How you choose a sample is crucial: Not all samples are equal. For example,

"That's the worst set of opinions I've heard in my entire life."

To attain their goal of objectivity and accuracy in their research, sociologists must put away their personal opinions.

TABLE 5.2 Three Ways to Measure "Average"

The Mean

The term *average* seems clear enough. As you learned in grade school, to find the average you add a group of numbers and then divide the total by the number of cases that you added. Assume that the following numbers represent men convicted of battering their wives.

EXAMPLE
321
229
57
289
136
57
1,795

The total is 2,884. Divided by 7 (the number of cases), the average is 412. Sociologists call this form of average the *mean*.

The mean can be deceptive because it is strongly influenced by extreme scores, either low or high. Note that six of the seven cases are less than the mean.

Two other ways to compute averages are the median and the mode.

The Median

To compute the second average, the *median*, first arrange the cases in order—either from the highest to the lowest or the lowest to the highest. That arrangement will produce the following distribution.

EXAMPLE		
57		1,795
57		321
136		289
229	or	229
289		136
321		57
1,795		57

Then look for the middle case, the one that falls halfway between the top and the bottom. That number is 229, for three numbers are lower and three numbers are higher. When there is an even numbers of cases, the median is the halfway mark between the two middle cases.

The Mode

The third measure of average, the *mode*, is simply the cases that occur the most often. In this instance the mode is 57, which is way off the mark.

EXAMPLE
57
57
136
229
289
321
1,795

Because the mode is often deceptive, and only by chance comes close to either of the other two averages, sociologists seldom use it. In addition, not every distribution of cases has a mode. And if two or more numbers appear with the same frequency, you can have more than one mode.

If sociologists were to study land diving on Pentecost Island in Vanuatu, they could use a variety of methods. Based on what you have learned in this chapter, how do you think this activity should be studied? Remember that there are both participants and observers.

married women enrolled in introductory sociology and engineering courses might have quite different experiences. If so, surveying just one or the other would produce skewed results.

Remember that your goal is to get findings that apply to your entire school. For this, you need a sample that represents the students. How can you get a *representative* sample?

The best way is to use a **random sample**. This does *not* mean that you stand on some campus corner and ask questions of any woman who happens to walk by. *In a random sample, everyone in your population (the target group) has the same chance of being included in the study.* In this case, because your population is every married woman enrolled in your college, all married women—whether first-year or graduate students, full- or part-time—must have the same chance of being included in your sample.

How can you get a random sample? First, you need a list of all the married women enrolled in your college. Then you assign a number to each name on the list. Using a table of random numbers, you then determine which of these women will become part of your sample. (Tables of random numbers are available in statistics books and online, or they can be generated by a computer.)

A random sample will represent your target population fairly—in this case, married women enrolled at your college. This means that you will be able to generalize your findings to *all* the married women students on your campus, even if they were not included in your sample.

What if you want to know only about certain subgroups, such as the freshmen and seniors? You could use a **stratified random sample**. You would need a list of the freshmen and senior married women. Then, using random numbers, you would select a sample from each group. This would allow you to generalize to all the freshmen and senior married women at your college, but you would not be able to draw any conclusions about the sophomores or juniors.

Asking Neutral Questions. After you have decided on your population and sample, the next task is to make certain that your questions are neutral. The questions must allow **respondents**, the people who answer your questions, to express their own opinions. Otherwise, you will end up with biased answers, which are worthless. For example, if you were to ask, "Don't you think that men who beat their wives should go to prison?" you would be tilting the answer toward agreement with a prison sentence. The *Doonesbury* cartoon illustrates another blatant example of biased questions. For other examples of flawed research, see the Down-to-Earth Sociology box on the next page.

Questionnaires and Interviews. There are two basic techniques for administering **questionnaires**, the list of questions to be asked. The first is to ask the respondents to fill them out. These **self-administered questionnaires** allow a larger number of people to be sampled at a lower cost, but the researchers lose control of the data collection.

survey the collection of data by having people answer a series of questions

population a target group to be studied

sample the individuals intended to represent the population to be studied

random sample a sample in which everyone in the target population has the same chance of being included in the study

Read on MySocLab
Document: Sense and Nonsense About Surveys

Improperly worded questions can steer respondents toward answers that are not their own, which produces invalid results.

Down-to-Earth Sociology

Loading the Dice: How *Not* to Do Research

The methods of science lend themselves to distortion, misrepresentation, and downright fraud. Consider these findings from surveys:

Americans overwhelmingly prefer Toyotas to Chryslers.
Americans overwhelmingly prefer Chryslers to Toyotas.

Obviously, these opposite conclusions cannot both be true. In fact, both sets of findings are misrepresentations, even though the responses came from surveys conducted by so-called independent researchers. It turns out that some consumer researchers load the dice. Hired by firms that have a vested interest in the outcome of the research, they deliver the results their clients are looking for (Armstrong 2007). Here are six ways to load the dice.

1. **Choose a biased sample.** If you want to "prove" that Americans prefer Chryslers over Toyotas, interview unemployed union workers who trace their job loss to Japanese imports. The answer is predictable. You'll get what you're looking for.
2. **Ask biased questions.** Even if you choose an unbiased sample, you can phrase questions in such a way that you direct people to the answer you're looking for. Suppose that you ask this question:

   We are losing millions of jobs to workers overseas who work for just a few dollars a day. After losing their jobs, some Americans are even homeless and hungry. Do you prefer a car that gives jobs to Americans, or one that forces our workers to lose their homes?

   This question is obviously designed to channel people's thinking toward a predetermined answer—quite contrary to the standards of scientific research. Look again at the *Doonesbury* cartoon.
3. **List biased choices.** Another way to load the dice is to use closed-ended questions that push people into the answers you want. Consider this finding:

   U.S. college students overwhelmingly prefer Levi's 501 to the jeans of any competitor.

   Sound good? Before you rush out to buy Levis, note what these researchers did: In asking students which jeans would be the most popular in the coming year, their list of choices included no other jeans but Levi's 501!
4. **Discard undesirable results.** Researchers can keep silent about results they don't like, or they can continue to survey samples until they find one that matches what they are looking for.
5. **Misunderstand the subjects' world.** This route can lead to errors every bit as great as those just cited. Even researchers who use an adequate sample and word their questions properly can end up with skewed results. They might, for example, fail to anticipate that people may be embarrassed to express an opinion that isn't "politically correct." For example, surveys show that 80 percent of Americans are environmentalists. Is this an accurate figure? Most Americans are probably embarrassed to tell a stranger otherwise. Today, that would be like going against the flag, motherhood, and apple pie.
6. **Analyze the data incorrectly.** Even when researchers strive for objectivity, the sample is good, the wording is neutral, and the respondents answer the questions honestly, the results can still be skewed. The researchers may make a mistake in their calculations, such as entering incorrect data into computer programs. This, too, of course, is inexcusable in science.

Of these six sources of bias, the first four demonstrate fraud. The final two reflect sloppiness, which is also not acceptable in science.

As has been stressed in this chapter, research must be objective if it is to be scientific. The underlying problem with the research cited here—and with so many surveys bandied about in the media as fact—is that survey research has become big business. Simply put, the money offered by corporations has corrupted some researchers.

The beginning of the corruption is subtle. Paul Light, dean at the University of Minnesota, put it this way: "A funder will never come to an academic and say, 'I want you to produce finding X, and here's a million dollars to do it.' Rather, the subtext is that if the researchers produce the right finding, more work—and funding—will come their way."

Sources: Based on Crossen 1991; Goleman 1993; Barnes 1995; Resnik 2000; Augoustinos et al. 2009.

The researchers don't know the conditions under which people answered the questions. For example, others could have influenced their answers.

The second technique is the **interview**. Researchers ask questions, often face to face, sometimes by telephone or e-mail. The advantage of this method is that the researchers can ask each question in the same way. The main disadvantage is that interviews are time-consuming, so researchers end up with fewer respondents. Interviews can also create **interviewer bias**; that is, the presence of interviewers can affect what people say. For example, instead of saying what they really feel, respondents might give "socially

stratified random sample a sample from selected subgroups of the target population in which everyone in those subgroups has an equal chance of being included in the research

respondents people who respond to a survey, either in interviews or by self-administered questionnaires

TABLE 5.3 Closed- and Open-Ended Questions

A. Closed-Ended Question	B. Open-Ended Question
Which of the following best fits your idea of what should be done to someone who has been convicted of spouse abuse? 1. Probation 2. Jail time 3. Community service 4. Counseling 5. Divorce 6. Nothing—It's a family matter	What do you think should be done to someone who has been convicted of spouse abuse?

acceptable" answers. Although they may be willing to write their true opinions on an anonymous questionnaire, they won't tell them to another person. Some respondents even shape their answers to match what they think the interviewer wants to hear.

In some cases, **structured interviews** work best. This type of interview uses **closed-ended questions**—each question is followed by a list of possible answers. Structured interviews are faster to administer, and they make it easier to code (categorize) answers so they can be fed into a computer for analysis. However, as you can see from Table 5.3, the choices listed on a questionnaire might fail to include the respondent's opinions. Because of this, some researchers prefer **unstructured interviews**. Here the interviewer asks **open-ended questions**, which allow people to answer in their own words. Open-ended questions let you tap the full range of people's opinions, but they make it difficult to compare answers. For example, how would you compare these answers to the question "Why do you think men abuse their wives?"

"They're sick."

"I think they must have had problems with their mother."

"We oughta string 'em up!"

Watch on **MySocLab**
Video: Sociological Theory and Research: Thinking Like a Sociologist

Establishing Rapport. Research on spouse abuse brings up a significant issue. You may have been wondering if women who have been abused will really give honest answers to strangers.

If your method of interviewing consists of walking up to women on the street and asking if their husbands have ever beaten them, there would be little reason to take your findings seriously. Researchers need to establish **rapport** (ruh-POUR), a feeling of trust, with their respondents, especially when it comes to sensitive topics—those that elicit feelings of embarrassment, shame, or other negative emotions.

Once rapport is gained (often by first asking nonsensitive questions), victims will talk about personal, sensitive issues. A good example is rape. To go beyond police statistics, researchers interview a random sample of 100,000 Americans each year. They ask them whether they have been victims of burglary, robbery, or other crimes. After establishing rapport, the researchers ask about rape. This National Crime Victimization Survey shows that rape victims will talk about their experiences (Weiss 2009; *Statistical Abstract* 2013:Tables 322, 323, 324).

To gather data on sensitive areas, some researchers use Computer-Assisted Self-Interviewing. In this technique, the interviewer gives the individual a laptop computer, then moves aside while he or she answers questions on the computer. In some versions of this method, the individual listens to the questions on headphones and answers on the computer screen. When he or she clicks the "Submit" button, the interviewer has no idea how any question was answered (Kaestle 2012). Although many people like the privacy that this technique provides, some prefer a live questioner even for sensitive areas of their lives. They say that they want positive feedback from interviewers (Estes et al. 2010).

questionnaires a list of questions to be asked of respondents

self-administered questionnaires questionnaires that respondents fill out

interview direct questioning of respondents

interviewer bias effects of interviewers on respondents that lead to biased answers

structured interviews interviews that use closed-ended questions

closed-ended questions questions that are followed by a list of possible answers to be selected by the respondent

unstructured interviews interviews that use open-ended questions

open-ended questions questions that respondents answer in their own words

rapport (ruh-POUR) a feeling of trust between researchers and the people they are studying

participant observation (or **fieldwork**) research in which the researcher participates in a research setting while observing what is happening in that setting

Participant Observation (Fieldwork)

In the second method, **participant observation** (or **fieldwork**), the researcher *participates* in a research setting while *observing* what is happening in that setting. But how is it possible to study spouse abuse by participant observation? Obviously, you would not sit around and watch someone being abused.

Let's suppose that you are interested in learning how spouse abuse affects wives. You might want to know how the abuse has changed their relationships with their husbands. Or how has it changed their hopes and dreams? Or their ideas about men? Certainly it has affected their self-concept as well. But how? By observing people as they live their lives, participant observation could provide insight into such questions.

For example, if your campus has a crisis intervention center, you might be able to observe victims of spouse abuse from the time they report the attack through their participation in counseling. With good rapport, you might even be able to spend time with them in other settings, observing further aspects of their lives. What they say and how they interact with others might help you understand how abuse has affected them. This, in turn, could give you insight into how to improve college counseling services.

Participant observers face two major dilemmas. The first is **generalizability**, the extent to which the findings from one setting apply to other groups. Although participant observation can stimulate hypotheses and theories that can be tested in other settings, most participant observation is exploratory, documenting in detail the experiences of people in a particular setting. Although such research suggests that other people who face similar situations react in similar ways, we don't know how far the findings apply beyond the original setting. A second dilemma is the extent to which participant observers should get involved in the lives of the people they are observing. Consider this as you read the Down-to-Earth Sociology box on the next page.

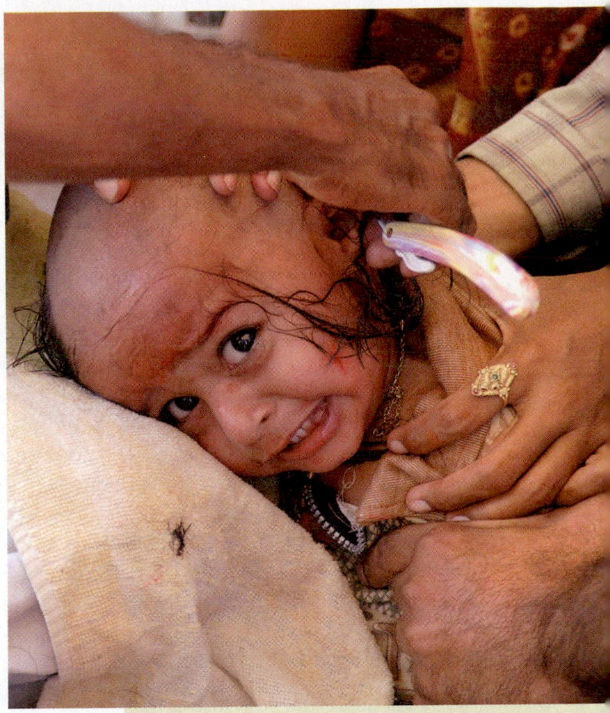

Participant observation, participating and observing in a research setting, is usually supplemented by interviewing, asking questions to better understand why people do what they do. In this instance, the sociologist would want to know what this hair removal ceremony in Gujarat, India, means to the child's family and to the community.

Case Studies

To do a **case study**, the researcher focuses on a single event, situation, or individual. The purpose is to understand the dynamics of relationships and power, or even the thinking that motivates people. Sociologist Ken Levi (1981/2009), for example, wanted to study hit men. He would have loved having many hit men to interview, but he had access to only one. He interviewed this man over and over, giving us an understanding of how someone can kill others for money. On another level entirely, sociologist Kai Erikson (1978) investigated the bursting of a dam in West Virginia that killed several hundred people. He focused on the events that led up to this disaster and how people tried to put their lives together after the devastation. For spouse abuse, a case study would focus on a single wife and husband, exploring the couple's history and relationship.

As you can see, the case study reveals a lot of detail about some particular situation, but the question always remains: How much of this detail applies to other situations? This problem of generalizability, which plagues case studies, is the primary reason that few sociologists use this method.

Secondary Analysis

In **secondary analysis**, a fourth research method, researchers analyze data that others have collected. For example, if you were to analyze the original interviews from a study of women who had been abused by their husbands, you would be doing secondary analysis. Researchers prefer to gather their own data, but the lack of resources, especially money, can make this impossible. In addition, existing data could contain a wealth of information that wasn't pertinent to the goals of the original researchers. You can analyze these for your own purposes.

Like the other methods, secondary analysis also poses its own problems, especially this question: How can a researcher who did not carry out the initial study be sure that the data were gathered systematically and recorded accurately?

Analysis of Documents

The fifth method that sociologists use is the study of **documents**, recorded sources. To investigate social life, they examine such diverse sources as books, newspapers, diaries,

generalizability the extent to which the findings from one group (or sample) can be generalized or applied to other groups (or populations)

case study an intensive analysis of a single event, situation, or individual

secondary analysis the analysis of data that have been collected by other researchers

documents in its narrow sense, written sources that provide data; in its extended sense, archival material of any sort, including photographs, movies, CDs, DVDs, and so on

Down-to-Earth Sociology

Gang Leader for a Day: Adventures of a Rogue Sociologist

Next to the University of Chicago is an area of poverty so dangerous that the professors warn students to avoid it. One graduate student in sociology, Sudhir Venkatesh, the son of immigrants from India, who was working on a research project with William Julius Wilson, ignored the warning.

With clipboard in hand, Sudhir entered "the projects." Ignoring the glares of the young men standing around, he went into the lobby of a high-rise. Seeing a gaping hole where the elevator was supposed to be, he decided to climb the stairs, where he was almost overpowered by the smell of urine. After climbing five flights, Sudhir came upon some young men shooting craps in a dark hallway. One of them jumped up, grabbed Sudhir's clipboard, and demanded to know what he was doing there.

Sudhir blurted, "I'm a student at the university, doing a survey, and I'm looking for some families to interview."

One man took out a knife and began to twirl it. Another pulled out a gun, pointed it at Sudhir's head, and said, "I'll take him."

Then came a series of rapid-fire questions that Sudhir couldn't answer. He had no idea what they meant: "You flip right or left? Five or six? You run with the Kings, right?"

Grabbing Sudhir's bag, two of the men searched it. They could find only questionnaires, pen and paper, and a few sociology books. The man with the gun then told Sudhir to go ahead and ask him a question.

Sweating despite the cold, Sudhir read the first question on his survey, "How does it feel to be black and poor?" Then he read the multiple-choice answers: "Very bad, somewhat bad, neither bad nor good, somewhat good, very good."

As you might surmise, the man's answer was too obscenity laden to be printed here.

As the men deliberated Sudhir's fate ("If he's here and he don't get back, you know they're going to come looking for him"), a powerfully built man with glittery gold teeth and a sizable diamond earring appeared. The man, known as J. T., who, it turned out, directed the drug trade in the building, asked what was going on. When the younger men mentioned the questionnaire, J. T. said to ask *him* a question.

Amidst an eerie silence, Sudhir asked, "How does it feel to be black and poor?"

Sudhir Venkatesh, who now teaches at Columbia University, New York City.

"I'm not black," came the reply.

"Well, then, how does it feel to be African American and poor?"

"I'm not African American either. I'm a nigger."

Sudhir was left speechless. Despite his naïveté, he knew better than to ask, "How does it feel to be a nigger and poor?"

As Sudhir stood with his mouth agape, J. T. added, "Niggers are the ones who live in this building. African Americans live in the suburbs. African Americans wear ties to work. Niggers can't find no work."

Not exactly the best start to a research project.

But this weird and frightening beginning turned into several years of fascinating research. Over time, J. T. guided Sudhir into a world that few outsiders ever see. Not only did Sudhir get to know drug dealers, crackheads, squatters, prostitutes, and pimps, but he also was present at beatings by drug crews, drive-by shootings done by rival gangs, and armed robberies by the police.

How Sudhir got out of his predicament in the stairwell, his immersion into a threatening underworld—the daily life for many people in "the projects"—and his moral dilemma at witnessing crimes are part of his fascinating experience in doing participant observation of the Black Kings.

Sudhir, who was reared in a middle-class suburb in California, even took over this Chicago gang for a day. This is one reason that he calls himself a rogue sociologist—the decisions he made that day were violations of law, felonies that could bring years in prison. There are other reasons, too: During the research, he kicked a man in the stomach, and he was present as the gang planned drive-by shootings.

Sudhir survived, completed his Ph.D., and now teaches at Columbia University.

Source: Based on Venkatesh 2008.

For Your Consideration

➔ From this report, what do you see as the advantages of participant observation? Its disadvantages? Do you think that doing sociological research justifies being present at beatings? At the planning of drive-by shootings?

bank records, police reports, immigration files, and records kept by organizations. The term *documents* is broad and also includes video and audio recordings. Sociologists have even used *Facebook* to study the race—ethnicity patterns of friendships among college students (Wimmer and Lewis 2011).

To study spouse abuse, you might examine police reports and court records. These could reveal what percentage of complaints result in arrest and what proportion of the men arrested are charged, convicted, or put on probation. If these were your questions, police statistics would be valuable.

But for other questions, those records would be useless. If you want to learn about the victims' social and emotional adjustment, for example, police and court records would tell you little. Other documents, however, might provide these answers. With the promise of confidentiality (no names or anything else to identify individuals), perhaps the director of a crisis intervention center might persuade victims to let you examine their counseling records. To my knowledge, no sociologist has yet studied spouse abuse in this way.

Of course, I am presenting an ideal situation: the director of a crisis intervention center who opens her arms to you. The actual situation might be quite different. To preserve the confidentiality of victims, she might not even let you near the center's records. *Access*, then, is another problem that researchers face. Simply put, you can't study a topic unless you can gain access to it.

The research methods that sociologists choose depend partially on the questions they want to answer. They might want to learn, for example, which forms of publicity are more effective in increasing awareness of spouse abuse as a social problem. This photo was taken in La Paz, Bolivia.

Experiments

Do you think there is a way to change a man who abuses his wife into a loving husband? No one has made this claim, but a lot of people say that abusers need therapy. Yet no one knows whether therapy really works. Because **experiments** are useful for determining cause and effect (discussed in Table 5.4 on the next page), let's suppose that you propose an experiment to a judge and she gives you access to men who have been arrested for spouse abuse. As in Figure 5.2 below, you would randomly divide the men into two groups. This helps to ensure that their individual characteristics (attitudes, number of arrests, severity of crimes, education, race–ethnicity, age, and so on) are distributed evenly between the groups. You then would arrange for the men in the **experimental group** to receive some form of therapy that the men in the **control group** would not get.

Your **independent variable**, something that causes a change in another variable, would be the therapy. Your **dependent variable**, the variable that might change, would be the men's behavior, whether they abuse women after they get out of jail. Unfortunately, your operational definition of the men's behavior will be sloppy: either reports from the wives or records indicating who has been rearrested for abuse. This is sloppy because some of the women will not report the abuse, and some of the men who abuse their wives will not be arrested. Yet it may be the best you can do.

Let's assume that you choose rearrest as your operational definition of the independent variable. If *fewer* of the men who received therapy are rearrested for abuse, you can attribute the difference to the therapy. If you find *no difference* in rearrest rates, you can conclude that the therapy was ineffective. If you find that the men who received the therapy have a *higher* rearrest rate, you can conclude that the therapy backfired.

Ideally, you would test different types of therapy. Perhaps only some types work. You could even test self-therapy by assigning articles, books, and videos.

experiment the use of control and experimental groups and dependent and independent variables to test causation

experimental group the group of subjects in an experiment who are exposed to the independent variable

control group the subjects in an experiment who are not exposed to the independent variable

independent variable a factor that causes a change in another variable, called the *dependent variable*

dependent variable a factor in an experiment that is changed by an independent variable

FIGURE 5.2 The Experiment

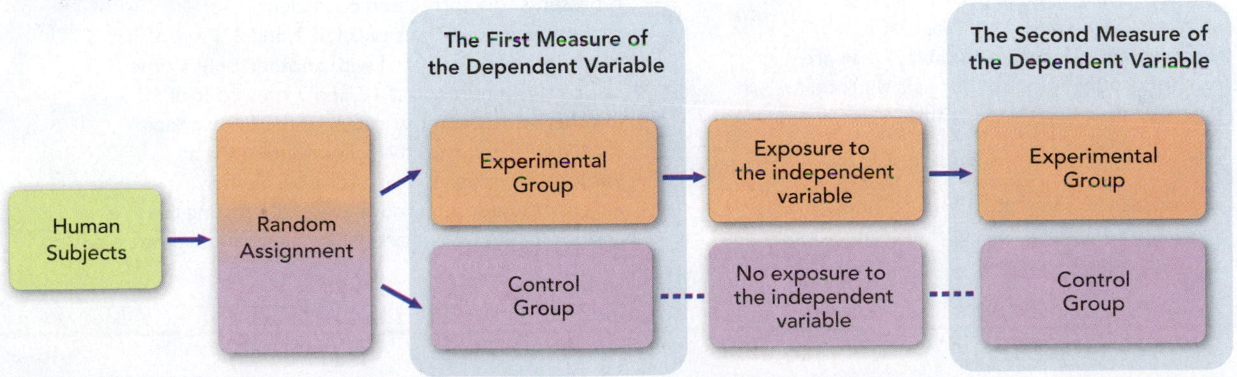

Source: By the author.

TABLE 5.4 Cause, Effect, and Spurious Correlations

Causation means that a change in one variable is caused by another variable. Three conditions are necessary for causation: correlation, temporal priority, and no spurious correlation. Let's apply each of these conditions to spouse abuse and alcohol abuse.

1 The first necessary condition is *correlation*

If two variables exist together, they are said to be correlated. If batterers get drunk, battering and alcohol abuse are correlated.

Spouse Abuse + Alcohol Abuse

People sometimes assume that correlation is causation. In this instance, they conclude that alcohol abuse causes spouse abuse.

Alcohol Abuse → Spouse Abuse

But *correlation never proves causation. Either* variable could be the cause of the other. Perhaps battering upsets men and they then get drunk.

Spouse Abuse → Alcohol Abuse

2 The second necessary condition is *temporal priority.*

Temporal priority means that one thing happens before something else does. For a variable to be a cause (*the independent variable*), it must *precede* that which is changed (*the dependent variable*).

Alcohol Abuse (**precedes**) **→ Spouse Abuse**

If the men had not drunk alcohol until after they beat their wives, obviously alcohol abuse could not be the cause of the spouse abuse. Although the necessity of temporal priority is obvious, in many studies this is not easy to determine.

3 The third necessary condition is *no spurious correlation.*

This is the necessary condition that really makes things difficult. Even if we identify the correlation of getting drunk and spouse abuse and can determine temporal priority, we still don't know that alcohol abuse is the cause. We could have a *spurious correlation;* that is, the cause may be some underlying third variable. These are usually not easy to identify. Some sociologists think that male culture is that underlying third variable.

Male Culture → Spouse Abuse

Socialized into dominance, some men learn to view women as objects on which to take out their frustration. In fact, this underlying third variable could be a cause of both spouse abuse and alcohol abuse.

Male Culture → Spouse Abuse
Male Culture → Alcohol Abuse

But since only some men beat their wives, while all males are exposed to male culture, other variables must also be involved. Perhaps specific subcultures that promote violence and denigrate women lead to both spouse abuse and alcohol abuse.

Male Subculture → Spouse Abuse
Male Subculture → Alcohol Abuse

If so, this does *not* mean that it is the only causal variable, for spouse abuse probably has many causes. Unlike the movement of amoebas or the action of heat on some object, human behavior is infinitely complicated. Especially important are people's *definitions of the situation*, including their views of right and wrong. To explain spouse abuse, then, we need to add such variables as the ways that men view violence and their ideas about the relative rights of women and men. It is precisely to help unravel such complicating factors in human behavior that we need the experiment method.

MORE ON CORRELATIONS

Correlation simply means that two or more variables are present together. The more often that these variables are found together, the stronger their relationship. To indicate their strength, sociologists use a number called a *correlation coefficient*. If two variables are always related, that is, they are always present together, they have what is called a *perfect positive correlation*. The number 1.0 represents this correlation coefficient. Nature has some 1.0's such as the lack of water and the death of trees. 1.0's also apply to the human physical state, such as the absence of nutrients and the absence of life. But social life is much more complicated than physical conditions, and there are no 1.0's in human behavior.

Two variables can also have a *perfect negative correlation*. This means that when one variable is present, the other is always absent. The number −1.0 represents this correlation coefficient.

Positive correlations of 0.1, 0.2, and 0.3 mean that one variable is associated with another only 1 time out of 10, 2 times out of 10, and 3 times out of 10. In other words, in most instances the first variable is *not* associated with the second, indicating a weak relationship. A strong relationship may indicate causation, but not necessarily. Testing the relationship between variables is the goal of some sociological research.

Source: By the author.

Unobtrusive Measures

Let's suppose you go to the mall, where you stop at an information kiosk. Unknown to you, a face-recognition camera has classified you by age and sex. As you stroll past stores, you are tracked by your smartphone and sent targeted ads (Ramstad 2012; Troianovski 2012). When you stop at a store, a bionic mannequin, one that looks like the regular ones, reports your age, sex, and race–ethnicity (Roberts 2012). Cameras follow you through the store, recording each item you touch, as well as every time you pick your nose (Singer 2010). The Web coupon you use to make a purchase is embedded with bar codes that contain your name and even Facebook information.

As in this photo from Tampa, Florida, hidden cameras now follow us almost everywhere we go. How do the unobtrusive measures of sociologists differ from hidden crime surveillance?

In our technological society, we are surrounded by **unobtrusive measures**, ways to observe people who are not aware that they are being studied. The face-recognition cameras, tracking services, and coupons, which raise ethical issues of invasion of privacy, are part of marketing, not sociological research. In contrast to these technological marvels, the unobtrusive measures used by sociologists are relatively primitive. To determine whiskey consumption in a town that was legally "dry," for example, sociologists counted the empty bottles in trashcans (Lee 2000).

How could we use unobtrusive measures to study spouse abuse? As you might surmise, sociologists would consider it unethical to watch someone being abused. If abused or abusing spouses held a public forum on the Internet, however, you could record and analyze their online conversations. Or you could analyze 911 calls. The basic ethical principle is this: To record the behavior of people in public settings, such as a crowd, without announcing that you are doing so is acceptable. To do this in private settings is not. Between public and private, however, lie semi-public/semi-private areas—such as the hallway just outside an instructor's office. Some say it is private, others that it is public (Hurdley 2010).

Read on **MySocLab**
Document: From Summer Camps to Glass Ceilings: The Power of Experiments

Deciding Which Method to Use

How do sociologists choose among these methods? Four primary factors affect the decision. The first is *access to resources.* Researchers may want to conduct a survey, for example, but if finances are not sufficient, they might analyze documents instead. The second is *access to subjects.* If the people who make up the sample live far away, researchers who would have preferred doing face-to-face interviews might mail them questionnaires instead. Or a researcher might conduct a survey by telephone or e-mail. The third is the *purpose of the research.* Each method is better for answering certain types of questions. Participant observation, for example, is good at uncovering people's attitudes, while experiments are better at resolving questions of cause and effect. Fourth, *the researcher's background or training* comes into play. In graduate school, sociologists study many methods, but they are able to practice only some of them. After graduate school, sociologists who were trained in quantitative research methods, which emphasize measurement and statistics, are likely to use surveys. Sociologists who were trained in qualitative research methods, which emphasize observing and interpreting people's behavior, lean toward participant observation.

Controversy in Sociological Research

Sociologists sometimes find themselves in the hot seat because of their research. Some researchers poke into private areas of life, which upsets people. Others investigate political matters, and their findings threaten those who have some stake in the situation. When researchers wanted to learn about how risky sexual practices are related to HIV infection, members of the U.S. Congress scoffed at the proposal and asked the National Institute of Health not to fund it (Kempner 2008). But it isn't just sex and politics. In the following Thinking Critically section, you can see how sociologists got in hot water just for wanting to count the homeless.

unobtrusive measures ways of observing people so they do not know they are being studied

Explore on **MySocLab**
Activity: Income Inequality in Chicago

THINKING CRITICALLY

Doing Controversial Research—Counting the Homeless

What could be less offensive than counting the homeless? As sometimes occurs, however, even basic sociology lands researchers in the midst of controversy. This is what happened to sociologist Peter Rossi and his associates.

The problem began with a dispute between advocates for the homeless and federal officials. The advocates claimed that 3 to 7 million Americans were homeless; the officials put the total at about 250,000. Each side accused the other of gross distortion—the one to place pressure on Congress, the other to keep the public from knowing how bad the situation really was. But each side was only guessing.

Only an accurate count could clear up the picture. Peter Rossi and the National Opinion Research Center took on that job. They had no vested interest in supporting either side, only in answering this question accurately.

The challenge was immense. The *population* was evident—the U.S. homeless. A *survey* would be appropriate, but how do you survey a *sample* of the homeless? No one has a list of the homeless, and only some of the homeless stay at shelters. As for *validity*, to make certain that they were counting only people who were really homeless, the researchers needed a good *operational definition* of homelessness. To include people who weren't really homeless would destroy the study's *reliability*. The researchers wanted results that would be consistent if others were to *replicate*, or repeat, the study.

As an operational definition, the researchers used "literally homeless," people "who do not have access to a conventional dwelling and who would be homeless by any conceivable definition of the term." With funds limited, the researchers couldn't do a national count, but they could count the homeless in Chicago.

By using a *stratified random sample*, the researchers were able to generalize to the entire city. How could they do this, since there is no list of the homeless? They did have a list of the city's shelters and a map of the city. A stratified random sample of the city's shelters gave them access to the homeless who sleep in the shelters. For those who sleep in the streets, parks, and vacant buildings, they used a stratified random sample of different city blocks.

Their findings? On an average night, 2,722 people are homeless in Chicago. Because people move in and out of homelessness, between 5,000 and 7,000 are homeless at some point during the year. On warm nights, only two out of five sleep in the shelters, and even during Chicago's cold winters, only three out of four do so. Seventy-five percent are men, and 60 percent are African Americans. One in four is a former mental patient, one in five a former prisoner. Projecting these findings to the United States yields a national total of about 350,000 homeless people.

The homeless, who used to be rare, have become a common sight in U.S. cities. The text describes how counting the homeless landed some sociologists in the midst of controversy.

This total elated government officials and stunned the homeless advocates. The advocates said that the number couldn't possibly be right, and they began to snipe at the researchers. This is one of the risks of doing research: Sociologists never know whose toes they will step on. The sniping made the researchers uncomfortable, and to let everyone know they weren't trying to minimize the problem, they stressed that these 350,000 Americans live desperate lives. They sleep on city streets, live in shelters, eat out of garbage cans, and suffer from severe health problems.

The controversy continues. With funding at stake for shelters and for treating mental problems and substance abuse, homeless advocates continue to insist that at least 2 million Americans are homeless. While the total is not in the millions, it has doubled recently to 650,000 or so, with over a million people using shelters during the course of a year. With the economic crisis, more families are homeless.

Sources: Based on Anderson 1986; Rossi 1989, 1991, 1999; National Coalition for the Homeless 2008; HUD 2012.

Gender in Sociological Research

5.5 Explain how gender is significant in sociological research.

You know how significant gender is in your own life, how it affects your orientations and attitudes. Because gender is also influential in social research, researchers take steps to prevent it from biasing their findings (Davis et al. 2009). For example, sociologists Diana Scully and Joseph Marolla (1984, 2014) interviewed convicted rapists in prison. They were concerned that gender might lead to *interviewer bias*—that the prisoners might shift their answers, sharing certain experiences or opinions with Marolla but saying something else to Scully. To prevent gender bias, each researcher interviewed half the sample. Later in this chapter, we'll look at what they found.

Gender certainly can be an impediment in research. In our imagined research on spouse abuse, for example, could a man even do participant observation of women who have been beaten by their husbands? Technically, the answer is yes. But because the women have been victimized by men, they might be less likely to share their experiences and feelings with men. If so, women would be better suited to conduct this research, more likely to achieve valid results. The supposition that these victims will be more open with women than with men, however, is just that—a supposition. Research alone would verify or refute this assumption.

Read on **MySocLab**
Document: Fraternities and Collegiate Rape Culture: Why Are Some Fraternities More Dangerous Places for Women?

Gender is significant in other ways, too. In the past, when almost all sociologists were men, women's experiences were neglected. Women's and men's lives differ significantly, and if we do research on just half of humanity, our research will be vastly incomplete. Today's huge number of female sociologists guarantees that women are not ignored in social research.

Gender issues can pop up in unexpected ways in sociological research. I vividly recall an incident in San Francisco.

> *The streets were getting dark, and I was still looking for homeless people. When I saw someone lying down, curled up in a doorway, I approached the individual. As I got close, I began my opening research line, "Hi, I'm Dr. Henslin from. . . ." The individual began to scream and started to thrash her arms and legs. Startled by this sudden, high-pitched scream and by the rapid movements, I quickly backed away. When I later analyzed what had happened, I concluded that I had intruded into a woman's bedroom.*

This incident also holds another lesson. Researchers do their best, but they make mistakes. Sometimes these mistakes are minor, even humorous. The woman sleeping in the doorway wasn't frightened. It was only just getting dark, and there were many people on the street. She was just assertively marking her territory and letting me know in no uncertain terms that I was an intruder. If we make a mistake in research, we pick up and go on. As we do so, we take ethical considerations into account, which is the topic of our next section.

Ethics in Sociological Research

5.6 Explain why it is vital for sociologists to protect the people they study; discuss the two cases that are presented.

In addition to choosing an appropriate research method, we must also follow the ethics of sociology (American Sociological Association 1999; Joungtrakul and Allen 2012). Research ethics require honesty, truth, and openness (sharing findings with the scientific community). Ethics clearly forbid the falsification of results. Rules also condemn plagiarism—that is, stealing someone else's work. Another ethical guideline states that, generally, people should be informed that they are being studied and that they never should be harmed by the research. Sociologists are also required to protect the anonymity of those who provide information. Sometimes people reveal things that are intimate, potentially embarrassing, or otherwise harmful to themselves or others. Finally, although not all sociologists agree, it generally is considered unethical for researchers to misrepresent themselves.

Sociologists take their ethical standards seriously. To illustrate the extent to which they will go to protect their respondents, consider the research conducted by Mario Brajuha.

Ethics in social research are of vital concern to sociologists. As discussed in the text, sociologists may disagree on some of the issue's finer points, but none would approve of slipping LSD to unsuspecting subjects like this Marine. This was done to U.S. soldiers in the 1960s under the guise of legitimate testing—just "to see what would happen."

Protecting the Subjects: The Brajuha Research

Mario Brajuha, a graduate student at the State University of New York at Stony Brook, was doing participant observation of restaurant workers. He lost his job as a waiter when the restaurant where he was working burned down—a fire of "suspicious origin," as the police said. When detectives learned that Brajuha had taken field notes, they asked to see them (Brajuha and Hallowell 1986). Because he had promised to keep the information confidential, Brajuha refused to hand them over. When the district attorney subpoenaed the notes, Brajuha still refused. The district attorney then threatened to put Brajuha in jail. By this time, Brajuha's notes had become rather famous, and unsavory characters—perhaps those who had set the fire—also wanted to know what was in them. They, too, demanded to see them, accompanying their demands with threats of a different nature. Brajuha found himself between a rock and a hard place.

For two years, Brajuha refused to hand over his notes, even though he grew anxious and had to appear at several court hearings. Finally, the district attorney dropped the subpoena. When the two men under investigation for setting the fire died, the threats to Brajuha, his wife, and their children ended.

Sociologists applaud the way Brajuha protected his respondents and the professional manner in which he handled himself.

Misleading the Subjects: The Humphreys Research

Another ethical problem involves what you tell participants about your research. Although it is considered acceptable for sociologists to do covert participant observation (studying some situation without announcing that they are doing research), to misrepresent oneself is considered unethical. Let's look at the case of Laud Humphreys, whose research forced sociologists to rethink and refine their ethical stance.

Laud Humphreys, a classmate of mine at Washington University in St. Louis, was an Episcopal priest who decided to become a sociologist. For his Ph.D. dissertation, Humphreys (1970/1975) studied social interaction in "tearooms," public restrooms where some men go for quick, anonymous oral sex with other men.

Humphreys found that some restrooms in Forest Park, just across from our campus, were tearooms. He began a participant observation study by hanging around these restrooms. He found that in addition to the two men having sex, a third man—called a "watch queen"—served as a lookout for police and other unwelcome strangers. Humphreys took on the role of watch queen, not only watching for strangers but also observing what the men did. He wrote field notes after the encounters.

Humphreys decided that he wanted to learn about the regular lives of these men. For example, what was the significance of the wedding rings that many of the men wore? He came up with an ingenious technique: Many of the men parked their cars near the tearooms, and Humphreys recorded their license plate numbers. A friend in the St. Louis police department gave Humphreys each man's address. About a year later, Humphreys arranged for these men to be included in a medical survey conducted by some of the sociologists on our faculty.

Disguising himself with a different hairstyle and clothing, Humphreys visited the men at home, supposedly to interview them for the medical study. He found that they led conventional lives. They voted, mowed their lawns, and took their kids to Little League games. Many reported that their wives were not aroused sexually or were afraid of getting pregnant because their religion did not allow birth control. Humphreys concluded that heterosexual men were also using the tearooms for a form of quick sex.

This research stirred controversy among sociologists and nonsociologists alike. Many sociologists criticized Humphreys, and a national columnist even wrote a scathing denunciation of "sociological snoopers" (Von Hoffman 1970). One of our professors even tried to get Humphreys' Ph.D. revoked. (This professor also hit Humphreys and kicked him after he was down—but that is another story.) As the controversy heated up and a court case loomed, Humphreys feared that his list of respondents might be subpoenaed. He gave me the list to take from Missouri to Illinois, where I had begun teaching. When he called and asked me to destroy it, I burned the list in my backyard.

Was this research ethical? This question is not decided easily. Although many sociologists sided with Humphreys—and his book reporting the research won a highly acclaimed award—the criticisms continued. At first, Humphreys defended his position vigorously, but five years later, in a second edition of his book (1975), he stated that he should have identified himself as a researcher.

How Research and Theory Work Together

5.7 Explain how research and theory work together in sociology.

Research cannot stand alone. Nor can theory. As sociologist C. Wright Mills (1959) argued so forcefully, research without theory is simply a collection of unrelated "facts." But theory without research, Mills added, is abstract and empty—it can't represent the way life really is.

Watch on **MySocLab**
Video: Sociological Theory and Research: The Basics

Research and theory, then, are both essential for sociology. Every theory must be tested, which requires research. And as sociologists do research, often coming up with surprising findings, those results must be explained: For this, we need theory. As sociologists study social life, then, they combine research and theory.

The Real World: When the Ideal Meets the Real

Although we can list the ideals of research, real-life situations often force sociologists to settle for something that falls short of the ideal. In the following Thinking Critically section, let's look at how two sociologists confronted the ideal and the real.

THINKING CRITICALLY

Are Rapists Sick? A Close-Up View of Research

Two sociologists, Diana Scully and Joseph Marolla, whose research was mentioned earlier, were not satisfied with the typical explanation that rapists are "sick," psychologically disturbed, or different mentally from other men. They developed the hypothesis that rape is like most human behavior—learned through interaction with others. That is, some men learn to think of rape as acceptable behavior.

To test this hypothesis, it would be best to interview a random sample of rapists. But this is impossible. There is no list of all rapists, so there is no way to give them all the same chance of being included in a sample. You can't even use prison populations to select a random sample, since many rapists have never been caught. And as we know from DNA testing, some men who have been convicted of rape are innocent. Scully and Marolla confronted the classic dilemma of sociologists—either to not do the research or to do it under less than ideal conditions.

They chose to do the research. When they had the opportunity to interview convicted rapists in prison, they jumped at it (Marolla and Scully 1986; Scully 1990; Scully and Marolla 1984, 2014). They knew that whatever they learned would be more than we already knew. They sent letters to 3,500 men serving time in seven prisons in Virginia, the state where they were teaching. About 25 percent of the prisoners agreed to be interviewed. The researchers matched these men on the basis of age, education, race–ethnicity, severity of offense, and previous criminal record. Their sample consisted of 98 prisoners who had been convicted of rape and a control sample of 75 men convicted of other crimes.

As mentioned, because the sex of the interviewer can bias research results, Scully and Marolla each interviewed half the sample. It took them 600 hours to gather information on the prisoners, including their psychological, criminal, and sexual history. To guard against lies, they checked what the individuals told them against their institutional records. They used twelve scales to measure the men's attitudes about women, rape, and themselves. In order to find out what circumstances the men defined as rape or when they viewed the victim as responsible, they also gave the men nine vignettes of forced sexual encounters and asked them to determine responsibility in each one.

Scully and Marolla discovered something that goes against common sense—that the psychological histories of the rapists and the nonrapists were similar. The rapists were neither sick nor had they been overwhelmed by uncontrollable urges. These men raped for a variety of reasons: to "blow off steam" over problems they were having with others, to get sex, to feel powerful, and to hurt women (Monahan et al. 2005). Some men raped spontaneously, while others planned their rapes. Some raped as a form of revenge, to get even with someone, although not necessarily their victim. For some, rape was a form of recreation, and they raped with friends on weekends.

Scully and Marolla also found support for what feminists had been pointing out for years, that power is a major element in rape. Here is what one man said:

> *Rape gave me the power to do what I wanted to do without feeling I had to please a partner or respond to a partner. I felt in control, dominant. Rape was the ability to have sex without caring about the woman's response. I was totally dominant.*

To discover that most rape is calculated behavior—that rapists are not "sick"; that a motivating force can be power, not passion; that the behavior stems from the criminal pursuit of pleasure, not from mental illness—is significant. It makes the sociological quest worthwhile.

Connecting Research and Theory

Watch on **MySocLab** **Video:** Sociology on the Job: Sociological Theory and Research

Some researchers have even interviewed rapists who have not been arrested (Jewkes 2012). Here are some of the patterns that are emerging from this research: hostility to women, cynicism about intimacy, sexual conquest as a source of self-esteem, and trauma during childhood. As indicated in Figure 5.1 on page 126, research stimulates both the development of theory and the need for more research. The theory and research that develop in this area may provide the basis for making changes that reduce rape. ■

Sociology needs more of this type of research—imaginative and sometimes daring investigations conducted under less than ideal conditions. This is really what sociology is all about. Sociologists study what people do—whether their behaviors are conforming or deviant, whether they please others or disgust them. No matter what behavior is studied, these research methods and the application of social theory take us beyond common sense. They allow us to penetrate surface realities so we can better understand human behavior. In the ideal case, they also serve as tools to make changes that help improve social life.

MySocLab

Study and **Review** on **MySocLab**

CHAPTER 5 Summary and Review

What Is a Valid Sociological Topic?

5.1 State what topics are valid for sociologists to study.

Any human behavior is a valid sociological topic, even disreputable behavior. Spouse abuse is an example. P. 125

Common Sense and the Need for Sociological Research

5.2 Explain why common sense can't replace sociological research.

Why isn't common sense adequate?

Common sense doesn't provide reliable information. When subjected to scientific research, commonsense ideas often are found to be limited or false. Pp. 125–126

A Research Model

5.3 Know the 8 steps of the research model.

What are the eight basic steps of sociological research?

(1) Selecting a topic, (2) Defining the problem, (3) Reviewing the literature, (4) Formulating a **hypothesis**, (5) Choosing a research method, (6) Collecting the data, (7) Analyzing the results, and (8) Sharing the results. These steps are explained in detail on pages 126–129.

Research Methods (Designs)

5.4 Know the main elements of the 7 research methods: surveys, participant observation, case studies, secondary analysis, analysis of documents, experiments, and unobtrusive measures; state why sociological research can lead to controversy.

How do sociologists gather data?

To collect data, sociologists use seven **research methods** (or research designs): **surveys**, **participant observation** (fieldwork), **case studies**, **secondary analysis**, **documents**, **experiments**, and **unobtrusive measures**. Pp. 129–137

How do sociologists choose a research method?

Sociologists choose their research method based on questions to be answered, their access to potential subjects, the resources available, and their training. The text explains each of the seven. Pp. 137–138

Controversy in Sociological Research

Why is sociological research often controversial?

There are two basic reasons that sociological research upsets people. Sociologists continuously probe below surface realities, which threatens people's interests. They also explore private or intimate areas of life. P. 138

Gender in Sociological Research

5.5 Explain how gender is significant in sociological research.

What is the relationship between gender and research?

Gender can affect research in two basic ways. The first is in doing research. Participants can shape their responses based on the gender of the researcher. The second is research findings. If a sample consists of only one sex, the results will not necessarily apply to the other sex. P. 139

Ethics in Sociological Research

5.6 Explain why it is vital for sociologists to protect the people they study; discuss the two cases that are presented.

How important are ethics in sociological research?

Ethics are of fundamental concern to sociologists, who are committed to openness, honesty, truth, and protecting their subjects from harm. The Brajuha research on restaurant workers and the Humphreys research on "tearooms" were cited to illustrate ethical issues that concern sociologists. Pp. 139–141

How Research and Theory Work Together

5.7 Explain how research and theory work together in sociology.

What is the relationship between theory and research?

Theory and research depend on one another. Theory generates questions that need to be answered by research, and sociologists use theory to interpret the data they gather. Research, in turn, helps to generate theory: Findings that don't match what is expected can indicate a need to modify theory. Pp. 141–142

Thinking Critically about Chapter 5

1. Should sociologists be allowed to do research on disreputable or disapproved behavior? On illegal behavior? Why or why not?
2. What are the differences between good and bad sociological research? How can biases be avoided?
3. What ethics govern sociological research?
4. Do you think that it is right (or ethical) for sociologists to not identity themselves when they do research? To misrepresent themselves? What if identifying themselves as researchers will destroy their access to a research setting or to informants?

Societies to Social Networks

6 CHAPTER

Listen to Chapter 6 on MySocLab

When Kody Scott joined the L.A. Crips, *his initiation had two parts. Here's the first:*

"How old is you now anyway?"

"Eleven, but I'll be twelve in November."

I never saw the blow to my head come from Huck. Bam! And I was on all fours. . . . Kicked in the stomach, I was on my back counting stars in the blackness. A solid blow to my chest exploded pain on the blank screen that had now become my mind. Bam! Blows rained on me from every direction. . . .

Then I just started swinging, with no style or finesse, just anger and the instinct to survive. . . . [This] reflected my ability to represent the set [gang] in hand-to-hand combat. The blows stopped abruptly. . . . My ear was bleeding, and my neck and face were deep red. . . .

Scott's beating was followed immediately by the second part of his initiation. For this, he received the name *Monster*, which he carried proudly:

"Give Kody the pump" [12-gauge pump action shotgun] . . . "Tonight we gonna rock they world." . . . Hand slaps were passed around the room. . . . "Kody, you got eight shots, you don't come back to the car unless they all are gone."

"Righteous," I said, eager to show my worth. . . .

Hanging close to buildings, houses, and bushes, we made our way, one after the other, to within spitting distance of the Bloods. . . . Huck and Fly stepped from the shadows simultaneously. . . . Boom! Boom! Heavy bodies hitting the ground, confusion, yells of dismay, running. . . . By my sixth shot I had advanced past the first fallen bodies and into the street in pursuit of those who had sought refuge behind cars and trees. . . .

Back in the shack we smoked more pot and drank more beer. . . .

Tray Ball said, "You got potential, 'cause you eager to learn. Bangin' [being a gang member] ain't no part-time thang, it's full-time, it's a career. . . . It's gettin' caught and not tellin'. Killin' and not caring, and dyin' without fear. It's love for your set and hate for the enemy. You hear what I'm sayin'?"

"Bangin'. . . . It's gettin' caught and not tellin'. Killin' and not caring, and dyin' without fear."

Kody adds this insightful remark:

. . . The supreme sacrifice was to "take a bullet for a homie" [fellow gang member]. Nothing held a light to the power of the set. If you died on the trigger you surely were smiled upon by the Crip God.

Excerpts from Scott 1994:8–13, 103.

Could you be like Kody and shoot strangers in cold blood—just because others tell you to pull the trigger? Although none of us want to think that we could, don't bet on it. In this chapter, you are going to read some surprising things about **groups**—people who interact with one another and who think of themselves as belonging together. As we move into this topic, let's first look at the big picture, how societies have changed over time.

Learning Objectives

After you have read this chapter, you should be able to:

6.1 Summarize the main characteristics of these types of societies: hunting and gathering, pastoral and horticultural, agricultural, industrial, postindustrial, and biotech. (p. 145)

6.2 Discuss the main characteristics of primary groups, secondary groups, in-groups and out-groups, reference groups, and social networks. (p. 152)

6.3 Be familiar with the effects of group size on stability, intimacy, attitudes, and behavior; types and styles of leaders; the Asch experiment on peer pressure; the Milgram experiment on authority; and the implications of groupthink. (p. 158)

group people who have something in common and who believe that what they have in common is significant; also called a *social group*

society people who share a culture and a territory

Societies and Their Transformation

6.1 Summarize the main characteristics of these types of societies: hunting and gathering, pastoral and horticultural, agricultural, industrial, postindustrial, and biotech.

The largest and most complex group that sociologists study is **society**, which consists of people who share a culture and a territory. Society, which surrounds us, sets the stage for our life experiences. *The sociological principle is that the type of society we live in is the fundamental reason for why we become who we are.* Not only does our society

As society—the largest and most complex type of group—changes, so, too, do the groups, activities, and, ultimately, the type of people who form that society. This photo is of Susi Kentikian and Sanae Jah in a world championship bout in Dusseldorf, Germany. What social changes can you identify from this photo?

lay the broad framework for our behavior, but it also influences the ways we think and feel. Its effects are so significant that if you had grown up in a different society, you would be a different type of person.

To see how our society developed, look at Figure 6.1. You can see that technology is the key to understanding the sweeping changes that produced our society. Let's review these broad changes. As we do, picture yourself as a member of each society. Consider how your life—even your thoughts and values—would be different as a member of these societies.

FIGURE 6.1 The Social Transformations of Society

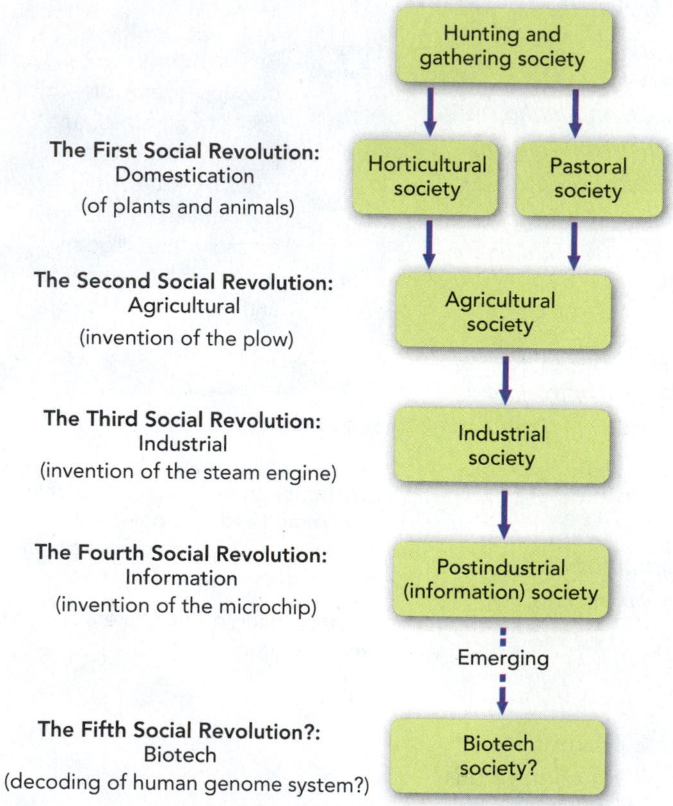

Note: Not all the world's societies will go through the transformations shown in this figure. Whether any hunting and gathering societies will survive, however, remains to be seen. A few might, perhaps kept on small "reserves" that will be off limits to developers—but open to guided "ethnotours" at a hefty fee.

Source: By the author.

Hunting and Gathering Societies

The members of **hunting and gathering societies** have few social divisions and little inequality. As the name implies, in order to survive, these groups depend on hunting animals and gathering plants. In some groups, the men do the hunting, and the women the gathering. In others, both men and women (and children) gather plants, the men hunt large animals, and both men and women hunt small animals. The groups usually have a **shaman**, an individual thought to be able to influence spiritual forces, but shamans, too, must help obtain food. Although these groups give greater prestige to the men hunters, who supply most of the meat, the women gatherers contribute about three-fourths of their total food supply (Hansen et al. 2012).

Because a region cannot support a large number of people who hunt animals and gather plants (group members do not plant—they only gather what is already there), hunting and gathering societies are small. They usually consist of only twenty-five to forty people. These groups are nomadic. As their food supply dwindles in one area, they move to another location. They place high value on sharing food, which is essential to their survival. Because of disease, drought, and pestilence, children have only about a fifty-fifty chance of surviving to adulthood (Lenski and Lenski 1987).

Of all societies, hunters and gatherers are the most egalitarian. Because what they hunt and gather is perishable, the people accumulate few personal possessions. Consequently, no one becomes wealthier than anyone else. There are no rulers, and most decisions are arrived at through discussion. Because their needs are basic and they do not work to store up material possessions, hunters and gatherers have the most leisure of all human groups (Sahlins 1972; Volti 1995).

As in the photo on the next page, all human groups were once hunters and gatherers. Until several hundred years ago, these societies were common, but only about 300 remain today (Stiles 2003). Some were wiped out when different groups took over their lands. Others moved to villages and took up a new way of life. The hunting and gathering groups that remain include the pygmies of central Africa, the aborigines of Australia, and various groups in South America.

shaman a tribe's healing specialist who attempts to control the spirits thought to cause a disease

hunting and gathering society a human group that depends on hunting and gathering for its survival

With today's expanding populations, these groups seem doomed to a similar fate, with their way of life disappearing from the human scene (Lenski and Lenski 1987; Bearak 2010).

pastoral society a society based on the pasturing of animals

Pastoral and Horticultural Societies

About ten thousand years ago, some groups found that they could tame and breed some of the animals they hunted—primarily goats, sheep, cattle, and camels. Others discovered that they could cultivate plants. As a result, hunting and gathering societies branched into two directions, each with different means of acquiring food.

The key to understanding the first branching is the word pasture; **pastoral societies** are based on the *pasturing of animals.* Pastoral (or herding) societies developed in regions where low rainfall made it impractical to build life around growing crops. Groups that took this turn remained nomadic: They follow their animals to fresh pasture. The key to understanding the second branching is the word *horticulture,* or plant cultivation. **Horticultural** (or gardening) **societies** are based on the *cultivation of plants by the use of hand tools.* Because they no longer had to abandon an area as the food supply gave out, these groups developed permanent settlements.

We can call the domestication of animals and plants the *first social revolution.* As shown in Figure 6.2, the **domestication revolution** changed human history. The changes, which occurred over thousands of years, touched almost every aspect of human life.

The simplest forms of societies are called hunting and gathering societies. Members of these societies have adapted well to their environments, and they have more leisure than the members of other societies. Not many hunting and gathering groups remain on earth. This Peul woman of Chad is moving her home.

FIGURE 6.2
Consequences of Animal Domestication and Plant Cultivation

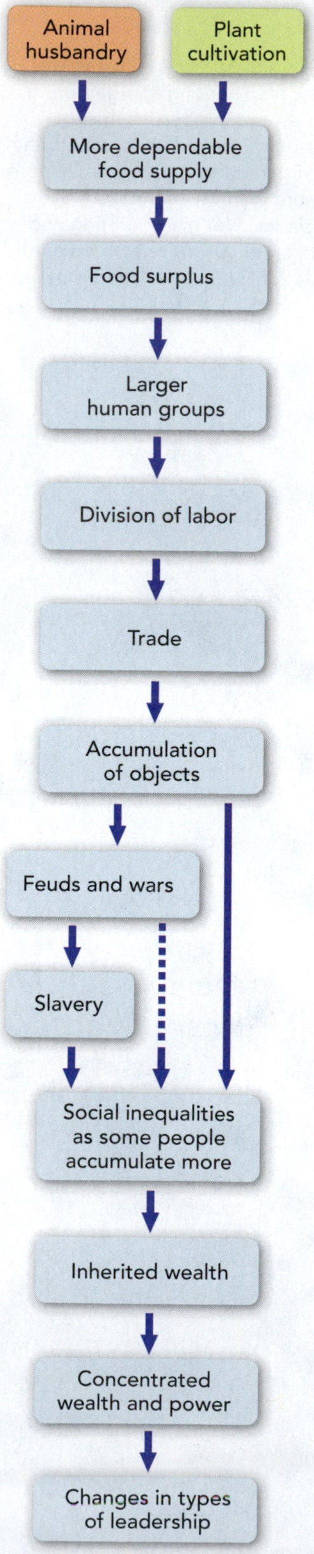

Source: By the author.

The more dependable food supply allowed groups to grow larger. With it no longer necessary for everyone to work at providing food, a *division of labor* developed. Some people began to make jewelry, others tools, others weapons, and so on. This led to a surplus of objects, which, in turn, stimulated trade. As groups traded with one another, they began to accumulate objects they prized, such as gold, jewelry, and utensils.

From Figure 6.2, you can see how these changes led to *social inequality*. Some families (or clans) acquired more goods than others. This led to feuds and war: Groups now possessed animals, pastures, croplands, jewelry, and other material goods to fight about. War, in turn, opened the door to slavery, since people found it convenient to let captives do the drudge work. Social inequality remained limited, however, because the surplus itself was limited. But as individuals passed their possessions on to their descendants, wealth grew more concentrated. So did power, and for the first time, some individuals became chiefs.

Note the pattern that runs through this transformation: *the change from fewer to more possessions and from more to less equality*. Just as it is now, where people were located *within* the hierarchy of a society became vital for determining what happened to them in life.

Agricultural Societies

The invention of the plow about five or six thousand years ago once again changed social life forever. Compared with hoes and digging sticks, using animals to pull plows is immensely more efficient. Plowing the earth returned more nutrients to the soil, making the land more productive. The food surplus of the **agricultural revolution** was unlike anything ever seen in human history. It allowed even more people to engage in activities other than farming. In this new **agricultural society**, people developed cities and what is popularly known as "culture," activities such as philosophy, art, music, literature, and architecture. Accompanied by other fundamental inventions, like the wheel, writing, and numbers, the changes were so profound that this period is sometimes referred to as "the dawn of civilization."

The social inequality of pastoral and horticultural societies turned out to be only a hint of what was to come. When some people managed to gain control of the growing surplus of resources in agricultural societies, *inequality became a fundamental feature of life in society*. To protect their expanding privileges and power, this elite surrounded itself with armed men. This small group even levied taxes on others, who now had become their "subjects." As conflict theorists point out, this concentration of resources and power—along with the oppression of people not in power—was the forerunner of the state.

No one knows exactly how it happened, but during this period, females also became subject to males. Sociologist Elise Boulding (1976) theorizes that this change occurred because men were in charge of plowing and the cows. She suggests that when metals were developed, men took on the new job of attaching the metal as tips to the wooden plows and doing the plowing. As a result,

> *the shift of the status of the woman farmer may have happened quite rapidly, once there were two male specializations relating to agriculture: plowing and the care of cattle. This situation left women with all the subsidiary tasks, including weeding and carrying water to the fields. The new fields were larger, so women had to work just as many hours as they did before, but now they worked at more secondary tasks. . . . This would contribute further to the erosion of the status of women.*

This explanation, however, raises more questions than it answers. Why, for example, did men take over metal work and plowing? Why didn't women? It also does not account for why men control societies in which women are in charge of the cattle. In short, we are left in the dark as to why and how men became dominant, a reason likely to remain lost in human history. This leaves us a topic perfect for endless speculation, as we try to tie together different strands of history. What do you think? We'll explore more theories in Chapter 11.

Industrial Societies

The *third* social revolution also turned society upside down. The **Industrial Revolution** began in Great Britain in 1765 when the steam engine was first used to run machinery. Before this, a few machines (such as windmills and water wheels) had helped to harness nature, but most machines depended on human and animal power. The resulting **industrial society** is defined by sociologist Herbert Blumer (1990) as one in which goods are produced by machines powered by fuels, instead of by the brute force of humans or animals.

The efficiency of the steam engine, greater than anything that preceded it, was another push toward even more social inequality. The cities held massive supplies of desperate labor, people who had been thrown off the lands that their ancestors had farmed as tenants for centuries. Homeless, they faced the choices of stealing, starving, or being paid the equivalent of a loaf of bread for a day of work. Some of the men who first harnessed the steam engine and employed these desperate workers accumulated such wealth that their riches outran the imaginations of royalty.

Workers had few legal rights. They could not unionize, and they didn't even have the right to safe working conditions. If workers protested, they were fired. If they returned to the factory, they were arrested for trespassing on private property. Strikes were illegal, and strikers were arrested—or beaten by the employer's private security force. During the early 1900s, some U.S. strikers were shot by private police and even by the National Guard. Against these odds, workers gradually won their fight to unionize and to improve their working conditions.

Industrialization brought an abundance of goods, and as workers won what we call basic rights, a surprising change occurred—*the pattern of growing inequality was reversed.* Home ownership became common, as did the ownership of automobiles and an incredible variety of consumer goods. Today's typical worker enjoys a high standard of living in terms of health care, food, housing, material possessions, and access to libraries and education. On an even broader scale of growing equality came the abolition of slavery, the shift from monarchies to more representative political systems, greater rights for women and minorities, and the rights to vote, to a jury trial, and to cross-examine witnesses. A recent extension of these equalities is the right to set up your own Internet blog where you can bemoan life in your school or criticize the president.

Postindustrial (Information) Societies

If you were to choose one word to characterize our society, what would it be? Of the many candidates, the word *change* would have to rank high. The primary source of the sweeping changes that are transforming our lives is the development of technology centering on the microchip. The change is so vast that sociologists say that a new type of society has emerged. They call it the **postindustrial** (or **information**) **society.**

What are the main characteristics of this new society? Unlike industrial society, its hallmark is not turning raw materials into products. Rather, its basic component is *information.* Teachers pass knowledge on to students, while lawyers sell their specialized understanding of law, physicians their expertise on the body, bankers their skills with money, and interior decorators their ideas regarding color schemes. Unlike the factory workers of an industrial society, these individuals don't *produce* anything. Rather, they transmit or apply information to provide services that others are willing to pay for.

The United States was the first country to have more than half of its workers in service industries: banking, counseling, education, entertainment, government, health, insurance, law, mass media, research, and sales. Australia, Japan, New Zealand, and

horticultural society a society based on cultivating plants by the use of hand tools

domestication revolution the first social revolution, based on the domestication of plants and animals, which led to pastoral and horticultural societies

agricultural revolution the second social revolution, based on the invention of the plow, which led to agricultural societies

agricultural society a society based on large-scale agriculture

Industrial Revolution the third social revolution, occurring when machines powered by fuels replaced most animal and human power

industrial society a society based on the harnessing of machines powered by fuels

postindustrial (information) society a society based on information, services, and high technology, rather than on raw materials and manufacturing western Europe soon followed. This trend away from manufacturing and toward selling information and services shows no sign of letting up.

The changes are so profound that they have led to a *fourth social revolution*. The surface changes of this new technology are obvious. Our purchases are scanned and billed in some remote place. While we ride in cars, trucks, boats, and airplanes, we can call home or talk to people on the other side of the globe. We probe remote regions of space and examine the surface of Mars. We pay out billions of dollars on Internet purchases, and millions of children (and adults) spend countless hours battling virtual video villains. Beyond these surface changes, the microchip is transforming relations among people. It is also uprooting our old perspectives and replacing them with new ones. In the Sociology and the New Technology box on the next page, we explore an extreme aspect of virtual reality.

Watch on **MySocLab**
Video: A Society of Consumers

Biotech Societies: Is a New Type of Society Emerging?

- Tobacco that fights cancer. ("Yes, smoke your way to health!")
- Tobacco that stops rabies. ("Dog bite you? Smoke our brand.")
- Corn that blocks herpes and prevents pregnancy. ("Cornflakes in the morning—and safe sex all day!")
- Goats' milk that contains spider silk to make body armor. ("Got milk? The best bulletproofing.")
- Part-human animals that produce medicines for humans. ("Ah, those liver secretions. Good for what ails you.")
- Bacteria that excrete diesel fuel. ("Put our germ droppings in your gas tank.")

I know that such products sound like science fiction, but we *already* have the goats that can make body armor. Human genes have been inserted into animals, and they do produce medicine (Kristoff 2002; Osborne 2002; Cowan 2010). We already have the bacteria that produce diesel fuel, but it isn't harvestable yet (Yarris 2012). And through the magic of biotransgenics, those nasty, death-producing cigarettes are being transformed into health aides (Saidak 2013).

The changes swirling around us are so extensive that we may be stepping into a new type of society. If so, the economy of this new **biotech society** will center on applying and altering genetic structures—both plant and animal—to produce food, medicine, and materials.

If there is a new society—and this is not certain—when did it begin? There are no firm edges to new societies, as each new one overlaps the one it is replacing. The opening to a biotech society could have been 1953, when Francis Crick and James Watson identified the double-helix structure of DNA. Or perhaps historians will trace the date to the decoding of the human genome in 2001.

Whether the changes that are engulfing our lives are part of a new type of society or just a continuation of the one before it is not the main point. Keep your eye on the *sociological significance of these changes: As society is transformed, it sweeps us along with it. The transformation we are experiencing is so fundamental that it will change even the ways we think about the self and life.* We might even see changes in the human species, an implication of the Sociology and the New Technology box on page 152.

In Sum: Each society sets boundaries around its members. Its framework of statuses, roles, groups, and social institutions establishes the prevailing behaviors and beliefs. These factors, along with social inequality, set the stage for relationships between men and women, racial–ethnic groups, the young and the elderly, the rich and the poor, and so on.

Consider how your life would be different if you lived in a hunting and gathering society. On the obvious level: You would not be listening to your favorite music, watching TV, playing video games—or taking this course. On a deeper level: You would not feel the same about life, have the beliefs you now have, or hold your particular aspirations for the future. Actually, no aspect of your life would be the same. You

biotech society a society whose economy increasingly centers on modifying genetics to produce food, medicine, and materials would be locked into the attitudes and views that come with a hunting and gathering way of life.

Introducing you to these major historical shifts in societies is just the beginning of what we want to do in this chapter. The goal is to help you understand how groups influence your life. So let's continue.

Sociology and the New Technology

Avatar Fantasy Life: The Blurring Lines of Reality

Dissatisfied with your current life? Would you like to become someone else? Maybe someone rich? You can. Join a world populated with virtual people and live out your fantasy.

Second Life and other Internet sites that offer an alternative virtual reality have exploded in popularity. Of the 27 million "residents" of *Second Life*, 450,000 spend twenty to forty hours a week in their alternative life (Alter 2007; "Second Life . . . " 2012).

To start your second life, select an avatar to be your persona in this virtual world. Your avatar, a kind of digital hand puppet, comes in just a basic form, although you can control its movements just fine. But that bare body certainly won't do. You will want to clothe it. For this, you have your choice of outfits for every occasion. Although you buy them from other avatars in virtual stores, you have to spend real dollars. You might want some hair, too. For that, too, you'll have your choice of designers. And again, you'll spend real dollars. And you might want to have a sex organ. There is even a specialty store for that.

A participant in Second Life posing next to her virtual self, her avatar, Misty Rhodes.

All equipped the way you want to be?

Then it is time to meet other avatars, the virtual personas of real-life people. As you interact with them in this virtual world, you will be able to share stories, talk about your desires in life, and have drinks in virtual bars. You can also buy property and open businesses.

Avatars flirt, too. Some even date and marry.

For most people, this second life is just an interesting game. They come and go, as if playing *Tomb Raider* or *World of Warcraft* now and then. Some people, though, get caught up in their virtual world. For some, everyday life shrinks in appeal, and they neglect friends and family. The virtual displaces the real, with the real fading into nonreality.

Ric Hoogestraat in Phoenix, Arizona, operates his avatar, Dutch—a macho motorcycle man, who is also filthy rich—from the time he gets up to the time he goes to bed. Dutch visits his several homes, where he can lounge on specially designed furniture. He pours his favorite drink and, from his penthouse, watches the sun setting over the ocean (Alter 2007).

Dutch met his wife, Tenaj, on *Second Life*. As courtships go, theirs went well. When they announced their wedding, about twenty avatar friends attended. They gave the newlyweds real congratulations, in a virtual sort of way.

Dutch and Tenaj have two dogs and pay the mortgage together. They love cuddling and intimate talks. Their love life is quite good, as avatars can have virtual sex.

But then there is Sue, who is not pleased that Ric spends so much time in his virtual world. Sue feels neglected. And she doesn't appreciate Tenaj. Sue, you see, is also Ric's wife, but in real life.

She says that the whole thing has become more than a little irritating. "I'll try to talk to him or bring him a drink, and he'll be having sex with a cartoon," she says.

The real life counterpart of Tenaj, the avatar, is Janet, who lives in Canada. Ric and Janet have never met—nor do they plan to meet. They haven't even talked on the phone as Ric and Janet—just a lot of sweet talking in their virtual world as Dutch and Tenaj.

For gamers, the virtual always overlaps the real to some extent, but for some, the virtual overwhelms the real. A couple from South Korea even let their 3-month-old daughter starve to death while they nurtured a virtual daughter online (Frayer 2010).

For Your Consideration

➤ How much time do you spend on computer games? Are you involved in any virtual reality? Do you think that Ric is cheating on Sue? (One wife divorced her husband when she caught a glimpse of his avatar having sex with an avatar prostitute ["Second Life Affair . . . " 2008].) Other than the sexual aspect, is having a second life really any different from people's involvement in fantasy football? (Keep in mind the term *football widows*.)

Sociology and the New Technology

"So, You Want to Be Yourself?" Cloning and the Future of Society

No type of society ends abruptly. The edges are fuzzy, as the old merges into the new. With time speeded up, our information society hasn't even matured, and it looks as though a biotech society is hard on its heels. Let's try to peer over the edge of today's society to glimpse the one that might be pressing in on us. If it arrives, what will life be like? We could examine many issues, but since space is limited, let's consider just one: cloning. Since human embryos have been cloned, it seems inevitable that some group somewhere will complete the process. If cloning humans becomes routine—well, consider these two scenarios:

It turns out that you can't have children. You go to your area's cloning clinic, pay the standard fee, and clone yourself. But is that little boy or girl, in effect, yourself as a child? Or instead of a daughter or son, is this child your sister or brother?

Or suppose that you love your mother dearly, and she is dying. With her permission, you decide to clone her. Who is the clone? Would you be rearing your own mother?

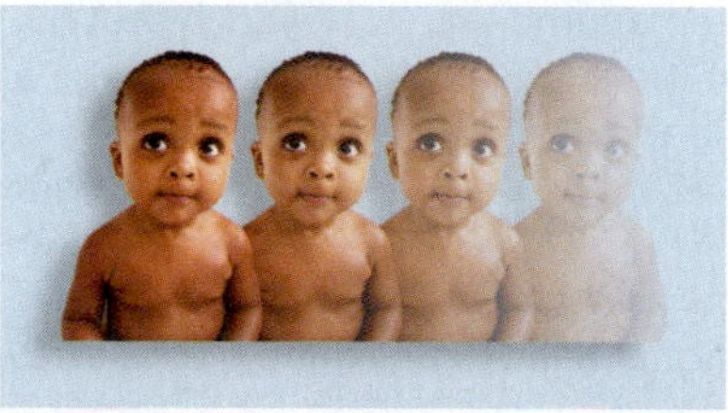

When we have genetic replicates, we will have to wrestle with new questions of human relationships: What is a clone's relationship to its "parents"? Indeed, what are "parents" and "children"?

Sources: Based on Davis 2001; Weiss 2004; Regalado 2005; Smith et al. 2012a; Baylis 2002.

For Your Consideration

➔ You might have heard people object that cloning is immoral. But have you heard the opposite, that cloning should be our moral choice? Let's suppose that mass cloning becomes possible. Let's also assume that geneticists trace great creative ability, high intelligence, compassion, and a propensity for peace to specific genes. They also identify a genetic base for the ability to create beautiful poetry, music, and architecture; to excel in mathematics, science, and other intellectual pursuits; even to be successful in love. Why, then, should we leave human reproduction to people who have inferior traits—genetic diseases, low IQs, perhaps even the propensity to be violent? Shouldn't we select people with the finer characteristics to reproduce—and to clone?

6.2 Discuss the main characteristics of primary groups, secondary groups, in-groups and out-groups, reference groups, and social networks.

Groups within Society

Our society is huge and dominating, sometimes even threatening and oppressive. This can create a bewildering sense of not belonging. Sociologist Emile Durkheim (1893/1933) called this condition *anomie* (AN-uh-mee). He said that small groups help prevent anomie by standing as a buffer between the individual and the larger society. By providing intimate relationships, small groups give us a sense of belonging, something that we all need. Because smaller groups are essential for our well-being, let's look at them in detail.

Watch on **MySocLab**
Video: Society, Groups, and Organizations: The Big Picture

But first, let's distinguish two terms that are sometimes confused with "group": *aggregate* and *category*. An **aggregate** consists of individuals who temporarily share the same physical space but who do not see themselves as belonging together. Shoppers standing in a checkout line or drivers waiting at a red light are an aggregate. A **category** is simply a statistic. It consists of people who share similar characteristics, such as all college women who wear glasses or all men over 6 feet tall. Unlike group members, the individuals who make up a category don't think of themselves as belonging together, and they don't interact with one another. These concepts are illustrated in the photos on the next page.

aggregate individuals who temporarily share the same physical space but who do not see themselves as belonging together

category people, objects, and events that have similar characteristics and are classified together

Primary Groups

As you will recall from Chapter 3, a major point about socialization is that you didn't develop "naturally" into a human adult. Your social experiences shaped you into what you have become. In this shaping process, it is hard to overestimate how significant your family has been. It was your family that laid down your basic orientations to life. Then

Categories, Aggregates, Primary and Secondary Groups

Groups have a deep impact on our actions, views, orientations, even what we feel and think about life. Yet, as illustrated by these photos, not everything that appears to be a group is actually a group in the sociological sense.

The outstanding trait that these three people have in common does not make them a group, but a **category**.

Primary groups such as the family play a key role in the development of the self. As a small group, the family also serves as a buffer from the often-threatening larger group known as society. The family has been of primary significance in forming the basic orientations of this couple, as it will be for their son.

Secondary groups are larger and more anonymous, formal, and impersonal than primary groups. Why are these cyclists lined up at the start of a race an example of a secondary group?

Aggregates are people who happen to be in the same place at the same time.

primary group a small group characterized by intimate, long-term, face-to-face association and cooperation

secondary group compared with a primary group, a larger, relatively temporary, more anonymous, formal, and impersonal group based on some interest or activity

in-group a group toward which one feels loyalty

out-group a group toward which one feels antagonism

came friends, where your sense of belonging expanded. Family and friends are what sociologist Charles Cooley called **primary groups**. By providing intimate, face-to-face interaction, your primary groups have given you an identity, a feeling of who you are. Here's how Cooley (1909) put it:

> *By primary groups I mean those characterized by intimate face-to-face association and cooperation. They are primary in several senses, but chiefly in that they are fundamental in forming the social nature and ideals of the individual.*

From our opening vignette, you can see that youth gangs are also primary groups.

Producing a Mirror Within. We humans have deep emotional needs. Among them are a sense of belonging and feelings of self-esteem. Through their intense face-to-face interaction as we are being introduced to the world, primary groups are uniquely equipped to meet these basic needs. They can make us feel appreciated—even that we are loved. When primary groups are dysfunctional, however, and fail to meet these basic needs, they produce dysfunctional adults, wounded people who make life difficult for others.

Regardless of the levels at which your primary groups have functioned—and none is perfect—their values and attitudes have become fused into your identity. You have internalized their views, which are now lenses through which you view life. Even as an adult—no matter how far you move away from your childhood roots—your early primary groups will remain "inside" you. There, they will continue to form part of the perspective from which you look out onto the world. Your primary groups have become your *mirror within*.

Read on **MySocLab**
Document: Gangstas, Thugs, and Hustlas: The Code of the Street in Rap Music

Secondary Groups

Compared with primary groups, **secondary groups** are larger, more anonymous, and more formal and impersonal. These groups are based on shared interests or activities, and their members are likely to interact on the basis of specific statuses, such as president, manager, worker, or student. Examples include college classes, the American Sociological Association, and political parties. Contemporary society could not function without secondary groups. They are part of the way we get our education, make our living, spend our money, and use our leisure time.

As necessary as secondary groups are for contemporary life, they often fail to satisfy our deep needs for intimate association. Consequently, *secondary groups tend to break down into primary groups*. At school and work, we form friendships. Our interaction with our friends is so important that we sometimes feel that if it weren't for them, school or work "would drive us crazy." The primary groups that we form within secondary groups, then, serve as a buffer between ourselves and the demands that secondary groups place on us.

How our participation in social groups shapes our self-concept is a focus of symbolic interactionists. In this process, knowing who we are *not* is as significant as knowing who we are.

"So long, Bill. This is my club. You can't come in."

In-Groups and Out-Groups

What groups do you identity with? Which groups in our society do you dislike?

We all have **in-groups**, groups toward which we feel loyalty. And we all have **out-groups**, groups toward which we feel antagonism. For Monster Kody in our opening vignette, the Crips were an in-group, while the Bloods were an out-group. That the Crips—and we—make such a fundamental division of the world has far-reaching consequences for our lives.

Implications for a Socially Diverse Society: Shaping Perception and Morality. You know the sense of belonging that some groups give you. This can bring positive consequences, such as our tendency to excuse the faults of people we love and to encourage them to do better. Unfortunately, dividing the world into a "we" and "them" also leads to discrimination, hatred, and, as we saw in our opening vignette, even murder. *From this, you can see the sociological significance of in-groups: They shape your perception of the world, your view of right and wrong, and your behavior.*

reference group a group whose standards we refer to as we evaluate ourselves

Let's look at two examples. The first you see regularly—prejudice and discrimination on the basis of sex. In-groups produce this fascinating double standard:

> *We tend to view the traits of our in-group as virtues, while we perceive those same traits as vices in out-groups. Men may perceive an aggressive man as assertive but an aggressive woman as pushy. They may think that a male employee who doesn't speak up "knows when to keep his mouth shut," while they consider a quiet woman as too timid to make it in the business world (Merton 1949/1968).*

The "we" and "they" division of the world can twist people's perception to such an extent that harming others comes to be viewed as right. The Nazis provide one of the most startling examples. For them, the Jews were an out-group who symbolized an evil that should be eliminated. Many ordinary, "good" Germans shared this view and defended the Holocaust as "dirty work" that someone had to do (Hughes 1962/2005).

Read on **MySocLab**
Document: Overview of U.S. White Supremacist Groups

An example from way back then, you might say—and the world has moved on. But our inclination to divide the world into in-groups and out-groups has not moved on—nor has the twisting of perception that accompanies it. After the terrorist attacks of September 11, 2001, al-Qaeda became Americans' number one out-group, so much so that top U.S. officials concluded that being "cruel, inhuman, and degrading" to al-Qaeda prisoners was not torture. Officials had one al-Qaeda leader waterboarded 180 times (Shane and Savage 2011). (None of us would want to be waterboarded even once.) Caught up in the torture hysteria of the times, Alan Dershowitz, a professor at Harvard Law School who usually takes very liberal views, said that we should make torture legal so judges could issue "torture warrants" (Dershowitz 2004; Allhoff 2011). Can you see how this works? Can you see that in-group/out-group thinking can be so severe that even "good people" can support torture? And with a good conscience. Shades of the Nazis!

In short, to divide the world into in-groups and out-groups, a natural part of social life, produces both functional and dysfunctional consequences.

All of us have *reference groups*—the groups we use as standards to evaluate ourselves. How do you think the reference groups of these members of the KKK who are demonstrating in Jaspar, Texas, differ from those of the police officer who is protecting their right of free speech? Although the KKK and this police officer use different groups to evaluate their attitudes and behaviors, the process is the same.

Reference Groups

> *Suppose you have just been offered a good job. It pays double what you hope to make even after you graduate from college. You have only two days to make up your mind. If you accept the job, you will have to drop out of college. As you consider the offer, thoughts like this may go through your mind: "My friends will say I'm a fool if I don't take the job . . . but Dad and Mom will practically go crazy. They've made sacrifices for me, and they'll be crushed if I don't finish college. They've always said I've got to get my education first, that good jobs will always be there. . . . But, then, I'd like to see the look on the faces of those neighbors who said I'd never amount to much!"*

Evaluating Ourselves. This is an example of how people use **reference groups**, the groups we refer to when we evaluate ourselves. Your reference groups may include your family, neighbors, teachers, classmates, co-workers, or the members of your church, synagogue, or mosque. If you were like Monster Kody in our opening vignette, the "set" would be your main reference group. Even a group you don't belong to can be a reference group. For example, if you are thinking about going to graduate school, graduate students or members of the profession you want to join may form a reference group. You would consider their standards as you evaluate your grades or writing skills.

Reference groups exert tremendous influence on us. For example, if you want to become a corporate executive, you might start to dress more formally, try to improve your vocabulary, read *The Wall Street Journal*, and change your major to business or law. In contrast, if you want to become a rock musician, you might get elaborate tattoos and body piercings, dress in ways your parents and even many of your peers consider extreme, read *Rolling Stone*, drop out of college, and hang around clubs and rock groups.

Explore on MySocLab
Activity: Women's Everyday Lives and the Importance of Education

Exposure to Contradictory Standards in a Socially Diverse Society. From these examples, you can see how you use reference groups to evaluate your life. When you see yourself as measuring up to a reference group's standards, you feel pleased. But you can experience inner turmoil if your behavior—or aspirations—does not match the group's standards. Although wanting to become a corporate executive would create no inner turmoil for most of us, it would for someone who had grown up in an Amish home. The Amish strongly disapprove of such aspirations for their children. They ban high school and college education, suits and ties, and corporate employment. Similarly, if you want to join the military and your parents are dedicated pacifists, you likely would feel deep conflict, because your parents would have quite different aspirations for you.

Contradictions that lead to inner turmoil are common because of two chief characteristics of our society: social diversity and social mobility. These expose us to standards and orientations that are inconsistent with those we learned during childhood. The "internal recordings" that play contrasting messages from different reference groups, then, are one price we pay for our social mobility.

Social Networks

Watch on MySocLab
Video: Sociology on the Job: Society, Groups, and Organizations

Although we live in a huge and diverse society, we don't experience social life as a sea of nameless, strange faces. This is because of the groups we have been discussing. Among these is our **social network**, people who are linked to one another. Your social network includes your family, friends, acquaintances, people at work and school, and even "friends of friends." Think of your social network as a spider's web. You are at the center, with lines extending outward, gradually encompassing more and more people.

social network the social ties radiating outward from the self that link people together

If you are a member of a large group, you probably associate regularly with a few people within that group. In a sociology class I was teaching at a commuter campus, six women who didn't know one another ended up working together on a project. They got along well, and they began to sit together. Eventually, they planned a Christmas party at one

The smallest part of *social networks* is our friends and acquaintances, the people we hang out with and do things together. This part of our social networks overlaps with and forms a core part of our *reference groups*. From these two photos, can you see how the *reference groups* and *social networks* of these youths are not likely to lead them to the same social destination?

of their homes. This type of social network, the clusters within a group, or its internal factions, is called a **clique** (cleek).

These L.A. high school football players are filing by the casket of a teammate who was shot by a gang member. How is network analysis being used to reduce such senseless deaths?

Applied Network Analysis. The analysis of social networks has become part of applied sociology. An interesting application is its use to reduce gang violence. When a gang member is shot, the gang retaliates by shooting members of the rival gang. This leads to endless violence, with each trying to even the score. To try to break this cycle of lethal violence, when they arrest a gang member, the Chicago police are adding the person's name to a program that links people. When a gang member is shot, the police click the name of the individual. This person appears at the center, with his associates and known enemies shown in concentric circles. Another click brings up the mug shots with their gang affiliations. The police then know who might be seeking to avenge the shooting (Belkin 2012).

The Small World Phenomenon. Social scientists have wondered just how extensive the connections are among social networks. If you list everyone you know, and each of those individuals lists everyone he or she knows, and you keep doing this, would almost everyone in the United States eventually be included on those lists?

It would be too cumbersome to test this hypothesis by drawing up such lists, but psychologist Stanley Milgram (1933–1984) came up with an interesting idea. In a classic study known as "the small world phenomenon," Milgram (1967) addressed a letter to "targets": the wife of a divinity student in Cambridge and a stockbroker in Boston. He sent the letter to "starters," who did not know these people. He asked them to send the letter to someone they knew on a first-name basis, someone they thought might know the "target." The recipients, in turn, were asked to mail the letter to a friend or acquaintance who might know the "target," and so on. The question was, Would the letters ever reach the "target"? If so, how long would the chain be?

Think of yourself as part of this study. What would you do if you were a "starter" and all you knew was the "target's" name and the state in which that person lives? In addition, you don't know anyone in that state. Remember that this is before the Internet. You would send the letter to someone that you think might know someone in that state.

This, Milgram reported, is just what happened. Although none of the senders knew the targets, the letters reached the designated individual in an average of just six jumps.

Milgram's study caught the public's fancy, leading to the phrase "six degrees of separation." This expression means that, on average, everyone in the United States is separated by just six individuals. Milgram's conclusions have become so popular that a game, "Six Degrees of Kevin Bacon," was built around it.

Is the Small World Phenomenon an Academic Myth? When psychologist Judith Kleinfeld (2002) decided to replicate Milgram's study, she went to the archives at Yale University Library to get more details. Going through Milgram's papers, she found that he had stacked the deck in favor of finding a small world. As mentioned, one of the "targets" was a Boston stockbroker. Kleinfeld found that this person's "starters" were investors in blue-chip stocks. She also found that on average, only 30 percent of the letters reached their "target."

Since most letters did *not* reach their targets, even with the deck stacked in favor of success, we can draw the *opposite* conclusion: People who don't know one another are

clique (cleek) a cluster of people within a larger group who choose to interact with one another

group dynamics the ways in which individuals affect groups and the ways in which groups influence individuals

small group a group small enough for everyone to interact directly with all the other members

dyad the smallest possible group, consisting of two persons

triad a group of three people

dramatically separated by social barriers. As Kleinfeld says, "Rather than living in a small world, we may live in a world that looks like a bowl of lumpy oatmeal, with many small worlds loosely connected and perhaps some small worlds not connected at all." Somehow, I don't think that the phrase "lumpy oatmeal phenomenon" will become standard, but it seems reasonable to conclude that we do *not* live in a small world where everyone is connected by six links.

But not so fast. The plot thickens. Although research with thousands of e-mail chains showed that only about 1 percent reached their targets (Dodds et al. 2003; Muhamad 2010), other research confirms Milgram's conclusions. Research on 250 million people who exchanged chat messages showed a link of less than seven, and a study of 700 million people on *Facebook* showed a connection of less than five (Markoff and Sengupta 2011).

Why such disparity? The problem seems to be the choice of samples and how researchers measure links. These definitions must be worked out before we can draw solid conclusions. But maybe Milgram did stumble onto the truth. We'll find out as the research continues.

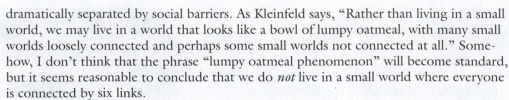

Read on **MySocLab**
Document: Georg Simmel, Dyads, Triads, and Larger Groups

Building Unintentional Barriers. Besides geography, the barriers that divide us into separate small worlds are primarily those of social class, gender, and race–ethnicity. Overcoming these social barriers is difficult because even our own social networks contribute to social inequality, a topic that we explore in the Cultural Diversity box on the next page.

6.3 Be familiar with the effects of group size on stability, intimacy, attitudes, and behavior; types and styles of leaders; the Asch experiment on peer pressure; the Milgram experiment on authority; and the implications of groupthink.

Group Dynamics

Group dynamics is a fascinating area of sociology. This term refers to how groups influence us and how we influence groups. Most of the ways that groups influence us lie below our sense of awareness, however, so let's see if we can bring some of this to the surface. Let's consider how even the size of a group makes a difference and then examine leadership, conformity, and decision making.

Before doing so, we should define **small group**, which is a group small enough so that each member can interact directly with all the others. Small groups can be either primary or secondary. A wife, husband, and children make up a *primary* small group, as do workers who take their breaks together. Students in a small introductory sociology class and bidders at an auction form *secondary* small groups. You might want to look again at the photos on page 153.

Similarity of appearance, activity, and belief help to fuse group identity and loyalty. These Buddhist monks in Myanmar are on their way to collect alms.

Effects of Group Size on Stability and Intimacy

Writing in the early 1900s, sociologist Georg Simmel (1858–1918) analyzed how group size affects people's behavior. He used the term **dyad** for the smallest possible group, which consists of two people. Dyads, which include marriages, love affairs, and close friendships, show two distinct qualities. First, they are the most intense or intimate of human groups. Because only two people are involved, the interaction is focused on both individuals. Second, dyads tend to be unstable. Because dyads require that both members participate, if one member loses interest, the dyad collapses. In larger groups, by contrast, if one person withdraws, the group can continue since its existence does not depend on any single member (Simmel 1950).

A **triad** is a group of three people. As Simmel noted, the addition of a third member

Cultural Diversity in the United States

Do Your Social Networks Perpetuate Social Inequality?

Suppose that an outstanding job—great pay, interesting work, opportunity for advancement—has just opened up where you work. Who are you going to tell?

Consider some of the principles we have reviewed. We are part of in-groups, people with whom we identify; we use reference groups to evaluate our attitudes and behavior; and we interact in social networks. Our in-groups, reference groups, and social networks are likely to consist of people whose backgrounds are similar to our own. For most of us, this means that just as social inequality is built into society, so it is built into our relationships. One consequence is that we tend to perpetuate social inequality.

Go back to the extract that opens this box. Who will you tell about the opening for this outstanding job? Most likely it will be someone you know, a friend or someone to whom you owe a favor. And most likely your social network is made up of people who look much like yourself—similar to your age, education, social class, race–ethnicity, and, probably also, gender. You can see how *our social networks both reflect the inequality in our society and help to perpetuate it.*

When people learn of opportunities, they share this information with their networks. Opportunities then flow to people whose characteristics are similar to theirs.

Consider a network of white men in some corporation. As they learn of opportunities (jobs, investments, real estate, and so on), they share this information with their networks. This causes opportunities and good jobs to flow to people whose characteristics are similar to theirs. This perpetuates the "good old boy"' network, bypassing people who have different characteristics—in this example, women and minorities. No intentional discrimination need be involved. It is just a reflection of our contacts, of our everyday interaction.

To overcome this barrier and advance their careers, women and minorities do networking. They try to meet "someone who knows someone" (Kantor 2009). Like the "good old boys," they go to parties and join clubs, religious organizations, and political parties. They also use *Facebook* and other online networking sites. The women's contacts have produced a "new girl" network in which they steer business to one another (Jacobs 1997). African American leaders have cultivated a network so tight that one-fifth of the entire national African American leadership knows one another personally. Add some "friends of a friend," and *three-fourths* of the entire leadership belong to the same network (Taylor 1992).

For Your Consideration

➔ You can see that the perpetuation of social inequality does not require intentional discrimination. Just as social inequality is built into society, so it is built into our personal relationships. How do you think your social network helps to perpetuate social inequality? How do you think we can break this cycle? How can we create diversity in our social networks?

fundamentally changes the group. With three people, interaction between the first two decreases. This can create strain. For example, with the birth of a child, hardly any aspect of a couple's relationship goes untouched. Attention focuses on the baby, and interaction between the husband and wife diminishes. Despite this, the marriage usually becomes stronger. Although the intensity of interaction is less in triads, they are inherently stronger and give greater stability to a relationship.

Yet, as Simmel noted, triads, too, are unstable. They tend to produce **coalitions**—two group members aligning themselves against one. This common tendency for two people to develop stronger bonds and prefer one another leaves the third person feeling hurt and excluded. Another characteristic of triads is that they often produce an arbitrator or mediator, someone who tries to settle disagreements between the other two. In one-child families, you can often observe both of these characteristics of triads—coalitions and arbitration.

coalition the alignment of some members of a group against others

Group size has a significant influence on how people interact. When a group changes from a dyad (two people) to a triad (three people), the relationships among the participants undergo a shift. How do you think the birth of this child affected the relationship between the mother and father?

The general principle is this: *As a small group grows larger, it becomes more stable, but its intensity, or intimacy, decreases.* To see why, look at Figure 6.3. As each new person comes into a group, the connections among people multiply. In a dyad, there is only 1 relationship; in a triad, there are 3; in a group of four, 6; in a group of five, 10. If we expand the group to six, we have 15 relationships, while a group of seven yields 21 relationships. If we continue adding members, we soon are unable to follow the connections: A group of eight has 28 possible relationships; a group of nine, 36; a group of ten, 45; and so on.

It is not only the number of relationships that makes larger groups more stable. As groups grow, they also tend to develop a more formal structure. For example, leaders emerge and more specialized roles come into play. This often results in such familiar offices as president, secretary, and treasurer. This structure provides a framework that helps the group survive over time.

Effects of Group Size on Attitudes and Behavior

You probably have observed the first consequence of group size. When a group is small, its members act informally, but as the group grows, the members lose their sense of intimacy and become more formal with one another. No longer can the members assume that the others are "insiders" who agree with their views. Now they must take a "larger audience" into consideration, and instead of merely "talking," they begin to "address" the group. As their speech becomes more formal, their body language stiffens.

FIGURE 6.3 The Effects of Group Size on Relationships

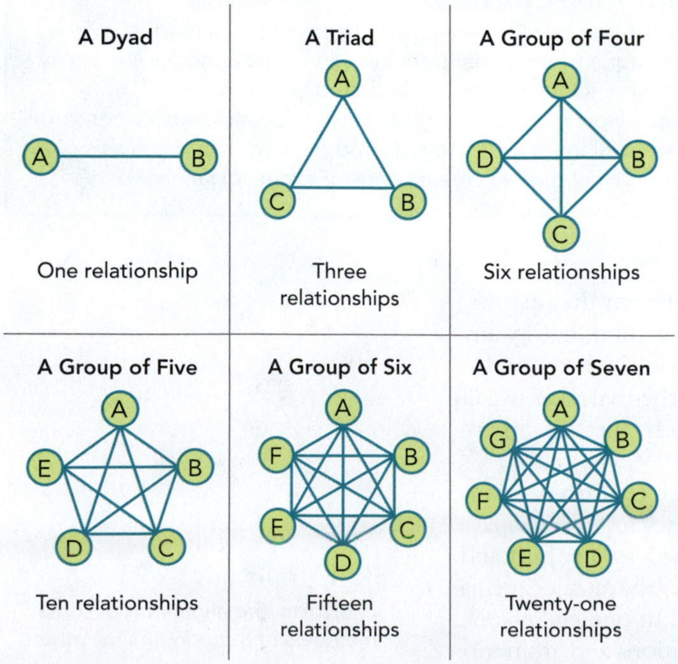

You probably have observed a second aspect of group dynamics, too. In the early stages of a party, when only a few people are present, almost everyone talks with everyone else. But as more people arrive, the guests break into smaller groups. Some hosts, who want their guests to mix together, make a nuisance of themselves trying to achieve *their* idea of what a group should be like. The division into small groups is inevitable, however: It follows the basic sociological principles that we have just reviewed. Because the addition of each person rapidly increases connections (in this case, "talk lines"), conversation becomes more difficult. The guests break into smaller groups in which they can look at each other directly and interact comfortably with one another.

Let's turn to a third consequence of group size:

Imagine that you are taking a team-taught course in social psychology and your professors have asked you to join a few students to discuss how you are adjusting to college life. When you arrive, they tell you that to make the discussion anonymous, they want you to sit unseen in a booth. You will participate in the discussion over an intercom, talking when your microphone comes on. The professors say that they will not listen to the conversation, and they leave.

> *You find the format somewhat strange, to say the least, but you go along with it. You have not seen the other students in their booths, but when they talk about their experiences, you find yourself becoming wrapped up in the problems that they are sharing. One student even mentions how frightening it is to be away from home because of his history of epileptic seizures. Later, you hear this individual breathe heavily into the microphone. Then he stammers and cries for help. A crashing noise follows, and you imagine him lying helpless on the floor.*
>
> *Nothing but an eerie silence follows. What do you do?*

Your professors, John Darley and Bibb Latané (1968), staged the whole thing, but you don't know this. No one had a seizure. In fact, no one was even in the other booths. Everything, except your comments, was on tape.

Some participants were told that they would be discussing the topic with just one other student, others with two, and still others with three, four, or five. Darley and Latané found that all students who thought they were part of a dyad rushed out to help. If they thought they were in a triad, only 80 percent went to help—and they were slower in leaving the booth. In six-person groups, only 60 percent went to see what was wrong—and they were even slower.

This experiment demonstrates how deeply group size influences our attitudes and behavior: It even affects our willingness to help one another. Students in the dyad knew that no one else could help the student in trouble. The professor was gone, and it was up to them. In the larger groups, including the triad, students felt a *diffusion of responsibility*: Giving help was no more their responsibility than anyone else's.

Laboratory Findings and the Real World. Experiments in social psychology can give insight into human behavior—but at the same time, they can woefully miss the mark. Darley and Latané's classic laboratory experiment has serious flaws when it comes to real life. Look at the photos on the next page that I snapped in Vienna, Austria, and you'll see something entirely different than what they reported. Many people—strangers to one another—were passing one another on the sidewalk. But as you can see, no diffusion of responsibility stopped them from immediately helping the man who had tripped and fallen. Other norms and values that people carry within them are also at work, ones that can trump the diffusion of responsibility.

Leadership

All of us are influenced by leaders, so it is important to understand leadership. Let's look at how people become leaders, the types of leaders, and different styles of leadership. Before we do this, though, it is important to clarify that leaders don't necessarily hold formal positions in a group. **Leaders** are people who influence the behaviors, opinions, or attitudes of others. Even a group of friends has leaders.

Who Becomes a Leader? Are leaders born with characteristics that propel them to the forefront of a group? No sociologist would agree with such an idea. In general, people who become leaders are perceived by group members as strongly representing their values or as able to lead a group out of a crisis (Trice and Beyer 1991). Leaders tend to be more talkative, outgoing, determined, and self-confident (Ward et al. 2010).

These findings may not be surprising, since such traits are related to what we expect of leaders. However, researchers have also discovered traits that seem to have no bearing on the ability to lead. For example, taller people and those judged better looking are more likely to become leaders (Stodgill 1974; Judge and Cable 2004). Some of the factors that go into our choice of leaders are quite subtle, as social psychologists Lloyd Howells and Selwyn Becker (1962) found in a simple experiment. They had five people who did not know one another sit at a small rectangular table. Three sat on one side, and two on the other. After discussing a topic for a set period of time, the group chose a leader. This was repeated with multiple groups. The findings are startling: Although only 40 percent of the people sat on the two-person side, 70 percent of the leaders emerged from there. The explanation is that we tend to interact more with people facing us than with people to our side.

leader someone who influences other people

THROUGH THE AUTHOR'S LENS

Helping a Stranger

Serendipity sometimes accompanies sociologists as they do their work, which was certainly the case here. The entire episode took no more than three minutes, and I was fortunate to capture it with my camera. Real life sometimes differs sharply from that portrayed in research laboratories.

As I was walking in Vienna, a city of almost 2 million people, I heard a crashing noise behind me. I turned, and seeing that a man had fallen to the sidewalk, quickly snapped this picture. You can see strangers beginning to help the man. This photo was taken about three seconds after the man fell.

Two strangers are helping the man, with another two ready to pitch in. They have all stopped whatever they were doing to help a man they did not know.

The man is now on his feet, but still a bit shaky. The two who have helped him up are still expressing their concern, especially the young woman.

By this point, the police officer has noticed that I have been taking photos. You can see him coming toward me, his hand on whatever he is carrying at his hip, his shoulders back, glowering and ready for a confrontation. He asked, "What are you doing?" I said, "I am taking pictures" (as though he couldn't see this). He asked, "Do you have to take pictures of this man?" I said, "Yes," and hoping to defuse the situation, added, "I'm a sociologist, and I'm documenting how people help each other in Vienna." He grunted and turned away.

This photo really completes the series, as this individual was acting as the guardian of the community, placing a barrier of protection around the participants in this little drama.

Types of Leaders. Groups have two types of leaders (Bales 1950, 1953; Cartwright and Zander 1968; Emery et al. 2013). The first is easy to recognize. This person, called an **instrumental leader** (or **task-oriented leader**), tries to keep the group moving toward its goals. These leaders try to keep group members from getting sidetracked, reminding them of what they are trying to accomplish. The **expressive leader** (or **socio-emotional leader**), in contrast, usually is not recognized as a leader, but he or she certainly is one. This person is likely to crack jokes, to offer sympathy, or to do other things that help to lift the group's morale. Both types of leadership are essential: the one to keep the group on track, the other to increase harmony and minimize conflicts.

It is difficult for the same person to be both an instrumental and an expressive leader, since these roles tend to contradict one another. Because instrumental leaders are task oriented, they sometimes create friction as they prod the group to get on with the job. Their actions often cost them popularity. Expressive leaders, in contrast, who stimulate personal bonds and reduce friction, are usually more popular (Olmsted and Hare 1978).

Leadership Styles. Let's suppose that the president of your college has asked you to head a task force to determine how to improve race relations on campus. You can adopt a number of **leadership styles**, or ways of expressing yourself as a leader. Of the three basic styles, you could be an **authoritarian leader**, one who gives orders; a **democratic leader**, one who tries to gain consensus; or a **laissez-faire leader**, one who is highly permissive. Which style should you choose?

Social psychologists Ronald Lippitt and Ralph White (1958) carried out a classic study of these leadership styles. After matching boys for IQ, popularity, physical energy, and leadership, they assigned them to "craft clubs" made up of five boys each. They

instrumental leader an individual who tries to keep the group moving toward its goals; also known as a *task-oriented leader*

expressive leader an individual who increases harmony and minimizes conflict in a group; also known as a *socioemotional leader*

leadership styles ways in which people express their leadership

authoritarian leader an individual who leads by giving orders

democratic leader an individual who leads by trying to reach a consensus

laissez-faire leader an individual who leads by being highly permissive

Adolf Hitler, shown here in Nuremberg in 1938, was one of the most influential—and evil—persons of the twentieth century. Why did so many people follow Hitler? This question stimulated the research by Stanley Milgram (discussed on pages 165–166).

trained men in the three leadership styles, and then peered through peepholes, took notes, and made movies as the men rotated among the clubs. To control possible influences of the men's personalities, each man played all three styles.

The *authoritarian* leaders assigned tasks to the boys and told them what to do. They also praised or condemned the boys' work arbitrarily, giving no explanation for why they judged it good or bad. The *democratic* leaders discussed the project with the boys, outlining the steps that would help them reach their goals. When they evaluated the boys' work, they gave "facts" as the bases for their decisions. The *laissez-faire* leaders, who gave the boys almost total freedom to do as they wished, offered help when asked, but made few suggestions. They did not evaluate the boys' projects, either positively or negatively.

The results? The boys under authoritarian leadership grew dependent on their leader. They also became either apathetic or aggressive, with the aggressive boys growing hostile toward their leader. In contrast, the boys in the democratic clubs were friendlier and looked to one another for approval. When the leader left the room, they continued to work at a steady pace. The boys with laissez-faire management goofed off a lot and were notable for their lack of achievement. The researchers concluded that the democratic style of leadership works best. This conclusion, however, may be biased, as the researchers favored a democratic style of leadership in the first place (Olmsted and Hare 1978). Apparently, this same bias in studies of leadership continues (Cassel 1999).

You may have noticed that only boys and men were involved in this experiment. It is interesting to speculate how the results might differ if we were to repeat the experiment with all-girl groups and with mixed groups of girls and boys—and if we used both men and women as leaders. Perhaps you will become the sociologist who studies such variations of this classic experiment.

Leadership Styles in Changing Situations. Different situations require different styles of leadership. Suppose that you are leading a dozen backpackers in the mountains, and it is time to make dinner. A laissez-faire style would be appropriate if the backpackers had brought their own food, or perhaps a democratic style if everyone is expected to pitch in. Authoritarian leadership—you telling the hikers how to prepare their meals—would create resentment. This, in turn, would likely interfere with meeting the primary goal of the group, which in this case is to have a good time while enjoying nature.

Read on **MySocLab**
Document: Solomon Asch, Opinions and Social Pressure

Now assume the same group but a different situation: One of your party is lost, and a blizzard is on its way. This situation calls for you to exercise authority. To simply shrug your shoulders and say "You figure it out" would invite disaster—and probably a lawsuit.

The Power of Peer Pressure: The Asch Experiment

How influential are groups in our lives? To answer this, let's look first at *conformity* in the sense of going along with our peers. Our peers have no authority over us, only the influence that we allow.

Imagine again that you are taking a course in social psychology, this time with Dr. Solomon Asch. You have agreed to participate in an experiment. As you enter his laboratory, you see seven chairs, five of them already filled by other students. You are given the sixth. Soon the seventh person arrives. Dr. Asch stands at the front of the room next to a covered easel. He explains that he will first show a large card with a vertical line on it, then another card with three vertical lines. Each of you is to tell him which of the three lines matches the line on the first card (see Figure 6.4).

Dr. Asch then uncovers the first card with the single line and the comparison card with the three lines. The correct answer is easy, for two of the lines are obviously wrong, and one is exactly right. Each person, in order, states his or her answer aloud. You all answer correctly. The second trial is just as easy, and you begin to wonder why you are there.

FIGURE 6.4 Asch's Cards

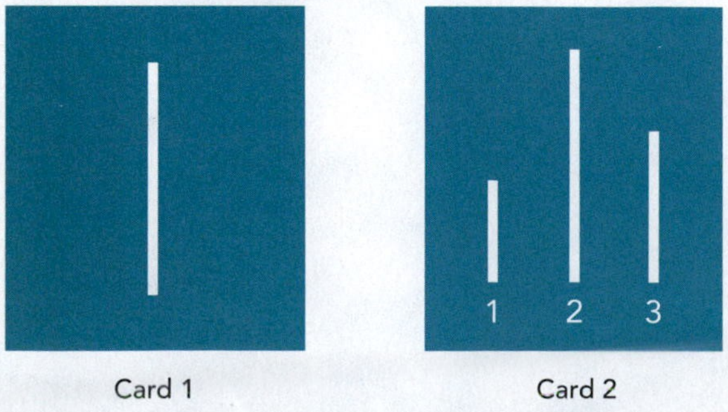

The cards used by Solomon Asch in his classic experiment on group conformity

Source: Asch 1952:452–453.

Then on the third trial, something unexpected happens. Just as before, it is easy to tell which lines match. The first student, however, gives a wrong answer. The second gives the same incorrect answer. So do the third and the fourth. By now, you are wondering what is wrong. How will the person next to you answer? You can hardly believe it when he, too, gives the same wrong answer. Then it is your turn, and you give what you know is the right answer. The seventh person also gives the same wrong answer.

On the next trial, the same thing happens. You know that the choice of the other six is wrong. They are giving what to you are obviously wrong answers. You don't know what to think. Why aren't they seeing things the same way you are? Sometimes they do, but in twelve trials they don't. Something is seriously wrong, and you are no longer sure what to do.

When the eighteenth trial is finished, you heave a sigh of relief. The experiment is finally over, and you are ready to bolt for the door. Dr. Asch walks over to you with a big smile on his face and thanks you for participating in the experiment. He explains that you were the only real subject in the experiment! "The other six were stooges. I paid them to give those answers," he says. Now you feel real relief. Your eyes weren't playing tricks on you after all.

What were the results? Asch (1952) tested fifty people. One-third (33 percent) gave in to the group half the time, providing what they knew to be wrong answers. Another two out of five (40 percent) gave wrong answers, but not as often. One-quarter (25 percent) stuck to their guns and always gave the right answer. I don't know how I would do on this test (if I knew nothing about it in advance), but I like to think that I would be part of the 25 percent. You probably feel the same way about yourself. But why should we feel that we wouldn't be like *most* people?

The results are disturbing, and researchers are still replicating Asch's experiment (Morl and Aral 2011). In our "land of individualism," the group is so powerful that most people are willing to say things that they know are not true. And this was a group of strangers! How much more conformity can we expect when our group consists of friends, people we value highly and depend on for getting along in life? Again, maybe you will become the sociologist who runs that variation of Asch's experiment, perhaps using both female and male subjects.

The Power of Authority: The Milgram Experiment

Let's look at the results of another experiment in the following Thinking Critically section.

Watch on **MySocLab**
Video: Milgram Obedience Study Today

THINKING CRITICALLY

If Hitler Asked You to Execute a Stranger, Would You? The Milgram Experiment

Imagine that Dr. Stanley Milgram (1963, 1965), a former student of Dr. Asch's, has asked you to participate in a study on punishment and learning. Assume that you do not know about the Asch experiment and have no reason to be wary. When you arrive at the laboratory, you and a second student draw lots for the roles of "teacher" and "learner." You are to be the teacher. When you see that the learner's chair has protruding electrodes, you are glad that you are the teacher. Dr. Milgram shows you the machine you will run. You see that one side of the control panel is marked "Mild Shock, 15 volts," while the center says "Intense Shock, 350 Volts," and the far right side reads "DANGER: SEVERE SHOCK."

"As the teacher, you will read aloud a pair of words," explains Dr. Milgram. "Then you will repeat the first word, and the learner will reply with the second word. If the learner can't remember the word, you press this lever on the shock generator. The shock will serve as punishment, and we can then determine if punishment improves memory." You nod, now very relieved that you haven't been designated the learner.

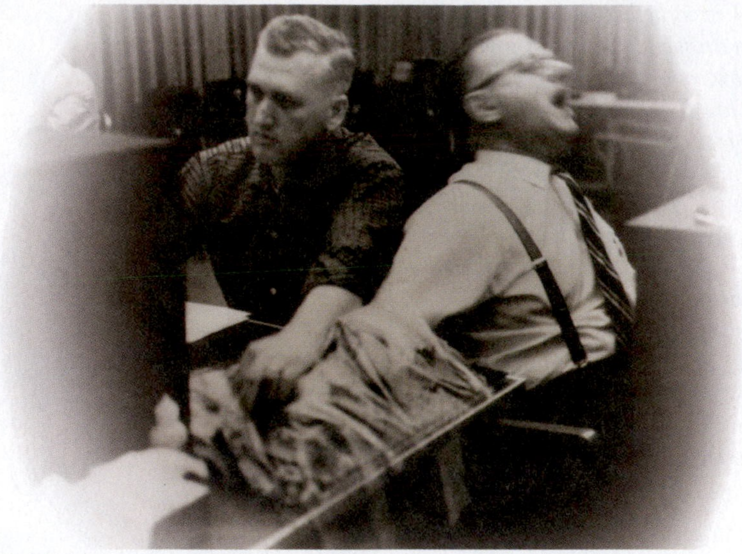

In the 1960s, social psychologists did highly creative but controversial experiments. This photo, taken during Stanley Milgram's experiment, should give you an idea of how convincing the experiment was to the "teacher."

"Every time the learner makes an error, increase the punishment by 15 volts," instructs Dr. Milgram. Then, seeing the look on your face, he adds, "The shocks can be very painful, but they won't cause any permanent tissue damage." He pauses, and then says, "I want you to see." You then follow him to the "electric chair," and Dr. Milgram gives you a shock of 45 volts. "There. That wasn't too bad, was it?" "No," you mumble.

The experiment begins. You hope for the learner's sake that he is bright, but, unfortunately, he turns out to be rather dull. He gets some answers right, but you have to keep turning up the dial. Each turn makes you more and more uncomfortable. You find yourself hoping that the learner won't miss another answer. But he does. When he received the first shocks, he let out some moans and groans, but now he is screaming in agony. He even protests that he suffers from a heart condition.

How far do you turn that dial?

By now, you probably have guessed that there was no electricity attached to the electrodes and that the "learner" was a stooge who only pretended to feel pain. The purpose of the experiment was to find out at what point people refuse to participate. Does anyone actually turn the lever all the way to "DANGER: SEVERE SHOCK"?

Milgram wanted the answer because millions of ordinary people did nothing to stop the Nazi slaughter of Jews, gypsies, Slavs, homosexuals, people with disabilities, and others whom the Nazis designated as "inferior." The cooperation of so many ordinary people in mass killing seemed bizarre, and Milgram wanted to see how Americans might react to orders from an authority (Russell 2010).

What he found upset Milgram. Some "teachers" broke into a sweat and protested that the experiment was inhuman and should be stopped. But when the experimenter calmly replied that the experiment must go on, this assurance from an "authority" ("scientist, white coat, university laboratory") was enough for most "teachers" to continue, even though the "learner" screamed in agony. Even "teachers" who were "reduced to twitching, stuttering wrecks" continued to follow orders.

Milgram varied the experiments. He used both men and women. In some experiments, he put the "teachers" and "learners" in the same room, so the "teacher" could see the suffering. In others, he put the "learners" in an adjacent room, and had them pound and kick the wall during the first shocks and then go silent. The results varied. When there was no verbal feedback from the "learner," 65 percent of the "teachers" pushed the lever all the way to 450 volts. Of those who could see the "learner," 40 percent turned the lever all the way. When Milgram added a second "teacher," a stooge who refused to go along with the experiment, only 5 percent of the "teachers" turned the lever all the way.

Milgram's research set off a stormy discussion about research ethics (Nicholson 2011). Researchers agreed that to reduce subjects to "twitching, stuttering wrecks" was unethical, and almost all deception was banned. Universities began to require that subjects be informed of the nature and purpose of social research.

Although researchers were itching to replicate Milgram's experiment, it took almost fifty years before they found a way to satisfy the committees that approve research. The findings: People today obey the experimenter at about the same rate that people did in the 1960s (Burger 2009). The results were even higher on The Game of Death, a fake game show in France, where the contestants were prodded by the show's host and a shouting audience to administer shocks and win prizes. The contestants kept turning up the dial, with 80 percent of them giving victims what they thought were near lethal 450-volt shocks (Crumley 2010).

For Your Consideration

➤ Taking into account the significance of Milgram's findings, do you think that the scientific community overreacted to these experiments? Should we allow such research? Consider both the Asch and Milgram experiments, and use symbolic interactionism, functionalism, and conflict theory to explain why groups have such influence over us. ■

Global Consequences of Group Dynamics: Groupthink

Suppose you are a member of the U.S. president's inner circle. It is midnight, and the president has called an emergency meeting. There has just been a terrorist attack, and you must decide how to respond to it. You and the others suggest several options. Eventually, these are narrowed to only a couple of choices, and at some point, everyone seems to agree on what now appears to be "the only possible course of action." To criticize the proposed solution at this point will bring you into conflict with all the other important people in the room and mark you as "not a team player." So you keep your mouth shut. As a result, each step commits you—and them—more and more to the "only" course of action.

Under some circumstances, as in this example, the influence of authority and peers can lead to **groupthink**. Sociologist Irving Janis (1972, 1982) used this term to refer to the collective tunnel vision that group members sometimes develop. As they begin to think alike, they become convinced that there is only one "right" viewpoint, just a single course of action to follow. They take any suggestion of alternatives as a sign of disloyalty. With their perspective narrowed, and fully convinced that they are right, they may even put aside moral judgments and disregard risk (Hart 1991; Flippen 1999).

Groupthink can bring catastrophe. Consider the *Columbia* space shuttle disaster of 2003.

Foam broke loose during launch, raising concerns that this might have damaged tiles on the nose cone, making reentry dangerous. Engineers sent e-mails to NASA officials, warning them about the risk. One suggested that the crew do a "space walk" to examine the tiles (Vartabedian and Gold 2003). The team in charge of the Columbia shuttle disregarded the warnings. Convinced that a piece of foam weighing less than 2 pounds could not seriously harm the shuttle, they refused to even consider the possibility (Wald and Schwartz 2003). The fiery results of their closed minds were transmitted around the globe.

Groupthink can lead to consequences even greater than this. In 1941, President Franklin D. Roosevelt and his chiefs of staff had evidence that the Japanese were preparing to attack Pearl Harbor. Refusing to believe it, they decided to continue naval operations as usual. The destruction of the U.S. naval fleet ushered the United States into World War II. During the Vietnam War, U.S. officials had evidence of the strength and determination of the North Vietnamese military. These officials arrogantly threw the evidence aside, refusing to believe that "little, uneducated, barefoot people in pajamas" could defeat the mighty U.S. military.

In each of these cases, options closed as officials committed themselves to a single course of action. Questioning the decisions would have indicated disloyalty and disregard for "team play." No longer did those in power try to weigh events objectively. Interpreting ongoing events as supporting their one "correct" decision, they plunged ahead, blind to disconfirming evidence and alternative perspectives.

One of the fascinating aspects of groupthink is how it can lead "good" people to do "bad" things. Consider the waterboarding I mentioned earlier. After 9/11, U.S. government officials defended torture as moral, "the lesser of two evils." Thought narrowed so greatly that the U.S. Justice Department ruled that the United States was not bound by the Geneva Convention that prohibits torture (Lewis 2005). Even medical professionals, supposedly trained to "help humanity," joined in. They advised the CIA interrogators, telling them when to stop waterboarding, slamming prisoners' heads into walls, or

groupthink a narrowing of thought by a group of people, leading to the perception that there is only one correct answer and that to even suggest alternatives is a sign of disloyalty shackling a prisoner's arms to the ceiling—so there wouldn't be "permanent damage" (Shane 2009).

Do you see the power of groups and groupthink?

Preventing Groupthink. The leaders of a government tend to surround themselves with an inner circle that closely reflects their own views. In "briefings," written summaries, and "talking points," this inner circle spoon-feeds the leaders information it has selected. As a result, the top leaders, such as the president, are largely cut off from information that does not support their own opinions. You can see how the mental captivity and intellectual paralysis known as groupthink is built into this arrangement.

Perhaps the key to preventing groupthink is the widest possible circulation—especially among a nation's top government officials—of research by social scientists independent of the government and information that media reporters have gathered freely. If this conclusion comes across as an unabashed plug for sociological research and the free exchange of ideas, it is. Giving free rein to diverse opinions can curb groupthink, which—if not prevented—can lead to the destruction of a society and, in today's world of nuclear, chemical, and biological weapons, the obliteration of Earth's inhabitants.

CHAPTER 6 Summary and Review

Societies and Their Transformation

6.1 Summarize the main characteristics of these types of societies: hunting and gathering, pastoral and horticultural, agricultural, industrial, postindustrial, and biotech.

What is a group?

Sociologists use many definitions of groups, but, in general, a **group** consists of people who interact with one another and who think of themselves as belonging together. **Societies** are the largest and most complex group that sociologists study. Pp. 145–146.

How is technology linked to the change from one type of society to another?

On their way to postindustrial society, humans passed through four types of societies. Each emerged from a social revolution that was linked to new technology. The **domestication revolution**, which brought the pasturing of animals and the cultivation of plants, transformed **hunting and gathering societies** into **pastoral** and **horticultural societies**. Then the invention of the plow ushered in **agricultural society**, while the **Industrial Revolution**, brought about by machines powered by fuels, led to **industrial society**. The computer chip ushered in a new type of society called **postindustrial** (or **information**) **society**. Another new type of society, the **biotech society**, may be emerging. Pp. 146–152.

How is social inequality linked to the transformation of societies?

Hunting and gathering societies had little social inequality, but as societies changed, social inequality grew. The root of the transition to social inequality was the accumulation of a food surplus, made possible through the domestication revolution. This surplus stimulated the division of labor, trade, the accumulation of material goods, the subordination of females by males, the emergence of leaders, and the development of the state. Social inequality increased with each new type of society. A reversal of this trend occurred in the latter part of the industrial society. Pp. 146–152.

Groups within Society

6.2 Discuss the main characteristics of primary groups, secondary groups, in-groups and out-groups, reference groups, and social networks.

How do sociologists classify groups?

Sociologists divide groups into primary groups, secondary groups, in-groups, out-groups, reference groups, and networks. The cooperative, intimate, long-term, face-to-face relationships provided by **primary groups** are fundamental to our sense of self. **Secondary groups** are larger, relatively temporary, and more anonymous, formal, and impersonal than primary groups. **In-groups** provide members with a strong sense of identity and belonging. **Out-groups** also foster identity by showing in-group members what they are *not*. **Reference groups** are groups whose standards we refer to as we evaluate ourselves. **Social networks** consist of social ties that link people together. Pp. 152–159.

Group Dynamics

6.3 Be familiar with the effects of group size on stability, intimacy, attitudes, and behavior; types and styles of leaders; the Asch experiment on peer pressure; the Milgram experiment on authority; and the implications of groupthink.

How does a group's size affect its dynamics?

The term **group dynamics** refers to how individuals affect groups and how groups influence individuals. In a **small group**, everyone can interact directly with everyone else. As a group grows larger, intimacy decreases but the group's stability increases. A **dyad**, consisting of two people, is the most unstable of human groups, but it provides the most intimacy. The addition of a third person, forming a **triad**, fundamentally changes relationships. Triads are unstable, as **coalitions** (the alignment of some members of a group against others) tend to form. Pp. 159–161.

What characterizes a leader?

A **leader** is someone who influences others. **Instrumental leaders** try to keep a group moving toward its goals, even though this causes friction and they lose popularity. **Expressive leaders** focus on creating harmony and raising group morale. Both types are essential to the functioning of groups. Pp. 161–163.

What are three leadership styles?

Authoritarian leaders give orders, **democratic leaders** try to lead by consensus, and **laissez-faire leaders** are highly permissive. An authoritarian style appears to be more effective in emergency situations, a democratic style works best for most situations, and a laissez-faire style is usually ineffective. Pp. 163–164.

How do groups encourage conformity?

The Asch experiment was cited to illustrate the influence of peer pressure, the Milgram experiment to show the power of authority. Both experiments demonstrate how easily we can succumb to **groupthink**, a kind of collective tunnel vision. Preventing groupthink requires the free circulation of diverse and opposing ideas. Pp. 164–168.

Thinking Critically about Chapter 6

1. How would your orientations to life (your ideas, attitudes, values, goals) be different if you had been reared in a hunting and gathering society? In an agricultural society?
2. Identify your in-groups and your out-groups. How have your in-groups influenced the way you see the world? How have out-groups affected your views?
3. Asch's experiments illustrate the power of peer pressure. How has peer pressure operated in your life? Think about something that you did, despite not wanting to, because of peer pressure.

Bureaucracy and Formal Organizations

7 CHAPTER

Listen to **Chapter 7** on **MySocLab**

Imagine for a moment that you have *just completed your first year at Eastern Michigan University at Ypsilanti. You have worked hard, but you also know you could have studied more. Your grades are so-so, but you've learned a lot about self-management during your first year in college.*

You have enrolled for your second-year classes. You hope to apply yourself and do better in the coming semester.

It's going to be a good year, you have told yourself over and over. You even know what you are going to major in. Sort of. At least a couple of maybes. You expect that things will come together as you take more courses.

As you look through your e-mail, you see a letter addressed to yourself from the Associate Director of Academic Advising. Strange, you think. You weren't expecting anything from her office.

"It must be a class schedule change for the fall," you say to yourself as you open the letter.

As you read the first paragraph, it's like someone hit you in the face. Your life doesn't exactly pass before your eyes, but they start to water. You can hardly finish the letter after reading this first paragraph.

> "Your nightmare has come true. You really have been kicked out of college."

As a result of your Winter academic performance, you have been dismissed from Eastern Michigan University. This dismissal action is in accordance with policies described in the University's undergraduate catalog (available online at EMU's Homepage, which is www.emich.edu, under the Student link). Any enrollment for upcoming terms will be cancelled and you will be ineligible to register for classes.

You sit down, hardly able to believe your eyes. You stare at the note again, then search for the sender's e-dress. You see that it's official. Your nightmare has come true. You really have been kicked out of college.

Your head is spinning as you mentally run through your grades. Not the best, you admit to yourself, but to be kicked out—this just doesn't make sense.

What are you going to tell your parents? They've been scrimping and saving for so many years for your college, and now this.

"There must be some mistake!" you say defiantly to the empty room. "I'm going to call EMU right now."

You grab the phone and make the call.

And you were right. It was a mistake, a horrible one. Instead of the dismissal letter going to the 100 students it was intended for, it had been sent to the entire student body.

Based on Baker 2012.

Some colleges have thousands of students. To make the job manageable, they have broken the administration of their students into separate steps. Each step is an integrated part of the entire procedure. Computer programs have facilitated this process, but, as this event indicates, things don't always go as planned. In this case, a low-level bureaucrat had mixed up the codes, releasing the dismissal letter to the entre student body.

Despite their flaws, we need bureaucracies, and in this chapter, we'll look at how society is organized to "get its job done." As you read this analysis, you may be able to trace the source of some of your frustrations to this social organization—as well as understand how your welfare depends on it.

Learning Objectives

After you have read this chapter, you should be able to:

7.1 Compare the explanations of Marx and Weber for why traditional societies rationalized. (p. 172)

7.2 Summarize the characteristics of bureaucracies, their dysfunctions, and goal displacement; also contrast ideal and real bureaucracy. (p. 174)

7.3 Discuss the functions of voluntary associations, why people join them, and the significance of the iron law of oligarchy. (p. 182)

7.4 Discuss humanizing the work setting, fads in corporate culture, the "hidden" corporate culture, and worker diversity. (p. 185)

7.5 Summarize major issues in the technological control of workers. (p. 188)

7.6 Explain how global competition is affecting corporations. (p. 188)

7.1 Compare the explanations of Marx and Weber for why traditional societies rationalized.

The Rationalization of Society

In the previous chapter, we discussed how societies have undergone transformations so extensive that whole new types of societies have emerged. We also saw that we are now caught up in one of those earth-shattering transformations. Underlying our information society (which may be merging into a biotech society) is an emphasis on **rationality**, the idea that efficiency and practical results should dominate human affairs. But it wasn't always this way. Let's examine how this approach to life—which today we take for granted—came about.

rationality using rules, efficiency, and practical results to determine human affairs

traditional society a society in which the past is thought to be the best guide for the present; tribal, peasant, and feudal societies

Why Did Society Make a Deep Shift in Human Relationships?

Life in Traditional Societies. Until recently, people lived in **traditional societies**. That way of life is so different from ours that I want you to take a moment to grasp what life in such a society is like. As Table 7.1 shows, personal relationships are the heart of this kind of society. Everything centers on deep obligation and responsibility. In producing goods, for example, what counts is not who is best at doing something but people's relationships, which are often lifelong. Based on origins that are lost in history, everyone has an established place in the society. A good part of socialization is learning one's place in the group, the obligations one has to others.

A second key aspect of traditional society is the idea that the past is the best guide for how to live life today. What exists is good because it has passed the test of time. Customs—and relationships based on them—have served people well, and these ways

TABLE 7.1 Production in Traditional and Nontraditional Societies

Traditional Societies (Horticultural, Agricultural)	Nontraditional Societies (Industrial, Postindustrial)
PRODUCING GOODS	
1. Production is done by family members and same-sex groups (men's and women's groups).	1. Production is done by workers hired for the job.
2. Production takes place in the home or in fields and other areas adjacent to the home.	2. Production takes place in a centralized location. (Some decentralization is occurring in the information society.)
3. Tasks are assigned according to personal relationships; men, women, and children do specific tasks based on custom.	3. Tasks are assigned according to agreements and training.
4. The "how" of production is not evaluated; the attitude is "We want to keep doing it the way we've always done it."	4. The "how" of production is evaluated; the attitude is "How can we make this more efficient?"
RELATIONSHIPS IN PRODUCTION	
5. Relationships are based on history ("the way it's always been").	5. Relationships are based on contracts, which change as the situation changes.
6. Relationships are diffuse (vague, covering many areas of life).	6. Relationships are specific; contracts (even if not written) specify conditions.
7. Relationships are long-term, often lifelong.	7. Relationships are short-term, for the length of the contract.
EVALUATING WORKERS	
8. It is assumed that arrangements will continue indefinitely.	8. Arrangements are evaluated periodically, to decide whether to continue or to change them.
9. People are evaluated informally according to how they fulfill their traditional roles, much as friends "evaluate" one another today.	9. People are evaluated formally according to the specific tasks they are assigned in the organization's goals.

Note: This model is an ideal type. Rationality is never totally absent from any society, and no society (or organization) is based entirely on rationality. Even the most rational organizations (those that most carefully and even ruthlessly compute the "bottom line") have traditional components. To properly understand this table, consider these nine characteristics as being "more" or "less" present.

Source: The author.

of doing things should be maintained. With the past prized, it rules the present. Change is viewed with suspicion and comes about slowly, if at all.

rationalization of society a widespread acceptance of rationality and social organizations that are built largely around this idea

The Shift to Rationality in Industrialized Societies. Because capitalism requires an entirely different approach to life, this traditional orientation is a roadblock to industrialization. If a society is to industrialize, a deep shift must occur in how people think about relationships. As you can see from Table 7.1, production in industrial societies is based on impersonal, short-term contracts, not personal relationships. The primary concern is the "bottom line" (explicitly measured results), not who will be affected by decisions to hire, fire, and assign tasks. Tradition ("This is the way we've always done it") must be replaced with *rationality* ("Let's find the most efficient way to do it").

This change to rationality is a fundamental divergence from all of human history. Yet we take it for granted that rationality should be the basis for much of social life, such as how schools and businesses are run. That we take rationality for granted makes it difficult for us to grasp the depths of this historical shift. The following illustration may help.

> *Let's suppose that family relationships change from personal to rational. If this were to occur, a wife might say to her husband, "Each year, I'm going to do a progress report. I will evaluate how much you've contributed to the family budget, how much time you've put in on child care and household tasks, and how you rank on this standardized list of sexual performance—and on that basis, I'll keep or replace you."*

I'm sure you'll agree that such a shift from tradition to rationality would bring about a fundamental change in human relationships. It probably would even produce a new type of marriage and family. This is just what happened when organizations shifted from tradition to rationality. Since such a profound change did occur, we are left with the question of what brought it about. Why did people shift from a traditional orientation to the **rationalization of society**—the widespread acceptance of rationality and the construction of social organizations largely around this idea?

To understand the sociological significance of this photo of a woman in Bangladesh applying fresh cow dung to jute sticks to be used as firewood, compare what you see here with the list of characteristics of traditional societies in Table 7.1.

Marx: Capitalism Broke Tradition

An early sociologist, Karl Marx (1818–1883), was one of the first to note that tradition was giving way to rationality. As Marx analyzed this change, he concluded that capitalism was breaking the bonds of tradition. People who tried capitalism were impressed with its greater efficiency. They found that it produced things in greater abundance and yielded high profits. This encouraged them to invest capital in manufacturing. As capitalism spread, traditional thinking receded. Gradually, the rationality of capitalism replaced the traditional approach to life. Marx's conclusion: The change to capitalism changed the way people thought about life.

Weber: Religion Broke Tradition

To sociologist Max Weber (1864–1920), this problem was as intriguing as an unsolved murder is to a detective. Weber wasn't satisfied with Marx's answer. He wanted to probe more deeply and find out what brought about capitalism. He found a clue when he noted that capitalism thrived only in certain parts of Europe. "There has to be a reason for this," he mused. As Weber pursued the matter, he noted that capitalism flourished in Protestant countries, while Roman Catholic countries held on to tradition and were relatively untouched by capitalism. "Somehow, then, religion holds the key," he thought.

But why did Roman Catholics cling to the past, while Protestants embraced change? Weber's solution to this puzzle has been a source of

capitalism an economic system characterized by the private ownership of the means of production, the pursuit of profit, and market competition

Read on MySocLab
Document: Max Weber, Asceticism and the Spirit of Capitalism

controversy ever since he first proposed it in his influential book *The Protestant Ethic and the Spirit of Capitalism* (1904–1905). Weber concluded that Roman Catholic doctrine emphasized the acceptance of present arrangements: "God wants you where you are. You owe allegiance to the Church, to your family, and to your king. Accept your lot in life and remain rooted." Weber argued that Protestant theology, in contrast, opened its followers to change. Weber was intimately familiar with Calvinism, his mother's religion. Calvinists (followers of the teachings of John Calvin, 1509–1564) believed that before birth, people are destined for either heaven or hell—and they do not know their destiny until after they die. Weber said that this teaching filled Calvinists with anxiety. Salvation became their chief concern—they wanted to know *now* where they were going after death.

To resolve their spiritual dilemma, Calvinists arrived at an ingenious solution: God surely did not want those chosen for heaven to be ignorant of their destiny. Therefore, those who were in God's favor would know it—they would receive a sign from God. But what sign? The answer, claimed Calvinists, would be found not in mystical, spiritual experiences but in things that people could see and measure. The sign of God's approval was success: Those whom God had predestined for heaven would be blessed with visible success in this life.

7.2 Summarize the characteristics of bureaucracies, their dysfunctions, and goal displacement; also contrast ideal and real bureaucracy

This idea transformed the lives of Calvinists. It motivated them to work hard, and because Calvinists also believed that thrift is a virtue, their dedication to work led to an accumulation of money. They could not spend this money on themselves, however. They considered the purchase of items beyond the basic necessities to be sinful. **Capitalism**, the investment of capital in the hope of making profits, became an outlet for their excess money. The success of their investments, in turn, became another sign of God's approval. In this way, Calvinists transformed worldly success into a spiritual virtue. Other branches of Protestantism, although not in agreement with the notion of predestination, also adopted the creed of thrift and hard work. Weber's conclusion: A changed way of thinking among Protestants (God will give a sign to the elect) produced capitalism.

The Two Views Today. Who is correct? Weber, who concluded that Protestantism produced rationality, which then paved the way for capitalism? Or Marx, who concluded that capitalism produced rationality? No analyst has yet reconciled these two opposing answers to the satisfaction of sociologists: The two views still remain side by side.

Today's armies, no matter what country they are from, are bureaucracies. They have a strict hierarchy of rank, division of labor, impersonality and replaceability (an emphasis on the office, not the person holding it), and they stress written records, rules, and communications—essential characteristics identified by Max Weber. This photo was taken in Pyongyang, North Korea.

Formal Organizations and Bureaucracies

Regardless of whether Marx or Weber was right about its cause, rationality profoundly changed how work is organized. When work is rooted in personal relationships, as in traditional society, a main purpose of business decisions is to maintain those relationships—for example, to make sure that your relatives and friends have jobs. In contrast, when work is rooted in rationality, business is centered around performing tasks efficiently and keeping an eye on the bottom line. As rationality gradually crowded out the traditional orientation, new types of organizations emerged. Let's look at these organizations and the impact they have on our lives today.

Formal Organizations

formal organization a secondary group designed to achieve explicit objectives

It is not surprising that **formal organizations**, secondary groups designed to achieve explicit objectives, are rare in traditional societies. As you have seen, life there is organized around personal relationships. There were three exceptions in traditional societies, however, that foreshadowed the changes ushered in by industrialization. An outstanding example is the twelfth-century guilds of western Europe. Men who performed the same type of work organized to control their craft in a local area. They set prices and standards of workmanship (Bridgwater 1953; "Guilds" 2008). Much like today's unions, guilds also prevented outsiders (nonmembers of the guild) from working at their particular craft. Two other examples of early formal organizations were the army and the Roman Catholic Church, each with its hierarchical structure. Although they use different names for their ranks (commander-in-chief/pope), (general/cardinal), (private/priest), in each, senior ranks are in charge of junior ranks.

Although formal organizations used to be rare, with rationality they have become a central feature of our life today. Society has changed so greatly that most of us are even born within a formal organization. We are also educated in formal organizations, we spend our working lives in them, and we are even buried by them. The change is so extensive that we can't even think of modern society without referring to formal organizations. One of the main characteristics of formal organizations is that they tend to develop into bureaucracies. As we examine them, let's start there.

The Characteristics of Bureaucracies

Do you know what the Russian army and the U.S. postal service have in common? Or the government of Mexico and your college?

When society began to be rationalized, production of items was broken into its components, with individuals assigned only specific tasks. Shown in this wood engraving is the production of glass in Great Britain in the early 1800s.

bureaucracy a formal organization with a hierarchy of authority and a clear division of labor; emphasis on impersonality of positions and written rules, communications, and records

Read on **MySocLab**
Document: Max Weber, Characteristics of Bureaucracy

Watch on **MySocLab**
Video: Frederick Taylor and Scientific Management

The sociological answer to these questions is that all four of these organizations are *bureaucracies*. As Weber (1913/1947) pointed out, **bureaucracies** have:

1. *Separate levels, with assignments flowing downward and accountability flowing upward.* Each level assigns responsibilities to the level beneath it, and each lower level is accountable to the level above it for fulfilling those assignments. Figure 7.1 below shows the bureaucratic structure of a typical university.
2. *A division of labor.* Each worker is assigned specific tasks, and the tasks of all the workers are coordinated to accomplish the purpose of the organization. In a college, for example, a teacher does not fix the heating system, the president does not approve class schedules, and a secretary does not evaluate textbooks. These tasks are distributed among people who have been trained to do them.
3. *Written rules.* In their attempt to become efficient, bureaucracies stress written procedures. In general, the longer a bureaucracy exists and the larger it grows, the more written rules it has. The rules of some bureaucracies cover just about every imaginable situation. In my university, for example, the rules are published in handbooks: separate ones for faculty, students, administrators, civil service workers, and perhaps others that I don't even know about.
4. *Written communications and records.* Records are kept for much of what occurs in a bureaucracy ("Be sure to CC all immediate supervisors"). Some workers must detail their activities in written reports. My university, for example, requires that each semester, faculty members produce a summary of the number of hours they spent performing specified activities. They must also submit an annual report listing what they accomplished in teaching, research, and service—all accompanied by copies of publications, evidence of service, and written teaching evaluations from each course. These materials go to committees that evaluate the performance of each faculty member.

FIGURE 7.1 The Typical Bureaucratic Structure of a Medium-Sized University

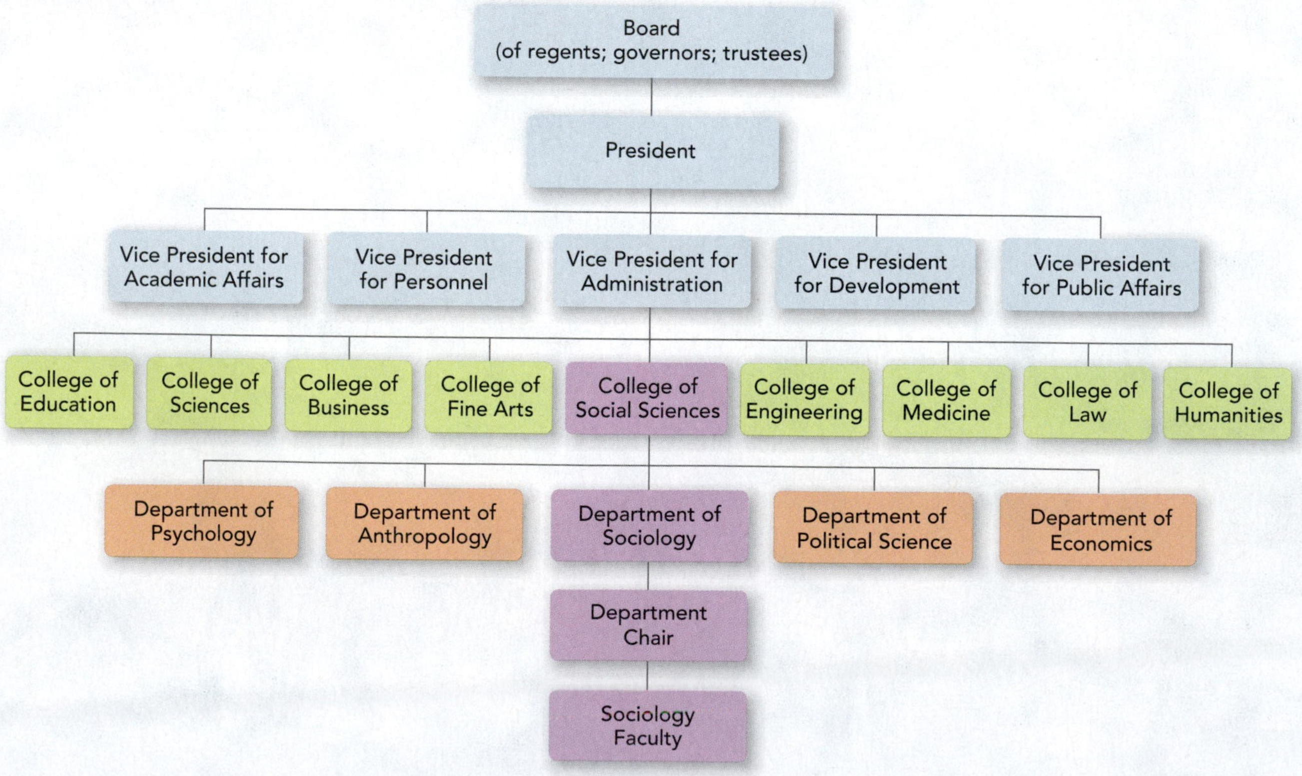

Source: By the author.

5. *Impersonality and replaceability.* The office is important, not the individual who holds the office. Each worker is a replaceable unit. You work for the organization, not for the replaceable person who holds some post in the organization. When a professor retires, for example, someone else is appointed to take his or her place. This makes each person a small cog in a large machine.

Read on **MySocLab**
Document: Hanging Tongues: A Social Encounter with the Assembly Line

These five characteristics help bureaucracies reach their goals. They also allow them to grow and endure. One bureaucracy in the United States, the postal service, has grown so large that 1 out of every 250 employed Americans works for it (*Statistical Abstract* 2013:Tables 626, 1137). If the head of a bureaucracy resigns, retires, or dies, the organization continues without skipping a beat, because unlike a "mom and pop" operation, its functioning does not depend on the individual who heads it.

McDonaldization of society the process by which ordinary aspects of life are rationalized and efficiency comes to rule them, including such things as food preparation

As we explore in the Down-to-Earth Sociology box below, bureaucracies have expanded to such an extent that they now envelop our entire lives.

Down-to-Earth Sociology

The McDonaldization of Society

The significance of the McDonald's restaurants that dot the United States—and, increasingly, the world—goes far beyond quick hamburgers, milk shakes, and salads. As sociologist George Ritzer (1993, 1998, 2012) says, our everyday lives are being "McDonaldized." Let's see what he means by this.

The **McDonaldization of society** does not refer just to the robotlike assembly of food. This term refers to the standardization of everyday life, a process that is transforming our lives. Want to do some shopping? Shopping malls offer one-stop shopping in controlled environments. Planning a trip? Travel agencies offer "package" tours. They will transport middle-class Americans to ten European capitals in fourteen days. All visitors experience the same hotels, restaurants, and other scheduled sites—and no one need fear meeting a "real" native. Want to keep up with events? *USA Today* spews out McNews—short, bland, non-analytical pieces that can be digested between gulps of the McShake or the McBurger.

McDonald's in Tel Aviv, Israel.

Efficiency brings dependability. You can expect your burger and fries to taste the same whether you buy them in Minneapolis or Moscow. Although efficiency also lowers prices, it does come at a cost. Predictability washes away spontaneity. It changes the quality of our lives by producing sameness—flat, bland versions of what used to be unique experiences. In my own travels, for example, had I taken packaged tours, I never would have had the eye-opening experiences that have added so much to my appreciation of human diversity. (Bus trips with chickens in Mexico, hitchhiking in Europe and Africa, sleeping on a granite table in a nunnery in Italy and in a cornfield in Algeria are not part of tour agendas.)

For good or bad, our lives are being McDonaldized, and the predictability of packaged settings seems to be our social destiny. When education is rationalized, no longer will our children have to put up with real professors, who insist on discussing ideas endlessly, who never come to decisive answers, and who come saddled with idiosyncrasies. At some point, such an approach to education is going to be, like quill pens and ink wells, a bit of quaint history.

Our programmed education will eliminate the need for discussion of social issues—we will have packaged solutions to social problems, definitive answers that satisfy our need for closure and the government's desire that we not explore its darker side. Computerized courses will teach the same answers to everyone—"politically correct" ways to think about social issues. Mass testing will ensure that students regurgitate the programmed responses. Like carcasses of beef, our courses will be stamped "U.S. government approved."

Our looming prepackaged society will be efficient. But we will be trapped in the "iron cage" of bureaucracy—just as Weber warned would happen.

For Your Consideration

➔ What do you like and dislike about the standardization of society? What do you think about the author's comments on the future of our educational system?

Technology has changed our lives fundamentally. The connection to *each* telephone call used to have to be made by hand. As in this 1939 photo from London, England, these connections were made by women. Long-distance calls, with their numerous hand-made connections, not only were slow, but also expensive. In 1927, a call from New York to London cost $25 a minute. In today's money, this comes to $300 a minute!

"Ideal" Versus "Real" Bureaucracy

Just as people often act differently from the way the norms say they should, so it is with bureaucracies. The characteristics of bureaucracies that Weber identified are *ideal types*; that is, they are a composite of characteristics based on many specific examples. Think of the judges at a dog show. They have a mental image of how each particular breed of dog should look and behave, and they judge each individual dog according to that mental image. Each dog will rank high on some characteristics and lower on others. In the same way, a particular organization will rank higher or lower on the traits of a bureaucracy, yet still qualify as a bureaucracy. Instead of labeling a particular organization as a "bureaucracy" or "not a bureaucracy," it probably makes more sense to consider the *extent* to which it is bureaucratized (Udy 1959; Hall 1963).

Bureaucracies often differ from their organizational charts. The real lines of authority ("going through channels"), for example, may be different from those portrayed on Figure 7.1 on page 176. For example, suppose that before being promoted, the university president taught in the history department. As a result, friends from that department may have direct access to him or her. If they wish to provide "input" (ranging from opinions about how to solve problems to personal grievances or even gossip), these individuals might be able to skip their chairperson or even the dean of their college and go directly to the president.

Goal Displacement and the Perpetuation of Bureaucracies

Bureaucracies are so good at harnessing people's energies to reach specific goals that they have become a standard feature of our lives. Once in existence, however, bureaucracies tend to take on a life of their own. In a process called **goal displacement**, even after an organization achieves its goal and no longer has a reason to continue, continue it does.

A classic example is the March of Dimes, organized in the 1930s with the goal of fighting polio (Sills 1957). At that time, the origin of polio was a mystery. The public was alarmed and fearful; overnight, a healthy child could be stricken with this crippling disease. To raise money to find a cure, the March of Dimes placed posters of children on crutches near cash registers in almost every store in the United States. The organization raised money beyond its wildest dreams. When Dr. Jonas Salk developed a vaccine for polio in the 1950s, the threat of polio was wiped out almost overnight.

Did the staff that ran the March of Dimes hold a wild celebration and then quietly fold up their tents and slip away? Of course not. They had jobs to protect, so they targeted a new enemy—birth defects. But then, in 2001, another ominous threat of success reared its ugly head. Researchers finished mapping the human genome system, a breakthrough that held the possibility of eliminating birth defects—and their jobs. Officials of the March of Dimes had to come up with something new—and something that would last. Their new slogan, "Stronger, healthier babies," is so vague that it should ensure the organization's existence forever: We are not likely to ever run out of the need for "stronger, healthier babies." This goal displacement is illustrated in the photos on the next page.

goal displacement an organization replacing old goals with new ones; also known as *goal replacement*

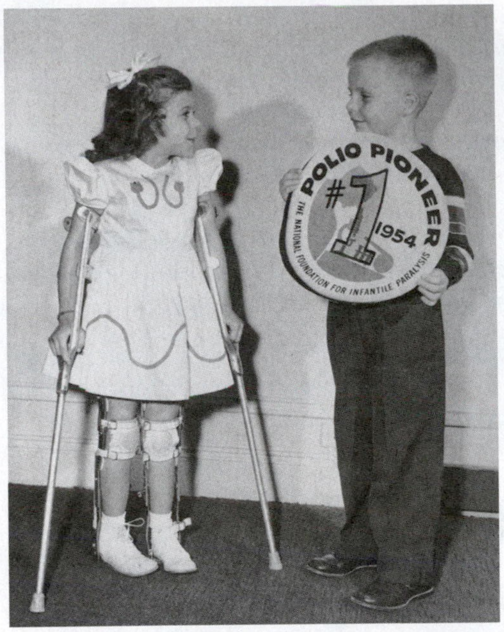

The March of Dimes was founded by President Franklin Roosevelt in the 1930s to fight polio. When a vaccine for polio was discovered in the 1950s, the organization did not declare victory and disband. Instead, its leaders kept the organization intact by creating new goals—first "fighting birth defects," and now "stronger, healthier babies." Sociologists use the term *goal displacement* to refer to this process of adopting new goals.

Then there is NATO (North Atlantic Treaty Organization), founded during the Cold War to prevent Russia from invading western Europe. The abrupt, unexpected end of the Cold War removed the organization's purpose. But why waste a perfectly good bureaucracy? As with the March of Dimes, the western powers found a new goal: to create "rapid response forces" to combat terrorism and "rogue nations" (Tyler 2002). They are still searching for goals—or, as they phrase it, to "define relationships with other organizations" (Kille and Hendrickson 2011).

Dysfunctions of Bureaucracies

Although in the long run no other form of social organization is more efficient, as Weber recognized, bureaucracies have a dark side. Let's look at some of their dysfunctions.

Red Tape: A Rule Is a Rule. Bureaucracies can be so bound by rules that the results defy logic. Here is what happened when I called American Express and reported that I had lost my credit card. The woman took the information and said that a new card would be overnighted to me at no cost. I was quite pleased. Then I said:

I: I need a card for my wife.
S: For that, you'll need the four-digit number above the card number.
I: Yes, I know what that is. It's 6465.
S: But I know you don't have the card. You told me it is lost.
I: Yes, but I know the number, and that's what you need.
S. But I know you don't have the card in front of you.
I: But I know the number, so—
S: It doesn't make any difference. I know you don't have the card.
I: How can I get a card for my wife then?
S: Call when the new card arrives and give us the four-digit number that is above the card number.

In Spain, I came across an example so ridiculous that it can make your head swim—if you don't burst from laughing first.

The Civil Registry of Barcelona recorded the death of a woman named Maria Antonieta Calvo in 1992. Apparently, Maria's evil brother had reported her dead so he could collect the family inheritance.

When Maria learned that she was supposedly dead, she told the Registry that she was very much alive. The bureaucrats at this agency looked at their records, shook their heads, and insisted that she was dead. Maria then asked lawyers to represent her in court. They all refused—because no dead person can bring a case before a judge.

When Maria's boyfriend asked her to marry him, the couple ran into a slight obstacle: No man in Spain (or most other places) can marry a dead woman—so these bureaucrats said, "So sorry, but no license."

After years of continuing to insist that she was alive, Maria finally got a hearing in court. When the judges looked at Maria, they believed that she really was a living person, and they ordered the Civil Registry to declare her alive.

The ending of this story gets even happier: Now that Maria was alive, she was able to marry her boyfriend. I don't know if the two lived happily ever after, but, after overcoming the bureaucrats, they at least had that chance ("Mujer 'resucite'" 2006).

Lack of Communication between Units. Each unit within a bureaucracy performs specialized tasks, which are designed to contribute to the organization's goals. This arrangement usually works quite well, but sometimes the units fail to communicate with one another and end up working at cross-purposes.

In Granada, Spain, the local government was concerned about the run-down appearance of buildings along one of its main streets. Officials assigned one unit of the government to fix the fronts of these buildings, to repair concrete and restore the decorations of iron and stone. The results were impressive, and the unit was proud of what it had accomplished. There was a problem, though. Another unit of the government had slated these same buildings for demolition (Arías 1993). Neither unit of this bureaucracy knew what the other was doing. One beautified the buildings while the other planned to turn them into a heap of rubble.

alienation Marx's term for workers' lack of connection to the product of their labor; caused by workers being assigned repetitive tasks on a small part of a product—this leads to a sense of powerlessness and normlessness; others use the term in the general sense of not feeling a part of something

Bureaucratic Alienation. Perceived in terms of roles, rules, and functions rather than as individuals, many workers begin to feel more like objects than people. Marx termed these reactions **alienation**, a result, he said, of workers being cut off from the finished product of their labor. He pointed out that before industrialization, workers used their own tools to produce an entire product, such as a chair or table. Now the capitalists own the tools (machinery, desks, computers) and assign each worker only a single step or

Bureaucracies have their dysfunctions and can be slow and even stifling. Most, however, are highly functional in uniting people's efforts toward reaching goals.

two in the entire production process. Relegated to performing repetitive tasks that seem remote from the final product, workers no longer identify with what they produce. They come to feel estranged not only from the results of their labor but also from their work environment.

Resisting Alienation. Because workers want to feel valued and to have a sense of control over their work, they resist alienation. A major form of that resistance is forming primary groups at work. Workers band together in informal settings—at lunch, around desks, or for a drink after work. There, they give one another approval for jobs well done and express sympathy for the shared need to put up with cantankerous bosses, meaningless routines, and endless rules. In these contexts, they relate to one another not just as workers but also as people who value one another. They flirt, laugh, tell jokes, and talk about their families and goals. Adding this multidimensionality to their work relationships helps them maintain their sense of being individuals rather than mere cogs in a machine.

As in the photo to the right, workers often decorate their work areas with personal items. The sociological implicatfion is that these workers are trying to resist alienation. By staking a claim to individuality, the workers are rejecting an identity as machines that exist to perform functions.

How is this worker trying to avoid becoming a depersonalized unit in a bureaucratic-economic machine?

The Alienated Bureaucrat. Not all workers succeed in resisting alienation. Some become alienated and quit. Others became alienated but remain in the organization because they see no viable alternative, or they wait it out because they have "only so many years until retirement." They hate every minute of work, and it shows—in their attitudes toward clients, toward fellow workers, and toward supervisors. The alienated bureaucrat does not take initiative, and uses company rules to justify doing as little as possible.

Despite poor attitude and performance, alienated workers often retain their jobs. Some keep their jobs because of seniority, while others threaten costly, time-consuming, and embarrassing legal action if anyone tries to fire them. Some alienated workers are shunted off into small bureaucratic corners, where they spend the day doing trivial tasks and have little chance of coming in contact with the public. This treatment, of course, only alienates them further.

Bureaucratic Incompetence. In a tongue-in-cheek analysis of bureaucracies, Laurence Peter proposed the **Peter Principle**: Each employee of a bureaucracy is promoted to his or her *level of incompetence* (Peter and Hull 1969, 2011). People who perform well in a bureaucracy come to the attention of those higher up the chain of command and are promoted. If they continue to perform well, they are promoted again. This process continues *until* they are promoted to a level at which they can no longer handle the responsibilities well—their level of incompetence. There they hide behind the work of others, taking credit for the accomplishments of employees under their direction. In our opening vignette, the employee who sent the wrong e-mail has already reached his or her level of incompetence.

Although the Peter Principle contains a grain of truth, if it were generally true, bureaucracies would be staffed by incompetents, and these organizations would fail. In reality, bureaucracies are so successful that they have come to dominate our society.

Since society is eternally evolving, could other forms replace the bureaucracy as the dominant form of organization? Of course they could, the topic of the Sociology and the New Technology box on the next page.

Peter Principle a tongue in-cheek observation that the members of an organization are promoted for their accomplishments until they reach their level of incompetence; there they cease to be promoted, remaining at the level at which they can no longer do good work

Sociology and the New Technology

Social Networking as the New Contender: A Cautious Prediction

There is no reason to assume that the bureaucracy is the ending point of organizational development. We might actually be seeing the newest contender emerging now. As you know, the Internet has become a major means by which many millions of people connect to others. Using iPhones, iPads, notebooks, and laptops, each day they transmit billions of verbal messages, photos, and real-time visuals to friends, family, and associates.

The microchip brought these new ways of communicating at the same time that transmitting information became a dominant aspect of society. As the significance of communicating information increased, factory production decreased as its share of the Gross Domestic Product. Bureaucracy receded in unexpected areas: Even the post office has started to reduce its work force. Millions of people who would have worked in bureaucracies, in factories and offices, now work independently through the Internet. They run businesses and manage careers without bricks-and-mortar locations, without a bureaucratic structure framing their activities. They depend on bureaucracies, such as Google, of course, but it is by means of online social networking, not within a bureaucracy, that they make a living.

Granted this change, it is possible that we are seeing the emergence of a form of social organization that will replace the dominance of the bureaucracy. Bureaucracies will not disappear. Their efficiency in producing goods and in distributing services will guarantee that they continue. But social networking outside the bureaucratic setting will become an increasingly significant way that people organize themselves to meet their goals. If this continues, bureaucracy might become a hazy "out there" sort of concept for our children.

As technology transforms society, it breaks down the "usual" ways of doing things. In one of the latest changes, some companies such as AKQA have opened virtual offices on Second Life. An AKQA avatar interviews avatars for real jobs. The real person, not the avatar, is actually hired and receives the real paycheck.

For Your Consideration

➔ Do you think that the author's prediction that social networking will replace the bureaucracy as the dominant form of social organization has any merit? Why or why not?

7.3 Discuss the functions of voluntary associations, why people join them, and the significance of the iron law of oligarchy.

Voluntary Associations

Although bureaucracies have become the dominant form of organization for large, task-oriented groups, even more common are voluntary associations. Let's examine their characteristics.

Back in the 1830s, Alexis de Tocqueville, a Frenchman, traveled across the United States, observing the customs of this new nation. His report, *Democracy in America* (1835/1966), was popular both in Europe and in the United States. It is still quoted for its insights into the American character. One of de Tocqueville's observations was that Americans joined a lot of **voluntary associations**, groups made up of volunteers who organize on the basis of some mutual interest.

voluntary associations groups made up of people who voluntarily organize on the basis of some mutual interest; also known as *voluntary memberships* and *voluntary organizations*

Americans have continued this pattern. A visitor entering one of the thousands of small towns that dot the U.S. landscape is often greeted by a sign proclaiming some of the town's voluntary associations: Girl Scouts, Boy Scouts, Kiwanis, Lions, Elks, Eagles, Knights of Columbus, Chamber of Commerce, American Legion, Veterans of Foreign Wars, and perhaps a host of others. One type of voluntary association is so prevalent that a separate sign sometimes indicates which varieties the town offers: Roman Catholic, Baptist, Lutheran, Methodist, Episcopalian, and so on. Not listed on these signs are many other voluntary associations, such as political parties, unions, health clubs, National Right to Life, National Organization for Women, Alcoholics Anonymous, Gamblers Anonymous, Association of Pinto Racers, and Citizens United For or Against This and That.

Americans love voluntary associations and use them to express a wide variety of interests. Some groups are local, consisting of only a few volunteers; others are national, with a paid professional staff. Some are temporary, organized to accomplish some specific task, such as arranging the Fourth of July fireworks. Others, such as the Scouts and political parties, are permanent—large, secondary organizations with clear lines of command—and they are also bureaucracies.

Functions of Voluntary Associations

Whatever their form, voluntary associations are numerous because they meet people's needs. People do not *have* to belong to these organizations. They join because they believe in "the cause" and obtain benefits from their participation. Functionalists have identified seven functions of voluntary associations.

1. They advance particular interests. For example, adults who are concerned about children's welfare volunteer for the Scouts because they think kids are better off joining this group than hanging out on the street. In short, voluntary associations get things done, whether this means organizing a neighborhood crime watch or a local arts association.
2. They offer people an identity. They give their members a feeling of belonging, and for many, a sense of doing something worthwhile. This function is so important for some individuals that the voluntary association even provides a sense of purpose in life.
3. They help maintain social order. This is easy to see in the case of organizations that focus on political action, such as those that "get out the vote" or those that promote patriotism. But to the extent that any organization helps to incorporate individuals into society, it helps to maintain social order.

Sociologist David Sills (1968) identified four other functions, which apply only to some voluntary associations.

4. Some voluntary groups mediate between the government and the individual. For example, some groups provide a way for people to put pressure on lawmakers or to promote candidates for political office.
5. By providing training in organizational skills, some groups help people climb the occupational ladder.
6. Other groups help bring people into the political mainstream. The National Association for the Advancement of Colored People (NAACP) is an example of such a group.
7. Finally, some voluntary associations pave the way for social change. As they challenge established ways of doing things, boundaries start to give way. The confrontations of Greenpeace and Sea Shepherds, for example, are reshaping taken-for-granted definitions of "normal" when it comes to the environment.

Motivations for Joining

People have many motivations for joining voluntary associations. Some join because they hold strong convictions about the purpose of the organization, and they want to help fulfill the group's goals. Others join because membership helps them politically or professionally—or looks good on a college or job application. Some may even join because they have romantic interests in a group member. With so many motivations for joining, and because their commitment is fleeting, some people move in and out of voluntary associations almost as fast as they change clothes.

Within each organization, however, is an *inner circle*—individuals who stand firmly behind the group's goals, who actively promote the group, and who are committed to maintaining the organization. If this inner circle loses its commitment, the group is likely to fold.

Let's look more closely at this inner circle.

The Inner Circle and the "Iron Law" of Oligarchy

The Inner Circle. A significant aspect of a voluntary association is that its key members, its inner circle, often grow distant from the regular members. They become convinced that only they can be trusted to make the group's important decisions. To see this principle at work, let's look at the Veterans of Foreign Wars (VFW).

Sociologists Elaine Fox and George Arquitt (1985) studied three local posts of the Veterans of Foreign Wars. They found that although the leaders of the VFW concealed their attitudes from the other members, the inner circle viewed the rank and file as a bunch of ignorant boozers. Because the leaders couldn't stand the thought that such people might represent them in the community and at national meetings, a curious situation arose. The rank-and-file members were eligible for top leadership positions, but they never became leaders. In fact, the inner circle was so effective in controlling these top positions that even before an election, they could tell you who was going to win. "You need to meet Jim," the sociologists were told. "He's the next post commander after Sam does his time."

At first, the researchers found this puzzling. The election hadn't been held yet. As they investigated further, they found that leadership was determined behind the scenes. The current leaders appointed their favored people to chair the key committees. This spotlighted their names and accomplishments, propelling the members to elect them. By appointing its own members to highly visible positions, then, the inner circle maintained control over the entire organization.

iron law of oligarchy Robert Michels' term for the tendency of formal organizations to be dominated by a small, self perpetuating elite

The Iron Law of Oligarchy. Like the VFW, in most voluntary associations, an elite inner circle keeps itself in power by passing the leadership positions among its members. Sociologist Robert Michels (1876–1936) coined the term the **iron law of oligarchy** to refer to how organizations come to be dominated by a small, self-perpetuating elite. (*Oligarchy* means a system in which many are ruled by a few.)

What many find disturbing about the iron law of oligarchy is that people are excluded from leadership because they don't represent the inner circle's values, or, in some instances, their background or even the way they look. This is true even of organizations that are committed to democratic principles. For example, U.S. political parties—supposedly the backbone of the nation's representative government—are run by an inner circle that passes leadership positions from one elite member to another. This principle also shows up in the U.S. Congress. With their control of political machinery and access to free mailing, 90 to 95 percent of U.S. senators and representatives who choose to run are reelected (*Statistical Abstract* 2006:Table 394; Friedman and Holden 2009).

The iron law of oligarchy is not without its limitations, of course. Regardless of their personal feelings, members of the inner circle must remain attuned to the opinions of the rank-and-file members. If the oligarchy gets too far out of line, it runs the risk of a grassroots rebellion that would throw the elite out of office. This threat softens the iron law of oligarchy by making the leadership responsive to the membership. The iron law of oligarchy, then, is actually more like a copper law of oligarchy. In addition, because not all organizations become captive to an elite, it is a strong tendency, not an inevitability.

In a process called the *iron law of oligarchy*, a small, self-perpetuating elite tends to take control of formal organizations. The text explains that the leaders of the local VFW posts separate themselves from the rank-and-file members, such as those shown here in Anaheim, California.

Working for the Corporation

Since you are likely to be working for a bureaucracy after college, let's examine some of its characteristics and how these might affect your career.

7.4 Discuss humanizing the work setting, fads in corporate culture, the "hidden" corporate culture, and worker diversity.

Humanizing the Work Setting

Bureaucracies have transformed society by harnessing people's energies to reach goals. Weber (1946) predicted that because bureaucracies were both efficient and had the capacity to replace themselves, they would come to dominate social life. All we have to do is look around us to see how this prediction in sociology has come true (Rothschild and Whitt 1986; Perrow 1991).

With most of us destined to spend our working lives in a bureaucracy, concern has grown that corporations can be rigid and impede people's abilities and relationships. To overcome this obstacle, called **humanizing the work setting**, some organizations have developed more flexible rules and open decision-making. They have also opened up greater access to power and opportunities for their workers.

humanizing the work setting organizing a workplace in such a way that it develops rather than impedes human potential

corporate culture the values, norms, and other orientation that characterize corporate work settings

But what about the cost of fostering a **corporate culture** that maximizes human potential? The United States faces formidable economic competitors—from Germany in Europe to Brazil in South America and Japan and China in Asia. Humanizing corporate culture, however, can actually increase profits. Sociologist Rosabeth Moss Kanter (1983) compared forty-seven companies that were rigidly bureaucratic with competitors of the same size that were more flexible. Kanter found that the more flexible companies were more profitable—probably because their greater flexibility encouraged creativity, productivity, and company loyalty.

Let's look at two ways that corporations have tried to humanize the work setting: worker empowerment and child care. Keep in mind that the companies are not motivated by some altruistic urge to make life better for their workers but by the same motivation as always—the bottom line. It is in management's self-interest to make their company more competitive.

Worker Empowerment. One way to give workers more power is to establish *work teams*, small groups of workers who set goals and develop solutions to reach them. These self-managed teams hold daily progress sessions and weekly reviews (Feiler 2013). Some teams even replace bosses, setting their own schedules and hiring and firing workers (Lublin 1991; Kanter 2009). Employees in work teams are absent less, are more productive, and are quicker to react to technological change and competitors' advances (Drucker 1992; Petty et al. 2008).

Why would empowering workers bring such positive results? Let's apply concepts we discussed in the last chapter. In small work groups, people form primary relationships, preventing their individuality from being lost in a bureaucratic maze. As their peers acknowledge their contributions, they come to feel appreciated. The group's successes become the individual's successes—as do its failures. With these personal ties creating face-to-face accountability, alienation is reduced, and workers make more of an effort. Not all teams work together well, however, and researchers are trying to determine what makes some teams succeed and others fail (Borsch-Supan et al. 2007).

Daycare for workers' children is one of the ways corporations attempt to humanize the work setting. This photo from Washington, D.C. is of emergency day care provided by Lipton.

Corporate Child Care. Some companies improve the work setting by offering on-site child care facilities. This eases the strain on parents, since they can keep in touch with their children while at work. They get to observe the quality of the child care, and they can even spend time with their children during breaks and lunch hours (Kantor 2006, 2009; Torres 2012). Some corporations that don't offer on-site child care offer *back-up care* for both children and dependent adults. This service helps employees avoid missing work even when they face emergencies, such as a sitter who can't make it.

As more women have become managers, their needs have found a greater voice in policy. A notable example is that the federal medical reform law requires employers to provide "lactation rooms" for nursing mothers who return to work. This must be a place other than a bathroom that is shielded from view and from the intrusion of others (Miller 2012). An issue that has arisen is how much time the employer must give the mothers to express milk for their babies (Shellenbarger 2011).

Conflict theorists would say that this cartoon is more realistic than the organization chart shown in Figure 7.1 (p. 176). They would revise the cartoon, however, to show one big fish (owners) eating a lot of little fish (workers).

"For the benefit of our new employees, we've simplified the corporate flow chart."

The Conflict Perspective. Conflict theorists point out that the term *humanizing the work setting* is camouflage for what is really going on. Workers and owners walk different paths in life, and their basic relationship is confrontational. Owners exploit workers to extract greater profits, and workers try to resist that exploitation. What employers call humanizing the work setting (or managing diversity) is just one of endless attempts to manipulate workers into cooperating in their own exploitation. Nice-sounding terms like *humanizing* are attempts to conceal the capitalists' goal of exploiting workers.

Fads in Corporate Culture

Ways to humanize the work setting—and, not coincidentally, to increase productivity—go through fads. Something that is hot one day may be cold the next. Twenty years ago, the rage was *quality circles*, workers and a manager or two who met regularly to try to improve both working conditions and the company's products. Because quality circles were used in Japan, U.S. managers embraced them, thinking they had discovered the secret of Japanese success. At their height of popularity in 1983, tens of thousands of U.S. firms were using quality circles, and sixty consultants specialized in teaching them (Strang and Macy 2001). Then quality circles were quietly shuffled into the corporate garbage bin.

Corporations continue to hop from one fad to another. They hold activities to build "emotional integration"—singing a company song or climbing a mountain together (Kanter 2009:201). They sponsor "cook-offs" with corporate teams going cleaver to cleaver, slicing, dicing, and sautéing against the clock (Hafner 2007). It seems safe to predict that, like quality circles, these team-building exercises will soon pass—to be replaced by still some other fad.

Self-Fulfilling Stereotypes in the "Hidden" Corporate Culture

As you might recall from Chapter 4, stereotypes can be self-fulfilling. That is, stereotypes can produce the very characteristics they are built around. The example used there was of stereotypes of appearance and personality. Sociologists have also uncovered **self-fulfilling stereotypes** in corporate life (Rivera 2012; Whiteley et al. 2012). Let's see how they might affect *your* career after college.

self-fulfilling stereotype
preconceived ideas of what someone is like that lead to the person's behaving in ways that match the stereotype

Self-Fulfilling Stereotypes and Promotions. Corporate and department heads have ideas of "what it takes" to get ahead. Not surprisingly, since they themselves got ahead, they look for people who have characteristics similar to their own. They feed better information to workers who have these characteristics, bring them into stronger networks, and put them in "fast-track" positions. With such advantages, these workers perform better and become more committed to the company. This, of course, confirms the supervisor's expectations, the initial stereotype of a successful person.

But for workers who don't look or act like the corporate leaders, the opposite happens. Thinking of these people as less capable, the bosses give them fewer opportunities and challenges. When these workers realize that they are working beneath their abilities and see others get ahead, they lose motivation, become less committed to the company, and don't perform as well. This, of course, confirms the stereotypes the bosses had of them.

In her research on U.S. corporations, Kanter (1977, 1983) found that such self-fulfilling stereotypes are part of a **"hidden" corporate culture**. That is, these stereotypes and their powerful effects on workers remain hidden to everyone, even the bosses. What bosses and workers see is the surface: Workers who have superior performance and greater commitment to the company get promoted. To bosses and workers alike, this seems to be just the way it should be. Hidden below this surface, however, are the higher and lower expectations and the opening and closing of opportunities that produce the attitudes and the accomplishments—or the lack of them.

Diversity in the Workplace

At one point in U.S. history, most workers were white men. Over the years, this gradually changed, and now 47 percent of workers are women and 31 percent are minorities (*Statistical Abstract* 2013:Tables 603, 604). With such extensive diversity, the stereotypes in the hidden corporate culture will give way, although only grudgingly. In the following Thinking Critically section, let's consider diversity in the workplace.

Explore on **MySocLab**
Activity: Age Discrimination on the Job

THINKING CRITICALLY

Managing Diversity in the Workplace

Times have changed. The San Jose, California, electronic phone book lists *ten* times more *Nguyens* than *Joneses* (Albanese 2010). More than half of U.S. workers are minorities, immigrants, and women. Diversity in the workplace is much more than skin color. Diversity includes age, ethnicity, gender, religion, sexual orientation, and social class (Bezrukova at al. 2012).

The cultural and racial–ethnic diversity of today's work force has led to the need for diversity training.

It used to be assumed that people would join the "melting pot." They would give up their distinctive traits and become like the dominant group. The civil rights and women's movements changed this idea, and people today are more likely to prize their distinctive traits. Realizing that assimilation (being absorbed into the dominant culture) is probably not the wave of the future, most large companies have "diversity training" (Bennett 2010). They hold lectures and workshops so that employees can learn to work with colleagues of diverse cultures and racial–ethnic backgrounds.

hidden corporate culture
stereotypes of the traits that make for high-performing and underperforming workers

Coors Brewery is a prime example. Coors went into a financial tailspin after one of the Coors brothers gave a racially charged speech in the 1980s. Today, Coors holds diversity workshops, sponsors gay dances, has paid for a corporate-wide mammography program, and has opposed an amendment to the Colorado constitution that would ban same-sex marriage. Coors has even sent a spokesperson to gay bars to promote its beer (Kim 2004). The company has also had rabbis certify its suds as kosher. Quite a change.

Coors even adopted the slogan "Coors cares." Cute, but this slogan does not mean that Coors cares about diversity. What Coors cares about is the same as other corporations, the bottom line. Blatant racism and sexism once made no difference to profitability. Today, they do. To promote profitability, companies must promote diversity—or at least give the appearance of doing so. The sincerity of corporate leaders is not what's important; diversity in the workplace is.

Pepsi provides a good example of a positive, effective approach to diversity training. Managers are given the assignment of sponsoring a group of employees who are unlike themselves. Men sponsor women, African Americans sponsor whites, and so on. The executives are expected to try to understand the work situation from the perspective of the people they sponsor, to identify key talent, and to personally mentor at least three people in their group. Accountability is built in: The sponsors have to give updates to executives even higher up (Terhune 2005).

Researchers have found that forcing workers to participate in diversity programs or doing the minimum to prevent lawsuits produces resentment. But setting goals for increasing diversity and making managers accountable for reaching these goals increase the diversity of a company's workers.

For Your Consideration

➤ Do you think that corporations and government agencies should offer diversity training? Can you suggest practical ways to develop workplaces that overcome divisions of gender and race–ethnicity? ■

7.5 Summarize major issues in the technological control of workers..

Scrutinizing the Workplace: The Technological Spy

Bosses want to know that their workers aren't goofing off. In many cases, this has been difficult to determine, but technology is coming to their rescue. Computers now monitor millions of workers. In some workplaces, cameras even analyze workers' facial expressions (Neil 2008). As with the workers in the Sociology and the New Technology box on the next page, few of us realize how extensively we are being monitored.

7.6 Explain how global competition is affecting corporations.

Global Competition in an Age of Uncertainty

A fierce competition has been unleashed across the globe. Major corporations are looking over their shoulders, fearful that competitors will discover cheaper ways to produce their products or sell their services. Each fears ending up as a corporate has-been, a business footnote, or even a forgotten nothing in economic history. The race may not always go to the swift, but organizations have to stay nimble if they are to survive. In the Cultural Diversity box with which we close this chapter, let's look at two of the main competitors in this global race to wealth and power.

Sociology and the New Technology

Cyberloafers and Cybersleuths: Surfing at Work

Few people work constantly at their jobs. Most of us take breaks and, at least once in a while, goof off. We meet fellow workers in the "break room," and we talk in the hallway. Much of this interaction is good for the company, since it bonds us to fellow workers and ties us to our jobs.

Sometimes our personal lives cross over into our workday. We check in with our child's school or make arrangements for a babysitter. Bosses expect such personal calls from the office. Some even wink as we make a date or nod as we arrange to have our car worked on. Bosses, too, make their own personal calls. These are the norm, the expected. It's the abuse that gets people fired.

Using computers at work for personal purposes is called *cyberslacking*. Many workers download music, gamble, and play games at work. They read books, shop, exchange jokes, send personal e-mail, trade stocks, and post messages in chat rooms. Some visit porno sites. Some cyberslackers even operate their own businesses online—when they're not battling virtual enemies during "work."

> *The master cyberslacker is a programmer who has become somewhat of a folk hero (Poole 2013). "Bob," as he is known, outsourced his own job to a company in China. Bob paid the Chinese one-fifth of his salary and spent his "work days" online. In his little cubicle, he would visit Facebook and eBay and watch cute cat videos. Bob's supervisors were pleased with Bob's work. He produced "clean code" and was always on time. Bob was even voted the best coder in the building.*

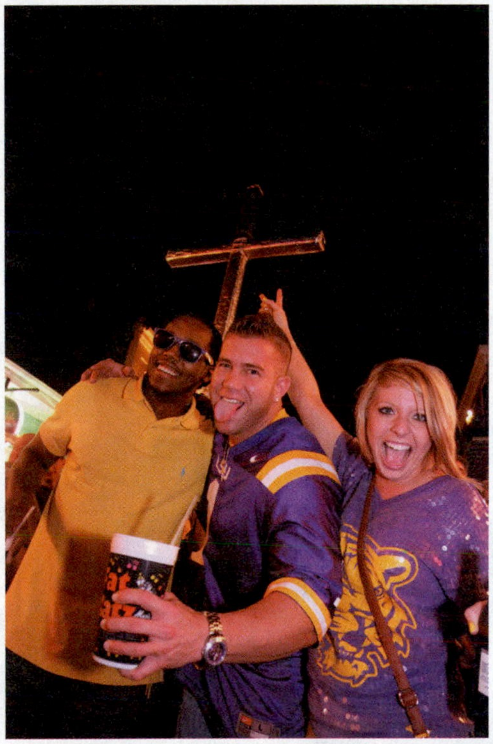

Candidates for jobs are sometimes rejected when the prospective employer finds negative images or information on social media sites.

Cyberslacking has given birth to *cybersleuths*. Investigators use software programs that can recover not just every note employees have written but also every Web site they have visited and even every keystroke they have made (Tokc-Wilde 2011). They can bring up every file that employees have deleted, every word they've erased. What some workers forget is that "delete" does not mean erase. Hitting the delete button simply pushes the text into the background of our hard drive. As if revealing invisible ink, cybersleuths can expose our "deleted" information with a few clicks. It's like opening a hidden diary for anyone to read. It was the company's cybersleuths who investigated "Bob" and found out how he really spent his days at work.

Then there are the social media sites, from Facebook to LinkedIn. When you delete a rant at the world or against some individual, is it gone? Or when you delete a photo that you posted solely for your close friends, does it disappear? So you might think. But they aren't gone. They seem to exist somewhere forever. Programs can seemingly grab them from back in time and expose them for the world to see.

For whatever reason, some people get a kick out of posting photos online of themselves drunk, naked, holding guns, or doing obnoxious things (Barrett and Saul 2011). These photos prevent many otherwise qualified applicants from landing a job. Let's suppose that an interviewer has done a little online searching. When he or she looks at the eager new college graduate with the solid academic record sitting on the other side of the desk, can you see why images of bongs, exposed breasts, or drooling, spaced-out looks will come to mind—and how those images can torpedo that job interview?

For Your Consideration

➤ Do you think that employers have a right to check what prospective employees have posted online? How about checking what their employees are doing with company computers on company time? How about checking on what their employees are doing on their own time?

Cultural Diversity around the World

Japanese and U.S. Corporations: Awkward Symbiosis

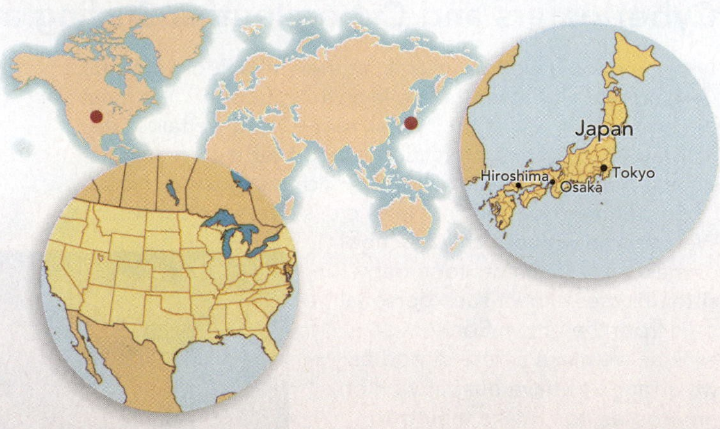

Do you know which of these statements is false?

The Japanese are more productive than Americans.
The living standard of Americans has fallen behind that of the Japanese.
Japanese workers enjoy lifetime job security.
The Japanese are paid less than Americans.

A while back, Japanese corporations seemed invincible. There was even talk that the United States had won World War II but had lost the economic war. Impressed with Japan's success, U.S. and European corporations sent executives to Japan to study their companies. They then copied parts of their model.

Then cracks in the Japanese corporate facade appeared. Small at first, the cracks grew until they destroyed some of Japan's major corporations. The change has been so extensive that all four of the statements above are false.

Unlike U.S. corporations, Japanese companies had been built on personal relationships. Mutual obligations transcended contracts. These personal relationships had created a fierce loyalty among production workers and executives. When workers were hired, they knew that they would remain with a company for life. As impressive as it was, this corporate strength turned out to be an Achilles heel. When Japan's economy went into a nosedive in the 1990s, companies did not lay off workers. Layoffs represented disloyalty, and they were not part of Japan's corporate culture. Labor costs mounted while profits disappeared, and companies sank in a sea of red ink.

In an abrupt turnabout, Japan turned to the United States to see why its companies were more efficient. Although following the U.S. model meant flying in the face of their traditions, Japanese companies began to offer merit pay and to lay off workers, acts that had previously been unthinkable in their culture (Tokoro 2005). Today, a third of Japanese factory workers are temporary workers who are paid just two-thirds of what regular workers earn. They have no job security and can be dismissed without severance pay (Murphy and Inada 2008).

Just as U.S. manufacturing and advertising have influenced Japan, so they are having an impact on China. Ford and Mazda have partnered with Changan Automobile to manufacture cars in China. As you can see from this photo taken at an automobile show in Beijing, China is adopting not just products but also Western culture, including some of its gender stereotypes.

When Mazda teetered on the edge of bankruptcy, its creditors decided that Ford knew more about building and marketing cars than Mazda. They invited Ford to take a controlling interest in and manage the company. In true U.S. fashion, Ford laid off workers and renegotiated contracts with suppliers. With its workforce slashed from 46,000 to 36,000, Mazda again became profitable. Similarly, when Sony's profits plummeted, an American who couldn't even speak Japanese became its CEO (Kane and Dvorak 2007).

In a continuing ironic twist of corporate evolution, the Japanese were learning their lessons just as their U.S. mentors began to stumble. Although Ford was able to turn Mazda to profitability, it failed to apply its own lessons to save itself from being swallowed in red ink. Under Ford's direction, Mazda turned in healthy profits, while Ford suffered its greatest losses since Henry Ford founded the company (Kageyama 2008). In a desperate bid to raise money to survive, Ford sold much of its stake in Mazda in 2008. With restructuring, Ford is again profitable (Seetharaman 2013).

In the economic shakeout that is rocking the world's economies as I write this, we don't know what companies will survive—but we do know this: Those that survive, whether thriving or hanging on by their corporate fingernails, will be bureaucracies.

CHAPTER 7

Summary and Review

The Rationalization of Society

7.1 Compare the explanations of Marx and Weber for why traditional societies rationalized.

How did the rationalization of society come about?

The term **rationalization of society** refers to a transformation in people's thinking and behaviors—one that shifts the focus from time-honored traditional ways to efficiency in producing results. Karl Marx attributed rationalization to capitalism. Max Weber, who developed this term, traced this change to Protestant (Calvinist) theology, which he said brought about capitalism. Pp. 172–174.

Formal Organizations and Bureaucracies

7.2 Summarize the characteristics of bureaucracies, their dysfunctions, and goal displacement; also contrast ideal and real bureaucracy

What are formal organizations?

Formal organizations are secondary groups designed to achieve specific objectives. Their dominant form is the **bureaucracy**, which Weber said consists of a hierarchy, division of labor, written rules and communications, impersonality, and replaceability of positions. **Goal displacement** is also common. These characteristics make bureaucracies efficient and enduring. Pp. 174–179.

What dysfunctions are associated with bureaucracies?

The dysfunctions of bureaucracies include red tape, lack of communication between units, alienation, and incompetence (as seen in the **Peter Principle**). In Weber's view, the impersonality of bureaucracies tends to produce **alienation** among workers—the feeling that no one cares about them and that they do not fit in. Marx's view of alienation is somewhat different: Workers do not identify with the product of their labor because they participate in only a small part of the production process. Pp. 179–182.

Voluntary Associations

7.3 Discuss the functions of voluntary associations, why people join them, and the significance of the iron law of oligarchy.

What are the functions of voluntary associations?

Voluntary associations are groups made up of volunteers who organize on the basis of common interests. These associations promote mutual interests, provide a sense of identity and purpose, help to govern and maintain order, mediate between the government and the individual, give training in organizational skills, provide access to political power, and pave the way for social change. Pp. 182–184.

What is "the iron law of oligarchy"?

Sociologist Robert Michels noted that inner circles usually run formal organizations, that they limit leadership to their own members. The dominance of a formal organization by an elite that keeps itself in power is called the **iron law of oligarchy**. P. 184.

Working for the Corporation

7.4 Discuss humanizing the work setting, fads in corporate culture, the "hidden" corporate culture, and worker diversity.

What does it mean to humanize the work setting?

Humanizing a work setting means to organize work in a way that it develops rather than impedes human potential. Among the attempts to make bureaucracies more humane are empowering workers and establishing corporate day care. Conflict theorists see attempts to humanize the work setting as a way of manipulating workers. Pp. 185–186.

How does a hidden corporate culture affect workers?

Within companies is a **hidden corporate culture**, stereotypes of the traits that produce successful and unsuccessful workers. People who match a corporation's hidden culture of success tend to be put on career tracks that enhance their chances of success. Those who do not match these **self-fulfilling stereotypes** are set on courses that minimize their performance. Pp. 186–188.

Scrutinizing the Workplace: The Technological Spy

7.5 Summarize major issues in the technological control of workers.

How is technology changing the surveillance of workers?

Computers and surveillance devices are increasingly used to monitor people, especially in the workplace. This intrusive technology is being extended to monitoring our everyday lives. Pp. 188–189.

Global Competition in an Age of Uncertainty

7.6 Explain how global competition is affecting corporations.

How do bureaucracies fit into global competition?

Of the corporations now in global competition, only the most efficient will survive. The rapid success of the Japanese corporations and their quick decline indicate the need for continuing innovation. Pp. 188–190.

Thinking Critically about Chapter 7

1. You are likely to work for a bureaucracy. How do you think that this will affect your orientations to life? How can you make the hidden corporate culture work to your advantage?
2. Do you think the Peter Principle is right? Why or why not?
3. Why do you think the iron law of oligarchy is such a common feature of voluntary organizations?
4. What do you think are the best ways to humanize the corporate culture?

CHAPTER 8

Deviance and Social Control

Listen to Chapter 8 on MySocLab

Learning Objectives

After you have read this chapter, you should be able to:

8.1 Summarize the relativity of deviance, the need of norms, and the types of sanctions; contrast sociobiological, psychological and sociological explanations of deviance. (p. 194)

8.2 Contrast three theories of deviance: differential association, control, and labeling. (p. 198)

8.3 Explain how deviance can be functional for society, how mainstream values can produce deviance (strain theory), and how social class is related to crime (illegitimate opportunities). (p. 204)

8.4 Explain how social class is related to the criminal justice system and how the criminal justice system is oppressive. (p. 210)

8.5 Be familiar with street crimes and prison, three-strikes laws, the decline in violent crime, recidivism, bias in the death penalty, the medicalization of deviance, and the need for a humane approach. (p. 211)

In just a few moments I was to meet my first Yanomamö, my first primitive man. What would it be like? . . . I looked up [from my canoe] and gasped when I saw a dozen burly, naked, filthy, hideous men staring at us down the shafts of their drawn arrows. Immense wads of green tobacco were stuck between their lower teeth and lips, making them look even more hideous, and strands of dark-green slime dripped or hung from their noses. We arrived at the village while the men were blowing a hallucinogenic drug up their noses. One of the side effects of the drug is a runny nose. The mucus is always saturated with the green powder, and the Indians usually let it run freely from their nostrils. . . . I just sat there holding my notebook, helpless and pathetic. . . .

The whole situation was depressing, and I wondered why I ever decided to switch from civil engineering to anthropology in the first place. . . . [Soon] I was covered with red pigment, the result of a dozen or so complete examinations. . . . These examinations capped an otherwise grim day. The Indians would blow their noses into their hands, flick as much of the mucus off that would separate in a snap of the wrist, wipe the residue into their hair, and then carefully examine my face, arms, legs, hair, and the contents of my pockets. I said [in their language], "Your hands are dirty"; my comments were met by the Indians in the following way: they would "clean" their hands by spitting a quantity of slimy tobacco juice into them, rub them together, and then proceed with the examination.

"They would "clean" their hands by spitting slimy tobacco juice into them."

This is how Napoleon Chagnon describes the culture shock he felt when he met the Yanomamö tribe of the rain forests of Brazil. His following months of fieldwork continued to bring surprise after surprise, and often Chagnon (1977) could hardly believe his eyes—or his nose.

If you were to list the deviant behaviors of the Yanomamö, what would you include? The way they appear naked in public? Use hallucinogenic drugs? Let mucus hang from their noses? Or the way they rub hands filled with mucus, spittle, and tobacco juice over a frightened stranger who doesn't dare to protest? Perhaps. But it isn't this simple. As we shall see, deviance is relative.

What Is Deviance?

8.1 Summarize the relativity of deviance, the need of norms, and the types of sanctions; contrast sociobiological, psychological and sociological explanations of deviance.

Sociologists use the term **deviance** to refer to any violation of norms, whether the infraction is as minor as driving over the speed limit, as serious as murder, or as humorous as Chagnon's encounter with the Yanomamö. This deceptively simple definition takes us to the heart of the sociological perspective on deviance, which sociologist Howard S. Becker (1966) described this way: *It is not the act itself, but the reactions to the act, that make something deviant.* What Chagnon saw disturbed him, but to the Yanomamö, those same behaviors represented normal, everyday life. What was deviant to Chagnon was *conformist* to the Yanomamö. From their viewpoint, you *should* check out strangers the way they did—and nakedness is good, as are hallucinogenic drugs. And it is natural to let mucus flow.

The Relativity of Deviance. Chagnon's abrupt introduction to the Yanomamö allows us to see the *relativity of deviance*, a major point made by symbolic interactionists. Because different groups have different norms, *what is deviant to some is not deviant to others.* This principle applies not just to cultures but also to groups within the same society. Look at the photo on the next page and the one on page 197. This principle also applies to norms of sexuality, the focus of the Cultural Diversity box on page 196.

deviance the violation of norms (or rules or expectations)

The relativity of deviance also applies to **crime**, the violation of rules that have been written into law. In the extreme, an act that is applauded by one group may be so despised by another group that it is punishable by death. Making a huge profit on business deals is one example. Americans who do this are admired. Like Donald Trump and Warren Buffet, they may even write books about their exploits. In China, however, until recently, this same act was considered a crime called *profiteering*. Those found guilty were hanged in a public square as a lesson to all.

The Chinese example also lets us see how even within the same society, the meaning of an act can change over time. With China's switch to capitalism, making large profits has changed from a crime punishable by death to an act to be admired.

A Neutral Term. Unlike the general public, sociologists use the term *deviance* nonjudgmentally, to refer to any act to which people respond negatively. When sociologists use this term, it does *not* mean that they are saying that an act is bad, just that people judge it negatively. To sociologists, then, *all* of us are deviants of one sort or another, since we all violate norms from time to time.

Stigma. To be considered deviant, a person does not even have to *do* anything. Sociologist Erving Goffman (1963) used the term **stigma** to refer to characteristics that discredit people. These include violations of norms of appearance (a facial birthmark, a huge nose, ears that stick out) and norms of ability (blindness, deafness, mental handicaps). Also included are involuntary memberships, such as being a victim of AIDS or the brother of a rapist. The stigma can become a person's master status, defining him or her as deviant. Recall from Chapter 4 that a master status cuts across all other statuses that a person occupies.

I took this photo on the outskirts of Hyderabad, India. Is this man deviant? If this were a U.S. street, he would be. But here? No houses have running water in his neighborhood, and the men, women, and children bathe at the neighborhood water pump. This man, then, would not be deviant in this culture. And yet, he is actually mugging for my camera, making the three bystanders laugh. Does this additional factor make this a scene of deviance?

How Norms Make Social Life Possible

No human group can exist without norms: *Norms make social life possible by making behavior predictable.* What would life be like if you could not predict what others would do? Imagine for a moment that you have gone to a store to purchase milk:

> *Suppose the clerk says, "I won't sell you any milk. We're overstocked with soda, and I'm not going to sell anyone milk until our soda inventory is reduced."*
>
> *You don't like it, but you decide to buy a case of soda. At the checkout, the clerk says, "I hope you don't mind, but there's a $5 service charge on every fifteenth customer." You, of course, are the fifteenth.*
>
> *Just as you start to leave, another clerk stops you and says, "We're not working anymore. We decided to have a party." Suddenly a CD player begins to blast, and everyone in the store begins to dance. "Oh, good, you've brought the soda," says a different clerk, who takes your package and passes sodas all around.*

Life is not like this, of course. You can depend on grocery clerks to sell you milk. You can also depend on paying the same price as everyone else and not being forced to attend a party in the store. Why can you depend on this? Because we are socialized to follow norms, to play the basic roles that society assigns to us.

Without norms, we would have social chaos. Norms lay out the basic guidelines for how we should play our roles and interact with others. In short, norms bring about **social order**, a group's customary social arrangements. Our lives are based on these arrangements, which is why deviance often is perceived as threatening: *Deviance undermines predictability, the foundation of social life.* Consequently, human groups develop a

crime the violation of norms written into law

stigma "blemishes" that discredit a person's claim to a "normal" identity

social order a group's usual and customary social arrangements, on which its members depend and on which they base their lives

Cultural Diversity around the World

Human Sexuality in Cross-Cultural Perspective

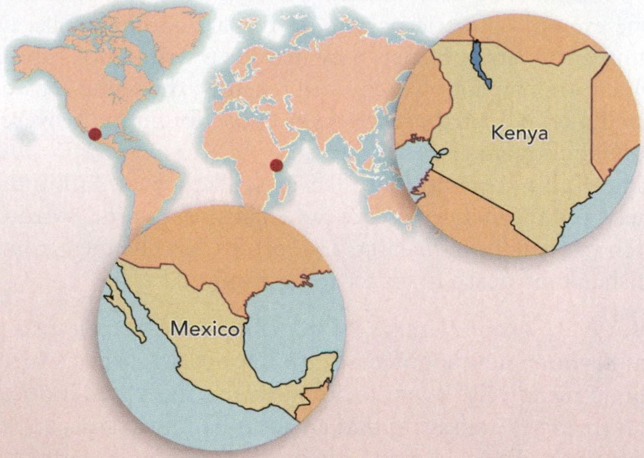

Human sexuality illustrates how a group's *definition* of an act, not the act itself, determines whether it will be considered deviant. Let's look at some examples reported by anthropologist Robert Edgerton (1976).

Norms of sexual behavior vary so widely around the world that what is considered normal in one society may be considered deviant in another. In Kenya, a group called the Pokot place high emphasis on sexual pleasure, and they expect that both a husband and wife will reach orgasm. If a husband does not satisfy his wife, he is in trouble—especially if she thinks that his failure is because of adultery. If this is so, the wife and her female friends will sneak up on her husband when he is asleep. The women will tie him up, shout obscenities at him, beat him, and then urinate on him. As a final gesture of their contempt, before releasing him they will slaughter and eat his favorite ox. The husband's hours of painful humiliation are intended to make him more dutiful concerning his wife's conjugal rights.

People can also become deviants for following their group's ideal norms instead of its real norms. As with many groups, the Zapotec Indians of Mexico profess that sexual relations should take place exclusively between husband and wife. However, the Zapotec also have a covert norm, an unspoken understanding, that married people will have affairs but that they will be discreet about them. In one Zapotec community, the *only* person who did not have an extramarital affair was condemned by everyone in the village. The reason was not that she did not have an affair but that she told the other wives who their husbands were sleeping with. It is an interesting case; if this virtuous woman had had an affair—and kept her mouth shut—she would not have become a deviant. Clearly, real norms can conflict with ideal norms—another illustration of the gap between ideal and real culture.

A Pokot married woman, Kenya

For Your Consideration

➤ How do the behaviors of the Pokot wives and husbands mentioned here look from the perspective of U.S. norms? What are those U.S. norms? What norms did the Zapotec woman break? How does cultural relativity apply to the Pokot and Zapotec? (We discussed this concept in Chapter 2, pages 37–41.)

system of **social control**—formal and informal means of enforcing norms. At the center of social control are sanctions.

social control a group's formal and informal means of enforcing its norms

negative sanction an expression of disapproval for breaking a norm, ranging from a mild, informal reaction such as a frown to a formal reaction such as a fine or a prison sentence

positive sanction an expression of approval for following a norm, ranging from a smile or a good grade in a class to a material reward such as a prize

Sanctions

As we discussed in Chapter 2, people do not enforce folkways strictly, but they become upset when people break mores (MO-rays). Expressions of disapproval for deviance, called **negative sanctions**, range from frowns and gossip for breaking folkways to imprisonment and death for violating mores. In general, the more seriously the group takes a norm, the harsher the penalty for violating it. In contrast, **positive sanctions**—from smiles to formal awards—are used to reward people for conforming to norms. Getting a raise is a positive sanction; being fired is a negative sanction. Getting an A in Intro to Sociology is a positive sanction; getting an F is a negative one.

Most negative sanctions are informal. You might stare if you observe someone dressed in what you consider to be inappropriate clothing, or you might gossip if a married person you know spends the night with someone other than his or her spouse. Whether you consider the breaking of a norm an amusing matter that warrants no sanction or a serious infraction that does, however, depends on your perspective. Let's suppose that a woman appears at your college graduation in a bikini. You might stare, laugh, and nudge the person next to you, but if this is *your* mother, you are likely to feel that different sanctions are appropriate. Similarly, if it is *your* father who spends the night with an 18-year-old college freshman, you are likely to do more than gossip.

In Sum: In sociology, the term deviance refers to all violations of social rules, regardless of their seriousness. The term is neutral, not a judgment about the behavior. Deviance is so relative that what is deviant in one group may be conformist in another. Because of this, we must consider deviance from within a group's own framework: It is their meanings that underlie their behavior.

Violating background assumptions is a common form of deviance. Although we have no explicit rule that says, "Do not put snakes through your nose," we all know that it exists (perhaps as a subcategory of "Don't do strange things in public"). Is this act also deviant for this man in Chennai, India?

Competing Explanations of Deviance: Sociobiology, Psychology, and Sociology

If social life is to exist, norms are essential. So why do people violate them? To better understand the reasons, it is useful to know how sociological explanations differ from biological and psychological ones. Let's compare them.

Biosocial Explanations. *Sociobiologists* explain deviance by looking for answers *within* individuals. They assume that **genetic predispositions** lead people to such behaviors as juvenile delinquency and crime (Lombroso 1911; Wilson and Herrnstein 1985; Barnes and Jacobs 2013). An early explanation was that men with an extra Y chromosome (the "XYY" theory) were more likely to become criminals. Another was that people with "squarish, muscular" bodies were more likely to commit **street crime**—acts such as mugging, rape, and burglary. These theories were abandoned when research did not support them.

With advances in the study of genetics, biosocial explanations are being proposed to explain differences in crime by sex, race-ethnicity, social class, and age (juvenile delinquency) (Walsh and Beaver 2009; Wiebe 2012). The basic explanation is that over the millennia, people with certain characteristics were more likely to survive than were people with different characteristics. As a result, different groups today inherit different propensities (tendencies) for empathy, self-control, and risk-taking.

A universal finding is that in all known societies, men commit more violent crimes than women do. There are no exceptions. Here is how sociobiologists explain this. It took only a few pelvic thrusts for men to pass on their genes. After that, they could leave if they wanted to. The women, in contrast, had to carry, birth, and nurture the children. Women who were more empathetic (inclined to nurture their children) engaged in less dangerous behavior. These women passed genes for more empathy, greater self-control, and less risk-taking to their female children. As a result, all over the world, men engage in more violent behavior, which comes from their lesser empathy, lower self-control, and greater tendency for taking risks.

But behavior, whether deviant or conforming, does not depend only on genes, add the biosocial theorists (Barnes and Jacobs 2013). Our inherited propensities (the *bio* part) are modified and stimulated by our environment (the *social* part). Biosocial research holds the potential of opening a new understanding of deviance.

Psychological Explanations. Psychologists focus on abnormalities *within* the individual. Instead of genes, they examine what are called **personality disorders**. Their supposition is that deviating individuals have deviating personalities (Mayer 2007; Yu et al. 2012) and that subconscious motives drive people to deviance.

Researchers have never found a specific childhood experience to be invariably linked with deviance. For example, some children who had "bad toilet training," "suffocating mothers," or "emotionally aloof fathers" do become embezzling bookkeepers—but others become good accountants. Just as college students and police officers represent a variety of bad—and good—childhood experiences, so do deviants. Similarly, people with "suppressed anger" can become freeway snipers or military heroes—or anything else. In short, there is no inevitable outcome of any childhood experience. Deviance is not associated with any particular personality.

genetic predisposition inborn tendencies (for example, a tendency to commit deviant acts)

street crime crimes such as mugging, rape, and burglary

personality disorders the view that a personality disturbance of some sort causes an individual to violate social norms

Sociological Explanations. Sociologists, in contrast with both sociobiologists and psychologists, search for factors *outside* the individual. They look for social influences that "recruit" people to break norms. To account for why people commit crimes, for example, sociologists examine such external influences as socialization, membership in subcultures, and social class. *Social class*, a concept that we discuss in depth in Chapter 10, refers to people's relative standing in terms of education, occupation, and especially income and wealth.

To explain deviance, sociologists apply the three sociological perspectives—symbolic interactionism, functionalism, and conflict theory. Let's compare these three explanations.

8.2 Contrast three theories of deviance: differential association, control, and labeling.

The Symbolic Interactionist Perspective

As we examine symbolic interactionism, it will become more evident why sociologists are not satisfied with explanations that are rooted in sociobiology or psychology. *A basic principle of symbolic interactionism is that we are thinking beings who act according to how we interpret situations.* Let's consider how our membership in groups influences how we view life and, from there, our behavior.

Differential Association Theory

The Theory. Going directly against the idea that biology or personality is the source of deviance, sociologists stress our experiences in groups (Deflem 2006; Chambliss 1973/2014). Consider an extreme: boys and girls who join street gangs and those who join the Scouts. Obviously, each will learn different attitudes and behaviors concerning deviance and conformity. Edwin Sutherland coined the term **differential association** to indicate this: From the *different* groups we *associate* with, we learn to deviate from or conform to society's norms (Sutherland 1924, 1947; McCarthy 2011).

Sutherland's theory is more complicated than this, but he basically said that the different groups with which we associate (our "*different*(ial) association") give us messages about conformity and deviance. We may receive mixed messages, but we end up with more of one than the other (an "excess of definitions," as Sutherland put it). The end result is an imbalance—attitudes that tilt us in one direction or another. Consequently, we learn to either conform or to deviate.

Families. You know how important your family has been in forming your views toward life, so it probably is obvious to you that the family makes a big difference in whether people learn deviance or conformity. Researchers have confirmed this informal observation. Of the many studies, this one stands out: Of all prison inmates across the United States, about *half* have a father, mother, brother, sister, or spouse who has served time in prison (*Sourcebook of Criminal Justice Statistics* 2003:Table 6.0011; Glaze and Maruschak 2008:Table 11). In short, families that are involved in crime tend to set their children on a lawbreaking path.

Friends, Neighborhoods, and Subcultures. Most people don't know the term *differential association*, but they do know how it works. Most parents want to move out of "bad" neighborhoods because they know that if their kids have delinquent friends, they are likely to become delinquent, too. Sociological research also supports this common observation (Miller 1958; Fabio et al. 2011).

In some neighborhoods, violence is so woven into the subculture that even a wrong glance can mean your death ("Why you lookin' at me?") (Gardiner and Fox 2010). If the neighbors feel that a victim deserved to be killed, they refuse to testify because "he got what was coming to him" (Kubrin and Weitzer 2003). Killing can even be viewed as honorable:

differential association Edwin Sutherland's term to indicate that people who associate with some groups learn an "excess of definitions" of deviance, increasing the likelihood that they will become deviant

Sociologist Ruth Horowitz (1983, 2005), who did participant observation in a lower-class Chicano neighborhood in Chicago, discovered how the concept of "honor" propels young

men to deviance. The formula is simple. "A real man has honor. An insult is a threat to one's honor. Therefore, not to stand up to someone is to be less than a real man."

Now suppose you are a young man growing up in this neighborhood. You likely would do a fair amount of fighting, since you would interpret many things as attacks on your honor. You might even carry a knife or a gun, because words and fists wouldn't always be sufficient. Along with members of your group, you would define fighting, knifing, and shooting quite differently from the way most people do.

Sociologist Victor Rios (2011), who did participant observation of young male African American and Latino gang members in Oakland, California, reports that these same ideas of masculinity continue. They also continue to produce high rates of violence, including homicide.

Members of the Mafia also intertwine ideas of manliness with killing. For them, *to kill is a measure of their manhood.* If some Mafia member were to seduce the *capo*'s wife or girlfriend, for example, the seduction would slash at the *capo*'s manliness and honor. This would require swift retaliation. The offender's body would be found in the trunk of a car somewhere with his penis stuffed in his mouth. Not all killings, however, receive the same respect, for "the more awesome and potent the victim, the more worthy and meritorious the killer" (Arlacchi 1980).

This Russian godfather is leaving a Moscow court just after he was acquitted of a double murder. Do you understand how the definitions of deviance that Mafia members use underlie their behavior?

From this example, you can again see the relativity of deviance. Killing is deviant in mainstream society, but for members of the Mafia, *not* to kill after certain rules are broken would be the deviant act.

Prison or Freedom? As was mentioned in Chapter 3, an issue that comes up over and over again in sociology is whether we are prisoners of socialization. Symbolic interactionists stress that we are not mere pawns in the hands of others. We are not destined to think and act as our groups dictate. Rather, we *help to produce our own orientations to life.* By joining one group rather than another (differential association), for example, we help to shape the self. One college student may join a feminist group that is trying to change ideas about fraternities and rape, while another associates with women who shoplift on weekends. Their choices point them in different directions. The one who joins the feminist group may develop an even greater interest in producing social change, while the one who associates with shoplifters may become even more oriented toward criminal activities.

control theory the idea that two control systems—inner controls and outer controls—work against our tendencies to deviate

Control Theory

Do you ever feel the urge to do something that you know you shouldn't, even something that would get you in trouble? Most of us fight temptations to break society's norms. We find that we have to stifle things inside us—urges, hostilities, raunchy desires of various sorts. And most of the time, we manage to keep ourselves out of trouble. The basic question that **control theory** tries to answer is, With the desire to deviate so common, why don't we all just "bust loose"?

The social control of deviance takes many forms, including the actions of the police. Shown here is a tug-of-war between police and sit-down protestors at a rally in Belfast, Ireland.

The Theory. Sociologist Walter Reckless (1973), who developed control theory, stressed that we have two control systems that work against our motivations to deviate. Our *inner controls* include our internalized morality—conscience, religious principles, ideas of right and wrong. Inner controls also include fears of punishment and the desire to be a "good" person (Hirschi 1969; McShane and Williams 2007). Our *outer controls* consist of people—such as family, friends, and the police—who influence us not to deviate.

The stronger our bonds are with society, the more effective our inner controls are (Hirschi 1969). These bonds are based on *attachments* (our affection and respect for people who conform to mainstream norms), *commitments* (having a stake in society that you don't want to risk, such as your place in your family, being a college student, or having a job), *involvements* (participating in approved activities), and *beliefs* (convictions that certain actions are wrong).

This theory is really about *self*-control, says sociologist Travis Hirschi. Where do we learn self-control? As you know, this happens during our childhood, especially in the family when our parents supervise us and punish our deviant acts (Gottfredson and Hirschi 1990; Church et al. 2009). Sometimes they use shame to keep us in line. You probably had that finger shaken at you. I certainly recall it aimed at me. Do you think that more use of shaming, discussed in the Down-to-Earth Sociology box on the next page, could help strengthen people's internal controls?

Read on **MySocLab**
Document: The Meaning of Social Control

Applying Control Theory.

Suppose that some friends invite you to go to a nightclub with them. When you get there, you notice that everyone seems unusually happy—almost giddy. They seem to be euphoric in their animated conversations and dancing. Your friends tell you that almost everyone here has taken the drug Ecstasy, and they invite you to take some with them.

What do you do?

Let's not explore the question of whether taking Ecstasy in this setting is a deviant or a conforming act. This is a separate issue. Instead, concentrate on the pushes and pulls you would feel. The pushes toward taking the drug: your friends, the setting, and perhaps your curiosity. Then there are your inner controls—those inner voices of your conscience and your parents, perhaps of your teachers, as well as your fears of arrest and the dangers of illegal drugs. There are also the outer controls—perhaps the uniformed security guard looking in your direction.

So, what *would* you decide? Which is stronger: your inner and outer controls or the pushes and pulls toward taking the drug? It is you who can best weigh these forces, since they differ with each of us. This little example puts you at the center of what control theory is all about.

Labeling Theory

Watch on **MySocLab**
Video: Sociology in Focus: Deviance

Suppose for one undesirable moment that people think of you as a "whore," a "pervert," or a "cheat." (Pick one.) What power such a reputation would have—over both how others would see you and how you would see yourself. How about if you became known as "very intelligent," "truthful in everything," or "honest to the core"? (Choose one.) You can see how this type of reputation would give people different expectations of your character and behavior—and how the label would also shape the way you see yourself.

This is what **labeling theory** focuses on: the significance of reputations, how reputations or labels help set us on paths that propel us into deviance or divert us away from it.

Rejecting Labels: How People Neutralize Deviance. Not many of us want to be called "whore," "pervert," or "cheat." We resist negative labels, even lesser ones than these that others might try to pin on us. Did you know that some people are so successful at rejecting labels that even though they beat people up and vandalize property, they consider themselves to be conforming members of society? How do they do it?

Sociologists Gresham Sykes and David Matza (1957/1988) studied boys like this. They found that the boys used five **techniques of neutralization** to deflect society's norms.

Denial of responsibility. Some boys said, "I'm not responsible for what happened because . . . " And they were quite creative about the "becauses." Some said that what happened was an "accident." Other boys saw themselves as "victims" of society. What else could you expect? "I'm like a billiard ball shot around the pool table of life."

degradation ceremony a term coined by Harold Garfinkel to refer to a ritual whose goal is to remake someone's self by stripping away that individual's self-identity and stamping a new identity in its place

labeling theory the view that the labels people are given affect their own and others' perceptions of them, thus channeling their behavior into either deviance or conformity

techniques of neutralization ways of thinking or rationalizing that help people deflect (or neutralize) society's norms

Down-to-Earth Sociology

Shaming: Making a Comeback?

Shaming can be effective, especially when members of a primary group use it. In some communities, where the individual's reputation was at stake, shaming was the centerpiece of the enforcement of norms. Violators were marked as deviant and held up for all the world to see. In Nathaniel Hawthorne's *The Scarlet Letter*, town officials forced Hester Prynne to wear a scarlet "A" sewn on her dress. The "A" stood for *Adulteress*. Wherever she went, Prynne had to wear this badge of shame—every day for the rest of her life.

As our society grew large and urban, the sense of community diminished, and shaming lost its effectiveness. Shaming is now starting to make a comeback.

- In Houston, Texas, a couple stole $265,000 from the crime victims' fund. The couple was sentenced to stand in front of a local mall for five hours every weekend for six years with a sign reading, "I am a thief." They also had to post a sign outside their house stating they were convicted thieves ("Woman Ordered to . . ." 2012).
- In Cleveland, Ohio, a judge ordered a woman who drove on a sidewalk in order to pass a school bus to hold a sign at the intersection reading, "Only an idiot would drive on the sidewalk to avoid a school bus" ("Woman Ordered to . . ." 2012).
- In Arizona, one sheriff makes the men in his jail wear pink underwear. The men also wear pink striped prison uniforms while they work in chain gangs. Women prisoners are paraded in chain gangs in public, where they are forced to pick up street trash (Billeaud 2008).
- Online shaming sites have also appeared. Captured on cell phone cameras are bad drivers, older men who leer at teenaged girls, and people who don't pick up their dog's poop (Saranow 2007).
- In Spain, where one's reputation with neighbors still matters, debt collectors, dressed in tuxedos and top hats, walk slowly to the front door. The sight shames debtors into paying (Catan 2008).

This 19-year-old in Wisconsin was given a reduced jail sentence for holding this sign in front of his former place of work.

Sociologist Harold Garfinkel (1956) gave the name **degradation ceremony** to an extreme form of shaming. The individual is called to account before the group, witnesses denounce him or her, the offender is pronounced guilty, and steps are taken to strip the individual of his or her identity as a group member. In some courts martial, officers who are found guilty stand at attention before their peers while others rip the insignia of rank from their uniforms. This procedure screams that the individual is no longer a member of the group. Although Hester Prynne was not banished from the group physically, she was banished morally; her degradation ceremony proclaimed her a *moral* outcast from the community. The scarlet "A" marked her as not "one of them."

Although we don't use scarlet "A"'s today, informal degradation ceremonies still occur. Consider what happened to this New York City police officer (Chivers 2001):

> *Joseph Gray had been a police officer in New York City for fifteen years. As with some of his fellow officers, alcohol and sex helped relieve the pressures of police work. After spending one afternoon drinking in a topless bar, bleary-eyed, Gray plowed his car into a vehicle carrying a pregnant woman, her son, and her sister. All three died. Gray was accused of manslaughter and drunk driving.*
>
> *The New York Times and New York television stations kept hammering this story to the public. Three weeks later, as Gray left police headquarters after resigning, an angry crowd surrounded him. Gray hung his head in public disgrace as Victor Manuel Herrera, whose wife and son were killed in the crash, followed him, shouting, "You're a murderer!" (Gray was later convicted of drunk driving and manslaughter.)*

For Your Consideration

→ How do you think law enforcement officials might use shaming to reduce law breaking?

→ How do you think school officials could use shaming?

→ Suppose that you were caught shoplifting at a store near where you live. Would you rather spend a week in jail with no one but your family knowing it or a week walking in front of the store you stole from wearing a placard that proclaims in bold red capital letters: "I AM A THIEF!" and in smaller letters: "I am sorry for stealing from this store and making you pay higher prices"? Why?

Denial of injury. A favorite explanation was "What I did wasn't wrong because no one got hurt." The boys would call vandalism "mischief," gang fights a "private quarrel," and stealing cars "borrowing." They might acknowledge that what they did was illegal but claim that they were "just having a little fun."

Denial of a victim. Some boys thought of themselves as avengers. Trashing a teacher's car was revenge for an unfair grade, while shoplifting was a way to get even with "crooked" store owners. In short, even if the boys did accept responsibility and admit that someone had gotten hurt, they protected their self-concept by claiming that the people "deserved what they got."

Condemnation of the condemners. Another technique the boys used was to deny that others had the right to judge them. They accused people who pointed their fingers at them of being "hypocrites": The police were "on the take," teachers had "pets," and parents cheated on their taxes. In short, they said, "Who are *they* to accuse *me* of something?"

Appeal to higher loyalties. A final technique the boys used to justify their activities was to consider loyalty to the gang more important than the norms of society. They might say, "I had to help my friends. That's why I got in the fight." Not incidentally, the boy may have shot two members of a rival group, as well as a bystander!

In Sum: These techniques of neutralization have implications far beyond this group of boys, since it is not only delinquents who try to neutralize the norms of mainstream society. Look again at these techniques—don't they sound familiar? (1) "I couldn't help myself"; (2) "Who really got hurt?"; (3) "Don't you think she deserved that, after what she did?"; (4) "Who are you to talk?"; and (5) "I had to help my friends—wouldn't you have done the same thing?" All of us attempt to neutralize the moral demands of society; neutralization helps us to sleep at night.

Embracing Labels: The Example of Outlaw Bikers. Although most of us resist attempts to label us as deviant, some people revel in a deviant identity. Some teenagers, for example, make certain by their clothing, music, hairstyles, and body art that no one misses their rejection of adult norms. Their status among fellow members of a subculture—within which they are almost obsessive conformists—is vastly more important than any status outside it.

One of the best examples of a group that embraces deviance is a motorcycle gang. Sociologist Mark Watson (1980/2006) did participant observation with outlaw bikers. He rebuilt Harleys with them, hung around their bars and homes, and went on "runs" (trips) with them. He concluded that outlaw bikers see the world as "hostile, weak, and effeminate." Holding this conventional world in contempt, gang members pride themselves on breaking its norms and getting in trouble, laughing at death, and treating women as lesser beings whose primary value is to provide them with services—especially sex. They take pleasure in shocking people by their appearance and behavior. They pride themselves in looking "dirty, mean, and generally undesirable." Outlaw bikers also regard themselves as losers, a view that becomes woven into their unusual embrace of deviance.

While most people resist labels of deviance, some embrace them. In what different ways do these photos illustrate the embracement of deviance?

Labels Can Be Powerful. To label a teenager a delinquent can trigger a process that leads to greater involvement in deviance (Lopes et al. 2012). Because of this, judges sometimes use *diversion*. To avoid the label of delinquent, they *divert* youthful offenders away from the criminal justice system. Instead of sending them to reform school or jail, they assign them to social workers and counselors. In the following Thinking Critically section, let's consider how powerful labeling can be.

THINKING CRITICALLY

The Saints and the Roughnecks: Labeling in Everyday Life

As you recall from Chapter 4, the Saints and the Roughnecks were high school boys. Both groups were "constantly occupied with truancy, drinking, wild parties, petty theft, and vandalism." Yet their teachers looked on the Saints as "headed for success" and the Roughnecks as "headed for failure." By the time they finished high school, not one Saint had been arrested, while the Roughnecks had been in constant trouble with the police.

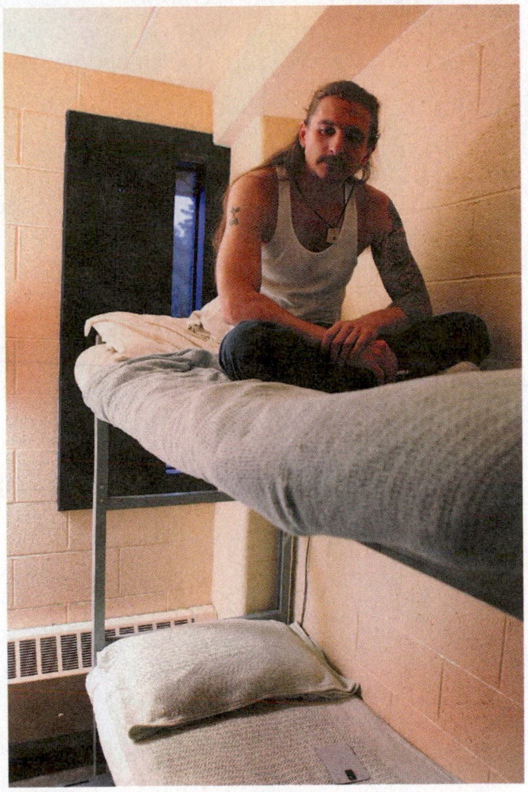

Stereotypes, both positive and negative, help to form the perception and reaction of authorities. What stereotypes come to mind when you look at this photo?

Why did the members of the community perceive these boys so differently? Chambliss (1973/2014) concluded that *social class* created this split vision. As symbolic interactionists emphasize, social class is like a lens that focuses our perceptions. The Saints came from respectable, middle-class families, while the Roughnecks were from less respectable, working-class families. These backgrounds led teachers and the authorities to expect good behavior from the Saints but trouble from the Roughnecks. And, like the rest of us, teachers and police saw what they expected to see.

The boys' social class also affected their visibility. The Saints had automobiles, and they did their drinking and vandalism out of town. Without cars, the Roughnecks hung around their own street corners. There, their drinking and boisterous behavior drew the attention of police, confirming the negative impressions that the community already had of them.

The boys' social class also equipped them with distinct *styles of interaction*. When police or teachers questioned them, the Saints were apologetic. Their show of respect for authority elicited a positive reaction from teachers and police, allowing the Saints to escape school and legal problems. The Roughnecks, said Chambliss, were "almost the polar opposite." When questioned, they were hostile. Even when these boys tried to assume a respectful attitude, everyone could see through it. As a result, the teachers and police let the Saints off with warnings, but they came down hard on the Roughnecks.

Certainly, what happens in life is not determined by labels alone, but the Saints and the Roughnecks did live up to the labels that the community gave them. As you may recall, all but one of the Saints went on to college. One earned a Ph.D., one became a lawyer, one a doctor, and the others business managers. In contrast, only two of the Roughnecks went to college. They earned athletic scholarships and became coaches. The other Roughnecks did not fare so well. Two of them dropped out of high school, later became involved in separate killings, and were sent to prison. Of the final two, one became a local bookie, and no one knows the whereabouts of the other.

For Your Consideration

➤ Did you see anything like this in your high school? If so, how did it work?

➤ Besides labels, what else could have been involved in the life outcomes of these boys?

➤ In what areas of life do you see the power of labels? ■

How do labels work? How labels work is complicated because it involves the self-concept and reactions that vary from one individual to another. To analyze this process would require a book. Here, let's just note that unlike its meaning in sociology, in everyday life the term *deviant* is emotionally charged with a negative judgment. This label closes doors of opportunity. It can lock people out of conforming groups and push them into almost exclusive contact with people who have been similarly labeled.

In Sum: Symbolic interactionists examine how people's definitions of the situation underlie their deviating from or conforming to social norms. They focus on group membership (differential association), how people balance pressures to conform and to deviate (control theory), and the significance of people's reputations (labeling theory).

8.3 Explain how deviance can be functional for society, how mainstream values can produce deviance (strain theory), and how social class is related to crime (illegitimate opportunities).

The Functionalist Perspective

When we think of deviance, its dysfunctions are likely to come to mind. Functionalists point out that deviance also has functions.

Can Deviance Really Be Functional for Society?

Most of us are upset by deviance, especially crime, and assume that society would be better off without it. In contrast to this common assumption, the classic functionalist theorist Emile Durkheim (1893/1933, 1895/1964) came to a surprising conclusion. Deviance, he said—including crime—is functional for society. Deviance contributes to the social order in these three ways:

1. *Deviance clarifies moral boundaries and affirms norms.* By *moral boundaries,* Durkheim referred to a group's ideas about how people should think and act. Deviant acts challenge those boundaries. To call a member into account is to say, in effect, "You broke an important rule, and we cannot tolerate that." Punishing deviants affirms the group's norms and clarifies what it means to be a member of the group.
2. *Deviance encourages social unity.* To affirm the group's moral boundaries by punishing deviants creates a "we" feeling among the group's members. By saying, "You can't get away with that," the group affirms the rightness of its ways.
3. *Deviance promotes social change.* Not everyone agrees on what to do with people who push beyond the accepted ways of doing things. Some group members may even approve of the rule-breaking behavior. Boundary violations that gain enough support become new, acceptable behaviors. Deviance, then, may force a group to rethink and redefine its moral boundaries, helping groups—and whole societies—to adapt to changing circumstances.

Every society has boundaries that divide what is considered socially acceptable from what is not acceptable. This woman in Great Britain is challenging those boundaries.

In the Down-to-Earth Sociology box on the next page, you can see these three functions of deviance, as well as the central point of symbolic interactionism, that *deviance* involves a clash of competing definitions.

Strain Theory: How Mainstream Values Produce Deviance

Functionalists argue that crime is a *natural* outcome of the conditions that people experience, not some alien element in our midst (Agnew 2012). Even mainstream values can generate crime. Consider what

Down-to-Earth Sociology

Running Naked with Pumpkins on Their Heads or Naked on a Bike: Deviance or Freedom of Self-Expression?

They can hardly sleep the night before Halloween, thinking about how they will carve their pumpkins and all the fun to come. When night falls, they put sneakers on their feet, the pumpkins on their heads, and run into the street. There is nothing between the pumpkins and the sneakers—except whatever nature endowed them with (Simon 2009).

They join one another for their annual chilly, late-night run. Do the gawkers bother them? Maybe a little, but it's all in good fun. The crowd is waiting, hooting and hollering and waving them on.

"Not so fast," reply the police in Boulder, Colorado, where the naked pumpkin run is held on the last day of each October. "You are breaking the law."

If the naked pumpkin run isn't enough, the Boulder police also have to deal with the annual World Naked Bike Ride, which has become so popular that it is held in 70 cities around the world (Vigil 2009). The naked bike rides seem to be a celebration of youth and freedom—and as older people join in, just freedom and maybe the joy of being alive.

World Naked Bike Ride, New Orleans, Louisiana.

Though the Boulder police have prided themselves on tolerance, they don't see the run and ride in quite the same way as the participants do. "The law," they say, "clearly states that no one can show genitalia in public."

"Are women's breasts genitalia?" they've been asked. "No, those are okay," replied the police. "But watch the rest of it—uh, that is, don't watch . . . uh, that is, don't show anything else. You know what we mean. If you do, we will arrest you, and you'll end up on the sexual offenders list."

"Bad sports," reply the naked pumpkin runners and the naked bike riders, pouting just a bit. "You're trying to ruin our fun."

"We didn't make the laws," the police reply, not pleased about the many who have become angry at their lack of understanding. "We just enforce them."

Trying to recover their tolerance, the police add, "Just wear a thong or a jock strap, and run and ride to your hearts' content."

The American Civil Liberties Union has stepped into the fray, too, saying that nakedness is a form of free speech. Participants should be able to express their, well, whatever it is they are expressing.

For Your Consideration

➔ Here is a basic principle of deviance: As people break rules, sometimes deliberately to test the boundaries of acceptable behavior, the group enforces its norms, or bends them to accommodate the deviants. How do the naked pumpkin runners and the naked bike riders illustrate this principle? What do you think the result will be in Boulder, Colorado?

sociologists Richard Cloward and Lloyd Ohlin (1960) identified as the crucial problem of the industrialized world: the need to locate and train talented people—whether they were born into wealth or into poverty—so that they can take over the key technical jobs of society. When children are born, no one knows which ones will have the ability to become dentists, nuclear physicists, or engineers. To get the most talented people to compete with one another, society tries to motivate *everyone* to strive for success.

We are quite successful in getting almost everyone to want **cultural goals**, success of some sort, such as wealth or prestige. But we are far from successful when it comes to providing everyone access to the **institutionalized means**, the legitimate ways to success. People who find their way to success blocked can come to see the institutionalized goals (such as working hard or pursuing higher education) as not applying to themselves. Sociologist Robert Merton (1956, 1949/1968) referred to this situation as *anomie*, a sense of normlessness. These people experience frustration, or what Merton called *strain*.

Table 8.1 on the next page presents a summary of Merton's **strain theory**. The most common reaction to means and goals is *conformity*. Most people find at least adequate access to the institutionalized means and use them to try to reach cultural goals. They try to get a quality education, good jobs, and so on. If well-paid jobs are unavailable,

cultural goals the objectives held out as legitimate or desirable for the members of a society to achieve

institutionalized means approved ways of reaching cultural goals

strain theory Robert Merton's term for the strain engendered when a society socializes large numbers of people to desire a cultural goal (such as success), but withholds from some the approved means of reaching that goal; one adaptation to the strain is crime, the choice of an innovative means (one outside the approved system) to attain the cultural goal

TABLE 8.1 How People Match Their Goals to Their Means

Do They Feel the Strain That Leads to Anomie?	Mode of Adaptation	Cultural Goals	Institutionalized Means
No	Conformity	Accept	Accept
	Deviant Paths:		
Yes	1. Innovation	Accept	Reject
	2. Ritualism	Reject	Accept
	3. Retreatism	Reject	Reject
	4. Rebellion	Reject/Replace	Reject/Replace

Source: Based on Merton 1968.

they take less desirable jobs. If they can't get into Harvard or Stanford, they go to a state university. Others take night classes and go to vocational schools. In short, most people take the socially acceptable path.

Four Deviant Paths. The remaining four responses, which are deviant, represent reactions to the gap that people find between the goals they want and their access to the institutionalized means to reach them. Let's look at each. *Innovators* are people who accept the goals of society but use illegitimate means to try to reach them. Embezzlers, for instance, accept the goal of achieving wealth, but they reject the legitimate avenues for doing so. Other examples are drug dealers, robbers, and con artists.

The second deviant path is taken by people who start out wanting the cultural goals but become discouraged and give up on achieving them. Yet they still cling to conventional rules of conduct. Merton called this response *ritualism*. Although ritualists have given up on getting ahead at work, they survive by rigorously following the rules of their job. Teachers whose idealism is shattered (who are said to suffer from "burnout"), for example, remain in the classroom, where they teach without enthusiasm. Their response is considered deviant because they cling to the job even though they have abandoned the goal, which may have been to stimulate young minds or to make the world a better place.

People who choose the third deviant path, *retreatism*, reject both the cultural goals and the institutionalized means of achieving them. Some people stop pursuing success and retreat into alcohol or drugs. Although their path to withdrawal is considerably different, women who enter a convent or men a monastery are also retreatists.

The final deviant response is *rebellion*. Convinced that their society is corrupt, rebels, like retreatists, reject both society's goals and its institutionalized means. Unlike retreatists, however, rebels seek to give society new goals, as well as new means for reaching them. Revolutionaries are the most committed type of rebels.

Merton either did not recognize *anarchy* as applying to his model or did not think of it. In either case, the angry *anarchist* who wants to destroy society is not shown on Table 8.1. Like the retreatist and the rebel, this frustrated individual has given up on both society's goals and means. Unlike the rebel, however, he or she does not want to replace the goals and means with anything. And unlike the retreatist, he or she does not want to withdraw and let others live in peace. Instead, he or she wants to annihilate everyone.

In Sum: Strain theory underscores the sociological principle that deviants are the product of society. Mainstream social values (cultural goals and institutionalized means to reach those goals) can produce strain (frustration, dissatisfaction). People who feel this strain are more likely than others to take deviant (nonconforming) paths.

Illegitimate Opportunity Structures: Social Class and Crime

Over and over in this text, you have seen the impact of social class on people's lives—and you will continue to do so in coming chapters. Let's look at how the social classes produce different types of crime.

Street Crime. In applying strain theory, functionalists point out that industrialized societies have no trouble socializing the poor into wanting to own things. Like others, the poor are bombarded with messages urging them to buy everything from iPhones and iPads to designer jeans and new cars. Television and movies are filled with images of middle-class people enjoying luxurious lives. The poor get the message—full-fledged Americans can afford society's many goods and services.

Yet, the most common route to success, education, presents a bewildering world. Run by the middle class, schools are at odds with the background of the poor. In the schools, what the poor take for granted is unacceptable, questioned, and mocked. Their speech, for example, is built around nonstandard grammar. It is also often laced with what the middle class considers obscenities. Their ideas of punctuality and their poor preparation in reading and paper-and-pencil skills also make it difficult to fit in. Facing such barriers, the poor are more likely than their more privileged counterparts to drop out of school. Educational failure, of course, slams the door on many legitimate avenues to success.

Not all doors slam shut, though. Woven into life in urban slums is what Cloward and Ohlin (1960) called an **illegitimate opportunity structure**. An alternative door to success opens: "hustles" such as robbery, burglary, drug dealing, prostitution, pimping, and gambling (Anderson 1978, 1990/2006; Duck and Rawls 2011). Pimps and drug dealers, for example, present an image of a glamorous life—people who are in control and have plenty of "easy money." For many of the poor, the "hustler" becomes a role model.

It should be easy to see, then, why street crime attracts disproportionate numbers of the poor. In the Down-to-Earth Sociology box on the next page, let's look at how gangs are part of the illegitimate opportunity structure that beckons disadvantaged youth.

White-Collar Crime. As with the poor, the *forms* of crime of the more privileged classes also match their life situation. And how different their illegitimate opportunities are! Physicians don't hold up cabbies, but they do cheat Medicare. Investment managers like Bernie Madoff run fraudulent schemes that cheat people around the world. Mugging, pimping, and burgling are not part of this more privileged world, but evading income tax, bribing public officials, and embezzling are. Sociologist Edwin Sutherland (1949) coined the term **white-collar crime** to refer to crimes that people of respectable and high social status commit in the course of their occupations.

A special form of white-collar crime is **corporate crime**, executives breaking the law in order to benefit their corporation. For example, to increase corporate profits, Sears executives defrauded $100 million from victims so poor that they had filed for bankruptcy. To avoid a criminal trial, Sears pleaded guilty. This frightened the parent companies of Macy's and Bloomingdales, which were doing similar things, and they settled out of court (McCormick 1999). *Not one of the corporate thieves at Sears, Macy's, or Bloomingdales spent even a day in jail.*

Citigroup, another household name, is notorious for breaking the law. In 2004, this firm was fined $70 million for stealing from the poor (O'Brien 2004). But, like a career criminal, this company continued its law-breaking ways. In 2008, Citigroup was caught red-handed "sweeping" money from its customers' credit cards, even from the cards of people who had died. For this, Citigroup paid another $18 million in penalties (Read 2008). Then, in 2010, Citigroup paid a $75 million penalty

illegitimate opportunity structure opportunities for crimes that are woven into the texture of life

white-collar crime Edwin Sutherland's term for crimes committed by people of respectable and high social status in the course of their occupations; for example, bribery of public officials, securities violations, embezzlement, false advertising, and price fixing

corporate crime crimes committed by executives in order to benefit their corporation

Explore on **MySocLab**
Activity: How are Crime and Punishment Distributed across the United States?

White collar crime usually involves only the loss of property, but not always. To save money, Ford executives kept faulty Firestone tires on their Explorers. The cost? The lives of over 200 people. Shown here in Houston is one of their victims. She survived a needless accident, but was left a quariplegic. Not one Ford executive spent even a single day in jail.

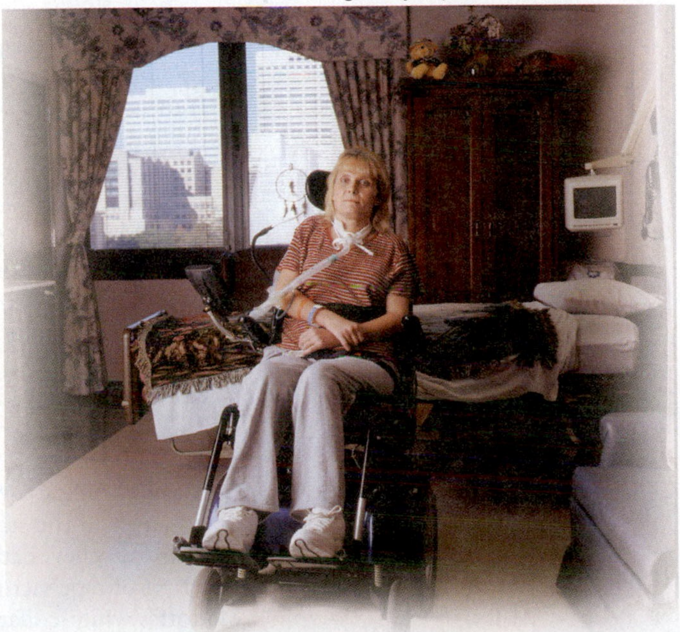

Down-to-Earth Sociology

Islands in the Street: Urban Gangs in the United States

Gangs, part of urban life around the world, can be ruthless. Just to gain respect, gang members can harm others (Densley 2012). Let's look at why people join gangs.

For more than ten years, sociologist Martín Sánchez-Jankowski (1991) did participant observation of thirty-seven African American, Chicano, Dominican, Irish, Jamaican, and Puerto Rican gangs in Boston, Los Angeles, and New York City. The gangs earned money through gambling, arson, mugging, armed robbery, and selling moonshine, drugs, guns, stolen car parts, and protection. Sánchez-Jankowski ate, slept, and fought with the gangs, but by mutual agreement he did not participate in drug dealing or other illegal activities. He was seriously injured twice during the study.

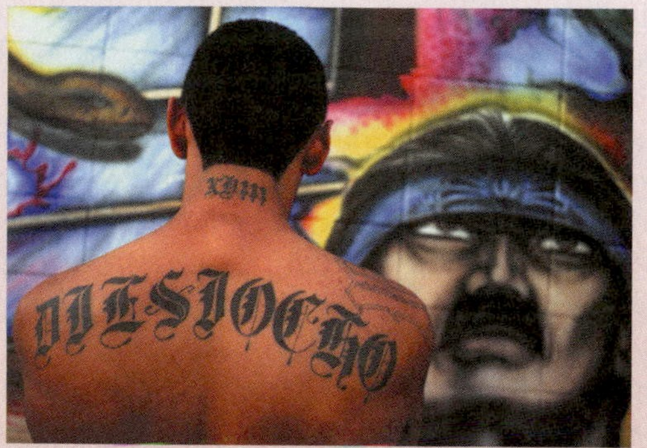

Contrary to stereotypes, Sánchez-Jankowski did not find that the motive for joining was to escape a broken home (there were as many members from intact families as from broken homes) or to seek a substitute family (the same number of boys said they were close to their families as those who said they were not). Rather, the boys joined to gain access to money, to have recreation (including sex and drugs), to maintain anonymity in committing crimes, to get protection, and to help the community. This last reason may seem surprising, but in some neighborhoods, gangs protect residents from outsiders and spearhead political change (Kontos et al. 2003). The boys also saw the gang as an alternative to the dead-end—and deadening—jobs held by their parents.

Neighborhood residents are ambivalent about gangs. On the one hand, they fear the violence. On the other hand, gang members are the children of people who live in the neighborhood, many of the adults once belonged to gangs, and some gangs provide better protection than the police.

Particular gangs will come and go, but gangs will likely always remain part of the city. As functionalists point out, gangs fulfill needs of poor youth who live on the margins of society.

For Your Consideration

- ➤ What functions do gangs fulfill (what needs do they meet)?
- ➤ Suppose that you have been hired as an urban planner for the city of Los Angeles. How could you arrange to meet the needs that gangs fulfill in ways that minimize violence and encourage youth to follow mainstream norms?

for misleading investors. In 2012, Citigroup paid a fine of over a *half billion dollars* for deceiving investors in subprime mortgages (Kapner 2012). Another big-name criminal is Bank of America, which paid *one billion dollars* for its lawbreaking (Raice and Timiraos 2012). Despite their many crimes, *not one of these corporate crime chiefs spent a day in jail.*

If these same executives had used guns to rob people on the street, you know what would have happened. White-collar crime, in contrast, is seldom taken seriously. This is unfortunately so even when those crimes result in death. In the 1930s, workers were hired to blast a tunnel through a mountain in West Virginia. The company knew the silica dust would kill the miners, and in just three months about 600 died (Dunaway 2008). No owner went to jail. In the 1980s, Firestone executives recalled faulty tires in Saudi Arabia and Venezuela but allowed them to remain on U.S. vehicles. When their tires blew out, about 200 Americans died (White et al. 2001). Not a single Firestone executive went to jail.

Consider this: Under federal law, causing the death of a worker by *willfully* violating safety rules is a misdemeanor punishable by up to six months in prison. Yet to harass a wild burro on federal lands is punishable by a year in prison (Barstow and Bergman 2003).

At $500 billion a year (Reiman and Leighton 2010), "crime in the suites" costs more than "crime in the streets." This refers only to dollar costs. The physical and emotional costs are another matter. For example, no one has figured out a way to compare the suffering of rape victims with the pain of elderly couples who lost their life savings to Madoff's white-collar fraud.

FIGURE 8.1 How Safe Is Your State? Violent Crime in the United States

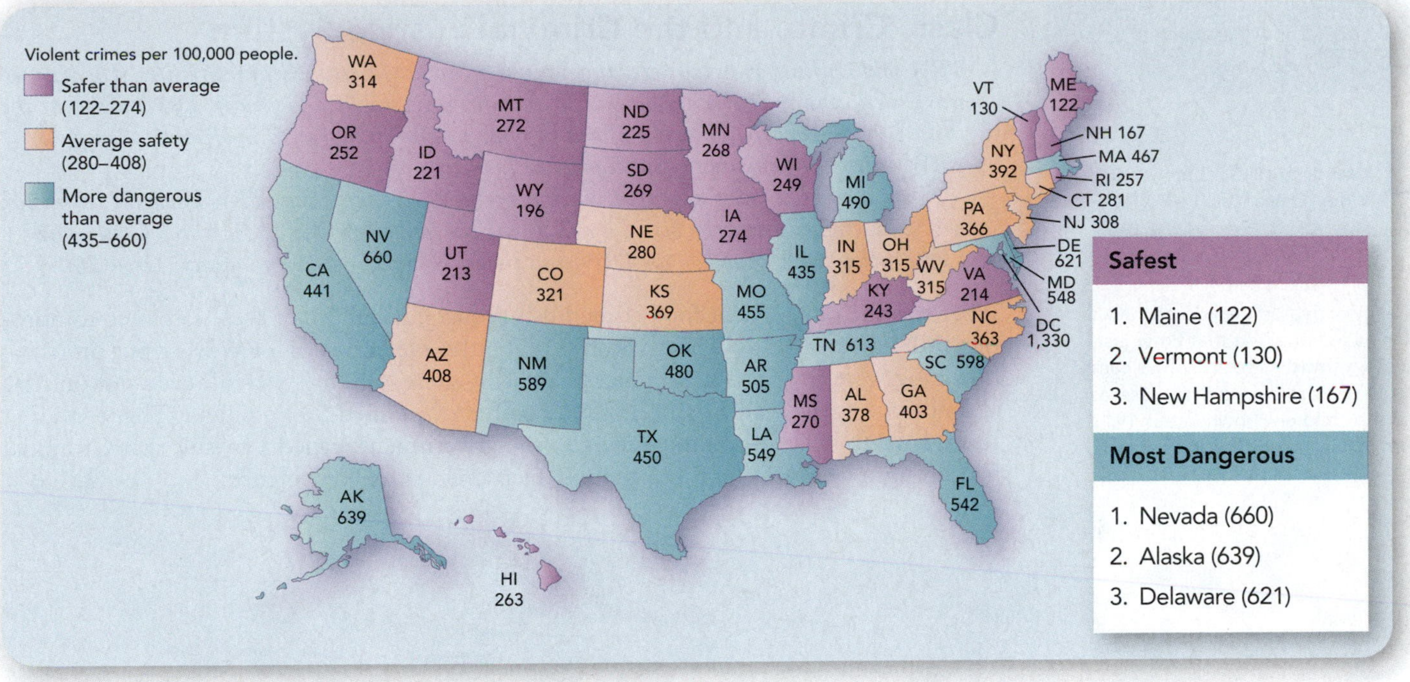

Note: Violent crimes are murder, rape, robbery, and aggravated assault. I estimated Minnesota's rate, based on earlier data and reduced rates since then. The chance of becoming a victim of a violent crime is more than five times higher in Nevada, the most dangerous state, than in Maine, the safest state. Washington, D.C., not a state, is in a class by itself. Its rate of 1,330 is *eleven* times higher than Maine's rate.

Source: By the author. Based on *Statistical Abstract of the United States* 2013:Table 314.

Fear, however, centers on street crime, especially the violent stranger who can change your life forever. As the Social Map above shows, the chances of such an encounter depend on where you live. You can see that entire regions are safer—or more dangerous—than others. In general, the northern states are safer, and the southern states more dangerous.

Gender and Crime. Gender is not just something we do. Gender is a feature of society that surrounds us from birth. Gender pushes us, as male or female, into different corners in life, offering and nurturing some behaviors while it withdraws others. The opportunity to commit crime is one of the many consequences of how society sets up a *gender order*. The social changes that opened business and the professions to women also brought new opportunities for women to commit crime. From stolen property to illegal weapons, Table 8.2 shows how women have taken advantage of this new opportunity.

In Sum: Functionalists stress that just as the social classes differ in opportunities for income and education, so they differ in opportunities for crime. As a result, street crime is greater among the lower social classes and white-collar crime greater among the higher social classes. The growing crime rates of women illustrate how changing gender roles have given women more access to what sociologists call "illegitimate opportunities."

TABLE 8.2 Women and Crime: What a Change

Of all those arrested, what percentage are women?

Crime	1992	2010	Change
Drunken driving	13.8%	23.7%	+72%
Burglary	9.2%	15.3%	+66%
Stolen property	12.5%	19.8%	+62%
Car theft	10.8%	17.5%	+58%
Aggravated assault	14.8%	21.5%	+45%
Robbery	8.5%	12.2%	+44%
Larceny/theft	32.1%	43.9%	+37%
Arson	13.4%	17.0%	+27%
Illegal drugs	16.4%	19.1%	+16%
Forgery and counterfeiting	34.7%	37.7%	+9%
Illegal weapons	7.5%	8.4%	+1%
Fraud	42.1%	41.4%	−3%

Source: By the author. Based on *Statistical Abstract of the United States* 2013:Table 338 and earlier years.

8.4 Explain how social class is related to the criminal justice system and how the criminal justice system is oppressive.

Watch on **MySocLab**
Video: Deviance: The Basics

The Conflict Perspective

Class, Crime, and the Criminal Justice System

TRW sold transistors to the federal government to use in its military satellites. The transistors failed, and the government had to shut down its satellite program. TRW said that the failure was a surprise, that it was due to some unknown defect. U.S. officials then paid TRW millions of dollars to investigate the failure.

Then a whistle blower appeared, informing the government that TRW knew the transistors would fail in satellites even before it sold them. The government sued Northrop Grumman Corporation, which had bought TRW, and the corporation was found guilty (Drew 2009).

What was the punishment for a crime this serious? The failure of these satellites compromised the defense of the United States. When the executives of TRW were put on trial, how long were their prison sentences? Actually, these criminals weren't even put on trial, and not one spent even a night in jail. Grumman was fined $325 million. Then—and this is hard to believe—on the same day, the government settled a lawsuit that Grumman had brought against it for $325 million. Certainly a rare coincidence.

In early capitalism, children worked alongside adults. At that time, just as today, most street criminals came from the *marginal working class*, as did the children shown in this 1911 yarn mill in Yazoo City, Mississippi.

Contrast this backdoor deal between influential people with what happens to the poor who break the law. A poor person who is caught stealing even a $1,000 car can end up serving years in prison. How can a legal system that proudly boasts "justice for all" be so inconsistent? According to conflict theory, this question is central to the analysis of crime and the **criminal justice system**—the police, courts, and prisons that deal with people who are accused of having committed crimes. Let's see what conflict theorists have to say about this.

criminal justice system the system of police, courts, and prisons set up to deal with people who are accused of having committed a crime

The Criminal Justice System as an Instrument of Oppression

Conflict theorists regard power and social inequality as the main characteristics of society. The criminal justice system, they stress, is a tool designed by the powerful to maintain their power and privilege. For the poor, in contrast, the law is an instrument of oppression (Spitzer 1975; Chambliss 2000, 1973/2014). The idea that the law operates impartially to bring justice, they say, is a cultural myth, promoted by the capitalist class to secure the cooperation of the poor in their own oppression.

The working class and those below them pose a special threat to the power elite. Receiving the least of society's material rewards, they hold the potential to rebel and overthrow the current social order (see Figure 10.5 on page 267). To prevent this, the law comes down hard on the poor and the underclass. They are the least rooted in society. They have only low-paying, part-time, or seasonal work—if they have jobs at all. Because their street crimes threaten the social order that keeps the elite in power, they are punished severely. From this class come *most* of the prison inmates in the United States.

The criminal justice system, then, does not focus on the executives of corporations and the harm they do through manufacturing unsafe products, creating pollution, and manipulating prices. Yet the violations of the capitalist class cannot be ignored totally; if they become too extreme, they might outrage the working class, encouraging them to rise up and revolt. To prevent this, a flagrant violation by a member of the capitalist class is occasionally prosecuted. The publicity given to the case provides evidence of the "fairness" of the criminal justice system, which helps to stabilize the social system—and keeps the powerful in their positions of privilege.

The cartoonist's hyperbole makes an excellent commentary on the social class disparity of our criminal justice system. Not only are the crimes of the wealthy not as likely to come to the attention of authorities as are the crimes of the poor, but when they do, the wealthy can afford legal expertise that the poor cannot.

"If you want justice, it's two hundred dollars an hour. Obstruction of justice runs a bit more."

The powerful are usually able to bypass the courts altogether, appearing instead before an agency that has no power to imprison (such as the Federal Trade Commission). These agencies are directed by people from wealthy backgrounds who sympathize with the intricacies of the corporate world. It is they who oversee most cases of price manipulation, insider stock trading, violations of fiduciary duty, and so on. Is it surprising, then, that the typical sanction for corporate crime is a token fine?

Read on MySocLab Document: The Rich Get Richer and the Poor Get Prison

In Sum: Conflict theorists stress that the power elite developed the legal system, which is used to stabilize the social order. They use it to control the poor, who pose a threat to the powerful. The poor hold the potential of rebelling as a group, which could dislodge the power elite from their place of privilege. To prevent this, the criminal justice system makes certain that heavy penalties come down on the poor.

Reactions to Deviance

8.5 Be familiar with street crimes and prison, three-strikes laws, the decline in violent crime, recidivism, bias in the death penalty, the medicalization of deviance, and the need for a humane approach.

Whether it involves cheating on a sociology quiz or holding up a liquor store, any violation of norms invites reaction. Before we examine reactions in the United States, let's take a little side trip to England. I think you'll enjoy this little excursion in the Cultural Diversity box on the next page.

Cultural Diversity **around the World**

"Dogging" in England

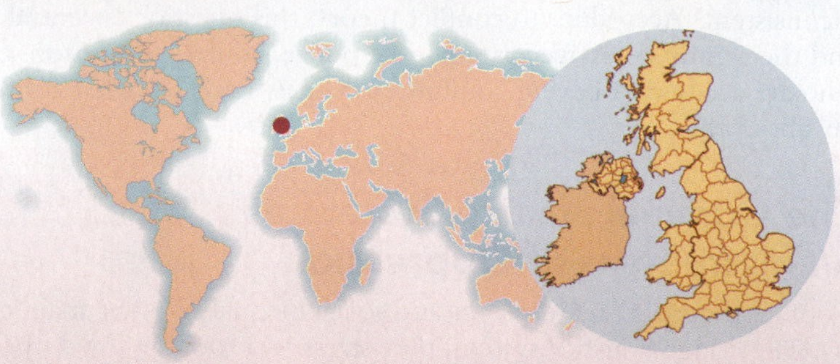

In some places in England, people like "dogging." This is their term for having sex in public so others can watch. The sex often is between strangers who have arranged to meet through the Internet.

"Dogging" is a strange term, and no one knows its origin. The term might come from voyeurs who doggedly follow people who are having sex. Or it might refer to the similarity to female dogs in heat that have sex with any dog around. Or it might even come from the statement "I'm just going to walk the dog," when they are really going out to do something else entirely.

Regardless of the term's origin, frolicking in the fields is popular. Internet sites even lay out basic rules, such as "Only join in if you are asked."

The Internet sites also rate England's dogging locations. The field in Puttenham, a village an hour's drive from London, is ranked Number 2 in England. The field is mostly used by homosexuals during the day, with heterosexuals taking over at night.

One motorist who stopped his car to use the bushes for a bathroom break was startled when a group of eager men surrounded him. He said that he took the quickest pee in his life.

Dogging isn't legal, but the police mostly ignore it. The police have even warned the public, but in a discreet English way. They have designated the field in Puttenham as a "public sex environment."

Some village residents are upset at the litter left behind, from condoms to tea cups. Others are upset that the dogging field is just 400 yards from the village nursery school. A woman who went to the police to complain showed them a pink vibrator she had found in the field. "What should we do with it?" asked the officer. Seeing that she was going to get nowhere, she said they could just put it in Lost and Found.

After listening to citizen complaints, the County Council Cabinet wanted to know if anyone had practical solutions. One suggested that the police patrol the site with dogs. Another said they should fill the field with bad-tempered bulls.

Distressed at such inconsiderate reactions, one empathetic cabinet member said, "If you close this site, they wouldn't have anywhere else to go. There might be an increase in suicides."

The citizens and Council members reached a compromise: They would put up a sign. "Don't have sex here" seemed too direct for the English, so the sign, much more polite and circuitous, says, "Do not engage in activities of an unacceptable nature."

Source: Based on Lyall 2010.

For Your Consideration

➤ What do you think the police would do if there were a "dogging" field in your town? What do you think the public's reaction would be? Why do you think the police are so "heavy handed" in the United States while those in England take such a lighter approach?

Street Crime and Prisons

Let's turn back to the United States. Figure 8.2 on the next page shows the surge in the U.S. prison population. Arrests and convictions have increased at such a torrid pace that the states and federal government haven't been able to build prisons fast enough to hold all of their incoming prisoners. To keep up, they hired corporations to operate private prisons for them. About 130,000 prisoners are held in these "for-profit" prisons (*Sourcebook of Criminal Justice Statistics* 2010:Table 6.32.2009). Actually, the United States has even more prisoners than shown in Figure 8.2, since this total does not include jail inmates. If we add them, the total comes to about 2.3 million people—about one out of every 135 citizens. Not only does the United States have more prisoners than any other country in the world but it also has a larger percentage of its population in prison (Massoglia et al. 2013). Another way of putting this is that the United States has only 5 percent of the world's population but about 25 percent of the world's prisoners (Brayne 2013).

As you can see from Figure 8.2, the number of prisoners peaked in 2009. In 2010, there was a slight decrease of prisoners (1,000), with a larger drop of 16,000 in 2011.

FIGURE 8.2 How Much Is Enough? The Explosion in the Number of U.S. Prisoners

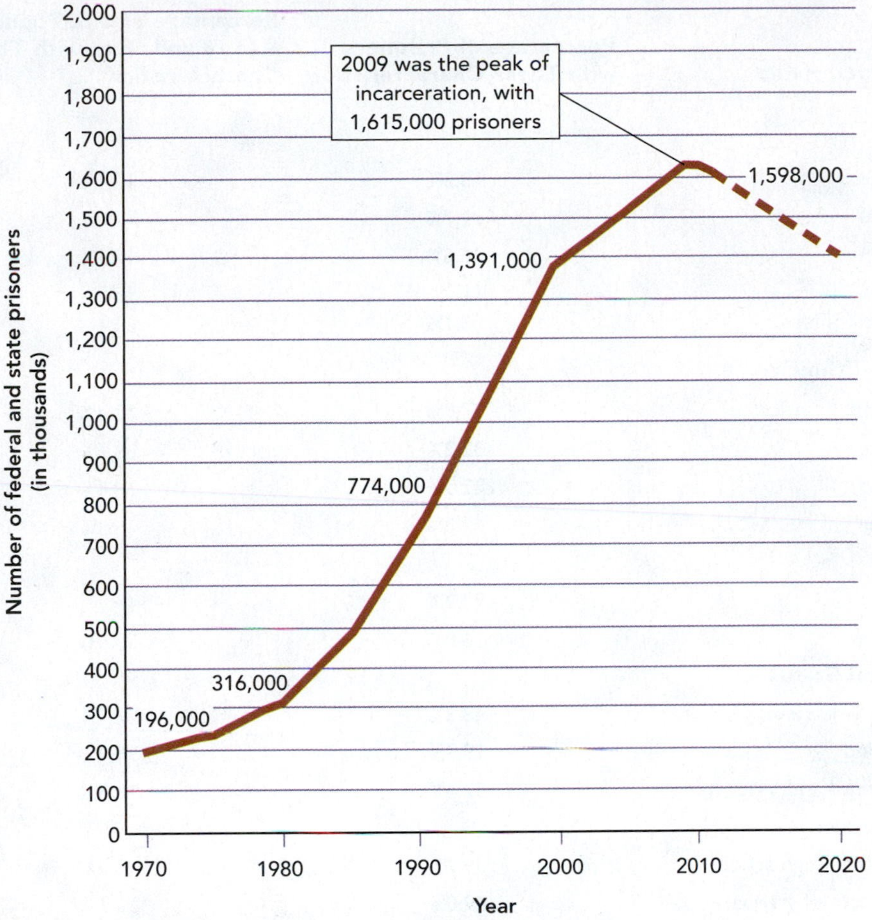

Between 1970 and 2011, the U.S. population increased 52 percent, while the number of prisoners increased 715 percent, *fourteen times faster* than population growth. If the number of prisoners had grown at the same rate as the U.S. population, we would have about 298,000 prisoners, about one-fifth of today's total. Or if the U.S. population had increased at the same rate as that of U.S. prisoners, the U.S. population would be 1,465,000,000—more than the population of China.

Sources: By the author. Based on Carson and Sabol 2012; *Statistical Abstract of the United States* 1995: Table 349; 2013:Tables 2, 6, 354. The broken line is the author's estimate.

With the state and federal governments running out of money, severe complaints about taxes, and an easing of the enforcement of marijuana laws, I predict that this decrease is not temporary. The broken line on this figure gives a rough indication of what the future might look like.

Who has been put in our prisons? Let's compare the prisoners with the U.S. population. As you look at Table 8.3 on the next page, several things may strike you. Close to half (46 percent) of all prisoners are younger than 35, and almost all prisoners are men. Then there is this remarkable statistic: There are more African American prisoners than there are white prisoners. On any given day, *one out of every nine* African American men ages 20 to 34 is in jail or prison. For Latinos, the rate is one of twenty-six; for whites, one of one hundred (Warren et al. 2008).

Read on **MySocLab**
Document: Beyond Crime and Punishment: Prisons and Inequality

Finally, note how marriage and education—two of the major ways that society "anchors" people into mainstream behavior—keep people out of prison. About

TABLE 8.3 Comparing Prison Inmates with the U.S. Population

Characteristics	Percentage of Prisoners with These Characteristics	Percentage of U.S. Population Age 18 and Over with These Characteristics[a]
Age		
18–24	13.3%	13.1%
25–34	32.7%	17.8%
35–44	26.6%	17.1%
45–54	19.2%	18.8%
55 and older	8.1%	33.4%
Race–Ethnicity		
African American	37.9%	12.4%
White	32.2%	66.7%
Latino	22.3%	14.6%
Other[b]	7.8%	6.3%
Sex		
Male	93.2%	49.2%
Female	6.8%	50.8%
Marital Status		
Never married	48.3%	27.4%
Married	19.3%	55.9%
Divorced and Widowed	32.4%	16.8%
Education		
Less than high school	39.7%	12.4%
High school graduate	49.0%	30.7%
Some college[c]	9.0%	26.5%
College graduate	2.4%	30.4%

[a]Because this column refers to Americans age 18 and over, the percentages will not agree with other totals in this book. For education, the percentages are based on Americans age 25 and over.

[b]*Sourcebook* places Asian Americans and Native Americans in this category.

[c]Includes associate's degrees.

Source: By the author. Based on *Sourcebook of Criminal Justice Statistics* 2004:Table 6.45.2003; 2011:Table 6.33.2010; *Statistical Abstract of the United States* 2013:Tables 11, 56, 236.

half of prisoners have never married. And look at the power of education, a major component of social class. As I mentioned earlier, social class funnels some people into the criminal justice system and diverts others away from it. You can see how people who drop out of high school have a high chance of ending up in prison—and how unlikely it is for a college graduate to have this unwelcome destination in life.

For about the past twenty years or so, the United States has followed a "get tough" policy. One of the most significant changes was "three-strikes-and-you're-out" laws, which have had unintended consequences, as you will see in the following Thinking Critically section.

THINKING CRITICALLY

"Three Strikes and You're Out!" Unintended Consequences of Well-Intended Laws

As the violent crime rate soared in the 1980s, Americans grew fearful. They demanded that their lawmakers do something. Politicians heard the message, and many responded by passing "three-strikes" laws in their states. Anyone who is convicted of a third felony receives an automatic mandatory sentence. Although some mandatory sentences carry life imprisonment, judges are not allowed to consider the circumstances. While few of us would feel sympathy if a man convicted of a third brutal rape or a third murder were sent to prison for life, in their haste to appease the public the politicians did not limit the three-strike laws to *violent* crimes.

And they did not consider that some minor crimes are considered felonies. As the functionalists would say, this has led to unintended consequences. Here are some actual cases:

- In Los Angeles, a 64-year-old man who stole a package of cigarettes was sentenced to 25-years-to-life in prison (Phillips 2013).
- In Sacramento, a man passed himself off as Tiger Woods and went on a $17,000 shopping spree. He was sentenced to *200 years* in prison (Reuters 2001).
- Also in California, Michael James passed a bad check for $94. He was sentenced to 25 years to life (Jones 2008).
- A Florida man put a lockbox with cocaine in his girlfriend's attic. He was sentenced to 15 years in prison, but his girlfriend, a 27-year-old mother of three, was sent to prison for life. The judge said the sentence was unjust, but he had no choice (Tierney 2012).
- In New York City, a man who was about to be sentenced for selling crack said to the judge, "I'm only 19. This is terrible." He then hurled himself out of a courtroom window, plunging to his death sixteen stories below (Cloud 1998).

For Your Consideration

➔ Apply the symbolic interactionist, functionalist, and conflict perspectives to the three-strikes laws. For *symbolic interactionism*, what do these laws represent to the public? How does your answer differ depending on what part of "the public" you are referring to? For *functionalism*, who benefits from these laws? What are some of the functions of three-strikes laws? Their dysfunctions? For the *conflict perspective*, which groups are in conflict? Who has the power to enforce their will on others?

➔ With the economic crisis, some states have concluded that they can't afford to lock so many people up. California is releasing some prisoners whose third crime was not violent (Phillips 2013). What is your opinion of this? ■

The Decline in Violent Crime

As you have seen, judges have put more and more people in prison, and legislators have passed the three-strikes laws. As these changes took place, the crime rate dropped sharply. Sociologists conclude that getting tough on criminals reduced crime, but it is only one of the reasons that violent crime dropped (Baumer and Wolff 2013). Other reasons include higher employment, less illegal drug use, a lower birth rate, and even abortion. There are even those who say that the best explanation is the elimination of lead in gasoline (Drum 2013). We can rule out employment: When the unemployment rate shot up with the economic crisis, the lower crime rates continued (Oppel 2011). This matter is not yet settled. We'll see what answers future research brings.

FIGURE 8.3 Recidivism of U.S. Prisoners

Of 272,000 prisoners released from U.S. prisons, what percentage were rearrested within three years?

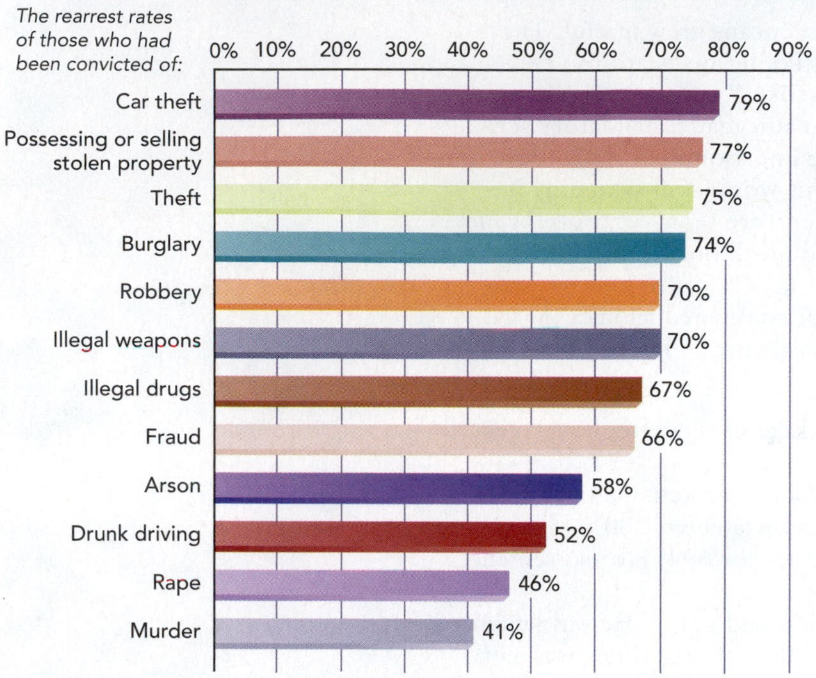

Note: The individuals were not necessarily rearrested for the same crime for which they had originally been imprisoned.

Source: By the author. Based on *Sourcebook of Criminal Justice Statistics* 2003:Table 6.50, the latest data available.

Recidivism

If a goal of prisons is to teach their clients to stay away from crime, they are colossal failures. We can measure their failure by the **recidivism rate**—the percentage of former prisoners who are rearrested. For people sent to prison for crimes of violence, within just three years of their release, two out of three (62 percent) are rearrested, and half (52 percent) are back in prison (*Sourcebook of Criminal Justice Statistics* 2003:Table 6.52). Since this research, the rates have dropped slightly ("State of Recidivism" 2011). Looking at Figure 8.3, which gives a breakdown of three-year recidivism by type of crime, it is safe to conclude that prisons do not teach people that crime doesn't pay.

The Death Penalty and Bias

As you know, **capital punishment**, the death penalty, is the most extreme measure the state takes. As you also know, the death penalty arouses both impassioned opposition and support. Advances in DNA testing have given opponents of the death penalty a strong argument: Innocent people have been sent to death row, and some have been executed. Others are just as passionate about retaining the death penalty. They point to such crimes as those of the serial killers discussed in the Down-to-Earth Sociology box on page 218.

Geography. Apart from anyone's personal position on the death penalty, it certainly is clear that the death penalty is not administered evenly. Consider geography: You can see from the Social Map on the next page that where people commit murder greatly affects their chances of being put to death.

Watch on **MySocLab**
Video: Deviance: Thinking Like a Sociologist

Social Class. The death penalty also shows social class bias. As you know from news reports, it is rare for a rich person to be sentenced to death. Although the government does not collect statistics on social class and the death penalty, this common observation is borne out by the education of the prisoners on death row. *Half* of the prisoners on death row (50 percent) have not finished high school (*Sourcebook of Criminal Justice Statistics* 2009:Table 6.81).

Explore on **MySocLab**
Activity: The Death Penalty

Gender. There is also a gender bias in the death penalty—so strong that it is almost unheard of for a woman to be sentenced to death, much less executed. Although women commit 9.6 percent of the murders, they make up only 1.8 percent of death row inmates (*Sourcebook of Criminal Justice Statistics* 2009:Table 6.81). Even on death row, the gender bias continues: Of those condemned to death, the state is more likely to execute a man than a woman. As Figure 8.5 on the next page shows, only 0.9 percent of the 5,093 prisoners executed in the United States since 1930 have been women. This gender bias could reflect the women's previous offenses and the relative brutality of their murders, but we need research to determine if this is so.

Race–Ethnicity. At one point, racial–ethnic bias was so flagrant that it put a stop to the death penalty. Donald Partington (1965), a lawyer in Virginia, was shocked by the bias he saw in the courtroom, and he decided to document it. He found that 2,798 men had been convicted for rape and attempted rape in Virginia between 1908 and 1963—56 percent whites and 44 percent blacks. For rape, 41 men had been executed.

recidivism rate the percentage of released convicts who are rearrested

capital punishment the death penalty

FIGURE 8.4 Executions in the United States

Executions since 1977, when the death penalty was reinstated.

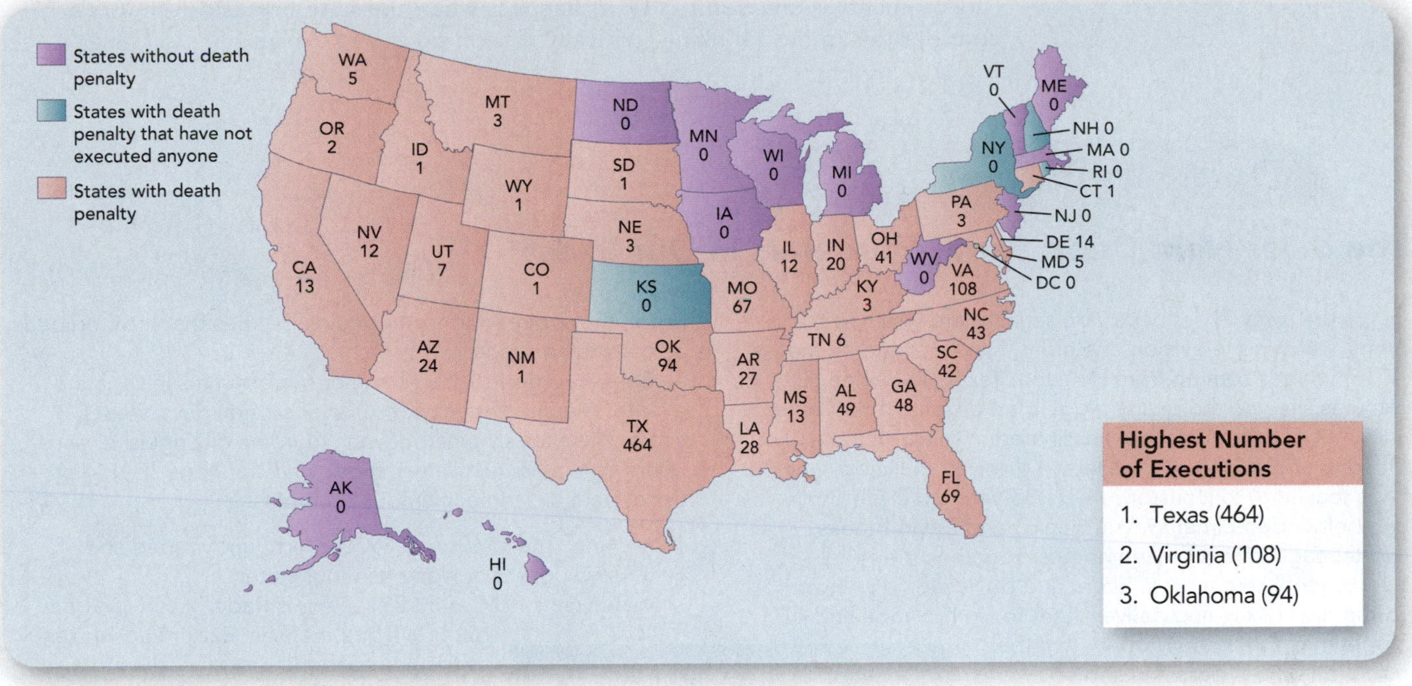

Source: By the author. Based on *Statistical Abstract of the United States* 2013:Table 360.

For attempted rape, 13 had been executed. *All those executed were black.* Not one of the whites was executed.

After listening to evidence like this, in 1972 the Supreme Court ruled in *Furman v. Georgia* that the death penalty, as applied, was unconstitutional. The execution of prisoners stopped—but not for long. The states wrote new laws, and in 1977, they again began to execute prisoners. On Table 8.4, you can see the race–ethnicity of the prisoners who are now on death row. Since the death penalty was reinstated, 65 percent of those put to death have been white and 35 percent African American (*Statistical Abstract* 2013:Table 359). (Latinos are evidently counted as whites in this statistic.)

TABLE 8.4 The Race–Ethnicity of the 3,170 Prisoners on Death Row

	Percentage	
	on Death Row	**in U.S. Population**[a]
Whites	43%	66.7%
African Americans	42%	12.4%
Latinos	12%	14.6%
Asian Americans	1%	5.1%
Native Americans	1%	1.1%

[a]Ages 18 and over.

Sources: By the author. Based on *Sourcebook of Criminal Justice Statistics* 2013:Table 6.80.2012; *Statistical Abstract of the United Sates* 2013:Table11.

FIGURE 8.5 Who Gets Executed? Gender Bias in Capital Punishment

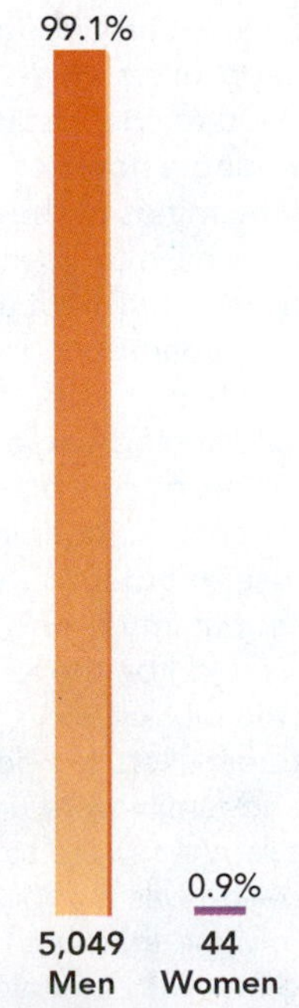

Source: By the author. Based on *Statistical Abstract of the United States* 2013:Table 359.

serial murder the killing of several victims in three or more separate events

In North Carolina, African Americans who kill whites are three times as likely to be sentenced to death as are whites who kill African Americans (Radelet and Pierce 2011). We don't have this statistic for other states.

The official responses to deviance that we have discussed assume that the state (government) is functioning. What happens when the state breaks down? Let's consider this in the Thinking Critically section on the next page.

Down-to-Earth Sociology

The Killer Next Door: Serial Murderers in Our Midst

Here is my experience with serial killers. As I was watching television one night, I was stunned by the images coming from Houston, Texas. Television cameras showed the police digging up dozens of bodies from under a boat storage shed. Fascinated, I waited impatiently for spring break. A few days later, I drove from Illinois, where I was teaching, to Houston, where 33-year-old Dean Corll had befriended Elmer Wayne Henley and David Brooks, two teenagers from broken homes. Together, they had killed twenty-seven boys. Elmer and David would pick up young hitchhikers and deliver them to Corll to rape and kill. Sometimes they even brought him their own high school classmates.

I talked to one of Elmer's neighbors, as he was painting his front porch. His 15-year-old son had gone to get a haircut one Saturday morning. That was the last time he saw his son alive. The police refused to investigate. They insisted that his son had run away. On a city map, I plotted the locations of the homes of the local murder victims. Many clustered around the homes of the teenage killers.

I decided to spend my coming sabbatical writing a novel on this case. To get into the minds of the killers, I knew that I would have to "become" them day after day. Corll kept a piece of plywood in his apartment. In each of its corners, he had cut a hole. He and the boys would spread-eagle their handcuffed victims on this board and torture them for hours. Sometimes, they would even pause to order pizza. I began to wonder about immersing myself in torture and human degradation. Would I be the same person afterward? I decided not to write the book.

The three killers led double lives so successfully that their friends and family were unaware of their criminal activities. Henley's mother swore to me that her son couldn't possibly be guilty—he was a good boy. Some of Elmer's high school friends told me that that his being involved in homosexual rape and murder was ridiculous—he was interested only in girls. I was interviewing them in Henley's bedroom, and for proof, they pointed to a pair of girls' panties that were draped across a lamp shade.

Ted Bundy is shown here on trial in Miami for killing two women, both college students. You can get a glimpse of his charm and wit and how, like most serial killers, he blended in with society. Bundy was executed for his murders.

Serial murder is killing three or more victims in separate events. The murders may occur over several days, weeks, or years. The elapsed time between murders distinguishes serial killers from *mass murderers*, those who do their killing all at once. Here are some infamous examples:

- During the 1960s and 1970s, Ted Bundy raped and killed dozens of women in four states.
- Between 1974 and 1991, Dennis Rader killed ten people in Wichita, Kansas. Rader had written to the newspapers, proudly calling himself the BTK (Bind, Torture, and Kill) strangler.
- In the late 1980s and early 1990s, Aileen Wuornos hitchhiked along Florida's freeways. She killed seven men after having had sex with them.
- The serial killer with the most victims appears to be Harold Shipman, a physician in Manchester, England. From 1977 to 2000, during house calls, Shipman gave lethal injections to 230 to 275 of his elderly female patients.
- In 2009, Anthony Sowell of Cleveland, Ohio, was discovered living with eleven decomposing bodies of women he had raped and strangled (UPI 2009).

Is serial murder more common now than it used to be? Not likely. In the past, police departments had little communication with one another, and seldom did anyone connect killings in different jurisdictions. Today's more efficient communications, investigative techniques, and DNA matching make it easier for the police to know when a serial killer is operating in an area. Part of the perception that there are more serial killers today is also due to ignorance of our history: In our frontier past, for example, serial killers went from ranch to ranch.

For Your Consideration

→ Do you think that serial killers should be given the death penalty? Why or why not? How does your social location influence your opinion?

THINKING CRITICALLY

Vigilantes: When the State Breaks Down

Many of us chafe under the coercive nature of the state: the IRS, Homeland Security, the many police agencies from the CIA, FBI, and NSA to who knows how many other groups summarized with three capital letters. Little cameras litter society, seemingly watching our every move.

We certainly have given up a lot of freedoms—and we are likely to give up many more in the name of security. We can chafe and complain all we want. This is the wave of the future, seemingly an unstoppable one.

There is another side to what is happening. As many fear, the many guns that the many uniformed and plainclothes men and women are carrying can be trained on us. But for now, they bring security. They indicate that the state is operating; perhaps overreacting, but operating effectively nonetheless.

What happens when the state fails, when men and women in an official capacity carry guns and shields but can't be effective in protecting citizens from the bad guys who are carrying guns—and using them to enforce their way?

A boy walks past a member of the unofficial "community police" in Cruz Grande, Guerrero, Mexico.

One reaction is vigilantism, people taking the law into their own hands. This is what happened in what we call the Wild West. Citizens armed themselves, formed posses, chased the bad guys, and dispensed quick justice at the end of a rope. You've seen the movies.

And this is what is happening in Mexico right now.

The state in Mexico has failed at all levels, from the local to the national. Citizens live in fear since the bad guys, in this case the drug lords, have gained much control. They have infiltrated the police, from the local cops to the *federales.* Even the head of Mexico's national drug enforcement agency was on the drug lords' payroll. Army generals, supposedly part of the war against drugs, take money to protect drug deals. They even use army vehicles to transport drugs. The corruption goes beyond belief, reaching even into the presidential palace. (But why the rush to judgment? Perhaps the president's brother was given a billion-dollar tip by some taxi driver who said he was a good passenger.)

The arrests are countless, the executions (shooting deaths by the police and the army) in the thousands. The death toll continues to mount, now over 60,000 police, drug dealers, and regular citizens.

The result, other than the many deaths? Failure to secure the people's safety.

The Mexican people, then, have begun to take the law into their own hands. In the state of Guerrero, country folk have grabbed their old hunting rifles, put on masks, raided the homes of drug dealers, and put them in makeshift jails. They have set up blockades on the roads leading to their little towns. They won't let drug dealers, or any strangers, in. They won't even let the federal police, the state police, or the army in. These "enforcers of the law" are too corrupt, they say. We can trust only the neighbors we grew up with.

The reaction of the local police, the honest ones? "Maybe they can do something about the problem. We can't. If we try, the drug dealers will go to our homes and kill our families. They don't know who these masked men are."

The reaction of the state governor? "Good job."

The reaction of the regular citizens? Relief. And pleasure at being able to go out at night again and drink a little tequila and dance in the town square.

The masked men are going to hold their own trials. They haven't strung anyone up yet. But what will they do? If they send the men they convict to prison, well, the prison guards and administrators are corrupt, too. In one prison (in Gomez Palacio), the administrators even loaned the prisoners their guns and cars, and let the prisoners out to kill members of a rival drug gang. Afterward, the men dutifully returned to the prison, turned in the cars and guns, and went back to their cells. Incredible, I know. But true.

Based on Sheridan 1998; Malkin 2010; Archibold 2012; Casey 2013.

For Your Consideration

➤ We don't yet know the consequences of this incipient vigilante movement in Mexico. But what else can the citizens do?

➤ How much freedom are you willing to give up to have security? Is there a balance somewhere? ■

The Trouble with Official Statistics

Read on **MySocLab**
Document: Rethinking Crime and Immigration

We must be cautious when it comes to official crime statistics. According to official statistics, working-class boys are more delinquent than middle-class boys. Yet, as we have seen, who actually gets arrested for what is influenced by social class, a point that has far-reaching implications. As symbolic interactionists point out, the police follow a symbolic system as they enforce the law. Ideas of "typical criminals" and "typical good citizens" permeate their work. The more a suspect matches their stereotypes of a lawbreaker (which they call "criminal profiles"), the more likely that person is to be arrested. **Police discretion**, the decision whether to arrest someone or even to ignore a matter, is a routine part of police work. Official crime statistics reflect these and many other biases.

Crime statistics do not have an objective, independent existence. They are not like oranges that you pick out in a grocery store. Rather, they are a human creation. If the police enforce laws strictly, crime statistics go up. Loosen up the enforcement, and crime statistics go down. New York City provides a remarkable example. To keep their crime statistics low, the police keep some crime victims waiting in the police station for hours. The victims give up and leave, and the crime doesn't enter any official record. In other cases, the police simply listen to crime victims but make no written record of the crime (Baker and Goldstein 2011). It is likely that such underreporting occurs in most places.

As a personal example, someone took my mailbox (rural, located on the street). When I called and reported the theft, a police officer arrived promptly. He was incredible friendly. He looked around and spotted the mailbox in the ditch. He retrieved it and then personally restored it to its post. He even used his tools to screw it back on. He then said, "I'm chalking this one up to the wind." I didn't object. I knew what he was doing. No crime to report, no paperwork for him, and the area has one less incident to go into the crime statistics.

The Medicalization of Deviance: Mental Illness

When the woman drove her car into the river, drowning her two small children strapped to their little car seats, people said that she had "gone nuts," "went bonkers," and just plain "lost it" because of her problems.

Neither Mental Nor Illness? When people cannot find a satisfying explanation for why someone does something weird or is "like that," they often say that a "sickness in the head" is causing the unacceptable behavior. To *medicalize* something is to make it a medical matter, to classify it as a form of illness that properly belongs in the care of physicians. For the past hundred years or so, especially since the time of Sigmund Freud (1856–1939), the Viennese physician who founded psychoanalysis, there has been a growing tendency toward the **medicalization of deviance**. In this view, deviance, including crime, is a sign of mental sickness. Rape, murder, stealing, cheating, and so on are external symptoms of internal disorders, consequences of a confused or tortured mind, one that should be treated by mental health experts.

police discretion the practice of the police, in the normal course of their duties, to either arrest or ticket someone for an offense or to overlook the matter

medicalization of deviance to make deviance a medical matter, a symptom of some underlying illness that needs to be treated by physicians

medicalization the transformation of a human condition into a matter to be treated by physicians

Thomas Szasz (1986, 1998, 2010), a renegade in his profession of psychiatry, disagrees. He argues that what are called *mental illnesses* are *neither mental nor illnesses. They are simply problem behaviors.* Szasz breaks these behaviors for which we don't have a ready explanation into two causes: physical illness and learned deviance.

Some behaviors that are called "mental illnesses" have physical causes. That is, something in an individual's body results in unusual perceptions or behavior. Some depression, for example, is caused by a chemical imbalance in the brain, which can be treated by drugs. The behaviors that are associated with depression—crying, long-term sadness, and lack of interest in family, work, school, or grooming—are only symptoms of a physical problem.

People whose behaviors violate norms are often called mentally ill. "Why else would they do such things?" is a common response to deviant behaviors that we don't understand. Mental illness is a label that contains the assumption that there is something wrong "within" people that "causes" their disapproved behavior. The surprise with this man, who changed his legal name to "Scary Guy," is that he speaks at schools across the country, where he promotes acceptance, awareness, love, and understanding.

Attention-deficit disorder (ADD) is an example of a new "mental illness" that has come out of nowhere. As Szasz says, "No one explains where this disease came from or why it didn't exist 50 years ago. No one is able to diagnose it with objective tests." ADD is diagnosed because a teacher or parent is complaining about a child misbehaving. Misbehaving children have been a problem throughout history, but now, with doctors looking to expand their territory, this problem behavior has become a sign of "mental illness" that they can treat.

All of us have troubles. Some of us face a constant barrage of problems as we go through life. Most of us continue the struggle, perhaps encouraged by relatives and friends and motivated by job, family responsibilities, religious faith, and life goals. Even when the odds seem hopeless, we carry on, not perfectly, but as best we can.

Some people, however, fail to cope well with life's challenges. Overwhelmed, they become depressed, uncooperative, or hostile. Some strike out at others, and some, in Merton's terms, become retreatists and withdraw into their apartments or homes, refusing to come out. These may be inappropriate ways of coping, stresses Szasz, but they are *behaviors, not mental illnesses.* Szasz concludes that "mental illness" is a myth foisted on a naive public. Our medical profession uses pseudoscientific jargon that people don't understand so it can expand its area of control and force nonconforming people to accept society's definitions of "normal."

Szasz's controversial claim forces us to look anew at the forms of deviance that we usually refer to as mental illness. To explain behavior that people find bizarre, he directs our attention not to causes hidden deep within the "subconscious" but, instead, to how people learn such behaviors. To ask, "What is the origin of someone's inappropriate or bizarre behavior?" then becomes similar to asking "Why do some women steal?" "Why do some men rape?" "Why do some teenagers cuss their parents and stalk out of the room, slamming the door?" *The answers depend on those people's particular experiences in life, not on an illness in their mind.* In short, some sociologists find Szasz's renegade analysis refreshing because it indicates that *social experiences*, not some illness of the mind, underlie bizarre behaviors—as well as deviance in general.

The Homeless Mentally Ill

Jamie was sitting on a low wall surrounding the landscaped courtyard of an exclusive restaurant. She appeared unaware of the stares elicited by her layers of mismatched clothing, her matted hair and dirty face, and the shopping cart that overflowed with her meager possessions.

After sitting next to Jamie for a few minutes, I saw her point to the street and concentrate, slowly moving her finger horizontally. I asked her what she was doing.

"I'm directing traffic," she replied. "I control where the cars go. Look, that one turned right there," she said, now withdrawing her finger.

"Really?" I said.

After a while she confided that her cart talked to her.

"Really?" I said again.

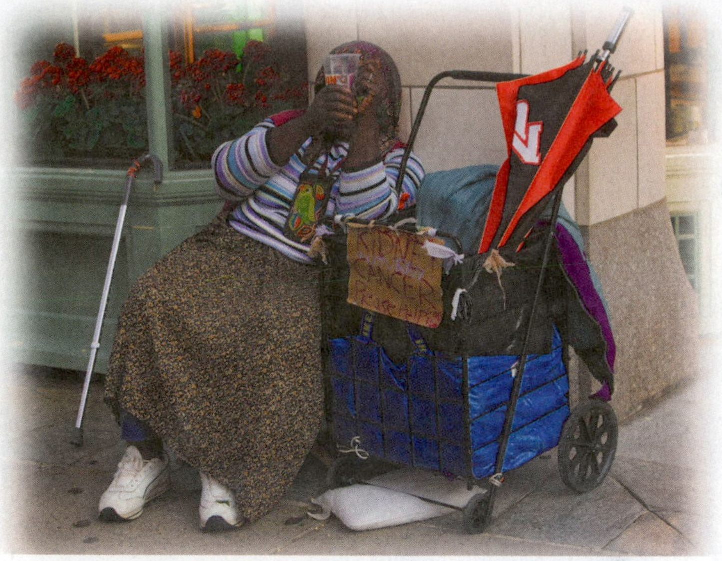

Mental illness is common among the homeless. This photo was taken in Boston, but it could have been taken in any large city in the United States.

"Yes," she replied. "You can hear it, too." At that, she pushed the shopping cart a bit.

"Did you hear that?" she asked.

When I shook my head, she demonstrated again. Then it hit me. She was referring to the squeaking wheels!

I nodded.

When I left Jamie, she was pointing a finger toward the sky, for, as she told me, she also controlled the flight of airplanes.

To most of us, Jamie's behavior and thinking are bizarre. They simply do not match any reality we know. Could you or I become like Jamie?

Suppose for a bitter moment that you are homeless and have to live on the streets. You have no money, no place to sleep, no bathroom. You do not know *if* you are going to eat, much less where. You have no friends or anyone you can trust. You live in constant fear of rape and other violence. Do you think this might be enough to drive you over the edge?

Consider just the problems involved in not having a place to bathe. (Shelters are often so dangerous that many homeless people prefer to sleep in public settings.) At first, you try to wash in the restrooms of gas stations, bars, the bus station, or a shopping center. But you are dirty, and people stare when you enter and call the management when they see you wash your feet in the sink. You are thrown out and told in no uncertain terms never to come back. So you get dirtier and dirtier. Eventually, you come to think of being dirty as a fact of life. Soon, maybe, you don't even care. The stares no longer bother you—at least not as much.

No one will talk to you, and you withdraw more and more into yourself. You begin to build a fantasy life. You talk openly to yourself. People stare, but so what? They stare anyway. Besides, they are no longer important to you.

Jamie might be mentally ill. Some organic problem, such as a chemical imbalance in her brain, might underlie her behavior. But perhaps not. How long would it take you to exhibit bizarre behaviors if you were homeless—and hopeless? The point is that *living on the streets can cause mental illness*—or whatever we want to label socially inappropriate behaviors that we find difficult to classify. *Homelessness and mental illness are reciprocal*: Just as "mental illness" can cause homelessness, so the trials of being homeless, of living on cold, hostile streets, can lead to unusual thinking and behaviors.

The Need for a More Humane Approach

As Durkheim (1895/1964:68) pointed out, deviance is inevitable—even in a group of saints.

> *Imagine a society of saints, a perfect cloister of exemplary individuals. Crimes, properly so called, will there be unknown; but faults which appear invisible to the layman will create there the same scandal that the ordinary offense does in ordinary society.*

With deviance inevitable, one measure of a society is how it treats its deviants. Our prisons certainly don't say much good about U.S. society. Filled with the poor, uneducated, and unskilled, they are warehouses of the unwanted. White-collar criminals continue to get by with a slap on the wrist while street criminals are punished severely. Some deviants, who fail to meet current standards of admission to either prison or mental hospital, take refuge in shelters, as well as in cardboard boxes tucked away in urban recesses. Although no one has *the* answer, it does not take much reflection to see that there are more humane approaches than these.

Because deviance is inevitable, the larger issues are to find ways to protect people from deviant behaviors that are harmful to themselves or others, to tolerate behaviors that are not harmful, and to develop systems of fairer treatment for deviants. In the absence of fundamental changes that would bring about an equitable society, most efforts are, unfortunately, like putting a Band-Aid on a gunshot wound. What we need is a more humane social system, one that would prevent the social inequalities that are the focus of the next four chapters.

MySocLab

Study and Review on MySocLab

CHAPTER 8 Summary and Review

What Is Deviance?

8.1 Summarize the relativity of deviance, the need of norms, and the types of sanctions; contrast sociobiological, psychological and sociological explanations of deviance.

Deviance (the violation of norms) is relative. What people consider deviant varies from one culture to another and from group to group within the same society. As symbolic interactionists stress, it is not the act but the reactions to the act that make something deviant. All groups develop systems of **social control** to punish **deviants**—those who violate their norms. Pp. 194–197.

How do sociological and individualistic explanations of deviance differ?

To explain why people deviate, sociobiologists and psychologists look for reasons *within* the individual, such as **genetic predispositions** or **personality disorders**. Sociologists, in contrast, look for explanations *outside* the individual, in social experiences. Pp. 197–198.

The Symbolic Interactionist Perspective

8.2 Contrast three theories of deviance: differential association, control, and labeling.

How do symbolic interactionists explain deviance?

Symbolic interactionists have developed several theories to explain deviance such as **crime** (the violation of norms that are written into law). According to **differential association** theory, people learn to deviate by associating with others. According to **control theory**, each of us is propelled toward deviance, but most of us conform because of an effective system of inner and outer controls. People who have less effective controls deviate. Pp. 198–200.

Labeling theory focuses on how labels (names, reputations) help to funnel people into or divert them away from deviance. People often use **techniques of neutralization** to deflect social norms. Pp. 200–204.

The Functionalist Perspective

8.3 Explain how deviance can be functional for society, how mainstream values can produce deviance (strain theory), and how social class is related to crime (illegitimate opportunities).

How do functionalists explain deviance?

Functionalists point out that deviance, including criminal acts, is functional for society. Functions include affirming norms and promoting social unity and social change. According to **strain theory**, societies socialize their members into desiring **cultural goals**. Many people are unable to achieve these goals in socially acceptable ways—that is, by **institutionalized means**. *Deviants*, then, are people who either give up on the goals or use disapproved means to attain them. Merton identified five types of responses to cultural goals and institutionalized means: conformity, innovation, ritualism, retreatism, and rebellion. Because of **illegitimate opportunity structures**, some people have easier access to illegal means of achieving goals. Pp. 204–209.

The Conflict Perspective

8.4 Explain how social class is related to the criminal justice system and how the criminal justice system is oppressive.

How do conflict theorists explain deviance?

Conflict theorists take the position that the group in power imposes its definitions of deviance on other groups. From this perspective, the law is an instrument of oppression used by the powerful to maintain their position of privilege. The ruling class, which developed the **criminal justice system**, uses it to punish the crimes of the poor while diverting its own criminal activities away from this punitive system. Pp. 210–211.

Reactions to Deviance

8.5 Be familiar with street crimes and prison, three-strikes laws, the decline in violent crime, recidivism, bias in the death penalty, the medicalization of deviance, and the need for a humane approach.

What are common reactions to deviance in the United States?

In following a "get-tough" policy, the United States has imprisoned millions of people. African Americans and Latinos make up a disproportionate percentage of U.S. prisoners. The death penalty shows biases by geography, social class, gender, and race–ethnicity. Pp. 211–220.

Are official statistics on crime reliable?

The conclusions of both symbolic interactionists (that the police operate with a large measure of discretion) and conflict theorists (that a power elite controls the legal system) indicate that we must be cautious when using crime statistics. P. 220.

What is the medicalization of deviance?

The medical profession has attempted to **medicalize** many forms of **deviance**, claiming that they represent mental illnesses. Thomas Szasz disagrees, asserting that these are problem behaviors, not mental illnesses. The situation of homeless people indicates that problems in living can lead to bizarre behavior and thinking. Pp. 220–222.

What is a more humane approach?

Deviance is inevitable, so the larger issues are to find ways to protect people from deviance that harms themselves and others, to tolerate deviance that is not harmful, and to develop systems of fairer treatment for deviants. Pp. 222–223.

Thinking Critically about Chapter 8

1. Select some deviance with which you are personally familiar. (It does not have to be your own—it can be something that someone you know did.) Choose one of the three theoretical perspectives to explain what happened.
2. As explained in the text, deviance can be mild. Recall some instance in which you broke a social rule in dress, etiquette, or speech. What was the reaction? Why do you think people reacted like that? What was your response to their reactions?
3. What do you think should be done about the U.S. crime problem? What sociological theories support your view?

CHAPTER 9

Global Stratification

Listen to Chapter 9 on MySocLab

Learning Objectives

After you have read this chapter, you should be able to:

Let's contrast two *"average" families from around the world:*

For Getu Mulleta, 33, and his wife, Zenebu, 28, of rural Ethiopia, life is a constant struggle to avoid starvation. They and their seven children live in a 320-square-foot manure-plastered hut with no electricity, gas, or running water. They have a radio, but the battery is dead. The family farms teff, a grain, and survives on $130 a year.

The Mulletas' poverty is not due to a lack of hard work. Getu works about eighty hours a week, while Zenebu puts in even more hours. "Housework" for Zenebu includes fetching water, cleaning animal stables, and making fuel pellets out of cow dung for the open fire over which she cooks the family's food. Like other Ethiopian women, she eats after the men.

In Ethiopia, the average male can expect to live to age 48, the average female to 50.

The Mulletas' most valuable possession is their oxen. Their wishes for the future: more animals, better seed, and a second set of clothing.

> They live in a 320-square-foot manure-plastered hut

* * * * *

Springfield, Illinois, is home to the Kellys—Rick, 36, Patti, 34, Julie, 10, and Michael, 7. The Kellys live in a three-bedroom, 2½-bath, 2,480-square-foot ranch-style house with a fireplace, central heating and air conditioning, a basement, and a two-car garage. Their home is equipped with a refrigerator, freezer, washing machine, clothes dryer, dishwasher, garbage disposal, vacuum cleaner, food processor, microwave, and convection stovetop and oven. They also own computers, cell phones, color televisions, a Kindle, digital cameras, a digital camcorder, an iPod, an iPad, a printer-scanner-fax machine, blow dryers, a juicer, an espresso coffee maker, a pickup truck, and an SUV.

Rick works forty hours a week as a cable splicer for a telephone company. Patti teaches school part-time. Together they make $60,395, plus benefits. The Kellys can choose from among dozens of superstocked supermarkets. They spend $5,218 for food they eat at home, and another $3,559 eating out, a total of 15 percent of their annual income.

In the United States, the average life expectancy is 76 for males, 81 for females.

On the Kellys' wish list are a hybrid car with satellite radio, a laptop computer (with solid-state drive, a terabyte of memory, and Bluetooth wi-fi), a 65-inch plasma TV with surround sound, a boat, a motor home, an ATV, and an in-ground heated swimming pool.

Menzel 1994; Statistical Abstract *2013:Tables 108, 701, 710, 984.*

Systems of Social Stratification

9.1 Compare and contrast slavery (including bonded labor), caste, estate, and class systems of social stratification.

Some of the world's nations are wealthy, others poor, and some in between. This division of nations, as well as the layering of groups of people within a nation, is called *social stratification*. Social stratification is one of the most significant topics we will discuss in this book, since, as you saw in the opening vignette, it profoundly affects our life chances—from our access to material possessions to the age at which we die.

Social stratification also affects the way we think about life. Look at the photo on the next page. If you were born into this family, you would expect hunger to be a part of life and would not expect all of your children to survive. You would also be illiterate and would assume that your children would be as well. In contrast, if you were one of the U.S. parents, you would expect your children not only to survive but to be well fed, not only to be able to read but to go to college. You can see that social stratification brings with it not just material things but also ideas of what we can expect out of life.

Social stratification is a system in which groups of people are divided into layers according to their relative property, power, and prestige. It is important to emphasize that social stratification does not refer to individuals. It is a way of ranking large groups of people into a hierarchy according to their relative privileges.

It is also important to note that *every society stratifies its members.* Some societies have greater inequality than others, but social stratification is universal. In addition, in every society of the world, *gender* is a basis for stratifying people. On the basis of their gender, people are either allowed or denied access to the good things offered by their society.

Let's consider four major systems of social stratification: slavery, caste, estate, and class.

social stratification the division of large numbers of people into layers according to their relative property, power, and prestige; applies to both nations and to people within a nation, society, or other group

slavery a form of social stratification in which some people own other people

Watch on **MySocLab**
Video: Social Stratification: The Big Picture

Slavery

Slavery, whose essential characteristic is that *some individuals own other people*, has been common throughout history. The Old Testament even lays out rules for how owners should treat their slaves. So does the Koran. The Romans had slaves, as did the Africans and Greeks. In classical Greece and Rome, slaves did the work, freeing citizens to engage in politics and the arts. Slavery was most widespread in agricultural societies and least common among nomads, especially hunters and gatherers (Landtman 1938/1968; Rowthorn et al. 2011). As we examine the major causes and conditions of slavery, you will see how remarkably slavery has varied around the world.

The Mulleta family of Ethiopia, described in the opening vignette.

A slave market in Marrakesh, Morocco. This lithograph is from the 1800s.

Causes of Slavery. Contrary to popular assumption, slavery was usually based not on racism but on one of three other factors. The first was *debt.* In some societies, creditors would enslave people who could not pay their debts. The second was *crime.* Instead of being killed, a murderer or thief might be enslaved by the victim's family as compensation for their loss. The third was *war.* When one group of people conquered another, they often enslaved some of the vanquished. Historian Gerda Lerner (1986) notes that women were the first people enslaved through warfare.

When tribal men raided another group, they killed the men, raped the women, and then brought the women back as slaves. The women were valued for sexual purposes, for reproduction, and for their labor.

Roughly twenty-five hundred years ago, when Greece was but a collection of city-states, slavery was common. A city that became powerful and conquered another city would enslave some of the vanquished. Both slaves and slaveholders were Greek. Similarly, when Rome became the supreme power of the Mediterranean area about two thousand years ago, following the custom of the time, the Romans enslaved some of the Greeks they had conquered. More educated than their conquerors, some of these slaves served as tutors in Roman homes. Slavery, then, was a sign of debt, of crime, or of defeat in battle. It was not a sign that the slave was viewed as inherently inferior.

Conditions of Slavery. The conditions of slavery have varied widely around the world. *In some places, slavery was temporary.* Slaves of the Israelites were set free in the year of jubilee, which occurred every fifty years. Roman slaves ordinarily had the right to buy themselves out of slavery. They knew what their purchase price was, and some were able to meet this price by striking a bargain with their owners and selling their services to others. In most instances, however, slavery was a lifelong condition. Some criminals, for example, became slaves when they were given life sentences as oarsmen on Roman warships. There they served until death, which often came quickly to those in this exhausting service.

Slavery was not necessarily inheritable. In most places, the children of slaves were slaves themselves. But in some instances, the child of a slave who served a rich family might even be adopted by that family, becoming an heir who bore the family name along with the other sons or daughters of the household. In ancient Mexico, the children of slaves were always free (Landtman 1938/1968:271).

Slaves were not necessarily powerless and poor. In almost all instances, slaves owned no property and had no power. Among some groups, however, slaves could accumulate property and even rise to high positions in the community. Occasionally, a slave might even become wealthy, loan money to the master, and, while still a slave, own slaves himself or herself (Landtman 1938/1968). This, however, was rare.

Bonded Labor in the New World. A gray area between slavery and contract labor is **bonded labor,** also called **indentured service.** People who wanted to start a new life in the American colonies but could not pay for their passage across the ocean would arrange for a ship captain to transport them on credit. When they arrived, wealthy colonists would pay the captain for the voyage, and these penniless people would become the colonists' servants for a set number of years. During this period, the servants were required by law to serve their masters. If they ran away, they became outlaws who were hunted down and forcibly returned. At the end of their period of indenture, they were free to sell their labor and to live where they chose (Main 1965; Post 2009).

bonded labor (indentured service) a contractual system in which someone sells his or her body (services) for a specified period of time in an arrangement very close to slavery, except that it is entered into voluntarily

Slavery in the New World. When there were not enough indentured servants to meet the growing need for labor in the American colonies, some colonists tried to enslave Native Americans. This attempt failed, in part because Indians who escaped knew how to survive in the wilderness and were able to make their way back to their tribes. The colonists then turned to Africans, who were brought to North and South America by the Dutch, English, Portuguese, and Spanish.

Because slavery has a broad range of causes, some analysts conclude that racism didn't lead to slavery but, rather, that slavery led to racism. To defend slavery, U.S. slave owners developed an **ideology,** beliefs that justify social arrangements, making those arrangements seem necessary and fair. They developed the view that their slaves were inferior. Some even said that they were not fully human. In short, the colonists wove elaborate justifications for slavery, built on the presumed superiority of their own group.

To make slavery even more profitable, slave states passed laws that made slavery *inheritable*; that is, the babies born to slaves became the property of the slave owners (Stampp 1956). These children could be sold, bartered, or traded. To strengthen their control, slave states passed laws making it illegal for slaves to hold meetings or to be away from the master's premises without carrying a pass (Lerner 1972). Sociologist W. E. B. Du Bois (1935/1992:12) noted that "gradually the entire white South became an armed camp to keep Negroes in slavery and to kill the black rebel."

The Civil War did not end legal discrimination. For example, until 1954, many states operated separate school systems for blacks and whites. Until the 1950s, in order to keep the races from "mixing," it was illegal in Mississippi for a white and an African American to sit together on the same seat of a car! There was no outright ban on blacks and whites being in the same car, however, so whites could employ African American chauffeurs.

During my research in India, I interviewed this 8-year-old girl. Mahashury is a *bonded laborer* who was exchanged by her parents for a 2,000 rupee loan (about $14). To repay the loan, Mahashury must do construction work for one year. She will receive one meal a day and one set of clothing for the year. Because this centuries-old practice is now illegal, the master bribes Indian officials, who inform him when they are going to inspect the construction site. He then hides his bonded laborers. I was able to interview and photograph Mahashury because her master was absent the day I visited the construction site.

Slavery Today. Slavery continues to rear its ugly head in several parts of the world (Crane 2012). The Ivory Coast, Mauritania, Niger, and Sudan have a long history of slavery, and not until the 1980s was slavery made illegal in Mauritania and Sudan (Ayittey 1998). It took until 2003 for slavery to be banned in Niger, where it still continues (Mwiti 2013).

The enslavement of children for work and sex is a problem in Africa, Asia, and South America (*Trafficking in Persons Report* 2012). A unique form of child slavery in some Mideast countries involves buying little boys around the ages of 4 or 6 to race camels. Their screams of terror are thought to make the camels run faster. In Qatar and the United Arab Emirates, which recently banned this practice, robots are supposed to replace the children (Nelson 2009; "Camel Racing . . ." 2011).

Caste

The second system of social stratification is caste. In a **caste system,** birth determines status, which is lifelong. Someone who is born into a low-status group will always have low status, no matter how much that person may accomplish in life. In sociological terms, a caste system is built on ascribed status (discussed on page 98). Achieved status cannot change an individual's place in this system.

Societies with this form of stratification try to make certain that the boundaries between castes remain firm. They practice **endogamy,** marriage within their own group, prohibiting the marriage of members of different castes. Rules about *ritual pollution* also keep contact between castes to a minimum. Touching a member of an inferior caste, for example, makes a member of the superior caste unclean.

India's Religious Castes. India provides the best example of a caste system. Based not on race but on religion, India's caste system has existed for almost three thousand years (Chandra 1993; Hnatkovska et al. 2012). Look at Table 9.1 on the next page, which lists India's four main castes. These castes are subdivided into about three

ideology beliefs about the way things ought to be that justify social arrangements

caste system a form of social stratification in which people's statuses are lifelong conditions determined by birth

endogamy the practice of marrying within one's own group

TABLE 9.1 India's Caste System

Caste	Occupation
Brahman	Priests and teachers
Kshatriya	Rulers and soldiers
Vaishya	Merchants and traders
Shudra	Peasants and laborers
Dalit (untouchables)	The outcastes; degrading or polluting labor

thousand subcastes, or *jati*. Each *jati* specializes in a particular occupation. For example, one subcaste washes clothes, another sharpens knives, and yet another repairs shoes.

The lowest group listed in Table 9.1, the Dalit, make up India's "untouchables." If a Dalit touches someone of a higher caste, that person becomes unclean. Even the shadow of an untouchable can contaminate. Early morning and late afternoons are especially risky, for the long shadows of these periods pose a danger to everyone higher up the caste system. Consequently, Dalits are not allowed in some villages during these times. Anyone who becomes contaminated must follow *ablution*, or washing rituals, to restore purity.

An untouchable summed up his situation this way:

> *At the tea stalls, we have separate cups to drink from, chipped and caked with dirt. We have to walk for 15 minutes to carry water to our homes, because we're not allowed to use the taps in the village that the upper castes use. We're not allowed into temples. When I attended school, my friends and I were forced to sit outside the classroom. The upper caste children would not allow us even to touch the football they played with. We played with stones instead. (Guru and Sidhva 2001)*

From personal observations in India, I can add that in some villages, Dalit children are not allowed in the government schools. If they try to enroll, they are beaten.

The Indian government formally abolished the caste system in 1949. However, these centuries-old practices continue, and the caste system remains part of everyday life in India. The ceremonies people follow at births, marriages, and deaths are dictated by caste (Chandra 1993). Caste is so ingrained in the Indian mind that when couples visit a sperm bank, they insist on knowing the caste of the donor (Tewary 2012).

India's caste system is changing, but only gradually. The federal government began an affirmative action plan that has increased education and jobs for the lower castes. Slowly, the caste system is giving way, being replaced by a social class system based on material wealth (Polgreen 2011).

In a *caste system*, status is determined by birth and is lifelong. At birth, these women received not only membership in a lower caste but also, because of their gender, a predetermined position in that caste. When I photographed these women, they were carrying sand to the second floor of a house being constructed in Andhra Pradesh, India.

South Africa. In South Africa, Europeans of Dutch descent, a numerical minority called Afrikaners, used to control the government, the police, and the military. They used these sources of power to enforce a system called **apartheid** (ah-PAR-tate), the separation of the races. Everyone was classified by law into one of four groups: Europeans (whites), Africans (blacks), Coloureds (mixed races), and Asians. These classifications determined where people could live, work, and go to school. It also established where they could swim or see movies; by law, whites and the others were not allowed to mix socially.

Listen to what an Anglican priest observed when he arrived in South Africa:

I went to the post office to send my mother a letter telling her that I had arrived safely. There were two entrances, one marked "Whites only" and the other, "Non-whites." . . . Durban is a seaside city and so I went off to explore the beach. There I discovered that even the sea was divided by race. The most beautiful beaches were where white people could swim; there was another for people of Indian descent, still another for people of mixed race, and far, far away, one for Africans. (Lapsley 2012)

After years of trade sanctions and sports boycotts, in 1990, Afrikaners began to dismantle their caste system, and in 1994, Nelson Mandela, a black, was elected president. Black Africans no longer have to carry special passes, public facilities are integrated, and all racial–ethnic groups have the right to vote and to hold office. Although apartheid has been dismantled, its legacy haunts South Africa. Whites still dominate the country's social institutions, and most blacks remain uneducated and poor. Many new rights—such as the rights to higher education, to eat in restaurants, even to see a doctor—are of little use to people who can't afford them. Political violence has been replaced by old-fashioned crime. Even though the U.S. murder rate is so high it intimidates foreigners, South Africa's murder rate is six times higher (South African Police Service 2013; *Statistical Abstract* 2013:Table 312). Apartheid's legacy of prejudice, bitterness, and hatred appears destined to fuel racial tensions for generations to come.

A U.S. Racial Caste System. Before leaving the subject of caste, we should note that when slavery ended in the United States, it was replaced by a *racial caste system*. From the moment of birth, race marked everyone for life (Berger 1963/2014). *All* whites, even if they were poor and uneducated, considered themselves to have a higher status than *all* African Americans. As in India and South Africa, the upper caste, fearing pollution from the lower caste, made intermarriage illegal. There were also separate schools, hotels, restaurants, and even toilets and drinking fountains for blacks and whites. In the South, when any white met any African American on a sidewalk, the African American had to move aside. The untouchables of India still must do this when they meet someone of a higher caste (Deliege 2001).

To see more parallels between the caste systems of the United States and India, see the Global Glimpse box on the next page.

Estate

During the middle ages, Europe developed an **estate stratification system.** There were three groups, or estates. The *first estate* was made up of the nobility, the wealthy families who ruled the country. This group owned the land, which was the source of wealth at that time. The nobility did no farming themselves, or any "work," for that matter. Work was considered beneath their dignity, something to be done by servants. The nobility's responsibility was to administer their lands, to defend the king (and, in doing so, their own position), and to live "genteel" lives worthy of their high position.

The *second estate* consisted of the clergy. The Roman Catholic Church was a political power at this time. It also owned vast amounts of land and collected taxes from everyone who lived within the boundaries of a parish. The church's power was so great that in order to be crowned, kings had to obtain the pope's permission.

apartheid the separation of racial–ethnic groups as was practiced in South Africa

estate stratification system the stratification system of medieval Europe, consisting of three groups or estates: the nobility, clergy, and commoners

Cultural Diversity around the World

Rape: Blaming the Victim and Protecting the Caste System

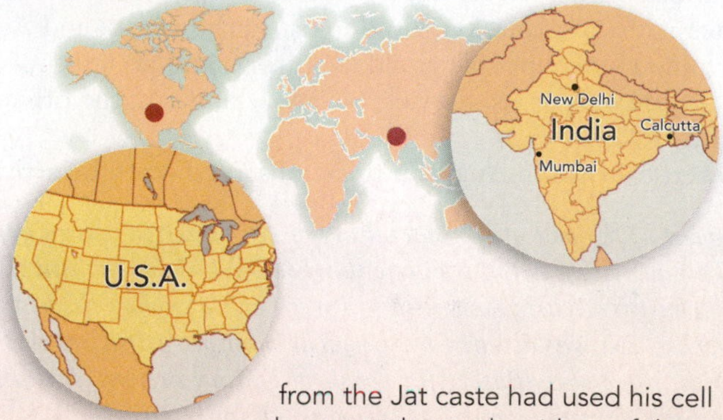

Shana, just 16 years old, was raped by four men. She was walking alongside the road leading to her house when a car stopped. The men got out, shoved her into the car, and drove about a mile down the road. For several hours, they took turns raping the terrified young woman. When the rape (and the other abuse that I won't describe) was over, they told Shana to keep her mouth shut. They would kill her if she told anyone.

Fearful of what her parents would say and how the neighbors would gossip, Shana told no one. She also knew that it would do no good to report the rape to the police, since they would do nothing. Shana carried the shame—and the anger—of her rape with her the rest of her life.

This is a composite story. Shana is a combined version of the many young black women who were raped by white men in the U.S. South years ago, at a time when rape brought shame to any woman, black or white, and the rape and the rapists were enshrouded in silence. For black women in the South at this time, it was useless to report a rape. The prosecutors, judges, and juries—all were white. And none was about to take a black woman's word over that of white men.

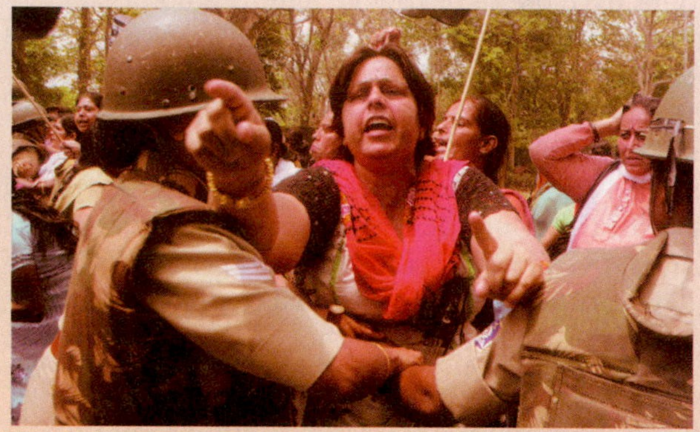

This woman in New Delhi, India, is protesting the lack of prosecution of rapists.

Now here's another event, one that just took place:

Shana, just 16 years old, was walking home when she was grabbed by several men and forced into a small stone shelter at the edge of a field. There, for three hours, eight men raped her. When they were finished, they told Shana to keep her mouth shut. They would kill her if she told anyone.

Shana told no one. The shame would bring severe dishonor to her family. Besides, what good would it do? Shana is a Dalit, formerly called an Untouchable. She is a poor member of a caste in poverty, one that is despised by the Jat caste that controls the society. (Yardley 2012)

I don't need to point out the parallels to you.

Then something unusual happened. One of the rapists from the Jat caste had used his cell phone to take trophy videos of the rape. As the video circulated, one man who saw it showed it to Shana's father. Dishonored by the rape of his daughter, he committed suicide.

His suicide and Shana's rape enraged the Dalits in the community. They marched to the police and demanded justice.

What did they get? One official said that the sexual drive of girls is causing rapes. He said that all girls should be married by the age of 16. Then there wouldn't be any "rapes." Another said that they never used to have any rapes, that it must be the new fast food the young people are eating. The fast food causes hormonal imbalance, creating sexual urges in young women.

I know that this reaction to Shana's rape sounds incredible, and frankly, it is. The problem is that this did happen.

For Your Consideration

➔ Can you compare the racial caste system that used to exist in the United States with the religious caste system that currently exists in India? Can you see how a caste system prevents people from receiving justice? In what ways other than rape does a caste system tolerate and perhaps encourage exploitation? Finally, do you see how the ruling Jat class "blamed the victim" instead of the rapists? How does this protect the caste system?

To prevent their vast land holdings from being carved into smaller chunks, members of the nobility practiced *primogeniture*, allowing only firstborn sons to inherit land. The other sons had to find some way to support themselves, and joining the clergy was a favorite way. (Other ways included becoming an officer in the military or practicing law.) The church was appealing because priests held lifetime positions and were guaranteed a comfortable living. At that time, the church sold offices, and, for example, a wealthy man could buy the position of bishop for his son, which guaranteed a high income.

The *third estate* consisted of the commoners. Known as *serfs*, they belonged to the land. If someone bought or inherited land, the serfs came with it. Serfs were born into the third estate, and they died within it, too. The rare person who made it out of the third estate was either a man who was knighted for extraordinary bravery in battle or someone "called" into a religious vocation.

In early industrialization, children worked alongside adults. They worked 12 hours a day Monday to Friday and 15 hours on Saturday, often in dangerous, filthy conditions. This photo was taken in 1908 at a West Virginia coal mine.

Women in the Estate System. Women belonged to the estate of their husbands. Women in the first estate had no occupation, since, as in the case of their husbands, work was considered beneath their dignity. Their responsibility was to administer the household, overseeing the children and servants. The women in the second estate, nuns, were the exception to the rule that women belonged to the estate of their husbands, as the Roman Catholic clergy did not marry. Women of the third estate shared the hard life of their husbands, including physical labor and food shortages. In addition, they faced the peril of rape by men of the first estate. A few commoners who caught the eye of men of the first estate did marry and join them in the first estate. This was rare.

Class

As we have seen, stratification systems based on slavery, caste, and estate are rigid. The lines drawn between people are firm, and there is little or no movement from one group to another. A **class system**, in contrast, is much more open, since it is based primarily on money or material possessions, which can be acquired. This system, too, is in place at birth, when children are ascribed the status of their parents. Unlike the other systems, however, individuals can change their social class by what they achieve (or fail to achieve) in life. In addition, no laws specify people's occupations on the basis of birth or prohibit marriage between the classes.

Watch on **MySocLab**
Video: Understanding Social Class

A major characteristic of the class system, then, is its relatively fluid boundaries. A class system allows **social mobility**, movement up or down the class ladder. The potential for improving one's life—or for falling down the class ladder—is a major force that drives people to go far in school and to work hard. In the extreme, the family background that a child inherits at birth may present such obstacles that he or she has little chance of climbing very far—or it may provide such privileges that it is almost impossible to fall down the class ladder. Because social class is so significant for our own lives, we will focus on class in the next chapter.

Global Stratification and the Status of Females

In *every* society of the world, gender is a basis for social stratification. In no society is gender the sole basis for stratifying people, but gender cuts across *all* systems of social stratification—whether slavery, caste, estate, or class (Huber 1990). In all these systems, on the basis of their gender, people are sorted into categories and given different access to the good things available in their society.

Apparently, these distinctions always favor males. It is remarkable, for example, that in *every* society of the world, men's earnings are higher than women's. Men's dominance is even more evident when we consider female circumcision (see the box on page 301). That most of the world's illiterate are females also drives home women's relative position in society. Of the several hundred million adults who cannot read, about two-thirds are women (UNESCO 2012). Because gender is such a significant factor in what happens to us in life, we shall focus on it more closely in Chapter 11.

The Global Superclass

The growing interconnections among the world's wealthiest people have produced a *global superclass*, one in which wealth and power are more concentrated than ever before. There are only about 6,000 members of this superclass. *The richest 1,000 of this superclass have more wealth than the $2\frac{1}{2}$ billion poorest people on this planet* (Rothkopf 2008:37). Almost all are white, and, except as wives and daughters, few women are an active part of the superclass. We will have more to say about the superclass in

class system a form of social stratification based primarily on the possession of money or material possessions

social mobility movement up or down the social class ladder

FIGURE 9.1 The Distribution of the Earth's Wealth

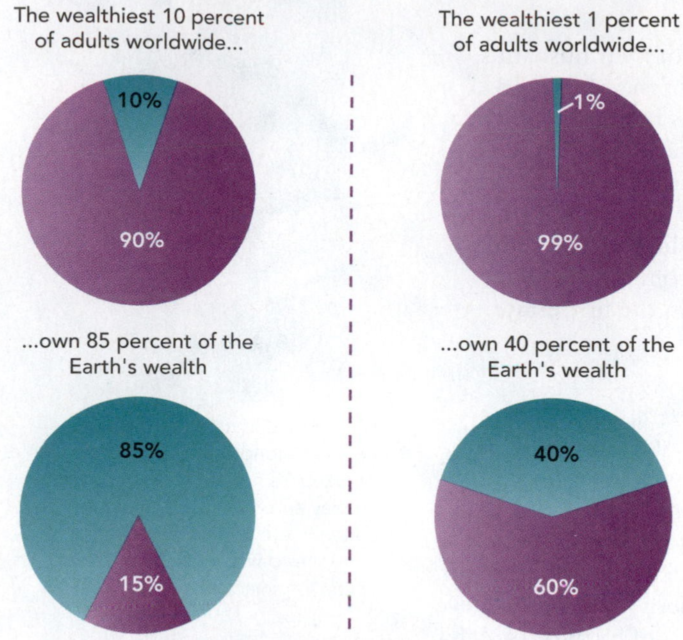
The wealthiest 10 percent of adults worldwide...
10%
90%
...own 85 percent of the Earth's wealth
85%
15%
The wealthiest 1 percent of adults worldwide...
1%
99%
...own 40 percent of the Earth's wealth
40%
60%

Source: By the author. Based on Rofthkopf 2008:37.

Chapter 14, but for now, let's just stress their incredible wealth. There is nothing in history to compare with what you see in Figure 9.1.

What Determines Social Class?

9.2 Contrast the views of Marx and Weber on what determines social class.

In the early days of sociology, a disagreement arose about the meaning of social class. Let's compare how Marx and Weber analyzed the issue.

Karl Marx: The Means of Production

As we discussed in Chapter 1, as agricultural society gave way to an industrial one, masses of peasants were displaced from their traditional lands and occupations. Fleeing to cities, they competed for the few available jobs. Paid only a pittance for their labor, they wore rags, went hungry, and slept under bridges and in shacks. In contrast, the factory owners built mansions, hired servants, and lived in the lap of luxury. Seeing this great disparity between owners and workers, Karl Marx (1818–1883) concluded that social class depends on a single factor: people's relationship to the **means of production**—the tools, factories, land, and investment capital used to produce wealth (Marx 1844/1964; Marx and Engels 1848/1967).

means of production the tools, factories, land, and investment capital used to produce wealth

bourgeoisie Marx's term for capitalists, those who own the means of production

Marx argued that the distinctions people often make among themselves—such as their clothing, speech, education, and paycheck, or the neighborhood they live in and the car they drive—are superficial matters. These things camouflage the only dividing line that counts. There are just two classes of people, said Marx: the **bourgeoisie** (*capitalists*), those who own the means of production, and the **proletariat** (*workers*), those who work for the owners. In short, people's relationship to the means of production determines their social class.

Marx did recognize other groups: farmers and peasants; a *lumpenproletariat* (people living on the margin of society, such as beggars, vagrants, and criminals); and a middle group of self-employed professionals. Marx did not consider these groups social classes,

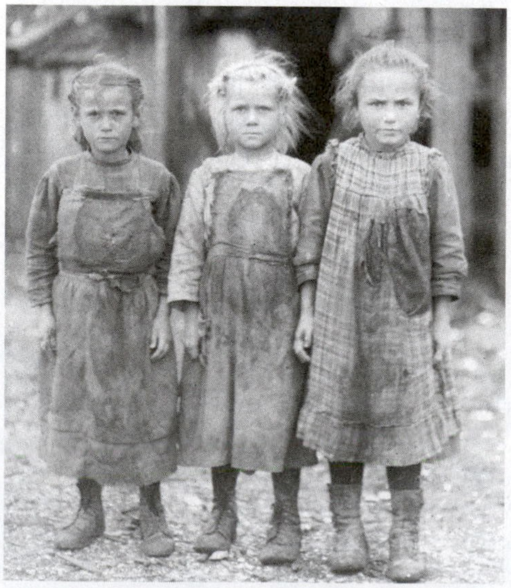

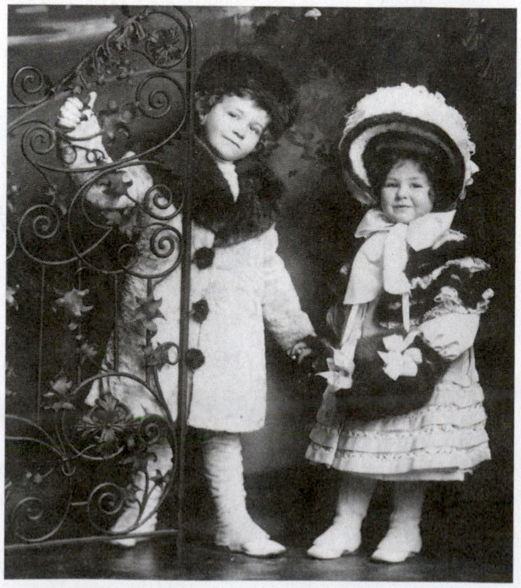

These photos illustrate the contrasting worlds of *social classes* produced by early capitalism. The photo on the left was taken in 1911 at a canning factory in Port Royal, South Carolina. The two girls on the left are 6 years old; the one on the right is 10. They worked full time shucking oysters and did not go to school. The photo on the right was taken in the late 1800s. The children on the right, Cornelius and Gladys Vanderbilt, are shown in front of their parents' estate. They went to school and did not work. You can see how the social locations illustrated in these photos would have produced different orientations to life and, therefore, politics, ideas about marriage, values, and so on—the stuff of which life is made.

however, because they lacked **class consciousness**—a shared identity based on their relationship to the means of production. In other words, they did not perceive themselves as exploited workers whose plight could be resolved by collective action. Marx thought of these groups as insignificant in the future he foresaw—a workers' revolution that would overthrow capitalism.

The capitalists will grow even wealthier, Marx said, and hostilities will increase. When workers come to realize that capitalists are the source of their oppression, they will unite and throw off the chains of their oppressors. In a bloody revolution, they will seize the means of production and usher in a classless society—and no longer will the few grow rich at the expense of the many. What holds back the workers' unity and their revolution is **false class consciousness,** workers mistakenly thinking of themselves as capitalists. For example, workers with a few dollars in the bank may forget that they are workers and instead see themselves as investors, or as capitalists who are about to launch a successful business.

The only distinction worth mentioning, then, is whether a person is an owner or a worker. This decides everything else, Marx stressed, because property determines people's lifestyles, establishes their relationships with one another, and even shapes their ideas.

proletariat Marx's term for the exploited class, the mass of workers who do not own the means of production

class consciousness Marx's term for awareness of a common identity based on one's position in the means of production

false class consciousness Marx's term to refer to workers identifying with the interests of capitalists

Max Weber: Property, Power, and Prestige

Max Weber (1864–1920) was an outspoken critic of Marx. Weber argued that property is only part of the picture. *Social class*, he said, has three components: property, power, and prestige (Gerth and Mills 1958; Weber 1922/1978). Some call these the three P's of social class. (Although Weber used the terms *class*, *power*, and *status*, some sociologists find *property*, *power*, and *prestige* to be clearer terms. To make them even clearer, you may wish to substitute *wealth* for *property*.)

Property (or wealth), said Weber, is certainly significant in determining a person's standing in society. On this point he agreed with Marx. But, added Weber, ownership is not the only significant aspect of property. For example, some powerful people, such as managers of corporations, *control* the means of production even though they do not *own* them. If managers can control property for their own benefit—awarding themselves huge bonuses and magnificent perks—it makes no practical difference that they do not own the property that they use so generously for their own benefit.

Power, the second element of social class, is the ability to control others, even over their objections. Weber agreed with Marx that property is a major source of power, but he added that it is not the only source. For example, prestige can be turned into power. Two well-known examples are actors Arnold Schwarzenegger, who became governor of California, and Ronald Reagan, who was elected governor of California and president of the United States. Figure 9.2 shows how property, power, and prestige are interrelated.

Prestige, the third element in Weber's analysis, is often derived from property and power, since people tend to admire the wealthy and powerful. Prestige, however, can be based on other factors. Olympic gold medalists, for example, might not own property or be powerful, yet they have high prestige. Some are even able to exchange their prestige for property—such as those who are paid a small fortune for endorsing a certain brand of sportswear or for claiming that they start their day with "the breakfast of champions." In other words, property and prestige are not one-way streets: Although property can bring prestige, prestige can also bring property.

In Sum: For Marx, the only distinction that counted was property, more specifically people's relationship to the means of production. Whether we are owners or workers decides everything else, since this determines our lifestyle and shapes our orientation to life. Weber, in contrast, argued that social class has three components—a combination of property, power, and prestige.

FIGURE 9.2 Weber's Three Components of Social Class

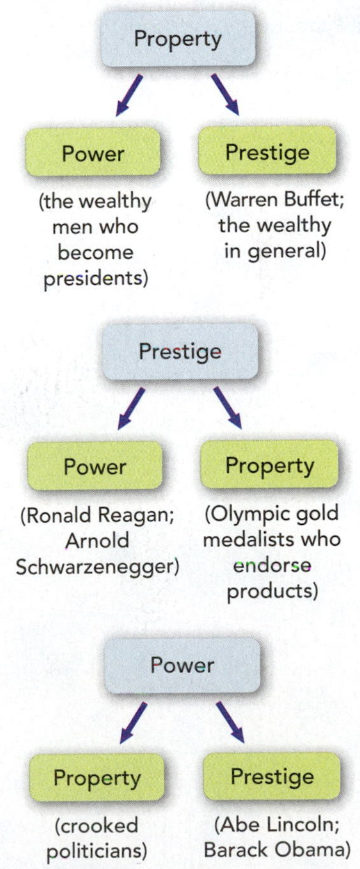

Source: By the author.

Prestige can sometimes be converted into property. Shown here is "Snooki" Polizzi, a reality television star, in one of her attempts to do this.

9.3 Contrast the functionalist and conflict views of why social stratification is universal.

Watch on **MySocLab**
Video: Stratification: The Basics

Why Is Social Stratification Universal?

What is it about social life that makes all societies stratified? We will first consider the explanation proposed by functionalists, which has aroused much controversy in sociology, and then explanations proposed by conflict theorists.

The Functionalist View: Motivating Qualified People

Functionalists take the position that the patterns of behavior that characterize a society exist because they are functional for that society. Because social inequality is universal, inequality must help societies survive. But how?

Davis and Moore's Explanation. Two functionalists, Kingsley Davis and Wilbert Moore (1945, 1953), wrestled with this question. They concluded that stratification of society is inevitable because:

1. For society to function, its positions must be filled.
2. Some positions are more important than others.
3. The more important positions must be filled by the more qualified people.
4. To motivate the more qualified people to fill these positions, they must offer greater rewards.

To flesh out this functionalist argument, consider college presidents and military generals. The position of college president is more important than that of student because the president's decisions affect a large number of people, including many students. College presidents are also accountable for their performance to boards of trustees. It is the same with generals. Their decisions affect many people and sometimes even determine life and death. Generals are accountable to superior generals and to the country's leader.

Why do people accept demanding, high-pressure positions? Why don't they just take easier jobs? The answer, said Davis and Moore, is that these positions offer greater rewards—more prestige, pay, and benefits. To get highly qualified people to compete with one another, some positions offer a salary of $2 million a year, country club membership, a private jet and pilot, and a chauffeured limousine. For less demanding positions, a $30,000 salary without fringe benefits is enough to get hundreds of people to compete. If a job requires rigorous training, it, too, must offer more salary and benefits. If you can get the same pay with a high school diploma, why suffer through the many tests and term papers that college requires?

Tumin's Critique of Davis and Moore. Davis and Moore did not attempt to justify social inequality. There were simply trying to explain *why* social stratification is universal. Nevertheless, their view makes many sociologists uncomfortable, because they see it as coming close to justifying the inequalities in society. Its bottom line seems to be: The people who contribute more to society are paid more, while those who contribute less are paid less.

Melvin Tumin (1953) was the first sociologist to point out what he saw as major flaws in the functionalist position. Here are three of his arguments.

First, how do we know that the positions that offer the higher rewards are more important? A heart surgeon, for example, saves lives and earns much more than a garbage collector, but this doesn't mean that garbage collectors are less important to society. By helping to prevent contagious diseases, garbage collectors save more lives than heart surgeons do. We need independent methods of measuring importance, and we don't have them.

Second, if stratification worked as Davis and Moore described it, society would be a **meritocracy;** that is, positions would be awarded on the basis of merit. But is this what we have? The best predictor of who goes to college, for example, is not ability but income: The more a family earns, the more likely their children are to go to college (Bailey and Dynarski 2011). Not merit, then, but money—another form of the inequality that is built into society. In short, people's positions in society are based on many factors other than merit.

Third, if social stratification is so functional, it ought to benefit almost everyone. Yet social stratification is *dysfunctional* for many. Think of the people who could have made valuable contributions to society had they not been born in slums, dropped out of school, and taken menial jobs to help support their families. Then there are the many who, born female, are assigned "women's work," thus ensuring that they do not maximize their mental abilities.

In Sum: Functionalists argue that some positions are more important to society than others. Offering higher rewards for these positions motivates more talented people to take them. For example, to get highly talented people to become surgeons—to undergo years of rigorous training and then cope with life-and-death situations, as well as malpractice suits—that position must provide a high payoff.

Venus and Serena Williams at the award ceremony at the Olympic Games in London. To determine the social class of athletes as highly successful as the Williams sisters presents a sociological puzzle. With their high prestige and growing wealth, what do you think their social class is? Why?

meritocracy a form of social stratification in which all positions are awarded on the basis of merit

Next, let's see how conflict theorists explain why social stratification is universal. Before we do, look at Table 9.2, which compares the functionalist and conflict views.

The Conflict Perspective: Class Conflict and Scarce Resources

Conflict theorists don't just criticize details of the functionalist argument. Rather, they go for the throat and attack its basic premise. Conflict, not function, they stress, is the reason that we have social stratification. Let's look at the major arguments.

Mosca's Argument. Italian sociologist Gaetano Mosca argued that every society will be stratified by power. This is inevitable, he said in an 1896 book titled *The Ruling Class*, because:

1. No society can exist unless it is organized. This requires leadership to coordinate people's actions.
2. Leadership requires inequalities of power. By definition, some people take leadership positions, while others follow.
3. Because human nature is self-centered, people in power will use their positions to seize greater rewards for themselves.

There is no way around these facts of life, added Mosca. Social stratification is inevitable, and every society will stratify itself along lines of power.

Marx's Argument. If he were alive to hear the functionalist argument, Karl Marx would be enraged. From his point of view, the people in power are not there because of superior traits, as

TABLE 9.2 Functionalist and Conflict Views of Stratification: The Distribution of Society's Resources

	Who Receive the Most Resources?	Who Receive the Least Resources?
The Functionalist View	Those who perform the more important functions (the more capable and more industrious)	Those who perform the less important functions (the less capable and less industrious)
The Conflict View	Those who occupy the more powerful positions	Those who occupy the less powerful positions

Source: By the author.

the functionalists would have us believe. This view is an ideology that members of the elite use to justify their being at the top—and to seduce the oppressed into believing that their welfare depends on keeping quiet and following authorities. What is human history, Marx asked, except the chronicle of class struggle? All of human history is an account of small groups of people in power using society's resources to benefit themselves and to oppress those beneath them—and of oppressed groups trying to overcome that domination.

Marx predicted that the workers will revolt. Capitalist ideology now blinds them, but one day, class consciousness will rip that blindfold off and expose the truth. When workers realize their common oppression, they will rebel. The struggle to control the means of production may be covert at first, taking such forms as work slowdowns and industrial sabotage. Ultimately, however, resistance will break out into the open. But the revolution will not be easy, since the bourgeoisie control the police, the military, and even the educational system, where they implant false class consciousness in the minds of the workers' children.

Current Applications of Conflict Theory. Just as Marx focused on overarching historic events—the accumulation of capital and power and the struggle between workers and capitalists—so do some of today's conflict sociologists. In analyzing global stratification and global capitalism, they look at power relations among nations, how national elites control workers, and how power shifts as capital is shuffled among nations (Jessop 2010; Sprague 2012).

Other conflict sociologists, in contrast, examine conflict wherever it is found, not just as it relates to capitalists and workers. They examine how groups *within the same class* compete with one another for a larger slice of the pie (Collins 1999; King et al. 2010). Even within the same industry, for example, union will fight against union for higher salaries, shorter hours, and more power. A special focus is conflict between racial–ethnic groups as they compete for education, housing, and even prestige—whatever rewards society has to offer. Another focus is relations between women and men, which conflict theorists say are best understood as a conflict over power—over who controls society's resources. Unlike functionalists, conflict theorists say that just beneath the surface of what may appear to be a tranquil society lies conflict that is barely held in check.

Lenski's Synthesis

As you can see, functionalist and conflict theorists disagree sharply. Is it possible to reconcile their views? Sociologist Gerhard Lenski (1966) thought so. He suggested that surplus is the key. He said that the functionalists are right when it comes to *groups that don't accumulate a surplus*, such as hunting and gathering societies. These societies give a greater share of their resources to those who take on important tasks, such as warriors who risk their lives in battle. It is a different story, said Lenski, with *societies that accumulate surpluses.* In them, groups fight over the surplus, and the group that wins becomes an elite. This dominant group rules from the top, controlling the groups below it. In the resulting system of social stratification, where you are born in that society, not personal merit, is what counts.

In Sum: Conflict theorists stress that in every society, groups struggle with one another to gain a larger share of their society's resources. Whenever a group gains power, it uses that power to extract what it can from the groups beneath it. This elite group also uses the social institutions to keep itself in power.

9.4 Discuss the ways that elites keep themselves in power.

How Do Elites Maintain Stratification?

Suppose that you are part of the ruling elite of your society. You want to make sure that you and your family and friends are going to be able to keep your privileged position for the next generation. How will you accomplish this?

You might think about passing laws and using the police and the military. After all, you are a member of the *ruling elite*, so you have this power. You could use force, but this can lead to resentment and rebellion. It is more effective to control people's ideas, information, and technology—which is just what the elite try to do. Let's look at some of their techniques.

Shown here is Pope Leo III crowning Charlemagne king of the Franks in 800.

Soft Control Versus Force

Let's start with medieval Europe, where we find an excellent example of "soft" control. At that time, land was the primary source of wealth—and only the nobility and the church could own land. Almost everyone was a peasant (a serf) who worked for these powerful landowners. The peasants farmed the land, took care of the livestock, and built the roads and bridges. Each year, they had to turn over a designated portion of their crops to their feudal lord. Year after year, for centuries, they did so. Why?

Controlling People's Ideas. Why didn't the peasants rebel and take over the land themselves? There were many reasons, not the least of which was that the nobility and church controlled the army. Coercion, however, goes only so far, because it breeds hostility and nourishes rebellion. How much more effective it is to get the masses to *want* to do what the ruling elite desires. This is where *ideology* (beliefs that justify the way things are) comes into play, and the nobility and clergy used it to great effect. They developed an ideology known as the **divine right of kings**—the idea that the king's authority comes directly from God. The king delegates authority to nobles, who, as God's representatives, must be obeyed. To disobey is to sin against God; to rebel is to merit physical punishment on earth and eternal suffering in hell.

Controlling people's ideas can be remarkably more effective than using brute force. Although this particular ideology governs few minds today, the elite in every society develops ideologies to justify its position at the top. For example, around the world, schools teach that their country's form of government—*no matter what form of government it has*—is good. Religious leaders teach that we owe obedience to authority, that laws are to be obeyed. To the degree that their ideologies are accepted by the masses, the elite remains securely in power.

Ideology is so powerful that it even sets limits on the elite. Although leaders use ideas to control people, the people can also insist that their leaders conform to those same ideas. Pakistan is an outstanding example. If Pakistani leaders depart from fundamentalist Islamic ideology, their position is in jeopardy. For example, regardless of their personal views, Pakistani leaders cannot support Western ideas of morality. If they were to allow women to wear short skirts in public, for example, not only would they lose their positions of leadership but perhaps also their lives. To protect their position within a system of stratification, leaders, regardless of their personal opinions, must also conform at least outwardly to the controlling ideas.

Controlling Information. To maintain their power, elites try to control information. Chinese leaders have put tight controls on Internet cafes and search engines, and they block access to Facebook and Twitter (Bradsher 2012; Mozur 2012). For watching a Jackie Chan movie, North Koreans can be sentenced to six months of back-breaking work in a labor camp (LaFraniere 2010). Lacking such power, the ruling elites of democracies rely on covert means. A favorite tactic of U.S. presidents is to withhold information "in the interest of national security," a phrase that usually translates as "in the interest of protecting me."

divine right of kings the idea that the king's authority comes from God; in an interesting gender bender, also applies to queens

Stifling Criticism. Like the rest of us, the power elite doesn't like to be criticized. But unlike the rest of us, they have the power to do something about it. Fear is a favorite tactic. In Thailand, you can be put in prison for criticizing the king or his family (Peck 2009). Poetry is dangerous, too. Judges in Qatar sentenced a poet to *life in prison* because one of his poems criticized "the ruling family" (Morgan 2012). It can be worse. In Saddam Hussein's Iraq, the penalty for telling a joke about Hussein was having your tongue cut out (Nordland 2003).

In a democracy, the control of critics takes a milder form. When the U.S. Defense Department found out that an author had criticized its handling of 9/11, it bought and destroyed 9,500 copies of his book (Thompson 2010).

Big Brother Technology. The new technology allows the elite to monitor citizens without anyone knowing they are being watched. Drones silently patrol the skies. The Picosecond laser scanner, able to read molecules, can sense from 150 feet away if you have gunpowder residue on your body, as well as report your adrenaline level (Compton 2012). Software programs can read the entire contents of a computer in a second—and not leave a trace. Security cameras—"Tiny Brothers"—have sprouted almost everywhere. Face-recognition systems can scan a crowd of thousands and instantly match the scans with digitized files of people's faces. It is likely that eventually the digitized facial image of every citizen will be on file. Dictators have few checks on how they use this technology, but democracies do have some, such as requiring court orders for search and seizure. Such restraints on power frustrate officials, so they are delighted with our new Homeland Security laws that allow them to spy on citizens without their knowledge.

The new technology, however, is a two-edged sword. Just as it gives the elite powerful tools for monitoring citizens, it also makes it more difficult for them to control information. With international borders meaning nothing to satellite communications, e-mail, and the Internet, information (both true and fabricated) flies around the globe in seconds. Internet users also have free access to some versions of PGP (Pretty Good Privacy), a code that no government has been able to break. The newest encryption that frustrates governments and excites privacy advocates is Silent Circle, an app that allows the transfer of files at the touch of a button. The photo or other file is shredded into thousands of pieces and stored in the cloud until the recipient downloads it. Only the recipient has the key, which is automatically deleted after the file is downloaded (Gallagher 2013).

In Sum: To maintain stratification, the elite tries to dominate its society's institutions. In a dictatorship, the elite makes the laws. In a democracy, the elite influences the laws. In both, the elite controls the police and military and can give orders to crush a rebellion—or to run the post office or air traffic control if workers strike. With force having its limits, especially the potential of provoking resistance, most power elites prefer to keep themselves in power by peaceful means, especially by influencing the thinking of their people.

9.5 Contrast social stratification in Great Britain and the former Soviet Union.

Comparative Social Stratification

Now that we have examined systems of social stratification, considered why stratification is universal, and looked at how elites keep themselves in power, let's compare social stratification in Great Britain and in the former Soviet Union. In the next chapter, we'll look at social stratification in the United States.

Social Stratification in Great Britain

Great Britain is often called England by Americans, but England is only one of the countries that make up the island of Great Britain. The others are Scotland and Wales. In addition, Northern Ireland is part of the United Kingdom of Great Britain and Northern Ireland.

Like other industrialized countries, Great Britain has a class system that can be divided into lower, middle, and upper classes. Great Britain's population is about evenly divided between the middle class and the lower (or working) class. A tiny upper class—wealthy, powerful, and highly educated—makes up perhaps 1 percent of the population.

Compared with Americans, the British are very class conscious (Aughey 2012). Like Americans, they recognize class distinctions on the basis of the type of car a person drives or the stores someone patronizes. But the most striking characteristics of the British class system are language and education. Because these often show up in distinctive speech, accent has a powerful impact on British life. Accent almost always betrays class. As soon as someone speaks, the listener is aware of that person's social class—and treats him or her accordingly (Sullivan 1998).

Education is the primary way by which the British perpetuate their class system from one generation to the next (Lindley and Machin 2013). Almost all children go to neighborhood schools. Great Britain's richest 5 percent, however—who own *half* the nation's wealth—send their children to exclusive private boarding schools. There the children of the elite are trained in subjects that are considered "proper" for members of the ruling class. An astounding 50 percent of the students at Oxford and Cambridge, the country's most elite universities, come from this 5 percent of the population. So do half of the prime minister's cabinet (Neil 2011). To illustrate how powerfully this system of stratified education affects the national life of Great Britain, sociologist Ian Robertson (1987) said,

> *Eighteen former pupils of the most exclusive of [England's high schools], Eton, have become prime minister. Imagine the chances of a single American high school producing eighteen presidents!*

Social Stratification in the Former Soviet Union

Heeding Karl Marx's call for a classless society, Vladimir Ilyich Lenin (1870–1924) and Leon Trotsky (1879–1940) led a revolution in Russia in 1917. They, and the nations that followed their banner, never claimed to have achieved the ideal of communism, in which all contribute their labor to the common good and receive according to their needs. Instead, they used the term *socialism* to describe the intermediate step between capitalism and communism, in which social classes are abolished but some inequality remains.

To tweak the nose of Uncle Sam, the socialist countries would trumpet their equality and point a finger at glaring inequalities in the United States. These countries, however, also were marked by huge disparities in privilege. Their major basis of stratification was membership in the Communist party. Party members decided who would gain admission to the better schools or obtain the more desirable jobs and housing. The equally qualified son or daughter of a nonmember would be turned down, since such privileges came with demonstrated loyalty to the party.

The Communist party, too, was highly stratified. Most members occupied a low level, where they fulfilled such tasks as spying on fellow workers. For this, they might get easier jobs in the factory or occasional access to special stores to purchase hard-to-find goods. The middle level consisted of bureaucrats who were given better than average access to resources and privileges. At the top level was a small elite: party members who enjoyed not only power but also limousines, imported delicacies, vacation homes, and even servants and hunting lodges. As with other stratification systems around the world, women held lower positions in the party. This was evident at each year's May Day, when the top members of the party reviewed the latest weapons paraded in Moscow's Red Square. Photos of these events show only men.

The leaders of the USSR became frustrated as they saw the West thrive. They struggled with a bloated bureaucracy, the inefficiencies of central planning, workers who did the minimum because they could not be fired, and a military so costly that it spent one of every eight of the nation's rubles (*Statistical Abstract* 1993:1432, table dropped in later editions). Socialist ideology did not call for their citizens to be deprived, and in an attempt to turn things around, the Soviet leadership initiated reforms. They allowed elections to be held in which more than one candidate ran for an office. (Before this, voters had a choice of only one candidate per office.) They also sold huge chunks of state-owned businesses to the public. Overnight, making investments to try to turn a profit changed from a crime into a respectable goal.

Russia's transition to capitalism took a bizarre twist. As authority broke down, a powerful Mafia emerged (Varese 2005; Elder 2013). These criminal groups are headed by gangsters, corrupt government officials (including members of the secret police, the FSB), and crooked businessmen. In some towns, they buy the entire judicial system—the police force, prosecutors, and judges. They assassinate business leaders, reporters, and politicians who refuse to cooperate. They amass wealth, launder money through banks they control, and buy luxury properties in popular tourist areas in South America, Asia, and Europe. A favorite is Marbella, a watering and wintering spot on Spain's Costa del Sol.

As Moscow reestablishes its authority, Mafia ties have brought wealth to some of the members of this central government. This group of organized criminals is taking its place as part of Russia's new capitalist class.

9.6 Compare the three worlds of global stratification: the Most Industrialized Nations, the Industrializing Nations, and the Least Industrialized Nations.

Read on **MySocLab**
Document: The Global Economy and the Privileged Class

Global Stratification: Three Worlds

The Problem with Terms. As was noted at the beginning of this chapter, just as the people within a nation are stratified by property, power, and prestige, so are the world's nations. Until recently, a simple model consisting of First, Second, and Third Worlds was used to depict global stratification. *First World* referred to the industrialized capitalist nations, *Second World* to the communist (or socialist) countries, and *Third World* to any nation that did not fit into the first two categories. The breakup of the Soviet Union in 1989 made these terms outdated. In addition, although *first, second,* and *third* did not mean "best," "better," and "worst," they implied it. An alternative classification that some now use—developed, developing, and undeveloped nations—has the same drawback. By calling ourselves "developed," it sounds as though we are mature and the "undeveloped" nations are somehow backward laggards.

To resolve this problem, I use more neutral, descriptive terms: *Most Industrialized, Industrializing,* and *Least Industrialized* nations. We can measure industrialization with no judgment implied as to whether a nation's industrialization represents "development," ranks it "first," or is even desirable at all. The intention is to depict on a global level the three primary dimensions of social stratification: property, power, and prestige. The Most Industrialized Nations have much greater property (wealth), power (they usually get their way in international relations), and prestige (they are looked up to as world leaders).

As you read this analysis, don't forget the sociological significance of the stratification of nations, its far-reaching effects on people's lives, as illustrated by the two families sketched in our opening vignette.

The Most Industrialized Nations

The Most Industrialized Nations are the United States and Canada in North America; Great Britain, France, Germany, Switzerland, and the other industrialized countries of western Europe; Japan in Asia; and Australia and New Zealand in the area of the world known as Oceania. Although there are variations in their economic systems, these countries are capitalistic. As Table 9.3 shows, although these nations have only 16 percent of the world's people, they possess 31 percent of the Earth's land. Their wealth is so enormous that even their poor live better and longer lives than do the average citizens of the Least Industrialized Nations. The Social Map on the next two pages shows the tremendous disparities in income among the world's nations.

TABLE 9.3 Distribution of the World's Land and Population

	Land	Population
Most Industrialized Nations	31%	16%
Industrializing Nations	20%	16%
Least Industrialized Nations	49%	68%

Sources: By the author. Computed from Kurian 1990, 1991, 1992.

FIGURE 9.3 Global Stratification: Income[1] of the World's Nations

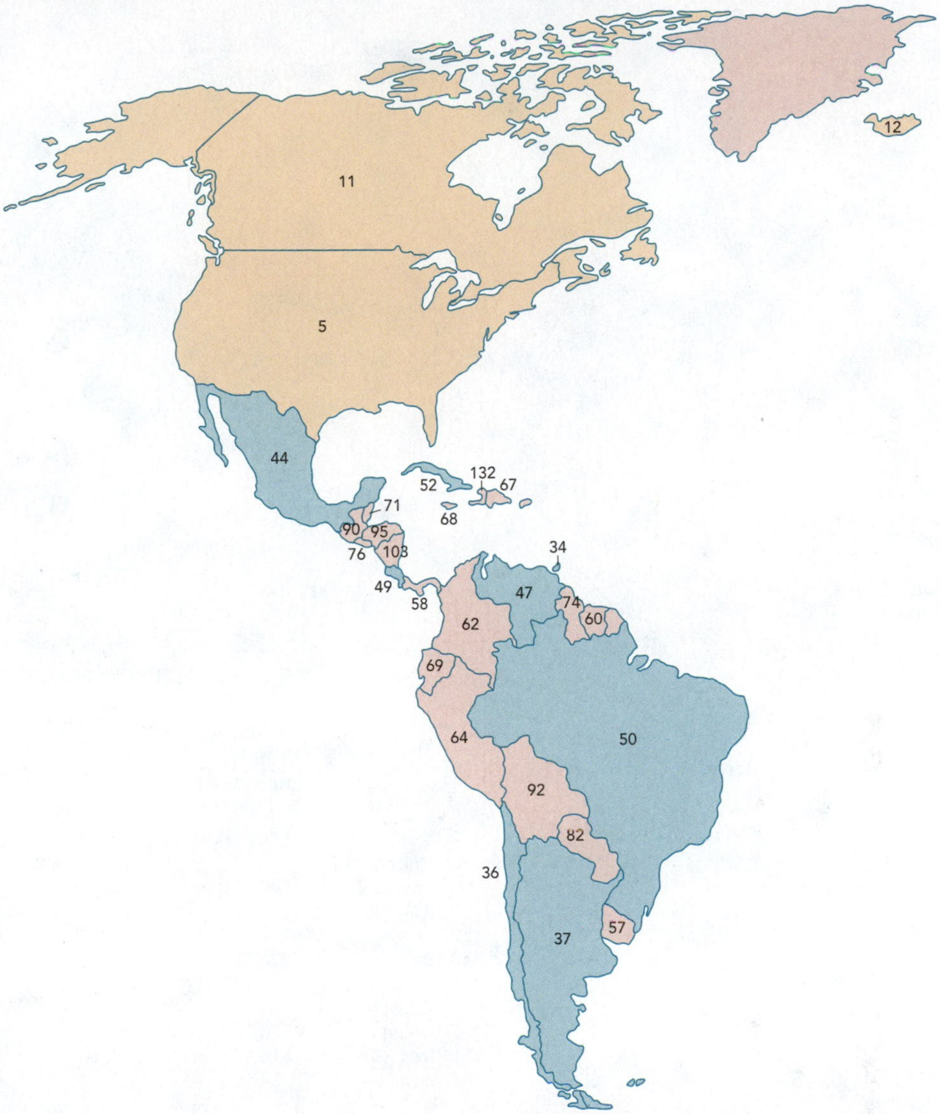

The Most Industrialized Nations

	Nation	Income per Person
1	Luxembourg	$80,700
2	Singapore	$60,900
3	Norway	$55,300
4	Hong Kong	$50,700
5	United States	$49,800
6	Switzerland	$45,300
7	Austria	$42,500
8	Australia	$42,400
9	Netherlands	$42,300
10	Sweden	$41,700
11	Canada	$41,500
12	Iceland	$39,400
13	Germany	$39,100
14	Taiwan	$38,500
15	Belgium	$38,100
16	Denmark	$37,700
17	United Kingdom	$36,700
18	Finland	$36,500
19	Japan	$36,200
20	France	$35,500
21	Korea, South	$32,400
22	Israel	$32,200
23	Italy	$30,100
24	New Zealand	$28,800
25	Slovenia	$28,600
26	Czech Republic	$27,200

The Industrializing Nations

	Nation	Income per Person
27	Ireland	$41,700
28	Spain	$30,400
29	Greece	$25,100
30	Slovakia	$24,300
31	Portugal	$23,000
32	Estonia	$21,200
33	Poland	$21,000
34	Trinidad	$20,400
35	Lithuania	$20,100
36	Chile	$18,400
37	Argentina	$18,200
38	Croatia	$18,100
39	Latvia	$18,100
40	Russia	$17,700
41	Gabon	$17,300
42	Malaysia	$16,900
43	Mauritius	$15,600
44	Mexico	$15,300
45	Turkey	$15,000
46	Bulgaria	$14,200
47	Venezuela	$13,200
48	Romania	$12,800
49	Costa Rica	$12,600
50	Brazil	$12,000
51	South Africa	$11,300
52	Cuba	$9,900
53	China	$9,100

The Least Industrialized Nations

	Nation	Income per Person
54	Botswana	$16,800
55	Belarus	$16,000
56	Lebanon	$15,900
57	Uruguay	$15,800
58	Panama	$15,300
59	Kazakhstan	$13,900
60	Suriname	$12,300
61	Azerbaijan	$10,700
62	Colombia	$10,700
63	Macedonia	$10,700
64	Peru	$10,700
65	Thailand	$10,000
66	Tunisia	$9,700
67	Dominican Republic	$9,600
68	Jamaica	$9,100
69	Ecuador	$8,800
70	Turkmenistan	$8,500

	Nation	Income per Person
71	Belize	$8,400
72	Bosnia	$8,300
73	Albania	$8,000
74	Guyana	$8,000
75	Namibia	$7,800
76	El Salvador	$7,700
77	Ukraine	$7,600
78	Algeria	$7,500
79	Egypt	$6,600
80	Bhutan	$6,500
81	Angola	$6,200
82	Paraguay	$6,100
83	Sri Lanka	$6,100
84	Jordan	$6,000
85	Georgia	$5,900
86	Armenia	$5,600
87	Mongolia	$5,400
88	Morocco	$5,300

(*continued*)

FIGURE 9.3 *(continued)*

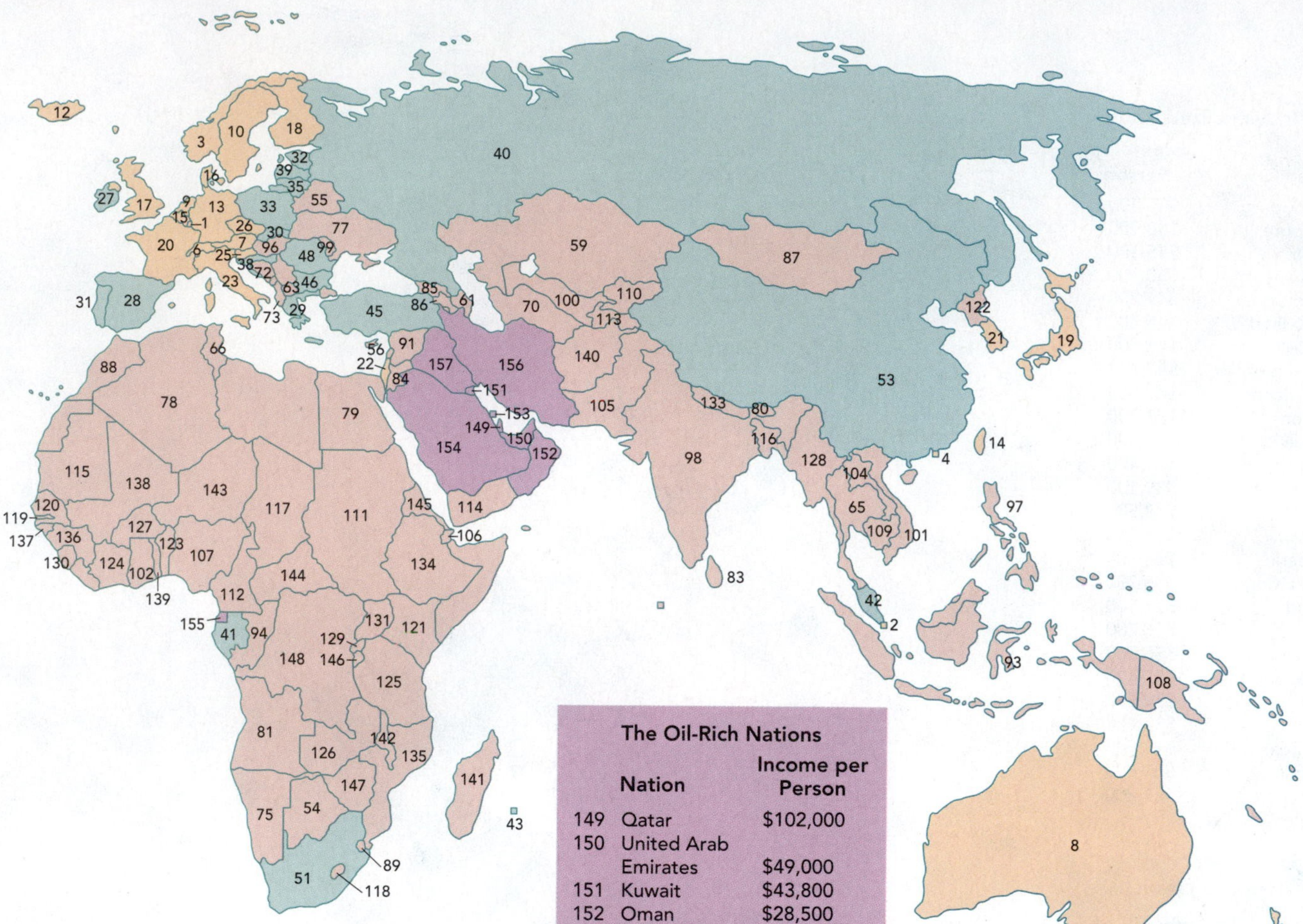

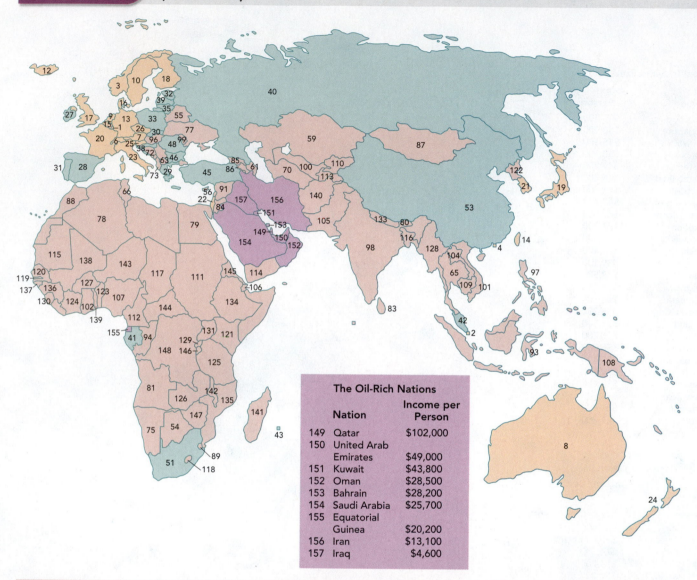

The Oil-Rich Nations

	Nation	Income per Person
149	Qatar	$102,000
150	United Arab Emirates	$49,000
151	Kuwait	$43,800
152	Oman	$28,500
153	Bahrain	$28,200
154	Saudi Arabia	$25,700
155	Equatorial Guinea	$20,200
156	Iran	$13,100
157	Iraq	$4,600

The Least Industrialized Nations

	Nation	Income per Person
89	Swaziland	$5,300
90	Guatemala	$5,200
91	Syria	$5,100
92	Bolivia	$5,000
93	Indonesia	$5,000
94	Congo	$4,700
95	Honduras	$4,600
96	Hungary	$4,600
97	Philippines	$4,300
98	India	$3,900
99	Moldova	$3,500
100	Uzbekistan	$3,500
101	Vietnam	$3,500
102	Ghana	$3,300
103	Nicaragua	$3,300
104	Laos	$3,000
105	Pakistan	$2,900
106	Djibouti	$2,700
107	Nigeria	$2,700
108	Papua-New Guinea	$2,700
109	Cambodia	$2,400
110	Krygyzstan	$2,400
111	Sudan	$2,400
112	Cameroon	$2,300
113	Tajikistan	$2,200
114	Yemen	$2,200
115	Mauritania	$2,100
116	Bangladesh	$2,000
117	Chad	$2,000
118	Lesotho	$2,000
119	Gambia	$1,900
120	Senegal	$1,900
121	Kenya	$1,800
122	Korea, North	$1,800
123	Benin	$1,700
124	Cote d'Ivoire	$1,700
125	Tanzania	$1,700
126	Zambia	$1,700
127	Burkina Faso	$1,400
128	Burma (Myanmar)	$1,400
129	Rwanda	$1,400
130	Sierra Leone	$1,400
131	Uganda	$1,400
132	Haiti	$1,300
133	Nepal	$1,300
134	Ethiopia	$1,200
135	Mozambique	$1,200
136	Guinea	$1,100
137	Guinea-Bissau	$1,100
138	Mali	$1,100
139	Togo	$1,100
140	Afghanistan	$1,000
141	Madagascar	$1,000
142	Malawi	$900
143	Niger	$900
144	Central African Republic	$800
145	Eritrea	$800
146	Burundi	$600
147	Zimbabwe	$500
148	Congo, Dem. Rep.	$400

Source: By the author. Based on *CIA World Factbook* 2013.

The Industrializing Nations

The Industrializing Nations include most of the nations of the former Soviet Union and its former satellites in eastern Europe. As Table 9.3 shows, these nations account for 20 percent of the Earth's land and 16 percent of its people.

The dividing points between the three "worlds" are soft, making it difficult to know how to classify some nations. This is especially the case with the Industrializing Nations. Exactly how much industrialization must a nation have to be in this category? Although soft, these categories do pinpoint essential differences among nations. Most people who live in the Industrializing Nations have much lower incomes and standards of living than do those who live in the Most Industrialized Nations. The majority, however, are better off than those who live in the Least Industrialized Nations. For example, on such measures as access to electricity, indoor plumbing, automobiles, telephones, and even food, most citizens of the Industrializing Nations rank lower than those in the Most Industrialized Nations but higher than those in the Least Industrialized Nations. As you saw in the opening vignette, stratification affects even life expectancy.

The benefits of industrialization are uneven. Large numbers of people in the Industrializing Nations remain illiterate and desperately poor. Conditions can be gruesome, as we explore in the following Thinking Critically section.

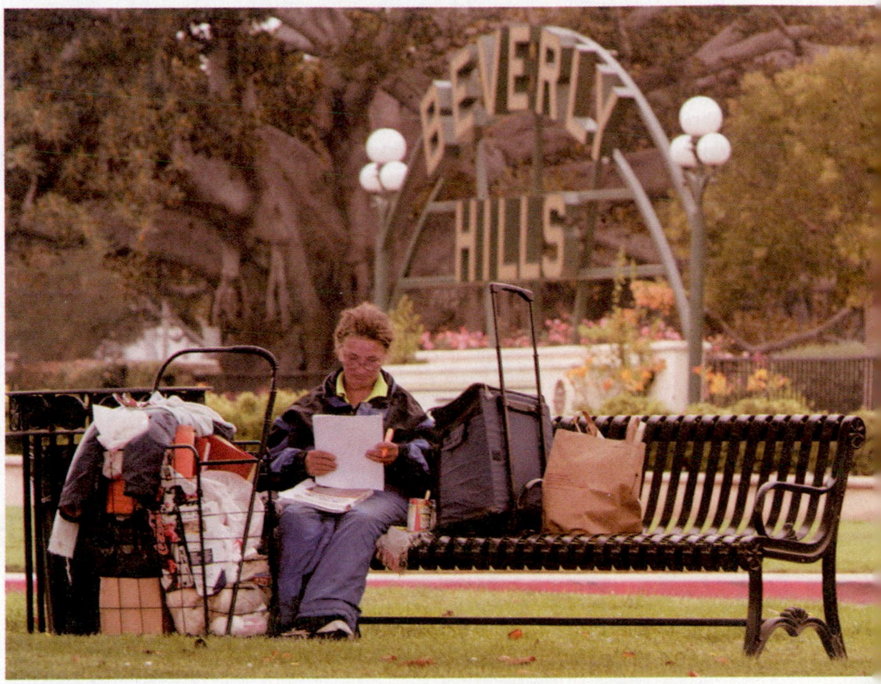

Homeless woman with her possessions on a park bench in Beverly Hills, California. The contrast between poverty and wealth is characteristic of all contemporary societies.

THINKING CRITICALLY

Open Season: Children as Prey

What is childhood like in the Industrializing Nations?

The answer depends on who your parents are. If you are the son or daughter of rich parents, childhood can be pleasant—a world filled with luxuries and servants. If you are born into poverty but live in a rural area where there is plenty to eat, life can still be good—although there may be no books, television, and little education. If you live in a slum, however, life can be horrible—worse even than in the slums of the Most Industrialized Nations (Auyero and de Lara 2012). Let's take a glance at a notorious slum in Brazil.

Not enough food—this you can take for granted—along with wife abuse, broken homes, alcoholism, drug abuse, and a lot of crime: From your knowledge of slums in the Most Industrialized Nations, you would expect these things. What you may not expect, however, are the brutal conditions in which Brazilian slum (*favela*) children live.

Sociologist Martha Huggins (Huggins et al. 2002) reports that poverty is so deep that children and adults swarm through garbage dumps to try to find enough decaying food to keep them alive. You might also be surprised to discover that the owners of some of these dumps hire armed guards to keep the poor out—so that they can sell the garbage for pig food. And you might be shocked to learn that some shop owners hire hit men, auctioning designated victims to the *lowest* bidder!

Life is cheap in the poor nations—but death squads for children? To understand this, we must first note that Brazil has a long history of violence. Brazil also has a high rate of poverty, has only a tiny middle class, and is controlled by a small group of families who, under a veneer of democracy, make the country's major decisions. Hordes of homeless children, with no schools or jobs, roam the streets. To survive, they wash windshields, shine shoes, beg, and steal (Huggins and Rodrigues 2004).

The "respectable" classes see these children as nothing but trouble. They hurt business: Customers feel intimidated when they see begging children—especially teenaged boys—clustered in front of stores. Some shoplift. Others break into stores. With no effective social institutions to care for these children, one solution is to kill them. As Huggins notes, murder sends a clear message—especially if it is accompanied by ritual torture: gouging out the eyes, ripping open the chest, cutting off the genitals, raping the girls, and burning the victim's body.

Not all life is bad in the Industrializing Nations, but this is about as bad as it gets.

For Your Consideration

➔ Do you think there is anything the Most Industrialized Nations can do about this situation? Or is it, though unfortunate, just an "internal" affair that is up to Brazil to handle as it wishes?

➔ Directed by the police, death squads in the Philippine slums also assassinate rapists and drug dealers ("You Can Die Anytime" 2009). What do you think about this? ■

The Least Industrialized Nations

Watch on **MySocLab** **Video:** Dubai Labor

In the Least Industrialized Nations, most people live on small farms or in villages, have large families, and barely survive. These nations account for 68 percent of the world's people but only 49 percent of the Earth's land.

Poverty plagues these nations to such an extent that some families actually *live* in city dumps. This is hard to believe, but look at the photos on pages 248–249, which I took in Phnom Penh, the capital of Cambodia. Although wealthy nations have their pockets of poverty, *most* people in the Least Industrialized nations are poor. *Most* of them have no running water, indoor plumbing, or access to trained teachers or doctors. As we will review in Chapter 20, most of the world's population growth occurs in these nations, placing even greater burdens on their limited resources and causing them to fall farther behind each year.

Modifying the Model

To classify countries into Most Industrialized, Industrializing, and Least Industrialized is helpful in that it pinpoints significant similarities and differences among groups of nations. But then there are the oil-rich nations of the Middle East, the ones that provide much of the gasoline that fuels the machinery of the Most Industrialized Nations. Although these nations are not industrialized, some are immensely wealthy. To classify them simply as Least Industrialized would gloss over significant distinctions, such as their modern hospitals, extensive prenatal care, desalinization plants, abundant food and shelter, high literacy, and computerized banking. On the Social Map on page 244, I classify them separately. Table 9.4 also reflects this distinction.

TABLE 9.4 An Alternative Model of Global Stratification

Four Worlds of Stratification
1. Most Industrialized Nations
2. Industrializing Nations
3. Least Industrialized Nations
4. Oil-rich, nonindustrialized nations

Source: By the author.

Kuwait is an excellent example. Kuwait is so wealthy that almost none of its citizens work for a living. The government simply pays them an annual salary just for being citizens. Everyday life in Kuwait still has its share of onerous chores, of course, but migrant workers from the poor nations do most of this work. To run the specialized systems that keep Kuwait's economy going, Kuwait imports trained workers from the Most Industrialized Nations.

9.7 Discuss how colonialism and world system theory explain how the world's nations became stratified.

How Did the World's Nations Become Stratified?

How did the globe become stratified into such distinct worlds? The commonsense answer is that the poorer nations have fewer resources than the richer nations. As with many commonsense answers, this one falls short. Many of the Industrializing and Least Industrialized Nations are rich in natural resources, while one Most Industrialized Nation, Japan, has few. Three theories explain how global stratification came about.

Colonialism

The first theory, **colonialism,** stresses that the countries that industrialized first got the jump on the rest of the world. Beginning in Great Britain about 1750, industrialization spread throughout western Europe. Plowing some of their profits into powerful armaments and fast ships, these countries invaded weaker nations, making colonies out of them (Harrison 1993). After subduing these weaker nations, the more powerful countries left behind a controlling force in order to exploit the nations' labor and natural resources. At one point, there was even a free-for-all among the industrialized European countries as they rushed to divide up an entire continent. As they sliced Africa into pieces, even tiny Belgium got into the act and acquired the Congo, which was *seventy-five* times larger than itself.

The purpose of colonialism was to establish *economic colonies*—to exploit the nation's people and resources for the benefit of the "mother" country. The more powerful European countries would plant their national flags in a colony and send their representatives to run the government, but the United States usually chose to plant corporate flags in a colony and let these corporations dominate the territory's government. Central and South America are prime examples. There were exceptions, such as the U.S. army's conquest of the Philippines, which President McKinley said was motivated by the desire "to educate the Filipinos, and uplift and civilize and Christianize them" (Krugman 2002).

Colonialism, then, shaped many of the Least Industrialized Nations. In some instances, the Most Industrialized Nations were so powerful that when dividing their spoils, they drew lines across a map, creating new states without regard for tribal or cultural considerations (Kifner 1999). Britain and France did just this as they divided up North Africa and parts of the Middle East—which is why the national boundaries of Libya, Saudi Arabia, Kuwait, and other countries are so straight. This legacy of European conquests is a background factor in much of today's racial–ethnic and tribal violence: By the stroke of a pen, groups with no history of national identity were incorporated within the same political boundaries.

Homeless people sleeping on the streets is a common sight in India's cities. I took this photo in Chennai (formerly Madras).

Explore on **MySocLab** **Activity:** Colonialism and Postcolonialism

World System Theory

The second explanation of how global stratification came about was proposed by Immanuel Wallerstein (1979, 1990, 2011). According to **world system theory**, industrialization led to four groups of nations. The first group consists of the *core nations*, the countries that industrialized first (Britain, France, Holland, and, later, Germany), which grew rich and powerful. The second group is the *semiperiphery*. The economies of these nations, located around the Mediterranean, stagnated because they grew dependent on trade with the core nations. The economies of the third group, the *periphery*, or fringe nations, developed even less. These are the eastern European countries, which sold cash crops to the core nations. The fourth group of nations includes most of Africa and Asia. Called the *external area*, these nations were left out of the

colonialism the process by which one nation takes over another nation, usually for the purpose of exploiting its labor and natural resources

world system theory how economic and political connections developed and now tie the world's countries together

THROUGH THE AUTHOR'S LENS

The Dump People: Working and Living and Playing in the City Dump of Phnom Penh, Cambodia

I went to Cambodia to inspect orphanages, to see how well the children are being cared for. While in Phnom Penh, Cambodia's capital, I was told about people who live in the city dump. *Live* there? I could hardly believe my ears. I knew that people made their living by picking scraps from the city dump, but I didn't know they actually lived among the garbage. This I had to see for myself.

I did. And there I found a highly developed social organization—an intricate support system. Because words are inadequate to depict the abject poverty of the Least Industrialized Nations, these photos can provide more insight into these people's lives than anything I could say.

The children who live in the dump also play there. These children are riding bicycles on a "road," a packed, leveled area of garbage that leads to their huts. The huge stacks in the background are piled trash. Note the ubiquitous Nike.

After the garbage arrives by truck, people stream around it, struggling to be the first to discover something of value. To sift through the trash, the workers use metal picks, like the one this child is holding. Note that children work alongside the adults.

This is a typical sight—family and friends working together. The trash, which is constantly burning, contains harmful chemicals. Why do people work under such conditions? Because they have few options. It is either this or starve.

One of my many surprises was to find food stands in the dump. Although this one primarily offers drinks and snacks, others serve more substantial food. One even has broken chairs salvaged from the dump for its customers.

The people live at the edge of the dump, in homemade huts (visible in the background). This woman, who was on her way home after a day's work, put down her sack of salvaged items to let me take her picture. She still has her pick in her hand.

I was surprised to learn that ice is delivered to the dump. This woman is using a hand grinder to crush ice for drinks for her customers. The customers, of course, are other people who also live in the dump.

At the day's end, the workers wash at the community pump. This hand pump serves all their water needs—drinking, washing, and cooking. There is no indoor plumbing. The weeds in the background serve that purpose. Can you imagine drinking water that comes from below this garbage dump?

Not too many visitors to Phnom Penh tell a cab driver to take them to the city dump. The cabbie looked a bit perplexed, but he did as I asked. Two cabs are shown here because my friends insisted on accompanying me.

I know my friends were curious themselves, but they had also discovered that the destinations I want to visit are usually not in the tourist guides, and they wanted to protect me.

Note the smoke from the smoldering garbage.

development of capitalism. The current expansion of capitalism has changed the relationships among these groups. Most notably, eastern Europe and Asia are no longer left out of capitalism.

The **globalization of capitalism**—the adoption of capitalism around the world—has created extensive ties among the world's nations. Production and trade are now so interconnected that events around the globe affect us all. Sometimes this is immediate, as happens when a civil war disrupts the flow of oil, or—perish the thought—as would be the case if terrorists managed to get their hands on nuclear or biological weapons. At other times, the effects are like a slow ripple, as when a government adopts some policy that gradually impedes its ability to compete in world markets. All of today's societies, then, no matter where they are located, are part of a world system.

The interconnections are most evident among nations that do extensive trading with one another. The following Thinking Critically section explores implications of Mexico's *maquiladoras.*

THINKING CRITICALLY

When Globalization Comes Home: *Maquiladoras* South of the Border

Two hundred thousand Mexicans rush to Juarez each year, fleeing the hopelessness of the rural areas in pursuit of a better life. They have no running water or plumbing, but they didn't have any in the country either, and here they have the possibility of a job, a weekly check to buy food for the kids.

The pay is $100 for a 48-hour work week, about $2 an hour (Harris 2008).

This may not sound like much, but it is more than twice the minimum daily wage in Mexico.

Assembly-for-export plants, known as *maquiladoras*, dot the Mexican border (Archibald 2011). The North American Free Trade Agreement (NAFTA) allows U.S. companies to import materials to Mexico without paying tax and to then export the finished products into the United States, again without tax. It's a sweet deal: few taxes and $16 a day for workers starved for jobs.

A worker at the Delphi Automotive *maquiladora* in Ciudad Juarez, Chihuahua, Mexico. She is assembling a dashboard harness for GM cars.

That these workers live in shacks, with no running water or sewage disposal, is not the employers' concern.

Nor is the pollution. The stinking air doesn't stay on the Mexican side of the border. Neither does the garbage. Heavy rains wash torrents of untreated sewage and industrial wastes into the Rio Grande (Lacey 2007).

There is also the loss of jobs for U.S. workers. Six of the fifteen poorest cities in the United States are located along the sewage-infested Rio Grande. NAFTA didn't bring poverty to these cities. They were poor before this treaty, but residents resent the transfer of jobs across the border (Thompson 2001).

What if the *maquilas* (*maquiladora* workers) organize and demand better pay? Farther south, even cheaper labor beckons. Workers in Guatemala and Honduras, even more desperate than those in Mexico, will gladly take these jobs (Brown 2008). China, too, is competing for them (Utar and Ruiz 2010).

globalization of capitalism capitalism (investing to make profits within a rational system) becoming the globe's dominant economic system

Inside the the home of a *maquiladora* worker.

Many Mexican politicians would say that this presentation is one-sided. "Sure there are problems," they would say, "but this is how it always is when a country industrializes. Don't you realize that the *maquiladoras* bring jobs to people who have no work? They also bring roads, telephone lines, and electricity to undeveloped areas." "In fact," said Vicente Fox, when he was the president of Mexico, "workers at the *maquiladoras* make more than the average salary in Mexico—and that's what we call fair wages" (Fraser 2001).

For Your Consideration

Let's apply our three theoretical perspectives.

➤ Some conflict theorists analyze how capitalists try to weaken the bargaining power of workers by exploiting divisions among them. In what is known as the *split labor market*, capitalists pit one group of workers against another to lower the cost of labor. How do you think *maquiladoras* fit this conflict perspective?

➤ When functionalists analyze a situation, they identify its functions and dysfunctions. What functions and dysfunctions of *maquiladoras* do you see?

➤ Symbolic interactionists analyze how people's experiences shape their views of the world. How would people's experiences in contrasting social locations lead to different answers to "Do *maquiladoras* represent exploitation or opportunity?" What multiple realities do you see here? ■

Culture of Poverty

The third explanation of global stratification is quite unlike colonialism and world system theory. Economist John Kenneth Galbraith (1979) claimed that the cultures of the Least Industrialized Nations hold them back. Building on the ideas of anthropologist Oscar Lewis (1966a, 1966b), Galbraith argued that some nations are crippled by a **culture of poverty,** a way of life that perpetuates poverty from one generation to the next. He explained it this way: Most of the world's poor people are farmers who live on little plots of land. They barely produce enough food to survive. Living on the edge of starvation, they have little room for risk—so they stick to tried-and-true, traditional ways. To experiment with new farming techniques is to court disaster, since failure would lead to hunger and death.

Their religion also encourages them to accept their situation. It teaches fatalism, the belief that an individual's position in life is God's will. For example, in India, the Dalits are taught that they must have done very bad things in a previous life to suffer so. They are supposed to submit to their situation, which they deserve—and in the next life, maybe they'll come back in a more desirable state.

culture of poverty the assumption that the values and behaviors of the poor make them fundamentally different from other people, that these factors are largely responsible for their poverty, and that parents perpetuate poverty across generations by passing these characteristics to their children

Evaluating the Theories

Most sociologists prefer colonialism and world system theory. To them, an explanation based on a culture of poverty places blame on the victim—the poor nations themselves. It points to characteristics of the poor nations, rather than to international political arrangements that benefit the Most Industrialized Nations at the expense of the poor nations. But even taken together, these theories yield only part of the picture. None of these theories, for example, would have led anyone to expect that after World War II, Japan would become an economic powerhouse: Japan had a religion that stressed fatalism, two of its major cities had been destroyed by atomic bombs, and it had been stripped of its colonies.

Each theory, then, yields but a partial explanation, and the grand theorist who will put the many pieces of this puzzle together has yet to appear.

9.8 Know how neocolonialism, multinational corporations, and technology account for how global stratification is maintained.

Maintaining Global Stratification

Regardless of how the world's nations became stratified, why do countries remain rich—or poor—year after year? Let's look at two explanations of how global stratification is maintained.

Read on MySocLab
Document: Citizenship and Inequality: Historical and Global Perspectives

Neocolonialism

Sociologist Michael Harrington (1977) argued that when colonialism fell out of style, it was replaced by **neocolonialism.** When World War II changed public sentiment about sending soldiers to conquer weaker countries and colonists to exploit them, the Most Industrialized Nations turned to the international markets as a way of controlling the Least Industrialized Nations. By selling them goods on credit—especially weapons that the local elites desire so they can keep themselves in power—the Most Industrialized Nations entrap the poor nations within a circle of debt.

As many of us learn the hard way, owing a large debt puts us at the mercy of our creditors. So it is with neocolonialism. The *policy* of selling weapons and other manufactured goods to the Least Industrialized Nations on credit turns those countries into eternal debtors. The capital they need to develop their own industries goes instead as payments toward the debt, which becomes bloated with mounting interest. Keeping these nations in debt forces them to submit to trading terms dictated by the neocolonialists (Carrington 1993; Smith 2001).

Relevance Today. Neocolonialism might seem remote from your life, but its heritage affects you directly. Consider the oil-rich Middle Eastern countries, our two wars in the Persian Gulf, and the terrorism that emanates from this region (*Strategic Energy Policy* 2001; Mouawad 2007). Although this is an area of ancient civilizations, the countries themselves are recent. Great Britain created Saudi Arabia, drawing its boundaries and even naming the country after the man (Ibn Saud) whom British officials picked to lead it. This created a debt for the Saudi family. For decades, this family repaid the debt by providing low-cost oil, which the Most Industrialized Nations need to maintain their way of life. When other nations pumped less oil—no matter the cause, whether revolution or an attempt to raise prices—the Saudis helped keep prices low by making up the shortfall. In return, the United States (and other nations) overlooked the human rights violations of the Saudi royal family, keeping them in power by selling them the latest weapons. This mutually sycophantic arrangement continues.

Multinational Corporations

Multinational corporations, companies that operate across many national boundaries, also help to maintain the global dominance of the Most Industrialized Nations. In some cases, multinational corporations exploit the Least Industrialized Nations directly. A prime example is the United Fruit Company, a U.S. corporation that used to run Central American nations as its own fiefdoms. The CIA would plot and overthrow elected, but uncooperative, governments (CIA 2003), and an occasional invasion by Marines would remind area politicians of the military power that backed U.S. corporations.

Most commonly, however, it is simply by doing business that multinational corporations help to maintain international stratification. A single multinational corporation may

neocolonialism the economic and political dominance of the Most Industrialized Nations over the Least Industrialized Nations

multinational corporations companies that operate across national boundaries; also called *transnational corporations* manage mining operations in several countries, manufacture goods in others, and market its products around the globe. No matter where the profits are made, or where they are reinvested, the primary beneficiaries are the Most Industrialized Nations, especially the one in which the multinational corporation has its world headquarters.

Buying Political Stability. In their pursuit of profits, the multinational corporations need cooperative power elites in the Least Industrialized Nations (Jessop 2010; Sprague 2012). In return for funneling money to the elites and selling them modern weapons, the corporations get a "favorable business climate"—that is, low taxes and cheap labor. The corporations politely call the money they pay to the elites "subsidies" and "offsets"—which ring prettier on the ear than "bribes." Able to siphon money from their country's tax collections and government budgets, these elites live a sophisticated upper-class life in the major cities of their home country. Although most of the citizens of these countries live a hard-scrabble life, the elites are able to send their children to prestigious Western universities, such as Oxford, the Sorbonne, and Harvard.

You can see how this cozy arrangement helps to maintain global stratification. The significance of these payoffs is not so much the genteel lifestyles that they allow the elites to maintain but the translation of the payoffs into power. They allow the elites to purchase high-tech weapons with which they preserve their positions of privilege, even though they must oppress their people to do so. The result is a political stability that keeps alive this diabolical partnership between the multinational corporations and the national elites.

Unanticipated Consequences. This, however, is not the full story. An unintentional by-product of the multinationals' global search for cheap resources and labor is to modify global stratification. When corporations move manufacturing from the Most Industrialized Nations to the Least Industrialized Nations, they not only exploit cheap labor but also bring jobs and money to these nations. Although workers in the Least Industrialized Nations are paid a pittance, it is more than they can earn elsewhere. With new factories come opportunities to develop skills, acquire technology, and accumulate a capital base from which local elites can launch their own factories.

The Pacific Rim nations provide a remarkable example. In return for providing the "favorable business climate" just mentioned, multinational corporations invested billions of dollars in the "Asian tigers" (Hong Kong, Singapore, South Korea, and Taiwan). These nations have developed such a strong capital base that, along with China, they have begun to rival the older capitalist countries. This has also made them subject to capitalism's "boom and bust" cycles. When capitalism suffers a downturn, investors and workers in these nations, including those in the *maquiladoras* that you just read about, have their dreams smashed.

Technology and Global Domination

The race between the Most and Least Industrialized Nations to develop and apply the new technologies might seem like a race between a marathon runner and someone with a broken leg. Can the outcome be in doubt? As the multinational corporations amass profits, they are able to invest huge sums in the latest technology while the Least Industrialized Nations are struggling to put scraps on the table.

So it would appear, but the race is not this simple. Although the Most Industrialized Nations have a seemingly insurmountable head start, some of the other nations are shortening the distance between themselves and the front-runners. With cheap labor making their manufactured goods inexpensive, China and India are exporting goods on a massive scale. They are using the capital from these exports to buy high technology so they can modernize their infrastructure (transportation, communication, electrical, and banking systems). Although global domination remains in the hands of the West, it could be on the verge of a major shift from West to East.

9.9 Identify strains in today's system of global stratification.

Strains in the Global System

It is never easy to maintain global stratification. At the very least, a continuous stream of unanticipated events forces the elite to stay on their toes, and at times, huge currents of history threaten to sweep them aside. No matter how secure a stratification system may seem, it always contains unresolved issues. These contradictions can be covered up for a while, but inevitably they rear up. Some are just little dogs nipping at the heels of the world's elites, bringing issues that can be resolved with a few tanks or bombs—or, better, with a scowl and the threat to bomb an opponent. Other issues are of a broader nature, part of huge historical shifts. Baring their teeth, both emerging and old unresolved contradictions snarlingly demand change, even the rearrangement of global power.

Historical shifts bring cataclysmic disruptions. We are now living through such a time. The far-reaching economic–political changes in Russia and China have been accompanied by huge cracks in a creaking global banking system. In desperation, the global powers have pumped trillions of dollars into their economic–political systems. As curious as we are about the outcome and as much as our lives are affected, we don't know the end point of this current strain in the global system and the power elites' attempts to patch up the most glaring inconsistencies in their global domination. As this process of realignment continues, however, it is likely to sweep all of us into its unwelcome net.

MySocLab — Study and Review on MySocLab

CHAPTER 9 Summary and Review

Systems of Social Stratification

9.1 Compare and contrast slavery (including bonded labor), caste, estate, and class systems of social stratification.

What is social stratification?

Social stratification refers to a hierarchy of privilege based on property, power, and prestige. Every society stratifies its members, and in every society, men-as-a-group are placed above women-as-a-group. Pp. 226–227.

What are four major systems of social stratification?

Four major stratification systems are slavery, caste, estate, and class. The essential characteristic of **slavery** is that some people own other people. Initially, slavery was based not on race but on debt, punishment for crime, or defeat in battle. Slavery could be temporary or permanent and was not necessarily passed on to the children. North American slavery was gradually buttressed by a racist **ideology**. In a **caste system**, people's status, which is lifelong, is determined by their caste's relation to other castes. The **estate system** of feudal Europe consisted of three estates: the nobility, clergy, and peasants (serfs). A **class system** is much more open than these other systems, since it is based primarily on money or material possessions. Industrialization encourages the formation of class systems. Gender cuts across all forms of social stratification. Pp. 227–234.

What Determines Social Class?

9.2 Contrast the views of Marx and Weber on what determines social class.

Karl Marx argued that a single factor determines social class: If you own the means of production, you belong to the **bourgeoisie**; if you do not, you are one of the **proletariat**. Max Weber argued that three elements determine social class: property, power, and prestige. Pp. 234–236.

Why Is Social Stratification Universal?

9.3 Contrast the functionalist and conflict views of why social stratification is universal.

To explain why stratification is universal, functionalists Kingsley Davis and Wilbert Moore argued that to attract the most capable people to fill its important positions, society must offer them greater rewards. Melvin Tumin said that if this view were correct, society would be a **meritocracy**, with positions awarded on the basis of merit. Gaetano Mosca argued that stratification is inevitable because every society must have leadership, which by definition means inequality. Conflict theorists argue that stratification is the outcome of an elite emerging as groups struggle for limited resources. Gerhard Lenski suggested a synthesis between the functionalist and conflict perspectives. Pp. 236–238.

How Do Elites Maintain Stratification?

9.4 Discuss the ways that elites keep themselves in power.

To maintain social stratification within a nation, the ruling class adopts an ideology that justifies its current arrangements. It also controls information and uses technology. When all else fails, it turns to brute force. Pp. 238–240.

Comparative Social Stratification

9.5 Contrast social stratification in Great Britain and the former Soviet Union.

What are key characteristics of stratification systems in other nations?

The most striking features of the British class system are speech and education. In Britain, accent reveals social class, and almost all of the elite attend private schools. In the former Soviet Union, communism was supposed to abolish class distinctions. Instead, it ushered in a different set of classes. Pp. 240–242.

Global Stratification: Three Worlds

9.6 Compare the three worlds of global stratification: the Most Industrialized Nations, the Industrializing Nations, and the Least Industrialized Nations.

How are the world's nations stratified?

The model presented here divides the world's nations into three groups: the Most Industrialized, the Industrializing, and the Least Industrialized. This layering represents relative property, power, and prestige. The oil-rich nations are an exception. Pp. 242–246.

How Did the World's Nations Become Stratified?

9.7 Discuss how colonialism and world system theory explain how the world's nations became stratified.

The main theories that seek to account for global stratification are **colonialism**, **world system theory**, and the **culture of poverty**. Pp. 246–252.

Maintaining Global Stratification

9.8 Know how neocolonialism, multinational corporations, and technology account for how global stratification is maintained.

How do elites maintain global stratification?

There are two basic explanations for why the world's countries remain stratified. **Neocolonialism** is the ongoing dominance of the Least Industrialized Nations by the Most Industrialized Nations. The second explanation points to the influence of **multinational corporations**. The new technology gives further advantage to the Most Industrialized Nations. Pp. 252–254.

Strains in the Global System

9.9 Identify strains in today's system of global stratification.

What strains are showing up in global stratification?

All stratification systems have contradictions that threaten to erupt, forcing the system to change. Currently, capitalism is in crisis, and we seem to be experiencing a global shift in economic (and, ultimately, political) power from the West to the East. P. 254.

Thinking Critically about Chapter 9

1. How do slavery, caste, estate, and class systems of social stratification differ?
2. Why is social stratification universal?
3. How do elites maintain stratification (keep themselves in power)?
4. What shifts in global stratification seem to be taking place? Why?

Social Class in the United States

10 CHAPTER

Listen to Chapter 10 on MySocLab

Ah, New Orleans, *that fabled city on the Mississippi Delta. Images from its rich past floated through my head—pirates, treasure, intrigue. Memories from a pleasant vacation stirred my thoughts—the exotic French Quarter with its enticing aroma of Creole food and sounds of earthy jazz floating through the air.*

The shelter for the homeless forced me back to an unwelcome reality. The shelter was like those I had visited in the North, West, and East—only dirtier. The dirt, in fact, was the worst that I had encountered during my research. On top of that, this was the only shelter to insist on payment in exchange for sleeping in one of its filthy beds.

The men here looked the same as the homeless anywhere in the country—disheveled and haggard, wearing that unmistakable expression of sorrow and despair. Except for the accent, you wouldn't know what region you were in. Poverty wears the same tired face wherever you are, I realized. The accent may differ, but the look remains the same.

I had grown used to the sights and smells of abject poverty. Those no longer surprised me. But after my fitful sleep with the homeless that night, I saw something that did. Just a block or so from the shelter, I was startled by a sight so out of step with the misery and despair I had just experienced that I stopped and stared.

I felt indignation swelling within me. Confronting me were life-size, full-color photos mounted on the transparent Plexiglas shelter of a bus stop. Staring back at me were images of finely dressed men and women, proudly strutting about as they modeled elegant suits, dresses, diamonds, and furs.

A wave of disgust swept over me. "Something is cockeyed in this society," I thought, as my mind refused to stop juxtaposing these images of extravagance with the suffering I had just seen.

"My mind refused to stop juxtaposing these images of extravagance with the suffering I had just seen."

The disjunction—the mental distress—that I felt in New Orleans was triggered by the ads, but it was not the first time that I had experienced this sensation. Whenever my research abruptly transported me from the world of the homeless to one of another social class, I experienced a sense of disjointed unreality. Each social class has its own way of thinking and behaving, and because these fundamental orientations to the world contrast so sharply, the classes do not mix well.

Learning Objectives

After you have read this chapter, you should be able to:

10.1 Explain the three components of social class—property, power, and prestige; distinguish between wealth and income; explain how property and income are distributed; and describe the democratic façade, the power elite, and status inconsistency. (p. 257)

10.2 Contrast Marx's and Weber's models of social class. (p. 264)

10.3 Summarize the consequences of social class for physical and mental health, family life, education, religion, politics, and the criminal justice system. (p. 269)

10.4 Contrast the three types of social mobility, and review gender issues in research on social mobility and why social mobility brings pain. (p. 272)

10.5 Explain the problems in drawing the poverty line, how poverty is related to geography, race-ethnicity, education, feminization, age, and the culture of poverty; analyze why people are poor; and discuss deferred gratification and the Horatio Alger myth. (p. 275)

What Is Social Class?

If you ask most Americans about their country's social class system, you are likely to get a blank look. If you press the matter, you are likely to get an answer like this: "There are the poor and the rich—and then there's us, neither poor nor rich." This is just about as far as most Americans' consciousness of social class goes. Let's try to flesh out this idea.

Our task is made somewhat difficult because sociologists have no clear-cut, agreed-on definition of social class (Sosnaud et al. 2013). As was noted in the last chapter, conflict sociologists (of the Marxist orientation) see only two social classes: those who own the means of production and those who do not. The problem with this view, say most sociologists, is that it lumps too many people together. Teenage "order takers" at McDonald's who work for $15,000 a year are lumped together with that company's executives who make $500,000 a year—because they both are workers at McDonald's, not owners.

Most sociologists agree with Weber that there is more to social class than just a person's relationship to the means of production. Consequently, most sociologists use the components Weber identified and define **social class** as a large group of people who rank closely to one another in property, power, and prestige. These three elements give people different chances in life, separate them into different lifestyles, and provide them with distinctive ways of looking at the self and the world.

Let's look at how sociologists measure these three components of social class.

10.1 Explain the three components of social class—property, power, and prestige; distinguish between wealth and income; explain how property and income are distributed; and describe the democratic façade, the power elite, and status inconsistency.

A mere one-half percent of Americans owns over a quarter of the entire nation's wealth. Very few minorities are numbered among this 0.5 percent. An exception is Oprah Winfrey, who has had an ultra-successful career in entertainment and investing. Worth $2.8 billion, she is the 215th richest person in the United States. Winfrey has given millions of dollars to help minority children.

Property

Property comes in many forms, such as buildings, land, animals, machinery, cars, stocks, bonds, businesses, furniture, jewelry, and bank accounts. When you add up the value of someone's property and subtract that person's debts, you have what sociologists call **wealth**. This term can be misleading, as some of us have little wealth—especially most college students. Nevertheless, if your net total comes to $10, then that is your wealth. (Obviously, *wealth* as a sociological term does not mean wealthy.)

Distinguishing Between Wealth and Income. Wealth and income are sometimes confused, but they are not the same. Where *wealth* is a person's net worth, **income** is a flow of money. Income has many sources: The most common is wages or a business, but other sources are rent, interest, and royalties. Even alimony, an allowance, and gambling winnings are part of income. Some people have much wealth and little income. For example, a farmer may own a lot of land (a form of wealth), but bad weather, combined with the high cost of gasoline, fertilizers, and machinery, can cause the income to dry up. Others have much income and little wealth. An executive with a $250,000 annual income may be debt-ridden. Below the surface prosperity—the exotic vacations, country club membership, private schools for the children, sports cars, and an elegant home—the credit cards may be maxed out, the sports cars in danger of being repossessed, and the mortgage payment "past due." Typically, however, wealth and income go together.

Distribution of Property. Who owns the property in the United States? One answer, of course, is "everyone." Although this statement has some merit, it overlooks how the nation's property is divided among "everyone."

Overall, Americans are worth a hefty sum, about $49 trillion (*Statistical Abstract* 2013:Table 735). This includes all real estate, stocks, bonds, and business assets in the entire country. This wealth is highly concentrated. From Figure 10.1, you can see that just *10 percent* of the nation's families own *75 percent* of the nation's wealth.

Explore on **MySocLab**
Activity: The Distribution of Wealth: Characteristics of Wealth in Southern Connecticut

FIGURE 10.1 Distribution of the Property of Americans

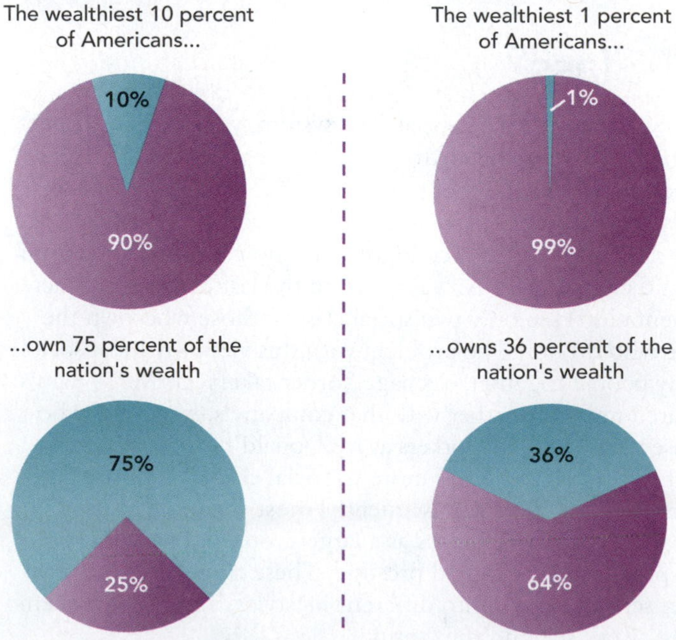
The wealthiest 10 percent of Americans...
10%
90%
...own 75 percent of the nation's wealth
75%
25%
The wealthiest 1 percent of Americans...
1%
99%
...owns 36 percent of the nation's wealth
36%
64%

Source: By the author. Based on Beeghley 2008.

social class according to Weber, a large group of people who rank close to one another in property, power, and prestige; according to Marx, one of two groups: capitalists who own the means of production or workers who sell their labor

property material possessions: animals, bank accounts, bonds, buildings, businesses, cars, cash, commodities, copyrights, furniture, jewelry, land, and stocks

wealth the total value of everything someone owns, minus the debts

income money received, usually from a job, business, or assets

As you can also see from this figure, 1 percent of Americans own more than one-third of all U.S. assets.

Distribution of Income. How is income distributed in the United States? Economist Paul Samuelson (Samuelson and Nordhaus 2005) put it this way: "If we made an income pyramid out of a child's blocks, with each layer portraying $500 of income, the peak would be far higher than Mount Everest, but most people would be within a few feet of the ground."

Actually, if each block were 1½ inches tall, the typical American would be just *12 feet off the ground*, since the average per capita income in the United States is about $42,000 per year. (This average income includes every American, even children.) The typical family climbs a little higher, since most families have more than one worker, and together, they average about $60,000 a year. Compared with the few families who are on the mountain's peak, the average U.S. family would still find itself only 15 feet off the ground. Figure 10.2 portrays these differences.

The fact that some Americans enjoy the peaks of Mount Everest while most—despite their efforts—make it only 12 to 15 feet up the slope presents a striking image of income inequality in the United States. Another picture emerges if we divide the U.S. population into five equal groups and rank them from highest to lowest income. As Figure 10.3 on the next page shows, the top 20 percent of the population receive *half* (50.2 percent) of all income in the United States. In contrast, the bottom 20 percent of Americans receive only 3.3 percent of the nation's income.

Two features of Figure 10.3 stand out. First, look at how income inequality decreased from 1935 to 1970. Then notice how inequality has increased since 1970. *Since 1970, the richest 20 percent of U.S. families have grown richer, while the poorest 20 percent have grown poorer.* Despite numerous government antipoverty programs, the poorest 20 percent of Americans receive *less* of the nation's income today than they did decades ago. The richest 20 percent, in contrast, are receiving more, about as much as they did in 1935.

The chief executive officers (CEOs) of the nation's largest corporations are especially affluent. *The Wall Street Journal* surveyed the 300 largest U.S. companies to find out what they paid their CEOs (Thurm 2013). Their median compensation (including salaries, bonuses, and stock options) came to $10,100,000 a year. (*Median* means that half received more than this amount, and half less.) On Table 10.1 on the next page, you can see the pay of the five highest paid CEOs.

The average income of these five CEOs is *1,225 times higher* than the average pay of U.S. workers (*Statistical Abstract* 2013:Table 693). This does *not* include their income from interest, dividends, or rents. Nor does it include the value of company-paid limousines and chauffeurs, airplanes and pilots, and private boxes at the symphony and sporting events. To really see the disparity, consider this:

> *Let's suppose that you started working the year Jesus was born and that you worked full time every year from then until now. Let's also assume that you earned today's average per capita income of $42,000 every year for all those years. You would still have to work another 250 years to earn the amount received by the highest-paid executive listed in Table 10.1.*

Imagine how you could live with an income like this. And this is precisely the point. Beyond these cold numbers lies a dynamic reality that profoundly affects people's lives. The difference in wealth between those at the top and those at the bottom of the U.S. class structure means that people experience vastly different lifestyles. For example,

> *a colleague of mine who was teaching at an exclusive Eastern university piqued his students' curiosity when he lectured on poverty in Latin America. That weekend, one of the students borrowed his parents' corporate jet and pilot, and in class on Monday, he and his friends related their personal observations on poverty in Latin America.*

FIGURE 10.2

Distribution of the Income of Americans

Some U.S. families have incomes that exceed the height of Mt. Everest, 29,028 feet
Average U.S. family income $60,000 or 15 feet
Average U.S. individual income $42,000 or 12 feet

If a 1½-inch child's block equals $500 of income, the average individual's annual income of $42,000 would represent a height of 12 feet, and the average family's annual income of $60,000 would represent a height of 15 feet. The income of some families, in contrast, would represent a height greater than that of Mt. Everest.

Source: By the author. Based on *Statistical Abstract of the United States* 2013:Tables 693, 711.

FIGURE 10.3 The More Things Change, the More They Stay the Same: Dividing the Nation's Income

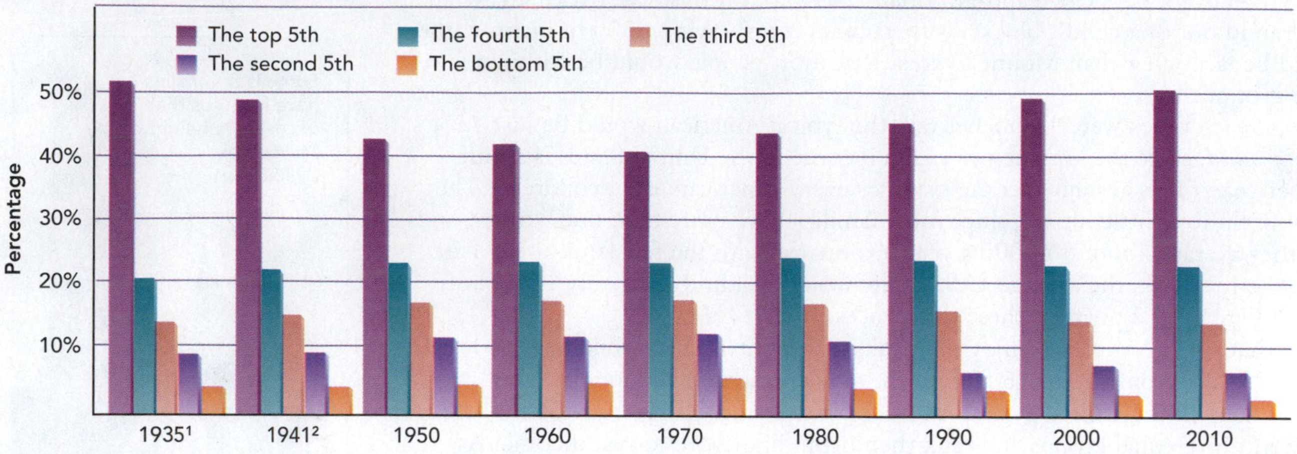

[1]Earliest year available. [2]No data for 1940.

Source: By the author. Based on *Statistical Abstract of the United States* 1960:Table 417; 1970:Table 489; 2013:Table 708.

Few of us could ever say, "Mom and Dad, I've got to do a report for my soc class, so I need to borrow the jet—and the pilot—to run down to South America for the weekend." What a lifestyle! Contrast this with Americans at the low end of the income ladder who lack the funds to travel even to a neighboring town for the weekend. For parents in poverty, choices may revolve around whether to spend the little they have at the laundromat or on milk for the baby. The elderly might have to choose between purchasing the medicines they need or buying food. In short, divisions of wealth represent not "empty" numbers but choices that make vital differences in people's lives. Let's explore this topic in the Down-to-Earth Sociology box on the next page.

Power

Let's look at the second component of social class: power.

The Democratic Facade. Like many people, you may have said to yourself, "The big decisions are always made despite what I might think. Certainly *I* don't make the decision to send soldiers to Afghanistan or Iraq. *I* don't order drones into Pakistan. *I* don't decide to raise taxes, lower interest rates, or spend $700 billion to bail out Wall Street fools and felons."

And then another part of you may say, "But I do participate in these decisions through my representatives in Congress, and by voting for president." True enough—as far as it goes. The trouble is, it just doesn't go far enough. Such views of being a

TABLE 10.1 The Five Highest-Paid CEOs

Executive	Company	Compensation
Lawrence Ellison	Oracle	$95 million
Leslie Moonves	CBS	$59 million
Robert Iger	Walt Disney	$36 million
Mark Parker	Nike	$34 million
Philippe Dauman	Viacom	$33 million

Note: Compensation is for 2012. It includes salary, bonuses, and stock options.

Source: Thurm 2013.

Down-to-Earth Sociology

How the Super-Rich Live

It's good to see how other people live. It gives us a different perspective on life. Let's take a glimpse at the life of John Castle (his real name). After earning a degree in physics at MIT and an MBA at Harvard, John went into banking and securities, where he made more than $100 million (Lublin 1999).

Wanting to be connected to someone famous, John bought President John F. Kennedy's "Winter White House," an oceanfront estate in Palm Beach, Florida. John spent $11 million to remodel the 13,000-square-foot house so that it would be more to his liking. Among those changes: adding bathrooms numbers 14 and 15. He likes to show off John F. Kennedy's bed and also the dresser that has the drawer labeled "black underwear," carefully hand-lettered by Rose Kennedy (Bloomfield 2012).

At his beachfront estate, John gives what he calls "refined feasts" to the glitterati ("On History . . ." 1999). If he gets tired of such activities—or weary of swimming in the Olympic-size pool where JFK swam the weekend before his assassination—John entertains himself by riding one of his thoroughbred horses at his nearby 10-acre ranch. If this fails to ease his boredom, he can relax aboard his custom-built 42-foot Hinckley yacht.

Participants in the regatta at Genoa, Italy, are dwarfed by Paul Allen's yacht.

The yacht is a real source of diversion. John once boarded it for an around-the-world trip. He didn't stay on board, though—just joined the cruise from time to time. A captain and crew kept the vessel on course, and whenever John felt like it he would fly in and stay a few days. Then he would fly back to the States to direct his business. He did this about a dozen times, flying perhaps 150,000 miles. An interesting way to go around the world.

How much does a custom-built Hinckley yacht cost? John can't tell you. As he says, "I don't want to know what anything costs. When you've got enough money, price doesn't make a difference. That's part of the freedom of being rich."

Right. And for John, being rich also means paying $1,000,000 to charter a private jet to fly Spot, his Appaloosa horse, back and forth to the vet. John didn't want Spot to have to endure a long trailer ride. Oh, and of course, there was the cost of Spot's medical treatment, another $500,000.

Other wealthy people spend extravagantly, too. Lee Tachman threw a four-day party for three friends. They had massages; ate well; took rides in a helicopter, a fighter jet, Ferraris, and Lamborghinis; and did a little paintballing—all for the bargain price of $50,000. At the 1Oak Lounge in New York City, some customers pay $35,000 for a bottle of champagne (Haughney and Konigsberg 2008). Of course, it is a large bottle.

Parties are fun, but what if you want privacy? You can buy that, too. Wayne Huizenga, the founder of Blockbuster, who sold a half ownership in the Miami Dolphins for $550 million ("Builder Stephen . . ." 2008), bought a 2,000-acre country club, complete with an 18-hole golf course, a 55,000-square-foot-clubhouse, and 68 slips for visiting vessels. The club is so exclusive that its only members are Wayne and his wife (Fabrikant 2005).

Withdrawing behind gated estates is one way to gain privacy, but Microsoft co-founder Paul Allen has found another way. He had a 414-foot yacht built. On the *Octopus* are two helicopters, a swimming pool, and a submarine (Freeland 2011).

While the length of Allen's yacht creates envy among the plutocracy that would make Freud break into a sweat, some might say that Charles Simonyi has even outdone this. He bought a $25 million ticket for a rocket ride to the International Space Station. Simonyi liked the experience so much that he bought a second ticket (Leo 2008). No frequent flyer miles included. But at the pace that prices are increasing, $50 million isn't worth what it used to be anyway.

For Your Consideration

➔ What effects has social class had on your life? (Go beyond possessions to values, orientations, and outlooks on life.) How do you think you would see the world differently if you were John Castle, Lee Tachman, Paul Allen, Charles Simonyi, or Mrs. Wayne Huizenga?

participant in the nation's "big" decisions are a playback of the ideology we learn at an early age—an ideology that is promoted by the elites to legitimate and perpetuate their power. Sociologists Daniel Hellinger and Dennis Judd (1991) call this the "democratic facade" that conceals the real source of power in the United States.

Let's try to get a picture of where that power is located.

Read on **MySocLab**
Document: C. Wright Mills, The Power Elite

The Power Elite. In Chapter 1, I mentioned that in the 1950s, sociologist C. Wright Mills pointed out that **power**—the ability to get your way despite resistance—was concentrated in the hands of a few. He met heavy criticism, because his analysis contradicted the dominant view that "the people" make the country's decisions. This ideology is still dominant, and Mills' analysis continues to ruffle some feathers. Some still choke on the term **power elite,** which Mills coined to refer to those who make the big decisions in U.S. society.

Mills and others have stressed how wealth and power coalesce in a group of people who look at the world in the same way—and view themselves as a special elite. They belong to the same private clubs, vacation at the same exclusive resorts, and even hire the same bands for their daughters' debutante balls (Domhoff 2006, 2010). This elite wields extraordinary power in U.S. society, so much so that *most* U.S. presidents have come from this group—millionaire white men from families with "old money" (Baltzell and Schneiderman 1988).

Continuing in the tradition of Mills, sociologist William Domhoff (2006, 2010) argues that this group is so powerful that the U.S. government makes no major decision without its approval. He analyzed how this group works behind the scenes with elected officials to determine both foreign and domestic policy—from setting Social Security taxes to imposing tariffs on imported goods. Although Domhoff's conclusions are controversial—and alarming—they certainly follow logically from the principle that wealth brings power and extreme wealth brings extreme power.

Prestige

Let's look at the third component of social class, occupational prestige.

Occupations and Prestige. What are you thinking about doing after college? Chances are, you don't have the option of lying in a hammock under palm trees in some South Pacific paradise. Almost all of us have to choose an occupation and go to work. Look at Table 10.2 to see how the career you are considering stacks up in terms of **prestige** (respect or regard). Because we are moving toward a global society, this table also shows how the rankings given by Americans compare with those of the residents of sixty other countries.

Why do people give more prestige to some jobs than to others? Look again at Table 10.2. The jobs at the top share four features:

1. They pay more.
2. They require more education.
3. They involve more abstract thought.
4. They offer greater autonomy (independence, or self-direction).

Now look at the bottom of the list. You can see that people give less prestige to jobs with the opposite characteristics: These jobs pay little, require less education, involve more physical labor, and are closely supervised. In short, the professions and the white-collar jobs are at the top of the list, the blue-collar jobs at the bottom.

One of the more interesting aspects of these rankings is how consistent they are across countries and over time. For example, people in every country rank college professors higher than nurses, nurses higher than social workers, and social workers higher than janitors. Similarly, the occupations that were ranked high 25 years ago still rank high today—and likely will rank high in the years to come.

Displaying Prestige. People want others to acknowledge their prestige. In times past, in some countries, only the emperor and his family could wear purple—it was the royal color. In France, only the nobility could wear lace. In England, no one could sit while the king was on his throne. Some kings and queens required that subjects walk backward as they left the room—so that they would not "turn their back" on the "royal presence."

Concern with displaying prestige has not let up. Military manuals specify who must salute whom. The U.S. president enters a room only after everyone else attending the function is present (to show that the president isn't waiting for others). Everyone must

power the ability to carry out your will, even over the resistance of others

power elite C. Wright Mills' term for the top people in U.S. corporations, military, and politics who make the nation's major decisions

prestige respect or regard

also be standing when the president enters. In the courtroom, bailiffs, some with a gun at the hip, make certain that everyone stands when the judge enters.

Status symbols vary with social class. Clearly, only the wealthy can afford certain items, such as yachts and huge estates—or the $35,000 bottle of champagne mentioned in the box on page 261. But beyond affordability lies a class-based preference in status symbols. For example, people who are striving to be upwardly mobile flaunt labels on their clothing or conspicuously carry shopping bags from prestigious stores to show that they have "arrived." The wealthy, who regard the symbols of the "common" classes as cheap and showy, flaunt their own status symbols, such as $75,000 Rolex watches and $50,000 diamond earrings. Like the other classes, they, too, try to outdo one another. They casually mention the length of their yacht or that a helicopter flew them to their golf game (Fabrikant 2005). Or they offhandedly bring up the $30,000-a-night suite at the Four Seasons in New York City, saying that it was "rather nice" (Feuer 2008).

Do you try to display prestige? Think about your clothing. How much more are you willing to pay for clothing that bears some hot "designer" label? Purses, shoes, jeans, and shirts—many of us pay more if they have some little symbol than if they don't. As we wear them proudly, aren't we actually proclaiming, "See, I had the money to buy this particular item!"? For many, prestige is a primary factor in deciding which college to attend. Everyone knows how the prestige of a generic sheepskin from Regional State College compares with a degree from Harvard, Princeton, Yale, or Stanford.

Status Inconsistency

Ordinarily, we have a similar rank on all three dimensions of social class—property, power, and prestige. The homeless men in the opening vignette are an example of these three dimensions lined up. Such people are **status consistent**. Some people, however, have a mixture of high and low ranks. This condition, called **status inconsistency**, leads to some interesting situations.

Sociologist Gerhard Lenski (1954, 1966) analyzed how people try to maximize their **status**, their position in a social group. Individuals who rank high on one dimension of social class but lower on others want people to judge them on the basis of their highest status. Others, however, are also trying to maximize their own positions, so they may respond according to these people's lowest rankings.

A classic study of status inconsistency was done by sociologist Ray Gold (1952). After apartment-house janitors unionized in Chicago, they made more money than some of the tenants whose garbage they carried out. Residents became upset when they saw janitors driving more expensive cars than they did. Some attempted to "put the janitor in his place" by making

TABLE 10.2 Occupational Prestige: How the United States Compares with Sixty Countries

Occupation	United States	Average of Sixty Countries
Physician	86	78
Supreme Court judge	85	82
College president	81	86
Astronaut	80	80
Lawyer	75	73
College professor	74	78
Airline pilot	73	66
Architect	73	72
Biologist	73	69
Dentist	72	70
Civil engineer	69	70
Clergy	69	60
Psychologist	69	66
Pharmacist	68	64
High school teacher	66	64
Registered nurse	66	54
Professional athlete	65	48
Electrical engineer	64	65
Author	63	62
Banker	63	67
Veterinarian	62	61
Police officer	61	40
Sociologist	61	67
Journalist	60	55
Classical musician	59	56
Actor or actress	58	52
Chiropractor	57	62
Athletic coach	53	50
Social worker	52	56
Electrician	51	44
Undertaker	49	34
Jazz musician	48	38
Real estate agent	48	49
Mail carrier	47	33
Secretary	46	53
Plumber	45	34
Carpenter	43	37
Farmer	40	47
Barber	36	30
Store sales clerk	36	34
Truck driver	30	33
Cab driver	28	28
Garbage collector	28	13
Waiter or waitress	28	23
Bartender	25	23
Lives on public aid	25	16
Bill collector	24	27
Factory worker	24	29
Janitor	22	21
Shoe shiner	17	12
Street sweeper	11	13

Note. The rankings are based on 1 to 100, from lowest to highest. For five occupations not located in the 1994 source, the 1991 ratings were used: Supreme Court judge, astronaut, athletic coach, lives on public aid, and street sweeper.

Sources: Treiman 1977: Appendices A and D; Nakao and Treas 1990, 1994: Appendix D.

"snotty" remarks to him. For their part, the janitors took delight in finding "dirty" secrets about the tenants in their garbage.

People who are status inconsistent, then, are likely to confront one frustrating situation after another (Dogan 2011). They claim the higher status but are handed the lower one. This is so frustrating that the resulting tension can affect people's health. Researchers who studied the health of thousands of Europeans over a decade found that men who were status inconsistent were twice as likely to have heart attacks as men who were status consistent. For reasons that no one knows, status inconsistent women do not have a higher risk of heart attacks (Braig et al. 2011).

How do you set yourself apart in a country so rich that of its 4.6 million people 79,000 are millionaires? Saeed Khouri (on the right), at an auction in Abu Dhabi paid $14 million for the license plate "1." His cousin was not as fortunate. His $9 million was enough to buy only "5."

There are other consequences as well. Lenski (1954) found that people who are status inconsistent tend to be more politically radical. An example is college professors. Their prestige is very high, as you saw in Table 10.2, but their incomes are relatively low. Hardly anyone in U.S. society is more educated, and yet college professors don't even come close to the top of the income pyramid. In line with Lenski's prediction, the politics of most college professors are left of center. This hypothesis may also hold true among academic departments; that is, the higher a department's average pay, the more conservative are the members' politics. Teachers in departments of business and medicine, for example, are among the most highly paid in the university—and they also are the most politically conservative.

Instant wealth, the topic of the Down-to-Earth Sociology box on the next page, provides an interesting case of status inconsistency.

Sociological Models of Social Class

10.2 Contrast Marx's and Weber's models of social class.

Watch on **MySocLab**
Video: Social Class in the United States: Fact or Fiction?

The question of how many social classes there are is a matter of debate. Sociologists have proposed several models, but no single one has gained universal support. There are two main models: One builds on Marx, the other on Weber.

Updating Marx

As Figure 10.4 illustrates, Marx argued that there are just two classes—capitalists and workers—with membership based solely on a person's relationship to the means of production. Sociologists have criticized this view, saying that these categories are too broad. For example, because executives, managers, and supervisors don't own the means of production, they would be classified as workers. But what do these people have in common with assembly-line workers? The category of "capitalist" is also too broad. Some people, for example, employ a thousand workers, and their decisions directly affect a thousand families. Others, in contrast, have very small businesses.

Consider a man I know in Godfrey, Illinois, who used to fix cars in his backyard. As Frank gained a following, he quit his regular job, and in a few years, he put up a building with five bays and an office. Frank is now a capitalist: He employs five or six mechanics and owns the tools and the building (the "means of production").

But what does this man have in common with a factory owner who controls the lives of one thousand workers? Not only is Frank's work different, so are his lifestyle and the way he looks at the world.

status consistency ranking high or low on all three dimensions of social class

status inconsistency ranking high on some dimensions of social class and low on others; also called *status discrepancy*

status the position that someone occupies in a social group

Down-to-Earth Sociology

The Big Win: Life after the Lottery

"If I just win the lottery, life will be good. These problems I've got, they'll be gone. I can just see myself now."

So goes the dream. And many Americans shell out megabucks every week, with the glimmering hope that "Maybe this week, I'll hit it big."

Most are lucky to get $20, or maybe just another scratch-off ticket.

But some do hit it big. What happens to these winners? Are their lives all wine, roses, and chocolate afterward?

We don't have any systematic studies of the big winners, so I can't tell you what life is like for the average winner. But several themes are apparent from reporters' interviews.

The most common consequence of hitting it big is that life becomes topsy-turvy (Bernstein 2007; Susman 2012). All of us are rooted somewhere. We have connections with others that provide the basis for our orientations to life and how we feel about the world. Sudden wealth can rip these moorings apart, and the resulting *status inconsistency* can lead to a condition sociologists call **anomie** (AN-uh-me).

First comes the shock. As Mary Sanderson, a telephone operator in Dover, New Hampshire, who won $66 million, said, "I was afraid to believe it was real, and afraid to believe it wasn't." Mary says that she never slept worse than her first night as a multimillionaire. "I spent the whole time crying—and throwing up" (Tresniowski 1999).

Dorice Moore, who swindled and then killed Abraham Shakespeare, one of the lottery winners mentioned here.

Reporters and TV crews appear on your doorstep. "What are you going to do with all that money?" they demand. You haven't the slightest idea, but in a daze you mumble something.

Then come the calls. Some are welcome. Your Mom and Dad call to congratulate you. But long-forgotten friends and distant relatives suddenly remember how close they really are to you—and strangely enough, they all have emergencies that your money can solve. You even get calls from strangers who have ailing mothers, terminally ill kids, sick dogs . . .

You have to get an unlisted number.

You might be flooded with marriage proposals. You certainly didn't become more attractive or sexy overnight—or did you? Maybe money makes people sexy.

You can no longer trust people. You don't know what their real motives are. Before, no one could be after your money because you didn't have any. You may even fear kidnappers. Before, this wasn't a problem—unless some kidnapper wanted the ransom of a seven-year-old car.

The normal becomes abnormal. Even picking out a wedding gift becomes a problem. If you give the usual juicer, everyone will think you're stingy. But should you write a check for $25,000? If you do, you'll be invited to every wedding in town—and everyone will expect the same.

Here is what happened to some lottery winners:

When Michael Klinebiel of Rahway, New Jersey, won $2 million, his mother, Phyllis, said that half of it was hers, that she and her son had pooled $20 a month for years to play the lottery. He said they had done this—but he had bought the winning ticket on his own. Phyllis sued her son ("Sticky Ticket" 1998).

Mack Metcalf, a forklift operator in Corbin, Kentucky, hit the jackpot for $34 million. To fulfill a dream, he built and moved into a replica of George Washington's Mount Vernon home. Then his life fell apart—his former wife sued him, his current wife divorced him, and his new girlfriend got $500,000 while he was drunk. Within three years of his "good" fortune, Metcalf had drunk himself to death (Dao 2005).

When Abraham Shakespeare, a dead-broke truck driver's assistant, won $31 million in the Florida lottery, he bought a million dollar home in a gated community. He lent money to friends to start businesses, even paid for funerals (McShane 2010). This evidently wasn't enough. His body was found buried in the yard of a "friend," who was convicted of his murder (Allen 2012).

Winners who avoid *anomie* seem to be people who don't make sudden changes in their lifestyle or their behavior. They hold onto their old friends and routines—the anchors in life that give them identity and a sense of belonging. Some even keep their old jobs—not for the money, of course, but because the job anchors them to an identity with which they are familiar and comfortable.

Sudden wealth, in other words, poses a threat that has to be guarded against.

And I can just hear you say, "I'll take the risk!"

For Your Consideration

➔ How do you think your life would change if you won a lottery jackpot of $10 million?

FIGURE 10.4

Marx's Model of the Social Classes

Capitalists (*Bourgeoisie*, those who own the means of production)
Workers (*Proletariat*, those who work for the capitalists)
Inconsequential Others (beggars, etc.)

Source: By the author.

To resolve this problem, sociologist Erik Wright (1985) suggests that some people are members of more than one class at the same time. They occupy what he calls **contradictory class locations**. By this, Wright means that a person's position in the class structure can generate contradictory interests. For example, the automobile-mechanic-turned-business-owner may want his mechanics to have higher wages because he, too, has experienced their working conditions. At the same time, his current interests—making profits and remaining competitive with other repair shops—lead him to resist pressures to raise their wages.

Because of such contradictory class locations, Wright modified Marx's model. As summarized in Table 10.3, Wright identifies four classes: (1) *capitalists*, business owners who employ many workers; (2) *petty bourgeoisie*, small business owners; (3) *managers*, who sell their own labor but also exercise authority over other employees; and (4) *workers*, who simply sell their labor to others. As you can see, this model allows finer divisions than the one Marx proposed, yet it maintains the primary distinction between employer and employee.

Problems persist, however. For example, in which category would we place college professors? And as you know, there are huge differences in the power of managers. An executive at Toyota, for example, may manage a thousand workers, while a shift manager at McDonald's may be responsible for only a handful. They, too, have little in common.

TABLE 10.3

Wright's Modification of Marx's Model of the Social Classes

1. Capitalists
2. Petty bourgeoisie
3. Managers
4. Workers

Source: By the author.

Explore on MySocLab **Activity:** Collars and Colors in America

Updating Weber

Sociologists Joseph Kahl and Dennis Gilbert (Gilbert and Kahl 1998; Gilbert 2011) developed a six-tier model to portray the class structure of the United States and other capitalist countries. Think of this model, illustrated in Figure 10.5 on the next page, as a ladder. Our discussion starts with the highest rung and moves downward. In line with Weber, on each lower rung, you find less property (wealth), less power, and less prestige. Note that in this model, education is also a primary measure of class.

The Capitalist Class. Sitting on the top rung of the class ladder is a powerful elite that consists of just 1 percent of the U.S. population. As you saw in Figure 10.1 on page 258, this capitalist class is so wealthy that it owns one-third of the entire nation's wealth. *This tiny 1 percent is worth more than the entire bottom 90 percent of the country* (Beeghley 2008).

Power and influence cling to this small elite. They have access to top politicians, and their decisions open or close job opportunities for millions of people. They even help to shape the consciousness of the nation: They own our major media and entertainment outlets—newspapers, magazines, radio and television stations, and sports franchises. They also control the boards of directors of our most influential colleges and universities. The super-rich perpetuate themselves in privilege by passing on their assets and social networks to their children.

The capitalist class can be divided into "old" and "new" money. The longer that wealth has been in a family, the more it adds to the family's prestige. The children of "old" money seldom mingle with "common" folk. Instead, they attend exclusive private schools where they learn views of life that support their privileged position. They don't work for wages; instead, many study business or become lawyers so that they can manage the family fortune. These old-money capitalists (also called "blue bloods") wield vast power as they use their extensive political connections to protect their economic empires (Sklair 2001; Domhoff 1990, 2006, 2010).

At the lower end of the capitalist class are the *nouveau riche*, those who have "new money." Although they have made fortunes in business, the stock market, inventions, entertainment, or sports, they are outsiders to the upper class. They have not attended the "right" schools, and they don't share the social networks that come with old money. Not blue bloods, they aren't trusted to have the right orientations to life. Even their "taste" in clothing and status symbols is suspect (Fabrikant 2005). Donald Trump, whose money is "new," is not listed in the *Social Register*, the "White Pages" of the blue bloods that lists the most prestigious and wealthy one-tenth of 1 percent of the U.S. population. Trump says he "doesn't care," but he reveals his true feelings by adding that

anomie Durkheim's term for a condition of society in which people become detached from the usual norms that guide their behavior

contradictory class locations Erik Wright's term for a position in the class structure that generates contradictory interests

FIGURE 10.5 The U.S. Social Class Ladder

Social Class	Education	Occupation	Income	Percentage of Population
Capitalist	Prestigious university	Investors and heirs, a few top executives	$1,000,000+	1%
Upper Middle	College or university, often with postgraduate study	Professionals and upper managers	$125,000+	15%
Lower Middle	High school or college; often apprenticeship	Semiprofessionals and lower managers, craftspeople, foremen	About $60,000	34%
Working	High school	Factory workers, clerical workers, low-paid retail sales, and craftspeople	About $36,000	30%
Working Poor	High school and some high school	Laborers, service workers, low-paid salespeople	About $19,000	15%
Underclass	Some high school	Unemployed and part-time, on welfare	Under $12,000	5%

Source: By the author. Based on Gilbert and Kahl 1998 and Gilbert 2011; income estimates are inflation-adjusted and modified from Duff 1995.

his heirs will be in it (Kaufman 1996). He is probably right, since the children of new money can ascend into the top part of the capitalist class—*if* they go to the right schools *and* marry old money.

Many in the capitalist class are philanthropic. They establish foundations and give huge sums to "causes." Their motives vary. Some feel guilty because they have so much while others have so little. Others seek prestige, acclaim, or fame. Still others feel a responsibility—even a sense of fate or destiny—to use their money for doing good. Bill Gates, who has given more money to the poor and to medical research than anyone else in history, seems to fall into this latter category.

The Upper Middle Class. Of all the classes, the upper middle class is the one most shaped by education. Almost all members of this class have at least a bachelor's degree, and many have postgraduate degrees in business, management, law, or medicine. These people manage the corporations owned by the capitalist class, operate their own businesses, or pursue professional careers. As Gilbert and Kahl (1998) say,

> *[These positions] may not grant prestige equivalent to a title of nobility in the Germany of Max Weber, but they certainly represent the sign of having "made it" in contemporary America. . . . Their income is sufficient to purchase houses and cars and travel that become public symbols for all to see and for advertisers to portray with words and pictures that connote success, glamour, and high style.*

With a fortune of $66 billion, Bill Gates, a cofounder of Microsoft Corporation, is the second wealthiest person in the world. His 40,000-square-foot home (sometimes called a "technopalace") in Seattle, Washington, was appraised at $110 million.

Sociologists use income, education, and occupational prestige to measure social class. For most people, this works well, but not for everyone, especially entertainers. To what social class do Di Caprio, Smith, Swift, and Carey belong? Leonard DiCaprio makes about $37 million a year, Will Smith $30 million, Taylor Swift $57 million, and Mariah Carey $60 million.

Watch on **MySocLab**
Video: Education and Financial Success

Consequently, parents and teachers push children to prepare for upper-middle-class jobs. Around 15 percent of the population belong to this class.

The Lower Middle Class. About 34 percent of the U.S. population are in the lower middle class. Their jobs require that they follow orders given by members of the upper middle class. With their technical and lower-level management positions, they can afford a mainstream lifestyle, although they struggle to maintain it. Many anticipate being able to move up the social class ladder. Feelings of insecurity are common, however, with the threat of inflation, recession, and job insecurity bringing a nagging sense that they might fall down the class ladder.

The distinctions between the lower middle class and the working class on the next rung below are more blurred than those between other classes. In general, however, members of the lower middle class work at jobs that have slightly more prestige, and their incomes are generally higher.

The Working Class. About 30 percent of the U.S. population belong to this class of relatively unskilled blue-collar and white-collar workers. Compared with the lower middle class, they have less education and lower incomes. Their jobs are also less secure, more routine, and more closely supervised. One of their greatest fears is that of being laid off during a recession. With only a high school diploma, the average member of the working class has little hope of climbing up the class ladder. Job changes usually bring "more of the same," so most concentrate on getting ahead by achieving seniority on the job rather than by changing their type of work. They tend to think of themselves as having "real jobs" and regard the "suits" above them as paper pushers who have no practical experience and don't do "real work" (Morris and Grimes 2005).

The Working Poor. Members of this class, about 15 percent of the population, work at unskilled, low-paying, temporary and seasonal jobs, such as sharecropping, migrant farm work, housecleaning, and day labor. Most are high school dropouts. Many are functionally illiterate, finding it difficult to read even the want ads. Believing that no matter what party is elected to office their situation won't change, they are not likely to vote (Beeghley 2008).

Although they work full time, millions of the working poor depend on food stamps and local food banks to survive on their meager incomes (O'Hare 1996b; Bello 2011). It is easy to see how you can work full time and still be poor. Suppose that you are married and have a baby 3 months old and another child 3 years old. Your spouse stays home to care for them, so earning the income is up to you. But as a highschool dropout, all you can get is a minimum wage job. At $7.25 an hour, you earn $290 for 40 hours. In a year, this comes to $15,080—before deductions. Your nagging fear—and recurring nightmare—is of ending up "on the streets."

The Underclass. On the lowest rung, and with next to no chance of climbing anywhere, is the **underclass**. Concentrated in the inner city, this group has little or no connection with the job market. Those who are employed—and some are—do menial, low-paying, temporary work. Welfare, if it is available, along with food stamps and food pantries, is their main support. Most members of other classes consider these people the "ne'er-do-wells" of society. Life is the toughest in this class, and it is filled with despair. About 5 percent of the population fall into this class.

The homeless men described in the opening vignette of this chapter, and the women and children like them, are part of the underclass. These are the people whom most Americans wish would just go away. Their presence on our city streets bothers passersby from the more privileged social classes—which includes just about everyone. "What are those obnoxious, dirty, foul-smelling people doing here, cluttering up my city?" appears to be a common response. Some people react with sympathy and a desire to do something. But what? Almost all of us just shrug our shoulders and look the other way, despairing of a solution and somewhat intimidated by their presence.

"There are plenty of jobs around. People just don't want to work."

A primary sociological principle is that people's views are shaped by their social location. Many people from the middle and upper classes cannot understand how anyone can work and still be poor.

The homeless are the "fallout" of our postindustrial economy. In another era, they would have had plenty of work. They would have tended horses, worked on farms, dug ditches, shoveled coal, and run the factory looms. Some would have explored and settled the West. The prospect of gold would have lured others to California, Alaska, and Australia. Today, however, with no frontiers to settle, factory jobs scarce, and farms that are becoming technological marvels, we have little need for unskilled labor.

Consequences of Social Class

10.3 Summarize the consequences of social class for physical and mental health, family life, education, religion, politics, and the criminal justice system.

The man was a C student in school. As a businessman, he ran an oil company (Arbusto) into the ground. A self-confessed alcoholic until age forty, he was arrested for drunk driving. With this background, how did he become president of the United States?

Accompanying these personal factors was the power of social class. George W. Bush was born the grandson of a wealthy senator and the son of a businessman who, after serving as a member of the House of Representatives and director of the CIA, was elected president of the United States. For high school, he went to an elite private prep school, Andover; for his bachelor's degree to Yale; and for his MBA to Harvard. He was given $1 million to start his own business. When that business (Arbusto) failed, Bush fell softly, landing on the boards of several corporations. Taken care of even further, he was made the managing director of the Texas Rangers baseball team and allowed to buy a share of the team for $600,000, which he sold for $15 million.

When it was time for him to get into politics, Bush's connections financed his run for governor of Texas and then for the presidency.

Does social class matter? And how! Think of each social class as a broad subculture with distinct approaches to life, so significant that it affects our health, family life, education, religion, politics, and even our experiences with crime and the criminal justice system. Let's look at some of the ways that social class affects our lives.

Physical Health

If you want to get a sense of how social class affects health, take a ride on Washington's Metro system. Start in the blighted Southeast section of downtown D.C. For every mile you travel to where the wealthy live in Montgomery County in Maryland, life expectancy rises about a year and a half. By the time you get off, you will find a twenty-year gap

underclass a group of people for whom poverty persists year after year and across generations

With tough economic times, a lot of people have lost their jobs—and their homes. If this happens, how can you survive? Maybe a smile and a sense of humor to tap the kindness of strangers. I took this photo outside Boston's Fenway Park.

between the poor blacks where you started your trip and the rich whites where you ended it. (Cohen 2004)

The principle is simple: As you go up the social-class ladder, health improves. As you go down the ladder, health gets worse (Masters et al. 2012). Age makes no difference. Infants born to the poor are more likely to die before their first birthday, and a larger percentage of poor people in their old age—whether 75 or 95—die each year than do the elderly who are wealthy.

How can social class have such dramatic effects? While there are many reasons, here are three. First, social class opens and closes doors to medical care. People with good incomes or with good medical insurance are able to choose their doctors and pay for whatever treatment and medications are prescribed. The poor, in contrast, don't have the money or insurance to afford this type of medical care. How much difference the new health reform will make is yet to be seen.

A second reason is lifestyle, which is shaped by social class. People in the lower classes are more likely to smoke, eat a lot of fats, be overweight, abuse drugs and alcohol, get little exercise, and practice unsafe sex (Chin et al. 2000; Dolnick 2010). This, to understate the matter, does not improve people's health.

There is a third reason, too. Life is hard on the poor. The persistent stresses they face weaken their immune systems and cause their bodies to wear out faster (Geronimus et al. 2010; John-Henderson et al. 2012). For the rich, life is so much better. They have fewer problems and vastly more resources to deal with the ones they have. This gives them a sense of control over their lives, a source of both physical and mental health.

Mental Health

Sociological research from as far back as the 1930s has found that the mental health of the lower classes is worse than that of the higher classes (Faris and Dunham 1939; Srole et al. 1978; Sareen et al. 2011). Greater mental problems are part of the higher stress that accompanies poverty. Compared with middle- and upper-class Americans, the poor have less job security and lower wages. They are more likely to divorce, to be the victims of crime, and to have more physical illnesses. Couple these conditions with bill collectors and the threat of eviction and you can see how they deal severe blows to people's emotional well-being.

People higher up the social class ladder experience stress in daily life, of course, but their stress is generally less, and their coping resources are greater. Not only can they afford vacations, psychiatrists, and counselors, but *their class position also gives them greater control over their lives, a key to good mental health.*

Family Life

Social class also makes a significant difference in our choice of spouse, our chances of getting divorced, and how we rear our children.

Choice of Husband or Wife. Members of the capitalist class place strong emphasis on family tradition. They stress the family's history, even a sense of purpose or destiny in life (Baltzell 1979; Aldrich 1989). Children of this class learn that their choice of husband or wife affects not just them but the entire family, that it will have an impact on the "family line." These background expectations shrink the field of "eligible" marriage partners, making it narrower than it is for the children of any other social class. As a result, parents in this class play a strong role in their children's mate selection.

Divorce. The more difficult life of the lower social classes, especially the many tensions that come from insecure jobs and inadequate incomes, leads to higher marital friction and a greater likelihood of divorce. Consequently, children of the poor are more likely to grow up in broken homes.

Child Rearing. As discussed on page 79, lower-class parents focus more on getting their children to follow rules and obey authority, while middle-class parents focus more on developing their children's creative and leadership skills (Lareau and Weininger 2008). Sociologists have traced this difference to the parents' occupations (Kohn 1977). Lower-class parents are closely supervised at work, and they anticipate that their children will have similar jobs. Consequently, they try to teach their children to defer to authority. Middle-class parents, in contrast, enjoy greater independence at work. Anticipating similar jobs for their children, they encourage them to be more creative. Out of these contrasting orientations arise different ways of disciplining children; lower-class parents are more likely to use physical punishment, while the middle classes rely more on verbal persuasion.

Education

In Figure 10.5 on page 267, you saw how education increases as one goes up the social class ladder. It is not just the amount of education that changes but also the type of education. Children of the capitalist class bypass public schools. They attend exclusive private schools where they are trained to take a commanding role in society. These schools teach upper-class values and prepare their students for prestigious universities (Beeghley 2008; Stevens 2009).

Keenly aware that private schools can be a key to upward social mobility, some upper-middle-class parents do their best to get their children into the prestigious preschools that feed into these exclusive prep schools. Although some preschools cost $37,000 a year, they have a waiting list (Anderson 2011). Figuring that waiting until birth to enroll a child is too late, some parents-to-be enroll their child as soon as the woman knows she is pregnant (Ensign 2012). Other parents hire tutors to train their 4-year-olds in test-taking skills so they can get into public kindergartens for gifted students. Experts teach these preschoolers to look adults in the eye while they are being interviewed for these limited positions (Banjo 2010). You can see how such parental involvement and

On the left is one of Jennifer Lopez's homes, this one in Miami Beach. She also has a home in California and a $10 million summer getaway in the Hamptons in New York. To the right is a middle-aged couple who live in an old motor home parked in Santa Barbara, one of the wealthiest communities in California.

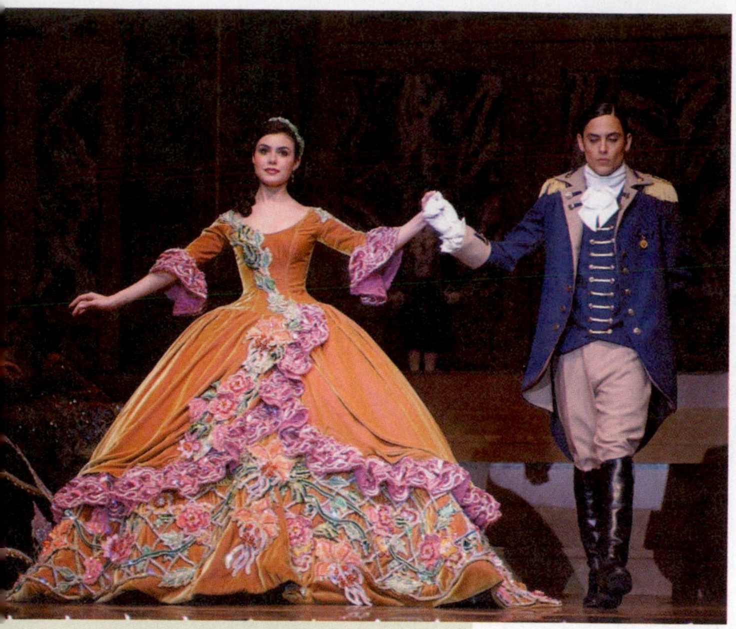

This debutante is making her formal entrance into society, announcing her eligibility for marriage. Like you she has learned from her parents, peers, and education, a view of where she belongs in life. How do you think her view is different from yours? (This photo was taken at the annual debutante ball of the Society of Martha Washington in Laredo, Texas.)

resources make it more likely that children from the more privileged classes go to college—and graduate.

Religion

One area of social life that we might think would not be affected by social class is religion. ("People are just religious, or they are not. What does social class have to do with it?") As we shall see in Chapter 18, however, the classes tend to cluster in different denominations. Episcopalians, for example, are more likely to attract the middle and upper classes, while Baptists draw heavily from the lower classes. Patterns of worship also follow class lines: The lower classes are attracted to more expressive worship services and louder music, while the middle and upper classes prefer more "subdued" worship.

Politics

As I have stressed throughout this text, people perceive events from their own corner in life. Political views are no exception to this symbolic interactionist principle, and the rich and the poor walk different political paths. The higher that people are on the social class ladder, the more likely they are to vote for Republicans (Hout 2008). In contrast, most members of the working class believe that the government should intervene in the economy to provide jobs and to make citizens financially secure. They are more likely to vote for Democrats. Although the working class is more liberal on *economic* issues (policies that increase government spending), it is more conservative on *social* issues (such as opposing abortion and the Equal Rights Amendment) (Houtman 1995; Hout 2008). People toward the bottom of the class structure are also less likely to be politically active—to campaign for candidates or even to vote (Gilbert 2003; Beeghley 2008).

Crime and Criminal Justice

If justice is supposed to be blind, it certainly is not when it comes to one's chances of being arrested (Henslin 2013). In Chapter 8 (pages 207–209), we discussed how the social classes commit different types of crime. The white-collar crimes of the more privileged classes are more likely to be dealt with outside the criminal justice system, while the police and courts deal with the street crimes of the lower classes. One consequence of this class standard is that members of the lower classes are more likely to be in prison, on probation, or on parole. In addition, since those who commit street crimes tend to do so in or near their own neighborhoods, the lower classes are more likely to be robbed, burglarized, or murdered.

10.4 Contrast the three types of social mobility, and review gender issues in research on social mobility and why social mobility brings pain.

Social Mobility

No aspect of life, then—from work and family life to politics—goes untouched by social class. Because life is so much more satisfying in the more privileged classes, people strive to climb the social class ladder. What affects their chances?

Watch on **MySocLab**
Video: Opportunity and Social Class

Three Types of Social Mobility

Janice's mom, a single mother, sold used cars at a Toyota dealership. Janice worked summers and part-time during the school year, earned her BA, and then her MBA. After college, she worked at IBM, but she missed her home town. When her mom's boss retired,

Janice grabbed the chance to put a down payment on the Toyota dealership. She has since paid the business off and has opened another at a second location.

When grown-up children like Janice end up on a different rung of the social class ladder from the one occupied by their parents, it is called **intergenerational mobility**. You can go up or down, of course. Janice experienced **upward social mobility**. If her mother had owned the dealership and Janice had dropped out of college and ended up selling cars, she would have experienced **downward social mobility**.

We like to think that individual efforts are the reason people move up the class ladder—and their faults the reason they move down. In this example, we can identify intelligence, hard work, and ambition. Although individual factors such as these do underlie social mobility, we must place Janice in the context of **structural mobility**. This second basic type of mobility refers to changes in society that allow large numbers of people to move up or down the class ladder.

Janice grew up during a boom time of easy credit and business expansion. Opportunities were abundant, and colleges were looking for women from working-class backgrounds. It is far different for people who grow up during an economic bust when opportunities are shrinking. As sociologists point out, in analyzing social mobility, we must always look at *structural mobility*, how changes in society (its *structure*) make opportunities plentiful or scarce.

The third type of social mobility is **exchange mobility**. This occurs when large numbers of people move up and down the social class ladder, but, on balance, the proportions of the social classes remain about the same. Suppose that a million or so working-class people are trained in some new technology, and they move up the class ladder. Suppose also that because of a surge in imports, about a million skilled workers have to take lower-status jobs. Although millions of people change their social class, there is, in effect, an exchange among them. The net result more or less balances out, and the class system remains basically untouched.

How much social mobility is there? For an overview of intergenerational social mobility today, read the Down-to-Earth Sociology box on the next page.

intergenerational mobility the change that family members make in social class from one generation to the next

upward social mobility movement up the social class ladder

downward social mobility movement down the social class ladder

structural mobility movement up or down the social class ladder that is due more to changes in the *structure* of society than to the actions of individuals

exchange mobility a large number of people moving up the social class ladder, while a large number move down; it is as though they have *exchanged* places, and the social class system shows little change

Read on **MySocLab**
Document: A Different Mirror

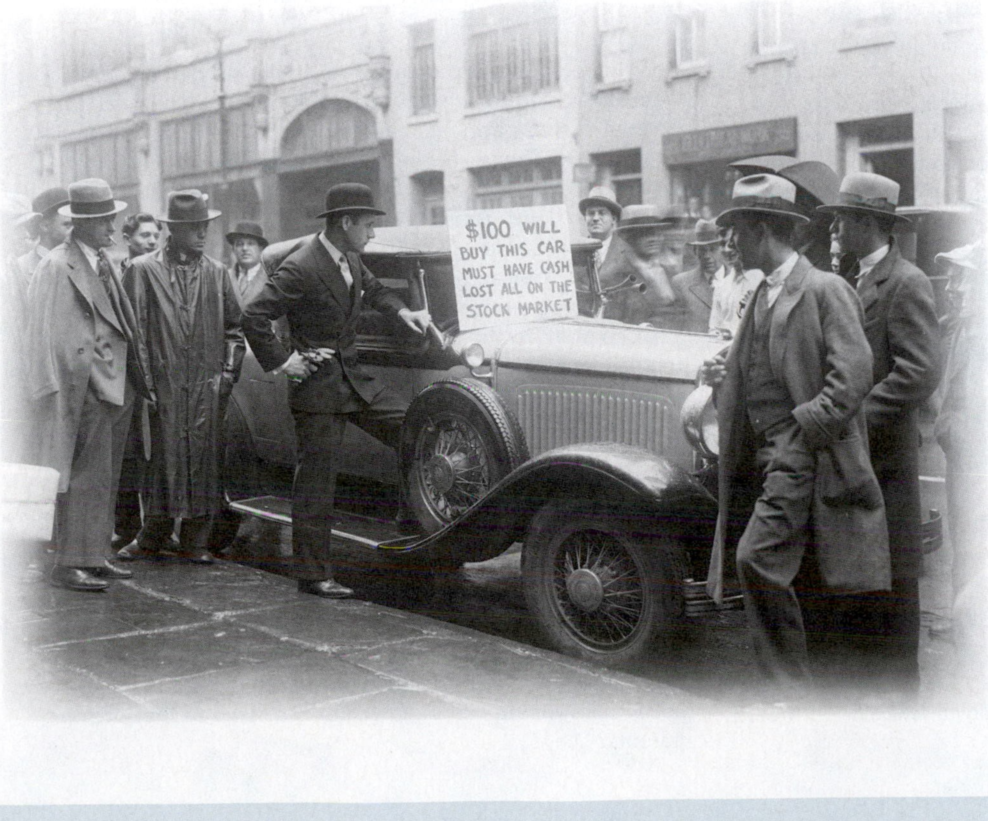

The term *structural mobility* refers to changes in society that push large numbers of people either up or down the social class ladder. A remarkable example was the stock market crash of 1929 when thousands of people suddenly lost their wealth. People who once "had it made" found themselves standing on street corners selling apples or, as depicted here, selling their possessions at fire-sale prices. The crash of 2008 brought similar problems to untold numbers of people.

Down-to-Earth **Sociology**

Researching "The American Dream": Social Mobility Today

"The American Dream" can mean many things. Sociologically, it refers to children being able to pass their parents as they climb the social class ladder. That children can do this is one of the attractions of the United States. It has been a driving force in immigration and American life. But just how much upward mobility is there today? We are fortunate to have national research that compares today's adult children with their parents (Lopoo and DeLeire 2012). As you look at the findings summarized in Figure 10.6, you will see that the United States has considerable upward mobility. Relative to their parents, one third (35 percent) of adult children have moved up at least one rung on the social class ladder. Contrary to the many dismal reports of current social life, the American Dream might be ailing, but it is still vibrant.

Some of the most interesting findings in this research concern changes in income. (The incomes of the parent and adult child generations were adjusted for inflation, so the dollars have the same base.) An impressive 84 percent of today's American adults have family incomes higher than their parents had at the same age. One of the surprises is that those most likely to surpass their parents are the children who were reared at the bottom of the income ladder. Of the adult children who started life there, *93 percent* have incomes higher than their parents did at the same age. With incomes stagnating and even going backward during the past several years, many fear that the "American dream" has been shattered. Certainly poverty has increased, but it is not likely that the Great Recession has crushed the dream, just deflated it a bit. We'll have to await the next round of social mobility research to find out.

Stickiness at the ends. Figure 10.6 summarizes the change in income from one generation to the next. Of children who were reared in the bottom fifth of the nation's income, as adults, 43 percent stayed where they started, while 57 percent moved upward. Four percent moved to the top quintile of the nation's income. Now look at the adult children who were reared in the top quintile. As adults, 40 percent stayed where they started, while 60 percent moved downward. Eight percent of these adult children moved to the bottom quintile.

FIGURE 10.6 Income of Adult Children Compared with That of Their Parents

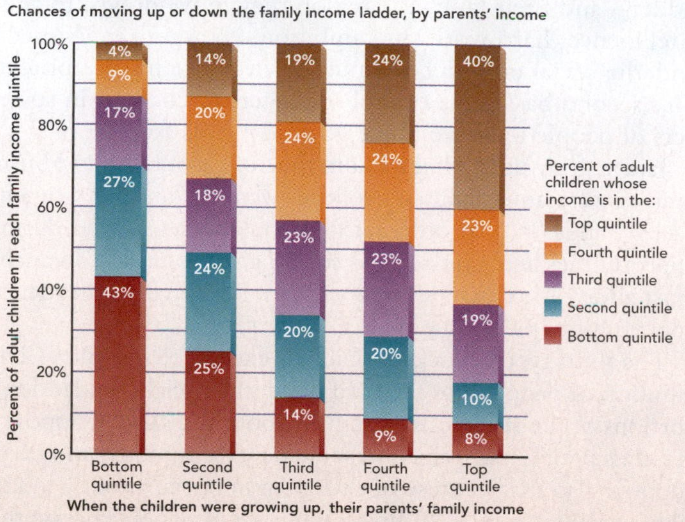

Source: Pursuing the American Dream: Economic Mobility Across Generations, p. 6. © July, 2013 the Pew Charitable Trusts.

Note: This figure is difficult to understand. Here is the explanation. Lopoo and DeLiere (2012) divided the parents' generation into five groups (quintiles) according to their share of the nation's income. The left bar represents the fifth of Americans of the parents' generation who had the lowest income, the bar on the right the quintile with the highest income. The divisions within the bars represent where the adult children ended up in terms of their own income.

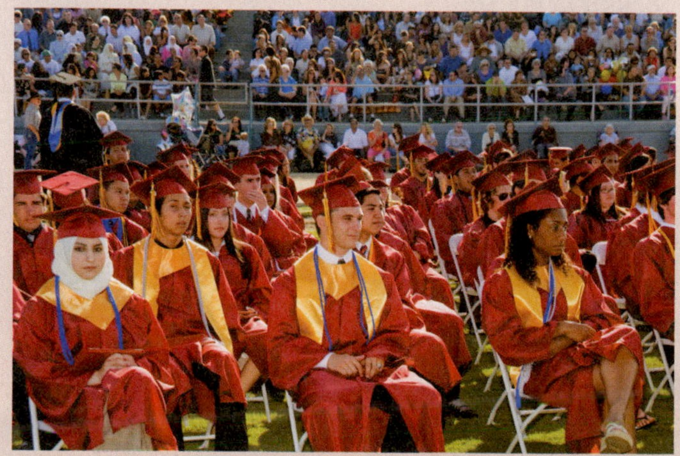

The main avenue to the upward social mobility reviewed here has been higher education.

What Do These Findings Mean? People have a lot of things they want to prove, and they like to use statistics to make their point. These findings will discourage some and elate others. Some will see a half-full glass, others one that is half empty. You can go either way. You can stress that 43 percent of the very poorest kids never got out of the bottom—or you can point to the 57 percent who did. It is the same with the richest kids: Forty percent stayed in the top quintile, and 60 percent dropped down.

No matter what your opinion, any way you look at it this is a lot of social mobility. Within all this, don't lose sight of the broader principle: The benefits that high-income parents enjoy tend to keep their children afloat, while the obstacles that low-income parents confront tend to weigh their children down. As you can see, though, the benefits don't keep most of the children up, nor do the obstacles keep most of the children down.

For Your Consideration

➔ What is your social class? In ten years, do you think your social class will be higher, lower, or the same as that of your parents? Why?

Women in Studies of Social Mobility

About half of sons pass their fathers on the social class ladder, about one-third stay at the same level, and about one-sixth fall down the ladder. (Blau and Duncan 1967; Featherman 1979)

"Only sons!" said feminists in response to these classic studies on social mobility. "Do you think it is good science to ignore daughters? And why do you assign women the class of their husbands? Do you think that wives have no social class position of their own?" (Davis and Robinson 1988; Western et al. 2012). The male sociologists brushed off these objections, replying that there were too few women in the labor force to make a difference.

These sociologists simply hadn't caught up with the times. The gradual but steady increase of women working for pay had caught them unprepared. Although sociologists now include women in their samples, research on the social class of married women is still in its infancy, and sons are sometimes still singled out in the research (Lopoo and DeLeire 2012).

Upwardly mobile women report how important their parents were in their success, how they were encouraged to achieve when they were just children. For upwardly mobile African American women, strong mothers are especially significant (Robinson and Nelson 2010). In their study of women from working-class backgrounds who became managers and professionals, sociologists Elizabeth Higginbotham and Lynn Weber (1992) found this recurring theme: parents encouraging their girls to postpone marriage and get an education. To these understandings from the micro approach, we need to add the macro level. Had there not been a *structural* change in society, the millions of new positions that women occupy would not exist.

Upward social mobility, though welcome, can place people in a world so different from their world of childhood orientation that they become strangers to their own family.

The Pain of Social Mobility

If you were to be knocked down the social class ladder, you know it would be painful. But are you aware that it also hurts to climb this ladder?

Sociologist Steph Lawler (1999) found that British women who had moved from the working class to the middle class were caught between two worlds—their working-class background and their current middle-class life. Their mothers found the daughters' middle-class ways "uppity." They criticized their preferences in furniture and food, their speech, even the way they reared their children. As you can expect, this strained the mother–daughter relationships. Studying working-class parents in Boston, sociologists Richard Sennett and Jonathan Cobb (1972/1988) found something similar. The parents had made deep sacrifices—working two jobs, even postponing medical care—so their children could go to college. They, of course, expected their children to appreciate their sacrifice. But again, the result was two worlds of experience. The children's educated world was so unlike that of their parents that even talking to one another became difficult. Not surprisingly, the parents felt betrayed and bitter. Their sacrifices had ripped their children from them.

Torn from their roots, some of those who make the jump from the working to the middle class never become comfortable with their new social class (Morris and Grimes 2005; Lacy 2007). The Cultural Diversity box on the next page discusses other costs that come with the climb up the social class ladder.

Poverty

10.5 Explain the problems in drawing the poverty line, how poverty is related to geography, race-ethnicity, education, feminization, age, and the culture of poverty; analyze why people are poor; and discuss deferred gratification and the Horatio Alger myth.

Many Americans find that the "limitless possibilities" of the American dream are quite elusive. As illustrated in Figure 10.5 on page 267, the working poor and underclass together form about one-fifth of the U.S. population. This translates into a huge number, over 60 million people. Who are these people?

Cultural Diversity in the United States

Social Class and the Upward Social Mobility of African Americans

The overview of social class presented in this chapter doesn't apply equally to all the groups that make up U.S. society. Consider geography: What constitutes the upper class of a town of 5,000 people will differ from that of a city of a million. In small towns, which have fewer extremes of wealth and occupation, family background and local reputation are more significant.

So it is with racial–ethnic groups. All racial–ethnic groups are marked by social class, but what constitutes a particular social class can differ from one group to another—as well as from one historical period to another. Consider social class among African Americans (Landry and Marsh 2011).

The earliest class divisions can be traced to slavery—to slaves who worked in the fields and those who worked in the "big house." Those who worked in the plantation home were exposed more to the customs, manners, and forms of speech of wealthy whites. Their more privileged position—which brought with it better food and clothing, as well as lighter work—was often based on skin color. Mulattos, lighter-skinned slaves, were often chosen for this more desirable work. One result was the development of a "mulatto elite," a segment of the slave population that, proud of its distinctiveness, distanced itself from other slaves. At this time, there also were free blacks. Not only were they able to own property but some even owned black slaves.

After the War Between the States (as the Civil War is known in the South), these two groups, the mulatto elite and the free blacks, formed an upper class that distanced itself from other blacks. From these groups came most of the black professionals. After World War II, the black middle class expanded as African Americans entered a wider range of occupations. Today, more than half of all African American adults work at white-collar jobs, about 22 percent at the professional or managerial level (Beeghley 2008).

An unwelcome cost greets many African Americans who move up the social class ladder: an uncomfortable distancing from their roots, a separation from significant others—parents, siblings, and childhood friends (hooks 2000; Lacy 2007). The upwardly mobile enter a world unknown to those left behind, one that demands not only different appearance and speech, but also different values, aspirations, and ways of viewing the world. These are severe challenges to the self and often rupture relationships with those left behind.

An additional cost is a subtle racism that lurks beneath the surface of some work settings, poisoning what could be easy, mutually respectful interaction. To be aware that white co-workers perceive you as different—as a stranger, an intruder, or "the other"—engenders frustration, dissatisfaction, and cynicism. To cope, many nourish their racial identity and stress the "high value of black culture and being black" (Lacy and Harris 2008). Some move to neighborhoods of upper-middle-class African Americans, where they can live among like-minded people who have similar experiences (Lacy 2007).

For Your Consideration

➔ In the box on upward social mobility on page 82, we discussed how Latinos face a similar situation. Why do you think this is? What connections do you see among upward mobility, frustration, and racial–ethnic identity? How do you think that the upward mobility of whites is different? Why?

Drawing the Poverty Line

Read on MySocLab
Document: The Compassion Gap in American Poverty Policy

To determine who is poor, the U.S. government draws a **poverty line**. This measure was set in the 1960s, when poor people were thought to spend about one-third of their incomes on food. On the basis of this assumption, each year, the government computes a low-cost food budget and multiplies it by 3. Families whose incomes are less than this amount are classified as poor; those whose incomes are higher—even by a dollar—are considered "not poor."

poverty line the official measure of poverty; calculated to include incomes that are less than three times a low-cost food budget

This official measure of poverty is grossly inadequate. Poor people actually spend only about 20 percent of their income on food, so to determine a poverty line, we ought to multiply their food budget by 5 instead of 3 (Uchitelle 2001). Another problem is that mothers who work outside the home and have to pay for child care are treated the same as mothers who don't have this expense. The poverty line is also the same for everyone across the nation, even though the cost of living is much higher in New York than in Alabama. On the other hand, much of the income of the poor is not counted: food stamps, rent assistance, subsidized child care, and the earned income tax credit (Short 2012). In the face of these criticisms, the Census Bureau has developed alternative ways to measure poverty. These show higher poverty, but the official measure has not changed.

That a change in the poverty line can instantly make millions of people poor—or take away their poverty—would be laughable, if it weren't so serious. Although this line is arbitrary, because it is the official measure of poverty, we'll use it to see who in the United States is poor. Before we do this, though, how do you think that your ideas of the poor match up with sociological findings? To find out, go to the Down-to-Earth Sociology box on the next page.

High rates of rural poverty have been a part of the United States from its origin to the present. This 1937 photo shows a 32-year old woman who had seven children and no food. She was part of a huge migration of people from the Dust Bowl of Oklahoma in search of a new life in California.

Down-to-Earth Sociology

Some Facts about Poverty: What Do You Know?

Can you tell which of these statements are true?

1. **Poverty is unusual.** *False.* Over a four-year period, *one-third* (32 percent) of all Americans experience poverty for at least two months (DeNavas-Walt et al. 2010. About *half* of the entire U.S. population will experience poverty at some time before they reach age 65 (Cellini et al. 2008).
2. **People with less education are more likely to be poor.** *True.* Most definitely.
3. **Most poor people are poor because they do not want to work.** *False.* About 40 percent of the poor are under age 18, and another 10 percent are age 65 or older. About 30 percent of the working-age poor work at least half the year (O'Hare 1996a, 1996b).
4. **The percentage of children who are poor is higher than that of adults.** *True.* Look at Figure 10.7.
5. **Most children who are born in poverty are poor as adults.** *False* (Ratcliffe and McKernan 2010). Also see Figure 10.6 on page 274.
6. **There is more poverty in urban than in rural areas.** *False.* We'll review this in the following section.
7. **Most African Americans are poor.** *False.* This one was easy. We just reviewed some statistics in the box on upward mobility on page 276—plus you have Figure 10.7.
8. **Most of the poor are African Americans.** *False.* There are more poor whites than any other group. Look at Part 2 of Figure 10.7.
9. **Most of the poor live in the inner city.** *False.* Most of the poor live in the suburbs (Kneebone and Garr 2010).
10. **Most of the poor are single mothers and their children.** *False.* About 38 percent of the poor match this stereotype, but 34 percent of the poor live in married-couple families, 22 percent live alone or with nonrelatives, and 6 percent live in other settings (O'Hare 1996a, 1996b).
11. **Most of the poor live on welfare.** *False.* Only about 25 percent of the income of poor adults comes from welfare. About half comes from wages and pensions, and about 22 percent from Social Security (O'Hare 1996a, 1996b).

For Your Consideration

➤ What stereotypes of the poor do you (or people you know) hold? How would you test these stereotypes?

FIGURE 10.7 Race–Ethnicity and U.S. Poverty

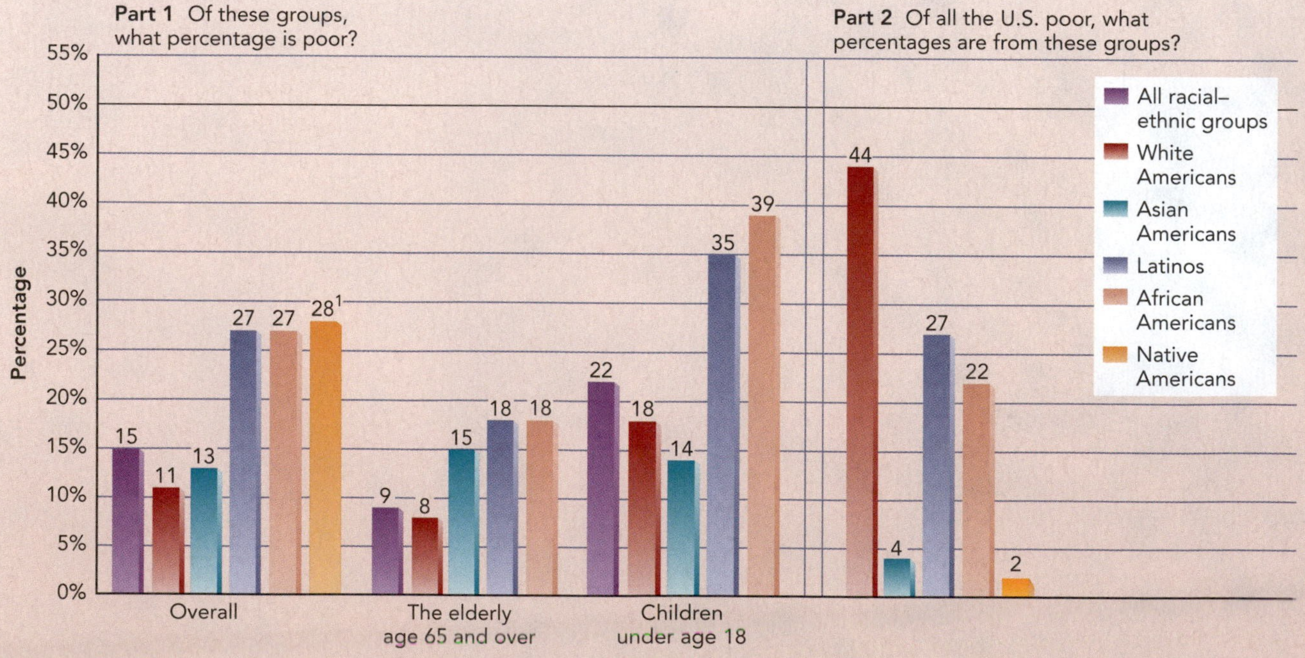

[1]The source does not break this total down by age.

Note: Only these groups are listed in the source. The poverty line is $22,314 for a family of four.

Source: By the author. Based on *Statistical Abstract of the United States* 2013:Tables 36, 722, and 724.

FIGURE 10.8 Patterns of Poverty

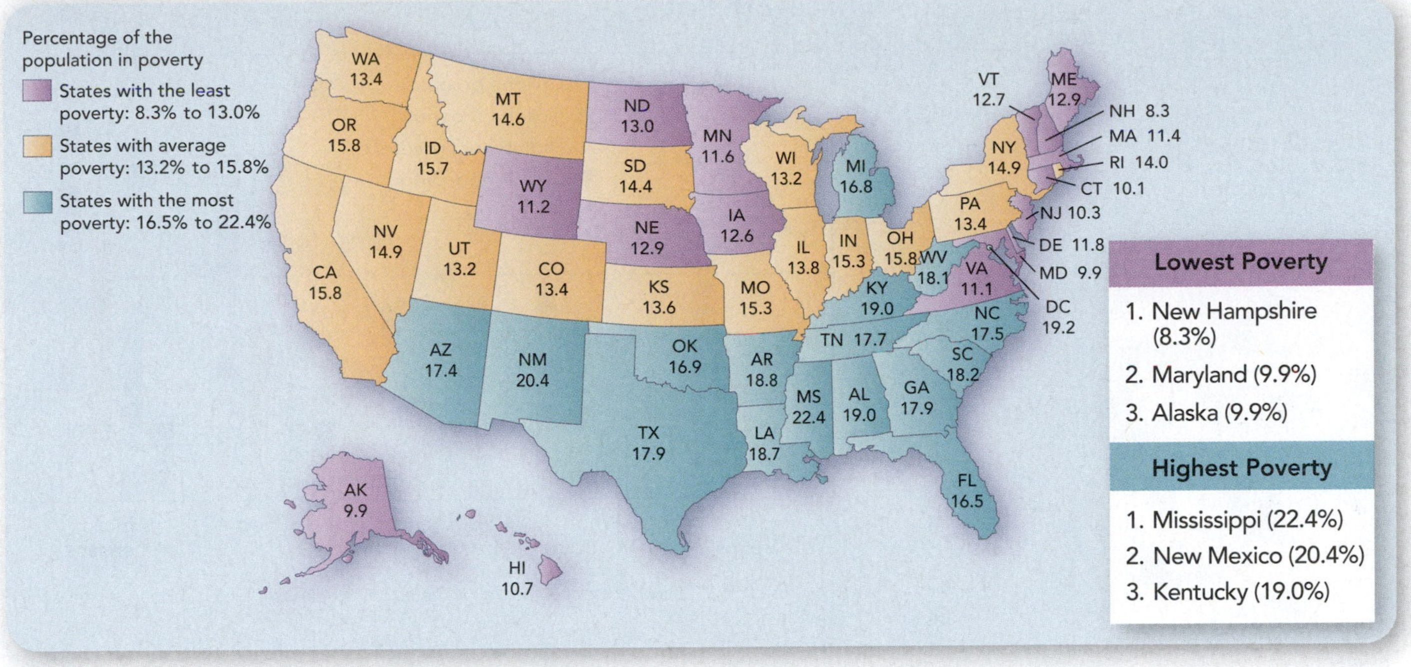

Source: By the author. Based on *Statistical Abstract of the United States* 2013:Table 721.

Who Are the Poor?

The Geography of Poverty. The Social Map above illustrates how poverty varies by *region*. The striking clustering of poverty in the South is a pattern that has prevailed for more than 150 years.

A second aspect of geography is *rural poverty*. At 16 percent, rural poverty is higher than the national average of 15 percent. Helping to maintain this higher rate are the lower education of the rural poor and the scarcity of rural jobs (Latimer and Woldoff 2010).

A third aspect of geography is the *suburbanization of poverty*. With the extensive migration from the cities to suburbs and the collapse of the housing market, poverty hit the suburbs—so hard that *most* of the nation's poor now live in the suburbs (Kneebone and Garr 2010). This major change is not likely to be temporary.

Geography, however, is not the main factor in poverty. The greatest predictors of poverty are race–ethnicity, education, and the sex of the person who heads the family. Let's look at these factors.

Race–Ethnicity. One of the strongest factors in poverty is race–ethnicity. As you can see from Figure 10.7, 11 percent of whites are poor, followed closely by Asian Americans at 13 percent. From there, the poverty rate jumps. Twenty-seven percent of Latinos and African Americans live in poverty. For Native Americans, it is 28 percent. Because whites are, by far, the largest group in the United States, their lower rate of poverty translates into larger numbers. As a result, there are many more poor whites than poor people of any other racial–ethnic group. As Part 2 of Figure 10.7 shows, 44 percent of all poor people are whites.

Watch on **MySocLab**
Video: Social Class: The Basics

Poverty comes in many forms. Families who go into debt to buy possessions squeak by month after month until a crisis turns their lives upside down. I took this photo of a family in Georgia, parked alongside a highway selling their possessions to survive our economic downturn.

Read on MySocLab
Document: Doubly Divided: The Racial Wealth Gap

FIGURE 10.9 Who Ends Up Poor? Poverty by Education and Race–Ethnicity

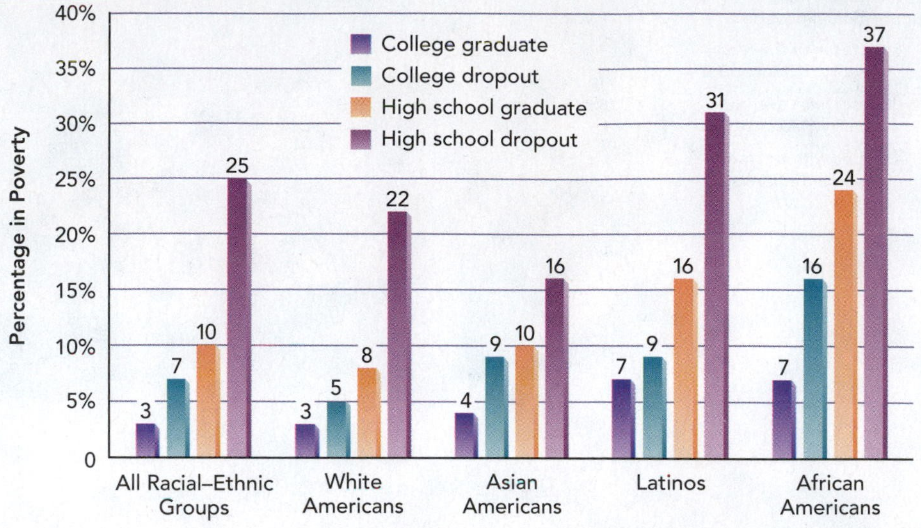

Source: By the author. Based on *Statistical Abstract of the United States* 2007:Table 694. Table dropped in later editions.

Education. You are aware that education is a vital factor in poverty, but you may not know just how powerful it is. Look at Figure 10.9, which shows that 1 of every 4 people who drop out of high school is poor, but only 3 of 100 people who finish college end up in poverty. As you can see, the chances that someone will be poor become less with each higher level of education. Although this principle applies regardless of race–ethnicity, you can also see that race–ethnicity makes an impact at every level of education.

The Feminization of Poverty. One of the best indicators of whether or not a family is poor is family structure. Families headed by both a mother and father are the least likely to be poor, while those headed by only a mother are the most likely to be poor (*Statistical Abstract* 2013:Table 728). The reason for this can be summed up in one statistic: Women average only 72 percent of what men earn. (If you want to jump ahead, go to Figure 11.8 on page 312.) With our high rate of divorce combined with the large number of births to single women, mother-headed families have become more common. Sociologists call this association of poverty with women the **feminization of poverty**.

Old Age. As Figure 10.7 on page 278 shows, the elderly are *less* likely than the general population to be poor. This is quite a change. It used to be that growing old increased people's chances of being poor, but government policies to redistribute income—Social Security and subsidized housing, food stamps, and medical care—slashed the rate of poverty among the elderly. Figure 10.7 also shows how the prevailing racial–ethnic patterns carry over into old age. You can see how much more likely elderly African Americans, Latinos, and Native Americans are to be poor than elderly whites. The exception is elderly Asian Americans, who show an unexplained jump in poverty.

Children of Poverty

Children are more likely to live in poverty than are adults or the elderly. This holds true regardless of race–ethnicity, but from Figure 10.7, you can see how much greater poverty is among Latino, African American, and Native American children. That millions of U.S. children are reared in poverty is shocking when one considers the wealth of this country and our supposed concern for the well-being of children. This tragic aspect of poverty is the topic of the following Thinking Critically section.

feminization of poverty a condition of U.S. poverty in which most poor families are headed by women

THINKING CRITICALLY

The Nation's Shame: Children in Poverty

One of the most startling statistics in sociology is shown in Figure 10.7 on page 278. Look at the rate of childhood poverty: For Asian Americans, one of seven children is poor; for whites, one of five or six; for Latinos, an astounding one of three; and for African Americans, an even higher total, with two of every five children living in poverty. These percentages translate into incredible numbers—approximately *16 million* children.

Why do so many U.S. children live in poverty? A major reason is the large number of births to women who are not married, about 1.7 million a year. This number has increased sharply, going from *one* out of twenty in 1960 to *eight* out of twenty today. With the total jumping eight times, single women now account for 41 percent of all U.S. births (*Statistical Abstract* 2013:Table 89).

But do births to single women actually cause poverty? Consider the obvious: Children born to wealthy single women don't live in poverty. Then consider this: In some industrialized countries, the birth rate of single women is higher than ours; *yet our rate of child poverty is higher than theirs* (Garfinkel et al. 2010). Their poverty rate is lower because their governments provide extensive support for rearing these children—from providing day care to health checkups. As the cause of the poverty of children born to single women, then, why can't we point to the lack of government support for children?

Apart from the matter of government policy, births to single women follow patterns that have a negative impact on their children's welfare. The less education a single woman has, the more likely she is to bear children. As you can see from Figure 10.10, births to single women drop with each gain in education. As you know, people with lower education earn less, so this means that the single women who can least afford children are those most likely to give birth. Their children are likely to face the obstacles to building a satisfying life that poverty brings. They are more likely to die in infancy, to go hungry, to be malnourished, and to have health problems. They also are more likely to drop out of school, to become involved in crime, and to have children while still in their teens—thus perpetuating a cycle of poverty.

FIGURE 10.10 Births to Single Mothers

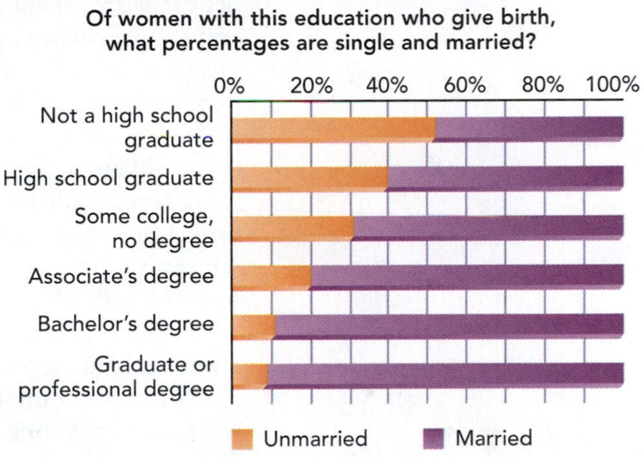

Note: Based on a national sample of all U.S. births in the preceding 12 months.
Source: Dye 2005.

For Your Consideration

➔ With education so important for obtaining jobs that pay well, in light of Figure 10.10, what programs would you suggest for helping women attain more education? What policies would you suggest for reducing child poverty? Be specific and practical. ■

The Dynamics of Poverty versus the Culture of Poverty

Some have suggested that the poor get trapped in a **culture of poverty** (Lewis 1966; Cohen 2010). They assume that the values and behaviors of the poor "make them fundamentally different from other Americans, and that these factors are largely responsible for their continued long-term poverty" (Ruggles 1989:7). Lurking behind this concept is the idea that the poor are lazy people who bring poverty on themselves. Certainly, some individuals and families do match this stereotype—many of us have known them. But is a self-perpetuating culture—one that poor people transmit across generations and that locks them in poverty—the basic reason for U.S. poverty?

culture of poverty the assumption that the values and behaviors of the poor make them fundamentally different from other people, that these factors are largely responsible for their poverty, and that parents perpetuate poverty across generations by passing these characteristics to their children

FIGURE 10.11

How Long Does Poverty Last?

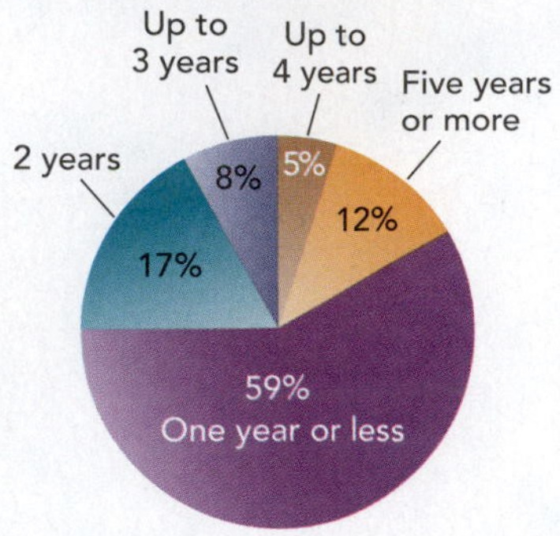

Source: Gottschalk et al. 1994:89.

Contrary to the stereotype of lazy people who contentedly sit back sucking welfare, poverty is dynamic. First, we should note that many people live on the edge of poverty. They manage to keep their heads above poverty, although barely, but then comes some dramatic life change such as a divorce, an accident, an illness, or the loss of a job. The *poverty trigger* propels them over the edge they were holding onto, and they find themselves in the poverty they fiercely had been trying to avoid (Western et al. 2012).

Second, most poverty is short-lived, lasting less than a year. As Figure 10.11 shows, only 12 percent of poverty lasts five years or longer. Yet from one year to the next, the number of poor people remains about the same. This means that the people who move out of poverty are replaced by people who move into poverty. Most of these newly poor will also move out of poverty within a year. Some people even bounce back and forth, never quite making it securely out of poverty.

Few poor people enjoy poverty—and they do what they can to avoid being poor. In the end, though, poverty touches a lot more people than the official totals indicate. Although 15 percent of Americans may be poor at any one time, for those under age 30, 40 percent will be poor in the next ten years (Western et al. 2012). Before they turn 65, about half of the U.S. population will experience poverty (Cellini et al. 2008).

Why Are People Poor?

Two explanations for poverty compete for our attention. The first, which sociologists prefer, focuses on *social structure.* Sociologists stress that *features of society* deny some people access to education or training in job skills. They emphasize racial–ethnic, age, and gender discrimination, as well as changes in the job market—fewer unskilled jobs, businesses closing, and manufacturing jobs moving overseas. In short, some people find their escape route from poverty blocked.

A competing explanation focuses on the *characteristics of individuals.* Sociologists reject explanations such as laziness and lack of intelligence, viewing these as worthless stereotypes. Individualistic explanations that sociologists reluctantly acknowledge include dropping out of school and bearing children in the teen years. Most sociologists are reluctant to speak of such factors in this context, since they appear to blame the victim, something that sociologists bend over backward not to do.

A third explanation is the *poverty triggers* that were just mentioned, the unexpected events in life that push people into poverty.

What do you think causes poverty? Your view is important because it not only affects your perception but also has practical consequences. To see why, read the following Thinking Critically section.

THINKING CRITICALLY

The Welfare Debate: The Deserving and the Undeserving Poor

Throughout U.S. history, Americans have divided the poor into two types: the deserving and the undeserving. The deserving poor are people who are thought to be poor through no fault of their own. Most of the working poor, such as the Lewises, are considered deserving:

Nancy and Ted Lewis are in their early 30s and have two children. Ted works three part-time jobs, earning $15,000 a year; Nancy takes care of the children and house and is not employed. To make ends meet, the Lewises rely on food stamps, Medicaid, and Section 8 (a federal housing subsidy).

The undeserving poor stand in sharp contrast. They are viewed as bringing poverty on themselves. They are considered freeloaders who waste their lives in laziness and alcohol and drug abuse. They revel in partying and promiscuous sex. They don't deserve help. If given anything, they will waste it on their immoral lifestyles. Some would see Joan as an example:

> *Joan, her mother, and her two brothers and two sisters lived on welfare. Joan started having sex at 13, bore her first child at 15, and, now, at 23, is expecting her fourth child. Her first two children have the same father, the third a different father, and Joan isn't sure who fathered her coming child. Joan parties most nights, using both alcohol and whatever drugs are available. Her house is filthy, the refrigerator is bare, and social workers have threatened to take away her children.*

This division of the poor into deserving and undeserving underlies the heated debate about welfare. "Why should we use *our* hard-earned money to help *them*? They are just going to waste it. Of course, there are others who want to get back on their feet, and helping them is okay."

For Your Consideration

➔ Why do people make a distinction between deserving and undeserving poor? Should we let some people starve because they "brought poverty upon themselves"? Should we let children go hungry because their parents are drug abusers? Does "unworthy" mean that we should not offer assistance to people who "squander" the help they are given?

➔ In contrast to thinking of poor people as deserving or undeserving, use the sociological perspective to explain poverty without blaming the victim. What *social* conditions (conditions of society) create poverty? Are there *social* conditions that produce the lifestyles that the middle class so despises? ■

Deferred Gratification

One consequence of a life of deprivation punctuated by emergencies—*and of viewing the future as promising more of the same*—is a lack of **deferred gratification**, giving up things in the present for the sake of greater gains in the future. It is difficult to practice this middle-class virtue of deferring gratification if you do not have a middle-class surplus—or middle-class hope.

In a classic 1967 study of black streetcorner men, sociologist Elliot Liebow noted that the men did not defer gratification. Their jobs were low-paying and insecure, their lives pitted with emergencies. With the future looking exactly like the present, and any savings they did manage gobbled up by emergencies, it seemed pointless to save for the future. The only thing that made sense from their perspective was to enjoy what they could at that moment. Immediate gratification, then, was not the cause of their poverty but, rather, its consequence. Cause and consequence loop together, however: Their immediate gratification helped perpetuate their poverty. For another look at this "looping," see the Down-to-Earth Sociology box on the next page, in which I share my personal experience with poverty.

If both structural and personal causes are at work, why do sociologists emphasize the structural explanation? Reverse the situation for a moment. Suppose that members of the middle class drove old cars that broke down, faced threats from the utility company to shut off the electricity and heat, and had to make a choice between paying the rent or buying medicine and food and diapers. How long would they practice deferred gratification? Their orientations to life would likely make a sharp U-turn.

Sociologists, then, do not view the behaviors of the poor as the cause of their poverty but, rather, as the result of their poverty. Poor people would welcome the middle-class opportunities that would allow them the chance to practice the middle-class virtue of deferred gratification. Without those opportunities, though, they just can't afford it.

deferred gratification going without something in the present in the hope of achieving greater gains in the future

Down-to-Earth **Sociology**

Poverty: A Personal Journey

I was born in poverty. My parents, who could not afford to rent either a house or an apartment, rented the tiny office in their minister's house. That is where I was born.

My father, who had only a seventh grade education, began to slowly climb the social class ladder. His fitful odyssey took him from laborer to truck driver to the owner of a series of small businesses (tire repair shop, bar, hotel), and from there to vacuum cleaner salesman, and back to bar owner. He converted a garage into a house. Although it had no indoor plumbing or insulation (on Minnesota's Canadian border!), it was a start. Later, he bought a house, and then he built a new home. After that we moved into a trailer, and then back to a house. Although he never became wealthy, poverty eventually became a distant memory for him.

My social class took a leap—from working class to upper middle class—when, after attending college and graduate school, I became a university professor. I entered a world that was unknown to my parents, one much more pampered and privileged. I had opportunities to do research, to publish, and to travel to exotic places. My reading centered on sociological research, and I read books in Spanish as well as in English. My father, in contrast, never read a book in his life, and my mother read only detective stories and romance paperbacks. One set of experiences isn't "better" than the other, just significantly different in determining what windows of perception it opens onto the world.

My interest in poverty, rooted in my own childhood experiences, stayed with me. I traveled to a dozen or so skid rows across the United States and Canada, talking to homeless people and staying in their shelters. In my own town, I spent considerable time with people on welfare, observing how they lived. I constantly marveled at the connections between *structural* causes of poverty (low education, low skills, low pay, the irregularity of unskilled jobs, undependable transportation) and *personal* causes (the *culture of poverty*—alcohol and drug abuse, multiple out-of-wedlock births, frivolous spending, all-night partying, domestic violence, criminal involvement, and a seeming incapacity to keep appointments—except to pick up the welfare check).

Sociologists haven't unraveled this connection, and as much as we might *like* for only structural causes to apply, *both* are at work (Duneier 1999:122). The situation can be illustrated by looking at the perennial health problems I observed among the poor—the constant colds, runny noses, backaches, and injuries. The health problems stem from the *social structure* (less access to medical care, less capable physicians, drafty houses, little knowledge about nutrition, and more dangerous jobs). At the same time, *personal* characteristics—hygiene, eating habits, and overdrinking—cause health problems. Which is the cause and which the effect? Both, of course: One loops into the other. The medical problems (which are based on both personal and structural causes) feed into the poverty these people experience, making them less able to perform their jobs successfully—or even to show up at work regularly. What an intricate puzzle for sociologists!

Where Is Horatio Alger? The Social Functions of a Myth

In the late 1800s, Horatio Alger was one of the country's most popular authors. The rags-to-riches exploits of his fictional boy heroes and their amazing successes in overcoming severe odds motivated thousands of boys of that period. Although Alger's characters have disappeared from U.S. literature, they remain alive and well in the psyche of Americans. From real-life examples of people of humble origin who climbed the social class ladder, Americans know that anyone who really tries can get ahead. In fact, they believe that most Americans, including minorities and the working poor, have an average or better-than-average chance of getting ahead—obviously a statistical impossibility (Kluegel and Smith 1986).

The accuracy of the **Horatio Alger myth** is less important than the belief that surrounds it—that limitless possibilities exist for everyone. Functionalists would stress that this belief is functional for society. On the one hand, it encourages people to compete for higher positions, or, as the song says, "to reach for the highest star." On the other hand, it places blame for failure squarely on the individual. If you don't make it—in the face of ample opportunities to get ahead—the fault must be your own. The Horatio Alger myth helps to stabilize society: Since the fault is viewed as the individual's, not society's, current social arrangements can be regarded as satisfactory. This reduces pressures to change the system.

Horatio Alger myth the belief that due to limitless possibilities anyone can get ahead if he or she tries hard enough

As Marx and Weber pointed out, social class penetrates our consciousness, shaping our ideas of life and our "proper" place in society. When the rich look at the world around them, they sense superiority and anticipate control over their own destiny. When the poor look around them, they are more likely to sense defeat and to anticipate that

A society's dominant ideologies are reinforced throughout the society, including its literature. Horatio Alger provided inspirational heroes for thousands of boys. The central theme of these many novels, immensely popular in their time, was rags to riches. Through rugged determination and self-sacrifice, a boy could overcome seemingly insurmountable obstacles to reach the pinnacle of success. (Girls did not strive for financial success, but were dependent on fathers and husbands.)

unpredictable forces will batter their lives. Both rich and poor know the dominant ideology: that their particular niche in life is due to their own efforts, that the reasons for success—or failure—lie solely with the self. Like fish that don't notice the water, people tend not to perceive the effects of social class on their own lives.

MySocLab

Study and Review on MySocLab

CHAPTER 10 Summary and Review

What Determines Social Class?

10.1 Explain the three components of social class—property, power, and prestige; distinguish between wealth and income; explain how property and income are distributed; and describe the democratic façade, the power elite, and status inconsistency.

What is meant by the term social class?

Most sociologists have adopted Weber's definition of **social class**: a large group of people who rank closely to one another in terms of property (wealth), power, and prestige. **Wealth**—consisting of the value of property and income—is concentrated in the upper classes. From the 1930s to the 1970s, the trend in the distribution of wealth in the United States was toward greater equality. Since that time, it has been toward greater inequality. **Power** is the ability to get your way even though others resist. C. Wright Mills coined the term **power elite** to refer to the small group that holds the reins of power in business, government, and the military. **Prestige** is linked to occupational status. Pp. 252–262.

How does occupational prestige differ around the world?

From country to country, people rank occupational prestige similarly. Globally, the occupations that bring greater prestige are those that pay more, require more education and abstract thought, and offer greater independence. Pp. 262–263.

What is meant by the term status inconsistency?

Status is social position. Most people are **status consistent**; that is, they rank high or low on all three dimensions of social class. People who rank higher on some dimensions than on others are status inconsistent. The frustrations of **status inconsistency** tend to produce political radicalism. Pp. 263–264.

Sociological Models of Social Class

10.2 Contrast Marx's and Weber's models of social class.

What models are used to portray the social classes?

Erik Wright developed a four-class model based on Marx: (1) capitalists (owners of large businesses), (2) petty bourgeoisie (small business owners), (3) managers, and (4) workers. Kahl and Gilbert developed a six-class model based on Weber. At the top is the capitalist class. In descending order are the upper middle class, the lower middle class, the working class, the working poor, and the **underclass**. Pp. 264–269.

Consequences of Social Class

10.3 Summarize the consequences of social class for physical and mental health, family life, education, religion, politics, and the criminal justice system.

How does social class affect people's lives?

Social class leaves no aspect of life untouched. It affects our chances of dying early, becoming ill, receiving good health care, and getting divorced. Social class membership also affects child rearing, educational attainment, religious affiliation, political participation, the crimes people commit, and their contact with the criminal justice system. Pp. 269–272.

Social Mobility

10.4 Contrast the three types of social mobility, and review gender issues in research on social mobility and why social mobility brings pain.

What are three types of social mobility?

The term **intergenerational mobility** refers to changes in social class from one generation to the next. **Structural mobility** refers to changes in society that lead large numbers of people to change their social class. **Exchange mobility** is the movement of large numbers of people from one social class to another, with the net result that the relative proportions of the population in the classes remain about the same. Pp. 272–275.

Poverty

10.5 Explain the problems in drawing the poverty line, how poverty is related to geography, race-ethnicity, education, feminization, age, and the culture of poverty; analyze why people are poor; and discuss deferred gratification and the Horatio Alger myth.

Who are the poor?

Poverty is unequally distributed in the United States. Racial–ethnic minorities (except Asian Americans), children, households headed by women, and rural Americans are more likely than others to be poor. The poverty line, although it has serious consequences, is arbitrary. The poverty rate of the elderly is less than that of the general population. Pp. 275–282.

Why are people poor?

Some social analysts believe that characteristics of *individuals* cause poverty. Sociologists, in contrast, stress the *structural* features of society, such as employment opportunities, to find the causes of poverty. There also are *poverty triggers*. Sociologists generally conclude that life orientations are a consequence, not the cause, of people's position in the social class structure. Pp. 282–284.

How is the Horatio Alger myth functional for society?

The **Horatio Alger myth**—the belief that anyone can get ahead if only he or she tries hard enough—encourages people to strive to get ahead. It also deflects blame for failure from society to the individual. Pp. 284–285.

Thinking Critically about Chapter 10

1. The belief that the United States is the land of opportunity draws millions of legal and illegal immigrants to the United States. How do the materials in this chapter support or undermine this belief?
2. In what three ways is social class having an ongoing impact on your life?
3. What social mobility has your own family experienced? In what ways has this affected your life?

CHAPTER 11

Sex and Gender

Listen to Chapter 11 on MySocLab

Learning Objectives

After you have read this chapter, you should be able to:

11.1 Distinguish between sex and gender; use research on Vietnam veterans and testosterone to explain why the door to biology is opening in sociology. (p. 288)

11.2 Discuss the origin of gender discrimination, sex typing of work, gender and the prestige of work, and global aspects of pay, violence, and education. (p. 294)

11.3 Review the rise of feminism; summarize gender inequality in everyday life, health care, and education. (p. 300)

11.4 Explain reasons for the pay gap; discuss the glass ceiling and sexual harassment. (p. 309)

11.5 Summarize violence against women: rape, murder, and violence in the home. (p. 315)

11.6 Discuss changes in gender and politics. (p. 317)

11.7 Explain why the future looks hopeful.(p. 318)

In Tunis, the capital of Tunisia, *on Africa's northern coast, I met some U.S. college students and spent a couple of days with them. They wanted to see the city's red light district, but I wondered whether it would be worth the trip. I already had seen other red light districts, including the unusual one in Amsterdam where a bronze statue of a female prostitute lets you know you've entered the area; the state licenses the women and men, requiring that they have medical checkups (certificates must be posted); and the prostitutes add sales tax to the receipts they give customers. The prostitutes sit behind lighted picture windows while customers stroll along the narrow canal side streets and "window shop" from the outside. Tucked among the brothels are day care centers, bakeries, and clothing stores. Amsterdam itself is an unusual place—in cafes, you can smoke marijuana but not tobacco.*

I decided to go with them. We ended up on a wharf that extended into the Mediterranean. Each side was lined with a row of one-room wooden shacks, crowded one against the next. In front of each open door stood a young woman. Peering from outside into the dark interiors, I could see that each door led to a tiny room with an old, well-worn bed.

The prostitutes sit behind lighted picture windows while customers stroll along the narrow canal side streets and "window shop" from the outside.

The wharf was crowded with men who were eyeing the women and negotiating prices. Many of the men wore sailor uniforms from countries that I couldn't identify.

As I looked more closely, I could see that some of the women had running sores on their legs. Incredibly, with such visible evidence of their disease, men still sought them out.

With a sick feeling in my stomach and the desire to vomit, I kept a good distance between the beckoning women and myself. One tour of the two-block area was more than sufficient.

Somewhere nearby, out of sight, I knew that there were men whose wealth derived from exploiting these women who were condemned to short lives punctuated by fear and misery.

In this chapter, we examine **gender stratification**—males' and females' unequal access to property, power, and prestige. Gender is especially significant because it is a *master status*; that is, it cuts across *all* aspects of social life. No matter what we attain in life, we carry the label *male* or *female*. These labels convey images and expectations about how we should act. Gender not only guides our behavior but also is a basis for making people unequal.

In this chapter's fascinating journey, we will look at inequality between the sexes both around the world and in the United States. We explore whether it is biology or culture that makes us the way we are and review sexual harassment, unequal pay, and violence against women. This excursion will provide a good context for understanding the power differences between men and women that lead to situations such as the one described in our opening vignette. It should also give you insight into your own experiences with gender.

Let's begin by considering the distinctions between sex and gender.

gender stratification males' and females' unequal access to property, power, and prestige

sex biological characteristics that distinguish females and males, consisting of primary and secondary sex characteristics

11.1 Distinguish between sex and gender; use research on Vietnam veterans and testosterone to explain why the door to biology is opening in sociology.

Issues of Sex and Gender

When we consider how females and males differ, the first thing that usually comes to mind is **sex**, the *biological characteristics* that distinguish males and females. *Primary sex characteristics* consist of a vagina or a penis and other organs related to reproduction. *Secondary sex characteristics* are the physical distinctions between males and females that are not directly connected with reproduction. These characteristics become clearly evident at puberty when males develop larger muscles, lower voices, more body hair, and greater height, while females develop breasts and form more fatty tissue and broader hips.

Gender, in contrast, is a *social*, not a biological characteristic. **Gender** consists of whatever behaviors and attitudes a group considers proper for its males and females. Sex refers to male or female, and *gender* refers to masculinity or femininity. In short, you inherit your sex, but you learn your gender as you learn the behaviors and attitudes your culture asserts are appropriate for your sex.

As the photo montage on the next page illustrates, the expectations associated with gender differ around the world. They vary so greatly that some sociologists replace the terms *masculinity* and *femininity* with *masculinities* and *femininities*.

Differences in how we display gender often lie below our awareness. How males and females use social space is an example. In this unposed photo from Grand Central Station in New York City, you can see how males tend to sprawl out, females to enclose themselves. Why do you think this difference exists? Biology? Socialization? Both?

The Sociological Significance of Gender. *The sociological significance of gender is that it is a device by which society controls its members.* Gender sorts us, on the basis of sex, into different life experiences. It opens and closes doors to property, power, and prestige. Like social class, gender is a structural feature of society.

Before examining inequalities of gender, let's consider why the behaviors of men and women differ.

Gender Differences in Behavior: Biology or Culture?

Why are most males more aggressive than most females? Why do women enter "nurturing" occupations, such as teaching young children and nursing, in far greater numbers than men? To answer such questions, many people respond with some variation of "They're born that way."

Watch on **MySocLab**
Video: The Basics: Gender

Is this the correct answer? Certainly biology plays a significant role in our lives. Each of us begins as a fertilized egg. The egg, or ovum, is contributed by our mother, the sperm that fertilizes the egg by our father. At the very instant the egg is fertilized, our sex is determined. Each of us receives twenty-three chromosomes from the ovum and twenty-three from the sperm. The egg has an X chromosome. If the sperm that fertilizes the egg also has an X chromosome, the result is a girl (XX). If the sperm has a Y chromosome, the result is a boy (XY).

The Dominant Position in Sociology

That's the biology. Now, the sociological question is, Does this biological difference control our behavior? Does it, for example, make females more nurturing and submissive and males more aggressive and domineering? Here is the quick sociological answer: The dominant sociological position is that *social* factors, not biology, are the reasons people do what they do.

Read on **MySocLab**
Document: If Men Could Menstruate

Let's apply this position to gender. If biology were the principal factor in human behavior, all around the world, we would find women behaving in one way and men in another. Men and women would be just like male spiders and female spiders, whose genes tell them what to do. In fact, however, ideas of gender vary greatly from one culture to another—and, as a result, so do male–female behaviors.

Despite this, to see why the door to biology is opening just slightly in sociology, let's consider a medical accident and a study of Vietnam veterans.

Opening the Door to Biology

A Medical Accident.

In 1963, 7-month-old identical twin boys were taken to a doctor for a routine circumcision. The physician, not the most capable person in the world, was using a heated needle. He turned the electric current too high and accidentally burned off the penis of one of the boys.

gender the behaviors and attitudes that a society considers proper for its males and females; masculinity or femininity

Standards of Gender

Each human group determines its ideas of "maleness" and "femaleness." As you can see from these photos of four women and four men, standards of gender are arbitrary and vary from one culture to another. Yet, in its ethnocentrism, each group thinks that its preferences reflect what gender "really" is. As indicated here, around the world men and women try to make themselves appealing by aspiring to their group's standards of gender.

Mexico

Jordan

Kenya

Ethiopia

Brazil

New Guinea

India

China

You can imagine the parents' disbelief—and then their horror—as the truth sank in. What could they do? After months of soul-searching and tearful consultations with experts, the parents decided that their son should have a sex-change operation (Money and Ehrhardt 1972). When he was 22 months old, surgeons castrated the boy, using the skin to construct a vagina. The parents then gave the child a new name, Brenda, dressed him in frilly clothing, let his hair grow long, and began to treat him as a girl. Later, physicians gave Brenda female steroids to promote female puberty (Colapinto 2001).

At first, the results were promising. When the twins were 4 years old, the mother said (remember that the children are biologically identical):

> *One thing that really amazes me is that she is so feminine. I've never seen a little girl so neat and tidy. . . . She likes for me to wipe her face. She doesn't like to be dirty, and yet my son is quite different. I can't wash his face for anything. . . . She is very proud of herself, when she puts on a new dress, or I set her hair. . . . She seems to be daintier. (Money and Ehrhardt 1972)*

If the matter were this clear-cut, we could use this case to conclude that gender is determined entirely by nurture. Seldom are things in life so simple, however, and a twist occurs in this story.

Despite this promising start and her parents' coaching, Brenda did not adapt well to femininity. She preferred to mimic her father shaving, rather than her mother putting on makeup. She rejected dolls, favoring guns and her brother's toys. She liked rough-and-tumble games and insisted on urinating standing up. Classmates teased her and called her a "cavewoman" because she walked like a boy. At age 14, she was expelled from school for beating up a girl who teased her. Despite estrogen treatment, she was not attracted to boys. At age 14, when despair over her inner turmoil brought her to the brink of suicide, her father, in tears, told Brenda about the accident and her sex change.

David Reimer, whose story is recounted here.

"All of a sudden everything clicked. For the first time, things made sense, and I understood who and what I was," the twin said of this revelation. David (his new name) was given testosterone shots and, later, had surgery to partially reconstruct a penis. At age 25, David married a woman and adopted her children (Diamond and Sigmundson 1997; Colapinto 2001). There is an unfortunate end to this story, however. In 2004, David committed suicide.

The Vietnam Veterans Study. Time after time, researchers have found that boys and men who have higher levels of testosterone tend to be more aggressive (Eisenegger et al. 2011). In one study, researchers compared the testosterone levels of college men in a "rowdy" fraternity with those of men in a fraternity that had a reputation for academic achievement. Men in the "rowdy" fraternity had higher levels of testosterone (Dabbs et al. 1996). In another study, researchers found that prisoners who had committed sex crimes and other crimes of violence had higher levels of testosterone than those who had committed property crimes (Dabbs et al. 1995). The samples were small, however, leaving the nagging uncertainty that these findings might be due to chance.

Then in 1985, the U.S. government began a health study of Vietnam veterans. To be certain that the study was representative, the researchers chose a random sample of 4,462 men. Among the data they collected was a measurement of testosterone. This sample supported the earlier studies. When the veterans with higher testosterone levels were boys, they were more likely to get in trouble with parents and teachers and to become delinquents. As adults, they were more likely to use hard drugs, to get into fights, to end up in lower-status jobs, and to have more sexual partners. Those who married were more likely to have affairs, to hit their wives, and, it follows, to get divorced (Dabbs and Morris 1990; Booth and Dabbs 1993).

This makes it sound like biology is the basis for behavior. Fortunately for us sociologists, there is another side to this research, and here is where *social class*, the topic of our previous chapter, comes into play. The researchers compared high-testosterone

Sociologists study the social factors that underlie human behavior, the experiences that mold us, funneling us into different directions in life. The research on Vietnam veterans indicates how the sociological door is opening slowly to also consider biological factors in human behavior. This February 14, 1966, photo shows soldiers of the 1st Cavalry Division carrying a buddy who had just been shot.

men from higher and lower social classes. The men from lower social classes were more likely to get in trouble with the law, do poorly in school, and mistreat their wives (Dabbs and Morris 1990). You can see, then, that *social* factors such as socialization, subcultures, life goals, and self-definitions were significant in these men's behavior.

More Research on Humans. Research on the effects of testosterone in humans continues. The results are intriguing. Not only do higher levels of testosterone lead to higher dominance but the reverse is also true: Dominance behavior, such as winning a game, also produces higher levels of testosterone. This has made it difficult to determine which causes which. Controlled studies in which cause can be determined help. When researchers administer single doses of testosterone, dominance behavior increases. This is true of *both* males and females. They seek higher status and show less concern for the feelings of others (Eisenegger et al. 2011). Researchers are investigating how the testosterone changes people's behaviors, which they think might be by triggering other hormones.

In Sum: Sociologists acknowledge that biological factors are involved in some human behavior other than reproduction and childbearing (Udry 2000). Alice Rossi, a feminist sociologist and former president of the American Sociological Association, suggested that women are better prepared biologically for "mothering" than are men. Rossi (1977, 1984) said that women are more sensitive to the infant's soft skin and to their nonverbal communications.

Perhaps Rossi expressed it best when she said that the issue is not either biology or society. Instead, whatever biological predispositions nature provides are overlaid with culture. A task of sociologists is to discover how social factors modify biology, especially, as sociologist Janet Chafetz (1990:30) said, to determine how "different" becomes translated into "unequal."

The sociological perspective—that of social factors in human behavior—dominates this book, and in the Thinking Critically section that follows, we will explore how gender is changing.

THINKING CRITICALLY

Making the Social Explicit: Emerging Masculinities and Femininities

Muscles rippling, a large male athlete strode into a class of 400 wearing a dress. The class broke into cheers, applauding his daring to break gender rules. The next week, a slightly-built, effeminate male student came into the same class wearing a dress. The class treated him like an outcast. As students moved away from him, he was surrounded by empty chairs (Anderson 2009:43).

People who are highly successful in meeting cultural standards of gender are given more leeway to temporarily transgress gender boundaries. The two men wearing dresses illustrate this principle at work. The students knew that the hypermasculine athlete was "just fooling around" or "making a point." But the effeminate man? No one was certain about him. His dress could have reflected a "real" violation of gender boundaries.

The Traditional Model of Gender. As you know, strength and dominance are central to the traditional model of masculinity in U.S. society. Expected of males are large muscles,

Watch on **MySocLab**
Video: The Big Picture: Gender

endurance and stamina, victory in competitive events, and achievement despite obstacles. For men, life has been cast as a form of competition in which they are pitted against one another. They are expected to mask compassion and avoid the appearance of weakness, fear, and vulnerability.

On the feminine side, the dominant model allows women to show—and probably to feel—more emotions than men. They can express greater compassion and feel and show fears and weaknesses. This feminine model also dictates that women meet the flip side of masculine dominance—making the real woman submissive to the strong man.

How do men who work in traditionally feminine nurturng jobs and women who work in jobs that give them authority over men reaffirm their gender at home?

Reclaiming Gender. A good part of "doing gender" is to show that we are *not* one of *them*. Most men try to avoid things that might be considered feminine or girlish. Most women try to do things defined as feminine, which they often manage by their clothing, makeup, speech, and gestures. Although this cultural boundary is often more difficult to locate than it was in previous generations, women manage it.

With doing gender so essential to our identities, what happens when women take jobs that give them authority at work, such as being supervisors, traditionally defined as masculine? Or to men who take nurturing jobs, such as nursing, traditionally defined as feminine? To find out, sociologist Daniel Schneider (2012) compared these women and men with people who work at jobs that match traditional ideas of gender. Compared with women who work at nurturing jobs, the women who exercise authority at work spend more time at home doing "feminine" activities, such as cleaning, cooking, and washing the dishes. And compared with men whose work gives them authority over others, the men who work at nurturing jobs spend more time at home doing "masculine" activities, such as making repairs and pruning the shrubbery. Gender is so locked into them that—beyond their awareness—they are reclaiming their gender, affirming that they are not one of "them."

Read on **MySocLab**
Document: How Subtle Sex Discrimination Works

New Models of Gender. Ideas of gender are changing, and new models are taking their place alongside the traditional ones. In the new models of softer masculinity, men can be masculine *and* still show tenderness, ask for help, diaper babies, form emotional bonds with others, and even tenderly touch both women and men. The emerging models of femininity encourage women to be more dominant. Women gain cultural approval for competing in business and the professions—and *winning* in what had been a men's arena. From action movies, you can even see the "tough femininity" that is emerging, one that incorporates masculine violence. This new femininity also shows up among female juvenile delinquents, with girls winning approval for attacking others, even men (Rios 2011).

Maria, a member of the male-dominated Chicanos por Vida in Yakima, Washington. A "tough femininity" that incorporates masculine violence is emerging among female juvenile delinquents.

As the new masculinities incorporate behaviors previously considered off limits or taboo, we can also expect a decrease of homophobia (dislike and fear of homosexuals). Homophobia seems to be based on a need to maintain gender boundaries, a need to mark a sharp distance from anyone who threatens the dominant model of masculinity or femininity. As cultural attitudes shift, no longer will there be this urgent need to show that "I'm not gay." As this model softens, then, so will attitudes toward homosexuals.

For Your Consideration

➔ Do you agree that the dominant form of masculinity and femininity is changing, that we are developing femininities and masculinities? What have you experienced to indicate that this is a correct or incorrect observation? How about the author's statement that homophobia will decrease? ■

11.2 Discuss the origin of gender discrimination, sex typing of work, gender and the prestige of work, and global aspects of pay, violence, and education.

Gender Inequality in Global Perspective

Around the world, gender is *the* primary division between people. Every society sorts men and women into separate groups and gives them different access to property, power, and prestige. These divisions *always* favor men-as-a-group. After reviewing the historical record, historian and feminist Gerda Lerner (1986) concluded that "there is not a single society known where women-as-a-group have decision-making power over men (as a group)." Consequently, sociologists classify females as a *minority group*. Because females outnumber males, you may find this strange. This term applies, however, because *minority group* refers to people who are discriminated against on the basis of physical or cultural characteristics, regardless of their numbers (Hacker 1951).

Around the world, women struggle against gender discrimination. For an extreme case, see the Mass Media in Social Life box on the next page.

How Did Females Become a Minority Group?

Have females always been a minority group? Some analysts speculate that in hunting and gathering societies, women and men were social equals (Leacock 1981; Hendrix 1994) and that horticultural societies also had less gender discrimination than is common today (Collins et al. 1993). In these societies,

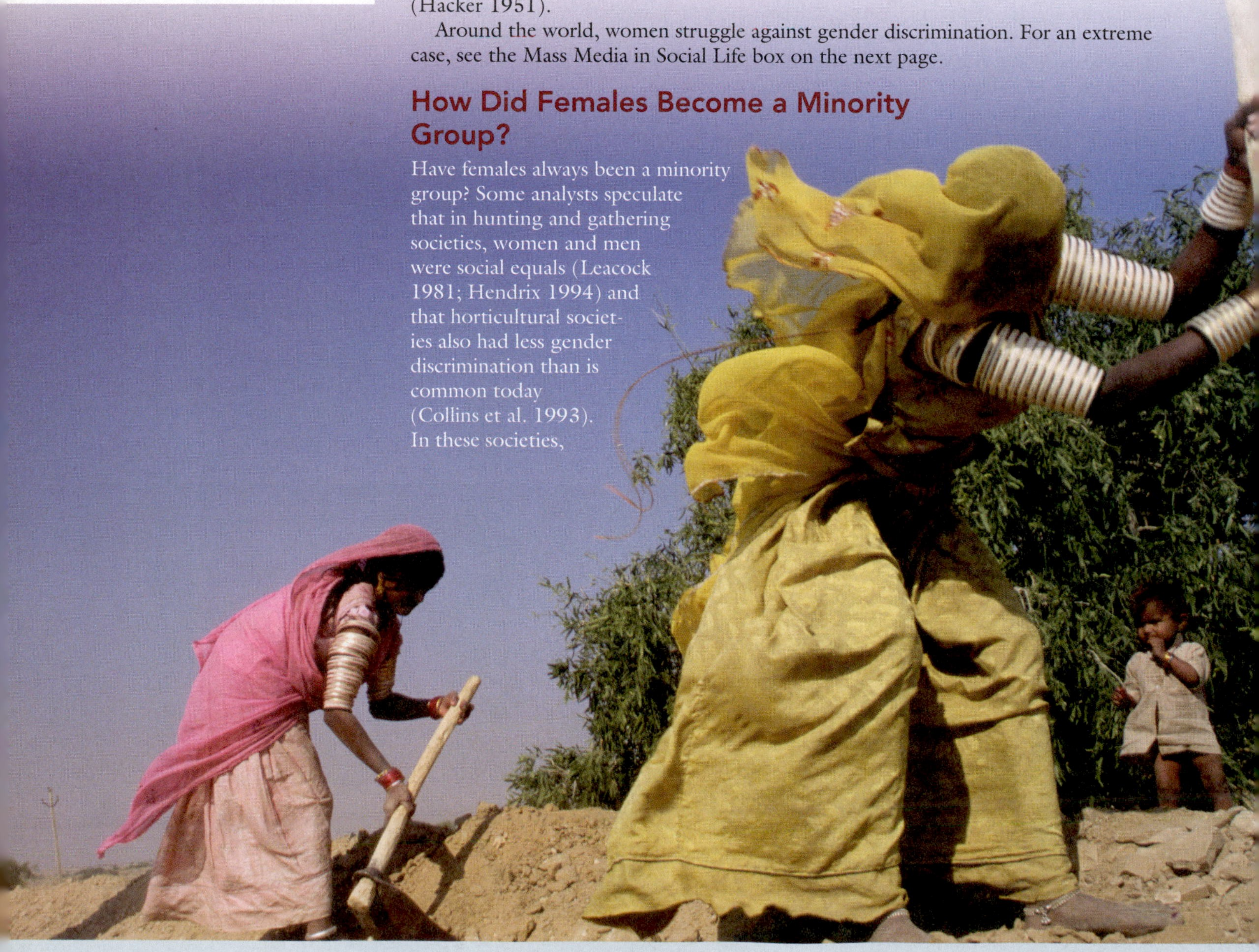

Men's work? Women's work? Customs in other societies can blow away stereotypes. As is common throughout India, these women are working on road construction.

Mass Media in **Social Life**

Women in Iran: The Times Are Changing, Ever So Slowly

A woman's testimony in court is worth half that of a man's testimony.

A woman may inherit from her parents only half what her brother inherits.

A woman who has sex with a man who is not her husband can be stoned to death.

A woman who refuses to cover her hair in public can receive 80 lashes with a whip.

Not exactly equality.

As you would expect, Iranian women don't like it. Until now, though, there was little they could do. Controlled by their fathers until they married and afterward by their husbands, women for the most part didn't know that life could be different.

The mass media and the new literacy are spearheading change in gender relations. Iranian women are logging onto the Internet, and they are reading books. Those who watch satellite television, which is illegal, are seeing pictures of other ways of life, an unfamiliar equality and mutual respect between women and men. Their eyes are being opened to the fact that not all the women in the world live under the thumbs of men. From this awareness is coming the realization that they don't have to live like this either, that there is a potential for new relationships.

This awareness and the glimmer of hope that another way of life can be theirs have stimulated a women's movement. The movement is small—and protest remains dangerous. Women are being arrested for being "feminists." Punishment is fines and prison. Security forces sometimes rape these offenders. Other protestors find brutality at home, from their husbands, fathers, or brothers.

Despite the danger, women are continuing to protest. They are even pressing for new rights in the Iranian courts. They are demanding divorce from abusive husbands—and some are getting it.

Not much has changed yet. Men can still divorce their wives whenever they want, while a woman must go through a lengthy procedure and cannot be sure that she will be granted a divorce. A husband also gets automatic custody of any children over the age of 7.

Change will come. The women are continuing their struggle. One small glimmer of hope: Embarrassed by the international outcry, Iranian politicians are allowing fewer women to be stoned to death. It is only a glimmer—women are still buried up to their necks in the ground and then stoned.

That there are fewer stonings, though, is, at least a beginning. The rest will follow.

A sign of fundamental change is Iranian women protesting in public. The Persian writing on this woman's hands says that women should have the same rights as men.

Sources: Based on Fathi 2009; Semple 2009. U.S. Department of State 2011.

For Your Consideration

➔ What do you think gender relations will be like in Iran ten years from now? Are you as confident of change as the author seems to be?

➔ If the women's movement in Iran continues, do you think that relationships between men and women will eventually be about the same as those in the United States? Why or why not?

women may have contributed about 60 percent of the group's total food. Yet, around the world, gender is the basis for discrimination.

How, then, did it happen that women became a minority group? Let's consider two theories that have been proposed to explain the origin of **patriarchy**—men dominating society.

Human Reproduction. The *first* theory—the major one—points to human reproduction (Lerner 1986; Friedl 1990). In early human history, life was short. Because people died young, if the group were to survive, women had to give birth to many children. This brought severe consequences for women. To survive, an infant needed a nursing mother. If there were no woman to nurse the child, it died. With a child at her breast or in her uterus, or one carried on her hip or on her back, women were not able to stay away from camp for as long as the men could. They also had to move slower. Around

patriarchy men-as-a-group dominating women-as-a-group; authority is vested in males

A theory of how *patriarchy* originated centers on childbirth. Because only women give birth, they assumed tasks associated with home and child care, while men hunted and performed other survival tasks that required greater strength, speed, and absence from home. This photo was taken in Bangladesh.

the world, then, women assumed the tasks that were associated with the home and child care, while men hunted the large animals and did other tasks that required greater speed and longer absences from the base camp (Huber 1990).

This led to men becoming dominant. When the men left the camp to hunt animals, they made contact with other groups. They traded with them, gaining new possessions—and they also quarreled and waged war with them. It was also the men who made and controlled the instruments of power and death, the weapons that were used for hunting and warfare. The men heaped prestige upon themselves as they returned triumphantly to the camp, leading captured prisoners and displaying their new possessions or the large animals they had killed to feed themselves and the women and children.

Contrast this with the women's activities, which were routine, dull, and taken for granted. The women kept the fire going, took care of the children, and did the cooking. There was nothing triumphant about what they did—and they were not perceived as risking their lives for the group. The women were "simply there," awaiting the return of their men, ready to acclaim their accomplishments.

Men, then, took control of society. Their sources of power were their weapons, items of trade, and the knowledge they gained from their contact with other groups. Women did not have access to these sources of power, which the men enshrouded in secrecy. The women became second-class citizens, subject to whatever the men decided.

Hand-to-Hand Combat. The *second* theory is short and simple, built around warfare and body strength. Anthropologist Marvin Harris (1977) pointed out that tribal groups did a lot of fighting with one another. Their warfare was personal and bloody. Unlike today, their battles were hand to hand, with groups fighting fiercely, trying to kill one another with clubs, stones, spears, and arrows. And when these weapons failed, they hit and strangled one another.

It is obvious, said Harris, that women were at a disadvantage in hand-to-hand combat. Because most men are stronger than most women, men became the warriors. And the women? The men needed strong motivation to risk their lives in combat, rather than just running into the bush when an enemy attacked. The women became the reward that enticed men to risk their lives in battle. The bravest men were allowed more wives—from the women at home and the women they captured. The women were valued for sex, labor, and reproduction.

Which One? Is either theory correct—the one built around human reproduction or the one built around warfare? With the answer buried in human history, there is no way to test these theories. Male dominance could even be the result of some entirely different cause. Gerda Lerner (1986) suggests that patriarchy could have had different origins in different places.

Continuing Dominance. We don't know the origins of patriarchy, then, but whatever its origins, a circular system of thinking evolved. Men came to think of themselves as inherently superior. And the evidence for their superiority? Their domination of society. (You can see how circular this reasoning is: Men dominate society because they are superior, and they know they are superior because they dominate society.) The men enshrouded many of their activities with secrecy and constructed rules and rituals to avoid "contamination" by females, whom they came to view as inferior. Even today, patriarchy is always accompanied by cultural supports designed to justify male dominance. A common support is to designate certain activities as "not appropriate" for women, such as playing football, driving race cars, mining coal, or being a soldier or astronaut.

Tribal societies eventually developed into larger groups, and the hunting and hand-to-hand combat ceased to be routine. Did the men then celebrate the end of their risky hunting and fighting and welcome the women as equals? You know the answer. Men enjoyed their power and privileges, and they didn't want to give them up. Male dominance in contemporary societies, then, is a continuation of a millennia-old pattern whose origin is lost in history.

Sex Typing of Work

Anthropologist George Murdock (1937) analyzed data that researchers had reported on 324 societies around the world. He found that all of them have *sex typed work*. In other words, every society associates certain work with one sex or the other. He also found that activities considered "female" in one society may be considered "male" in another. In some groups, for example, taking care of cattle is women's work, while other groups assign this task to men.

Vedda hunters in Sri Lanka. Anthropologist George Murdock surveyed 324 traditional societies worldwide. In all of them, some work was considered "men's work," while other tasks were considered "women's work." He found that hunting is almost universally considered "men's work."

There was one exception, metalworking, which was considered men's work in all of the societies that Murdock examined. Making weapons, pursuing sea mammals, and hunting came close to being exclusively male activities, but there were a few exceptions. Although Murdock discovered no specific work that was universally assigned only to women, he did find that making clothing, cooking, carrying water, and grinding grain were almost always female tasks. In a few societies, however, such activities were regarded as men's work.

From Murdock's cross-cultural survey, we can conclude that nothing about biology requires men and women to be assigned different work. Anatomy does not have to equal destiny when it comes to occupations; as we have seen, pursuits that are considered feminine in one society may be deemed masculine in another, and vice versa. The photo essay on the next two pages showing women at work in India underscores this point.

Gender and the Prestige of Work

Read on **MySocLab**
Document: Sex Segregation in the U.S. Labor Force

You might ask whether dividing work by sex really illustrates social inequality. Perhaps it simply represents each group's arbitrary ways of deciding how to do work, not gender discrimination?

This could be the case, except for this finding: *Universally, greater prestige is given to male activities—regardless of what those activities are* (Linton 1936; Rosaldo 1974). If taking care of goats is men's work, then the care of goats is considered important and carries high prestige, but if it is women's work, it is considered less important and given less prestige. Let's take an example closer to home. When delivering babies was "women's work" done by midwives, it was given low prestige. But when men took over this task, they became "baby doctors" with high prestige (Ehrenreich and English 1973; Rothman 1994). In short, *it is not the work that provides the prestige, but the sex with which the work is associated.*

Other Areas of Global Discrimination

Let's briefly consider four additional aspects of global gender discrimination. Later, when we focus on the United States, we will examine these topics in greater detail.

THROUGH THE AUTHOR'S LENS

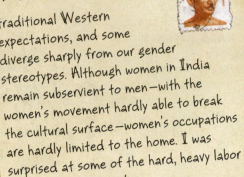

Work and Gender: Women at Work in India

Traveling through India was both a pleasant and an eye-opening experience. The country is incredibly diverse, the people friendly, and the land culturally rich. For this photo essay, wherever I went—whether city, village, or countryside—I took photos of women at work.

From these photos, you can see that Indian women work in a wide variety of occupations. Some of their jobs match traditional Western expectations, and some diverge sharply from our gender stereotypes. Although women in India remain subservient to men—with the women's movement hardly able to break the cultural surface—women's occupations are hardly limited to the home. I was surprised at some of the hard, heavy labor that Indian women do.

The villages of India have no indoor plumbing. Instead, each village has a well with a hand pump, and it is the women's job to fetch the water. This is backbreaking work, for, after pumping the water, the women wrestle the heavy buckets onto their heads and carry them home. This was one of the few kinds of work I saw that was limited to women.

Indian women are highly visible in public places. A storekeeper is as likely to be a woman as a man. This woman is selling glasses of water at a beach on the Bay of Bengal. The structure on which her glasses rest is built of sand.

I visited quarries in different parts of India, where I found men, women, and children hard at work in the tropical sun. This woman works 8 ½ hours a day, six days a week. She earns 40 rupees a day (about ninety cents). Men make 60 rupees a day (about $1.35). Like many quarry workers, this woman is a bonded laborer. She must give half of her wages to her master.

Women also take care of livestock. It looks as though this woman dressed up and posed for her photo, but this is what she was wearing and doing when I saw her in the field and stopped to talk to her. While the sheep are feeding, her job is primarily to "be" there, to make certain the sheep don't wander off or that no one steals them.

Sweeping the house is traditional work for Western women. So it is in India, but the sweeping has been extended to areas outside the home. These women are sweeping a major intersection in Chennai. When the traffic light changes here, the women will continue sweeping, with the drivers swerving around them. This was one of the few occupations that seems to be limited to women.

As in the West, food preparation in India is traditional women's work. Here, however, food preparation takes an unexpected twist. Having poured rice from the 60-pound sack onto the floor, these women in Chittoor search for pebbles or other foreign objects that might be in the rice.

When I saw this unusual sight, I had to stop and talk to the workers. From historical pictures, I knew that belt-driven machines were common on U.S. farms 100 years ago. This one in Tamil Nadu processes sugar cane. The woman feeds sugar cane into the machine, which disgorges the stalks on one side and sugar cane juice on the other.

This woman belongs to the Dhobi subcaste, whose occupation is washing clothes. She stands waist deep at this same spot doing the same thing day after day. The banks of this canal in Hyderabad are lined with men and women of her caste, who are washing linens for hotels and clothing for more well-to-do families.

A common sight in India is women working on construction crews. As they work on buildings and on highways, they mix cement, unload trucks, carry rubble, and, following Indian culture, carry loads of bricks atop their heads. This photo was taken in Raipur, Chhattisgarh.

The Global Gap in Education. Almost 1 billion adults around the world cannot read; two-thirds are women (UNESCO 2012). Illiteracy is especially common in Africa and the Middle East, although certainly not limited to those areas. In North America, only about half of the women in Haiti can read and write. As bad as these totals are, they underestimate the problem. Some people are counted as literate if they can write their names (Falkenberg 2008).

The Global Gap in Politics. It is typical for women to be underrepresented in politics. On average, women make up just 20 percent of the world's national legislative bodies. At 18 percent, the United States is below the average. The United States has the same percentage as Asia, but is below Africa and Europe (Inter-Parliamentary Union 2013). In 2008, Rwanda became the first country in the world to elect more women (56 percent) than men to its national legislature (Pflanz 2008).

The Global Gap in Pay. In every nation, women earn less than men. As we will see later, full-time working women in the United States average only 72 percent of what men make. (If you want to jump ahead, go to Figure 11.8 on page 312.) In some countries, women make much less than this.

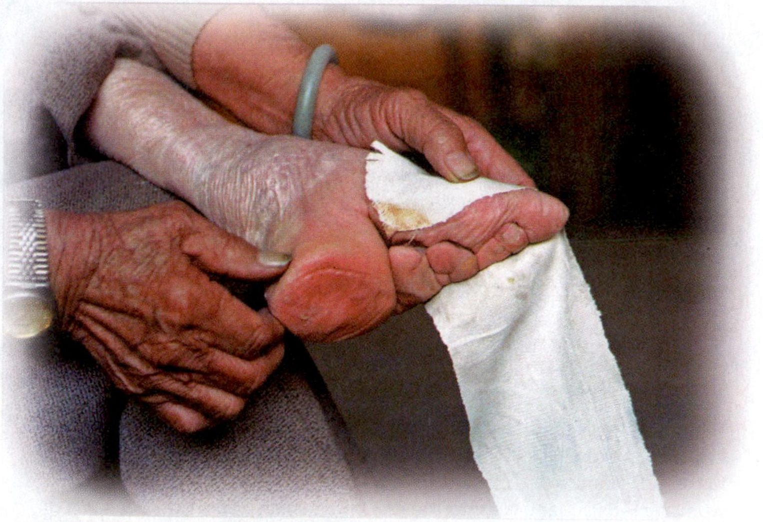

Photo of Xiao Xiuxiang, taken in 2002. Tiny feet were a status symbol. Making it difficult for a woman to walk; small feet indicated that a woman's husband did not need his wife's labor. To make the feet even smaller, sometimes the baby's feet were broken and wrapped tightly. Some baby's toes were cut off. Footbinding was banned by the Chinese government in 1911, but continued to be practiced in some places for several decades.

Global Violence against Women. A global human rights issue is violence against women. Historical examples include foot binding in China, witch burning in Europe, and, in India, *suttee,* burning the living widow with the body of her dead husband. Today, we have rape, wife beating, female infanticide, and the kidnapping of women to be brides. There is also forced prostitution, which was probably the case in our opening vignette. Another notorious example is female circumcision, the topic of the Cultural Diversity box on the next page.

"Honor killings" are another form of violence against women (Yardley 2010). In some societies, such as India, Jordan, Kurdistan, and Pakistan, a woman who is thought to have brought disgrace on her family is killed by a male relative—usually a brother or her husband, but sometimes her father or uncles. What threat to a family's honor can be so severe that a man would kill his own daughter, wife, or sister? The usual reason is sex outside of marriage. Virginity at marriage is so prized in these societies that even a woman who has been raped is in danger of becoming the victim of an honor killing (Zoepf 2007; Falkenberg 2008). Killing the girl or woman—even one's own sister or mother—removes the "stain" she has brought to the family and restores its honor in the community. Sharing this view, the police generally ignore honor killings, viewing them as private family matters.

In Sum: Gender inequality is not some accidental, hit-or-miss affair. Rather, each society's institutions work together to maintain the group's particular forms of inequality. Customs, often venerated throughout history, both justify and maintain these arrangements. In some cases, the prejudice and discrimination directed at females is so extreme that it results in their enslavement and death.

11.3 Review the rise of feminism; summarize gender inequality in everyday life, health care, and education.

Gender Inequality in the United States

As we review gender inequality in the United States, let's begin by taking a brief look at how change in this vital area of social life came about.

Cultural Diversity **around the World**

Female Circumcision

"Lie down there," the excisor suddenly said to me [when I was 12], pointing to a mat on the ground. No sooner had I laid down than I felt my frail, thin legs grasped by heavy hands and pulled wide apart. . . . Two women on each side of me pinned me to the ground . . . I underwent the ablation of the labia minor and then of the clitoris. The operation seemed to go on forever. I was in the throes of agony, torn apart both physically and psychologically. It was the rule that girls of my age did not weep in this situation. I broke the rule. I cried and screamed with pain . . . !

Afterwards they forced me, not only to walk back to join the other girls who had already been excised, but to dance with them. I was doing my best, but then I fainted. . . . It was a month before I was completely healed. When I was better, everyone mocked me, as I hadn't been brave, they said. (Walker and Parmar 1993:107–108)

Worldwide, about 140 million females have been circumcised, mostly in Muslim Africa and in some parts of Malaysia and Indonesia (Lazaro 2011). In Egypt and Indonesia, about 95 percent of the women have been circumcised (Slackman 2007; Leopold 2012). In most cultures, the surgery takes place between the ages of 4 and 8, but in some, it is not performed until the girls reach adolescence. Because the surgery is usually done without anesthesia, the pain is excruciating and adults hold the girls down. In urban areas, physicians sometimes perform the operation; in rural areas, a neighborhood woman usually does it, often with a razor blade.

In some cultures, only the girl's clitoris is cut off; in others, more is removed. In Sudan, the Nubians cut away most of the girl's genitalia, then sew together the outer edges. They bind the girl's legs from her ankles to her waist for several weeks while scar tissue closes up the vagina. They leave a small opening the diameter of a pencil for the passage of urine and menstrual fluids. When a woman marries, the opening is cut wider to permit sexual intercourse. Before she gives birth, the opening is enlarged further. After birth, the vagina is again sutured shut. This cycle of surgically closing and opening begins anew with each birth.

Why are girls circumcised? Some groups believe that it reduces sexual desire, making it more likely that a woman will be a virgin at marriage and, afterward, remain faithful to her husband. Others think that women can't bear children if they aren't circumcised.

Feminists have campaigned against female circumcision, calling it a form of ritual torture to control female sexuality. They point out that men dominate the societies that practice it.

An excisor (cutter) in Uganda holding the razor blades she is about to use to circumcise teenage girls.

Change is on the way. Responding to a social movement to ban female circumcision, the World Health Organization has declared that female circumcision is a human rights issue. Fifteen African countries have made the circumcision of females illegal. Without sanctions, though, these laws accomplish little. Egypt prohibited female circumcision in 1996, but almost all girls continue to be circumcised (Leopold 2012).

Some mothers and grandmothers even insist that this custom continue. Their concern is that their daughters marry well, and in some of these societies, uncircumcised women are considered impure and are not allowed to marry.

Health workers have hit upon a strategy that is meeting with some success. To overcome resistance to change, they begin by teaching village women about germs and hygiene. They then trace the women's current health problems such as incontinence to female circumcision. When enough support has been gained, an entire village will publicly abandon the practice. As other villages do the same, the lack of circumcision no longer remains an obstacle to marriage.

Sources: As cited, and Lightfoot-Klein 1989; Merwine 1993; Chalkley 1997; Tuhus-Dubrow 2007; UNIFEM 2008; Lazaro 2011; Sacirbey 2012.

For Your Consideration

➔ Do you think that the members of one culture have the right to judge the customs of another culture as inferior or wrong and to then try to get rid of them? If so, under what circumstances? What makes us right and them wrong?

➔ Let's go further. Some are trying to ban the circumcision of boys. Already, one court in Germany has ruled that the circumcision of boys "amounts to bodily harm even if the parents consent to the circumcision" ("German Court . . ." 2012). Do you think the same principle should apply to both female and male circumcision? Why or why not?

feminism the philosophy that men and women should be politically, economically, and socially equal; organized activities on behalf of this principle

Watch on **MySocLab**
Video: Feminism - The F Word

Fighting Back: The Rise of Feminism

In the early history of the United States, the second-class status of women was taken for granted. A husband and wife were legally one person—him (Chafetz and Dworkin 1986). Women could not vote, buy property in their own names, make legal contracts, or serve on juries. How could relationships have changed so much in the last hundred years that these examples sound like fiction?

A central lesson of conflict theory is that power yields privilege. Like a magnet, power draws society's best resources to the elite. Because men tenaciously held onto their privileges and used social institutions to maintain their dominance, basic rights for women came only through prolonged and bitter struggle.

Feminism—the view that biology is not destiny, that stratification by gender is wrong and should be resisted, and that men and women should be equal—met with strong opposition, both by men who had privilege to lose and by women who accepted their status as morally correct. In 1894, for example, Jeannette Gilder said that women should not have the right to vote: "Politics is too public, too wearing, and too unfitted to the nature of women" (Crossen 2003).

Feminists, known at that time as suffragists, struggled against such views. In 1916, they founded the National Woman's Party, and in 1917, they began to picket the White House. After picketing for six months, the women were arrested. Hundreds were sent to prison, including Lucy Burns, a leader of the National Woman's Party. The extent to which these women had threatened male privilege is demonstrated by how they were treated in prison.

> *Two men brought in Dorothy Day [the editor of a periodical that promoted women's rights], twisting her arms above her head. Suddenly they lifted her and brought her body down twice over the back of an iron bench. . . . They had been there a few minutes when Mrs. Lewis, all doubled over like a sack of flour, was thrown in. Her head struck the iron bed and she fell to the floor senseless. As for Lucy Burns, they handcuffed her wrists and fastened the handcuffs over [her] head to the cell door.* (Cowley 1969)

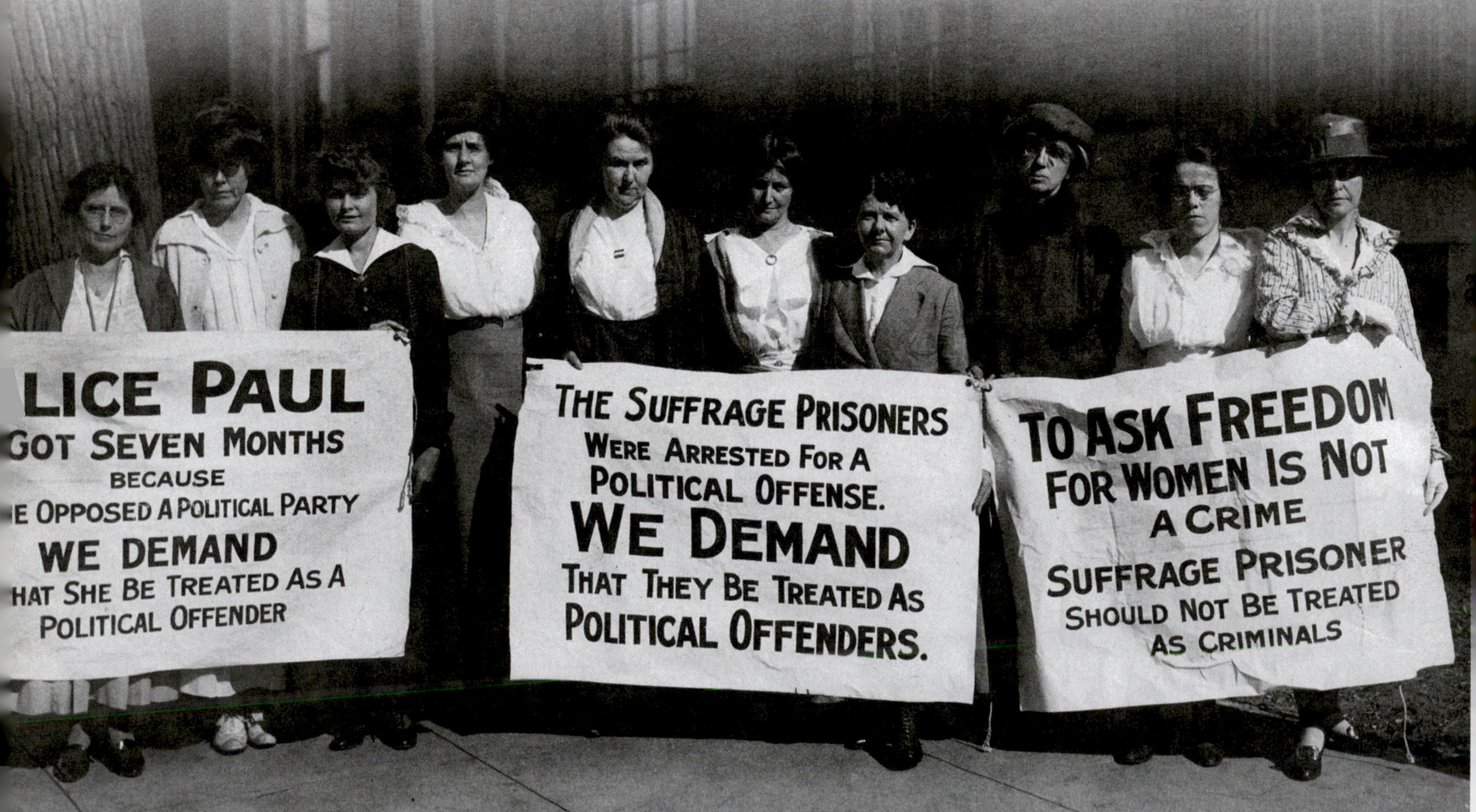
LICE PAUL
GOT SEVEN MONTHS
BECAUSE
E OPPOSED A POLITICAL PARTY
WE DEMAND
HAT SHE BE TREATED AS A
POLITICAL OFFENDER
THE SUFFRAGE PRISONERS
WERE ARRESTED FOR A
POLITICAL OFFENSE.
WE DEMAND
THAT THEY BE TREATED AS
POLITICAL OFFENDERS.
TO ASK FREEDOM
FOR WOMEN IS NOT
A CRIME
SUFFRAGE PRISONER
SHOULD NOT BE TREATED
AS CRIMINALS

The "first wave" of the U.S. women's movement met enormous opposition. The women in this 1920 photo had just been released after serving two months in jail for picketing the White House. Lucy Burns, mentioned on this page, is the second woman on the left. Alice Paul, who was placed in solitary confinement and is a subject of this 1920 protest, is featured in the photo circle of early female sociologists in Chapter 1, page 16.

This *first wave* of the women's movement had a radical branch that wanted to reform all the institutions of society and a conservative branch whose goal was to win the vote for women (Freedman 2001). The conservative branch dominated, and after winning the right to vote in 1920, the movement basically dissolved.

Inequality continued, of course, and even social science was part of the problem. In what is historically humorous, male social scientists paraded themselves as experts on the essence of womanhood. Here is what a renowned psychologist wrote, the paternalism oozing out of his well-intentioned statement: "We must start with the realization that, as much as we want women to be good scientists or engineers, they want first and foremost to be womanly companions of men and to be mothers" (Bettelheim 1965:15 in Eagly et al. 2012).

This man knew what women wanted—and in the 1960s, almost everyone else made the same assumption. From infancy, women were immersed in this idea that their purpose in life was to be "mothers and womanly companions of men." Even children's books reinforced such thinking, as you can see from Figure 11.1.

Reared with this idea, most women thought of work as a temporary activity intended to fill the time between completing school—usually high school—and getting married (Chafetz 1990). Then, as more women took jobs, they began to regard them as careers. This fundamental shift in perspective ushered in huge discontent. Women compared their working conditions with those of men, and they didn't like what they saw. The result was a *second wave* of protest against gender inequalities, roughly from the 1960s to the 1980s (Eagly et al. 2012). The goals of this second wave (which continues today) were broad, ranging from raising women's pay to changing policies on violence against women and legalizing abortion.

About 1990, the second wave gradually merged into a *third wave* (Byers and Crocker 2012). This current wave has many divisions, but three main aspects are apparent. The first is a greater focus on the problems of women in the Least Industrialized Nations

FIGURE 11.1 **Teaching Gender**

Mother and Sally
Mother can sew.
Jane can sew.
"I will help," said Dick.
"I will help you with the pigs."
Father

The "Dick and Jane" readers were the top selling readers in the United States in the 1940s and 1950s. In addition to reading, they taught "gender messages." What gender message do you see here?

What gender lesson is being taught here?

Besides learning words like "pigs" (relevant at that historical period), boys and girls also learned that rough outside work was for men.

What does this page teach children other than how to read the word "Father"? (Look to the left to see what Jane and Mother are doing.)

Source: From *Dick and Jane: Fun with Our Family,* Illustrations © copyright 1951, 1979, and *Dick and Jane: We Play Outside*, copyright © 1965, Pearson Education, Inc., published by Scott, Foresman and Company. Used with permission.

(Spivak 2000; Hamid 2006). Women there are fighting battles against conditions long since overcome by women in the Most Industrialized Nations. The second is a criticism of the values that dominate work and society. Some feminists argue that competition, toughness, calloused emotions, and independence represent "male" qualities and need to be replaced with cooperation, connection, openness, and interdependence (England 2000). A third aspect is an emphasis on women's sexual pleasure (Swigonski and Raheim 2011).

Sharp disagreements have arisen among feminists (Kantor 2013). Some center on male–female relationships. Some feminists, for example, say that to get ahead at work, women should use their "erotic capital," their sexual attractiveness and seductiveness. Other feminists deplore this as a denial of women's ability to compete with men and a betrayal of the equality women have fought for (Hakim 2010).

Although U.S. women enjoy fundamental rights today, gender inequality continues to play a central role in social life. Let's first consider everyday life, the most pervasive form of gender inequality.

Gender Inequality in Everyday Life

Gender discrimination is common in everyday life. Let's look at how femininity is devalued, something so frequent that it is often invisible, assumed as a background factor of social interaction.

Devaluation of Things Feminine. In general, with masculinity symbolizing strength and success, a higher value is placed on things considered masculine. Femininity, in contrast, is often perceived as weakness and lack of accomplishment. People are often unaware that they make these evaluations, but if you listen carefully, you can hear them pop up in everyday speech. Let's take a quick historical glance at one of these indicators. It might even be one that you have used:

> *Sociologist Samuel Stouffer headed a research team that produced* The American Soldier *(Stouffer et al. 1949), a classic study of World War II combat soldiers. To motivate their men, officers used feminine terms as insults. If a man showed less-than-expected courage or endurance, an officer might say, "Whatsa matter, Bud—got lace on your drawers?" ["Drawers" was a term for shorts or underpants.] A generation later, as officers trained soldiers to fight in Vietnam, they, too, used accusations of femininity to motivate their men. Drill sergeants would mock their troops by saying, "Can't hack it, little girls?" (Eisenhart 1975). The practice continues. Male soldiers who show hesitation during maneuvers are mocked by others, who call them girls. (Miller 1997/2007)*

It is the same in sports. Anthropologist Douglas Foley (1990/2006), who studied high school football in Texas, reports that coaches insult boys who don't play well by shouting that they are "wearing skirts." In her research, sociologist Donna Eder (1995) heard junior high boys call one another "girl" when they didn't hit hard enough in football. In basketball, boys of this age also call one another a "woman" when they miss a basket (Stockard and Johnson 1980). If professional hockey players are not rough enough on the ice, their teammates call them "girls" (Gallmeier 1988:227).

In the ghetto, too, boys are under pressure to prove their manhood, and a boy who won't react violently to an insult is said to be "wearing a skirt" (Jones 2010).

How do these insults, which roll so easily off the tongues of men, represent a devaluation of femininity? Sociologists Stockard and Johnson (1980:12) hit the nail on the head when they pointed out, "There is no comparable phenomenon among women, for young girls do not insult each other by calling each other 'man.'"

Gender Inequality in Health Care

Medical researchers were perplexed. Reports were coming in from all over the country: Women were twice as likely as men to die after coronary bypass surgery. Researchers at

Cedars-Sinai Medical Center in Los Angeles checked their own records. They found that of 2,300 coronary bypass patients, 4.6 percent of the women died as a result of the surgery, compared with 2.6 percent of the men.

The researchers faced a sociological puzzle. To solve it, they first turned to biology (Bishop 1990). In coronary bypass surgery, a blood vessel is taken from one part of the body and stitched to an artery on the surface of the heart. Perhaps the surgery was more difficult to do on women because of their smaller arteries. To find out, researchers measured the amount of time that surgeons kept patients on the heart-lung machine. They were surprised to learn that women spent *less* time on the machine than men. This indicated that the surgery was not more difficult to perform on women.

As the researchers probed further, a surprising answer unfolded: unintended sexual discrimination. When women complained of chest pains, their doctors took them only *one tenth as seriously* as when men made the same complaints. How do we know this? Doctors were *ten* times more likely to give men exercise stress tests and radioactive heart scans. They also sent men to surgery on the basis of abnormal stress tests, but they waited until women showed clear-cut symptoms of heart disease before sending them to surgery. Patients with more advanced heart disease are more likely to die during and after heart surgery.

Although these findings have been publicized, the problem continues (Jackson et al. 2011). Perhaps as more women become physicians, the situation will change, since female doctors are more sensitive to women's health problems (Tabenkin et al. 2010). For example, they are more likely to order Pap smears and mammograms (Lurie et al. 1993). In addition, as more women join the faculties of medical schools, we can expect women's health problems to receive more attention in the training of physicians. Even this might not do it, however, as women, too, hold our cultural stereotypes.

In contrast to unintentional sexism in heart surgery, there is a type of surgery that is a blatant form of discrimination against women. This is the focus of the Down-to-Earth Sociology box on the next page.

Gender Inequality in Education

The Past.

Until 1832, women were not allowed to attend college with men. When women were admitted to colleges attended by men—first at Oberlin College in Ohio—they had to wash the male students' clothing, clean their rooms, and serve them their meals (Flexner 1971/1999).

How the times have changed—so much so that this quote sounds like it is a joke. But there is more. The men who controlled education were bothered by female organs. They said that women's minds were dominated by their organs, making women less qualified than men for higher education. The men considered menstruation to be a special obstacle to women's success in education: It made women so feeble that they could hardly continue with their schooling, much less anything else in life. Here is how Dr. Edward Clarke, of Harvard University, put it:

A girl upon whom Nature, for a limited period and for a definite purpose, imposes so great a physiological task, will not have as much power left for the tasks of school, as the boy of whom Nature requires less at the corresponding epoch. (Andersen 1988)

Because women are so much weaker than men, Clarke urged them to study only one-third as much as young men. And, of course, in their weakened state, they were advised to not study at all during menstruation.

Down-to-Earth Sociology

Cold-Hearted Surgeons and Their Women Victims

While doing participant observation in a hospital, sociologist Sue Fisher (1986) was surprised to hear surgeons recommend total hysterectomy (removal of both the uterus and the ovaries) *when no cancer was present.* When she asked why, the male doctors explained that the uterus and ovaries are "potentially disease producing." They also said that these organs are unnecessary after the childbearing years, so why not remove them? Doctors who reviewed hysterectomies confirmed this gender-biased practice. *Ninety percent* of hysterectomies are avoidable. Only ten percent involve cancer (Costa 2011).

Greed is a powerful motivator in many areas of social life, and it rears its ugly head in surgical sexism (Domingo and Pellicer 2009). Surgeons make money when they do hysterectomies. The more hysterectomies they do, the more money they make. Since women, to understate the matter, are reluctant to part with these organs, surgeons have to "sell" this operation. Here is how one resident explained the "hard sell" to sociologist Diana Scully (1994):

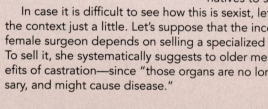

> *You have to look for your surgical procedures; you have to go after patients. Because no one is crazy enough to come and say, "Hey, here I am. I want you to operate on me." You have to sometimes convince the patient that she is really sick—if she is, of course [laughs], and that she is better off with a surgical procedure.*

Used-car salespeople would love to have the powerful sales weapon that surgeons have at their disposal: To "convince" a woman to have this surgery, the doctor puts on a serious face and tells her that the examination has turned up *fibroids* in her uterus—and these lumps might turn into *cancer.* This statement is often sufficient to get the woman to buy the surgery. She starts to picture herself lying at death's door, her sorrowful family gathered at her death bed. Then the used car salesperson—I mean, the surgeon—moves in to clinch the sale. Keeping a serious face and displaying an "I-know-how-you-feel" look, the surgeon starts to make arrangements for the surgery. What the surgeon withholds is the rest of the truth—that uterine fibroids are common, that they usually do *not* turn into cancer, and that the patient has several alternatives to surgery.

In case it is difficult to see how this is sexist, let's change the context just a little. Let's suppose that the income of some female surgeon depends on selling a specialized operation. To sell it, she systematically suggests to older men the benefits of castration—since "those organs are no longer necessary, and might cause disease."

For Your Consideration

➔ Hysterectomies have become so common that by age 60, one of three U.S. women has had her uterus surgically removed (Rabin 2013). Why do you think that surgeons are so quick to operate? How can women find alternatives to surgery?

The Change. Like out-of-fashion clothing, such ideas were discarded. As Figure 11.2 on the next page shows, by 1900, one-third of college students were women. Today, far more women than men attend college, but the overall average differs with racial–ethnic groups. As you can see from Figure 11.3 on the next page, African Americans have the most women relative to men, and Asian Americans the least. Another indication of how extensive the change is: Women now earn 57 percent of all bachelor's degrees and 60 percent of all master's degrees (*Statistical Abstract* 2013:Table 299). As discussed in the Down-to-Earth Sociology box on page 308, could it be time to apply affirmative action to men?

FIGURE 11.2 Changes in College Enrollment, by Sex

What percentages of U.S. college students are female and male?

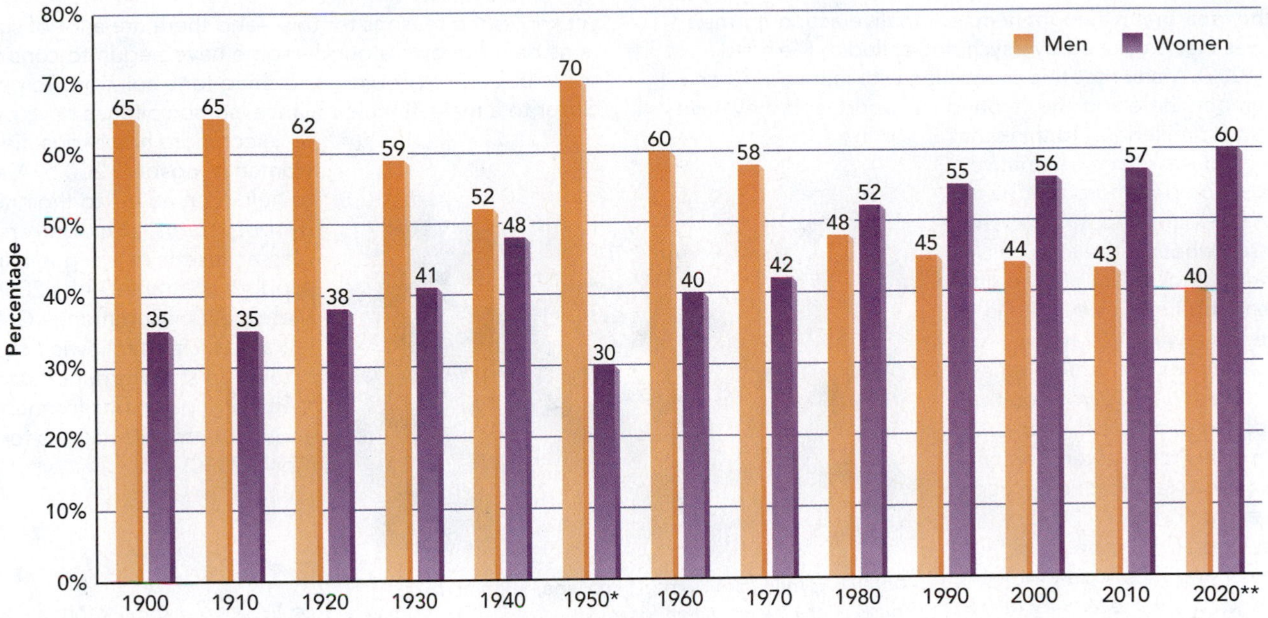

*This sharp drop in women's enrollment occurred when large numbers of male soldiers returned from World War II and attended college under the new GI Bill of Rights.

**Author's estimate.

Source: By the author. Based on *Statistical Abstract of the United States* 1938:Table 114; 1959:Table 158; 1991:Table 261; 2013:Table 278.

Figure 11.4 on page 308 illustrates another major change—how women have increased their share of professional degrees. The greatest change is in dentistry: In 1970, across the entire United States, only 34 women earned degrees in dentistry. Today, that total has jumped to 2,300 a year. As you can also see, almost as many women as men now become dentists, lawyers, and physicians. It is likely that women will soon outnumber men in earning these professional degrees.

Gender Tracking. With such extensive change, it would seem that gender equality has been achieved, or at least almost so. In some instances—as with the changed sex ratio in college—we even have a new form of gender inequality. If we look closer, however, we can see *gender tracking*. That is, college degrees tend to follow gender, which reinforces male–female distinctions. Here are two extremes: Men earn 94 percent of the associate's degrees in the "masculine" field of construction trades, while women are awarded 95 percent of the associate's degrees in the "feminine" field of "family and consumer sciences" (*Statistical Abstract* 2013:Table 302). Because gender socialization gives men and women different orientations to life, they enter college with gender-linked aspirations. Socialization—not some presumed innate characteristic—channels men and women into different educational paths.

Graduate School and Beyond. If we follow students into graduate school, we see that with each passing year, the

FIGURE 11.3 College Students, by Sex and Race–Ethnicity

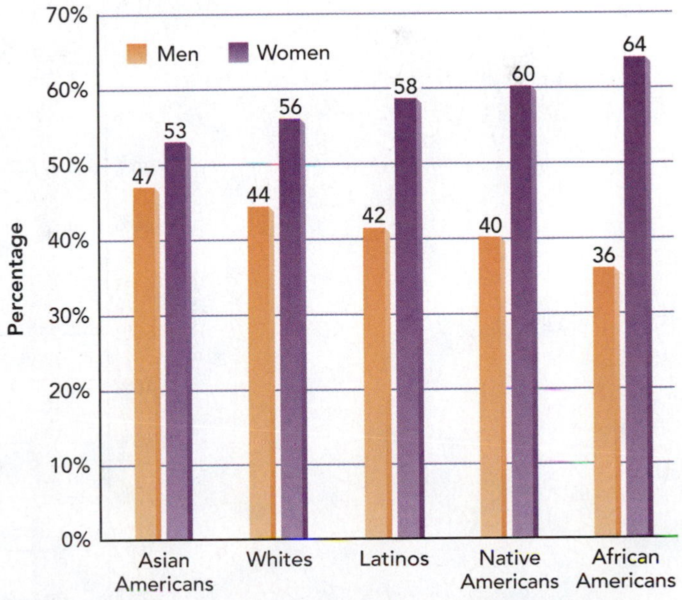

Note: This figure can be confusing. To read it, ask, What percentage of a particular group in college are men or women? (For example, what percentage of Asian American college students are men or women?)

Source: By the author. Based on *Statistical Abstract of the United States* 2013:Table 279.

Down-to-Earth Sociology

Affirmative Action for Men?

The idea that we might need affirmative action *for men* was first proposed by psychologist Judith Kleinfeld (2002). Many met this suggestion with laughter. After all, men dominate societies around the world, and they have done so for millennia. To think that men would ever need affirmative action seemed humorous at best.

But let's pause, step back, and try to see whether the idea has any merit. Look again at Figures 11.2 and 11.3 on page 307. Do you see that women have not only caught up with men but have passed them by? Do you see that this applies to all racial–ethnic groups? This is not a temporary situation, like lead cars changing place at the Indy 500. For decades, women have been adding to their share of college enrollment and the degrees they earn.

With colleges open to both women and men, why don't enrollment and degree totals match the relative proportions of women and men in the population (51 percent and 49 percent)? Although no one yet knows the reasons for this—and there are a lot of suggestions being thrown around—some have begun to consider the imbalance a problem searching for a solution. To get closer to a male–female balance, some colleges have begun to reject more highly qualified women (Kingsbury 2007). And to help men adjust to their new minority status, Clark University in Massachusetts has begun a men's support program (Gibbs 2008). Metropolitan Community College in Kansas City is following suit, setting up study groups for men, mentoring programs for men, and students associations for men (Rosin 2010).

With fewer men than women in college, is it time to consider affirmative action for men?

For Your Consideration

➔ Why do you think that men have fallen behind? What implications could this have for the future of society? Do you think anything should be done about this imbalance? If so, why? And if so, what?

FIGURE 11.4 Gender Changes in Professional Degrees

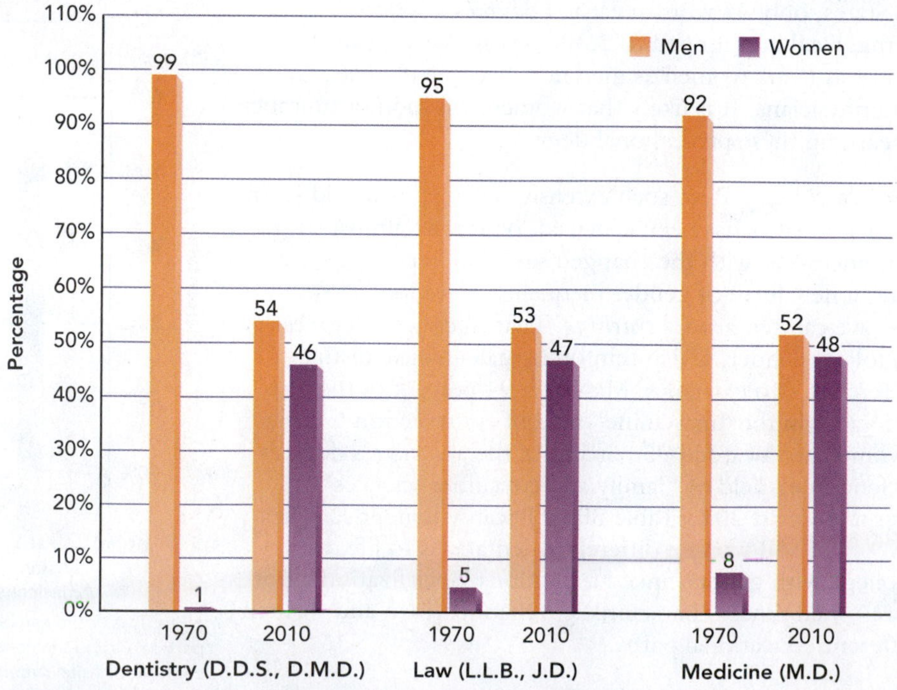

Source: By the author. Based on *Digest of Education Statistics* 2007:Table 269; *Statistical Abstract of the United States* 2013:Table 304.

TABLE 11.1 Doctorates in Science, By Sex

	Students Enrolled		Doctorates Conferred		Completion Ratio[1] Higher (+) or Lower (–) Than Expected	
Field	Women	Men	Women	Men	Women	Men
Engineering	23%	77%	23%	77%	−0	+0
Psychology	75%	25%	70%	30%	−7	+20
Agriculture	49%	51%	45%	55%	−8	+8
Biological sciences	57%	43%	52%	48%	−9	+12
Physical sciences	33%	67%	30%	70%	−9	+4
Social sciences	53%	47%	48%	52%	−9	+11
Computer sciences	24%	76%	21%	79%	−13	+4
Mathematics	34%	66%	29%	71%	−15	+8

[1]The formula for the completion ratio is *X* minus *Y* divided by *Y* times 100, where *X* is the doctorates conferred and *Y* is the proportion enrolled in a program.
Source: By the author. Based on *Statistical Abstract of the United States* 2013:Tables 821, 825.

proportion of women drops. Table 11.1 above gives us a snapshot of doctoral programs in the sciences. Note how aspirations (enrollment) and accomplishments (doctorates earned) are sex-linked. In five of these doctoral programs, men outnumber women, and in three, women outnumber men. In all but one, however, women are less likely to complete the doctorate.

If we follow those who earn doctoral degrees to their teaching careers at colleges and universities, we find gender stratification in rank and pay. Throughout the United States, women are less likely to become full professors, the highest-paying and most prestigious rank. In both private and public colleges, the average pay of full professors is more than twice that of instructors (*Statistical Abstract* 2013:Table 295). Even when women do become full professors, their average pay is less than that of men who hold the same rank (AAUP 2013:Table 5).

Gender Inequality in the Workplace

11.4 Explain reasons for the pay gap; discuss the glass ceiling and sexual harassment.

To examine the work setting is to make visible basic relations between men and women. Let's begin with one of the most remarkable areas of gender inequality at work, the pay gap.

Read on **MySocLab**
Document: Detours on the Road to Equality: Women, Work, and Higher Education

The Pay Gap

After college, you might like to take a few years off, travel around Europe, sail the oceans, or maybe sit on a beach in some South American paradise and drink piña coladas. But chances are, you are going to go to work instead. Since you have to work, how would you like to make an extra $688,000 on your job? If this sounds appealing, read on. I'm going to reveal how you can make an extra $1,435 a month between the ages of 25 and 65.

Historical Background. First, let's get a broad background to help us understand today's situation. One of the chief characteristics of the U.S. workforce is the steady increase in the numbers of women who work for wages outside the home.

FIGURE 11.5 Proportion of Women and Men in the U.S. Labor Force

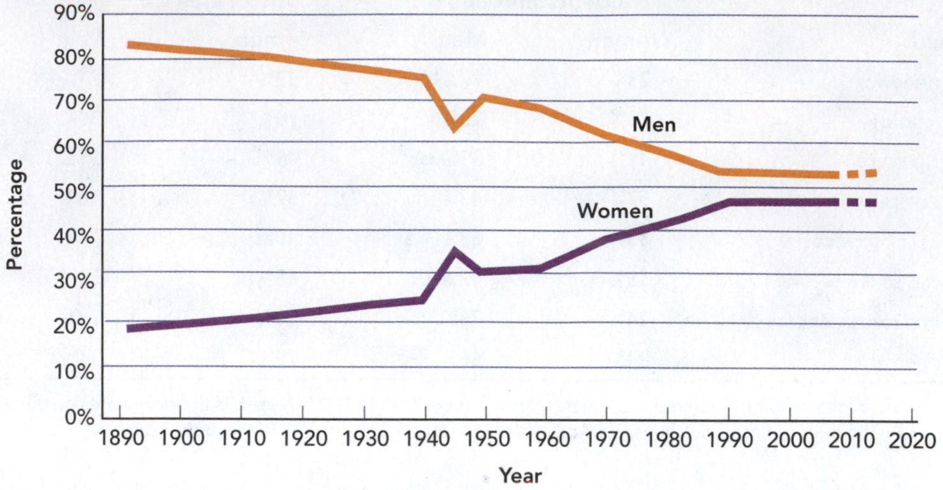

Note: Pre-1940 totals include women 14 and over; totals for 1940 and after are for women 16 and over. Broken lines are the author's projections.

Sources: By the author. Based on Women's Bureau of the United States 1969:10; *Manpower Report to the President*, 1971:203, 205; Mills and Palumbo 1980:6, 45; *Statistical Abstract of the United States* 2013:Table 597.

Figure 11.5 shows that in 1890, about one of every five paid workers was a woman. By 1940, this ratio had grown to one of four; by 1960 to one of three; and today, it is almost one of two. As you can see from this figure, 53 percent of U.S. workers are men, and 47 percent are women. During the next few years, we can expect little change in this ratio.

Geographical Factors. Women who work for wages are not distributed evenly throughout the United States. From the Social Map on the next page, you can see that where a woman lives makes a difference in how likely she is to work outside the home. Why is there such a clustering among the states? The geographical patterns that you see on this map reflect regional subcultural differences about which we currently have little understanding.

Explore on **MySocLab**
Activity: Sex and Occupation

The "Testosterone Bonus." Now, back to how you can make an extra $688,000 at work—maybe even more. You might be wondering if this is hard to do. Actually, it is simple for some and impossible for others. As Figure 11.7 on the next page shows, all you have to do is be born a male. If we compare full-time workers, based on current differences in earnings, this is how much more money the *average male* can expect to earn over the course of his career. Now, if you want to boost that difference by $28,900 a year for a whopping career total of $1,155,000, be both a male and a college graduate. Hardly any single factor pinpoints gender discrimination better than these totals. As you can see from Figure 11.7, the pay gap shows up at *all* levels of education.

For college students, the gender gap in pay begins with the first job after graduation. You might know of a particular woman who was offered a higher salary than most men in her class, but she would be an exception. On average, employers start men out at higher salaries than women, and although women advance in salary at roughly the same rate as men, they never catch up from the men's starting "testosterone bonus" (Carter 2010; Weinberger 2011; Smith 2012). Depending on your sex, then, you will either benefit from the pay gap or be victimized by it.

The pay gap is so great that U.S. women who work full time average *only 72 percent* of what men are paid. As you can see from Figure 11.8 on page 312, the pay gap used to be even worse. A gender gap in pay occurs not only in the United States but also in *all* industrialized nations.

FIGURE 11.6 Women in the Workforce

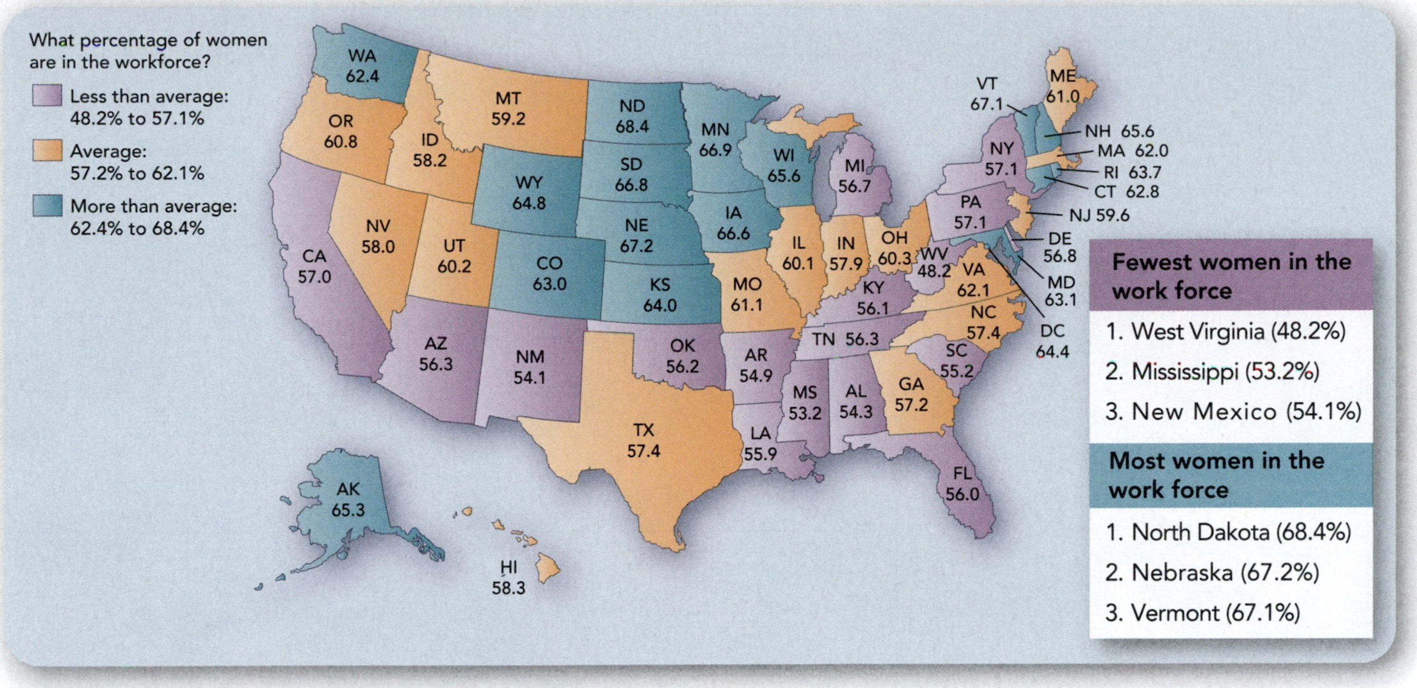

Note: This is the women's *labor participation rate*, the proportion of women of working age who are in the labor force.

Source: By the author. Based on *Statistical Abstract of the United States* 2013:Table 604.

FIGURE 11.7 The Gender Pay Gap, by Education[1]

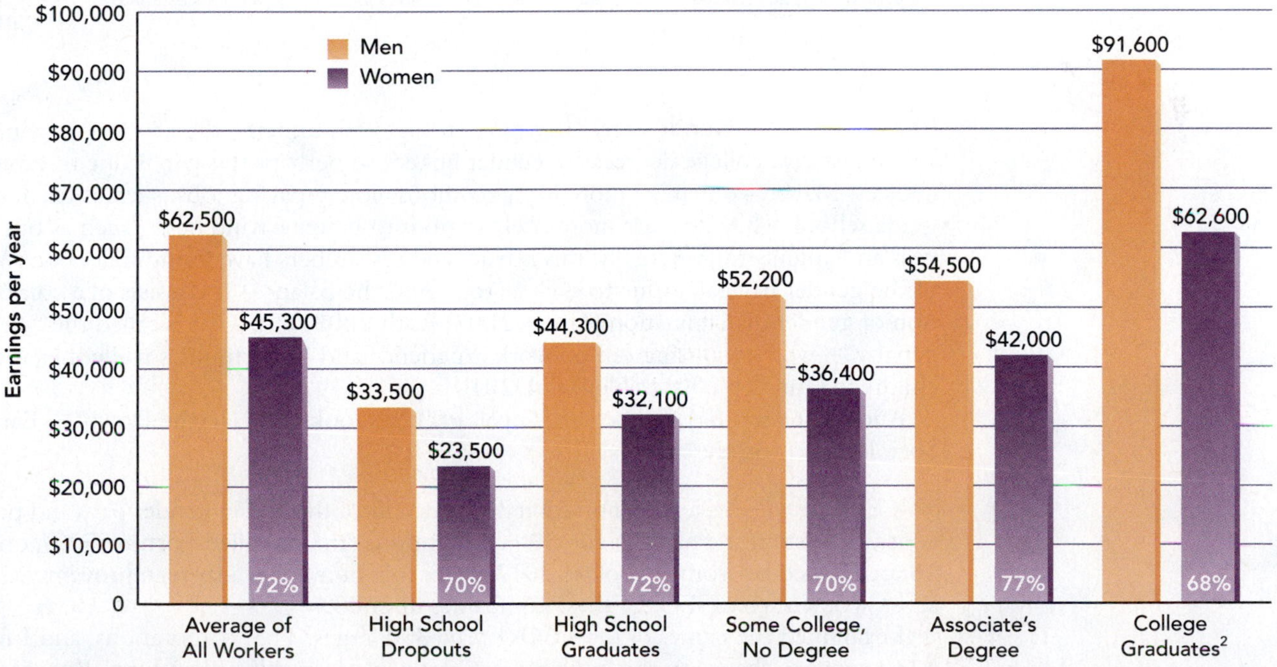

[1]Full-time workers in all fields. Dollars rounded to the nearest hundred. The percentage at the bottom of each purple bar indicates the women's average percentage of the men's income.

[2]Bachelor's and all higher degrees, including professional degrees.

Source: By the author. Based on *Statistical Abstract of the United States* 2013:Table 717.

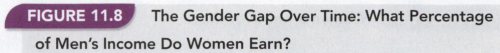

FIGURE 11.8 The Gender Gap Over Time: What Percentage of Men's Income Do Women Earn?

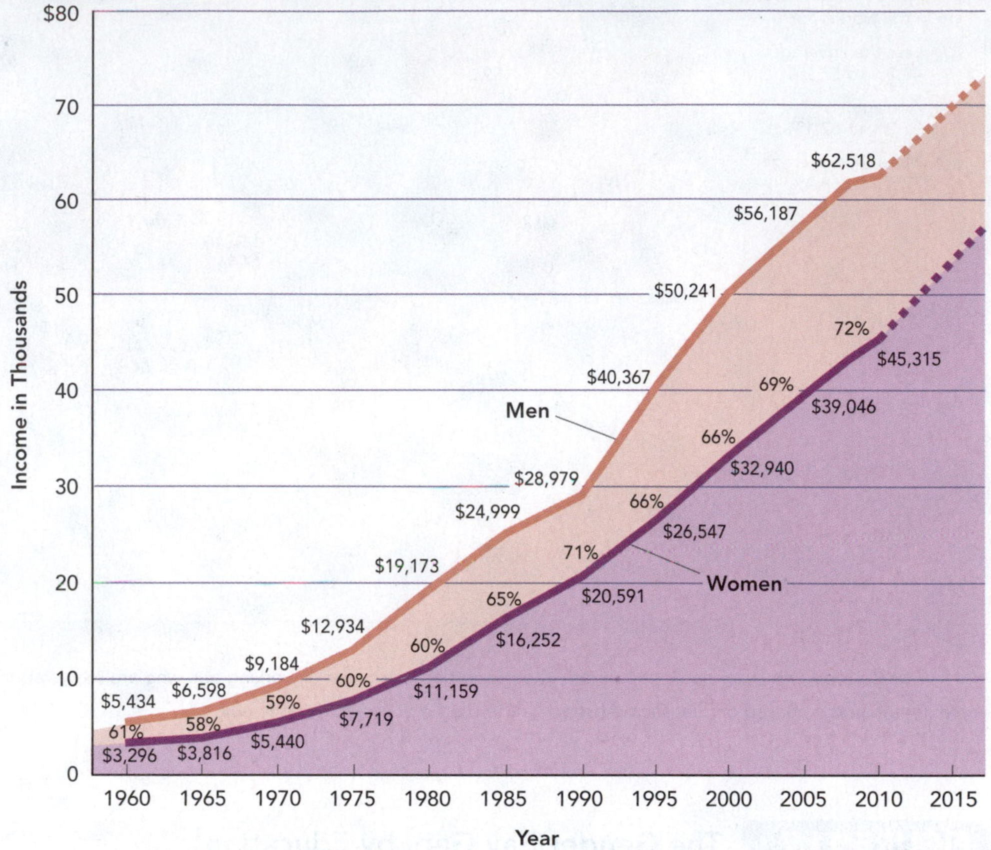

Source: By the author. Based on *Statistical Abstract of the United States* 1995:Table 739; 2002:Table 666; 2008:Table 681; 2013:Table 717, and earlier years. Broken lines indicate the author's estimate.

Reasons for the Gender Pay Gap. What logic can underlie the gender pay gap? As we just saw, college degrees are gender linked, so perhaps this gap is due to career choices. Maybe women are more likely to choose lower-paying jobs, such as teaching grade school, while men are more likely to go into better-paying fields, such as business and engineering. Actually, this is true, and researchers have found that about *half* of the gender pay gap is due to such factors. And the balance? It consists of a combination of gender discrimination (Jacobs 2003; Roth 2003) and what is called the "child penalty"—women missing out on work experience and opportunities while they care for children (Hundley 2001; Wilde et al. 2010).

Another reason has also become apparent. Let's look at this in the Down-to-Earth Sociology box on the next page.

The CEO Gap. As a final indication of the extent of the gap in gender pay (and power), consider this. Of the nation's top 500 corporations (the so-called Fortune 500), only 18 are headed by women (Bosker 2012). This low number is a large improvement! Just seven women were CEOs of these companies in 2003.

I examined the names of the CEOs of the 350 largest U.S. corporations, and I found that your best chance to reach the top is to be named (in this order) John, Robert, James, William, or Charles. Edward, Lawrence, and Richard are also advantageous names. Amber, Katherine, Leticia, and Maria apparently draw a severe penalty. Naming your baby girl John or Robert might seem a little severe, but it could help her reach the

Down-to-Earth Sociology

Applying Sociology: How to Get a Higher Salary

It will take years of united effort to overcome the powerful structural factors that hold down women's pay at work. But to increase your own pay, you don't have to wait for this to happen.

Let's apply sociology to see what steps you can take. As you just read, when college students take their first jobs, most women start at lower salaries than men do. Apart from the structural reasons such as men being perceived as more valuable workers, another factor is that women aren't as good as men at negotiating salaries. Women are more likely to accept the first offer, or to negotiate a little and be happy with the small increase that comes with a second offer (Babcock and Laschever 2008; Bennett 2012).

Why be satisfied with less? If you are a woman, remember that the first offer is usually negotiable. The hiring agent will be happy if you accept the offer, but usually is willing to add considerably to it if you negotiate strongly. Negotiating is like riding a bike. It is simply a skill that you can learn. So learn it. Read books on how to negotiate. Also, practice with a partner. Role-play until you are good at it.

Then, during your career, continue to promote yourself. You might think that the system will automatically reward hard work. It should, but things don't work this way in real life. Don't be afraid to bring your accomplishments to the attention of your supervisors. You need to show them that you deserve higher raises. If you don't, you run the risk of what you have done getting lost in the shuffle of the many accomplishments of the workers around you.

On top of this, be bold and ask for larger raises. If this makes you feel uncomfortable, then overcome that discomfort. Again, read books on how to negotiate, and practice your negotiating skills with others. (And copy this page and put it in practice.)

Does this application of sociology apply only to women? Of course not. Even though men on average are less reluctant to bring their accomplishments to the attention of supervisors and to ask for and negotiate salaries, many men also hesitate to do so. They can use these same techniques to overcome their reluctance. All workers, male and female, can hone up on their negotiating skills. It's worth the time you put into improving this skill. It can pay off in your weekly paycheck.

Sociology isn't something to be locked up in an ivory tower. Sociology is about life. As you can see, you can even apply its insights into increasing your standard of living.

For Your Consideration

➤ How do you think you can improve your negotiating skills?

➤ For practice, what partner do you think you should choose? How can you evaluate what you are learning?

➤ What other insights of sociology do you think you can apply to your career?

top. (I say this only slightly tongue in cheek. One of the few women to head a Fortune 500 company—before she was fired and given $21 million severance pay—had a man's first name: Carleton Fiorina of Hewlett-Packard. Carleton's first name is actually Cara, but knowing what she was facing in the highly competitive business world, she dropped this feminine name to go by her masculine middle name.)

Is the Glass Ceiling Cracking?

"First comes love, then comes marriage, then comes flex time and a baby carriage."
—Said by a supervisor at Novartis who refused to hire women (Carter 2010)

This supervisor's statement reflects blatant discrimination. Most gender discrimination in the workplace, however, seems to be unintentional, with much of it based on gender stereotypes.

Apart from cases of discrimination, then, what keeps women from breaking through the **glass ceiling**, the mostly invisible barrier that prevents women from reaching the executive suite? Stereotypes are part of the reason (Isaac 2012). It is common for men, who dominate leadership, to have the stereotype that women are good at "support" but less capable than men of leadership. They steer women into human resources or public

glass ceiling the mostly invisible barrier that keeps women from advancing to the top levels at work

As the glass ceiling slowly cracks, women are gaining entry into the top positions of society. Shown here is Marissa Mayer, CEO of Yahoo! as she announces Yahoo's purchase of Tumblr.

relations. This keeps many away from the "pipelines" that lead to the top of a company—marketing, sales, and production—positions that produce profits for the company and bonuses for the managers (Hymowitz 2004; DeCrow 2005).

Another reason that the glass ceiling is so strong is that women lack mentors—successful executives who take an interest in them and teach them the ropes. Lack of a mentor is no trivial matter, since mentors can provide opportunities to develop leadership skills that open the door to the executive suite (Hymowitz 2007; Yakaboski and Reinert 2011).

The Women Who Break Through. As you would expect, the women who have broken through the glass ceiling are highly motivated individuals with a fierce competitive spirit. They are willing to give up sleep, recreation, and family responsibilities for the sake of advancing their careers (Sellers 2012). Hannah Bowles (2012), who interviewed fifty women who had reached top positions of responsibility in their companies, reports that these women

1. have a great deal of confidence in their abilities;
2. set goals for themselves and measure their progress;
3. promote themselves;
4. identified "gatekeepers" to advancement and made themselves noticeable; and
5. identified a need, sold management on it, and successfully met that need.

These keys to success apply to both women and men.

sexual harassment the abuse of one's position of authority to force unwanted sexual demands on someone

And the Future? Will the glass ceiling crack open? Some think so. They point out that women who began their careers twenty to thirty years ago are now running major divisions within the largest companies, and from them, some will emerge as the new CEOs. Others reply that these optimists have been saying this same thing for years. They point out that the glass ceiling continues to be so strong that most of these women have already reached their top positions (Carter 2010).

Although crassly put by the cartoonist, behind the glass ceiling lies this background assumption.

"Of course it isn't a case of sexual discrimination. We just don't think you're the right man for the job."

Sexual Harassment—and Worse

Sexual harassment—unwelcome sexual attention at work or at school, which may affect job or school performance or create a hostile environment—was not recognized as a problem until the 1970s. Before this, a woman considered unwanted sexual comments, touches, looks, and pressure to have sex as a personal matter, something between her and some "turned on" man—or an obnoxious one.

With the prodding of feminists, women began to perceive unwanted sexual advances at work and school as part of a *structural* problem. That is, they began to realize that the issue was more than a man here or there doing obnoxious things because he was attracted to a woman; rather, men were using their positions of authority to pressure women for sex.

Labels and Perception. As symbolic interactionists stress, labels affect the way we see things. Because we have the term *sexual harassment*, we perceive actions in a different light than people used to. We are now more apt to perceive the sexual advances of a supervisor toward a worker not as sexual attraction but as a misuse of authority.

Not Just a "Man Thing." It is important to add that sexual harassment is not just a "man thing." Unlike the past, many women today are in positions of authority, and in those positions, they, too, sexually harass subordinates

(McLaughlin et al. 2012). With most authority still vested in men, however, most sexual harassers are men.

Sexual Orientation. Originally, sexual desire was an element of sexual harassment, but no longer. This changed when the U.S. Supreme Court considered the lawsuit of a homosexual who had been tormented by his supervisors and fellow workers. The Court ruled that sexual desire is not necessary—that sexual harassment laws also apply to homosexuals who are harassed by heterosexuals while on the job (Felsenthal 1998; Ramakrishnan 2011). By extension, the law applies to heterosexuals who are sexually harassed by homosexuals.

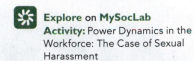

Explore on MySocLab
Activity: Power Dynamics in the Workforce: The Case of Sexual Harassment

Gender and Violence

11.5 Summarize violence against women: rape, murder, and violence in the home.

One of the consistent characteristics of violence in the United States—and the world—is its gender inequality. That is, females are more likely to be the victims of males, not the other way around. Let's briefly review this almost one-way street in gender violence as it applies to the United States.

Read on MySocLab
Document: Is Violence against Women about Women or about Violence?

Violence against Women

We have already examined violence against women in other cultures; on page 306, we reviewed a form of surgical violence in the United States; and in Chapter 16, we will review violence in the home. Here we briefly review some primary features of gender violence.

Forcible Rape. The fear of rape is common among U.S. women, a fear that is far from groundless. The U.S. rate is 0.52 per 1,000 females (*Statistical Abstract* 2013:Table 320). If we exclude the very young and women over 50, those who are the least likely rape victims, the rate comes to about 1 per 1,000. This means that 1 of every 1,000 U.S. girls and women between the ages of 12 and 50 is raped *each year*. Despite this high number, women are safer now than they were ten and twenty years ago. The rape rate in 1990 was 50 percent higher than it is today.

Although any woman can be a victim of sexual assault—and victims include babies and elderly women—the typical victim is 16 to 19 years old. As you can see from Table 11.2, sexual assault peaks at those ages and then declines.

Women's most common fear seems to be an attack by a stranger—a sudden, violent abduction and rape. However, contrary to the stereotypes that underlie these fears, most victims know their attackers. As you can see from Table 11.3, about one of three rapes is committed by strangers.

Watch on MySocLab
Video: Sexual Violence Billboards

TABLE 11.2 Rape Victims

Age	Rate per 1,000 Females
12–15	1.6
16–19	2.7
20–24	2.0
25–34	1.3
35–49	0.8
50–64	0.4
65 and Older	0.1

Sources: By the author. A ten-year average, based on *Statistical Abstract of the United States* 2004:Table 322; 2005:Table 306; 2006:Table 308; 2007:Table 311; 2008:Table 313; 2009:Table 305; 2010:Table 305; 2011:Table 312; 2012:Table 316; 2013:Table 322.

TABLE 11.3 Relationship of Victims and Rapists

Relationship	Percentage
Relative	6%
Known Well	33%
Casual Acquaintance	23%
Stranger	34%
Not Reported	3%

Sources: By the author. A ten-year average, based on *Statistical Abstract of the United States* 2004:Table 323; 2005:Table 307; 2006:Table 311; 2007: Table 315; 2008:Table 316; 2009:Table 306; 2010:Table 306; 2011:Table 313; 2012:Table 317; 2013:Table 323.

The most common drug used to facilitate date rape is alcohol, not GHB.

Males are also victims of rape, which is every bit as devastating for them as it is for female victims (Choudhary et al. 2010). The rape of males in jails and prisons is a special problem, sometimes tolerated by guards, at times even encouraged as punishment for prisoners who have given them trouble (Donaldson 1993; Buchanan 2010). A devastating finding is that about as many prisoners are raped by prison staff as by other prisoners (Holland 2012).

Date (Acquaintance) Rape. What has shocked so many about date rape (also known as *acquaintance rape*) are studies showing how common it is (Littleton et al. 2008). Researchers who used a nationally representative sample of women enrolled in U.S. colleges and universities with 1,000 students or more found that 1.7 percent had been raped during the preceding six months. Another 1.1 percent had been victims of attempted rape (Fisher et al. 2000).

Think about how huge these numbers are. With 12 million women enrolled in college, 2.8 percent (1.7 plus 1.1) means that over a quarter of a million college women were victims of rape or of attempted rape *in just the past six months.* (This conclusion assumes that the rate is the same in colleges with fewer than 1,000 students, which has not been verified.)

Most of the women told a friend what happened, but only *5 percent* reported the crime to the police (Fisher et al. 2003). The most common reason was thinking that the event "was not serious enough." The next reason given most often was uncertainty about whether a crime had been committed. Many women were embarrassed and didn't want others, especially their families, to know what had happened. Others felt there was no proof ("It would be my word against his"), feared reprisal from the man, or mistrusted the police (Fisher et al. 2000). Sometimes a rape victim feels partially responsible because she knows the person, was drinking with him, went to his place voluntarily, or invited him to her place. However, as a physician who treats victims of date rape said, "Would you feel responsible if someone hit you over the head with a shovel—just because you knew the person?" (Carpenito 1999).

Murder. All over the world, men are more likely than women to be killers. Figure 11.9 illustrates this gender pattern in U.S. murders. Note that although females make up about 51 percent of the U.S. population, they don't even come close to making up 51 percent of the nation's killers. As you can see from this figure, when women are murdered, about nine times out of ten the killer is a man.

FIGURE 11.9 Killers and Their Victims

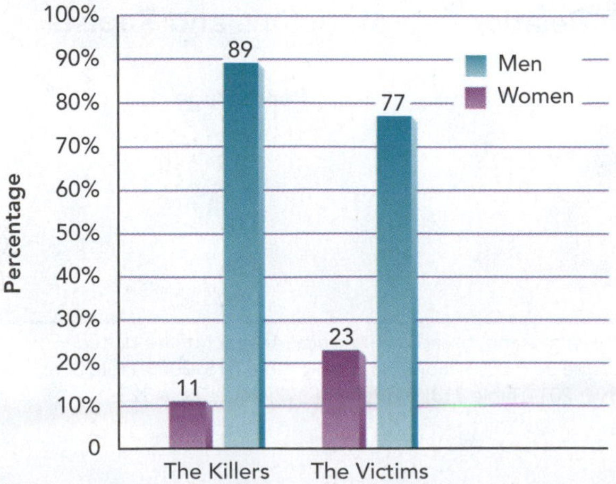

Source: By the author. Based on *Statistical Abstract of the United States* 2013:Tables 317, 338.

Violence in the Home. In the family, too, women are the typical victims. Spouse battering, marital rape, and incest are discussed in Chapter 16, pages 480–481. Two forms of violence against women—honor killings and female circumcision—are discussed on pages 300 and 301.

Feminism and Gendered Violence. Feminist sociologists have been especially effective in bringing violence against women to the public's attention. Some use symbolic interactionism, pointing out that to associate strength and virility with violence—as is done in many cultures—is to promote violence. Others employ conflict theory. They argue that men are losing power, and that some men turn violently against women as a way to reassert their declining power and status (Reiser 1999; Xie et al. 2011).

Solutions. There is no magic bullet for the problem of gendered violence, but to be effective, any solution must break the connection between violence and masculinity. This would require an educational program that encompasses schools, churches, homes, and the media. Given the gunslinging heroes of the Wild West and other American icons, as well as the violent messages that are so prevalent in the mass media, including video games, it is difficult to be optimistic that a change will come any time soon.

Our next topic, women in politics, however, gives us much more reason for optimism.

The Changing Face of Politics

11.6 Discuss changes in gender and politics.

Women could take over the United States! Think about it. There are eight million more women than men of voting age. But look at Table 11.4. Although women voters greatly outnumber men voters, men greatly outnumber women in political office. The remarkable gains women have made in recent elections can take our eye off the broader picture. Since 1789, about 2,000 men have served in the U.S. Senate. And how many women? Only 44, including the 20 current senators. Not until 1992 was the first African American woman (Carol Brown) elected to the U.S. Senate. It took until 2013 for the first Asian American woman (Mazie Hirono) to be sworn in to the Senate. No Latina has yet been elected to the Senate (National Women's Political Caucus 1998, 2013; *Statistical Abstract* 2013:Table 421).

We are in the midst of fundamental change. In 2002, Nancy Pelosi was the first woman to be elected by her colleagues as minority leader of the House of Representatives. Five years later, in 2007, they chose her as the first female Speaker of the House. These posts made her the most powerful woman ever in Congress. Another significant event occurred in 2008 when Hillary Clinton came within a hair's breadth of becoming the presidential nominee of the Democratic party. That same year, Sarah Palin was chosen as the Republican vice-presidential candidate. We can also note that more women are becoming corporate executives, and, as indicated in Figure 11.4 on page 308, more women are also becoming lawyers. In these positions, women are traveling more and making statewide and national contacts. Along with other societal changes that give women more freedom, such as more people seeing child care as the responsibility of both mother and father, it is only a matter of time until a woman occupies the Oval Office.

Hillary Clinton broke through the glass ceiling in politics when she was elected senator from New York. She also came close to being the Democratic nominee for president. She is shown here in her position as Secretary of State, meeting with Arab leaders in United Arab Emirates.

TABLE 11.4 U.S. Women in Political Office

	Offices Held by Women (Percentage)	Offices Held By Women (Number)
National Office		
U.S. Senate	20%	20
U.S. House of Representatives	18%	77
State Office		
Governors	10%	5
Lt. Governors	22%	11
Attorneys General	16%	8
Secretaries of State	24%	12
Treasurers	16%	8
State Auditors	12%	6
State Legislators	24%	1,779

Source: Center for American Women and Politics 2013.

11.7 Explain why the future looks hopeful.

Glimpsing the Future—with Hope

Women's fuller participation in the decision-making processes of our social institutions has shattered stereotypes that tended to limit females to "feminine" activities and push males into "masculine" ones. As structural barriers continue to fall and more activities are deggendered, both males and females will have greater freedom to pursue activities that are more compatible with their abilities and desires as individuals.

As females and males develop a new consciousness both of their capacities and of their potential, relationships will change. Distinctions between the sexes will not disappear, but there is no reason for biological differences to be translated into social inequalities. The potential, as sociologist Alison Jaggar (1990) observed, is for gender equality to become less a goal than a background condition for living in society.

MySocLab

Study and Review on MySocLab

CHAPTER 11 Summary and Review

Issues of Sex and Gender

11.1 Distinguish between sex and gender; use research on Vietnam veterans and testosterone to explain why the door to biology is opening in sociology.

What is gender stratification?

The term **gender stratification** refers to unequal access to property, power, and prestige on the basis of sex. Each society establishes a structure that, on the basis of sex and gender, opens and closes doors to its privileges. P. 288.

How do sex and gender differ?

Sex refers to biological distinctions between males and females. It consists of both primary and secondary sex characteristics. **Gender**, in contrast, is what a society considers proper behaviors and attitudes for its male and female members. Sex physically distinguishes males from females; gender refers to what people call "masculine" and "feminine." Pp. 288–291.

Why do the behaviors of males and females differ?

The "nature versus nurture" debate refers to whether differences in the behaviors of males and females are caused by inherited (biological) or learned (cultural) characteristics. Almost all sociologists take the side of nurture. In recent years, however, sociologists have begun to cautiously open the door to biology. Pp. 289–293.

Gender Inequality in Global Perspective

11.2 Discuss the origin of gender discrimination, sex typing of work, gender and the prestige of work, and global aspects of pay, violence, and education.

Is gender stratification universal?

George Murdock surveyed information on tribal societies and found that all of them have sex-linked activities and give greater prestige to male activities. **Patriarchy**, or male dominance, appears to be universal. Besides work, male dominance is seen in education, politics, and everyday life. P. 294.

How did females become a minority group?

The origin of discrimination against females is lost in history, but the primary theory of how females became a minority group in their own societies focuses on the physical limitations imposed by childbirth. Pp. 294–297.

What forms does gender inequality take around the world?

Its many variations include inequalities in education, politics, and pay. It also includes domination in the form of violence, including female circumcision. Pp. 297–300.

Gender Inequality in the United States

11.3 Review the rise of feminism; summarize gender inequality in everyday life, health care, and education.

Is the feminist movement new?

In what is called the "first wave," feminists made political demands for change in the early 1900s—and were met with hostility, even violence. The "second wave" began in the 1960s and continues today. An overlapping "third wave" is in process. Pp. 300–304.

What forms does gender inequality take in everyday life, health care, and education?

In everyday life, a lower value is placed on things feminine. In health care, physicians don't take women's health complaints as seriously as those of men. They also exploit women's fears, performing unnecessary hysterectomies. In education, more women than men attend college, but many choose fields that are categorized as "feminine." More women than men also earn college degrees. However, women are less likely to complete the doctoral programs in science. Fundamental change is indicated by the growing numbers of women in law and medicine. Pp. 304–309.

Gender Inequality in the Workplace

11.4 Explain reasons for the pay gap; discuss the glass ceiling and sexual harassment.

How does gender inequality show up in the workplace?

All occupations show a gender gap in pay. For college graduates, the lifetime pay gap runs over a million dollars in favor of men. **Sexual harassment** also continues to be a reality of the workplace. Pp. 309–315.

Gender and Violence

11.5 Summarize violence against women: rape, murder, and violence in the home.

What is the relationship between gender and violence?

Overwhelmingly, the victims of rape and murder are females. Female circumcision and honor killing are special cases of violence against females. Conflict theorists point out that men use violence to maintain their power and privilege. Pp. 315–317.

The Changing Face of Politics

11.6 Discuss changes in gender and politics.

What is the trend in gender inequality in politics?

A traditional division of gender roles—women as child care providers and homemakers, men as workers outside the home—used to keep women out of politics. Women continue to be underrepresented in politics, but the trend toward greater political equality is firmly in place. P. 317.

Glimpsing the Future—with Hope

11.7 Explain why the future looks hopeful.

How might changes in gender roles and stereotypes affect our lives?

In the United States, women are increasingly involved in the decision-making processes of our social institutions. Men, too, are reexamining their traditional roles. New ideas of gender are developing, allowing both males and females to pursue more individual, less stereotypical interests. P. 318.

Thinking Critically about Chapter 11

1. What is your position on the "nature versus nurture" (biology or culture) debate? What materials in this chapter support your position?
2. Why do you think that the gender gap in pay exists all over the world?
3. What do you think can be done to reduce gender inequality?

12 CHAPTER

Race and Ethnicity

Listen to Chapter 12 on MySocLab

Imagine that you are an African American *man living in Macon County, Alabama, during the Great Depression of the 1930s. Your home is a little country shack with a dirt floor. You have no electricity or running water. You never finished grade school, and you make a living, such as it is, by doing odd jobs. You haven't been feeling too good lately, but you can't afford a doctor.*

Then you hear incredible news. You rub your eyes in disbelief. It is just like winning the lottery! If you join Miss Rivers' Lodge *(and it is free to join), you will get free physical examinations at Tuskegee University* for life. *You will even get free rides to and from the clinic, hot meals on examination days, and a lifetime of free treatment for minor ailments.*

You eagerly join Miss Rivers' Lodge.

After your first physical examination, the doctor gives you the bad news. "You've got bad blood," he says. "That's why you've been feeling bad. Miss Rivers will give you some medicine and schedule you for your next exam. I've got to warn you, though. If you go to another doctor, there's no more free exams or medicine."

> "You have just become part of one of the most callous experiments of all time."

You can't afford another doctor anyway. You are thankful for your treatment, take your medicine, and look forward to the next trip to the university.

What has really happened? You have just become part of what is surely slated to go down in history as one of the most callous experiments of all time, outside of the infamous World War II Nazi and Japanese experiments. With heartless disregard for human life, the U.S. Public Health Service told 399 African American men that they had joined a social club and burial society called Miss Rivers' Lodge. *What the men were* not *told was that they had syphilis, that there was no real* Miss Rivers' Lodge, *that the doctors were just using this term so they could study what happened when syphilis went untreated. For forty years, the "Public Health Service" allowed these men to go without treatment for their syphilis—and kept testing them each year—to study the progress of the disease. The "public health" officials even had a control group of 201 men who were free of the disease (Jones 1993).*

By the way, the men did receive a benefit from "Miss Rivers' Lodge," a free autopsy to determine the ravages of syphilis on their bodies.

Learning Objectives

After you have read this chapter, you should be able to:

12.1 Contrast the myth and reality of race, race and ethnicity, and minority and dominant groups; discuss ethnic work. (p. 321)

12.2 Contrast prejudice and discrimination and individual and institutional discrimination; discuss learning prejudice, internalizing dominant norms, and institutional discrimination. (p. 328)

12.3 Contrast psychological and sociological theories of prejudice: include functionalism, conflict, and symbolic interactionism. (p. 332)

12.4 Explain genocide, population transfer, internal colonialism, segregation, assimilation, and multiculturalism. (p. 335)

12.5 Summarize the major patterns that characterize European Americans, Latinos, African Americans, Asian Americans, and Native Americans. (p. 339)

12.6 Discuss immigration, affirmative action, and a multicultural society. (p. 352)

Laying the Sociological Foundation

As unlikely as it seems, this is a true story. Rarely do racial–ethnic relations degenerate to this point, but reports of troubled race relations surprise none of us. Today's newspapers, TV, and Internet regularly report on racial problems. Sociology can contribute greatly to our understanding of this aspect of social life—and this chapter may be an eye-opener for you. To begin, let's consider to what extent race itself is a myth.

Race: Myth and Reality

12.1 Contrast the myth and reality of race, race and ethnicity, and minority and dominant groups; discuss ethnic work.

The Reality of Human Variety. With its 7 billion people, the world offers a fascinating variety of human shapes and colors. Skin colors come in all shades between black and white, heightened by reddish and yellowish hues. Eyes come in shades of blue, brown, and green. Lips are thick and thin. Hair is straight, curly, kinky, black, blonde, and red—and, of course, all shades of brown.

As humans spread throughout the world, their adaptations to diverse climates and other living conditions resulted in this profusion of colors, hair textures, and other physical variations. Genetic mutations added distinct characteristics to the peoples of the globe. In this sense, the concept of **race**—a group of people with inherited physical

race a group whose inherited physical characteristics distinguish it from other groups characteristics that distinguish it from another group—is a reality. Humans do, indeed, come in a variety of colors and shapes.

Humans show remarkable diversity. Shown here is just one example—He Pingping, from China, who at 2 feet 4 inches, was the world's shortest man, and Svetlana Pankratova, from Russia, who, according to the *Guinness Book of World Records,* is the woman with the longest legs. Race–ethnicity shows similar diversity.

The Myth of Pure Races. Humans show such a mixture of physical characteristics that there are no "pure" races. Instead of falling into distinct types that are clearly separate from one another, human characteristics—skin color, hair texture, nose shape, head shape, eye color, and so on—flow endlessly together. The mapping of the human genome system shows that the so-called racial groups differ from one another only once in a thousand subunits of the genome (Angler 2000; Frank 2007). As you can see from the example of Tiger Woods, discussed in the Cultural Diversity box on the next page, these minute gradations make any attempt to draw lines of pure race purely arbitrary.

The Myth of a Fixed Number of Races. Although large groupings of people can be classified by blood type and gene frequencies, even these classifications do not uncover "race." Rather, the term is so arbitrary that biologists and anthropologists cannot even agree on how many "races" there are (Smedley and Smedley 2005). Ashley Montagu (1964, 1999), a physical anthropologist, pointed out that some scientists have classified humans into only two "races," while others have found as many as two thousand. Montagu (1960) himself classified humans into forty "racial" groups.

"Race" is so fluid that even a plane ride can change someone's race. If you want to see how, read the Down-to-Earth Sociology box on page 324.

The Myth of Racial Superiority. Regardless of what anthropologists, biologists, and sociologists say, however, people do divide one another into races, and we are stuck with this term. People also tend to see some races (mostly their own) as superior and others as inferior. As with language, however, no race is better than another. All races have their geniuses—and their idiots. Yet the myth of racial superiority abounds, a myth that is particularly dangerous. Adolf Hitler, for example, believed that the Aryans were a superior race, destined to establish an advanced culture and a new world order. This destiny required them to avoid the "racial contamination" that would come from breeding with inferior races. The Aryans, then, had a "cultural duty" to isolate or destroy races that threatened their racial purity and culture.

Put into practice, Hitler's views left an appalling legacy—the Nazi slaughter of those they deemed inferior: Jews, Slavs, gypsies, homosexuals, and people with mental and physical disabilities. Horrific images of gas ovens and emaciated bodies stacked like cordwood have haunted the world's nations. At Nuremberg, the Allies, flush with victory, put the top Nazis on trial, exposing their heinous deeds to a shocked world. Their public executions, everyone assumed, marked the end of such grisly acts.

Watch on **MySocLab**
Video: Race and Ethnicity: The Big Picture

Obviously, they didn't. Fifty years later in Rwanda, in the summer of 1994, Hutus slaughtered about 800,000 Tutsis—mostly with machetes (Gettleman and Kron 2010). In the same decade, Serbs in Bosnia massacred Muslims, giving us a new term, *ethnic cleansing*. As these events sadly attest, **genocide**, the attempt to destroy a group of people because of their presumed race or ethnicity, remains alive and well. Although more recent killings are not accompanied by swastikas and gas ovens, the perpetrators' goal is the same.

Read on **MySocLab**
Document: Race Matters

The Myth Continues. The *idea* of race, of course, is far from a myth. Firmly embedded in our culture, it is a powerful force in our everyday lives. That no race is superior and that even biologists cannot decide how people should be classified into races is not what counts. "I know what I see, and you can't tell me any different" seems to be the common attitude. As was noted in Chapter 4, sociologists W. I. and D. S. Thomas (1928) observed, "If people define situations as real, they are real in their consequences." In other words, people act on perceptions and beliefs, not facts. As a result, we will always have people like Hitler and, as illustrated in our opening vignette, officials like those in the U.S. Public Health Service who thought that it was fine to experiment with people whom they deemed inferior. While few people hold such extreme views, most people appear to be ethnocentric enough to believe that their own race is—at least just a little—superior to others.

genocide the annihilation or attempted annihilation of a people because of their presumed race or ethnicity

Cultural Diversity in the United States

Tiger Woods: Mapping the Changing Ethnic Terrain

Tiger Woods, perhaps the top golfer of all time, calls himself *Cablinasian*. Woods invented this term as a boy to try to explain to himself just who he was—a combination of Caucasian, Black, Indian, and Asian (Leland and Beals 1997; Hall 2001). Woods wanted to embrace all sides of his family.

Like many of us, Tiger Woods' heritage is difficult to specify. Analysts who like to quantify ethnic heritage put Woods at one-quarter Thai, one-quarter Chinese, one-quarter white, an eighth Native American, and an eighth African American. From this chapter, you know how ridiculous such computations are, but the sociological question is why many people consider Tiger Woods an African American. The U.S. racial scene is indeed complex, but a good part of the reason is that Woods has dark skin and this is the label the media placed on him. The attitude seems to be "Everyone has to fit somewhere." And for Tiger Woods, the media chose African American.

The United States once had a firm "color line"—barriers between racial–ethnic groups that you didn't dare cross, especially in dating or marriage. This invisible barrier has broken down, and today such marriages are common (*Statistical Abstract* 2013:Table 60). Children born in these marriages have a difficult time figuring out how to classify themselves (Saulney 2011). To help them make an adjustment in college, some colleges have interracial student organizations.

Tiger Woods as he answers questions at a news conference.

As we enter unfamiliar ethnic terrain, our classifications are bursting at the seams. Here is how Kwame Anthony Appiah, of Harvard's Philosophy and Afro-American Studies Departments, described his situation:

> *"My mother is English; my father is Ghanaian. My sisters are married to a Nigerian and a Norwegian. I have nephews who range from blond-haired kids to very black kids. They are all first cousins. Now according to the American scheme of things, they're all black—even the guy with blond hair who skis in Oslo."* (Wright 1994)

I marvel at what racial experts the U.S. census takers once were. When they took the national census, which is done every ten years, they looked at people and assigned them a race. At various points, the census contained these categories: mulatto, quadroon, octoroon, Negro, black, Mexican, white, Indian, Filipino, Japanese, Chinese, and Hindu. Quadroon (one-fourth black and three-fourths white) and octoroon (one-eighth black and seven-eighths white) proved too difficult to "measure," and these categories were used only in 1890. Mulatto appeared in the 1850 census, and lasted until 1920. The Mexican government complained about Mexicans being treated as a race, and this category was used only in 1930. I don't know whose idea it was to make Hindu a race, but it lasted for three censuses, from 1920 to 1940 (Bean et al. 2004; Tafoya et al. 2005).

In the 2010 census, we were first asked to declare whether we were or were not "Spanish/Hispanic/Latino." After this, we were asked to check "one or more races" that we "consider ourselves to be." We could choose from White; Black, African American, or Negro; American Indian or Alaska Native; and Asian Indian, Chinese, Filipino, Japanese, Korean, Vietnamese, Native Hawaiian, Guamanian or Chamorro, or Samoan. There were boxes for Other Asian and Other Pacific Islander, with examples that listed Hmong, Pakistani, and Fijian as races. If these didn't do it, we could check a box called "Some Other Race" and then write whatever we wanted.

Perhaps the census should list Cablinasian, after all. We could also have ANGEL for African-Norwegian-German-English-Latino Americans, DEVIL for those of Danish-English-Vietnamese-Italian-Lebanese descent, and STUDENT for Swedish-Turkish-Uruguayan-Danish-English-Norwegian-Tibetan Americans. As you read farther in this chapter, you will see why these terms make as much sense as the categories we currently use.

For Your Consideration

➔ Just why do we count people by "race" anyway? Why not eliminate race from the U.S. census? (Race became a factor in 1790 during the first census. To determine the number of representatives from each state, a slave was counted as three-fifths of a person!) Why is race so important to some people? Perhaps you can use the materials in this chapter to answer these questions.

Down-to-Earth Sociology

Can a Plane Ride Change Your Race?

At the beginning of this text (pages 7–9), I mentioned that common sense and sociology often differ. This is especially so when it comes to race. According to common sense, our racial classifications represent biological differences between people. Sociologists, in contrast, stress that what we call races are *social* classifications, not biological categories.

Sociologists point out that *our "race" depends more on the society in which we live than on our biological characteristics.* For example, the racial categories common in the United States are only one of *numerous* ways by which people around the world classify physical appearances. Although various groups use different categories, each group assumes that its categories are natural, merely a response to visible biology.

To better understand this essential sociological point—that race is more social than it is biological—consider this: In the United States, children born to the same parents are all of the same race. "What could be more natural?" Americans assume. But in Brazil, children born to the same parents may be of different races—if their appearances differ. "What could be more natural?" assume Brazilians.

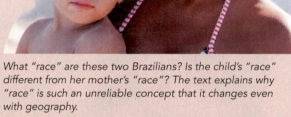

What "race" are these two Brazilians? Is the child's "race" different from her mother's "race"? The text explains why "race" is such an unreliable concept that it changes even with geography.

Consider how Americans usually classify a child born to a "black" mother and a "white" father. Why do they usually say that the child is "black"? Wouldn't it be equally as logical to classify the child as "white"? Similarly, if a child has one grandmother who is "black," but all her other ancestors are "white," the child is often considered "black." Yet she has much more "white blood" than "black blood." Why, then, is she considered "black"? Certainly not because of biology.

Such thinking is a legacy of slavery. In an attempt to preserve the "purity" of their "race" in the face of the many children whose fathers were white slave masters and whose mothers were black slaves, whites classified anyone with even a "drop of black blood" as black. They actually called this the "one-drop" rule.

Even a plane trip can change a person's race. In the city of Salvador in Brazil, people classify one another by color of skin and eyes, breadth of nose and lips, and color and curliness of hair. They use at least seven terms for what we call white and black. Consider again a U.S. child who has "white" and "black" parents. If she flies to Brazil, she is no longer "black"; she now belongs to one of their several "whiter" categories (Fish 1995).

If the girl makes such a flight, would her "race" actually change? Our common sense revolts at this, I know, but it actually would. We want to argue that because her biological characteristics remain unchanged, her race remains unchanged. This is because we think of race as biological, when *race is actually a label we use to describe perceived biological characteristics.* Simply put, the race we "are" depends on our social location—on who is doing the classifying.

"Racial" classifications are also fluid, not fixed. Even now, you can see change occurring in U.S. classifications. The category "multiracial," for example, indicates changing thought and perception.

For Your Consideration

→ How would you explain to someone that race is more a social classification than a biological one? Can you come up with any arguments to refute this statement?

→ How do you think our racial–ethnic categories will change in the future?

Ethnic Groups

In contrast to *race*, which people use to refer to supposed biological characteristics that distinguish one group of people from another, **ethnicity** and **ethnic** refer to cultural characteristics. Derived from the word *ethnos* (a Greek word meaning "people" or "nation"), *ethnicity* and *ethnic* refer to people who identify with one another on the basis of common ancestry and cultural heritage. Their sense of belonging may center on their nation or region of origin, distinctive foods, clothing, language, music, religion, or family names and relationships.

ethnicity (and ethnic) having distinctive cultural characteristics

People often confuse the terms *race* and *ethnic group*. For example, many people, including many Jews, consider Jews a race. Jews, however, are more properly

The reason I selected these photos is to illustrate how seriously we must take all preaching of hatred and of racial supremacy, even though it seems to come from harmless or even humorous sources. The strange-looking person with his hands on his hips, who is wearing *lederhosen*, traditional clothing of Bavaria, Germany, is Adolf Hitler. He caused this horrific carnage at the Landsberg concentration camp.

considered an ethnic group, since it is their cultural characteristics, especially their religion, that bind them together. Wherever Jews have lived in the world, they have intermarried. Consequently, Jews in China may have Chinese features, while some Swedish Jews are blue-eyed blonds. The confusion of race and ethnicity is illustrated in the photo on the next page.

Minority Groups and Dominant Groups

Sociologist Louis Wirth (1945) defined a **minority group** as people who are singled out for unequal treatment and who regard themselves as objects of collective discrimination. Worldwide, minorities share several conditions: Their physical or cultural traits are held in low esteem by the dominant group, which treats them unfairly, and they tend to marry within their own group (Wagley and Harris 1958). These conditions tend to create a sense of identity among minorities (a feeling of "we-ness"). In some instances, even a sense of common destiny emerges (Chandra 1993).

Not Size, But Dominance and Discrimination. Surprisingly, a minority group is not necessarily a *numerical* minority. For example, before India's independence in 1947, a handful of British colonial rulers dominated tens of millions of Indians. Similarly, when South Africa practiced apartheid, a smaller group of Afrikaners, primarily Dutch, discriminated against a much larger number of blacks. And all over the world, as we discussed in the previous chapter, females are a minority group. Because of this, sociologists refer to those who do the discriminating not as the *majority* but, rather, as the **dominant group**. Regardless of its numbers, the dominant group has the greater power and privilege.

Possessing political power and unified by shared physical and cultural traits, the dominant group uses its position to discriminate against those with different—and supposedly inferior—traits. The dominant group considers its privileged position to be the result of its own innate superiority.

Emergence of Minority Groups. A group becomes a minority in one of two ways. The *first* is through the expansion of political boundaries. With the exception of females, tribal societies contain no minority groups. In them, everyone shares the same culture, including the same language, and belongs to the same group. When a group expands its political boundaries, however, it produces minority groups if it incorporates people with different customs, languages, values, or physical characteristics into

minority group people who are singled out for unequal treatment and who regard themselves as objects of collective discrimination

dominant group the group with the most power, greatest privileges, and highest social status

Assumptions of race-ethnicity can have unusual consequences. In this photo, Ethiopian Jews in Gondar, Ethiopia, are checking to see if they have been given a date to immigrate to Israel. Because Ethiopian Jews look so different from other Jews, it took Israeli authorities several years to acknowledge that the Ethiopian Jews were "real Jews" and allow them to immigrate.

the same political entity and discriminates against them. For example, in 1848, after defeating Mexico in war, the United States took over the Southwest. The Mexicans living there, who had been the dominant group prior to the war, were transformed into a minority group, a master status that has influenced their lives ever since. Referring to his ancestors, one Latino said, "We didn't move across the border—the border moved across us."

A *second* way in which a group becomes a minority is by migration. This can be voluntary, as with the Mexicans and South Americans who have chosen to move to the United States, or involuntary, as with the Africans who were brought in chains to the United States. (The way females became a minority group represents a third way, but, as discussed in the previous chapter, no one knows just how this occurred.)

Ethnic Work: Constructing Our Racial–Ethnic Identity

Some of us have a greater sense of ethnicity than others, and we feel firm boundaries between "us" and "them." Others of us have assimilated so extensively into the mainstream culture that we are only vaguely aware of our ethnic origins. With interethnic marriage common, some do not even know the countries from which their families originated—nor do they care. If asked to identify themselves ethnically, they respond with something like "I'm Heinz 57—German and Irish, with a little Italian and French thrown in—and I think someone said something about being one-sixteenth Indian, too."

Why do some people feel an intense sense of ethnic identity, while others feel hardly any? Figure 12.1 portrays four factors, identified by sociologist Ashley Doane, that heighten or reduce our sense of ethnic identity. From this figure, you can see that the keys are relative size, power, appearance, and discrimination. If your group is relatively small, has little power, looks different from most people in society, and is an object of discrimination, you will have a heightened sense of ethnic identity. In contrast, if you belong to the dominant group that holds most of the power, look like most people in the society, and feel no discrimination, you are likely to experience a sense of "belonging"—and to wonder why ethnic identity is such a big deal.

We can use the term **ethnic work** to refer to the way we construct our ethnicity. For people who have a strong ethnic identity, this term refers to how they enhance and maintain their group's distinctions—from clothing, food, and language to religious practices and holidays. For people whose ethnic identity is not as firm, it refers to attempts to recover their ethnic heritage, such as trying to trace family lines or visiting the country or region of their family's origin. As illustrated by the photo essay on the next page, many Americans do ethnic work. This has confounded the experts, who thought that the United States would be a *melting pot*, with most of its groups blending into a sort of ethnic stew. Because so many Americans have become fascinated with their "roots," some analysts have suggested that "tossed salad" is a more appropriate term than "melting pot."

ethnic work activities designed to discover, enhance, maintain, or transmit an ethnic or racial identity

FIGURE 12.1 A Sense of Ethnicity

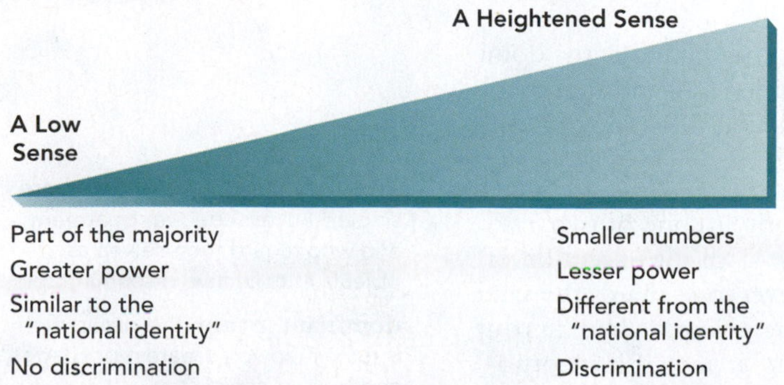

Source: By the author. Based on Doane 1997.

Ethnic Work

Explorations in Cultural Identity

Ethnic work refers to the ways that people establish, maintain, and transmit their ethnic identity. As shown here, among the techniques people use to forge ties with their roots are dress, dance, and music.

As some groups do ethnic work, they produce a mythical long-lost heritage, as in this photo of "1500s Spanish" that I took in St. Augustine, Florida.

Many African Americans are trying to get in closer contact with their roots. To do this, some use musical performances. This photo was taken in Philadelphia, Pennsylvania.

Many European Americans are involved in ethnic work, attempting to maintain an identity more precise than "from Europe." These women of Czech ancestry are performing for a Czech community in a small town in Nebraska.

Many Native Americans have maintained continuous identity with their tribal roots. You can see the blending of cultures in this photo taken at the March Pow Wow in Denver, Colorado.

The Cinco de Mayo celebration is used to recall roots and renew ethnic identities. This one was held in Los Angeles, California.

12.2 Contrast prejudice and discrimination and individual and institutional discrimination; discuss learning prejudice, internalizing dominant norms, and institutional discrimination.

Prejudice and Discrimination

With prejudice and discrimination so significant in social life, let's consider the origin of prejudice and the extent of discrimination.

Watch on **MySocLab**
Video: Racial Stereotypes and Discrimination

Learning Prejudice

Distinguishing between Prejudice and Discrimination. Prejudice and discrimination are common throughout the world. In Mexico, Mexicans of Hispanic descent discriminate against Mexicans of Native American descent; in Israel, Ashkenazi Jews, primarily of European descent, discriminate against Sephardic Jews from the Middle East; in China, the Han and the Uighurs discriminate against each other. In some places, the elderly discriminate against the young; in others, the young discriminate against the elderly. And all around the world, men discriminate against women.

Discrimination is an *action*—unfair treatment directed against someone. Discrimination can be based on many characteristics: age, sex, height, weight, skin color, clothing, speech, income, education, marital status, sexual orientation, disease, disability, religion, and politics. When the basis of discrimination is someone's perception of race, it is known as **racism**. Discrimination is often the result of an *attitude* called **prejudice**—a prejudging of some sort, usually in a negative way. There is also *positive prejudice*, which exaggerates the virtues of a group, as when people think that some group is superior to others. Most prejudice, however, is negative and involves prejudging a group as inferior.

Learning Prejudice from Associating with Others. As with our other attitudes, we are not born with prejudice. Rather, we learn prejudice from the people around us. You probably know this, but here is a twist that sociologists have found. Michael Kimmel (2007), who interviewed neo-Nazi skinheads in Sweden, found that the young men were attracted mostly by the group's tough masculinity, not its hatred of immigrants. Kathleen Blee (2005, 2011), who interviewed female members of the Ku Klux Klan (KKK) and Aryan Nations in the United States, found something similar. They were attracted to the hate group because someone they liked belonged to it. They learned to be racists *after* they joined the group. Both Blee and Kimmel found that the members' racism was not the *cause* of their joining but, rather, joining was the cause of their racism.

Just as our associations can increase prejudice, so they can reduce prejudice, the topic of our Down-to-Earth Sociology box on the next page.

discrimination an act of unfair treatment directed against an individual or a group

racism prejudice and discrimination on the basis of race

prejudice an attitude or prejudging, usually in a negative way

This photo, taken in Birmingham, Alabama, provides a glimpse into the determination and bravery of the civil rights demonstrators of the 1960s and the severe opposition they confronted.

Down-to-Earth Sociology

Living in the Dorm: Contact Theory

From your own experience, you know that friends influence one another. Much of this influence comes from talking. As friends talk about their experiences and share their ideas, they help give shape to one another's views of life.

It is no different for friends who are from different racial–ethnic groups. As they interact with one another, their understandings change and their perspectives broaden. Over time, if they cannot see the world through each other's eyes, they at least get a glimpse of what that world looks like.

If one of the goals of college is to increase students' understanding of the world and change their attitudes while helping to integrate racial–ethnic groups—and this is a big if—then why do some colleges have separate dorms for African American students, Jewish students, and so on? And when there aren't separate dorms, why do some colleges assign roommates so blacks will room with blacks and whites with whites?

The goal of such room assignments, of course, is to make minority students feel comfortable and help prevent them from feeling lost in a sea of white faces and suffering from *anomie*, feelings of not belonging.

These good intentions have an unanticipated result. As African American students interact in these "little corners" of the campus, their interracial friendships decrease. At the end of their freshman year in college, African American students have about 10 percent fewer interracial friends than when they began college. They are the only group to experience a decline in interracial–ethnic friendships.

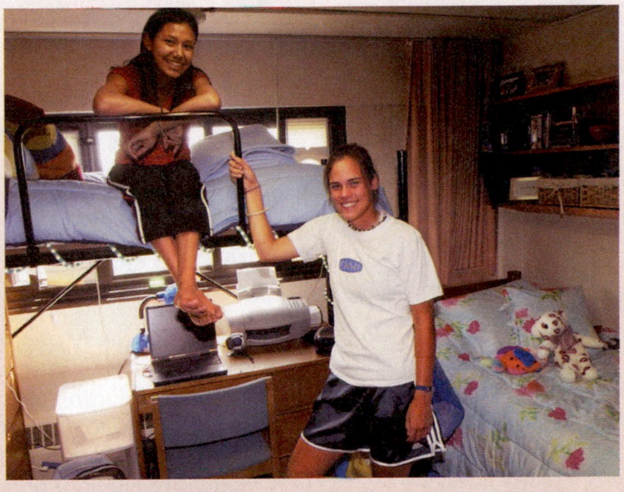

Contact theory indicates that prejudice decreases and relations improve when individuals of different racial–ethnic backgrounds who are of equal status interact frequently. These two freshmen are roommates at DePaul University in Chicago.

What happens if colleges assign students of different racial–ethnic groups to the same dorm rooms? These students end up with more interracial friendships than those who have roommates of their own race–ethnicity.

On the negative side, these mixed pairing arrangements are more likely to fail. About 17 percent end during the school year, compared to 10 percent of white–white pairings and 9 percent of black–black pairings. The dissatisfactions cut both ways, with blacks and whites requesting transfers at about the same rate.

But note that the vast majority of these interracial pairings last. They don't always blossom into friendships, of course, and like other roommate assignments, some roommates can barely tolerate one another. But contacts and cross-racial friendships do increase in most cases, changing understandings and perspectives. We need in-depth research to uncover who is changed in what ways.

To summarize the sociological research: Mutual understandings increase, prejudice decreases, and relations improve when people of different racial–ethnic backgrounds interact frequently and work toward mutual goals with equal status. The shorthand for these findings is **contact theory**.

Source: Based on Riley 2009.

For Your Consideration

➜ Do you think colleges should eliminate racially and ethnically themed dormitories? What is your opinion about colleges assigning students of different racial–ethnic groups to the same dorm rooms?

The Far-Reaching Nature of Prejudice. It is amazing how much prejudice people can learn. In a classic article, psychologist Eugene Hartley (1946) asked people how they felt about several racial–ethnic groups. Besides Negroes, Jews, and so on, he included the Wallonians, Pireneans, and Danireans—names he had made up. Most people who expressed dislike for Jews and Negroes showed similar contempt for these three fictitious groups.

Hartley's study shows that prejudice does not depend on negative experiences with others. It also reveals that people who are prejudiced against one racial or ethnic group also tend to be prejudiced against other groups. People can be, and are, prejudiced against people they have never met—and even against groups that do not exist!

The neo-Nazis and the KKK base their existence on prejudice. These groups believe that race is real, that white is best, and that beneath society's surface is a murky river of

contact theory the idea that prejudice and negative stereotypes decrease and racial-ethnic relations improve when people from different racial-ethnic backgrounds, who are of equal status, interact frequently mingling conspiracies (Ezekiel 1995). What would happen if a Jew attended their meetings? Would he or she survive? In the Down-to-Earth Sociology box below, sociologist Raphael Ezekiel reveals some of the insights he gained during his remarkable study of these groups.

Internalizing Dominant Norms. People can even learn to be prejudiced against their own group. A national survey found that African Americans think that lighter-skinned African American women are more attractive than those with darker skin (Hill 2002). Participant observation in the inner city also reveals a preference for lighter skin (Jones 2010). Sociologists call this *internalizing the norms of the dominant group.*

To study the internalization of dominant norms, psychologists Mahzarin Banaji and Anthony Greenwald created the *Implicit Association Test.* In one version of this test,

Down-to-Earth Sociology

The Racist Mind

Sociologist Raphael Ezekiel wanted to get a close look at the racist mind. The best way to study racism from the inside is to do participant observation (see pages 132–133). But Ezekiel is a Jew. Could he study these groups by participant observation? To find out, Ezekiel told Ku Klux Klan (KKK) and neo-Nazi leaders that he wanted to interview them and attend their meetings. He also told them that he was a Jew. Surprisingly, they agreed. Ezekiel published his path-breaking research in a book, *The Racist Mind* (1995). Here are some of the insights he gained during his fascinating sociological adventure:

> *[The leader] builds on mass anxiety about economic insecurity and on popular tendencies to see an Establishment as the cause of economic threat; he hopes to teach people to identify that Establishment as the puppets of a conspiracy of Jews. . . . [He has a] belief in exclusive categories. For the white racist leader, it is profoundly true . . . that the socially defined collections we call races represent fundamental categories. A man is black or a man is white; there are no in-betweens. Every human belongs to a racial category, and all the members of one category are radically different from all the members of other categories. Moreover, race represents the essence of the person. A truck is a truck, a car is a car, a cat is a cat, a dog is a dog, a black is a black, a white is a white. . . . These axioms have a rock-hard quality in the leaders' minds; the world is made up of racial groups. That is what exists for them.*
>
> *Two further beliefs play a major role in the minds of leaders. First, life is war. The world is made of distinct racial groups; life is about the war between these groups. Second, events have secret causes, are never what they seem superficially. . . . Any myth is plausible, as long as it involves intricate plotting. . . . It does not matter to him what others say. . . . He lives in his ideas and in the little world he has created where they are taken seriously. . . . Gold can be made from the tongues of frogs; Yahweh's call can be heard in the flapping swastika banner. (pp. 66–67)*

Raphael Ezekiel

Who is attracted to the neo-Nazis and KKK? Here is what Ezekiel discovered:

> *[There is a] ready pool of whites who will respond to the racist signal. . . . This population [is] always hungry for activity—or for the talk of activity—that promises dignity and meaning to lives that are working poorly in a highly competitive world. . . . Much as I don't want to believe it, [this] movement brings a sense of meaning—at least for a while—to some of the discontented. To struggle in a cause that transcends the individual lends meaning to life, no matter how ill-founded or narrowing the cause. For the young men in the neo-Nazi group . . . membership was an alternative to atomization and drift; within the group they worked for a cause and took direct risks in the company of comrades. . . .*
>
> *When interviewing the young neo-Nazis in Detroit, I often found myself driving with them past the closed factories, the idled plants of our shrinking manufacturing base. The fewer and fewer plants that remain can demand better educated and more highly skilled workers. These fatherless Nazi youths, these high-school dropouts, will find little place in the emerging economy . . . a permanently underemployed white underclass is taking its place alongside the permanent black underclass. The struggle over race merely diverts youth from confronting the real issues of their lives. Not many seats are left on the train, and the train is leaving the station. (pp. 32–33)*

For Your Consideration

→ Use functionalism, conflict theory, and symbolic interaction to explain how the leaders and followers of these hate groups view the world. Use these same perspectives to explain why some people are attracted to the message of hate.

good and bad words are flashed on a screen along with photos of African Americans and whites (Blair et al. 2013). Most subjects are quicker to associate positive words (such as "love," "peace," and "baby") with whites and negative words (such as "cancer," "bomb," and "devil") with blacks. Here's the clincher: This is true for *both* whites and blacks (Dasgupta et al. 2000; Greenwald and Krieger 2006). Apparently, we all learn the *ethnic maps* of our culture and, along with them, their route to biased perception.

Individual and Institutional Discrimination

Sociologists stress that we should move beyond thinking in terms of **individual discrimination**, the negative treatment of one person by another. Although such behavior creates problems, it is primarily an issue between individuals. With their focus on the broader picture, sociologists encourage us to examine **institutional discrimination**, that is, to see how discrimination is woven into the fabric of society. Let's look at two examples.

Watch on **MySocLab**
Video: Race and Ethnicity: The Basics

Home Mortgages. Bank lending provides an excellent illustration of institutional discrimination (Ropiequet et al. 2012). Earlier studies using national samples showed that bankers were more likely to reject the loan applications of minorities. When bankers defended themselves by saying that whites had better credit history, researchers retested their data. They found that even when applicants had identical credit, African Americans and Latinos were *60 percent* more likely to be rejected (Thomas 1991, 1992). Look at Figure 12.2 below. You can see that *minorities are still more likely to be turned down for a loan—whether their incomes are below or above the median income of their community.*

In the Great Recession that we have suffered through, African Americans and Latinos were hit harder than whites. The last set of bars on Figure 12.2 shows one of the reasons for this: *Banks purposely charged minorities higher interest rates, a practice called predatory lending.* The results were devastating. When the economic crisis hit, many African

FIGURE 12.2 Buying a House: Institutional Discrimination and Predatory Lending

This figure, based on a national sample, illustrates *institutional discrimination.* Rejecting the loan applications of minorities and gouging them with higher interest rates are a nationwide practice, not the acts of a rogue banker here or there. Because the discrimination is part of the banking system, it is also called *systemic discrimination.*

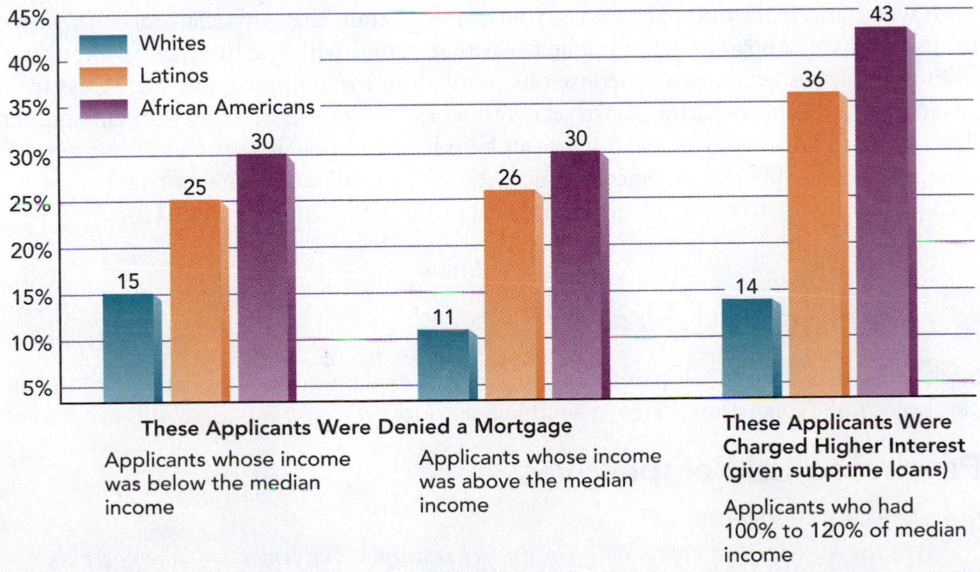

Source: By the author. Based on Kochbar and Gonzalez-Barrera 2009.

individual discrimination person-to-person or face-to-face discrimination; the negative treatment of people by other individuals

institutional discrimination negative treatment of a minority group that is built into a society's institutions; also called *systemic discrimination*

Americans and Latinos who could have continued to make their house payments if they had the lower interest rates lost their homes (Ropiequet et al. 2012).

Would nice bankers really do predatory lending? After checking data like these, the Justice Department accused Countrywide Financial, a major mortgage lender, of discriminating against 200,000 Latino and African American borrowers. Countrywide agreed to pay a fine of $335 million, the largest fair-lending settlement in history (Savage 2011).

Health Care. Losing your home is devastating. Losing your mother or baby is even worse. Look at Table 12.1. You can see that institutional discrimination can be a life-and-death matter. In childbirth, African American mothers are almost *three* times as likely to die as white mothers, while their babies are more than *twice* as likely to die during their first year of life. This is not a matter of biology, as though African American mothers and children are more fragile. It is a matter of *social* conditions, primarily nutrition and medical care.

TABLE 12.1 Health and Race–Ethnicity

	Infant Deaths[1]	Maternal Deaths[1]	Life Expectancy	
			Male	Female
Whites	5.5	10.0	75.9	80.8
African Americans	12.7	26.5	70.9	77.4

[1]The death rates given here are the number per 1,000. Infant deaths refer to the number of infants under 1 year old who die in a year per 1,000 live births. The source does not provide data for other racial–ethnic groups.
Source: By the author. Based on *Statistical Abstract of the United States* 2013:Tables 110, 118.

Discrimination is not always deliberate. In some ***unintentional discrimination***, no one is aware of it—neither those being discriminated against nor those doing the discriminating (Harris et al. 2011). Researchers studied the race–ethnicity of people who receive knee replacements and coronary bypass surgery. They found that white patients are more likely than Latino or African American patients to receive these procedures (Skinner et al. 2003; Popescu 2007). They found a similar pattern in treatment after a heart attack: Whites are more likely than blacks to be given cardiac catheterization, a test to detect blockage of blood vessels. This study of 40,000 patients held a surprise: Both black and white doctors are more likely to give this preventive care to whites (Stolberg 2001).

Researchers do not know why race–ethnicity is a factor in medical decisions. With both white and black doctors involved, we can be certain that physicians do not *intend* to discriminate. Apparently, the implicit bias that comes with the internalization of dominant norms becomes a subconscious motivation for giving or denying access to advanced medical procedures. Race seems to work like gender: Just as women's higher death rates in coronary bypass surgery can be traced to implicit attitudes about gender (see pages 304–305), so also race–ethnicity becomes a subconscious motivation for giving or denying access to advanced medical procedures (Blair et al. 2013).

12.3 Contrast psychological and sociological theories of prejudice: include functionalism, conflict, and symbolic interactionism.

Theories of Prejudice

Social scientists have developed several theories to explain prejudice. Let's first look at psychological explanations, then at sociological ones.

Read on MySocLab
Document: Color-Blind Privilege: The Social and Political Functions of Erasing the Color Line in Post-Race America

Psychological Perspectives

Frustration and Scapegoats.

"Why are we having a depression? The answer is simple. The Jews have taken over the banking system, and they want to suck every dollar out of us."

This was a common sentiment in Germany in the 1930s during the deep depression that helped bring Hitler to power. People often unfairly blame their troubles on a **scapegoat**—often a racial–ethnic or religious minority. Why do they do this? Psychologist John Dollard (1939) suggested that prejudice is the result of frustration. People who are unable to strike out at the real source of their frustration (such as unemployment) look for someone to blame. This person or group becomes a target on which they vent their frustrations. Gender and age are also common targets of scapegoating. So are immigrants.

Prejudice and frustration often are related. A team of psychologists led by Emory Cowen (1959) measured the prejudice of a group of students. They then gave the students two puzzles to solve, making sure the students did not have enough time to finish. After the students had worked furiously on the puzzles, the experimenters shook their heads in disgust and expressed disbelief that the students couldn't complete such a simple task. They then retested the students. The results? Their scores on prejudice increased. The students had directed their frustrations outward, transferring them to people who had nothing to do with the contempt they had experienced.

The Authoritarian Personality.

"I don't like Swedes. They're too rigid. And I don't like the Italians. They're always talking with their hands. I don't like the Walloneans, either. They're always smiling at something. And I don't like librarians. And my job sucks. Hitler might have had his faults, but he put people to work during the Great Depression."

Have you ever wondered whether some people's personalities make them more inclined to be prejudiced, and others more fair-minded? For psychologist Theodor Adorno, who had fled from the Nazis, this was no idle speculation. With the horrors he had observed still fresh in his mind, Adorno wondered whether there might be a certain type of person who is more likely to fall for the racist spewings of people like Hitler, Mussolini, and those in the KKK.

To find out, Adorno gave three tests to about two thousand people, ranging from college professors to prison inmates (Adorno et al. 1950). He measured their ethnocentrism, anti-Semitism (bias against Jews), and support for strong, authoritarian leaders. People who scored high on one test also scored high on the other two. For example, people who agreed with anti-Semitic statements also said that governments should be authoritarian and that foreign customs pose a threat to the "American" way.

Adorno concluded that highly prejudiced people have deep respect for authority and are submissive to authority figures. He termed this the **authoritarian personality**. These people believe that things are either right or wrong. Ambiguity disturbs them, especially in matters of religion or sex. They become anxious when they confront norms and values that are different from their own. To view people who differ from themselves as inferior assures them that their own positions are right.

Adorno's research stimulated more than a thousand research studies. In general, the researchers found that people who are older, less educated, less intelligent, and from a lower social class are more likely to be authoritarian. Critics say that this doesn't indicate a particular personality, just that the less educated are more prejudiced—which we already knew (Yinger 1965; Ray 1991). Nevertheless, researchers continue to study this concept (Solt 2012).

Sociological Perspectives

Sociologists find psychological explanations inadequate. They stress that the key to understanding prejudice cannot be found by looking *inside* people but, rather, by examining conditions *outside* them. For this reason, sociologists focus on how social environments influence prejudice. With this background, let's compare functionalist, conflict, and symbolic interactionist perspectives on prejudice.

Functionalism.

In a television documentary, journalist Bill Moyers interviewed Fritz Hippler, a Nazi who at age 29 was put in charge of the entire German film industry. When Hitler came

scapegoat an individual or group unfairly blamed for someone else's troubles

authoritarian personality Theodor Adorno's term for people who are prejudiced and rank high on scales of conformity, intolerance, insecurity, respect for authority, and submissiveness to superiors *to power, Hippler said, the Germans were no more anti-Semitic than the French. Hippler was told to increase anti-Semitism in Germany. Obediently, he produced movies that contained vivid scenes comparing Jews to rats—with their breeding threatening to infest the population.*

Why was Hippler told to create hatred? Prejudice and discrimination were functional for the Nazis. Defeated in World War I and devastated by fines levied by the victors, Germany was on its knees. Runaway inflation was destroying its middle class. To help unite this fractured Germany, the Nazis created a scapegoat to blame for their troubles. In addition, the Jews owned businesses, bank accounts, fine art, and other property that the Nazis could confiscate. Jews also held key positions (as university professors, reporters, judges, and so on), which the Nazis could give as prizes to their followers. In the end, hatred also showed its dysfunctional face, as the Nazi officials hanged at Nuremberg discovered.

Prejudice becomes practically irresistible when state machinery is used to advance the cause of hatred. To produce prejudice, the Nazis harnessed government agencies, the schools, police, courts, and mass media. The results were devastating. Recall the identical twins featured in the Down-to-Earth Sociology box on page 63. Jack and Oskar had been separated as babies. Jack was brought up as a Jew in Trinidad, while Oskar was reared as a Catholic in Czechoslovakia. Under the Nazi regime, Oskar learned to hate Jews, unaware that he himself was a Jew.

That prejudice is functional and is shaped by the social environment was demonstrated by psychologists Muzafer and Carolyn Sherif (1953). In a boys' summer camp, the Sherifs assigned friends to different cabins and then had the cabin groups compete in sports. In just a few days, strong in-groups had formed. Even lifelong friends began to taunt one another, calling each other "crybaby" and "sissy."

The Sherif study teaches us important lessons about social life. Note how it is possible to arrange the social environment to generate either positive or negative feelings about people, and how prejudice arises if we pit groups against one another in an "I win, you lose" situation. You can also see that prejudice is functional, how it creates in-group solidarity. And, of course, it is obvious how dysfunctional prejudice is, when you observe the way it destroys human relationships.

Conflict Theory.

"The Japanese have gone on strike? They're demanding a raise? And they even want a rest period? We'll show them who's boss. Hire those Koreans who keep asking for work."

This did happen. When Japanese workers in Hawaii struck, owners of plantations hired Koreans (Jeong and You 2008). The division of workers along racial–ethnic and gender lines is known as a **split labor market** (Du Bois 1935/1992; Alimahomed-Wilson 2012). Although today's exploitation of these divisions is more subtle, whites are aware that other racial–ethnic groups are ready to take their jobs, African Americans often perceive Latinos as competitors (Glanton 2013), and men know that women are eager to get promoted. All of this helps to keep workers in line.

Conflict theorists, as you will recall, focus on how groups compete for scarce resources. Owners want to increase profits by holding costs down, while workers want better food, health care, housing, education, and leisure. Divided, workers are weak, but united, they gain strength. The *split labor market* is one way that owners divide workers so they can't take united action to demand higher wages and better working conditions.

Another tactic that owners use is the **reserve labor force**. This is simply another term for the unemployed. To expand production during economic booms, companies hire people who don't have jobs. When the economy contracts, they lay off unneeded workers. That there are desperate people looking for work is a lesson not lost on those who have jobs. They fear eviction and worry about having their cars and furniture repossessed. Many know they are just one or two paychecks away from ending up "on the streets."

Just like the boys in the Sherif experiment, African Americans, Latinos, whites, and others see themselves as able to make gains only at the expense of other groups.

split labor market workers split along racial–ethnic, gender, age, or any other lines; this split is exploited by owners to weaken the bargaining power of workers

reserve labor force the unemployed; unemployed workers are thought of as being "in reserve"—capitalists take them "out of reserve" (put them back to work) during times of high production and then put them "back in reserve" (lay them off) when they are no longer needed

Sometimes this rivalry shows up along very fine racial–ethnic lines, such as that in Miami between Haitians and African Americans, who distrust each other as competitors. Divisions among workers deflect anger and hostility away from the power elite and direct these powerful emotions toward other racial–ethnic groups. Instead of recognizing their common class interests and working for their mutual welfare, workers learn to fear and distrust one another.

Symbolic Interactionism.

> *"I know her qualifications are good, but yikes! She's ugly. I don't want to have to look at her every day. Let's hire the one with the nice curves."*

While conflict theorists focus on the role of the owner (or capitalist) class in exploiting racial–ethnic divisions, symbolic interactionists examine how labels affect perception and create prejudice.

How Labels Create Prejudice. Symbolic interactionists stress that *the labels we learn affect the ways we perceive people.* Labels create **selective perception**; that is, they lead us to see certain things while they blind us to others. If we apply a label to a group, we tend to perceive its members as all alike. We shake off evidence that doesn't fit (Simpson and Yinger 1972; Drakulich 2012). Shorthand for emotionally charged stereotypes, some racial–ethnic labels are especially powerful. As you know, the term *nigger* is not neutral. Nor are *cracker, dago, guinea, honky, kike, kraut, limey, mick, spic,* or any of the other scornful words people use to belittle other groups. As in the statement above, *ugly* can work in a similar way. Such words overpower us with emotions, blocking out rational thought about the people to whom they refer (Allport 1954).

Labels and Self-Fulfilling Stereotypes. Some stereotypes not only justify prejudice and discrimination but also produce the behavior depicted in the stereotype. We examined this principle in Chapter 4 in the box on beauty (page 109). Let's consider Group X. According to stereotypes, the members of this group are lazy, so they don't deserve good jobs. ("They are lazy and wouldn't do the job well.") Denied the better jobs, most members of Group X do "dirty work," the jobs few people want. ("That's the right kind of work for that kind of people.") Since much "dirty work" is sporadic, members of Group X are often seen "on the streets." The sight of their idleness reinforces the original stereotype of laziness. The discrimination that created the "laziness" in the first place passes unnoticed.

To apply these three theoretical perspectives and catch a glimpse of how amazingly different things were in the past, read the Down-to-Earth Sociology box on the next page.

Global Patterns of Intergroup Relations

12.4 Explain genocide, population transfer, internal colonialism, segregation, assimilation, and multiculturalism.

In their studies of racial–ethnic relations around the world, sociologists have found six basic ways that dominant groups treat minority groups. These patterns are shown in Figure 12.3 on page 337. Let's look at each.

Genocide

> *When gold was discovered in northern California in 1849, the fabled "Forty-Niners" rushed in. In this region lived 150,000 Native Americans. To get rid of them, the white government put a bounty on their heads. It even reimbursed the whites for their bullets. The result was the slaughter of 120,000 Native American men, women, and children. (Schaefer 2004)*

Could you ever participate in genocide? Don't be too quick in answering. Gaining an understanding of how ordinary people take part in genocide will be our primary goal in this section. In the events depicted in the little vignette above, those who did the killing were regular people—people like you and me. The killing was promoted by calling

selective perception seeing certain features of an object or situation, but remaining blind to others

Down-to-Earth Sociology

The Man in the Zoo

The Bronx Zoo in New York City used to keep a 22-year-old pygmy in the Monkey House. The man—and the orangutan he lived with—became the most popular exhibit at the zoo. Thousands of visitors would arrive daily and head straight for the Monkey House. Eyewitnesses to what they thought was a lower form of human in the long chain of evolution, the visitors were fascinated by the pygmy, especially by his sharpened teeth.

To make the exhibit even more alluring, the zoo director had animal bones scattered in front of the man.

I know it sounds as though I must have made this up, but this is a true story. The World's Fair was going to be held in St. Louis in 1904, and the Department of Anthropology wanted to show villages from different cultures. They asked Samuel Verner, an explorer, if he could bring some pygmies to St. Louis to serve as live exhibits. Verner agreed, and on his next trip to Africa, in the Belgian Congo, he came across Ota Benga (or Otabenga), a pygmy who had been enslaved by another tribe. Benga, then about age 20, said he was willing to go to St. Louis. After Verner bought Benga's freedom for some cloth and salt, Benga recruited another half dozen pygmies to go with them.

Ota Benga, 1906, on exhibit in the Bronx Zoo.

After the World's Fair, Verner took the pygmies back to Africa. When Benga found out that a hostile tribe had wiped out his village and killed his family, he asked Verner if he could return with him to the United States. Verner agreed.

When they returned to New York, Verner ran into financial trouble and wrote some bad checks. No longer able to care for Benga, Verner left him with friends at the American Museum of Natural History. After a few weeks, they grew tired of Benga's antics and turned him over to the Bronx Zoo. The zoo officials put Benga on display in the Monkey House, with this sign:

> *The African Pygmy, 'Ota Benga.' Age 23 years. Height 4 feet 11 inches. Weight 103 pounds. Brought from the Kasai River, Congo Free State, South Central Africa by Dr. Samuel P. Verner. Exhibited each afternoon during September.*

Exhibited with an orangutan, Benga became a sensation. An article in *The New York Times* said it was fortunate that Benga couldn't think very deeply, or else living with monkeys might bother him.

When the Colored Baptist Ministers' Conference protested that exhibiting Benga was degrading, zoo officials replied that they were "taking excellent care of the little fellow." They added that "he has one of the best rooms at the primate house." (I wonder what animal had *the* best room.)

Not surprisingly, this reply didn't satisfy the ministers. When they continued to protest, zoo officials decided to let Benga out of his cage. They put a white shirt on him and let him walk around the zoo. At night, Benga slept in the monkey house.

Benga's life became even more miserable. Zoo visitors would follow him, howling, jeering, laughing, and poking at him. One day, Benga found a knife in the feeding room of the Monkey House and flourished it at the visitors. Unhappy zoo officials took the knife away.

Benga then made a little bow and some arrows and began shooting at the obnoxious visitors. This ended the fun for the zoo officials. They decided that Benga had to leave.

After living in several orphanages for African American children, Benga ended up working as a laborer in a tobacco factory in Lynchburg, Virginia.

Always treated as a freak, Benga was desperately lonely. In 1916, at about the age of 32, in despair that he had no home or family to return to in Africa, Benga ended his misery by shooting himself in the heart.

Source: Based on Bradford and Blume 1992; Crossen 2006; Richman 2006.

For Your Consideration

➤ 1. See what different views emerge as you apply the three theoretical perspectives (functionalism, symbolic interactionism, and conflict theory) to exhibiting Benga at the Bronx Zoo.

2. How does the concept of ethnocentrism apply to this event?

3. Explain how the concepts of prejudice and discrimination apply to what happened to Benga.

the Native Americans "savages," making them seem inferior, somehow less than human. Killing them, then, didn't seem the same as killing whites in order to take their property.

It is true that most Native Americans died not from bullets but from the diseases the whites brought with them. Measles, smallpox, and the flu came from another continent, and the Native Americans had no immunity against them (Dobyns 1983). But disease wasn't enough. To accomplish the takeover of the Native Americans' resources, the settlers and soldiers destroyed their food supply (crops and buffalo). From all causes,

FIGURE 12.3 Global Patterns of Intergroup Relations: A Continuum

INHUMANITY ↔ HUMANITY

REJECTION ↔ ACCEPTANCE

Genocide	Population Transfer	Internal Colonialism	Segregation	Assimilation	Multiculturalism (Pluralism)
The dominant group tries to destroy the minority group (e.g., Germany and Rwanda)	The dominant group expels the minority group (e.g., Native Americans forced onto reservations)	The dominant group exploits the minority group (e.g., low-paid, menial work)	The dominant group structures the social institutions to maintain minimal contact with the minority group (e.g., the U.S. South before the 1960s)	The dominant group absorbs the minority group (e.g., American Czechoslovakians)	The dominant group encourages racial and ethnic variation; when successful, there is no longer a dominant group (e.g., Switzerland)

Source: By the author.

about *95 percent* of Native Americans died (Thornton 1987; Schaefer 2012). Ordinary, "good" people were intent on destroying the "savages."

Now consider last century's two most notorious examples of genocide. In Germany during the 1930s and 1940s, Hitler and the Nazis attempted to destroy all Jews. In the 1990s, in Rwanda, the Hutus tried to destroy all Tutsis. One of the horrifying aspects of these two slaughters is that the killers did not crawl out from under a rock someplace. In some cases, it was even the victims' neighbors and friends who did the killing. *Their killing was facilitated by labels that marked the victims as enemies who deserved to die* (Huttenbach 1991; Browning 1993; Gross 2001).

In Sum: Labels are powerful; dehumanizing ones are even more so. They help people to **compartmentalize**—to separate their acts of cruelty from their sense of being good and decent people. To regard members of some group as inferior opens the door to treating them inhumanely. In some cases, these labels help people to kill—and to still retain a good self-concept (Bernard et al. 1971). In short, *labeling the targeted group as inferior or even less than fully human facilitates genocide.*

Population Transfer

There are two types of **population transfer**: indirect and direct. *Indirect transfer* is achieved by making life so miserable for members of a minority that they leave "voluntarily." Under the bitter conditions of czarist Russia, for example, millions of Jews made this "choice." *Direct transfer* occurs when a dominant group expels a minority. Examples include the U.S. government relocating Native Americans to reservations and transferring Americans of Japanese descent to internment camps during World War II.

In the 1990s, a combination of genocide and population transfer occurred in Bosnia and Kosovo, parts of the former Yugoslavia. A hatred nurtured for centuries had been kept under wraps by Tito's iron-fisted rule from 1944 to 1980. After Tito's death, these suppressed, smoldering hostilities soared to the surface, and Yugoslavia split into warring factions. When the Serbs gained power, Muslims rebelled and began guerilla warfare. The Serbs vented their hatred by what they termed **ethnic cleansing**: They terrorized villages with killing and rape, forcing survivors to flee in fear.

Internal Colonialism

In Chapter 9, the term *colonialism* was used to refer to one way that the Most Industrialized Nations exploit the Least Industrialized Nations (page 247). Conflict theorists use the term **internal colonialism** to describe how a country's dominant group exploits

compartmentalize to separate acts from feelings or attitudes

population transfer the forced transfer of a minority group

ethnic cleansing a policy of eliminating a population; includes forcible expulsion and genocide

internal colonialism the policy of exploiting minority groups for economic gain minority groups for its economic advantage. The dominant group manipulates the social institutions to suppress minorities and deny them full access to their society's benefits. Slavery, reviewed in Chapter 9, is an extreme example of internal colonialism, as was the South African system of *apartheid*. Although the dominant Afrikaners despised the minority, they found its presence necessary. As Simpson and Yinger (1972) put it, who else would do the hard work?

Amid fears that Japanese Americans were "enemies within" who would sabotage industrial and military installations on the West Coast, in the early days of World War II Japanese Americans were transferred to "relocation camps." To make sure they didn't get lost, the children were tagged like luggage.

This is one of two major examples of population transfer in the United States. The other is transferring Native Americans to reservations.

Segregation

Internal colonialism is often accompanied by **segregation**—the separation of racial or ethnic groups. Segregation allows the dominant group to maintain social distance from the minority and yet to exploit their labor as cooks, cleaners, chauffeurs, nannies, farm workers, and so on. Even today, in some villages of India, an ethnic group, the Dalits (untouchables), is forbidden to use the village pump. Dalit women must walk long distances to streams or pumps outside of the village to fetch their water (author's notes).

Do you recall from Chapter 9 the account of *apartheid* in South Africa, where the beaches were divided by racial groups? It was once like this in parts of the United States, too. In St. Augustine, Florida, Butler Beach was reserved for blacks, while the area's many other beaches were for whites (author's notes). Until the 1960s, in the U.S. South, by law, African Americans and whites had to stay in separate hotels, go to separate schools, and use separate bathrooms and even drinking fountains. In thirty-eight states, laws prohibited marriage between blacks and whites. The punishment for violating these marriage laws? Prison. The last law of this type was repealed in 1967 (Baars 2009).

Assimilation

Assimilation is the process by which a minority group is absorbed into the mainstream culture. There are two types. In *forced assimilation*, the dominant group refuses to allow the minority to practice its religion, to speak its language, or to follow its customs. Before the fall of the Soviet Union, for example, the dominant group, the Russians, required that Armenian children attend schools where they were taught in Russian. Armenians could celebrate only Russian holidays, not Armenian ones. *Permissible assimilation*, in contrast, allows the minority to adopt the dominant group's patterns in its own way and at its own speed.

Multiculturalism (Pluralism)

A policy of **multiculturalism**, also called **pluralism**, permits or even encourages racial–ethnic variation. The minority groups are able to maintain their separate identities, yet participate freely in the country's social institutions, from education to politics. Switzerland provides an outstanding example of multiculturalism. The Swiss population includes four ethnic groups: French, Italians, Germans, and Romansh. These groups have kept their own languages, and they live peacefully in political and economic unity. Multiculturalism has been so successful that none of these groups can properly be called a minority.

segregation the policy of keeping racial–ethnic groups apart

assimilation the process of being absorbed into the mainstream culture

multiculturalism (or **pluralism**) a policy that permits or encourages ethnic differences

Racial–Ethnic Relations in the United States

12.5 Summarize the major patterns that characterize European Americans, Latinos, African Americans, Asian Americans, and Native Americans.

Writing about race–ethnicity is like stepping onto a minefield: One never knows where to expect the next explosion. Serbian students have written to me, saying that I have been unfair to their group. So have American whites. Even basic terms are controversial. Some people classified as *African Americans* reject this term because they identify themselves as blacks. Similarly, some Latinos prefer the term *Hispanic American*, but others reject it, saying that it ignores the Native American side of their heritage. Some would limit the term *Chicanos*—commonly used to refer to Americans from Mexico—to those who have a sense of ethnic oppression and unity; they say that it does not apply to those who have assimilated.

No term that I use here, then, will satisfy everyone. Racial–ethnic identity is fluid, constantly changing, and all terms carry a risk as they take on politically charged meanings. Nevertheless, as part of everyday life, we classify ourselves and one another as belonging to distinct racial–ethnic groups. As Figures 12.4 and 12.5

FIGURE 12.4 Race–Ethnicity of the U.S. Population

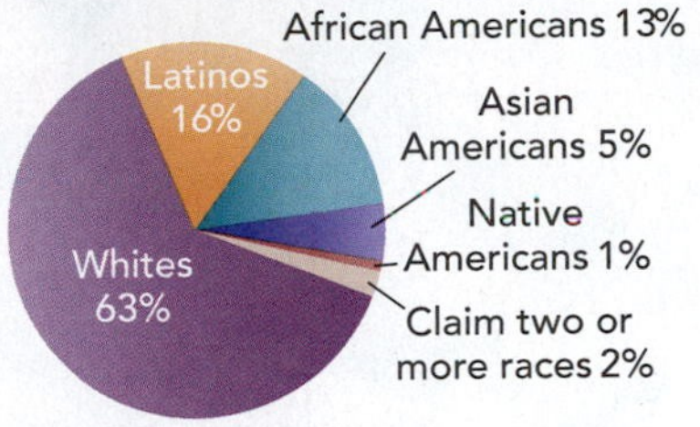

Source: By the author. See Figure 12.5.

FIGURE 12.5 U.S. Racial–Ethnic Groups

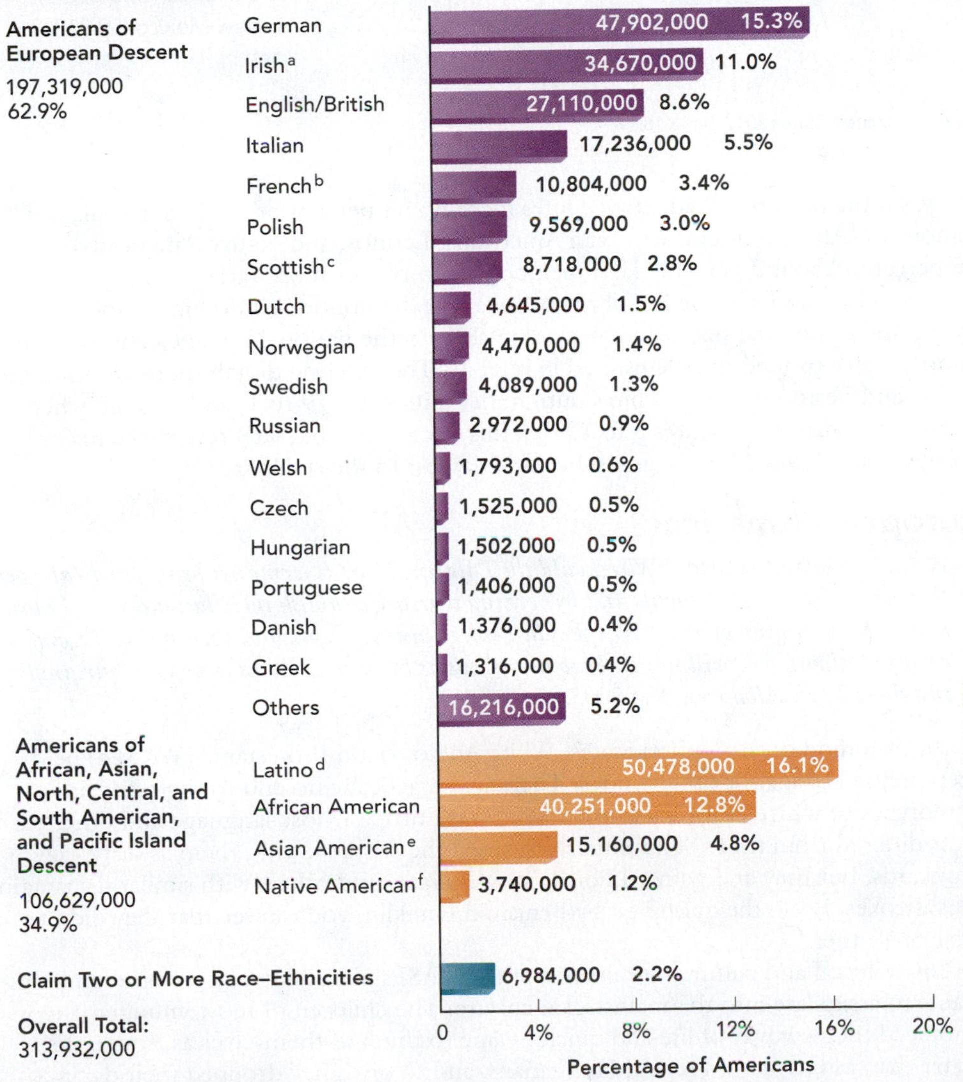

[a]Interestingly, this total is six times higher than all the Irish who live in Ireland.
[b]Includes French Canadian.
[c]Includes "Scottish—Irish."
[d]Most Latinos trace at least part of their ancestry to Europe.
[e]In descending order, the largest groups of Asian Americans are from China, the Philippines, India, Korea, Vietnam, and Japan. See Figure 12.9 on page 348. Also includes those who identify themselves as Native Hawaiian or Pacific Islander.
[f]Includes Native Alaskan.

Source: By the author. Based on *Statistical Abstract of the United States* 2013:Tables 10, 52.

Explore on **MySocLab**
Activity: Diversity in American Society

USA—the land of diversity.

FIGURE 12.6 The Distribution of Dominant and Minority Groups

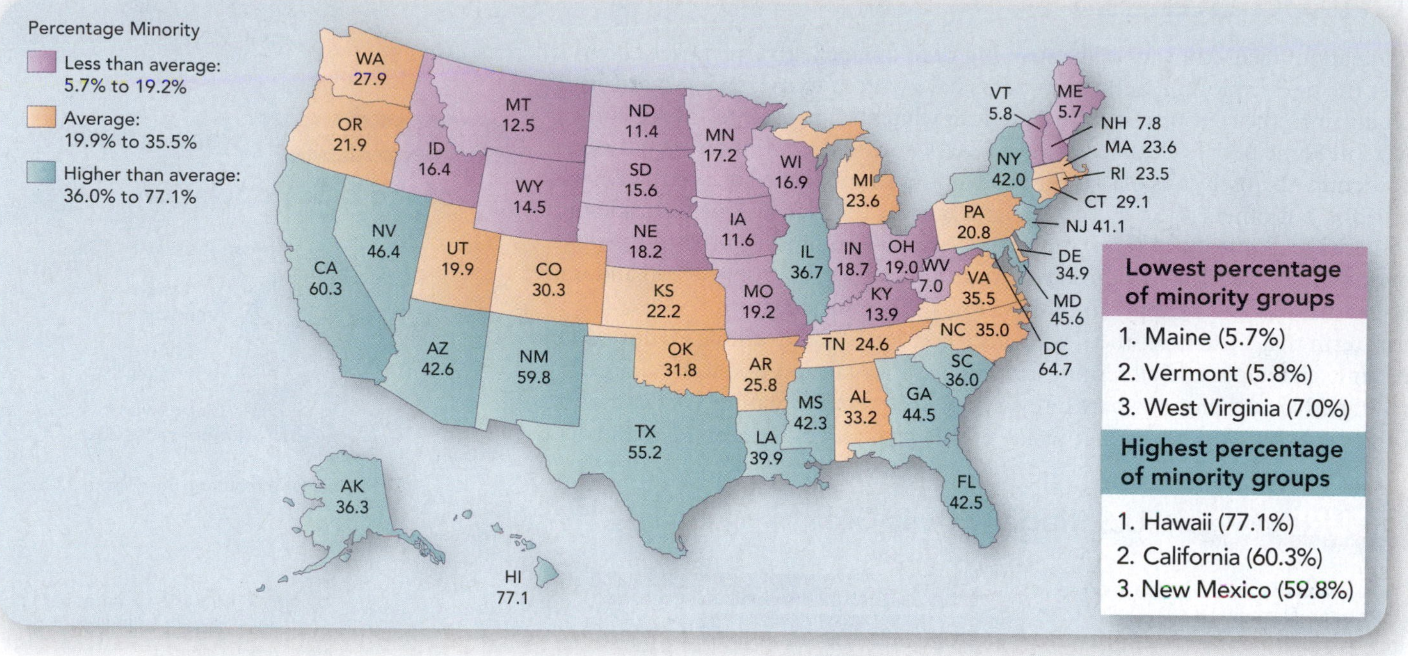

Source: By the author. Based on *Statistical Abstract of the United States* 2013:Table 18.

WASP white anglo saxon protestant

white ethnics white immigrants to the United States whose cultures differ from WASP culture

As immigrants assimilate into a new culture, they learn and adapt new customs. This photo was taken at the Arab International Festival in Dearborn, Michigan.

show, on the basis of self-identity, whites make up 63 percent of the U.S. population, minorities (African Americans, Asian Americans, Latinos, and Native Americans) 35 percent. About 2 percent claim membership in two or more racial–ethnic groups.

As you can see from the Social Map above, the distribution of dominant and minority groups among the states does not come close to the national average. This is because minority groups tend to be clustered in regions. The extreme distributions are found in Maine and Vermont, where whites outnumber minorities 19 to 1, and Hawaii, where minorities outnumber whites 3 to 1.With this as background, let's review the major groups in the United States, going from the largest to the smallest.

European Americans

Benjamin Franklin said, "Why should the Palatine boors (Germans) be suffered (allowed) to swarm into our settlements and by herding together establish their language and manners to the exclusion of ours? Why should Pennsylvania, founded by the English, become a colony of aliens, who will shortly be so numerous as to germanize us instead of our anglifying them?" (in Alba and Nee 2003:17)

At the founding of the United States, White Anglo Saxon Protestants (**WASPs**) held deep prejudices against other whites. There was practically no end to their disdainful stereotypes of **white ethnics**—immigrants from Europe whose language and other customs differed from theirs. The English despised the Irish, viewing them as dirty, lazy drunkards, but they also painted Poles, Jews, Italians, and others with similar disparaging brushstrokes. From the quotation by Benjamin Franklin, you can see that they didn't like Germans either.

The political and cultural dominance of the WASPs placed intense pressure on immigrants to assimilate into the mainstream culture. The children of most immigrants embraced the new way of life and quickly came to think of themselves as Americans rather than as Germans, French, Hungarians, and so on. They dropped their distinctive customs, especially their languages, often viewing them as symbols of shame. This second generation of immigrants was sandwiched between two worlds: "the old country" of their parents and their new home. Their children, the third generation, had an easier adjustment, since they had fewer customs to discard. As white ethnics assimilated into this Anglo-American culture, the meaning of WASP expanded to include them.

And for those who weren't white? Perhaps the event that best illustrates the racial view of the nation's founders occurred when Congress passed the Naturalization Act of 1790, declaring that only white immigrants could apply for citizenship. Relationships between the various racial–ethnic groups since the founding of the nation have been, at best, a rocky one.

In Sum: Because Protestant English immigrants settled the colonies, they established the culture—from the dominant language to the dominant religion. Highly ethnocentric, they regarded the customs of other groups as inferior. Because white Europeans took power, they determined the national agenda to which other ethnic groups had to react and conform. Their institutional and cultural dominance still sets the stage for current racial–ethnic relations, a topic that we explore in the Down-to-Earth Sociology box below.

Read on **MySocLab**
Document: Beyond the Melting Pot Reconsidered

Latinos (Hispanics)

Umbrella Term. *Latino* is an umbrella term that lumps people from many cultures into a single category. Taken together, these people, who trace their origins to the Spanish-speaking countries of Latin America, form the largest ethnic group in the United States.

Down-to-Earth Sociology

Unpacking the Invisible Knapsack: Exploring Cultural Privilege

Overt racism in the United States has dropped sharply, but doors still open and close on the basis of the color of our skins. Whites have a difficult time grasping the idea that good things come their way because they are white. They usually fail to perceive how "whiteness" operates in their own lives.

Peggy McIntosh, of Irish descent, began to wonder why she was so seldom aware of her race–ethnicity, while her African American friends were so conscious of theirs. She realized that people are not highly aware of things that they take for granted—and that "whiteness" is a "taken-for-granted" background assumption of U.S. society. (You might want to review Figure 12.1 on page 326.) To explore this, she drew up a list of taken-for-granted privileges that come with her "whiteness," what she calls her "invisible knapsack." Because she is white, McIntosh (1988) says:

1. When I go shopping, store detectives don't follow me.
2. If I don't do well as a leader, I can be sure people won't say that it is because of my race.
3. When I watch television or look at the front page of the paper, I see people of my race presented positively.
4. When I study our national heritage, I see people of my color and am taught that they made our country great.
5. To protect my children, I do not have to teach them to be aware of racism.
6. I can talk with my mouth full and not have people put this down to my color.
7. I can speak at a public meeting without putting my race on trial.
8. I can achieve something and not be "a credit to my race."
9. If a traffic cop pulls me over, I can be sure that it isn't because I'm white.
10. I can be late to a meeting without people thinking I was late because "That's how *they* are."

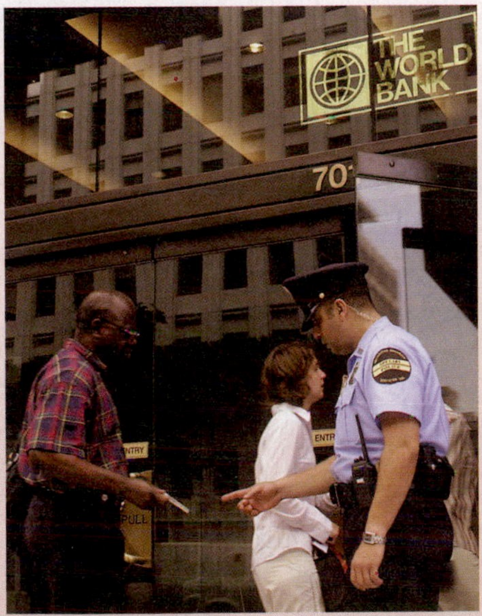

One of the cultural privileges of being white in the United States is less suspicion of wrongdoing.

For Your Consideration

➔ Can you think of other "background privileges" that come to whites because of their skin color? (McIntosh's list contains forty-six items.) Why are whites seldom aware that they carry an "invisible knapsack"?

FIGURE 12.7 Geographical Origins of U.S. Latinos

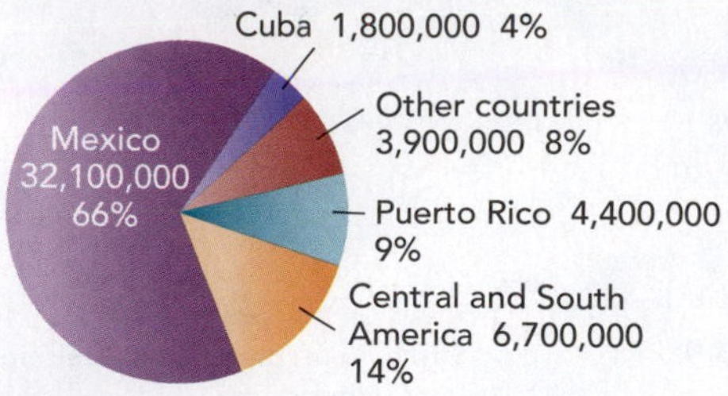

Source: By the author. Based on *Statistical Abstract of the United States* 2013:Table 37.

Few people who are classified as Latino, however, consider themselves to be part of a single ethnic group. Instead, they think of themselves as Americans of Mexican origin (*Mexicanos*), Americans of Cuban origin (*Cubanos*), Americans from Puerto Rico (*Puertoricanos*), and so on. Nor do most identify with the umbrella term *Hispanic*, another artificial grouping of peoples. It is also important to stress that neither *Latino* nor *Hispanic* refers to race. Latinos may identify themselves as African American, white, or Native American. Some even refer to themselves as *Afro Latino*.

Countries of Origin. As shown in Figure 12.7, about 32 million people trace their origin to Mexico, 7 million to Central and South America, 4 million to Puerto Rico, and 2 million to Cuba (*Statistical Abstract* 2013:Table 37). Although most Latinos of Mexican origin live in the Southwest, most Latinos from Puerto Rico live in New York City, and those from Cuba live primarily in Florida.

Unauthorized Immigrants. Officially tallied at 50 million, the number of Latinos in the United States is considerably higher than this. Although most Latinos are U.S. citizens, about 9 million have entered the country illegally (7 million from Mexico and 2 million from Central and South America) (*Statistical Abstract* 2013:Table 45). Although the economic crisis slowed the number of unauthorized immigrants (Jordan 2012), each year about 500,000 people are returned to Mexico or Central and South America (*Statistical Abstract* 2013:Table 541). Some come to the United States for temporary work and then return home. Most do not.

This massive unauthorized entry into the United States has aroused intense public concern. One reaction has been to open paths to citizenship or work permits. In 1986, the federal government passed the Immigration Reform and Control Act, which permitted unauthorized immigrants to apply for U.S. citizenship. Over 3 million people applied, the vast majority from Mexico (Espenshade 1990). In 2012, President Obama signed an Executive Order allowing work permits to unauthorized immigrants who are not over the age of 30, who arrived here before the age of 16, who are in school or are high school graduates, and who have no criminal record (Preston and Cushman 2012).

Another reaction has been to try to prevent illegal entry. The primary one is to check documents at entry points and to patrol the borders. A more unusual prevention measure was to start building a wall along the 2,000-mile border between Mexico and the Untied States. After building just 53 miles of the wall at the horrendous cost of $1 billion, the wall was cancelled (Preston 2011). With many dissatisfied at the effectiveness of the U.S. Border Patrol, citizen groups have jumped in to offer their often unwelcome help. One group, the Minutemen, patrols the border, quite unofficially. Another group, the Techno Patriots, monitors the border by computers and thermal imaging cameras. When they confirm illegal crossings, they call the Border Patrol to make the arrests (Marino 2008).

Arizona, where many of the illegal crossings take place, gave still another response. That state's legislature passed a law that gives its police the power to detain anyone suspected of being in the country illegally. When the law was reviewed by the U.S. Supreme Court, the justices threw out some aspects of it but upheld the state's right to check the immigration status of anyone they stop or arrest (Liptak 2012).

To gain insight into why this vast subterranean migration exists and will continue, see the Cultural Diversity box on the next page.

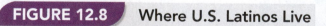

FIGURE 12.8 Where U.S. Latinos Live

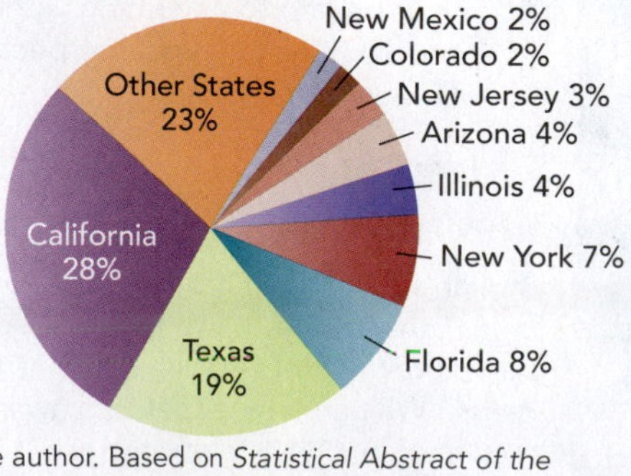

Source: By the author. Based on *Statistical Abstract of the United States* 2013:Table 18.

Residence. As Figure 12.8 shows, seven of every ten Latinos live in just six states—California, Texas, Florida, New York, Illinois, and Arizona. With its prominent Latino presence, Miami has been called "the capital of South America."

Spanish. The factor that clearly distinguishes Latinos from other U.S. minorities is the Spanish language. Although not all Latinos speak Spanish, most do. About 37 million Latinos speak Spanish at

Cultural Diversity in the United States

The Illegal Travel Guide

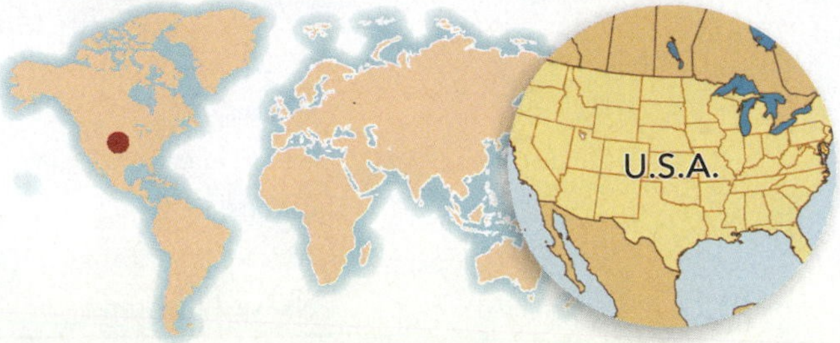

Manuel was a drinking buddy of José, a man I had met in Colima, Mexico. At 45, Manuel was friendly, outgoing, and enterprising.

Manuel, who had lived in the United States for seven years, spoke fluent English. Preferring to live in his hometown in Colima, where he palled around with his childhood friends, Manuel always seemed to have money and free time.

When Manuel invited me to go on a business trip with him, I accepted. I never could figure out what he did for a living or how he could afford a car, a luxury that none of his friends had. As we traveled from one remote village to another, Manuel would sell used clothing that he had heaped in the back of his older-model Ford station wagon.

At one stop, Manuel took me into a dirt-floored, thatched-roof hut. While chickens ran in and out, Manuel whispered to a slender man who was about 23 years old. The poverty was overwhelming. Juan, as his name turned out to be, had a partial grade school education. He also had a wife, four hungry children under the age of 5, and two pigs—his main food supply. Although eager to work, Juan had no job; there was simply no work available in this remote village.

Crossing the border at Calexico, California.

As we were drinking a Coke, which seems to be the national beverage of Mexico's poor, Manuel explained to me that he was not only selling clothing—he was also lining up migrants to the United States. For a fee, he would take a man to the border and introduce him to a "wolf," who would help him cross into the promised land.

When I saw the hope in Juan's face, I knew nothing would stop him. He was borrowing every cent he could from every friend and relative to scrape the money together. Although he risked losing everything if apprehended and would be facing unknown risks, Juan would make the trip: Beckoning to him was a future with opportunity, perhaps even with wealth. He knew people who had been to the United States and spoke glowingly of its opportunities. Manuel, of course, salesman that he was, stoked the fires of hope.

Looking up from the children playing on the dirt floor with chickens pecking about them, I saw a man who loved his family. In order to make the desperate bid for a better life, he would suffer an enforced absence, as well as the uncertainties of a foreign culture whose language he did not know.

Juan opened his billfold, took something out, and slowly handed it to me. I looked at it curiously. I felt tears as I saw the tenderness with which he handled this piece of paper. It was his passport to the land of opportunity: a Social Security card made out in his name, sent by a friend who had already made the trip and who was waiting for Juan on the other side of the border.

It was then that I realized that the thousands of Manuels scurrying about Mexico and the millions of Juans they are transporting can never be stopped, since only the United States can fulfill their dreams of a better life.

For Your Consideration

➔ The vast stream of immigrants illegally crossing the Mexican–U.S. border has become a national issue. What do you think is the best way to deal with this issue? Why?

➔ How does your social location affect your view?

home (*Statistical Abstract* 2013:Table 53). Many cannot speak English or can do so only with difficulty. Being fluent only in Spanish in a society where English is spoken almost exclusively remains an obstacle.

Despite the 1848 Treaty of Hidalgo, which guarantees Mexicans the right to maintain their culture, from 1855 until 1968, California banned teaching in Spanish in school. In a 1974 decision (*Lau v. Nichols*), the U.S. Supreme Court ruled that using only English to teach Spanish-speaking students violated their civil rights. This decision paved the way for bilingual instruction for Spanish-speaking children (Vidal 1977; Lopez 1980).

TABLE 12.2 Indicators of Relative Economic Well-Being

	Family Income		Families In Poverty	
	Median Family Income	Percentage of White Income	Percentage Below Poverty	Compared to Whites
Whites	$67,900		10.6%	
Asian Americans	$76,700	113%	12.5%	18% higher
Latinos	$41,100	61%	24.8%	233% higher
African Americans	$39,900	59%	27.1%	256% higher
Native Americans	$39,700	58%	28.4%	268% higher

Note: These totals are for families, which have less poverty than "persons," the unit of the tables in Chapter 7.
Source: By the author. Based on *Statistical Abstract of the United States* 2013:Table 36.

The use of Spanish has provoked an "English-only" movement. Although the constitutional amendment that was proposed never got off the ground, thirty states have passed laws that declare English their official language (Newman et al. 2012).

Economic Well-Being. To see how Latinos are doing on major indicators of well-being, look at Table 12.2. Their family income averages only three-fifths that of whites, and they are more than twice as likely as whites to be poor. On the positive side, one of every eight Latino families has an income higher than $100,000 a year.

From Table 12.3, you can see that Latinos are the most likely to drop out of high school and the least likely to graduate from college. In a postindustrial society that increasingly requires advanced skills, these totals indicate that huge numbers of Latinos are being left behind.

Politics. Because of their huge numbers, we might expect about 16 of the 100 U.S. senators to be Latino. How many are there? *Three.* In addition, Latinos hold only 7 percent of the

TABLE 12.3 Race–Ethnicity and Education

	Education Completed				Doctorates		
Racial–Ethnic Group	Less Than High School	High School	Some College	College (BA or Higher)	Number Awarded	Percentage of all U.S. Doctorates[1]	Percentage of U.S. Population
Whites	9.3%	29.3%	21.9%	31.4%	39,648	78.0%	62.9%
Latinos	37.8%	26.5%	17.2%	13.0%	2,540	5.0%	16.1%
Country or Area of Origin							
Cuba	NA[2]	NA	NA	26.2%	NA	NA	0.6%
Puerto Rico	NA	NA	NA	17.5%	NA	NA	1.4%
Central and South America	NA	NA	NA	18.9%	NA	NA	2.2%
Mexico	NA	NA	NA	10.6%	NA	NA	10.4%
African Americans	18.1%	31.7%	24.9%	17.9%	4,434	8.7%	12.8%
Asian Americans	14.6%	16.0%	13.1%	49.9%	3,875	7.6%	4.8%
Native Americans	22.7%	30.7%	25.6%	13.4%	332	0.7%	1.2%

[1]The percentage after the doctorates awarded to nonresidents have been deducted from the total.
[2]Not Available.
Source: By the author. I used 2009 data, as the 2010 data show an unexplained jump of 134% in doctorates awarded. Based on *Statistical Abstract of the United States* 2013:Tables 36, 37, 300, and Figure 12.5 of this text.

seats in the U.S. House of Representatives (*Statistical Abstract* 2013:Table 421). Yet, compared with the past, even these small totals represent substantial gains. On the positive side, several Latinos have been elected as state governors. The first Latina to become a governor is Susana Martinez of New Mexico, who was elected in 2010.

It is likely that Latinos soon will play a larger role in U.S. politics, perhaps one day even beyond their overall numbers. This is because the six states in which they are concentrated hold one-third of the country's 538 electroral votes: California (55), Texas (38), Florida (29), New York (29), Illinois (20), and Arizona (11). Latinos have received presidential appointments to major federal positions, such as Secretary of the Interior, Secretary of Transportation, and Secretary of Housing and Urban Development.

For millions of people, the United States represents a land of opportunity and freedom from oppression. Shown here are Cubans who reached the United States by transforming their 1950s truck into a boat.

Divisions based on country of origin hold back the potential political power of Latinos. As I mentioned, Latinos do not think of themselves as a single people, and national origin remains highly significant. People from Puerto Rico, for example, feel little sense of unity with people from Mexico. It is similarly the case with those from Venezuela, Colombia, or El Salvador. It used to be the same with European immigrants. Those who came from Germany and Sweden or from England and France did not identify with one another. With time, the importance of the European country of origin was lost, and they came to think of themselves as Americans. Perhaps this will happen to Latinos as well, but for now, these distinctions nourish disunity and create political disagreements.

Explore on **MySocLab**
Activity: Social Constructions of Race and Ethnicity

Social class divisions also obstruct unity among Latinos. In some cases, even when they come from the same country, the differences in their backgrounds are severe. Most of the half million Cubans who fled their homeland after Fidel Castro came to power in 1959 were well-educated, financially comfortable professionals or businesspeople. In contrast, the 100,000 "boat people" who arrived 20 years later were mainly lower-class refugees to whom the earlier arrivals would hardly have spoken in Cuba. The earlier arrivals have prospered in Florida and control many businesses and financial institutions: There continues to be a vast gulf between them and those who came later.

African Americans

It was 1955, in Montgomery, Alabama. As specified by law, whites took the front seats of the bus, and blacks went to the back. As the bus filled up, blacks had to give up their seats to whites.

When Rosa Parks, a 42-year-old African American woman and secretary of the Montgomery NAACP, was told that she would have to stand so that white folks could sit, she refused (Bray 1995). She stubbornly sat there while the bus driver raged and whites felt insulted. Her arrest touched off mass demonstrations, led 50,000 blacks to boycott the city's buses for a year, and thrust an otherwise unknown preacher into a historic role.

Reverend Martin Luther King, Jr., who had majored in sociology at Morehouse College in Atlanta, Georgia, took control. He organized car pools and preached nonviolence. Incensed at this radical organizer and at the stirrings in the normally compliant black community, segregationists also put their beliefs into practice—by bombing the homes of blacks and dynamiting their churches.

After slavery was abolished, the Southern states passed legislation (*Jim Crow* laws) to segregate blacks and whites. In 1896, the U.S. Supreme Court ruled in *Plessy v. Ferguson* that it was a reasonable use of state power to require "separate but equal" accommodations

rising expectations the sense that better conditions are soon to follow, which, if unfulfilled, increases frustration

for blacks. Whites used this ruling to strip blacks of the political power they had gained after the Civil War. Declaring political primaries to be "white," they prohibited blacks from voting in them. Not until 1944 did the Supreme Court rule that political primaries were not "white" and were open to all voters. White politicians then passed laws that restricted voting only to people who could read—and they determined that most African Americans were illiterate. Not until 1954 did African Americans gain the legal right to attend the same public schools as whites, and, as recounted in the vignette, even later to sit where they wanted on a bus.

Rising Expectations and Civil Strife. The barriers came down, but they came down slowly. In 1964, Congress passed the Civil Rights Act, making it illegal to discriminate on the basis of race. African Americans were finally allowed in "white" restaurants, hotels, theaters, and other public places. Then in 1965, Congress passed the Voting Rights Act, banning the fraudulent literacy tests that the Southern states had used to keep African Americans from voting.

African Americans then experienced what sociologists call **rising expectations**. They expected that these sweeping legal changes would usher in better conditions in life. However, the lives of the poor among them changed little, if at all. Frustrations built up, exploding in Watts in 1965, when people living in that ghetto of central Los Angeles took to the streets in the first of what were termed the *urban revolts*. When a white supremacist assassinated King on April 4, 1968, inner cities across the nation erupted in fiery violence. Under threat of the destruction of U.S. cities, Congress passed the sweeping Civil Rights Act of 1968.

Until the 1960s, the South's public facilities were segregated. Some were reserved for whites, others for blacks. This *apartheid* was broken by blacks and whites who worked together and risked their lives to bring about a fairer society. Shown here is a 1963 sit-in at a Woolworth's lunch counter in Jackson, Mississippi. Sugar, ketchup, and mustard are being poured over the heads of the demonstrators.

Continued Gains. Since then, African Americans have made remarkable gains in politics, education, and jobs. At 10 percent, the number of African Americans in the U.S. House of Representatives is *two to three times* what it was a generation ago (*Statistical Abstract* 1989:Table 423; 2013:Table 421). As college enrollments increased, the middle class expanded, and today a little over half (54 percent) of all African American families make more than $35,000 a year. Two in five earn more than $50,000 a year. As you can see from Table 12.4, one in eight has an income over $100,000 a year.

African Americans have become prominent in politics. Jesse Jackson (another sociology major) competed for the Democratic presidential nomination in 1984 and 1988. In 1989, L. Douglas Wilder was elected governor of Virginia, and in 2006, Deval Patrick became governor of Massachusetts. These accomplishments, of course, pale in comparison to the election of Barack Obama as president of the United States in 2008 and his re-election in 2012.

In 2008, Barack Obama was elected president of the United States, the first minority to achieve this office. In 2012, he was reelected.

Current Losses. Despite these remarkable gains, African Americans continue to lag behind in politics, economics, and education. According to their share of the population, we would expect twelve or thirteen African American senators. How many are there? *Zero.* There have been only six in U.S. history. As Tables 12.2 and 12.3 on page 344 show, African Americans average only 59 percent of white income, experience much more poverty, and are less likely to have a college education. That two of five of African American families have incomes over $50,000 is only part of the story. Table 12.4 shows the other part—that one of every five African American families makes less than $15,000 a year.

Watch on **MySocLab**
Video: Sociology in Focus: Race and Ethnicity

Race or Social Class? A Sociological Debate. Let's turn to an ongoing disagreement in sociology. Sociologist William Julius Wilson (1978, 2000, 2007) argues that social class is more important than race in determining the life chances of African Americans. Some other sociologists disagree.

Read on **MySocLab**
Document: Race as Class

For background on why Wilson makes this argument, let's start with civil rights legislation. Prior to the civil rights laws, African Americans were excluded from avenues of economic advancement: good schools and good jobs. When civil rights laws opened new opportunities, African Americans seized them, and millions entered the middle class. As the better-educated African Americans obtained white-collar jobs, they moved to better areas of the city and to the suburbs.

Left behind in the inner city were the less educated and less skilled, who depended on blue-collar jobs. At this time, a second transition was taking place: Manufacturing was moving from the city to the suburbs. This took away those blue-collar jobs. Without work, those in the inner city have the least hope, the most despair, and the violence that so often dominates the evening news.

This is the basis of Wilson's argument. The upward mobility of millions of African Americans into the middle class created two worlds of African American experience—one educated and affluent, the other uneducated and poor. Those who have moved up the social class ladder live in comfortable homes in secure neighborhoods. Their jobs provide decent incomes, and they send their children to good schools. Those who are stuck in the inner city live in depressing poverty, attend poor schools, and have little

TABLE 12.4 Race–Ethnicity and Income Extremes

	Less than $15,000	Over $100,000
Asian Americans	6.6%	37.6%
Whites	5.8%	30.3%
African Americans	19.4%	12.5%
Latinos	15.6%	12.1%

Note: These are family incomes. Only these groups are listed in the source.
Source: By the author: Based on *Statistical Abstract of the United States* 2013:Table 710.

Sociologists disagree about the relative significance of race and social class in determining social and economic conditions of African Americans. William Julius Wilson, shown here, is an avid proponent of the social class side of this debate.

opportunity for work. They are filled with hopelessness and despair, combined with apathy or hostility.

Our experiences shape our views on life, our attitudes, our values, and our behavior. Look at how vastly different these two worlds of experiences are. Those who learn middle-class views, with its norms, aspirations, and values, have little in common with the orientations to life that arise from living in neighborhoods of deep poverty. Wilson, then, stresses that social class—not race—has become the more significant factor in the lives of African Americans.

Some sociologists reply that this analysis overlooks the discrimination that continues to underlie the African American experience. They note that African Americans who do the same work as whites average less pay (Willie 1991; Herring 2002) and even receive fewer tips (Lynn et al. 2008). Others document how young black males experience daily indignities and are objects of suspicion and police brutality (Rios 2011). These, they argue, point to racial discrimination, not to social class.

What is the answer to this debate? Wilson would reply that it is not an either-or question. My book is titled *The **Declining** Significance of Race*, he would say, not *The **Absence** of Race*. Certainly racism is still alive, he would add, but today, social class is more central to the African American experience than is racial discrimination. He stresses that we need to provide jobs for the poor in the inner city—because work provides an anchor to a responsible life (Wilson 1996, 2007, 2009).

Read on **MySocLab**
Document: Dumping in Dixie: Race, Class, and the Politics of Place

Racism as an Everyday Burden.

Researchers sent out 5,000 résumés in response to help wanted ads in the Boston and Chicago Sunday papers. The résumés were identical, except some applicants had white-sounding names, such as Emily and Brandon, while others had black-sounding names, such as Lakisha and Jamal. Although the qualifications of these supposed job applicants were identical, the white-sounding names elicited 50 percent more callbacks than the black-sounding names (Bertrand and Mullainathan 2002).

Certainly racism continues as a regular feature of society, often something that whites, not subjected to it, are only vaguely aware of. But for those on the receiving end, racism can be an everyday burden. Here is how an African American professor describes his experiences:

Read on **MySocLab**
Document: Racisim Without "Racists"

> *[One problem with] being black in America is that you have to spend so much time thinking about stuff that most white people just don't even have to think about. I worry when I get pulled over by a cop. . . . I worry what some white cop is going to think when he walks over to our car, because he's holding on to a gun. And I'm very aware of how many black folks accidentally get shot by cops. I worry when I walk into a store, that someone's going to think I'm in there shoplifting. . . . And I get resentful that I have to think about things that a lot of people, even my very close white friends whose politics are similar to mine, simply don't have to worry about. (Feagin 1999:398)*

FIGURE 12.9 Countries of Origin of Asian Americans

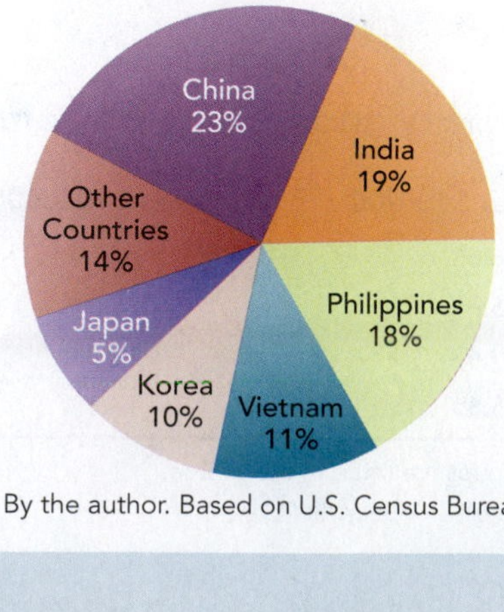

Source: By the author. Based on U.S. Census Bureau 2010.

Asian Americans

I have stressed in this chapter that our racial–ethnic categories are based more on social factors than on biological ones. This point is again obvious when we examine the category Asian American. As Figure 12.9 shows, those who are called Asian Americans came to the United States from many nations. *With no unifying culture or "race," why should people from so many backgrounds be clustered together and assigned a single label?* Think about it. What culture or race–ethnicity do Samoans and Vietnamese have in common? Or Laotians and Pakistanis? Or people from Guam and those from China? Those from Japan and those from India? Yet all these groups—and more—are lumped together and called Asian Americans. Apparently, the U.S. government is not satisfied until it is able to pigeonhole everyone into some racial–ethnic category.

Since *Asian American* is a standard term, however, let's look at the characteristics of the 15 million people who are lumped together and assigned this label.

Mazie Hirono, the first Japanese American woman to be elected a U.S. senator.

A Background of Discrimination.

> *Lured by gold strikes in the West and an urgent need for unskilled workers to build the railroads, 200,000 Chinese immigrated between 1850 and 1880. When the famous golden spike was driven at Promontory, Utah, in 1869 to mark the completion of the railroad to the West Coast, white workers prevented Chinese workers from being in the photo—even though Chinese made up 90 percent of Central Pacific Railroad's labor force (Hsu 1971).*

After the transcontinental railroad was complete, the Chinese competed with whites for other jobs. Anglos then formed vigilante groups to intimidate them. They also used the law. California's 1850 Foreign Miners Act required Chinese (and Latinos) to pay $20 a month in order to work—when wages were a dollar a day. The California Supreme Court ruled that Chinese could not testify against whites (Carlson and Colburn 1972). In 1882, Congress passed the Chinese Exclusion Act, suspending all Chinese immigration for ten years. Four years later, the Statue of Liberty was dedicated. The tired, the poor, and the huddled masses it was intended to welcome were obviously not Chinese.

When immigrants from Japan arrived, they encountered *spillover bigotry*, a stereotype that lumped Asians together, depicting them as sneaky, lazy, and untrustworthy. After Japan attacked Pearl Harbor in 1941, conditions grew worse for the 110,000 Japanese Americans who called the United States their home. U.S. authorities feared that Japan would invade the United States and that the Japanese Americans would fight on Japan's side. They also feared that Japanese Americans would sabotage military installations on the West Coast. Although no Japanese American had been involved in even a single act of sabotage, on February 19, 1942, President Franklin D. Roosevelt ordered that everyone who was *one-eighth Japanese or more* be confined in detention centers (called "internment camps"). These people were charged with no crime, and they had no trials. Japanese ancestry was sufficient cause for being imprisoned.

Diversity. As you can see from Tables 12.2 and 12.4 on pages 334 and 347, the income of Asian Americans has outstripped that of all groups, including whites. This has led to the stereotype that all Asian Americans are successful. Are they? Their poverty rate is actually slightly higher than that of whites, as you can also see from Table 12.2. As with Latinos, country of origin is significant: Poverty is low for Chinese and Japanese Americans, but it clusters among Americans from Southeast Asia. Altogether, between 1 and 2 million Asian Americans live in poverty.

Reasons for Financial Success. The high average incomes of Asian Americans can be traced to three major factors: family life, educational achievement, and assimilation into mainstream culture. Of all ethnic groups, including whites, Asian American children are the most likely to grow up with two parents and the least likely to be born to a single mother (*Statistical Abstract* 2013:Table 69). Common in these families is a stress on self-discipline, thrift, and hard work (Suzuki 1985; Bell 1991). This early socialization provides strong impetus for the other two factors.

The second factor is their unprecedented rate of college graduation. As Table 12.3 on page 344 shows, 50 percent of Asian Americans complete college. To realize how stunning this is, compare their rate with those of the other groups shown on this table. Educational achievement, in turn, opens doors to economic success.

The most striking indication of the third factor, assimilation, is a high rate of intermarriage. Of all racial–ethnic groups, Asian Americans are the most likely to marry someone of a different racial–ethnic group (Wang 2012). Of Asian Americans who graduate from college, about 40 percent of the men and 60 percent of the women marry a non–Asian American (Qian and Lichter 2007). The intermarriage of Japanese Americans is so extensive that two of every three of their children have one parent who is not of Japanese descent (Schaefer 2012). The Chinese are close behind (Alba and Nee 2003).

Politics. Asian Americans are becoming more prominent in politics. With about half of its citizens being Asian American, Hawaii has elected Asian American governors and sent several Asian American senators to Washington, including the one now serving there (Lee 1998; *Statistical Abstract* 2013:Table 421). The first Asian American governor outside of Hawaii was Gary Locke, who served from 1997 to 2005 as governor of Washington, a state in which Asian Americans make up less than 6 percent of the population. In 2008, Bobby Jindal became the first Indian American governor when he was elected governor of Louisiana, a state in which Asian Americans make up less than 2 percent of the population.

Native Americans

"I don't go so far as to think that the only good Indians are dead Indians, but I believe nine out of ten are—and I shouldn't inquire too closely into the case of the tenth.

—Teddy Roosevelt, President of the United States 1901–1909
(As cited in "Past Imperfect" 2012)

Diversity of Groups. This quotation from Teddy Roosevelt provides insight into the rampant racism of earlier generations. Yet, even today, thanks to countless grade B Westerns, some Americans view the original inhabitants of what became the United States as uncivilized savages, a single group of people subdivided into separate tribes. The European immigrants to the colonies, however, encountered diverse groups of people who spoke over 700 languages. Their variety of cultures ranged from nomadic hunters and gatherers to farmers who lived in wooden houses (Schaefer 2004). Each group had its own norms and values—and the usual ethnocentric pride in its own culture. Consider what happened in 1744 when the colonists of Virginia offered college scholarships for "savage lads." The Iroquois replied:

"Several of our young people were formerly brought up at the colleges of Northern Provinces. They were instructed in all your sciences. But when they came back to us, they were bad runners, ignorant of every means of living in the woods, unable to bear either cold or hunger, knew neither how to build a cabin, take a deer, or kill an enemy. . . . They were totally good for nothing."

They added, "If the English gentlemen would send a dozen or two of their children to Onondaga, the great Council would take care of thfeir education, bring them up in really what was the best manner and make men of them." (Nash 1974; in McLemore 1994)

This depiction breaks stereotypes, but is historically accurate. Shown here is an Iroquois fort. Can you guess who the attackers are?

Native Americans, who numbered about 10 million, had no immunity to the diseases the Europeans brought with them. With deaths due to disease—and warfare, a much lesser cause—their population plummeted (Schaefer 2012). The low point came in 1890, when the census reported only 250,000 Native Americans. If the census and the estimate of the original population are accurate, Native Americans had been reduced to about *one-fortieth* their original size. The population has never recovered, but Native Americans now number about 4 million (see Figure 12.5 on page 339). Native Americans, who today speak 169 different languages, do not think of themselves as a single people who fit neatly within a single label (Siebens and Julian 2011).

From Treaties to Genocide and Population Transfer. At first, the Native Americans tried to accommodate the strangers, since there was plenty of land for both the few newcomers and themselves. Soon, however, the settlers began to raid Indian villages and pillage their food supplies (Horn 2006). As wave after wave of settlers arrived, Pontiac, an Ottawa chief, saw the future—and didn't like it. He convinced several tribes to unite in an effort to push the Europeans into the sea. He almost succeeded, but failed when the English were reinforced by fresh troops (McLemore 1994).

A pattern of deception evolved. The U.S. government would make treaties to buy some of a tribe's land, with the promise to honor forever the tribe's right to what it had not sold. European immigrants, who continued to pour into the United States, would then disregard these boundaries. The tribes would resist, with death tolls on both sides. The U.S. government would then intervene—not to enforce the treaty it had made but to force the tribe off its lands. In its relentless drive westward, the U.S. government embarked on a policy of genocide. It assigned the U.S. cavalry the task of "pacification," which translated into slaughtering Native Americans who "stood in the way" of this territorial expansion.

The acts of cruelty perpetrated by the Europeans against Native Americans appear endless, but two are especially notable. The first is the Trail of Tears. The U.S. government adopted a policy of population transfer (see Figure 12.3 on page 337), which it called *Indian Removal.* The goal was to confine Native Americans to specified areas called *reservations.* In the winter of 1838–1839, the U.S. Army rounded up 15,000 Cherokees and forced them to walk a thousand miles from the Carolinas and Georgia to Oklahoma. Conditions were so brutal that about 4,000 of those who were forced to make this midwinter march died along the way. The second notable act of cruelty also marked the symbolic end of Native American resistance to the European expansion. In 1890 at Wounded Knee, South Dakota, the U.S. cavalry gunned down 300 men, women, and children of the Dakota Sioux tribe. After the massacre, the soldiers threw the bodies into a mass grave (Thornton 1987; Lind 1995; DiSilvestro 2006).

The Invisible Minority and Self-Determination. Native Americans can truly be called the invisible minority. Because about half live in rural areas and one-third in just three states—Oklahoma, California, and Arizona—most other Americans are hardly aware of a Native American presence in the United States. The isolation of about one-third of Native Americans on reservations further reduces their visibility (Schaefer 2012).

The systematic attempts of European Americans to destroy the Native Americans' way of life and their forced resettlement onto reservations continue to have deleterious effects. The rate of suicide among Native Americans is higher than that of any other group, and their life expectancy is lower than that of the nation as a whole (Murray et al. 2006; Crosby et al. 2011). Table 12.3 on page 344 shows that their educational attainment also lags behind most groups: Only 13 percent graduate from college.

Native Americans are experiencing major changes. In the 1800s, U.S. courts ruled that Native Americans did not own the land on which they had been settled and had no right to develop its resources. They made Native Americans wards of the state, and the Bureau of Indian Affairs treated them like children (Mohawk 1991; Schaefer 2012). Then, in the 1960s, Native Americans won a series of legal victories that gave them control over reservation lands. With this legal change, many Native American tribes have opened businesses—ranging from fish canneries to industrial parks that serve metropolitan areas. The Skywalk, opened by the Hualapai, which offers breathtaking views of the Grand Canyon, gives an idea of the varieties of businesses to come (Audi 2012).

The Casinos. It is the casinos, though, that have attracted the most attention. In 1988, the federal government passed a law that allowed Native Americans to operate gambling establishments on reservations. Now over 200 tribes have casinos. *They bring in $27 billion a year, more than all the casinos in Las Vegas combined* (Pratt 2011; *Statistical Abstract* 2013:Table 1273). The United Auburn tribe of California, which has only 200 adult members, runs a casino that nets $30,000 *a month* for each member (Onishi 2012). This huge amount, however, pales in comparison with that of the Mashantucket Pequot tribe of Connecticut. With only 700 members, the tribe brings in more than $2

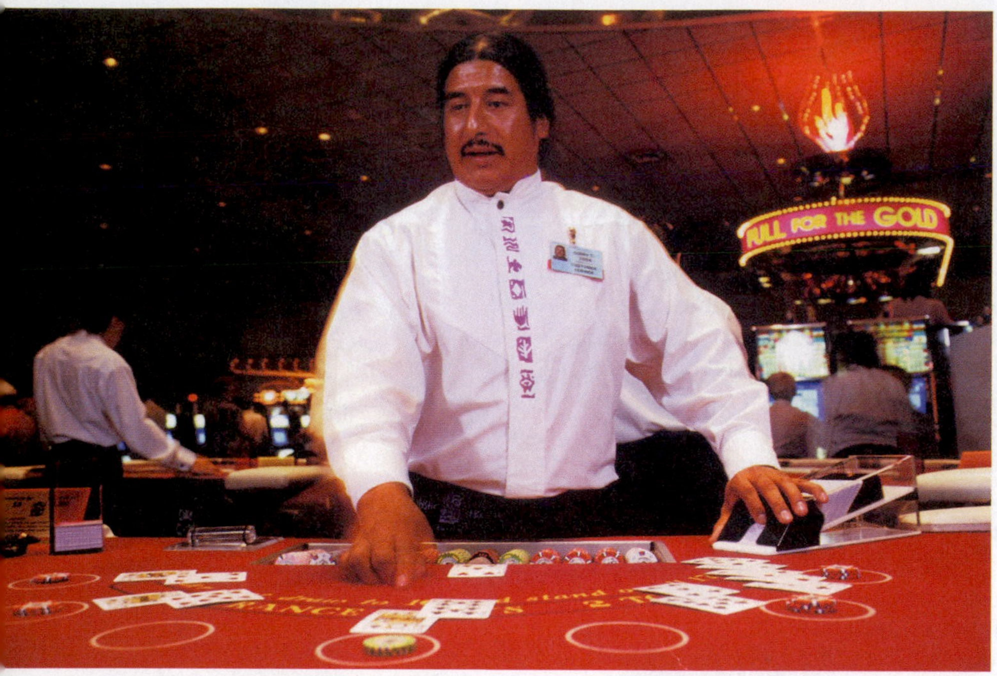

Native American casinos remain a topic of both controversy and envy. Shown here is Corey Two Crow as he deals blackjack in a casino in Minnesota.

million a day just from slot machines (Rivlin 2007). Incredibly, one tribe has only *one* member: She has her own casino (Bartlett and Steele 2002).

Separatism. Preferring to travel a different road, some Native Americans embrace the highly controversial idea of *separatism.* Because Native Americans were independent peoples when the Europeans arrived and they never willingly joined the United States, many tribes maintain the right to remain separate from the U.S. government. The chief of the Onondaga tribe in New York, a member of the Iroquois Federation, summarized the issue this way:

> *For the whole history of the Iroquois, we have maintained that we are a separate nation. We have never lost a war. Our government still operates. We have refused the U.S. government's reorganization plans for us. We have kept our language and our traditions, and when we fly to Geneva to UN meetings, we carry Hau de no sau nee passports. We made some treaties that lost some land, but that also confirmed our separate-nation status. That the U.S. denies all this doesn't make it any less the case. (Mander 1992)*

Pan-Indianism. One of the most significant changes for Native Americans is **pan-Indianism**. This emphasis on common elements that run through their cultures is an attempt to develop an identity that goes beyond the tribe. Pan-Indianism ("We are all Indians") is a remarkable example of the plasticity of ethnicity. It embraces and substitutes for individual tribal identities the label "Indian"—originally imposed by Spanish and Italian sailors who thought they had reached the shores of India. As sociologist Irwin Deutscher (2002:61) put it, "The peoples who have accepted the larger definition of who they are, have, in fact, little else in common with each other than the stereotypes of the dominant group which labels them."

Determining Identity and Goals. Native Americans say that it is they who must determine whether to establish a common identity and work together as in pan-Indianism or to stress separatism and identify solely with their own tribes. It is up to us, they say, whether we want to assimilate into the dominant culture or to stand apart from it; to move to cities or to remain on reservations; or to operate casinos or to engage only in traditional activities. "We are sovereign nations," they point out, "and we will not take orders from the victors of past wars."

12.6 Discuss immigration, affirmative action, and a multicultural society.

Looking Toward the Future

pan-Indianism an attempt to develop an identity that goes beyond the tribe by emphasizing the common elements that run through Native American cultures

Back in 1903, sociologist W. E. B. Du Bois said, "The problem of the twentieth century is the problem of the color line—the relation of the darker to the lighter races." Incredibly, over a hundred years later, the color line remains one of the most volatile topics facing the United States. From time to time, the color line takes on a different complexion, as with the war on terrorism and the corresponding discrimination directed against people of Middle Eastern descent.

In another hundred years, will yet another sociologist lament that the color of people's skins still affects human relationships? Given our past, it seems that although racial–ethnic walls will diminish, some even crumbling, the color line is not likely to disappear. Let's close this chapter by looking at two issues we are currently grappling with, immigration and affirmative action.

The Immigration Debate

Throughout its history, the United States has both welcomed immigration and feared its consequences. The gates opened wide (numerically, if not in attitude) for waves of immigrants in the 1800s and early 1900s. During the past twenty years, a new wave of immigration has brought close to a million new residents to the United States each year. Today, more immigrants (38 million) live in the United States than at any other time in the country's history (*Statistical Abstract* 2007:Table 5; 2013:Table 40).

Read on **MySocLab**
Document: Illegal Immigration: Gaps Between and Within Parties

In contrast to earlier waves, in which immigrants came almost exclusively from western Europe, the current wave of immigrants is so diverse that it is changing the U.S. racial–ethnic mix. If current trends in immigration (and birth) persist, in about fifty years, the "average" American will trace his or her ancestry to Africa, Asia, South America, the Pacific Islands, the Middle East—almost anywhere but white Europe. This change is discussed in the Cultural Diversity box on the next page.

In some states, the future is arriving much sooner than this. In California, racial–ethnic minorities have become the majority. California has 23 million minorities and 15 million whites (*Statistical Abstract* 2013:Table 18). Californians who request new telephone service from Pacific Bell can speak to customer service representatives in Spanish, Korean, Vietnamese, Mandarin, Cantonese—or English.

As in the past, there is concern that "too many" immigrants will change the character of the United States. "Throughout the history of U.S. immigration," write sociologists Alejandro Portés and Rubén Rumbaut (1990), "a consistent thread has been the fear that the 'alien element' would somehow undermine the institutions of the country and would lead it down the path of disintegration and decay." A hundred years ago, the widespread fear was that the immigrants from southern Europe would bring communism with them. Today, some fear that Spanish-speaking immigrants threaten the primacy of the English language. In addition, the age-old fear that immigrants will take jobs away from native-born Americans remains strong. Finally, minority groups that struggled for political representation fear that newer groups will gain political power at their expense.

Affirmative Action

Affirmative action in our multicultural society lies at the center of a national debate about racial–ethnic relations. In this policy, initiated by President Kennedy in 1961, goals based on race (and sex) are used in hiring, promotion, and college admission. Sociologist Barbara Reskin (1998) examined the results of affirmative action. She concluded that although it is difficult to separate the results of affirmative action from economic booms and busts and the greater number of women in the workforce, affirmative action has had a modest impact.

The results may have been modest, but the reactions to this program have been anything but modest. Affirmative action has been at the center of controversy for two generations. Liberals, both white and minority, say that this program is the most direct way to level the playing field of economic opportunity. If whites are passed over, this is an unfortunate cost that we must pay if we are to make up for past discrimination. In contrast, conservatives, both white and minority, agree that opportunity should be open to all, but claim that putting race (or sex) ahead of an individual's training and ability to perform a job is reverse discrimination. Because of their race (or sex), qualified people who had nothing to do with past inequality are discriminated against. They add that affirmative action stigmatizes the people who benefit from it, because it suggests that they hold their jobs because of race (or sex), rather than merit.

This national debate crystallized with a series of controversial rulings. One of the most significant was *Proposition 209*, a 1996 amendment to the California state

Cultural Diversity **in the United States**

Glimpsing the Future: The Shifting U.S. Racial–Ethnic Mix

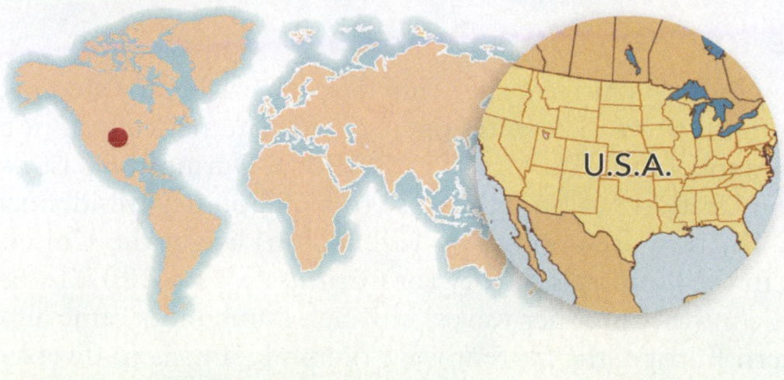

During the next twenty-five years, the population of the United States is expected to grow by about 22 percent. To see what the U.S. population will look like at that time, can we simply add 22 percent to our current racial–ethnic mix? The answer is a resounding no. As you can see from Figure 12.10, some groups will grow much more than others, giving us a different-looking United States. Some of the changes in the U.S. racial–ethnic mix will be dramatic. In twenty-five years, one of every nineteen Americans is expected to have an Asian background, and, in the most dramatic change, about one of four is expected to be of Latino ancestry.

The basic causes of this fundamental shift are the racial–ethnic groups' different rates of immigration and birth. Both will change the groups' proportions of the U.S. population, but immigration is by far the more important. From Figure 12.10, you can see that the proportion of non-Hispanic whites is expected to shrink, that of African Americans and Native Americans to remain about the same, and that of Latinos to increase sharply.

For Your Consideration

➤ This shifting racial–ethnic mix is one of the most significant events occurring in the United States. To better understand its implications, apply the three theoretical perspectives. Use the *conflict perspective* to identify the groups that are likely to be threatened by this change. Over what resources are struggles likely to develop? What impact do you think this changing mix might have on European Americans? On Latinos? On African Americans? On Asian Americans? On Native Americans? What changes in immigration laws (or their enforcement) can you anticipate?

To apply the *symbolic interactionist perspective*, consider how groups might perceive one another differently as their proportions of the population change. How do you think that these changed perceptions will affect people's behavior?

To apply the *functionalist perspective*, try to determine how each racial–ethnic group will benefit from this changing mix. How will other parts of society (such as businesses) benefit? What functions and dysfunctions can you anticipate for politics, economics, education, or religion?

FIGURE 12.10 **Projections of the Racial–Ethnic Makeup of the U.S. Population**

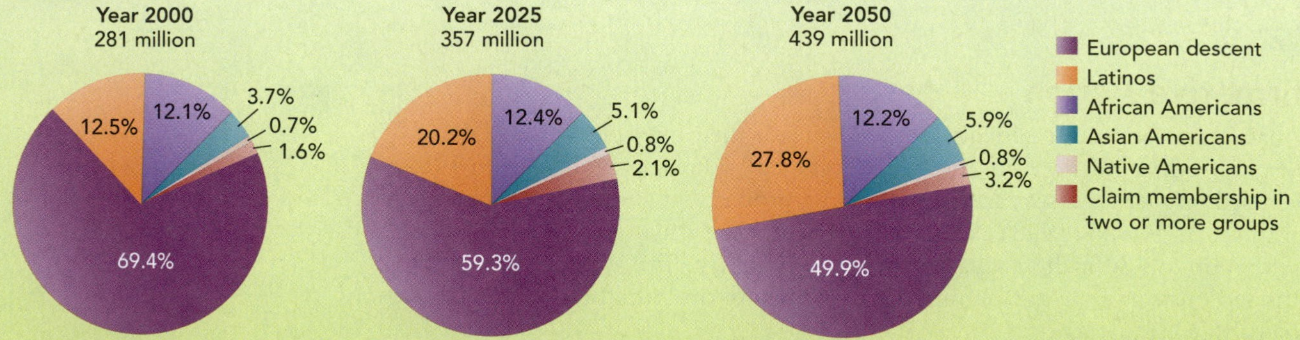

Source: By the author. Based on U.S. Census Bureau 2009; *Statistical Abstract of the United States* 2013:Tables 5, 12. I modified the projections based on the new census category of membership in two or more groups and trends in interethnic marriage.

constitution. This amendment made it illegal to give preference to minorities and women in hiring, promotion, and college admissions. Despite appeals by a coalition of civil rights groups, the U.S. Supreme Court upheld this California law.

A second significant ruling was made by the U.S. Supreme Court in 2003. White students who had been denied admission to the University of Michigan claimed that they had been discriminated against because less qualified applicants had been admitted on the basis of their race. Again, the Court's ruling was ambiguous. The Court ruled that universities can give minorities an edge in admissions, but they cannot use a point system to do so. Race can be a "plus factor," but in the Court's words, there must be "a meaningful individualized review of applicants."

Officials found this ruling murky. To remove ambiguity, voters in California, Michigan, and Nebraska added amendments to their state constitutions that make it illegal for public institutions to consider race or sex in hiring, in awarding contracts, or in college admissions (Espenshade and Radford 2009; Pérez-Peña 2012).

With constitutional battles continuing and whites increasingly feeling that they are being discriminated against (Norton and Sommers 2011), the issue of affirmative action in a multicultural society is likely to remain center stage for quite some time.

The United States is the most racially–ethnically diverse society in the world. This can be our central strength, with our many groups working together to build a harmonious society, a stellar example for the world. Or it can be our Achilles heel, with us breaking into feuding groups, a Balkanized society that marks an ill-fitting end to a grand social experiment. Our reality will probably fall somewhere between these extremes.

Toward a True Multicultural Society

The United States has the potential to become a society in which racial–ethnic groups not only coexist but also respect one another—and thrive—as they work together for mutually beneficial goals. In a true multicultural society, the minority groups that make up the United States would participate fully in the nation's social institutions while maintaining their cultural integrity. Reaching this goal will require that we understand that "the biological differences that divide one race from another add up to a drop in the genetic ocean." For a long time, we have given racial categories an importance they never merited. Now we need to figure out how to reduce them to the irrelevance they deserve. In short, we need to make real the abstraction called equality that we profess to believe (Cose 2000).

MySocLab — Study and Review on MySocLab

CHAPTER 12 Summary and Review

Laying the Sociological Foundation

12.1 Contrast the myth and reality of race, race and ethnicity, and minority and dominant groups; discuss ethnic work.

How is race both a reality and a myth?

In the sense that different groups inherit distinctive physical traits, race is a reality. There is no agreement regarding what constitutes a particular race, however, or even how many races there are. In the sense of one race being superior to another and of there being pure races, race is a myth. The *idea* of race is powerful, shaping basic relationships among people. Pp. 321–324.

How do race and ethnicity differ?

Race refers to inherited biological characteristics, **ethnicity** to cultural ones. Members of ethnic groups identify with one another on the basis of common ancestry and cultural heritage. Pp. 324–325.

What are minority and dominant groups?

Minority groups are people who are singled out for unequal treatment by members of the **dominant group**, the group with more power and privilege. Minorities originate with migration or the expansion of political boundaries. Pp. 325–326.

What heightens ethnic identity, and what is "ethnic work"?

A group's ethnic identity is heightened or reduced by its relative size, power, and physical characteristics, as well as the amount of discrimination it faces. **Ethnic work** is the process of constructing and maintaining an ethnic identity. For people without a firm ethnic identity, ethnic work is an attempt to recover their ethnic heritage. For those with strong ties to their culture of origin, ethnic work involves enhancing group distinctions. Pp. 326–327.

Prejudice and Discrimination

12.2 Contrast prejudice and discrimination and individual and institutional discrimination; discuss learning prejudice, internalizing dominant norms, and institutional discrimination.

Why are people prejudiced?

Prejudice is an attitude, and **discrimination** is an action. Like other attitudes, prejudice is learned in association with others. Prejudice is so extensive that people can show prejudice against groups that don't even exist. Minorities also internalize the dominant norms, and some show prejudice against their own group. Pp. 328–331.

How do individual and institutional discrimination differ?

Individual discrimination is the negative treatment of one person by another, while **institutional discrimination** is negative treatment that is built into social institutions. Institutional discrimination can occur without the awareness of either those who do the discriminating or those who are discriminated against. Discrimination in health care is one example. Pp. 331–332.

Theories of Prejudice

12.3 Contrast psychological and sociological theories of prejudice: include functionalism, conflict, and symbolic interactionism.

How do psychologists explain prejudice?

Psychological theories of prejudice stress the **authoritarian personality** and frustration displaced toward **scapegoats**. Pp. 332–333.

How do sociologists explain prejudice?

Sociological theories focus on how different social environments increase or decrease prejudice. *Functionalists* stress the benefits and costs that come from discrimination. *Conflict theorists* look at how the groups in power exploit racial–ethnic divisions in order to control workers and maintain power. *Symbolic interactionists* stress how labels create **selective perception** and self-fulfilling prophecies. Pp. 333–335.

Global Patterns of Intergroup Relations

12.4 Explain genocide, population transfer, internal colonialism, segregation, assimilation, and multiculturalism.

What are the major patterns of minority and dominant group relations?

Beginning with the least humane, they are **genocide**, **population transfer**, **internal colonialism**, **segregation**, **assimilation**, and **multiculturalism** (**pluralism**). Pp. 335–339.

Racial–Ethnic Relations in the United States

12.5 Summarize the major patterns that characterize European Americans, Latinos, African Americans, Asian Americans, and Native Americans.

What are the major racial–ethnic groups in the United States?

From largest to smallest, the major groups are European Americans, Latinos, African Americans, Asian Americans, and Native Americans. Pp. 339–341.

What are some issues in racial–ethnic relations and characteristics of minority groups?

Latinos are divided by social class and country of origin. African Americans are increasingly divided into middle and lower classes, with two sharply contrasting worlds of experience. On many measures, Asian Americans are better off than white Americans, but their well-being varies with country of origin. For Native Americans, the primary issues are poverty, nationhood, and settling treaty obligations. The overarching issue for minorities is overcoming discrimination. Pp. 341–352.

Looking Toward the Future

12.6 Discuss immigration, affirmative action, and a multicultural society.

What main issues dominate U.S. racial–ethnic relations?

The main issues are immigration, affirmative action, and how to develop a true multicultural society. The answers are significant for our future. Pp. 352–355.

Thinking **Critically** about Chapter 12

1. How many races do your friends or family think there are? Do they think that one race is superior to the others? What do you think their reaction would be to the sociological position that racial categories are primarily social?
2. A hundred years ago, sociologist W. E. B. Du Bois said, "The problem of the twentieth century is the problem of the color line—the relation of the darker to the lighter races." Why do you think that the color line remains one of the most volatile topics facing the nation?
3. If you were appointed head of the U.S. Civil Service Commission, what policies would you propose to reduce racial–ethnic strife in the United States? Be ready to explain the sociological principles that might give your proposals a higher chance of success.

13 CHAPTER

The Elderly

Listen to Chapter 13 on MySocLab

In 1928, Charles Hart, *who was working on his Ph.D. in anthropology, did fieldwork with the Tiwi, a people who live on an island off the northern coast of Australia. Because every Tiwi belongs to a clan, they assigned Hart to the bird (Jabijabui) clan and told him that a particular woman was his mother. Hart described the woman as "toothless, almost blind, withered." He added that she was "physically quite revolting and mentally rather senile." He then recounted this remarkable event:*

> *Toward the end of my time on the islands an incident occurred that surprised me because it suggested that some of them had been taking my presence in the kinship system much more seriously than I had thought. I was approached by a group of about eight or nine senior men. . . . They were the senior members of the Jabijabui clan and they had decided among themselves that the time had come to get rid of the decrepit old woman who had first called me son and whom I now called mother. . . . As I knew, they said, it was Tiwi custom, when an old woman became too feeble to look after herself, to "cover her up." This could only be done by her sons and brothers and all of them had to agree beforehand, since once it was done, they did not want any dissension among the brothers or clansmen, as that might lead to a feud. My "mother" was now completely blind, she was constantly falling over logs or into fires, and they, her senior clansmen, were in agreement that she would be better out of the way. Did I agree?*
>
> *I already knew about "covering up." The Tiwi, like many other hunting and gathering peoples, sometimes got rid of their ancient and decrepit females. The method was to dig a hole in the ground in some lonely place, put the old woman in the hole and fill it in with earth until only her head was showing. Everybody went away for a day or two and then went back to the hole to discover to their great surprise, that the old woman was dead, having been too feeble to raise her arms from the earth. Nobody had "killed" her; her death in Tiwi eyes was a natural one. She had been alive when her relatives last saw her. I had never seen it done, though I knew it was the custom, so I asked my brothers if it was necessary for me to attend the "covering up."*
>
> *They said no and that they would do it, but only after they had my agreement. Of course I agreed, and a week or two later we heard in our camp that my "mother" was dead, and we all wailed and put on the trimmings of mourning. (C. W. M. Hart in Hart and Pilling 1979:125–126)*

[They would] put the old woman in the hole and fill it in with earth until only her head was showing.

Learning Objectives

After you have read this chapter, you should be able to:

13.1 Understand the social construction of aging; explain how industrialization led to a graying globe and how race-ethnicity is related to aging. (p. 359)

13.2 Explain how people decide when they are old and discuss changes in perceptions of the elderly. (p. 364)

13.3 Summarize theories of disengagement, activity, and continuity. (p. 368)

13.4 Explain the conflict perspective on Social Security and discuss intergenerational competition and conflict. (p. 370)

13.5 Review findings on the living arrangements of the elderly, nursing homes, elder abuse, and the elderly poor. (p. 375)

13.6 Explain how industrialization changed death practices, how death is a process, why hospices emerged, suicide and age, and adjusting to death. (p. 380)

13.7 Discuss developing views of aging and the impact of technology on how long people live. (p. 382)

Watch on **MySocLab**
Video: Planning for the End of Life

Aging in Global Perspective

13.1 Understand the social construction of aging; explain how industrialization led to a graying globe and how race-ethnicity is related to aging.

We won't deal with the question of whether it was moral or ethical for Hart to agree that the old woman should be "covered up." What is of interest for our purposes is how the Tiwi treated their frail elderly—or, more specifically, their frail *female* elderly. You probably noticed that the Tiwi "covered up" only old women. As was noted in Chapter 11, females are discriminated against throughout the world. As this incident makes evident, gender discrimination can even bring death.

Every society must deal with the problem of people growing old, and of some becoming frail. Although few societies choose to bury old people alive, all societies must decide how to allocate limited resources among their citizens. With more people around the world making it to old age, these decisions are producing tensions between the generations on a global level.

The Social Construction of Aging

The way the Tiwi treated frail elderly women reflects one extreme of how societies cope with aging. Another extreme, one that reflects a sharply different attitude, is illustrated

This 80-year old man in a village in Hubei, China, has slowed down, but he has not retired. He is still making rope for straw sandals and remains integrated in his community.

by the Abkhasians, an agricultural people who live in Georgia, a republic of the former Soviet Union. The Abkhasians pay their elderly high respect and look to them for guidance. They would no more dispense with their elderly by "covering them up" than we would "cover up" a sick child in our culture.

The Abkhasians may be the longest-lived people on Earth. Many claim to live past 100—some beyond 120 and even 130 (Benet 1971; Robbins 2006). Although researchers have concluded that the extreme claims are bogus (Young et al. 2010), government records indicate that many Abkhasians do live to a very old age.

Three main factors appear to account for their long lives. The first is their diet, which consists of little meat and much fresh fruit, vegetables, garlic, goat cheese, cornmeal, buttermilk, and wine. The second is their lifelong physical activity. They do slow down after age 80, but even after the age of 100, they still work about four hours a day. The third factor—a highly developed sense of community—lies at the very heart of the Abkhasian culture. From childhood, each individual is integrated into a primary group and remains so throughout life. There is no such thing as a nursing home, nor do the elderly live alone. Because they continue to work and contribute to the group's welfare, the elderly aren't a burden to anyone. They don't vegetate, nor do they feel the need to "fill time" with bingo and shuffleboard. In short, the elderly feel no sudden rupture between what they "were" and what they "are."

In Sum. The examples of the Tiwi and the Abkhasians reveal an important sociological principle: Like gender, aging is *socially constructed*. That is, nothing in the nature of aging summons forth any particular viewpoint. Rather, attitudes toward the aged are rooted in society. They differ with groups around the world. As we shall see, even the age at which people are considered old depends not on biology but on culture.

Industrialization and the Graying of the Globe

As was noted in previous chapters, industrialization is occurring worldwide. With industrialization comes a higher standard of living: more food, a purer water supply, better housing, more material goods, and more effective ways of fighting the diseases that kill children. As a result, when a country industrializes, more of its people reach older ages. The Social Map on the next page illustrates this principle.

From this global map, you can see that the industrialized countries have the highest percentage of elderly. The range among nations is broad, from just 1 of 45 citizens in nonindustrialized Uganda to *nine* times more—1 of 4 or 5—in postindustrial Japan (*Statistical Abstract* 2013:Table 1350). In another ten years, *half* the population of Italy and Japan will be older than 50 (U.S. Census Bureau 2013). The graying of the globe is so new that *two-thirds of all people who have ever passed age 50 in the history of the world are alive today* (Zaslow 2003).

As the number of elderly continues to grow, analysts have become alarmed about future liabilities for their care. This issue is especially troubling in western Europe and Japan, which have the largest percentage of citizens over age 60. The basic issue is, How can nations provide high-quality care for growing numbers of elderly people without burdening future generations with impossible taxes? Although more and more nations around the world are confronting this issue, no one has found a solution yet.

life expectancy the number of years that an average person at any age, including newborns, can expect to live

The Graying of America

From Figure 13.2 on the next page, you can see how the United States is part of this global trend. This figure shows how U.S. **life expectancy**, the number of years people

FIGURE 13.1 The Graying of the Globe

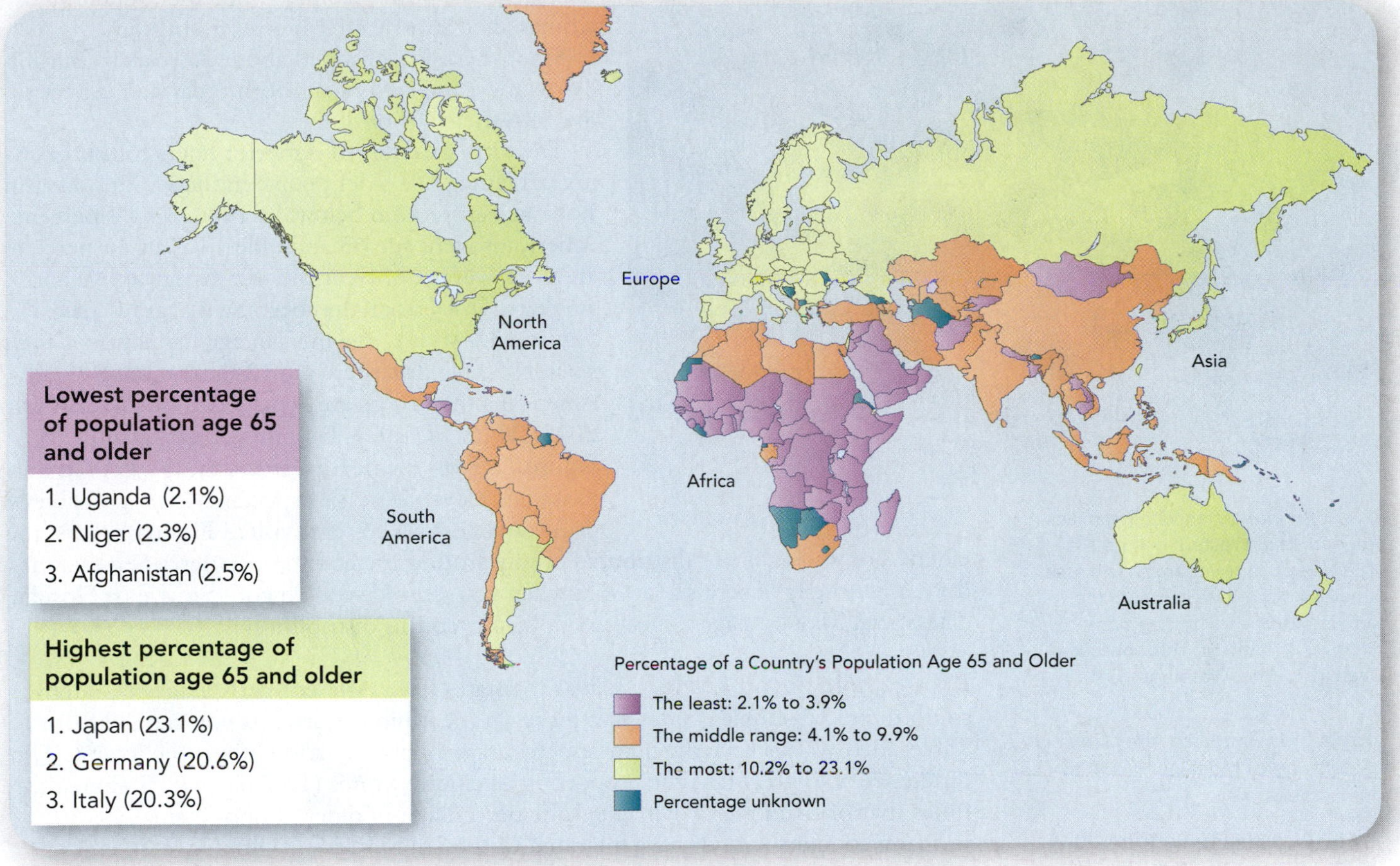

Source: By the author. Based on *Statistical Abstract of the United States*; 2013:Table 1350.

FIGURE 13.2 U.S. Life Expectancy by Year of Birth

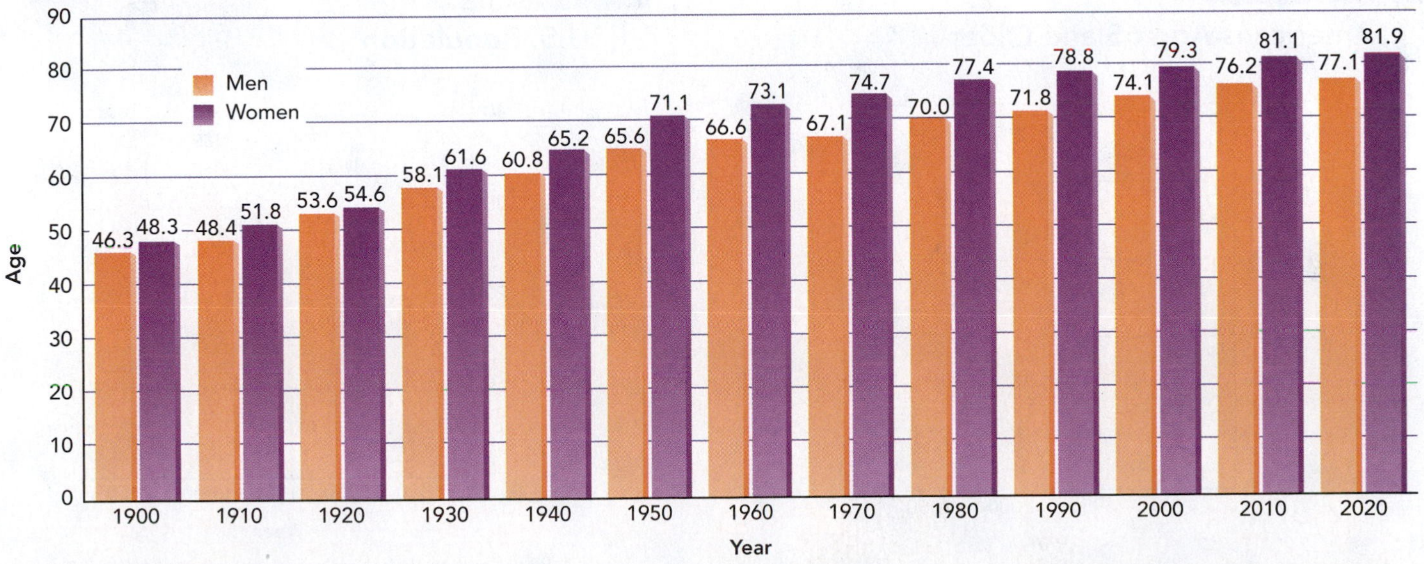

Sources: By the author. Based on *Historical Statistics of the United States, Colonial Times to 1970*, Bicentennial Edition, Part I, Series B, 107–115; *Statistical Abstract of the United States* 2013:Table 108.

Except for interaction within families, age groups in Western culture are usually kept fairly separate. The idea of having a day care center in the same building as a nursing home breaks this tradition. This photo was taken in Seattle, Washington.

graying of America the growing percentage of older people in the U.S. population

life span the maximum length of life of a species; for humans, the longest that a human has lived

can expect to live, has increased since 1900. To me, and perhaps to you, it is startling to realize that a little over a hundred years ago, the average U.S. man didn't make it to his 50th birthday, while the average U.S. woman died shortly after her 50th birthday.

Since then, we've added about *30* years to our life expectancy, and Americans born today can expect to live into their 70s or 80s.

The term **graying of America** refers to this growing percentage of older people in the U.S. population. Look at Figure 13.3 below. In 1900, only 4 percent of Americans were age 65 and older. Today, 13 percent are. The average 65-year-old can expect to live another 19 years. U.S. society has become so "gray" that, as Figure 13.4 shows, the median age has almost *doubled* since 1850. Today, there are 12 million *more* elderly Americans than there are teenagers (*Statistical Abstract* 2013:Tables 11, 107). Despite this vast change, as Figure 13.5 on the next page shows, the United States ranks just eleventh in life expectancy on a global level.

As anyone who has ever visited Florida knows, the elderly population is not distributed evenly around the country. (As Jerry Seinfeld sardonically noted, "There's a law that when you get old, you've got to move to Florida.") The Social Map on page 364 shows how uneven this distribution is.

Race–Ethnicity and Aging. Just as the states have different percentages of elderly, so do the racial–ethnic groups that make up the United States. As you can see from Table 13.1, whites have the highest percentage of elderly, and Latinos the lowest. The difference is so great that the proportion of elderly whites (16.7 percent) is almost three times that of Latinos (5.7 percent). The percentage of older Latinos is small because so many younger Latinos have migrated to the United States. Differences in cultural attitudes about aging, family relationships, work histories, and health practices will be important areas of sociological investigation in coming years.

FIGURE 13.3 The Graying of America: Americans Age 65 and Older

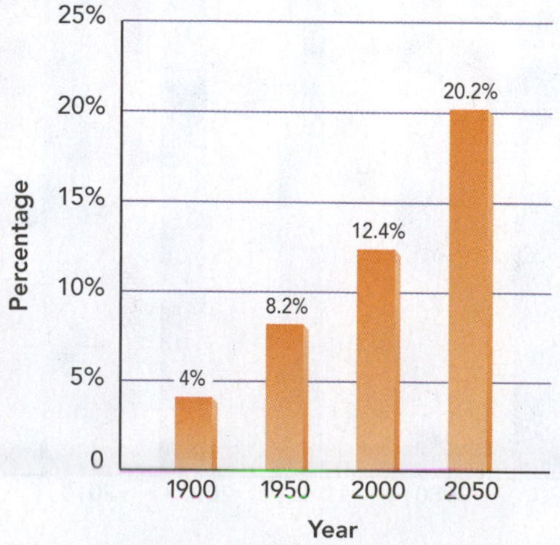

Source: By the author. Based on *Statistical Abstract of the United States* 2013:Table 9, and earlier years.

FIGURE 13.4 The Median Age of the U.S. Population

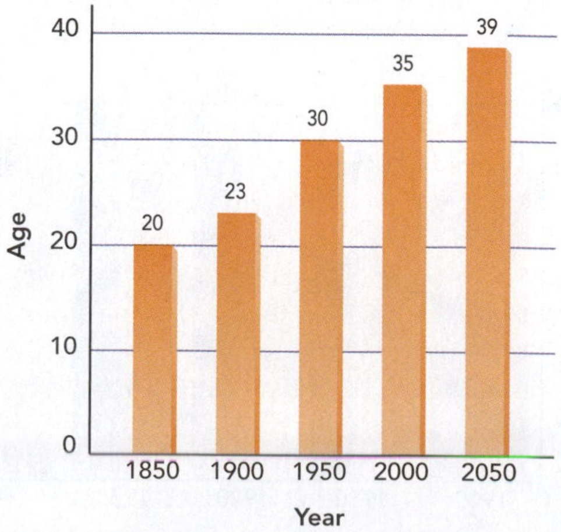

Source: By the author. Based on *Statistical Abstract of the United States* 2000:Table 14; 2013:Table 9, and earlier years.

FIGURE 13.5 Life Expectancy in Global Perspective

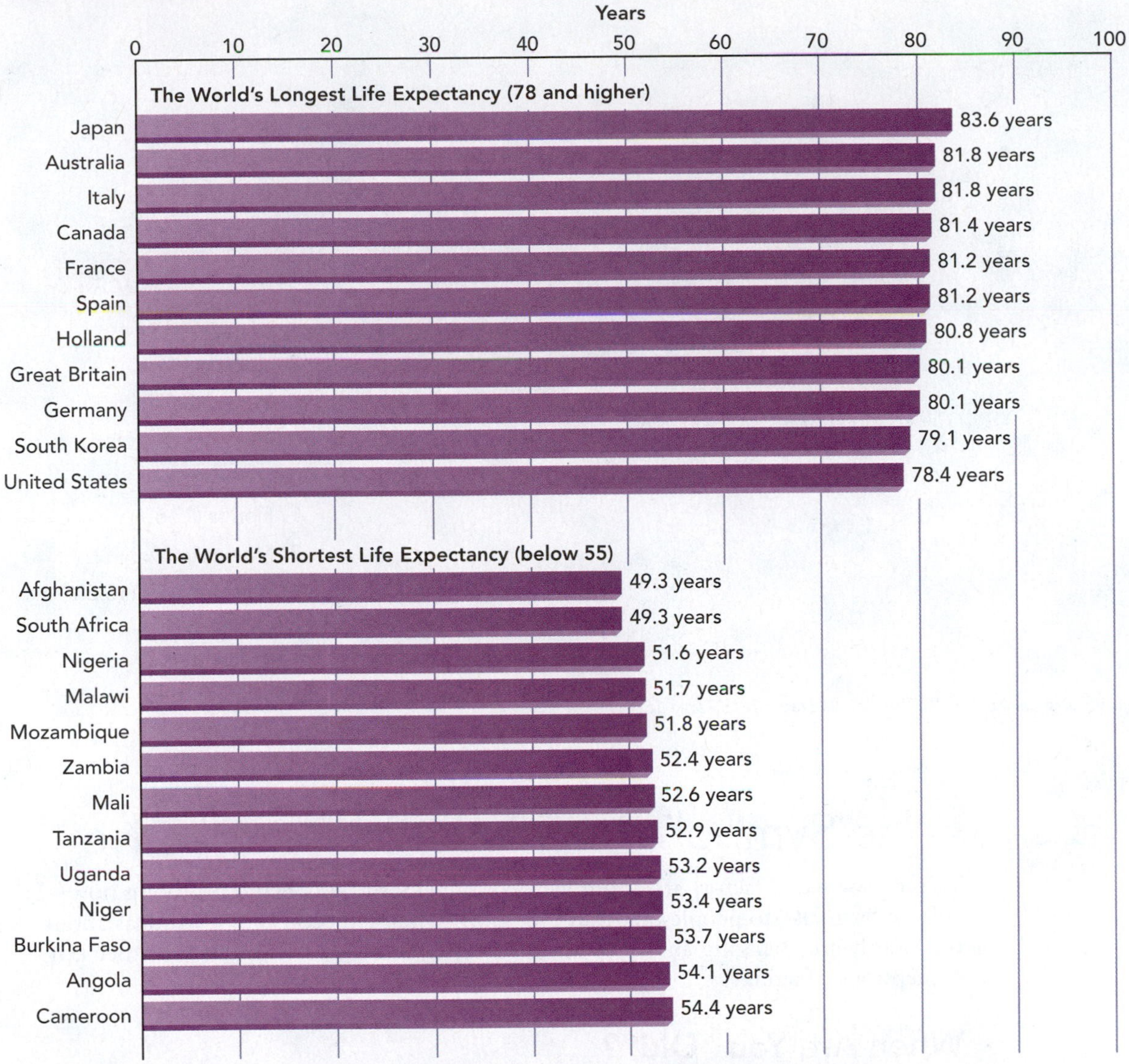

Note: The countries listed in the source with a life expectancy longer than the United States and those with a life expectancy less than 55 years. All the countries in the top group are industrialized, and none of those in the bottom group are.

Source: By the author. Based on *Statistical Abstract of the United States* 2013:Table 1355.

Although more people are living to old age, the maximum length of life possible, the **life span**, has not increased. No one knows, however, just what that maximum is. We do know that it is at least 122: This was the well-documented age of Jeanne Louise Calment of France at her death in 1997. If the birth certificate of Tuti Yusupova in Uzbekistan proves to be genuine, which shows her birth year as 1880, then the human life span exceeds even this number by a comfortable margin. It is also likely that advances in genetics will extend the human life span—maybe even to hundreds of years—a topic we will return to later. For now, let's see the different pictures of aging that emerge when we apply the three theoretical perspectives.

TABLE 13.1 Race–Ethnicity and Aging

	Median Age	65 and Over	75 and Over	85 and Over
Whites	42.3	16.7%	7.8%	2.5%
Asian Americans	35.5	9.7%	3.9%	1.0%
African Americans	32.3	8.9%	3.7%	1.0%
Native Americans	29.4	6.6%	2.4%	0.6%
Latinos	27.6	5.7%	2.3%	0.6%
U.S. Average	37.3	13.3%	6.1%	1.8%

Source: By the author. Based on *Statistical Abstract of the United States* 2013:Table 10.

FIGURE 13.6 As Florida Goes, So Goes the Nation

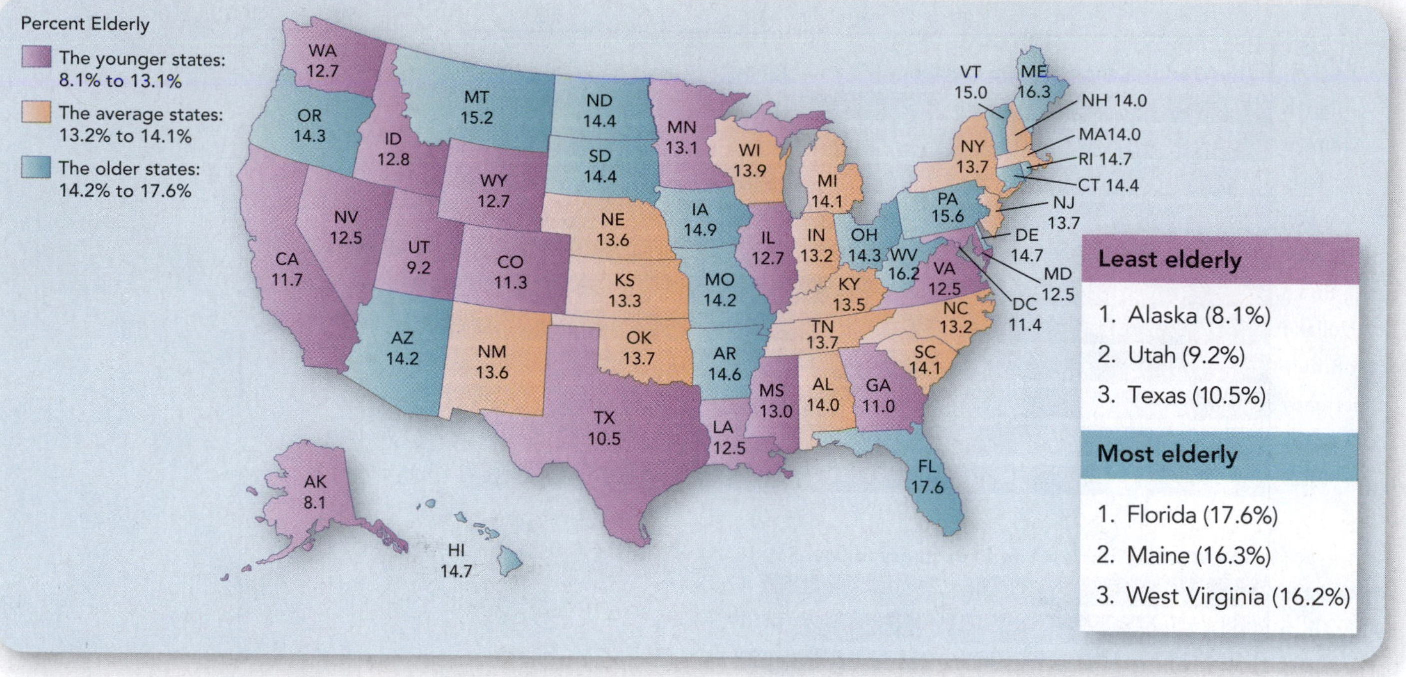

Source: By the author. Based on *Statistical Abstract of the United States* 2013:Table 16.

13.2 Explain how people decide when they are old and discuss changes in perceptions of the elderly.

The Symbolic Interactionist Perspective

To see how social factors affect our views of the elderly, let's begin by asking how culture "signals" to people that they are "old." Then let's consider how ideas about the elderly are changing and the ways stereotypes and the mass media influence our perceptions of aging.

Watch on **MySocLab**
Video: U.S. Seniors Gym

When Are You "Old"?

Changing Perceptions as You Age. You probably can remember when you thought that a 12-year-old was "old"—and anyone older than that, beyond reckoning. You probably were 5 or 6 at the time. Similarly, to a 12-year-old, someone who is 21 seems "old." To someone who is 21, 30 may mark the point at which one is no longer "young," and 40 may seem very old. As people add years, "old" gradually recedes farther from the self. To people who turn 40, 50 seems old; at 50, the late 60s look old—not the early 60s, for the passing of years seems to accelerate as we age, and at 50, age 60 doesn't seem so far away.

In Western culture, most people have difficulty applying the label "old" to themselves. In the typical case, they have become used to what they see in the mirror. The changes have taken place gradually, and each change, if it has not exactly been taken in stride, has been accommodated. Consequently, it comes as a shock to meet a long-lost friend and see how much that person has changed. At class reunions, *each* person can hardly believe how much older *the others* appear!

Four Factors in Our Decision. If there is no fixed age line that people cross, what makes someone "old"? Sociologists have identified several factors that spur people to apply the label of "old" to themselves.

At age 115, Misao Okawa of Osaka, Japan, is the world's oldest living person. The world's record for age that has been documented by a birth certificate is held by Jeanne Calment of France who died in 1997 at the age of 122.

The first factor is *biology*. One person may experience "signs" of aging earlier than others: wrinkles, balding, aches, difficulty in doing something that he or she used to take for granted. Consequently, some people *feel* "old" at an earlier or later age than others.

A second factor is *personal history* or biography. An accident that limits someone's mobility, for example, can make that person feel old sooner than others. Or consider actress Whoopi Goldberg, who became a grandmother at age 34. She gave birth to her daughter Alexandrea when she was 18, and her daughter gave birth to her own daughter, Amarah, at age 16. Although Goldberg became a biological grandmother at age 34, she certainly did not play a stereotypical role. But *knowing* at 34 that she had become a grandmother had to have an impact on her self-concept. At a minimum, she had to *deny to herself* that she was old.

Then there is **gender age**, the relative value that a culture places on men's and women's ages. For example, graying hair on a man, and even a few wrinkles, may be perceived as signs of "maturity," while on a woman, these same features may indicate that she is getting "old." "Mature" and "old," of course, carry different meanings; most of us like to be called mature, but few of us like to be called old. Similarly, around the world, most men are able to marry younger spouses than women can. Maria might be an exception and marry Bill, who is twenty years younger than she. But in most marriages in which there is a twenty-year age gap, the odds greatly favor the wife being the younger of the pair. This is not biology in action; rather, it is the social construction of appearance and gender age.

The fourth factor in deciding when people label themselves as "old" is timetables, the signals societies use to inform their members that old age has begun. Since there is no automatic age at which people become "old," these timetables vary around the world. One group may choose a particular birthday, such as the 60th or 65th, to signal the onset of old age. Other groups do not even have birthdays, making such numbers meaningless. In the West, retirement is sometimes a cultural signal of the beginning of old age—which is one reason that some people resist retirement.

Read on **MySocLab**
Document: Growing Old in an Arab American Family

Changing Perceptions of the Elderly

At first, the audience sat quietly as the developers explained their plans to build a high-rise apartment building. After a while, people began to shift uncomfortably in their seats. Then they began to show open hostility.

"That's too much money to spend on those people," said one.

"You even want them to have a swimming pool?" asked another incredulously.

Finally, one young woman put their attitudes in a nutshell when she asked, "Who wants all those old people around?"

When physician Robert Butler (1975, 1980) heard these complaints about plans to build apartments for senior citizens, he began to realize how deeply antagonistic feelings toward the elderly can run. He coined the term **ageism** to refer to prejudice and discrimination directed against people because of their age. Let's see how ageism developed in U.S. society.

Shifting Meanings. As we have seen, there is nothing inherent in old age to produce any particular attitude, negative or not. Some historians point out that in early U.S. society, old age was regarded positively (Cottin 1979; Fleming et al. 2003). In colonial times, growing old was seen as an accomplishment because so few people made it to old age.

gender age the relative value placed on men's and women's ages

ageism prejudice and discrimination directed against people because of their age; can be directed against any age group, including youth

When does old age begin? And what activities are appropriate for the elderly? From this photo that I took of Munimah, a 65-year-old bonded laborer in Chennai, India, you can see how culturally relative these questions are. No one in Chennai thinks it is extraordinary that this woman makes her living by carrying heavy rocks all day in the burning, tropical sun. Working next to her in the quarry is her 18-year-old son, who breaks the rocks into the size that his mother carries.

With no pensions, the elderly continued to work. Their jobs changed little over time, and they were viewed as storehouses of knowledge about work skills and sources of wisdom about how to live a long life.

The coming of industrialization eroded these bases of respect. With better sanitation and medical care, more people reached old age, and being elderly lost its uniqueness and the honor it had brought. Industrialization's new forms of mass production also made young workers as productive as the elderly. Coupled with mass education, this stripped away the elderly's superior knowledge (Cowgill 1974; Lee 2009). In the Cultural Diversity box on the next page, you can see how a similar process is now occurring in China as it, too, industrializes.

A basic principle of symbolic interactionism is that we perceive both ourselves and others according to the symbols of our culture. When the meaning of old age changed from an asset to a liability, not only did younger people come to view the elderly differently but the elderly also began to perceive themselves in a new light. This shift in meaning is demonstrated in the way people lie about their age: They used to say that they were older than they were but now claim to be younger than their true ages (Clair et al. 1993).

Today, the meaning of old age is shifting once again—this time in a positive direction. More positive images of the elderly are developing, largely because most of today's U.S. elderly enjoy good health and can take care of themselves financially. If this symbolic shift continues, the next step—now in process—will be to view old age not as a period that precedes death but, rather, as a new stage of growth.

Even theories of old age have taken a more positive tone. A theory that goes by the mouthful *gerotranscendence* was developed by Swedish sociologist Lars Tornstam. The thrust of this theory is that as people grow old, they transcend their limited views of life. They become less self-centered and begin to feel more at one with the universe. Coming to see things as less black and white, they develop subtler ways of viewing right and wrong and tolerate more ambiguity (Manheimer 2005; Hyse and Tornstam 2009). However, this theory seems to miss the mark. Some elderly people do grow softer and more spiritual, but I have seen others turn bitter, close up, and become even more judgmental of others. The theory's limitations should become apparent shortly.

The Influence of the Mass Media

In Chapter 3 (pages 77–79), we noted that the mass media help to shape our ideas about both gender and relationships between men and women. As a powerful source of symbols, the media also influence our ideas of the elderly, the topic of the Mass Media box on page 368.

Stereotypes, which play such a profound role in social life, are a basic area of sociological investigation. In contemporary society, the mass media are a major source of stereotypes.

Cultural Diversity **around the World**

China: Changing Sentiment about the Elderly

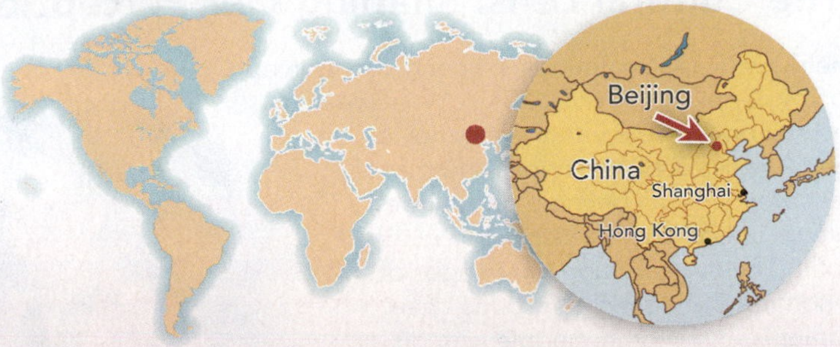

Zhao Chunlan, a 71-year-old widow, smiles with satisfaction. She has heard how sons are abandoning their aged parents. But Zhao has no such fears.

It is not that her son is so devoted that he would never swerve from his traditional duty to his mother. Rather, it is a piece of paper that has eased Zhao's mind. Her 51-year-old son has just signed a support agreement: He will cook her special meals, take her to medical checkups, even give her the largest room in his house and put the family's color television in it.

"I'm sure he would do right by me, anyway," says Zhao, "but this way I know he will." (Sun 1990)

The high status of the elderly in China is famed around the world: The elderly are considered a source of wisdom and given honored seating at both family and public gatherings. They are even venerated after death in ancestor worship.

Or at least, this is how it used to be. But now, China is shedding its slow-moving rural heritage, exchanging it for a fast-paced urban way of life. This change affects most areas of life—including the way the younger view and treat the elderly (Tatlow 2012).

This woman in Shandong, China, who is celebrating her 111th birthday, is surrounded by family and friends. As discussed in this box, attitudes toward the elderly are changing.

The traditional respect for the elderly was grounded in a rural society that stayed much the same year after year. Under those circumstances, the elderly's knowledge remained valuable throughout their lives. In addition, families, which spanned generations, lived together in the same house.

City life is far different, and the structural changes are tearing at the bonds that united the generations. For urban dwellers, apartments are small, and more life is lived within their walls. For some, the adult children's success in the new market economy places them in a world unknown to their parents (Chen 2005; Fan 2008). The longer lives that industrialization has brought make the duty to dependent parents span decades. The change is startling: In 1950, China's life expectancy was 41 years. It has now jumped to 70 years (Li 2004). China's elderly population is growing so rapidly that the country has 120 million elderly—8.9 percent of its population (*Statistical Abstract* 2013:Table 1350).

China's policy that allows each married couple only one child has also created a problem for the support of the elderly. With such small families, the responsibility for supporting aged parents falls on fewer shoulders. Some younger couples must now support *four* elderly parents (Zhang and Goza 2007). Try putting yourself in that situation. If you and your spouse were supporting all four of your parents, how would it interfere with your plans for life? Can you see how it might affect your attitudes toward your aging parents, who constantly depend on you? How about your attitude toward your in-laws?

Alarmed by the weakening of parent–child bonds, the National People's Congress passed a law that requires adult children to visit their parents and pay them respect. The law doesn't specify how often the children need to visit their parents, but it is a sign of concern over the changing sentiment (Tejada 2012).

One province has gone farther than the national legislature. To get a marriage license, a couple must sign a contract pledging to support their parents after they reach age 60 (Sun 1990).

For Your Consideration

→ Do you think we could solve our Social Security crisis by requiring adult children to sign a parental support agreement in order to get a marriage license? Why or why not? What do you think Chinese officials can do to solve the problem of supporting their huge and growing number of elderly?

In Sum: Symbolic interactionists stress that old age has no inherent meaning. There is nothing about old age to automatically summon forth responses of honor and respect, as with the Abkhasians, or any other response. Culture shapes how we perceive the elderly, including the ways we view our own aging. In short, the social modifies the biological.

Mass Media in Social Life

The Cultural Lens: Shaping Our Perceptions of the Elderly

The mass media profoundly influence our perception of people (Levy et al. 2013). What we hear and see on television and in the movies, the songs we listen to, the books and magazines we read—all become part of the cultural lens through which we view the world. The media shape our images of minorities and dominant groups; men, women, and children; people with disabilities; those from other cultures—and the elderly.

The shaping of our images and perception of the elderly is subtle, so much so that it usually occurs without our awareness. The elderly, for example, are underrepresented on television and in most popular magazines. This leaves a covert message—that the elderly are of little consequence and can be safely ignored.

The media also reflect and reinforce stereotypes of *gender age*. Older male news anchors are likely to be retained, while female anchors who turn the same age are more likely to be transferred to less visible positions. Similarly, in movies, older men are more likely to play romantic leads—and to play them opposite much younger rising stars.

The message might be subtle, but it is not lost. The more television that people watch, the more they perceive the elderly in negative terms. The elderly, too, internalize these negative images, which, in turn, influences the ways they view themselves. These images are so powerful that they affect the elderly's health, even the way they walk (Donlon et al. 2005).

Aging is more than biology. In some cultures, Jennifer Lopez, 43, would be considered elderly. Lopez is shown here with her boyfriend, Casper Smart, 25.

We become fearful of growing old, and we go to great lengths to deny that we are losing our youth. Fear and denial play into the hands of advertisers, of course, who exploit our concerns. They help us deny this biological reality by selling us hair dyes, skin creams, and other products that are designed to conceal even the appearance of old age. For these same reasons, plastic surgeons do a thriving business as they remove telltale signs of aging.

The elderly's growing number and affluence translate into economic clout and political power. It is inevitable, then, that the media's images of the elderly will change. An indication of that change is shown in the photo at left.

For Your Consideration

➤ What other examples of fear and denial of growing old are you familiar with? What examples of older men playing romantic leads with younger women can you give? Of older women and younger men? Why do you think we have gender age stereotypes?

13.3 Summarize theories of disengagement, activity, and continuity.

The Functionalist Perspective

Functionalists analyze how the parts of society work together. Among the components of society are **age cohorts**—people who were born at roughly the same time and who pass through the life course together. This term might strike you as something divorced from your life, but age cohorts actually affect your life deeply. For example, when you finish college, if the age cohort that is retiring is large (a "baby boom" generation), jobs will be plentiful. In contrast, if the age cohort is small (a "baby bust" generation), your opportunities for the kind of job you really want will shrink.

Let's consider people who are about to retire or who have retired recently. We will review theories that focus on how people adjust to retirement.

age cohort people born at roughly the same time who pass through the life course together

Disengagement Theory

Think about how disruptive it would be if the elderly left their jobs only when they died or became incompetent. How does society get the elderly to leave their positions so younger people can take them? According to **disengagement theory**, developed by Elaine Cumming and William Henry (1961), this is the function of pensions. Pensions get the elderly to *disengage* from their positions and hand them over to younger people. Retirement, then, is a mutually beneficial arrangement between two parts of society.

Cumming (1976) also examined disengagement from the individual's perspective. She pointed out that people start to disengage long before retirement. During middle age, they sense that the end of life is closer than its start. As they realize that their time is limited, they begin to assign priority to goals and tasks. Disengagement begins in earnest when their children leave home and increases with retirement and eventually widowhood.

Among the factors that influence health in old age are exercise, diet, and a sense of belonging. Shown here is a senior women's aqua-fitness class in Alameda, California.

Evaluation of the Theory. Certainly pensions do entice the elderly to leave their jobs so a younger generation can step in. I think we all know this, so it isn't much of a theory. Critics have also pointed out that the elderly don't really "disengage." People who quit their jobs don't sit in rocking chairs and watch the world go by. Instead of disengaging, the retired *exchange* one set of roles for another (Tadic et al. 2012). They find these new ways of conducting their lives, which often center on friendship, no less satisfying than their earlier roles. In addition, the meaning of retirement has changed since this "theory" was developed. Less and less does retirement mean an end to work. Many people stay at their jobs, but they slow down, putting in fewer hours. Others remain as part-time consultants. Some use the Internet to explore new areas of work. Some switch careers, even in their 60s, some even in their 70s. If disengagement theory is ever resurrected, it must come to grips with our new patterns of retirement.

Activity Theory

Are retired people more satisfied with life? (All that extra free time and not having to kowtow to a boss must be nice.) Are intimate activities more satisfying than formal ones? Such questions are the focus of **activity theory**. Although we could consider this theory from other perspectives, we are examining it from the functionalist perspective because its focus is how disengagement is functional or dysfunctional.

Evaluation of the Theory. When it comes to retired people, it is the same as with young people: There is no one size that fits all. Some people are happier when they are more active, but others prefer less involvement (Keith 1982; Levy et al. 2013). Similarly, many people find informal, intimate activities, such as spending time with friends, to be more satisfying than formal activities. But not everyone does. In one study, 2,000 retired U.S. men reported formal activities to be just as satisfying as informal ones. Even solitary tasks, such as doing home repairs, had about the same impact as intimate activities on these men's life satisfaction (Beck and Page 1988). It is the same for spending time with adult children. "Often enough" for some parents is "not enough" or even "too much" for others. In short, researchers have discovered the obvious: What makes life satisfying for one person doesn't work for another. (This, of course, can be a source of intense frustration for retired couples.)

Continuity Theory

Another theory of aging called **continuity theory** focuses, as its name implies, on how the elderly continue ties with their past (Wang and Shultz 2010). When they retire, many people take on new roles that are similar to the ones they give up. For example, a former CEO might serve as a consultant, a retired electrician might do small electrical repairs, or a pensioned banker might take over the finances of her church. Researchers have found that people who are active in multiple roles (wife, author, mother, intimate

disengagement theory the view that society is stabilized by having the elderly retire (disengage from) their positions of responsibility so the younger generation can step into their shoes

activity theory the view that satisfaction during old age is related to a person's amount and quality of activity

continuity theory a theory focusing on how people adjust to retirement by continuing aspects of their earlier lives friend, church member, etc.) are better equipped to handle the changes that come with growing old. Social class is also significant: With their greater resources, people from higher social classes adjust better to the challenges of aging.

Evaluation of the Theory. The basic criticism of continuity theory is that it is too broad (Hatch 2000). We all have anchor points based on our particular experiences in life, and we all rely on them to make adjustments to what we confront in life. This applies to people of all ages beyond infancy. This theory is really a collection of loosely connected ideas, with no specific application to the elderly.

In Sum: The *broader* perspective of the functionalists is how society's parts work together to keep society running smoothly. If younger workers had to fight to take over the jobs of the elderly, it would be disruptive to society. To make this a smooth transition, the elderly are offered pensions, which entice them to leave their positions. Functionalists also use a *narrower* perspective, focusing on how individuals adjust to their retirement. The findings of this narrower perspective are too mixed to be of much value—except that people who have better resources and are active in multiple roles adjust better to old age (Thomas 2012).

Because U.S. workers do not have to retire by any certain age, it is also important to study how people decide to keep working or to retire in the first place. After they retire, how do they reconstruct their identities and come to terms with their changed lives? As the United States grows even grayer, this should prove a productive area of sociological theory and research.

13.4 Explain the conflict perspective on Social Security and discuss intergenerational competition and conflict.

The Conflict Perspective

As you know, the conflict perspective's guiding principle is how social groups struggle to control power and resources. How does this apply to society's age groups? Regardless of whether the young and old recognize it, say conflict theorists, they are opponents in a struggle that threatens to throw society into turmoil. Let's look at how the passage of Social Security legislation fits the conflict view.

Read on **MySocLab**
Document: A Gradual Goodbye: If People Are Living Longer, They Will Have to Work Longer Too

Fighting for Resources: Social Security Legislation

In the 1920s, before Social Security provided an income for the aged, two-thirds of all citizens over 65 had no savings and could not support themselves (Holtzman 1963; Crossen 2004). Destitution in old age loomed even larger for workers during the Great Depression, and in 1930, Francis Townsend, a physician, started a movement to rally older citizens. He soon had one-third of all Americans over age 65 enrolled in his Townsend Clubs. They demanded that the federal government impose a national sales tax of 2 percent to provide $200 a month for every person over 65 ($2,100 a month in today's money). In 1934, the Townsend Plan went before Congress. Because it called for such high payments and many were afraid that it would destroy people's incentive to save for the future, members of Congress looked for a way to reject the plan without appearing to oppose the elderly. When President Roosevelt announced his own, more modest Social Security plan in 1934, Congress embraced it (Schottland 1963; Amenta 2006).

To provide jobs for younger people, the new Social Security law required that workers retire at age 65. It did not matter how well people did their work, or how much they needed the pay. For decades, the elderly protested. Finally, in 1986, Congress eliminated mandatory retirement. Today, almost 90 percent of Americans retire by age 65, but most do so voluntarily. No longer can they be forced out of their jobs simply because of age.

In the following Thinking Critically section, let's look at what has happened to this groundbreaking legislation since it was passed.

THINKING CRITICALLY

Social Security: The Magical Money Machine

The Social Security trust fund isn't a fund, and you shouldn't trust it. (Sloan 2001)

The system is simple: The Social Security Administration (SSA) takes money from the pay of about 200 million U.S. workers and sends checks to about 55 million retired and disabled people or their dependents (*Statistical Abstract* 2013:Tables 554, 555). The taking and sending goes like clockwork. What could go wrong?

The first problem is well known. Social Security is not like a bank. None of us has a Social Security savings account. At retirement, we don't withdraw the money we paid into Social Security. The government spent that money as fast as it came in. Instead, the government will write us checks on money that it collects from people who are working at that time. When these workers retire, they, too, will be paid, not from their own savings but from money collected from others who are still working.

The Social Security system is like a giant chain letter or Ponzi scheme—it works as long as it recruits enough new people. (In a Ponzi scheme, early investors are paid from the investments of later investors. Eventually the scam runs out of money and collapses.) If you join early enough, you'll collect more than you paid in—but if you join toward the end, you're out of luck. And we seem to be nearing the end of the chain. The shift in the **dependency ratio**—the number of people who collect Social Security compared with the number of workers who pay into it—is troubling. As Figure 13.7 shows, at the beginning of the Ponzi scheme, sixteen workers supported each person who collected Social Security. The dependency ratio has now dropped to four to one. In another generation, it could hit two to one—that is, every two workers will have to support one retired worker. If it comes to this, Social Security taxes could stifle the country's economy.

The second problem, to be blunt about it, is that the U.S. government is lying to us. They tell us that the Social Security system has a trust fund, trillions of excess dollars it has collected from workers. But does it?

This question takes us to the root of the crisis, or, perhaps better phrased, the fraud. In 1965, President Lyndon Johnson was bogged down with a war in Vietnam. To conceal the war's costs from the public, he hit upon a diabolical scheme. He got Congress to pass a law that said the SSA could invest only in government IOUs called U.S. Treasury bonds. This transferred all the money that workers pay into Social Security to the government's general fund. This allowed Johnson to use this money to finance the war.

What a politicians' dream this was. They fell in love with the easy money, and they continue the fraud today. They have even developed a term for their theft of the workers' Social Security money, and surprise!—the term doesn't even rhyme with the word *stealing*. Their term? They call it "off-budget spending." That certainly is softer on the ears than "theft from workers." And *every year, they spend every cent they confiscate from U.S. workers.*

FIGURE 13.7 Fewer Workers to Support the Retired

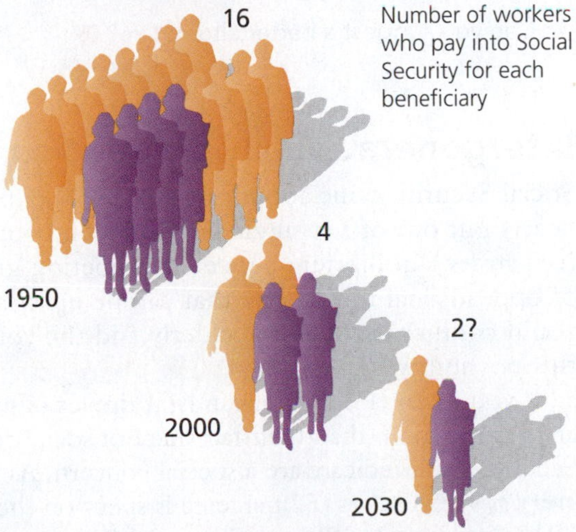

Source: By the author. Based on Social Security Administration; *Statistical Abstract of the United States* 2013:Tables 554, 555.

dependency ratio the number of workers who are required to support each dependent person—those 65 and older and those 15 and under

Here is a mental diagram of the Ponzi scheme that has been forced on us. The SSA collects the money from workers. It pays what is required to the retired, disabled, and survivors of deceased workers, then hands the excess to the U.S. government. The government, in turn, hands IOUs to the SSA in the form of U.S. Treasury bonds. The government spends the money on whatever it wants—good things, like building roads, parks, and schools, and bad things, like subsidizing tobacco crops, buying bombs, and fighting wars in far-off places. Anything it wants.

Here's another analogy.

Suppose you have spent more money than you make, and your credit is running low. You talk to your Aunt Mary, who is suffering from Alzheimer's disease. She arranges to transfer money from her bank account to your account each month. And in her confused state of mind, she says it is okay with her if you just give her IOUs each month.

What a deal! You have loads of money to spend, and Mary thinks that those IOUs are real money.

This is just what the U.S. government does. It fills a database with IOUs and then reports a nonexistent trust fund to the public.

Wouldn't such an arrangement be a dream for you (forgetting, of course, that it is immoral to steal from Aunt Mary)? It is the same for the politicians—who are not bothered by the immorality of stealing from workers. They simply grab the money from the workers, give them giant IOUs, and then pretend that they haven't even spent the money.

What a magical money machine Social Security is for politicians!

Sources: Smith 1986; Hardy 1991; Genetski 1993; Stevenson 1998; *Statistical Abstract* 2013. Government publications that list Social Security receipts as deficits can be found in *Monthly Treasury Statement of Receipts and Outlays*, the *Winter Treasury Bulletin*, and the *Statement of Liabilities and Other Financial Commitments of the United States Government.*

For Your Consideration

➔ What do you think about this proposal: that a worker's Social Security taxes be put into his or her own individual retirement account? Most proposals to do this lack controls to make the system work. Here is one idea for adding those missing controls: A board, *independent* of the government, selects money managers to invest the workers' funds in natural resources, real estate, stocks, and bonds—both foreign and domestic. Annually, this independent board reviews the performance of each money management team, retaining those who do the best job and replacing the others. All investment results are published on the Internet, and individuals can select the management team that they prefer. No one can withdraw funds before retirement for any reason.

➔ Can you suggest a better alternative? ■

Intergenerational Competition and Conflict

Social Security came about not because the members of Congress had generous hearts but out of a struggle between competing interest groups. As conflict theorists stress, equilibrium between competing groups is only a temporary balancing of oppositional forces, one that can be upset at any time. Following this principle, could conflict between the elderly and the young be in our future? Let's consider this possibility.

If you listen closely, you can hear ripples of grumbling—complaints that the elderly are getting more than their fair share of society's resources. The huge costs of Social Security and Medicare are a special concern. As incredible as it may seem, *one of every two* tax dollars (52 percent) is spent on these two programs (*Statistical Abstract* 2013:Tables 481, 488). As Figure 13.8 shows, Social Security payments were $781 million in 1950; now they run *1,000 times* higher. Now look at Figure 13.9 on page 374, which shows the nation's huge—and growing—medical bill to care for the elderly.

Like gasoline poured on a bonfire, these soaring costs may well fuel an intergenerational showdown.

Figure 13.10 on the next page shows another area of concern that can provoke an intergenerational conflict. You can see how greatly the poverty rate of the elderly dropped as the government transferred resources to them. Their poverty rate is now just a *third* of what it used to be. Now compare the path of the children's poverty. You can see that it is *higher* now than it was in 1967—and in all the years in between. Our economic crisis has taken a severe toll on the nation's children.

Did the sharp decline in the elderly's rate of poverty come at the expense of the nation's children? Of course not. Congress could have decided to finance the welfare of children just as it did that of the elderly. It chose not to. Why? Following conflict theorists, the reason is that the elderly, not the children, launched a broad assault on Congress. The lobbyists for the elderly put a lot of grease in the politicians' reelection machine. The children didn't offer them a payoff, a silence that has cost them dearly.

Figure 13.10 could indicate another reason for a coming intergenerational conflict. If we take a 9 percent poverty rate as a goal for the nation's children—to match what the government has accomplished for the elderly—where would the money come from? If the issue gets pitched as a case of taking money from the elderly to give to the children, it can divide the generations. To get people to think that they must choose between pathetic children and suffering old folks can splinter voters into opposing groups. Would improving the welfare of children ever be presented in such a crass way? Ask yourself this: Do politicians ever try to manipulate our emotions to get elected?

FIGURE 13.8 Social Security Payments to Beneficiaries

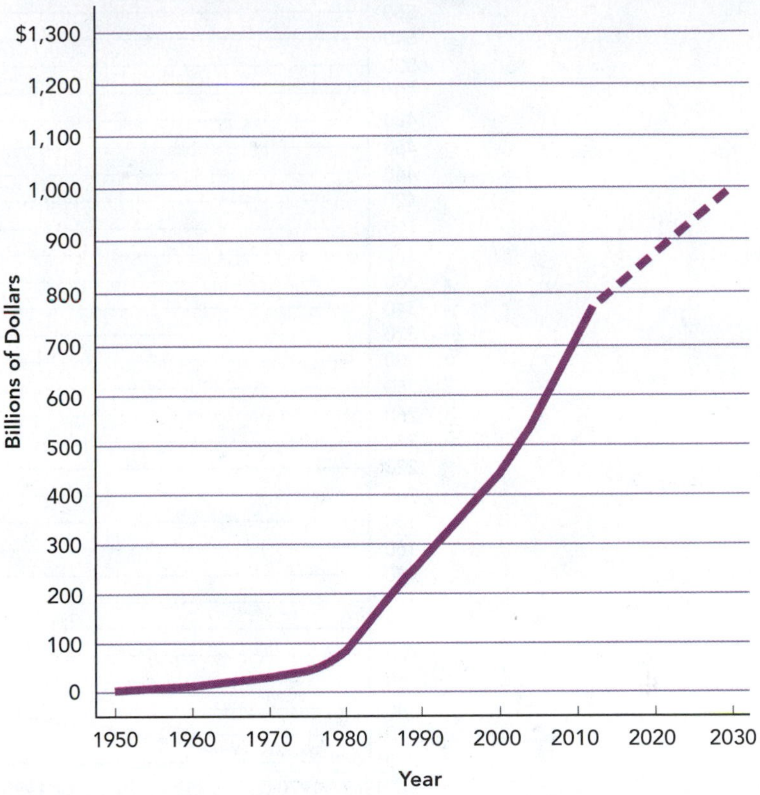

Source: By the author. Based on *Statistical Abstract of the United States* 1997: Table 518; 2013:Table 481. Broken line indicates the author's projections.

A few politicians, but a rare few, say what they really feel. Taro Aso, the finance minister of Japan, said that the elderly are "tax burdens who should hurry up and die" (Bennett-Smith 2013). On Figure 13.1, you saw that 23 percent of Japan's population is elderly. Evidently, the intergenerational conflict has begun there.

The Down-to-Earth Sociology box on page 375 highlights a significant change that might pour even more fuel on a coming intergenerational conflict for limited resources.

Fighting Back

Some organizations are fighting to make life better for the elderly and to protect the gains they have made. Let's consider two.

The Gray Panthers. The Gray Panthers, an organization of 20,000 members, are aware how easily the public can be split along age lines (Gray Panthers n.d.). This group encourages people of all ages to work for the welfare of both the old and the young. On the micro level, their goal is to help people develop positive self-concepts (Dychtwald 2013), and on the macro level, to challenge institutions that oppress the poor. One indication of their effectiveness is that Gray Panthers frequently testify before congressional committees concerning pending legislation.

The American Association of Retired Persons. The AARP also champions legislation to benefit the elderly. With 39 million members, this organization has political clout. It monitors federal and state legislation and mobilizes its members to act on issues affecting their welfare. A statement of displeasure from the AARP about some proposed

FIGURE 13.9 Health Care Costs for the Elderly and Disabled

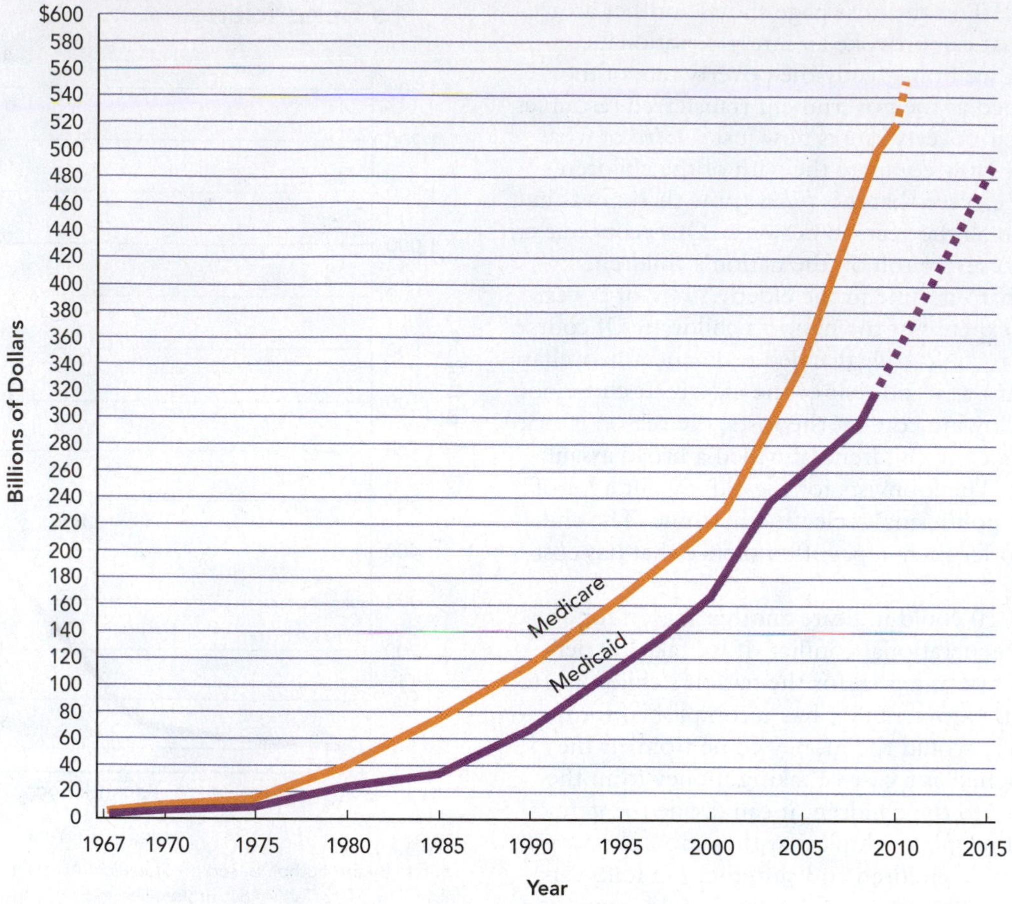

Note: Medicare is intended for the elderly and disabled, Medicaid for the poor. About 72 percent of Medicare ($373 billion) and 20 percent of Medicaid payments ($61 billion) go for medical care for the elderly (*Statistical Abstract* 2013:Tables 147, 154).

Source: By the author. Based on *Statistical Abstract of the United States* various years, and 2013:Tables 147, 154. Broken lines indicate the author's projections.

FIGURE 13.10 Age and Trends in Poverty

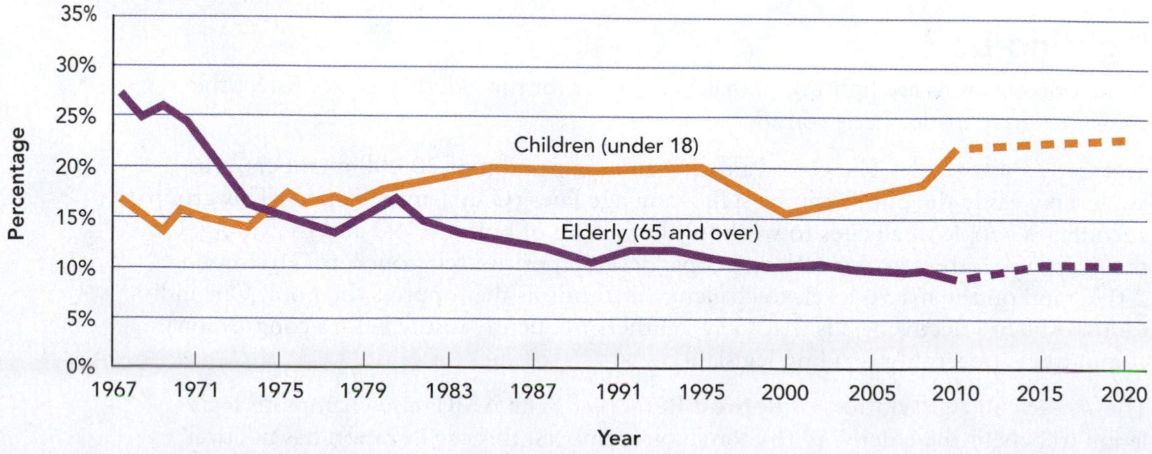

Source: By the author. Based on *Statistical Abstract of the United States*, various years, and 2013:Table 725. Broken lines indicate the author's projections.

Down-to-Earth Sociology

The New Centenarians

The oxymoron *new centenarians* may seem strange, since the word *centenarians* refers to someone who has reached age 100 or beyond. But apparently centenarians are new to the world. Some population experts think that before 1900, only one person a century made it to age 100 or beyond (Himes 2001).

Although age 100 isn't exactly common today, it is frequent. About 80,000 Americans have reached their hundredth birthday or more (Arrison 2011). However, the number may be somewhat inflated by people's tendency to fudge a bit about their age when they get to be very old. Census officials think that pride about making it that far may lead some to tack on a few years. But even if we lop off 10,000 people, this still leaves us with about 70,000 folks who have managed to reach age 100 or more.

As you probably would expect, more women than men reach 100. In fact, women centenarians outnumber men centenarians *four to one*. (The men have quite a choice of mates, but little interest.) Because the average woman outlives the average man, about 25 percent of the men who become centenarians are married, but only about 4 percent of the women are. Then there is this surprising statistic: About 20 percent of centenarians report no disabilities (Himes 2001). They are still healthy and feeling good.

No one knows exactly why the "new" centenarians have appeared at this point in world history, but our improved public health, modern medicines, and ample food supply certainly play a part. On the individual level—why Dick and Jane make it to 100 while Bill and Mary do not—there appear to be three main reasons: genetics, lifestyle, and just plain luck. With regard to genetics, some people inherit physical problems that bring an earlier death. For lifestyle, some people take better care of their bodies, while some like to drive motorcycles, dive out of airplanes, and smoke. Then there is the matter of luck—or the lack of it. You can simply be in the wrong place at the wrong time, such as visiting the World Trade Center on September 11, 2001. Or driving on an interstate highway when a boat unhooks from a trailer in the oncoming lane and smashes into your car, taking your head with it, as happened to two friends of mine in St. Louis.

We are experiencing a tidal wave of new centenarians. Centenarians are so new that of all who have ever lived on earth, most are still alive. This new centenarian is throwing out the ceremonial first pitch at a baseball game in Boston.

This continuing trend toward longer life has brought with it a new term, the *supercentenarians*, those who have made it to 110 or beyond (Murabito et al. 2012). There are about 75 to 80 supercentenarians in the United States.

And geneticists are working to bring even more centenarians and supercentenarians onto the world scene. If they improve their techniques of manipulating genes, we may one day be talking about the new centenarians and a half, or even the double centenarians.

For Your Consideration

➤ Centenarians are one of the fastest growing segments of our population. Although still relatively rare today, they are destined to become more common. What do you think the consequences will be for society? How about the medical bill?

law can trigger tens of thousands of telephone calls, telegrams, letters, and e-mails from irate elderly citizens. To protect their chances of reelection, politicians try not to cross swords with the AARP. As you can expect, critics claim that this organization is too powerful, that it muscles its way to claim more than its share of the nation's resources.

In Sum: People of different ages (cohorts) are among society's many interest groups that are competing for scarce resources. As more demands are placed on these resources, the opposing interests of these groups will become more apparent.

Recurring Problems

13.5 Review findings on the living arrangements of the elderly, nursing homes, elder abuse, and the elderly poor.

"When I get old, will I be able to take care of myself? Will I become frail and unable to get around? Will I end up in some nursing home, in the hands of strangers who don't care about me, maybe even abuse me?" These are common concerns of people as they age. Let's first examine gender and the elderly and then the problems of nursing homes, abuse, and poverty.

FIGURE 13.11

The Elderly Who Are Widowed

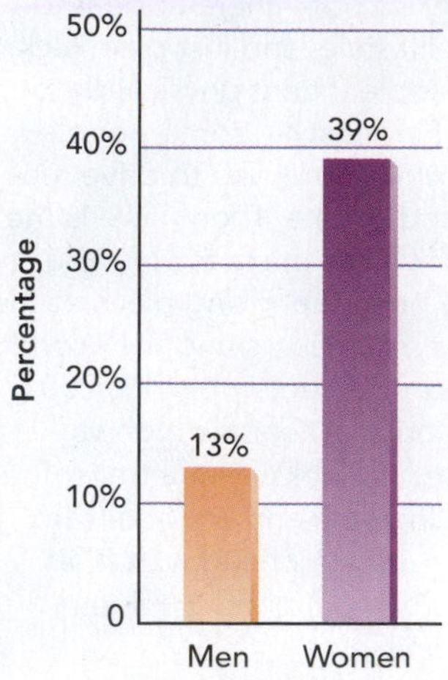

Source: By the author. Based on *Statistical Abstract of the United States* 2013:Table 34.

FIGURE 13.12

The Elderly Who Live with a Spouse

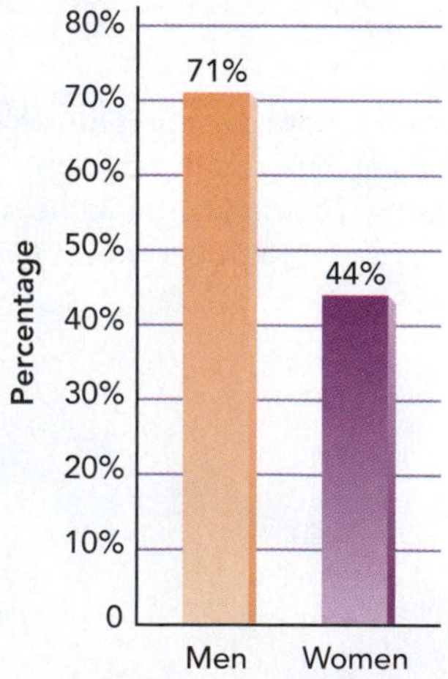

Source: By the author. Based on *Statistical Abstract of the United States* 2013:Table 34.

Explore on **MySocLab**
Activity: The Graying of America: Life Expectancies and the Senior Citizen Population

Gender and Living Arrangements of the Elderly

As you know, the average woman lives longer than the average man. Whether this is biological or biosocial (a combination of biology and social factors) is a matter of debate. Regardless of its cause, men having shorter lives brings with it consequences. You can see the first in Figure 13.11. Because most men die younger than most women, they are less likely to experience widowhood. This means that the loneliness and isolation that widowhood brings are more likely to be a woman's burden. Another consequence is different living arrangements in old age. From Figure 13.12, you can see how much more likely elderly men are to be living with their wives than elderly women are to be living with their husbands.

Another "living arrangement" is nursing homes. Let's take a brief look at them. But before we do, let's try to break a stereotype. Some people paint the elderly with the same brush, as though all old people are alike. This seems to be especially true of young people, who sometimes thrust the elderly into a general, catch-all category. Old people, in contrast, are individuals. They come from different backgrounds, have different needs, and exhibit contrasting personalities. I think you will enjoy the Down-to-Earth Sociology box on the next page. It will give you a glimpse of some of the variety that exists among the elderly, as well as how people carry gender roles into old age.

Nursing Homes

In one nursing home, the nurses wrote in the patient's chart that she had a foot lesion. She actually had gangrene and maggots in her wounds (Rhone 2001). In another nursing home—supposedly a premier retirement home in Southern California—a woman suffered a stroke in her room. Her "caretakers" didn't discover her condition for 15 hours. She didn't survive. (Morin 2001)

Most elderly are cared for by their families, but at any one time, about a million and a half Americans age 65 and over are in nursing homes. This comes to about 3 percent of the nation's elderly (*Statistical Abstract* 2013:Tables 10, 198). Some patients return home after only a few weeks or months. Others die after a short stay. Overall, about one-half of elderly women and one-third of elderly men spend at least some time in nursing homes.

Nursing home residents are *not typical* of the elderly. Three of four are age 75 or older. Almost all (80 percent) are widowed or divorced, or have never married, leaving them without family to provide care. Most of these elderly are in such poor health that they need help to bathe, dress, and eat (Harrington et al. 2011).

Understaffing, Dehumanization, and Death. It is difficult to say good things about nursing homes. The literature on nursing homes, both popular and scientific, is filled with horror stories of neglected and abused patients. One-fourth of nursing homes have conditions that jeopardize their residents' health (Harrington et al. 2011). In nursing homes that are understaffed, patients are more likely to have bedsores and urinary tract infections (Hagerty 2013). Most nursing homes are understaffed.

It is easy to see why nursing homes are understaffed. Who—if he or she has a choice—would work for poverty-level wages in a place that smells of urine, where you have to change adults' diapers and you are surrounded by dying people? Each year, 40 to 75 percent of nursing home staff quit (Hagerty 2013).

But all the criticisms of nursing homes pale in comparison with this finding: Compared with the elderly who have similar health conditions but remain home, those who go to nursing homes tend to get sicker and to die sooner (Wolinsky et al. 1997). This is a remarkable finding. Could it be, then, that a function of nursing homes is to dispose of the frail and unwanted elderly? If so, could we consider nursing homes the Western equivalent of the Tiwi's practice of "covering up," which we reviewed in this chapter's opening vignette?

Perhaps this judgment is too harsh. But despite alternatives, we continue to have the depressing nursing homes that all of us want to avoid. Among the many attempts to make nursing homes center more on the needs of their patients rather than on the needs

Down-to-Earth Sociology

Feisty to the End: Gender Roles among the Elderly

This image of my father makes me smile—not because he was arrested as an old man but, rather, because of the events that led to his arrest. My dad had always been a colorful character, ready with endless ribald jokes and a hearty laugh. He carried these characteristics into his old age.

In his late 70s, my dad was living in a small apartment in a complex for the elderly in Minnesota. The adjacent building was a nursing home, the next destination for the residents of these apartments. None of them liked to think about this "home," because no one survived it—yet they all knew that this would be their destination. Under the watchful eye of these elderly neighbors, care in the nursing home was fairly good. Until they were transferred to this unwelcome last stopping-place, life for them went on "as usual" in the complex for the elderly.

According to the police report and my dad's account, here is what happened:

Dad was sitting in the downstairs lounge with other residents, waiting for the mail to arrive, a daily ritual that the residents looked forward to. For some reason known only to him, my dad hooked his cane under the dress of an elderly woman, lifted up her skirt, and laughed. Understandably, this upset her, as well as her husband, who was standing next to her. Angry, the man moved toward my father, threatening him.

I say "moved," rather than "lunged," because this man was using a walker. My dad started to run away from this threat. Actually, "run" isn't quite the right word. "Hobbled" would be more appropriate.

My dad fled as fast as he could using his cane, while the other man pursued him as fast as he could using his walker. Wheezing and puffing, the two went from the lounge into the long adjoining hall, pausing now and then to catch their breath. Tiring the most, the other man gave up the pursuit. He then called the police.

When the police officer arrived, he said, "Uncle Marv, I'm sorry, but I'm going to have to arrest you." (This event occurred in a small town, and the officer assigned this case turned out to be Dad's nephew.)

Dad went before a judge, who could hardly keep a straight face. He gave Dad a small fine and warned him to behave himself. The apartment manager also gave Dad a warning: One more incident and he would have to move out of the complex.

Dad's wife wasn't too happy about the situation, either.

During their elderly years, men and women continue to exhibit aspects of the gender roles that they learned and played in their younger years. This man is about to surprise his invalid wife with a bouquet of flowers.

This event was brought to mind by a newspaper account of a fight that broke out at the food bar of a retirement home ("Melee Breaks . . ." 2004). It seems that one elderly man criticized the way another man was picking through the salad. When a fight broke out between the two, several elderly people were hurt as they tried either to intervene or to flee.

For Your Consideration

➔ People carry their personalities, values, and other traits into old age. Among these characteristics are gender roles. What examples of gender roles do you see in the events related here? Are you familiar with how old people continue to show their femininity or masculinity?

of the bureaucracy is one that is highly controversial. We explore it in the Down-to-Earth Sociology box on next page.

Elder Abuse

You've probably heard stories of elder abuse, about residents of nursing homes being pushed, grabbed, shoved, or shouted at. Some of the elderly in nursing homes are also abused sexually (Phillips et al. 2013). Others are mistreated at home, by family members who exploit them financially or harm them physically.

Although abuse of the elderly is a genuine problem, it is not typical. Less than 4 percent of the U.S. elderly experience financial abuse, and less than 1 percent are injured physically (Laumann et al. 2008). Few of the abusers are "mean" people. One of the

Down-to-Earth Sociology

What Do You Think about the Red Sock? Sex in Nursing Homes

"Those old guys are grabbing at us! What are we going to do?"

This was the female staff's complaint at Chaseley, a nursing home in Eastbourne, England. The women had to keep swatting the hands of the male patients, and they were growing tired of it.

Something had to be done. The groping called for a meeting. The director knew that she could sedate the men, but she also knew that the drugs would have negative effects on the men's bodies and minds. "We are here to help our patients, not hurt them," she thought. "But what can we do? It isn't fair for our women to have to put up with this."

"Sex is a basic human need," she told her staff, "a primeval one. And we want humane, holistic treatment for our patients. So how can we meet this need?"

"Prostitution is legal, so why not have prostitutes visit the men?" This solution seemed good. It didn't take much planning to implement. They just needed to set a room aside. They did this, and then they added one little detail: They put a little red sock on the doorknob, a polite reminder not to enter because a man was having what they called a "special visit."

Everyone was pleased with the solution. The men apparently smiled a lot more, they kept their hands to themselves, and the sex workers had a dependable source of income.

Then some reporters heard about the situation, and the quiet arrangement didn't remain quiet. The news created a little stir, but in a low-key British sort of way. The nursing home manager defended her arrangement as part of quality patient care. The County Council that oversees the nursing home got into the act, too. They said they would check into the matter to make sure that the men weren't being harmed.

The meaning of this photo will become apparent as you read the box.

For Your Consideration

➤ What do you think about the red sock? That is, do you think that satisfying the sexual needs of nursing home patients should be part of patient care? Why or why not? Did you notice the sexism in this event? It was only the men's sexual needs that were being gratified. Granted that it was only the men whose hands were wandering, but what about the sexual needs of the women patients?

➤ Whether prostitution should be legal or not is a separate matter, but not irrelevant. When reporters learned that a nursing home in Denmark was having call girls come in, the matter of women being used by men was the main issue.

Based on Wienberg 2008; Croydon 2009; Hawkins 2013; Whipple 2013.

most common reasons for abuse is that a family member has run out of patience. The husband of a woman who was suffering from Alzheimer's disease said this to the social scientists who interviewed him:

> *Frustration reaches a point where patience gives out. I've never struck her, but sometimes I wonder if I can control myself. . . . This is . . . the part of her care that causes me the frustration and the loss of patience. What I tell her, she doesn't register. Like when I tell her, "You're my wife." "You're crazy," she says. (Pillemer and Suitor 1992)*

This quotation is not intended to excuse any abuse but, rather, to provide insight into why someone would mistreat a family member. The husband's admission can help us understand the stress that comes with caring for a person who is dependent, demanding, and uncomprehending—and whose care takes 24 hours a day 7 days a week. Since most people who undergo this stress are not violent toward those they care for, however, we do not have the answer to why some do become violent. For this, we must await future research.

More important than understanding the causes of mistreatment, however, is preventing the elderly from being abused in the first place. There is little that can be done about abuse at home by relatives—except to enforce current laws when problems come to the attention of authorities. For home-care and nursing home workers, in contrast, we can require background checks to screen out people who have been convicted of robbery, rape, and other violence. This is similar to requiring background checks of preschool workers in order to eliminate applicants who have been convicted of molesting children. Such laws are only a first step to solving this problem, however, because they will not completely prevent abuse, only avoid the obvious.

The Elderly Poor

A problem that the retired elderly face is that they don't know if they will outlive their pension or savings and end up in poverty. As we reviewed earlier, Social Security has lifted most elderly Americans out of poverty, and today's elderly are less likely than the average American to be poor. When we look at the poverty that does exist among the elderly, however, we see two recurring patterns.

Race–Ethnicity and Poverty. The first pattern is that poverty in old age mirrors the racial–ethnic patterns of the general society. From Figure 13.13, you can see that, as with all younger groups, elderly whites are less likely to be poor than are African Americans and Latinos.

FIGURE 13.13 Race–Ethnicity and Poverty in Old Age

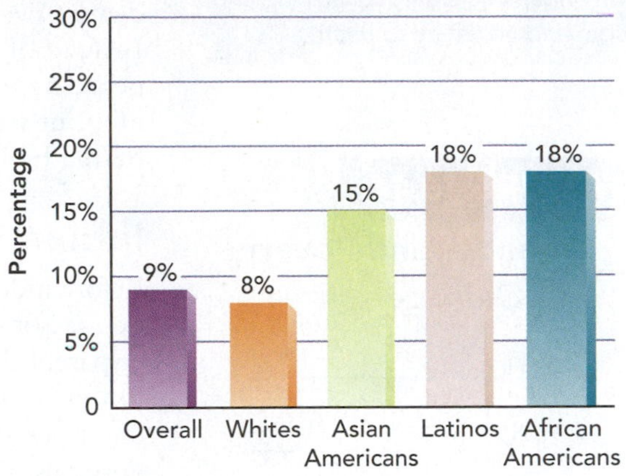

Source: By the author. Only the groups are listed in the source. Based on *Statistical Abstract of the United States* 2013:Table 725.

Gender and Poverty. Figure 13.14 on the next page shows the second pattern, that poverty in old age follows gender lines. That women are more likely than men to be poor in their elderly years goes back to what we reviewed in Chapter 11: During their working years, most women earn less than men.

In old age, as in all other stages of the life course, people find life more pleasant if they have friends and enough money to meet their needs. How do you think the elderly man to the left finds life? How about the elderly men in the photo to the right? While neither welcomes old age, you can see what a difference social factors make in how people experience this time of life.

13.6 Explain how industrialization changed death practices, how death is a process, why hospices emerged, suicide and age, and adjusting to death.

The Sociology of Death and Dying

Have you ever noticed how people use language to try to distance themselves from death? We use *linguistic masks*, ways to refer to death without using the word itself. Instead of dead, we might say "gone," "passed on," "no longer with us," or "at peace now." We don't have space to explore this fascinating characteristic of social life, but we can take a brief look at why sociologists emphasize that dying is more than a biological event.

FIGURE 13.14

Gender and Poverty in Old Age

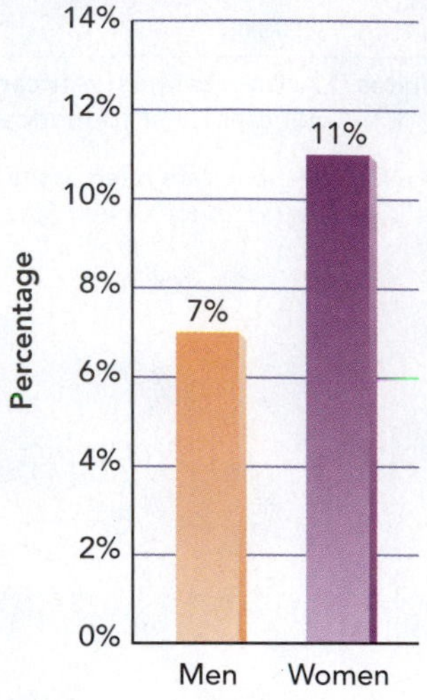

The percentage of Americans aged 65 and older who are poor

Source: By the author. Based on *Statistical Abstract of the United States* 2013:Table 34.

Industrialization and the New Technology

Before industrialization, death was no stranger to family life. The family took care of the sick at home, and the sick died at home. Because life was short, *most* children saw a sibling or parent die (Carr 2012). As noted in Chapter 1 (p. 26), the family even prepared corpses for burial. Industrialization changed this. As secondary groups came to dominate society, the process of dying was taken from the family and placed in the hands of professionals in hospitals. Dying now takes place behind closed doors—isolated, remote, and managed by strangers. For most of us, death has now become something strange and alien.

Not only did new technologies lead to the dying being removed from our presence, but they also created *technological life*—a form of existence that lies between life and death, but is neither (Cerulo and Ruane 1996). The "brain dead" in our hospitals have no selves. The "person" is gone—dead—yet our technology keeps the body alive. This muddles the boundary between life and death, which used to seem so certain.

For most of us, however, that boundary will remain firm, and we will face a definite death. Some of us will even learn in advance that we will die shortly. If so, how are we likely to cope with this unwelcome knowledge? Let's look at what researchers have found.

Death as a Process

Let me share an intimate event from my own life.

> *When my mother was informed that she had inoperable lung cancer, she went into a vivid stage of denial. If she later went through anger or negotiation, she kept it to herself. After a short depression, she experienced a longer period of questioning why this was happening to her. After coming to grips with the fact that she was going to die soon, she began to make her "final arrangements." The extent of those preparations soon became apparent.*
>
> *After her funeral, my two brothers and I went to her apartment, as she had instructed us. There, to our surprise, attached to each item in every room—from the bed and the television to the boxes of dishes and knickknacks—was a piece of masking tape with one of our names on it. At first we found this strange. We knew she was an orderly person, but to this extent? As we sorted through her things, reflecting on why she had given certain items to whom, we began to appreciate the "closure" she had given to this aspect of her material life.*

Psychologist Elisabeth Kübler-Ross (1969/2008) studied how people cope during the *living–dying interval*, that period between discovering they are going to die soon and death itself. After interviewing people who had been informed that they had an incurable illness, she concluded that people who come face to face with their own death go through five stages:

1. *Denial*. At first, people cannot believe that they are going to die. ("The doctor must have made a mistake. Those test results can't be right.") They avoid the topic of death and situations that remind them of it.
2. *Anger*. After a while, they acknowledge that they are going to die, but they view their death as unjust. ("I didn't do anything to deserve this. So-and-so is much worse than I am, and she's in good health. It isn't right that I should die.")
3. *Negotiation*. Next, the individual tries to get around death by making a bargain with God, with fate, or even with the disease itself. ("I need one more Thanksgiving with

my family. I never appreciated them as much as I should have. Let me just hold out until then.")

4. *Depression.* During this stage, people become resigned to their death, but they grieve because life is about to end, and they have no power to change the course of events.
5. *Acceptance.* In this final stage, people come to terms with impending death. They put their affairs in order—make wills, pay bills, instruct their children to take care of the surviving parent. They also express regret at not having done certain things when they had the chance. Devout Christians are likely to talk about the hope of salvation and their desire to be in heaven with Jesus.

Dying is more individualized than this model indicates. Not everyone, for example, tries to make bargains. What is important sociologically is that *death is a process*, not just an event. People who expect to die soon face a reality quite different from the one experienced by those of us who expect to be alive years from now. Impending death powerfully affects their thinking and behavior.

hospice a place (or services brought to someone's home) for the purpose of giving comfort and dignity to a dying person

Hospices

What a change. In earlier generations, life was short, and people took death at an early age for granted. Today, we take it for granted that most people will see old age. Due to advances in medical technology and better public health practices, three of four deaths in the United States occur after age 65 (Carr 2012). Most of these deaths take place in hospitals. People want to die with dignity, in the comforting presence of friends and relatives, but hospitals, to put the matter bluntly, are awkward places in which to die. In hospitals, people experience what sociologists call *institutional death*—they die surrounded by strangers in formal garb, in sterile rooms filled with machines, in an organization that puts its routines ahead of patients' needs.

Hospices emerged as a way to reduce the emotional and physical burden of dying—and to lower the costs of death. Hospice care is built around the idea that the people who are dying and their families should control the process of dying. The term **hospice** originally described a place, but now it generally refers to home care. Services are brought into a dying person's home—from counseling and managing pain to providing transportation to doctors. During the course of a year, more than a million people are in hospice care in the United States. These services have become so popular that almost half of Americans receive hospice care prior to death (*Statistical Abstract* 2013:Tables 116, 183).

Hospitals are dedicated to prolonging life, but hospice care is meant to provide dignity in death and make people comfortable during the *living–dying interval.* In the hospital, attention is centered on treating the patient or saving the patient's life. In hospice care, the focus switches to both the dying person and that person's friends and family. The hospital's goal is to make the patient well, with the focus on the individual's physical welfare; hospice care seeks to relieve pain and suffering and make death easier to bear. Although medical needs are met, the primary concern of hospices is the individual's personal comfort and social—and, in some instances, spiritual—well-being.

Among the reasons for hospices are providing comfort and dignity to people in their last days. Shown here is a music therapist with a woman and her dying mother.

Suicide and Age

We noted in Chapter 1 how Durkheim stressed that suicide is much more than an individual act, that it has a *social* basis. Let's explore the *social* basis of suicide a little more. Each country has its own suicide rate, which remains quite stable year after year. In the United States, we can predict that 31,000 people will commit suicide this year. If we are off by more than 1,000, it would be a surprise. As we saw in Figure 1.1 (p. 12), we can also predict that Americans will choose firearms as the most common way to kill themselves and that hanging will come in second. We can also be certain that this year more men than women will kill themselves, and more people in their 60s than in their 20s will make this same decision. It is this way year after year.

To explore the ages of people who take their own lives reveals more about the *social* part of suicide. As you know, the suicides of young people are given much publicity, but such deaths are comparatively rare. The suicide rate of adolescents is *lower* than that of adults of any age, just half that of the elderly (15 per 100,000 for the elderly and 7.5 for adolescents). Because adolescents have such a low overall death rate, however, suicide ranks as their third leading cause of death—after accidents and homicide (*Statistical Abstract* 2013:Tables 125, 130). Occasionally, you will hear that there is an "epidemic" of suicide among the youth. There isn't.

These findings on suicide are an example of the primary sociological point stressed throughout this text: Recurring patterns of human behavior—whether education, marriage, work, crime, use of the Internet, or even suicide—represent underlying social forces. Consequently, if no basic change takes place in the social conditions of the groups that make up U.S. society, you can expect these same patterns of suicide to continue.

Adjusting to Death

After the death of a loved one, people experience a jumble of feelings. Along with grief and loneliness, they may feel guilt, anger, or even relief. During the period of mourning that follows, usually one or two years, they sort out their feelings and come to terms with the death. They also reorganize their family system to deal with the absence of the person who was so important to it.

Although there is some disagreement among researchers, in general, when death is expected, family members find it less stressful (Carr 2012). They have already begun to cope with the coming death by managing a series of smaller losses, including the person's inability to fulfill his or her usual roles or to do specific tasks. They also have been able to say tender goodbyes to their loved one. In contrast, unexpected deaths—accidents, suicides, and murders—bring greater emotional shock. The family members have had no time to get used to the idea that the individual is going to die. One moment, the person is here; the next, he or she is gone. The sudden death gave them no chance to say goodbye or to bring any form of "closure" to their relationship.

13.7 Discuss developing views of aging and the impact of technology on how long people live.

Looking toward the Future

Let's not lose sight of one of the major changes stressed in this chapter—that for the first time in human history, huge numbers of people are becoming elderly. It is inevitable that such a fundamental change will have a powerful impact on societies around the world, so much so that it might even transform them. We don't have space to explore such potential transformations, which are only speculative at the moment, so let's try to catch a glimpse of what is happening with the elderly themselves.

New Views of Aging

As huge numbers of Americans move into old age, the elderly have begun not only to challenge the demeaning stereotypes of the aged but also to develop new models of aging. These new approaches build on the idea that old age should not be viewed as "a-time-close-to-death" but, rather, as a new period of life, one with its specific challenges, to be sure, but also one to be enjoyed, even celebrated. This new time of life provides unique opportunities to pursue interests, to develop creativity, and to enhance the appreciation of life's beauty and one's place in it. Let's look at how this new model is being applied.

More and more, the goal of the elderly is to enjoy themselves—and with more resources at their disposal, more and more are able to do so. The goal of the Red Hat Society, with chapters around the nation, is simply for older women to have fun.

Creative Aging. In the 1970s, as larger numbers of people became elderly, many said that having endless amounts of leisure time was not their idea of how to enjoy being old. Pioneering the view that old age is a time to embark on new learning, they promoted free, space-available, noncredit attendance at colleges and universities, group travel to historical sites around the world, and the writing of memoirs about the past.

In the second phase, which we are just entering, emphasis is being placed on mental growth and enhancing people's creative abilities. An example is The Colony, a retirement home in Hollywood, where the emphasis is on the arts. Residents write and perform plays, make sculptures, write and record songs, paint, and write novels (Brown 2006). Some residents, who did none of these things during their preretirement years, now perform on radio and television.

Creative aging is new, so we don't know the directions it will take. But if this emphasis continues, it will change how younger people view the elderly—as well as how the elderly view themselves. The stereotype of despondent, disengaged old people might even be replaced with a stereotype of robust, engaged, thriving older adults (Manheimer 2005). No stereotype will encompass the reality of the elderly, of course, as the aged differ among themselves as much as younger people do. Cultural differences will remain, as will those of social class. The Colony, for example, with its emphasis on developing creativity, is directed toward the middle class. It seems certain that the poor, with their fewer resources, will not be affected as directly by creative aging.

The Impact of Technology

Throughout this text, we have examined some of the deep impacts that technology is having on our lives. To close this chapter, I would like you to reflect on how technological breakthroughs might affect your own life as you grow older.

THINKING CRITICALLY

How Long Do You Want to Live?

Would you like to live to 200? To 500? To 1,000?

Such a question may strike you as absurd. But new and still-developing technology might stretch the life span to limits unheard of since biblical days.

We are just at the beginning stages of genetic engineering, and ahead of us may lie a brave new world. Technicians may be able to snip out our bad DNA and replace it with more compliant bits. The caps at the ends of our chromosomes, the telomeres, shrink as we age, causing the cells to die. An enzyme called telomerase may be able to modify this process, allowing cells to reproduce many more times than they currently are able to (Demidov 2005).

By manipulating genes, scientists have been able to extend the life spans of worms by six times. Humans have these same genes. A sixfold increase in the human life span would take the longest-living people to over 600 (Arrison 2011). We are only peering over the edge of the future, glimpsing what might be possible. Life spans of 150 years may become possible fairly soon. Some wild-eyed geneticists are predicting future life spans of 1,000 years (Arrison 2011).

Some geneticists compare the human body to a house (Gorman 2003). A house keeps standing not because it is built to last forever but because people keep repairing it. In this envisioned future of scientific advances, we will use stem cells to grow spare body parts—livers, hearts, kidneys, fingers, and so on. As parts of our body wear out, we will place orders for replacements as we need them.

In grade school, many of us heard stories about Ponce de Leon, an explorer from Spain who searched for the fountain of youth. He eventually "discovered" Florida, but never located the fountain of youth. In our perpetual search for immortality, could we be discovering what eluded Ponce de Leon?

For Your Consideration

➔ Let's assume that biomedical science does stretch the human life span, that living to be 150 or 200 becomes common. If people retire at age 65, how could society afford to support them for 100 years or so? People can't work much past 70, because—and this may be the basic flaw in this scenario of a brave new world—even with new body parts, the world would not be filled with 200-year-olds who functioned as though they were 25. They would be very old people, subject to the diseases and debilities that come with advanced age. If Medicare costs are bulging at the seams now, what would they be like in such a world?

➔ Finally, how would you answer this question: Is the real issue how we can live longer, or how we can live better? Because of medical advances, public health, and better nutrition, millions of today's elderly enjoy good health. This is leading to a new view of old age—from a time of decay and death to a time of opportunity to pursue interests and develop talents, to obtain fresh perspectives and a growing sense of satisfaction with life. ■

MySocLab

Study and Review on MySocLab

CHAPTER 13 Summary and Review

Aging in Global Perspective

13.1 Understand the social construction of aging; explain how industrialization led to a graying globe and how race-ethnicity is related to aging.

How are the elderly treated around the world?

No single set of attitudes, beliefs, or policies regarding the aged characterizes the world's nations. Rather, they vary from exclusion and killing to integration and honor. The global trend is for more people to live longer. Pp. 359.

What does the social construction of aging mean?

Nothing in the nature of aging produces any particular set of attitudes. Rather, attitudes toward the elderly are rooted in culture and differ from one social group to another. Pp. 359–362.

What does the phrase "graying of America" mean?

The phrase **graying of America** refers to the growing percentage of Americans who reach old age. The costs of Social Security and health care for the elderly have become major social issues. Pp. 362–363.

The Symbolic Interactionist Perspective

13.2 Explain how people decide when they are old and discuss changes in perceptions of the elderly.

What factors influence perceptions of aging?

Symbolic interactionists stress that aging is *socially constructed*. That is, no age has any particular built-in meaning; rather, we use cultural cues to define age. Four factors influence when people label themselves as "old": biological changes, biographical events, **gender age**, and cultural timetables. Cross-cultural comparisons demonstrate how culture shapes the ways that people experience aging. **Ageism**, negative reactions to the elderly, is based on stereotypes. Pp. 364–368.

The Functionalist Perspective

13.3 Summarize theories of disengagement, activity, and continuity.

How is retirement functional for society?

Functionalists focus on how the withdrawal of the elderly from positions of responsibility benefits society. **Disengagement theory** examines retirement as a device for ensuring that a society's positions of responsibility are passed smoothly from one generation to the next. **Activity theory** examines how people adjust when they retire. **Continuity theory** focuses on how people adjust to growing old by continuing their roles and coping techniques. Pp. 368–370.

The Conflict Perspective

13.4 Explain the conflict perspective on Social Security and discuss intergenerational competition and conflict.

How do the younger and the elderly compete for scarce resources?

Social Security legislation is an example of one generation making demands on another generation for limited resources. As the number of retired people grows, there are relatively fewer workers to support them. The Social Security Trust Fund may be viewed as a gigantic fraud perpetrated by the power elite on the nation's workers. Organizations such as the Gray Panthers and the AARP watch out for the interests of the elderly. Pp. 370–375.

Recurring Problems

13.5 Review findings on the living arrangements of the elderly, nursing homes, elder abuse, and the elderly poor.

What are some of the problems that today's elderly face?

Women are more likely to live alone and to be poor. At any one time, about 3 percent of the elderly live in nursing homes. Nursing homes are understaffed, and patient neglect is common. Those most likely to abuse the elderly are members of their own families. Poverty in old age, greatly reduced through government programs, reflects the gender and racial–ethnic patterns of poverty in the general society. Pp. 375–379.

The Sociology of Death and Dying

13.6 Explain how industrialization changed death practices, how death is a process, why hospices emerged, suicide and age, and adjusting to death.

How does culture affect the way we experience death and dying?

Like old age, death is much more than a biological event. Industrialization brought with it modern medicine, hospitals—and dying in a formal setting surrounded by strangers. Kübler-Ross identified five stages in the dying process, which, though insightful, do not characterize all people. **Hospices** are a cultural device designed to overcome the negative aspects of dying in hospitals. The suicide rate of the elderly is double that of adolescents. Pp. 380–382.

Looking toward the Future

13.7 Discuss developing views of aging and the impact of technology on how long people live.

What technological developments can be a wild card in social planning for the aged?

The huge number of elderly who are in good health is fostering a new view of old age—as a time of creativity and personal development. Technological breakthroughs may stretch the human **life span**. If so, it is difficult to see how younger workers would be able to support retired people for 100 years or longer. Pp. 382–384.

Thinking Critically about Chapter 13

1. How does culture influence people's ideas about the elderly and when old age begins? Can you identify cultural changes that are likely to affect your own perceptions of the onset of old age and of the elderly?
2. How do the symbolic interactionist, functionalist, and conflict perspectives on the elderly differ?
3. If you were appointed to head the U.S. Department of Health and Human Services, how would you improve the nation's nursing homes?

CHAPTER 14

The Economy

Listen to Chapter 14 on MySocLab

Learning Objectives

After you have read this chapter, you should be able to:

14.1 Summarize the broad historical shifts in economic systems; emphasize inequality. (p. 388)

14.2 Summarize historical changes in the medium of exchange. (p. 391)

14.3 Contrast capitalism and socialism: their components, ideologies, criticisms, and convergence. (p. 393)

14.4 Discuss corporate capitalism, ownership and management, and global functions and dysfunctions of capitalism. (p. 399)

14.5 Summarize shifts in corporate capitalism, concentration of power, the global superclass, and global investing. (p. 402)

14.6 Discuss types of work, women at work, the underground economy, stagnant paychecks, and work and leisure. (p. 409)

14.7 Explain how our economic transition is affecting the national income distribution. (p. 415)

If you are like most students, *you are wondering how changes in the economy are going to affect your chances of getting a good job. Let's see if we can shed some light on this question. We'll begin with this story:*

"Not Monday already," Kim groaned as the alarm went off. "There must be a better way of starting the week." With her eyes still closed, she pressed the snooze button on the clock (from Germany) to sneak another ten minutes' sleep. In what seemed like just thirty seconds, the alarm once again shrilly insisted that she get up and face the week.

Still bleary-eyed after her shower, Kim peered into her closet and picked out a silk blouse (from China), a plaid wool skirt (from Scotland), and leather shoes (from Italy). She nodded, satisfied, as she added a pair of simulated pearls (from Taiwan). Running late, she hurriedly ran a brush (from Mexico) through her hair. As Kim wolfed down a bowl of cereal (from the United States) topped with milk (from the United States), bananas (from Costa Rica), and sugar (from the Dominican Republic), she turned on her kitchen television (from Korea) to listen to the weather forecast.

> She said to herself, "If people were more like me, this country would be in better shape."

Gulping the last of her coffee (from Brazil), Kim grabbed her briefcase (from India), purse (from Spain), and jacket (from Malaysia), left her house, and quickly climbed into her car (from Japan). As she glanced at her watch (from Switzerland), she hoped that the traffic would be in her favor. She muttered to herself as she pulled up at a stoplight (from Great Britain) and eyed her gas gauge. She muttered again when she pulled into a station and paid for gas (from Saudi Arabia), because the price had risen over the weekend. "My paycheck never keeps up with prices," she moaned.

When Kim arrived at work, she found the office abuzz. Six months ago, New York headquarters had put the company up for sale, but there had been no takers. The big news was that both a Chinese company and a Canadian company had put in bids over the weekend. No one got much work done that day, as the whole office speculated about how things might change.

As Kim walked to the parking lot after work, she saw a tattered "Buy American" bumper sticker on the car next to hers. "That's right," she said to herself. "If people were more like me, this country would be in better shape."

The Transformation of Economic Systems

14.1 Summarize the broad historical shifts in economic systems; emphasize inequality.

Although this vignette may be slightly exaggerated, many of us are like Kim: We use a multitude of products from around the world, and yet we're concerned about our country's ability to compete in global markets. Today's **economy**—our system of producing and distributing goods and services—differs radically from past economies. The products that Kim uses make it apparent that today's economy knows no national boundaries. To better understand how global forces affect the U.S. economy—and your life—let's begin by summarizing the sweeping historical changes we reviewed in Chapter 6.

Preindustrial Societies: The Birth of Inequality

The earliest human groups, *hunting and gathering societies*, had a **subsistence economy**. In small groups of about twenty-five to forty, people lived off the land. They gathered plants and hunted animals in one location and then moved to another place as these sources of food ran low. Having few possessions, they did little trading with one another. With no excess to accumulate, as was mentioned in Chapter 6, everybody owned as much (or, really, as little) as everyone else.

economy a system of producing and distributing goods and services

subsistence economy a type of economy in which human groups live off the land and have little or no surplus

Then people discovered how to breed animals and cultivate plants. The more dependable food supply in what became *pastoral and horticultural societies* allowed humans to settle down in a single place. Human groups grew larger, and for the first time in history, it was no longer necessary for everyone to work at producing food. Some people became leather workers, others weapon makers, and so on. This new division of labor produced a surplus, and groups traded items with one another. The primary sociological significance of surplus and trade is this: They fostered *social inequality*, since some people accumulated more possessions than others. The effects of that change remain with us today.

The plow brought the next major change, ushering in *agricultural societies.* Plowing the land made it more productive, allowing even more people to specialize in activities other than producing food. More specialized divisions of labor followed, and trade expanded. Trading centers then developed, which turned into cities. As power passed from the heads of families and clans to a ruling elite, social, political, and economic inequalities grew.

The commonsense meaning of market is a place where people exchange or buy and sell goods. Such old-fashioned markets remain common in the Least Industrialized Nations, such as this one in Peshawar, Pakistan. Here people find the social interaction every bit as rewarding as the goods and money that they exchange.

Industrial Societies: The Birth of the Machine

The steam engine, invented in 1765, ushered in *industrial societies.* Based on machines powered by fuels, these societies created a surplus unlike anything the world had seen. This, too, stimulated trade among nations and brought even greater social inequality. A handful of individuals opened factories and exploited the labor of many.

Then came more efficient machines. As the surpluses grew even greater, the emphasis gradually changed—from producing goods to consuming them. In 1912, sociologist Thorstein Veblen coined the term **conspicuous consumption** to describe this fundamental change in people's orientations. By this term, Veblen meant that the Protestant ethic identified by Weber—an emphasis on hard work, savings, and a concern for salvation (discussed on pages 173–174)—was being replaced with an eagerness to show off wealth by the "elaborate consumption of goods."

Postindustrial Societies: The Birth of the Information Age

In 1973, sociologist Daniel Bell noted that *a new type of society was emerging.* This new society, which he called the *postindustrial society*, has six characteristics: (1) a service sector so large that *most* people work in it, (2) a vast surplus of goods, (3) even more extensive trade among nations, (4) a wider variety and quantity of goods available to the average person, (5) an information explosion, and (6) an interconnected *global village*—that is, the world's nations are linked by fast communications, transportation, and trade.

Biotech Societies: The Merger of Biology and Economics

As discussed in Chapter 6, we may be on the verge of yet another new type of society. This one is being ushered in by advances in biology, especially the deciphering of the human genome system. Although the specifics of this new society have yet to unfold, the marriage of biology and economics is likely to yield even greater surpluses and more extensive trade. The technological advances that will emerge in this new society may allow us to lead longer and healthier lives. Its effects on inequality between the nations are likely to be spotty. Some poorer nations may be able to import the new technology and develop their economies, while others will remain in poverty. We discuss global realignment in the next chapter.

Implications for Your Life

The broad changes in societies that I have just sketched may seem to be merely abstract matters, but they are far from irrelevant to your life. Changes in society directly affect you. Consider the information explosion. When you graduate from college, you will

conspicuous consumption
Thorstein Veblen's term for a change from the thrift, savings, and investments of the Protestant ethic to showing off wealth through spending and the display of possessions

most likely do some form of "knowledge work." Instead of working in a factory, you will manage information or design, sell, or service products. The type of work you do has profound implications for your life. It produces social networks, creates attitudes, and even affects how you view yourself and the world. To better understand this, consider how vastly different your outlook on life would be if you were one of the children discussed in the Cultural Diversity box below.

Watch on **MySocLab** **Video:** Global Wealth and Poverty

It is the same with the global village. Think of the globe as being divided into three neighborhoods—the three worlds of industrialization and postindustrialization that we reviewed in Chapter 9. Some nations are located in the poor part of the village. Their

Cultural Diversity **around the World**

The Child Workers

In Afghanistan, Zar Muhammad expresses guilt and sorrow that his 7- and 8-year-old sons work 12 hours a day making bricks in the mud. Zar borrowed 10,000 rupees to get married. He now owes 150,000 rupees. The children have to work alongside him to try to pay the debt. But the debt continues to grow: rent to the kiln owner for their mud house, electricity, and food, and sometimes emergency medicine for the children. They are locked in a cycle that makes Zar and his sons servants/slaves forever (Kamber 2011).

Does the government know about this situation? Of course it knows. When asked about the 5,000 children who work in the kilns in his area, the district governor said, "I know this is not good for kids, but we have to build our buildings, build our country. The work provides income for the children's families" (Kamber 2011).

*****

In Zambia, 9-year-old Alone Banda works in an abandoned quarry. Using a bolt, he breaks rocks into powder. In a week, he makes enough powder to fill half a cement bag. Alone gets $3 for the half bag.

It is a slow death for Alone. Robbed of his childhood and breathing rock dust continuously, Alone is likely to come down with what the quarry workers call a "heavy chest," an early sign of silicosis.

The amount Alone makes is pitiful, but without it, he and his grandmother would starve to death. As one mother said, "If I feel pity for them, what are they going to eat?" (Wines 2006a.)

*****

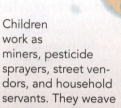

As in the photo I took of an 8-year-old girl in India (page 229), some children work in construction, others in factories. Children work as miners, pesticide sprayers, street vendors, and household servants. They weave carpets in India, race camels in the Middle East, and, all over the world, work as prostitutes. In the poverty-stricken areas of some of these countries, people live on less than $1 a day. The few dollars the children earn make the difference between life and death.

Besides poverty, there is also a cultural factor (Hilson 2012). In many parts of the world, people view children differently than we do in the West. The idea that children have the right to be educated and to be spared from adult burdens is fairly new in history. A major factor shaping our views of life is economics, and when prosperity comes to these other countries, so will this new perspective.

The answer to "What is the proper role of children in an economy?" varies by social class, culture, economic development, and historical period. On the left is a boy working in a Pennsylvania coal mine about 1908. On the right is a girl working in a rice field in Madagascar today.

For Your Consideration

➔ How do you think the wealthier nations can help alleviate the suffering of child workers? Before industrialization, and for a period afterward, having children work was also common in the West. Just because our economic system has changed, bringing with it different ideas of childhood and of the rights of children, why do we have the right to impose our changed ideas on other nations?

citizens do menial work and barely eke out a living. Life is so precarious that some even starve to death, while their fellow villagers in the rich neighborhood feast on steak and lobster, washed down with vintage Chateau Lafite Rothschild. It's the same village, but what a difference the neighborhood makes.

Now visualize any one of the three neighborhoods. Again you will see gross inequalities. Not everyone who lives in the poor neighborhood is poor, and some areas of the rich neighborhood are packed with poor people. The United States is the global economic leader, occupying the most luxurious mansion in the best neighborhood and spearheading the new biotech society.

The Transformation of the Medium of Exchange

14.2 Summarize historical changes in the medium of exchange.

As each type of economy evolved, so, too, did the means by which people valued and exchanged goods and services—the **medium of exchange** used for transactions. As we review the changes summarized in the time–event line at the bottom of this page, you'll see how the medium of exchange reflects a country's economy.

Earliest Mediums of Exchange

Hunting and gathering and pastoral and horticultural societies produced little surplus, and people **bartered**, directly exchanging one item for another. As surpluses grew and trade expanded, barter became too cumbersome. People then developed new ways of placing values on goods and services so they could trade them. Let's look at how the medium of exchange was transformed.

Medium of Exchange in Agricultural Societies

Although bartering continued in agricultural societies, people increasingly came to use **money**, items that serve as a medium of exchange. In most places, money consisted of gold and silver coins. A coin's weight and purity determined the amount of goods or services it could purchase. In some places, people made purchases with **deposit receipts**. These receipts transferred ownership of a specified amount of goods—ounces of gold or silver, bushels of grain, and so on—that were on deposit in a warehouse or bank. Toward the end of the agricultural period, deposit receipts became formalized into **currency** (paper money). Each piece of paper represented a specific amount of gold or silver stored in a warehouse. Currency and deposit receipts represented **stored value**. No more currency or deposit receipts could be issued than the total amount of gold or silver or other items in the warehouse. Gold and silver coins continued to circulate alongside deposit receipts and currency.

Medium of Exchange in Industrial Societies

With few exceptions, bartering became a thing of the past in industrial societies. Gold was replaced by paper currency, which, in the United States, could be exchanged for gold stored at Fort Knox. This policy was called the **gold standard**. As long as each

medium of exchange the means by which people place a value on goods and services in order to make an exchange—for example, currency, gold, and silver

barter the direct exchange of one item for another

money any item (from sea shells to gold) that serves as a medium of exchange

deposit receipt a receipt stating that a certain amount of goods are on deposit in a warehouse or bank; the receipt is used as a form of money

currency paper money

stored value the goods that are stored and held in reserve that back up (or provide the value for) a deposit receipt or a currency

gold standard paper money backed by gold

FIGURE 14.1 Changes in the Medium of Exchange

Note: This figure depicts a general course of development, not a sequence of events with firm edges. Credit cards are not shown, as they are not a medium of exchange but an IOU, a version of merchants' charge accounts.

Source: By the author.

dollar represented a specified amount of gold, the number of dollars that could be issued was limited. In 1971, the U.S. government stopped exchanging its paper money for gold. At this point, U.S. dollars became **fiat money**, currency issued by a government that is not backed by stored value. When there is no stored value, a government can print as much currency as it desires.

When fiat money replace stored value, coins made of precious metals disappeared from circulation. People considered these coins to be more valuable than their face value, and they were unwilling to part with them. The gold coins disappeared first, followed by the silver coins. Today's coins are made of inferior metals—copper, zinc, and nickel. Yet with metal prices increasing, people have begun to pull these out of circulation, too. The older gold and silver coins are sold by collectors for many times their face value in fiat money. A worn $20 gold piece brings $2,000, 100 times its original value.

Even without a gold standard that restricts the total currency issued to the amount of stored value, governments do have a practical limit on how much paper money they can print. In general, prices increase if a government issues currency at a rate higher than the growth of its **gross domestic product (GDP)**, the total goods and services that a country produces. This condition, **inflation**, means that each unit of currency will purchase fewer goods and services. Governments try to control inflation, since high inflation can destabilize a society and sweep away the ruling class.

As you can see from Figure 14.2 below, as long as the gold standard limited the amount of currency, the purchasing power of the dollar remained relatively stable. When the United States left the gold standard in 1937, the dollar no longer represented stored value, and it plunged in value. Today's dollar is but a skinny shadow of its former self, retaining only about 5 percent of its earlier purchasing power. And it is getting skinnier by the moment.

fiat money currency issued by a government that is not backed by stored value

gross domestic product (GDP) the amount of goods and services produced by a nation

inflation an increase in prices; technically, an increase in the amount of money in circulation, which leads to an increase in prices

FIGURE 14.2 Declining Value of the U.S. Dollar

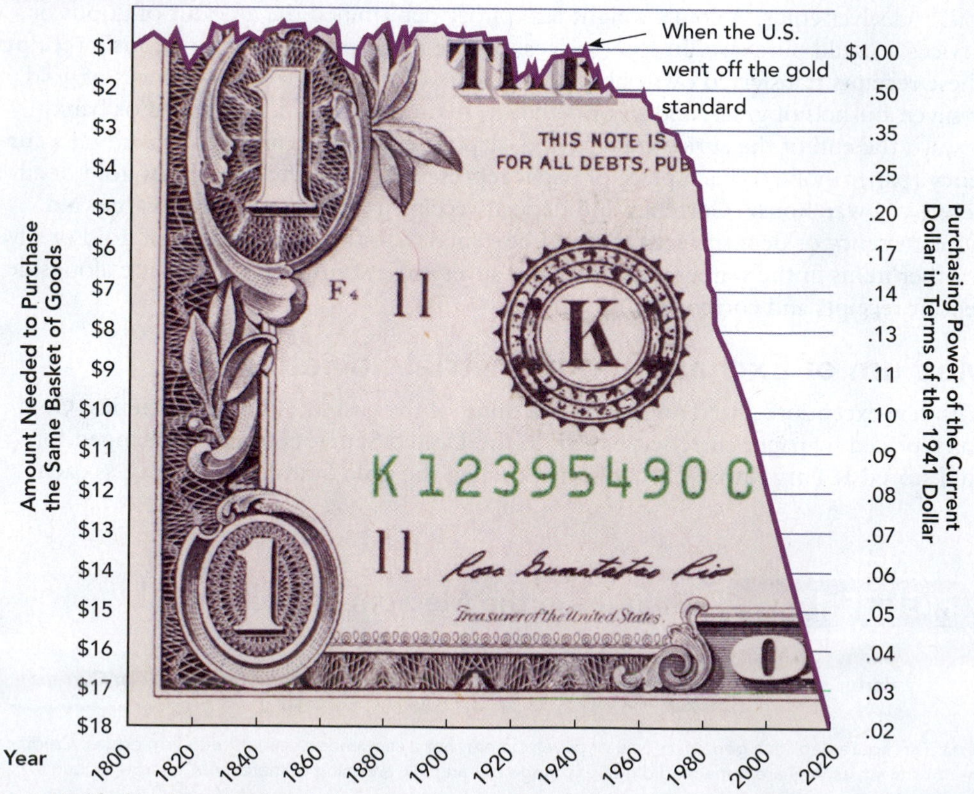

Source: Modified by the author from "Alternative Investment Market Letter," November 1991.

Inflation in the United States is usually mild, about 3 percent a year. People get used to gradual increases in prices. High inflation, in contrast, makes life difficult, and when inflation goes wild, it upsets everything. How would you like to pay $800,000 for a little bread roll? Or $1,000,000 for a chicken? How about $417 for a single piece of scratchy toilet paper? These were prices in Zimbabwe when inflation ran wild in 2008 (Wines 2006b; Bearak 2008). A Coke cost $15,000,000,000 (Walker and Higgins 2008). That was at noon. By dinner, it cost a few million more (all prices in Zimbabwean money, not U.S. dollars).

After World War I, Germany was ravaged by high inflation, which helped to usher Hitler into power. Look at the photos to the right. The large, beautiful bill at the top—which I bought in an antique shop—looks and feels as though it were engraved. Although it is only 100 marks, with this 1908 bill you could have bought a car. The smaller bills of 200,000 and 1 million marks, churned out by the German mint at the height of inflation in 1923, look and feel like Monopoly money. With them, you could buy a loaf of bread—if you rushed to the store before the price rose.

In industrialized societies, checking accounts became common. A check is a type of deposit receipt, a promise that the check writer has deposited enough currency in the warehouse (the bank or credit union) to cover the check. The latter part of the industrial period saw the invention of the **credit card**. This device allows someone who has been approved for a specified amount of credit to purchase goods without an immediate exchange of money. Instead, the owner of the credit card is billed for the purchase.

Medium of Exchange in Postindustrial Societies

During the first part of the postindustrial (or information) society, paper money circulated freely, only gradually being replaced by checks and credit cards. The next development was the **debit card**, a device that electronically withdraws the cost of an item from the cardholder's bank account. Like the check, the debit card is a type of deposit receipt, for it transfers ownership of currency on deposit.

The latest evolution of money is **e-cash**, money stored on a company's computer that can be transferred over the Internet to anyone who has an account with that company. The most common form of e-cash is *e-currency*, an amount recorded in a government's paper money, such as so many dollars or euros. Governments dislike the development of e-cash, because the transactions bypass banks, making it difficult to monitor the financial activities of their citizens.

Another form of e-cash that governments also view as a threat is *electronic gold*, which represents a balance in units of gold. A transaction in e-gold is actually the transfer of ownership of a specified amount of gold, which the owner has stored in a bank's vault. E-gold takes us back to the time when people made transactions in gold and silver—this time, in contrast, using an electronic form for the exchange. The value of an electronic gold account goes up or down depending on the price of gold. Because electronic gold is not issued by a national government, it does not represent the transfer of euros or dollars or any other fiat currency. This makes electronic gold a non-national money that can be used by people in any country. Because electronic gold bypasses government-issued currencies, we can expect extensive legislation as governments try to keep their control over money.

credit card a device that allows its owner to purchase goods and to be billed later

debit card a device that electronically withdraws the cost of an item from the cardholder's bank account

e-cash digital money that is stored on computers

World Economic Systems

14.3 Contrast capitalism and socialism: their components, ideologies, criticisms, and convergence.

Now that we have sketched the major historical changes in world economic systems and their means of exchange, let's compare capitalism and socialism, the two main economic systems in force today. This will help us to understand where the United States stands in the world economic order.

Capitalism

Listen on MySocLab
Audio: NPR: In Africa, No Coke Can Mean No Stability

What Capitalism Is. People who live in a capitalist society may not understand its basic tenets, even though they see them reflected in their local shopping malls and fast-food chains. Table 14.1 distills the many businesses of the United States down to their basic components. As you can see, **capitalism** has three essential features: (1) *private ownership of the means of production* (individuals own the land, machines, and factories), (2) *market competition* (competing with one another, the owners decide what to produce and set the prices for their products), and (3) *the pursuit of profit* (the owners try to sell their products for more than they cost).

TABLE 14.1 Comparing Capitalism and Socialism

Capitalism	Socialism
1. Individuals own the means of production.	1. The public owns the means of production.
2. Based on competition, the owners determine production and set prices.	2. Central committees plan production and set prices; no competition.
3. The pursuit of profit is the reason for distributing goods and services.	3. No profit motive in the distribution of goods and services.

Source: By the author.

What State Capitalism Is. No country has pure capitalism. Pure capitalism, known as **laissez-faire capitalism** (literally "hands off" capitalism), means that the government doesn't interfere in the market. The current form of U.S. capitalism is *state* (or *welfare*) *capitalism*. Private citizens own the means of production and pursue profits, but they do so within a vast system of laws designed to protect the welfare of the population, and—not incidentally—ensure that the government can collect taxes.

Consider this example:

Suppose that you discover what you think is a miracle tonic: It will grow hair, erase wrinkles, and dissolve excess fat. If your product works, you will become an overnight sensation—not only a multimillionaire but also the toast of television talk shows and the darling of Hollywood.

But don't count on your money or fame yet. You still have to reckon with market restraints, the laws and regulations of welfare capitalism that limit your capacity to produce and sell. First, you must comply with local and state laws. You must obtain a business license and a state tax number that allows you to buy your ingredients without paying sales taxes. Then come the federal regulations. You cannot simply take your product to local stores and ask them to sell it; you first must seek approval from federal agencies that monitor compliance with the Pure Food and Drug Act. This means that you must prove that your product will not cause harm to the public. Your manufacturing process is also subject to federal, state, and local laws concerning fraud, hygiene, and the disposal of hazardous wastes.

Suppose that you overcome these obstacles, and your business prospers. Other federal agencies will monitor your compliance with laws concerning minimum wages, Social Security taxes, and discrimination on the basis of race, gender, religion, or disability. State agencies will examine your records to see whether you have paid unemployment and sales taxes. Finally, as your shadowy but ever-present business partner, the Internal Revenue Service will look over your shoulder and demand about 35 percent of your profits.

In short, the U.S. economic system is highly regulated and is far from an example of laissez-faire capitalism.

The Development of State Capitalism. To see how state (or welfare) capitalism developed in the United States, let's go back to an earlier era. Back in the 1800s, when capitalism was in its infancy, you could have made your "magic" potion at home

capitalism an economic system built around the private ownership of the means of production, the pursuit of profit, and market competition

laissez-faire capitalism literally "hands off" capitalism, meaning that the government doesn't interfere in the market and sold it at any store willing to handle it. You could have advertised that it cured baldness, erased wrinkles, and dissolved fat; no agency existed to monitor your product or your claims. As you can see from the 1885 poster, this is precisely what thousands of individuals did at that time. They made "elixirs" in their basements and gave them whimsical names such as "Granny's Miracle Medicine" and "Elixir of Health and Happiness." They might claim that their product could restore sexual potency, purge the intestines, and make people more intelligent. These tonics often made people feel better, since many were braced with alcohol and cocaine (Ashley 1975). (The *Coca* in Coca-Cola refers to cocaine, which this "pick-me-up" drink contained until 1903.) To protect the public's health, in 1906 the federal government passed the Pure Food and Drug Act and began to regulate products.

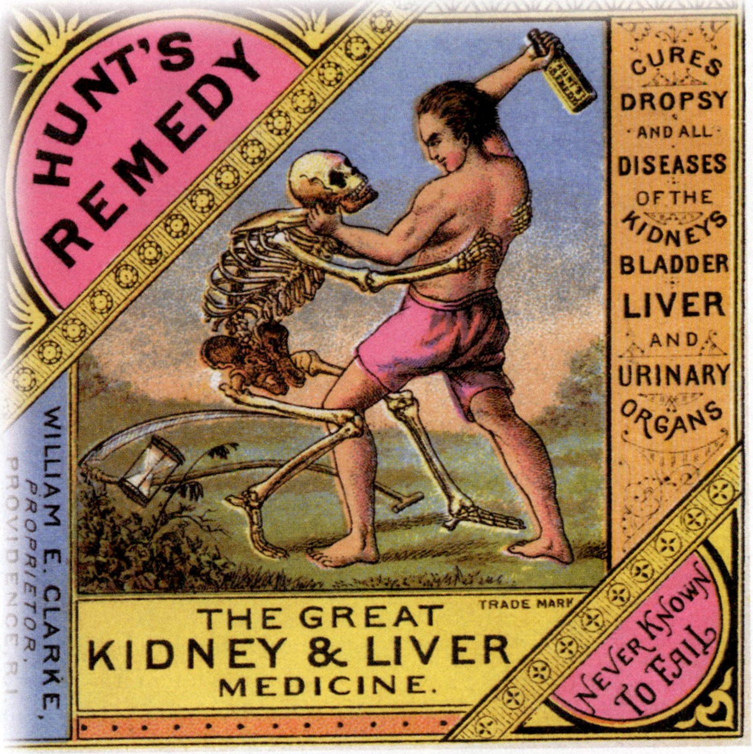

This advertisement from about 1885 represents an early stage of capitalism when individuals were free to manufacture and market products with little or no interference from the government. Today, the production and marketing of goods take place under detailed, complicated government laws and regulations.

John D. Rockefeller's remarkable success in unregulated markets helps to explain why the government began to regulate capitalism. After a ruthless drive to eliminate competition, Rockefeller managed to corner the U.S. oil and gasoline market (Spence and Prentice 2012). He slashed prices to drive out competitors and even sabotaged their pipelines and refineries (Josephson 1949). With his competitors crippled or eliminated, his company, Standard Oil, was able to dictate prices to the entire nation. Rockefeller had achieved the capitalist's dream, a **monopoly**, the control of an entire industry by a single company.

Rockefeller had played the capitalist game too well, however. He had wiped out one of its essential components: competition. Consequently, to protect this cornerstone of capitalism, the federal government passed antimonopoly legislation and broke Standard Oil into 34 separate companies (Spence and Prentice 2012). Today, the top firms in each industry—such as General Electric in household appliances—must obtain federal approval before acquiring another company in the same industry. If the government determines that one firm dominates a market, it can force that company to *divest* (sell off) some of the businesses it owns.

Although monopolies are illegal in state capitalism, the government establishes its own monopoly over what it calls "common good" items. These are items and services presumed essential for the common good of the citizens, such as armed forces, highways, and sewers.

Socialism

What Socialism Is. As Table 14.1 on the previous page shows, **socialism** also has three essential components: (1) public ownership of the means of production, (2) central planning, and (3) the distribution of goods without a profit motive.

In socialist economies, the government owns the means of production—not only the factories but also the land, railroads, oil wells, and gold mines. Unlike capitalism, in which **market forces**—supply and demand—determine both what will be produced and the prices that will be charged, a central committee decides that the country needs X number of toothbrushes, Y toilets, and Z shoes. The committee decides how many of each will be produced, which factories will produce them, what price will be charged for the items, and where they will be distributed.

Socialism is designed to eliminate competition: Goods are sold at predetermined prices regardless of the demand for an item or the cost of producing it. The goal is not to make a profit, nor is it to encourage the consumption of goods that are in low

monopoly the control of an entire industry by a single company

socialism an economic system built around the public ownership of the means of production, central planning, and the distribution of goods without a profit motive

market forces the law of supply and demand

The wealthy, whether capitalist or socialist, can afford most anything, including trophy spouses. It is usually successful men who marry women much younger than themselves, such as such as Bruce Willis, age 58, and his wife, Emma Heming, age 35. This pattern will continue, but with changing norms we can expect more financially successful women to marry younger men.

demand (by lowering the price) or to limit the consumption of hard-to-get goods (by raising the price). Rather, the goal is to produce goods for the general welfare and to distribute them according to people's needs, not their ability to pay.

In a socialist economy, *everyone* in the economic chain works for the government. The members of the central committee who set production goals are government employees, as are the supervisors who implement their plans, the factory workers who produce the merchandise, the truck drivers who move it, and the clerks who sell it. Those who buy the items may work at different jobs—in offices, on farms, or in day care centers—but they, too, are government employees.

Socialism in Practice. Just as capitalism does not exist in a pure form, neither does socialism. Although the ideology of socialism calls for resources to be distributed according to need and not the ability to pay, socialist countries found it necessary to pay higher salaries for some jobs in order to entice people to take on greater responsibilities. Factory managers, for example, always earned more than factory workers. These differences in pay follow the functionalist argument of social stratification presented in Chapter 9 (pages 236–237). By narrowing the huge pay gaps that characterize capitalist nations, however, socialist nations established considerably greater equality of income.

Democratic Socialism. Dissatisfied with the greed and exploitation of capitalism and the lack of freedom and individuality of socialism, Sweden and Denmark developed **democratic socialism** (also called *welfare socialism*). In this form of socialism, both the state and individuals produce and distribute goods and services. The government owns and runs the steel, mining, forestry, and energy concerns, as well as the country's telephones, television stations, and airlines. Remaining in private hands are the retail stores, farms, factories, and most service industries.

Ideologies of Capitalism and Socialism

Watch on **MySocLab** **Video:** The Big Picture: Economy and Work

Not only do capitalism and socialism have different approaches to producing and distributing goods, but they also represent opposing belief systems. *Capitalists* believe that market forces should determine both products and prices. They also believe that profits are good for humanity. The potential to make money stimulates people to produce and distribute goods, as well as to develop new products. Society benefits, as the result is a more abundant supply of goods at cheaper prices.

Socialists take an opposite view of profits. They consider profits to be immoral. An item's value is based on the work that goes into it, said Karl Marx (1906). The only way there can be profit, he stressed, is by paying workers less than the value of their labor. Profit, he said, is the *excess value* that has been withheld from workers. Socialists believe that the government should protect workers from this exploitation. To do so, the government should own the means of production, using them not to generate profit but to produce items that match people's needs, not their ability to pay.

Capitalists and socialists paint each other in such stark colors that *each perceives the other system as one of exploitation.* Capitalists believe that socialists violate people's basic right to make their own decisions and to pursue opportunity. Socialists believe that capitalists violate people's basic right to be free from poverty. With each side claiming moral superiority while viewing the other as a threat to its very existence, the last century

democratic socialism a hybrid economic system in which the individual ownership of businesses is mixed with the state ownership of industries thought essential to the public welfare, such as the postal service, natural resources, the medical delivery system, and mass transportation

Propaganda to influence public opinion surrounds us, but most propaganda is covert, difficult to recognize. During economic-political conflicts, much propaganda moves into the open. The anti-German poster on the left is from Russia. It reads: "Father, kill the Germans" (who have just killed my mother). The anti-Russian poster on the right is from Germany. It reads: "Bolshevism means the world will drown in blood." To arouse their people, each accuses the other of the same acts.

witnessed the world split into two main blocs. In what was known as the *Cold War*, the West armed itself to defend and promote capitalism, the East to defend and promote socialism.

Criticisms of Capitalism and Socialism

In India, an up-and-coming capitalist giant, the construction of a 27-story building is almost complete (Yardley 2010). It comes with a grand ballroom, nine elevators, a fifty-seat theater, a six-story garage and three helipads on the roof.

The occupants are ready to move in—all five of them—a husband and wife and their three children. From their elegant perch, they will be able to view the teeming mass of destitute people below.

Watch on **MySocLab**
Video: UN World Inequality

The primary criticism leveled against capitalism is that it leads to social inequality. Capitalism, say its critics, produces a tiny top layer of wealthy people who exploit an immense bottom layer of poorly paid workers. Another criticism is that the tiny top layer wields vast political power. Those few who own the means of production reap huge profits, accrue power, and get legislation passed that goes against the public good.

The first criticism leveled against socialism is that it does not respect individual rights. Others (in the form of some government agency) control people's lives. They decide where people will live, work, and go to school. In China, government officials even determine how many children women may bear (Mosher 1983, 2006). Critics make a second point—that central planning is grossly inefficient and that socialism is not capable of producing much wealth. They say that its greater equality really amounts to giving almost everyone an equal chance to be poor.

The Convergence of Capitalism and Socialism

Regardless of the validity of these mutual criticisms, as nations industrialize they come to resemble one another. They urbanize, encourage higher education, and produce similar divisions of labor (such as professionals and skilled technicians; factory workers and factory managers). Similar values also emerge (Kerr 1983). By itself, this tendency would make capitalist and socialist nations grow more alike, but another factor also brings them closer to one another (Form 1979): Despite their incompatible ideologies, both capitalist and socialist systems have adopted features from the other.

That capitalism and socialism are growing similar is known as **convergence theory**. Fundamental changes in socialist countries give evidence for this coming hybrid, or mixed, economy. For example, Russians suffered from shoddy goods and shortages, and their standard of living lagged severely behind that of the West. To try to catch up, in the 1980s and 1990s the rulers of Russia made the private ownership of property legal and abandoned communism. Making a profit—which had been a crime—was encouraged. China joined the change, but kept a communist government. In its converged form of "capunism," capitalists joined the Communist party. The convergence is so great that when the Western governments instituted stimulus plans to counter the economic crisis, China joined in with a huge stimulus plan of its own (Batson 2009). Even Western banks are now welcome in China. Among other things, they provide specialized services to China's 960,000 new millionaires (Yenfang 2011)—and, of course, to China's 117 new billionaires (Harris 2012b). The change is so remarkable that some textbooks in China now give more space to Bill Gates than to Mao (Guthrie 2008). The Cultural Diversity box on the next page provides a glimpse of the new capitalism in China.

Changes in capitalism also support this theory. The United States has adopted many socialist practices. One of the most obvious is that the government collects money from some individuals to pay for benefits given to others. It had none of these when the country was founded: unemployment compensation (taxes paid by workers are distributed to those who no longer produce a profit); subsidized housing, food, and medical care (paid for by the many and given to the poor and elderly with no motive of profit); welfare (taxes from the many are distributed to the needy); a minimum wage (the government, not the employer, determines the minimum that workers are paid); and Social Security (the retired do not receive what they paid into the system but, rather, money that the government collects from current workers).

Convergence is continuing. In 2008, when Wall Street and auto firms started to buckle, the U.S. government stepped in to shore up these businesses. In some cases, the government even bought the companies, fired CEOs, and set salary limits. Such an extended embrace of socialist principles indicates that the United States has produced its own version of a mixed economy.

In Sum: Convergence is unfolding before our very eyes. On the one hand, capitalists have assumed, reluctantly, that their system should provide workers with at least minimal support during unemployment, extended illness, and old age—and, in some instances, that the government should buy company stock. On the other hand, socialist leaders have admitted, also reluctantly, that profit and private ownership do motivate people to work harder.

Possible Transmergence. Social life is sometimes stranger than fiction, and here is a fascinating possibility. Like two cars heading toward each other, these two economic systems do not converge. Rather, each passes the other, continuing in the direction where the other was. The capitalist nations end up adopting so many features of socialism while the former socialist nations embrace so many aspects of capitalism that each is transformed into a version of what the other was.

Could this idea, which we can call *transmergence theory*, indicate something that is even possible? Consider this. An article in *Pravda*, Russia's main newspaper and the former propaganda organ of the Soviet Communist Party, warned the United States not to travel farther on the road to socialism (Mishin 2009). These new capitalists said that by bailing out private companies—such as banks and automobile manufacturers—the United States is choosing a path that is "dangerously Marxist."

convergence theory the view that as capitalist and socialist economic systems each adopt features of the other, a hybrid (or mixed) economic system will emerge

Cultural Diversity around the World

The New Competitor: The Chinese Capitalists

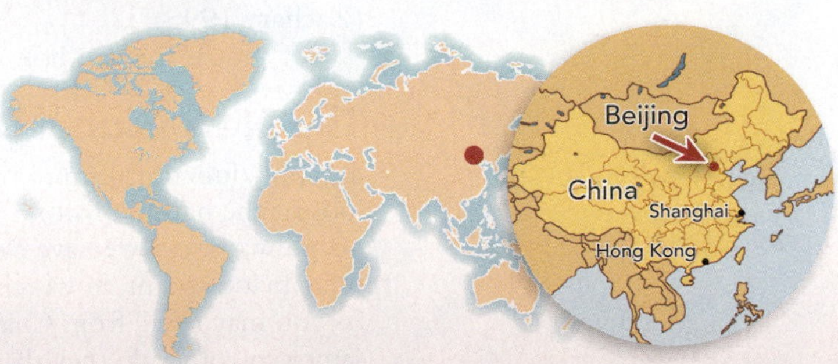

Socialism has the virtue of making people more equal. Socialism's equality, however, translates into distributing poverty throughout a society. Under socialism, almost everyone becomes equally poor.

Capitalism has the virtue of producing wealth. A lot of people remain poor, however, leaving deep gaps between wealth and poverty, which produces envy and sometimes creates social unrest.

Chinese leaders realized the wealth-producing capacity of capitalism and wanted this for their people (Karon 2011). In the Chinese version they produced—capitalism directed by communists—wealth has increased at an astonishing rate. In all the world's history, this new capitalism has lifted the largest number of people—*a half billion*—out of poverty in the shortest time. The poor farmers who are left behind, however, aren't happy when their land is taken from them to help make others wealthy. The anger and resentment have kept the Party busy sending out the army to squelch riots.

As China has embraced its version of capitalism, wealth has grown, as has consumption. Luxury goods from the United States are considered prestigious and are highly desired.

In Beijing, the capital of China, stands a mansion built by Zhang Yuchen. This is no ordinary mansion, like those built by China's other newly rich. This imposing building is a twin of the Chateau de Maisons-Laffitte, an architectural landmark on the Seine River outside Paris. At a cost of $50 million, the Beijing replica matches the original edifice detail for detail. The architects even used the original blueprints of the French chateau. The building also features the same Chantilly stone (Kahn 2004, 2007).

Eight hundred farmers were made landless to build the chateau and its nearby luxury homes. But if they get angry, the spiked fence, the moat, and the armed guards—looking sharp in their French-style uniforms complete with capes and kepis—will keep the peasants out of the chateau.

In most places, you need connections to become wealthy. In China, this means connections with the Communist Party, since this group holds the power. Yuchen has those connections. As a member of the Party, it was his job to direct Beijing's construction projects. With his deep connections, Yuchen was able to get the wheat fields that were farmed by the peasants rezoned from farmland to a "conservation area." He was even able to divert a river so he could build the moat around the chateau, one of the finishing touches on his architectural wonder.

Beneath such ostentatious examples of capitalistic excess lies this irony: China is doing capitalism better than the capitalist countries are. Using the state machinery, their leaders have proven themselves more nimble in reacting to competition, in seizing opportunities for profit, and in accumulating vast amounts of capital. The capitalist nations have become envious, especially as the Chinese model of capitalism—at least at this historical point—is proving competitively superior (Bremer 2011; Karon 2011).

For Your Consideration

➔ When China has completed its transition to capitalism, what do you think the final version will look like (that is, what characteristics do you think it will have)? Where will the top Party leaders fit in the class system that is emerging? Why? (To answer this, consider the connections and resources of the Chinese elite.)

The Functionalist Perspective on the Globalization of Capitalism

14.4 Discuss corporate capitalism, ownership and management, and global functions and dysfunctions of capitalism.

Capitalism has made the world's countries part of the same broad economic unit. When the economic crisis hit the United States, it spread quickly around the world. To decide what they should do, the leaders of the top 20 producers of consumer goods met in Washington. The Chinese leaders said that no one should worry about them not being a team player; they knew that their actions would affect other nations. (Yardley and Bradsher 2008)

The globalization of capitalism is so significant that its ultimate impact on our lives may rival that of the Industrial Revolution. As Louis Galambos, a historian of business, says, "This new global business system will change the way everyone lives and works" (Zachary 1995).

Let's look, then, at how capitalism is changing the face of the globe.

The New Global Division of Labor

Watch on **MySocLab** **Video:** The Basics: Economy and Work

To apply functionalism to the globalization of capitalism, let's step back a moment and look at the nature of work. You know that work is functional for society. Only because people work can we have electricity, hospitals, schools, automobiles, and homes. Beyond this obvious point, however, lies a basic sociological principle: *Work binds us together*. As you may recall from Chapter 4, Emile Durkheim noted that because farmers do the same type of work, they share a similar view of life. Durkheim used the term **mechanical solidarity** to refer to the sense of unity that comes from doing similar activities.

When an agricultural society industrializes, people work at many different types of jobs. As the division of labor grows, people come to feel less solidarity with one another. Grape pickers in California, for example, feel little in common with workers who make aircraft in Missouri. Yet, what each worker does contributes to the economic system and, therefore, to the welfare of the others. Because they are *like the separate organs that make up the same body*, Durkheim called this type of unity **organic solidarity**.

Durkheim was observing the early stages of a *global division of labor*. Since then, the division of labor has evolved so greatly that today each of us depends on workers around the globe. If we live in California or New York—or even Michigan—we depend on workers in Tokyo to produce cars. Tokyo workers, in turn, depend on Saudi Arabian workers to pump oil and South American workers to operate ships that deliver the oil. We may not feel a sense of unity with one another, but the same global economic web links us together.

As you know, these interconnections of our developing global village offer vast opportunities for corporations to reap profits. Their attempts to do so, however, sometimes hit unexpected cultural hurdles, the topic of the Cultural Diversity box on the next page.

Capitalism in a Global Economy

Corporate Capitalism. The dominance that capitalism currently enjoys can be traced to a social invention called the corporation. A **corporation** is a business that is treated legally as a person. A corporation can make contracts, incur debts, sue, and be sued. Its liabilities and obligations, however, are separate from those of its owners. For example, each shareholder of Ford Motor Company—whether that person has 1 or 100,000 shares—owns a portion of the company. However, Ford, not its individual owners, is responsible for fulfilling its contracts and paying its debts. The term **corporate capitalism** is used to indicate that corporations dominate an economy.

Separation of Ownership and Management. One of the most surprising aspects of corporations is their separation of ownership and management. Unlike most businesses, it is not the owners—those who own the company's stock—who run the day-to-day affairs of the company (Sklair 2001). Instead, managers run the corporation, and they are able to treat it *as though it were their own*. Sociologist Michael Useem (1984) put it this way:

> *When few owners held all or most of a corporation's stock, they readily dominated its board of directors, which in turn selected top management and ran the corporation. Now that a firm's stock [is] dispersed among many unrelated owners, each holding a tiny fraction of the total equity, the resulting power vacuum allow[s] management to select the board of directors; thus management [becomes] self-perpetuating and thereby acquire[s] de facto control over the corporation.*
>
> *Management determines its own salaries, sets goals and awards itself bonuses for meeting them, authorizes market surveys, hires advertising agencies, determines marketing strategies, and negotiates with unions. The management's primary responsibility to the owners is to produce profits.*

mechanical solidarity Durkheim's term for the unity (a shared consciousness) that people feel as a result of performing the same or similar tasks

organic solidarity Durkheim's term for the interdependence that results from the division of labor; as part of the same unit, we all depend on others to fulfill their jobs

corporation a business enterprise whose assets, liabilities, and obligations are separate from those of its owners; as a legal entity, it can enter into contracts, assume debt, and sue and be sued

corporate capitalism the domination of an economic system by giant corporations

Cultural Diversity around the World

Doing Business in the Global Village

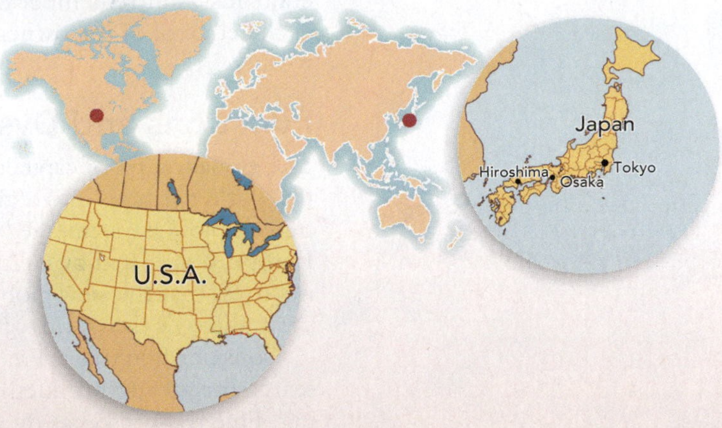

As capitalism globalizes, businesspeople face cultural hurdles. Some of the cultural mistakes they make as they market products in other countries are downright humorous.

In trying to reach Spanish-speaking Americans and Latin and South America's growing middle classes, some companies have stumbled over their Spanish. Parker Pen was using a slogan "It won't leak in your pocket and embarrass you." The translation, however, came out as "It won't leak in your pocket and make you pregnant." Frank Perdue's cute chicken slogan "It takes a strong man to make a tender chicken" didn't fare any better in Spanish. It came out as "It takes an aroused man to make a chicken affectionate." And when American Airlines launched a "Fly in Leather" campaign to promote its leather seats in first class, the Mexican campaign stumbled just a bit. "Fly in Leather" (*vuela en cuero*), while literally correct, came out as "Fly Naked"—which certainly must have appealed to some (Archbold and Harmon 2001).

The huge Spanish market keeps enticing companies to run marketing campaigns. The American Dairy Association made a hit in the United States with its humorous campaign, "Got Milk?" In Mexico, though, the Spanish translation read "Are you lactating?" All those mouths with white milk on them suddenly took on new meaning. Coors didn't fare any better. Their slogan, "Turn It Loose," was a hit in the United States, but in Spanish it came out as "Get Diarrhea."

Hershey's came out with a candy bar, *Cajeta Elegancita*, marketed to Spanish-speaking customers. While *cajeta* can mean nougat, its more common meaning is "little box." The literal translation of *cajeta elegancita* is elegant or fancy little box. Some customers are snickering about this one, too, for *cajeta* is also slang for an intimate part of the female anatomy ("Winner . . . " 2006).

It isn't only Spanish that has given U.S. companies problems. Vicks decided to sell its cough drops in Germany. In German, "v" is pronounced "f." Unfortunately, this made Vicks sound like the "f" word in English, which is just what *ficks* means in German.

Cultural mistakes are a two-way street, of course. A Swedish company makes Electrolux, a vacuum cleaner. Their slogan is cute in Swedish, but the translation for their U.S. audience was "Nothing sucks like an Electrolux."

The Unites States version

The Japanese version

Some businesspeople have overcome language hurdles and successfully seized profit opportunities in cultural differences. For example, Japanese women are embarrassed by the sounds they make in public toilets. To drown out the offensive sounds, they flush the toilet an average of 2.7 times a visit (Iori 1988). This wastes a lot of water, of course. Seeing this cultural trait as an opportunity, a U.S. entrepreneur developed a battery-powered device that is mounted in the toilet stall. When a woman activates the device, it emits a twenty-five-second flushing sound. A toilet-sound duplicator may be useless in our culture, but the Japanese have bought thousands of them.

To be accepted in another culture, sometimes the product has to be changed. In a process called *transcreation*, cartoons designed originally for one audience are modified to match the tastes of an audience in another culture. The illustration in this box shows this process. At the top is the U.S. version of the Powerpuff Girls; at the bottom is how the Powerpuff Girls appear on Japanese television. Portraying Blossom, Buttercup, and Bubbles as leggy and dressed in skimpy outfits has broadened their appeal considerably: Not only do little girls look forward to this cartoon on Saturday mornings, but so do many adult Japanese men (Fowler and Chozick 2007).

For Your Consideration

➔ 1. Why is it often difficult to do business across cultures?

➔ 2. How can businesspeople avoid cross-cultural mistakes?

➔ 3. If a company makes a cultural blunder, what should it do?

Because of this power vacuum, at their annual meetings the stockholders usually rubber-stamp management's recommendations. It is so unusual for this *not* to happen that when it occurs it is called a **stockholders' revolt**. The irony of this term is generally lost, but remember that in such cases, it is not the workers who are rebelling at the control of the owners but the owners who are rebelling at the control of the workers!

Functions and Dysfunctions on a Global Scale

Read on **MySocLab**
Document: The Uses of Global Poverty: How Economic Inequality Benefits the West

The globalization of capitalism is producing a new world structure, one that integrates the world's nations into a global production and distribution system. Three primary trading blocs have emerged: North and South America, dominated by the United States; Europe, dominated by Germany; and Asia, dominated by China and Japan. Functionalists stress that this new global division benefits not only the multinational giants but also the citizens of the world.

Consider free trade. Free trade increases competition, which, in turn, drives the search for greater productivity. This lowers prices and brings a higher standard of living. Free trade also has dysfunctions. As production moves to countries where labor costs are lower, millions of U.S., U.K., French, and Spanish workers lose their jobs. Functionalists point out that this is a temporary dislocation. As the Most Industrialized Nations lose factory jobs, their workers shift into service and high-tech jobs. Perhaps. But the millions of workers searching in vain for jobs that no longer exist would disagree.

The adjustment is not easy. As the U.S. steel industry lost out to global competition, for example, the closings of plants created "rust belts" in the northern states. The globalization of capitalism has also brought special challenges to small towns, which were already suffering long-term losses because of urbanization. Their struggle to survive is the topic of the photo essay on pages 404–405.

14.5 Summarize shifts in corporate capitalism, concentration of power, the global superclass, and global investing.

The Conflict Perspective on the Globalization of Capitalism

Although the leaders of the world's top corporations compete with one another, they are united by a common interest—making capitalism flourish (Rothkopf 2008; Harris 2012a). Let's look at how some of their mutual interests work out in practice. To understand the implications of what you are going to read, you should note that it makes no difference whether a Democrat or a Republican is president.

Close Corporate-Political Connections. The interests of the heads of corporations and politicians overlap to such a degree that even U.S. presidents get involved in selling products. Seldom is this relationship spelled out, but occasionally it is, such as in this report from the Associated Press ("Saudis Sign" 1995):

> *The White House celebrated Saudi Arabia's $6 billion purchase of U.S.-made airplanes Thursday, calling it a victory for both American manufacturers and the Clinton administration. . . . Clinton personally pitched the quality of the U.S. planes to Saudi King Fahd. . . . The Clinton administration worked this sale awfully hard because of the president's commitment to promoting U.S. business abroad. . . . He has done that routinely, instructed his ambassadors and his diplomats to put the economic interests of Americans forward as they conduct their diplomacy.*

If enough bottles were at stake, the president probably would help sell underarm deodorant. I doubt that this is an exaggeration, as Obama helped make certain that Tyson was able to sell chickens to Russia (Nichol 2011).

stockholders' revolt refusal by stockholders at their annual meetings to approve management's recommendations

Corporate Power and Conspiracies. Cooperation, not working at cross-purposes, benefits both corporations and politicians. Selling products together is not the usual form of their cooperation. The typical form of "one hand washing the other" is campaign contributions matched by legislation that benefits big business, with perhaps a few under-the-table payoffs. Sometimes, however, the cooperation takes more sinister forms. Here are two examples:

In the 1950s, the newly elected president of Guatemala, Jacobo Árbenz, wanted workers to get higher wages. The largest employer in Guatemala was the United Fruit Company, and this U.S. corporation wanted to keep wages low. The CIA funded and trained an army, which overthrew Árbenz (Shefner 2008). In 1973, another U.S. company, the International Telephone & Telegraph Company (ITT), joined the CIA in a plot that led to the assassination of Salvador Allende, the president of Chile (Coleman 1995; Rohter 2002).

Shifting Dominance. Finally, let's look at one of the most significant changes in global capitalism. Table 14.2 below lists the world's twenty-five largest **multinational corporations**—companies that operate across national borders. You can see that the largest multinationals are spread among nine countries. You can also see the dominance of the United States. What is not apparent from this list is the decline of the United States and the rapid

multinational corporations companies that operate across national boundaries; also called *transnational corporations*

TABLE 14.2 The World's Largest Corporations

Rank	Company	Country	Industry	Sales ($bil)	Profits ($bil)	Assets ($bil)
1	ICBC	China	Banking	135	38	2,814
2	China Construction Bank	China	Banking	113	31	2,241
3	JP Morgan Chase	United States	Banking	108	21	2,359
4	General Electric	United States	Conglomerates	147	14	685
5	Exxon Mobil	United States	Oil & Gas	421	45	334
6	HSBC Holdings	United Kingdom	Banking	105	14	2,684
7	Royal Dutch Shell	Netherlands	Oil & Gas	467	27	360
8	Agricultural Bank of China	China	Banking	103	23	2,124
9	Berkshire Hathaway	United States	Diversified	163	15	426
10	PetroChina	China	Oil & Gas	309	18	348
11	Bank of China	China	Banking	98	22	2,034
12	Wells Fargo	United States	Banking	91	19	1,423
13	Chevron	United States	Oil & Gas	223	26	233
14	Volkswagen Group	Germany	Manufacturing	254	29	408
15	Apple	United States	Electronics	165	42	196
16	Wal-Mart Stores	United States	Retailing	469	17	203
17	Gazprom	Russia	Oil & Gas	144	41	339
18	BP	United Kingdom	Oil & Gas	371	12	301
19	Citigroup	United States	Banking	91	8	1,865
20	Petrobas	Brazil	Oil & Gas	144	11	332
21	Samsung Electronics	South Korea	Electronics	188	22	196
22	BNP Paribas	France	Banking	126	9	2,504
23	Total	France	Oil & Gas	241	14	224
24	AT&T	United States	Telecommunications	127	7	272
25	Allianz	Germany	Insurance	140	7	916

Source: "Global 2000," 2013.

Through the Author's Lens

Small Town USA: Struggling to Survive

All across the nation, small towns are struggling to survive. Parents and town officials are concerned because so few young adults remain in their home town. There is little to keep them there, and when they graduate from high school, most move to the city. With young people leaving and old ones dying, the small towns are shriveling.

How can small towns contend with cut-throat global competition when workers in some countries are paid just a few dollars a day? Even if you open a store, down the road Wal-Mart sells the same products for about what you pay for them—and offers much greater variety.

There are exceptions: Some small towns are located close to a city, and they receive the city's spillover. A few possess a rare treasure—some unique historical event or a natural attraction—that draws visitors with money to spend. Most of the others, though, are drying up, left in a time warp as history shifts around them. This photo essay tells the story.

People do whatever they can to survive. This enterprising proprietor uses the building for an unusual combination of purposes: a "plant world", along with the sale of milk, eggs, bread, and, in a quaint southern touch, cracking pecans.

I was struck by the grandiosity of people's dreams, at least as reflected in the names that some small-towners give their businesses. Donut Palace has a nice ring to it—inspiring thoughts of wealth and royalty (note the crowns). Unfortunately, like so many others, this business didn't make it.

The small towns are filled with places like this—small businesses, locally owned, that have enough clientele for the owner and family to eke out a living. They have to offer low prices because there is a fast-food chain down the road. Fixing the sign? That's one of those "I'll get-to-its."

In striking contrast to the grandiosity of some small town business names is the utter simplicity of others. Cafe tells everyone that some type of food and drinks are served here. Everyone in this small town knows the details.

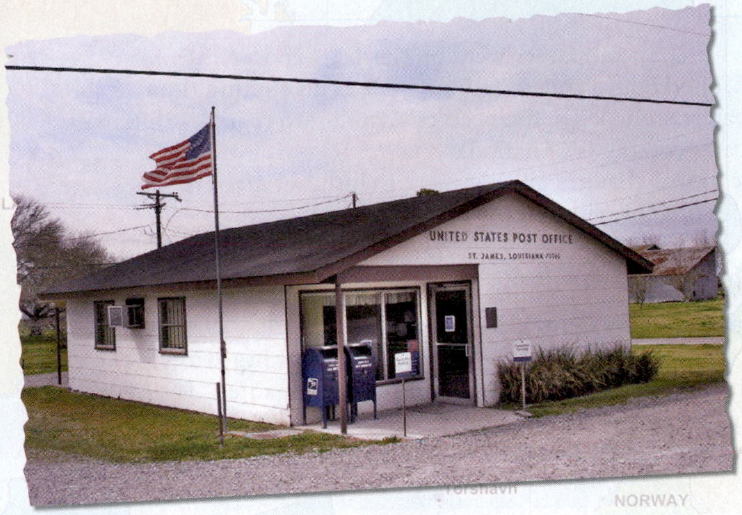

One of the few buildings consistently in good repair in the small towns is the U.S. Post Office. Although its importance has declined in the face of telecommunications, for "small towners" the post office still provides a vital link with the outside world.

With little work available, it is difficult to afford adequate housing. This house, although cobbled together and in disrepair, is a family's residence.

There is no global competition for this home-grown business. Shirley has located her sign on a main highway just outside Niceville, Florida. By the looks of the building, business could be better.

s general store used to be the main business in the area: it even
s a walk-in safe. It has been owned by the same family since the
20s, but is no longer successful. To get into the building, I had to
d out where the owner (shown here) lived, knock on her door, and
en wait while she called around to find out who had the keys.

This is a successful business. The store goes back to the early 1900s, and the proprietors have capitalized on the "old timey" atmosphere.

rise of China. Six years ago, twelve U.S. companies were on this list—and *none* from China. Now it is ten from the United States and *five* from China. This shifting dominance of global capitalism indicates, at the least, the need of adapting to regional shifts in power, but perhaps it also indicates coming international conflict.

You can see, then, that these global changes are not mere theoretical matters. They affect both your future and those of your children.

Concentration of Power

Conflict theorists stress how power is concentrated in the capitalist class described on pages 266–267. Helping to consolidate their power are **interlocking directorates**, individuals serving on the boards of directors of multiple companies. These overlapping memberships, which join the top companies into a single network, are like a spider's web that starts at the center and fans out in all directions. As one chief executive said:

> *If you serve on, say, six outside boards, each of which has, say . . . five experts in one or another subject, you have a built-in panel of thirty friends who are experts who you meet regularly, automatically each month, and you really have great access to ideas and information. You're joining a club, a very good club. (Useem 1984)*

This is not just a characteristic of capitalism in the United States, but of capitalism throughout the world.

The Global Superclass

Read on **MySocLab**
Document: The Global Economy and the Privileged Class

The overlapping memberships of the globe's top multinational companies enfold their leaders into a small circle that we can call the **global superclass** (Rothkopf 2008). This group is also called the *transnational elite* (Robinson 2012) and the *transnational ruling class* (Phillips and Soeiro 2012). The global superclass is not only extremely wealthy, as we reviewed in Chapter 9, but it is also extremely powerful. These people have access to the top circles of political power around the globe.

This group shies away from researchers, but here is your chance to listen to a member of the global superclass describe their tight connections:

> *Every country has its large financial institutions that are central to the development of that country, and everyone else in finance knows somebody who will know the head of one of those companies. That person knows a senior person in their government that could be useful in a situation. . . . the key is the network. . . . it is twenty, thirty, fifty people worldwide who ultimately drive the decisions. (Rothkopf 2008:129–130)*

Twenty to fifty individuals who make the world's major decisions! Could this possibly be true? The individual who said this, Stephen Schwarzman, is an insider who is worth about $9 billion (Freeland 2011). Here is a real-life example of how this interconnected global power works out in practice:

> *When Schwarzman, a co-founder of Blackstone, an investment company, had a problem with some policy of the German government, he called a German friend. The friend arranged for Schwarzman to meet with the Chancellor of Germany. After listening to Schwarzman, the Chancellor agreed to support a change in Germany's policy.*

interlocking directorates the same people serving on the boards of directors of several companies

global superclass the top members of the capitalist class, who, through their worldwide interconnections, make the major decisions that affect the world

Do you see the power that is concentrated in this small group? The U.S. members can call the U.S. president, the English members can ring up the British prime minister, and so on. They know how to get and give favors, to move vast amounts of capital from country to country, and to open and close doors to investments around the world. This concentration of power is new to the world scene. Working behind the scenes, the global superclass affects our present and our future.

Before turning to the United States, let's take a quick look at global investing.

Global Investing

"Fill up at Shell!"—Thanks to Shell, a Dutch oil company

"This Bud's for you!"—Thanks to InBev, a Belgian brewer

"Aren't you glad you use Dial?"—Thanks to Henkel, a German company

"Fuel the Fun!" (with Skippy Peanut Butter)—Thanks to Unilever, a Dutch conglomerate

These quotations provide a brief glimpse into how multinationals affect our lives, usually without us even being aware of it. For another glimpse, look at the Social Maps below and on the next page. Cross-border investments are so extensive that about 1 of every 21 U.S. employees—over 5 million people—works for a business owned by people in other countries (*Statistical Abstract* 2013:Table 1308).

Although we take multinational corporations—as well as their cornucopia of products—for granted, their presence and power are new to the world scene. These global giants move investments and production from one part of the globe to another—with no concern for consequences other than profits. How opening or closing factories affects workers is of no concern to them; their moral guide is profit, and their conscience is written in dollar signs.

Sure seems American, doesn't it? Dotting the landscape from coast to coast for decades, Shell is a global giant from a little country better known for its tulips and windmills.

FIGURE 14.3 The Globalization of Capitalism: U.S. Ownership in Other Countries

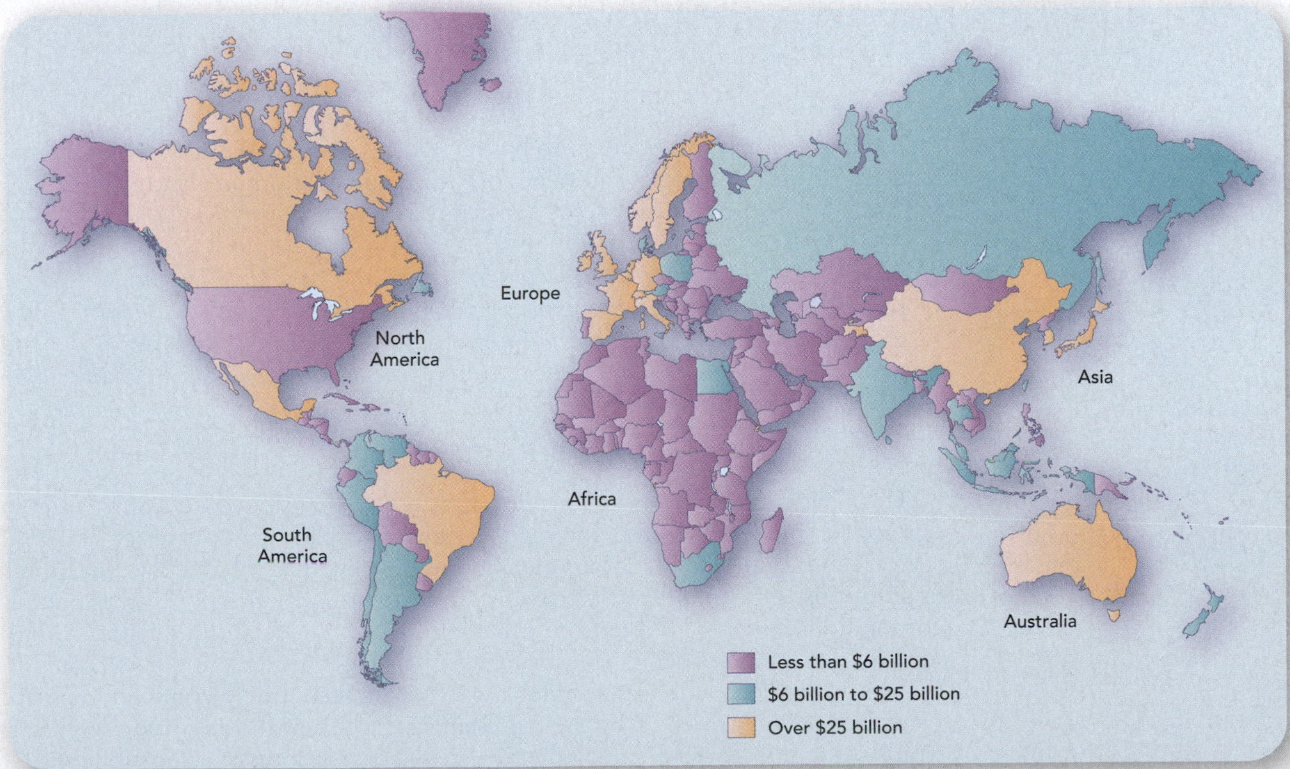

Source: By the author. Based on *Statistical Abstract of the United States* 2013:Table 1311.

FIGURE 14.4 **The Globalization of Capitalism: U.S. Workers Who Work for Foreign-Owned Businesses**

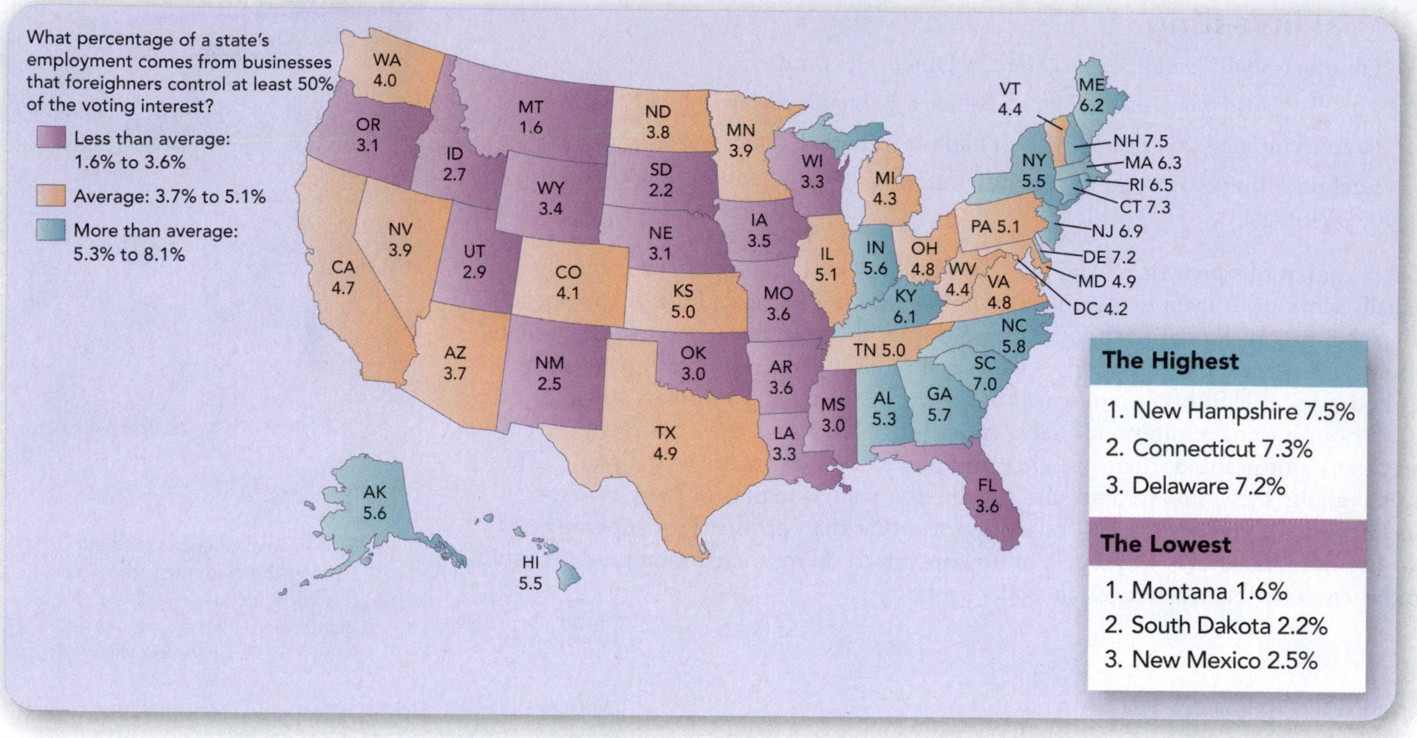

*"Controlled by foreign owners" means that non-U.S. citizens have 50% or more of the voting rights of a business.

Source: By the author. Based on *Statistical Abstract of the United States* 2013:Table 1308.

As multinational corporations do business across national borders, they become detached from the interests and values of their country of origin (Harris 2012a). Here's how one member of the global superclass put it:

> *The circles we move in are defined by "interests" and "activities" rather than "geography": Beijing has a lot in common with New York, London, or Mumbai. You see the same people, you eat in the same restaurants, you stay in the same hotels. But most important, we are engaged as global citizens in crosscutting commercial, political, and social matters of common concern. We are much less place-based than we used to be (Freeland 2011).*

The allegiance to profits and market share rather than to workers or even to country, accompanied by a web of interconnections that span the globe, is of high sociological significance. This shift in orientation is so new that we don't yet know its implications. But we can consider two stark contrasts. The first: With the multinational corporations largely removed from tribal loyalties and needing fluid national borders for easy movement of capital and materials, their global interconnections could unite the world's nations and produce global peace. The second: We could end up with a New World Order directed by the representatives of the world's corporate giants. We would be at their mercy, bent to their desires. We will discuss this possibility in the next chapter.

Work in U.S. Society

14.6 Discuss types of work, women at work, the underground economy, stagnant paychecks, and work and leisure.

With this global background, let's focus on work in U.S. society.

The Transition to Postindustrial Society

Analysts often use the term *postindustrial society* to describe the United States. Figure 14.5 illustrates why this term is appropriate. The change shown in this figure is without parallel in human history. In the 1800s, most U.S. workers were farmers. Today, farmers make up about 1 percent of the workforce. With the technology of the 1800s, a typical farmer produced enough food to feed five people. With today's powerful machinery and hybrid seeds, a farmer now feeds about eighty. In 1940, about half of U.S. workers wore a blue collar. As changing technology shrank the market for blue-collar jobs, white-collar work continued its ascent, reaching the dominant position it holds today.

When you look at Figure 14.5, the change in type of work is readily apparent, but what you see here is merely the surface. The significance of this change in work is that it indicates the arrival of a new type of society. To live in an industrialized or a postindustrial society is to live in different worlds. Not only is your work different but so are your lifestyle, your relationships, the age at which you marry, the amount of education you attain, the number of children you have, your attitudes and values, and even the way you view the world.

FIGURE 14.5 The Revolutionary Change in the U.S. Workforce

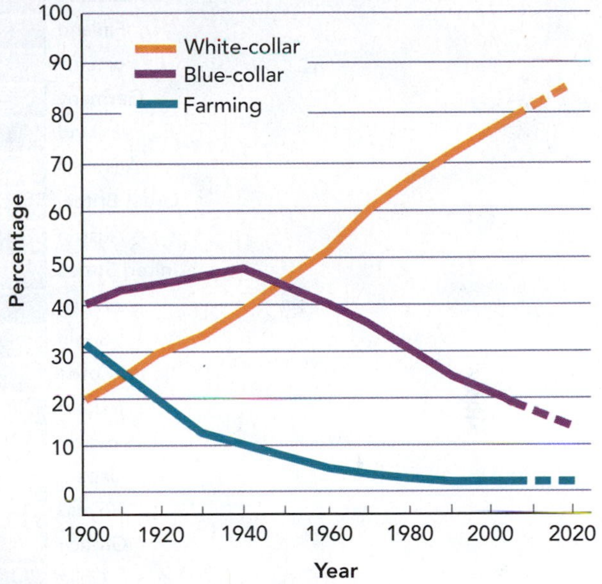

Source: By the author. Based on *Statistical Abstract of the United States*, various years, and 2013:Tables 626, 631.

Women and Work

Let's look at another major change that has transformed our world, the unprecedented increase in the numbers of women who work for wages. In Chapter 11 (Figure 11.5, page 310), you saw how this number has increased so greatly that today, almost half of all U.S. workers are women. From Figure 14.6 on the next page, you can see how the United States ranks among other nations in the percentage of women who are employed.

Work Styles. Researchers have found two primary distinctions between women and men in the world of work. First, women seem to be more concerned than men with maintaining a balance between their work and family lives (Statham et al. 1988; Caproni 2004). Second, men and women tend to follow different models for success: Men seem to place more emphasis on individualism, power, and competition, while women seem more likely to stress collaboration, encouragement, and helping (Miller-Loessi 1992; Mayer et al. 2008).

Note the caution with which I have presented these findings—the use of *seem to* and *tend to*. I am not convinced that there are any essential differences between women's and men's orientations to work. It is possible that the few studies we have on this topic are tapping core differences—but they could be measuring temporary tendencies owing to women's more recent entrance into the paid workforce. If so, as women gain more extensive work experience, these differences will disappear. It will be interesting to see what happens as more women reach the top levels of their professions and attain more powerful positions in the business world.

How likely is it that a woman will be in the labor force? Figure 14.7(a) on page 411 shows how working for wages increases with each level of education. This is probably because women who have more education find more satisfying work—and get higher pay. Figure 14.7(b) shows the influence of marital status. You can see that single

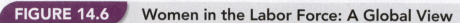

FIGURE 14.6 Women in the Labor Force: A Global View

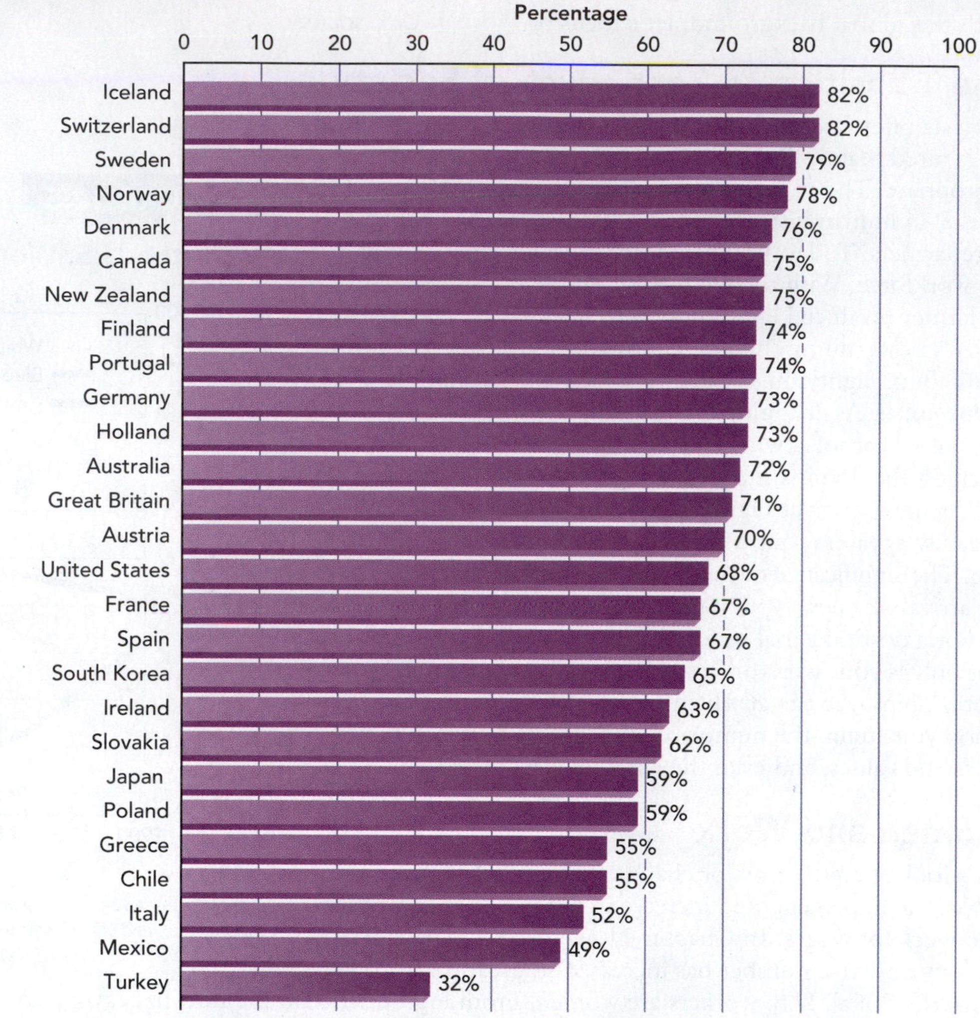

Note: Female labor force participation rates are derived by dividing the female labor force of all ages by the female population ages 15–64. These totals include women who work part-time.

Source: By the author. Based on *Statistical Abstract of the United States* 2013:Table 1383.

women are the most likely to work for wages; married women follow closely behind; and divorced, widowed, and separated women are the least likely to be in the workforce. From Figure 14.7(c) on the next page, you can see that African American women are more likely than women from other racial–ethnic groups to be in the workforce, but that race–ethnicity makes little difference in whether women work for wages. You can also see that the racial–ethnic groups have been following a parallel course.

Sociologists use the term **quiet revolution** to refer to the consequences of so many women joining the ranks of paid labor. This quiet revolution has transformed self-concepts, spending patterns, and relations at work. It has also changed relationships with boyfriends, husbands, and children. It has even transformed views of life. I'll give just one example. Unless a woman with preschoolers had the utmost necessity—being widowed or divorced—it used to be considered immoral for her to work for wages. Believing that they would be neglecting their children and that neighbors would talk, mothers of preschoolers took jobs only as a last resort. Now, as Figure 14.7(d) shows, *most* mothers of preschoolers have paid jobs—even those with children under age 3. The neighbors don't gossip, since what was once considered wrong is now considered right—and most of the mothers in the neighborhood are at work.

quiet revolution the fundamental changes in society that follow when vast numbers of women enter the workforce

FIGURE 14.7 Women in the Labor Force: The U.S. Experience

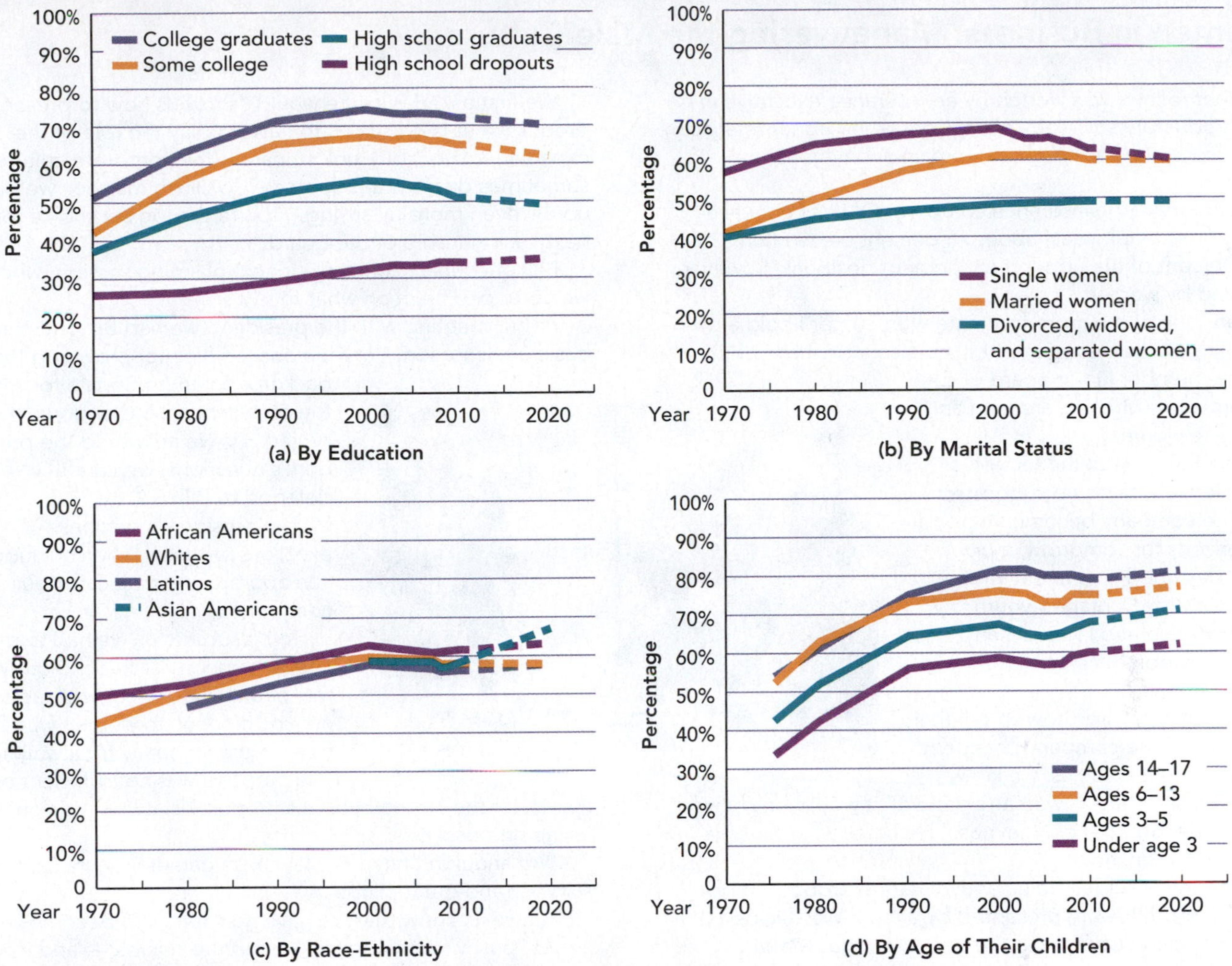

Note: To understand this figure, ask, "What percentage of Group X is working for wages?" The broken are the author's projections.

Sources: By the author. Based on *Statistical Abstract of the United States* 1989:Tables 638, 639, 640; 1990:Tables 625, 627, 637; 2001:Table 578; 2013:Tables 597, 603, 607, 610.

As discussed in Chapter 11, women face discrimination at work. The Down-to-Earth Sociology box on the next page explores how some women cope with this discrimination.

The Underground Economy

> *The underground economy. The term has a sinister ring—suggestive of dope deals struck in alleys and wads of bills hastily exchanged. The underground economy is this, but it is a lot more—and it is usually a lot more innocent. If you pay the plumber with a check made out to "Cash," if you purchase a pair of sunglasses from a street vendor or a kitchen gadget at a yard sale, if you so much as hand a neighbor's kid a $20 bill to mow the lawn or to babysit, you are participating in the underground economy. (Pennar and Farrell 1993)*

Also known as the *informal economy* and the *off-the-books economy*, the **underground economy** consists of economic activities—whether legal or illegal—that people don't report to the government. What interests most of us is not unreported babysitting money, but the illegal activities that people could not report even if they wanted to. As a 20-year-old child care worker in one of my classes who also worked as a prostitute two or three nights a week told me, "Why do I do this? For the money! Where else can I make this kind of money in a few hours? And it's all tax free."

underground economy exchanges of goods and services that escape taxes because they are not reported to the government

Down-to-Earth Sociology

Women in Business: Maneuvering the Male Culture

What follows was written by an insurance executive in my introductory sociology class. Concerned about retaliation at work, she has chosen to remain anonymous.

I work for a large insurance company. Of its twenty-five-hundred employees, about 75 percent are women. Only 5 percent of the upper management positions, however, are held by women.

I am one of the more fortunate women, for I hold a position in middle management. I am also a member of the twelve-member junior board of directors, of whom nine are men and three are women.

Recently, one of the female members of the board suggested that the company become involved in Horizons for Tomorrow, a program designed to provide internships for disadvantaged youth. Two other women and I spent many days developing a proposal for our participation.

The problem was how to sell the proposal to the company president. From past experiences, we knew that if he saw it as a "woman's project" it would be shelved into the second tier of "maybes." He hates what he calls "aggressive bitches."

We three decided, reluctantly, that the proposal had a chance only if it were presented by a man. We decided that Bill was the logical choice. We also knew that we had to "stroke" Bill if we were going to get his cooperation.

We first asked Bill if he would "show us how to present our proposal." (It is ridiculous to have to play the role of the "less capable female," but, unfortunately, the corporate culture sometimes dictates this strategy.) To clinch matters, we puffed up Bill even more by saying, "You're the logical choice for the next chairmanship of the board."

Bill, of course, came to our next planning session, where we "prepped" *him* on what to say.

At our meeting with the president, we had Bill give the basic presentation. We then backed *him* up, providing the background and rationale for why the president should endorse the project. As we answered the president's questions, we carefully deferred to Bill.

The president's response? "An excellent proposal," he concluded, "an appropriate project for our company."

To be successful, we had to maneuver through the treacherous waters of the "hidden culture" (actually not so "hidden" to women who have been in the company for a while). The proposal was not sufficient on its merits, for the "who" behind a proposal is at least as significant as the proposal itself.

"We shouldn't have to play these games," Laura said, summarizing our feelings.

But we all know that we have no choice. To become labeled "pushy" is to commit "corporate suicide"—and we're no fools.

The largest source of illegal income is probably drug dealing. Fourteen million Americans currently use illegal drugs (*Statistical Abstract* 2013:Tables 7, 209). To serve them, billions of dollars flow from users to sellers and to their networks of growers, importers, processors, transporters, dealers, and enforcers. These particular networks are so huge that each year the police arrest more than one million Americans for illegal drug activities (*Statistical Abstract* 2013:Table 338).

Explore on **MySocLab**
Activity: Global Inequality: Chasing the American Dream: US Immigration Patterns

The illegal immigrants who enter the United States each year are also part of the underground economy. Often called *undocumented workers* (referred to as *los sin documentos* in Mexico), they work for employers who either ignore their fake Social Security cards or pay them in cash. I asked a housekeeper from Mexico who had entered the United States illegally if she had a "green card" (the card given to immigrants who enter the country legally). She said that she did, adding, "They're sold on the street like candy."

When terrorists struck the World Trade Center, forty-three restaurant workers were killed—twelve of them with fake Social Security cards (Cleeland 2001). Undocumented workers from China are employed primarily in Chinese restaurants and in New York's garment industry. Many from India work in motels and fast-food restaurants. Those from Mexico and Central and South America do housework, pick lettuce on farms, sew garments in clandestine sweatshops, clean rooms in hotels, and serve food at restaurants. For the most part, the undocumented workers do the low-paying and dirty jobs that U.S. citizens try to avoid. The rest of us benefit from their labor, since they bring us cheaper goods and services.

Because of its subterranean nature, no one knows the exact size of the underground economy, but it probably runs around 9 percent of the regular economy (Barta 2009). Since the official gross domestic product of the United States is about $15 trillion (*Statistical Abstract* 2013:Table 679), the underground economy probably totals well over $1 trillion a year. It is so huge that it distorts the official statistics of the country's gross domestic product. It also costs the IRS billions of dollars a year in lost taxes.

Stagnant Paychecks

With extensive automation, the productivity of U.S. workers has increased year after year, making them some of the most productive in the world (*Statistical Abstract* 2013:Tables 1368, 1370). One might think, therefore, that their pay would be increasing. This brings us to a disturbing trend, one that bothers Americans and is an underlying reason that so many workers lost their homes to foreclosure.

Listen on **MySocLab**
Audio: NPR: Anheuser-Busch Takeover Talk Shakes St. Louis

Look at Figure 14.8. The gold bars show current dollars. These are the dollars the average worker finds in his or her paycheck. You can see that since 1970 the average pay of U.S. workers has soared from just over $3 an hour to over $19 an hour. Workers today are bringing home *six* times as many dollars as workers used to.

But let's strip away the illusion. Look at the purple bars, which show the dollars adjusted for inflation, the *buying power* of those paychecks. You can see how inflation has suppressed the value of the dollars that workers earn. Today's workers, with their $19 an hour, can buy little more than workers in 1970 could with their "measly" $3 an hour. The question is not "How could workers live on just $3 an hour back then?" but, rather, *"How can workers get by on a 50-cent-an-hour raise that took 41 years to get?"* That's only slightly more than a penny an hour per year! Incredibly, despite workers having more years of college and more technical training, despite the use of computers, and much higher productivity, the workers' purchasing power increased just 50 cents an hour between 1970 and 2010. What can you buy with those 50 cents?

Actually, after taxes and Social Security deductions, we should ask, What can you buy with the 35 or 40 cents?

FIGURE 14.8 Average Hourly Earnings of U.S. Workers in Current and Constant Dollars

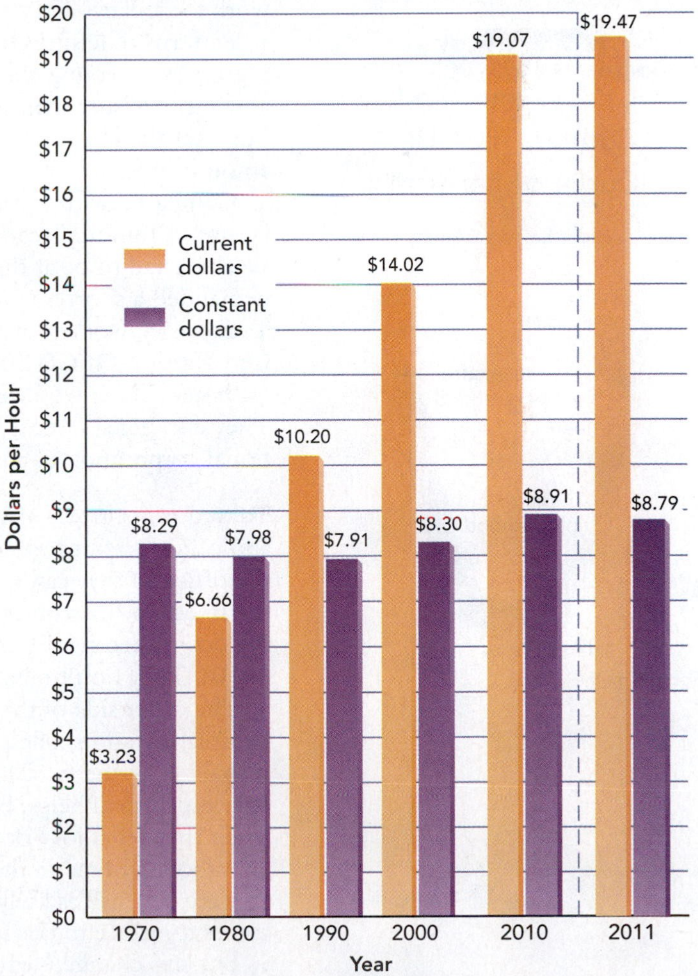

Note: Constant dollars are dollars adjusted for inflation with 1982–1984 as the base.

Source: By the author. Based on *Statistical Abstract of the United States* 1992:Table 650; 1999:Table 698; 2013:Table 656.

Patterns of Work and Leisure

Suppose that it is 1860 and you work for a textile company in Lowell, Massachusetts. When you arrive at work one day, you find that the boss has posted a new rule: "All workers will have to come in at the same time and remain until quitting time." Like the other workers, you feel outrage. You join them as they shout, "This is slavery!" and march out of the plant, indignant at such a preposterous rule. (Zuboff 1991)

This is a true story. The workers were angry because up until then, they had been able to come and go whenever they wanted. Let's consider how patterns of work and leisure are related to the transformation of economies.

Effects of Industrialization. Hunting and gathering societies provide enormous amounts of leisure, time not taken up by work or necessary activities such as eating and sleeping. Assuming they didn't live in a barren place or have to deal with some calamitous event, such as drought or pestilence, it did not take long for people to hunt and gather what they needed for the day. In fact, *most of their time was leisure*, and the rhythms of nature were an essential part of their lives. Agricultural economies also allowed much leisure, because, at least in the northern hemisphere, work peaked with the spring planting, let up in the summer, and then peaked again with the fall harvest. During the winter, work again receded, since by this time the harvest was in, animals had been slaughtered, food had been preserved and stored, and wood had been laid up.

Industrialization, however, broke this harnessing of work to seasonal rhythms. Going against all of human history, bosses and machines began to dictate when work was to be done. Workers resisted, clinging to their traditional patterns. After working for several weeks—or even just a few days—a worker would disappear, only to reappear when money ran out. For most workers, enjoying leisure was considerably more important than amassing money (Weber 1958/1904–1905). Since regular, efficient production brought more profits, bosses began to insist that all workers start work at the same time. To workers of that period, this seemed like slavery. Today, in contrast, work patterns that corporations and bosses impose on us have become part of the taken-for-granted cultural rhythms that coordinate our lives.

Trends in Leisure. It is not the activity itself that makes something leisure but the purpose for which it is done. Consider driving a car. If you do it for pleasure, it is leisure, but if you are a cabbie or if you must commute to the office, it is work. If done for enjoyment, horseback riding and reading a book are leisure—but these activities are work for jockeys and students.

Patterns of leisure change with the life course, following the U-curve shown on Figure 14.9. Young children enjoy the most leisure, but teenagers still have considerably more leisure than their parents. Parents with small children have the least leisure, but after the children leave home, leisure picks up again. After the age of 60 or so, the amount of leisure for adults peaks.

FIGURE 14.9
Leisure and the Life Course: The "U" Curve of Leisure

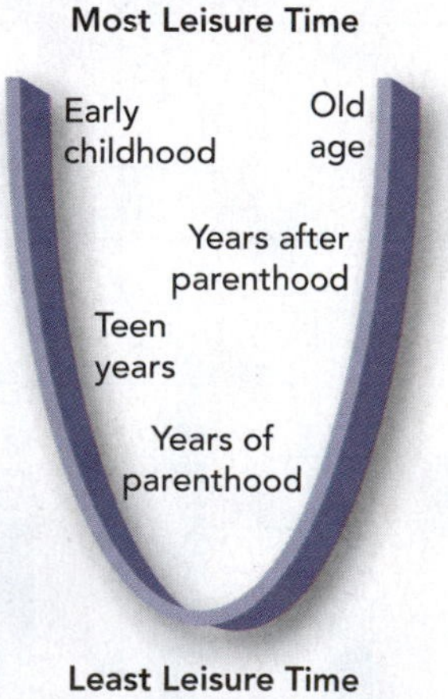

Source: By the author.

Compared with workers during early industrialization, today's workers have far more leisure. A hundred years ago, the work week was one and a half times as long as today's: Workers had to be at their machines sixty hours a week. When workers unionized, they demanded a shorter workweek. Over the years, the workweek has gradually shrunk. Today, U.S. workers average 1,787 hours per year, the highest of any Most Industrialized Nation (OECD 2013). At 1,399 hours a year, workers in Germany put in the fewest hours. Their workweek is thirty-five hours, with Friday afternoons usually taken off. They also get six weeks of paid vacation a year. Volkswagen is the world's first multinational corporation to adopt a thirty-hour workweek.

Telecommuting. Just as the Industrial Revolution took workers from home to factory and office, so our technological revolution has allowed several million workers to leave the office so they can work at home (Silverman and Fottrell 2013). Many workers love the freedom that comes with telecommuting—not having to dress up, no bosses breathing down their necks, and being there when the kids come home from school (Marino 2010). They don't miss the traffic jams, either.

The other side of the telecommuting experience is that some find work at home to be isolating and soulless. They miss the camaraderie of co-workers. And the lack of nonverbal cues—the facial expressions and body language—makes some communications difficult. E-mail helps, but it isn't the same as seeing the look on Bob's and Mary's faces when they tell a joke or repeat the latest office gossip.

Although home workers seem to be just as productive as those who come in to the office, they are only half as likely to be promoted. The reason? Teleworkers lack the bonding that comes from face to face interaction with management (Silverman and Fottrell 2013).

But this change is extensive and unrelenting. Here is the future looking back at you:

A subscriber to a newsletter: "I would love to just 'drop in' on your offices in Baltimore to see what it's like behind the scenes and maybe even meet some of you in person to thank you for your help."

The newsletter owner's reply: "You won't find us there. I live most of the time in Miami Beach. Sean lives in New York City. Brian lives near Ft. Lauderdale. Dan lives in Oregon. And Jeff lives near San Francisco. My three staff analysts live in Barcelona, Atlanta, and Seattle."

He added, "We all work on the Internet . . . And where we are physically is irrelevant" (Stansberry 2012).

Global Capitalism and Our Future

14.7 Explain how our economic transition is affecting the national income distribution.

We are immersed in global capitalism's constant changes. They vitally affect all of us, and they will continue to do so. Let's look at just one more aspect of our fast-changing economic times.

The New Economic System and the Old Divisions of Wealth

Suppose that you own a business that manufactures widgets. You are paying your workers an average $156 a day *($19.47 an hour including vacation pay, sick pay, unemployment benefits, Social Security, and so on). Widgets similar to yours are being manufactured in Thailand, where workers are paid* $8 a day. *Those imported widgets are being sold in the same stores that feature your widgets.*

We are in the midst of the globalization of capitalism. The explosion that is sending products around the world brings new ways of thinking to people in the Least Industrialized Nations. Many ideas are subtle, such as what refreshing drinks are.

What happens when oil tankers wear out? They go to Bangladesh, where they are turned into scrap. These workers, an expendable part of the global economic system that we are all a part of, are exposed to PCBs, asbestos, and other toxins. For this, they earn $1 a day.

How long do you think you could stay in business? Even if your workers were willing to cut their pay in half—which they aren't willing to do—you still couldn't compete.

What do you do? Your choices are simple. You can continue as you are and go broke, try to find some other product to manufacture (which, if successful, will soon be made in Thailand or India or China)—or you can close up your plant here and manufacture your widgets in Thailand.

These are not easy times for workers. One disruption after another. High insecurity with layoffs, plant closings, and the prospect of more of the same. The insecurity is especially hard-hitting on the most desperate of workers, the less skilled and those who live from paycheck to paycheck. How can they compete with people overseas who work for peanuts? They suffer the wrenching adjustments that come from having their jobs pulled out from under them, looking for work and finding only jobs that pay lower wages—if that—watching their savings go down the drain, postponing their retirement, and seeing their children disillusioned about the future. The photo above indicates some of the effects on the workers in the Least Industrialized Nations.

What about the wealthy? In these tough economic times, aren't they being hurt, too? Some rich individuals do get on the wrong side of investments and lose their collective shirts. In general, though, the wealthy do just fine in these challenging times.

How can I be so sure?, you probably wonder. Take a look at Figure 14.10. Each rectangle on the left of this figure represents a fifth of the U.S. population, about 62 million people. The rectangles of the inverted pyramid on the right show the percentage of the

FIGURE 14.10 The Inverted Income Pyramid: The Proportion of Income Received by Each Fifth of the U.S. Population

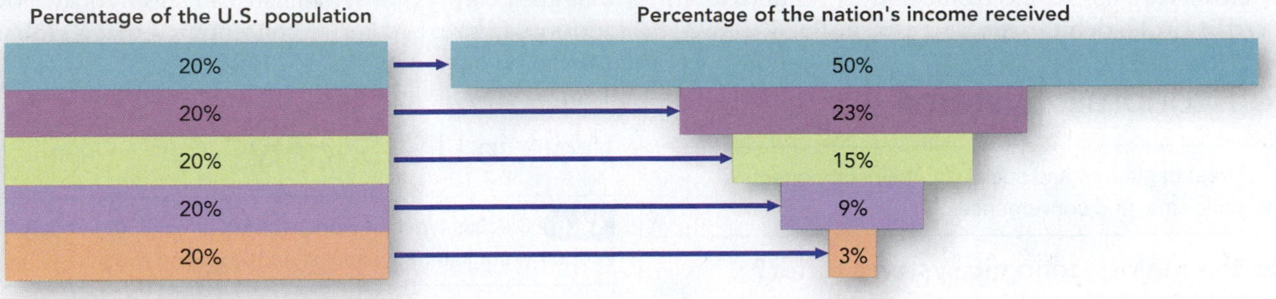

Source: By the author. Based on *Statistical Abstract of the United States* 2013:Table 708.

nation's income that goes to each fifth of the population. You can see that half of the entire country's income goes to the richest fifth of Americans. Only 3 percent goes to the poorest fifth.

This gap has been growing over the years, and it is now *greater* than it has been in generations. The transition to a postindustrial economy and the globalization of capitalism have increased our income inequalities. The common folk saying that the rich are getting richer and the poor are getting poorer is certainly an apt observation, well supported by social research. What implications of this division of the nation's wealth do you see for our future?

MySocLab — Study and Review on MySocLab

CHAPTER 14 Summary and Review

The Transformation of Economic Systems

14.1 Summarize the broad historical shifts in economic systems; emphasize inequality.

How are economic systems linked to types of societies?

In early societies (hunting and gathering), small groups lived off the land and produced little or no surplus. Economic systems grew more complex as people discovered how to domesticate animals and grow plants (pastoral and horticultural societies), farm (agricultural societies), and manufacture (industrial societies). As people produced a surplus, trade developed. Trade, in turn, brought social inequality as some people accumulated more than others. Service industries dominate the postindustrial societies. If a biotech society is emerging, it is too early to know its consequences for our economy. Pp. 388–391.

The Transformation of the Medium of Exchange

14.2 Summarize historical changes in the medium of exchange.

How has the medium of exchange evolved?

A **medium of exchange** is any means by which people exchange goods and services. In hunting and gathering and pastoral and horticultural societies, people **bartered** goods and services. In agricultural societies, **money** came into use, and evolved into **currency**, or paper money, representing a specific amount of gold or silver on deposit. Postindustrial societies rely increasingly on electronic transfer of funds in the form of **credit cards**, **debit cards**, and **e-cash.** Pp. 391–393.

World Economic Systems

14.3 Contrast capitalism and socialism: their components, ideologies, criticisms, and convergence.

How do the major economic systems differ?

The world's two major economic systems are capitalism and socialism. In **capitalism**, private citizens own the means of production and pursue profits. In **socialism**, the state owns the means of production and has no goal of profit. Adherents of each have developed ideologies that defend their own systems and paint the other as harmful or even evil. As expected from **convergence theory**, each system has adopted features of the other. Pp. 393–399.

The Functionalist Perspective on the Globalization of Capitalism

14.4 Discuss corporate capitalism, ownership and management, and global functions and dysfunctions of capitalism.

How does functionalism apply to the globalization of capitalism?

From the functionalist perspective, work is a basis of social solidarity. Traditional societies have **mechanical solidarity**; people perform similar tasks and identify with one another. Industrialization brings **organic solidarity**, interdependence based on the division of labor. This process has continued to the point that we now are developing a global division of labor. **Corporations**, with their separation of ownership and management, underlie the success of capitalism. Pp. 399–402.

The Conflict Perspective on the Globalization of Capitalism

14.5 Summarize shifts in corporate capitalism, concentration of power, the global superclass, and global investing.

How does a conflict perspective apply to the globalization of capitalism?

Conflict theorists, who focus on power, note that global capitalism is a means by which capitalists exploit workers. From the major owners of the **multinational corporations** comes an *inner circle*. While workers lose jobs to automation, the inner circle maintains its political power and profits from the new technology. The term **corporate capitalism** indicates that giant corporations dominate capitalism today. Power and wealth have become so concentrated that a **global superclass** has arisen. Pp. 402–408.

Work in U.S. Society

14.6 Discuss types of work, women at work, the underground economy, stagnant paychecks, and work and leisure.

How has the workforce changed?

In the transition to a postindustrial society, the number of farm workers has plummeted, blue-collar work has shrunk, and most people work at service jobs. More women are in the workforce. Pp. 409–411.

What is the underground economy?

The **underground economy** consists of any money-making enterprise not reported to the government, from babysitting to prostitution. The size of the underground economy runs about 9 percent of the regular economy. Pp. 411–413.

What are stagnant paychecks?

In constant dollars, workers' average pay has increased just 50 cents an hour since 1970. See Figure 14.8. P. 413

How have patterns of work and leisure changed?

In hunting and gathering societies, most time was **leisure**. In agricultural societies, work was dictated by the seasons. Industrialization reduced workers' leisure, but workers have now regained some leisure. Americans work more hours per week than do the workers of any other industrialized nation. Pp. 413–415.

Global Capitalism and Our Future

14.7 Explain how our economic transition is affecting the national income distribution.

How are the old divisions of wealth changing?

The wealthy can make mistakes that jeopardize their economic welfare, but it is primarily the workers who face the most precarious survival during our current economic dislocations. Global capitalism has brought more of the old inequalities, with the wealthy getting a larger share of the economic pie and the poorest even less than previously. Pp. 415–417.

Thinking Critically about Chapter 14

1. What global forces are affecting the U.S. economy? What consequences are they having? How do they affect your life?
2. What are the major characteristics and ideologies of capitalism and socialism? What changes are taking place in these economic systems?
3. How can anyone say that the average U.S. worker hasn't gotten ahead in recent years, when the average hourly wage has jumped from about $3 an hour in 1970 to about $19 an hour today? What implications does this have for your own future?

CHAPTER 15
Politics

Listen to Chapter 15 on MySocLab

In 1949, George Orwell wrote *1984, a book about a time in the future when a government known as "Big Brother" spies on everyone and dictates almost every aspect of each individual's life. Even loving someone is considered sinister—a betrayal of the supreme love and total allegiance that all citizens owe Big Brother.*

Despite the danger, Winston and Julia fall in love. They delight in each other, but they must meet furtively, always with the threat of discovery hanging over their heads. When informers turn them in, interrogators separate Julia and Winston and try to destroy their affection and restore their loyalty to Big Brother.

Winston's tormentor is O'Brien, who straps Winston into a chair so tightly that he can't even move his head. O'Brien explains that inflicting pain is not always enough to break a person's will, but everyone has a breaking point. There is some worst fear that will push anyone over the edge.

O'Brien tells Winston that he has discovered his worst fear. Then he sets a cage with two starving giant sewer rats on the table next to Winston. O'Brien picks up a hood connected to the door of the cage and places it over Winston's head. He then explains that when he presses the lever, the door of the cage will slide up, and the rats will shoot out like bullets and bore straight into Winston's face. Winston's eyes, the only part of his body that he can move, dart back and forth, revealing his terror. Speaking so quietly that Winston has to strain to hear him, O'Brien adds that the rats sometimes attack the eyes first, but sometimes they burrow through the cheeks and devour the tongue. When O'Brien places his hand on the lever, Winston realizes that the only way out is for someone else to take his place. But who? Then he hears his own voice screaming, "Do it to Julia! . . . Tear her face off. Strip her to the bones. Not me! Julia! Not me!"

Even loving someone is considered sinister—a betrayal of the supreme love and total allegiance that all citizens owe Big Brother.

Orwell does not describe Julia's interrogation, but when Julia and Winston see each other later, they realize that each has betrayed the other. Their love is gone. Big Brother has won.

Winston's and Julia's misplaced loyalty had made them political heretics, a danger to the state. Every citizen had the duty to place the state above all else in life. Pledging love and loyalty to an individual was a threat to the state's dominance. Their allegiance to one another had to be stripped from them. As you see, it was.

Although seldom as dramatic as the interrogations of Winston and Julia, politics is always about power and authority. Let's explore this topic that is so significant for our lives.

Learning Objectives

After you have read this chapter, you should be able to:

15.1 Distinguish between micropolitics and macropolitics. (p. 421)

15.2 Contrast power, authority, and violence; compare traditional, rational–legal, and charismatic authority; explain authority as an ideal type. (p. 422)

15.3 Compare monarchies, democracies, dictatorships, and oligarchies. (p. 426)

15.4 Compare the U.S. political system with other democratic systems; discuss voting patterns, lobbyists, and PACs. (p. 428)

15.5 Compare the functionalist (pluralist) and conflict (power elite) perspectives on U.S. power. (p. 435)

15.6 Distinguish between war and terrorism; explain how common war is, why countries go to war, the role of profits, and the costs of war. (p. 438)

15.7 Explain how the globalization of capitalism might be bringing a New World Order. (p. 447)

Micropolitics and Macropolitics

15.1 Distinguish between micropolitics and macropolitics.

The images that come to mind when we think of *politics* are associated with government: kings, queens, coups, dictatorships, people running for office, voting. These are examples of politics, but the term actually has a much broader meaning. **Politics** refers to *power relations wherever they exist*, including those in everyday life.

As Max Weber (1922/1978) said, **power** is the ability to get your way even over the resistance of others. You can see the struggle for power all around you. When workers try to gain the favor of their bosses, they are attempting to maneuver into a stronger position. Students do the same with their teachers. Power struggles are also part of family life, such as when parents try to enforce a curfew over the protests of a reluctant daughter or son. Ever have a struggle over the remote control to the TV? These examples are also attempts to gain or keep power, so they, too, are political actions.

politics the exercise of power and attempts to maintain or to change power relations

power the ability to carry out one's will, even over the resistance of others

Every group, then, is political, since in every group, there are power struggles of some sort. Symbolic interactionists use the term **micropolitics** to refer to the exercise of power in everyday life (Anderson and Kennedy 2012).

As interesting as micropolitics is, in this chapter, we are focusing on the broader view. We will look at **macropolitics**, the exercise of power over a large group. Governments—whether dictatorships or democracies—are examples of macropolitics. Because authority is essential to macropolitics, let's begin with this topic.

15.2 Contrast power, authority, and violence; compare traditional, rational–legal, and charismatic authority; explain authority as an ideal type.

Watch on **MySocLab**
Video: The Basics: Politics and Government

Power, Authority, and Violence

To exist, every society must have a system of leadership. Some people must have power over others. As Weber (1913/1947) pointed out, we perceive power as either legitimate or illegitimate. *Legitimate* power is called **authority**. This is power that people accept as right. In contrast, *illegitimate* power—called **coercion**—is power that people do not accept as just.

Imagine that you are on your way to buy the hot new cell phone that is on sale for $250. As you approach the store, a man jumps out of an alley and shoves a gun in your face. He demands your money. Frightened for your life, you hand over your $250. After filing a police report, you head back to college to take a sociology exam. You are running late, so you step on the gas. As you hit 85, you see flashing blue and red lights in your rearview mirror. Your explanation about the robbery doesn't faze the officer—or the judge who hears your case a few weeks later. She first lectures you on safety and then orders you to pay $50 in court costs plus $10 for every mile over 65. You pay the $250.

The mugger, the police officer, and the judge—all have power, and in each case you part with $250. What, then, is the difference? The difference is that the mugger has no authority. His power is *illegitimate*—he has no *right* to do what he did. In contrast, you acknowledge that the officer has the right to stop you and that the judge has the right to fine you. They have authority, or *legitimate* power.

micropolitics the exercise of power in everyday life, such as deciding who is going to do the housework or use the remote control

macropolitics the exercise of large-scale power, the government being the most common example

authority power that people consider legitimate, as rightly exercised over them; also called *legitimate power*

coercion power that people do not accept as rightly exercised over them; also called *illegitimate power*

Authority and Legitimate Violence

As sociologist Peter Berger observed, it makes little difference whether you willingly pay the fine that the judge levies against you or refuse to pay it. The court will get its money one way or another.

There may be innumerable steps before its application [of violence], in the way of warnings and reprimands. But if all the warnings are disregarded, even in so slight a matter

The ultimate foundation of any political order is violence, no more starkly demonstrated than when a government takes a human life. This iconic photo from the war in Vietnam shows the chief of the national police shooting a suspected Viet Cong officer.

as paying a traffic ticket, the last thing that will happen is that a couple of cops show up at the door with handcuffs and a Black Maria [paddy wagon]. Even the moderately courteous cop who hands out the initial traffic ticket is likely to wear a gun—just in case. (Berger 1963)

state a political entity that claims monopoly on the use of violence in some particular territory; commonly known as a country

revolution armed resistance designed to overthrow and replace a government

traditional authority authority based on custom

The *government,* then, also called the **state**, claims a monopoly on legitimate force or violence. This point, made by Max Weber (1946, 1922/1978)—that the state claims both the exclusive right to use violence and the right to punish everyone else who uses violence—is crucial to our understanding of politics. If someone owes you $100, you cannot take the money by force, much less imprison that person. The state, in contrast, can. The ultimate proof of the state's authority is that you cannot kill someone because he or she has done something that you consider absolutely horrible—but the state can. As Berger (1963) summarized this matter, "*Violence is the ultimate foundation of any political order.*"

Before we explore the origins of the modern state, let's first look at a situation in which the state loses legitimacy.

The Collapse of Authority. Sometimes the state oppresses its people, and they resist their government just as they do a mugger. The people cooperate reluctantly—with a smile if that is what is required—while they eye the gun in the hand of the government's representatives. But as they do with a mugger, when they get the chance, they take up arms to free themselves. **Revolution**, armed resistance with the intent to overthrow and replace a government, is not only a people's rejection of a government's claim to rule over them but also their rejection of its monopoly on violence. In a revolution, people assert that right for themselves. If successful, they establish a new state in which they claim the right to monopolize violence.

What some see as coercion, however, others see as authority. Consequently, while some people are ready to take up arms against a government, others remain loyal to it, willingly defend it, and perhaps even die for it. *The more that a government's power is seen as legitimate, then, the more stable a government is.*

But just why do people accept power as legitimate? Max Weber (1922/1978) identified three sources of authority: traditional, rational–legal, and charismatic. Let's examine each.

Traditional Authority

Throughout history, the most common basis for authority has been tradition. **Traditional authority**, which is based on custom, is the hallmark of tribal groups. In these societies, custom dictates basic relationships. For example, birth into a particular family makes an individual the chief, king, or queen. As far as members of that society are concerned, this is the right way to determine who rules because "We've always done it this way."

Gender relations often open a window on traditional authority. For example, as shown in the photo to the right, in the villages around the Mediterranean, widows were expected to wear only black until they remarried. This generally meant that they wore black for the rest of their lives. By law, a widow was free to wear any color she wanted to, but custom dictated otherwise. Tradition was so strong that if a widow violated this dress code by wearing a color other than black, she was perceived as having profaned the memory of her deceased husband and became an outcast in the community.

When a traditional society industrializes, its transformation undermines traditional authority. Social change brings with it new experiences. This opens up new perspectives on life, and no longer

For centuries, widows in the Mediterranean countries, such as thise widow in Greece, were expected to dress in black and to mourn for their husbands the rest of their lives. Widows conformed to this expression of lifetime sorrow not because of law, but because of custom. As industrialization erodes traditional authority, fewer widows follow this practice.

rational–legal authority authority based on law or written rules and regulations; also called *bureaucratic authority*

charismatic authority authority based on an individual's outstanding traits, which attract followers

does traditional authority go unchallenged. In some villages of Italy and Portugal, for example, you can still see old women dressed in black from head to toe—and you immediately know their marital status. Younger widows, however, are likely to be indistinguishable from other women.

Although traditional authority declines with industrialization, it never dies out. Even though we live in a postindustrial society, parents continue to exercise authority over their children *because* parents always have had such authority. From generations past, we inherit the idea that parents should discipline their children, choose their doctors and schools, and teach them religion and morality.

Rational–Legal Authority

The second type of authority, **rational–legal authority**, is based not on custom but on written rules. *Rational* means reasonable, and *legal* means part of law. Thus *rational–legal* refers to matters that have been agreed to by reasonable people and written into law (or regulations of some sort). The matters that are agreed to may be as broad as a constitution that specifies the rights of all members of a society or as narrow as a contract between two individuals. Because bureaucracies are based on written rules, rational–legal authority is also called *bureaucratic authority.*

Rational–legal authority comes from the *position* that someone holds, not from the person who holds that position. In the United States, for example, the president's authority comes from the legal power assigned to that office, as specified in a written constitution, not from custom or the individual's personal characteristics. In rational–legal authority, everyone—no matter how high the office held—is subject to the organization's written rules. In governments based on traditional authority, the ruler's word may be law; but in those based on rational–legal authority, the ruler's word is subject to the law.

One of the best examples of charismatic authority is Joan of Arc. In this painting from the early 1900s, she is shown holding the standard and leading her men. The artist has maintained her femininity by adding a skirt.

Charismatic Authority

A few centuries back, in 1429, the English controlled large parts of France. When they prevented the coronation of a new French king, a farmer's daughter heard a voice telling her that God had a special assignment for her—that she should put on men's clothing, recruit an army, and go to war against the English. Inspired, Joan of Arc raised an army, conquered cities, and defeated the English. Later that year, her visions were fulfilled as she stood next to Charles VII while he was crowned king of France. (Bridgwater 1953)

Joan of Arc is an example of **charismatic authority**, the third type of authority Weber identified. (*Charisma* is a Greek word that means a gift freely and graciously given [Arndt and Gingrich 1957].) People are drawn to a charismatic individual because they believe that individual has been touched by God or has been endowed by nature with exceptional qualities (Lipset 1993). The armies did not follow Joan of Arc because it was the custom to do so, as in traditional authority. Nor did they risk their lives fighting alongside her because she held a position defined by written rules, as in rational–legal authority. Instead, people followed her because they were attracted by her outstanding traits. They saw her as a messenger of God, fighting on the side of justice, and they accepted her leadership because of these appealing qualities.

The Threat Posed by Charismatic Leaders. Kings and queens owe allegiance to tradition, and presidents to written laws. To what, however, do charismatic leaders owe allegiance? Their authority resides in their ability to attract followers, which is often based on their sense of a special mission or calling. Not tied to tradition or the regulation of law, charismatic leaders pose a threat to the established political order. Following their personal inclination, charismatic leaders can inspire followers to disregard—or even to overthrow—traditional and rational–legal authorities.

This threat does not go unnoticed, and traditional and rational–legal authorities often oppose charismatic leaders. If they are not careful, however, their opposition can arouse even more positive sentiment in favor of the charismatic leader, who might be viewed as an underdog persecuted by the powerful. Occasionally, the Roman Catholic Church faces such a threat, as when a priest claims miraculous powers that appear to be accompanied by amazing healings. As people flock to this individual, they bypass parish priests and the formal ecclesiastical structure. This transfer of allegiance from the organization to an individual threatens the church hierarchy. Consequently, church officials may encourage the priest to withdraw from the public eye, perhaps to a monastery, to rethink matters. This defuses the threat, reasserts rational–legal authority, and maintains the stability of the organization.

Charismatic authorities can be of any morality, from the saintly to the most bitterly evil. Like Joan of Arc, Adolf Hitler attracted throngs of people, providing the stuff of dreams and arousing them from disillusionment to hope. This poster from the 1930s, titled *Es Lebe Deutschland* ("Long Live Germany"), illustrates the qualities of leadership that Germans of that period saw in Hitler.

Authority as Ideal Type

Weber's classifications—traditional, rational–legal, and charismatic—represent ideal types of authority. As noted on page 178, *ideal type* does not refer to what is ideal or desirable, but to a composite of characteristics found in many real-life examples. A particular leader, then, may show a combination of characteristics.

An example is John F. Kennedy, who combined rational–legal and charismatic authority. As the elected head of the U.S. government, Kennedy represented rational–legal authority. Yet his mass appeal was so great that his public speeches aroused large numbers of people to action. When in his inaugural address Kennedy said, "Ask not what your country can do for you; ask what you can do for your country," millions of Americans were touched. When Kennedy proposed a Peace Corps to help poorer countries, thousands of idealistic young people volunteered for challenging foreign service.

Charismatic and traditional authority can also overlap. The Ayatollah Khomeini of Iran, for example, was a religious leader, holding the traditional position of ayatollah. His embodiment of the Iranian people's dreams, however, as well as his austere lifestyle and devotion to principles of the Koran, gave him such mass appeal that he was also a charismatic leader. Khomeini's followers were convinced that God had chosen him, and his speeches could arouse tens of thousands of followers to action.

In rare instances, then, traditional and rational–legal leaders possess charismatic traits. This is unusual, however, and most authority is clearly one type or another.

The Transfer of Authority

The orderly transfer of authority from one leader to another is crucial for social stability. Under traditional authority, people know who is next in line. Under rational–legal authority, people might not know who the next leader will be, but they do know how that person will be selected. South Africa provides a remarkable example of the orderly transfer of authority under a rational–legal organization. This country had been ripped apart by decades of racial–ethnic strife, including horrible killings committed by each side. Yet, by maintaining its rational–legal authority, the country was able to transfer power peacefully from the dominant group led by President de Klerk to the minority group led by Nelson Mandela.

Charismatic authority has no rules of succession, making it less stable than either traditional or rational–legal authority. Because charismatic authority is built around a single individual, the death or incapacitation of a charismatic leader can mean a bitter struggle for succession. To avoid this, some charismatic leaders make arrangements for an orderly transition of power by appointing a successor. This step does not guarantee orderly succession, since the followers may not share the leader's confidence in the designated heir. A second strategy is for the charismatic leader to build an organization. As the organization develops rules or regulations, it transforms itself into a rational–legal organization.

routinization of charisma the transfer of authority from a charismatic figure to either a traditional or a rational–legal form of authority

Weber used the term **routinization of charisma** to refer to the transition of authority from a charismatic leader to either traditional or rational–legal authority.

The transfer of authority in Cuba after Fidel Castro became ill is a remarkable example. Castro was a charismatic leader, attracting enough followers to overthrow Cuba's government. He ruled through a combination of personal charisma and bureaucratic machinery. Castro set up an organized system to transfer authority to his non-charismatic brother, Raul, who, in turn, made certain that authority was transferred in an orderly manner to the state bureaucracies (Hoffman 2011).

15.3 Compare monarchies, democracies, dictatorships, and oligarchies.

Types of Government

How do the various types of government—monarchies, democracies, dictatorships, and oligarchies—differ? As we compare them, let's also look at how the state arose and why the concept of citizenship was revolutionary.

This classic painting, "Siege at Yorktown" by Louis Coulder, depicts George Washington and Jean de Rochambeau giving the final orders for the attack on Yorktown in 1781. This turned out to be the decisive battle of the American Revolution, allowing the fledgling U.S. democracy to proceed.

Monarchies: The Rise of the State

Early societies were small and needed no extensive political system. They operated more like an extended family. As surpluses developed and societies grew larger, cities evolved—perhaps around 3500 B.C. (Ur 2010). **City-states** then came into being, with power radiating outward from the city like a spider's web. Although the ruler of each city controlled the immediate surrounding area, the land between cities remained in dispute. Each city-state had its own **monarchy**, a king or queen whose right to rule was passed on to the monarch's children. If you drive through Spain, France, or Germany, you can still see evidence of former city-states. In the countryside, you will see only scattered villages. Farther on, your eye will be drawn to the outline of a castle on a faraway hill. As you get closer, you will see that the castle is surrounded by a city. Several miles farther, you will see another city, also dominated by a castle. Each city, with its castle, was once a center of power.

City-states often quarreled, and wars were common. The victors extended their rule, and eventually a single city-state was able to wield power over an entire region. As the size of these regions grew, the people slowly began to identify with the larger region. That is, they began to see distant inhabitants as "we" instead of "they." What we call the *state*—the political entity that claims a monopoly on the use of violence within a territory—came into being.

city-state an independent city whose power radiates outward, bringing the adjacent area under its rule

monarchy a form of government headed by a king or queen

democracy a government whose authority comes from the people; the term, based on two Greek words, translates literally as "power to the people"

direct democracy a form of democracy in which the eligible voters meet together to discuss issues and make their decisions

representative democracy a form of democracy in which voters elect representatives to meet together to discuss issues and make decisions on their behalf

citizenship the concept that birth (and residence or naturalization) in a country imparts basic rights

Democracies: Citizenship as a Revolutionary Idea

The United States had no city-states. Each colony, however, was small and independent like a city-state. After the American Revolution, the colonies united. With the greater strength and resources that came from political unity, they conquered almost all of North America, bringing it under the power of a central government.

The government formed in this new country was called a **democracy**. (Derived from two Greek words—*demos* [common people] and *kratos* [power]—democracy literally means "power to the people.") Because of the bitter antagonisms associated with the revolution against the British king, the founders of the new country were distrustful of monarchies. They wanted to put political decisions into the hands of the people.

This was not the first democracy the world had seen, but such a system had been tried before only with smaller groups. Athens, a city-state of Greece, practiced democracy 2,500 years ago, with each free male above a certain age having the right to be heard and to vote. Members of some Native American tribes, such as the Iroquois, also elected their chiefs, and in some, women were able to vote and to hold the office of chief. (The Incas and Aztecs of Mexico and Central America had monarchies.)

Because of their small size, tribes and cities were able to practice **direct democracy**. That is, they were small enough for the eligible voters to meet together, express their opinions, and then vote publicly—much like a town hall meeting today. As populous and spread out as the United States was, however, direct democracy was impossible, and the founders invented **representative democracy**. Certain citizens (at first only white men who owned property) voted for other white men who owned property to represent them. Later, the vote was extended to men who didn't own property, then to African American men, and, finally, to women.

Today we take the concept of citizenship for granted. What is not evident to us is that this idea had to be envisioned in the first place. There is nothing natural about citizenship; it is simply one way in which people choose to define themselves. Throughout most of human history, people were thought to *belong* to a clan, to a tribe, or even to a ruler. The idea of **citizenship**—that by virtue of birth and residence, people have basic rights—is quite new to the human scene.

The concept of representative democracy based on citizenship—perhaps the greatest gift the United States has given to the world—was revolutionary. Power was to be vested in the people themselves,

Democracy (or "democratization") is a global social movement. People all over the world yearn for the freedoms that are taken for granted in the Western democracies. Shown here is a tribal leader voting in the Philipines.

universal citizenship the idea that everyone has the same basic rights by virtue of being born in a country (or by immigrating and becoming a naturalized citizen)

dictatorship a form of government in which an individual has seized power

oligarchy a form of government in which a small group of individuals holds power; the rule of the many by the few

totalitarianism a form of government that exerts almost total control over people

Watch on **MySocLab**
Video: ABC Nightline: Old-Fashioned Democracy

and government was to flow from the people. That this concept was revolutionary is generally forgotten, but its implementation meant *the reversal of traditional ideas. It made the government responsive to the people's will, rather than the people being responsive to the government's will.* To keep the government responsive to the needs of its citizens, people were expected to express dissent. In a widely quoted statement, Thomas Jefferson observed:

> *A little rebellion now and then is a good thing. . . . It is a medicine necessary for the sound health of government. . . . God forbid that we should ever be twenty years without such a rebellion. . . . The tree of liberty must be refreshed from time to time with the blood of patriots and tyrants. (In Hellinger and Judd 1991)*

The idea of **universal citizenship**—of *everyone* having the same basic rights by virtue of being born in a country (or by immigrating and becoming a naturalized citizen)—flowered slowly, and came into practice only through fierce struggle. When the United States was founded, for example, this idea was still in its infancy. Today, it seems inconceivable to Americans that sex or race–ethnicity should be the basis for denying anyone the right to vote, hold office, make a contract, testify in court, or own property. For earlier generations of property-owning white American men, however, it seemed just as inconceivable that women, racial–ethnic minorities, and the poor should be *allowed* such rights.

Over the years, then, rights have been extended, and in the United States, citizenship and its privileges now apply to all. No longer do sex, race–ethnicity, or owning property determine someone's right to vote, testify in court, and so on. These characteristics, however, do influence whether people vote, as you will see later in this chapter.

Dictatorships and Oligarchies: The Seizure of Power

If an individual seizes power and then dictates his will to the people, the government is known as a **dictatorship**. If a small group seizes power, the government is called an **oligarchy**. The occasional coups in Central and South America and Africa, in which military leaders seize control of a country, are often oligarchies. Although one individual may be named president, often it is military officers, working behind the scenes, who make the decisions. If their designated president becomes uncooperative, they remove him from office and appoint another.

Monarchies, dictatorships, and oligarchies vary in the amount of control they wield over their citizens. **Totalitarianism** is almost *total* control of a people by the government. In Nazi Germany, Hitler organized a ruthless secret police force, the Gestapo, which searched for any sign of dissent. Spies even watched how moviegoers reacted to newsreels, reporting those who did not respond "appropriately" (Hippler 1987). Saddam Hussein acted just as ruthlessly toward Iraqis. The lucky ones who opposed Hussein were shot; the unlucky ones had their eyes gouged out, were bled to death, or were buried alive (Amnesty International 2005).

People around the world find great appeal in the freedom that is inherent in citizenship and representative democracy. Those who have no say in their government's decisions, or who face prison, torture, or death for expressing dissent, find in these ideas the hope for a brighter future. With today's electronic communications, people no longer remain ignorant of whether they are more or less politically privileged than others. This knowledge produces pressure for greater citizen participation in government—and for governments to respond to their citizens' concerns. The communist rulers of China are sensitive to online communications and are known to change course if they sense strong sentiment in some direction (Areddy 2012). As electronic communications develop further, this pressure will increase.

15.4 Compare the U.S. political system with other democratic systems; discuss voting patterns, lobbyists, and PACs.

The U.S. Political System

With this global background, let's examine the U.S. political system. We shall consider the two major political parties, compare the U.S. political system with other democratic systems, and examine voting patterns and the role of lobbyists and PACs.

Political Parties and Elections

After the founding of the United States, numerous political parties emerged. By the time of the Civil War, however, two parties dominated U.S. politics: the Democrats and the Republicans (Burnham 1983). Each party draws from all social classes, but the working class leans toward the Democrats, and wealthier people toward the Republicans. In pre-elections, called *primaries*, the voters decide who will represent their party. The candidates chosen by each party then campaign, trying to appeal to the most voters. The Social Map below shows how Americans align themselves with political parties.

Although the Democrats and the Republicans represent slightly different slices of the center, those differences arouse extreme emotions, pandered to by both parties.

Slices from the Center. Although the Democrats and Republicans have somewhat contrasting philosophical principles, each party represents *slightly different slices of the center*. Each party may ridicule the other and promote different legislation—and they do fight hard battles—but they both firmly support such fundamentals of U.S. political philosophy as free public education; a strong military; freedom of religion, speech, and assembly; and, of course, capitalism—especially the private ownership of property. This makes it difficult to distinguish a conservative Democrat from a liberal Republican.

Explore on **MySocLab** **Activity:** Majority-Minoritiy States

FIGURE 15.1 Which Political Party Dominates?

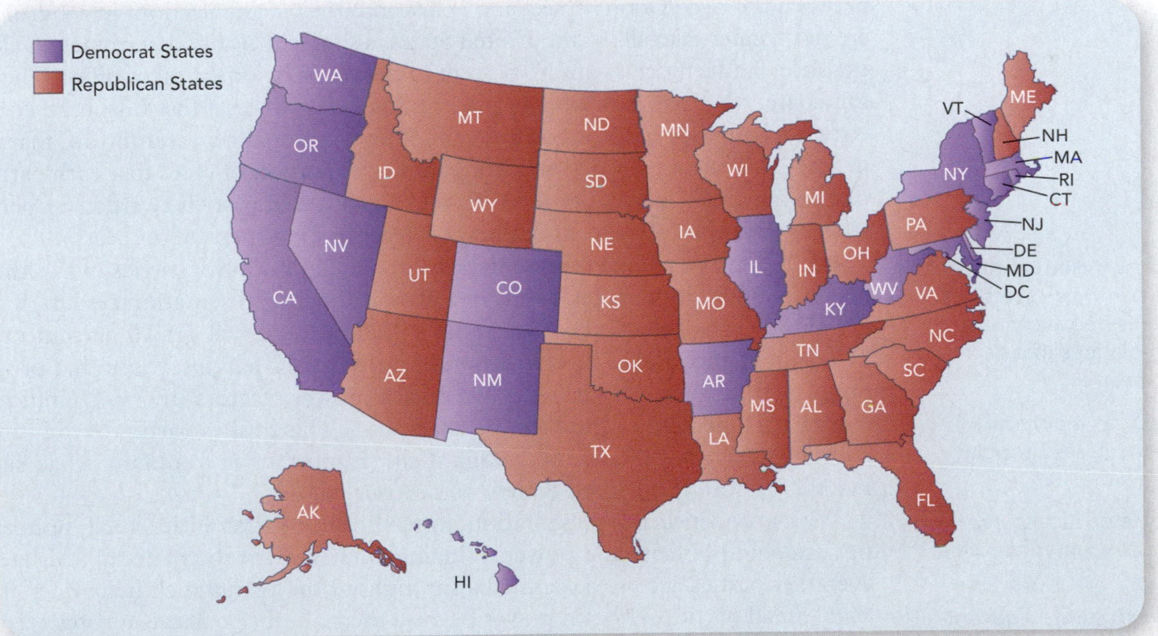

Note: Domination by a political party does not refer to votes for president or Congress. This social map is based on the composition of the states' upper and lower houses. When different parties dominate a state's houses, the total number of legislators was used. In Nebraska, where no parties are designated, the percentage vote for president was the determining factor.

Source: By the author. Based on *Statistical Abstract of the United States* 2013:Table 427.

From The Wall Street Journal, permission Cartoon Features Syndicate

The extremes are easy to see, however. Deeply committed Democrats support legislation that transfers income from those who are richer to those who are poorer or that controls wages, working conditions, and competition. Deeply committed Republicans, in contrast, oppose such legislation.

Those who are elected to Congress may cross party lines. That is, some Democrats vote for legislation proposed by Republicans, and vice versa. This happens because officeholders support their party's philosophy but not necessarily its specific proposals. When it comes to a particular bill, such as raising the minimum wage, some conservative Democrats may view the measure as unfair to small employers and vote with the Republicans against the bill. At the same time, liberal Republicans—feeling that the proposal is just, or sensing a dominant sentiment in voters back home—may side with its Democratic backers.

Third Parties. Third parties sometimes play a role in U.S. politics, but, to gain power, they must also support these centrist themes. Any party that advocates radical change is doomed to a short life. Because most Americans consider votes for them as wasted, third parties do not do well at the polls. Two exceptions are the Bull Moose party, whose candidate, Theodore Roosevelt, won more votes in 1912 than William Howard Taft, the Republican presidential candidate, and the United We Stand (Reform) party, founded by billionaire Ross Perot, which won 19 percent of the vote in 1992. Amidst internal bickering, the Reform Party declined rapidly and fell off the political map (Bridgwater 1953; *Statistical Abstract* 1995:Table 437; 2013:Table 411).

Watch on **MySocLab**
Video: Thinking Like a Sociologist: Politics and Government

Contrast with Democratic Systems in Europe

We tend to assume that other democracies looks like ours—even down to having two major parties. This is not the case. To gain a comparative understanding, let's look at the European system.

Although both their system and ours are democracies, there are fundamental distinctions between the two (Doorenspleet and Pellikaan 2013). First, elections in most of Europe are not winner-take-all. In the United States, a simple majority determines an election. For example, if a Democrat wins 51 percent of the votes, he or she takes office. The Republican candidate, who may have won 49 percent, loses everything. Most European countries, in contrast, base their elections on a system of **proportional representation**; that is, the seats in the legislature are divided according to the proportion of votes that each party receives. If one party wins 51 percent of the vote, for example, that party is awarded 51 percent of the seats; a party with 49 percent of the votes receives 49 percent of the seats.

Second, proportional representation encourages minority parties, while the winner-take-all system discourages them. In a proportional representation system, if a party can get 10 percent of the voters to support its candidate, it will get 10 percent of the seats. This system encourages the formation of **noncentrist parties**, those that propose less popular ideas, such as shutting down nuclear power reactors. In the United States, in contrast, 10 percent of the votes means 0 seats. This pushes parties to the center: If a party is to have any chance of "taking it all," it must strive to obtain broad support. For this reason, the United States has **centrist parties**.

With proportional representation, instead of being cast aside, small, noncentrist parties can gain publicity and power. Winning a few seats in the national legislature gives even tiny parties access to the media throughout the year, which helps keep its issues alive. Small parties also gain power beyond their numbers. Because votes are fragmented among the many parties that compete in elections, seldom does a single party gain a majority of the seats in the legislature. To muster the required votes, the party with the most seats must form a **coalition government** by aligning itself with one or more of the smaller parties. A party with only 10 or 15 percent of the seats, then, may be able to

proportional representation an electoral system in which seats in a legislature are divided according to the proportion of votes that each political party receives

noncentrist party a political party that represents less popular ideas

centrist party a political party that represents the center of political opinion

coalition government a government in which a country's largest party does not have enough votes to rule, and to do so aligns itself with one or more smaller parties trade its vote on some issues for the larger party's support on others. However, because coalitions often fall apart, these arrangements tend to be unstable. Italy, for example, has had sixty-four different governments since World War II (some lasting as little as two weeks, none longer than four years) (Fisher and Provoledo 2008; 2013 events). During this same period, the United States has had twelve presidents. Seeing the greater stability of the U.S. government, the Italians modified their system, and now, three-fourths of their Senate seats are decided on the winner-take-all system (Katz 2006).

Voting Patterns

Year after year, Americans show consistent voting patterns. From Table 15.1 below, you can see how the percentage of people who vote increases with age. This table also shows

TABLE 15.1 Who Votes for President?

	1988	1992	1996	2000	2004	2008	2012
Overall							
Americans Who Voted	57%	61%	54%	55%	58%	58%	57%
Age							
18–20	33%	39%	31%	28%	41%	41%	33%
21–24	38%	46%	33%	35%	43%	47%	47%
25–34	48%	53%	43%	44%	47%	49%	46%
35–44	61%	64%	55%	55%	57%	55%	53%
45–64	68%	70%	64%	64%	67%	65%	63%
65 and older	69%	70%	67%	68%	69%	68%	69%
Sex							
Male	56%	60%	53%	53%	56%	56%	54%
Female	58%	62%	56%	56%	60%	60%	59%
Race–Ethnicity							
Whites	59%	64%	56%	56%	60%	60%	58%
African Americans	52%	54%	51%	54%	56%	61%	62%
Asian Americans	NA	NA	NA	25%	30%	32%	31%
Latinos	29%	29%	27%	28%	28%	32%	32%
Education							
Some high school	41%	41%	34%	34%	35%	34%	32%
High school graduates	55%	58%	49%	49%	52%	51%	49%
Some college	65%	69%	61%	60%	66%	65%	62%
College graduates	78%	81%	73%	72%	74%	73%	72%
Marital Status							
Married	NA	NA	66%	67%	71%	70%	69%
Divorced	NA	NA	50%	53%	58%	59%	59%
Labor Force							
Employed	58%	64%	55%	56%	60%	60%	59%
Unemployed	39%	46%	37%	35%	46%	49%	46%
Income[1]							
Under $20,000	NA	NA	NA	NA	48%	52%	48%
$20,000 to $30,000	NA	NA	NA	NA	58%	56%	56%
$30,000 to $40,000	NA	NA	NA	NA	62%	62%	58%
$40,000 to $50,000	NA	NA	NA	NA	69%	65%	63%
$50,000 to $75,000	NA	NA	NA	NA	72%	71%	68%
$75,000 to $100,000	NA	NA	NA	NA	78%	76%	74%
Over $100,000	NA	NA	NA	NA	81%	92%	79%

[1]The primary source changed the income categories in 2004, making the data from earlier presidential election years incompatible.

Sources: By the author. Based on Casper and Bass 1998; Jamieson et al. 2002; Holder 2006; *Current Population Survey*: Voting and Registration Supplement 2012; *Statistical Abstract of the United States* 1991:Table 450; 1997:Table 462; 2013:Table 407.

how significant race–ethnicity is. Although African Americans are less likely to vote than non-Hispanic whites, when Barack Obama ran for president, African Americans voted at higher rates than whites. You can also see that both whites and African Americans are much more likely to vote than are Latinos and Asian Americans.

Look at education on Table 15.1. Notice how voting increases with each level of education. Education is so significant that college graduates are twice as likely to vote as are high school dropouts. You can also see how much more likely the employed are to vote. And look at how powerful income is in determining voting. At each higher income level, people are more likely to vote. Finally, note that women are more likely than men to vote.

The voting of immigrants also has its distinctive patterns, the topic of the Cultural Diversity box on page 434.

Social Integration. How can we explain these voting patterns? It is useful to look at the extremes. You can see from this table that those who are most likely to vote are the older, more educated, affluent, and employed. Those who are least likely to vote are the younger, less educated, poor, and unemployed. From these extremes, we can draw this principle: The more that people feel they have a stake in the political system, the more likely they are to vote. They have more to protect, and they feel that voting can make a difference. In effect, people who have been rewarded more by the political and economic system feel more socially integrated. They vote because they perceive that elections make a difference in their lives, including the type of society in which they and their children live.

Alienation. In contrast, those who gain less from the system—in terms of education, income, and jobs—are more likely to feel alienated from politics. Perceiving themselves as outsiders, many feel hostile toward the government. Some feel betrayed, believing that politicians have sold out to special-interest groups. They ask, "How can you tell when politicians are lying?" and reply, "When you see their lips moving."

Watch on **MySocLab**
Video: Democracy: Those Who Don't Participate

Apathy. But we must go beyond this. From Table 15.1, you can see that many highly educated people with good incomes also stay away from the polls. They are not alienated, but many do not vote because of **voter apathy**, or indifference. Their view is that "next year will just bring more of the same, regardless of who is in office." A common attitude of those who are apathetic is "What difference will my one vote make when there are millions of voters?" Many also see little difference between the two major political parties. Only about *half* of the nation's eligible voters cast ballots in presidential elections (*Statistical Abstract* 2013:Table 406).

The Gender and Racial–Ethnic Gaps in Voting. Historically, men and women voted the same way, but now we have a *political gender gap*. That is, men and women are somewhat more likely to vote for different presidential candidates. As you can see from Table 15.2 on the next page, men are more likely to favor the Republican candidate, while women are more likely to vote Democratic. This table also illustrates the much larger racial–ethnic gap in politics. Note how few African Americans vote for a Republican presidential candidate.

As we saw in Table 15.1, voting patterns reflect life experiences, especially people's economic conditions. On average, women earn less than men, and African Americans earn less than whites. As a result, at this point in history, women and African Americans tend to look more favorably on government programs that redistribute income, and they are more likely to vote for Democrats. As you can see in this table, Asian American voters, with their higher average incomes, are an exception to this pattern. Attempted explanations are far from satisfactory (Logan et al. 2012), but the reason could be a lesser emphasis on individualism in the Asian American subculture.

Watch on **MySocLab**
Video: Lobbying and Special Interest Groups

Lobbyists and Special-Interest Groups

voter apathy indifference and inaction on the part of individuals or groups with respect to the political process

Suppose that you are president of the United States, and you want to make milk more affordable for the poor. As you check into the matter, you find that part of the reason prices are high is because the government is paying farmers billions of dollars a year in price supports. You propose to eliminate these subsidies.

TABLE 15.2 How the Two-Party Presidential Vote is Split

	1988	1992	1996	2000	2004	2008	2012
Women							
Democrat	50%	61%	65%	56%	53%	57%	55%
Republican	50%	39%	35%	44%	47%	43%	44%
Men							
Democrat	44%	55%	51%	47%	46%	52%	45%
Republican	56%	45%	49%	53%	54%	48%	52%
African Americans							
Democrat	92%	94%	99%	92%	90%	99%	93%
Republican	8%	6%	1%	8%	10%	1%	6%
Whites							
Democrat	41%	53%	54%	46%	42%	44%	39%
Republican	59%	47%	46%	54%	58%	56%	59%
Latinos							
Democrat	NA	NA	NA	61%	58%	66%	71%
Republican	NA	NA	NA	39%	42%	34%	27%
Asian Americans							
Democrat	NA	NA	NA	62%	77%	62%	73%
Republican	NA	NA	NA	38%	23%	38%	26%

Sources: By the author. Based on Gallup Poll 2008; *Statistical Abstract of the United States* 1999:Table 464; 2002: Table 372; 2013:Table 412; Roper 2013.

special-interest group a group of people who support a particular issue and who can be mobilized for political action

lobbyists people who influence legislation on behalf of their clients

Immediately, large numbers of people leap into action. They contact their senators and representatives and hold news conferences. Your office is flooded with calls, faxes, and e-messages.

Reuters and the Associated Press distribute pictures of farm families—their Holsteins grazing contentedly in the background—and inform readers that your harsh proposal will destroy these hard-working, healthy, happy, good Americans who are struggling to make a living. President or not, you have little chance of getting your legislation passed.

Lobbying by Special-Interest Groups. What happened? The dairy industry went to work to protect its special interests. A **special-interest group** consists of people who think alike on a particular issue and can be mobilized for political action. The dairy industry is just one of thousands of such groups that employ **lobbyists**, people who are paid to influence legislation on behalf of their clients. Members of Congress who want to be reelected must pay attention to them, since they represent blocs of voters who share an interest in some proposed legislation. Well financed and able to contribute huge sums, lobbyists can deliver votes to you—or to your opponent.

Lobbying has led to a *revolving door*. People who served as assistants to the president or to powerful senators are sought after as lobbyists (Vidal et al. 2010). With their contacts swinging open the doors of the powerful, some even go to work for the same companies they regulated when they worked for the president (Delaney 2010).

To try to reign in some of this influence peddling, Congress made it illegal for former senators to lobby for two years after they leave office. Yet senators do lobby immediately after leaving office.

Cultural Diversity in the United States

The Politics of Immigrants: Power, Ethnicity, and Social Class

That the United States is the land of immigrants is a truism. Every schoolchild knows that since the English Pilgrims landed on Plymouth Rock, group after group has sought relief from hardship by reaching U.S. shores. Some, such as the Irish immigrants in the late 1800s and early 1900s, left to escape brutal poverty and famine. Others, such as the Jews of czarist Russia, fled religious persecution. Some sought refuge from lands ravaged by war. Others, called entrepreneurial immigrants, came primarily for better economic opportunities. Still others were sojourners who planned to return home after a temporary stay. Some, not usually called immigrants, came in chains, held in bondage by earlier immigrants.

Today, the United States is in the midst of its second largest wave of immigration. In the largest wave, immigrants accounted for 15 percent of the U.S. population. Almost all of those immigrants in the late 1800s and early 1900s came from Europe. In our current wave, immigrants make up 13 percent of the U.S. population, with a mix that is far more diverse: Immigration from Europe has slowed to a trickle, with twice as many of our recent immigrants coming from Asia as from Europe (*Statistical Abstract* 2013:Table 41). In the past 20 years, about 20 million immigrants have settled legally in the United States, and another 12 million are here illegally (*Statistical Abstract* 2013:Tables 43, 45).

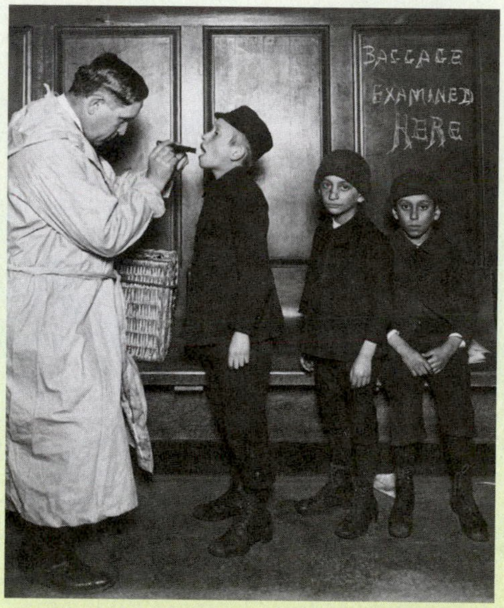

This photo from 1911 shows immigrants arriving at Ellis Island, New York. They are being inspected for signs of disease. If any disease is detected, they will be refused entry. Sociologists have studied the process by which immigrants are assimilated.

In the last century, U.S.-born Americans feared that immigrants would bring socialism or communism with them. Today's fear is that the millions of immigrants from Spanish-speaking countries threaten the primacy of the English language. Last century brought a fear that immigrants would take jobs away from U.S.-born citizens. This fear has returned. In addition, African Americans fear a loss of political power as immigrants from Mexico and Central and South America swell the Latino population.

What path do immigrants take to political activity? In general, immigrants first organize as a group on the basis of *ethnicity* rather than *class*. They respond to common problems, such as discrimination and issues associated with adapting to a new way of life. This first step in political activity reaffirms their cultural identity. As sociologists Alejandro Portes and Rubén Rumbaut (1990) note, "By mobilizing the collective vote and by electing their own to office, immigrant minorities have learned the rules of the democratic game and absorbed its values in the process."

Immigrants, then, don't become "American" overnight. Instead, they begin by fighting for their own interests as an ethnic group—as Irish, Italians, and so on. However, as Portes and Rumbaut noted, once a group gains representation somewhat proportionate to its numbers, a major change occurs: At this point, social class becomes more significant than race–ethnicity. Note that the significance of race–ethnicity in politics does not disappear, but it recedes in importance.

Irish immigrants to Boston illustrate this pattern. Banding together on the basis of ethnicity, they built a power base that put the Irish in political control of Boston. As the significance of ethnicity faded, social class became prominent. Ultimately, they saw John F. Kennedy, one of their own, from the upper class, sworn in as president of the United States. Even today, being "Irish" continues to be a significant factor in Boston politics.

For Your Consideration

➔ Try to project the path to political participation of the many millions of new U.S. immigrants. Just as the immigrants before them, today's Latino immigrants prefer candidates of their ethnicity, even if they are less qualified (Manzano and Sanchez 2010). Why do you think the path of Latinos and others will or will not be similar to that of earlier U.S. immigrants?

How do you suppose they get around this law? It's all in the name. They hire themselves out to lobbying firms as *strategic advisors*. They then lobby—excuse me—"strategically advise" their former colleagues ("It's So Much Nicer . . . " 2008). And they laugh all the way to the bank.

The Money. Buying votes is what especially bothers people. In response to publicity, Congress passed laws that limit the amount that corporations and individuals can give to candidates. To get around this law, special-interest groups form **political action committees (PACs)** to solicit contributions from many, and then hand over huge sums to politicians. The amounts are mind-boggling. Each year, about 4,500 PACs shell out almost a half billion dollars to politicians (*Statistical Abstract* 2013:Tables 430, 431). A few PACs represent broad social interests such as environmental protection. Most, however, represent the financial interests of specific groups, such as the banking, dairy, defense, and oil industries.

In 2010, the Supreme Court opened the floodgates to bankrolling politicians. In *Citizens United v. Federal Election Commission*, the Court ruled that laws that limit the amount corporations can contribute to politicians violate the First Amendment, which guarantees the right to political speech (Liptak 2010). This has led to the creation of *Super PACS* that raise huge amounts for a single candidate (Confessore 2011). At this point in the strange history of politics, corporations have more legal rights to fund candidates than individuals do.

Read on **MySocLab**
Document: Campaign Finance (Super PACs)

Read on **MySocLab**
Document: Is Congress Really for Sale?

Who Rules the United States?

15.5 Compare the functionalist (pluralist) and conflict (power elite) perspectives on U.S. power.

With lobbyists and PACs wielding such influence, just whom do U.S. senators and representatives really represent? This question has led to a lively debate among sociologists. Let's look at the functionalist and conflict perspectives.

The Functionalist Perspective: Pluralism

Functionalists view the state as having arisen out of the basic needs of the social group. To protect themselves from oppressors, people formed a government and gave it the monopoly on violence. The risk is that the state can turn that force against its own citizens. To return to the example used earlier, states have a tendency to become muggers. Thus, people must find a balance between having no government—which would lead to **anarchy**, a condition of disorder and violence—and having a government that protects them from violence, but that also may turn against them. When functioning well, then, the state is a balanced system that protects its citizens both from one another *and* from government.

What keeps the U.S. government from turning against its citizens? Functionalists say that **pluralism**, a diffusion of power among many special-interest groups, prevents any one group from gaining control of the government and using it to oppress the people (Bentley 1908; Dahl 1961, 1982; McKay 2012). To keep the government from coming under the control of any one group, the founders of the United States set up three branches of government: the executive branch (the president), the judiciary branch (the courts), and the legislative branch (the Senate and House of Representatives). Each is sworn to uphold the Constitution, which guarantees rights to citizens, and each can nullify the actions of the other two. This system, known as **checks and balances**, was designed to ensure that no one branch of government dominates the others.

In Sum: Our pluralist society has many parts—women, men, racial–ethnic groups, farmers, factory and office workers, religious organizations, bankers, bosses, the unemployed, the retired—as well as such broad categories as the rich, middle class, and poor. No group dominates. Rather, as each group pursues its own interests, it is balanced by other groups that are pursuing theirs. To attain their goals, groups must make compromises and work together. Because these many groups have political

political action committee (PAC) an organization formed by one or more special-interest groups to solicit and spend funds for the purpose of influencing legislation

anarchy a condition of lawlessness or political disorder caused by the absence or collapse of governmental authority

pluralism the diffusion of power among many interest groups that prevents any single group from gaining control of the government

checks and balances the separation of powers among the three branches of U.S. government—legislative, executive, and judicial—so that each is able to nullify the actions of the other two, thus preventing any single branch from dominating the government muscle to flex at the polls, politicians try to design policies that please as many groups as they can. This, say functionalists, makes the political system responsive to the people, and no one group rules.

The Conflict Perspective: The Power Elite

If you focus on the lobbyists scurrying around Washington, stress conflict theorists, you get a blurred image of superficial activities. What really counts is the big picture, not its fragments. The important question is, Who holds the power that determines the country's overarching policies? For example, who determines interest rates—and their impact on the price of our homes? Who sets policies that encourage the transfer of jobs from the United States to countries where labor costs less? And the ultimate question of power: Who is behind the decision to go to war?

Sociologist C. Wright Mills (1956) took the position that the country's most important matters are not decided by lobbyists or even by Congress. Rather, the decisions that have the greatest impact on the lives of Americans—and people across the globe—are made by a **power elite**. As depicted in Figure 15.2, the power elite consists of the top leaders of the largest corporations, the most powerful generals and admirals of the armed forces, and certain elite politicians—the president, the president's cabinet, and senior members of Congress who chair the major committees. It is they who wield power, who make the decisions that direct the country and shake the world.

FIGURE 15.2 Power in the United States: The Model Proposed by C. Wright Mills

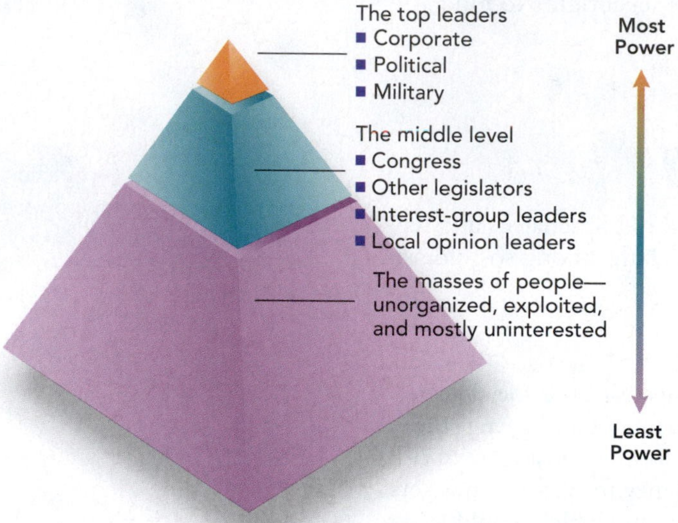

Source: By the author. Based on Mills 1956.

Are the three groups that make up the power elite—the top business, political, and military leaders—equal in power? Mills said that they were not, but he didn't point to the president and his staff or even to the generals and admirals as the most powerful. Instead, he said that the corporate leaders are the most dominant. Because all three segments of the power elite view capitalism as essential to the welfare of the country, Mills said that business interests take center stage in setting national policy. (Remember the incident mentioned in the previous chapter [page 406] of a U.S. president selling airplanes.)

Sociologist William Domhoff (2010) uses the term **ruling class** to refer to the power elite. He focuses on the 1 percent of Americans who belong to the super-rich, the powerful capitalist class analyzed in Chapter 10 (pages 266–267). Members of this class control our top corporations and foundations, even the boards that oversee our major universities. It is no accident, says Domhoff, that from this group come most members of the president's cabinet and the ambassadors to the most powerful countries of the world.

To explore these ideas further, read the Down-to-Earth Sociology box on the next page.

In Sum: Conflict theorists take the position that a *power elite* dominates the United States. With connections that extend to the highest centers of power, this ruling class determines the economic and political conditions under which the rest of the country operates. They say that we should not think of the power elite (or ruling class) as some secret group that meets to agree on specific matters. Rather, the group's unity springs from the members having similar backgrounds and orientations to life. They have attended prestigious private schools, belong to exclusive clubs, and are millionaires many times over. Their behavior stems not from some grand conspiracy to control the country but from a mutual interest in solving the problems that face big business.

power elite C. Wright Mills' term for the top people in U.S. corporations, military, and politics who make the nation's major decisions

ruling class another term for the power elite

Down-to-Earth Sociology

Who Opens the Door of Power?

It's hard to put your finger on it. You can see power in action. The president orders soldiers to some far-off country. The top military leaders of the United States, called the Joint Chiefs of Staff, meet with the president in the White House. Major congressional leaders are "briefed" on the latest threat to the country and our planned response to it. Business leaders contribute huge funds for the presidential and congressional campaigns. Big Wall Street names are tapped to head the Department of the Treasury and the Federal Reserve Board.

But how power works is elusive. Its interconnections and behind-the-scenes maneuvering seldom come to our attention. We are vaguely aware that something is going on, but it is hard to say just who is doing what and why they are doing it.

Some even say, "Nothing is going on behind the scenes except the usual horse trading. Governors and senators jockey to keep a military base open or to get some sort of financial relief from Washington. Businesses try to get bills passed that favor them. This sort of thing. Anything beyond this is conspiracy theory, built on nothing but conjecture and suspicions."

This general of the U.S. Air Force is promoting this weapon of war made by Lockheed Martin. Notice how the weapon is made to look appealing, as though it were wrapped with a bow.

Could be, of course. But then, every once in a while, some revelation bursts on us that blows the cover back just a bit, revealing that there really are high-powered interconnections that drive major decisions.

Here's one:

What do our top generals do after they retire from the military? They have generous pensions, and they could relax, golf or fish a bit, and write their memoirs. They could, but what do they actually do? Between 70 percent and 80 percent of three- and four-star generals go to work for defense contractors, companies that manufacture things to sell to the military ("Strategic Maneuvers" 2012).

Does this mean anything other than that these powerful men don't like to golf or fish or write memoirs? To understand the implications, we need to realize that these companies hire the generals because of their contacts. The companies they go to work for—Lockheed Martin, Boeing, General Dynamics, Raytheon, and Northrop Grumman—make things to sell to the military: armored vehicles, planes, bombs, ships, guns, ammunition, guidance systems, and missiles. These are outrageously expensive, specialized items, not something you pick up at your local hardware store or car dealership.

Hiring these top generals pays off. Their retirement doesn't end their contacts in the military. When they pick up a phone, their calls get through. They call people they have worked with for years. Some of these people are getting close to their own retirement, waiting for their own turn at high-paying, cushy jobs that consist of little more than attending parties and making a few phone calls.

Not all officers are allowed through this door that leads from the military to the lush corporate suite. Just those at the top of the power pyramid are given the key. To see who enters is to catch a glimpse of the interconnections of power.

For Your Consideration

➔ This analysis focuses on how the military is connected with corporate power. How do you think the politicians fit into this picture?

Which View Is Right?

The functionalist and conflict views of power in U.S. society cannot be reconciled. Either competing interests block any single group from being dominant, as functionalists assert, or a power elite oversees the major decisions of the United States, as conflict theorists maintain. The answer may have to do with the level you look at. Perhaps at the middle level of power depicted in Figure 15.2, the competing groups do keep each other at bay, and none can dominate. If so, the functionalist view would apply to this level. But which level holds the key to U.S. power? Perhaps the functionalists have not looked high enough, and activities at the peak remain invisible to them. On that level, does an elite

war armed conflict between nations or politically distinct groups

dominate? To protect its mutual interests, does a small group make the major decisions of the United States?

Sociologists passionately argue this issue, but with mixed data, we don't yet know the answer. We await further research.

15.6 Distinguish between war and terrorism; explain how common war is, why countries go to war, the role of profits, and the costs of war.

War and Terrorism: Implementing Political Objectives

Some students have asked why I include war and terrorism as topics of politics. The reason is that war and terrorism are tools used to pursue political goals. The Prussian military analyst Carl von Clausewitz, who entered the military at the age of 12 and rose to the rank of major-general, put it best when he said "War is merely a continuation of politics by other means."

Let's look at this aspect of politics.

Is War Universal?

Although human aggression and individual killing characterize all human groups, war does not. **War**, armed conflict between nations (or politically distinct groups), is simply *one option* that groups have for dealing with disagreements, but not all societies choose this option. The Mission Indians of North America, the Arunta of Australia, the Andaman Islanders of the South Pacific, and the Inuit (Eskimos) of the Arctic, for example, had procedures to handle aggression and quarrels, but they did not have organized battles that pitted one tribe or group against another. These groups do not even have a word for war (Lesser 1968).

How Common Is War?

One of the contradictions of humanity is that people long for peace while at the same time they glorify war. "Do people really glorify war?" you might ask. If you read the history of a nation, you will find a recounting of a group's major battles—and the exploits of the heroes of those battles. And if you look around a country, you are likely to see monuments to generals, patriots, and battles scattered throughout the land. From May Day parades in Moscow's Red Square to the Fourth of July celebrations in the United States and the Cinco de Mayo victory marches in Mexico, war and revolution are interwoven into the fabric of national life.

Few want to say that we honor war, but we do. Its centrality in the teaching of history and the honoring of the patriots who founded a country are two indications. A third is the display of past weapons in parks and museums. A fourth is the monuments that commemorate wars and battles. I took this photo in Washington, D.C., a memorial of the war in Vietnam.

War is so common that a cynic might say it is the normal state of society. Sociologist Pitirim Sorokin (1937–1941) counted the wars in Europe from 500 B.C. to A.D. 1925. He documented 967 wars, an average of one war every two to three years. Counting years or parts of a year in which a country was at war, Germany, at 28 percent, had the lowest record of warfare. Spain's 67 percent gave it the dubious distinction of being the most war-prone. Sorokin found that Russia, the land of his birth, had experienced only one peaceful quarter-century during the entire previous thousand years. Since the time of William the Conqueror, who took power in 1066, England had been at war an average of fifty-six out of each hundred years. It is worth noting the history of the United States: Since 1850, it has intervened militarily around the world about 160 times, an average of *once a year* (Kohn 1988).

Why Countries Go to War

Why do countries choose war as a means to handle disputes? As usual, sociologists answer this question not by focusing on factors *within* humans, such as aggressive impulses, but by looking for *social* causes—conditions in society that encourage or discourage combat between nations.

Sociologist Nicholas Timasheff (1965) identified three essential conditions for war. The *first* is an antagonistic situation in which two or more states confront incompatible objectives. For example, each may want the same land or resources. The *second* is a cultural tradition of war. Because their nation has fought wars in the past, the leaders of a group see war as an option for dealing with serious disputes with other nations. The *third* is a "fuel" that heats the antagonistic situation to a boiling point, so that politicians cross the line from thinking about war to actually waging it.

Timasheff identified seven such "fuels." He found that war is likely if a country's leaders see the antagonistic situation as an opportunity to achieve one or more of these objectives:

1. *Power*: dominating a weaker nation
2. *Unity*: uniting rival groups within their country
3. *Revenge*: settling "old scores" from earlier conflicts
4. *Prestige*: defending the nation's "honor"
5. *Leaders*: protecting or exalting the leaders' positions
6. *Ethnicity*: bringing under their rule "our people" who are living in another country
7. *Beliefs*: converting others to religious or political beliefs

You can use these three essential conditions and seven fuels to analyze any war. They will help you understand why politicians at that time chose this political action.

The War Machine and the Profits of War

Watch on **MySocLab**
Video: NPR: The Long War in Afghanistan

Two "fuels" of war that Timasheff did not analyze are the war machine and the profits of war. These two work together. If a country becomes dominant in world affairs, it accumulates enemies, and, as with the Romans, it takes a war machine to defend its far-flung interests. Just having a large military encourages war. It is there to be used, and war provides military leaders a way to prove their worth, to reap honor and acclaim, and to show that the country will back up its threats.

To operate a large military, as the United States is doing, requires a vast, efficient system to produce and distribute war goods. The profits involved in these goods are also a "fuel" for war, a topic we explore in the *Mass Media in Social Life* box on the next page.

Costs of War

One side effect of the new technologies stressed in this text is a higher capacity to inflict death. During World War I, bombs claimed fewer than 3 of every 100,000 people in England and Germany. With World War II's more powerful airplanes and bombs, these deaths increased a hundredfold, to 300 of every 100,000 civilians (Hart 1957). Our killing capacity has increased so greatly that if a nuclear war were fought, the death rate could be 100 percent. War is also costly in terms of money. As shown in Table 15.3, the United States has spent about $7 trillion on twelve of its wars.

Despite its massive costs in lives and property, war remains a common way to pursue political objectives. For about seven years, the United States fought in Vietnam—at a cost of 59,000 American and about 2 million Vietnamese lives (Hellinger and Judd 1991). For nine years, the Soviet Union waged war in Afghanistan—with a death toll of about 1 million Afghans and about 14,000 Soviet soldiers (Kalinovsky 2012). An eight-year war between Iran and Iraq cost about 400,000 lives. Cuban mercenaries fighting in Africa and South America brought an unknown number of deaths. Civil wars in Africa, Asia, and South America claimed hundreds of thousands

TABLE 15.3 What U.S. Wars Cost

American Revolution	$2,407,000,000
War of 1812	$1,553,000,000
Mexican War	$2,376,000,000
Civil War	$79,742,000,000
Spanish-American War	$9,034,000,000
World War I	$334,000,000,000
World War II	$4,104,000,000,000
Korean War	$341,000,000,000
Vietnam War	$738,000,000,000
Gulf War	$102,000,000,000
Iraq War	$784,000,000,000
Afghanistan	$321,000,000,000
Total	$6,820,000,000,000

Note: These totals are in 2011 dollars. Not included are veterans' benefits, which run about $110 billion a year; interest payments on war loans; and the ongoing expenditures of the military, currently about $700 billion a year. Nor are these costs reduced by the financial benefits to the United States, such as the acquisition of California, Arizona, and New Mexico during the Mexican War.

The military costs for the numerous U.S. involvements in "small" clashes such as the Barbary Coast War of 1801–1805 and others more recently in Grenada, Panama, Somalia, Haiti, and Kosovo are not listed in the sources.

Sources: Daggett 2010:Table 1; *Statistical Abstract of the United States* 2013:Table 480.

Mass Media in Social Life

The Propaganda and Profits of War

WARNING: Regardless of your political views, the contents of this box might make you angry.

The top executives of Lockheed Martin, Boeing, General Dynamics, Raytheon, and Northrop Grumman face a dilemma. They have huge investments in factories that spew out vast quantities of armored vehicles, guns, ammunition, bombs, planes, and missiles. *They sell these items to the military for a profit.* If the military stops buying, production will stop, workers will be laid off, and these war machines will turn into dust collectors. And, not incidentally, the firms won't need these highly paid top executives.

On the other hand, if the items that these companies manufacture are destroyed, then they must be replaced. This keeps the profits rolling in. Without this cycle—production, destruction, and replacement—it wouldn't take long for the military to possess more of these war items than they would ever need.

It is not unreasonable, then, to assume that the executives of the war industry welcome war. War is the basis of their prosperity. It is only through the destruction of what their companies produce that their factories keep humming along, and with them, the ongoing pay and bonuses that flow to the executives and stockholders.

Fortunately for these large businesses that depend on war for their existence, the U.S. government manages to find one enemy after another. And each bullet that is fired, each missile that is launched, each armored vehicle that is destroyed, each helicopter that is shot down means more profits for these companies.

For the war industry (euphemistically called the defense industry), war isn't real, although the profits are. To the executives who sell the weapons of destruction and the politicians who fund these purchases, war has become something that resembles a video game. The fighting takes place in an unfamiliar, distant "over there" somewhere, similar to the abstract, mythical locations of the battles in video games. And with drone strikes controlled by young men in the United States, who hit targets displayed on computer screens, the nastiness of war has grown even dimmer. Only a few of our soldiers get involved in the real thing. And only a tiny percentage of them die. As long as deaths are held within "acceptable limits," there is no public outcry. For the distracted public, the fighting is relegated to short news items sandwiched between the latest baseball and football scores.

To keep the public acquiescent, the media release a steady dosage of fear. *Those* people over there threaten *our* lives here. While we the public don't know precisely how this or that group threatens us, we are sure that our government has secret, classified information that they can't share with us. We are assured that we must attack them before they attack us. The distortions are sometimes brazen, but effective. And it makes no difference if it is a Democrat or a Republican who is the president. In the infamous "Gulf of Tonkin incident," President Johnson, a Democrat, prepared Americans for our invasion of Vietnam by announcing that the North Vietnamese had attacked one of our naval ships, an attack that never took place (Hallin 1986; Wells 2005). To prepare the public for the invasion of Iraq, which became our longest war, President Bush, a Republican, reported that Saddam Hussein had WMDs (weapons of mass destruction). No such weapons were found (Hughes 2006). When the powers that be decide that we should invade a country, whatever the particular threat they say is brewing, they insist that we've got to strike now.

The media's propaganda buildup prior to our launching an attack is an essential part of this orchestrated drama. Prior to an attack, the media hype the threat, sometimes even featuring reports about the utter depravity of the enemy. When no WMDs

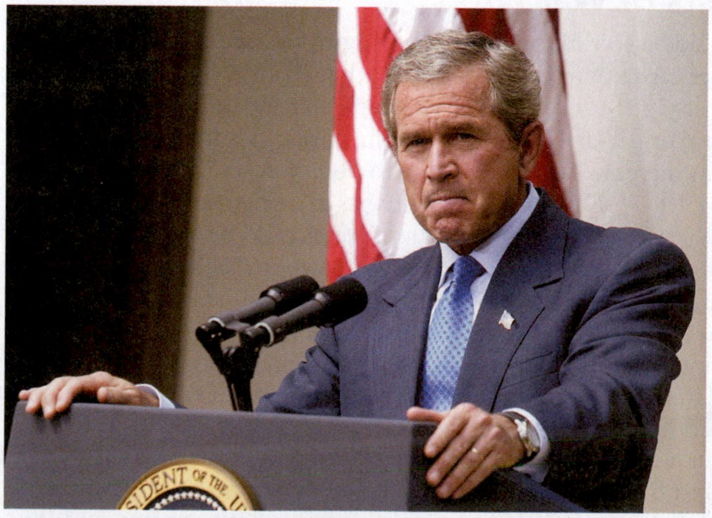

Regardless of political party, power operates the same. Prior to an invasion, presidents try to rouse the public. In an amazing coincidence, President Johnson announced an attack that didn't exist, and President Bush announced weapons that didn't exist.

were found in Iraq, the media feasted the public on the depravity of Saddam Hussein's son, Uday, who apparently exhausted himself raping several women a week. For his evil diversion, to satisfy his endlessly depraved passions, Uday once fed a living woman feet-first into a huge meat grinder that he apparently kept for such nefarious purposes. Another time, after raping a woman, he rubbed her naked body with steak and pushed her into a pack of ravenous dogs who ate her alive (Bennett and Weisskopf 2003; "Tales of Saddam's Brutality" 2003).

We probably never will know the truth about such emotionally inflammatory stories that our media have fed us, but we can note that Goebbels under Hitler would love to have used such stories to prepare the German people for war. His shortcoming was that he didn't let his imagination roam far enough.

As servants of the government, the media are paid well. It isn't that the defense contractors and their political handmaidens slip them envelopes filled with cash. Rather, the more the media hype a coming war, or publicize the evils of a targeted regime, the more their advertising revenues increase. And the more viewers or readers they attract, the more they can charge for each ad.

Waving the flag for war is just plain good business all around. The profits roll in.

For Your Consideration

➤ Do you agree with this provocative and controversial analysis? How is your answer related to your social location? Do you think that if we could remove profits from war, we would have fewer wars? How could we ever do this?

of lives, mostly of civilians. The war in Iraq cost the lives of 112,000 Iraqi civilians, 8,000 police, and 4,400 U.S. soldiers (O'Hanlon and Livingston 2010; "Casualties in Iraq" 2011; U.S. Department of Defense 2013). The death tolls continue, one "hot spot" following another, an endless cycle of U.S. interventions.

dehumanization the act or process of reducing people to objects that do not deserve the treatment accorded humans

A Special Cost of War: Dehumanization

Proud of his techniques, the U.S. trainer was demonstrating to the South American soldiers how to torture a prisoner. As the victim screamed in anguish, the trainer was interrupted by a phone call from his wife. His students could hear him say, "A dinner and a movie tonight? I'll see you after work." Hanging up the phone, he continued the lesson. (Stockwell 1989)

War exacts many costs in addition to killing people and destroying property. One of the most remarkable is its effect on morality. Exposure to brutality and killing often causes **dehumanization**, the process of reducing people to objects that do not deserve to be treated as humans. From the quotation above, you can see how numb people's consciences can become, allowing them to participate in acts they would ordinarily condemn.

The hatred and vengeance of adults become the children's heritage. The headband of this 4-year-old Palestinian boy reads: "Friends of Martyrs."

Success and Failure of Dehumanization. Dehumanization can be remarkably effective in protecting people's mental adjustment. During World War II, surgeons who were highly sensitive to patients' needs in ordinary medical settings became capable of mentally denying the humanity of Jewish prisoners. By thinking of Jews as "lower people" (*untermenschen*), they were able to mutilate them just to study the results. For a remarkable account of dehumanization, read the Down-to-Earth Sociology box on the next page.

Dehumanization does not always insulate the self from guilt, however, and its failure to do so can bring severe consequences. During the war, while soldiers are surrounded by buddies who agree that the enemy is less than human and deserves to be brutalized, it is easier for such definitions to remain intact. After returning home, the dehumanizing definitions can break down, and many soldiers find themselves disturbed by what they did during the war. Although most eventually adjust, some cannot, such as this soldier from California who wrote this note before putting a bullet through his brain (Smith 1980):

I can't sleep anymore. When I was in Vietnam, we came across a North Vietnamese soldier with a man, a woman, and a three- or four-year-old girl. We had to shoot them all. I can't get the little girl's face out of my mind. I hope that God will forgive me . . . I can't.

Down-to-Earth Sociology

The Rape of Nanking: A Report on Dehumanization

For Americans, World War II began with the Japanese attack on Pearl Harbor on December 7, 1941. For the Chinese, the war began with the Japanese attack on Manchuria in 1931. One of the most brutal and infamous events of the Japanese invasion was the treatment of the people of Nanking. You can read about these events in Iris Chang's *The Rape of Nanking* (1997), from which this account is taken. I chose the following because it is one of the best illustrations of dehumanization that I have ever read.

How then do we explain the raw brutality carried out day after day after day in the city of Nanking? Unlike their Nazi counterparts, who have mostly perished in prisons and before execution squads or, if alive, are spending their remaining days as fugitives from the law, many of the Japanese war criminals are still alive, living in peace and comfort, protected by the Japanese government. They are therefore some of the few people on this planet who, without concern for retaliation in a court of international law, can give authors and journalists a glimpse of their thoughts and feelings while committing World War II atrocities.

Here is what we learn. The Japanese soldier was not simply hardened for battle in China; he was hardened for the task of murdering Chinese combatants and noncombatants alike. Indeed, various games and exercises were set up by the Japanese military to numb its men to the human instinct against killing people who are not attacking.

For example, on their way to the capital, Japanese soldiers were made to participate in killing competitions, which were avidly covered by the Japanese media like sporting events. The most notorious one appeared in the December 7 issue of the Japan Advertiser under the headline "Sub-Lieutenants in Race to Fell 100 Chinese Running Close Contest."

> *Sub-Lieutenant Mukai Toshiaki and Sub-Lieutenant Noda Takeshi, both of the Katagiri unit at Kuyung, in a friendly contest to see which of them will first fell 100 Chinese in individual sword combat before the Japanese forces completely occupy Nanking, are well in the final phase of their race, running almost neck to neck. On Sunday [December 5] . . . the "score," according to the Asahi, was: Sub-Lieutenant Mukai, 89, and Sub-Lieutenant Noda, 78.*

A week later the paper reported that neither man could decide who had passed the 100 mark first, so they upped the goal to 150. "Mukai's blade was slightly damaged in the competition," the Japan Advertiser reported. He explained that this was the result of cutting a Chinese in half, helmet and all. The contest was 'fun' he declared."

For new soldiers, horror was a natural impulse. One Japanese wartime memoir describes how a group of green Japanese recruits failed to conceal their shock when they witnessed seasoned soldiers torture a group of civilians to death. Their commander expected this reaction and wrote in his diary: "All new recruits are like this, but soon they will be doing the same things themselves."

But new officers also required desensitization. A veteran officer named Tominaga Shozo recalled vividly his own transformation from innocent youth to killing machine. Tominaga had been a fresh second lieutenant from a military academy when assigned to the 232nd Regiment of the 39th Division from Hiroshima. When he was introduced to the men under his command, Tominaga was stunned. "They had evil eyes," he remembered. "They weren't human eyes, but the eyes of leopards or tigers."

On the front Tominaga and other new candidate officers underwent intensive training to stiffen their endurance for war. In the program an instructor had pointed to thin, emaciated Chinese in a detention center and told the officers: "These are the raw materials for your trial of courage." Day after day the instructor taught them how to cut off heads and bayonet living prisoners.

> *On the final day, we were taken out to the site of our trial. Twenty-four prisoners were squatting there with their hands tied behind their backs. They were blindfolded. A big hole had been dug—ten meters long, two meters wide, and more than three meters deep. The regimental commander, the battalion commanders, and the company commanders all took the seats arranged for them. Second Lieutenant Tanaka bowed to the regimental commander and reported, "We shall now begin." He ordered a soldier on fatigue duty to haul one of the prisoners to the edge of the pit; the prisoner was kicked when he resisted. The soldiers finally dragged him over and forced him to his knees. Tanaka turned toward us and looked into each of our faces in turn. "Heads should be cut off like this," he said, unsheathing his army sword. He scooped water from a bucket with a dipper, then poured it over both sides of the blade. Swishing off the water, he raised his sword in a long arc. Standing behind the prisoner, Tanaka steadied himself, legs spread apart, and cut off the man's head with a shout, "Yo!" The head flew more than a meter away. Blood spurted up in two fountains from the body and sprayed into the hole.*
>
> *The scene was so appalling that I felt I couldn't breathe.*

But gradually, Tominaga Shozo learned to kill. And as he grew more adept at it, he no longer felt that his men's eyes were evil. For him, atrocities became routine, almost banal. Looking back on his experience, he wrote: "We made them like this. Good sons, good daddies, good elder brothers at home were brought to the front to kill each other. Human beings turned into murdering demons. Everyone became a demon within three months." . . .

"Few know that soldiers impaled babies on bayonets and tossed them still alive into pots of boiling water," Nagatomi (a soldier who became a doctor after the war) said. "They gang raped women from the ages of twelve to eighty and then killed them when they could no longer satisfy sexual requirements. I beheaded people, starved them to death, burned them, and buried them alive, over two hundred in all. It is terrible that I could turn into an animal and do these things. There are really no words to explain what I was doing. I was truly a devil."

For Your Consideration

➔ Do you understand the process of dehumanization by which ordinary men are turned into "killing and torture machines"? If you had been a soldier in the 232nd Regiment of the 39th Division from Hiroshima, what would you have done?

Terrorism

Mustafa Jabbar, in Najaf, Iraq, is proud of his first born, a baby boy. Yet he said, "I will put mines in the baby and blow him up." (Sengupta 2004)

Can feelings really run so deep that a father would sacrifice his only son? Some groups nourish hatred, endlessly chronicling the injustices and atrocities of their archenemy. Stirred in a cauldron of bitter hatred, antagonism can span generations, its embers sometimes burning for centuries. The combination of perceived injustice and righteous hatred fuels the desire to strike out—but what can a group do if it is weaker than its enemy? Unable to meet its more powerful opponent on the battlefield, one option is **terrorism**, violence intended to create fear in order to bring about political objectives. And, yes, if the hatred is strong enough, that can mean blowing up your only child.

terrorism the use of violence or the threat of violence to produce fear in order to attain political objectives

Watch on **MySocLab**
Video: Bin Laden Tape

Suicide terrorism, a weapon sometimes chosen by the weaker group, captures headlines around the world. Among the groups that have used suicide terrorism are the Palestinians against the Israelis and the Iraqis against U.S. troops. The suicide terrorism that has had the most profound effects on our lives is the attack on the World Trade Center and the Pentagon under the direction of Osama bin Laden. What kind of sick people become suicide terrorists? This is the topic of the Down-to-Earth Sociology box on the next page.

It is sometimes difficult to tell the difference between war and terrorism. This is especially so in civil wars when the opposing sides don't wear uniforms and attack civilians. Africa is embroiled in such wars. In the Down-to-Earth Sociology box on page 445, we look at one aspect of these wars—child soldiers.

Targeted Killings

To U.S. officials, al-Qaeda has been like a multi-headed snake. Over and over, the head of some al-Qaeda group has been targeted and killed. In each instance, a replacement head pops up and takes over. Although this process of targeting and killing seems endless, it continues. A new element has been added, however, which we explore in the following Thinking Critically section.

THINKING CRITICALLY

Targeted Killings

"I wonder if I should kill her?" the president of the United States asks himself as he sits in the Oval Office. "Let's see the record," he says to his advisor whose job it is to add names to the president's "kill list."

"She's only 17," says the president.

"She's young, but a killer—and a threat to the security of our troops," replies the advisor.

"Yes, she's a valid target. Keep her on the list. But remember—no collateral damage. If she's with her family, no strike. That goes for all."

For the record, not to be revealed to the public, the president initials the list and the date.

The advisor leaves the office, the "kill list" carefully tucked in his briefing book.

"Did he approve the list?"

The advisor nods.

"Did he keep her on it?"

"Who?"

"You know who I mean. Don't play games."

"Yes. She's still on it."

"I wonder why he wants to approve each kill himself?"

"He said something about 'The buck stops here,'" said the advisor.

"Right. Truman's statement will live forever."

(Continued on page 446)

A BQM-74E drone as it leaves the flight deck of a missile frigate.

Down-to-Earth Sociology

Who Are the Suicide Terrorists? Testing Your Stereotypes

We carry a lot of untested ideas around in our heads, and we use those ideas to make sense out of our experiences. When something happens, we place the event into a mental file of "similar events," which gives us a way of interpreting it. This is a normal process. We all do it all the time. Without stereotypes—ideas of what people, things, and events are like—we could not get through everyday life.

As we traverse society, our files of "similar people" and "similar events" are usually adequate. That is, the explanations we get from our interpretations usually satisfy our "need to understand." Sometimes, however, our files for classifying people and events leave us perplexed, not knowing what to make of things. For most of us, suicide terrorism is like this. We don't know any terrorists or suicide bombers, so it is hard to imagine someone becoming one.

Let's see if we can flesh out our mental files a bit.

Sociologist Marc Sageman (2008a, 2008b) wondered about terrorists, too. Finding that his mental files were inadequate to understand them, he decided that research might provide the answer. Sageman had an unusual advantage for gaining access to data—he had been in the CIA. Through his contacts, he studied 400 al-Qaeda terrorists who had targeted the United States. He was able to examine thousands of pages of their trial records.

So let's use Sageman's research to test some common ideas. I think you'll find that the data blow away stereotypes of terrorists.

What does a suicide bomber look like? This 16-year old blew herself up in a supermarket in west Jerusalem. Two others were killed and 16 were injured.

- Here's a common stereotype.
  Terrorists come from backgrounds of poverty. Cunning leaders take advantage of their frustration and direct it toward striking out at an enemy.

Not true. Three-quarters of the terrorists came from the middle and upper classes.

- How about this image, then—the deranged loner? We carry around images like this concerning serial and mass murderers. It is a sort of catch-all stereotype that we have. These people can't get along with anyone; they stew in their loneliness and misery, and all this bubbles up in misapplied violence. You know, the workplace killer sort of image, loners "going postal."

Not true, either. Sageman found that 90 percent of the terrorists came from caring, intact families. On top of this, 73 percent were married, and most of them had children.

- Let's try another one. Terrorists are uneducated, ignorant people, so those cunning leaders can manipulate them easily.

We have to drop this one, too. Sageman found that 63 percent of the terrorists had gone to college. Three-quarters worked in professional and semi-professional occupations. Many were scientists, engineers, and architects.

What? Most terrorists are intelligent, educated, family-oriented, professional people? How can this be? Sageman found that these people had gone through a process of radicalization. Here was their trajectory:

1. *Moral outrage*. They became angry, even enraged, about something that they felt was terribly wrong.
2. *Ideology*. They interpreted their moral outrage within a radical, militant understanding of Islamic teachings.
3. *Shared outrage and ideology*. They found like-minded people, often on the Internet, especially in chat rooms.
4. *Group support for radical action*. They decided that thinking and talking were not enough. The moral wrong needed dramatic action. The choice was an act of terrorism.

To understand terrorists, then, it is not the individual that we need to look at. We need to focus on *group dynamics*, how the group influences the individual and how the individual influences the group (as we studied in Chapter 6).

In one sense, however, the image of the loner does come close. Seventy percent of these terrorists committed themselves to extreme acts while they were living away from the country where they grew up. They became homesick, sought out people like themselves, and ended up at radical mosques where they learned a militant script.

Constantly, then, sociologists seek to understand the relationship between the individual and the group. This fascinating endeavor sometimes blows away stereotypes.

For Your Consideration

1. How do you think we can reduce the process of radicalization that turns people into terrorists?
2. Sageman concludes that this process of radicalization has produced networks of homegrown, leaderless terrorists, who don't need al-Qaeda to direct them. He also concludes that this process will eventually wear itself out. Do you agree? Why or why not?

Down-to-Earth **Sociology**

Child Soldiers

When rebels entered 12-year-old Ishmael Beah's village in Sierra Leone, they lined up the boys (Beah 2007). One of the rebels said, "We are going to initiate you by killing these people. We will show you blood and make you strong."

Before the rebels could do the killing, shots rang out and the rebels took cover. In the confusion, Ishmael escaped into the jungle. When he returned, he found his family dead and his village burned.

With no place to go and rebels attacking the villages, killing, looting, and raping, Ishmael continued to hide in the jungle. As he peered out at a village one day, he saw a rebel carrying the head of a man, which he held by the hair. With blood dripping from where the neck had been, Ishmael said that the head looked as though it were still feeling its hair being pulled.

Months later, government soldiers found Ishmael. The "rescue" meant that he had to become a soldier—on their side, of course.

Ishmael's indoctrination was short but to the point. Hatred is a strong motivator.

A boy soldier in Liberia.

> *"You can revenge the death of your family, and make sure that more children do not lose their parents," the lieutenant said. "The rebels cut people's heads off. They cut open pregnant women's stomachs and take the babies out and kill them. They force sons to have sex with their mothers. Such people do not deserve to live. This is why we must kill every single one of them. Think of it as destroying a great evil. It is the highest service you can perform for your country."*

Along with thirty other boys, most of whom were ages 13 to 16, with two just 7 and 11, Ishmael was trained to shoot and clean an AK-47.

Banana trees served for bayonet practice. With thoughts of disemboweling evil rebels, the boys would slash at the leaves.

The things that Ishmael had seen, he did.

Killing was difficult at first, but after a while, as Ishmael says, "killing became as easy as drinking water."

The corporal thought that the boys were sloppy with their bayonets. To improve their performance, he held a contest. He chose five boys and placed them opposite five prisoners with their hands tied. He told the boys to slice the men's throats on his command. The boy whose prisoner died the quickest would win the contest.

> *"I stared at my prisoner," said Ishmael. "He was just another rebel who was responsible for the death of my family. The corporal gave the signal with a pistol shot, and I grabbed the man's head and sliced his throat in one fluid motion. His eyes rolled up, and he looked me straight in the eyes before they suddenly stopped in a frightful glance. I dropped him on the ground and wiped my bayonet on him. The corporal, who was holding a timer, proclaimed me the winner. The other boys clapped at my achievement."*
>
> *"No longer was I running away from the war," adds Ishmael. "I was in it. I would scout for villages that had food, drugs, ammunition, and the gasoline we needed. I would report my findings to the corporal, and the entire squad would attack the village. We would kill everyone."*

Ishmael was one of the lucky ones. Of the approximately 300,000 child soldiers worldwide, Ishmael is one of the few who has been rescued and given counseling at a UNICEF rehabilitation center. Ishmael has also had the remarkable turn of fate of graduating from college in the United States and becoming a permanent U.S. resident.

Source: Based on Beah 2007; quotations are summaries.

For Your Consideration

➔ 1. What can be done to prevent the recruitment of child soldiers? Why don't we just pass a law that requires a minimum age to serve in the military?
2. How can child soldiers be helped? Which agencies should be involved, taking what actions?
3. How was Ishmael's training in dehumanization like that of Tominaga Shozo's reported in the box on page 442?

The order was given. The drones flew to their target. And to the next one. And to the next. Each killing personally approved by the president of the United States.

The advisor watched the monitor, much like a video game. The explosions were silent.

He nodded, grim-faced, then went to his office to prepare the next kill list. This one had an American on it. The president approved this list, too.

Based on Savage 2011; Becker and Shane 2012; Savage 2012.

For Your Consideration

➔ This is not a transcript of a recording, so the conversation in the Oval Office will differ from this vignette. But it is based on actual events. The president of the United States personally authorizes the names of the people he wants killed in other countries. Some are American citizens. No trial. No lawyers. Just some men, and an occasional woman, I presume, poring over reports and deciding what names to suggest to the president. The president reviews the report and approves or disapproves each name. Never in the history of the United States have we had something like this. The president is both judge and jury.

➔ The rationale? It's necessary to cripple al-Qaeda and protect the United States.

➔ What do you think? ■

Sowing the Seeds of Future Violence

Selling War Technology. Selling weapons to the Least Industrialized Nations sows the seeds of war and terrorism. When a Least Industrialized Nation buys high-tech weapons, its neighbors get nervous, which sparks an arms race among them (Broad and Sanger 2007). The chief merchant of death, as you can see from Table 15.4, is the United States. Russia and Great Britain place a distant second and third.

This table also shows the major customers in the business of death. You can see that several of the top four spenders have low standards of living, and certainly could use the money for other purchases. The top buyer is of special interest. Saudi Arabia's huge purchases of arms indicate that many of the U.S. dollars spent on oil return to the United States. There is, in reality, an exchange of arms for oil, with dollars the medium of exchange. As mentioned in Chapter 9 (page 252), Saudi Arabia cooperates with the United States by trying to keep oil prices down and, in return, the United States props up its dictators.

TABLE 15.4 The Business of Death

The Top 10 Arms Sellers		The Top 10 Arms Buyers	
1. United States	$64 billion	1. Saudi Arabia	$25 billion
2. Russia	$46 billion	2. India	$18 billion
3. Great Britain	$15 billion	3. China	$13 billion
4. France	$12 billion	4. Egypt	$11 billion
5. China	$13 billion	5. Pakistan	$10 billion
6. Germany	$6 billion	6 Israel	$10 billion
7. Israel	$5 billion	7. U.A.E.	$9 billion
8. Italy	$3 billion	8. South Korea	$7 billion
9. Sweden	$3 billion	9. Taiwan	$7 billion
10. Spain	$3 billion	10. Algeria	$7 billion

Note: For years 2004–2011. U.A.E. is United Arab Emirates.
Source: By the author. Based on Grimmett and Kerr 2012:Tables 20, 23.

Nuclear proliferation also sows the seeds of wars and terrorism. The head of nuclear development in Pakistan, which has the bomb, sold blueprints for atomic bombs to Libya, North Korea, and Iran (Perry et al. 2007). The United States eliminated Libya from the nuclear race, but as I write this, Iran and North Korea are furiously following Pakistan's blueprints to develop their own nuclear weapons. In the hands of terrorists or a dictator who wants to settle grudges—whether nationalistic or personal—these weapons can mean nuclear blackmail or nuclear destruction, or both.

Making Alignments and Protecting Interests. The current alignments of the powerful nations also sow the seeds of future conflicts. The seven richest, most powerful, and most technologically advanced nations (Canada, France, Germany, Great Britain, Italy, Japan, and the United States) formed a loose alliance that they called G7 (the Group of 7). The goal was to coordinate their activities so they could perpetuate their global dominance, divide up the world's markets, and regulate global economic activity. Fearing Russia's nuclear arsenal and wanting to tame its ambitions, G7 invited Russia as an observer at its annual summits. Russia became a full member in 2002, and the organization is now called G8. China, which has increased its economic clout and nuclear arsenal, has been invited to be an observer—a form of trial membership.

G8, soon to be G9, may be a force for peace—if these nations can agree on how to divide up the world's markets and force weaker nations to cooperate. But opposition always arises. As I write this, the growing nuclear capability of Iran poses a special threat to G8's dominance. If G8 does not act through the United Nations, the United States, with the support of Great Britain and Israel, might bomb Iran's nuclear facilities. An alternative course of action is for the United States to give the go-ahead for Israel to do the bombing. One way or the other, the United States will protect its interests in this oil-rich region of the world.

It does not take much imagination to foresee the implications of these current alignments: the propping up of cooperative puppet governments that support the interests of G8, the threat of violence to those that do not cooperate, and the inevitable resistance—including the use of terrorism—of various ethnic groups to the domination of these more powerful countries. With these conditions in place, the perpetuation of war and terrorism is guaranteed.

Where do non-industrialized tribal and clan-oriented people get such weapons? What you read in this chapter is significant for understanding many current events. This photo was taken in Libya.

A New World Order?

15.7 Explain how the globalization of capitalism might be bringing a New World Order.

War and terrorism are tools by which some nations dominate other nations. So far, their use to control the globe has failed. A New World Order, however, might be ushered in, not by war, but by nations cooperating for economic reasons. Perhaps the key political event in our era is the globalization of capitalism. Why the term *political*? Because politics and economics are twins, with each setting the stage for the other.

Listen on **MySocLab**
Audio: NPR: Analysts: By 2025, U.S. Won't Be Top Power

This is the Enemy
WINNER R. HOE & CO., INC. AWARD – NATIONAL WAR POSTER COMPETITION

Hinter den
Feindmächten:
der Jude

All governments—all the time—use propaganda to influence public opinion. During times of war, the propaganda becomes more obvious. The World War II propaganda poster on the left, from the United States, is intended to encourage Americans to sacrifice and soldiers to fight: The Nazis are killers. The propaganda poster on the right, from Nazi Germany, is intended to encourage Germans to sacrifice and soldiers to fight: The words read, "Behind the fiendish enemy, the Jew."

Trends toward Unity

As discussed in the previous chapter, the world's nations are almost frantically embracing capitalism. In this pursuit, they are forming cooperative economic–political units. The United States, Canada, and Mexico entered into a North American Free Trade Agreement (NAFTA). Eventually, all of North and South America may belong to such an organization. Ten Asian countries with a combined population of a half billion people have formed a regional trading partnership called ASEAN (Association of Southeast Asian Nations). Struggling for dominance is the even more encompassing World Trade Organization. These coalitions of trading partners, along with the Internet, are making national borders increasingly insignificant.

The European Union (EU) may indicate a unified future. Transcending their national boundaries, twenty-seven European countries (with a combined population of 450 million) now make up this economic and political unit. These nations have adopted a single currency, the Euro, which replaced their marks, francs, liras, lats, and pesetas. The EU has also established a military staff in Brussels, Belgium (Mardell 2007).

Could this process continue until there is just one state or empire that envelops the earth? It is possible. The United Nations (UN) is striving to become the legislative body of the world, wanting its decisions to supersede those of any individual nation. The UN operates a World Court (formally titled the International Court of Justice). It also has a rudimentary army and has sent "peacekeeping" troops to several nations. There is even a *World Bank*.

Inevitable Changes

If we take a broad historical view, we see that a particular group or culture can dominate only so long. Its dominance always comes to an end, to be replaced by another group or culture. The process of decline can be slow, sometimes taking even hundreds of years (Toynbee 1946). Life today, though, is so speeded-up that the future invades the present at a furious pace. The decline of U.S. dominance—like that of Great Britain—could come fairly quickly, although certainly not without resistance and bloodshed. What the new political arrangements of world power will look like is anyone's guess, but it certainly will include an ascendant China (Kissinger 2011).

nationalism strongly identifying with a nation (a people) accompanied by desiring that nation to be dominant

We can be certain that whatever the shape of future global stratification, an economic–political elite will direct it. This small group of wealthy, powerful people, whose main goal is to continue its dominance, will make alliances around the globe. Perhaps this process will lead to a one-world government. Only time will tell.

MySocLab

Study and Review on MySocLab

CHAPTER 15 Summary and Review

Micropolitics and Macropolitics

15.1 Distinguish between micropolitics and macropolitics.

What is the difference between micropolitics and macropolitics?

The essential nature of **politics** is **power**, and every group is political. The term **micropolitics** refers to the exercise of power in everyday life. **Macropolitics** refers to large-scale power, such as governing a country. Pp. 421–422.

Power, Authority, and Violence

15.2 Contrast power, authority, and violence; compare traditional, rational-legal, and charismatic authority; explain authority as an ideal type.

How are authority and coercion related to power?

Authority is power that people view as legitimately exercised over them, while **coercion** is power they consider unjust. The **state** is a political entity that claims a monopoly on violence over some territory. If enough people consider a state's power illegitimate, **revolution** is possible. P. 422.

What kinds of authority are there?

Max Weber identified three types of authority. In **traditional authority**, power is derived from custom: Patterns set down in the past serve as rules for the present. In **rational–legal authority** (also called *bureaucratic authority*), power is based on law and written procedures. In **charismatic authority**, power is derived from loyalty to an individual to whom people are attracted. Charismatic authority, which undermines traditional and rational–legal authority, has built-in problems in transferring authority to a new leader. Pp. 422–426.

Types of Government

15.3 Compare monarchies, democracies, dictatorships, and oligarchies.

How are the types of government related to power?

In a **monarchy**, power is based on hereditary rule; in a **democracy**, power is given to the ruler by citizens; in a **dictatorship**, power is taken by an individual; and in an **oligarchy**, power is seized by a small group. Pp. 426–428.

The U.S. Political System

15.4 Compare the U.S. political system with other democratic systems; discuss voting patterns, lobbyists, and PACs.

What are the main characteristics of the U.S. political system?

The United States has a "winner take all" system, in which a simple majority determines the outcome of elections. Most European democracies, in contrast, have **proportional representation**: Legislative seats are allotted according to the percentage of votes each political party receives. Pp. 428–431.

Voter turnout is higher among people who are more socially integrated—those who sense a greater stake in the outcome of elections, such as the more educated and well-to-do. **Lobbyists** and **special-interest groups**, such as **political action committees** (PACs), play a significant role in U.S. politics. Pp. 431–435.

Who Rules the United States?

15.5 Compare the functionalist (pluralist) and conflict (power elite) perspectives on U.S. power.

Is the United States controlled by a ruling class?

In a view known as **pluralism**, functionalists say that no one group holds power, that the country's many competing interest groups balance one another. Conflict theorists, who focus on the top level of power, say that the United States is governed by a **power elite**, a **ruling class** made up of the top corporate, political, and military leaders. At this point, the matter is not settled. Pp. 435–438.

War and Terrorism: Implementing Political Objectives

15.6 Distinguish between war and terrorism; explain how common war is, why countries go to war, the role of profits, and the costs of war.

How are war and terrorism related to politics—and what are their costs?

War and **terrorism** are both means of pursuing political objectives. Timasheff identified three essential conditions of war and seven fuels that ignite antagonistic situations into war. His analysis can be applied to terrorism. Because of technological advances in killing, the costs of war in terms of money spent and human lives lost have escalated. Another cost is **dehumanization**, whereby people no longer see others as worthy of human treatment. This paves the way for torture and killing. Pp. 438–447.

A New World Order?

15.7 Explain how the globalization of capitalism might be bringing a New World Order.

Is humanity headed toward a world political system?

The globalization of capitalism and the trend toward regional economic and political unions may indicate that a world political system is developing. Oppositional forces include rivalries, global economic crises, ethnic loyalties, and **nationalism**. Pp. 447–448.

Thinking Critically about Chapter 15

1. What are the three sources of authority, and how do they differ from one another?
2. What does terrorism have to do with politics? What does the globalization of capitalism have to do with politics?
3. Apply the findings in the section "Why Countries Go to War" (pages 438–439) to a recent war that the United States has been a part of.

16 CHAPTER

Marriage and Family

Listen to Chapter 16 on MySocLab

I was living in a remote village in the state of Colima, *Mexico. I had chosen this nondescript town a few kilometers from the ocean because it had no other Americans, and I wanted to immerse myself in the local culture.*

The venture was successful. I became friends with my neighbors, who were curious about why a gringo was living in their midst. After all, there was nothing about their drab and dusty town to attract tourists. So why was this gringo there, this guy who looked so different from them and who had the unusual custom of jogging shirtless around the outskirts of town and among the coconut and banana trees? This was their burning question, while mine was "What is your life like?"

We satisfied one another. I explained to them what a sociologist is. Although they never grasped why I would want to know about their *way of life, they accepted my explanation. And I was able to get my questions answered. I was invited into their homes—by the men. The women didn't talk to men outside the presence of their husbands, brothers, or other women. The women didn't even go out in public unless they were accompanied by someone. Another woman would do, just so they weren't alone. The women did the cooking, cleaning, and child care. The men worked in the fields.*

> "It was his wife's job to pick up the used toilet paper."

I was culturally startled one day at my neighbor's house. The man had retired from the fields, and he and his wife, as the custom was, were being supported by their sons who worked in the fields. When I saw the bathroom, with a homemade commode made of clay—these were poor people—I asked him about the used toilet paper thrown into a pile on the floor. He explained that the sewer system couldn't handle toilet paper. He said that I should just throw mine onto the pile, adding that it was his wife's job to pick up the used toilet paper and throw it out.

I became used to the macho behavior of the men. This wasn't too unlike high school behavior—a lot of boisterous man-to-man stuff—drinking, joking, and bragging about sexual conquests. The sex was vital for proving manhood. When the men took me to a whorehouse (to help explain their culture, they said), they couldn't understand why I wouldn't have sex with a prostitute. Didn't I find the women attractive? Yes, they were good looking. Weren't they sexy? Yes, very much so. Was I a real man? Yes. Then why not? My explanation about being married didn't faze them one bit. They were married, too—and a real man had to have sex with more women than just his wife.

Explanations of friendship with a wife and respect for her fell on deaf cultural ears.

Learning Objectives

After you have read this chapter, you should be able to:

16.1 Define marriage and family and summarize their common cultural themes. (p. 451)

16.2 Contrast the functionalist, conflict, and symbolic interactionist perspectives on marriage and family. (p. 455)

16.3 Summarize research on love and courtship, marriage, childbirth, child rearing, and family transitions. (p. 458)

16.4 Summarize research on families: African American, Latino, Asian American, Native American, one-parent, couples without children, blended, and gay and lesbian. (p. 465)

16.5 Discuss changes in the timetable of family life, cohabitation, and elder care. (p. 472)

16.6 Summarize problems in measuring divorce, research findings on children and grandchildren of divorce, fathers' contact after divorce, ex-spouses, and remarriage. (p. 474)

16.7 Summarize the dark and bright sides of family life. (p. 480)

16.8 Explain the likely future of marriage and family. (p. 482)

Marriage and Family in Global Perspective

16.1 Define marriage and family and summarize their common cultural themes.

These men and I were living in the same physical space, but our cultural space—which we carry in our heads and show in our behavior—was worlds apart. My experiences with working-class men in this remote part of Mexico helped me understand how marriage and family can differ vastly from one culture to another. To broaden our perspective for understanding this vital social institution, let's look at how marriage and family customs differ around the world.

What Is a Family?

"What is a family, anyway?" *Family* should be easy to define, since it is so significant to humanity that it is universal. Although every human group organizes its members in families, the world's cultures display an incredible variety of family forms. The Western world regards a family as a husband, wife, and children, but in some groups, men have more than one wife (**polygyny**) or women more than one husband (**polyandry**). How about the obvious? Can we define the family as the approved group into which children

polygyny a form of marriage in which men have more than one wife

polyandry a form of marriage in which women have more than one husband

family two or more people who consider themselves related by blood, marriage, or adoption

household people who occupy the same housing unit

nuclear family a family consisting of a husband, wife, and child(ren)

extended family a family in which relatives, such as the "older generation" or unmarried aunts and uncles, live with the partents and their children

family of orientation the family in which a person grows up

family of procreation the family formed when a couple's first child is born

are born? If so, we would overlook the Banaro of New Guinea. In this group, a young woman must give birth *before* she can marry—and she *cannot* marry the father of her child (Murdock 1949).

What if we were to define the family as the unit in which parents are responsible for disciplining children and providing for their material needs? This, too, seems obvious, but it is not universal. Among the Trobriand Islanders, it is not the parents but the wife's eldest brother who is responsible for providing the children's discipline and their food (Malinowski 1927).

Such remarkable variety means that we have to settle for a broad definition. A **family** consists of people who consider themselves related by blood, marriage, or adoption. A **household**, in contrast, consists of people who occupy the same housing unit—a house, apartment, or other living quarters.

We can classify families as **nuclear** (husband, wife, and children) and **extended** (including people such as grandparents, aunts, uncles, and cousins in addition to the nuclear unit). Sociologists also refer to the **family of orientation** (the family in which an individual grows up) and the **family of procreation** (the family that is formed when a couple has its first child).

What Is Marriage?

We have the same problem in defining marriage. For just about every element you might regard as essential to marriage, some group has a different custom.

Consider the sex of the bride and groom. Until recently, opposite sex was taken for granted. Then in the 1980s and 1990s, several European countries legalized same-sex marriages. Canada and several U.S. states soon followed.

Same-sex marriages sound so new, but when Columbus landed in the Americas, some Native American tribes already had same-sex marriages. Through a ceremony called the *berdache*, a man or woman who wanted to be a member of the opposite sex was officially *declared* to have his or her sex changed. The "new" man or woman put on the clothing and performed the tasks associated with his or her new sex, and was allowed to marry.

Even sexual relationships don't universally characterize marriage. The Nayar of Malabar never allow a bride and groom to have sex. After a three-day celebration of the marriage, they send the groom packing—and never allow him to see his bride again (La Barre 1954). This can be a little puzzling to figure out, but it works like this: The groom is "borrowed" from another tribe for the ceremony. Although the Nayar bride can't have sex with her husband, after the wedding, she can have approved lovers from her tribe. This system keeps family property intact—along matrilineal lines.

At least one thing has to be universal in marriage: We can at least be sure that the bride and groom are alive. So you would think. But even for this there is an exception. On the Loess Plateau in China, if a son dies without a wife, his parents look for a dead woman to be his bride. After buying one—from the parents of a dead unmarried daughter—the dead man and woman are married and then buried together. Happy that their son will have intimacy in the afterlife, the parents throw a party to celebrate the marriage (Fremson 2006).

With such tremendous cultural variety, we can define **marriage** this way: a group's approved mating arrangements, usually marked by a ritual of some sort (the wedding) to indicate the couple's new public status.

Often one of the strongest family bonds is that of mother–daughter. The young artist, an eleventh grader, wrote: "This painting expresses the way I feel about my future with my child. I want my child to be happy and I want her to love me the same way I love her. In that way we will have a good relationship so that nobody will be able to take us apart. I wanted this picture to be alive; that is why I used a lot of bright colors."

Common Cultural Themes

Despite this diversity, several common themes run through marriage and family. As Table 16.1 illustrates, all societies use marriage and family to establish patterns of mate selection, descent, inheritance, and authority. Let's look at these patterns.

TABLE 16.1 Common Cultural Themes: Marriage in Traditional and Industrialized Societies

Characteristic	Traditional Societies	Industrial (and Postindustrial) Societies
What is the structure of marriage?	*Extended* (marriage embeds spouses in a large kinship network of explicit obligations)	*Nuclear* (marriage brings few obligations toward the spouse's relatives)
What are the functions of marriage?	Encompassing (see the six functions listed on page 455)	More limited (many functions are fulfilled by other social institutions)
Who holds authority?	*Patriarchal* (authority is held by males)	Although some patriarchal features remain, authority is divided more equally
How many spouses at one time?	Most have one spouse (*monogamy*), while some have several (*polygamy*)	One spouse
Who selects the spouse?	Parents, usually the father, select the spouse	Individuals choose their own spouses
Where does the couple live?	Couples usually reside with the groom's family (*patrilocal residence*), less commonly with the bride's family (*matrilocal residence*)	Couples establish a new home (*neolocal residence*)
How is descent figured?	Usually figured from male ancestors (*patrilineal kinship*), less commonly from female ancestors (*matrilineal kinship*)	Figured from male and female ancestors equally (*bilineal kinship*)
How is inheritance figured?	Rigid system of rules; usually patrilineal, but can be matrilineal	Highly individualistic; usually bilineal

Source: By the author.

Mate Selection. Each human group establishes norms to govern who marries whom. If a group has norms of **endogamy,** it specifies that its members must marry *within* their group. For example, some groups prohibit interracial marriage. In some societies, these norms are written into law, but in most cases, they are informal. In the United States, most whites marry whites, and most African Americans marry African Americans—not because of any laws but because of informal norms. In contrast, norms of **exogamy** specify that people must marry *outside* their group. The best example of exogamy is the **incest taboo**, which prohibits sex and marriage among designated relatives.

As you can see from Table 16.1, how people find mates varies around the world, from fathers selecting them to the highly personal choices common in Western cultures. Changes in mate selection are the focus of the Sociology and the New Technology box on the next page.

Descent. How are you related to your father's father or to your mother's mother? You would think that the answer to this question would be the same all over the world—but it isn't. Each society has a **system of descent**, the way people trace kinship over generations. We use a **bilineal system**; that is, we think of ourselves as related to both our mother's and our father's sides of the family. As obvious as this seems to us, when we look around the world, we find that ours is only one way that people reckon descent. Some groups use a **patrilineal system**, tracing descent only on the father's side—they don't think of children as being related to their mother's relatives. Others don't consider children to be related to their father's relatives and follow a **matrilineal system**, tracing descent only on the mother's side. The Naxi of China don't even have a word for father (Hong 1999).

Inheritance. Marriage and family are also used to determine rights of inheritance. In a bilineal system, property is passed to both males and females, in a patrilineal system, only to males, and in a matrilineal system (the rarest form), only to females. No system is natural. Rather, each matches a group's ideas of justice and logic.

Authority. Some form of **patriarchy,** men-as-a-group dominating women-as-a-group, runs through all societies. Contrary to what some think, there are no historical

Read on **MySocLab**
Document: Mate Selection and Marriage Around the World

marriage a group's approved mating arrangements, usually marked by a ritual of some sort

endogamy the practice of marrying within one's own group

exogamy the practice of marrying outside of one's group

incest taboo the rule that prohibits sex and marriage among designated relatives

system of descent how kinship is traced over the generations

bilineal system (of descent) a system of reckoning descent that counts both the mother's and the father's side

patrilineal system (of descent) a system of reckoning descent that counts only the father's side

matrilineal system (of descent) a system of reckoning descent that counts only the mother's side

patriarchy men-as-a-group dominating women-as-a-group; authority is vested in males

Sociology and the New Technology

Online Dating: Risks and Rewards

There are over 1,000 online dating sites. Some are general—they try to appeal to everyone. Others are niche, targeting people by age, race, or religion. Still others are super-niche. There are sites for Goths, military widows, and pet lovers (Broughton 2013). One targets "green singles," people for whom environmental, vegetarian, and animal rights are central. Another targets women who like men with mustaches (Cole 2012; Webb 2013).

Electronic matchmaking is changing the way we find mates. Online dating has become so popular that one-fifth (22 percent) of heterosexual couples now meet online. For homosexuals, the total swells to three-fifths of couples (Rosenfeld and Thomas 2012).

This is from an interview I did with Brenda, who is in her late 20s:

> *I had just moved to Colorado, and I didn't know anyone. I decided to go on the matchmaking Web site. I filled out the profile, but I didn't have high expectations. I searched for someone who liked similar activities and had a similar taste in music.*
>
> *I could weed through the profiles and eliminate the Wackos, the Desperates, and the Shady. I e-mailed three men. Pedro seemed interesting. We wrote back and forth for a while. It was a little scary when he asked to meet somewhere. It was out of my comfort zone—I had never seen him, and none of my friends knew him.*
>
> *We met at a neighborhood bar, where a local band was playing. We talked for hours. I knew so much about him before we met.*
>
> *Then we started dating normally.*

Brenda's last statement is especially significant. Although Internet dating has lost most of its stigma, a residue remains. You can see how Brenda expresses her feeling that Internet dating is not quite normal. She also asked that I not use her real name. Eventually, Internet dating will shed all stigma.

It isn't difficult to see the appeal of the dating sites. They offer thousands of potential companions, lovers, or spouses. For a low monthly fee, you can meet the person of your dreams—or so they promise.

The photos on these sites are fascinating. Some seem to be lovely people—warm, attractive, and vivacious. Others seem okay, although perhaps a bit needy. Then there are the desperate, begging for someone—anyone—to contact them: women who try for sexy poses, their exposed flesh suggesting the promise of a good time, and men who do their best to look like hulks, their muscular presence promising the same.

If you want to meet a mate online, though, you can expect to be fed a few lies. Researchers have found that to "put their best foot forward," women say that they weigh less than they do. And men? They say they are taller than they are (Rosenbloom 2011). But this seems to be in line with what you could expect in meeting someone at a bar, or wherever you would meet someone for the first time. To make a good impression, most people stretch the truth. (Do they really scuba dive, or is this something they would just like to do?)

Are there dangers? The Craig's List rapists and all that? Certainly there are, and you have to watch out for shady characters lurking on the Net. How do you know that the engaging person you are corresponding with is not already married, does not have a dozen kids, or is not a child molester or a rapist? But what makes such concerns unique to Internet dating? Aren't these the same kind of issues you need to be concerned about when meeting someone at school, a party, or even in the supermarket?

Even though the form is changing, the substance appears to be about the same. Maybe Internet dating is just tradition dressed up in more technological clothing.

Snapshots

© Jason Love/www.CartoonStock.com

Tall, Dark, and Handsome chats with Buxom Blonde.

For Your Consideration

➔ Have you used an online dating site? Would you consider using one (if you were single and unattached)? Why or why not?

records of a society that was a true **matriarchy**, where women-as-a-group dominated men-as-a-group. Although U.S. family patterns are becoming more **egalitarian**, or equal, some of today's customs still reflect their patriarchal origin. One of the most obvious is the U.S. naming pattern: Despite some changes, the typical bride still takes the groom's last name, and children usually receive the father's last name.

Marriage and Family in Theoretical Perspective

16.2 Contrast the functionalist, conflict, and symbolic interactionist perspectives on marriage and family.

As we have seen, human groups around the world have many forms of mate selection, ways to view the parent's responsibility, and ways to trace descent. Although these patterns are arbitrary, each group perceives its own forms of marriage and family as natural. Now let's see what pictures emerge when we view marriage and family theoretically.

The Functionalist Perspective: Functions and Dysfunctions

Functionalists stress that to survive, a society must fulfill basic functions (that is, meet its basic needs). When functionalists look at marriage and family, they examine how they are related to other parts of society, especially the ways that marriage and family contribute to the well-being of society.

Why the Family Is Universal. Although the form of marriage and family varies from one group to another, the family is universal. The reason for this, say functionalists, is that the family fulfills six needs that are basic to the survival of every society. These needs, or functions, are (1) economic production, (2) socialization of children, (3) care of the sick and aged, (4) recreation, (5) sexual control, and (6) reproduction. To make certain that these functions are performed, every human group has adopted some form of the family.

Watch on **MySocLab** **Video:** How a Family Is Defined

Functions of the Incest Taboo. Functionalists note that the incest taboo helps families avoid *role confusion*. This, in turn, helps parents socialize children. For example, if father–daughter incest were allowed, how should a wife treat her daughter—as a daughter or as a second wife? Should the daughter consider her mother as a mother or as the first wife? Would her father be a father or a lover? And would the wife be the husband's main wife or the "mother of the other wife"? And if the daughter had a child by her father, what relationships would everyone have? Maternal incest would also lead to complications every bit as confusing as these.

The incest taboo also forces people to look outside the family for marriage partners. Anthropologists theorize that *exogamy* was especially functional in tribal societies, because it forged alliances between tribes that otherwise might have killed each other off. Today, exogamy still extends both the bride's and the groom's social networks by building relationships with their spouse's family and friends.

Isolation and Emotional Overload. As you know, functionalists also analyze dysfunctions. The relative isolation of today's nuclear family creates one of those dysfunctions. Because they are embedded in a larger kinship network, the members of extended families can count on many people for material and emotional support. In nuclear families, in contrast, the stresses that come with crises—the loss of a job, a death, or even family quarrels—are spread among fewer people. This places greater strain on each family member, creating *emotional overload*. In addition, the relative isolation of the nuclear family makes it vulnerable to a "dark side"—incest and other forms of abuse, matters that we examine later in this chapter.

matriarchy a society in which women-as-a-group dominate men-as-a-group; authority is vested in females

egalitarian authority more or less equally divided between people or groups (in heterosexual marriage, for example, between husband and wife

The Conflict Perspective: Struggles between Husbands and Wives

Explore on MySocLab **Activity:** Domestic Life: A Battle of the Sexes?

Anyone who has been married or who has seen a marriage from the inside knows that—despite a couple's best intentions—conflict is a part of marriage. Conflict inevitably arises between two people who live intimately and who share most everything in life—from their goals and checkbooks to their bedroom and children. At some point, their desires and approaches to life clash, sometimes mildly, at other times quite harshly. Conflict among married people is so common that it is the grist of soap operas, movies, songs, and novels.

Power is the source of much conflict in marriage. Who has it? And who resents not having it? Throughout history, husbands have had more power, and wives have resented it. In the United States, as I'm sure you know, wives have gained more and more power in marriage. Do you think that one day, wives will have more power than their husbands?

You probably are saying that such a day will never come. But maybe wives have *already* reached this point. From time to time, you've seen some surprising things in this book. Now look at Figure 16.1. Based on a national sample, this figure shows who makes decisions concerning the family's finances and purchases, what to do on the weekends, and even what to watch on television. As you can see, wives now have *more* control over the family purse and make *more* of these decisions than do their husbands. These findings are such a surprise that we await confirmation by future studies.

FIGURE 16.1 Who Makes the Decisions at Home?

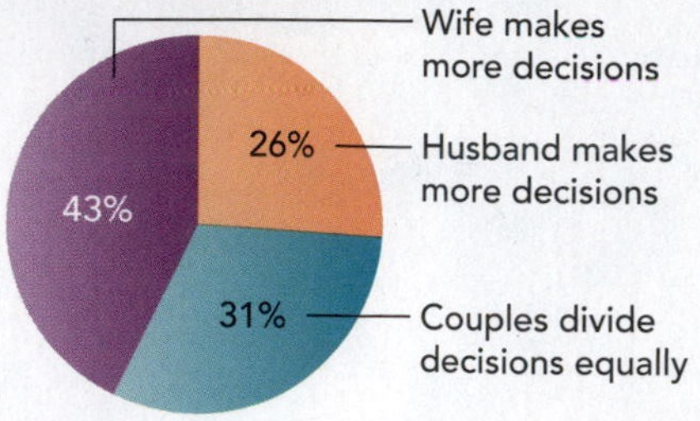

Note: Based on a nationally representative sample, with questions on who chooses weekend activities, buys things for the home, decides what to watch on television, and manages household finances.

Source: Morin and Cohn 2008.

The Symbolic Interactionist Perspective: Gender, Housework, and Child Care

Changes in Traditional Gender Orientations. This chapter's opening vignette gave you a glimpse into extreme gender roles. Apart from the specifics mentioned there, throughout the generations, housework and child care have been regarded as "women's work." As times changed and women put in more hours at paid work, men gradually did more housework and took more responsibility for the care of their children. Ever so slowly, cultural ideas shifted, with housework, care of children, and paid labor coming to be regarded as the responsibilities of both men and women. Let's examine this shift.

Paid Work and Housework. Figure 16.2 on the next page illustrates significant changes that have taken place in U.S. families. The first is startling—how wives have traded housework for paid work. They have cut down the amount of time they spend doing housework by 14.5 hours a week, while they have increased the time they spend at paid work by 14.9 hours a week. From this figure, you can see that husbands have done just the opposite. They have increased the time they spend on housework and child care, while they have dropped their paid work hours slightly.

From Figure 16.2, you can see that the total hours husbands and wives spend on housework have dropped by 9.4 hours a week. That is a lot less housework. Does this mean that today's homes are dirtier and messier than those of the past? This is one possibility. But it is likely that the explanation lies in changed technology (Bianchi et al. 2006). Our microwaves, dishwashers, washing machines, clothes dryers, and wrinkle-free clothing save hours of drudgery. The "McDonaldization" we discussed in Chapter 7, which has led to so many "fast-food" meals, also reduces the time

In Hindu marriages, the roles of husband and wife are firmly established. Neither this woman, whom I photographed in Chittoor, India, nor her husband question whether she should carry the family wash to the village pump. Women here have done this task for millennia. As India industrializes, as happened in the West, who does the wash will be questioned—and may eventually become a source of strain in marriage.

FIGURE 16.2 In Two-Paycheck Marriages, How Do Wives and Husbands Divide Their Responsibilities?

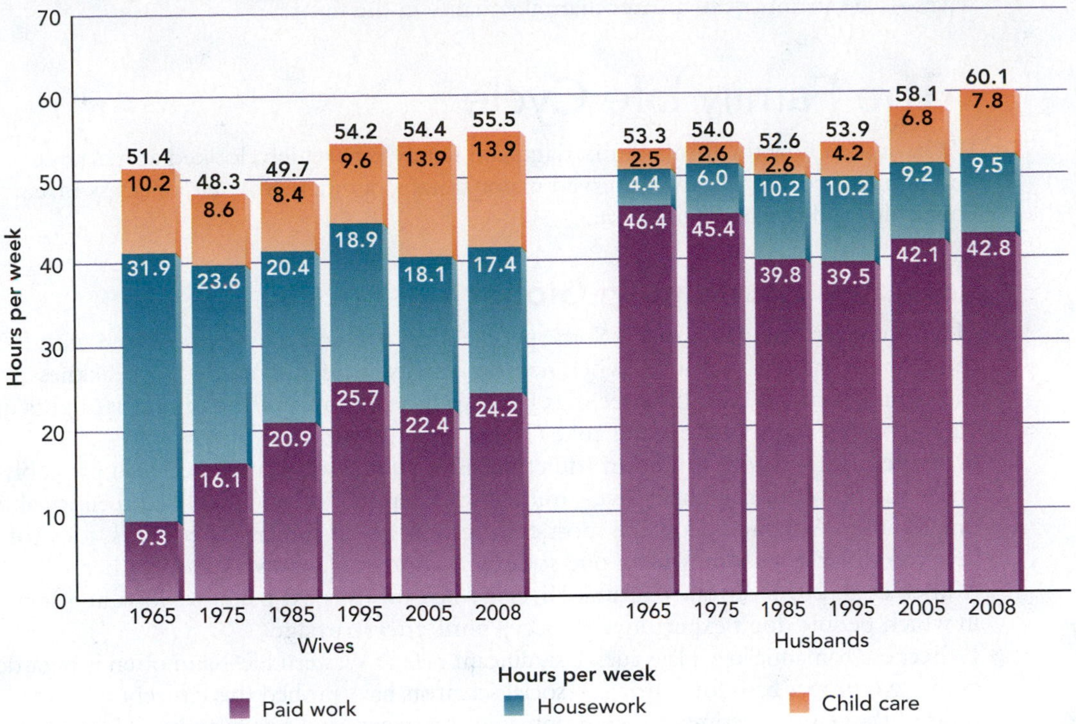

Source: By the author. Based on Bianchi 2010:Tables 1, 2.

family members spend on food preparation and cleanup. Home hygiene could well be about the same as in years past.

More Child Care. From this figure, you can see another significant change: *Both* husbands and wives are spending more time on child care. How can children be getting *more* attention from their parents than they used to? This flies in the face of our mythical past, the *Leave It to Beaver* images that color our perception of the present. We know that today's families are not leisurely strolling through life as huge paychecks flow in. So if parents are spending more time with their children, just where is that time coming from?

Read on **MySocLab**
Document: Women and Men in the Caregiving Role

The answer isn't very exciting, but researchers know what it is. Today's parents have squeezed out some of the extra time for their children by cutting down on their reading and the time they spend on preparing meals. However, the main way that parents are getting the extra time is by spending about 5 hours a week less visiting with friends and relatives (Bianchi 2010). We don't yet know the implications of this change, but if the individual family is withdrawing more into itself, it could be increasing the "emotional overload" that was just mentioned.

Total Hours. Figure 16.2 holds another surprise. You can see that *both* husbands and wives are now putting in more hours taking care of family responsibilities. However, each week husbands average 4.6 hours more than their wives. This comes to 240 hours a year, the equivalent of today's husbands spending *30 8-hour days* a year more than their wives.

A Gendered Division of Labor. Something else is evident from Figure 16.2. Look at how differently husbands and wives spend their time. Sociologists call this a *gendered division of labor*. You can see that husbands still take the primary responsibility for earning the income and wives the primary responsibility for taking care of the house and children. You have seen, however, the major shift that is taking place in this traditional gender orientation: Wives are spending more time earning the family income, while husbands are spending more time on housework and child care. In light of these trends and with changing ideas of gender—of what is considered appropriate for husbands and wives—we can anticipate greater marital equality in the future.

16.3 Summarize research on love and courtship, marriage, childbirth, child rearing, and family transitions.

The Family Life Cycle

We have seen how the forms of marriage and family vary widely, looked at marriage and family theoretically, and observed major shifts in gender. Now let's discuss love, courtship, and the family life cycle.

Love and Courtship in Global Perspective

Watch on **MySocLab** **Video:** Robert Sternberg: Triangular Theory of Love

Have you ever been "love sick"? Some people can't eat, and they are obsessed with thoughts of the one they love. When neuroscientists decided to study "love sickness," they found that it is real: Love feelings light up the same area of the brain that lights up when cocaine addicts are craving coke (Fisher et al. 2010).

Evidently, then, love can be an addiction. From your own experience, you probably know the power of **romantic love**—mutual sexual attraction and idealized feelings about one another. Although people in most cultures talk about similar experiences, ideas of love can differ dramatically from one society to another (Jankowiak and Fischer 1992; Munck et al. 2011). In the Cultural Diversity box on the next page, we look at a society in which people don't expect love to occur until *after* marriage.

Because romantic love plays such a significant role in Western life—and often is regarded as the *only* proper basis for marriage—social scientists have probed this concept with the tools of the trade: experiments, questionnaires, interviews, and observations (Hatfield et al. 2012). In a fascinating experiment, psychologists Donald Dutton and Arthur Aron discovered that fear can produce romantic love (Rubin 1985). Here's what they did.

> *About 230 feet above the Capilano River in North Vancouver, British Columbia, a rickety footbridge sways in the wind. It makes you feel like you might fall into the rocky gorge below. A more solid footbridge crosses only 10 feet above the shallow stream.*
>
> *The experimenters had an attractive woman approach men who were crossing these bridges. She told them she was studying "the effects of exposure to scenic attractions on creative expression." She showed them a picture, and they wrote down their associations. The sexual imagery in their stories showed that the men on the unsteady, frightening bridge were more sexually aroused than were the men on the solid bridge. More of these men also called the young woman afterward—supposedly to get information about the study.*

You may have noticed that this research was really about sexual attraction, not love. The point, however, is that romantic love usually begins with sexual attraction. Finding ourselves sexually attracted to someone, we spend time with that person. If we discover mutual interests, we may label our feelings "love." Apparently, then, *romantic love has two components.* The first is emotional, a feeling of sexual attraction. The second is cognitive, a label that we attach to our feelings. If we attach this label, we describe ourselves as being "in love."

Marriage

Read on **MySocLab** **Document:** What is Marriage For?

Ask Americans why they married, and they will say that they were "in love." Contrary to folklore, whatever love is, it certainly is not blind. That is, love does not hit us willy-nilly, as if Cupid had shot darts blindly into a crowd. If it did, marital patterns would be unpredictable. When we look at who marries whom, however, we can see that love follows social channels.

The Social Channels of Love and Marriage. The most highly predictable social channels are age, education, social class, and race–ethnicity. For example, a Latina with a college degree whose parents are both physicians is likely to fall in love with and marry a Latino slightly older than herself who has graduated from college. Similarly, a girl who drops out of high school

romantic love feelings of erotic attraction accompanied by an idealization of the other

Cultural Diversity around the World

East Is East and West Is West: Love and Arranged Marriage in India

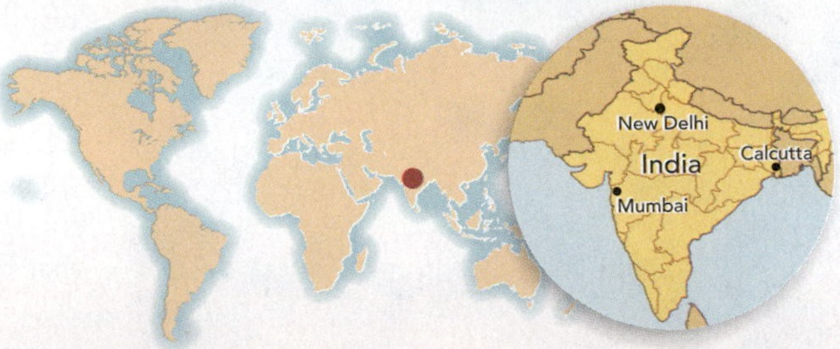

After Arun Bharat Ram returned to India with a degree from the University of Michigan, his mother announced that she wanted to find him a wife. Arun would be a good catch anywhere: 27 years old, educated, intelligent, handsome—and, not incidentally, heir to a huge fortune.

Arun's mother already had someone in mind. Manju came from a middle-class family and was a college graduate. Arun and Manju met in a coffee shop at a luxury hotel—along with both sets of parents. He found her pretty and quiet. He liked that. She was impressed that he didn't boast about his background.

After four more meetings, including one at which the two young people met by themselves, the parents asked their children whether they were willing to marry. Neither had any major objections.

The Prime Minister of India and 1,500 other guests came to the wedding.

"I didn't love him," Manju says. "But when we talked, we had a lot in common." She then adds, "But now I couldn't live without him. I've never thought of another man since I met him."

This billboard in India caught my attention. As the text indicates, even though India is industrializing, most of its people still follow traditional customs. This billboard is a sign of changing times.

Despite India's many changes, parents still arrange about 90 percent of marriages. Unlike the past, however, today's couples have veto power over their parents' selection. Another innovation is that the prospective bride and groom are allowed to talk to each other before the wedding—unheard of a generation or two ago.

Why do Indians have arranged marriages? And why does this practice persist, even among the educated and upper classes? We can also ask why the United States has such an individualistic approach to marriage.

The answers to these questions take us to two sociological principles. First, *a group's marriage practices match its values.* Individual mate selection matches U.S. values of individuality and independence, while arranged marriages match the Indian value of children deferring to parental authority. To Indians, allowing unrestricted dating would mean entrusting important matters to inexperienced young people.

Second, *a group's marriage practices match its patterns of social stratification.* Arranged marriages in India affirm caste lines by channeling marriage within the same caste. Unchaperoned dating would encourage premarital sex, which, in turn, would break down family lines. Virginity at marriage, in contrast, assures the upper castes that they know who fathered the children. Consequently, Indians socialize their children to think that parents have superior wisdom in these matters. In the United States, where family lines are less important and caste is an alien concept, the practice of young people choosing their own dating partners mirrors the relative openness of our social class system.

These different backgrounds have produced contrasting ideas of love. Americans idealize love as something mysterious, a passion that suddenly seizes an individual. Indians view love as a peaceful feeling that develops when a man and a woman are united in intimacy and share life's interests and goals. For Americans, love just "happens," while for Indians, the right conditions create love. Marriage is one of those right conditions.

The end result is this startling difference: *For Americans, love produces marriage—while for Indians, marriage produces love.*

Sources: Based on Gupta 1979; Bumiller 1992; Sprecher and Chandak 1992; Dugger 1998; Gautham 2002; Swati 2008; Harris 2013; Berger 1963/2014.

For Your Consideration

➤ What advantages do you see to the Indian approach to love and marriage? Could the Indian system work in the United States? Why or why not? Do you think that love can be created? Or does love suddenly "seize" people? What do you think love is, anyway?

Taye Diggs and Idina Menzel are an example of the most common pattern of marriages between African Americans and whites.

and whose parents are on welfare is likely to fall in love with and marry a man who comes from a background similar to hers.

Sociologists use the term **homogamy** to refer to the tendency of people who have similar characteristics to marry one another. Homogamy occurs largely as a result of *propinquity*, or spatial nearness. This is a sociological way of saying that we tend to "fall in love" with and marry someone who lives near us or someone we meet at school, church, work, or a neighborhood bar. The people with whom we associate are far from a random sample of the population, since social filters produce neighborhoods, schools, and places of worship that follow racial–ethnic and social class lines.

homogamy the tendency of people with similar characteristics to marry one another

As with all social patterns, there are exceptions. Although most married Americans choose someone of their same racial–ethnic background, 8 percent do not. Eight percent is a lot of people. With 60 million married couples in the United States, this comes to close to 5 million couples (*Statistical Abstract* 2013:Table 60).

One of the more dramatic changes in U.S. marriage is the increase in marriages between African Americans and whites. Today it is difficult to realize how norm-shattering such marriages used to be, but they were once illegal in 40 states (Staples 2008). In Mississippi, the penalty for interracial marriage was *life in prison* (Crossen 2004). Despite the risks, a few couples crossed the "color line," but it took the social upheaval of the 1960s to shatter this barrier. In 1967, the U.S. Supreme Court struck down the state laws that prohibited such marriages.

Figure 16.3 shows this change. Look at the race–ethnicity of the husbands and wives in these marriages, and you will see that here, too, Cupid's arrows don't hit

Read on **MySocLab**
Document: Breaking the Last Taboo: Interracial Marriage in America

FIGURE 16.3 Marriages between Whites and African Americans: The Race–Ethnicity of the Husbands and Wives

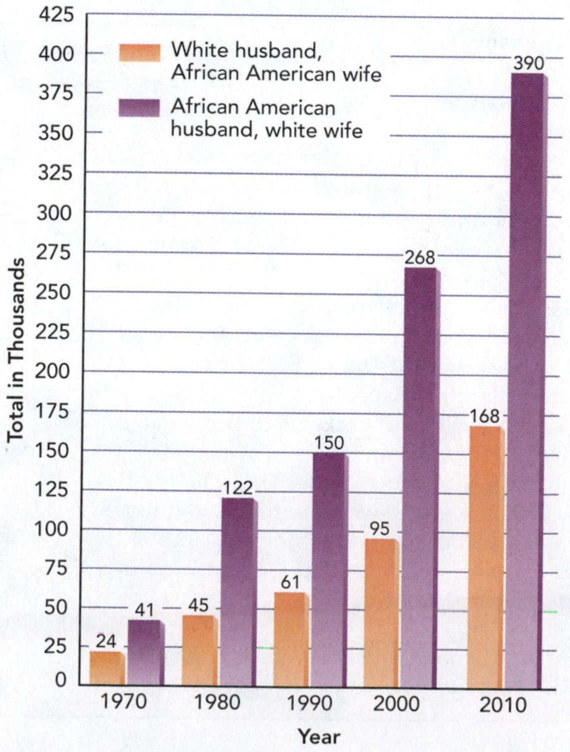

Source: By the author. *Based on Statistical Abstract of the United States* 1990:Table 53; 2013:Table 60.

random targets. Why do you think this particular pattern exists? Why do you think it is changing?

For a surprising effect of marriage—that it helps people live longer—look at the Down-to-Earth Sociology box below.

Watch on **MySocLab**
Video: Is Marriage Good for Your Health?

Down-to-Earth Sociology

Health Benefits of Marriage: Living Longer

An old joke goes like this.

JOE: Do married people really live longer?

MARY: Not really. Marriage is so boring that it just seems like it.

Jokes about marriage aside, marriage brings health benefits, and the married really do live longer than the unmarried. This has been observed since the 1800s and confirmed in study after study. Look at Figure 16.4 to see the results of recent research. The follow-up years shown on this figure began at age 18.

From this figure, you can see that marriage's greatest health benefits go to those who marry and stay married, but that getting remarried is also highly beneficial for health. Both those who remain married and those who remarry and stay married live considerably longer. Getting divorced and staying single shortens life, but even though marriage ends in divorce, it adds years to people's lives. As you can see, the worst for health is never getting marred. At each age, people who remain single all of their lives are the most likely to die.

Why does marriage help people live longer? Beyond practical matters, such as husbands and wives encouraging one another to exercise and eat regularly, the primary reason seems to be social support. The married have someone significant to help them get through the problems of everyday life. The touches, kisses, sex, reassurances, and encouragements are good for health.

FIGURE 16.4 Health Benefits of Marriage

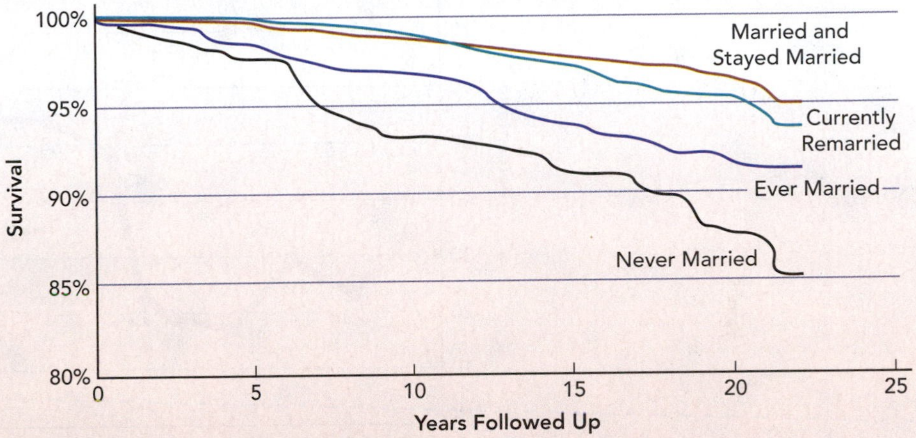

Note: Based on the University of North Carolina Alumni Heart Study, follow-up research on a cohort of 4,802 men and women.

Source: Siegler et al. 2013.

Among the health benefits of marriage is a longer life.

For Your Consideration

→ With more people staying single longer, how do you think this might affect the data shown in Figure 16.4? How about cohabitation? Singles also develop social support systems. Why do you think they fall so short when compared with the social support of marriage?

Childbirth

Ideal Family Size. The number of children that Americans consider ideal has changed over the years. You can track these changes in Figure 16.5 Note the sharp change in the 1970s. I can't specify with certainty the reason for this sudden change of wanting fewer children, but I expect that it has to do with three major events of that time: the birth control pill, the sexual revolution, and women's changed perception of work, from a temporary activity before marriage to long-term careers.

FIGURE 16.5 The Number of Children Americans Think Are Ideal

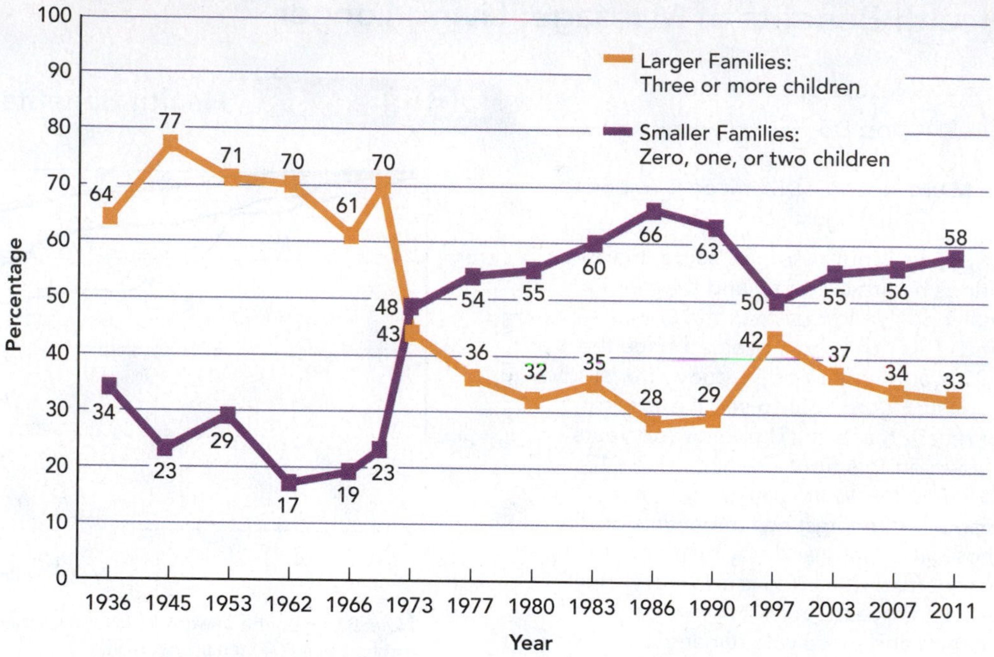

Source: Gallup Poll 2011b.

The research shows an interesting religious divide in the number of children that people want—not between Protestants and Roman Catholics, who give the same answers, but by church attendance. Those who attend services more often prefer larger families than those who attend less often. The last couple of polls reveal an unexpected change: Younger Americans (ages 18 to 34) prefer larger families than do those who are older than 34 (Gallup Poll 2011a).

If they had their way, some couples would specify not just the number of children but also their characteristics, the topic of the Sociology and the New Technology box on the next page.

Marital Satisfaction. Sociologists have found that after the birth of a child, marital satisfaction usually decreases (Twenge et al. 2003; Dew and Wilcox 2011). To understand why, recall from Chapter 6 that a dyad (two persons) provides greater intimacy than a triad (after adding a third person, interaction must be shared). In addition, the birth of a child unbalances the life that the couple has worked out. To move from the abstract to the concrete, think about the implications for marriage of coping with a fragile newborn's 24-hour-a-day needs of being fed, soothed, and diapered—while the parents have less sleep and greater expenses.

Marital happiness increases when the last child reaches age 6, when the child starts school and is away from home a lot. This happiness is short-lived, though, and takes a nosedive when the child reaches age 12 or 13. You can figure this one out—the devil years of adolescence. But those years don't last forever (although many parents think they will), and happiness increases again when the last child gets through the troubled, rebellious years (Senior 2010).

Sociology and the New Technology

What Color Eyes? How Tall? Designer Babies on the Way

You can't carry a tune, but you want your daughter to be a musical? You're short, but you want to make sure that your son is tall? You want your child to be a basketball star or a scientist?

Welcome to the world of Designer Baby Clinics, where you can put in your order. Not like fast food, of course, since it will still take the usual nine months. But you will get what you ordered.

Or at least this is the promise. A few technical details must still be worked out, but these hurdles are falling rapidly (Hanlon 2012).

The allure of designer babies is apparent. To pick superior qualities for your child—this is sort of like being able to pick a superior college. To be able to do so much good for your child!

But with this allure come moral dilemmas. Let's suppose that a couple wants a green-eyed blond girl. As Figure 16.6 shows, the technicians will fertilize several eggs, test the embryos, and plant the one(s) with the desired characteristics in a uterus. And the ones that are not used? They will be flushed down the drain. Some people find this objectionable.

Others are concerned that selecting certain characteristics represents a bias against people who have different characteristics. To order a tall designer baby, for example, is this a bias against short people?

If the bias isn't quite clear, perhaps this will help. If there is a preference for boys, a lot of female embryos will be discarded.

There is also the issue of a super race. If we can produce people who are superior physically, intellectually, and emotionally, would it be wrong to do so? Or would it be immoral *not* to do this if it were within our capacity?

Or consider this: Two deaf parents want their child to share their subculture, not to be a part of the hearing world, which they fear will drive a wedge between them and their child (Fordham 2011). Would it be moral or immoral to produce a deaf child?

Oh, the moral dilemmas our new technologies bring!

For Your Consideration

➔ What are your answers to the questions raised in this box? On what do you base your answers?

FIGURE 16.6 On the Way to Designer Babies

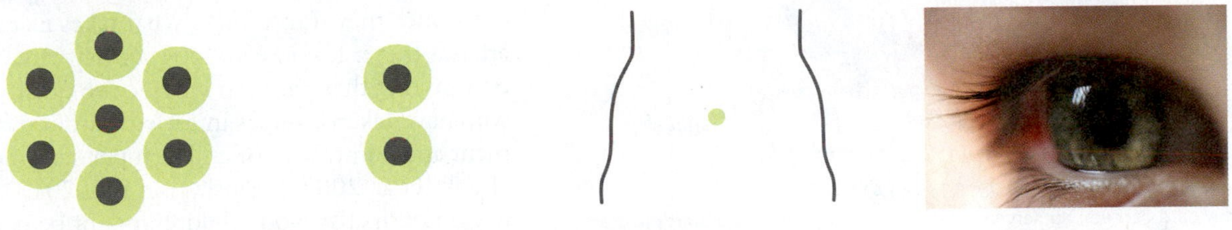

A woman's eggs are fertilized with sperm in a lab, creating several embryos.

A single cell is removed from each embryo, and then tested for biomarkers associated with females, green eyes, and blond hair.

Only embryos with the biomarkers for the required traits are placed in the woman's womb.

The procedure virtually guarantees that the child will be female and increases the probability she will have green eyes and blond hair.

Source: Adapted from Naik 2009. Reproduced with permission.

Husbands and wives have children because of biological urges and because of the satisfactions they expect. New parents bubble over with joy, saying things like "There's no feeling to compare with holding your own child in your arms. Those little hands, those tiny feet, those big eyes, that little nose, that sweet face . . ." and they gush on and on.

There really is no equivalent to parents. It is *their* child, and no one else takes such delight in the baby's first steps, its first word, and so on. Let's turn, then, to child rearing.

Child Rearing

As you saw in Figure 16.2 on page 457, today's parents—both mothers and fathers—are spending more time with their children than parents did in the 1970s and 1980s. Despite this trend, with mothers and fathers spending so many hours away from home at work, we must ask: Who's minding the kids while the parents are at work?

FIGURE 16.7 Who Takes Care of the Children While Their Mothers Are at Work?

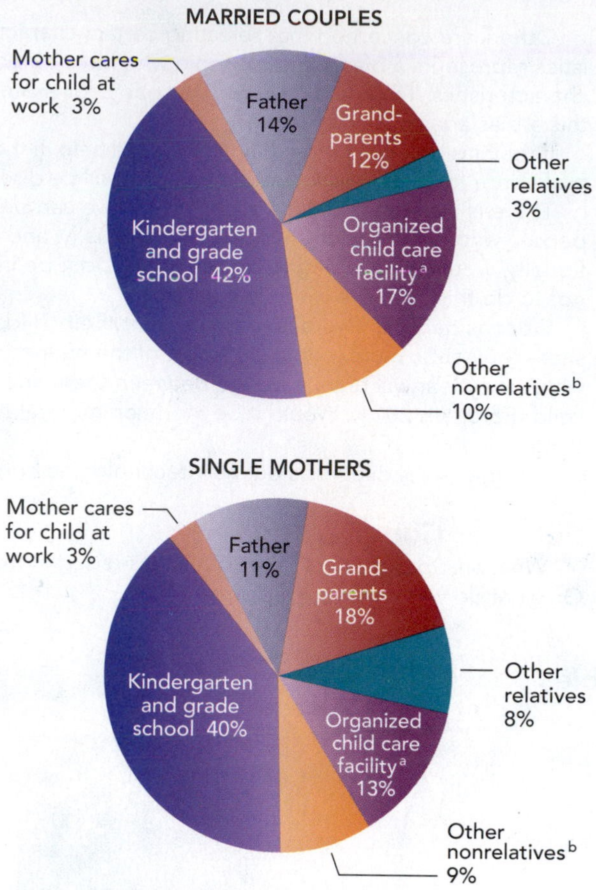

Source: *America's Children in Brief 2010*:Table FAM3A.

[a]Includes day care centers, nursery schools, preschools, and Head Start programs.

[b]Includes in-home babysitters and other nonrelatives providing care in either the child's or the provider's home.

Married Couples and Single Mothers. Figure 16.7 compares the child care arrangements of single and married mothers. As you can see, their overall arrangements are similar. A main difference, though, is that when married women are at work, the child is more likely to be under the father's care or in day care. For single mothers, grandparents and other relatives are more likely to fill in for the absent father.

Day Care. From Figure 16.7, you can see that about one of six or seven children is in day care. The broad conclusions of research on day care were reported in Chapter 3 (pages 80–81). Apparently only a minority of U.S. day care centers offer high-quality care as measured by whether they provide stimulating learning activities, emotional warmth, and attentiveness to children's needs (Bergmann 1995; Blau 2000; Belsky 2009). A primary reason for this dismal situation is the low salaries paid to day care workers, who average only about $10 an hour ("Child Care Workers" 2013).

With many parents doing shift work (evening and midnight work), some "day care" centers are open 24 hours a day. The workers brush the children's teeth, read them bedtime stories, and tuck them in. The parents pick their children up whenever they get off work, whether this is midnight or 6 A.M. (Tavernise 2012).

It is difficult for parents to judge the quality of day care, since they don't know what takes place when they are not there. If you ever look for day care, two factors best predict that children will receive quality care: staff who have taken courses in early childhood development and a low ratio of children per staff member (Belsky et al. 2007; Sosinsky and Kim 2013). If you have nagging fears that your children might be neglected or even abused, choose a center that streams live Web cam images on the Internet. While at work, you can "visit" each room of the day care center via cyberspace and monitor your toddler's activities and care.

Watch on **MySocLab** **Video:** Working Women and Childcare

Read on **MySocLab** **Document:** The Nanny Chain

Nannies. For upper-middle-class parents, nannies have become a popular alternative to day care centers. Parents love the one-on-one care. They also like the convenience of in-home care, which eliminates the need to transport the child to an unfamiliar environment, reduces the chances that the child will catch illnesses, and eliminates the hardship of parents having to take time off from work when their child becomes ill. A recurring problem, however, is tensions between the parents and the nanny: jealousy that the nanny might see the first step, hear the first word, or—worse yet—be called "mommy." There are also tensions over different discipline styles. Feelings of guilt or envy can be high if the child cries when the nanny leaves but not when the mother goes to work.

Social Class. Do you think that social class makes a difference in how people rear their children? If you answered "yes," you are right. But what difference? And why? Sociologists have found that working-class parents tend to think of children as wildflowers that develop naturally, while in the middle-class mind, children are like garden flowers that need a lot of nurturing if they are to bloom (Lareau 2002). These contrasting views make a world of difference in how people rear their children (Colarco 2011; Sherman and Harris 2012). Working-class parents are more likely to set limits for their children and then let them choose their own activities, while middle-class parents are more likely to try to push their children into activities that they think will develop their thinking and social skills.

Sociologist Melvin Kohn (1963, 1977; Kohn and Schooler 1969) also found that the type of work that parents do has an impact on how they rear their children. Because members of the working class are closely supervised on their jobs, where they are expected to follow explicit rules, their concern is less with their children's motivation and more with their outward conformity. These parents are more apt to use physical punishment—which brings about outward conformity without regard for internal attitudes. Middle-class workers, in contrast, are expected to take more initiative on the job. Consequently, middle-class parents have more concern that their children develop curiosity and self-expression. They are also more likely to withdraw privileges or affection than to use physical punishment.

Family Transitions

The later stages of family life bring their own pleasures to be savored and problems to be solved. Let's look at two transitions—children staying home longer and adults adjusting to widowhood.

Transitional Adulthood and the Not-So-Empty Nest. Adolescents, especially young men, used to leave home after finishing high school. When the last child left home at about age 17 to 19, the husband and wife were left with what was called an *empty nest*. Today's nest is not as empty as it used to be. With prolonged education and the higher cost of establishing a household, U.S. children are leaving home later. Many stay home during college, while others who strike out on their own find the cost or responsibility too great and return home. Much to their own disappointment, some even leave and return to the parents' home several times. As a result, 18 percent of all U.S. 25- to 29-year-olds are living with their parents. About 11 percent of this still-at-home group have children (U.S. Census Bureau 2012:Table A2).

This major historical change in how people become adults, which we call *transitional adulthood*, is playing out before our eyes. With the path to adulthood changing abruptly, its contours—its roadmap—are still being worked out. Although "adultolescents" enjoy the protection of home, they have to work out issues about privacy, authority, and responsibilities—items that both the children and parents thought were resolved long ago. You might want to look again at Figure 3.2 on page 88.

Widowhood. As you know, women are more likely than men to become widowed. There are two reasons for this: On average, women live longer than men, and they usually marry men older than they are. For either women or men, the death of a spouse tears at the self, clawing at identities that merged through the years. With the one who had become an essential part of the self gone, the survivor, as in adolescence, once again confronts the perplexing question "Who am I?"

The death of a spouse produces what is called the *widowhood effect*: The impact of the death is so strong that surviving spouses tend to die earlier than expected. The widowhood effect is not even across the board, however. It is stronger for men. "Excess deaths," as sociologists call them, are almost twice as high among widowed men as among widowed women (Shor et al 2012). This seems to indicate that marriage brings greater health benefits to elderly men.

Diversity in U.S. Families

16.4 Summarize research on families: African American, Latino, Asian American, Native American, one-parent, couples without children, blended, and gay and lesbian.

As we review some of the vast diversity of U.S. families, it is important to note that we are not comparing any of them to *the* American family. There is no such thing. Rather, family life varies widely throughout the United States. In several contexts, we have seen how significant social class is in our lives. Its significance will continue to be evident as we examine diversity in U.S. families.

There is no such thing as *the* African American family, any more than there is *the* Native American, Asian American, Latino, or Irish American family. Rather, each racial–ethnic group has different types of families, with the primary determinant being social class.

African American Families

Note that the heading reads African American *families*, not *the* African American family. There is no such thing as *the* African American family any more than there is *the* white family or *the* Latino family. The primary distinction is not between African Americans and other groups but between social classes (Willie and Reddick 2003). Because African Americans who are members of the upper class follow the class interests reviewed in Chapter 10—preservation of privilege and family fortune—they are especially concerned about the family background of those whom their children marry (Gatewood 1990). To them, marriage is viewed as a merger of family lines. Children of this class marry later than children of other classes.

Middle-class African American families focus on achievement and respectability. Both husband and wife are likely to work outside the home. A central concern is that their children go to college, get good jobs, and marry well—that is, marry people like themselves, respectable and hardworking, who want to get ahead in school and pursue a successful career.

African American families in poverty face all the problems that cluster around poverty (Smith-Bynum 2013). Because the men have few marketable skills and few job prospects, it is difficult for them to fulfill the cultural roles of husband and father. Consequently, these families are likely to be headed by a woman and to have a high rate of births to single women. Divorce and desertion are also more common than among other classes. Sharing scarce resources and "stretching kinship" are primary survival mechanisms. People who have helped out in hard times are considered brothers, sisters, or cousins to whom one owes obligations as though they were blood relatives. Men who are not the biological fathers of their children are given fatherhood status (Stack 1974; Nelson 2013). Sociologists use the term *fictive kin* to refer to this stretching of kinship.

Read on **MySocLab**
Document: African American Families: A Legacy of Vulnerability and Resilience

From Figure 16.8 on the next page, you can see that, compared with other groups, African American families are the least likely to be headed by married couples and the most likely to be headed by women. Because African American women tend to go farther in school than African American men, they face a *marriage squeeze*. That is, their pool of eligible partners with characteristics that match theirs has shrunk, and they are more likely than women in other racial–ethnic groups to marry men who are less educated than themselves (Smith-Bynum 2013).

Latino Families

As Figure 16.8 shows, the proportion of Latino families headed by married couples and women falls in between that of whites and Native Americans. The effects of social class on families, which I just sketched, also apply to Latinos. In addition, families differ by country of origin. Families from Mexico, for example, are more likely to be headed by a married couple than are families from Puerto Rico (*Statistical Abstract* 2013:Table 37). It is important to note that the longer that Latinos live in the United States, the more their families resemble those of middle-class Americans (Falicov 2010).

Researchers disagree on what is distinctive about Latino families (Cabrera and Bradley 2012). Some point to the strong role that Latino husbands/fathers play in family life, but others find great diversity in their involvement. Some indicate that Latino families are set apart by the Spanish language, the Roman Catholic religion, and a strong family orientation coupled with a disapproval of divorce. True in a mild, general sort of way, but this overlooks the Latino families that are Protestants, don't

machismo an emphasis on male strength and dominance

FIGURE 16.8 Family Structure: U.S. Families with Children under Age 18 Headed by Mothers, Fathers, and Both Parents

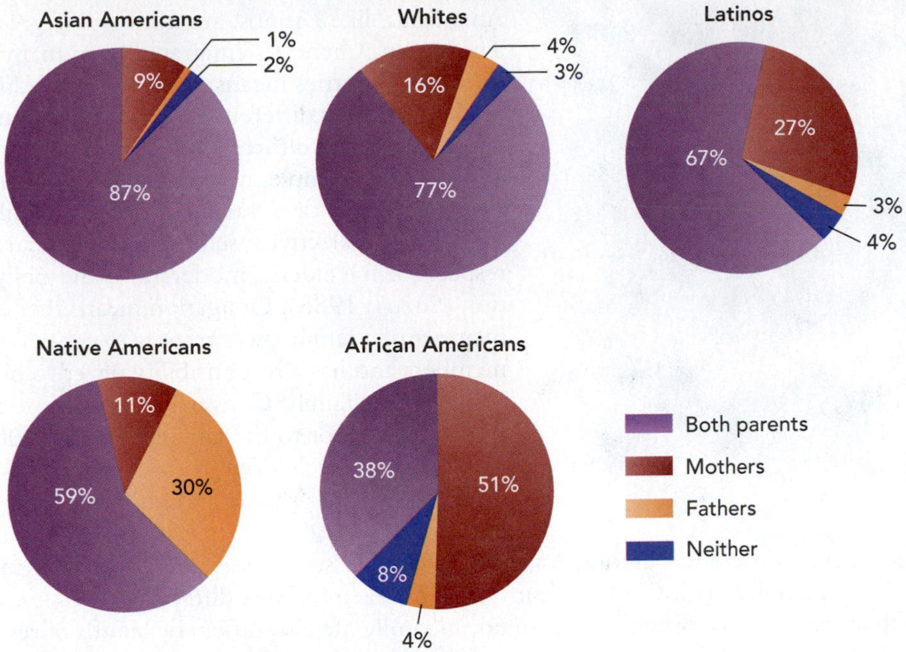

Sources: By the author. For Native Americans, Kreider and Elliott 2009:Table 1. For other groups, *Statistical Abstract of the United States* 2013:Table 69.

speak Spanish, and so on. Still others emphasize loyalty to the extended family, with an obligation to support relatives in times of need (Cauce and Domenech-Rodriguez 2002). This, too, is hardly unique to Latino families. Descriptions of Latino families used to include **machismo**—an emphasis on male strength, sexual vigor, and dominance, like that recounted in the chapter's opening vignette—but *machismo* decreases with each generation in the United States and is certainly not limited to Latinos (Hurtado et al. 1992; Wood 2001; Torres et al. 2002). Some point out that compared to their husbands, Latina wives/mothers tend to be more family centered and display more warmth and affection for their children. Maybe. But hardly unique to Latinos.

With such diversity among Latino families, you can see why researchers are unable to generalize about all or even most Latino families. However, there is a central sociological point that runs through the studies of Latino families: Social class is more important in determining family life than is either being Latino or a family's country of origin.

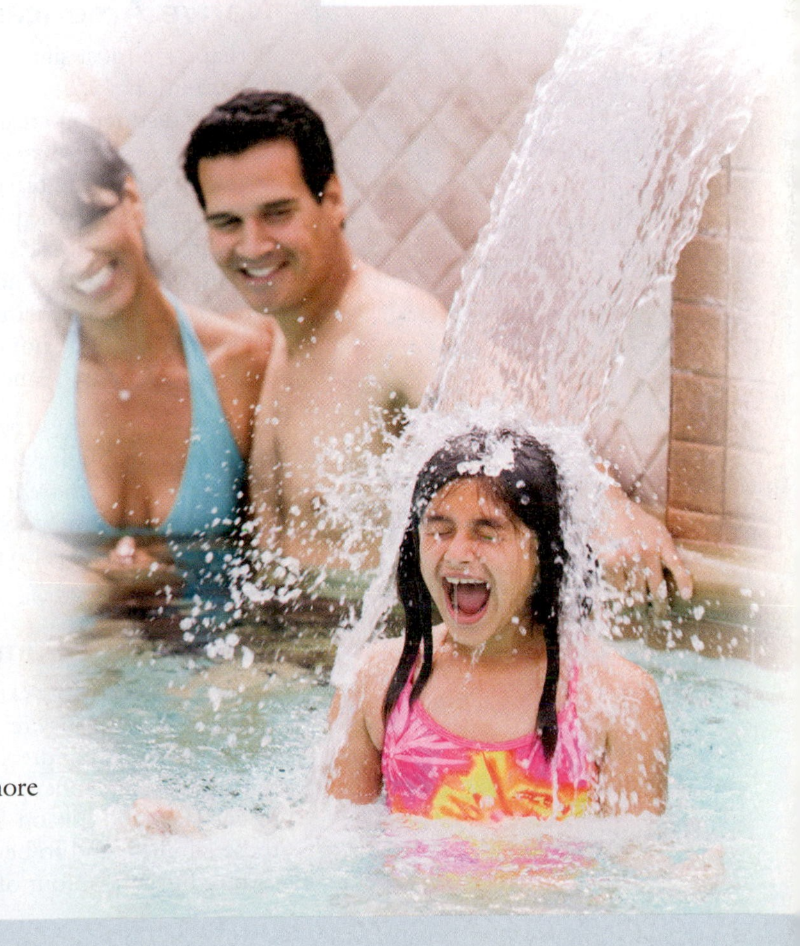

As with other groups, there is no such thing as *the* Latino family. Some Latino families speak little or no English, while others have assimilated into U.S. culture to such an extent that they no longer speak Spanish.

Asian American Families

As you can see from Figure 16.8, Asian American children are more likely than children in the other racial–ethnic groups to grow up with both parents. This significant difference is a foundation

To search for *the* Native American family would be fruitless. There are rural, urban, single-parent, extended, nuclear, rich, poor, traditional, and assimilated Native American families, to name just a few. This photo was taken on the Big Cypress Reservation near Hollywood, Florida.

for the higher educational and income attainments of Asian Americans that we discussed in Chapter 12.

In Chapter 12, I also emphasized how Asian Americans, like Latinos, are not a single group. That Asian Americans emigrated from many different countries means that their family life reflects not only differences of social class but also a variety of cultures. Families whose origin is Japan, for example, tend to retain Confucian values that provide a framework for family life: humanism, collectivity, self-discipline, hierarchy, respect for the elderly, moderation, and obligation (Suzuki 1985). Obligation means that each member of a family owes respect to other family members and has a responsibility never to bring shame to the family. Conversely, a child's success brings honor to the family (Zamiska 2004). To control their children, these parents are more likely to use shame and guilt than physical punishment.

The cultural differences among Asian Americans are so extensive, however, that many are not even familiar with Confucianism. In addition to the vast differences stemming from their countries of origin, Asian American family life also differs by length of residence in the United States. As with immigrants everywhere, recent immigrants continue their old patterns, while the family life of Asian Americans who have been here for generations reflects few of the patterns of their country of origin.

Native American Families

Perhaps the most significant issue that Native American families face is whether to follow traditional values or to assimilate into the dominant culture (Frosch 2008). This primary distinction creates vast differences among families. The traditionals speak native languages and emphasize distinctive Native American values and beliefs. Those who have assimilated into the broader culture do not.

Figure 16.8 on the previous page depicts the structure of Native American families. You can see that it is closest to that of Latinos. In general, Native American parents are permissive with their children and avoid physical punishment. Elders play a much more active role in their children's families than they do in most U.S. families: Elders, especially grandparents, not only provide child care but also teach and discipline children. Like others, Native American families differ by social class.

In Sum: From this brief review, you can see that race–ethnicity signifies little for understanding family life. Rather, social class and culture hold the keys. The more resources a family has, the more it assumes the characteristics of a middle-class nuclear family. Compared with the poor, middle-class families have fewer children and fewer unmarried mothers. They also place greater emphasis on educational achievement and deferred gratification.

One-Parent Families

An indication of how extensively U.S. families are changing is the increase in one-parent families. Look at Figure 16.9 on the next page. There you can see the decline in the percentage of U.S. children who live with two parents. Divorce is not the only reason for this fundamental change. Another is that single women who give birth are taking longer to get married (Gibson-Davis 2011). Because women head most one-parent families, these families tend to be poor. Even though most divorced women earn less than their former husbands, four of five children of divorce live with their mothers (U.S. Census

Bureau 2013:Table C3). The concerns—even alarm—that many express about one-parent families may have more to do with their poverty than with children being reared by one parent.

For a glimpse of why family structure is important, read the Down-to-Earth Sociology box on the next page.

blended family a family whose members were once part of other families

Couples without Children

While most married women give birth, about one of five do not (Livingston and Cohn 2010). This is *double* what it was thirty years ago. As you can see from Figure 16.10, childlessness varies by racial–ethnic group, with whites representing the extreme. From this figure, you can also see that, except for women with Ph.D.s, the more education women have, the less likely they are to have children.

Some couples are infertile, but most childless couples have made a *choice* to not have children—and they prefer the term *childfree* rather than *childless*. Some decide before marriage that they will never have children, often to attain a sense of freedom—to pursue a career, to travel, and to have less stress. Other couples keep postponing the time they will have their first child until either it is too late to have children or it seems too uncomfortable to add a child to their lifestyle.

With trends firmly in place—more education and careers for women, advances in contraception, legal abortion, the high cost of rearing children, and an emphasis on possessing more material things—the proportion of women who never bear children is likely to increase. Here is how one woman expressed her view:

> *I'd rather continue traveling the world, running my business, getting massages, getting pedicures and manicures, working out with my trainer, enjoying great dining experiences and enjoying life to the fullest.*

FIGURE 16.9 The Decline of Two-Parent Families

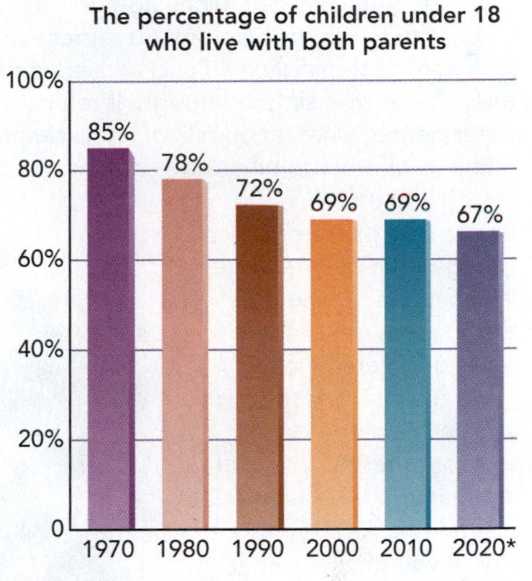

*Author's estimate.

Source: By the author. Based on *Statistical Abstract of the United States* 1995:Table 79; 2013:Table 69.

A couple summed up their reasons for choosing not to have children this way:

> *We are DINKS (Dual Incomes, No Kids). We are happily married. I am 43; my wife is 42. We have been married for almost twenty years. . . . Our investment strategy has a lot to do with our personal philosophy: "You can have kids—or you can have everything else!" (in a newsletter)*

FIGURE 16.10 What Percentage of U.S. Married Women Ages 40-44 Have Never Given Birth?

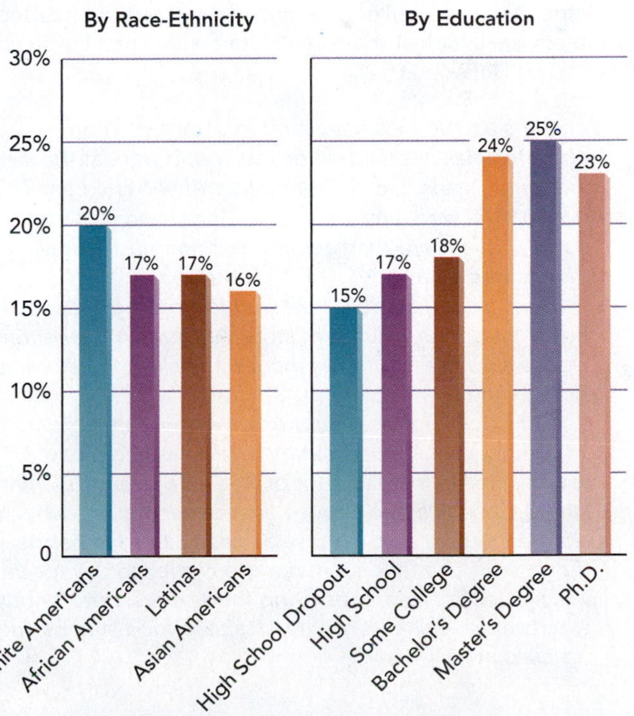

Source: By the Author. Based on Livingston and Cohn 2010.

Blended Families

The **blended family**, one whose members were once part of other families, is an increasingly important type of family in the United States. Two divorced people who marry and each bring their children into a new family unit form a blended family. With divorce common, millions of children spend some of their childhood in blended families. I've never seen a better explanation of how blended families can complicate family relationships than this description written by one of my freshman students:

> *I live with my dad. I should say that I live with my dad, my brother (whose mother and father are also my mother and father), my half sister (whose father is my dad, but whose mother is my father's last wife), and two stepbrothers and stepsisters (children of my father's current wife). My father's wife (my current stepmother, not to be confused with his second wife who, I guess, is no*

Down-to-Earth Sociology

Family Structure: Single Moms and Married Moms

Some of the terms that sociologists use seem "dry," theoretical, and unconnected to "real life." The term *family structure* ranks high among such terms. It certainly is not likely to get your juices going.

But the terms of sociology do represent "real life." Let's look at the seemingly cold and antiseptic term *family structure*. The term is simple enough. It refers to the way a family is put together, what it consists of. In its simplest form, the term refers to whether families have one or two parents and how many children are in the family. And granted recent changes in legal marriage, it also refers to whether the spouses are of the same or different sex.

At this point in the text, you've been introduced to a lot of terms. Like others that you have learned, this one packs a lot into it. And if you think about it (which I know you might or might not do), *family structure* is a short-hand way of saying a lot of relevant things. Yes—*relevant.* To see why, let's look at just one aspect of family structure—whether or not a husband-father is present. Single-parent families also consist of father-headed families, but since four of five are headed by mothers, we'll look at these. Let's start with a real-life situation (based on DeParle 2012):

Chris and Jessica have a lot in common. They are both white females in their late twenties who work at the same day care center. Each is the mother of two children. They both juggle work and child care. Chris, who is the boss, earns a little more than Jessica, but not much. They are friends who even got tattoos together.

During the workday, their worlds are almost identical. But night brings a different story. After work, they enter worlds so different, it is as though they live on opposite sides of the Grand Canyon.

Chris goes home to an attractive house in the suburbs, Jessica to a small apartment in a less desirable part of town. Chris' kids go to a lot of weekend events: swimming, karate, baseball, and Scouts. Jessica very much wants her children to take part in these activities, but she has neither the time to take them nor the money to pay for the activities. Chris bemoans rising food prices, but she buys whatever food she wants. Jessica uses food stamps and watches every penny.

What's the difference? Chris is married and lives on two paychecks. Jessica is single and lives on one paycheck.

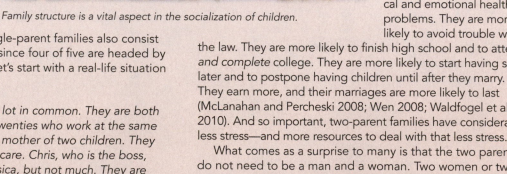

Family structure is a vital aspect in the socialization of children.

Married parents enjoy tremendous advantages that elude single parents. Just the time factor is significant. Two parents can divide up the housework, shopping, and taking the kids to after-school and weekend activities. Where does the time come from for one parent to do it all? How about supervising homework? Handling the children's inevitable bickering? Or encouraging the "constant little things" that children are involved in and for which they want their parents' attention and approval? The needs are endless, and one parent can't double her time simply by wishing it.

Does this distinction make any real difference? Yes, it certainly does. Children get a lot of benefits from living with two parents. The additional attention, encouragement, supervision, and opportunities go a long way. Children who live with two parents are less likely to have physical and emotional health problems. They are more likely to avoid trouble with the law. They are more likely to finish high school and to attend *and complete* college. They are more likely to start having sex later and to postpone having children until after they marry. They earn more, and their marriages are more likely to last (McLanahan and Percheski 2008; Wen 2008; Waldfogel et al. 2010). And so important, two-parent families have considerably less stress—and more resources to deal with that less stress.

What comes as a surprise to many is that the two parents do not need to be a man and a woman. Two women or two men who rear children together apparently do as well as a husband and wife (Farr et al. 2010).

As you probably noticed, the distinction is not only whether children have one or two parents. At least as significant is family income. Higher and lower incomes create huge divisions, offering lifestyles of opportunity for some while forcing others into tiny corners of highly limited choices.

You can see, then, why sociologists are so interested in *family structure*—and why this term refers to "real life."

For Your Consideration

→ What is your family structure? Has your family structure changed over your lifetime? What effects has family structure had on your life?

longer my stepmother) is pregnant, and soon we all will have a new brother or sister. Or will it be a half brother or half sister?

If you can't figure this out, I don't blame you. I have trouble myself. It gets very complicated around Christmas. Should we all stay together? Split up and go to several other homes? Who do we buy gifts for, anyway?

Gay and Lesbian Families

Watch on **MySocLab Video:** Thinking Like a Sociologist: Same-Sex Marriage

Most gay and lesbian couples lack legal rights to support their relationship. As I write this, 13 states allow same-sex marriages, 35 states prohibit them, and the laws of two states are ambiguous ("U.S. Supreme Court. . ." 2013). A handful of U.S. states allow people of the same sex to marry, but 41 states have laws that prohibit same-sex marriages. The U.S. Supreme Court ruled in 2013 that the federal government cannot deny benefits to same-sex married couples but did not rule on the constitutionality of laws that ban same-sex marriage.

What are same-sex relationships like? Researchers have found that the main struggles of same-sex couples are housework, money, careers, problems with relatives, and sexual adjustment (Blumstein and Schwartz 1985). If these sound familiar, they should, as they are the same problems that heterosexual couples face. A major difference is that many same-sex couples face a stigma, sometimes accompanied by discrimination. As you can imagine, this complicates a couple's relationship.

Just as with heterosexual couples, for same-sex couples, marriage is a big step. No longer is the relationship a casual thing. Instead, it becomes immersed in legal ties and obligations. Like others, gay and lesbian couples who marry hope that marriage will make their relationship even more solid. One problem that same-sex couples face is social acceptance, including acceptance by their families of origin. Researchers have found that after marriage, most families of origin are more accepting of the couple. Surprisingly, though, in some instances, the marriage brings less acceptance (Ocobock 2013). Apparently, some disapproving relatives had told themselves that their son, daughter, nephew, or niece was not in a sexual relationship with "the friend"—even though the couple had been living together for years. When the couple married, the relatives could no longer keep up this pretense, and the relationship with the family of origin fell apart.

As with heterosexual couples, same-sex relationships also sour—and for all the same reasons: disagreements about sex, how to spend money, how to rear children, romantic triangles, and so on. Since about 30 percent of lesbian couples and 17 percent of gay couples are rearing children, breakups bring the usual problems of custody and visitation (Gartrell et al. 2011).

Except for the sex of the individuals, same-sex and heterosexual relationships are quite similar. There is no "exotic difference" that some people expect to exist. Major differences center on social acceptance and discrimination.

After years of struggle, including numerous court cases and lobbying of legislatures, the U.S. Supreme Court ruled that federal benefits apply equally to gay couples.

Adoption by Gay and Lesbian Couples.

Adoption by same-sex couples has been a hot-button issue across the United States. A fear of heterosexuals is that children reared by same-sex parents will be pressured into becoming homosexuals (Lewin 2009). Researchers have compared the children adopted by heterosexual and gay and lesbian couples. The results: The children reared by same-sex parents have about the same adjustment as children reared by heterosexual parents (Gelderen et al. 2012). Their children are not more likely to have a gay or lesbian sexual orientation (Farr et al. 2010; Tasker 2010).

Sociologist Paul Amato (2012) points out that these studies have statistical flaws that make them unusable for discovering differences in the children's adjustment. The one study that passes statistical standards shows that children reared by gay and lesbian parents are slightly less well adjusted. He adds that this finding is not clear, because parents of many of these children were divorced, and children of divorce show slightly worse emotional adjustment. Regardless, he says, we would not deny adoption to heterosexual couples who had divorced because the children of divorced parents do slightly less well. Future research in this area will be interesting—and destined to land in the midst of controversy.

Why do gay and lesbian couples want to adopt children? When anthropologist Ellen Lewin (2009) interviewed homosexual couples who had adopted, she found the same reasons that you would expect of heterosexual couples: to establish a family, love of children, wanting to give parentless children a home, to feel more adult, and to give meaning to one's life.

16.5 Discuss changes in the timetable of family life, cohabitation, and elder care.

Trends in U.S. Families

As is apparent from our discussion, marriage and family life in the United States are undergoing fundamental change. Let's look at some of the other major trends.

The Changing Timetable of Family Life: Marriage and Childbirth

Figure 16.11 on the next page illustrates a profound change in U.S. marriage. As you can see, the average age of first-time brides and grooms declined from 1890 to about 1950. In 1890, the typical first-time bride was 22, but by 1950, she had just left her

FIGURE 16.11 When Do Americans Marry? The Changing Age at First Marriage

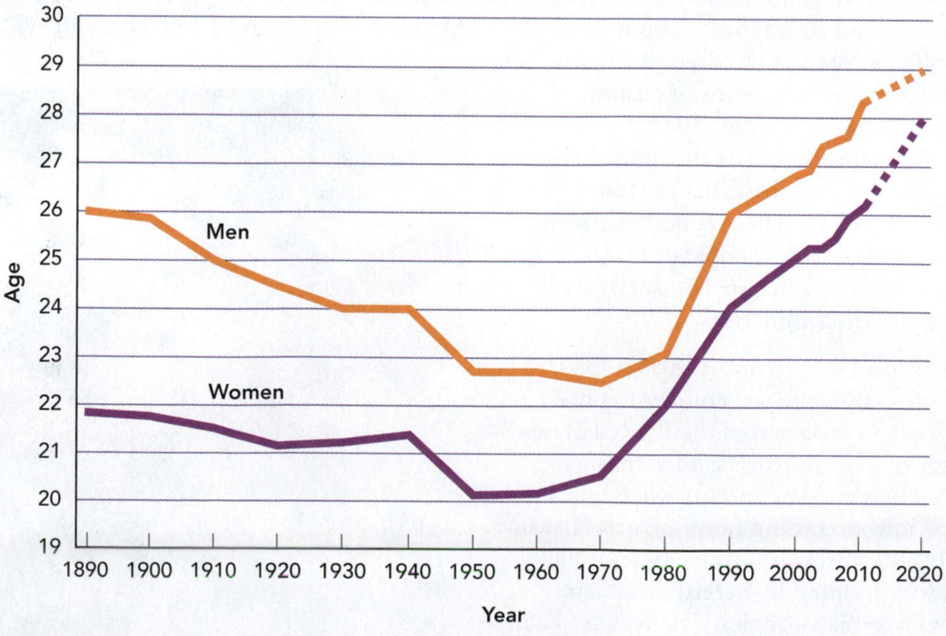

Note: This is the median age at first marriage. The broken lines indicate the author's estimate.

Sources: By the author. Based on U.S. Census Bureau 2010; Elliott et al. 2012.

cohabitation unmarried couples living together in a sexual relationship

FIGURE 16.12 Americans Ages 20–24 Who Have Married*

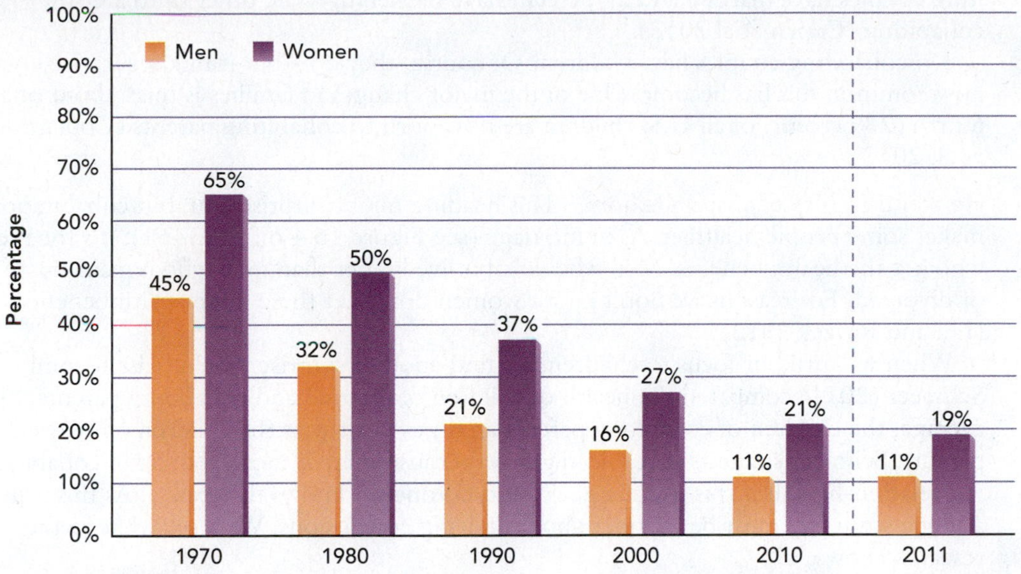

*Includes widowed and divorced.

Source: By the author. Based on *Statistical Abstract of the United States* 1993:Table 60; 2002: Table 48; 2012:Table 57; 2013:Table 57.

teens. For about twenty years, there was little change. Then in 1970, the average age took a sharp turn upward, and *today's average first-time bride and groom are older than at any other time in U.S. history.*

Since postponing marriage is today's norm, it may surprise you to learn that *most* U.S. women used to marry before they turned 24. To see this remarkable change, look at Figure 16.12 on the next page. The percentage of women between 20 and 24 who are married is now *less than a third* of what it was in 1970. For men, it is *less than a fourth.* Just as couples are postponing marriage, so they are putting off having children. Today's average U.S. woman now has her first child at age 25, the highest age in U.S. history (Mathews and Hamilton 2009).

Why have these changes occurred? The primary reason is cohabitation. Although Americans have postponed the age at which they first marry, they have *not* postponed the age at which they first set up housekeeping with someone of the opposite sex. Let's look at this trend.

Cohabitation

To see one of the most remarkable trends in the United States, look at Figure 16.13. This figure shows the remarkable increase in **cohabitation**, adults living together in a sexual relationship without being married. I know of no other social trend that has risen this steeply and consistently. From a furtive activity, cohabitation has moved into the mainstream. Today, somewhere between one-half and two-thirds of couples have cohabited before their marriage (Huang et al. 2011; Copen et al 2013).

Cohabitation and Marriage: The Essential Difference. The essential difference between cohabitation and marriage is *commitment.* In marriage, the assumption is permanence; in cohabitation, couples agree to remain together for "as long as it works out." For marriage, individuals make public vows that legally bind them as a couple; for cohabitation, they simply move in together. Marriage requires a judge to authorize its termination, but if a cohabiting relationship sours, the couple separates, telling friends and family that "it didn't work out."

FIGURE 16.13 Cohabitation in the United States

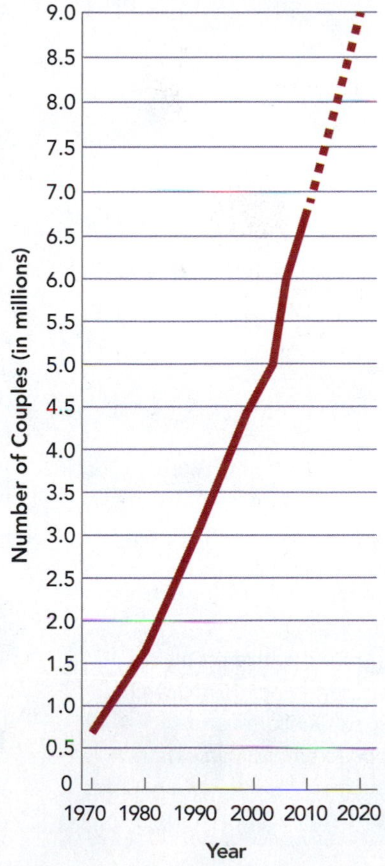

Note: Broken line indicates author's estimate

Source: By the author. Based on U.S. Census Bureau 2007 and *Statistical Abstract of the United States* 1995:Table 60; 2013:Table 63.

After Cohabitation. Sociologists have studied a national sample of people who cohabit. What happens to their relationship? Within three years, 40 percent of cohabiting couples have married and 27 percent have broken up. The other third are still cohabiting (Copen et al 2013).

Do cohabiting couples have children? Of course, they do—but it might surprise you how common this has become. One of the major changes in families is this: About one-fourth (23 percent) of all U.S. children are now born to cohabiting parents (Copen et al. 2013).

Health Benefits of Cohabitation. This heading might surprise you, but cohabitation makes some people healthier. As in marriage (see Figure 16.4 on page 461), it's the men who get the health benefits. Men who cohabit live longer than men who remain single or divorced. For reasons we don't know, women don't get these same health benefits (Liu and Reczek 2012).

When we turn our focus to children, we find another surprise. Sociologist Kammi Schmeer (2011) compared the health of children of married and cohabiting parents. On average, the children of cohabiting parents aren't as healthy as the children of married parents. Schmeer suggests that this might be because there is more conflict in cohabiting relationships. But this is just a guess, and no one yet knows the reason. As this is just a single study, we must be cautious about drawing conclusions. We'll see what further research shows.

Does Cohabitation Make Marriage Stronger? Are couples who live together before marriage less likely to divorce than couples who did not cohabit before marriage? It would seem that cohabitation would make marriage stronger. Cohabiting couples have the chance to work out many real-life problems before marriage—and they marry only after sharing these experiences. A few years ago, researchers found that couples who cohabited before marriage were *more* likely to divorce (Osborne et al. 2007; Lichter and Qian 2008). Now that cohabitation is more common, these initial findings have changed. The latest research shows that of the recently married, the divorce rate of those who did and did not cohabit before marriage is about the same (Manning and Cohen 2011). If this finding holds, we can conclude that cohabitation neither weakens nor strengthens marriage.

The "Sandwich Generation" and Elder Care

The "sandwich generation" refers to people who find themselves sandwiched between and responsible for two other generations, their children and their own aging parents. Typically between the ages of 40 and 55, these people find themselves pulled in two directions. Many feel overwhelmed as these competing responsibilities collide. Some are plagued with guilt and anger because they can be in only one place at a time and are left with little time to pursue personal interests—or just to "get away from it all." As during the child-rearing years, women provide more emotional support than men to both grown children and aging parents (Parker and Patten 2013).

With people living longer, this issue is likely to become increasingly urgent.

16.6 Summarize problems in measuring divorce, research findings on children and grandchildren of divorce, fathers' contact after divorce, ex-spouses, and remarriage.

Divorce and Remarriage

The topic of family life would not be complete without considering divorce. Let's first try to determine how much divorce there is.

Watch on **MySocLab** **Video:** Thinking Like a Sociologist: Marriage, Divorce, and Families in the U.S.

Ways of Measuring Divorce

You probably have heard that the U.S. divorce rate is 50 percent, a figure that is popular with reporters. The statistic is true in the sense that each year about half as many divorces are granted as there are marriages performed. The totals are about 2 million marriages and 1 million divorces (*Statistical Abstract* 2013:Table 135).

What is wrong, then, with saying that the divorce rate is about 50 percent? Think about it for a moment. Why should we compare the number of divorces and marriages that take place during the same year? The couples who divorced do not—with rare exceptions—come from the group that married that year. The one number has *nothing* to do with the other, so in no way do these two statistics reveal the divorce rate.

What figures should we compare, then? Couples who divorce come from the entire group of married people in the country. Since the United States has 60,000,000 married couples, and about 1 million of them get divorced in a year, the divorce rate for any given year is less than 2 percent. A couple's chances of still being married at the end of a year are over 98 percent—not bad odds—and certainly much better odds than the mass media would have us believe. As the Social Map on the next page shows, the "odds"—if we want to call them that—depend on where you live.

Over time, of course, each year's small percentage adds up. A third way of measuring divorce, then, is to ask, "Of all U.S. adults, what percentage are divorced?" Figure 16.15 on the next page answers this question. You can see how divorce has increased over the years and how race–ethnicity makes a difference for the likelihood that couples will divorce.

Figure 16.15 shows us the percentage of Americans who are currently divorced, but we get yet another answer if we ask the question, "What percentage of Americans have ever been divorced?" This percentage increases with each age group, peaking when people reach their 50s ("Marital History . . ." 2004). Overall, about 43 to 46 percent of marriages end in divorce (Amato 2010), so a divorce rate of 50 percent is actually fairly accurate.

National statistics are fine, but you probably want to know if sociologists have found anything that will tell you about *your* chances of divorce. This is the topic of the Down-to-Earth Sociology box on page 477.

S. Harris
" I NOW PRONOUNCE YOU SECOND HUSBAND AND FOURTH WIFE."

This fanciful depiction of marital trends may not be too far off the mark.

Divorce and Intermarriage

It is "common knowledge" that people who marry outside their racial–ethnic group have a higher divorce rate. This is true in general, but it is not quite this simple (Wang 2012). Researchers have found that it depends on "who marries whom." Marriages between African American men and white women are the most likely to break up. Their rate is much higher than the national average. For marriages between Latinos and whites, the divorce rate is less than that of African American men and white women but still higher than the U.S. average.

The researchers also came up with a major surprise: Some mixed marriages, as they are called, have a *lower* divorce rate than the U.S. average. The marriages that are more durable than the national average are those between Asian Americans and whites and those in which the husband is white and the wife is African American. Why these marriages are stronger is not known at present.

Children of Divorce

Emotional Problems. Children whose parents divorce are more likely than children reared by both parents to experience emotional problems, both during childhood and after they grow up (Amato and Sobolewski 2001; Weitoft et al. 2003). They are also more likely to become juvenile delinquents (Wallerstein et al. 2001) and less likely to complete high school, to attend college, or to graduate from college (McLanahan and Schwartz 2002). Finally, the children of divorce are themselves more likely to divorce, perpetuating a marriage–divorce cycle (Cui and Fincham 2010).

Read on **MySocLab**
Document: Life Without Father: What Happens to the Children?

FIGURE 16.14 The "Where" of U.S. Divorce

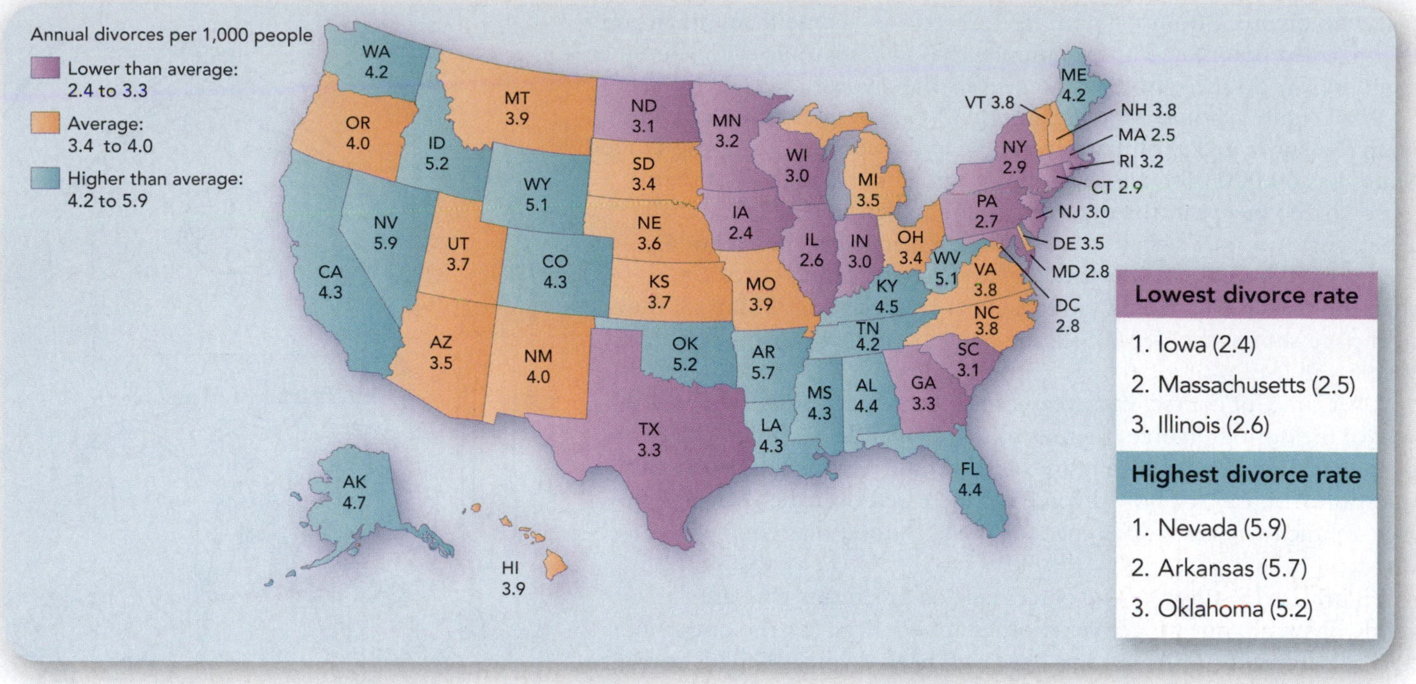

Source: By the author. Based on *Statistical Abstract of the United States* 1995:Table 149; 2002:Table 111; 2013:Table 134.

Note: Data for Indiana and Louisiana, based on the earlier editions in the source, have been decreased by the average decrease in U.S. divorce.

FIGURE 16.15 The Increase in Divorce

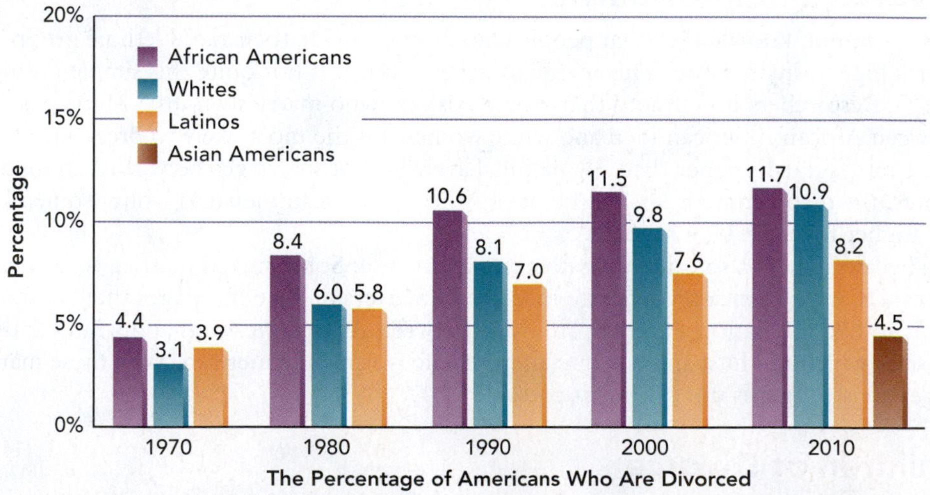

Note: This figure shows the percentage of those who are divorced and have not remarried, not the percentage of those who have ever divorced. Only these racial–ethnic groups are listed in the source. The source only recently added data on Asian Americans.

Source: By the author. Based on *Statistical Abstract of the United States* 1995:Table 58; 2013:Table 56.

Down-to-Earth Sociology

"What Are *Your* Chances of Getting Divorced?"

As you have seen, over a lifetime, about half of all marriages fail. If you have that 50 percent figure dancing in your head while you are getting married, you might as well make sure that you have an escape hatch open even while you're saying "I do."

Not every group carries the same risk of divorce. For some, the risk is much higher; for others, much lower. Let's look at some factors that reduce people's risk. As Table 16.2 shows, sociologists have worked out percentages that you might find useful. As you can see, people who go to college, participate in a religion, wait until marriage before having children, and earn higher incomes have a much better chance that their marriages will last. You can also see that having parents who did not divorce is significant. If you reverse these factors, you will see how the likelihood of divorce increases for people who have a baby before they marry, who marry in their teens, and so on. It is important to note, however, that these factors reduce the risk of divorce for *groups* of people, not for any particular individual.

Divorces are often messy. To settle the question of who gets the house, a couple in Cambodia sawed their house in half.

Other factors increase the risk for divorce, but sociologists have not computed percentages for them. Here is one that might strike you as strange: Divorce is higher among couples whose firstborn child is a girl (Ananat and Michaels 2007; Dahl and Moretti 2008). The reason is probably that men prefer sons, and if the firstborn is a boy, the father is more likely to stick around (Gallup Poll 2011b). A second factor is more obvious: The more co-workers you have who are of the opposite sex, the more likely you are to get divorced (McKinnish 2007). (I'm sure you can figure out why.) Another factor is marrying someone of a different race–ethnicity, which leads to more incompatible backgrounds. (But page 475 gives exceptions.) Another factor that no one knows the reason for is working with people who are recently divorced (Aberg 2003). It could be that divorced people are more likely to "hit on" their fellow workers—and human nature being what it is. . . .

For Your Consideration

➔ Why do you think that people who go to college have a lower risk of divorce? How would you explain the other factors shown in Table 16.2 or discussed in this box?

➔ Why can't you figure your own chances of divorce by starting with some percentage (say 14 percent less likelihood of divorce if your parents are not divorced, another 13 percent for going to college, and so on)? To better understand this, you might want to read the section on the misuse of statistics on page 482.

TABLE 16.2 What Reduces the Risk of Divorce?

Factors That Reduce People's Chances of Divorce	How Much Does This Decrease the Risk of Divorce?
Some college (vs. high school dropout)	–13%
Affiliated with a religion (vs. none)	–14%
Parents not divorced	–14%
Age 25 or over at marriage (vs. under 18)	–24%
Having a baby 7 months or longer after marriage (vs. before marriage)	–24%
Annual income over $25,000 (vs. under $25,000)	–30%

Note: These percentages apply to the first ten years of marriage.

Source: Whitehead and Popenoe 2004; Copen et al. 2012.

It is difficult to capture the anguish of the children of divorce, but when I read these lines by the fourth-grader who drew these two pictures, my heart was touched:

Me alone in the park . . .
All alone in the park.
My Dad and Mom are divorced
that's why I'm all alone.

This is me in the picture with my son.
We are taking a walk in the park.
I will never be like my father.
I will never divorce my wife and kid.

Is the greater maladjustment of the children of divorce a serious problem? This question initiated a lively debate between two psychologists. Judith Wallerstein claims that divorce scars children, making them depressed and leaving them with insecurities that follow them into adulthood (Wallerstein et al. 2001). Mavis Hetherington replies that 75 to 80 percent of children of divorce function as well as children who are reared by both of their parents (Hetherington and Kelly 2003).

Without meaning to weigh in on either side of this debate, it doesn't seem to be a simple case of the glass being half empty or half full. If 75 to 80 percent of children of divorce don't suffer long-term harm, this leaves one-fourth to one-fifth who do. Any way you look at it, one-fourth or one-fifth of a million children *each year* is a lot of kids who are having a lot of problems.

What helps children adjust to divorce? The children who feel close to both parents make the best adjustment, and those who don't feel close to either parent make the worst adjustment (Richardson and McCabe 2001). Children have an especially difficult time when one parent tries to undermine the other. These children are more likely to be depressed and insecure—even after they are grown up (Ben-Ami and Baker 2012). Children adjust well if they experience little conflict, feel loved, live with a parent who is making a good adjustment, and have consistent routines. It also helps if their family has adequate money to meet its needs. Children also adjust better if a second adult can be counted on for support (Hayashi and Strickland 1998). Urie Bronfenbrenner (1992) says this person is like the third leg of a stool, giving stability to the smaller family unit. Any adult can be the third leg, he says—a relative, friend, or even a former mother-in-law—but the most powerful stabilizing third leg is the father, the ex-husband. (For children living with their father, it is the mother, of course.)

Perpetuating Divorce. When the children of divorce grow up and marry, they are more likely to divorce than are adults who grew up in intact families. Have researchers found any factors that increase the chances that the children of divorce will have successful marriages? Actually, they have. Children of divorce are more likely to have a lasting marriage if they marry someone whose parents did not divorce. These marriages have more trust and less conflict. If both husband and wife come from broken families, however, it is not good news. Those marriages tend to have less trust and more conflict, leading to a higher chance of divorce (Wolfinger 2003).

Grandchildren of Divorce

Paul Amato and Jacob Cheadle (2005), the first sociologists to study the grandchildren of couples who had divorced, found that the effects of divorce continue across generations. Using a national sample, they compared grandchildren—those whose grandparents had divorced with those whose grandparents had not divorced. Their findings are astounding. The grandchildren of divorce have weaker ties to their parents, don't go as far in school, and don't get along as well with their spouses. As these researchers put it, when parents divorce, the consequences ripple through the lives of children who are not yet born.

Fathers' Contact with Children after Divorce

With most children living with their mothers after divorce, how often do fathers see their children? As you can see from Table 16.3, researchers have found four main patterns. The most common pattern is for fathers to see their children frequently after the divorce, and to keep doing so. But as you can see, a similar number of fathers have little contact with their children both right after the divorce and in the following years.

Which fathers are more likely to see and talk often to their children? It is men who were married to the mothers of the children, especially those who are older, more educated, and have higher incomes. In contrast, men who were cohabiting with the mothers, as well as younger, less educated men with lower incomes, tend to have less contact with their children. If his former wife marries, the father tends to see his children less (Berger et al. 2012).

TABLE 16.3 Fathers' Contact with Their Children after Divorce

Frequent[1]	Minimal[2]	Decrease[3]	Increase[4]
38%	32%	23%	8%

[1]Maintains contact once a week or more through the years.
[2]Little contact after the divorce, maybe 2 to 6 times a year.
[3]Has frequent contact after the divorce but decreases it through the years.
[4]Has little contact after the divorce but increases it through the years. Sometimes called the "divorce activated" father.

Source: By the author: Based on Cheadle et al. 2010.

The Ex-Spouses

Anger, depression, and anxiety are common feelings at divorce. But so is relief. Women are more likely than men to feel that divorce is giving them a "new chance" in life. A few couples manage to remain friends through it all—but they are the exception. The spouse who initiates the divorce usually gets over it sooner (Kelly 1992; Wang and Amato 2000) and remarries sooner (Sweeney 2002).

Divorce does not necessarily mean the end of a couple's relationship. Many divorced couples maintain contact because of their children. For others, the *continuities*, as sociologists call them, represent lingering attachments (Vaughan 1985; Masheter 1991; author's file 2005). The former husband may help his former wife paint a room or move furniture; she may invite him over for a meal or to watch television. They might even go to dinner or to see a movie together. Some couples even continue to make love after they divorce.

FIGURE 16.16 The Marital History of U.S. Brides and Grooms

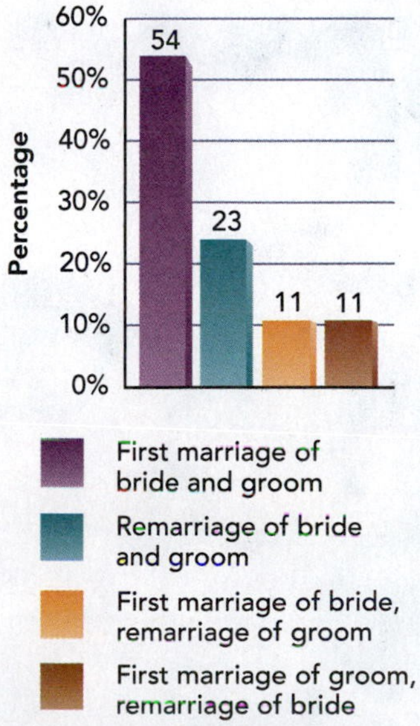

Source: By the author. Based on *Statistical Abstract of the United States* 2000: Table 145. Table dropped in later editions.

Remarriage

Remarriage is now so common that one-fourth (24 percent) of married couples are on their second (or more) marriage (Elliott and Lewis 2010). As you can see in Figure 16.16, divorced people are as likely to marry other divorced people as someone who has not been married before. How do remarriages work out? The divorce rate of remarried people *without* children is the same as that of first marriages. For those who bring children into a new marriage, however, marriage and family life are more complicated and stressful, and these couples are more likely to divorce (MacDonald and DeMaris 1995). A lack of clear norms may also undermine these marriages (Coleman et al. 2000). As sociologist Andrew Cherlin (1989) noted, we lack satisfactory names for stepmothers, stepfathers, stepbrothers, stepsisters, stepaunts, stepuncles, stepcousins, and stepgrandparents. Not only are these awkward terms to use, but they also represent ill-defined relationships.

16.7 Summarize the dark and bright sides of family life.

Two Sides of Family Life

Let's first look at situations in which marriage and family have gone seriously wrong and then try to answer the question of what makes marriage work.

Explore on **MySocLab**
Activity: Violence over the Life Course

The Dark Side of Family Life: Battering, Child Abuse, Marital Rape, and Incest

The dark side of family life involves events that people would rather keep in the dark. We will look at spouse battering, child abuse, rape, and incest.

Spouse Battering. From his own research and his review of the research of others, sociologist Murray Straus (2011) concludes that wives attack their husbands as often as husbands attack their wives. Gender equality may exist in *initiating* marital violence, but it certainly vanishes when it comes to the *effects* of violence. As you know, women are much more likely to be injured. You also know that the primary reason is that most husbands are bigger and stronger than their wives, putting women at a physical disadvantage in this literal battle of the sexes.

Gender equality in initiating violence goes against the dominant idea of our society, which generally lays the blame at the feet of men. This is another of the surprising findings in sociology. And it has serious implications: If we want to curb violence, we should *not* concentrate on men but, instead, on both men and women. The basic sociological question, then, is how to socialize *both* males and females to handle frustration and disagreements without resorting to violence. We do not yet have this answer.

Child Abuse.

I answered an ad about a lakeside house in a middle-class neighborhood that was for sale by owner. As the woman showed me through her immaculate house, I was surprised to see a plywood box in the youngest child's bedroom. About 3 feet high, 3 feet wide, and 6 feet long, the box was perforated with holes and had a little door with a padlock. Curious, I asked what it was. The woman replied matter-of-factly that her son had a behavior problem, and this was where they locked him for "time out." She added that other times, they would tie him to a float, attach a line to the dock, and put him in the lake.

I left as soon as I could. With thoughts of a terrorized child filling my head, I called the state child abuse hotline.

Wives and husbands are equally as likely to initiate violence, but unlike this photo, wives are more likely to be injured.

As you can tell, what I saw upset me. Most of us are bothered by child abuse—helpless children being victimized by their parents and other adults who are supposed to love, protect, and nurture them. The most gruesome of these cases make the evening news: The 4-year-old girl who was beaten and raped by her mother's boyfriend, passed into a coma, and three days later passed out of this life; the 6- to 10-year-old children whose stepfather videotaped them engaging in sex acts. Unlike these cases, which made headlines in my area, most child abuse is never brought to our attention: the children who live in filth, who are neglected—left alone for hours or even days at a time—or who are beaten with extension cords—cases like the little boy I learned about when I went house hunting.

Child abuse is extensive. Each year, U.S. authorities receive about 2 million reports of children being abused or neglected. Over 3 million children are involved in these reports. After investigating, authorities find that that about 750,000 of the children have been abused or neglected (*Statistical Abstract* 2013:Table 353). The excuses that parents make are incredible.

Of those I have read, the most fantastic is what a mother said to a Manhattan judge: "I slipped in a moment of anger, and my hands accidentally wrapped around my daughter's windpipe" (LeDuff 2003).

incest sexual relations between specified relatives, such as brothers and sisters or parents and children

Marital or Intimacy Rape. Marital rape seems to be more common than is usually supposed, but we have no national totals. Sociologist Diana Russell (1990) used a sampling technique that allows generalization, but only to San Francisco. Fourteen percent of married women told her that their husbands had raped them. In interviews with a representative sample of Boston women, 10 percent reported that their husbands had used physical force to compel them to have sex (Finkelhor and Yllo 1985, 1989). Compared with victims of rape by strangers or acquaintances, victims of marital rape are less likely to report the rape (Mahoney 1999).

With the huge numbers of couples who are cohabiting, we need a term that includes sexual assault in these relationships. Perhaps, then, we should use the term *intimacy rape*. And intimacy rape is not limited to men who sexually assault women. Sociologist Lori Girshick (2002) interviewed lesbians who had been sexually assaulted by their female partners. Girshick points out that if the pronoun "he" were substituted for "she" in her interviews, a reader would believe that the events were being told by women who had been raped by their husbands. Just as in heterosexual rape, these victims suffered from shock, depression, and self-blame.

Incest. Sexual relations between certain relatives (for example, between brothers and sisters or between parents and children) constitute **incest**. Incest is most likely to occur in families that are socially isolated (Smith 1992). Sociologist Diana Russell (n.d.) found that incest victims who experience the greatest trauma are those who were victimized the most often, whose assaults occurred over longer periods of time, and whose incest was "more intrusive"—for example, sexual intercourse as opposed to sexual touching.

Incest can occur between any family members, but apparently the most common form is sex between children. An analysis of 13,000 cases of sibling incest showed that three-fourths of the incest was initiated by a brother who was five years older than his sister (Krienert and Walsh 2011). In one-fourth of the cases, the victim was a younger brother, and in 13 percent of the cases, it was an older sister who was the offender. Most offenders are between the ages of 13 and 15, and most victims are age 12 or younger. Most parents treat the incest as a family matter to be dealt with privately.

This couple, a brother and sister in Germany and the proud parents of this child, are challenging their country's laws against incest.

The Bright Side of Family Life: Successful Marriages

Successful Marriages. After examining divorce and family abuse, one could easily conclude that marriages seldom work out. This would be far from the truth, however, since about three of every five married Americans report that they are "very happy" with their marriages (Whitehead and Popenoe 2004). (Keep in mind that each year, divorce eliminates about a million unhappy marriages.) To find out what makes marriage successful, sociologists Jeanette and Robert Lauer (1992) interviewed 351 couples who had been married fifteen years or longer. Fifty-one of these marriages were unhappy, but the couples stayed together for religious reasons, because of family tradition, or "for the sake of the children."

Of the others, the 300 happy couples, all

1. Think of their spouses as best friends
2. Like their spouses as people

3. Think of marriage as a long-term commitment
4. Believe that marriage is sacred
5. Agree with their spouses on aims and goals
6. Believe that their spouses have grown more interesting over the years
7. Strongly want the relationship to succeed
8. Laugh together

Sociologist Nicholas Stinnett (1992) used interviews and questionnaires to study 660 families from all regions of the United States and parts of South America. He found that happy families

1. Spend a lot of time together
2. Are quick to express appreciation
3. Are committed to promoting one another's welfare
4. Do a lot of talking and listening to one another
5. Are religious
6. Deal with crises in a positive manner

Here are three more important factors: Marriages are happier when the partners get along with their in-laws (Bryant et al. 2001), find leisure activities that they both enjoy (Crawford et al. 2002), and agree on how to spend money (Bernard 2008).

Symbolic Interactionism and the Misuse of Statistics

Many students are concerned that divorce statistics mean they won't have a successful marriage. Because sociology is not just about abstract ideas but is really about our lives, it is important to stress that you are an individual, not a statistic. That is, if the divorce rate were 33 percent or 50 percent, this would *not* mean that if you marry, your chances of getting divorced are 33 percent or 50 percent. This is a misuse of statistics—and a common one at that. Divorce statistics represent all marriages and have absolutely *nothing* to do with any individual marriage. Our own chances depend on our own situations—especially the way we approach marriage.

To make this point clearer, let's apply symbolic interactionism. From a symbolic interactionist perspective, we create our own worlds. That is, because our experiences don't come with built-in meanings, we interpret our experiences and act accordingly. As we do so, we can create a self-fulfilling prophecy. For example, if we think that our marriage might fail, we are more likely to run when things become difficult. If we think that our marriage is going to work out, we are more likely to stick around and to do things to make the marriage successful. The folk saying "There are no guarantees in life" is certainly true, but it does help to have a vision that a good marriage is possible and that it is worth the effort to work things out.

16.8 Explain the likely future of marriage and family.

The Future of Marriage and Family

What can we expect of marriage and family in the future? We can first note that marriage is so functional that it exists in every society. Despite its many problems, then, marriage is in no danger of becoming a relic of the past, and the vast majority of Americans will continue to find marriage vital to their welfare.

As we have discussed, changes in society have an impact on the family. Technology is no exception. In the Sociology and the New Technology box on the next page, let's catch a glimpse of a change in its infancy, the use of software to manage the family.

Sociology and the New Technology

"How Should We Handle Family Disagreements?" Use Your App

Families are messy. Family members are constantly negotiating with one another—from who does what task to how to settle disagreements. What is worked out one day can fall apart the next. From the pleasures of satisfaction to the bitterness of disappointment; from love and consideration to selfishness and spite; from lifelong commitment to lifetime divorce—these are what families are made of.

We want success. For school, we do our homework and prepare for tests. At work, we improve our skills and try to please others. But when it comes to the family, we largely assume that it will take care of itself.

But then comes the inevitable in our technological, software-driven society. Some families have begun to use software to coordinate activities, to solve problems, and, in general, to tidy up the messiness of families.

They are using a program called Agile Development, software that was developed to manage small teams at work (Feiler 2013). Agile provides a way to organize daily progress sessions and weekly reviews. As some saw how effective the software was at work, they began to think "If the members of our family were broken into teams, and we had progress sessions and reviews. . . ."

Throughout history, technology has had an impact on families. Today is no exception.

So they tried the program at home. From the initial reports, those who are successful

1. Start with the assumption that teams require teamwork. Because successful teams aren't dominated by a single leader, the parents are guides, not dictators.
2. Empower the children. The children set weekly goals and pick their own rewards and punishments for meeting or not meeting them.
3. Develop morning checklists.
4. Build in flexibility. Situations change, but they keep each family member accountable.
5. Hold weekly family meetings. They ask what went well during the week, what didn't go well, and, after discussion, agree on two things to improve during the coming week.

For Your Consideration

➔ Small teams are one of the more successful techniques for organizing work. As we discussed in Chapter 7, small teams give group members a sense of belonging and improve productivity. What do you think about organizing the family into a small team? Do you think that using software to manage the family is a wave of the future, or just a little passing fad? Why?

We can get a glimpse of the future by considering trends that are firmly in place. Cohabitation, births to single women, and the age at first marriage will increase. As more married women join the workforce, wives will continue to gain marital power. As the number of elderly increase, more couples will find themselves sandwiched between caring for their parents and rearing their own children.

Our culture will continue to be haunted by distorted images of marriage and family: the bleak ones portrayed in the mass media and the rosy ones perpetuated by cultural myths. Sociological research can help correct these distortions and allow us to see how our own family experiences fit into the patterns of our culture. Sociological research can also help to answer the big question: How do we formulate social policies that support and enhance the quality of family life?

MySocLab ✓ Study and Review on MySocLab

CHAPTER 16 Summary and Review

Marriage and Family in Global Perspective

16.1 Define marriage and family and summarize their common cultural themes.

What is a family—and what themes are universal?

Family is difficult to define because there are exceptions to every element that one might consider essential. Consequently, **family** is defined broadly—as people who consider themselves related by blood, marriage, or adoption. Universally, **marriage** and family are mechanisms for governing mate selection, reckoning descent, and establishing inheritance and authority. Pp. 451–455.

Marriage and Family in Theoretical Perspective

16.2 Contrast the functionalist, conflict, and symbolic interactionist perspectives on marriage and family.

What is a functionalist perspective on marriage and family?

Functionalists examine the functions and dysfunctions of family life. Examples include the **incest taboo** and how weakened family functions increase divorce. P. 455.

What is a conflict perspective on marriage and family?

Conflict theorists focus on inequality in marriage, especially unequal and changing power between husbands and wives. P. 456.

What is a symbolic interactionist perspective on marriage and family?

Symbolic interactionists examine the contrasting experiences and perspectives of men and women in marriage. They stress that only by grasping the perspectives of wives and husbands can we understand their behavior. Pp. 456–457.

The Family Life Cycle

16.3 Summarize research on love and courtship, marriage, childbirth, child rearing, and family transitions.

What are the major elements of the family life cycle?

The major elements are love and courtship, marriage, childbirth, child rearing, and the family in later life. Most mate selection follows patterns of age, social class, and race–ethnicity. Child-rearing patterns vary by social class. Pp. 458–465.

Diversity in U.S. Families

16.4 Summarize research on families: African American, Latino, Asian American, Native American, one-parent, couples without children, blended, and gay and lesbian.

How significant is race–ethnicity in family life?

The primary distinction is social class, not race–ethnicity. Families of the same social class are likely to be similar, regardless of their race–ethnicity. P. 465.

What other diversity do we see in U.S. families?

Also discussed are one-parent, childless, **blended**, and gay and lesbian families. Each has its unique characteristics, but social class is important in determining their primary characteristics. Poverty is especially significant for one-parent families, most of which are headed by women. Pp. 466–472.

Trends in U.S. Families

16.5 Discuss changes in the timetable of family life, cohabitation, and elder care.

What major changes characterize U.S. families?

Three major changes are postponement of first marriage, an increase in **cohabitation**, and having the first child at a later age. With more people living longer, many middle-aged couples find themselves sandwiched between rearing their children and taking care of their aging parents. Pp. 472–474.

Divorce and Remarriage

16.6 Summarize problems in measuring divorce, research findings on children and grandchildren of divorce, fathers' contact after divorce, ex-spouses, and remarriage.

What is the current divorce rate?

Depending on what numbers you choose to compare, you can produce rates between 2 percent and 50 percent. Pp. 474–475.

How do children and their parents adjust to divorce?

Divorce is difficult for children, whose adjustment problems often continue into adulthood. Consequences of divorce are passed on to grandchildren. Fathers who have frequent contact with their children after a divorce are likely to maintain it. Pp. 475–479.

Two Sides of Family Life

16.7 Summarize the dark and bright sides of family life.

What are the two sides of family life?

The dark side is abuse—spouse battering, child abuse, marital rape, and **incest**, all a misuse of family power. The bright side is that most people find marriage and family to be rewarding. Pp. 480–482.

The Future of Marriage and Family

16.7 Explain the likely future of marriage and family.

What is the likely future of marriage and family?

We can expect cohabitation, births to unmarried women, and age at first marriage to increase. The growing numbers of women in the workforce are likely to continue to shift the balance of marital power. Pp. 482–483.

Thinking Critically about Chapter 16

1. Functionalists stress that the family is universal because it provides basic functions for individuals and society. What functions does *your* family provide? *Hint:* In addition to the section "The Functionalist Perspective," also consider the section "Common Cultural Themes."
2. Explain why social class is more important than race–ethnicity in determining a family's characteristics.
3. Apply this chapter's contents to your own experience with marriage and family. What social factors affect your family life? In what ways is your family life different from that of your grandparents when they were your age?

CHAPTER 17

Education

Listen to Chapter 17 on MySocLab

Kathy Spiegel was upset. *Horace Mann, the school principal in her hometown in Oregon, had asked her to come to his office. He explained that Kathy's 11-year-old twins had been acting up in class. They were disturbing other children and the teacher—and what was Kathy going to do about this?*

Kathy didn't want to tell Mr. Mann what he could do with the situation. That would have gotten her kicked out of the office. Instead, she bit her tongue and said she would talk to her daughters.

* * * * *

"Kathy's 11-year-old twins were disturbing other children and the teacher—and what was Kathy going to do about this?"

On the other side of the country, Jim and Julia Attaway were pondering their own problem. When they visited their son's school in the Bronx, they didn't like what they saw. The boys looked like they were little gangsta wannabes, and the girls dressed and acted as though they were sexually active. Their own 13-year-old son had started using street language at home, and it was becoming increasingly difficult to talk to him.

* * * * *

In Minneapolis, Denzil and Tamika Jefferson were facing a much quieter crisis. They found life frantic as they hurried from one school activity to another. Their 13-year-old son attended a private school, and the demands were so intense that it felt like the junior year in high school. They no longer seemed to have any relaxed family time together.

* * * * *

In Atlanta, Jaime and Maria Morelos were upset at the ideas that their 8-year-old daughter had begun to express at home. As devout first-generation Protestants, Jaime and Maria felt moral issues were a top priority, and they didn't like what they were hearing.

* * * * *

Kathy talked the matter over with her husband, Bob. Jim and Julia discussed their problem, as did Denzil and Tamika and Jaime and Maria. They all came to the same conclusion: The problem was not their children. The problem was the school their children attended. All four sets of parents also came to the same solution: home schooling for their children.

Home schooling might seem to be a radical solution to today's education problems, but it is one that the parents of 1½ million U.S. children have chosen. We'll come back to this topic, but, first, let's take a broad look at education.

Learning Objectives

After you have read this chapter, you should be able to:

17.1 Discuss education in earlier societies and how education is related to industrialization. (p. 487)

17.2 To understand how education is related to a nation's culture and economy, compare education in Japan, Russia, and Egypt. (p. 491)

17.3 Explain the functions of education: knowledge and skills, values, social integration, gatekeeping, and replacing family functions. (p. 493)

17.4 Explain how the educational system reproduces the social class structure. (p. 496)

17.5 Explain the significance of teacher expectations and give examples. (p. 502)

17.6 Discuss mediocrity in education, grade inflation, social promotion, rising standards, cheating by administrators, and violence in schools. (p. 504)

17.7 Explain how technology is changing education. (p. 509)

The Development of Modern Education

To provide a background for understanding our educational system, let's look first at education in earlier societies, then trace the development of universal education.

Education in Earlier Societies

17.1 Discuss education in earlier societies and how education is related to industrialization.

Earlier societies had no separate social institution called education. They had no special buildings called schools and no people who earned their livings as teachers. Rather, as an ordinary part of growing up, children learned what was necessary to get along in life. If hunting or cooking were the essential skills, then parents and other relatives taught these skills to the children. *Education was the same as acculturation*, learning a culture. It still is in today's tribal groups.

In some societies—such as China, Greece, and North Africa—when a sufficient surplus developed, a separate institution for education appeared. Some people then devoted themselves to teaching, while those who had the leisure—the children of the wealthy—became their students. In ancient China, for example, Confucius taught a few select pupils, while in Greece, Aristotle, Plato, and Socrates taught science and philosophy

In hunting and gathering societies, there is no separate social institution called *education*. Instead, children learn from their parents and elders. This father in Thailand is teaching his son how to use a blowgun. The dart shot from the blowgun has been dipped in a poison that kills the prey.

to upper-class boys. Education, then, came to be something distinct from informal acculturation. **Education** is a group's *formal* system of teaching knowledge, values, and skills. Such instruction stood in marked contrast to the learning of traditional skills such as farming or hunting, since it was intended to develop the mind.

Education flourished during the period roughly marked by the birth of Christ, then slowly died out. During the Dark Ages of Europe, monks kept the candle of enlightenment burning. Except for a handful of the wealthy and some members of the nobility, only the monks could read and write. Although the monks delved into philosophy, they focused on learning Greek, Latin, and Hebrew so they could study the Bible and writings of early church leaders. The Jews also kept formal learning alive as they studied the Torah. In the Arab world, the center of learning was Baghdad, where the focus was on the Koran, poetry, philosophy, linguistics, and astronomy.

Formal education remained limited to those who had the leisure to pursue it. (The word *school* comes from the Greek word *scholé,* meaning "leisure.") Industrialization transformed education, because some of the machinery and new types of jobs required workers to read, write, and work accurately with numbers—the classic "three R's" of the nineteenth century (Readin', 'Ritin', 'n 'Rithmetic).

Industrialization and Universal Education

Watch on **MySocLab**
Video: The Big Picture: Education

After the American Revolution, the founders of the new republic were concerned that the many contrasting religious and ethnic groups (nationalities) would make the nation unstable. To help create a uniform national culture, Thomas Jefferson and Noah Webster proposed universal schooling. Standardized texts would instill patriotism and teach the principles of representative government (Hellinger and Judd 1991). If this new political experiment of democracy were to succeed, they reasoned, it would need educated citizens who were capable of making informed decisions and voting wisely. A national culture remained elusive, however, and the country remained politically fragmented into the 1800s. Many states considered themselves to be near-sovereign nations.

Education reflected this national disunity. There was no comprehensive school system, just a hodgepodge of independent schools. Public schools even charged tuition. Lutherans, Presbyterians, and Roman Catholics operated their own schools (Hellinger and Judd 1991). Children of the rich attended private schools. Children of the poor received no formal education—nor did slaves. High school was considered higher education (hence the name *high* school), and only a few could afford it. College was beyond the reach of almost everyone.

Horace Mann, an educator from Massachusetts, found it deplorable that parents with an average income could not afford to send their children even to grade school. In 1837, he proposed that "common schools," supported through taxes, be established throughout his state. Mann's idea spread, and other states began to provide free public education.

By 1918, all U.S. states had **mandatory education laws** requiring children to attend school, usually until they completed the eighth grade or turned 16, whichever came first. By this time, schooling had become widespread, and graduation from the eighth grade marked the end of education for most people. "Dropouts" at that time were students who did not complete grade school.

education a formal system of teaching knowledge, values, and skills

mandatory education laws laws that require all children to attend school until a specified age or until they complete a minimum grade in school

It is no coincidence that universal education and industrialization occurred at the same time. As political and civic leaders observed the transformation of the economy, they recognized the need for an educated workforce. They also feared the influx of "foreign" values and, like the founders of the country, looked at public education as a way to "Americanize" immigrants (Jones and Meyer 2010).

As industrialization progressed and fewer people made their living from farming, even more years of formal education came to be regarded as essential to the well-being of society. Graduation from high school became more common, and more students wanted a college education. Free education stopped with high school, however, and with the distance to the nearest college too far and the cost of tuition and lodging too great, few high school graduates were able to attend college. As discussed in the Down-to-Earth Sociology box on the next page, this predicament gave birth to community colleges. Figure 17.1 below shows the incredible change in educational achievement. As you can see, receiving a bachelor's degree is now more than *twice* as common as completing high school used to be. Two of every three (68 percent) high school graduates enter college (*Statistical Abstract* 2013: Table 276).

One of eight Americans has not made it through high school, however, which leads to economic problems for most of them throughout their lives (*Statistical Abstract* 2013:Table 236). The Social Map on page 491 shows how unevenly distributed high school graduation is among the states. You may want to compare this Social Map with the Social Map on page 279 that shows how poverty is distributed among the states.

In this 1921 photo of a one-room schoolhouse in Marey, West Virginia, you can see how public education had spread to even poor, rural areas of the United States. Notice the barefoot children.

Watch on **MySocLab**
Video: Current Issues in U.S. Education

Watch on **MySocLab**
Video: Thinking Like a Sociologist: Graduation Rates

FIGURE 17.1 Educational Achievement in the United States

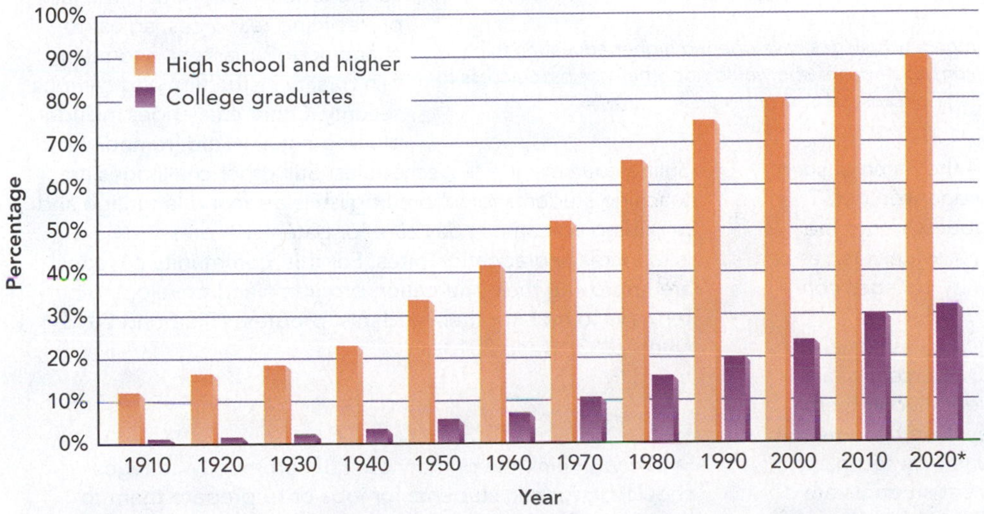

Note: Americans 25 years and over. Asterisk indicates author's estimate. College graduates are included in both categories (High school and higher, and College graduates).

Sources: By the author. Based on National Center for Education Statistics 1991:Table 8; *Statistical Abstract of the United States* 2013:Table 236.

Down-to-Earth Sociology

Community Colleges: Facing Old and New Challenges

I attended a junior college in Oakland, California. From there, with fresh diploma in hand, I transferred to a senior college—a college in Fort Wayne, Indiana, that had no freshmen or sophomores.

I didn't realize that my experimental college matched the vision of some of the founders of the community college movement. In the early 1900s, they foresaw a system of local colleges that would be accessible to the average high school graduate—a system so extensive that it would be unnecessary for universities to offer courses at the freshman and sophomore levels (Handel 2013).

A group with an equally strong opinion questioned whether preparing high school graduates for entry to four-year colleges and universities should be the goal of junior colleges. They insisted that the purpose of junior colleges should be vocational preparation, to equip people for the job market as electricians and other technicians. In some regions, where the proponents of transfer dominated, the admissions requirements for junior colleges were higher than those of Yale (Pedersen 2001). This debate was never won by either side, and you can still hear its echoes today (Handel 2013).

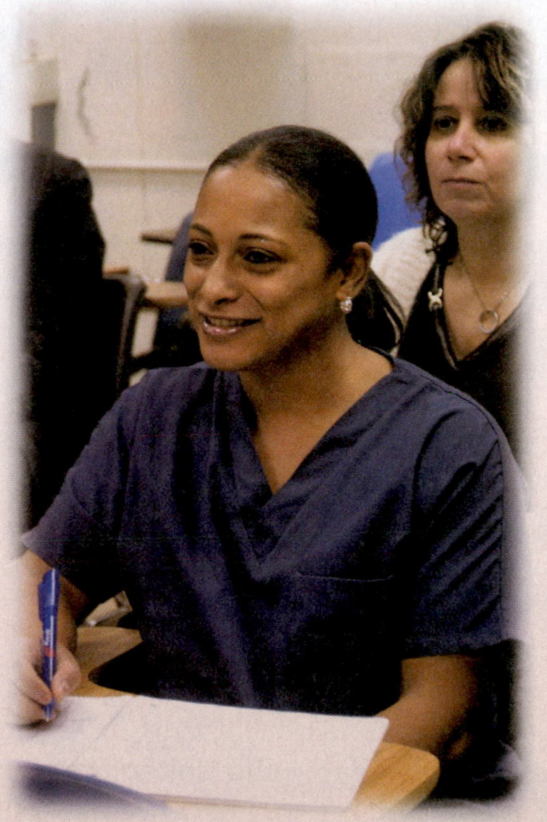

Community colleges have opened higher education to millions of students who would not otherwise have access to college because of cost or distance.

The name *junior* college also became a problem. Some felt that the word *junior* made their institution sound as though it weren't quite a real college. A struggle to change the name ensued, and several decades ago, *community* college won out. The name change didn't settle the debate about whether the purpose was preparing students to transfer to universities or training them for jobs, however. Community colleges continue to serve this dual purpose.

Community colleges have become such an essential part of the U.S. educational system that 37 percent of all undergraduates in the United States are enrolled in them (*Statistical Abstract* 2013:Table 279). They have become the major source of the nation's emergency medical technicians, firefighters, nurses, and police officers. Most students are *nontraditional* students: Many are age 25 or older, come from the working class, have jobs and children, and attend college part-time (Osterman 2010; Jackson et al. 2013).

To help students who are not seeking occupational certificates transfer to four-year colleges and universities, many community colleges work closely with four-year public and private universities. Some provide admissions guidance on how to enter flagship state schools. Others coordinate courses, making sure they match the university's title and numbering system, as well as its rigor of instruction and grading. Many offer honors programs that prepare talented students to transfer with ease into these schools.

An emerging trend is for community colleges to become four-year colleges without changing their names. Some are now granting work-related baccalaureate degrees in such areas as teaching, nursing, and public safety (Hanson 2010). This raises questions: Will these community colleges eventually develop into full four-year colleges? If they do, will this create the need to establish community colleges to replace them?

Community colleges face continuing challenges. They must secure adequate budgets in the face of declining resources, adjust to changing job markets, and maintain quality instruction and campus security. Other challenges include offering financial aid, remedial and online courses, and flex schedules. Still other challenges are teaching students for whom English is a second language and providing on-campus day care for parents. A pressing need is to increase graduation rates. For this, community colleges are improving their orientation programs and developing better ways to monitor their students' progress (Diamond 2013; Dunn 2013; Wang 2013).

For Your Consideration

➔ Do you think the primary goal of community colleges should be to train students for jobs or to prepare them to transfer to four-year colleges and universities? Why?

FIGURE 17.2 Not Making It: Dropping Out of High School

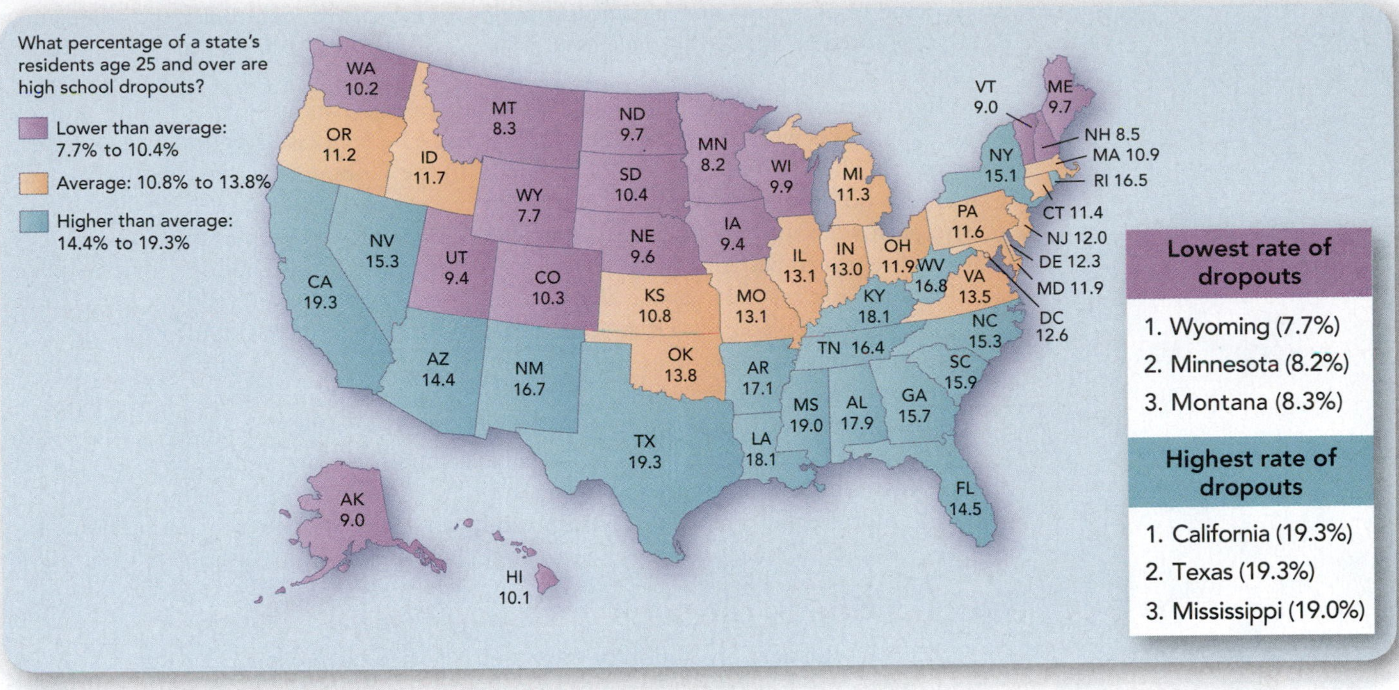

Source: By the author. Based on *Statistical Abstract of the United States* 2013:Table 238.

Read on **MySocLab**
Document: The Hispanic Dropout Mystery

Education in Global Perspective

17.2 To understand how education is related to a nation's culture and economy, compare education in Japan, Russia, and Egypt.

To place our own educational system in global perspective, let's look at education in three countries at different levels of industrialization. This will help us see how education is related to a nation's culture and its economy.

Education in the Most Industrialized Nations: Japan

> *The yells of children pierce the night, belting out the elements—"Lithium! Magnesium!"—as an instructor displays abbreviations from the periodic table. Next, two dozen flags stream by as the ten-year-olds shout out the names of the corresponding countries. Later they identify 20 constellations they have committed to memory. Timers on desks push older students as they practice racing through different tests. The scene at this* juku *(cram school) on the edge of Tokyo, repeats itself nightly at 50,000 cram schools across Japan. ("Testing Times" 2011)*

What an emphasis on education. Japanese parents pay over $3,000 a year to enroll a child in a cram school. And one in five first graders is enrolled in these schools, which operate after the regular school day.

Another unique aspect of Japanese education is that during the regular school day, all grade school children study the same page from the same textbook ("Less Rote . . ." 2000). This vast uniformity is accompanied by a personal touch: Teachers are required to visit each student's home once a year (Yamamoto and Brinton 2010).

School is over—but not for this student. After the regular school day, hundreds of thousands in Japan attend 50,000 cram (*juku*) schools.

Watch on **MySocLab**
Video: Sociology in Focus: Education

A central sociological principle of education is that a nation's education reflects its culture. Studying the same materials at the same time reflects the core Japanese value of solidarity with the group. In the workforce, people who are hired together are not expected to compete with one another for promotions. Instead, they work as a team and are promoted as a group (Ouchi 1993). Japanese education reflects this group-centered approach to life.

In a fascinating cultural contradiction, college admission in Japan is highly competitive, and this is where the cram schools come in. The Scholastic Assessment Test (SAT), taken by college-bound high school students in the United States, is voluntary. Japanese seniors who want to attend college, however, must take a national test. U.S. students who perform poorly on their tests can usually find some college to attend—as long as their parents can pay the tuition. Until recently, in Japan, only the top scorers—rich and poor alike—were admitted to college. Because Japan's birth rate has dropped so low, more space is available, and it is becoming easier for students to get into college. Competition for entrance to the best colleges remains intense (Okada 2012).

As in the United States, children from Japan's richer families score higher on college admission tests and are more likely to attend the nation's elite colleges (Okada 2012). In both countries, children born in richer families inherit privileges that give them advantages over others. Among these privileges, which sociologists call **cultural capital**, are having more highly educated parents, encouragement and pressure to bring home top grades, and cultural experiences that translate into higher test scores.

Education in the Industrializing Nations: Russia

Listen on **MySocLab**
Audio: NPR: U.S. Universities No Longer Only Game in Town

Prior to the Russian Revolution of 1917, the czar had been expanding Russia's educational system beyond the children of the elite (Andreev 2012). The Soviet Communist party continued this expansion until education encompassed all children. Following the sociological principle that education reflects culture, the new government made certain that socialist values dominated its schools, because it saw education as a means to undergird the new political system. As a result, schoolchildren were taught that capitalism was evil and communism was the salvation of the world. Every classroom was required to prominently display photographs of Lenin and Stalin.

Education under the Soviets, including college, was free. Just as the economy was directed from central headquarters in Moscow, so was education. Schools stressed mathematics and the natural sciences. Each school followed the same state-prescribed curriculum, and all students in the same grade used the same textbooks. To prevent critical thinking, which might lead to criticisms of communism, there were few courses in the social sciences. Students memorized course materials, repeating lectures on oral exams (Deaver 2001).

Russia's switch from communism to capitalism brought a change in culture—especially new ideas about profit, private property, and personal freedom. This, in turn, meant that the educational system had to adjust to the country's changing values and views of the world. Not only did the photos of Lenin and Stalin come down, but also, for the first time, private, religious, and even foreign-run schools were allowed. For the first time as well, teachers were able to encourage students to think for themselves.

The problems that Russia confronted in "reinventing" its educational system are mind-boggling. Tens of thousands of teachers who had been teaching students to memorize Party-dictated political answers had to learn new methods of instruction. As the economy faltered during Russia's early transition to capitalism, school budgets dwindled. Some teachers went unpaid for months; instead of money, at one school, teachers were paid in toilet paper and vodka (Deaver 2001). Teachers are now paid regularly (and in money), but the salaries are low. University professors average only $1,000 a month (Agranovich 2012). The economic crisis is global, and Russia's education is again feeling the pinch as budgets shrink (Filatova et al. 2012).

For obvious reasons, politicians are interested in their country's educational system, and Russia is no exception. The president of Russia, Vladimir Putin, declared that the

cultural capital privileges accompanying a social location that help someone in life; included are more highly educated parents, from grade school through high school being pushed to bring home high grades, and enjoying cultural experiences that translate into higher test scores, better jobs, and higher earnings new history books did not do justice to Russia's glorious past. Educational bureaucrats immediately jumped into action, and now officials inspect the content of history books to make certain they are sufficiently patriotic (Rapoport 2009). We can confidently predict that Russia's educational system will continue to glorify Russia's historical exploits and reinforce its values and world views—no matter what direction those values and views may take.

Education in the Least Industrialized Nations: Egypt

Education in the Least Industrialized Nations stands in sharp contrast to that in the industrialized world. Because most of the citizens of these nations work the land or take care of families, there is little emphasis on formal schooling. Mandatory attendance laws are not enforced. As we saw in Figure 9.3 (pages 233–234), many people in the Least Industrialized Nations live on less than $1,000 a year.

Consequently, in some of these nations, few children go to school beyond the first couple of grades. As was once common around the globe, it is primarily the wealthy in the Least Industrialized Nations who have the means and the leisure for formal education—especially anything beyond the basics. As an example, let's look at education in Egypt.

The poverty of the Least Industrialized Nations carries over to their educational system. These students in Zimbabwe are being taught outside because their school has run out of space.

Several centuries before the birth of Christ, Egypt's centers of learning were world-renowned. They produced such acclaimed scientists as Archimedes and Euclid. During this classical period, the primary areas of study during this classic period were astronomy, geography, geometry, mathematics, medicine, philosophy, and physics. The largest library in the world was at Alexandria. Fragments from the papyrus manuscripts of this library, which burned to the ground, have been invaluable in deciphering ancient manuscripts. After Rome defeated Egypt, however, education declined and has never regained its former prominence.

Although the Egyptian constitution guarantees six years of free school for all children, many poor children receive no education at all. For those who do attend school, qualified teachers are few, and classrooms are crowded. As a result, one-third to one-half of Egyptians are illiterate, with more men than women able to read and write (UNESCO 2012). After the six years of grade school, students are tracked. Most study technical subjects for three years and at about the age of 14 are done with school. Others go on to high school for three years, with those who score the highest on national exams admitted to college. All education is free (British Council 2013).

The emphasis is on memorizing facts to pass national tests. With concerns that this approach leaves minds less capable of evaluating life and opens the door to religious extremism, Egyptian educators have pressed for critical thinking to be added to the curriculum (Gauch 2006). The general low quality of education, including university classes, leaves Egypt uncompetitive in the global economy (Loveluck 2012). Without fundamental reforms, Egypt will continue to lag behind in the global race for economic security.

manifest functions the intended beneficial consequences of people's actions

latent functions unintended beneficial consequences of people's actions

The Functionalist Perspective: Providing Social Benefits

17.3 Explain the functions of education: knowledge and skills, values, social integration, gatekeeping, and replacing family functions.

A central position of functionalism is that when the parts of a society are working properly, each contributes to the well-being or stability of that society. The positive things that people intend their actions to accomplish are known as **manifest functions**. The positive consequences they did not intend are called **latent functions**. Let's begins by looking at the functions of education.

©Robert Mankoff/The New Yorker Collection/www.cartoonbank.com

"Hey, how come no diplomas?" "Oh, I'm self-taught."

The cartoonist captures a primary reason that we have become a credential society.

Teaching Knowledge and Skills

Education's most obvious manifest function is to teach knowledge and skills—whether the traditional three R's or their more contemporary counterparts, such as computer literacy. Each generation must train the next to fill the group's significant positions. Because our postindustrial society needs highly educated people, the schools supply them.

But testing in algebra or paragraph construction to sell sheets at K-Mart or gizmos at Radio Shack? As sociologist Randall Collins (1979) said, industrialized nations have become **credential societies**. By this, he meant that employers use diplomas and degrees as *sorting devices* to determine who is eligible for a job. Because employers don't know potential workers, they depend on schools to weed out the incapable. For example, when you graduate from college, potential employers will presume that you are a responsible person—that you have shown up for numerous classes, have turned in scores of assignments, and have demonstrated basic writing and thinking skills. They will then graft their particular job skills onto this foundation, which has been certified by your college.

In some cases, job skills must be mastered before you are allowed to do the work. On-the-job training was once adequate for someone to become a physician, an engineer, or an airline pilot, but with changes in information and technology, this training falls far short of what is needed today. This is precisely why doctors display their credentials so prominently. Their framed degrees declare that an institution of higher learning has certified them to work on your body.

Cultural Transmission of Values

Another manifest function of education is the **cultural transmission of values**, a process by which schools pass on a society's core values from one generation to the next. Schools in a socialist society stress values that support socialism, while schools in a capitalist society teach values that support capitalism. U.S. schools, for example, stress the significance of private property, individualism, and competition.

Regardless of a country's economic system, loyalty to the state is a cultural value, and schools around the world teach patriotism. U.S. schools—as well as those of Russia, France, China, and other countries around the world—extol the society's founders, their struggle for freedom from oppression, and the goodness of the country's social institutions. Seldom is this function as explicit as it is in Japan, where the law requires that schools "cultivate a respect for tradition and culture, and love for the nation and homeland" (Nakamura 2006).

To visualize what the functionalists mean, consider how differently a course in U.S. history would be taught in Cuba, Iran, and Muncie, Indiana.

Social Integration

Schools also bring about *social integration*. Among the ways they promote a sense of national identity is by having students salute the flag and sing the national anthem.

Integrating Immigrants.

One of the best examples of how U.S. schools promote political integration is their teaching of mainstream ideas and values to tens of millions of immigrants. The schools help the immigrants regard themselves as Americans and give up their earlier national and cultural identities (Carper 2000; Thompson 2009).

Stabilizing Society: Maintaining the Status Quo.

This integrative function of education goes far beyond making people similar in their appearance, speech, or even ways of thinking. *To forge a national identity is to stabilize the political system.* If people identify with a society's institutions and *perceive them as the basis of their own welfare*, they have no reason to rebel. This function of education is especially significant when it comes to

credential society the use of diplomas and degrees to determine who is eligible for jobs, even though the diploma or degree may be irrelevant to the actual work

cultural transmission of values the process of transmitting values from one group to another; often refers to how cultural traits are transmitted across generations; in education, the ways in which schools transmit a society's culture, especially its core values the lower social classes, from which most social revolutionaries emerge. The wealthy already have a vested interest in maintaining the status quo, but getting the lower classes to identify with a social system *as it is* goes a long way toward preserving the system as it is.

Integrating People with Disabilities. People with disabilities often have found themselves left out of the mainstream of society. As a matter of routine policy, students with special needs used to be placed in special classes or schools. There, however, they learned to adjust to a specialized situation, leaving them ill prepared to cope with the dominant world. To overcome this, U.S. schools have added a manifest function, **inclusion**, or mainstreaming. As in the photo to the rights, this means that educators try to incorporate students with disabilities into regular school activities. Wheelchair ramps are provided for people who cannot walk; interpreters who use sign language may attend classes with students who cannot hear. Exceptions include most blind students, who attend special schools, as well as people with severe learning disabilities. Most inclusion goes fairly smoothly, but mainstreaming students with serious emotional and behavioral problems disrupts classrooms, frustrates teachers, and increases teacher turnover (Tomsho and Golden 2007). About 90 percent of students with disabilities now spend at least some of their days in regular classrooms, with over half there most of the time (IES 2010).

Children with disabilities used to be sent to special schools. In a process called *mainstreaming* or inclusion, they now attend regular schools. This photo was taken in Detroit, Michigan.

Gatekeeping (Social Placement)

Sociologists Talcott Parsons (1940), Kingsley Davis, and Wilbert Moore (Davis and Moore 1945) pioneered a view called **social placement**. They pointed out that some jobs require few skills and can be performed by people of lesser intelligence. Other jobs, such as that of physician, require high intelligence and advanced education. It is up to the schools to sort the capable from the incapable. They do this, say the functionalists, on the basis of merit, that is, the students' abilities and ambitions.

As you can see, social placement, more commonly known as **gatekeeping**, means to open the doors of opportunity for some and to close them to others. The question is what opens and closes those doors. Is it merit, as the functionalists argue? To accomplish gatekeeping, schools use some form of **tracking**, sorting students into different educational "tracks" or programs on the basis of their perceived abilities. Some U.S. high schools funnel students into one of three tracks: general, college prep, or honors. Students on the lowest track are likely to go to work after high school, or to take vocational courses. Those on the highest track usually attend prestigious colleges. Those in between usually attend a local college or regional state university.

The impact of gatekeeping is lifelong. Tracking affects people's opportunities for jobs, income, and lifestyle. When tracking was challenged—that it is based more on social class than merit, which perpetuates social inequality—schools retreated from formal tracking. Placing students in "ability groups" and "advanced" classes, however, serves the same purpose (Loveless 2013).

Replacing Family Functions

Over the years, the functions of U.S. schools have expanded, and they now rival some family functions. Child care, for example, has always been a latent function of formal education, since it was an unintended consequence. Now, however, with two wage earners in most families, child care has become a manifest function, and some schools offer

inclusion helping people to become part of the mainstream of society; also called *mainstreaming*

social placement a function of education—funneling people into a society's various positions

gatekeeping the process by which education opens and closes doors of opportunity; another term for the *social placement* function of education

tracking the sorting of students into different programs on the basis of real or perceived abilities child care both before and after the school day. Some high schools even provide nurseries for the children of their teenaged students (Bosman 2007).

Another function is providing sex education, and, in some school-based health centers, birth control (Elliott 2007). This has stirred controversy, since some families resent schools taking this function away from them. Disagreement over values has fueled the social movement for home schooling, featured in our opening vignette and in the Down-to-Earth Sociology box on the next page.

Other Functions

Schools also help to *reduce the unemployment rate.* U.S. education is big business. Schools—from elemetary to college—provide jobs for 5 million teachers (*Statistical Abstract* 2013:Tables 247, 278). There are also vast numbers of secretaries, janitors, bus drivers, and administrative staff. Others earn their living in industries that service schools—from publishing textbooks to building schools and manufacturing pencils, paper, desks, and computers.

Not only do schools employ millions of teachers and support personnel, but the millions of young people in the classroom are kept out of the job market. With 15 million students in high school and another 13 million full-time college students, this helps to *stabilize society* (*Statistical Abstract* 2013:Tables 248, 278). These 28 million young people are kept off the streets, where many might be demonstrating and demanding jobs and changes in the political system.

Read on **MySocLab**
Document: School Failure as an Adolescent Turning Point

A Surprising Latent Function. Researchers have found a surprising effect of education: On average, the farther that people go in school, the longer they live. Americans who drop out of high school live to an average age of 75, but those who go beyond high school live to an average age of 82 (Meara et al. 2008). The most likely reasons are that the more educated have healthier lifestyles (better diets, less smoking) and better jobs, higher pay, and superior medical services.

In Sum: Functionalists analyze the functions, the benefits, that schools provide to society. Not only do schools teach the knowledge and skills needed by the next generation, but they also stabilize society by forging a national identity, providing employment, and keeping young adults out of the labor market. A controversial function is gatekeeping, sorting students for various levels of jobs. Schools have expanded their domain, taking over some functions formerly performed by families.

17.4 Explain how the educational system reproduces the social class structure.

The Conflict Perspective: Perpetuating Social Inequality

Unlike functionalists, who look at the benefits of education, conflict theorists examine how *the educational system reproduces the social class structure*. By this, they mean that schools perpetuate the social divisions of society and help members of the elite maintain their dominance.

Let's look, then, at how education is related to social classes, how it helps people inherit *cultural capital*, the life opportunities that were laid down before they were born.

Read on **MySocLab**
Document: Racial Stratification and Education in the United States: Why Inequality Persists

Watch on **MySocLab**
Video: Thinking Like a Sociologist: Dollars and Degrees

The Hidden Curriculum: Reproducing the Social Class Structure

The term **hidden curriculum** refers to the attitudes, values, and unwritten rules of behavior that schools teach in addition to the formal curriculum. Examples are obedience to authority and conformity to mainstream norms. Conflict theorists stress that the hidden curriculum helps to perpetuate social inequalities.

hidden curriculum the unwritten goals of schools, such as teaching obedience to authority and conformity to cultural norms

To understand this central point, consider the way English is taught. Schools for the middle class—whose teachers know where their students are headed—stress "proper"

Down-to-Earth Sociology

Home Schooling: The Search for Quality and Values

"You're doing WHAT? You're going to teach your kids at home?" is the typical, incredulous response to parents who decide to home school their children. The unspoken questions are "How can you teach? You're not trained. And taking your kids out of the public schools—Do you want your kids to be dumb and social misfits?"

The home-schooling movement was small at first, just a trickle of parents who were dissatisfied with the school bureaucracy, lax discipline, incompetent teachers, low standards, lack of focus on individual needs, and, in some instances, hostility to their religion. That trickle grew into a social movement, and now 1,500,000 U.S. children are being taught at home (*Statistical Abstract* 2013:Table 245).

Home schooling is far from new. In the colonial era, home schooling was the *typical* form of education (Gaither 2009). Today's home-schooling movement is restoring this earlier pattern, but it also reflects a fascinating shift in U.S. politics. Political and religious *liberals* began the contemporary home-schooling movement in the 1950s and 1960s. Their objection was that the schools were too conservative. Then the schools changed, and in the 1970s and 1980s, political and religious *conservatives* embraced home schooling (Stevens 2001; Gaither 2009). Their objection was that the schools were too liberal. Some home-schooling parents have no political motivation. Their concerns are their children's safety at school, boring classes, and the lack of individual attention (MacFarquhar 2008; Lewin 2011).

Homeschooling has come a long way. These children are performing in a musical at the annual Homeschool Theater Workshop in Lexington, Kentucky.

Does home schooling work? Can parents who are not trained as teachers actually teach? To find out, researchers tested 21,000 home schoolers across the nation (Rudner 1999). The results were astounding. With median scores for every test at every grade in the 70th to 80th percentiles, the home schoolers vastly outscored students in both public and Catholic schools. Follow-up studies have confirmed the initial research (Ray 2010).

The basic reason for this stunning success appears to be the parents' involvement in their children's education. Home schoolers receive intense, one-on-one teaching. Their curriculum—although it includes the subjects that are required by the state—is designed around the students' interests and needs. Mothers do most of the teaching—90 percent of students versus 10 percent by fathers (Lines 2000). The parents' income is also above average.

We do not know what these home schoolers' test scores would have been if they had been taught in public schools. With their parents' involvement in their education, they likely would have done very well there, too. In addition, although the Rudner study was large, it was not a random sample, and we cannot say how the *average* home schooler is doing. But, then, we have no random sample of all public school students, either.

What about the children's social skills? Since they don't attend school with dozens and even hundreds of other students, do they become social misfits? Contrary to stereotypes, home-schooled children are not isolated. As part of their educational experience, their parents take them to libraries, museums, factories, and nursing homes (Weiner 2012). Some home schoolers also participate in the physical education and sports programs of the public schools (Longman 2012). Parents have also formed regional and national home-schooling associations and hold national sports championships (Drape 2008). Some get together and hold group graduations (Lewin 2011).

Slowly coming to terms with home schooling, some public schools have begun to offer hybrid programs (Gaither 2009). Some offer dual enrollment: The home-schooled child can attend public school part of the day, such as to gain access to specific classes, and learn the rest of the day at home. Others offer "cyber schools," full public education delivered at home via the Internet.

How about getting into college? How can home-schooled children be admitted without official transcripts? This has been a problem, but as home schooling has become widespread, colleges have adjusted. Now three of four colleges have procedures for admitting home schoolers (Gloeckner and Jones 2013).

For Your Consideration

➔ Why do you think that home schooling has become so popular? Do you think this social movement could eventually become a threat to U.S. public schools? Would you consider home schooling your children? Why or why not?

Stressing that education reproduces a country's social class system, conflict theorists point out that the social classes attend separate schools. There they learn perspectives of the world that match their place in it. Show here are students at a private school in Argentina. What do you think this school's *hidden curriculum* is?

English and "good" manners. In contrast, the teachers in inner-city schools—who also know where *their* students are headed—allow ethnic and street language in the classroom. *Each type of school is helping to reproduce the social class structure.* That is, each is preparing students to work in positions similar to those of their parents. The social class of some children destines them for higher positions. For these jobs, they need "refined" speech and manners. The social destiny of others is low-status jobs. For this type of work, they need only to obey rules (Bowles and Gintis 1976, 2002). Teaching these students "refined" speech and manners would be wasted effort. In other words, even the teaching of English and manners helps keep the social classes intact across generations.

For a humorous but serious account of how teachers perpetuate social classes even though they do not intend to do so, read the Down-to-Earth Sociology box on the next page.

Tilting the Tests: Discrimination by IQ

Even intelligence tests help to keep the social class system intact. Let's look at an example. How would you answer this question?

A symphony is to a composer as a book is to a(n) ___
___ *paper* ___ *sculptor* ___ *musician* ___ *author* ___ *man*

You probably had no difficulty coming up with "author" as your choice. Wouldn't any intelligent person have done so?

In point of fact, this question raises a central issue in intelligence testing. Not all intelligent people would know the answer. This question contains *cultural biases.* Children from some backgrounds are more familiar with the concepts of symphonies, composers, and sculptors than are other children. This tilts the test in their favor.

To make the bias clearer, try to answer this question:

If you throw two dice and "7" is showing on the top, what is facing down?
___ *seven* ___ *snake eyes* ___ *box cars* ___ *little Joes* ___ *eleven*

Adrian Dove (n.d.), a social worker in Watts, a poor area of Los Angeles, suggested this question. Its cultural bias should be obvious—that it allows children from some social backgrounds to perform better than others. Unlike the first question, this one is not tilted to the middle-class experience. In other words, IQ (intelligence quotient) tests measure not only intelligence but also acquired knowledge.

You should now be able to perceive the bias of IQ tests that use such words as *composer* and *symphony*. A lower-class child may have heard about rap, rock, gangsta, or jazz, but not about symphonies. One consequence of this bias to the middle-class experience is that the children of the poor score lower on IQ tests. Then, to match their supposedly inferior intelligence, these children are assigned to less demanding courses. Their inferior education helps them reach their social destiny, their lower-paying jobs in adult life. As conflict theorists view them, then, IQ tests are another weapon in an arsenal designed to maintain the social class structure across the generations.

Stacking the Deck: Unequal Funding

Explore on **MySocLab**
Activity: High School Dropouts and Educational Funding

As you can see from the Social Map on page 500, the amount spent on educating children varies widely among the states. Although there is no one-to-one match, in general, the states that spend more on education have higher-quality schools. A main reason is that they attract more highly qualified teachers. Conflict theorists

Down-to-Earth Sociology

How I Became a Fairy: Education and the Perpetuation of Social Inequality

I was excited about going to school. With its scissors, glue, and coloring, kindergarten had turned out to be fun. Like the other boys, recess and rough and tumble games on the playground were perhaps my favorite activities.

First grade whizzed by, and I looked forward to second grade. Those big second graders had told me about how they were learning to read. How magical to be able to make out words from those strange marks on paper.

My second-grade teacher took her job seriously. She taught us how to sound out each letter. I couldn't figure out how s-a-i-d could be pronounced sed. It didn't seem to fit with what I was being taught about the sounds of letters, but I accepted it.

I liked learning. Each lesson seemed to reveal a different part of the world.

I tried my best. And I learned and did well.

Then my teacher divided our class into two groups. She called the slower readers Elves, and the better readers Fairies. (These were simpler times.)

I was an elf.

Disappointment flooded over me! In the fairy group were my friends, the boys I played with during recess and after school—Jerry, the lawyer's son; Jon, the doctor's son; and Jacky, our principal's son. Roseau was a small town on the Canadian border in Minnesota, and we all lived just a few blocks from one another.

The teacher took turns teaching each group. She would go around the circle, having each student read aloud. As I heard the fairies read, I knew that my reading was just as good as theirs, actually better than some. I had to get this across to the teacher. But how?

The next time my turn came, I decided to read loudly and deliberately. She had no or few corrections for me, and would then move on to the other elves, explaining to them over and over how to attach the right sounds to the letters, and from there, how to form words.

After several reading lessons, with me continuing the loud reading, she looked at me and said, "I think you belong in the other group." I happily moved my chair into their little circle.

And I went home, triumphantly announcing to my mother, "I'm a fairy!"

From your experiences in grade school, can you tell if or how your teachers unintentionally helped perpetuate social class divisions?

For Your Consideration

➤ Please don't get lost in the humor of this little story. My parents were ill educated and poor, farmers' children who had moved into town. Everyone in this little town knew precisely how everyone else ranked. Hidden within the teacher's awareness was this perception of social class. She thought that the students from advantaged homes—the children of professionals and those who had more money (there were no really wealthy people in town) could read better—and for the most part, she was right. She pegged the poorer students as poor readers, and here, too, for the most part, she was right.

➤ But not entirely. What had happened in this instance was a misclassification of ability based on social class. This same process—perpetrated throughout the U.S. school system by well-meaning teachers—continues today (Loveless 2013). It is an essential part of, as we sociologists are fond of saying, how the educational system perpetuates the social class structure.

➤ Did you see anything like this in "ability groups" in your grade school or "advanced placement classes" in your high school?

go beyond this, however, and stress the significance of *how* U.S. schools are funded. Because public schools are supported largely by local property taxes, the richer communities (where property values and incomes are higher) have more to spend on their children's schools, and the poorer communities have less to spend on theirs. The richer communities, then, can offer higher salaries and take their pick of the most highly qualified and motivated teachers. They can also afford to buy the latest textbooks, computers, and software, as well as offer courses in foreign languages, music, and the arts. This, stress conflict theorists, means that in *all* states, the deck is stacked against the poor.

FIGURE 17.3 The Unequal Funding of Education

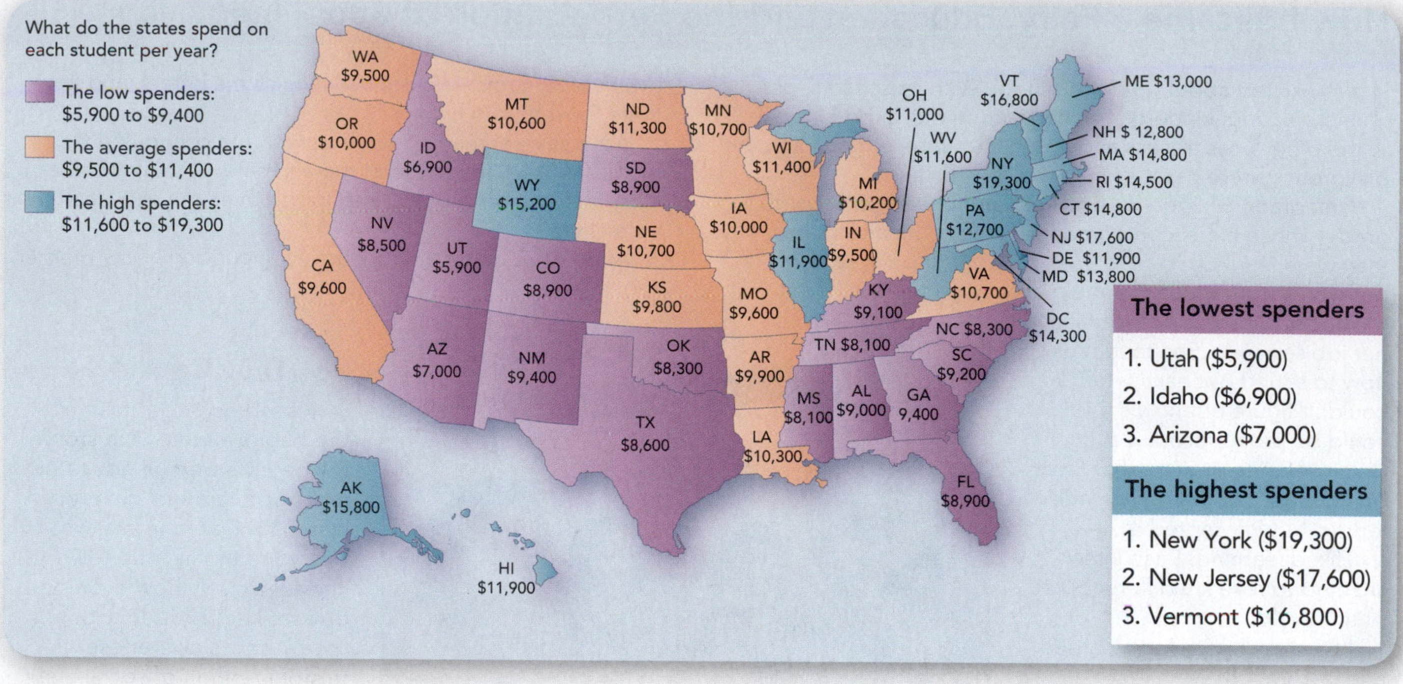

Source: By the author. Based on *Statistical Abstract of the United States* 2013:Table 275.

The Correspondence Principle

In a classic analysis, conflict sociologists Samuel Bowles and Herbert Gintis (1976, 2002) used the term **correspondence principle**. This term means that a nation's schools *correspond* to (or reflect) the characteristics of their society. Here are some examples.

Characteristics of Society	Characteristics of Schools
1. Capitalism	1. Encourage competition
2. Social inequality	2. Unequal funding of schools
3. Social class bias	3. Funnel children of the poor into job training programs that demand little thinking
4. Bureaucratic structure of corporations	4. Provide a model of authority in the classroom
5. Need for submissive workers	5. Make students submissive to teachers
6. Need for dependable workers	6. Enforce punctuality in attendance and homework
7. Need to maintain armed forces	7. Promote patriotism

Conflict theorists conclude that the correspondence principle demonstrates that the U.S. educational system is designed to turn students into dependable workers who will not question their bosses. It also is intended to produce some who are innovators in thought and action, but who can still be counted on to be loyal to the social system as it exists (Olneck and Bills 1980).

correspondence principle the sociological principle that schools correspond to (or reflect) the social structure of their society

The Bottom Line: Family Background

Reproducing the Social Class Structure. The end result of unequal funding, IQ testing, and the other factors we have discussed is this: Family background is more important than test scores in predicting who attends college. In a classic study, sociologist Samuel Bowles (1977) compared the college attendance of high school students who were the most and least intellectually prepared for college. Figure 17.4 shows the results. Of the students who scored the highest on tests, 90 percent of those from affluent homes went to college, but only half of the high scorers from low-income homes went to college. Of the least prepared—those who scored the lowest—26 percent from affluent homes went to college, while only 6 percent from poorer homes did so.

Other sociologists have confirmed this classic research (Carnevale and Rose 2003; Bailey and Dynarski 2011). Regardless of personal abilities, children from more well-to-do families are more likely not only to go to college but also to attend the nation's most elite schools. This, in turn, piles advantage upon advantage, because they get higher-paying and more prestigious jobs when they graduate. The elite colleges are the icing on the cake of these students' more privileged births.

FIGURE 17.4 Who Goes to College? Comparing Social Class and Ability in Determining College Attendance

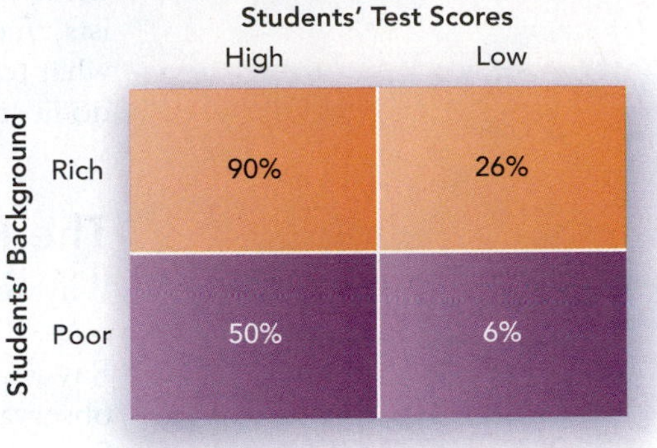

Source: Bowles 1977.

Reproducing the Racial–Ethnic Structure. Conflict theorists point out that the educational system reproduces not only the U.S. social class structure but also its racial–ethnic divisions. From Figure 17.5, you can see that, compared with whites, African Americans and Latinos are less likely to complete high school and, for those who do, less likely to go to college. Because adults with only a high school diploma usually end up with low-paying, dead-end jobs, you can see how this supports the conflict view—that education is helping to reproduce the racial–ethnic structure for the next generation.

Table 17.1 below gives us another snapshot of the significance of race–ethnicity and college attendance. From this table, you can see African Americans are the most likely to attend private colleges. This does not support the conflict perspective. You can also see that Latinos are the least likely to go to four-year colleges. This supports the conflict view. The primary exception that conflict theorists have a difficult time explaining is the success of Asian Americans. Their success in education and their attaining incomes that surpass that of whites, as you saw on Tables 12.2 and 12.3 on page 344, do not fit their model.

In Sum: U.S. schools closely reflect the U.S. social class system. They equip the children of the elite with the tools they need to maintain their dominance, while they prepare the children of the poor for lower-status positions. Because education's doors of opportunity swing wide open for some but have to be pried open by others, conflict theorists stress that the educational system perpetuates social inequality across generations (or, as they often phrase it, helps to reproduce the social class structure). In fact, they add, this is one of its primary purposes.

FIGURE 17.5 The Funneling Effects of Education: Race–Ethnicity

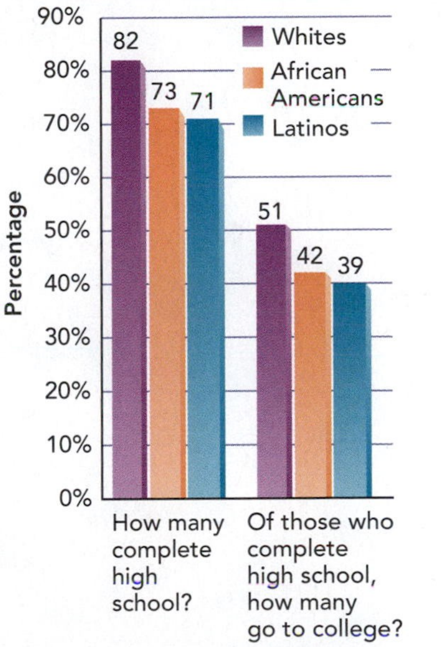

Note: The source gives totals only for these three groups.

Source: By the author. Based on *Statistical Abstract of the United States* 2013:Table 272.

TABLE 17.1 Types of College and Race–Ethnicity

	Public	Private	Two-Year	Four-Year
Whites	72%	28%	34%	66%
African Americans	65%	35%	39%	61%
Asian Americans	76%	24%	36%	64%
Latinos	79%	21%	51%	49%
Native Americans	77%	23%	44%	56%

Source: By the author. Based on *Statistical Abstract of the United States* 2013:Table 279.

17.5 Explain the significance of teacher expectations and give examples.

The Symbolic Interactionist Perspective: Teacher Expectations

As you have seen, functionalists look at how education benefits society, and conflict theorists examine how education perpetuates social inequality. Symbolic interactionists, in contrast, study face-to-face interaction in the classroom. They have found that what teachers expect of their students has profound consequences for how students do in school.

The Rist Research

Watch on MySocLab
Video: Pygmalion Experiment

Why do some people get tracked into college prep courses and others into vocational ones? There is no single answer, but in what has become a classic study, sociologist Ray Rist came up with some intriguing findings. Rist (1970, 2007) did participant observation in an African American grade school with an African American faculty. He found that after only eight days in the classroom, the kindergarten teacher felt that she knew the children's abilities well enough to assign them to three separate worktables. To Table 1, Mrs. Caplow assigned those she considered to be "fast learners." They sat at the front of the room, closest to her. Those whom she saw as "slow learners," she assigned to Table 3, located at the back of the classroom. She placed "average" students at Table 2, in between the other tables.

This seemed strange to Rist. He knew that the children had not been tested for ability, yet their teacher was certain that she could identify the bright and slow children. Investigating further, Rist found that social class was the underlying basis for assigning the children to the different tables. Middle-class students were separated out for Table 1, and children from poorer homes were assigned to Tables 2 and 3. The teacher paid the most attention to the children at Table 1, who were closest to her, less to Table 2, and the least to Table 3. It didn't take long for the children at Table 1 to perceive that they were treated better and come to see themselves as smarter. They became the leaders in class activities and even called children at the other tables "dumb." Eventually, the children at Table 3 disengaged themselves from many classroom activities. At the end of the year, only the children at Table 1 had completed the lessons that prepared them for reading.

This early tracking stuck. Their first-grade teacher looked at the work these students had done, and she placed students from Table 1 at her Table 1. She treated her tables much as the kindergarten teacher had, and the children at Table 1 again led the class.

The children's reputations continued to follow them. The second-grade teacher reviewed their scores and also divided her class into three groups. The first she named the "Tigers" and, befitting their name, gave them challenging readers. Not surprisingly, the Tigers came from the original Table 1 in kindergarten. The second group she called the "Cardinals." They came from the original Tables 2 and 3. Her third group consisted of children she had failed the previous year, whom she called the "Clowns." The Cardinals and Clowns were given less advanced readers.

Rist concluded that *each child's journey through school was determined by the eighth day of kindergarten!* As we saw with the Saints and Roughnecks, in Chapter 4, labels can be so powerful that they can set people on courses of action that affect the rest of their lives.

What occurred was a **self-fulfilling prophecy**. This term, coined by sociologist Robert Merton (1949/1968), refers to a false assumption of something that is going to happen but which then comes true simply because it was predicted. For example, if people believe an unfounded rumor that a credit union is going to fail because its officers have embezzled their money, they all rush to the credit union to demand their money. The prediction—although originally false—is now likely to come true.

self-fulfilling prophecy Robert Merton's term for an originally false assertion that becomes true simply because it was predicted

The Rosenthal-Jacobson Experiment

Let's look at another classic example of how teacher expectations lead to a self-fulfilling prophecy. This one, too, holds surprises. Social psychologists Robert Rosenthal and Lenore Jacobson (1968) told the teachers in a San Francisco grade school that they had developed a predictive test of children's abilities. After testing their students, they told them which students would probably "spurt" ahead during the year. They told the teachers to watch these students' progress, but not to let the students or their parents know about the test results. At the end of the year, they tested the students again. As they predicted, the "spurters" had spurted: Their IQs had jumped ten to fifteen points!

Did Rosenthal and Jacobson become world-famous for developing a powerful scholastic aptitude test? Actually, they hadn't developed any test at all, much less something this astounding. They had just done another of those covert experiments. They had given routine IQ tests to the children and then had *randomly* chosen 20 percent of the students as "spurters." These students were *no* different from their classmates. The "spurting," though, was real. What had happened was a self-fulfilling prophecy: The teachers expected more from those particular students, and responding to subtle cues, these students learned more and performed better on the tests.

A good deal of research confirms that, *regardless of their abilities,* students who are expected to do better generally do better, and those who are expected to do poorly do poorly (Rosenthal 1998; McKown and Weinstein 2002, 2008). In short, expect dumb, and you get dumb. Expect smart, and you get smart.

How Do Teacher Expectations Work?

Sociologist George Farkas (Farkas et al. 1990a; Farkas et al. 1990b; Farkas 1996) became interested in how teacher expectations affect grades. Using a stratified sample of students in a large school district in Texas, he found that teacher expectations produce gender and racial–ethnic biases. *On the gender level:* When boys and girls have the *same* test scores, girls, on average, are given higher course grades. *On the racial–ethnic level:* Asian Americans who have the *same* test scores as the other groups average higher grades.

At first, this may sound like more of the same old news—another case of discrimination. But this explanation doesn't fit, which is what makes the finding fascinating. Look at who the victims are. It is most unlikely that the teachers would be prejudiced against boys and whites. To interpret these unexpected results, Farkas used symbolic interactionism. He observed that some students "signal" to their teachers that they are "good students." They show an eagerness to cooperate, and they quickly agree with what the teacher says. They also show that they are "trying hard." The teachers pick up these signals and reward these "good students" with better grades. Girls and Asian Americans, Farkas concluded, are better at giving these signals so coveted by teachers.

So much for Texas. How about the other states? Their interest piqued, other researchers examined data from a national sample of students from kindergarten to the fifth grade. The results? The same. Regardless of race–ethnicity, if girls and boys have the same test scores, the girls, on average, receive higher grades (Cornwell et al. 2013). The researchers had another measure. They had the teachers rank their students on their "interpersonal skills," how often they "lose control," and how "engaged" they are in the classroom. The teachers reported that the girls had a "better attitude toward learning." Like the Texas researchers, these researchers conclude that the teachers are responding to the children's behavior.

We do not have enough information on how teachers communicate their expectations to students. Nor do we know much about how students "signal" messages to their teachers. Perhaps you will become the educational sociologist who sheds more light on this interesting area of human behavior.

17.6 Discuss mediocrity in education, grade inflation, social promotion, rising standards, cheating by administrators, and violence in schools.

Problems in U.S. Education—and Their Solutions

Now that we've looked at some of the dynamics within the classroom, let's turn to three problems facing U.S. education—mediocrity, cheating, and violence—and consider potential solutions.

Mediocrity

The Rising Tide of Mediocrity. Since I know you love taking tests, let's see how you do on these three questions:

1. *How many goals are on a basketball court? a. 1 b. 2 c. 3 d. 4*
2. *How many halves are in a college basketball game? a.1 b. 2 c. 3 d. 4*
3. *How many points does a three-point field goal account for in a basketball game? a. 1 b. 2 c. 3 d. 4*

I know this sounds like a joke, but it isn't. Sociologist Robert Benford (2007) got his hands on a copy of a twenty-question final examination given to basketball players who took a credit course on coaching principles at the University of Georgia. It is often difficult to refer to athletes, sports, and academics in the same breath, but this is about as mediocre as mediocrity can get.

Let's move to a broader view of the mediocrity that plagues our educational system like pollution plagues gasoline engines:

- Arizona officials gave their high school sophomores a math test covering the math that sophomores should know. One of ten passed.
- To get its students out of high school, Arkansas dropped its passing score in math to 24 out of 100 (Urbina 2010).
- In Washington, D.C., most of the students who graduate from high school operate at about the *fifth grade* level. How do they graduate? When they fail a course, they take something called "Credit Recovery," which does not require a test (Rossiter 2012).
- In Florida, only 27 percent of the state's fourth graders passed the reading test. That didn't sound good, so the state dropped the passing grade. Then 80 percent passed (Kristoff 2012). Much better.

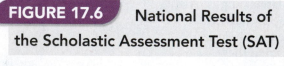

FIGURE 17.6 National Results of the Scholastic Assessment Test (SAT)

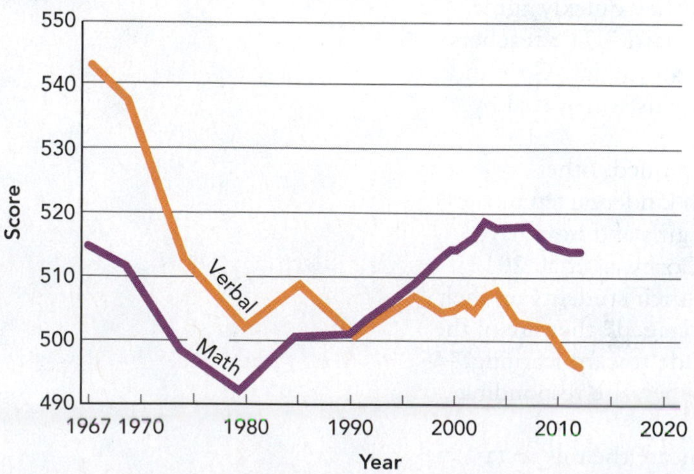

Note: Possible scores range from 200 to 800.

Sources: By the author. Based on College Board 2012; *Statistical Abstract of the United States* 2013:Table 266.

The SATs. How are we doing on the SATs? Look at Figure 17.6. You can see how fast and far the scores dropped from the 1960s to 1980. At that point, educators sounded an alarm—and even Congress expressed concern. School officials decided that they had better do something if they didn't want to lose their jobs.

Here's the *good* news. When school officials raised their standards, the math scores started to climb, and they continued going up for the next 20 years. Although scores have dropped recently, today's high school seniors score the same in math as seniors did in the 1960s. Administrators are requiring more of math teachers, who, in turn, are demanding more of students. Each is performing according to these higher expectations.

But there is also the *bad* news. Look at the verbal scores on Figure 17.6. Their drop from the 1960s was even larger than the drop in math. They have stayed down, and now have dropped even more. No one knows why these scores are so low, but the usual suspects have been rounded up: "dummied down" textbooks, less rigorous teaching, and less reading because of television, videos, and computer games.

The news is actually worse than what you see on this figure. To accommodate today's less prepared students, those who develop the SAT have made it easier. They shortened the test, dropped the section on analogies and antonyms, and gave students more time to take the test. The test makers then "rescored" the totals of previous years to match the easier test. This "dummying down" of the SAT is a form of grade inflation, the topic to which we shall now turn.

grade inflation higher grades given for the same work; a general rise in student grades without a corresponding increase in learning

social promotion passing students on to the next level even though they have not mastered basic materials

functional illiterate a high school graduate who has difficulty with basic reading and math

Grade Inflation, Social Promotion, and Functional Illiteracy.

Some graduates of prestigious law schools were having difficulty getting jobs. This reflected badly on these proud law schools—Georgetown, Golden Gate University, Loyola Law School, Tulane University, and New York University. They couldn't have this—so they found a quick solution. To make their graduates look better when recruiters came to campus, they raised everyone's grades (Rampell 2010). Much better-looking transcripts—all in a flash.

The letter grade C used to indicate average. Since more students are average than superior, high school teachers used to give about twice as many C's as A's. Now they give more A's than C's. Students aren't smarter—grading is just easier. **Grade inflation** is so pervasive that *50 percent* of all college freshmen have an overall high school grade point average of A. This is about twice what it was in 1980 (*Statistical Abstract* 2013:Table 286). Unfortunately, some of today's A's are the C's of years past.

Easy grades and declining standards have been accompanied by **social promotion**, passing students from one grade to the next despite their failure to learn the basic materials. One result is **functional illiteracy**, high school graduates who have never mastered things they should have learned in grade school. They even have difficulty with reading and writing. Some high school graduates can't fill out job applications; others can't even figure out whether they get the right change at the grocery store.

Raising Standards

Raising Standards for Teachers. It is one thing to identify problems, quite another to find solutions for them. How can we solve mediocrity? To offer a quality education, we need quality teachers. Don't we already have them? Most teachers are qualified and, if motivated, can do an excellent job. But a large number of teachers are not qualified. Consider what happened in California, where teachers must pass an educational skills test. The teachers did so poorly that to fill the classrooms, officials had to drop the passing grade to the tenth-grade level. These are college graduates who are teachers—and they are expected to perform at the tenth-grade level (Schemo 2002). I don't know about you, but I think this situation is a national disgrace. If we want to improve teaching, we need to insist that teachers meet high standards.

Watch on **MySocLab** **Video:** Attracting and Retaining Good Teachers

Our schools compete with private industry for the same pool of college graduates. If the starting salary in other fields is higher than it is in education, those fields will attract brighter, more energetic graduates. Figure 17.7 on the next page highlights the abysmal job we are doing in this competition for talent. On the SATs, education majors score lower than average for both reading and math (Shaw et al. 2012:Table 3).

On average, students in Roman Catholic schools score higher on national tests than students in public schools. Is it because Roman Catholic schools have better students, or because they do better teaching? The text reports the sociological findings.

Raising Standards for Students. What else can we do to improve the quality of education? An older study by sociologists James Coleman and Thomas Hoffer (1987) provides helpful guidelines. They wanted to see why the test scores of students in Roman Catholic schools average 15 to 20 percent higher than those of students in public schools. Is it because Catholic schools attract better students, while public schools have to put up with everyone? To find out, they tested 15,000 students in public and Catholic high schools.

Their findings? From the sophomore through the senior years, students at Catholic schools pull ahead of public school students by a full grade in verbal and math skills. The superior test

FIGURE 17.7 Starting Salaries of U.S. College Graduates, BA or BS Degree: Public School Teachers Compared with Private Industry

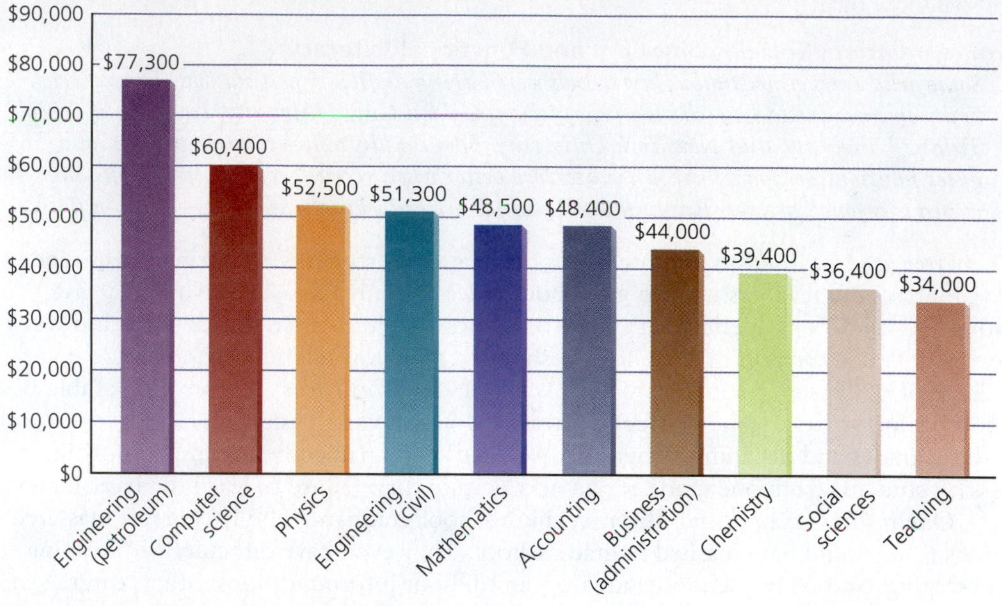

Note: Starting salaries for BA or BS degree.

Sources: By the author. Based on *Teacher Average Starting Salaries by State*, National Education Association, 2011; *Statistical Abstract of the United States* 2013:Table 298.

Listen on **MySocLab**
Audio: NPR: Chicago Charter School Network Defies Expectations

performance of students in Catholic schools, they concluded, is not due to better students, but to higher standards. Catholic schools have not watered down their curricula as have public schools. The researchers also underscored the importance of parental involvement. Parents and teachers in Catholic schools reinforce each other's commitment to learning.

These findings support the basic principle reviewed earlier about teacher expectations: Students perform better when they are expected to meet higher standards. To this, you might want to reply, "Of course. I knew that. Who wouldn't?" Somehow, however, this basic principle is lost on many teachers, who expect little of their students and have supervisors who accept low performance from students. The reason, actually, is probably not their lack of awareness of such basics but, rather, the organization that entraps them, a bureaucracy in which ritual replaces performance. To understand this point better, you may want to review Chapter 7.

A Warning about Higher Standards. If we raise standards, we can expect to upset students and their parents. It is soothing to use low standards and to pat students on the head and tell them they are doing well. But it upsets people if you do rigorous teaching and use high standards to measure performance. When Florida decided that its high school seniors needed to pass an assessment test in order to receive a diploma, 13,000 students across the state failed the test. Parents of failed students protested. Did they demand better teaching? No. What they wanted was for the state to drop the test. In their anger, they asked people to boycott Disney World and to not buy Florida orange juice (Canedy 2003). What positive steps to improve their children's learning!

Let's look at a second problem in education.

Cheating

The cheating I'm referring to is not what you saw in your social studies or math class in high school. I'm referring to cheating by *teachers and school administrators.* Listen to this:

> *The state school board of Georgia ordered an investigation after computer scanners showed that teachers in* 191 schools *had erased students' answers on reading and math tests and*

penciled in correct ones (Gabriel 2010). The cheating was apparently led by the superintendent *of Atlanta's school system. She was charged with several crimes, including theft for taking $500,000 in bonuses for producing good test scores (Winerip 2013).*

The school district was facing pressure to show that their teaching had improved, and this was a quick way to do it. It is not far-fetched to think that these same teachers cheated on tests when they were students to show that their own learning had improved.

Now look at this:

Mississippi keeps two sets of books: The one sent to Washington reports the state's graduation rate at 87 percent. The other, which the state keeps, reports that 63 percent of its students graduate. Other states do the same. California reports its totals at 83 percent and 67 percent. (Dillon 2008)

Why do high school administrators across the nation fake their graduation rates? The reason is that federal agencies publish these reports, and states don't want to look bad. Also, Washington might reduce the money it gives them. It's like a girl telling her parents that she received a B in English when she really received a D. She doesn't want to look bad, and her allowance might be cut.

School administrators can be quite creative in faking their numbers. Some count the number of students who begin their senior year, and report the percentage of these seniors who graduate. This conveniently overlooks those who drop out in their freshman, sophomore, and junior years. Some even encourage high school students who are doing poorly to drop out before they reach their senior year. This way, they won't be counted as dropouts (Dillon 2008).

The Solution to Cheating. The solution to this cheating is fairly simple. Zero tolerance. Require all states to follow the same measurement of high school graduation, and fire teachers and administrators who cheat. A simple measure is to compare the number of those who graduate from high school with the number who entered high school in the ninth grade, minus those who died and those who transferred out, plus those who transferred in. Federal officials can spot-check records across the nation. With loss of job the punishment, we could expect honesty in reporting to jump immediately. Real graduation rates could help pinpoint where the problems are, letting us know where to focus solutions. If you don't know where it's broken, you don't know where to fix it.

Let's turn to the third problem.

Violence

The man stalked the high school's hallways. He pressed his ear against a door, trying to determine if students were in the classroom. Hearing nothing, he moved silently to another classroom and did the same thing. Going from one locked door to another, he proceeded down the length of the entire hallway. Students were behind each door, but they remained absolutely quiet.

Still hearing nothing, the man smiled.

The man smiled? Yes, because he was not a sociopath seeking random victims. This was a teacher checking how well the school was performing in a "Code Blue" drill. In some schools, the safety of students and teachers is so precarious that armed guards, metal detectors, and drug-sniffing dogs are permanent fixtures. In an era of bomb threats and armed sociopaths, some states require lockdown, or "Code Blue," drills: The classrooms—each equipped with a phone—are locked. Shades or blinds on the windows are closed. The students are told to remain absolutely silent, while a school official wanders the halls, like an armed intruder, listening for the slightest sound that would indicate that someone is in a classroom (Kelley 2008).

Certainly, a good teaching-learning environment starts with safety, and school shootings have become a national concern. Are they getting worse? The answer—in the Mass Media box on school shootings on the next page—might surprise you.

Mass Media in Social Life

School Shootings: Exploding a Myth

This frame from a home video shows Eric Harris (on the left) and Dylan Klebold (on the right) as they pretend that they are searching for victims. They put their desires into practice in the infamous Columbine High School shootings.

The media sprinkle their reports of school shootings with such dramatic phrases as "alarming proportions," "outbreak of violence," and "out of control." They give us the impression that wackos walk our hallways, ready to spray our schools with gunfire. Parents used to consider schools safe havens, but no longer. Those naïve thoughts have been shattered by the media accounts of bullets ripping through our schools, children hovering in fear, and little bodies strewn across classroom floors.

Have our schools really become war zones, as the mass media would have us believe? Certainly events such as those at Sandy Hook Elementary School, Columbine High School, and Virginia Tech are disturbing, but we need to probe deeper than screaming headlines and startling images.

When we do, we find that the media's sensationalist reporting has created a myth. Contrary to "what everyone knows," *there is no trend toward greater school violence*. In fact, we find just the opposite—*the trend is toward greater safety at school*. Despite the dramatic school shootings that make the screaming headlines, as you can see from Table 17.2, shooting deaths at schools are *decreasing*. Because school homicides are high one year and low another, to see trends, we need to average them out. Here is where we get the surprising results. The average number of annual shooting deaths for 1992 to 2000 is twenty-eight. This is more than *twice* as high as the annual average of thirteen for 2000 to 2010.

School shootings are a serious problem. Even one student being wounded or killed is too many. But contrary to the impression fostered by the media, school shooting deaths have dropped. Headlines like "No Shootings This Month!" or "Schools Safer Than Ever!" simply don't get much attention—nor bring in much advertising revenue.

This is one reason that we need sociology: to quietly, dispassionately search for facts so we can better understand the events that shape our lives. The first requirement for solving any problem is accurate data. How can we create solutions based on hysteria? The information presented in this box may not make for sensational headlines, but it does serve to explode one of the myths that the media have created.

For Your Consideration

→ How do you think we can reduce school shootings? How about school violence of any sort? Why are people's ideas often based more on headlines than facts?

TABLE 17.2 Exploding a Myth: Deaths at U.S. Schools[1]

School Year	Deaths: Shooting Deaths	Deaths: Other Deaths[2]	Victims: Boys	Victims: Girls	Total
1992–1993	45	11	49	7	56
1993–1994	41	12	41	12	53
1994–1995	16	5	18	3	21
1995–1996	29	7	26	10	36
1996–1997	15	11	18	8	26
1997–1998	36	8	27	17	44
1998–1999	25	6	24	7	31
1999–2000	16	16	26	6	32
2000–2001	19	5	20	4	24
2001–2002	4	2	6	0	6
2002–2003	14	8	16	6	22
2003–2004	29	13	37	5	42
2004–2005	20	8	20	8	28
2005–2006	5	0	4	1	5
2006–2007	16	4	13	7	20
2007–2008	3	0	3	0	3
2008–2009	10	3	11	2	13
2009–2010	5	2	4	3	7
Total deaths 1992–2010	348	121	363	106	469
Mean 1992–2010	19.3	6.7	20.2	5.9	26.1

[1]Includes all school-related homicides, even those that occurred on the way to or from school. Includes suicides, school personnel killed at school by other adults, and even adults who had nothing to do with the school but who were found dead on school property. Source does not report on deaths at colleges, only K–12 (kindergarten through high school).

[2]Beating, hanging, jumping, stabbing, slashing, strangling, or heart attack.

Source: By the author. Based on National School Safety Center 2013. The CDC (Centers for Disease Control and Prevention) also reports data on school deaths, but they, too, go only to 2010 and do not include a breakdown by sex. The killings at Sandy Hook will change the totals but likely not the long-term trend of fewer school deaths.

Technology and Education

17.7 Explain how technology is changing education.

Let's end this chapter with a brief look at how technology is changing education. Most changes in education are merely minor adjustments to a flawed system. Teachers give this test instead of that test or require more memorization or less memorization. Administrators measure progress this way instead of that way, tinker with the curriculum, or use different carrots to try to motivate teachers and students. Each might be important in its own way, but each is but a cosmetic adjustment to the details of a flawed system that needs to be overhauled from top to bottom. In the meantime, as illustrated by the Thinking Critically section, technology is transforming education, changing what we learn and the way we learn it.

THINKING CRITICALLY

Internet University: No Walls, No Ivy, No All-Night Parties

Distance learning, courses taught to students who are not physically present with their instructor, is transforming education. Millions of students a year take at least one class online. Many of these students aren't really very "distant," some just across the campus in a college dorm. Distance learning has jumped in popularity. Amazing numbers of students are signing up for some classes. The photo to the right features a class that enrolled 180,000 students.

MOOCs (Massive Online Open Courses) are one way that technology is transforming education. The philosophy course taught by this professor at Duke University enrolled an amazing number of students.

Using video links, students attend lectures, watching the professor on their computers. They click an icon to "raise their hands" and ask questions. Tucked deep within the networking programs are little spies to let these instructors of low-enrolled courses know who is e-mailing others—and who is holding back. The programs also let deans (supervisors) scrutinize these instructors, sending them reports, for example, about how long an instructor takes to answer e-mail from students.

A fascinating potential of distance learning is to broaden the experience of both students and instructors through cultural diversity. With distance learning, students can enjoy stimulating international experiences without leaving the country. For example, sociology professors at the State University of New York and the State University of Belarus (Minsk, Russia) jointly taught an online course on Social Control. Coming from such different political backgrounds, the American and Russian students found that the course opened their eyes to different perspectives (Beaman 2003). A U.S. firefighter who took another course was impressed with being able to talk to a student in Siberia (Lewin 2012).

Why should formal education be limited to walled classrooms? Think of the possibilities the Net opens to us. We could study human culture and compare notes on eating, dating, or burial customs with fellow students in Thailand, Iceland, South Africa, Germany, Egypt, China, and Australia. We could write a joint paper in which we compare our experiences with one another, within the context of theories and research taught in the text, and then submit our paper to our mutual instructor.

As distance learning expands, will we eventually go from kindergarten to grad school with classmates from around the world? While this may sound intriguing, having no walls also means no joking in the hallway or dorm, no flirting after class, no getting together over a cup of coffee. . . .

And more seriously (at least for me), it also means no give-and-take conversations with fellow students and instructors, a type of learning essential to good classroom teaching that is impossible to replicate online.

Something is gained, but certainly something is also lost.

For Your Consideration

→ Do you think that at some point, online teaching might replace traditional classrooms? Why or why not? What do you see as the advantages of online learning? Its disadvantages? If you were able to take all your college classes online and receive the same degree from the same college, would you? Why or why not? ■

MySocLab

Study and Review on MySocLab

CHAPTER 17 Summary and Review

The Development of Modern Education

17.1 Discuss education in earlier societies and how education is related to industrialization.

How did modern education develop?

For most of human history, **education** consisted of informal learning, equivalent to learning the culture. In some earlier societies, centers of formal education did develop, such as among the Arabs, Chinese, Greeks, and Egyptians. Because free public education came about in response to industrialization, formal education is much less common in the Least Industrialized Nations. Pp. 487–491.

Education in Global Perspective

17.2 To understand how education is related to a nation's culture and economy, compare education in Japan, Russia, and Egypt.

How does education compare among the Most Industrialized, Industrializing, and Least Industrialized Nations?

Formal education reflects a nation's economy and culture. Education is extensive in the Most Industrialized Nations, undergoing vast change in the Industrializing Nations, and spotty in the Least Industrialized Nations. Japan, Russia, and Egypt provide examples of education in countries at three levels of industrialization. Pp. 491–493.

The Functionalist Perspective: Providing Social Benefits

17.3 Explain the functions of education: knowledge and skills, values, social integration, gatekeeping, and replacing family functions

What is the functionalist perspective on education?

Among the functions of education are the teaching of knowledge and skills, providing credentials, **cultural transmission of values**, social integration, **gatekeeping**, and **mainstreaming**. Functionalists also note that education has replaced some traditional family functions. Pp. 493–496.

The Conflict Perspective: Perpetuating Social Inequality

17.4 Explain how the educational system reproduces the social class structure.

What is the conflict perspective on education?

The basic view of conflict theorists is that *education reproduces the social class structure;* that is, through such mechanisms as unequal funding and operating different schools for the elite and for the masses, education perpetuates a society's basic social inequalities from one generation to the next. Pp. 496–501.

The Symbolic Interactionist Perspective: Teacher Expectations

17.5 Explain the significance of teacher expectations and give examples.

What is the symbolic interactionist perspective on education?

Symbolic interactionists focus on face-to-face interaction. In examining what occurs in the classroom, they have found that student performance tends to conform to teacher expectations, whether they are high or low. Pp. 501–503.

Problems in U.S. Education—and Their Solutions

17.6 Discuss mediocrity in education, grade inflation, social promotion, rising standards, cheating by administrators, and violence in schools.

What are the chief problems that face U.S. education?

The major problems are mediocrity (low achievement as shown by SAT scores), **grade inflation**, **social promotion**, **functional illiteracy**, faked data reported by school administrators, and violence. P. 504.

What are the potential solutions to these problems?

To restore high educational standards, we must expect more of *both* students and teachers. School administrators can be required to use a single reporting measure based on objective, verifiable data. Although we cannot prevent all school violence, for an effective learning environment, we must provide basic security for students and teachers. Pp. 504–508.

Technology and Education

17.7 Explain how technology is changing education.

What development indicates the future of U.S. education?

Most changes in education represent minor, even trivial, tinkering with an existing system. Distance learning, in contrast, indicates a major change in education, one that will transform the way students are educated and, likely, the content of their learning. Pp. 509–510.

Thinking Critically about Chapter 17

1. How does education in the United States compare with education in Japan, Russia, and Egypt?
2. How have your experiences in education (including classmates, teachers, and assignments) influenced your goals, attitudes, and values? Be specific.
3. How do you think that U.S. schools can be improved?

Religion

CHAPTER 18

Listen to Chapter 18 on MySocLab

Learning Objectives

After you have read this chapter, you should be able to:

18.1 Explain what Durkheim meant by sacred and profane; discuss the three elements of religion. (p. 513)

18.2 Apply the functionalist perspective to religion: functions, dysfunctions, and functional equivalents. (p. 514)

18.3 Apply the symbolic interactionist perspective to religion: symbols, rituals, beliefs, religious experience, and community. (p. 518)

18.4 Apply the conflict perspective to religion: opium of the people and legitimating social inequalities. (p. 521)

18.5 Explain Weber's analysis of how religion broke tradition and brought capitalism. (p. 524)

18.6 Discuss the origins and development of Judaism, Islam, Hinduism, Buddhism, and Confucianism. (p. 525)

18.7 Compare cult, sect, church, and ecclesia; discuss the conflict between religion and culture. (p. 530)

18.8 Summarize main features of religion in the United States and discuss the secularization of religion and culture. (p. 534)

18.9 Discuss the likely future of religion. (p. 541)

Yearning for Zion—Who would give such a strange name to a ranch?

And what are those strange people doing behind their locked gates? A 1,700-acre ranch with its own temple. Women who come into town wearing homemade prairie dresses—like women wear in Western movies.

The rumors swirled. "Those are Mormons, and the men have a lot of wives."

Those aren't real Mormons," someone said. "They're a breakaway group of some sort. They've got armed guards at the ranch gates, and they won't let anyone in."

But they did let someone in. In fact, they let a lot of outsiders in.

The telephone call was anonymous. A female, claiming to be 16 years old, said she had been forced to marry a 50-year-old man, and he was abusing her. Ordinarily, an anonymous call doesn't merit much action, but the authorities jumped at this one. This was their chance to get behind those gates.

> "A female, claiming to be 16 years old, said she had been forced to marry a 50-year-old man."

State troopers, officials from Child Protective Services, and even the famed Texas Rangers rushed to those locked gates. They were concerned that they might have another Waco on their hands (another place in Texas, where federal officials who raided the compound of a religious group met armed resistance, and eighty-two of the sect's members were burned alive).

The police set up roadblocks and brought in an armored vehicle. The leaders of Yearning for Zion, also aware of Waco, offered no resistance. They didn't relish being shot and having their wives and children burned to death.

The officials rushed in and carried off fifty-two girls. Then they came back, seizing another four hundred children, this time both girls and boys.

It took a couple of months of protest, but the parents finally got their children back. Authorities were stunned when an appeals court ruled that snatching babies from their mothers' arms is illegal. The authorities won another matter, though. They charged the group's leaders with bigamy and the sexual assault of minors.

The group, which broke off from the Latter Day Saints in 1890, still believes that to reach heaven's highest realms, a man must have three wives in this life.

Based on Blumenthal 2008a, 2008b; Hylton 2008; Vergakis 2010.

Seldom does the government swoop down on a religious group, but it does happen. One of the topics we will consider in this chapter is the relationship of the dominant culture to cults, or new religions. Let's begin by asking what religion is.

What Is Religion?

18.1 Explain what Durkheim meant by sacred and profane; discuss the three elements of religion.

All human societies are organized by some form of the family, as well as by some kind of economic system and political order. As we have seen, these key social institutions touch on aspects of life that are essential to human welfare. In this chapter, we focus on religion, another universal social institution.

What does sociology have to do with something so personal and intimate as religion? As you'll recall, in Chapter 16, we focused on the family, also personal and intimate. As with the family, sociologists do two primary things: They analyze the relationship between society and religion, and they study the role that religion plays in people's lives.

It is also important to ask what sociologists do *not* do in their research on religion. Just as sociologists do not try to prove that one family form is better than another, so they do not try to prove that one religion is better than another. As was mentioned in Chapter 1, sociologists don't even have tools for deciding that one course of action is more moral than another, much less that one religion is the "correct" one. Religion is

Parents around the world teach their children their religious beliefs and practices. This photo is of Sikh children in India.

a matter of faith—and sociologists deal with empirical matters, things they can observe or measure. Sociologists can study how religious beliefs and practices affect people's lives, but unlike theologians, they have nothing to say about the truth of a religion's teachings.

Religion was a major interest of Emile Durkheim, probably because he was reared in a mixed-religion family, by a Protestant mother and a Jewish father. Durkheim decided to find out what all religions have in common. After surveying religions around the world, he published his findings in *The Elementary Forms of the Religious Life*. This 1912 book is complicated, but let's summarize Durkheim's three main findings. The first is that the world's religions have no specific belief or practice in common. The second is that all religions develop a community centering on their beliefs and practices. The third is that all religions separate the sacred from the profane. By **sacred**, Durkheim referred to aspects of life having to do with the supernatural that inspire awe, reverence, deep respect, or even fear. By **profane**, he meant the aspects of life that are not concerned with religion but, instead, are part of ordinary, everyday life.

Durkheim (1912/1965) summarized his conclusions by saying,

> *A religion is a unified system of beliefs and practices relative to sacred things, that is to say, things set apart and forbidden—beliefs and practices which unite into one single moral community called a Church, all those who adhere to them.*

Religion, then, has three elements:

1. *Beliefs* that some things are sacred (forbidden, set apart from the profane)
2. *Practices* (rituals) centering on the things considered sacred
3. *A moral community* (a church), which results from a group's beliefs and practices

Durkheim used the word **church** in an unusual sense, to refer to any "moral community" centered on beliefs and practices regarding the sacred. In Durkheim's sense, *church* refers to Buddhists bowing before a shrine, Hindus dipping in the Ganges River, and Confucians offering food to their ancestors. Similarly, the term *moral community* does not imply morality in the sense familiar to most of us—of ethical conduct. Rather, a moral community is simply a group of people who are united by their religious practices—and that would include sixteenth-century Aztec priests who each day gathered around an altar to pluck out the beating heart of a virgin.

To better understand the sociological approach to religion, let's see what pictures emerge when we apply the three theoretical perspectives.

sacred Durkheim's term for things set apart or forbidden that inspire fear, awe, reverence, or deep respect

profane Durkheim's term for common elements of everyday life

religion according to Durkheim, beliefs and practices that separate the profane from the sacred and unite its adherents into a moral community

church according to Durkheim, one of the three essential elements of religion—a moral community of believers; also refers to a large, highly organized religious group that has formal, sedate worship services with little emphasis on evangelism, intense religious experience, or personal conversion

18.2 Apply the functionalist perspective to religion: functions, dysfunctions, and functional equivalents.

The Functionalist Perspective

Functionalists stress that religion is universal because it meets universal human needs. What are religion's functions and dysfunctions?

Functions of Religion

Questions about Ultimate Meaning. Around the world, religions provide answers to perplexing questions about ultimate meaning. What is the purpose of life? Why do people suffer? Is there an afterlife? The answers to questions like these give followers a

Watch on **MySocLab**
Video: The Big Picture: Religion

sense of purpose, a framework for living. Instead of seeing themselves buffeted by random events in an aimless existence, believers see their lives as fitting into a divine plan.

One of the many functions of religion is providing emotional support. This photo was taken in Newark, New Jersey.

Emotional Comfort. The answers that religion provides about ultimate meaning bring comfort by assuring people that there is a purpose to life, even to suffering. The religious rituals that enshroud crucial events such as illness and death assure the individual that others care.

Social Solidarity. Religious teachings and practices unite believers into a community that shares values and perspectives ("we Jews," "we Christians," "we Muslims"). The religious rituals that surround marriage, for example, link the bride and groom with a broader community that wishes them well. So do other religious rituals, such as those that celebrate birth and mourn death.

Guidelines for Everyday Life. The teachings of religion are not all abstractions. They also provide practical guidelines for everyday life. For example, four of the ten commandments delivered by Moses to the Israelites concern God, but the other six contain instructions for getting along with others, from how to avoid problems with parents and neighbors to warnings about lying, stealing, and having affairs.

Many consequences for people who follow these guidelines can be measured. For example, people who attend church are less likely to abuse alcohol, nicotine, and illegal drugs than are people who don't go to church. They are also more likely to exercise (Gillum 2005; Wallace et al. 2007; Newport et al. 2012). In general, churchgoers follow a healthier lifestyle than people who don't go to church—and they live longer. How religion affects health is discussed in the Down-to-Earth Sociology box on the next page.

Read on **MySocLab**
Document: Religion and the Domestication of Men

Social Control. Although a religion's guidelines for everyday life usually apply only to its members, nonmembers feel a spillover. Religious teachings, for example, are incorporated into criminal law. In the American colonial period, people could be arrested for blasphemy and adultery. As a carryover today, some states have laws that prohibit the sale of alcohol before noon on Sunday. The original purpose of these laws was to get people out of the saloons and into the churches.

Adaptation. Religion can help people adapt to new environments. For example, it isn't easy for immigrants to adjust to the customs of a new land. By keeping their native language alive within a community of people who are going through similar experiences, religion serves as a bridge between the old and new: It provides both continuity with the immigrants' cultural past and encouragement to adapt to the new culture. This was the case for earlier U.S. immigrants from Europe, and it remains true for today's immigrants from around the globe. The many mosques and thousands of Spanish-speaking churches around the United States are outstanding examples.

Support for the Government. Most religions provide support for the government. An obvious example is the way some churches prominently display the U.S. flag. Some fly it in front of the church building, and many display both the U.S. flag and a church flag on stands at the front of the worship center. Religions that become hostile to the government—or even seem strange—can run into trouble, as in the example of our opening vignette.

For their part, governments reciprocate by supporting churches. Some governments sponsor a particular religion and ban or place a heavy hand on others. They provide financial support for building churches, synagogues, mosques, and seminaries, and even

Down-to-Earth **Sociology**

Religion and Health: What We Know and Don't Know

"After seeing the data, I think I should go to church," said Lynda Powell, an epidemiologist at Rush University Medical Center in Chicago (Helliker 2005).

This was the response of a non-churchgoing scientist when she saw the data on health and religion. Although scientists cannot determine the truth of any religion, they can study the effects of religion on people's lives. Health is one of those areas that can be measured, and the research is bringing some surprises.

Powell, along with two colleagues, evaluated the published research on the effects of religion on health. They evaluated only research that met rigid criteria. For example, they threw out studies that didn't control for age, income, gender, or race–ethnicity, significant variables in health (Powell et al. 2003). Their most outstanding finding? *People who attend religious services once a week or more have 25 percent fewer deaths in a given time period than people who don't go to church*. Think about it: For every hundred deaths of non-churchgoers, there are only 75 deaths of people who attend church weekly.

Religious activity brings surprising health benefits. This photo was taken in New York City.

How could this possibly be? Perhaps the churchgoers were already healthier. This wasn't the reason, though, because the researchers compared people who were at the same levels of health.

How about healthier lifestyles? Churchgoers are less likely to smoke, to get drunk, and so on. Not this either. The researchers also controlled for lifestyle and social class. The weekly churchgoers actually had 30 percent less mortality, but when the researchers adjusted for lifestyle and social class, the difference was 25 percent (Powell et al. 2003).

What explanation could there be, then? Remember that the researchers are scientists, so they aren't going to say "God." They suggest three mechanisms that might account for the lower mortality of churchgoers: finding a sense of self-worth and purpose in life, learning calming ways of coping with crises, and experiencing positive emotions. Other researchers have documented the power of positive emotions: People who have a positive world view and those who believe that God is loving have better health (Campbell et al. 2010). And religious people do have fewer negative emotions (Newport et al. 2010).

What else might account for this remarkable reduction in mortality? Some researchers think it might be prayer. Prayer (or meditation) seems to change people's brain activity in a way that improves their immune response. Scientists are investigating this hypothesis (Kalb 2003).

One researcher points to another possibility—the practice of forgiveness. It turns out that people who forgive easily are more likely to be in good emotional health. They are less likely to be angry, sad, or depressed (Krause and Ellison 2003; Newport et al. 2010, 2012). To forgive someone who has done you wrong apparently brings release from feelings of resentment, bitterness, and hatred—but holding on to grudges can rip you apart inside.

One study shows that mortality is not less among the highly educated who are active in a religion (Moulton and Sherkat 2012). We certainly need more research, but at this initial stage of research on religion and health, we have this remarkable finding: People who go to religious services more than once a week live an average of seven and a half years longer than those who don't attend religious services (Hummer et al. 1999; Hummer et al. 2004).

So, if you want to live longer . . .

For Your Consideration

➔ If you attend a church, synagogue, or mosque, what difference do you think that your attendance makes in your life? How does your religion affect your lifestyle? What decisions would you have made differently if you did not practice your religion?

state religion a government–sponsored religion; also called *ecclesia*

civil religion Robert Bellah's term for religion that is such an established feature of a country's life that its history and social institutions become sanctified by being associated with God

pay salaries to the clergy. These religions are known as **state religions**. During the sixteenth and seventeenth centuries in Sweden, the government sponsored Lutheranism; in Switzerland, Calvinism; and in Italy, Roman Catholicism. Some Arab countries today make Islam their official religion.

Even though a government sponsors no particular religion, religious beliefs can be embedded in a nation's life. This is called **civil religion** (Bellah 1970). For example, in their inaugural speeches, U.S. presidents—regardless of whether or not they are believers—invariably ask God to bless the nation. U.S. officials take office by swearing in the name of God that they will fulfill their duty. Similarly, Congress opens each session with a prayer led by its own chaplain. The Pledge of Allegiance includes the phrase "one nation under God," and coins bear the inscription "In God We Trust."

functional equivalent a substitute that serves the same functions (or meets the same needs) as religion; for example, psychotherapy

Social Change. Although religion is often so bound up with the prevailing social order that it resists social change, religious activists sometimes spearhead change. In the 1960s, for example, the civil rights movement, whose goals were to desegregate public facilities and abolish racial discrimination in southern voting, was led by religious leaders. African American churches served as centers at which demonstrators were trained and rallies were organized. Other churches were centers for resisting this change.

Functional Equivalents of Religion

If a group that is not a religion answers questions about ultimate meaning and provides emotional comfort and guidelines for daily life, sociologists call it a **functional equivalent** of religion. For some people, Alcoholics Anonymous is a functional equivalent of religion (Chalfant 1992). Other functional equivalents are psychotherapy, humanism, transcendental meditation, and even political parties.

Some functional equivalents are difficult to distinguish from a religion (Brinton 1965; Luke 1985). For example, communism had its prophets (Marx and Lenin), sacred writings (everything written by Marx, Engels, and Lenin, but especially the *Communist Manifesto*), high priests (the heads of the Communist Party), sacred buildings (the Kremlin), shrines (Lenin's body on display in Red Square), rituals (the annual May Day parade in Red Square), and even martyrs (Cuba's Ché Guevara). Avowedly atheistic, Soviet communism tried to wipe out all traces of Christianity, Judaism, and Islam from its midst. The Communist Party devised its own rituals for weddings and funerals and replaced baptisms and circumcisions with state-sponsored rituals that dedicated children to the state.

As sociologist Ian Robertson (1987) pointed out, however, there is a fundamental distinction between a religion and its functional equivalents. The equivalent may perform similar functions, but its activities are not directed toward God, gods, or the supernatural.

Religion can promote social change, as was evident in the U.S. civil rights movement. Dr. Martin Luther King, Jr., a Baptist minister, shown here in his famous "I have a dream" speech, was the foremost leader of this movement.

Dysfunctions of Religion

Functionalists also examine ways in which religion is *dysfunctional*, that is, how religion can bring harmful results. Two dysfunctions are persecution and war and terrorism.

Religion as Justification for Persecution. Beginning in the 1100s and continuing into the 1800s, in what has become known as the Inquisition, special commissions of the Roman Catholic Church tortured and burned at the stake hundreds of accused heretics. In 1692, Protestant leaders in Salem, Massachusetts, executed twenty-one women and men who were accused of being witches. In 2001, in the Democratic Republic of the Congo, about 1,000 alleged witches were hacked to death (Jenkins 2002). In Papua New Guinea, accused witches are tortured, doused with gasoline, and set on fire (Chumley 2013). Similarly, it seems fair to say that the Aztec religion had its dysfunctions—at least for the virgins who were offered to appease angry gods. In short, religion has been used to justify oppression and any number of brutal acts.

War and Terrorism. History is filled with wars based on religion—commingled with politics. Between the eleventh and fourteenth centuries, for example, Christian monarchs conducted nine bloody Crusades in an attempt to wrest control of the region they called the Holy Land from the Muslims. Terrorist acts, too, are sometimes committed in the name of religion, as discussed in the Down-to-Earth Sociology box on the next page.

18.3 Apply the symbolic interactionist perspective to religion: symbols, rituals, beliefs, religious experience, and community.

The Symbolic Interactionist Perspective

Symbolic interactionists focus on the meanings that people give their experiences, especially how they use symbols. Let's apply this perspective to religious symbols, rituals, and beliefs to see how they help to forge a community of like-minded people.

Religious Symbols

Suppose that it is about two thousand years ago and you have just joined a new religion. You have come to believe that a recently crucified Jew named Jesus is the Messiah, the Lamb of God offered for your sins. The Roman leaders are persecuting the followers of Jesus. They hate your religion because you and your fellow believers will not acknowledge Caesar as God.

Christians are few in number, and you are eager to have fellowship with other believers. But how can you tell who is a believer? Spies are everywhere. The government has sworn to destroy this new religion, and you do not relish the thought of being fed to lions in the Colosseum.

You use a simple technique. While talking with a stranger, as though doodling absentmindedly in the sand or dust, you casually trace the outline of a fish. Only fellow believers know the meaning—that, taken together, the first letter of each word in the Greek sentence "Jesus (is) Christ the Son of God" spell the Greek word for fish. If the other person gives no response, you rub out the outline and continue the interaction as usual. If there is a response, you eagerly talk about your new faith.

Symbolic interactionists stress that a basic characteristic of humans is that they attach meaning to objects and events and then use representations of those objects or events to communicate with one another. Michelangelo's *Pietà*, depicting Mary tenderly holding her son, Jesus, after his crucifixion, is one of the most acclaimed symbols in the Western world. It is admired for its beauty by believers and nonbelievers alike.

All religions use symbols to provide identity and create social solidarity for their members. For Muslims, the primary symbol is the crescent moon and star; for Jews, the Star of David; for Christians, the cross. For members, these are not ordinary symbols, but sacred emblems that evoke feelings of awe and reverence. In Durkheim's terms, religions use symbols to represent what the group considers sacred and to separate the sacred from the profane.

A symbol is a condensed way of communicating. Worn by a fundamentalist Christian, for example, the cross says, "I am a follower of Jesus Christ. I believe that he is the Messiah, the promised Son of God, that he loves me, that he died to take away my sins, that he rose from the dead and is going to return to Earth, and that through him I will receive eternal life."

Down-to-Earth Sociology

Terrorism and the Mind of God

WARNING: The "equal time" contents of this box are likely to offend just about everyone.

"There is just enough truth in the ideas held by religiously motivated terrorists to keep the delusion alive."

After September 11, 2001, the question on many people's minds was some form of "How can people do such evil in the name of God?"

To answer this question, we need to broaden the context. The question is fine, but to direct the question solely at Islamic terrorists misses the point.

We need to consider other religions, too. For Christians, we don't have to go back centuries to the Inquisition or to the Crusades. We only have to look at Ireland and the bombings in Belfast. There, Protestants and Catholics killed each other in the name of God.

In the United States, we can consider the killing of abortion doctors. Paul Hill, a minister who was executed for killing a doctor in Florida, was convinced that his act was good, that he had saved the lives of unborn babies. Before his execution, he said that he was looking forward to heaven.

Religious violence goes back thousands of years. This woman's house was burned in bloodshed between Muslims and Buddhists in Myanmar.

Since I want to give equal time to the major religions, we can't forget the Jews. Dr. Baruch Goldstein was convinced that Yahweh wanted him to take an assault rifle, go to the Tomb of the Patriarchs, and shoot into a crowd of praying Palestinian men and boys. His admirers built a monument on his grave (Juergensmeyer 2000).

Finally, for the sake of inclusivity, we can't let the Hindus, Buddhists, and Sikhs off the hook. In India, in the name of their gods, they have attacked the houses of worship of others and blown one another up. The Hindus are actually equal opportunists—they kill Christians, too. I visited Orissa, a state in India where Hindus had doused a jeep with gasoline and burned alive an Australian missionary and his two sons. This dysfunctional aspect of religion came alive for me in 2008 when Hindu leaders orchestrated riots throughout Orissa. Violently sweeping through the state, the rioters burned down churches and orphanages. People I know had to flee into the nearby jungles. When they returned, they found their homes looted and burned.

None of these terrorists—Islamic, Christian, Jew, Sikh, Buddhist, or Hindu—represent the mainstream of their religions, but they do commit violence for religious reasons. How can they do so? Here are five elements that religious terrorists seem to have in common.

First, the individuals believe that they are under attack. Evil forces are bent on destroying the good of their world—whether their religion, their way of life, or unborn babies.

Second, they become convinced that God wants the evil destroyed.

Third, they conclude that only violence will resolve the situation.

Fourth, they become convinced that God has chosen them for this task.

Fifth, these perspectives are nurtured by a community, a group in which the individuals find identity. This group may realize that most members of their faith do not support their views, but they conclude that those others are mistaken. The smaller community holds the truth.

Under these conditions, morality is turned upside down. Killing becomes moral, a good deed done for a greater cause.

There is just enough truth in these points of view to keep the delusion alive. After all, wouldn't it have been better for the millions of victims of Hitler, Stalin, and Pol Pot if someone had had the foresight—and the bravery—to kill them? Wouldn't their deaths and the assassins' self-sacrifice have been a greater good? Today, there are those bad Protestants, those bad Catholics, those bad Jews, those bad Palestinians, those bad Muslims, those bad abortionists, those bad Americans—an endless list. And the violence is for the Greater Good: what God wants.

Once people buy into this system of thought, they become convinced that they have access to the mind of God.

For Your Consideration

→ How do you think the type of thinking that leads to religiously motivated violence can be broken?

That is a lot to pack into one symbol—and it is only part of what this symbol means to a fundamentalist believer. To people in other traditions of Christianity, the cross conveys somewhat different meanings—but to all Christians, the cross is a shorthand way of expressing many meanings. So it is with the Star of David, the crescent moon and star, the cow (expressing to Hindus the unity of all living things), and the various symbols of the world's many other religions.

Rituals

Rituals, ceremonies or repetitive practices, are also symbols that help to unite people into a moral community. Some rituals, such as the bar mitzvah of Jewish boys and the holy communion of Christians, are designed to create in devout believers a feeling of closeness with God and unity with one another. Rituals include kneeling and praying at set times; bowing; crossing oneself; singing; lighting candles and incense; reading scripture; and following prescribed traditions at processions, baptisms, weddings, and funerals. The photo essay on pages 522–523 features photos I took of annual rituals held in Spain during Holy Week (the week that leads into the Christian holiday of Easter).

Beliefs

Symbols, including rituals, develop from beliefs. The belief may be vague ("God is") or highly specific ("God wants us to prostrate ourselves and face Mecca five times each day"). Religious beliefs include not only *values* (what is considered good and desirable in life—how we ought to live) but also a **cosmology**, a unified picture of the world. For example, the Jewish, Christian, and Muslim belief that there is only one God, the creator of the universe, who is concerned about the actions of humans and who will hold us accountable for what we do, is a cosmology. It presents a unifying picture of the universe.

Religious Experience

The term **religious experience** refers to becoming suddenly aware of the supernatural or a feeling of coming into contact with God. Some people undergo a mild version, such as feeling closer to God when they look at a mountain, watch a sunset, or listen to a certain piece of music. Others report a life-transforming experience. St. Francis of Assisi, for example, said that he became aware of God's presence in every living thing.

Some Protestants use the term **born again** to describe people who have undergone such a life-transforming religious experience. These people say that they came to the realization that they had sinned, that Jesus had died for their sins, and that God wants them to live a new life. Their worlds become transformed. They look forward to the Resurrection and to a new life in heaven. They see relationships with spouses, parents, children, and even bosses in a new light. They also report a need to change how they interact with people so that their lives reflect their new, personal commitment to Jesus as their "Savior and Lord." They describe a feeling of beginning life anew—which is why they use the term *born again*.

Community

Unity. Finally, the shared meanings that come through symbols, rituals, and beliefs (and for some, a religious experience) unite people into a moral community. Their beliefs and rituals bind them together—and at the same time separate them from those who do not share their unique symbolic world. Mormons, for example, feel a "kindred spirit" (as it is often known) with other Mormons. Baptists, Jews, Jehovah's Witnesses, and Muslims feel similar bonds with members of their respective faiths.

As a symbol of their unity, members of some religious groups address one another as "brother" or "sister." "Sister Luby, we are going to meet at Brother and Sister Maher's on Wednesday" is a common way of expressing a message. The terms *brother* and *sister* are intended to symbolize a relationship so close that the individuals consider themselves members of the same family.

rituals ceremonies or repetitive practices; in religion, observances or rites often intended to evoke a sense of awe of the sacred

cosmology teachings or ideas that provide a unified picture of the world

religious experience a sudden awareness of the supernatural or a feeling of coming in contact with God

born again a term describing Christians who have undergone a religious experience so lifetransforming that they feel they have become new persons

Exclusion. Community is powerful. Not only does it bind people together through mutual identity, but it also establishes compelling norms. People either conform to them or they lose their membership in the group. In Christian churches, for example, an individual whose adultery becomes known, and who refuses to admit wrongdoing and ask forgiveness, may be banned from the church. He or she may be formally excommunicated, as in the Catholic tradition, or more informally "stricken from the rolls," as is the usual Protestant practice.

Sociologists John Hostetler (1980, 2013), Richard Schaefer, and William Zellner (Schaefer and Zellner 2011) describe the Amish practice of *shunning*—ignoring an offender in all situations. Persons who are shunned are treated as though they do not exist. (If they do not repent publicly for their act—acknowledging that they have sinned and are sorry—they cease to exist as members of the community.) The shunning is so thorough that even family members, who themselves remain in good standing in the congregation, are not allowed to talk to the person being shunned. This obviously makes for some interesting times at the dinner table.

The Conflict Perspective

18.4 Apply the conflict perspective to religion: opium of the people and legitimating social inequalities.

In general, conflict theorists are highly critical of religion. They stress that religion supports the status quo and helps to maintain social inequalities. Let's look at some of their analyses.

Opium of the People

Watch on **MySocLab**
Video: Religion: The Basics

Karl Marx, an avowed atheist who believed that the existence of God was impossible, set the tone for conflict theorists with this statement: "Religion is the sigh of the oppressed creature, the sentiment of a heartless world. . . . It is the opium of the people" (Marx 1844/1964). Marx meant that for oppressed workers, religion is like a drug that helps addicts forget their misery. By diverting thoughts toward future happiness in an afterlife, religion takes the workers' eyes off their suffering in this world. This reduces the possibility that they will throw off their chains, overthrow their oppressors, and usher in a new society of equality.

Legitimating Social Inequalities

Conflict theorists stress that religion legitimates social inequalities. By this, they mean that religion teaches that the existing social arrangements represent what God desires. For example, during the Middle Ages, Christian theologians decreed the *divine right of kings*. This doctrine meant that God determined who would become king and set him on the throne. The king ruled in God's place, and it was the duty of a king's subjects to be loyal to him (and to pay their taxes). To disobey the king was to disobey God.

In what was perhaps the supreme technique of legitimating the social order (one that went even farther than the divine right of kings), the religion of ancient Egypt held that the Pharaoh was a *god*. The emperor of Japan was similarly declared divine. If this were so, who could ever question his decisions? Today's politicians would give their right arms for such a religious teaching.

Conflict theorists point to many other examples of how religion legitimates the social order. In India, Hinduism supports the caste system by teaching that anyone who tries to change caste will come back in the next life as a member of a lower caste—or even as an animal. In the decades before the American Civil War, southern ministers used scripture to defend slavery, saying that it was God's will—while northern ministers legitimated *their* region's social structure by using scripture to denounce slavery as evil (Ernst 1988; White 1995; Riley 2012).

THROUGH THE AUTHOR'S LENS

Holy Week in Spain

Religious groups develop rituals designed to evoke memories, create awe, inspire reverence, and stimulate social solidarity. One of the primary means by which groups, religious and secular, accomplish these goals is through the display of symbols.

I took these photos during Holy Week in Spain—in Malaga and Almuñecar. Throughout Spain, elaborate processions feature *tronos* that depict the biblical account of Jesus' suffering, death, and resurrection. During the processions in Malaga, the participants walk slowly for about two minutes; then because of the weight of the *tronos*, they rest for about two minutes. They repeat this process for about six hours a day.

Bands, sometimes several of them, are part of the processions.

The procession in the village was more informal. This Roman soldier has an interesting way of participating—and keeping tabs—on his little daughter. The girl is distributing candy.

A group of participants exiting the Church of the Incarnation for Malaga's Easter procession.

Parents gave a lot of attention to their children both during the preparations and during the processions. This photo was taken during one of the repetitive two-minute breaks.

Beneath the costumes are townspeople and church members who know one another well. They enjoy themselves prior to the procession. This man is preparing to put on his hood.

During the short breaks at the night processions, children from the audience would rush to collect dripping wax to make wax balls. This was one way that the audience made themselves participants in the drama.

Some *tronos* are so heavy that they require many men to carry them. (Some were carried by over 100 men.) This photo was taken in Malaga, on Monday of Holy Week.

For the Good Friday procession, I was fortunate to be able to photograph the behind-the-scenes preparations, which are seldom seen by visitors. Shown here are finishing touches being given to the Mary figure.

The town square was packed with people awaiting the procession. From one corner of the square, the *trono* of Jesus was brought in. Then from another, that of Mary ("reuniting" them, as I was told). During this climactic scene, the priest on the balcony on the left read a message.

© Robert Weber/The New Yorker Collection/www.cartoonbank.com

"We're thinking maybe it's time you started getting some religious instruction. There's Catholic, Protestant, and Jewish—any of those sound good to you?"

For some Americans, religion is an "easy-going, makes-little-difference" matter, as expressed in this cartoon. For others, religious matters are firmly held, and followers find even slight differences of faith to be significant.

Religion and the Spirit of Capitalism

Max Weber disagreed with the conflict perspective. Religion, he said, does not merely reflect and legitimate the social order and impede social change. Rather, religion's focus on the afterlife is a source of profound social change.

Like Marx, Weber observed the early industrialization of Europe. As he did so, he began to wonder why some societies embraced capitalism while others held onto their traditional ways. Tradition was strong in all these countries, yet capitalism transformed some while others remained untouched. As Weber explored this puzzle, he concluded that religion held the key to **modernization**—the transformation of traditional societies to industrial societies.

To explain his conclusions, Weber wrote *The Protestant Ethic and the Spirit of Capitalism* (1904–1905, 2011). Because his argument was presented in Chapter 7 (pages 173–174), it is only summarized here.

18.5 Explain Weber's analysis of how religion broke tradition and brought capitalism.

1. Capitalism represents a fundamentally different way of thinking about work and money. *Traditionally, people worked just enough to meet their basic needs, not so that they could have a surplus to invest.* To accumulate money (capital) as an end in itself, not just to spend it, was a radical departure from traditional thinking. People even came to consider it a duty to invest money so they could make profits. They reinvested these profits to make even more profits. Weber called this new approach to work and money the **spirit of capitalism**.
2. Why did the spirit of capitalism develop in Europe and not, for example, in China or India, where people had similar material resources and education? According to Weber, *religion was the key.* The religions of China and India, and indeed Roman Catholicism in Europe, encouraged a traditional approach to life, not thrift and investment. Capitalism appeared when Protestantism came on the scene.
3. What was different about Protestantism, especially Calvinism? John Calvin taught that God had predestined some people to go to heaven, and others to hell. Neither church membership nor feelings about your relationship with God could assure you that you were saved. You wouldn't know your fate until after you died.
4. "Am I predestined to hell or to heaven?" Calvin's followers wondered. As they wrestled with this question, they concluded that church members have a duty to live as though they are predestined to heaven—for good works are a demonstration of salvation.
5. This conclusion motivated Calvinists to lead moral lives *and* to work hard, to use their time productively, and to be frugal—since idleness and needless spending were signs of worldliness. Weber called this self-denying approach to life the **Protestant ethic**.
6. As people worked hard and spent money only on necessities (a pair of earrings or a second pair of dress shoes would have been defined as sinful luxuries), they had money left over. Because it couldn't be spent, this capital was invested, which led to a surge in production.
7. Weber's analysis can be summed up this way: The change in religion (from Catholicism to Protestantism, especially Calvinism) led to a fundamental change in thought and behavior (the *Protestant ethic*). The result was the *spirit of capitalism*. For this reason, capitalism originated in Europe and not in places where religion did not encourage capitalism's essential elements: the accumulation of capital and its investment and reinvestment.

modernization the transformation of traditional societies into industrial societies

spirit of capitalism Weber's term for the desire to accumulate capital—not to spend it, but as an end in itself—and to constantly reinvest it

Protestant ethic Weber's term to describe the ideal of a self-denying, highly moral life accompanied by thrift and hard work

Although Weber's analysis has been influential, it has not lacked critics. Hundreds of scholars have attacked it, some for overlooking the lack of capitalism in Scotland (a Calvinist country), others for failing to explain why the Industrial Revolution was born in England (not a Calvinist country). Hundreds of other scholars have defended Weber's argument, and sociologists continue to test Weber's theory (Becker 2009; Basten and Betz 2011). Currently, sociologists are not in agreement on this matter.

At this point in history, the Protestant ethic and the spirit of capitalism are not confined to any specific religion or even to any one part of the world. Rather, they have become cultural traits that have spread to societies around the globe (Greeley 1964; Yinger 1970). U.S. Catholics have about the same approach to life as do U.S. Protestants. In addition, Hong Kong, Japan, Malaysia, Singapore, South Korea, and Taiwan—not exactly Protestant countries—have embraced capitalism. China, Russia, and Vietnam are in the midst of doing so.

monotheism the belief that there is only one God

polytheism the belief that there are many gods

animism the belief that all objects in the world have spirits, some of which are dangerous and must be outwitted

The World's Major Religions

18.6 Discuss the origins and development of Judaism, Islam, Hinduism, Buddhism, and Confucianism.

The largest of the thousands of religions in the world are listed in Figure 18.1. Let's briefly review six of them.

Judaism

The origin of Judaism is traced to Abraham, who lived about four thousand years ago in Mesopotamia. Jews believe that God (Yahweh) made a covenant with Abraham, selecting his descendants as a chosen people—promising to make them "as numerous as the sands of the seashore" and to give them a special land that would be theirs forever. The sign of this covenant was the circumcision of males, which was to be performed when a boy was eight days old. Descent is traced through Abraham and his wife, Sarah, their son Isaac, and their grandson Jacob (also called Israel).

Joseph, a son of Jacob, was sold by his brothers into slavery and taken to Egypt. Following a series of hair-raising adventures, Joseph became Pharaoh's right-hand man. When a severe famine hit Canaan, where Jacob's family was living, Jacob and his eleven other sons fled to Egypt. Under Joseph's leadership, they were welcome. A subsequent Pharaoh, however, enslaved the Israelites. After about four hundred years, Moses, an Israelite who had been adopted by Pharaoh's daughter, confronted Pharaoh. He persuaded Pharaoh to release the slaves, who at that time numbered about 2 million. Moses led the Israelites out of Egypt, but before they reached their Promised Land, they spent forty years wandering in the desert. Sometime during those years, Moses delivered the Ten Commandments from Mount Sinai. Abraham, Isaac, Jacob, and Moses hold revered positions in Judaism. The events of their lives and the recounting of the early history of the Israelites are contained in the first five books of the Bible, called the Torah.

FIGURE 18.1 The World's Largest Religions

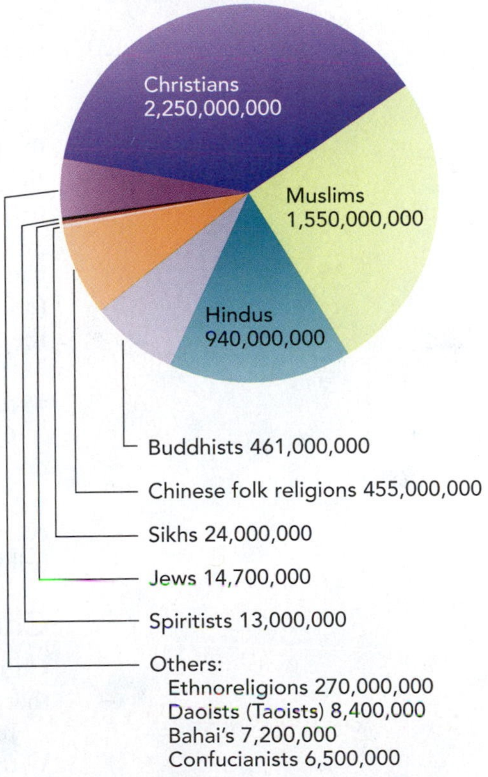

Note: With the various classifications of religions, it is sometimes difficult to tell what groups are included in what categories. Ethnoreligions, for example, is a catch-all category that refers to folk religions that are limited to specific ethnic groups.

Source: Turner 2011.

The founding of Judaism marked a fundamental change in religion; It was the first religion based on **monotheism**, the belief that there is only one God. Prior to Judaism, religions were based on **polytheism**, the belief that there are many gods. In ancient Greek religion, for example, Zeus was the god of heaven and earth, Poseidon the god of the sea, and Athena the goddess of wisdom. Other groups followed **animism**, believing that all objects in the world have spirits, some of which are dangerous and must be outwitted.

Contemporary Judaism in the United States has three main branches: Orthodox, Reform, and Conservative. Orthodox Jews adhere to the laws espoused by Moses. They eat only foods prepared in a designated manner (kosher), observe the Sabbath in a traditional way, and segregate males and females in their religious services. During the 1800s, a group that wanted to make their practices

Religion, which provides community and identity, is often passed from the older to the younger. Shown here are Hasidic Jews in Brooklyn. Differences among religious groups are often incomprehensible to outsiders. The man on the left is carrying a pouch under his left arm, considered by the men on the right to be a violation of the Sabbath.

Read on **MySocLab** **Document:** Are American Jews Vanishing Again?

more compatible with U.S. culture broke from this tradition. This liberal group, known as Reform Judaism, mostly uses English in its religious ceremonies and has much less ritual. The third branch, Conservative Judaism, falls somewhere between the other two. No branch has continued to practice polygyny (allowing a man to have more than one wife), the original marriage custom of the Jews, which was outlawed by rabbinic decree about a thousand years ago.

The history of Judaism is marked by conflict and persecution. The Israelites conquered the peoples who lived in the lands they settled, and they, in turn, were conquered by the Babylonians. After returning from Babylonian slavery to Israel and rebuilding the Temple, they were conquered by the Romans. After the Romans destroyed the Second Temple in A.D. 70, most Jews left Israel and were exiled for almost two thousand years into other nations. During those centuries, they faced prejudice, discrimination, and persecution (called **anti-Semitism**) by many peoples and rulers. The most horrendous example was the Nazi Holocaust of World War II, when Hitler attempted to eliminate the Jews as a people. Under the Nazi occupation of Europe and North Africa, about 6 million Jews were slaughtered. Many died in gas ovens that were constructed for this purpose.

Central to Jewish teaching is the requirement to love God and do good deeds. Good deeds begin in the family, where each member has an obligation toward the others. Sin is a conscious choice to do evil and must be atoned for by prayers and good works. Jews consider Jerusalem a holy city and believe that one day, the Messiah will appear there, bringing redemption for them.

Christianity

Christianity, which developed out of Judaism, is also monotheistic. Christians believe that Jesus is the Christ, the Messiah whom God promised the Jews.

Jesus was born in poverty, and traditional Christians believe his mother was a virgin. Within two years of his birth, Herod—named king of Palestine by Caesar, the ruler of the Roman Empire—was informed that people were saying a new king had been born. When they realized Herod had sent soldiers to kill the baby, Jesus' parents fled with him to Egypt. After Herod died, they returned, settling in the small town of Nazareth.

At about the age of 30, Jesus began a preaching and healing ministry. His teachings challenged the contemporary religious establishment, and as his popularity grew, the

anti-Semitism prejudice, discrimination, and persecution directed against Jews religious leaders plotted to have him killed by the Romans. Christians interpret the death of Jesus as a blood sacrifice made to atone for their sins. They believe that through his death, they have peace with God and will inherit eternal life.

The twelve main followers of Jesus, called *apostles*, believed that Jesus rose from the dead. They preached the need to be "born again," that is, to accept Jesus as Savior, give up selfish ways, and live a devout life. The new religion spread rapidly, and after an initial period of hostility on the part of imperial Rome—during which time believers were fed to the lions in the Colosseum—in A.D. 317, Christianity became the empire's official religion.

During the next 700 years, there was only one church organization, directed from Rome. During the eleventh century, after disagreement over doctrine and politics, the Greek branch declared itself independent of Rome and made its headquarters in Constantinople (now Istanbul, Turkey). During the Middle Ages, the Roman Catholic Church, which was aligned with the political establishment, became corrupt. Some Church offices, such as that of bishop, were sold for a set price. The Reformation, which was led by Martin Luther in the sixteenth century, was sparked by Luther's outrage that the forgiveness of sins (including those not yet committed) could be purchased by buying an "indulgence."

Although Martin Luther's original goal was to reform the Church, not divide it, the Reformation began a splintering of Christianity. The Reformation coincided with the breakup of feudalism, and as the ancient political structure came apart, people clamored for independence in both political and religious thought.

Today, Christianity is the most popular religion in the world, with more than 2 billion adherents. Christians are divided into hundreds of groups, some with doctrinal differences so slight that only members of the group can appreciate the extremely fine distinctions that they feel significantly separate them from others. The Social Map below shows how some of these groups are distributed in the United States.

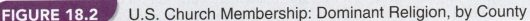

FIGURE 18.2 U.S. Church Membership: Dominant Religion, by County

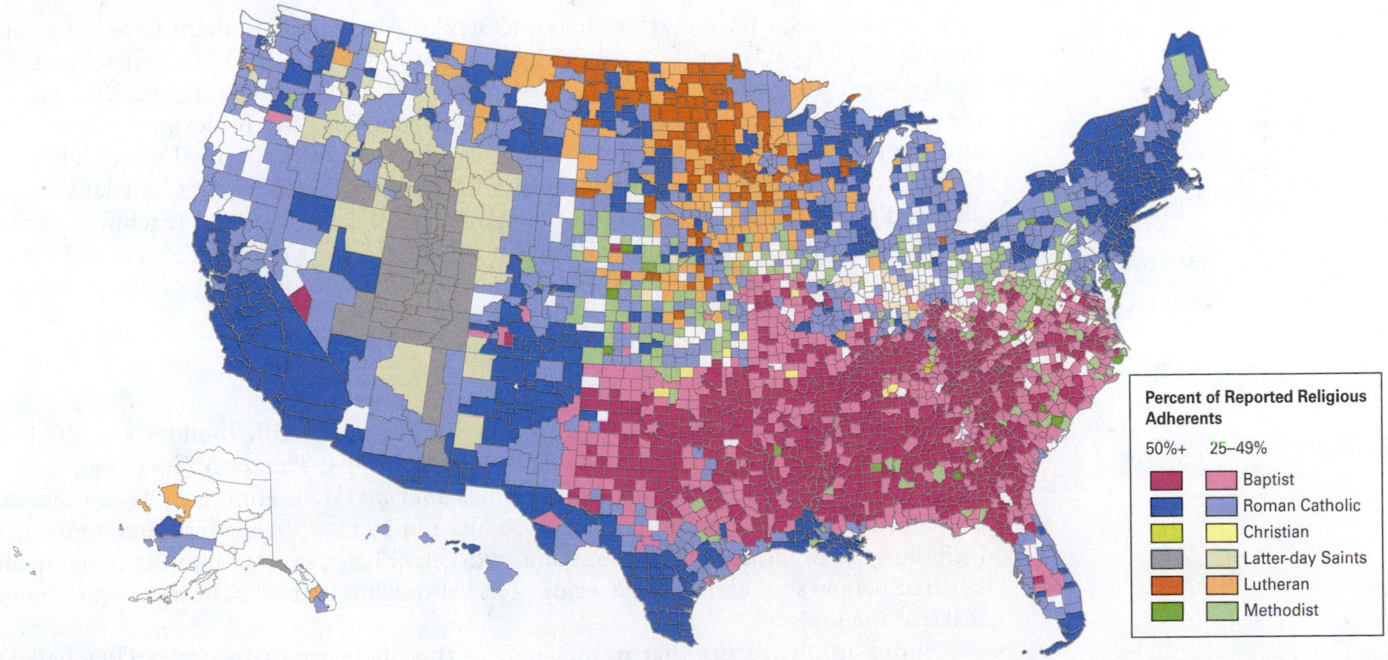

Note: When no religious group has 25 percent of the total membership in a county, that county is left blank. When two or more religious groups have 25–49 percent of the membership in a county, the largest is shown.

Source: Reprinted with permission from Grammich et al. *2010 U.S. Religious Census: Religious Congregations & Membership Study.* Fairfield, Ohio: Glenmary Research Center, 2012. © Association of Statisticians of American Religious Bodies (ASARB). All rights reserved.

The annual Hajj pilgrimage to Mecca, the birthplace of the prophet Muhammad. About two million Muslims make this pilgrimage each year.

Islam

Islam, whose followers are known as Muslims, began in the same part of the world as Judaism and Christianity. Islam, the world's third monotheistic religion, has about a billion and a half followers. It was founded by Muhammad, who was born in Mecca (now in Saudi Arabia) in about A.D. 570. Muhammad married Khadija, a wealthy widow. At about the age of 40, Muhammad reported that he had revelations from God. These, and his teachings, were later written down in a book called the Qur'an (Koran). Few paid attention to Muhammad, although Ali, his son-in-law, believed him. When Muhammad found out that there was a plot to murder him, he fled to Medina, where he found a more receptive audience. There he established a *theocracy* (a government based on the principle that God is king, God's laws are the statutes of the land, and priests are the earthly administrators of God). In A.D. 630, he returned to Mecca, this time as a conqueror (Bridgwater 1953).

After Muhammad's death, a struggle for control over the empire he had founded split Islam into two main branches that remain today, the Sunni and the Shi'ite. The Shi'ites believe that Islamic leadership should be traced through the descendants of Muhammad and that the *imam* (the religious leader) is inspired as he interprets the Qur'an. The Sunnis followed different leadership after Muhammad's death and developed different prayer and legal traditions. Despite their differences, both groups accept the fundamental teachings of Islam.

Like the Jews, Muslims trace their ancestry to Abraham. Abraham fathered a son, Ishmael, by Hagar, his wife Sarah's Egyptian maid (Genesis 25:12). Ishmael had twelve sons, from whom a good portion of today's Arab world is descended. For them also, Jerusalem is a holy city. The Muslims consider the Bibles of the Jews and the Christians to be sacred, but they take the Qur'an as the final word. They believe that the followers of Abraham and Moses (Jews) and Jesus (Christians) changed the original teachings and that Muhammad restored these teachings to their initial purity. It is the duty of each Muslim to make a pilgrimage to Mecca during his or her lifetime. Unlike the Jews, the Muslims continue to practice polygyny. They limit a man to four wives.

Hinduism

Unlike Judaism, Christianity, and Islam, Hinduism has no specific founder. For about 3,000 years, Hinduism has been the chief religion of India. The term *Hinduism*, though, is Western. In India the closest term is *dharma* (law). Hinduism has no canonical scripture, that is, no texts thought to be inspired by God. Instead, several books, including the Brahmanas, Bhagavad-Gita, and Upanishads, expound on the moral qualities that people should strive to develop. They also delineate the sacrifices people should make to the gods.

Hindus are *polytheists*; that is, they believe that there are many gods. They believe that one of these gods, Brahma, created the universe. Brahma, Shiva (the Destroyer), and Vishnu (the Preserver) form a triad that is at the center of modern Hinduism. A central belief is *karma*, spiritual progress. Instead of a final judgment, there is **reincarnation**, a cycle of life, death, and rebirth. Death involves only the body. The soul continues its existence, coming back in a form that matches the individual's moral progress in the previous life (which centers on proper conduct in following the rules of one's caste). If an individual reaches spiritual perfection, he or she has attained *nirvana*. This marks the end of the cycle of death and rebirth, when the soul is reunited with the universal soul. When this occurs, *maya*, the illusion of time and space, has been conquered.

Because of social protest, some Hindu practices have changed—especially child marriage and *suttee*, the practice of cremating a surviving widow along with her deceased husband (Bridgwater 1953). Other ancient rituals remain unchanged, including ***kumbh mela***, a purifying washing in the Ganges River in which millions participate.

When I visited a Hindu temple in Chattisgargh, India, I was impressed by the colorful and expressive statues on its roof. Here is a close-up of some of those figures, which represent some of the millions of gods that Hindus worship.

Buddhism

In about 600 B.C., Siddhartha Gautama founded Buddhism. (Buddha means the "enlightened one," a term Gautama was given by his disciples.) Gautama was the son of an upper-caste Hindu ruler in an area north of Benares, India. At the age of 29, he renounced his life of luxury and became an ascetic. Through meditation, he discovered the "four noble truths," which emphasize self-denial and compassion:

1. Existence is suffering.
2. The origin of suffering is desire.
3. Suffering ceases when desire ceases.
4. The way to end desire is to follow the "noble eightfold path."

The noble eightfold path consists of

1. Right understanding
2. Right speech
3. Right occupation or living
4. Right concentration
5. Right mindedness (or contemplation)
6. Right effort
7. Right conduct
8. Right intention (to renounce carnal pleasure and to harm no living creature)

reincarnation in Hinduism and Buddhism, the return of the soul (or self) after death in a different form

The central symbol of Buddhism is the eight-spoked wheel, illustrated in Figure 18.3. Each spoke represents one aspect of the noble eightfold path. As with Hinduism, the ultimate goal of Buddhism is the cessation of rebirth and with it, the end of suffering. Buddhists teach that there is no soul and that all things are temporary and destined to pass away (Reat 1994).

FIGURE 18.3 Buddhism's Eight-Spoked Wheel

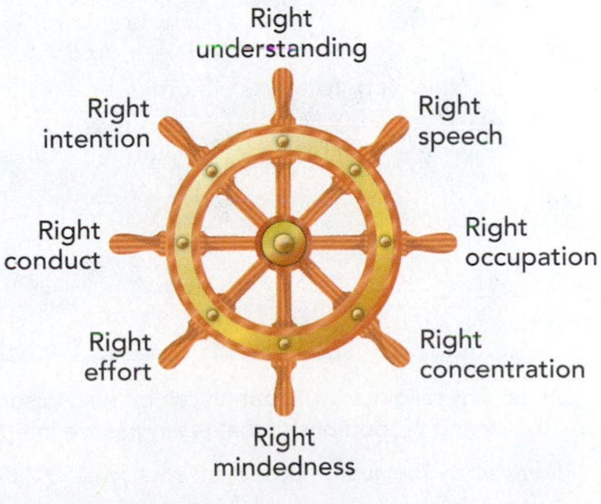

Buddhism spread rapidly. In the third century B.C., the ruler of India adopted Buddhism and sent missionaries throughout Asia to spread the new teaching (Bridgwater 1953). By the fifth century A.D., Buddhism reached the height of its popularity in India, after which it died out. Buddhism, however, had spread to Ceylon, Burma, Tibet, Laos, Cambodia, Thailand, China, Korea, and Japan, where it still flourishes. With increased immigration from Asian nations, communities of Buddhists have developed in the United States (Grammich et al. 2012).

Confucianism

About the time that Gautama lived, K'ung Fu-tsu (551–479 B.C.) was born in China. Confucius (his name strung together in English), a public official, was distressed by the corruption that he saw in government. Unlike Gautama, who emphasized withdrawal from social activities, Confucius urged social reform and developed a system of moral principles based on peace, justice, and universal order. His teachings were incorporated into writings called the *Analects.*

The basic moral principle of Confucianism is to maintain *jen*, sympathy or concern for other humans. The key to *jen* is to sustain right relationships—being loyal and placing morality above self-interest. In what is called the "Confucian Golden Rule," Confucius stated a basic principle for *jen*: to treat those who are subordinate to you as you would like to be treated by people superior to yourself. Confucius taught that right relationships within the family (loyalty and respect) should be the model for society. He also taught the "middle way," an avoidance of extremes.

Confucianism was originally atheistic, simply a set of moral teachings without reference to the supernatural. As the centuries passed, however, local gods were added to the teachings, and Confucius himself was declared a god. Confucius' teachings became the basis for the government of China. About A.D. 1000, the emphasis on meditation gave way to a stress on improvement through acquiring knowledge. This emphasis remained dominant until the twentieth century. By that time, the government had become rigid, and respect for the existing order had replaced respect for relationships (Bridgwater 1953). Following the Communist revolution of 1949, political leaders attempted to weaken the people's ties with Confucianism. They succeeded in part, but Confucianism remains embedded in Chinese culture.

18.7 Compare cult, sect, church, and ecclesia; discuss the conflict between religion and culture.

Types of Religious Groups

Sociologists have identified four types of religious groups: cult, sect, church, and ecclesia. Why do some of these groups meet with hostility, while others tend to be accepted? For an explanation, look at Figure 18.4.

FIGURE 18.4 Religious Groups: From Hostility to Acceptance

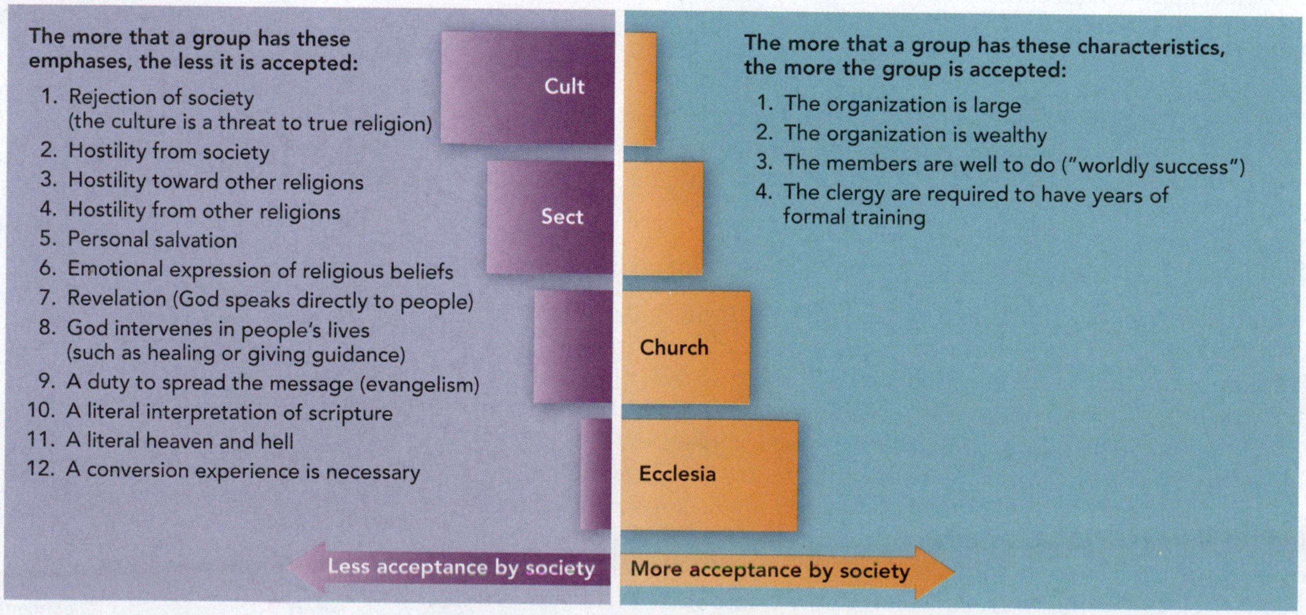
The more that a group has these emphases, the less it is accepted:
1. Rejection of society (the culture is a threat to true religion)
2. Hostility from society
3. Hostility toward other religions
4. Hostility from other religions
5. Personal salvation
6. Emotional expression of religious beliefs
7. Revelation (God speaks directly to people)
8. God intervenes in people's lives (such as healing or giving guidance)
9. A duty to spread the message (evangelism)
10. A literal interpretation of scripture
11. A literal heaven and hell
12. A conversion experience is necessary
Cult
Sect
Church
Ecclesia
The more that a group has these characteristics, the more the group is accepted:
1. The organization is large
2. The organization is wealthy
3. The members are well to do ("worldly success")
4. The clergy are required to have years of formal training
Less acceptance by society
More acceptance by society

Note: Any religious organization can be placed somewhere on this continuum, based on its having "more" or "less" of these characteristics and emphases. The varying proportions of the rectangles are intended to represent the group's relative characteristics and emphases.

Sources: By the author. Based on Troeltsch 1931; Pope 1942; Johnson 1963.

Let's explore what sociologists have found about these four types of religious groups. The summary that follows is a modification of analyses by sociologists Ernst Troeltsch (1931), Liston Pope (1942), and Benton Johnson (1963).

cult a new religion with few followers, whose teachings and practices put it at odds with the dominant culture and religion

Cult

The word *cult* conjures up bizarre images. Shaven heads, weird music, brainwashing—even ritual suicide—may come to mind. Cults, however, are not necessarily weird, and few practice "brainwashing" or bizarre rituals. In fact, *all religions began as cults* (Stark 1989). A **cult** is simply a new or different religion whose teachings and practices put it at odds with the dominant culture and religion. Because the term *cult* arouses negative associations in the public mind, however, some scholars prefer to use the term *new religion* instead. As is evident from the Cultural Diversity box below, "new" can mean that an old religion is making its appearance in a culture that is not familiar and is uncomfortable with it.

Cultural Diversity in the United States

Human Heads and Animal Blood: Testing the Limits of Tolerance

As the U.S. customs officials looked over the line of people who had just gotten off the plane from Haiti, there was nothing to make this particular woman stand out. She would have passed through without a problem, except for one thing: A routine search turned up something that struck the custom agents as somewhat unusual—a human head.

The head had teeth, hair, pieces of skin, and some dirt. It had evidently been dug up from some grave, probably in Haiti.

The 30-year-old woman, who lives in Florida, practiced voodoo. The head was for her religious rituals.

The woman was arrested. Her crime? Not filing a report that she was carrying "organic material" ("Mujer con Cabeza . . ." 2006).

* * * * *

The Santeros from Cuba who live in Florida sacrifice animals. They meet in apartments, where, following a Yoruba religion, they kill goats and chickens. Calling on their gods, they first ask permission to sacrifice the animals. After sacrificing them, they pour out the animals' blood, which opens and closes the doors of their destiny. They also cut off the animals' heads and place them at locations in the city that represent the four directions of the compass. This is done to terrorize their enemies and give them safety. The heads also protect the city from hurricanes and other destructive forces.

When city officials in Hialeah, Florida, learned that the Santeros were planning to build a church in their city, they passed a law against the sacrifice of animals within the city limits. The Santeros appealed to the U.S. Supreme Court, claiming discrimination, because the law was directed against them. The Court ruled in their favor.

City officials of Euless, Texas, were shocked when they learned that Jose Merced was sacrificing goats in his home. They sent in the police (Rassbach 2009). Merced appealed to the federal circuit court, saying that the officials were violating his rights as a Santeria priest. He can now sacrifice goats at home.

Animal sacrifice is part of many religions. This man in Pakistan is transporting a goat to be sacrificed to celebrate the Islamic festival of Eid al-Adha.

For Your Consideration

➜ What do you think the limitations on religious freedom should be? Should people be allowed to sacrifice animals as part of their religious practices?

➜ If the Santeros can sacrifice animals, why shouldn't people who practice voodoo be able to use human heads in their rituals if they want to? (Assume that the relatives of the dead person have given their permission.)

charismatic leader literally, someone to whom God has given a gift; in its extended sense, someone who exerts extraordinary appeal to a group of followers

charisma literally, an extraordinary gift from God; more commonly, an outstanding, "magnetic" personality

sect a religious group larger than a cult that still feels substantial hostility from and toward society

evangelism an attempt to win converts

Cults often originate with a **charismatic leader**, an individual who inspires people because he or she seems to have extraordinary gifts, qualities, or abilities. **Charisma** refers to an outstanding gift or to some exceptional quality. People feel drawn to both the person and the message because they find something highly appealing about the individual—in some instances, almost a magnetic charm.

The most popular religion in the world began as a cult. Its handful of followers believed that an unschooled carpenter who preached in remote villages in a backwater country was the Son of God, and that he was killed and came back to life. Those beliefs made the early Christians a cult, setting them apart from the rest of their society. Persecuted by both religious and political authorities, these early believers clung to one another for support. Many cut off associations with friends who didn't accept the new message. To others, the early Christians must have seemed deluded and brainwashed.

So it was with Islam. When Muhammad revealed his visions and said that God's name was really Allah, only a few people believed him. To others, he must have seemed crazy, deranged.

Each cult (or new religion) is met with rejection on the part of society. Its message is considered bizarre, its approach to life strange. Its members antagonize the majority, who are convinced that they have a monopoly on the truth. The new religion may claim messages from God, visions, visits from angels—some form of enlightenment or seeing the true way to God. The cult demands intense commitment, and its followers, who are confronting a hostile world, pull together in a tight circle, separating themselves from nonbelievers. As you saw, this was the situation of Yearning for Zion in the chapter's opening vignette.

Most cults fail. Not many people believe the new message, and the cult fades into obscurity. Some, however, succeed and make history. Over time, large numbers of people may come to accept the message and become followers of the religion. If this happens, the new religion changes from a cult to a sect.

Sect

A **sect** is larger than a cult, but its members still feel tension between their views and the prevailing beliefs and values of the broader society. A sect may even be hostile to the society in which it is located. At the very least, its members remain uncomfortable with many of the emphases of the dominant culture; in turn, nonmembers tend to be uncomfortable with members of the sect.

Ordinarily, sects are loosely organized and fairly small. They emphasize personal salvation and an emotional expression of one's relationship with God. Clapping, shouting, dancing, and extemporaneous prayers are hallmarks of sects. Like cults, sects also stress **evangelism**, the active recruitment of new members.

Like other aspects of culture, religion is filled with background assumptions that usually go unquestioned. In this photo, which I took in Amsterdam, what background assumption of religion is this woman violating? (See page 538.)

If a sect grows, its members tend to gradually make peace with the rest of society. To appeal to a broader base, the sect shifts some of its doctrines, redefining matters to remove some of the rough edges that create tension between it and the rest of society. As the members become more respectable in the eyes of the society, they feel less hostility and little, if any, isolation. If a sect follows this course, as it grows and becomes more integrated into society, it changes into a church.

Church

At this point, the religious group is highly bureaucratized—probably with national and international headquarters that give direction to the local congregations, enforce rules about who can be ordained, and control finances. The relationship with God has grown less intense. The group is likely to have less emphasis on personal salvation and emotional expression. Worship services are likely to be more sedate, with formal sermons and written prayers read before the congregation. Rather than being recruited from the outside by personal evangelism, most new members now come from within, from children born to existing members. Rather than joining through conversion—seeing the new truth—children may be baptized, circumcised, or dedicated in some other way. At some designated age, children may be asked to affirm the group's beliefs in a ceremony, such as a confirmation or bar mitzvah.

Ecclesia

Finally, some groups become so well integrated into a culture, and allied so strongly with their government, that it is difficult to tell where one leaves off and the other takes over. In these *state religions*, also called **ecclesia**, the government and religion work together to try to shape society. Since citizenship makes everyone a member, there is no recruitment of members. For most people in the society, the religion is part of a cultural identity, not an eye-opening experience. Sweden provides a good example of how extensively religion and government intertwine in an ecclesia. In the 1860s, all citizens had to memorize Luther's *Small Catechism* and be tested on it annually (Anderson 1995). Today, Lutheranism is still associated with the state, but most Swedes come to church only for baptisms, marriages, and funerals.

Unlike cults and sects, which perceive God as personally involved with and concerned about people, ecclesias envision God as more impersonal and remote. Reflecting this view of the supernatural, church services tend to be highly formal, directed by ministers or priests who, after undergoing training in approved schools or seminaries, follow prescribed rituals.

Examples of ecclesia include the Church of England (whose very name expresses alignment between church and state), the Lutheran church in Norway and Denmark, Islam in Iran and Iraq, and, during the time of the Holy Roman Empire, the Roman Catholic Church, which was the official religion for the region that is now Europe.

Variations in Patterns

Obviously, not all religious groups go through all these stages—from cult to sect to church to ecclesia. Some die out because they fail to attract enough members. Others, such as the Amish, remain sects. And, as is evident from the few countries that have state religions, it is rare for a religion to become an ecclesia.

In addition, these classifications are not perfectly matched in the real world. For example, although the Amish are a sect, they place little or no emphasis on recruiting others—and they don't like loud music. The early Quakers, another sect, also shied away from emotional expressions of their beliefs. They would quietly meditate in church, with no one speaking, until God gave someone a message to share with others. Finally, some groups that become churches may retain a few characteristics of sects, such as an emphasis on evangelism or a personal relationship with God.

Read on **MySocLab**
Document: The Amish: A Small Society

Although all religions began as cults, not all varieties of a particular religion begin that way. For example, some **denominations**—"brand names" within a major religion, such as Baptists or Reform Judaism—begin as splinter groups. Some members of a church disagree with *particular* aspects of the church's teachings (not its main message), and they break away to form their own organization.

When Religion and Culture Conflict

As you have seen, cults and sects represent a break with the past. This challenge to the social order often generates hostility. When religion and the culture in which it is embedded find themselves in conflict, how do they adapt?

First, the members of the religion may reject the dominant culture and have little to do with people who aren't members of their group. As noted in the Cultural Diversity box in Chapter 4 (page 105), the Amish withdraw into closed communities where they try to preserve the culture of their ancestors. They follow traditional male and female

ecclesia a religious group so integrated into the dominant culture that it is difficult to tell where the one begins and the other leaves off; also called a *state religion*

denomination a "brand name" within a major religion; for example, Methodist or Baptist roles, wear the same style of clothing as their ancestors wore three hundred years ago, light their homes with oil lamps, and speak German at home and in church. They do mingle with non-Amish when they shop in town—where their transportation (horse-drawn carriages), clothing, and speech set them apart.

In the *second* pattern, the cult or sect rejects only specific elements of the prevailing culture. Wearing makeup or going to the movies might be prohibited. Or an emphasis might be on avoiding immodest clothing—short skirts, skimpy swimsuits, low-cut dresses, and so on. Although specific activities are forbidden, members of the group participate in most aspects of the broader society.

In the *third* pattern, the society rejects the religious group. In the extreme, as with the early Christians, political leaders may even try to destroy the group. The Roman emperor declared the followers of Jesus to be enemies of Rome and ordered them to be hunted down and destroyed. In the United States, after mobs killed Joseph Smith and hounded his followers out of several communities, the Mormons decided to escape the dominant culture altogether. In 1847, they settled in a wilderness, in what is today Utah's Great Salt Lake Valley (Bridgwater 1953). The most remarkable example in the United States within the past couple of decades occurred in 1993 when U.S. authorities attacked and destroyed a cult called the Branch Davidians. Including the twenty-five children found huddled next to their dead mothers, more than eighty people died.

18.8 Summarize main features of religion in the United States and discuss the secularization of religion and culture.

Religion in the United States

To better understand religion in the United States, let's look at some of its major features.

Watch on **MySocLab**
Video: Thinking Like a Sociologist: Religious Diversity in America

Explore on **MySocLab**
Activity: Where Are Different Religions Practiced Across the United States?

Characteristics of Members

About 65 percent of Americans belong to a church, synagogue, or mosque. What are the characteristics of people who hold formal membership in a religion?

Social Class and Religious Participation. Religion in the United States is stratified by social class. As you can see from Figure 18.5 on the next page, some religious groups are "top-heavy" and others are "bottom-heavy." The most top-heavy are Jews and Episcopalians; the most bottom-heavy are Assembly of God, Southern Baptists, and Jehovah's Witnesses. This figure provides further confirmation that churchlike groups tend to appeal to people who have more "worldly" success, while the more sectlike groups attract people who have less "worldly" success.

From this figure, you can see how *status consistency* (a concept we reviewed in Chapter 10, page 263–264) applies to religious groups. If a group ranks high (or low) on education, it is also likely to rank high (or low) on income and occupational prestige. Jews, for example, rank the highest on education, income, and occupational prestige, while Jehovah's Witnesses rank the lowest on these three measures of social class. As you can see, the Mormons are status inconsistent. They rank second in income, fourth in education, and tie for sixth in occupational prestige. Even more status inconsistent is the Assembly of God. Their members tie for third in occupational prestige but rank only eighth in income and ninth in education. This inconsistency is so jarring that there could be a problem with the sample.

Americans who change their social class also tend to change their religion. Their new social class experiences create changes in their ideas about the world, molding new preferences for music and styles of speech. Upwardly mobile people are likely to seek a religion that draws more affluent people. An upwardly mobile Baptist, for example, may become a Methodist or a Presbyterian. For Roman Catholics, the situation is somewhat different. Because each parish is a geographical unit, Catholics who move into more affluent neighborhoods are also likely to be moving to a congregation that has a larger proportion of affluent members.

FIGURE 18.5 Social Class and Religious Affiliation

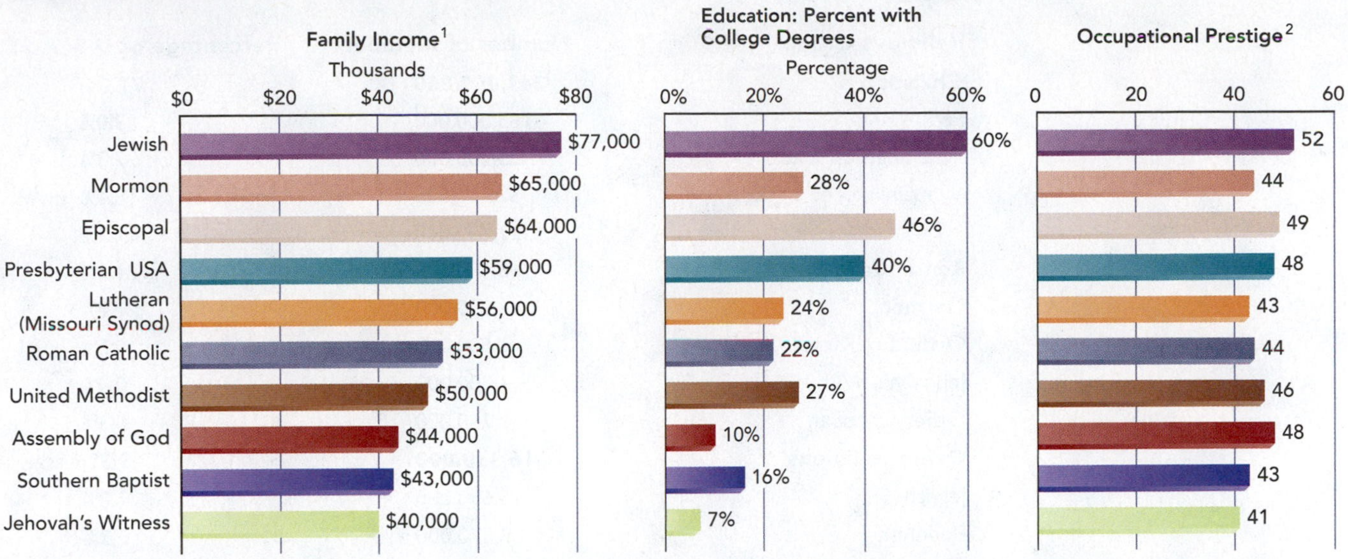

[1]The family incomes reported here must be taken as approximate. The original totals were from 1996. I increased them by 48 percent, the inflation rate reported by the Bureau of Labor Statistics for 1996 to 2013.

[2]Higher numbers mean that more of the group's members work at occupations that have higher prestige, generally those that require more education and offer higher pay. For more information on occupational prestige, see Table 10.2 on page 263.

Source: By the author. Based on Smith and Faris 2005.

Race–Ethnicity. Many religions are associated with race–ethnicity: Islam with Arabs, Judaism with Jews, Hinduism with Indians, and Confucianism with Chinese. In the United States, all major religious groups draw from the nation's many racial–ethnic groups. Like social class, however, race–ethnicity tends to cluster. People of Irish descent are likely to be Roman Catholics; those with Greek ancestors are likely to belong to the Greek Orthodox Church. African Americans are likely to be Protestants—more specifically, Baptists—or to belong to fundamentalist sects.

Although many churches are integrated, it is with good reason that Sunday morning between 10 and 11 A.M. has been called "the most segregated hour in the United States." African Americans tend to belong to African American churches, while most whites see only whites in their churches. The segregation of churches is based on custom, not on law.

Characteristics of Religious Groups

Let's examine features of the religious groups in the United States.

Diversity. About 65 percent of Americans hold formal membership in church, synagogue, or mosque, but with their 300,000 congregations and hundreds of denominations, no religious group even comes close to being a dominant religion in the United States (*Statistical Abstract* 2013:Tables 78, 79). Table 18.1 on the next page illustrates some of this remarkable diversity.

Pluralism and Freedom. It is the U.S. government's policy not to interfere with religions. The government's position is that its obligation is to ensure an environment in which people can worship as they see fit. Religious freedom is so extensive that anyone can start a church and proclaim himself or herself a minister, revelator, or any other desired term. The exceptions to this hands-off policy are startling. The most notorious exception in recent times was mentioned earlier, the attack by the Bureau of Alcohol, Tobacco, and Firearms on the Branch Davidians, an obscure religious group in Waco,

TABLE 18.1 How Americans Identify with Religion

Religious Group	Number of Members	Percentage of U.S. Adults
Christian	**243,060,000**	**77.8%**
Protestant	165,000,000	53.0%
Evangelical churches	85,200,000	27.3%
Mainline churches	57,000,000	18.4%
Historic black churches	22,800,000	7.3%
Roman Catholic	68,400,000	21.7%
Mormon	6,200,000	1.9%
Orthodox: Greek, Russian	1,500,000	0.5%
Jehovah's Witness	1,200,000	0.4%
Other Christian	760,000	0.3%
Other Religions	**16,350,000**	**5.3%**
Jewish	5,690,000	1.8%
Buddhist	3,570,000	1.2%
Muslim	2,770,000	0.9%
Hindu	1,790,000	0.6%
Other faiths (Unitarians, New Age, Native American religions, Liberal)	2,530,000	0.8%
No Identity with a Religion	**50,980,000**	**16.3%**
Nothing in particular	36,196,000	11.6%
Agnostic	8,667,000	2.7%
Atheist	6,118,000	1.9%
Don't Know or Refused	**1,863,000**	**0.6%**

Note: Due to rounding, totals may not add to 100.

Sources: The Global Religious Landscape 2012:Table 12; *Yearbook of American & Canadian Churches* 2012.

Texas. The eighty-two victims remain a dark blot on the history of the United States. A second example is the focus of this chapter's opening vignette. A third is the government's infiltration of mosques to monitor the activities of Arab immigrants (ACLU 2010; Mohajer 2012). Other limitations to this policy were discussed in the Cultural Diversity box on page 531.

Competition and Recruitment. The many religious groups of the United States compete for clients. They even advertise in the Yellow Pages of the telephone directory and insert appealing advertising—under the guise of news—in the religion section of the weekend editions of the local newspapers.

Commitment. Americans are a religious people, and 45 percent report that they attend religious services each week or "almost weekly" (Funk and Smith 2012). Sociologists have questioned this statistic, suggesting that the high total is due to an *interviewer effect.* Because people want to please interviewers, they stretch the truth a bit. To find out, sociologists Stanley Presser and Linda Stinson (1998) examined people's written reports (no interviewer present) on how they spend their Sundays. They concluded that about 30 percent or so attend church each week.

Whether the percentage of weekly church attendance is 30 or 45, Americans are a religious people, and they back up their commitment with generous support for religion and its charities. Each year, Americans donate about $30 billion to religious causes

(*Yearbook of American & Canadian Churches* 2012). To appreciate the significance of this huge figure, keep in mind that, unlike a country in which there is an ecclesia, those billions of dollars are not forced taxes but money that people give away.

Toleration. The general religious toleration of Americans can be illustrated by three prevailing attitudes: (1) "All religions have a right to exist—as long as they don't try to brainwash or hurt anyone." (2) "With all the religions to choose from, how can anyone tell which one—if any—is true?" (3) "Each of us may be convinced about the truth of our religion—and that is good—but don't be obnoxious by trying to convince others that you have the exclusive truth."

Fundamentalist Revival. As discussed in the Cultural Diversity box on the next page, the fundamentalist Christian churches are undergoing a revival. They teach that the Bible is literally true and that salvation comes only through a personal relationship with Jesus Christ. They also denounce what they see as the degeneration of U.S. culture: flagrant sex on television, in movies, and in videos; abortion; corrupt politicians; premarital sex and cohabitation; and drug abuse. Their answer to these problems is firm, simple, and direct: People whose hearts are changed through religious conversion will change their lives. The mainstream churches, which offer a more remote God and less emotional involvement, fail to meet the basic religious needs of large numbers of Americans.

One result is that mainstream churches are losing members while the fundamentalists are gaining them. Figure 18.6 depicts this change. One exception is the Roman Catholic Church, whose growth in the United States comes primarily from the immigrants from Mexico and other Roman Catholic countries.

The Electronic Church. What began as a ministry to shut-ins and those who do not belong to a church blossomed into its own type of church. Its preachers, called "televangelists," reach millions of viewers and raise millions of dollars. Some of its most famous ministers are Joel Osteen, Kenneth Copeland, Creflo Dollar, Benny Hinn, Joyce Meyers, and Pat Robertson.

Many local ministers view the electronic church as a competitor. They complain that it competes for the attention and dollars of their members. Leaders of the electronic church reply that the money goes to good causes and that through its conversions, the electronic church feeds members into the local churches, strengthening, not weakening them.

FIGURE 18.6 U.S. Churches: Gains and Losses in Ten Years

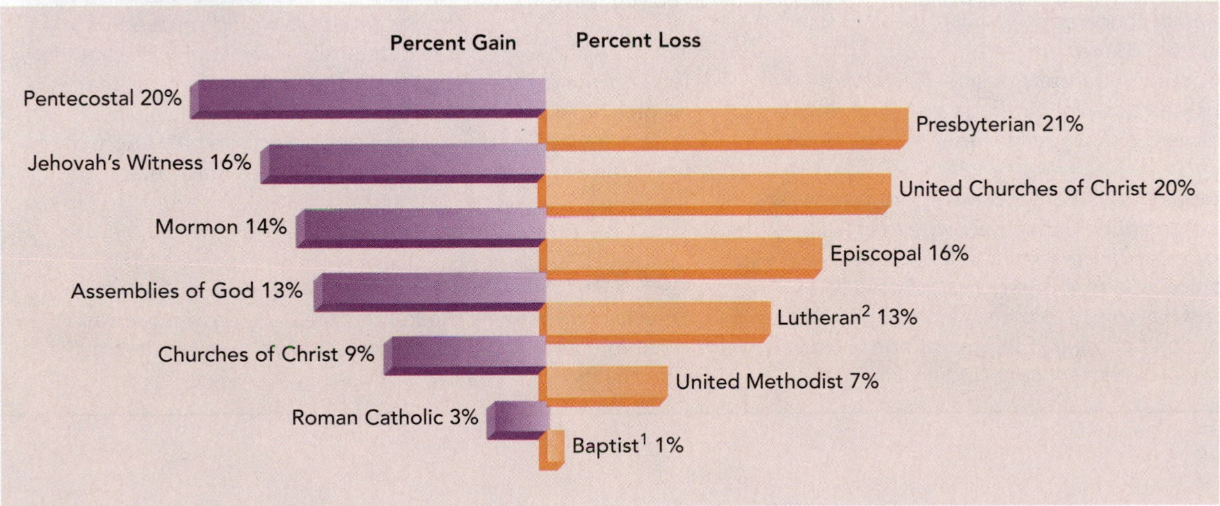

[1]National Baptist Convention and Southern Baptist Convention.

[2]Evangelical Lutheran Church of America and Lutheran Church-Missouri Synod.

Source: By the author. Based on *Yearbook of American & Canadian Churches* 2002 and 2012.

Cultural Diversity in the United States

The New Face of Religion: Pentecostals and Spanish-Speaking Immigrants

The preachers know what they are talking about. Some work at factory jobs during the day. They know what it is to sweat for a living and that J-O-B is really spelled B-R-O-K-E. Cantankerous bosses, unpaid bills, and paychecks that run out before the week does are part of their own lives.

As the preacher preaches, the congregation breaks out into Amens. "Amen, brother! Bring it on!" shouts one person, while another says, "Amen. Tell it like it is!"

As people clap and sway to the sounds of the drums and guitars—like salsa music with religious lyrics—some pray silently. Others shout out strange sounds. "Speaking in tongues," they call it.

That there are millions of immigrants from Spanish-speaking countries in the United States is not news. That most of them are poor isn't news, either. Almost all the immigrants who came before them were poor, too.

What is news is that many Latinos are abandoning the Roman Catholic religion to embrace Protestantism (Newport 2013). Many are joining the Pentecostals. Taking the Bible literally, Pentecostals believe there is a real heaven and a real hell. They expect God to act in their lives in a personal way. They lay hands on each other and pray for healings.

And they are noisily joyful about their faith.

Go into any of the thousands of little churches that have sprung up around the country. You'll hear music and clapping. The preachers talk about a God who is concerned about people's troubles. They warn the congregation about the dangers of sin—the adultery that seductively beckons, the downfall of drugs and alcohol, the dead end of laziness and extravagance. They also extol thrift and hard work.

"Speaking in tongues" sets Pentecostals apart from most religions. These strange sounds, they believe, are messages from God. But no one can understand them unless someone gives the interpretation. When this happens, people listen intently for what God has to say to them personally.

The worshippers don't come just for an hour on Sunday mornings. They come night after night, finding comfort in community, spiritual warmth in praying for one another, and encouragement in the message and music. They revel in the freedom of being able to express their emotions among like-minded people.

Religion often helps immigrants adapt to their new culture. What indications of this do you see in this photo?

This religious movement isn't limited to storefronts and immigrants. Pentecostalism is the fastest-growing religion in the United States, and there are perhaps 400 million Pentecostals worldwide. Although there are middle-class and college-educated Pentecostals, the middle-class arms don't open as wide. The appeal is mainly to the poor. When the poor make the transition to the middle class—as their religion's emphasis on work and thrift will help them do—they are likely to seek less expressive religions.

When this happens, we can expect the form of Pentecostalism to remain recognizable but the fervor to be lost. For now, though, the driving force of this religion is its fervor—the intensity that connects the individuals to God and to one another. The Pentecostals would phrase this a little differently. They would say that the fervor is merely the expression of the driving force of their religion, which is the Holy Spirit.

Either way you put it, these people are on fire. And that fire is burning a new imprint on the face of religion.

For Your Consideration

➔ Why do you think the Pentecostals are growing so fast? What effect do you think this might have on mainstream Christianity?

Secularization of Religion and Culture

The term *secularization* refers to the process by which worldly affairs replace spiritual interests. (The term **secular** means "belonging to the world and its affairs.") As we shall see, both religions and cultures can become secularized.

The Secularization of Religion.

> *As the model, fashionably slender, paused before the head table of African American community leaders, her gold necklace glimmering above the low-cut bodice of her emerald-green dress, the hostess, a member of the Church of God in Christ, said, "It's now OK to wear more revealing clothes—as long as it's done in good taste." Then she added, "You couldn't do this when I was a girl, but now it's OK—and you can still worship God." (Author's files)*

Read on **MySocLab**
Document: Abiding Faith

When I heard these words, I grabbed a napkin and quickly jotted them down, my sociological imagination stirred by their deep implication. As strange as it may seem, this simple event pinpoints the essence of why the Christian churches in the United States have splintered. Let's see how this could possibly be.

The simplest explanation for why Christians don't have just one church, or at most several, instead of the hundreds of sects and denominations that dot the U.S. landscape, is disagreements about doctrine (church teaching). As theologian and sociologist H. Richard Niebuhr pointed out, however, there are many ways of settling doctrinal disputes besides splintering off and forming other religious organizations. Niebuhr (1929) suggested that the answer lies more in *social* change than it does in *religious* conflict.

The explanation goes like this. As was noted earlier, when a sect becomes more churchlike, its members feel less tension with the mainstream culture. Quite likely, when a sect is established, its founders and early members are poor, or at least not very successful in worldly pursuits. Feeling like strangers in the dominant culture, they derive a good part of their identity from their religion. In their church services and lifestyle, they stress how different their values are from those of the dominant culture. They are also likely to emphasize the joys of the coming afterlife, when they will be able to escape from their present pain.

As time passes, the group's values—such as frugality and the avoidance of gambling, alcohol, and drugs—help the members become successful. As their children attain more education and become more middle class, members of this group grow more respectable in the eyes of society. They no longer experience the alienation that was felt by the founders of their group. Life's burdens don't seem as heavy, and the need for relief through an afterlife becomes less pressing. Similarly, the pleasures of the world no longer appear as threatening to the "truth." As with the woman at the fashion show, people then attempt to harmonize their religious beliefs with their changing ideas about the culture.

This process is called the **secularization of religion**—shifting the focus from spiritual matters to the affairs of this world. Anyone familiar with today's mainstream Methodists would be surprised to know that they once were a sect. Methodists used to ban playing cards, dancing, and going to movies. They even considered circuses to be sinful. As Methodists grew more middle class, however, they began to change their views on sin. They started to dismantle the barriers that they had constructed between themselves and the outside world (Finke and Stark 1992).

Secularization leads to a splintering of the group. Adjusting to the secular culture displeases some of the group's members, especially those who have had less worldly success. These people still feel a gulf between themselves and the broader culture. For them, tension and hostility continue to be real. They see secularization as a desertion of the group's fundamental truths, a "selling out" to the secular world.

After futile attempts by die-hards to bring the group back to its senses, the group splinters. Those who protested the secularization of Methodism, for example, were kicked out—even though *they* represented the values around which the group had organized in the first place. The dissatisfied—who come to be viewed as complainers—then

secular belonging to the world and its affairs

secularization of religion the replacement of a religion's spiritual or "other worldly" concerns with concerns about "this world"

In its technical sense, to evangelize means to "announce the Good News" (that Jesus is the Savior). In its more common usage, to evangelize means to make converts. As *Peanuts* so humorously picks up, evangelization is sometimes accomplished through means other than preaching.

form a sect that once again stresses its differences from the world; the need for more personal, emotional religious experience; and salvation from the pain of living in this world. As time passes, the cycle repeats: adjustment to the dominant culture by some, continued dissatisfaction by others, and further splintering.

This process is not limited to sects but also occurs in churches. When U.S. Episcopalians elected a gay bishop in 2003, some pastors and congregations splintered from the U.S. church and affiliated with the more conservative African archbishops. In an ironic twist, this made them mission congregations from Africa. Sociologists have not yet compared the income or wealth of those who stayed with the group that elected the gay bishop and those who joined the splinter groups. If such a study is done and it turns out that there is no difference, we will have to modify the secularization thesis.

The Secularization of Culture. Just as religion can secularize, so can culture. Sociologists use the term **secularization of culture** to refer to a culture that was once heavily influenced by religion but no longer retains much of that influence. The United States provides an example.

Despite attempts to reinterpret history, the Pilgrims and most of the founders of the United States were highly religious people. The Pilgrims were even convinced that God had guided them to establish a new religious community whose members would follow the Bible. Similarly, many of the framers of the U.S. Constitution felt that God had guided them to develop a new form of government.

The clause in the Constitution that mandates the separation of church and state was not an attempt to keep religion out of government, but a (successful) device to avoid the establishment of a state religion like that in England. Here, people were to have the freedom to worship as they wished. The assumption of the founders was even more specific—that Protestantism represented the true religion.

The phrase in the Declaration of Independence, "All men are *created* equal," refers to a central belief in God as the creator of humanity. A member of the clergy opened Congress with prayer. Many colonial laws were based on principles derived explicitly from the Old and New Testaments. In some colonies, blasphemy was a crime, as was failing to observe the Sabbath. Similarly, sexual affairs were a crime; in some places adultery carried the death penalty. Even public kissing between husband and wife was punished by placing the offenders in the public stocks (wooden yokes that locked the individual's head and arms in place) (Frumkin 1967). In other words, religion permeated U.S. culture. It was part and parcel of how the colonists saw life. Their lives, laws, and other aspects of the culture reflected their religious beliefs.

As U.S. culture secularized, religion's influence on public affairs diminished. No longer are laws based on religious principles. Ideas of what is "generally good" have replaced religion as an organizing principle for the culture. The secularization has been so complete that it is now illegal to post the Ten Commandments in civic buildings.

secularization of culture the process by which a culture becomes less influenced by religion

Underlying the secularization of culture is *modernization*, a term that refers to a society industrializing, urbanizing, developing mass education, and adopting science and advanced technology. Science and advanced technology bring with them a secular view of the world, explanations for aspects of life that people traditionally attributed to God. People come to depend much less on religion to explain life's events. Birth and death—and everything in between, from life's problems to its joys—are attributed to natural causes. When a society has secularized thoroughly, even religious leaders may turn to answers provided by biology, philosophy, psychology, sociology, and so on.

As U.S. culture secularized, religion became less important in public life. *Personal* religious involvement among Americans, however, has not diminished. Rather, it has increased (Finke and Stark 1992). About 86 percent of Americans believe there is a God, and 81 percent believe there is a heaven. Not only do 63 percent claim membership in a church or synagogue, but, as we saw, on any given weekend, somewhere between 30 and 44 percent of all Americans attend a worship service (Gallup 1990, 2010).

Table 18.2 underscores the paradox. While the culture secularized, church membership increased. The proportion of Americans who belong to a church or synagogue is now about *three and a half* times higher than it was when the country was founded. As you can see, membership peaked in 1975. Church membership, of course, is only a rough indicator of how significant religion is in people's lives. Some church members are not particularly religious, while many intensely religious people—Lincoln, for one—never join a church.

TABLE 18.2 Change in Religious Membership

Year	Americans Who Belong to a Church or Synagogue
1776	17%
1860	37%
1890	45%
1926	58%
1975	71%
2000	68%
2011	61%

Note: The sources do not contain data on mosque membership.
Sources: Finke and Stark 1992; *Statistical Abstract of the United States* 2002:Table 64; Gallup Poll 2007 and 2011.

The Future of Religion

18.9 Discuss the likely future of religion.

Religion thrives in the most advanced scientific nations—and, as officials of Soviet Russia and communist China were disheartened to learn—even in ideologically hostile climates. Although the Soviet and Chinese authorities threw believers into prison, they continued to practice their religion. Humans are inquiring creatures. As they reflect on life, they ask, What is the purpose of it all? Why are we born? Is there an afterlife? If so, where are we going? Out of these concerns arises this question: If there is a God, what does God want of us in this life? Does God have a preference about how we should live?

Science, including sociology, cannot answer such questions. By its very nature, science cannot tell us about four main concerns that many people have:

Read on **MySocLab**
Document: Religion and Spirituality Among Scientists

1. *The existence of God*. About this, science has nothing to say. No test tube has either isolated God or refuted God's existence.
2. *The purpose of life*. Although science can provide a definition of life and describe the characteristics of living organisms, it has nothing to say about ultimate purpose.
3. *An afterlife*. Science can offer no information on this at all, since it has no tests to prove or disprove a "hereafter."
4. *Morality*. Science can demonstrate the consequences of behavior, but not the moral superiority of one action compared with another. This means—to use an extreme example—that science cannot even prove whether loving your family and neighbor is superior to hurting and killing them.

There is no doubt that religion will last as long as humanity lasts—what could replace it? And if something did, and answered such questions, would it not be religion under a different name?

To close this chapter, let's try to glimpse the cutting edge of religious change.

Mass Media in Social Life

God on the Net: The Online Marketing of Religion

In Thailand: *Teenaged Buddhist monks post videos of themselves on YouTube playing air guitar and reciting religious chants to hip-hop beats. This upsets older Buddhists who feel that the young monks are being disrespectful (Hookway 2012).*

In Israel: *You want to pray here at the Holy Land, but you can't leave home? No problem. Buy our special telephone card—available at your local 7-11. Just record your prayer, and we'll broadcast it via the Internet at the site you choose. Press 1 for the holy site of Jerusalem, press 2 for the holy site of the Sea of Galilee, press 3 for the birthplace of Jesus, press 4 for. . . . (Rhoads 2007)*

In India: *You moved to Kansas, but you want to pray in Chennai? No problem. Order your pujas (prayers), and a priest will say them in the temple of your choice. Just click how many you want. Food offerings for Vishnu included in the price. All major credit cards accepted (Sullivan 2007).*

In Rome: *The Pope tries to reach out to younger Roman Catholics by tweeting, little religious messages in 145 characters or less. The Pope doesn't actually write the tweets, but he "is involved" in what they say (Moloney 2012).*

In the United States: *Erin Polzin, a 20-year-old college student, listens to a Lutheran worship service on the radio, confesses online, and uses PayPal to tithe. "I don't like getting up early," she says. "This is like going to church without really having to" (Bernstein 2003).*

In Europe: *Muslims download sermons and join an invisible community of worshippers at virtual mosques. Jews type messages that fellow believers in Jerusalem download and insert in the Western Wall.*

Everywhere: No matter where you are, virtual church services are available. Just choose an avatar, and you can sing, kneel, pray, and listen to virtual sermons. And if you get bored, you don't have to continue to sit. You can walk around the virtual church and talk to other avatars (Feder 2004). And, of course, you can use your credit card—a real one, not the virtual kind.

Some people have begun to "attend" church as avatars.

The changes certainly are far reaching. One rabbi celebrates Rosh Hashana, a high Holy Day service, by having congregants use their cell phones to text anonymous messages regarding their reactions to what is being discussed. The messages are projected onto a screen in front of the congregation (Alvarez 2012).

Some say that the microchip has put us on the verge of a religious reformation that will turn out to be as big as the one set off by Gutenberg's invention of the printing press. This is likely an exaggeration, but perhaps not.

For Your Consideration

➤ We are gazing into the future of religious practices changing with technology. How do you think that the Internet might change religion? Do you think it can replace the warm embrace of fellow believers? Will tweets bring comfort to someone who is grieving for a loved one?

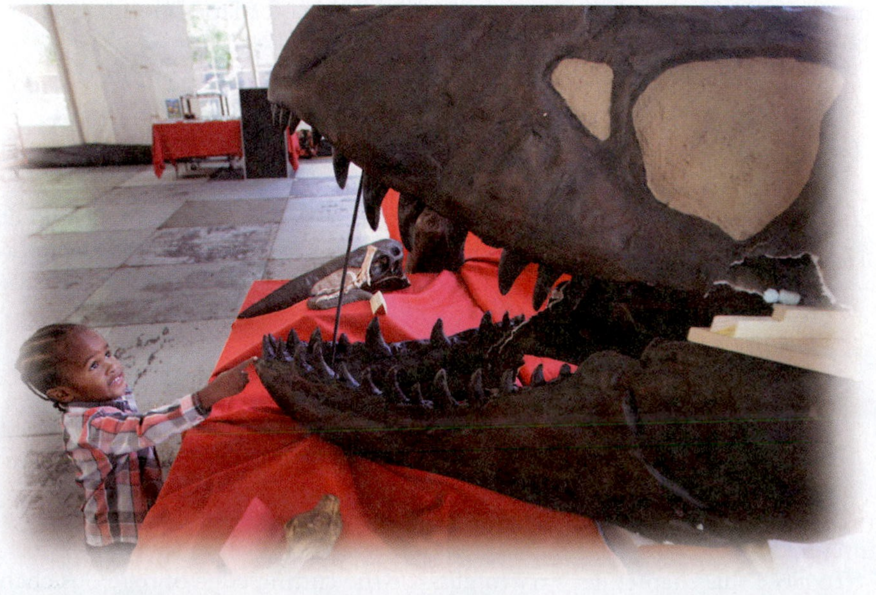

A basic principle of symbolic interactionism is that meaning is not inherent in an object or event, but is determined by people as they interpret the object or event. Does this dinosaur fossil "prove" evolution? Does it "disprove" creation? Such "proof" and "disproof" lie in the eye of the beholder, based on the background assumptions by which it is interpreted.

MySocLab

Study and Review on MySocLab

CHAPTER 18 Summary and Review

What Is Religion?

18.1 Explain what Durkheim meant by sacred and profane; discuss the three elements of religion.

Durkheim identified three essential characteristics of **religion**: beliefs that set the **sacred** apart from the **profane**, **rituals**, and a moral community (a **church**). Pp. 513–514.

The Functionalist Perspective

18.2 Apply the functionalist perspective to religion: functions, dysfunctions, and functional equivalents.

What are the functions and dysfunctions of religion?

Among the functions of religion are answering questions about ultimate meaning; providing emotional comfort, social solidarity, guidelines for everyday life, social control, help in adapting to new situations, and support for the government; and fostering social change. Nonreligious groups or activities that provide these functions are called **functional equivalents** of religion. Among the dysfunctions of religion are religious persecution and war and terrorism. Pp. 514–518.

The Symbolic Interactionist Perspective

18.3 Apply the symbolic interactionist perspective to religion: symbols, rituals, beliefs, religious experience, and community.

What aspects of religion do symbolic interactionists study?

Symbolic interactionists focus on the meanings of religion for its followers. They examine religious symbols, **rituals**, beliefs, **religious experiences**, and the sense of community that religion provides. Pp. 518–523.

The Conflict Perspective

18.4 Apply the conflict perspective to religion: opium of the people and legitimating social inequalities.

What aspects of religion do conflict theorists study?

Conflict theorists examine the relationship of religion to social inequalities, especially how religion reinforces a society's stratification system. P. 521.

Religion and the Spirit of Capitalism

18.5 Explain Weber's analysis of how religion broke tradition and brought capitalism.

What does the spirit of capitalism have to do with religion?

Max Weber saw religion as a primary source of social change. He analyzed how Calvinism gave rise to the **Protestant ethic**, which stimulated what he called the **spirit of capitalism**. The result was capitalism, which transformed society. Pp. 524–525.

The World's Major Religions

18.6 Discuss the origins and development of Judaism, Islam, Hinduism, Buddhism, and Confucianism.

What are the world's major religions?

Judaism, Christianity, and Islam, all **monotheistic** religions, can be traced to the same Old Testament roots. Hinduism, the chief religion of India, has no specific founder, but Judaism (Abraham), Christianity (Jesus), Islam (Muhammad), Buddhism (Gautama), and Confucianism (K'ung Fu-tsu) do. Specific teachings and histories of these religions are reviewed in the text. Pp. 525–530.

Types of Religious Groups

18.7 Compare cult, sect, church, and ecclesia; discuss the conflict between religion and culture.

What types of religious groups are there?

Sociologists divide religious groups into cults, sects, churches, and ecclesia. All religions began as **cults**. Those that survive tend to develop into **sects** and eventually into **churches**. Sects, often led by **charismatic leaders**, are unstable. Some are perceived as threats and are persecuted by the state. **Ecclesia**, or a **state religion**, is rare. Pp. 530–534.

Religion in the United States

18.8 Summarize main features of religion in the United States and discuss the secularization of religion and culture.

What are the main characteristics of religion in the United States?

Membership of religious groups varies by social class and race–ethnicity. The major characteristics are diversity, pluralism and freedom, competition, commitment, and toleration. There is currently a fundamentalist revival, while at the same time the electronic church is gaining in influence. Pp. 534–538.

What is the connection between secularization of religion and the splintering of churches?

Secularization of religion, a change in a religion's focus from spiritual matters to concerns of "this world," is the key to understanding why churches divide. Basically, as a cult or sect adjusts to accommodate its members' upward social class mobility, it changes into a church. Left dissatisfied are members who are not upwardly mobile. They tend to splinter off and form a new cult or sect, and the cycle repeats itself. Cultures permeated by religion also secularize. This, too, leaves many people dissatisfied and promotes social change. Pp. 538–541.

The Future of Religion

18.9 Discuss the likely future of religion.

What can we anticipate in the future?

Although industrialization led to the **secularization of culture**, this did not spell the end of religion, as many social analysts assumed it would. Because science cannot answer questions about ultimate meaning, prove the existence of God or an afterlife, or offer guidelines for morality, the need for religion will remain. In any foreseeable future, religion will prosper. The Internet is likely to have far-reaching consequences for religion. Pp. 541–542.

Thinking Critically about Chapter 18

1. Since 9/11 especially, many people have wondered how anyone can use religion to defend or promote terrorism or other violence. How does the Down-to-Earth Sociology box on terrorism and the mind of God on page 519 help to answer this question? How do the analyses of groupthink in Chapter 6 (pages 167–168) and dehumanization in Chapter 15 (pages 441–446) fit into your analysis?
2. How has secularization affected religion and culture in the United States (or in your country of birth)?
3. Why is religion likely to remain a strong feature of U.S. life—and remain strong in people's lives around the globe?

CHAPTER 19

Medicine and Health

Listen to Chapter 19 on MySocLab

Learning Objectives

After you have read this chapter, you should be able to:

19.1 Explain why health and illness are culturally relative, not absolute matters. (p. 546)

19.2 Summarize the sick role: its elements, ambiguity, gatekeepers, and gender differences. (p. 547)

19.3 Explain how health care is part of the struggle over scarce resources. (p. 548)

19.4 Discuss changes in causes of death and whether Americans were healthier in the past. (p. 553)

19.5 Discuss medical care as a right or a commodity, increasing costs, social inequality, lawsuits, incompetence, fraud, conflict of interest, depersonalization, sexism, racism, the medicalization of society, physician assisted suicide, and attempts to reduce cost. (p. 554)

19.6 Discuss threats to health: HIV/AIDS, weight, alcohol and nicotine, disabling environments, medical experiments, globalization of disease and treatment or prevention. (p. 564)

19.7 Explain why it is difficult to change people's focus from the treatment of illness to the prevention of illness. (p. 572)

19.8 Discuss how technology and alternative medicine are likely to affect the future of medicine. (p. 574)

I decided that it was not enough to just study the homeless—*I had to help them. I learned that a homeless shelter in St. Louis, just across the river from where I was teaching, was going to help poor people save on utilities by installing free wood stoves in their homes. When their utilities are cut off, the next step is eviction and being forced onto the streets. It wasn't exactly applied sociology, but I volunteered.*

I was a little anxious about the coming training session on how to install stoves, as I had never done anything like this. Sociology hadn't trained me to be "handy with my hands," but with the encouragement of a friend, I decided to participate. As I entered the homeless shelter on that Saturday morning, I found the building in semidarkness. "They must be saving on electricity," I thought. Then I was greeted with an unnerving scene. Two police officers were chasing a naked man, who was running through the halls. They caught him. I watched as the elderly man, looking confused, struggled to put on his clothing. From the police, I learned that this man had ripped the wires out of the shelter's main electrical box; that was why there were no lights on.

> "He was crawling under cars at a traffic light—and they let him out in two days."

I asked the officers where they were going to take the man, and they replied, "To Malcolm Bliss" (the state hospital). When I said, "I guess he'll be in there for quite a while," they replied, "Probably just a day or two. We picked him up last week—he was crawling under cars at a traffic light—and they let him out in two days."

The police then explained that the man must be a danger to himself or to others to be admitted as a long-term patient. Visualizing this old man crawling under stopped cars at an intersection, and considering how he had risked electrocution by ripping out the electrical wires with his bare hands, I marveled at the definition of "danger" that the psychiatrists must be using.

Sociology and the Study of Medicine and Health

In this chapter, we will examine why the poor often receive second-rate medical care and, as in this instance, abysmal treatment. We'll also look at how skyrocketing costs have created ethical dilemmas such as the discharge of patients from hospitals before they are well and the potential rationing of medical care.

As we consider these issues, the role of sociology in studying **medicine**—a society's standard ways of dealing with illness and injury—will become apparent. For example, because medicine in the United States is a profession, a bureaucracy, and a big business, sociologists study how it is influenced by self-regulation, a bureaucratic structure, and the profit motive. Sociologists also study how illness and health are much more than biological matters—how they are related to cultural beliefs, lifestyle, and social class. Because of these emphases, the sociology of medicine is one of the applied fields of sociology. Many medical schools and even hospitals have sociologists on their staffs.

19.1 Explain why health and illness are culturally relative, not absolute matters.

The Symbolic Interactionist Perspective

Let's begin, then, by examining how culture influences health and illness. This takes us to the heart of the symbolic interactionist perspective.

The Role of Culture in Defining Health and Illness

Suppose that one morning you look in the mirror and you see strange blotches covering your face and chest. Hoping against hope that it is not serious, you rush to a doctor. If the doctor said that you had "dyschromic spirochetosis," your fears would be confirmed.

Wouldn't everyone around the world draw the same conclusion—that your spots indicate a disease? Not everybody. In one South American tribe, this skin condition is so common that the few individuals who *aren't* spotted are seen as the unhealthy ones. They are even excluded from marriage because they are "sick" (Ackernecht 1947; Hausman 2012).

Consider mental "illness" and mental "health." People aren't automatically "crazy" because they do certain things. Rather, they are defined as "crazy" or "normal" according to cultural guidelines. If an American talks aloud to spirits that no one else can see or hear, he or she is likely to be defined as insane—and, for everyone's good, locked up in a mental hospital. In some tribal societies, in contrast, someone who talks to invisible spirits might be honored for being in close contact with the spiritual world—and, for everyone's good, be declared a **shaman**, or spiritual intermediary. The shaman would then diagnose and treat medical problems.

"Sickness" and "health," then, are not absolutes, as we might suppose. Rather, they are matters of cultural definition. Around the world, each culture provides guidelines that its people use to determine whether they are "healthy" or "sick."

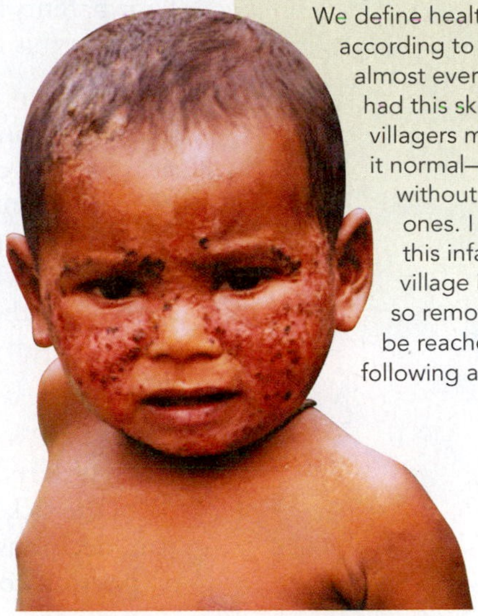

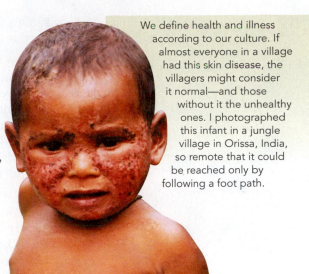

We define health and illness according to our culture. If almost everyone in a village had this skin disease, the villagers might consider it normal—and those without it the unhealthy ones. I photographed this infant in a jungle village in Orissa, India, so remote that it could be reached only by following a foot path.

medicine one of the social institutions that sociologists study; a society's organized ways of dealing with sickness and injury

shaman the healing specialist of a tribe who attempts to control the spirits thought to cause a disease or injury; commonly called a witch doctor

health a human condition measured by four components: physical, mental, social, and spiritual

The Components of Health

Back in 1941, international "health experts" identified three components of **health**: physical, mental, and social (World Health Organization 1946). They missed the focus of our previous chapter, however, and I have added a spiritual component to Figure 19.1. Even the dimensions of health, then, are subject to debate.

Even if we were to agree on the components of health, we would still be left with the question of what makes someone physically, mentally, socially, or spiritually healthy. Again, as symbolic interactionists stress, these are not objective matters. Rather, what is considered "health" or "illness" varies from culture to culture and, in a pluralistic society, even from group to group.

As with religion in the previous chapter, then, the concern of sociologists is not to define "true" health or "true" illness. Instead, it is to analyze how lifestyle affects health, how ideas about health and illness affect people's lives, and even how people determine that they are sick.

FIGURE 19.1 A Continuum of Health and Illness

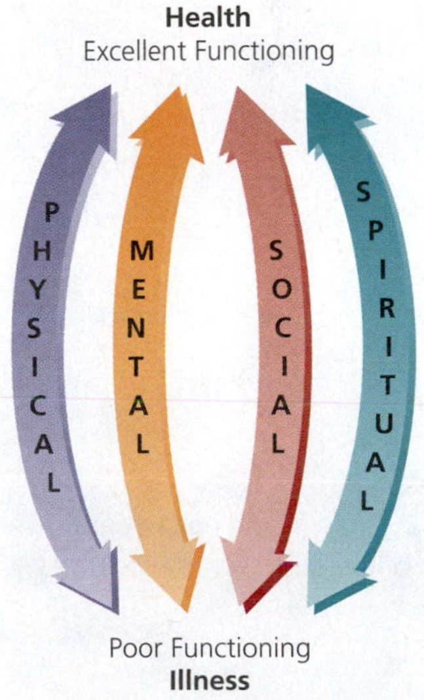

The Functionalist Perspective

Functionalists begin with an obvious point: If society is to function well, its people need to be healthy enough to perform their normal roles. This means that societies must set up ways to control sickness. One way they do this is to develop a system of medical care. Another way is to make rules that help keep too many people from "being sick." Let's look at how this works.

19.2 Summarize the sick role: its elements, ambiguity, gatekeepers, and gender differences.

The Sick Role

Do you remember a time when your throat began to hurt, and when your mom or dad took your temperature, the thermometer registered 102°F? Your parents took you to the doctor, and despite your protests that tomorrow was the first day of summer vacation (or some other important event), you had to spend the next three days in bed taking medicine.

Read on **MySocLab**
Document: The Sick Role and the Role of the Physician Reconsidered

Your parents forced you to play what sociologists call the "sick role." What do they mean by this term?

Elements of the Sick Role. Talcott Parsons, the functionalist who first analyzed the sick role, pointed out that it has four elements: You are not held responsible for being sick, you are exempt from normal responsibilities, you don't like the role, and you will get competent help so you can return to your routines. People who seek approved help are given sympathy and encouragement; those who do not are given the cold shoulder. People who don't get competent help are considered responsible for being sick, are refused the right to claim sympathy from others, and are denied permission to be excused from their normal routines. They are considered to be wrongfully claiming the sick role.

Ambiguity in the Sick Role. Instead of a fever of 102°F, suppose that the thermometer registers 99.5°F. Do you then "become" sick—or not? That is, do you decide to claim the sick role? Because most instances of illness are not as clear-cut as, say, a broken arm, decisions to claim the sick role often are based more on social considerations than on physical conditions. To make this clear, consider this:

> *Along with your 99.5°F temperature, let's suppose that you are also facing a midterm that you are unprepared for. The more you think about the test (which you can make up if you are ill), the worse you are likely to feel—which makes the need to claim the sick role seem more legitimate. Now assume that the thermometer still shows 99.5°F, but you have no test and your friends are on their way to take you out to celebrate your twenty-first birthday.*

For your twenty-first birthday party, you are not likely to play the sick role at all. But in both cases your physical condition is the same.

Gatekeepers to the Sick Role. To keep too many people from claiming the sick role, *gatekeepers* guard the door. Before parents call the school to excuse a child from class, they decide whether their child is faking or has genuine symptoms. If they determine that the symptoms are real, then they decide whether the symptoms are serious enough to keep the child home from school or even severe enough to take the child to a doctor. For adults, the gatekeepers to the sick role are physicians. Adults can bypass the gatekeeper for a few days, but eventually employers will insist on a "doctor's excuse," perhaps in the form of insurance claims signed by the doctor. In sociological terms, these are ways of getting permission to play the sick role.

Gender Differences in the Sick Role. Women are more willing than men to claim the sick role: They go to doctors more frequently, and they visit hospital emergency rooms more often. Women also are hospitalized more often (*Statistical Abstract* 2013:Tables 169, 171, 172, 179). No one knows the reason for sure, but it is likely that it is related to gender. The sick role does not match the ideal that most men try to project—being strong, keeping pain to themselves, and "toughing it out." The woman's model, in contrast, is more likely to involve sharing feelings and seeking help from others, characteristics that are compatible with the sick role.

19.3 Explain how health care is part of the struggle over scarce resources.

The Conflict Perspective

As we stressed in earlier chapters, the primary focus of the conflict perspective is the struggle over scarce resources. Health care is one of those resources. Let's first take a global perspective on medical care. Then, turning our attention to the United States, we will analyze how one group secured a monopoly on U.S. health care.

Watch on **MySocLab**
Video: Health Care Outside the United States

Global Stratification and Health Care

In Chapter 9 (page 247), we saw how the first nations to industrialize gained the economic and military power that allowed them to dominate other nations. The global stratification that resulted includes medical care, starkly evident in the photo to the right. Other examples are open heart surgery and organ transplants, which have become routine in the Most Industrialized Nations. The Least Industrialized Nations, in contrast, have neither the trained surgeons nor the money to buy the technologies that these surgeries require.

Global stratification in health care is starkly evident in this photo from a mental health center in Mogadishu, Somalia. They really are bound by chains.

Life expectancy and infant mortality rates also tell the story. Most people in the industrialized world can expect to live to about age 75, but most people in Afghanistan, Nigeria, and South Africa don't make it to 55. Look at Figure 19.2 below, which shows the world's countries in which fewer than 7 of every 1,000 babies die before they are a year old. They are all Most Industrialized Nations. The infant mortality rates of some of the Least Industrialized Nations are incredibly high. Afghanistan's rate is *fifty* times higher than that of Japan (*Statistical Abstract* 2013:Table 1355).

Global stratification even helps to determine what diseases we get. Suppose that you had been born in a Least Industrialized Nation located in the tropics. During your much shorter life, you would face four major causes of illness and death: malaria (from mosquitoes), internal parasites (from contaminated water), diarrhea (from food and soil contaminated with human feces), and malnutrition. You would not face heart disease and cancer. As strange as it sounds, these are "luxury" diseases—they are part of the world where people live long enough to get them. As nations industrialize, health care and nutrition improve, and their citizens live longer. The diseases that used to be their primary killers decline, and residents begin to worry about cancer and heart attacks instead.

Watch on **MySocLab**
Video: The Basics: Health and Medicine

FIGURE 19.2 **How Many Babies Die before Their First Birthday?**

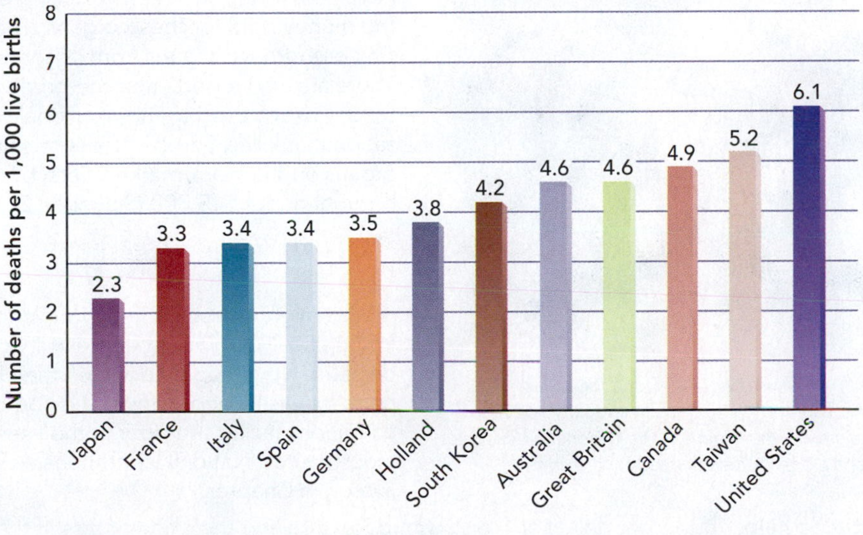

Note: Infant mortality is the number of babies that die before their first birthday, per 1,000 live births. Belgium, Czech Republic, and Greece, with lower infant mortality rates than that of the United States, have been dropped from recent editions of the source. Italy must have experienced a miracle: Its rate of 5.4 in 2010 plummeted to 3.4 in 2011.

Source: By the author. Based on *Statistical Abstract of the United States* 2013:Table 1355.

Keep in mind that death rates are averages for a population. Not everyone dies young in the Least Industrialized Nations, especially the rich. As it does in ours, social stratification shows up *within* the Least Industrialized Nations. In these countries, the elite, who have garnered the lion's share of the country's resources, lavish it on themselves. To have advanced medical technology for their own medical treatment, they even send a few students to top medical schools in the West. The poor of these nations, in contrast, go without even basic medical services and continue to die at an early age.

Before turning to medical care in the United States, let's consider the international black market in human organs. This stunning example of the inequality that arises from global stratification is the topic of the Down-to-Earth Sociology box below.

Down-to-Earth Sociology

José's Old Kidney: The International Black Market in Human Body Parts

One of José da Silva's memories from childhood is the morning when seven children shared a single egg for breakfast.

Da Silva is one of twenty-three children of a woman in Brazil who sold her flesh to survive. As an adult, da Silva works for the Brazilian minimum wage, making $80 a month. When he heard that he could sell a kidney for $6,000, it was like a dream come true. It would take six years of hard work to make $6,000.

How did da Silva's kidney become part of an international black market in human organs? The story starts in Brooklyn, where a woman had been on dialysis for fifteen years. The woman was on waiting lists for organ transplants—but so were another 80,000 Americans (Suddath and Altman 2009). By the time there would be a kidney for her, she would be dead and buried. Her doctor told her, "If you want to live, get a kidney any way you can" (Rohter 2004).

Selling human organs is illegal in all countries except Iran, so making this arrangement wasn't easy (Carney 2011). The woman's husband "heard from someone who heard from someone" that a group in Israel might be able to help. The man had relatives in Tel Aviv, and they made contact with this group. The charge would be $60,000 for a kidney. This group's middleman in Brazil made arrangements to buy one of da Silva's kidneys. They paid da Silva $6,000 and flew him to South Africa, where he was lodged in a safe house. The U.S. woman also flew to South Africa, where she was put up at a beach house.

South African surgeons don't participate in the illegal traffic in human organs, but then, like surgeons in many places, including those in some of the finest hospitals in the United States, they don't ask a lot of questions (Interlandi 2009). Hospital administrators accepted the statement signed by da Silva saying that the woman was his cousin.

The ability to transplant livers, lungs, kidneys, and even hearts and faces is one of the marvels of modern medicine. But the shortage of donated organs and the long list of people who need organs have led to underground transactions. You never know who is on the receiving end of the money paid for these organs. The Chinese remove organs from prisoners. There are also reports that the prime minister of Kosovo used to run a criminal organization that killed Serbs in order to sell their organs on the black market. Each body brought about $45,000 (Schmidle 2013).

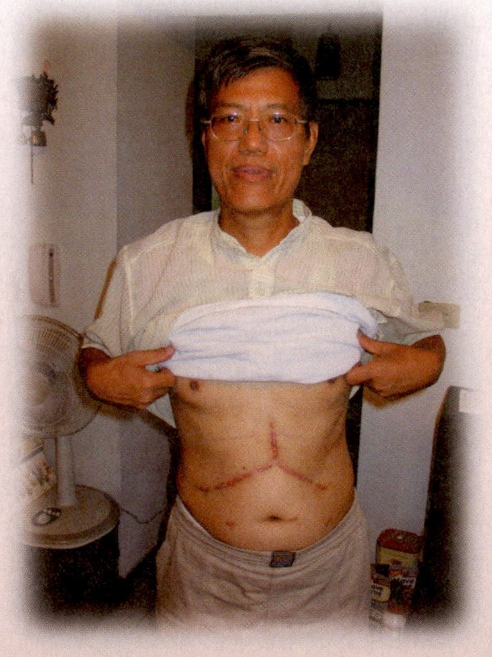

This man from Taiwan went to China for a liver transplant. The liver came from an executed prisoner. China "harvests" the organs of the prisoners it executes. The organs are resources claimed by the state.

For Your Consideration

➔ You might not sell one of your kidneys for $6,000, but a lot of people will. To understand why people "donate" their body parts for cash, keep in mind the horrible conditions facing the poor in the Least Industrialized Nations, conditions we discussed in Chapter 9. What is wrong with people selling their body parts, if they want to? Aren't poor people better off with one kidney and six years of extra earnings to buy a home, start a business, get out of debt, or take care of their families than with two kidneys and no such opportunities?

Establishing a Monopoly on U.S. Health Care

Did you know that health care is the largest business in the United States? And did you know that it is the country's only legal monopoly? To understand how these remarkable facts developed, we first need to see how medicine became professionalized.

The Professionalization of Medicine.

Imagine that you are living in the American colonies in the 1700s and you want to become a physician. Will the entrance exams and required courses be difficult? Not really. You won't have any. Because there is neither licensing nor medical school, you won't need any formal education. You can simply ask a physician to train you. In return for the opportunity to learn, you'll be his assistant and help him with menial tasks. When you think that you have learned enough, you can hang out a sign and proclaim yourself a doctor. If you want to, you can even skip the apprenticeship. If you can convince people you are a good doctor, you'll make a living. If not, you'll have to turn to something else. The process was similar to how people can become automobile mechanics today.

In the 1800s, things began to change. A few medical schools opened, and there was some licensing of physicians. The medical schools of this period were like religions are today: They competed for clients and made different claims to the truth. One medical school would teach a particular idea about what causes illness and how to treat it, while another medical school would teach something else. Training was short, and often not even a high school diploma was required. There was no clinical training. The medical school at Harvard University took only two school years to complete—and each school year lasted only four months (Starr 1982; Rosenberg 1987; Riessman 1994).

Watch on **MySocLab**
Video: The Big Picture: Health and Medicine

Then came the 1900s. By 1906, the United States had 160 medical schools. The Carnegie Foundation asked Abraham Flexner, an educator, to evaluate them. Thinking that funds from the Carnegie Foundation would follow, even the most inadequate schools opened their doors to Flexner (Pescosolido 2013). In some schools, the laboratories consisted only of "a few vagrant test tubes squirreled away in a cigar box." Other schools had libraries with no books. On Flexner's advice, philanthropies funded the most promising schools. Upgrading their facilities, these schools attracted more capable faculty and students. Facing these higher standards and greater competition, most of the other schools had to close their doors.

professionalization of medicine the development of medicine into a specialty that requires physicians to (1) obtain a rigorous education, (2) regulate themselves, (3) take authority over clients, (4) claim a theoretical understanding of illness, and (5) present themselves as doing a service to society (rather than just following self-interest)

The Flexner report (1910) led to the **professionalization of medicine**. When sociologists use the term *profession*, they mean something quite specific. What happened was that physicians began to (1) undergo a rigorous education, (2) claim a theoretical understanding of illness, (3) regulate themselves, (4) assert that they were performing a service for society (rather than just following self-interest), and (5) take authority over clients (Freidson 2001; Dingwall 2008).

The Monopoly of Medicine.

The key to understanding our current situation is this: Medicine became not only a profession but also a monopoly. The American Medical Association (AMA), the group that gained control over U.S. medicine, managed to get laws passed that limited medical licenses to graduates of schools they controlled. This put other groups out of business and silenced most competing philosophies of medicine. At first, the men in charge of the AMA refused to admit women to medical schools, but in 1915, they began to admit women on a limited basis (Campbell and McCammon 2005).

You just read about medical training in the 1800s. This ad from that period illustrates the state of medical treatment at that time.

HAGAN'S
MAGNOLIA BALM
LYON MFG. CO.
NEW YORK
Its praise Columbia loudly chants,
"And so do her sisters, and her cousins and her aunts,
Especially her cousins whom she reckons by the dozens."

The monopoly gained by the AMA was thorough. By law, only this approved group—a sort of priesthood of medicine—was allowed to diagnose and treat medical problems. Only they knew what was right for people's health. Only they could scribble the secret language (Latin) on pieces of parchment (prescription forms) for translators (pharmacists) to decipher (Miner 1956/2007). This group of men grew so powerful that it was even able to take childbirth away from midwives—the focus of the Down-to-Earth Sociology box below.

fee-for-service payment to a physician to diagnose and treat a patient's medical problems

In Sum: From its humble origins (no training or licensing required), medicine has become the largest business in the United States. It is so powerful that it lobbies all state legislatures and the U.S. Congress. The AMA, which practices **fee-for-service**—payment to a physician in exchange for diagnosis and treatment—has become the only legal monopoly in the United States. The medical business consists not only of physicians but also of nurses, physician assistants, hospital personnel,

Down-to-Earth Sociology

Having Babies Is Men's Work

Delivering babies used to be a matter of women helping women. Some midwives were neighborhood women who had experience in childbirth. Others were trained to deliver babies.

Physicians—almost all of whom were men—wanted to expand their business, and taking over childbirth was one way to do it. The men confronted two major obstacles, however. The first you can expect: The midwives didn't want men to cut into their business. The second was ignorance. The men knew nothing about delivering babies. It was considered indecent for a man to even know much about pregnancy, and unheard of for a man to help a woman give birth.

Some physicians bribed midwives to sneak them into the bedrooms where women were giving birth. To say "sneaked" is no exaggeration: They crawled on their hands and knees so that the mother-to-be wouldn't know that a man was present. Most physicians, however, weren't fortunate enough to find such cooperative midwives, and they trained with mannequins. Eventually, physicians were allowed to be present at births, but this was still considered indecent, because it meant that a man who was not a woman's husband might see the woman's private parts. To prevent this, the physician had to fumble blindly under a sheet in a darkened room, his head decorously turned aside.

As physicians gained political power, they launched a ruthless campaign against their competitors. They attacked the midwives as "dirty, ignorant, and incompetent." They even called them a "menace to the health of the community." After physicians formed their union, the American Medical Association, they persuaded many states to pass laws that made it illegal for anyone but physicians to deliver babies. Some states, however, continue to allow nurse-midwives to practice. Even today, this struggle is not over; nurse-midwives and physicians sometimes still clash over who has the right to deliver babies.

Conflict theorists emphasize that this was not just a business matter but gender conflict—men sought to take control over what had been women's work. Symbolic interactionists stress that to win this struggle, the physicians manipulated symbols. They convinced the public that pregnancy and childbirth were not natural processes but medical conditions that required the assistance of able men. This new definition flew in the face of human history, since it had always been women who had helped women have babies. The symbolic change created a new reality, transforming childbirth into "men's work." When this happened, the prestige of the work went up—and so did the price.

Tension between midwives and physicians continues today over who should have what authority in childbirth.

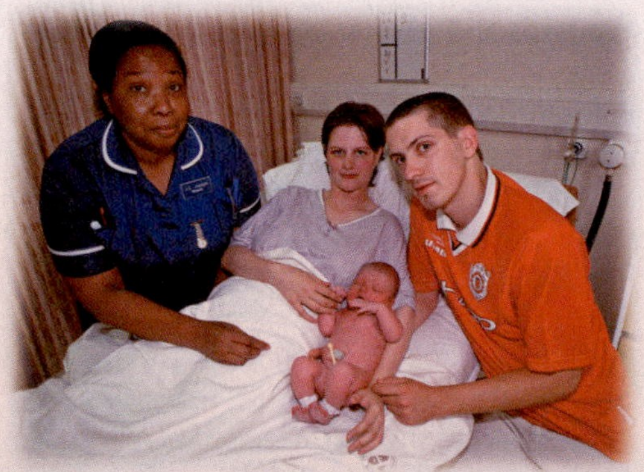

This midwife, who works in a hospital, integrated the husband into the delivery process.

Sources: Wertz and Wertz 1981; Rothman 1994; Phillips 2007; Cheyney 2011.

For Your Consideration

➤ In Chapter 11, we learned an interesting principle of gender: Activities that are associated with women are given lower prestige than activities that are associated with men. Managing childbirth is an example. If women come to dominate medicine, which seems likely, do you think the prestige of practicing medicine will decline? How about the income of physicians?

pharmacists, insurance companies, corporations that own hospitals and nursing homes, and the research, manufacturing, and sales force that lies behind the drug industry.

epidemiology the study of patterns of disease and disability in a population

Historical Patterns of Health

19.4 Discuss changes in causes of death and whether Americans were healthier in the past.

Let's look at how health and illness in the United States have changed. This will take us into the field of **epidemiology**, the study of how medical problems are distributed throughout a population.

Explore on **MySocLab**
Activity: Health across the United States

Physical Health

Leading Causes of Death. To see how the physical health of Americans has changed, we can compare the leading causes of death in two time periods. As you can see from Figure 19.3, the change is dramatic. Today's two leading causes of death, heart disease and cancer, placed only fourth and eighth in 1900. Two of the top three killers in 1900, tuberculosis and diarrhea, don't even show up in today's top ten. Similarly, diabetes and Alzheimer's disease didn't make the top ten in 1900, but they do now. From this figure, you can see that disease and death are not just biological events; they change as society changes. These shifts reveal the *social* nature of disease and death.

FIGURE 19.3 The Top Ten Causes of Death in the United States, 1900 and Now

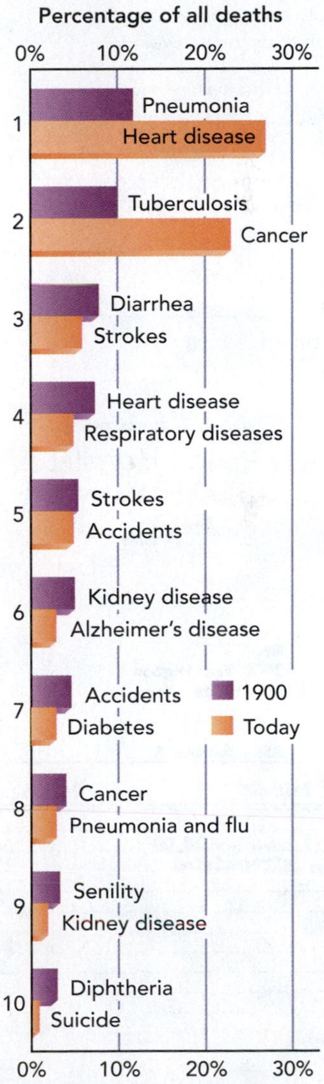

Sources: By the author. 1900 data from CDC 2009. Current data from *Statistical Abstract of the United States* 2013:Table 125.

Were Americans Healthier in the Past? A second way to see how the physical health of Americans has changed is to ask if they are healthier—or sicker—than they used to be. This question brings us face to face once again with the problem of how we define things: "Healthy"—by whose standards? "Sicker"—by what measures? One way around this problem is to look at mortality rates. If Americans lived longer in the past, we can assume they used to be healthier. Because most people today live longer than their ancestors, however, we can conclude that contemporary Americans are healthier.

Some may think that this conclusion flies in the face of our polluted air and water—and of the heart disease and cancer shown in Figure 19.3. And it does. Sometimes older people say, "When I was a kid, hardly anyone died from cancer, and now it seems almost everyone does." What they say is true, but what this statement overlooks is that most cancers strike older people. When life expectancy is shorter, fewer people live long enough to die from cancer. Also, past physicians lacked today's diagnostic tests, and most cancer went unrecognized. Doctors often said that people died from "old age," "heart failure," or the "senility" you see on Figure 19.3.

Mental Health

In the past, there was little mental illness because almost everyone grew up with two loving parents. They enjoyed a harmonious life in close-knit families. Everyone seemed to bend over backward to help one another.

Some people seem to paint an idyllic past in colors similar to this. But what facts do we have? We can conclude that Americans today are physically healthier than earlier generations, but when it comes to mental health, we have no way to make good comparisons with earlier times. We need solid measures of mental illness or mental health, not stories of how things used to be. It is easy to make the past look better than it was, to

Were Americans healthier in the past? As this photo from the 1920s shows, some people even worked out. But longevity gives us the answer.

gloss over its hardships and struggles. Idyllic pasts never existed—except in people's imaginations. Beliefs that mental illness is worse today represent a perception, not measured reality. Perhaps there was less mental illness in the past—but perhaps there was *more* mental illness in the past. Since we don't even know how much mental illness there is today (Scheff 1999), how can we judge how much there was in the past?

Issues in Health Care

19.5 Discuss medical care as a right or a commodity, increasing costs, social inequality, lawsuits, incompetence, fraud, conflict of interest, depersonalization, sexism, racism, the medicalization of society, physician assisted suicide, and attempts to reduce cost.

Let's turn to health care in the United States.

Medical Care: A Right or a Commodity?

Nataline Sarkisyan, a 17-year-old cancer patient, waited for a liver transplant that never came. Livers were available, but her health insurer refused to pay for the transplant. Nataline's hospital, UCLA Medical Center, said it would do the transplant, but only if the family paid $75,000 up front.

The family managed to get the $75,000, but then the hospital demanded $300,000 to care for Nataline after surgery. The family could not raise the money, and Nataline died. (Martinez 2008)

Here is a primary controversy in the United States: Is medical care a right or a commodity? If medical care is a right, then all citizens should have access to similar medical care. If medical care is a commodity, then it is like cars and clothing. The natural outcome is that the rich will have access to one type of medical care, and the poor to another.

But why should we even bother asking this question? Nataline's death makes it starkly clear that medical care in the United States is *not* the right of citizens. Medical care *is* a commodity for sale. Those who have more money can buy quality health care; those who have little money have to settle for less, or even for none.

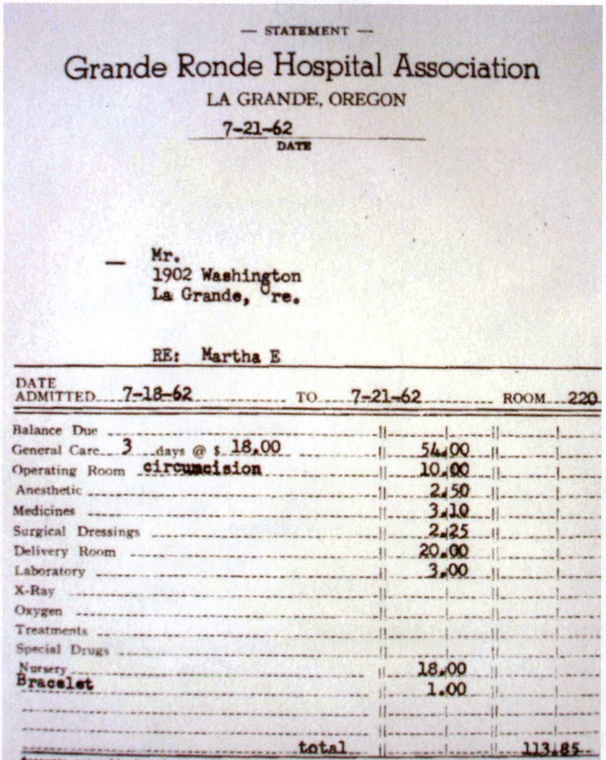

— STATEMENT —

Grande Ronde Hospital Association
LA GRANDE, OREGON

7-21-62
DATE

Mr.
1902 Washington
La Grande, Ore.

RE: Martha E

DATE ADMITTED 7-18-62 TO 7-21-62 ROOM 220

Balance Due	
General Care 3 days @ $ 18.00	54.00
Operating Room circumcision	10.00
Anesthetic	2.50
Medicines	3.10
Surgical Dressings	2.25
Delivery Room	20.00
Laboratory	3.00
X-Ray	
Oxygen	
Treatments	
Special Drugs	
Nursery	18.00
Bracelet	1.00
total	113.85

Accounts not paid when due are subject to interest charge.

Skyrocketing Costs

To see how the cost of medical care has skyrocketed, look at Figure 19.4 on the next page. In 1960, health care cost the average American $150 a year. Today, the total has jumped to $8,400. Consider this: In 1960, a 17-inch black-and-white television cost $150. If the cost of televisions had risen at the same rate as the cost of health care, a *17-inch black-and-white* television would now cost $8,400. However, the jump in medical costs includes more advanced technology and medicines, so to keep this comparison accurate, assume that the television is also more advanced, say 60 inches, thin-screen, color, plasma, high definition, and Internet connected. But don't forget this startling aspect of the comparison: The average American would have to pay $8,400 for a new television every year!

It is difficult to grasp how reasonable medical costs used to be. Look at the hospital bill to the left. This is the entire amount billed by a private hospital for the delivery of a child. The $113.85 included a three-day stay in the hospital. The delivery room cost $20, the circumcision $10, and the anesthetic $2.50.

Social Inequality

In the opening vignette, you read about the naked man in the homeless shelter who was being taken to the state mental hospital. This event lays bare our **two-tier system of medical care**. A middle-class or rich person who had mental problems would visit a private counselor, not be sent to a state mental hospital—or to jail, where poor people with mental illnesses often end up. Of course, he or she would not have been in that shelter in the first place. Because health care is a commodity—and, today, a costly one—those who can afford it buy superior health care, while, for the most part, the poor get leftovers. In short, medical care is like automobiles—new sports cars for the wealthy and old, worn-out cars for the poor.

Since 1939, sociologists have found that people's emotional wellbeing gets worse the lower they are on the social class ladder. Those in the lower social classes are more likely to be depressed, anxious, nervous, and phobic (fearful). Numerous studies have confirmed this finding (Faris and Dunham 1939; Srole et al. 1978; Muntaner et al. 2013).

With the many stresses that poverty thrusts on the lower social classes, it isn't difficult to understand why they have greater mental problems. Compared with middle- and upper-class Americans, the poor have less job security and lower wages, and are hounded by bill collectors. They also are more likely to divorce, to be victims of violent crime, and to abuse alcohol. Such conditions deal severe blows to emotional well-being.

These same stresses are bad for physical health. Unlike the middle and upper classes, few poor people have a personal physician, and some of them spend hours waiting in emergency rooms and public health clinics. After waiting most of a day, some don't even get to see a doctor; they are simply told to come back the next day (Fialka 1993; Goldstein 2008). When hospitalized, the poor are likely to find themselves in understaffed and underfunded public hospitals, where they are treated by rotating interns who do not know them and do not follow up on their progress.

For a quick snapshot of how health improves with income, look at Figure 19.5.

Reducing Inequalities: Health Care Reform

In 2010, after rancorous debate that extended over a year, Congress passed the Patient Protection and Affordable Care Act. The intention of this law is to reduce the inequalities in health care by requiring all U.S. citizens and legal residents to have medical insurance. Those who cannot afford it will be provided health insurance by raising taxes on those with higher incomes ("Focus on Health . . ." 2010).

FIGURE 19.4 The Soaring Cost of Medical Care: Annual Costs per American

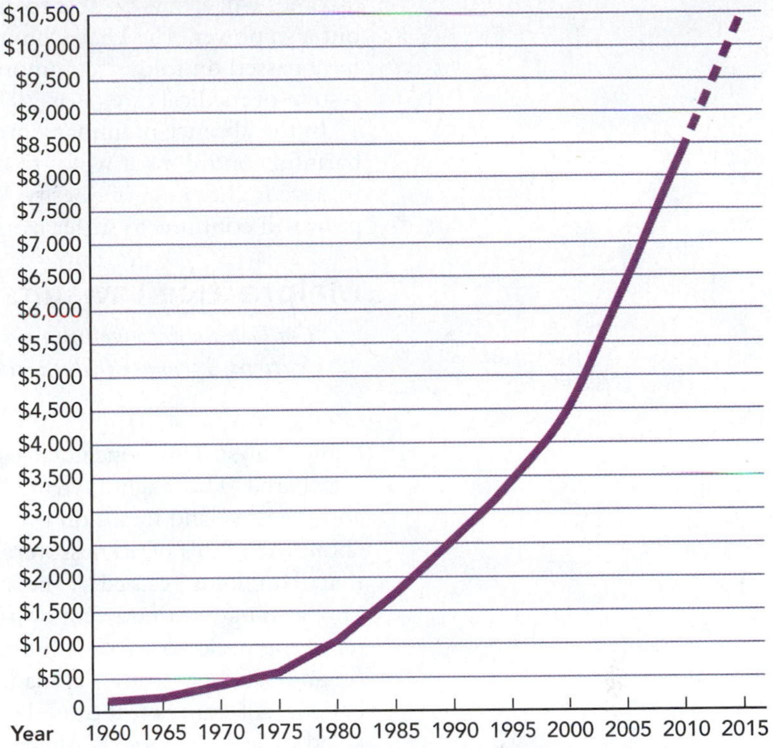

Note: This is the national medical bill divided by the total population. The average American pays 37 percent of this amount out of pocket and by insurance.

Source: By the author. Based on *Statistical Abstract of the United States* 2013:Table 137, and earlier years.

two-tier system of medical care a system of medical care in which the wealthy receive superior medical care and the poor inferior medical care

FIGURE 19.5 Income and Days Sick in Bed

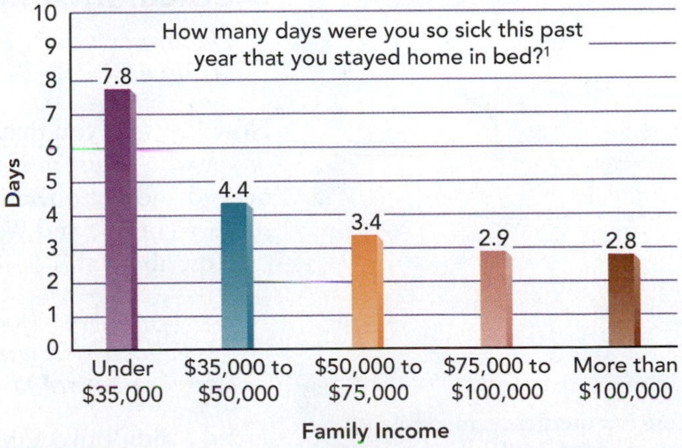

[1]A nationally representative sample of adults age 18 and over was asked some form of this question.

Source: By the author. Based on CDC 2012:Table 17.

Watch on **MySocLab**
Video: Medical Ethics and Morality

Only as the years pass will we see what impact this law has on inequalities in health care. In advance, however, we can be certain that this law will *not* eliminate the inequalities in medical care. Inequalities are built into our social structure. People with higher incomes will always be able to afford higher-quality medical care. It is not just money, but also power. The U.S. Congress has exempted itself from the medical system they have passed on to the "common" people, keeping their own luxurious, government-paid system of medical care (Roy 2013).

In the absence of fundamental change, the poor will continue to be exposed to more harmful conditions at work, to eat unhealthier food, to exercise less, to smoke more, and to have higher rates of obesity. With such change most unlikely, we can expect that the poor will continue to suffer from more health problems and to die at younger ages.

Malpractice Lawsuits and Defensive Medicine

"I'm looking for something else to do, because medicine is no longer fun. Every time I treat a patient, I wonder if this is the one who is going to turn around and sue me."

—Said by an anxious physician to the author

Some analysts have concluded—seriously—that physicians used to kill more patients than they cured. This might be true. Physicians did leave a trail of death. They didn't know about germs, and they didn't wash their hands before surgery or childbirth. Their beliefs about the causes of sickness were not exactly helpful either. In the 1800s, doctors thought that "bad fluids" caused sickness. To get rid of these bad fluids, they used four techniques: (1) bleeding (cutting a vein or using leeches to drain out "bad" blood); (2) blistering (applying packs so hot they burned the skin, causing the "bad pus" to drain); (3) vomiting (giving patients liquids that made them vomit up the bad fluids); and (4) purging (giving patients substances that caused diarrhea). Not surprisingly, these treatments sometimes killed patients. George Washington was just one in that long line of medical victims.

We have a paradox. Back then, with such inferior medical care, there were no medical malpractice suits. But today, with our vastly superior health care, malpractice suits are common. Why? The thinking used to be, "People make mistakes, including doctors," and the law didn't allow patients to recover damages. Today's physicians, in contrast, are held to much higher standards—and they are not excused for making mistakes. As indicated by the quotation that opened this section, malpractice suits are like a sword dangling over the heads of physicians. Suspended only by a rotting thread, the sword will fall, but doctors don't know when. To protect themselves, they practice **defensive medicine**—consulting with colleagues and ordering lab tests not because the patient needs them but because the doctors want to leave a paper trail in case they are sued. These consultations and tests—done for the doctor's benefit, not the patient's—run medical bills up even higher.

Medical Incompetence

The surgeon was the innovative type. When he saw that no one had brought the titanium rod that he needed for the back surgery, he spotted a screwdriver nearby and inserted it instead.

Now I'm sure you think that I must be exaggerating. I mean, we all know that a screwdriver would rust inside someone's body. Unfortunately, this did happen. The patient needed another operation—to remove the screwdriver, of course. He died during that surgery (Levine and Wolfe 2009).

How about this one?

The surgeon was frustrated. The surgery was taking longer than expected, and the bank was going to close soon. He excused himself and left to cash his paycheck. A half hour or so later, he returned to complete the surgery.

No I didn't make this one up either (Levine and Wolfe 2009). Nor these:

When ultrasound showed that one of the twins had defects, the woman asked her doctor to abort it. He removed the healthy one.

defensive medicine medical practices done not for the patient's benefit but in order to protect physicians from malpractice suits

Another woman went into the hospital with a lung problem. Her surgeon removed her uterus.

A man went into the hospital for a circumcision. The surgeon removed both of his testicles.

Some physicians even operate on the wrong patient.

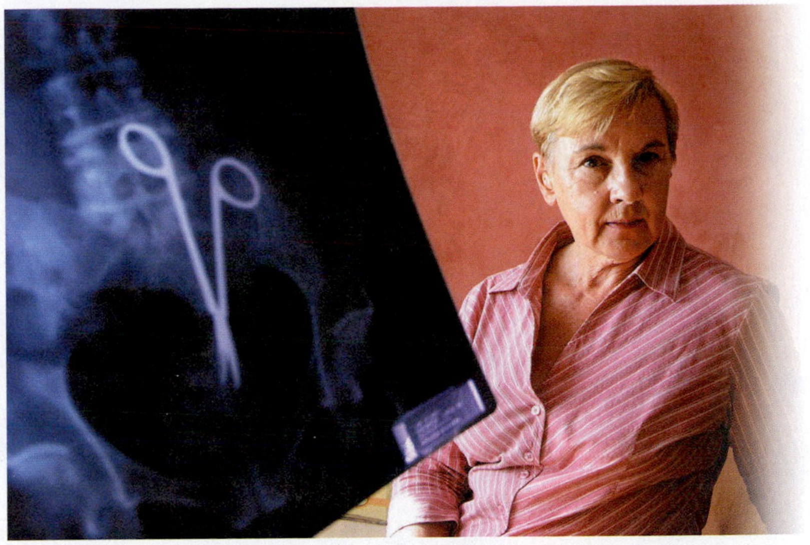

When this woman complained of pain after surgery, she was told that the pain was normal. After 18 months' of complaints, the hospital took an X-ray. The surgical scissors had been "lost" inside her.

Each day in the United States, there are about a dozen wrong-patient, wrong-side, or wrong-procedure surgeries (Steinhauer and Fessenden 2001; Seiden and Barach 2006; Senders and Kanzki 2008; Associated Press 2010). Some hospitals have grown so desperate that before an operation, they require the surgeon to mark the patient's body where the incision is to be made. Then at that spot, both the surgeon and the patient sign their names in indelible ink.

Death by Doctors. About 98,000 patients die each year from mistakes made in U.S. hospitals (Makary 2012). *If deaths from medical errors were an official classification, it would rank as the sixth leading cause of death in the United States* (*Statistical Abstract* 2013:Table 125). Doctors have even developed a term to refer to these deaths. Do you think it is "death by incompetence" or "killed by doctors"? Understandably, they have chosen a more innocuous term: "adverse events." These deaths and the many more injuries certainly are "adverse" to the patient and family.

Using a Checklist. In an interesting experiment, surgeons in eight countries were required to use a simple checklist ("Did you check the patient's identification bracelet? Did you check for allergies. Did you. . . ."). The results were dramatic. *Patient deaths dropped by 40 percent* (Goldstein 2009). If surgeons used checklists worldwide, about 500,000 needless deaths could be avoided each year (Borchard et al. 2012). Physicians are gradually discovering what airline pilots learned long ago: With lives at stake, don't rely on your memory to make sure you've done everything before takeoff.

Federal Center for Patient Safety. The Institute of Medicine has proposed that we establish a Federal Center for Patient Safety. All medical deaths and injuries would be reported to the Center. Just as the Federal Aviation Agency investigates each plane crash, the Center would investigate each medical injury or death. Based on the cause it pinpoints, the Center would set up guidelines to reduce similar events. With prospective patients able to check out the hospital they are thinking of using—to see how many people their doctors have injured or killed through incompetence or negligence—I anticipate that this number would drop sharply.

Depersonalization: The Medical Cash Machine

As Mary Duffy lay in her hospital bed in San Jose, California, a group of white-coated strangers came in. Without a word, a man leaned over, pulled back her blanket, and stripped her nightgown from her shoulders, exposing her breasts. He then began to lecture about carcinomas to the group standing around the bed. As the half dozen medical students stared at Mrs. Duffy's naked body, the doctor spoke his first words to Mrs. Duffy, asking, "Have you passed gas yet?" (Carey 2005)

Depersonalization is one of the main complaints that patients have about their medical treatment. As was the case with Mrs. Duffy, patients often feel as though they are treated like cases and diseases, not as individuals. Some also get the impression that doctors and hospitals view them as cash machines, as walking (or bed-ridden) ATMs. While talking to patients, some physicians seem to be counting minutes so that they can move on to the next ATM and extract more money. After all, any extra time spent with a patient is money down the drain.

depersonalization dealing with people as though they were objects; in the case of medical care, as though patients were merely cases and diseases, not people

Although some students start medical school with lofty motives, desiring to "treat the whole person," it doesn't take long for them to learn to depersonalize patients. Sociologists Jack Haas and William Shaffir (1993), who did participant observation at McMaster University in Canada, discovered how this happens. As vast amounts of information are thrown at medical students, their feelings for patients are overpowered by the need to be efficient. Here is what one student told the researchers:

Somebody will say, "Listen to Mrs. Jones's heart. It's just a little thing flubbing on the table." And you forget about the rest of her . . . and it helps in learning in the sense that you can go in to a patient, put your stethoscope on the heart, listen to it, and walk out. . . . The advantage is that you can go in a short time and see a patient, get the important things out of the patient, and leave.

Unconscious patients, the dying, and the dead are even transformed into objects for practicing medical skills (Berger et al. 2002). Listen to what this student said to Haas and Shaffir.

You don't know the people that are under anesthesia—just practice putting the tube in, and the person wakes up with a sore throat, and well, it's just sort of a part of the procedure. . . . Someone comes in who has croaked [and you say], "Well, come on. Here is a chance to practice your intubation" [inserting a tube in the throat].

Conflict of Interest

1. You depend on the medicine you take to be safe.
2. Your doctor depends on clinical trials to know the medicine is safe.
3. The clinical trials are done by the company that makes the medicine.

It doesn't take a brain surgeon to see the conflict of interest. But at least we know that no drug company will fake test results, especially when lives are at stake.

Or do we?

GlaxoSmithKline manufactures Avandia, a medicine to treat diabetes. To show that Avandia was safe, GlaxoSmithKline provided data on clinical trials to the Food and Drug Administration. The data looked good. The only problem was that the report didn't mention some patients who had adverse reactions—such as the patient whose brain began to bleed or the one who suffered a stroke so severe she had to be hospitalized for sixty-seven days. These patients miraculously disappeared from the data reported to the Food and Drug Administration (Harris 2010).

Now consider the doctor with his or her patient. The doctor is figuring out what medicine to prescribe. When a used car salesperson steers a customer to a car that brings more money, it is no surprise. In the practice of medicine, money talks in the same way. Analysts have reviewed thousand upon thousands of cases. They have found that if physicians make more money by prescribing one medicine or medical treatment rather than another, they tend to prescribe the more profitable one (Robertson et al. 2012). If they make money from X-rays or a particular test or drug, they recommend more X-rays or give that test or drug more often. Some surgeons invest in medical supply companies that sell the products they use in surgery. The screws used in spinal fusion surgery cost just $100 to manufacture, but they sell for $1,000 to $2,000 each (Carreyrou and McGinty 2010).

You can see the conflict of interest. Did the physician use an extra screw in surgery because the patient needed it or to get a share of the additional $900 to $1,900 profit? Is the doctor recommending X-rays because the patient needs the X-rays or because the doctor has invested in the x-ray company?

Some reform has begun. At Harvard University, medical students protested that professors who receive money from drug companies are not objective in their teaching. Reacting to the protest, Harvard passed a rule that teachers in the medical school must inform their students of any ties they have with drug companies (Wilson 2009). Medical journals now require the same disclosure.

Medical Fraud

A doctor who billed Medicare for treating a patient's eye slipped up just a bit—the patient was missing that eye (Levy 2003). A dentist charged Medicare for 991 procedures in a single day. This would come to one procedure every 36 seconds (Levy and Luo 2005). A Brooklyn proctologist charged Medicare $6.5 million for removing hemorrhoids. He slipped up when he billed for removing the same patient's hemorrhoids 10 times ("111 Health-Care" 2011). Then there is the psychiatrist in California who had sex with his patient—and charged Medicaid for the time (Geis et al. 1995). I'm sure he thought the sex was a form of treatment.

These are not isolated incidents—they are just some of the most outrageous. With 4 million Medicare claims filed every day, physicians are not likely to be audited (C. Parker 2013). Many doctors have not been able to resist the temptation to cheat.

Do you recall the section on white-collar crime in Chapter 8, where I pointed out that the harm of some white-collar crime goes far beyond the loss of money, that it even kills people? So it is with medical fraud. A pharmacist in Kansas City was so driven by greed that he diluted the drugs he sold for patients in chemotherapy (Belluck 2001). And what do you think Guidant Corporation did when it discovered that its heart defibrillators, which are surgically implanted in patients, could short-circuit and kill patients? Immediately tell the patients and doctors? You would think so. Instead, the company kept selling the defective model while it developed a new one. Several patients died when their defibrillators short-circuited (Meier 2005, 2006).

Then there is Bayer, that household name you trust when you reach for aspirin. Bayer also makes Trasylol, a drug given after heart surgery. Bayer found that its drug had a few slight side effects—increased risk of strokes, heart failure, and death. Did Bayer warn doctors that their medicine might be killing patients? Not at all. In Bayer's own words, it "mistakenly did not inform" the Federal Drug Administration of the study (Harris 2006). In the same vein as Bayer's statement, I will assume that the $200 million annual sales of Trasylol had nothing to do with making this "mistake."

Greed can be so enticing that it ensnares even outstanding individuals, distorting both their ethics and their sense of reality. A top medical researcher at Harvard who also held the prestigious position of head of pediatric research at Massachusetts General Hospital told a drug company, Johnson & Johnson, that if they funded his research, his findings would benefit the company (Harris 2009). No honest researcher knows in advance what research findings will be.

Sexism and Racism in Medicine

Read on **MySocLab**
Document: Health Care Reform: A Woman's Issue

In Chapter 11 (pages 304–305), we saw that physicians don't take women's health complaints as seriously as they do those of men. As a result, surgeons operate on women after the women's heart disease has progressed farther, making it more likely that women die from the disease. This sexism is so subtle that the physicians are not aware that they are discriminating against women. Some sexism in medicine, in contrast, is blatant. One of the best examples is the bias against women's reproductive organs that we reviewed in Chapter 11 (page 306).

Racism is also an unfortunate part of medical practice. In Chapter 12, we reviewed racism in surgery and in health care after heart attacks. You might want to review these materials on page 332.

The Medicalization of Society

As we have seen, childbirth and women's reproductive organs have come to be defined as medical matters. Sociologists use the term **medicalization** to refer to the process of turning something that was not previously considered an issue for physicians into a medical matter. "Bad" behavior is an example. If a psychiatric model is followed, crime becomes not willful behavior that should be punished but a symptom of unresolved mental problems that were created during childhood. These problems need to be treated

medicalization the transformation of a human condition into a medical matter to be treated by physicians by doctors. The human body is a favorite target of medicalization. Characteristics that once were taken for granted—such as wrinkles, acne, balding, sagging buttocks and chins, bulging stomachs, and small breasts—have become medical problems, all in need of treatment by physicians. Drug companies are even trying to turn "deficient eyebrows" into a medical problem (Singer 2009).

Theoretical Perspectives. As usual, the three theoretical perspectives give us contrasting views of the medicalization of human conditions. Symbolic interactionists would stress changing symbols. There is nothing inherently medical about wrinkles, acne, balding, sagging chins, or "deficient" eyebrows. People used to consider such matters as normal problems of life, but now they are being redefined as medical problems. Functionalists would stress that by broadening its customer base, the medicalization of such conditions is functional for the medical establishment. Conflict sociologists would argue that the medicalization indicates the growing power of the medical establishment: The more conditions of life that physicians and drug companies can medicalize, the greater their profits and power.

Medically Assisted Suicide

Do you think doctors should be able to write prescriptions to end the life of terminally ill patients? As you explore medically assisted suicide in the following Thinking Critically section, you will come face to face with issues that are difficult to resolve.

euthanasia mercy killing

THINKING CRITICALLY

Your Vote, Please: Should Doctors Be Allowed to Kill Patients?

Should doctors be able to help people commit suicide? The issue is emotionally charged.

Bill Simpson, in his 70s, had battled leukemia for years. After his spleen was removed, he developed an abdominal abscess. Despite operation after operation, the abscess continued to fill. Simpson began to go in and out of consciousness. When Simpson's brother-in-law suggested euthanasia, the surgeon injected a lethal dose of morphine into Simpson's intravenous feeding tubes.

At a medical conference in which euthanasia, mercy killing, was discussed, a cancer specialist announced that he had kept count of the patients who had asked him to help them die. "There were 127 men and women," he said. He paused, and then added, "And I saw to it that 25 of them got their wish" (Nuland 1995).

When a doctor ends a patient's life, such as by injecting a lethal drug, it is called *active euthanasia*. To end life by withholding life support (nutrients or liquids) is called *passive euthanasia*. To remove life support, such as disconnecting a patient from oxygen, falls somewhere in between. The result, of course, is the same.

Two images seem to dominate the public's ideas of **euthanasia**: One is of an individual devastated by chronic pain. The doctor mercifully helps to end that pain by performing euthanasia. The second is of a brain-dead individual—a human vegetable—who lies in a hospital bed, kept alive only by machines. How accurate are these images?

We have the example of Holland. There, along with Albania, Belgium, and Luxembourg, euthanasia is legal. Each year, Dutch physicians kill about 1,000 patients without the patients' express consent. One doctor ended the life of a woman because he thought she would have wanted him to do so but was afraid to ask because she was a nun. Another physician killed a patient with breast cancer who said that she did *not* want euthanasia. In the doctor's words, "It could have taken another week before she died. I needed this bed" (Hendin 1997, 2000).

Concerned that they could be euthanized if they have a medical emergency, some Dutch carry "passports" that instruct medical personnel that they want to live. Most Dutch, however, support euthanasia, and many carry "passports" that instruct medical personnel to end their lives if warranted (Shapiro 1997).

In Michigan, Dr. Jack Kevorkian, a pathologist (he didn't treat patients—he studied diseased tissues) decided that regardless of laws, he had the right to help people commit suicide. He did, 120 times. Here is how he described one of those times:

> *I started the intravenous dripper, which released a salt solution through a needle into her vein, and I kept her arm tied down so she wouldn't jerk it. This was difficult as her veins were fragile. And then once she decided she was ready to go, she just hit the switch and the device cut off the saline drip and through the needle released a solution of thiopental that put her to sleep in ten to fifteen seconds. A minute later, through the needle flowed a lethal solution of potassium chloride.* (Denzin 1992)

Kevorkian provided the poison, as well as a "death machine" that he developed to administer the poison, but he was careful to never touch the lever that released the poison. He taunted authorities by leaving some bodies in vans. Michigan prosecutors tried Kevorkian for murder four times, but four times, juries refused to convict him. Then Kevorkian slipped up. On national television, he played a videotape showing him giving a lethal injection to a man who was dying from Lou Gehrig's disease. Prosecutors put Kevorkian on trial again. This time, he was convicted of second-degree murder and sentenced to ten to twenty-five years in prison. After eight years, Kevorkian was released, but to get out, he had to promise not to kill anyone else (Wanzer 2007).

In some states, supporters and opponents of medically assisted suicide are fighting hard battles, but only in Oregon (since 1997) and Washington (since 2008) is it legal for doctors to assist in suicide. If Kevorkian had lived in Oregon or Washington, and he hadn't begun killing patients until those years, he would never have been convicted.

To end pain does not seem to be the main reason that terminally ill Americans request lethal prescriptions. Rather, it seems to be their desire to control the circumstances of their death. As a patient who suffers from the progressive and incurable Lou Gehrig's disease said, "I don't know if I'll use the medication to end my life. But I do know that it is my life, it is my death, and it should be my choice" (Hafner 2012).

For Your Consideration

➔ Do you think Oregon and Washington are right? Why? In the future, do you think other states will approve medically assisted suicide?

➔ In addition to what is reported here, Dutch doctors also kill newborn babies who have serious birth defects (Smith 1999; "Piden en Holanda" 2004). Their justification is that if these children live, they will not have "quality of life." Would you support this? Why or why not? ■

Reducing the Costs of Medical Care

With the costs of health care soaring, both the public and politicians have demanded that something be done. Let's look at some attempts to reduce costs.

Health maintenance organizations. Some medical companies—health maintenance organizations (HMOs)—charge an annual fee in exchange for providing medical care to a company's employees. This reduces medical costs because HMOs bid against one another. Whatever money is left over at the end of the year is the HMO's profit. While this arrangement eliminates unnecessary medical treatment, it can also reduce *necessary* treatment. The results are anything but pretty.

Watch on **MySocLab**
Video: Managed Care

> *Over her doctor's objections, a friend of mine was discharged from the hospital even though she was still bleeding and running a fever. Her HMO representative said he would not authorize another day in the hospital.*
>
> *Some doctors also have HMOs. One doctor, who works for a hospital, noticed a lump in her breast. She went to the X-ray department to get a mammogram, but her own hospital*

The cartoonist has captured an unfortunate reality of U.S. medicine.

"Frank and Ernest" © Thaves. All Right Reserved. Used with the permission of the Thaves family in conjuction with the Cartoonist Group.

said she couldn't have one. Her HMO allowed one mammogram every two years, and she had had one 18 months before. After a formal appeal, she was granted an exception. She had breast cancer. ("What Scares Doctors?" 2006)

If we don't reduce medical costs, they can bankrupt us. But the dilemma is, At what human cost do we reduce spending on medical treatment?

Diagnosis-Related Groups. To curb costs, the federal government has classified all illnesses into diagnosis-related groups (DRGs), setting a fixed amount that it will pay for the treatment of each illness. Hospitals make a profit if they discharge patients before the allotted amount is spent and lose money if the patient stays longer. As a consequence, some patients are discharged before they have recovered. Others are refused admittance because they appear to have a "worse than average" case of a particular illness: If they take longer to treat, they will cost the hospital money instead of bringing a profit.

Pay-as-You-Go Clinics.

Single ear infections $40
Simple cuts with suture removal $95
Ingrown toenail corrections $150

The Tennessee doctor who advertised these prices had grown tired of insurance claims: hiring people to fill them out, waiting to get paid, having the forms rejected and having to resubmit them (Brown 2007). To avoid these frustrations and the cost, this doctor, like a few others, opened a *pay-as-you-go* clinic: Cash or credit card only.

Group Care. Some doctors are lowering costs by replacing individual consultations with *group care*. They meet with a group of patients who have similar medical conditions. Eight or ten pregnant women, for example, go in for their checkup together. The doctor can charge each patient less and have more time to discuss symptoms and treatments. The patients also receive support and encouragement from people who have the same medical problem (Herba et al. 2013).

Workplace Care. The principle is simple: The sooner people get examined by medical personnel, the sooner they get treated, and the sooner they get back to work. This reduces absenteeism and increases productivity. With these benefits, large businesses are setting up medical clinics at the workplace (Mathews 2012a). This also allows medical problems to be detected earlier, before they turn into larger ones, which further reduces costs.

Dumping.

The van from Hollywood Presbyterian Hospital pulled up to the curbside in skid row in Los Angeles, California. The driver got out and walked to the passenger side. As several people watched, she opened the door and helped a paraplegic man out. As she drove away, leaving the befuddled man behind, people shouted at her, "Where's his wheelchair? Where's his walker?"

Someone called 911. The police found the man crawling in the gutter, wearing a soiled hospital gown and trailing a broken colostomy bag.

"I can't think of anything colder than that," said an L.A. detective. "It's the worst area of skid row." (Blankstein and Winton 2007)

dumping private hospitals sending unprofitable patients to public hospitals or any hospital discharging unprofitable patients before they are well

This is a blatant example of **dumping**, hospitals discharging unprofitable patients. Seldom is dumping as dramatic as in this instance, but it happens. Dumping, an attempt by hospitals to reduce costs, is a consequence of a system that puts profits ahead of patient care.

Rationing Medical Care. A controversial suggestion for reducing costs is to ration medical care. The argument is simple: We cannot afford to provide all the expensive technology to everyone, so we have to ration it. No easy answer has been found for this dilemma, the focus of the Sociology and the New Technology box below.

Sociology and the New Technology

Talking to Medical Machines and Making Virtual House Calls

"Hi. Thanks for coming," the medical assistant says, greeting a mother with her 5-year-old son. "Are you here for your child or yourself?"

"My boy," the mother replies. "He has diarrhea."

"Oh, sorry to hear that," the assistant says, looking down at the boy. "Has your tummy been hurting?" "Yes," he replies.

The assistant then asks the mother about fever ("slight") and abdominal pain ("He hasn't been complaining").

After a few more questions, the assistant says, "I'm not concerned at this point. I would like you to see the doctor tomorrow at, let's see, yes, she is free at two." The mother leads her son from the room, holding his hand. But he keeps looking back at the assistant, fascinated, as if reluctant to leave.

Maybe this is because the assistant is only a woman's face on a computer screen. The avatar's words of sympathy are jerky and mechanical, but she has the right stuff—the ability to understand speech and recognize pediatric conditions. She can reason according to simple rules and make an initial diagnosis of a childhood ailment and its seriousness. And she can win the trust of a little boy (Lohr and Markoff 2010).

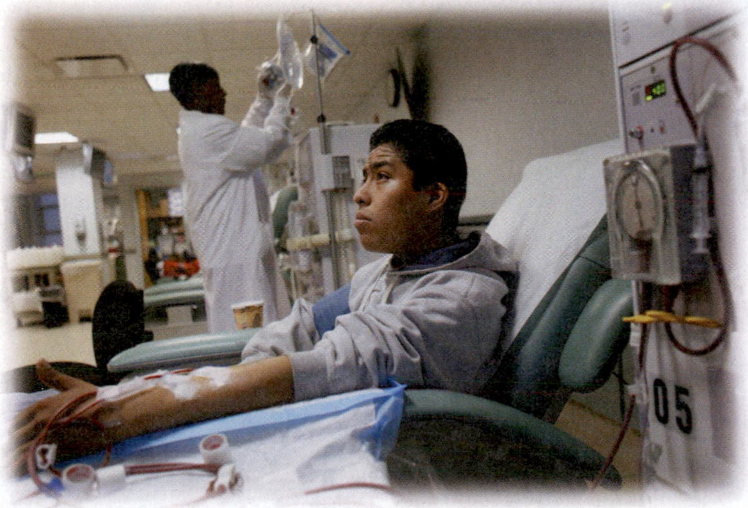

Dialysis is a costly medical treatment that saves lives. On what basis could it be rationed?

One day, avatars may be so advanced that they do the doctoring. Behind the face will be a vast computerized system of knowledge that will allow the accurate diagnosis of almost all medical problems (Cohn 2013).

Time moves fast in the digital age, and telemedicine is advancing quickly. More people are logging on online and having "face-to-face" consultations with their doctors. Via webcams or video-enabled tablets and smartphones, they show the doctor what hurts. The teledoctor looks at the image, listens to the patient's heart through an electronic stethoscope, and calls a prescription in to the patient's local drugstore (Freudenheim 2010; Mathews 2012b).

The change is remarkable. Some surgeons operate on wounded soldiers who are thousands of miles away, while the battle is still raging. Sitting in New York or Los Angeles, the surgeon peers at electronic images and manipulates a remote surgical device.

Most of us, though, haven't yet experienced even a virtual house call. When we do, we will be able to avoid germ-infested doctors' offices and, of course, those outdated magazines. Telemedicine brings advantages to doctors, too. Online physicians save the expense of running an office, hiring nurses, and paying utilities. Another nice side benefit is avoiding contact with sick people. And getting paid is no problem. Patients don't get to "see" the doctor until after their credit cards have been approved (Costello 2008; Baum 2013).

For Your Consideration

→ Which would you prefer—visiting your doctor online or in his or her office? Why?

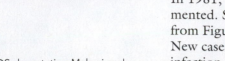

19.6 Discuss threats to health: HIV/AIDS, weight, alcohol and nicotine, disabling environments, medical experiments, globalization of disease and treatment or prevention.

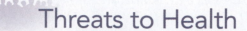

Threats to Health

Let's look at major threats to health, both in the United States and worldwide.

HIV/AIDS

In 1981, the first case of AIDS (acquired immune deficiency syndrome) was documented. Since then, about 600,000 Americans have died from AIDS. As you can see from Figure 19.6, in the United States, this disease has been brought under control. New cases peaked in 1993, and deaths hit their highest level in 1995. Although the infection and death rates are much lower today, the HIV virus continues to be a deadly disease. For the 700,000 Americans who receive treatment, however, HIV/AIDS has become a chronic disease that they live with (Centers for Disease Control and Prevention [CDC] 2013a, 2013b).

With AIDS devastating Malawi and other areas of Africa, orphans have become a common sight. This photo was taken in Karonga, Malawi.

Globally, in contrast, the epidemic is exploding, with 7,000 new HIV infections every day, 2.5 million a year (UNAIDS 2012). Over 40 million people have died from AIDS, but the worst is yet to come. As Figure 19.7 illustrates, Africa is the hardest-hit region of the world, with sub-Saharan Africa the most devastated area. The death toll in this region is so high that the average person dies at age 55. The lowest life expectancy in the world is in Sierra Leone, where the average person is dead by age 47 (Haub and Kaneda 2012).

Let's look at some of the major characteristics of this disease.

Origin. The question of how HIV/AIDS originated baffled scientists for two decades, but they finally traced its genetic sequences back to monkeys and apes in the Congo (Kolata 2001; McNeil 2010a). Apparently, the virus was present in these animals for millennia. How the crossover to humans occurred is not known, but the best guess

FIGURE 19.6 The Path of AIDS in the United States

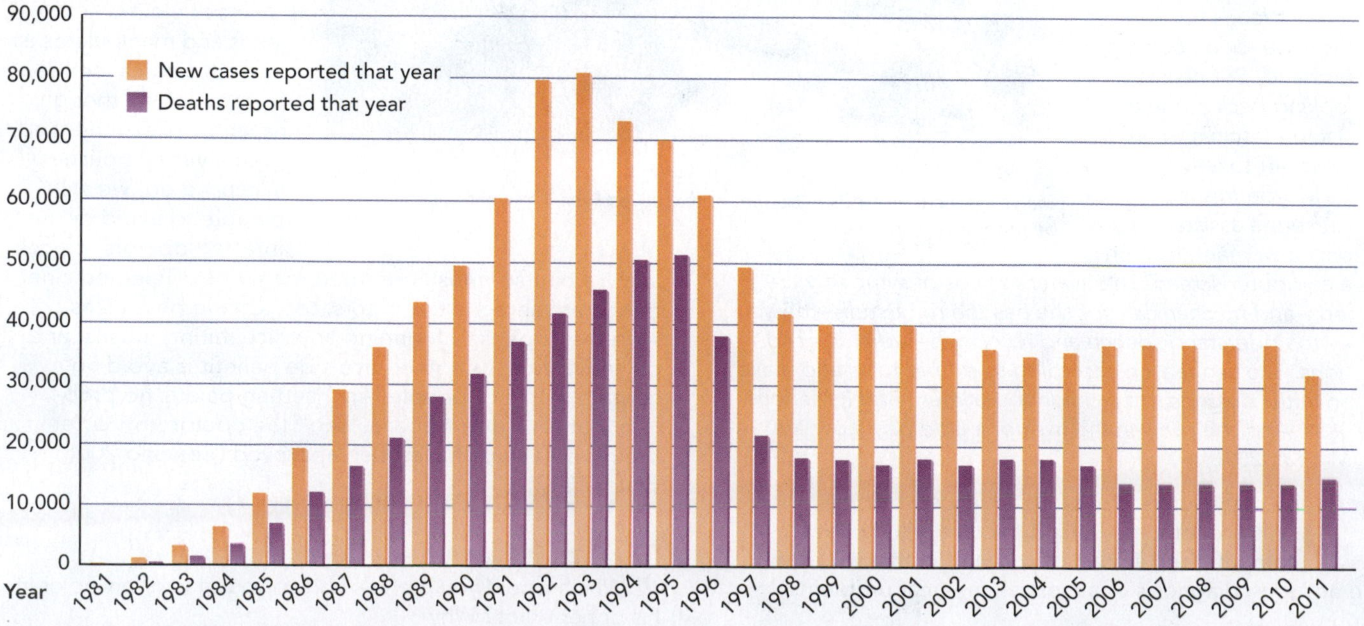

Sources: By the author. Based on CDC 2003:Table 21; 2013a, 2013b.

is that hunters were exposed to the animals' blood as they slaughtered them for meat.

The Transmission of HIV/AIDS. The only way a person can become infected with the HIV virus is by bodily fluids passing from one person to another. HIV is most commonly transmitted through blood, semen, and vaginal secretions. Nursing babies can also get HIV through the milk of their infected mothers. Since the HIV virus is present in all bodily fluids (including sweat, tears, spittle, and urine), some people think that HIV can also be transmitted in these forms. The U.S. Centers for Disease Control and Prevention, however, stresses that HIV cannot be transmitted by casual contact in which traces of these fluids would be exchanged. Figure 19.8 compares how U.S. men and women get infected.

FIGURE 19.7 AIDS: A Global Glimpse

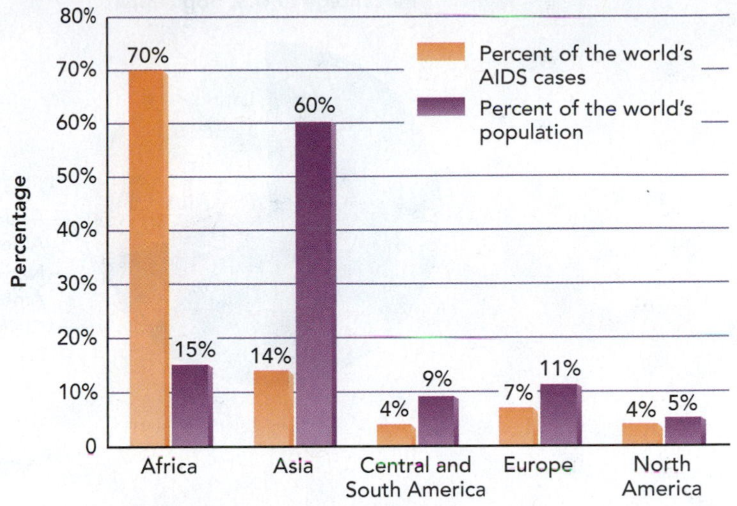

Sources: By the author. Based on UNAIDS 2012; Haub and Kaneda 2012.

Gender, Circumcision, and Race–Ethnicity. In the United States, AIDS hits men the hardest, but the proportion of women has been growing. In 1982, only 6 percent of AIDS cases were women, but today it is 21 percent (CDC 1997, 2013a, 2013b). In sub-Saharan Africa, AIDS is more common among women (UNAIDS 2010). Researchers have found that circumcision cuts a man's chance of getting infected with HIV by about half (Park 2013). Because circumcision is not widely practiced in sub-Saharan Africa, to help stem the epidemic, Israel has sent circumcision teams (Kraft 2008). Israeli doctors have also developed a plastic device that does circumcisions (Sifferlin 2012).

Watch on **MySocLab** **Video:** ABC Primetime: AIDS in Black America

HIV infections are related to race ethnicity. One of the most startling examples is this: African American women are *fifteen times* more likely to come down with AIDS than are white women (CDC 2010c). Figure 19.9 on the next page summarizes HIV infections by race ethnicity. The reason for the differences shown on this figure is *not* genetic. No racial–ethnic group is more susceptible to AIDS because of biological factors. Rather, the rates of infection differ because of social factors, such as the use of condoms and the number of drug users who share needles.

FIGURE 19.8 How Americans Get AIDS

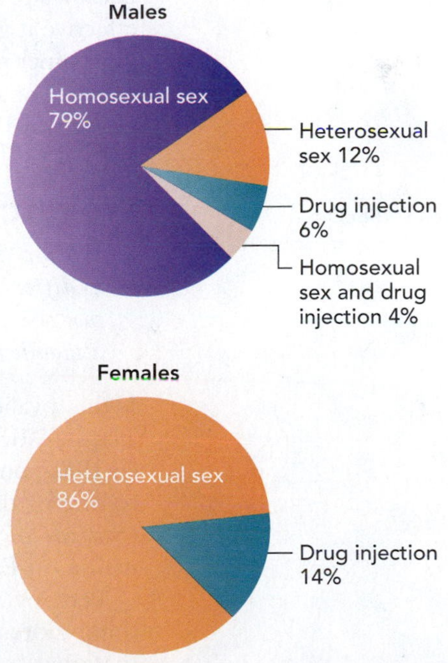

Note: There is another category, "Other," consisting of blood transfusions and unknown, but it is too small to show: 36 for males and 15 for females.
Source: CDC 2013b.

The Stigma of AIDS. Do you recall how I stressed at the beginning of this chapter that social factors are essential to understanding health and illness? The stigma associated with AIDS is a remarkable example. Some people refuse even to be tested because they fear the stigma they would bear if they test HIV-positive. One unfortunate consequence is the continuing spread of AIDS by people who "don't want to know." Even some governments have put their heads in the sand. Chinese officials, for example, at first refused to admit that they had an AIDS problem, but now they are more open about it. If this disease is to be brought under control, its stigma must be overcome: AIDS must be viewed like any other lethal disease—as the work of a destructive biological organism.

Is There a Cure for AIDS? For about twenty years, thousands of scientists have been doing research on a cure for AIDS. The drop in deaths that you saw in Figure 19.6 came about when *antiretroviral therapy* was discovered. If those who are in the

FIGURE 19.9 New Diagnoses of HIV by Race–Ethnicity

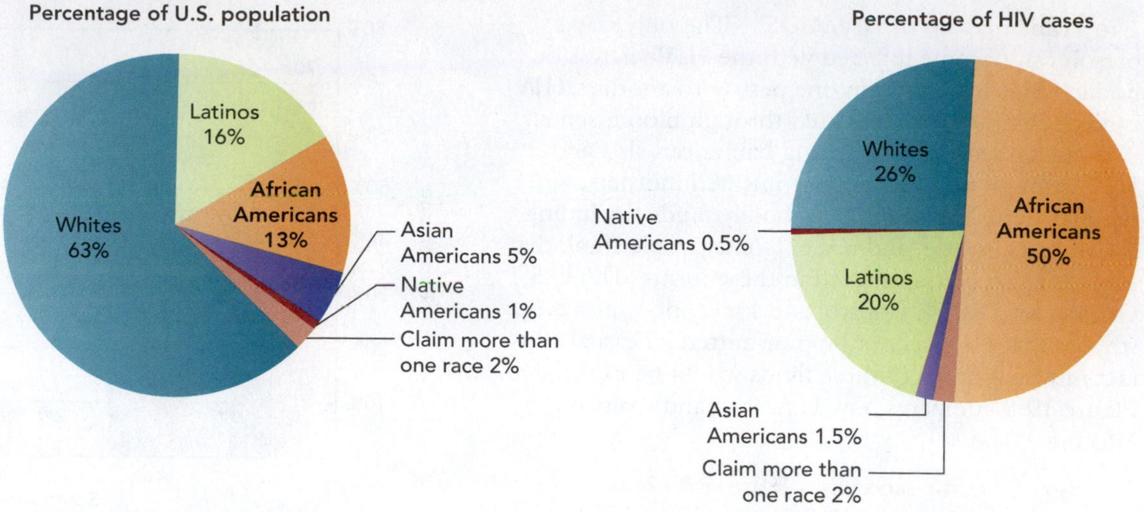

Source: By the author. Based on Figure 12.4 of this text and CDC 2013b.

early stages of the disease take a "cocktail" of drugs (a combination of protease, fusion, and integrase inhibitors), their immune systems rebound. The virus remains, however, ready to flourish if the drugs are withdrawn.

Then in 2010, it was found that if men who have sex with men take an antiretroviral pill daily, they are up to 90 percent less likely to become infected with HIV (Mermin 2013). The pill, called Truvada, is a combination of two antiretroviral drugs. There is also a vaginal microbicide that cuts a woman's chance of getting HIV by half (Schoofs 2011). These breakthroughs could indicate that a vaccination that will save millions of lives is on the way, but we are not there yet.

Some researchers have issued a dire warning that these treatments could become this decade's penicillin. When penicillin was introduced, everyone was ecstatic about how effective it was. But over the years, the microbes that penicillin targets mutated, producing "super germs" against which we have little protection. If this happens with AIDS, a tsunami of a "super-AIDS" virus could hit the world with more fury than the first devastating wave.

Watch on MySocLab
Video: Sociology in Focus: Health and Medicine

Weight: Too Much and Too Little

When a friend from Spain visited, I asked him to comment on the things that struck him as different. He mentioned how surprised he was to see people living in metal houses. It took me a moment to figure out what he meant, but then I understood: He had never seen a mobile home. Then he added, "And there are so many fat Americans."

Is this a valid perception, or just some twisted ethnocentric observation by a foreigner? The statistics bear out his observation. Americans have added weight—and a lot of it. In 1980, one of four Americans was overweight. By 1990, this percentage had jumped to one of three. Now about *two-thirds* (67 percent) of Americans are overweight (*Statistical Abstract* 1998:Table 242; 2013:Table 213). We have become the fattest nation on Earth.

Perhaps we should just shrug our shoulders and say, "So what?" Is obesity really anything more than someone's arbitrary idea of how much we should weigh? It turns out that obesity has significant costs. Obese people are more likely to come down with diabetes, heart and kidney disease, and some types of cancer. They also die younger. There are also the additional health care costs, perhaps $2,000 a year for each obese person (Lehnert at al. 2013).

A surprising side effect of being overweight is that it helps some people live longer (Flegal and Hunter 2013). Being seriously overweight (obese) increases people's chances of dying, but being a little overweight is good. No one yet knows the reason for this.

The moderate consumption of alcohol brings health benefits. Its heavy consumption harms health. Mixing alcohol with other drugs can be lethal.

Alcohol and Nicotine

Many drugs, both legal and illegal, harm their users. Let's examine some of the health consequences of alcohol and nicotine, the two most frequently used legal drugs in the United States.

Alcohol. Alcohol is *the* standard recreational drug of Americans. The *average* adult American drinks 26 gallons of alcoholic beverages per year—about 22 gallons of beer, 3 gallons of wine, and 1 gallon of whiskey, vodka, or other distilled spirits. Beer is so popular that Americans drink more beer than they do milk (*Statistical Abstract* 2011:Table 211).

As you know, despite laws that ban alcohol consumption before the age of 21, underage drinking is common. Table 19.1 shows that almost two-thirds of all high school students drink alcohol during their senior year. If getting drunk is the abuse of alcohol, then, without doubt, among high school students abusing alcohol is popular. As this table shows, almost half of all high school seniors have been drunk during the past year, with 28 percent getting drunk during just the past month. From this table, you can also see what other drugs high school seniors use.

In Table 19.2 on the next page, we turn to college students. Among them, too, alcohol is the most popular drug. About three of four of all college students have drunk alcohol during the past year, almost two-thirds in the past month. About three of five have been drunk during the past year, about two of five in just the past month.

TABLE 19.1 What Drugs Do High School Seniors Use?

	In the Past Month?	In the Past Year?
Alcohol	41.5%	63.5%
How many have been drunk?	28.1%	45.0%
Marijuana	22.9%	36.4%
Nicotine (cigarettes)	17.1%	NA
Amphetamines	3.3%	7.9%
Tranquilizers	2.1%	5.3%
Barbiturates (sedatives)	2.0%	4.5%
Hallucinogens[1]	1.6%	4.8%
Cocaine	1.1%	2.7%
Ecstasy (MDMA)	0.9%	3.8%
Steroids	0.9%	1.3%
LSD	0.8%	2.4%
PCP	0.5%	0.9%
Heroin	0.3%	0.6%
OxyContin	NA	4.3%

[1]Other than LSD. NA = Not Available.

Source: By the author. Based on Johnston et al 2013:Tables 2, 17.

TABLE 19.2 What Drugs Do Full-Time College Students Use?

	In the Past Month?		In the Past Year?	
	Men	Women	Men	Women
Alcohol	64.6%	62.8%	76.21%	78.1%
How many have been drunk?	43.7%	37.4%	63.4%	58.1%
Marijuana	24.8%	16.1%	39.9%	29.0%
Nicotine (cigarettes)	16.09%	14.6%	29.5%	23.4%
Amphetamines	5.4%	4.0%	11.1%	8.2%
Hallucinogens*	2.6%	0.3%	7.5%	1.9%
Tranquilizers	2.0%	1.3%	4.9%	3.8%
Cocaine	1.9%	0.8%	4.5%	2.6%
Ecstasy (MDMA)	1.1%	0.5%	4.7%	3.6%
LSD	0.9%	0.2%	3.8%	0.8%
Barbiturates (sedatives)	0.5%	0.9%	1.2%	2.0%
Heroin	0.0%**	0.0%**	0.1%	0.1%
OxyContin	NA	NA	3.5%	1.7%

*Other than LSD.
**Not actually zero, but too small to show up.
NA = Not Available

Source: By the author. Based on Johnston et al. 2012. Tables 8-2, 8-3.

Is alcohol bad for health? This beverage cuts both ways. One to two drinks a day for men and one drink a day for women reduces the risk of heart attacks, strokes, gallstones, and diabetes ("Alcohol" 2009). (Women get this health benefit with less alcohol because on average they weigh less than men.) Beyond these amounts, however, alcohol scars the liver, damages the heart, and increases the risk of cancer, breast and other types. It also raises the likelihood that a woman will give birth to a child with birth defects.

Driving drunk is also perilous. Here is a remarkable statistic: One-third of the 33,000 Americans who die in vehicle accidents each year are drunk (*Statistical Abstract* 2013:Table 1117).

Nicotine.

Let's suppose that you are on your way to the airport to leave for a long-awaited vacation in Hawaii. You are listening to the radio and thinking about the palm trees and ocean waves when an announcer breaks into your reverie with a flash bulletin: "Homeland Security has just discovered that terrorists have hidden bombs aboard five passenger jets scheduled for takeoff today. They have not been able to find the bombs." The announcer pauses, and then adds, "Because they don't know which flights will crash, all flights will depart on schedule."

Five jets are going to crash. On each jet will be 200 passengers and crew. They will plummet from the skies, leaving a trail of agonizing screams as they meet their fiery destiny.

What would you do? My guess is that you would turn your car around and go home. Adios to Hawaii's beaches, and hello to your own backyard.

Nicotine use—with its creeping side effects of emphysema and cancer—kills about 400,000 Americans each year (CDC 2011). This is the equivalent of five fully loaded, 200-passenger jets with full crews crashing each and every day—leaving no survivors. Who in their right mind would take the risk that *their* plane will not be among those that crash?

Smokers take this risk, even though nicotine is, by far, the most lethal of all recreational drugs. Smoking causes cancer of the bladder, cervix, esophagus, kidneys, larynx, lungs, and other body organs. Smokers are more likely to have heart attacks and strokes, and even to come down with cataracts and pneumonia (Surgeon General 2005; CDC 2010a). The list of health problems related to smoking goes on and on.

Then there is secondhand smoke, which is estimated to kill 45,000 nonsmokers a year (Surgeon General 2006; CDC 2010b). This is the equivalent of another fully loaded jet going down every two days.

An antismoking campaign that stresses tobacco's health hazards has been so successful that smoking is banned on public transportation and in most offices, restaurants, and, in some states, even bars. From Figure 19.10, you can see how this antismoking message has hit home. As you look at this figure, you might be surprised to see that *most* men used to smoke.

FIGURE 19.10 **Who Is Still Smoking?** ***The Percentage of Americans Age 18 and over Who Smoke Cigarettes***

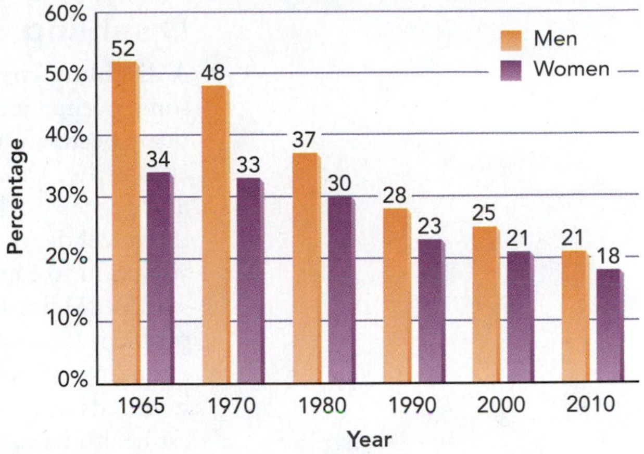

Note: The first year these data were reported was 1965; 1970 and 1980 are averages of the closest preceding years where data were available.

Source: By the author. Based on *Statistical Abstract of the United States* 1996:Table 222; 2013:Table 206.

Millions of Americans wouldn't think of flying if they knew that even one jet was going to crash—yet they continue to smoke. Why? The two major reasons are addiction and advertising. Nicotine may be as addictive as heroin (Britt and McGehee 2008). While this may sound far-fetched, consider Buerger's disease:

> *In this disease, the blood vessels, especially those supplying the legs, become so constricted that circulation is impaired whenever nicotine enters the bloodstream.*
>
> *If a patient continues to smoke, gangrene may eventually set in. First a toe may have to be amputated, then the foot at the ankle, then the leg at the knee, and ultimately at the hip. . . . Patients are informed that if they will only stop smoking, it is virtually certain that the otherwise inexorable march of gangrene up the legs will be curbed. Yet surgeons report that some patients with Buerger's disease vigorously puff away in their hospital beds following a second or third amputation. (Brecher et al. 1972)*

The second reason is advertising. Cigarette ads were banned from television and radio in 1970, but cigarettes continue to be advertised in newspapers and magazines and on billboards. Cigarette companies spend huge amounts to encourage Americans to smoke—about $12 billion a year. This comes to $43 for every man, woman, and child in the entire country (CDC 2010a). Although the tobacco industry denies it, they target youth, often by associating cigarette smoking with success, high fashion, independence, and having fun. Look at Joe Camel below. He has since been banned from advertising.

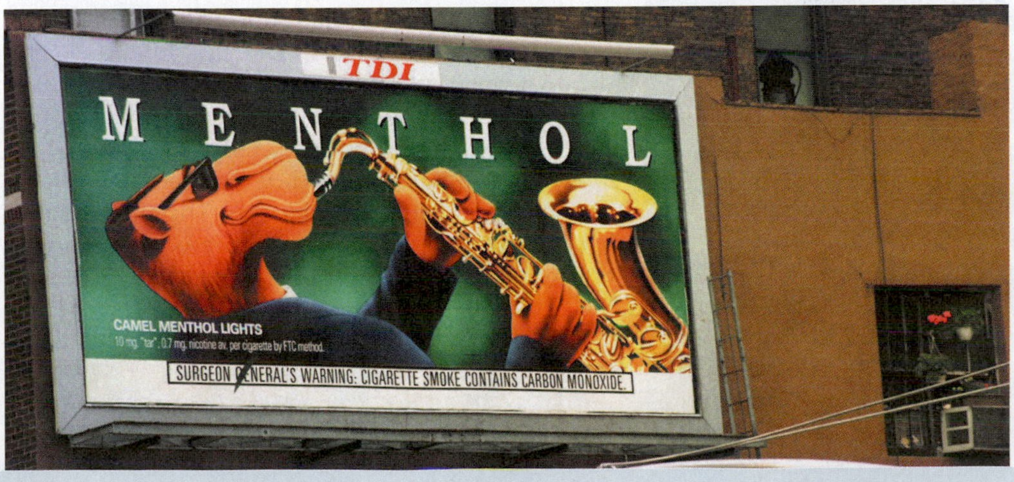

Do you think that this magazine ad is designed to make cigarettes appealing to male youth? Tobacco industry officials denied that they were trying to entice youth to smoke, and it took pressure from the U.S. Congress to get R.J. Reynolds Tobacco Company to stop its Joe Camel ads.

disabling environment an environment that is harmful to health

With fewer smokers in the United States, the tobacco companies have had to search for victims elsewhere. They have found them in the Least Industrialized Nations. Their efforts to produce more addicts there have been quite successful, making nicotine deaths a serious problem in countries such as China (Wilson 2010).

Disabling Environments

A **disabling environment** is one that is harmful to people's health. The health risk of some occupations is evident: lumberjacking, riding rodeo bulls, or training lions. In many occupations, however, people become aware of the risk only years after working at jobs they thought were safe. For example, during and after World War II, several million people worked with asbestos. The federal government estimates that one-quarter of them will die of cancer from having breathed asbestos particles. Many other substances also seem to cause slowly developing cancers—including, ironically, some asbestos substitutes (Meier 1987; Hawkes 2001). Illnesses and deaths from asbestos are a global problem (Stayner et al. 2013).

Industrialization increased the world's standard of living and brought better health to hundreds of millions of people. Ironically, industrialization poses what may be the greatest health hazard of all time, one so great that it threatens to disable the basic environment of the human race. The burning of carbon fuels has led to the greenhouse effect, a warming of the Earth that may melt the polar ice caps and flood the Earth's coastal shores. Additional risks to life on our planet come from the pollution of land, air, and water, especially through nuclear waste, pesticides, herbicides, and other chemicals. We discuss these problems in Chapter 22.

Medical Experiments: Callous and Harmful

At times, physicians and government officials behave so arrogantly that they callously disregard people's health. Harmful medical experiments, though well-intentioned, are an excellent example. We can trace these experiments to 1895, with an attempt to find a way to immunize people against syphilis. In that year, Albert Neisser, a physician in Germany, injected young prostitutes—one was just 10 years old—with syphilis. Many came down with the disease (Proctor 1999).

How about American doctors? Let's see.

You trust your doctor, don't you? But of course. So did this man in Guatemala as the doctor gave him an injection. Unknown to him, the U.S. doctor from the U.S. Public Health Service was injecting him with a sexually transmitted disease.

The Tuskegee Syphilis Experiment. To review this horrible experiment conducted by the U.S. Public Health Service, read the opening vignette for Chapter 12 (page 321). To summarize here, the U.S. Public Health Service did not tell 399 African American men in Mississippi that they had syphilis. Doctors examined them once a year, recording their symptoms and letting the disease kill them.

The Guatemalan Experiment. The Tuskegee experiment was not enough. U.S. health researchers did even worse with Guatemalans (McNeil 2010b). In the 1940s, they purposely infected hundreds of prisoners, psychiatric patients, and sex workers with syphilis and gonorrhoea so they could determine how good the new drug, penicillin, was. The photo to the left shows one of the smiling doctors as he injects an unsuspecting Guatemalan.

The Cold War Experiments.

Assume that you are a soldier stationed in Nevada. The U.S. Army orders your platoon to march through an area in which an atomic bomb has just exploded.

> *Nobody knows much about radiation, and you don't know that the army is using you as a guinea pig: It wants to see if you'll be able to withstand the fallout—without radiation equipment.*
>
> *Now suppose you are a patient at the University of Rochester in 1946. Your doctor, whom you trust implicitly, says, "I am going to give you something to help you." You are pleased. But the injection, it turns out, is uranium (Noah 1994). He and a team of other doctors are conducting an experiment to find out how much uranium it will take to damage your kidneys. (U.S. Department of Energy 1995)*

Like the Tuskegee syphilis experiment, radiation experiments like these were conducted on unsuspecting subjects simply because government officials wanted information. There were others, too. Some soldiers were given LSD. In Palmetto, Florida, officials released whooping cough viruses into the air, killing a dozen children (Conahan 1994). In other tests, deadly chemical and biological agents, such as sarin, were sprayed onto naval ships to see if the sailors' new protective clothing worked. The sailors in these tests were unaware that they had become white mice (Shanker 2002). In 2003, Congress approved a bill to provide health care for 5,842 soldiers harmed by these secret tests.

The Department of Veterans Affairs never learned its lesson, and it is still using veterans for testing drugs. But this time it gets permission—by offering $30 a month to down-and-out veterans of Iraq and Afghanistan. When a drug turns out to have serious side effects, department officials delay telling their guinea pig veterans ("VA Testing" 2008).

Playing God. To most of us, it is incredible that government officials and medical personnel would callously disregard human life, but it happens. And, obviously, the most expendable citizens are the poor and powerless. *It is inconceivable that the doctors who did the syphilis studies would have used wealthy and powerful subjects.* The elite are protected from such callous disregard of human rights and life. The only way the poor can be protected against such abuse of professional power is if we publicize each known instance of abuse and insist on vigorous prosecution of those who plan, direct, and carry out such experiments.

Do medical researchers still play God? You can decide for yourself. Consider how fetal surgery developed. Surgeons were intrigued with the idea of operating on unborn children. Not only did such surgery hold the possibility of extending medical knowledge, but the pioneers would also get their names in prestigious medical journals and be applauded by their peers. Such experimental surgery, though, could cost lives. To reduce the risk, the researchers first experimented on animals. Their next step in refining their skills was to operate on pregnant Puerto Rican women. Now that the procedures are proven, the main patients are the unborn of the white and affluent (Casper 1998). The steps taken in this process expose an underlying assumption about the value of life—from animals to Puerto Rican women to white women. It is almost as though the researchers viewed themselves as climbing an evolutionary ladder.

Chicken Bones and the Globalization of Disease

> *The year was 1918. Men and women, seemingly healthy the day before, collapsed and were soon dead. In the morning, men wheeled carts down the streets to pick up corpses that were left on porches like last night's trash. In a matter of months, a half million Americans died. Worldwide, the death toll reached about 30 million. (Phillips 1998)*

What silent killer had hovered over the world, dropping its deadly poison on unsuspecting victims? Incredibly, it was just the flu. For some reason, out of nowhere, a particularly deadly variety of the common flu bug had appeared.

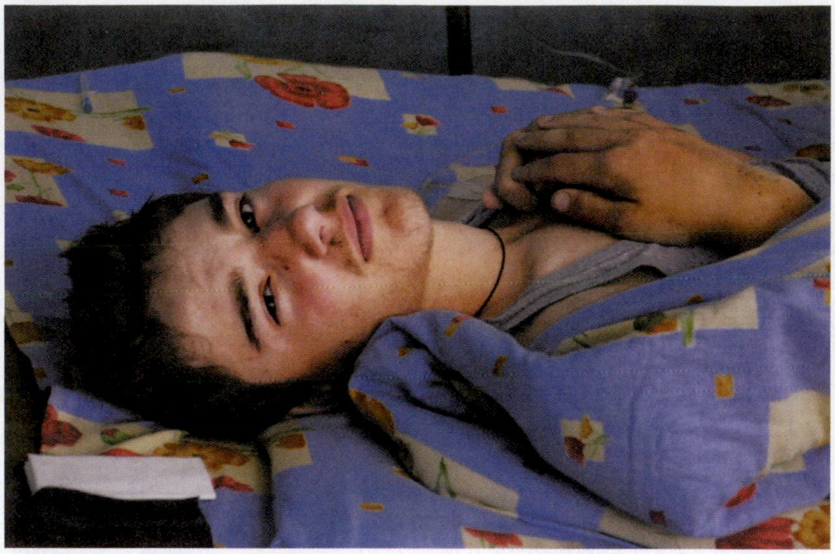

Multi Drug Resistant Turberculosis is appearing in many parts of the world. This 16-year old is in a hospital in Tbillisi, Georgia, a former Russian colony.

From time to time, entirely new deadly diseases appear on the world scene. In 1976, the Ebola virus made its surprise appearance. This disease, which causes uncontrollable bleeding, was contained by isolating an entire region of Zaire (Quammen 2012). In 2003, SARS (Severe Acute Respiratory Syndrome) appeared in Angola, followed by the Asian bird flu (avian influenza) and the Marburg virus. In 2012, Ebola reappeared, this time in the Democratic Republic of Congo ("Ebola Virus" 2012). When deadly diseases for which there is no cure break out, emergency medical teams seal off the area. So far, this has worked.

There are also old diseases that suddenly show up in a more deadly form. Tuberculosis (TB), once thought to be under control, has mutated to the point that there is now a strain that is resistant to all drugs (Anand and McKay 2012). Officials fear the spread of this new form of lethal TB.

Global travel has destroyed the natural frontiers that used to contain diseases, and in just a matter of hours, airline passengers can spread a disease around the world. If this happens, today's global jet travel could make the 1918 death toll seem puny by comparison.

Rubbing Chicken Bones Together.

"We're back to dancing around a bubbling cauldron while rubbing two chicken bones together."

Will superbugs roll around the Earth killing tens of millions of people? The short answer is: Quite likely. The main culprit is that some infectious diseases are becoming resistant to the antibiotics that brought them under control. Physicians are growing alarmed. During their stay in hospitals, so many patients pick up MRSA (methicillin-resistant staphylococcus aureus) that MRSA now kills more Americans than AIDS.

And it isn't just MRSA. Other killers are showing up. A germ called CRK (carbapenem resistant Klebsiella) is lethal to about half the people it hits. CRK even had the nerve to strike the medical center at the National Institutes of Health, where people who came in for routine treatment left in body bags. More would have died except the medical staff—realizing that CRK is deadlier than AIDS, and easier to get—quickly put in emergency preventive measures (McCaughey 2013).

But rubbing chicken bones together? We could pass off such a statement—except that it was said by Brad Spellberg, a top disease specialist (Pollack 2010). He is using exaggeration to get the point across, but only to draw attention to a vital problem facing medical care—and perhaps your life. Not yet chicken bones, but maybe soon.

19.7 Explain why it is difficult to change people's focus from the treatment of illness to the prevention of illness.

Treatment or Prevention?

Let's turn our attention again to the U.S. medical system. One promising alternative to the way U.S. medicine is usually practiced is to change the focus from the treatment of disease to its prevention. Let's consider this in the following Thinking Critically section.

THINKING CRITICALLY

How Will Your Lifestyle Affect Your Health?

Let's contrast health conditions in Utah and Nevada. Utah is home of the Mormons, who disapprove of alcohol, tobacco, extramarital sex, and even caffeine. Nevada, an adjacent state, is home of a gambling industry that fosters rather different values and lifestyles. The two states have similar levels of income, education, urbanization, and medical care, but Nevadans are more likely to die from cancer, heart attacks, kidney disease, lung diseases, and strokes. They are also more likely to commit suicide and to die in accidents. On the other hand, Utahans are more likely to die from Alzheimer's disease and diabetes. (Statistical Abstract 2013:Table 126)

As you can tell from this example, lifestyle is vital for health. Your lifestyle can lead you down a road to disease and illness—or to health and wellness. Of course, you know this. Our schools and the mass media publicize the message that healthy living—exercising, eating nutritious food, maintaining optimal weight, not smoking, avoiding alcohol and other drug abuse, and not having a lot of sexual partners—leads to better health and a longer life. It doesn't take much reading to know that processed fatty, sugary foods bring disease and that a diet rich in fresh fruits, vegetables, nuts, and extra-virgin olive oil stimulates health (Estruch et al. 2013). Yet the message of lifestyle and health often falls on deaf ears.

Although millions of Americans follow a healthy lifestyle, with the self-control that this requires, more millions still gorge on potato chips, cookies, and soft drinks during their mesmerized hours of watching television and wielding joy sticks. Strokes, heart attacks, diabetes, a shorter life, and the misery of sickness are not on people's minds while snacks, video games, soap operas, nip slips, and the latest events in the lives of Hollywood's celebrities beckon. Prevention demands work. Why make the effort? Just get a doctor's prescription when you need one.

Most doctors, too, are trained to write prescriptions for health problems, not to focus on preventive medicine and "wellness." When patients see their doctors, they don't want to hear "Lose weight, exercise, and don't forget to eat your vegetables." Who wants to pay for that? You can get that message from your mother free. Patients want to leave their doctor's office with the message "You've got such and such"—and a comforting prescription in hand to relieve such and such.

For Your Consideration

➤ First, place the focus on yourself. How can you apply this information to live a healthier life?

➤ Second, doctors make money writing prescriptions for sick people. Under our fee-for-service system, if doctors and hospitals prevent illness, they lose money. Getting the medical establishment to turn its focus to "wellness," then, requires making "wellness" profitable. Do you think we should pay doctors and hospitals a fee for keeping people well? "Wellness" programs can be profitable. Many companies have found that their medical bills are lower if they help their employees stay healthy so they don't become patients (Conlin 2007).

➤ Third, consider the broader picture of "wellness" and disease prevention. How can we decrease the use of harmful drugs and stop industry from spewing their wastes into the air and using our rivers and oceans as industrial sewers?

➤ Finally, since we live in a global village, how can we establish international controls and cooperation so we can create a global wellness-producing environment? ■

19.8 Discuss how technology and alternative medicine are likely to affect the future of medicine.

The Future of Medicine

What will the practice of medicine be like in the future? You can expect current issues to remain, especially disagreements about the extent that medical care should be an individual or governmental responsibility. Other issues mentioned in this chapter will also remain, such as social inequality in health care, malpractice lawsuits, and depersonalization. Some, such as conflicts of interest and incompetence, will continue to scandalize the medical profession. New diseases will also appear, for which we will have to find new treatments. Beyond such carryover issues, two trends seem to be shaping the future of medicine: alternative medicine and technology.

Alternative Medicine

Despite attempts by the American Medical Association to enforce a single, conforming view of illness and health, competing views and practices are demanding equal time. An outstanding example is **alternative medicine**, also called *nontraditional medicine.* In addition to the use of herbs and food supplements, this term often refers to medical practices imported from Asian cultures. From the perspective of traditional Western medical theory and practice, most alternative medicine makes no sense. Regarding it as the superstitious practices of ignorant people, Western doctors usually turn a scornful and hostile eye to alternative medicine. They first ridiculed acupuncture, for example, because it violated their understanding of how the body works. But with patients reporting results such as pain relief, acupuncture has slowly been accepted in U.S. medical practice.

This model is publicizing the use of leeches in medical treatment. Researchers have found that when leeches suck blood they secrete chemicals that relieve symptoms of arthritis and other conditions.

Many U.S. patients have begun to demand alternatives, and the U.S. medical establishment has started to listen. Although the change is slow, in some places, the Western and Eastern approaches to medical care are being combined. In two hospitals in Savannah, Georgia, standard and alternative doctors work alongside one another. Patients are given traditional treatment accompanied by yoga, meditation, and shirodhara, in which warm herbalized sesame oil is slowly dripped onto the patient's forehead. Patients may also choose polarity therapy (to unblock energy), biofeedback, Chinese face-lifting, and aromatherapy (Abelson and Brown 2002). Harvard Medical School has opened a division that specializes in alternative (complementary) medicine ("Harvard Medical School" 2011).

The change is just a trickle at this point, but what is sociologically significant is that alternative medicine has begun to make inroads into the exclusive club run by the U.S. medical establishment.

alternative medicine medical treatment other than that of standard Western medicine; often refers to practices that originate in Asia, but may also refer to taking vitamins not prescribed by a doctor

Technology

Technology is certainly destined to have profound effects on medicine. Let's close this chapter with a look at these changes.

Sociology and the New Technology

Who Should Live, and Who Should Die? The Dilemma of Rationing Medical Care

A 75-year old woman enters the emergency room, screaming and in tears from severe pain. Cancer has spread through her body. She has only weeks to live, and she needs to be admitted to the intensive care unit.

At this same moment, a 20-year-old woman, severely injured in a car wreck, is wheeled into the emergency room. To survive, she must be admitted to the intensive care unit.

There is only one unoccupied bed left in intensive care. What do the doctors do?

This story distills a pressing situation that faces U.S. medical health care. Even though particular treatments are essential to care for medical problems, they are too expensive to provide to everyone who needs them. They are so costly that they could bankrupt the nation if they were made available to everyone who has those particular medical problems. Who, then, should receive the benefits of our new medical technology?

In the vignette that opened this box, medical care would be rationed. The young woman would be admitted to intensive care, and the elderly woman would be sent to some ward in the hospital. But what if the elderly woman had already been admitted to intensive care? Would physicians pull her out? This is not as easily done, but perhaps.

Consider the much more routine case of dialysis, the use of machines to cleanse the blood of people who are suffering from kidney disease. With dialysis currently available to anyone who needs it, the cost runs several billion dollars a year. With the nation broke and in debt, many wonder how we can afford to continue to pay this medical bill. Physicians in Great Britain reduce costs by acting much like doctors would in our opening vignette. They ration dialysis, but they do this informally. They exclude most older patients from dialysis. For others, they make bedside assessments of their chances of survival (Aaron et al. 2005).

Modern medical technology is marvelous. People walk around with the hearts, kidneys, livers, lungs, and faces of deceased people. Eventually, perhaps, surgeons will be able to transplant brains. The costs are similarly astounding. Look again at Figure 19.4 on page 555. Our national medical bill is approaching $3 trillion a year (*Statistical Abstract* 2013:Table 137). This is even more than the total amount that the country raises in income taxes (*Statistical Abstract* 2013:Table 468).

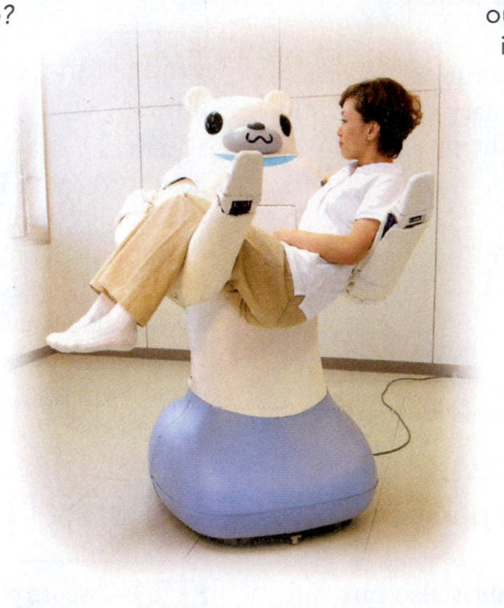

Medical technology is taking many forms, including this robot nurse developed in Japan. The robot is designed to help nurses lift patients in and out of their beds.

Frankly, I can't understand what a trillion of anything is. I've tried, but the number is just too high for me to grasp. Now there are three of these trillions to pay each year.

How long can we continue to pay such fantastic amounts of money? This question haunts our medical system, making the possibility of medical rationing urgent.

The nation's medical bill will not level off. Medical technology, including new drugs, continues to advance—and to be costly. The number of elderly is growing rapidly, and it is the elderly who need the most medical care, especially during their last months of life. It is fine to discuss limiting medical technology on a theoretical level, but when we are sick, we all want the latest, most advanced treatment.

The dilemma is harsh: If we ration medical treatment, many sick people will die. If we don't, we will burden future generations with even more debt.

For Your Consideration

→ At the heart of this issue lie questions not only of cost but also of fairness. If all of us can't have the latest, best, and most expensive medical care, then who should get it? Use ideas, concepts, and principles from this and other chapters to develop a proposal for solving this dilemma. How does the picture change if you view it from the contrasting perspectives of functionalism, symbolic interactionism, and conflict theory?

→ If we ration medical care, what factors should we consider? If age is a factor, for example, should the younger or the older get preferred treatment? If you are about 20 years old, your answer is likely to be a quick "the younger." But is the matter really this simple? What about a 40-year-old who has a 5-year-old child, for example? Or a 55-year-old nuclear physicist? Or the U.S. president? OK, why bring that up? He or she will never get the same medical treatment as we get. But, wait, isn't this the point?

MySocLab

Study and Review on MySocLab

CHAPTER 19 Summary and Review

Sociology and the Study of Medicine and Health

What is the role of sociology in the study of medicine?

Sociologists study **medicine** as a social institution. As practiced in the United States, three of its primary characteristics are professionalization, bureaucracy, and the profit motive. P. 546.

The Symbolic Interactionist Perspective

19.1 Explain why health and illness are culturally relative, not absolute matters.

What is the symbolic interactionist perspective on health and illness?

Health is not only a biological matter but is also intimately related to society. Illness is also far from an objective condition, since health and illness are always viewed through the framework of culture. How people define physical and mental conditions varies from one group to another. Pp. 546–547.

The Functionalist Perspective

19.2 Summarize the sick role: its elements, ambiguity, gatekeepers, and gender differences.

What is the functionalist perspective on health and illness?

Functionalists stress that in return for being excused from their usual activities, people have to accept the **sick role**. They must assume responsibility for seeking competent medical help and cooperate in getting well so they can quickly resume normal activities. Pp. 547–548.

The Conflict Perspective

19.3 Explain how health care is part of the struggle over scarce resources.

What is the conflict perspective on health and illness?

Health care is one of the scarce resources for which a society's groups compete. In 1910, the education of U.S. physicians came under the control of a group of men who eliminated most of their competition and turned medicine into a monopoly that has become the largest business in the United States. On a global level, health care follows the stratification that we studied in Chapter 9. The best health care is available in the Most Industrialized Nations, the worst in the Least Industrialized Nations. Pp. 548–553.

Historical Patterns of Health

19.4 Discuss changes in causes of death and whether Americans were healthier in the past.

How have health patterns changed over time?

Patterns of disease in the United States have changed so extensively that of today's top ten killers, four did not even show up on the 1900 top ten list. Because most Americans live longer than their ancestors did, we can conclude that contemporary Americans are healthier. For mental illness, we have no baselines from which to make comparisons, so we have no idea how the current rate of mental illness compares with that of the past. Pp. 553–554.

Issues in Health Care

19.5 Discuss medical care as a right or a commodity, increasing costs, social inequality, lawsuits, incompetence, fraud, conflict of interest, depersonalization, sexism, racism, the medicalization of society, physician assisted suicide, and attempts to reduce cost.

How does treating health care as a commodity lead to social inequalities?

Because health care is a commodity to be sold to the highest bidder, the United States has a **two-tier system of medical care** in which the poor receive inferior health care for both their mental and physical illnesses. Pp. 554–556.

What are some other problems in U.S. health care?

One problem is **defensive medicine**, which refers to medical procedures that are done for the physician's benefit, not for the benefit of the patient. Intended to protect physicians from lawsuits, these tests and consultations add huge amounts to the nation's medical bill. Other problems are incompetence, **depersonalization**, conflict of interest, medical fraud, and racism and sexism. Pp. 556–560.

What is the controversy over physicians helping people end their lives?

Major concerns surround **euthanasia**, mercy killing in cases of chronic, intense pain or incurable, debilitating diseases. Among them is fear that if euthanasia is legal, physicians will misuse it, as happens in Holland. Pp. 560–561.

What attempts have been made to cut medical costs?

Health maintenance organizations (**HMOs**), diagnosis-related groups (DRGs), group care, and pay-as-you-go clinics are among the measures that have been taken to reduce medical costs. **Dumping** is a radical action taken by some hospitals to reduce costs. The most controversial proposal is to ration medical care. Pp. 561–563.

Threats to Health

19.6 Discuss threats to health: HIV/AIDS, weight, alcohol and nicotine, disabling environments, medical experiments, globalization of disease and treatment or prevention.

What are some threats to the health of Americans?

Threats to the health of Americans include HIV/AIDS, which has stabilized in the United States but is devastating sub-Saharan Africa; obesity; abuse of alcohol and nicotine; **disabling environments**; unethical experiments; and the globalization of disease. Pp. 564–572.

Treatment or Prevention

19.7 Explain why it is difficult to change people's focus from the treatment of illness to the prevention of illness.

How is treatment or prevention an issue in medicine?

Many medical problems can be traced to lifestyle and are preventable. U.S. medicine focuses on treating existing medical problems, not preventing them. To change this focus, prevention must be made profitable. Pp. 572–573.

The Future of Medicine

19.8 Discuss how technology and alternative medicine are likely to affect the future of medicine.

What is the future of medicine?

Current practices and issues will continue for years, slightly changing the shape of medicine as they are modified. The major stimulants for change will come from technology and **alternative medicine**. Pp. 574–575.

Thinking Critically about Chapter 19

1. A major issue running through this chapter is the tension between medicine as a right and medicine as a commodity. What arguments support each side of this issue?
2. How does lifestyle affect health? What does this have to do with sociology?
3. Have you had an experience with alternative medicine? Or do you know someone who has? If so, how did the treatment (and the theory underlying the cause of the health problem) differ from standard medical practice?

CHAPTER 20

Population and Urbanization

Listen to Chapter 20 on MySocLab

The image still haunts me. *There stood Celia, age 30, her distended stomach visible proof that her thirteenth child was on its way. Her oldest was only 14 years old! A mere boy by our standards, he had already gone as far in school as he ever would. Each morning, he joined the men to work in the fields. Each evening around twilight, I saw him return home, exhausted from hard labor in the subtropical sun.*

I was living in Colima, Mexico, and Celia and her husband Angel had invited me for dinner. Their home clearly reflected the family's poverty. A thatched hut consisting of only a single room served as home for all fourteen members of the family. At night, the parents and younger children crowded into a double bed, while the eldest boy slept in a hammock. As in many homes in the village, the other children slept on mats spread on the dirt floor—despite the crawling scorpions.

The home was meagerly furnished. It had only a gas stove, a table, and a cabinet where Celia stored her few cooking utensils and clay dishes. There were no closets; clothes hung on pegs in the walls. There also were no chairs, not even one. I was used to the poverty in the village, but this really startled me. The family was too poor to afford even a single chair.

"There stood Celia, age 30, her distended stomach visible proof that her thirteenth child was on its way."

Celia beamed as she told me how much she looked forward to the birth of her next child. Could she really mean it? It was hard to imagine that any woman would want to be in her situation.

Yet Celia meant every word. She was as full of delighted anticipation as she had been with her first child—and with all the others in between.

How could Celia have wanted so many children—especially when she lived in such poverty? This question bothered me. I couldn't let it go until I understood why.

This chapter helps to provide an answer.

Learning Objectives

After you have read this chapter, you should be able to:

20.1 Contrast the views of the New Malthusians and Anti-Malthusians on population growth and the food supply; explain why people are starving. (p. 579)

20.2 Explain why the Least Industrialized Nations have so many children, consequences of rapid population growth, population pyramids, the three demographic variables, and problems in forecasting population growth. (p. 586)

20.3 Summarize the development of cities, the process of urbanization, U.S. urban patterns, and the rural rebound. (p. 595)

20.4 Compare the models of urban growth. (p. 602)

20.5 Discuss alienation and community, types of people who live in the city, the norm of noninvolvement and the diffusion of responsibility. (p. 604)

20.6 Explain the effects of suburbanization, disinvestment and deindustrialization, and the potential of urban revitalization. (p. 608)

Population in Global Perspective

Celia's story takes us to the heart of **demography**, the study of the size, composition, growth (or decline), and distribution of human populations. It brings us face to face with the question of whether we are doomed to live in a world so filled with people that there will be little space for anybody. Will our planet be able to support its growing population? Or are chronic famine and mass starvation the sorry fate of most earthlings?

Let's look at how concern about population growth began.

A Planet with No Space for Enjoying Life?

20.1 Contrast the views of the New Malthusians and Anti-Malthusians on population growth and the food supply; explain why people are starving.

The story begins with the lowly potato. When the Spanish *conquistadores* found that people in the Andes Mountains ate this vegetable, which was unknown in Europe, they brought some home with them. At first, Europeans viewed the potato with suspicion, but gradually it became the main food of the lower classes. With a greater abundance of food, fertility increased, and the death rate dropped. Europe's population soared, almost doubling during the 1700s (McKeown 1977; McNeill 1999).

Thomas Malthus (1766–1834), an English economist, became alarmed at this surging growth, seeing it as a sign of doom. In 1798, he wrote *An Essay on the Principle of Population* (1798/1926). In this book, which became world famous, Malthus proposed what became known as the **Malthus theorem**. He argued that although population grows geometrically (from 2 to 4 to 8 to 16 and so forth), the food supply increases only arithmetically (from 1 to 2 to 3 to 4 and so on). This meant, he claimed, that if births go unchecked, the population will outstrip its food supply.

demography the study of the size, composition, growth (or shrinkage), and distribution of human populations

Malthus theorem an observation by Thomas Malthus that although the food supply increases arithmetically (from 1 to 2 to 3 to 4 and so on), population grows geometrically (from 2 to 4 to 8 to 16 and so forth)

exponential growth curve a pattern of growth in which numbers double during approximately equal intervals, showing a steep acceleration in the later stages

The New Malthusians

Was Malthus right? This question has provoked heated debate among demographers. One group, which can be called the *New Malthusians*, is convinced that today's situation is at least as grim as—if not grimmer than—Malthus ever imagined. For example, *the world's population is growing so fast that in just the time it takes you to read this chapter, another 20,000 to 40,000 babies will be born!* By this time tomorrow, Earth will have about 231,000 more people to feed. This increase goes on hour after hour, day after day, without letup. For an illustration of this growth, see Figure 20.1.

The New Malthusians point out that the world's population is following an **exponential growth curve**. This means that if growth doubles during approximately equal intervals of time, it suddenly accelerates. To illustrate the far-reaching implications of exponential growth, sociologist William Faunce (1981) retold an old parable about a poor man who saved a rich man's life. The rich man was grateful and said that he wanted to reward the man for his heroic deed.

> *The man replied that he would like his reward to be spread out over a four-week period, with each day's amount being twice what he received on the preceding day. He also said he would be happy to receive only one penny on the first day. The rich man immediately handed over the penny and congratulated himself on how cheaply he had gotten by.*
>
> *At the end of the first week, the rich man checked to see how much he owed and was pleased to find that the total was only $1.27. By the end of the second week he owed only $163.83. On the twenty-first day, however, the rich man was surprised to find that the total had grown to $20,971.51. When the twenty-eighth day arrived the rich man was shocked to discover that he owed $1,342,177.28 for that day alone and that the total reward had jumped to $2,684,354.56!*

This is precisely what alarms the New Malthusians. They claim that humanity has just entered the "fourth week" of an exponential growth curve. To see why they think the day of reckoning is just around the corner, look at Figure 20.2. *It took from the beginning of time until 1800 for the world's population to reach its first billion.* It then took only

Large families on U.S. farms used to be common. Children helped plant and harvest crops, take care of animals, and prepare food. As the country industrialized and urbanized, children became nonproducers, making them expensive to have around. Consequently, the size of families shrank as we entered Stage 3 of the demographic transition. The two adult sons in this 1890s Minnesota farm family are likely from their father's first wife who died.

FIGURE 20.1 How Fast Is the World's Population Growing?

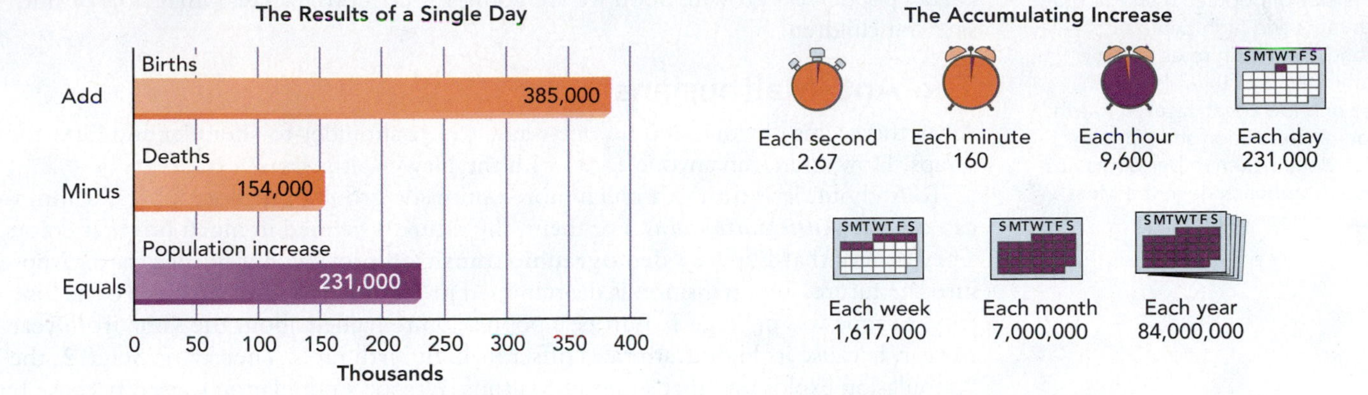

Source: By the author. Based on Haub and Kaneda 2012.

130 years (1930) to add the second billion. Just 30 years later (1960), the world population hit 3 billion. The time it took to reach the fourth billion was cut in half, to only 15 years (1975). Then just 12 years later (in 1987) the total reached 5 billion, in another 12 years it hit 6 billion (in 1999), and in yet another 12 years it hit 7 billion (in 2011).

Another way to put this is that in the past 43 years, the world's population has doubled—going from 3.5 billion to 7 billion.

On average, every minute of every day, 160 babies are born. As Figure 20.1 shows, at each sunset, the world has 231,000 more people than it did the day before. In a year, this comes to 84 million people. During the next four years, this increase will total more than the entire U.S. population. Think of it this way: *In the next dozen years, the world will add as many people as it did during the entire time from when the first humans began to walk the earth until the year 1800.*

These totals terrify the New Malthusians. They are convinced that we are headed toward a showdown between population and food. In the year 2050, the population

FIGURE 20.2 World Population Growth

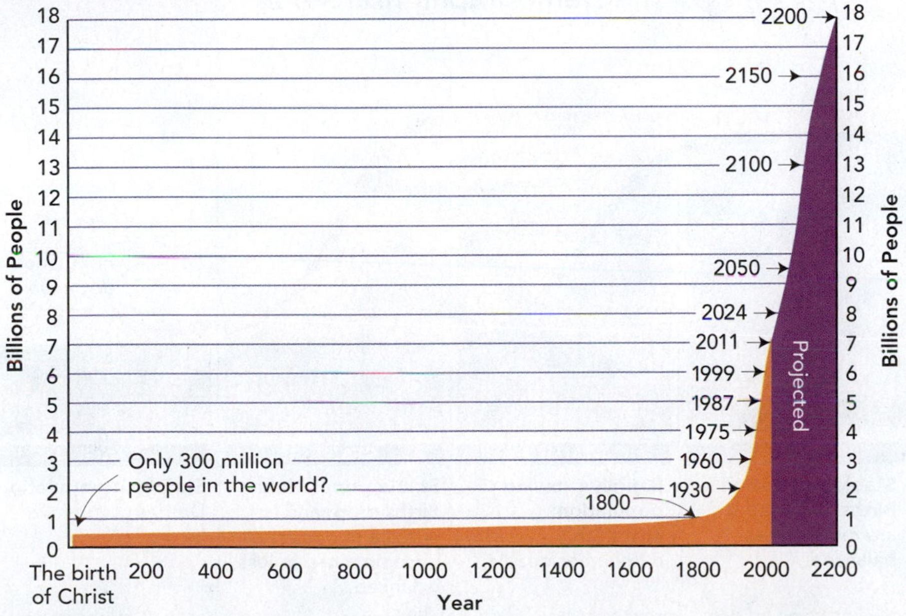

Sources: Modified from Piotrow 1973; McFalls 2007; based on projections from Haub and Kaneda 2012.

Watch on **MySocLab**
Video: Population Growth and Decline

demographic transition a three-stage historical process of change in the size of populations: first, high birth rates and high death rates; second, high birth rates and low death rates; and third, low birth rates and low death rates; a fourth stage of population shrinkage in which deaths outnumber births has made its appearance in the Most Industrialized Nations

of just India and China is expected to be as large as the entire world population was in 1960 (Haub and Kaneda 2012). It is obvious that we will run out of food if we don't curtail population growth. Soon we are going to see more televised images of pitiful, starving children.

The Anti-Malthusians

All of this seems obvious, and no one wants to live shoulder-to-shoulder and fight for scraps. How, then, can anyone argue with the New Malthusians?

To find out, let's turn to a much more optimistic group of demographers, whom we can call the *Anti-Malthusians.* For them, the future is painted in much brighter colors. They believe that Europe's **demographic transition** provides a more accurate glimpse into the future. This transition is diagrammed in Figure 20.3. During most of its history, Europe was in Stage 1. Europe's population remained about the same from year to year, because its high death rates offset its high birth rates. Then came Stage 2, the "population explosion" that so upset Malthus. Europe's population surged because birth rates remained high while death rates went down. Finally, Europe made the transition to Stage 3: The population stabilized as people brought their birth rates into line with their lower death rates.

This, say the Anti-Malthusians, will also happen in the Least Industrialized Nations. Their current surge in population growth simply indicates that they have reached Stage 2 of the demographic transition. Hybrid seeds, medicine from the Most Industrialized Nations, and purer public drinking water have cut their death rates, while their birth rates have remained high. When they move into Stage 3, as surely they will, we will wonder what all the fuss was about. In fact, their growth is already slowing.

Who Is Correct?

As you can see, both the New Malthusians and the Anti-Malthusians have looked at historical trends and projected them onto the future. The New Malthusians project continued world growth and are alarmed. The Anti-Malthusians project Stage 3 of the demographic transition onto the Least Industrialized Nations and are reassured.

There is no question that the Least Industrialized Nations are in Stage 2 of the demographic transition. The question is, Will these nations enter Stage 3? After World War II,

FIGURE 20.3 The Demographic Transition

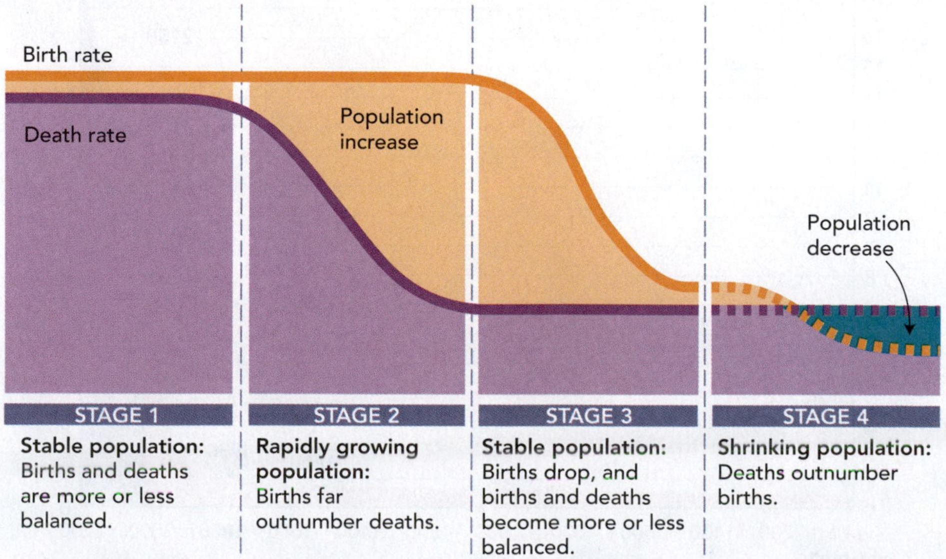

Birth rate
Death rate
Population increase
Population decrease
STAGE 1
Stable population: Births and deaths are more or less balanced.
STAGE 2
Rapidly growing population: Births far outnumber deaths.
STAGE 3
Stable population: Births drop, and births and deaths become more or less balanced.
STAGE 4
Shrinking population: Deaths outnumber births.

Note: The standard demographic transition is depicted by Stages 1–3. Stage 4 has been suggested by some Anti-Malthusians.

the West exported its hybrid seeds, herbicides, and techniques of public hygiene around the globe. Death rates plummeted in the Least Industrialized Nations as their food supply increased and health improved. Because their birth rates stayed high, their populations mushroomed. This alarmed demographers, just it had Malthus 200 years earlier. Some predicted worldwide catastrophe if something were not done immediately to halt the population explosion (Ehrlich and Ehrlich 1972, 1978).

We can use the conflict perspective to understand what happened when this message reached the leaders of the industrialized world. They saw the mushrooming populations of the Least Industrialized Nations as a threat to the global balance of power they had so carefully worked out. With swollen populations, the poorer countries might demand a larger share of Earth's resources. The leaders found the United Nations to be a willing tool, and they used it to spearhead efforts to reduce world population growth. The results have been remarkable. The annual growth of the Least Industrialized Nations has dropped one third (33 percent), from an average of 2.1 percent a year in the 1960s to 1.4 percent today (Haub and Yinger 1994; Haub and Kaneda 2012).

The New Malthusians and Anti-Malthusians have greeted this news with incompatible interpretations. For the Anti-Malthusians, this slowing of growth is the signal they were waiting for: Stage 3 of the demographic transition has begun. First, the death rates in the Least Industrialized Nations fell; now, just as they predicted, birth rates are also falling. Did you notice, they would say if they looked at Figure 20.2, that it took twelve years to add the fifth billion to the world's population—and also twelve years to add the sixth billion—and also twelve years to add the seventh billion? Despite millions upon millions of more women of childbearing age, population growth has leveled off. The New Malthusians reply that a slower growth rate still spells catastrophe—it will just take longer for it to hit.

The Anti-Malthusians also argue that our future will be the *opposite* of what the New Malthusians worry about: There are going to be too few children in the world, not too many. The world's problem will not be a population explosion, but **population shrinkage**—populations getting smaller. Births in seventy-seven countries have already dropped so low that these countries no longer produce enough children to maintain their populations. Another nine countries are on the verge of dropping this low. If it weren't for immigration from Africa, all the countries of Europe would fill more coffins than cradles (Haub and Kaneda 2012).

Some Anti-Malthusians even predict a *demographic free fall* (Mosher 1997). As more nations enter Stage 4 of the demographic transition, the world's population will peak and then begin to grow smaller. Two hundred years from now, they say, we will have a lot fewer people on Earth.

Who is right? It simply is too early to tell. Like the proverbial pessimists who see the glass of water half empty, the New Malthusians interpret changes in world population growth negatively. And like the eternal optimists who see the same glass half full, the Anti-Malthusians view the figures positively. Sometime during our lifetimes, we should know the answer.

Why Are People Starving?

Pictures of starving children gnaw at our conscience. We live in such abundance, while these children and their parents starve before our very eyes. Why don't they have enough food? Is it because there isn't enough food in the world to feed them, or because the abundant food the world produces does not reach them?

The Anti-Malthusians make a point that seems irrefutable. As Figure 20.4 on page 585 shows, *there is much more food for each person in the world now than there was in 1950. Despite the billions of additional people who now live on this planet*, improved seeds and fertilizers have made more food available for *each* person on Earth. And, with bioengineers making breakthroughs in agriculture, even more food is on the way.

But will bioengineered foods live up to their promise? A slight problem seems to be emerging, the focus of our Down-to-Earth Sociology box on the next page.

population shrinkage the process by which a country's population becomes smaller because its birth rate and immigration are too low to replace those who die and emigrate

Down-to-Earth Sociology

BioFoods: What's in *Your* Future?

Luddites are all around us. They oppose anything new. They can't stand change.

You can expect the Luddites to complain about bioengineered foods. Biofoods, also called genetically modified organisms (GMOs), are a radical departure from the past. Until a few years ago, biofoods were just a gleam in the eyes of scientists. They experimented and came up with seeds that vastly increased harvests. Good enough. Then they came up with seeds that could withstand drought. Then seeds whose added genetic materials could even produce insecticides.

Crops kept increasing. And the Luddites kept shouting warnings about contaminating nature, about humans playing God. Scientists and the public shrugged them off. And Monsanto and the other agricultural conglomerates kept doing their research, developing new seeds that would allow the worlds' population—and their profits—to keep growing.

But a little matter seems to have popped up. Scientists love to test things, just about anything. Now that we have genetically modified plants, they are testing them. The first tests were not conclusive, and scientists called for more tests. We now have the results of the first research on rats that were fed GMO corn all of their lives.

The photo to the right shows one of the rats in the study. This is not a pretty sight.

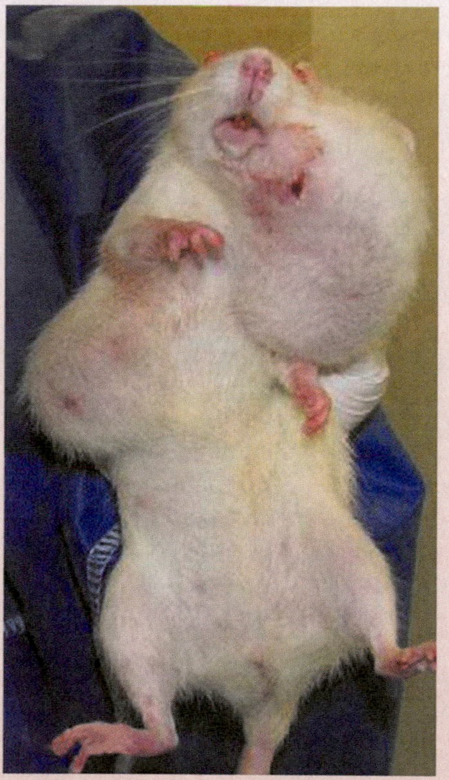

One of the rats in the research reported here.

Basically, the researchers divided the rats into control and experimental groups (Seralini et al. 2012). The control group was fed non-GMO corn, while the experimental group ate only GMO corn. Compared with the control group, a lot of the rats in the experimental group came down with tumors. Like the tumors in the photo, some growths were large enough to block the rats' breathing and digestion. The rats' kidneys and livers were also damaged. Their sex hormones were also disturbed. And female rats tended to come down with breast tumors.

With such damage to essential organs and functioning, the death rate of the experimental group was two to three times higher than that of the control group. The researchers suggest that the GMO corn disturbs the subnuclear structure of body cells.

There's a lot at stake—billions of dollars. You can be sure that Monsanto and other companies are doing research to try to disprove this study. They will not report research that shows that GMOs are harmful. The law doesn't require it. If they have positive results from some sample, however, you can be sure that the media will trumpet them—especially the media in which these companies pay for expensive ads.

This research touched an exposed nerve, and criticism and defense have flown fast and furious (Bardocz et al. 2012; Butler 2012). After the dust settles, we can see what future researchers come up with. I am referring to objective scientists whose own research has not been funded by the agricultural companies.

In the meantime, no GMO for me. My wife looked at the photo as I was writing this box.

For Your Consideration

➤ How do you think we can make our food safe? Do you think companies should be required to put labels on food that informs the consumer if the product contains GMO plants? Do you think all research on GMOs should be required to be posted to a centralized site?

If the Earth is so productive, then why do people die of hunger? Look again at Figure 20.4 on the next page. You can see that people don't starve because the Earth produces too little food. The reason people starve is that particular places lack food. Droughts and wars are the main reasons. Just as droughts slow or stop food production, so does war. In nations ravaged by civil war, opposing sides confiscate and burn crops, and farmers flee to the cities (Thurow 2005; Gettleman 2009).

The New Malthusians counter with the argument that the world's population is still growing and that we don't know how long Earth will continue to produce enough food. They add that the recent policy of turning food (such as corn and sugar cane) into biofuels (such as gasoline and diesel) is short-sighted, posing a serious threat to the world's food supply. *A bushel of corn that goes into someone's gas tank is a bushel of corn that does not go on people's dinner plates.*

FIGURE 20.4 How Much Food Does the World Produce per Person?

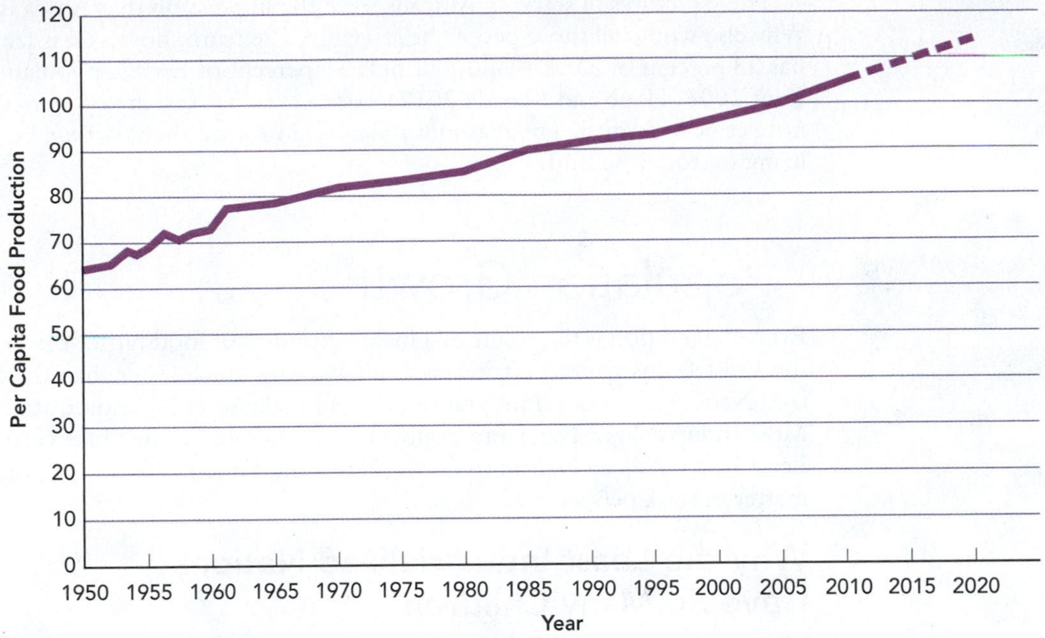

Note: 2004-2006 equals 100. Projections by the author.

Sources: By the author. Based on Simon 1981; *Statistical Abstract of the United States* 2010:Table 1335; Food and Agriculture Organization of the United Nations, January 27, 2012.

Both the New Malthusians and the Anti-Malthusians have contributed significant ideas, but theories will not eliminate famines. Starving children are going to continue to peer out at us from our televisions and magazines, their tiny, shriveled bodies and bloated stomachs nagging at our consciences, imploring us to do something. Regardless of the underlying causes of this human misery, the solution is twofold: first, to transfer

Photos of starving children, such as this child in Somalia, haunt Americans and other members of the Most Industrialized Nations. Many of us wonder why, when some are starving, we should live in the midst of such abundance, often overeating and even casually scraping excess food into the garbage. As in this photo I took in San Antonio, Texas, we even have eating contests to see who can eat the most food in the least time.

food from nations that have a surplus to those that have a shortage, and second, where needed, to teach more efficient farming techniques.

These pictures of starving Africans leave the impression that Africa is overpopulated. Why else would all those people be starving? The truth, however, is far different. Africa has 23 percent of Earth's land, but only 15 percent of Earth's population (Haub and Kent 2008; Haub and Kaneda 2012). Africa even has vast areas of fertile land that have not yet been farmed. The reason for famines in Africa, then, *cannot* be too many people living on too little land.

20.2 Explain why the Least Industrialized Nations have so many children, consequences of rapid population growth, population pyramids, the three demographic variables, and problems in forecasting population growth.

Population Growth

Even if starvation is the result of a maldistribution of food rather than overpopulation, the Least Industrialized Nations are still growing much faster than the Most Industrialized Nations. Without immigration, it would take several hundred years for the average Most Industrialized Nation to double its population, but just fifty years for the average Least Industrialized Nation to do so (Haub and Kaneda 2012). Figure 20.5 puts the matter in stark perspective.

Why the Least Industrialized Nations Have So Many Children

Read on **MySocLab**
Document: Sixteen Impacts of Population Growth

Why do people in the countries that can least afford it have so many children? Let's go back to the chapter's opening vignette and try to figure out why Celia was so happy about having her thirteenth child. It will help if we apply the symbolic interactionist perspective. We must take the role of the other so that we can understand the world of Celia and Angel as *they* see it. As our culture does for us, their culture provides a perspective on life that guides their choices. Celia and Angel's culture tells them that twelve children are *not* enough, that they ought to have a thirteenth—as well as a fourteenth and fifteenth. How can this be? Let's consider three reasons why bearing many children is important to Celia and Angel—and to millions upon millions of poor people around the world.

First is the status of parenthood. In the Least Industrialized Nations, motherhood is the most prized status a woman can achieve. The more children a woman bears, the more she is thought to have achieved the purpose for which she was born. Similarly, a man proves his manhood by fathering children. The more children he fathers, especially sons, the better: Through them, his name lives on.

Second, the community supports this view. Celia and those like her live in *Gemeinschaft* communities, where people share similar views of life. To them, children are a sign of God's blessing. By producing children, people reflect the values of their community, achieve status, and are assured that they are blessed by God. It is the barren woman, not the woman with a dozen children, who is to be pitied.

You can see how these factors provide strong motivations for bearing many children. There is also another powerful incentive: For poor people in the Least Industrialized Nations, children are *economic assets.* Look at Figure 20.6. Like Celia's and Angel's eldest son, children begin contributing to the family income at a young age. But even more important: *Children are their equivalent of our Social Security.* In the Least Industrialized Nations, the government does not provide social security or medical and unemployment insurance. This motivates people to bear *more* children, because when parents become too old to work, or when no work is to be found, their children take care of them. The more children they have, the broader their base of support and the more secure their future.

FIGURE 20.5 World Population Growth, 1750–2150

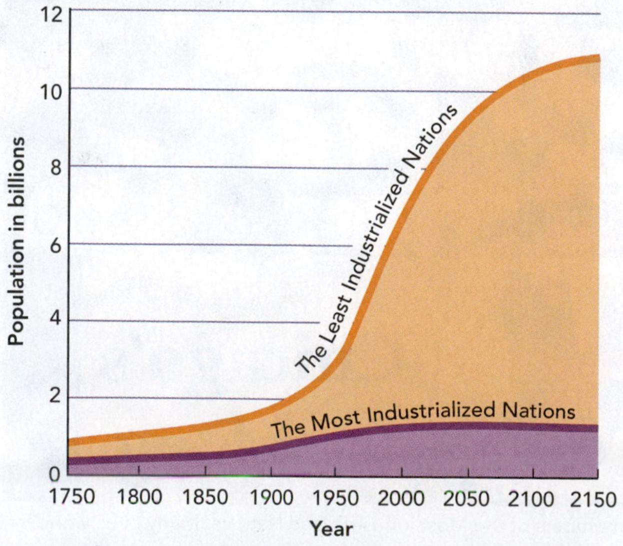

Sources: "The World of the Child 6 Billion" 2000; Haub and Kaneda 2012.

FIGURE 20.6 Why the Poor Need Children

Children are an economic asset in the Least Industrialized Nations. Based on a survey in Indonesia, this figure shows that boys and girls can be net income earners for their families by the age of 9 or 10.

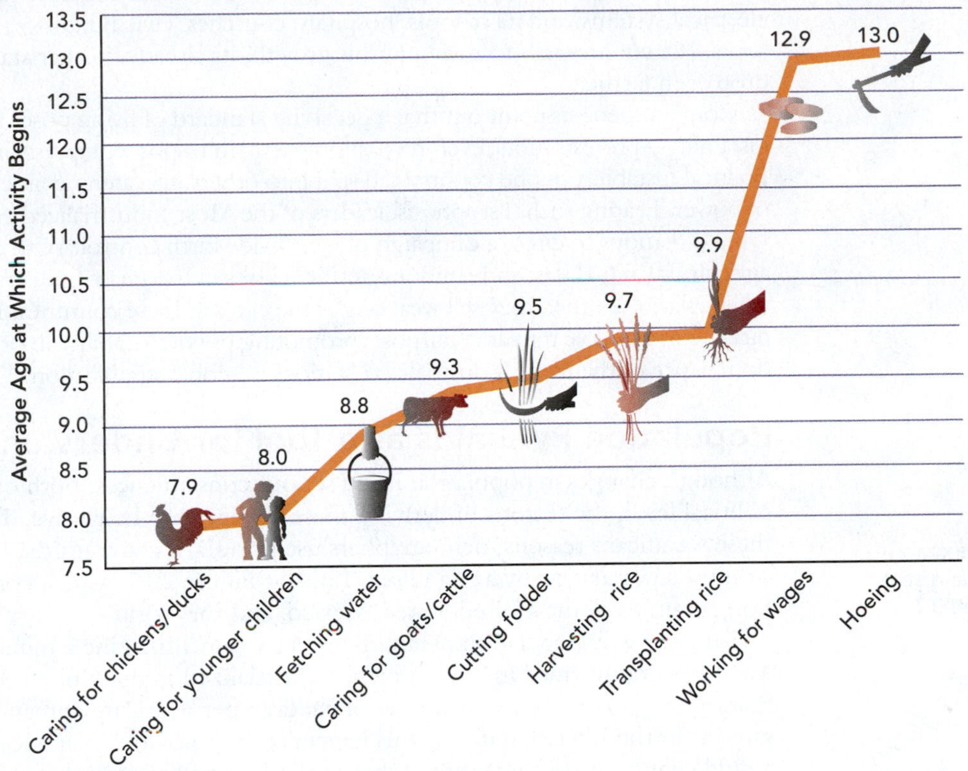

Source: U.N. Fund for Population Activities.

To those of us who live in the Most Industrialized Nations, it seems irrational to have many children. And *for us, it would be*. Understanding life from the framework of people who are living it, however—the essence of the symbolic interactionist perspective—reveals how it makes perfect sense to have many children. Consider this report by a government worker in India:

> *Thaman Singh (a very poor man, a water carrier) ... welcomed me inside his home, gave me a cup of tea (with milk and "market" sugar, as he proudly pointed out later), and said: "You were trying to convince me that I shouldn't have any more sons. Now, you see, I have six sons and two daughters and I sit at home in leisure. They are grown up and they bring me money. One even works outside the village as a laborer. You told me I was a poor man and couldn't support a large family. Now, you see, because of my large family I am a rich man."* (Mamdani 1973)

Conflict theorists offer a different view of why women in the Least Industrialized Nations bear so many children. Feminists argue that women like Celia have internalized values that support male dominance. In Latin America, *machismo*—an emphasis on male virility and dominance—is common. To father many children, especially sons, shows that a man is *macho*, strong and sexually potent, a real man, which earns him higher status in the community. From a conflict perspective, then, the reason poor people have so many children is that men control women's reproductive choices.

Consequences of Rapid Population Growth

The result of Celia's and Angel's desire for many children—and of the millions of Celias and Angels like them—is that the population of the average Least Industrialized Nation will double in fifty years. In contrast, women in the United States are having so few children that if it weren't for immigration, the U.S. population would be shrinking.

The implications of a doubling population are mind-boggling. *Just to stay even*, within fifty years, a country must double the number of available jobs and housing facilities; its food production; its transportation and communication facilities; its water, gas, sewer, and electrical systems; and its schools, hospitals, churches, civic buildings, theaters, stores, and parks. If a country fails to maintain this growth, its already meager standard of living will drop even farther.

Conflict theorists point out that a declining standard of living poses the threat of political instability—protests, riots, even revolution—and, in response, repression by the government. Political instability in one country can spill into others, threatening an entire region's balance of power. Fearing such disruptions, leaders of the Most Industrialized Nations are using the United Nations to direct a campaign of worldwide birth control. With one hand, they give agricultural aid, IUDs, and condoms to the masses in the Least Industrialized Nations—while, with the other, they sell weapons to the elites in these countries. Both actions, say conflict theorists, serve the same purpose: promoting political stability in order to maintain the dominance of the Most Industrialized Nations in global stratification.

Population Pyramids as a Tool for Understanding

population pyramid a graph that represents the age and sex of a population (see Figure 20.7)

Although changes in population bring serious consequences, both on a personal and a political level, the reasons underlying these changes can be elusive. To illustrate one of these significant reasons, demographers use **population pyramids**, figures that depict a country's population by age and sex. Look at Figure 20.7, which compares the population pyramids of the United States, Mexico, and the world.

Let's see why population pyramids are important. Imagine a miracle—that overnight, Mexico is transformed into a nation as industrialized as the United States. Imagine also that overnight, the average number of children per Mexican woman drops to 2.0, the same as in the United States. If this happened, it is obvious that Mexico's population would change at the same rate as that of the United States, right?

But this isn't what would happen. Instead, the population of Mexico would continue to grow rapidly. To see why, look again at the population pyramids. Notice that a much higher percentage of Mexican women are in their childbearing years. This means that even if Mexico and the United States had the same birth rate, a larger percentage of Mexican women would be giving birth, and Mexico's population would grow rapidly while, without

FIGURE 20.7 Three Population Pyramids

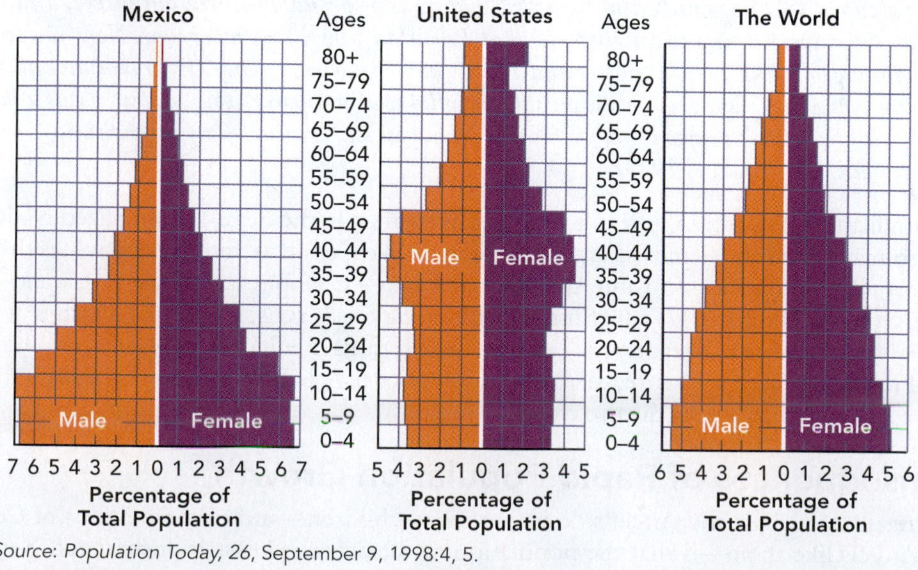

Source: *Population Today, 26*, September 9, 1998:4, 5.

immigration, that of the United States would be standing still or decreasing. As demographers like to phrase this, Mexico's *age structure* gives it greater *population momentum*.

The Three Demographic Variables

How many people will live in the United States fifty years from now? What will the world's population be then? These are important questions. Educators want to know how many schools to build. Manufacturers want to anticipate changes in the market for their products. The government needs to know how many doctors, engineers, and executives to train. Politicians want to know how many people will be paying taxes—and how many young people will be available to fight their wars.

To project the future of populations, demographers use three **demographic variables:** fertility, mortality, and migration. Let's look at each.

Fertility. The number of children that the average woman bears is called the **fertility rate**. The world's overall fertility rate is 2.4, which means that during her lifetime, the average woman in the world bears 2.4 children (Haub and Kaneda 2012). A term that is sometimes confused with fertility is **fecundity**, the number of children that women are *capable* of bearing. This number is rather high, as some women have given birth to 30 children (McFalls 2007).

Watch on MySocLab
Video: The Basics: Population, Urbanization, and Environment

To see which countries have the highest and lowest low birth rates, look at Table 20.1. You can see that two countries tie for the world's lowest fertility rate. There, the average woman gives birth to only 1.1 children. Five of the lowest-birth countries are in Europe. The other five are located in Asia. Now look at the countries with the highest birth rates. Four of them are in Africa, and one is in Asia. Niger in West Africa holds the record for the world's highest birth rate. There, the average woman gives birth to 7.1 children, over six times as many children as the average woman in Latvia and Taiwan.

To compute the fertility rate of a country, demographers analyze the government's records of births. From these, they figure the country's **crude birth rate**, the annual number of live births per 1,000 people.

TABLE 20.1 Extremes in Childbirth

Where Do Women Give Birth to the Fewest Children?		Where Do Women Give Birth to the Most Children?	
Country	Number of Children	Country	Number of Children
Latvia	1.1	Niger	7.1
Taiwan	1.1	Burundi	6.4
Andorra	1.2	Somalia	6.4
Bosnia-Herzegovina	1.2	Angola	6.3
Hong Kong	1.2	Congo, Dem. Republic	6.3
Hungary	1.2	Mali	6.3
Macao	1.2	Zambia	6.3
San Marino	1.2	Afghanistan	6.2
Singapore	1.2	Uganda	6.2
South Korea	1.2	Burkina Faso	6.0

Source: Haub and Kaneda 2012.

Mortality. The second demographic variable is measured by the **crude death rate**, the annual number of deaths per 1,000 people. Its extremes are even greater than the extremes of the birth rate. The highest death rate is 17, a record held by two African countries, the Democratic Republic of Congo and Guinea-Bissau. The lowest death rate is 1, a record held by two Asian countries, Qatar and United Arab Emirates (Haub and Kaneda 2012).

Migration. The third demographic variable is *migration*, the movement of people from one area to another. There are two types of migration. The first type occurs when people move from one region to another within the same country. During and after World War II, in what U.S. demographers call "The Great Migration," millions of African Americans moved from the South to the North. In a historical shift, many are now returning to the South to participate in its growing economy, to enjoy its warmer climate, and to renew ties with family roots (Bilefsky 2011).

The second type of migration occurs when people move from one country to another. Demographers use the term **net migration rate** to refer to the difference between the number of *immigrants* (people moving into a country) and *emigrants* (people moving out of a country) per 1,000 people. Unlike fertility and mortality, migration does not

demographic variables the three factors that change the size of a population: fertility, mortality, and net migration

fertility rate the number of children that the average woman bears

fecundity the number of children that women are capable of bearing

crude birth rate the annual number of live births per 1,000 population

crude death rate the annual number of deaths per 1,000 population

net migration rate the difference between the number of immigrants and emigrants per 1,000 population

Current U.S. immigration shows great diversity. During this ceremony on Ellis Island, New York, over 100 people from 44 countries were sworn in as American citizens.

affect the global population: People are simply shifting their residence from one country or region to another.

What motivates people to give up the security of their family and friends to move to a country with a strange language and unfamiliar customs? To understand migration, we need to look at both "pushes" and "pulls." The *pushes* are the things people want to escape: poverty, violence, war, or persecution for their religious and political ideas. The *pulls* are the magnets that draw people to a new land, such as opportunities for education, better jobs, the freedom to worship or to discuss political ideas, and a more promising future for their children. After "migrant paths" are established, immigration often accelerates—networks of kin and friends attract more people from the same nation, even from the same villages.

Around the world, the flow of migration is from the Least Industrialized Nations to the industrialized countries. By far, the United States is the world's number one choice. The United States admits more immigrants each year than all the other nations of the world combined. Thirty-eight million residents—one of every eight Americans—were born in other countries (*Statistical Abstract* 2013:Table 41). Table 20.2 below shows where recent U.S. immigrants were born. With the economic crisis, this flow has slowed somewhat (Chishti and Bergeron 2010).

Explore on **MySocLab**
Activity: Where in the United States Do You Find the Largest Minority Populations?

To escape grinding poverty, such as that which surrounds Celia and Angel, millions of people also enter the United States illegally. Although it may seem surprising, as Figure 20.8 shows, U.S. officials have sufficient information on these approximately 12 million people to estimate their countries of origin.

Experts cannot agree on whether immigrants are a net contributor to the U.S. economy or a drain on it. Adding what immigrants produce in jobs and taxes and subtracting what they cost in welfare and the medical and school systems, some economists conclude that

TABLE 20.2 Country of Birth of Authorized U.S. Immigrants

Asia	**3,785,000**	El Salvador	252,000	**South America**	**906,000**
China	663,000	Haiti	214,000	Colombia	251,000
India	663,000	Jamaica	181,000	Peru	146,000
Philippines	587,000	Canada	168,000	Brazil	124,000
Vietnam	306,000	Guatemala	161,000	Ecuador	113,000
Korea	222,000	**Europe**	**1,264,000**	Venezuela	85,000
Pakistan	157,000	Ukraine	149,000	Guyana	76,000
Iran	126,000	United Kingdom	154,000	Argentina	51,000
Bangladesh	107,000	Russia	140,000	**Africa**	**860,000**
Taiwan	88,000	Poland	117,000	Nigeria	111,000
Japan	76,000	Bosnia and Herzegovina	89,000	Ethiopia	110,000
North America	**3,605,000**	Germany	78,000	Egypt	73,000
Mexico	1,693,000	Romania	54,000	Somalia	64,000
Cuba	318,000	Albania	51,000	Ghana	65,000
Dominican Republic	329,000				

Note: Totals are for the top countries of origin for 2001–2010, the latest years available.
Source: By the author. Based on *Statistical Abstract of the United States* 2013:Table 50.

immigrants produce more than they cost (Council of Economic Advisers; Parker 2013). Other economists conclude that immigrants cost taxpayers trillions of dollars (Davis and Weinstein 2002; Rector and Richwine 2013). Determining the costs or benefits of immigrants has become a highly-charged political matter. I shake my head in wonder as I see political liberals and conservatives look at the same data and arrive at opposite conclusions. In the midst of this controversy, the fairest conclusion seems to be that the more educated immigrants produce more than they cost, while the less educated cost more than they produce.

FIGURE 20.8 Countries of Origin of Unauthorized Immigrants to the United States

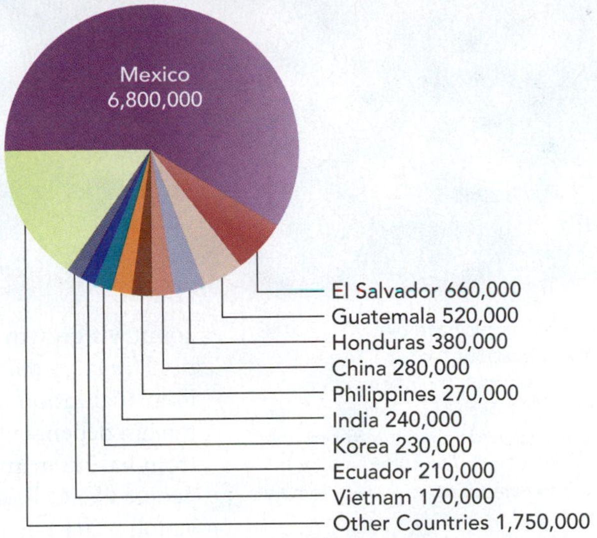

Source: Statistical Abstract of the United States 2013:Table 45.

Problems in Forecasting Population Growth

> *Russia's population is falling. We've got to do something. Let's give $5,000 to every woman who has a first child—and $15,000 to women who have a second child. And let men have two wives.*
> *—Vladimir Zhirinovsky, Russian politician, January 2010*

> *Here's a better idea. Let's have a National Day of Conception. Workers can go home early and make love. Any woman who has a child 9 months later will get a free refrigerator.*
> *—Another politician in Russia*

How politicians complicate the demographer's job. Russians in Ulyanovsk now celebrate a Day of Conception. Women who give birth on Russia Day, June 12, win prizes—video cameras, TVs, refrigerators. The grand prize is a car ("Russians Given Day Off" 2007; Salyer 2013).

If population growth depended only on biology, making projections of the future population would be easier. Just use the **basic demographic equation**. Add and subtract the three demographic variables—fertility, mortality, and net migration—and you get a country's **growth rate**, the net change after people have been added to and subtracted from a population. Here is how demographers put it:

basic demographic equation the growth rate equals births minus deaths plus net migration

growth rate the net change in a population after adding births, subtracting deaths, and either adding or subtracting net migration; can result in a negative number

Growth rate equals births minus deaths plus net migration.

Then you just project the results into the future—because current rates indicate future rates.

Or they *usually* do, and here is the rub. Some politician comes along and pushes those rates in an unexpected direction. When Hitler decided that Germany needed more "Aryans," the government outlawed abortion and offered not refrigerators but cash to women who gave birth. Germany's population increased.

This couple is sitting in the grand prize they won for participating in the Day of Conception and giving birth on Russia Day.

Some politicians go in the other direction and try to slow births. The Indian government is offering $106 to each newlywed woman who waits two years to get pregnant (Yardley 2010). As you probably know, China has a "one couple, one child" policy, but you might not know how ruthlessly officials have enforced this policy. Steven Mosher (2006), an anthropologist who did fieldwork in China, reports that if a woman gets pregnant without government permission (yes, you read that right!), doctors abort the fetus—even if the woman is nine months pregnant. The woman has no say in the matter. After the birth of her first child, each woman—whether she wants it or not—is fitted with an IUD (intrauterine device). Every three months, she must have a sonogram to

Chinese officials have become concerned about the lopsided gender ratio that their "one couple, one child" policy has produced. Their recent billboards continue to promote this policy, but by featuring a female child they are trying to reduce female infanticide.

verify that she is not pregnant (Chang 2013). If a woman has a second child, she is sterilized.

Chinese officials are easing up a bit. Concerned that there will not be enough young workers to support their rapidly aging population, officials allow rural couples to have a second child—if their first one was a girl (Greenhalgh 2009). Another exception is allowing a second child if both the husband and wife are only children (LaFraniere 2011). Some couples with higher-paying jobs are having a second child and paying the fine (Chang 2013).

As you might suppose, wars, economic booms and busts, plagues, and famines also affect population growth. As we discuss in the Cultural Diversity box on the next page, so does infanticide.

As you can see, government policies can change a country's growth rate. The main factor, though, is not the government, but industrialization. *In every country that industrializes, the birth rate declines.* Why? One reason is that industrialization makes rearing children more expensive. They require more education and remain dependent longer. Another reason is that the basis for conferring status changes—from having many children to attaining education and displaying material wealth. As people like Celia and Angel in our opening vignette begin to see life differently, their motivation to have many children drops sharply. Not knowing how rapidly industrialization will progress or how quickly changes in values and reproductive behavior will follow adds to the difficulty of making accurate projections.

Consider how difficult it is to estimate U.S. population growth. During the next fifty years, will we have **zero population growth**? (Every 1,000 women would give birth to 2,100 children, the extra 100 children making up for those who do not survive or reproduce.) Will more women go to college? (Educated women bear fewer children.) How many immigrants will we have? Will some devastating disease appear? Because of these many unknowns, demographers play it safe by making several projections of population growth, each depending on an "if" scenario. Figure 20.9 shows three projections of the U.S. population.

zero population growth women bearing only enough children to reproduce the population

FIGURE 20.9 Population Projections of the United States

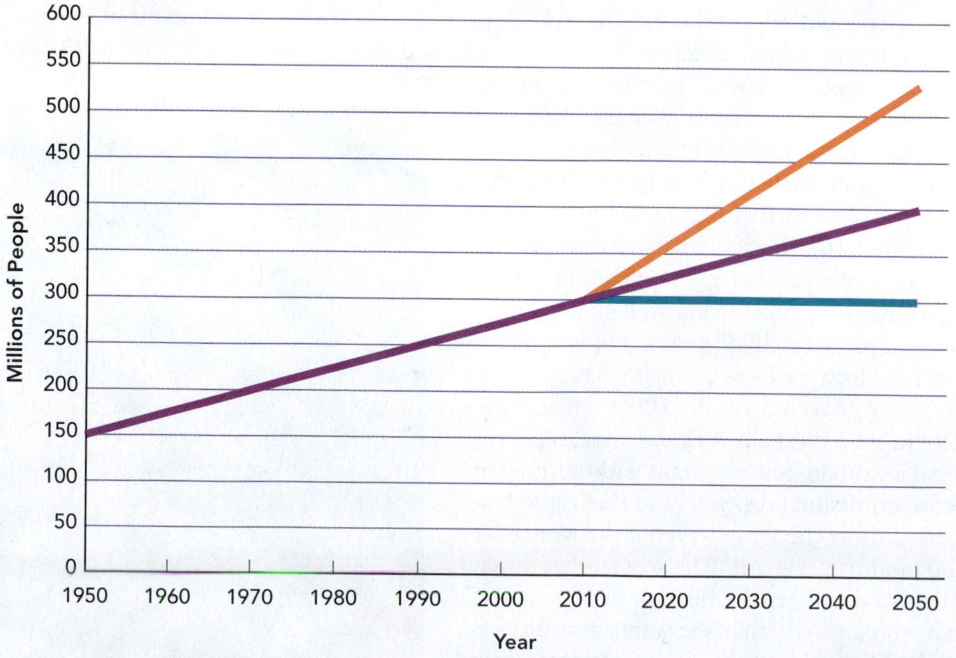

Note: The projections are based on different assumptions of fertility, mortality, and especially migration.
Source: By the author. Based on Day 2010.

Cultural Diversity **around the World**

Killing Little Girls: An Ancient and Thriving Practice

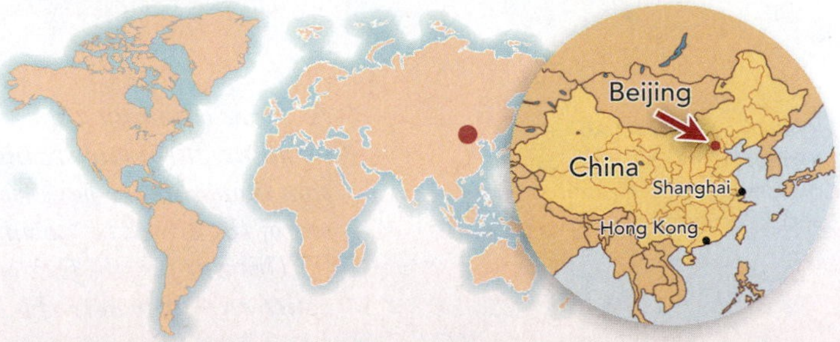

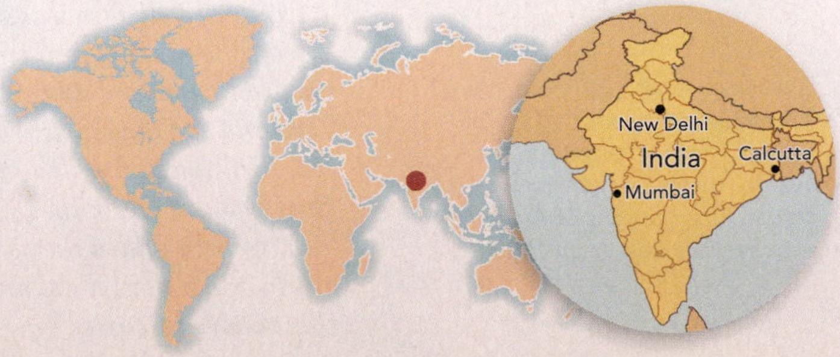

"The Mysterious Case of the Missing Girls" could have been the title of this box. Around the globe, for every 100 births of girls, about 105 boys are born. In China, however, for every 100 baby girls, the total jumps to 121 baby boys (Last 2011). Given China's huge population, this means that China has about *30 million* fewer females than males under the age of 20 (Yardley 2010). What happened to the 30 million girls?

The answer is *female infanticide*, the killing of baby girls. When a Chinese woman goes into labor, the village midwife sometimes grabs a bucket of water. If the newborn is a girl, she is plunged into the water before she can draw her first breath.

At the root of China's sexist infanticide is economics. The people are poor, and they have no pensions. When parents can no longer work, sons support them. In contrast, a daughter must be married off, at great expense, and at that point, her obligations transfer to her husband and his family.

"Raising a girl is like watering someone else's plant," as they say in India, where female infanticide is also common.

In China, the past few years have brought even larger percentages of boy babies. The reason, again, is economics, but this time with a new twist. When China adopted capitalism, travel and trade opened up—but primarily to men, since it is not thought appropriate for women to travel alone. With men finding themselves in a better position to bring money home, parents have one more reason to want boys.

The gender ratio is so lopsided that for Chinese in their 20s, there are six bachelors for every five potential brides. Politicians fear that the men who cannot marry—"bare branches," as they call them—will become disgruntled. Lacking the stabilizing influences of marriage and children, these bare branches might become a breeding ground for political dissent. To head this off, officials have begun a campaign to stop the drowning of girl babies and the aborting of female fetuses.

We find a similar situation in India. For the same reasons, India has an extra 37 million men. Officials there, too, are concerned. These additional men who cannot find wives, they say, are a major reason for sexual harassment and rape.

Targeting female fetuses for abortion has become a main issue of the emerging feminist movement in India.

Sources: Jordan 2000; Dugger 2001; Riley 2004; Yardley 2007, 2011; Harney 2011; Sharma 2013.

For Your Consideration

➔ What do you think can be done to reduce female infanticide? Why do you think this issue receives so little publicity and is not a priority with world leaders?

Let's turn to a different aspect of population: where people live. Because more and more people around the world are living in cities, let's look at urban trends and urban life.

Urbanization

Watch on **MySocLab**
Video: Sociology in Focus: Population, Urbanization, and Environment

As I was climbing a steep hill in Medellin, Colombia, in a district called El Tiro, my informant, Jaro, said, "This used to be a garbage heap." I stopped to peer through the vegetation alongside the path we were on, and sure enough, I could see bits of refuse still sticking out of the dirt. The "town" had been built on top of garbage.

This was just the first of my many revelations that day. The second was that the Medellin police refused to enter El Tiro because it was so dangerous. I shuddered for a moment, but I had good reason to trust Jaro. He had been a pastor in El Tiro for several years, and he knew the people well. I was confident that if I stayed close to him, I would be safe.

Actually, El Tiro was safer now than it had been. A group of young men had banded together to make it so, Jaro told me. A sort of frontier justice prevailed. The vigilantes told the prostitutes and drug dealers that there would be no prostitution or drug dealing in El Tiro and to "take it elsewhere." They killed anyone who robbed or murdered someone. And they even made families safer—they would beat up any man who got drunk and battered "his" woman. With the threat of instant justice, the area had become much safer.

Jaro then added that each household had to pay the group a monthly fee, which turned out to be less than a dollar in U.S. money. Each business had to pay a little more. For this, they received security.

As we wandered the streets of El Tiro, it did look safe—but I still stayed close to Jaro. And I wondered about this group of men who had made the area safe. What kept them from turning on the residents? Jaro had no answer. When Jaro pointed to two young men, who he said were part of the ruling group, I asked if I could take their picture. They refused. I did not try to snap one on the sly.

My final revelation was El Tiro itself. On pages 596 and 597, you can see some of the things I saw that day.

Early cities were small economic centers surrounded by walls to keep out enemies. These cities had to be fortresses, for they were constantly under threat. This photo is of Ávila, Spain, whose walls date from 1090.

In this second part of the chapter, I will try to lay the context for understanding urban life—and El Tiro. Let's begin by first finding out how the city itself came about.

20.3 Summarize the development of cities, the process of urbanization, U.S. urban patterns, and the rural rebound.

The Development of Cities

Cities are not new to the world scene. Perhaps as early as 7,000 years ago, people built small cities with massive defensive walls, such as biblically famous Jericho (Homblin 1973). Cities on a larger scale appeared about 3500 B.C., around the time that writing was invented (Chandler and Fox 1974; Hawley 1981). The earliest cities emerged in several parts of the world—in Asia (China, India, Iran, and Iraq), West Africa (Egypt), Europe, and Central and South America (Fischer 1976; Palen 2012).

About 6,500 years ago, Bulgaria was home to the oldest town in Europe (Toshkov 2012). Its massive walls were 10 feet high and 6 feet thick. Its 350 residents made their living producing salt for trade. Another city that goes back 5,500 years was discovered in 2010 in Norway (Goll 2010). The city had been buried under sand. In the Americas, the first city was Caral, in what is now Peru (Fountain 2001). It was also discovered recently, covered by jungle growth.

The key to the origin of cities is the development of more efficient agriculture (Lenski and Lenski 1987). Only when farming produces a surplus can some people stop producing food and gather in cities to spend time in other economic pursuits. A **city**, in fact, can be defined as a place in which a large number of people are permanently based and do not produce their own food. The invention of the plow about 5,000 years ago created widespread agricultural surpluses, stimulating the development of towns and cities.

Most early cities were small, merely a collection of a few thousand people in agricultural centers or on major trade routes. The most notable exceptions are two cities that reached 1 million residents for a brief period of time before they declined—Changan (Xi'an) in China about A.D. 800 and Baghdad in Persia (Iraq) about A.D. 900 (Chandler and Fox 1974). Even Athens at the height of its power in the fifth century B.C. had only about 250,000 inhabitants. Rome, at its peak, may have had a million people or more, but as the Roman Empire declined, the city of Rome became only a collection of villages (Palen 2012).

Two hundred years ago, the only city in the world that had a population of more than a million was Peking (Beijing), China (Chandler and Fox 1974). But today, as you can see from Figure 20.10, the world has about 500 cities with more than a million residents. Behind this urban surge lies the Industrial Revolution, which not only drew people to cities by providing work but also stimulated rapid transportation and communication. These, in turn, allowed the efficient movement of people, resources, products, and, especially today, information—essential factors (called *infrastructure*) that allow large cities to exist.

FIGURE 20.10 A Global Boom: Cities with over One Million Residents

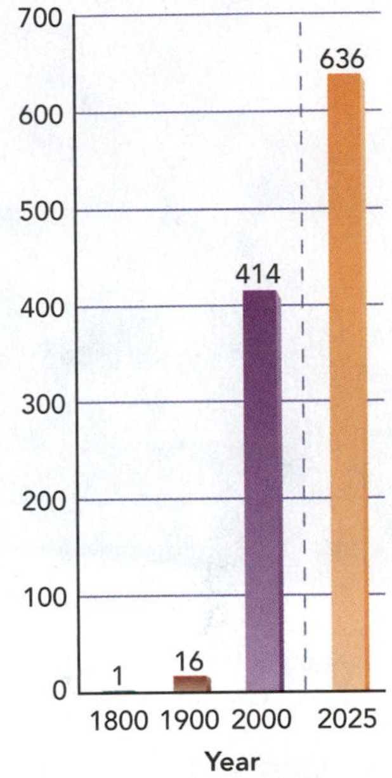

Sources: By the author. Based on Chandler and Fox 1974; Brockerhoff 2000; United Nations 2008. *World Population Prospects* 2012.

urbanization the process by which an increasing proportion of a population lives in cities and has a growing influence on the culture

The Process of Urbanization

Although cities are not new to the world scene, quite recent in world history is **urbanization**—the movement of masses of people to cities, which then have a growing influence on society. In 1800, only 3 percent of the world's population lived in cities (Hauser and Schnore 1965). The watershed year was 2008, when for the first time in history, more people lived in cities than in rural areas. From Figure 20.11, you can see how urbanization has accelerated—and how uneven it is. Note especially the rapid increase of urbanization in the Least Industrialized Nations.

FIGURE 20.11 How the World Is Urbanizing

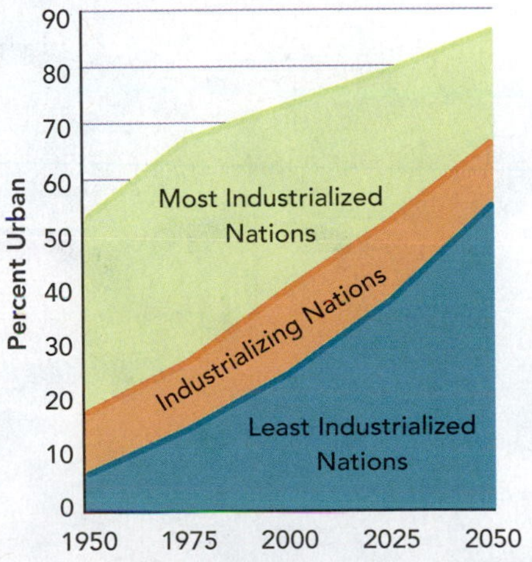

Source: By the author. Based on United Nations 2010

To understand the city's attraction, we need to consider the "pulls" of urban life. Because of its exquisite division of labor, the city offers incredible variety—music ranging from rap and salsa to death metal and classical, shops that feature imported delicacies from around the world and those that sell special foods for

THROUGH THE AUTHOR'S LENS

Medellin, Colombia: A Walk Through El Tiro

One of the most significant changes in our time is the global rush of poor, rural people to the cities of the Least Industrialized Nations. Some of these settlements are dangerous. I was fortunate to be escorted by an insider through this section of Medellin, Colombia.

Almost at the top of the garbage heap, I saw this boy in front of his house. His mother hung out the family's wash to dry.

Kids are kids the world over. These children don't know they are poor. They are having a great time playing on a pile of dirt in the street.

This is the "richer" area below El Tiro. As you can see, some of the residents own cars.

This is one of my favorite photos. The woman is happy that she has a home—and proud of what she has done with it. What I find remarkable is the flower garden she so carefully tends, and has taken great effort to protect from children and dogs. I can see the care she would take of a little suburban home.

The road to El Tiro. On the left, going up the hill, is a board walk. To the right is a meat market (carnicería). Note the structure above the meat market, where the family that runs the store lives.

El Tiro has home delivery.

It doesn't take much skill to build your own house in El Tiro. A hammer and saw, some nails, and used lumber will provide most of what you need. This man is building his house on top of another house.

An infrastructure has developed to serve El Tiro. This woman is waiting in line to use the only public telephone.

"What does an El Tiro home look like inside? I kept wondering. Then Jaro, my guide (on the left), took me inside the home of one of his parishioners. Amelia keeps a neat house, with everything highly organized.

What do people do to make a living in El Tiro? Anything they can. This man is sharpening a saw in front of his home.

vegetarians and diabetics. Cities also offer anonymity, which so many find refreshing in light of the tighter controls of village and small-town life. And, of course, the city offers work.

Explore on **MySocLab**
Activity: Where Do Americans Live?

Some cities have grown so large and have so much influence over a region that the term *city* is no longer adequate to describe them. The term **metropolis** is used instead, referring to a central city surrounded by smaller cities and their suburbs. They are linked by transportation and communication and connected economically, and sometimes politically, through county boards and regional governing bodies. St. Louis is an example.

Although this name, St. Louis, properly refers to a city of 350,000 people in Missouri, it also refers to another 3 million people who live in more than a hundred separate towns in both Missouri and Illinois. Altogether, the region is known as the "St. Louis or Bi-State Area." Although these towns are independent politically, they form an economic unit. They are linked by work (many people in the smaller towns work in St. Louis or are served by industries from St. Louis), by communications (they share the same area newspaper and radio and television stations), and by transportation (they use the same interstate highways, the Bi-State Bus system, and international airport). As symbolic interactionists would note, shared symbols (the Arch, the Mississippi River, Busch Brewery, the Cardinals, the Rams, and the Blues—both the hockey team and the music) provide the residents a common identity.

Most of the towns run into one another, and if you were to drive through this metropolis, you would not know that you were leaving one town and entering another—unless you had lived there for some time and were aware of the fierce small-town loyalties and rivalries that coexist within this overarching identity.

Some metropolises have grown so large and influential that the term **megalopolis** is used to describe them. This term refers to an overlapping area consisting of at least two metropolises and their many suburbs. Of the twenty or so megalopolises in the United States, the three largest are the Eastern seaboard running from Maine to Virginia, the area in Florida between Miami, Orlando, and Tampa, and California's coastal area between San Francisco and San Diego. The California megalopolis extends into Mexico and includes Tijuana and its suburbs.

This process of urban areas turning into a metropolis, and a metropolis developing into a megalopolis, is occurring worldwide. When a city's population hits 10 million, it is called a **megacity**. In 1950, New York City and Tokyo were the only megacities in the world. Today, as you can see from Figure 20.12, the world has twenty-two megacities, most of which are located in the Least Industrialized Nations. Megacities are growing so fast that by the year 2025, there will be twenty-nine (United Nations 2010).

U.S. Urban Patterns

From Country to City. In its early years, the United States was almost exclusively rural. In 1790, only about 5 percent of Americans lived in cities. By 1920, this figure had jumped to 50 percent. Urbanization has continued without letup, and today, about 80 percent of Americans live in cities.

The U.S. Census Bureau divides the country into 274 **metropolitan statistical areas (MSAs).** Each MSA consists of a central city of at least 50,000 people and the urbanized areas linked to it. About three of five Americans live in just fifty or so MSAs. As you can see from the Social Map on the next page, like our other social patterns, urbanization is uneven across the United States.

From City to City. As Americans migrate in search of work and better lifestyles, some cities grow while others shrink. Table 20.3 on page 600 compares the fastest-growing U.S. cities with those that are losing people. This table reflects a major shift of people, resources, and power between regions of the United States. As you can see, six of the ten fastest-growing cities are in the West, and four are in the South. Of the ten shrinking

city a place in which a large number of people are permanently based and do not produce their own food

metropolis a central city surrounded by smaller cities and their suburbs

megalopolis an urban area consisting of at least two metropolises and their many suburbs

megacity a city of 10 million or more residents

metropolitan statistical area (MSA) a central city and the urbanized counties adjacent to it

FIGURE 20.12 The World's Megacities

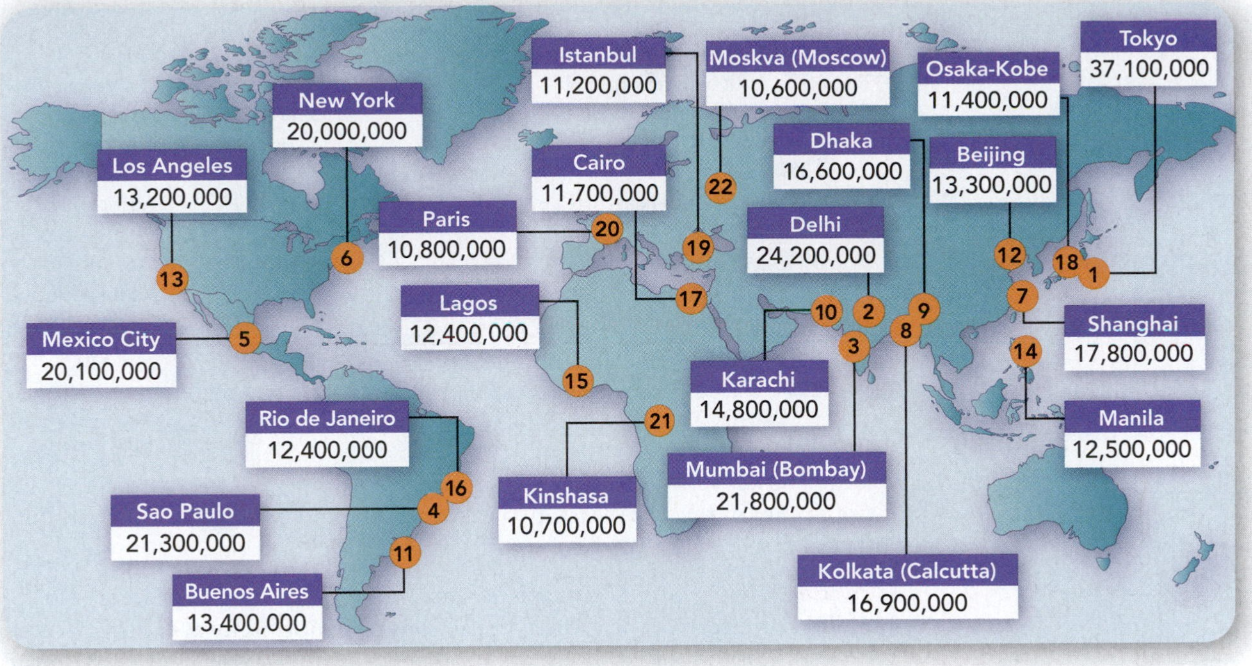

Sources: By the author. Based on projected *2015* populations by United Nations.

FIGURE 20.13 How Urban Is Your State? The Rural–Urban Makeup of the United States

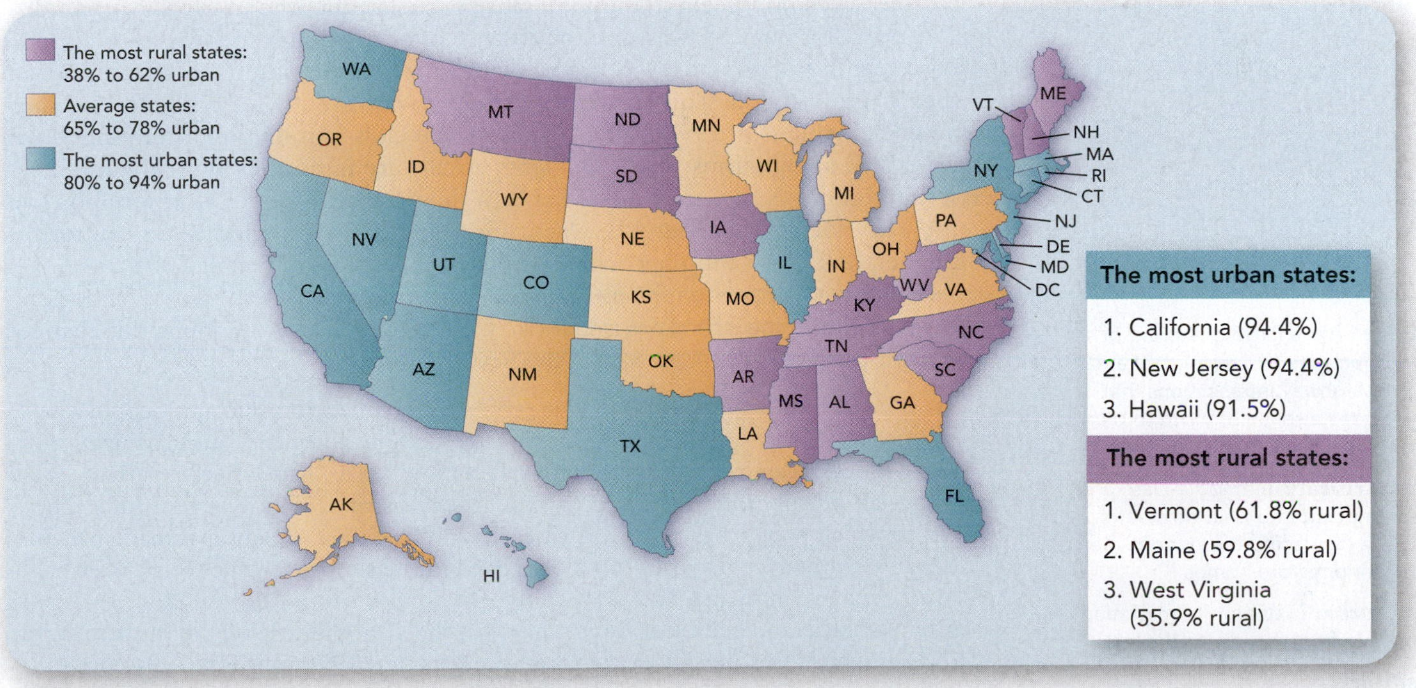

Source: By the author. Based on *Statistical Abstract of the United States* 2013:Table 29.

TABLE 20.3 The Shrinking and the Fastest-Growing Cities

The Shrinking Cities		The Fastest-Growing Cities	
1. −9.3%	New Orleans, LA	1. +44.7%	Raleigh, NC
2. −6.7%	Youngstown, OH	2. +42.8%	Las Vegas, NV
3. −3.7%	Cleveland, OH	3. +42.5%	Provo, UT
4. −3.7%	Detroit, MI	4. +42.3%	Cape Coral–Ft. Myers, FL
5. −3.3%	Flint, MI	5. +42.0%	Greeley, CO
6. −3.1%	Buffalo–Niagara Falls, NY	6. +41.2%	Austin, TX
7. −3.0%	Pittsburgh, PA	7. +39.6%	Myrtle Beach, SC
8. −1.9%	Charleston, WV	8. +39.1%	McAllen, TX
9. −1.4%	Toledo, OH	9. +36.4%	Kennewick, WA
10. −0.5%	Utica-Rome, NY	10. +35.7%	Fayetteville, AR

Note: Population change from 2000 to 2011, the latest years available.
Source: By the author. Based on *Statistical Abstract of the United States* 2013:Table 20.

cities, six are in the Northeast, two in the South, and two in the Midwest. New Orleans, a special case, has not yet recovered from Hurricane Katrina.

Between Cities. As Americans migrate, **edge cities** have appeared—clusters of buildings and services near the intersections of major highways. These areas of shopping malls, hotels, office parks, and apartment complexes are not cities in the traditional sense. Rather than being political units with their own mayors or city managers, they overlap political boundaries and include parts of several cities or towns. Yet, edge cities—such as Tysons Corner near Washington, D.C., and those clustering along the LBJ Freeway near Dallas, Texas—provide a sense of place to those who live or work there.

Read on **MySocLab** **Document:** Death of a Neighborhood

Within the City. Another U.S. urban pattern is **gentrification**, the movement of middle-class people into rundown areas of a city. What draws the middle class are the low prices for large houses that, although deteriorated, can be restored. With gentrification comes an improvement in the appearance of the neighborhood—freshly painted buildings, well-groomed lawns, and the absence of boarded-up windows.

As a neighborhood improves, property prices go up, driving many of the poor out of their neighborhood. This creates tensions between the poorer residents and the newcomers (Anderson 1990, 2006). These social class tensions are often tinged with racial–ethnic antagonisms, as the residents usually are minorities while the middle-class newcomers usually are whites. Beneath this surface, though, is a more positive factor. Sociologists have found that gentrification also draws middle-class minorities to the neighborhood and improves their incomes (McKinnish et al. 2008).

Among the exceptions to the usual pattern of the gentrifiers being whites and the earlier residents being minorities is Harlem in New York City. We examine this change in the Down-to-Earth Sociology box on the next page.

From City to Suburb and Back. The term **suburbanization** refers to people moving from cities to **suburbs**, the communities located just outside a city. Suburbanization is not new. The Mayan city of Caracol (in what is now Belize) had suburbs, perhaps even with specialized subcenters, the equivalent of today's strip malls (Wilford 2000). The extent to which people have left U.S. cities in search of their dreams is remarkable. In 1920, only about 15 percent of Americans lived in the suburbs, while today, over half of all Americans live in them (Palen 2012).

After the racial integration of U.S. schools in the 1950s and 1960s, suburbanization sped up as whites fled the city. A few years later, around 1970, minorities also began to move to the suburbs. This, too, has been extensive, and in some suburbs, minorities have become the majority. Whites are now returning to the city. In a remarkable switch,

edge city a large clustering of service facilities and residential areas near highway intersections that provides a sense of place to people who live, shop, and work there

gentrification middle-class people moving into a rundown area of a city, displacing the poor as they buy and restore homes

suburbanization the migration of people from the city to the suburbs

suburb a community adjacent to a city

Down-to-Earth Sociology

Reclaiming Harlem: A Twist in the Invasion–Succession Cycle

The story is well known. The inner city is filled with crack, crime, and corruption. It stinks from foul, festering filth strewn on its dangerous streets and piled up around burned-out buildings. Only people who have no choice live in these despairing areas where predators stalk their prey. Danger lurks around every corner.

What is not so well known is that affluent African Americans are reclaiming some of these areas.

Howard Sanders was living the American Dream. After earning a degree from Harvard Business School, he took a position with a Manhattan investment firm. He lived in an exclusive apartment on Central Park West, but he missed Harlem, where he had grown up. He moved back, along with his wife and daughter.

African American lawyers, doctors, professors, and bankers are doing the same.

What's the attraction? The first is nostalgia, a cultural yearning for Harlem past, the time of legend and folklore. It was here that black writers and artists lived in the 1920s, here that the blues and jazz attracted young and accomplished musicians.

One indication of the remarkable transformation of Harlem is town hall meetings. This one was held to discuss a rezoning issue.

The second reason is that Harlem offered housing values. Some homes, built in the 1800s, boasted five bedrooms and 6,000 square feet. They sold for a song, even with Honduran mahogany. Some brownstones were in good condition, although others were only shells and had to be rebuilt from the inside out.

What happened was the rebuilding of a community. Some people who had succeeded in business and the professions wanted to be role models. They wanted children in the community to see them going to and returning from work.

When the middle class moved out of Harlem and the area was taken over by drug dealers and prostitutes, the amenities moved out, too. When the young professionals moved back in, the amenities returned. There were no coffee shops, restaurants, jazz clubs, florists, copy centers, dentist and optometrist offices, or art galleries—the types of things urbanites take for granted. Now there are.

The police have also helped to change Harlem. No longer do they just rush in, sirens wailing and guns drawn, to confront emergencies and shootouts. Instead, the police have become a normal part of this urban scene. Not only did they shut down the open-air drug markets, but they also began enforcing laws against urinating on the streets, something they used to ignore as too trivial to matter for "that area." The greater safety of the area has attracted even more of the middle class. The change is so extensive that former president Clinton chose to locate his office there, and Magic Johnson opened a Starbucks and a multiplex.

Another side of the story has emerged—tension between the people who were already living in Harlem and the newcomers. Social class is often the source of the irritation. Each class has its own ways, and the classes often grate on each other's nerves. The old-timers like loud music, for example, while the newcomers prefer a more sedate lifestyle. Then there is the old power establishment. They feel slighted if the newcomers don't ask their approval before they open a business. For their part, the new business owners feel they don't need to get those old people's permission to open anything.

There is another issue as well. Remember those large houses that sold for a song? No longer. Vacant lots now bring a million dollars. Rents have shot upward, of course. Tenants' associations protest, their moans mostly muffled and unheard.

And the poor? The same as happened in other gentrified areas. Most are pushed out, block by block, forced into adjoining rundown streets.

The in-fighting of this emerging drama mostly involves African Americans. The issue is not race but social class. The "invasion–succession cycle," as sociologists call it, is continuing, but this time with a twist—a flight back in.

Sources: Based on Leland 2003; Hyra 2006; Williams 2008; Haughney 2009; Barnard 2012.

For Your Consideration

➔ Would you be willing to move into an area of high crime in order to get a good housing bargain? How do you think the current residents of an area being gentrified can be protected from rising rents and allowed to continue to live in the area? Should they be?

some black churches and businesses in Washington, D.C., and San Francisco, California, are making the switch to a white clientele. In another reversal of patterns, some black churches are fleeing the city, following their parishioners to the suburbs.

Smaller Centers. Another trend is the development of *micropolitan areas.* A *micropolis* is a city of 10,000 to 50,000 residents that is not a suburb (McCarthy 2004), such as Gallup, New Mexico, or Carbondale, Illinois. Most micropolises are located "next to nowhere." They are fairly self-contained in terms of providing work, housing, and entertainment, and few of their residents commute to urban centers for work. Micropolises are growing, as residents of both rural and urban areas find their cultural attractions and conveniences appealing, especially less crime and pollution.

The Rural Rebound

The desire to retreat to a safe haven has led to a migration to rural areas that is without precedent in the history of the United States. Some small farming towns are making a comeback, their boarded-up stores and schools once again open for business and learning. Some towns have even become too expensive for families that had lived there for decades (Dougherty 2008).

The "push" factors for this fundamental shift are fears of urban crime and violence. The "pull" factors are safety, lower cost of living, and more living space. Interstate highways have made airports—and the city itself—accessible from longer distances. With satellite communications, cell phones, fax machines, and the Internet, people can be "plugged in"—connected with others around the world—even though they live in what just a short time ago were remote areas.

Listen to the wife of one of my former students as she explains why she and her husband moved to a rural area, three hours from the international airport that they fly out of each week:

> *I work for a Canadian company. Paul works for a French company, with headquarters in Paris. He flies around the country doing computer consulting. I give motivational seminars to businesses. When we can, we drive to the airport together, but we often leave on different days. I try to go with my husband to Paris once a year.*
>
> *We almost always are home together on the weekends. We often arrange three- and four-day weekends, because I can plan seminars at home, and Paul does some of his consulting from here.*
>
> *Sometimes shopping is inconvenient, but we don't have to lock our car doors when we drive, and the new Wal-Mart superstore has most of what we need. E-commerce is a big part of it. I just type in www—whatever, and they ship it right to my door. I get make-up and books online. I even bought a part for my stove.*
>
> *Why do we live here? Look at the lake. It's beautiful. We enjoy boating and swimming. We love to walk in this parklike setting. We see deer and wild turkeys. We love the sunsets over the lake. (author's files)*

She added, "I think we're ahead of the learning curve," referring to the idea that their lifestyle is a wave of the future.

Models of Urban Growth

20.4 Compare the models of urban growth.

human ecology Robert Park's term for the relationship between people and their environment (such as land and structures); also known as *urban ecology*

In the 1920s, Chicago was a vivid mosaic of immigrants, gangsters, prostitutes, the homeless, the rich, and the poor—much as it is today. Sociologists at the University of Chicago studied these contrasting ways of life. One of these sociologists, Robert Park, coined the term **human ecology** to describe how people adapt to their environments (Park and Burgess 1921; Park 1936). (This concept is also known as *urban ecology.*) The process of urban growth is of special interest to sociologists. Let's look at four main models they developed.

FIGURE 20.14 How Cities Develop: Models of Urban Growth

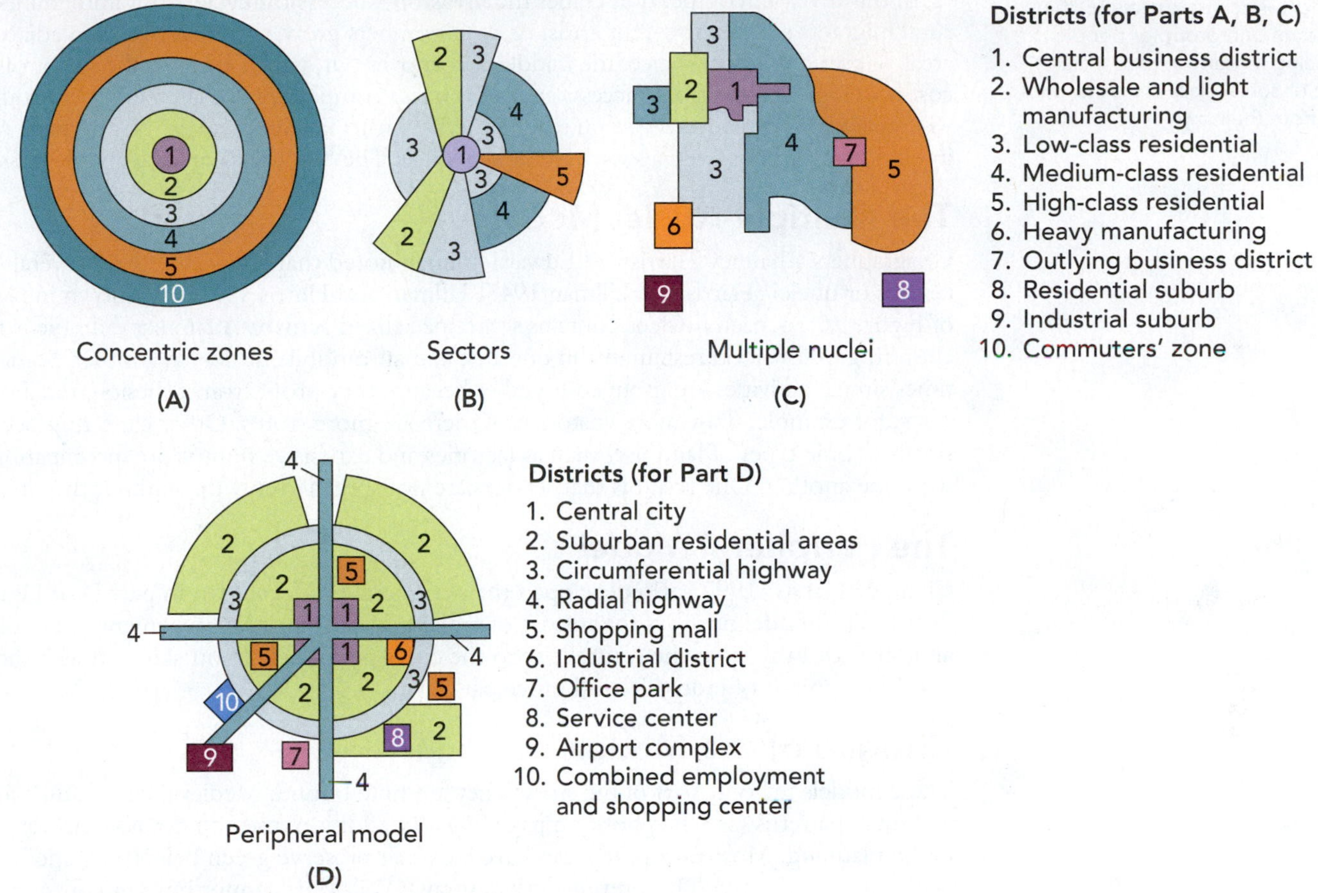

Source: Cousins and Nagpaul 1970; Harris 1997.

The Concentric Zone Model

To explain how cities expand, sociologist Ernest Burgess (1925) proposed a *concentric-zone model.* As shown in part A of Figure 20.14, Burgess noted that a city expands outward from its center. Zone 1 is the central business district. Zone 2, which encircles the downtown area, is in transition. It contains rooming houses and deteriorating housing, which Burgess said breed poverty, disease, and vice. Zone 3 is the area to which thrifty workers have moved in order to escape the zone in transition and yet maintain easy access to their work. Zone 4 contains more expensive apartments, residential hotels, single-family homes, and exclusive areas where the wealthy live. Commuters live in Zone 5, which consists of suburbs or satellite cities that have grown up around transportation routes.

Burgess said that no "city perfectly fits this ideal scheme." Some cities have physical obstructions such as a lake, river, or railroad that cause their expansion to depart from the model. Burgess also noticed another deviation from the model, that businesses were beginning to locate in outlying zones (see Zone 10). This was in 1925. Burgess didn't know it, but he was seeing the beginning of a major shift that led businesses away from downtown areas to suburban shopping malls. Today, these malls account for most of the country's retail sales.

The Sector Model

Sociologist Homer Hoyt (1939, 1971) modified Burgess' model of urban growth. As shown in part B of Figure 20.14, he noted that a concentric zone can contain several sectors—one of working-class housing, another of expensive homes, a third of businesses, and so on—all competing for the same land.

invasion–succession cycle the process of one group of people displacing a group whose racial–ethnic or social class characteristics differ from their own

In this dynamic competition comes the **invasion–succession cycle.** Poor immigrants and rural migrants settle in low-rent areas. As their numbers grow, they spill over into adjacent areas. Upset by their presence, the middle class moves out, which expands the sector of low-cost housing. The invasion–succession cycle is never complete, since later, another group will replace this earlier one. As you read in the Down-to Earth Sociology box on page 601, in Harlem, there has been a switch in the sequence: The "invaders" are the middle class.

The Multiple-Nuclei Model

Geographers Chauncy Harris and Edward Ullman noted that some cities have several centers or nuclei (Harris and Ullman 1945; Ullman and Harris 1970). As shown in part C of Figure 20.14, each nucleus contains some specialized activity. A familiar example is the clustering of fast-food restaurants in one area and automobile dealers in another. Sometimes similar activities are grouped together because they profit from cohesion; retail districts, for example, draw more customers if there are more stores. Other clustering occurs because some types of land use, such as factories and expensive homes, are incompatible with one another. One result is that services are not spread evenly throughout the city.

The Peripheral Model

Chauncy Harris (1997) also developed the peripheral model shown in part D of Figure 20.14. This model portrays the impact of radial highways on the movement of people and services away from the central city to the city's periphery, or outskirts. It also shows the development of industrial and office parks.

Critique of the Models

These models tell only part of the story. They are time bound: Medieval cities didn't follow these patterns (see the photo on page 594). In addition, they do not account for urban planning. Most European cities have laws that preserve green belts (trees and farmlands) around the city. This prevents urban sprawl: Wal-Mart cannot buy land outside the city and put up a store; instead, it must locate in the downtown area with the other stores. Norwich has 250,000 people—yet the city ends abruptly in a green belt where pheasants skitter across plowed fields while sheep graze in verdant meadows (Milbank 1995).

If you were to depend on these models, you would be surprised when you visit the cities of the Least Industrialized Nations. There, the wealthy often claim the inner city, where fine restaurants and other services are readily accessible. Tucked behind walls and protected from public scrutiny, they enjoy luxurious homes and gardens. The poor, in contrast, especially rural migrants, settle in areas outside the city—or, as in the case of El Tiro, featured in the photo essay on pages 596–597, on top of piles of garbage in what used to be the outskirts of a city. The vast movement of rural migrants to the city is the topic of the Cultural Diversity box on the next page.

alienation Marx's term for workers' lack of connection to the product of their labor; caused by workers being assigned repetitive tasks on a small part of a product—this leads to a sense of powerlessness and normlessness; others use the term in the general sense of not feeling a part of something

City Life

20.5 Discuss alienation and community, types of people who live in the city, the norm of noninvolvement, and the diffusion of responsibility.

Life in cities is filled with contrasts. Let's look at two of those contrasts, alienation and community.

Alienation in the City

In a classic essay, sociologist Louis Wirth (1938) noted that urban dwellers live anonymous lives marked by segmented and superficial encounters. This type of relationship, he said, undermines kinship and neighborhood, the traditional bases of social control and feelings of solidarity. Urbanites then grow aloof and indifferent to other people's problems. In short, the price of the personal freedom that the city offers is **alienation**.

Cultural Diversity around the World

Why City Slums Are Better Than the Country: Urbanization in the Least Industrialized Nations

At the bottom of a ravine near Mexico City is a bunch of shacks. Some of the parents have 14 children. "We used to live up there," Señora Gonzalez gestured toward the mountain, "in those caves. Our only hope was one day to have a place to live. And now we do." She smiled with pride at the jerry-built shacks . . . each one had a collection of flowers planted in tin cans. "One day, we hope to extend the water pipes and drainage—perhaps even pave. . . ."

And what was the name of her community? Señora Gonzalez beamed. "Esperanza!" (McDowell 1984:172)

Esperanza means hope in Spanish.

What started as a trickle has become a torrent. In 1930, only one Latin American city had over a million people—now fifty do. The world's cities are growing by more than one million people each week (Moreno et al. 2012). The rural poor are flocking to the cities at such a rate that, as you saw in Figure 20.12 on page 599, the Least Industrialized Nations now contain most of the world's largest cities.

It is difficult for Americans to grasp the depth of the poverty that is the everyday life of hundreds of millions of people across the globe. This man in Cambodia lives in this unused concrete drain pipe.

When migrants move to U.S. cities, they usually settle in rundown housing near the city's center. The wealthy live in suburbs and luxurious city enclaves. Migrants to cities of the Least Industrialized Nations, in contrast, establish illegal squatter settlements outside the city. There, they build shacks from scrap boards, cardboard, and bits of corrugated metal. Even flattened tin cans are scavenged for building material. The squatters enjoy no city facilities—roads, public transportation, water, sewers, or garbage pickup. After thousands of squatters have settled an area, the city reluctantly acknowledges their right to live there and adds bus service and minimal water lines. Hundreds of people use a single spigot. About 5 million of Mexico City's residents live in such squalid conditions, with hundreds of thousands more pouring in each year.

Why this rush to live in the city under such miserable conditions? On the one hand are the "push" factors that come from the breakdown of traditional rural life. More children are surviving because of a safer water supply and modern medicine. As rural populations multiply, the parents no longer have enough land to divide among their children. With neither land nor jobs, there is hunger and despair. On the other hand are the "pull" factors that draw people to the cities—jobs, schools, housing, and even a more stimulating life.

How will the Least Industrialized Nations adjust to this vast migration? Removing the migrants by force doesn't work. Authorities in Brazil, Guatemala, Venezuela, and other countries have sent in the police and even the army to evict the settlers. After a violent dispersal, the settlers return—and others stream in. The roads, water and sewer lines, electricity, schools, and public facilities must be built. But these poor countries don't have the resources to build them. As wrenching as the adjustment will be, these countries must—and somehow will—make the transition. They have no choice.

For Your Consideration

➜ What solutions do you see for this river of migration to the cities of the Least Industrialized Nations?

Alienation takes many forms, such as the "road rage" that makes the evening news. You can be following your usual routine, such as driving home from work, when the unexpected erupts, changing your life forever.

In crowded traffic on a bridge going into Detroit, Deletha Word bumped the car ahead of her. The damage was minor, but the driver, Martell Welch, jumped out. Cursing, he pulled Deletha from her car, pushed her onto the hood, and began beating her. Martell's friends got out to watch. One of them held Deletha down while Martell took a car jack and smashed Deletha's car. Scared for her life, Deletha broke away, fleeing to the bridge's railing. Martell and his friends taunted her, shouting, "Jump, bitch, jump!" Deletha plunged to her death (Stokes and Zeman 1995). Welch was convicted of second-degree murder and sentenced to 16 to 40 years in prison.

This certainly is not an ordinary situation, but anyone who lives in a large city knows that even a minor traffic accident can explode into road rage. And you never know who that stranger in the mall—or even next door—really is. The most common reason for impersonality and self-interest is not fear of danger, however, but the impossibility of dealing with crowds as individuals and the need to tune out many of the stimuli that come buzzing in from the bustle of the city (Berman et al. 2008).

Community in the City

Read on **MySocLab**
Document: Life and Death in the City: Neighborhoods in Context

I don't want to give the impression that the city is inevitably alienating. Far from it. Many people find community in the city. There are good reasons that millions around the globe are rushing to the world's cities. And there is another aspect of the attack on Deletha Word. After Deletha went over the railing, two men jumped in after her, risking injury and their own lives in a futile attempt to save her.

Sociologist Herbert Gans, a symbolic interactionist who did participant observation in the West End of Boston, was so impressed with the area's sense of community that he titled his book *The Urban Villagers* (1962). In this book, which has become a classic in sociology, Gans said:

Read on **MySocLab**
Document: Community Building: Steps Toward a Good Society

After a few weeks of living in the West End, my observations—and my perceptions of the area—changed drastically. The search for an apartment quickly indicated that the individual units were usually in much better condition than the outside or the hallways of the buildings. Subsequently, in wandering through the West End, and in using it as a resident, I developed a kind of selective perception, in which my eye focused only on those parts of the area that were actually being used by people. Vacant buildings and boarded-up stores were no longer so visible, and the totally deserted alleys or streets were outside the set of paths normally traversed, either by myself or by the West Enders. The dirt and spilled-over garbage remained, but, since they were concentrated in street gutters and empty lots, they were not really harmful to anyone and thus were not as noticeable as during my initial observations.

Since much of the area's life took place on the street, faces became familiar very quickly. I met my neighbors on the stairs and in front of my building. And, once a shopping pattern developed, I saw the same storekeepers frequently, as well as the area's "characters" who wandered through the streets everyday on a fairly regular route and schedule. In short, the exotic quality of the stores and the residents also wore off as I became used to seeing them.

In short, Gans found a *community*, people who identified with the area and with one another. Its residents enjoyed networks of friends and acquaintances. Despite the area's substandard buildings, most West Enders had chosen to live here. *To them, this was a low-rent district, not a slum.*

Most West Enders had low-paying, insecure jobs. Other residents were elderly, living on small pensions. Unlike the middle class, these people didn't care about their "address." The area's inconveniences were something they put up with in exchange for cheap housing. In general, they were content with their neighborhood.

Who Lives in the City?

Whether people find alienation or community in the city depends on whom you are talking about. As with almost everything in life, social class is especially significant. The greater security enjoyed by the city's wealthier residents reduces alienation and increases satisfaction with city life (Santos 2009). There also are different types of urban dwellers, each with distinctive experiences. As we review the five types that Gans (1962, 1968, 1991) identified, try to see where you fit.

The Cosmopolites. These are the intellectuals, professionals, artists, and entertainers who have been attracted to the city. They value its conveniences and cultural benefits.

The Singles. Usually in their early 20s to early 30s, the singles have settled in the city temporarily. For them, urban life is a stage in their life course. Businesses and services, such as singles bars and apartment complexes, cater to their needs and desires. After they marry, many move to the suburbs.

The Ethnic Villagers. Feeling a sense of identity, working-class members of the same ethnic group band together. They form tightly knit neighborhoods that resemble villages and small towns. Family- and peer-oriented, they try to isolate themselves from the dangers and problems of urban life.

The Deprived. Destitute, emotionally disturbed, and having little income, education, or work skills, the deprived live in neighborhoods that are more like urban jungles than urban villages. Some of them stalk those jungles in search of prey. Neither predator nor prey has much hope for anything better in life—for themselves or for their children.

The Trapped. These people don't live in the area by choice, either. Some were trapped when an ethnic group "invaded" their neighborhood and they could not afford to move. Others found themselves trapped in a downward spiral. They started life in a higher social class, but because of personal problems—mental or physical illness or addiction to alcohol or other drugs—they drifted downward. There also are the elderly who are trapped by poverty and not wanted elsewhere. Like the deprived, the trapped suffer from high rates of assault, mugging, and rape.

Where do you think these people fit in Gans' classification of urban dwellers?

Critique. You probably noticed this inadequacy in Gans' categories, that you can be both a cosmopolite and a single. You might have noticed also that you can be these two things and an ethnic villager as well. Gans also seems to have missed an important type of city dweller—the people living in the city who don't stand out in any way. They work and marry there and quietly raise their families. They aren't cosmopolites, singles, or ethnic villagers. Neither are they deprived nor trapped. Perhaps we can call these the "Just Plain Folks."

In Sum: Within the city's rich mosaic of social diversity, not all urban dwellers experience the city in the same way. Each group has its own lifestyle, and each has distinct experiences. Some people welcome the city's cultural diversity and mix with several groups. Others find community by retreating into the security of ethnic enclaves. Still others feel trapped and deprived. To them, the city is an urban jungle. It poses threats to their health and safety, and their lives are filled with despair.

The Norm of Noninvolvement and the Diffusion of Responsibility

Tuning Out: The Norm of Noninvolvement. To avoid intrusions from strangers, urban dwellers follow a *norm of noninvolvement*.

> *To do this, we sometimes use props such as newspapers to shield ourselves from others and to indicate our inaccessibility for interaction. In effect, we learn to "tune others out." In this regard, we might see the [iPod] as the quintessential urban prop in that it allows us to be tuned in and tuned out at the same time. It is a device that allows us*

to enter our own private world and thereby effectively to close off encounters with others. The use of such devices protects our "personal space," along with our body demeanor and facial expression (the passive "mask" or even scowl that persons adopt on subways). (Karp et al. 1991)

Social psychologists John Darley and Bibb Latané (1968) ran the series of experiments featured in Chapter 6 (page 160–161). They uncovered the *diffusion of responsibility*—the more bystanders there are, the less likely people are to help. As a group grows, people's sense of responsibility becomes diffused, with each person assuming that *another* will do the responsible thing. "With these other people here, it is not *my* responsibility," they reason.

The diffusion of responsibility helps to explain why people can ignore the plight of others. Those who did nothing to intervene in the attack on Deletha Word were *not* uncaring people. Each felt that others might do something. Then, too, there was the norm of noninvolvement—helpful for getting people through everyday city life but, unfortunately, dysfunctional in some crucial situations.

As mentioned in Chapter 6, laboratory experiments can give insight into human behavior—but they can also woefully miss the mark. Recall the photo sequence I took in Vienna of the man who fell in Vienna, Austria (see page 162). That these people were strangers who were simply passing one another on the sidewalk didn't stop them from immediately helping the man who tripped and fell. We carry many norms within us, some of which can trump the diffusion of responsibility and norm of noninvolvement.

20.6 Explain the effects of suburbanization, disinvestment and deindustrialization, and the potential of urban revitalization.

Urban Problems and Social Policy

To close this chapter, let's look at the primary reasons that U.S. cities have declined, and then consider how they can be revitalized.

As cities evolve, so does architecture. This photo is of the Exhibition and Conference Center in Glasgow, Scotland.

Suburbanization

We have discussed the transition to the suburbs. The U.S. city has been the loser in this transition. As people moved out of the city, businesses and jobs followed. Insurance companies and others that employ white-collar workers were the first to move their offices to the suburbs. They were soon followed by manufacturers and their blue-collar workers. This process has continued so relentlessly that today, twice as many manufacturing jobs are located in the suburbs as in the city (Palen 2012). This transition hit the city's tax base hard, leaving a budget squeeze that affected not only parks, zoos, libraries, and museums but also the city's basic services—its schools, streets, sewer and water systems, and police and fire departments.

Left behind were people who had no choice but to stay in the city. As we reviewed in Chapter 12, sociologist William Julius Wilson says that this exodus transformed the inner city into a ghetto. Individuals who lacked training and skills were trapped by poverty, unemployment, and welfare dependency. Also left behind were those who prey on others through street crime. The term *ghetto*, says Wilson, "suggests that a fundamental social transformation has taken place ... that groups represented by this term are collectively different from and much more socially isolated from those that lived in these communities in earlier years" (quoted in Karp et al. 1991).

City versus Suburb. Suburbanites want the city to keep its problems to itself. They reject proposals to share suburbia's revenues with the city and oppose measures that would allow urban and suburban governments joint control over what has become a contiguous mass of people and businesses (Innes et al. 2011). They do not mind going to the city to work, or venturing there on weekends for the diversions it offers, but they do not want to help pay the city's expenses.

It is likely that the mounting bill ultimately will come due, however, and that suburbanites will have to pay for their uncaring attitude toward the urban disadvantaged. Sociologist David Karp and colleagues (1991) put it this way:

> *It may be that suburbs can insulate themselves from the problems of central cities, at least for the time being. In the long run, though, there will be a steep price to pay for the failure of those better off to care compassionately for those at the bottom of society.*

Our occasional urban riots may be part of that bill—perhaps just the down payment.

Suburban Flight. In some places, the bill is coming due quickly. As they age, some suburbs are becoming mirror images of the city that their residents so despise. Suburban crime, the flight of the middle class, a shrinking tax base, and eroding services create a spiraling sense of insecurity, stimulating more middle-class flight (Katz and Bradley 2009; Palen 2012). Figure 20-15 illustrates this process, which is new to the urban–suburban scene.

redlining a decision by the officers of a financial institution not to make loans in a particular area

disinvestment the withdrawal of investments by financial institutions, which seals the fate of an urban area

deindustrialization the process of industries moving out of a country or region

Disinvestment and Deindustrialization

As the cities' tax bases shrank and their services declined, neighborhoods deteriorated and banks began **redlining**: Afraid of loans going bad, bankers would draw a line around a problem area on a map and refuse to make loans for housing or businesses there (Ropiequet et al. 2012). This **disinvestment** (withdrawal of investment) pushed these areas into further decline. Youth gangs, muggings, and murders are common in these areas, but good jobs are not. All are woven into this process of disinvestment.

The globalization of capitalism has also left a heavy mark on U.S. cities. As we reviewed in Chapter 14, to compete in the global market, many U.S. companies moved their factories to countries where labor costs are lower. This process, called **deindustrialization**, made U.S. industries more competitive, but it eliminated millions of U.S. manufacturing jobs. Lacking training in the new information technologies, many poor people are locked out of the benefits of the postindustrial economy that is engulfing the United States. Left behind in the inner cities, many live lives of quiet and not-so-quiet despair.

Watch on **MySocLab**
Video: Challenges Facing Cities

FIGURE 20.15 Urban Growth and Urban Flight

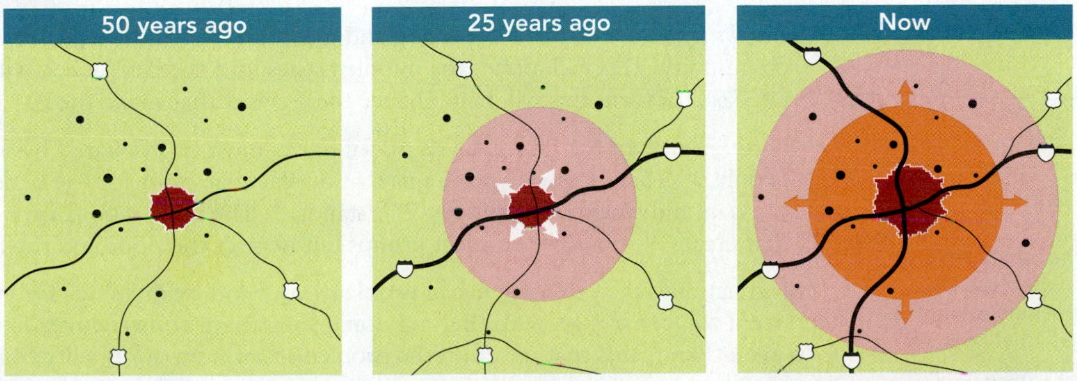

At first, the city and surrounding villages grew independently.

As city dwellers fled urban decay, they created a ring of suburbs.

As middle-class flight continues outward, urban problems are arriving in the outer rings.

U.S. suburbs were once unplanned, rambling affairs that took irregular shapes as people moved away from the city. Today's suburbs are planned to precise details even before the first foundation is laid. This photo is of a suburb in Maryland.

The Potential of Urban Revitalization

Social policy usually takes one of two forms. The first is to tear down and rebuild—something that is fancifully termed **urban renewal**. The result is the renewal of an area—but *not* for the benefit of its inhabitants. Stadiums, high-rise condos, luxury hotels, and boutiques replace run-down, cheap housing. Outpriced, the area's inhabitants are displaced into adjacent areas.

The second is to attract businesses to an area by offering them reduced taxes. This program, called **enterprise zones**, usually fails because most businesses refuse to locate in high-crime areas. They know that the high costs of security and the losses from crime can eat up the tax savings.

A highly promising form of the enterprise zone, called the *Federal Empowerment Zone*, is the opposite of disinvestment. It targets the redevelopment of an area by adding low-interest loans to the tax breaks. The renaissance of Harlem, featured in the Down-to-Earth Sociology box on page 601, was stimulated by designating Harlem a Federal Empowerment Zone. The low-interest loans brought grocery stores, dry cleaners, and video stores, attracting the middle class. As they moved back in, the demand for more specialty shops followed. A self-feeding cycle of investment and hope replaced the self-feeding cycle of despair and crime that accompanies disinvestment.

If they become top agenda items of the government, U.S. cities can be turned into safe and decent places to live and enjoy. This will require not just huge sums of money but also creative urban planning. That we are beginning to see success in Harlem, Chicago's North Town, and even in formerly riot-torn East Los Angeles indicates that we can accomplish this transformation.

Public Sociology. Replacing old buildings with new ones is certainly not the answer. Instead, we need to do *public sociology* (discussed on page 20) and apply sociological principles to build community. Here are three guiding principles suggested by sociologist William Flanagan (1990):

> *Scale.* Regional and national planning is necessary. Local jurisdictions, with their many rivalries, competing goals, and limited resources, end up with a hodgepodge of mostly unworkable solutions.
>
> *Livability.* Cities must be appealing and meet human needs, especially the need for community. This will attract the middle classes into the city, which will increase its tax base. In turn, this will help finance the services that make the city more livable.
>
> *Social justice.* In the final analysis, social policy must be evaluated by how it affects people. "Urban renewal" programs that displace the poor for the benefit of the middle class and wealthy do not pass this standard. The same would apply to solutions that create "livability" for select groups but neglect the poor and the homeless.

Most actions taken to solve urban problems are window dressings for politicians who want to *appear* as though they are doing something constructive. The solution is to avoid Band-Aids that cover up the problems that hurt our quality of life and to address their *root* causes—poverty, poor schools, crimes of violence, lack of jobs, and an inadequate tax base to provide the amenities that enhance our quality of life and attract people to the city.

urban renewal the rehabilitation of a rundown area, which usually results in the displacement of the poor who are living in that area

enterprise zone the use of economic incentives in a designated area to encourage investment

CHAPTER 20 Summary and Review

A Planet with No Space for Enjoying Life?

20.1 Contrast the views of the New Malthusians and Anti-Malthusians on population growth and the food supply; explain why people are starving.

What debate did Thomas Malthus initiate?

In 1798, Thomas Malthus analyzed the surge in Europe's population. He concluded that the world's population will outstrip its food supply. The debate between today's New Malthusians and those who disagree, the Anti-Malthusians, continues. Pp. 579–583.

Why are people starving?

Starvation is not due to a lack of food in the world: There is now *more* food for each person in the entire world than there was fifty years ago. Rather, starvation is the result of a maldistribution of food, which is primarily due to drought and civil war. Pp. 583–586.

Population Growth

20.2 Explain why the Least Industrialized Nations have so many children, consequences of rapid population growth, population pyramids, the three demographic variables, and problems in forecasting population growth.

Why do people in the poor nations have so many children?

In the Least Industrialized Nations, children are often viewed as gifts from God. In addition, they cost little to rear, contribute to the family income at an early age, and provide the parents' social security. These are powerful motivations to have large families. Pp. 586–589.

What are the three demographic variables?

To compute population growth, demographers use *fertility*, *mortality*, and *migration*. They follow the **basic demographic equation**, births minus deaths plus net migration equals the growth rate. Pp. 589–591.

Why is forecasting population difficult?

A nation's growth rate is affected by changing conditions—from economic cycles, wars, and famines to industrialization and government policies. Pp. 591–593.

The Development of Cities

20.3 Summarize the development of cities, the process of urbanization, U.S. urban patterns, and the rural rebound.

How are cities related to farming and the Industrial Revolution?

Cities can develop only if there is an agricultural surplus large enough to free people from food production. The primary impetus to the development of cities was the invention of the plow. After the Industrial Revolution stimulated rapid transportation and communication, cities grew quickly. Today, **urbanization** is so extensive that some cities have become **metropolises**, dominating the areas adjacent to them. Some metropolises spill over into each other, forming a **megalopolis**. Pp. 594–602.

What is the rural rebound?

As people flee cities and suburbs, the population of many U.S. rural counties is growing. This is a fundamental departure from a trend that had been in place for a couple of hundred years. P. 602.

Models of Urban Growth

20.4 Compare the models of urban growth.

What models of urban growth have been proposed?

The primary models are concentric zone, sector, multiple-nuclei, and peripheral. These models fail to account for ancient and medieval cities, many European cities, cities in the Least Industrialized Nations, and urban planning. Pp. 602–606.

City Life

20.5 Discuss alienation and community, types of people who live in the city, the norm of noninvolvement, and the diffusion of responsibility.

Who lives in the city?

Some people experience **alienation** in the city; others find **community** in it. What people find depends largely on their backgrounds and urban networks. Five types of people who live in cities are cosmopolites, singles, ethnic villagers, the deprived, and the trapped. Pp. 606–608.

Urban Problems and Social Policy

20.6 Explain the effects of suburbanization, disinvestment and deindustrialization, and the potential of urban revitalization.

Why have U.S. cities declined?

Three primary reasons for the decline of U.S. cities are **suburbanization** (as people moved to the suburbs, the tax base of cities eroded and services deteriorated), **disinvestment** (banks withdrew their financing), and **deindustrialization** (which caused a loss of jobs). Pp. 608–609.

What social policy can salvage U.S. cities?

Three guiding principles for developing urban social policy are scale, livability, and social justice. P. 610.

Thinking Critically about Chapter 20

1. Do you think that the world is threatened by a population explosion? Use data from this chapter to support your position.
2. Why do people find alienation or community in the city?
3. What are the causes of urban problems, and what can we do to solve those problems?

CHAPTER 21

Collective Behavior and Social Movements

Listen to **Chapter 21** on **MySocLab**

Learning Objectives

After you have read this chapter, you should be able to:

21.1 Explain what early theorists meant about crowds transforming people; summarize the 5 stages of an acting crowd. (p. 614)

21.2 Explain why sociologists today view crowds as rational and what is meant by emergent norms. (p. 616)

21.3 Describe the forms of collective behavior: riots, rumors, panics, mass hysteria, moral panics, fads and fashions, and urban legends. (p. 618)

21.4 Analyze the types and tactics of social movements; include the use of propaganda. (p. 627)

21.5 To explain why people join social movements, use relative deprivation theory, declining privilege theory, and morality and ideology; include agents provocateur. (p. 631)

21.6 Explain why most social movements fail, why some succeed, and why some continue for decades. (p. 633)

The news spread like wildfire. *A police officer had been killed. In just twenty minutes, the white population was armed and heading for the cabin. Men and mere boys, some not more than 12 years old, carried rifles, shotguns, and pistols.*

The mob, now swollen to about four hundred, surrounded the log cabin. Tying a rope around the man's neck, they dragged him to the center of town. While the men argued about the best way to kill him, the women and children shouted their advice—some to hang him, others to burn him alive.

Someone pulled a large wooden box out of a store and placed it in the center of the street. Others filled it with straw. Then they lifted the man, the rope still around his neck, and shoved him head first into the box. One of the men poured oil over him. Another lit a match.

As the flames shot upward, the man managed to lift himself out of the box, his body a mass of flames. Trying to shield his face and eyes from the fire, he ran the length of the rope, about twenty feet, when someone yelled, "Shoot!" In an instant, dozens of shots rang out. Men and boys walked to the lifeless body and emptied their guns into it.

> "I could smell the poor man's burning flesh. No one tried to hide their identity."

They dragged the man's body back to the burning box, then piled on more boxes from the stores, and poured oil over them. Each time someone threw on more oil and the flames shot upward, the crowd roared shouts of approval.

Standing about seventy-five feet away, I could smell the poor man's burning flesh. No one tried to hide their identity. I could clearly see town officials help in the burning. The inquest, dutifully held by the coroner, concluded that the man met death "at the hands of an enraged mob unknown to the jury." What else could he conclude? Any jury from this town would include men who had participated in the man's death.

They dug a little hole at the edge of the street, and dumped in it the man's ashes and what was left of his body.

The man's name was Sam Pettie, known by everybody to be quiet and inoffensive. I can't mention my name. If I did, I would be committing suicide.

Based on a May 1914 letter to The Crisis

Collective Behavior

Why did people in this little town "go mad"? These men—and the women who shouted suggestions about how to kill the captured man—were ordinary, law-abiding citizens. Even some of the "pillars of the community" joined in the vicious killing of Sam Pettie, who may have been innocent.

Lynching is a form of **collective behavior**, actions by a group of people who bypass the usual norms governing their behavior and do something unusual (Turner and Killian 1987; Harper and Leicht 2002). Collective behavior is a broad term. It includes not only such violent acts as lynchings and riots but also rumors, panics, fads, and fashions. Before examining its specific forms, let's look at theories that seek to explain collective behavior.

collective behavior extraordinary activities carried out by groups of people; includes lynchings, rumors, panics, urban legends, fads, and fashions

Early Explanations: The Transformation of People

21.1 Explain what early theorists meant about crowds transforming people; summarize the 5 stages of an acting crowd.

When people can't figure something out, they often resort to using "madness" as an explanation. People may say, "She went 'off her rocker'—that's why she drove her car into the river." "He must have 'gone nuts,' or he wouldn't have shot into the crowd."

Early explanations of collective behavior were linked to such assumptions. Let's look at how these ideas developed.

How Crowds Change People

The study of collective behavior began when Charles Mackay (1814–1889), a British journalist, noticed that "country folks," who ordinarily are reasonable sorts of people, sometimes "went mad" and did "disgraceful and violent things" when they formed a crowd. The best explanation Mackay (1852) could come up with was that people had a "herd mentality"—they were like a herd of cows that suddenly stampede.

About fifty years later, Gustave LeBon (1841–1931), a French psychologist, built on this initial idea. In an 1895 book, LeBon stressed how people feel anonymous in crowds, less accountable for what they do. Some even develop feelings of invincibility and come to think that they can do almost anything. A **collective mind** develops, he said, and people are swept up by almost any suggestion. Then contagion, something like mass hypnosis, takes over, releasing the destructive instincts that society so carefully represses.

These students in Brazil, who are tearing down a traffic light, are participating in a national protest against the government. If you were demonstrating, how do you think you might get "carried away" and do things you wouldn't usually do?

Robert Park (1864–1944), a U.S. sociologist who studied in Germany and wrote a 1904 dissertation on the nature of the crowd, was influenced by LeBon (McPhail 1991). After Park joined the faculty at the University of Chicago, he added the idea of social unrest. He said,

> *Social unrest . . . is transmitted from one individual to another . . . so that the manifestations of discontent in A [are] communicated to B, and from B reflected back to A. (Park and Burgess 1921)*

Watch on **MySocLab**
Video: Grievances, Anger, and Hope

Park used the term **circular reaction** to refer to this back-and-forth communication between members of a crowd. He said that circular reaction creates a "collective impulse" that comes to "dominate all members of the crowd." If you think that Park's "collective impulse" sounds like LeBon's "collective mind," you are right. They are the same thing. Park's slightly different term did not change the basic idea at all.

The Acting Crowd

Herbert Blumer (1900–1987), who studied under Park, synthesized LeBon's and Park's ideas. As you can see from Figure 21.1 on the next page, Blumer (1939) identified five stages that precede what he called an **acting crowd**, an excited group that moves toward a goal. This model still dominates today's police manuals on crowd behavior (McPhail 1989). Let's apply it to the killing of Sam Pettie.

1. *A background of tension or unrest.* At the root of collective behavior is a background condition of tension or unrest. In the early 1900s when Sam Pettie was killed, the country was industrializing and southern life was in upheaval. In their search for jobs, millions of Americans were moving from farm to city and from South to North. Left behind were many poor, rural southerners, white and black, who faced a bleak future. In addition, African Americans were questioning the legitimacy of their low status and deprivation.
2. *Exciting event.* An exciting event occurs, one so startling that people become preoccupied with it. In this instance, that event was the killing of a police officer.
3. *Milling.* Next comes **milling**, people standing or walking around, talking about the exciting event. A circular reaction then sets in. Picking up cues about the "right"

collective mind Gustave LeBon's term for the tendency of people in a crowd to feel, think, and act in extraordinary ways

circular reaction Robert Park's term for a back-and-forth communication among the members of a crowd whereby a "collective impulse" is transmitted

acting crowd an excited group of people who move toward a goal

milling a crowd standing or walking around as they talk excitedly about some event

FIGURE 21.1 Blumer's Model of How an Acting Crowd Develops

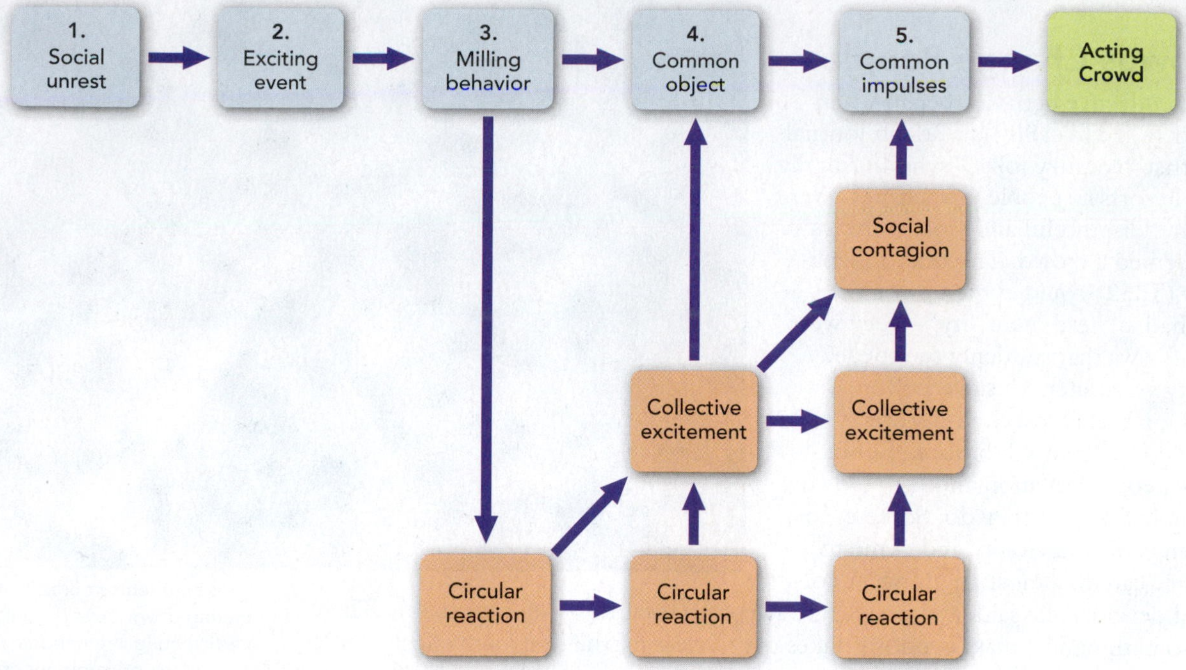

Source: Based on McPhail 1991:11.

way to think and feel about the event, people reinforce them in one another. Members of the mob that killed Sam Pettie milled only a short time, but while they did, they became increasingly agitated as they discussed the officer's death.

4. *A common object of attention.* As people's attention becomes riveted on some aspect of the event, they get caught up in collective excitement. In this case, people's attention turned to Sam Pettie. Someone may have said that he had been talking to the officer or that they had been arguing.
5. *Common impulses.* People get the feeling that they are in agreement about what should be done. These common impulses are stimulated by *social contagion*, a sense of excitement that is passed from one person to another. In this instance, people concluded that only the killer's immediate death would be adequate vengeance.

Acting crowds aren't always negative or destructive, as this one was. In Spain, crowds of government employees, including firefighters, have demonstrated against massive layoffs (Emsden and Dalton 2013). Nor are all acting crowds concerned about serious matters: Students having a food fight in a cafeteria are also an acting crowd.

21.2 Explain why sociologists today view crowds as rational and what is meant by emergent norms.

The Contemporary View: The Rationality of the Crowd

If we were to see a lynching—or a screaming mob—most of us might agree with LeBon that some sort of "madness" had swept over the crowd. Sociologists today, however, point out that beneath the chaotic surface, crowds are actually quite rational (Martin et al. 2009; Franzosi et al. 2012). They point out that crowd participants take deliberate steps to reach some goal. As sociologist Clark McPhail (1991) says, even a lynch mob is cooperative—someone gets the rope while others hold the victim, some tie the knot, and others hoist the body. This is exactly what you saw in Pettie's execution—the men working together: the rope, the boxes, the straw, and the oil.

Watch on **MySocLab**
Video: Collective Behavior and Social Movements: The Basics

The Minimax Strategy

A general principle of human behavior is that we try to minimize our costs and maximize our rewards. Sociologist Richard Berk (1974) called this a **minimax strategy**. The fewer costs and the more rewards we anticipate from something, the more likely we are to do it. For example, if we think that others will approve an act, the chances increase that we will do it. Whether someone is yelling for the referee's blood after a bad call in a football game or shouting for real blood as a member of a lynch mob, this principle applies. In short, whether in the fun of a video game with friends or the wrath of a mob, the principles of human behavior remain the same.

Emergent Norms

Since collective behavior is unusual behavior, however, could it also involve unusual norms? Sociologists Ralph Turner and Lewis Killian (1987) use the term **emergent norms** to express this idea. They point out that life usually proceeds pretty much as we expect it to, making our usual norms adequate for dealing with everyday events. If something disrupts our usual life, however, ordinary norms may not cover the new situation. To deal with new events, new norms may emerge. People may even develop novel definitions of right and wrong, feeling that the new circumstances justify actions that they otherwise would consider wrong.

To understand how new norms emerge, we need to keep in mind that not everyone in a crowd shares the same point of view (Surowiecki 2005; Wilkinson 2009). As Turner and Killian (1987) point out, crowds have at least five kinds of participants:

1. The *ego-involved* feel a personal stake in the unusual event.
2. The *concerned* also have a personal interest in the event, but less so than the ego-involved.
3. The *insecure* care little about the matter; they join the crowd because it gives them a sense of power, security, or belonging.
4. The *curious spectators* also care little about the issue; they are simply curious about what is going on.
5. The *exploiters* don't care about the event; they use it for their own purposes, such as selling food or T-shirts. For them, a rock concert would serve just as well.

The "ego-involved" set the crowd on a course of action. Some make suggestions about what should be done; others simply start doing something. As the "concerned" join in, they, too, influence the crowd. If things get heated up, the "insecure" and the "curious spectators" may also join in. Although the "exploiters" are unlikely to participate, they do lend passive support to the crowd. A common mood completes the stage for new norms to emerge: Activities that are "not okay" in everyday life now may seem "okay"—whether they involve throwing bottles at the cops or shouting obscenities at the college president.

To consider how new norms emerge is to see that collective behavior is *rational.* For a suggested action to be accepted, for example, it must match the crowd's predispositions. If not, it will be rejected. You can see that this current view is a far cry from the earlier interpretation that crowds transform people, driving them out of their minds.

How Sociologist Study Collective Behavior

From this review of crowds and emergent norms, it is probably apparent to you that sociologists analyze collective behavior the same way they do other forms of behavior. And this is precisely what they do. They ask their usual questions about interaction, such as, How do people influence one another? What is the significance of the participants' age, gender, race–ethnicity, and social class? How did the participants perceive the situation? How did their perceptions get translated into action? In other words, sociologists view collective behavior as the actions of ordinary people who are responding to extraordinary situations.

minimax strategy Richard Berk's term for the efforts people make to minimize their costs and maximize their rewards

emergent norms Ralph Turner and Lewis Killian's term for the idea that people develop new norms to cope with a new situation; used to explain crowd behavior

riot violent crowd behavior directed at people and property

21.3 Describe the forms of collective behavior: riots, rumors, panics, mass hysteria, moral panics, fads and fashions, and urban legends.

Forms of Collective Behavior

In addition to lynchings, collective behavior includes riots, rumors, panics, mass hysteria, moral panics, fads, fashions, and urban legends. Let's look at each.

Riots

A passerby had videotaped white police officers in Los Angeles as they beat an African American with their nightsticks. Television stations around the United States—and the world—broadcast the pictures to stunned audiences.

The officers were put on trial for beating the man identified as Rodney King. With such dramatic evidence, how could the verdict be anything but guilty? Yet a jury consisting of eleven whites and one Asian American found the officers innocent of using excessive force. Within minutes of the verdict, angry crowds began to gather in Los Angeles. That night, mobs set fire to businesses, and looting and arson began in earnest. The rioting spread to other cities, including Atlanta, Tampa, Las Vegas, and even Madison, Wisconsin. Whites and Koreans were favorite targets of violence.

Americans sat transfixed before their television sets as they saw parts of Los Angeles go up in flames. Looters lugged television sets and sofas in full view of the Los Angeles Police, which took no steps to stop them. Seared into the public's collective consciousness was the sight of Reginald Denny, a 36-year-old white truck driver who had been yanked from his truck. As Denny sat dazed in the street, Damian Williams, laughing, broke the truck driver's skull with a piece of concrete.

In this photo from the Los Angeles riots of 1992, can you identify emergent norms?

On the third night, after 4,000 fires had been set and more than thirty people killed, President George H. W. Bush announced that the U.S. Department of Justice would pursue federal charges against the police officers. He ordered the Seventh Infantry, SWAT teams, and the FBI into Los Angeles. He also federalized the California National Guard and placed it under the command of General Colin Powell, the chairman of the Joint Chiefs of Staff. Rodney King went on television and tearfully pleaded for peace.

The Los Angeles riot was the bloodiest since the Civil War. Before it was over, fifty-one people lost their lives, thousands of businesses were burned, and about $1 billion of property was destroyed. Two of the police officers were later sentenced to two years in prison, and King was awarded $3.8 million in damages. (Rose 1992; Stevens and Lubman 1992; Cannon 1998; Hunt 2012)

Frustration and anger precede a **riot**, violent crowd behavior directed at people and property. These *background conditions* often center around a sense of injustice. Especially frustrating is being singled out by the police for the crime of "driving while black," as some victims put it. A *precipitating event* can bring these pent-up feelings to a boiling point, and they erupt in collective violence. These background conditions preceded the Los Angeles riot. The jury's verdict was the precipitating event.

Participants in Riots. The deprived, of course, participate in riots. But so do others. The first outbursts over the Rodney King verdict came from stable working-class neighborhoods, not the poorest ones. Similarly, after the assassination of Dr. Martin Luther King, Jr., in 1968, even people with good jobs rioted (McPhail 1991). Why would middle-class people participate in riots? The answer is the same, says sociologist Victor Rodríguez (1994): frustration and anger. Minorities with good jobs and middle-class lifestyles can also be treated as second-class citizens. The right precipitating event can bring their resentments to the surface.

Opportunists also participate in riots. These participants aren't smoldering over their situation in life, nor do they feel outrage about the precipitating event. For them, a riot is handy. It gives them the chance to participate in something exciting. They even get to loot stores. This is likely the type of participant shown in the photo on the page to the left.

In Sum: *The event that precipitates a riot is important, but so is the riot's general context.* The precipitating event is the match that lights the fuel, but the fuel is anger, resentment, and tension. To be set ablaze, this fuel takes but a match, such as the Rodney King verdict. Opportunists participate for other reasons.

Rumors

"I felt as though I had entrusted my kids to pedophiles," said Ann Runge, a mother of eight (Bannon 1995). What set her off? She had just learned that the Magic Kingdom was giving obscene, subliminal messages to children. This would bother any parent—and look at the examples:

> *In* Aladdin, *the title character murmurs, "All good children, take off your clothes."*
>
> *In* The Lion King, *Simba, the lion star, stirs up a cloud of dust that spells S-E-X.*

Rumor is unverified information that one person passes to another. Rumors thrive on ambiguity. They fill in missing information (Fine and Ellis 2010; DiFonzo et al. 2013). When Disney officials heard this rumor about their movies, they knew they had to squelch it. The company reported that Aladdin really says, "Scat, good tiger, take off and go." The line is hard to understand, though, and its ambiguity lets people hear what they want to hear, even to insist that the line is an invitation to a teenage orgy. Similar ambiguity remains with Simba's dust.

Most rumors are short-lived. They arise in a situation of ambiguity, only to dissipate when they are replaced by factual information—or by another rumor. Occasionally, however, a rumor has a long life. Let's look at one that probably will strike you as rather strange.

> *In the eighteenth and nineteenth centuries, for no known reason, healthy people would grow weak and slowly waste away. People said they had consumption (now called tuberculosis). They were terrified as they saw their loved ones wither into shells of their former selves. No one knew when the disease would strike or who its next victim would be.*
>
> *Within this terrifying context arose a terrifying rumor: The dead had turned into vampire-like beings. At night, these undead came out of their graves and drained the life out of the living. To kill these ghoulish undead, people began to sneak into cemeteries and dig up bodies. They would remove the leg bones and place them crossed on the skeleton's chest. They would lay the skull at the feet, forming a skull and crossbones. They would then rebury the remains. In New England, the rumors and "killing the undead" continued off and on until the 1890s. (Sledzik and Bellantoni 1994)*

Why do rumors thrive? Besides ambiguity, importance and source are significant. Rumors deal with subjects that are important to people. The information that clarifies the ambiguity is thought to have come from a credible source. An office rumor may be preceded by "Jane overheard the boss say that . . ."

Rumors are killed by facts. But if something important remains unexplained, it provides fertile ground for rumor. The New Englanders speculated about why their loved ones wasted away. Their conclusion seems bizarre to us, but for them, it provided answers to bewildering events. The Disney rumor may have arisen from fears that the moral fabric of modern society is decaying.

Most rumors are short-lived and of little consequence. But they can be highly significant. The rumor you will read about in the Down-to-Earth Sociology box on the next page led to the destruction of a community.

rumor unfounded information spread among people

Down-to-Earth Sociology

Rumors and Riots: An Eyewitness Account of the Tulsa Riot

In 1921, a race riot ripped Tulsa, Oklahoma, apart. And it all began with a rumor (Gates 2004). At this time, Tulsa's black community was vibrant and prosperous. Many blacks owned their own businesses and competed successfully with whites. Then on May 31, everything changed after a black man was accused of assaulting a white girl.

Buck Colbert Franklin (Franklin and Franklin 1997), a black attorney in Tulsa at the time, was there. Here is what he says:

> *Hundreds of men with drawn guns were approaching from every direction, as far I could see as I stood at the steps of my office, and I was immediately arrested and taken to one of the many detention camps. Even then, airplanes were circling overhead dropping explosives upon the buildings that had been looted, and big trucks were hauling all sorts of furniture and household goods away.*

Martial law was declared in Tulsa after the riots. Pictured here are national guardsmen taking injured prisoners to a hospital.

Unlike recent U.S. riots, these were white looters who were breaking into and burning the homes and businesses of blacks.

Franklin continues:

> *Soon I was back upon the streets, but the building where I had my office was a smoldering ruin, and all my lawbooks and office fixtures had been consumed by flames. I went to where my roominghouse had stood a few short hours before, but it was in ashes, with all my clothes and the money to be used in moving my family. As far as one could see, not a Negro dwellinghouse or place of business stood. . . . Negroes who yesterday were wealthy, living in beautiful homes in ease and comfort, were now beggars, public charges, living off alms.*

The rioters burned all black churches, including the Zion Baptist church, which had just been completed. They destroyed over 1,000 homes. When they finished destroying homes and businesses, it looked as though a tornado had swept through the area. Overnight, the formerly prosperous had become homeless, spending the next year in tents pitched in the ruins of their neighborhoods (Sulzberger 2011).

And what about the young man who had been accused of assault, the event that precipitated the riot? Franklin says that the police investigated and found that there had been no assault. All the man had done was accidentally step on a lady's foot in a crowded elevator, and, as Franklin says, "She became angry and slapped him, and a fresh, cub newspaper reporter, without any experience and no doubt anxious for a byline, gave out an erroneous report through his paper that a Negro had assaulted a white girl."

For Your Consideration

➔ It is difficult to place ourselves in a historical mind-set where stepping on someone's foot could lead to such destruction, but it did. Can you apply the sociological findings on both rumors and riots to explain the riot in Tulsa? Why do you think that so many whites believed this rumor, and why were some of them so intent on destroying this thriving black community? If "seething rage" underlies riots, it should apply to this one, too. What "seething rage" (or resentments or feelings of injustice) do you think were involved?

Panics

The Classic Panic.

In 1938, on the night before Halloween, a radio program of dance music was interrupted by a report that explosions had been observed on the surface of Mars. The announcer added that a cylinder of unknown origin had been discovered embedded in the ground on a farm in New Jersey. The radio station then switched to the farm, where a breathless reporter gave details of horrible-looking Martians climbing out of the cylinder. They were carrying death-ray weapons that had destructive powers unknown to humans. An astronomer then confirmed that Martians had invaded the Earth.

Perhaps six million Americans heard this radio program. Many missed the announcement at the beginning and somewhere in the middle that this was a dramatization of H. G. Wells' *The War of the Worlds*. Thinking that Martians had really invaded Earth, thousands grabbed weapons and hid in their basements or ran into the streets. Hundreds bundled up their families and jumped into their cars, jamming the roads as they headed to who knows where.

I think you and I would both panic in this situation. The normal—iPads, purses, whatever—would not be a concern. But note the order that is also here. The father dressed in white is protecting his son from the bull. Look also at the father on the left with his son. If you look closely you can also see the mother's arm tugging at the boy.

Panic occurs when people become so fearful that they cannot function normally and may even flee a situation they perceive as threatening. The reaction to this radio program seems humorous, but we need to ask why these people panicked. Psychologist Hadley Cantril (1941) attributed the reaction to widespread anxiety about world conditions. The Nazis were marching in Europe, and millions of Americans (correctly, as it turned out) were afraid that the United States would get involved in the conflict. War jitters, he said, created fertile ground for the broadcast to touch off a panic.

But was there a panic? The story is good, but the facts are few. Some people did become frightened, and a few did get in their cars and drive like maniacs. Sociologist William Bainbridge (1989) says that most of this famous panic was an invention of the news media, with reporters milking the few cases to manufacture headlines.

Bainbridge points to a 1973 event in Sweden. To dramatize the dangers of atomic power, Swedish Radio broadcast a play about an accident at a nuclear power plant. Knowing about the 1938 broadcast in the United States, Swedish sociologists were waiting to see what would happen. Might some people fail to realize that it was a dramatization and panic at the threat of ruptured reactors spewing out radioactive gases? The sociologists found no panic. A few people did become frightened. Some telephoned family members and the police; others shut windows to keep out the radioactivity—reasonable responses, considering what they thought had occurred.

In the midst of this calm, the Swedish media reported a panic! Apparently, a reporter had telephoned two police departments and learned that each had received calls from concerned citizens. With a deadline hanging over his head, the reporter decided to gamble. He reported that police and fire stations were jammed with citizens, people were flocking to the shelters, and others were fleeing south (Bainbridge 1989).

Although these "panics" were more humorous than real, panics can have devastating consequences.

> *On November 22, 2010, tens of thousands of people were at a concert at Diamond Island in Phnom Penh, Cambodia. As the crowd pressed hard together, some people lost consciousness. Seeing these people drop, others tried to rush away from the unknown danger. As they pushed away, it made others fearful, and they did the same. The pushing grew into a stampede, with people trampling one another. It was especially the women and children who fell under foot, leaving hundreds of bodies stacked upon bodies (Cheang 2010).*

The fear that underlies panics can be anything, even something unknown, as in this Cambodian panic. Fear of getting trapped by fire sometimes sets off panics as people frantically try to escape, all lunging for the same narrow exit. Here is what happened on Memorial Day weekend in 1977 at the Beverly Hills Supper Club in Southgate, Kentucky.

panic the condition of being so fearful that one cannot function normally and may even flee

> *About half of the Club's 2,500 patrons were crowded into the Cabaret Room. A fire, which began in a small banquet room near the front of the building, burned undetected until it*

was beyond control. When employees discovered the fire and warned patrons, people began to exit in orderly fashion. But when flames rushed in, they trampled one another in a furious attempt to reach the exits. The exits were blocked by masses of screaming people trying to push their way through all at once. The writhing bodies at the exits created further panic among the remainder, who pushed even harder to force their way through the bottlenecks. One hundred sixty-five people died. All but two were within thirty feet of two exits in the Cabaret Room.

Sociologists who studied this panic found the same thing that researchers have discovered in analyzing other disasters. *Not everyone panics.* Many people continue to act responsibly (Clarke 2002). Especially important are primary bonds. Parents help their children, for example (Morrow 1995). Gender roles also persist, and more men help women than women help men (Johnson 1993). Even work roles continue to guide people. As you can see from Table 21.1, most of the workers at the Beverly Hills Supper Club helped customers and fought the fire.

Sociologists use the term **role extension** to describe the actions of these employees. By this term, they mean that the workers extended their occupational role so that it included other activities. Servers, for example, extended their role to include helping people to safety. How do we know that giving help was an extension of their occupational role and not simply a general act of helping? Sociologists Drue Johnston and Norris Johnson (1989) found that servers who were away from their assigned stations returned to them in order to help *their* customers.

In some life-threatening situations in which we might expect panic, we find a sense of order. During the attack on the World Trade Center, at peril to their own lives, people helped injured friends and even strangers escape down many flights of stairs. These people, it would seem, were highly socialized into the collective good, and had a well-developed sense of empathy. But even this is a weak answer. We simply don't know why these people didn't panic when so many others do under threatening situations.

TABLE 21.1 Employees' First Action after Learning of the Fire

Action	Percentage
Left the building	29%
Helped others to leave	41%
Fought or reported the fire	17%
Continued routine activities	7%
Other (e.g., looked for a friend or relative)	5%

Note: Based on interviews with 95 of the 160 employees present at the time of the fire: 48 men and 47 women.

Source: Based on Johnston and Johnson 1989.

Mass Hysteria

Let's look at **mass hysteria**, where an imagined threat causes physical symptoms among large numbers of people. I think you'll enjoy the Down-to-Earth Sociology box on the next page.

Moral Panics

"They touched me down there. Then they cut the head off a little kittie. They said if I told they would kill my sister."

"They took off my clothes. Then they got in a space ship and flew away."

"It was awful when they killed the baby. There was blood all over."

What would you think if you heard little children saying things like this? You probably would shake your head and wonder what kind of TV shows they had been watching.

But not if you were an investigator during the 1980s in the United States. At that time, rumors swept the country that day care centers were run by monsters who were sexually molesting the little kids.

Prosecutors believed the children who told these fantastic stories. They knew their statements about space ships and aliens weren't true, but maybe little pets had been killed and families threatened. There was no evidence, but interrogators kept hammering away at the children. They said that the kids who insisted nothing had happened were "in denial."

Prosecutors took their flimsy but dramatic cases to court. Juries believed the kids. That there was no evidence bothered some jury members, but the startling emotional

role extension a role being stretched to include activities that were not originally part of that role

mass hysteria an imagined threat that causes physical symptoms among a large number of people

Down-to-Earth Sociology

Dancing, Sex, and Monkey Men

Let's look at five events.

Several hundred years ago, something strange happened near Naples, Italy. When people were bitten by tarantulas, they felt unusual sexual urges and an irresistible desire to dance—and to keep dancing until they were exhausted.

The disease was contagious. Even people who hadn't been bitten by tarantulas started to experience the same symptoms. The contagion was so severe that instead of gathering the summer harvest, whole villages would dance in a frenzy.

Of the remedies that were tried, nothing worked except music. Bands of musicians traveled from village to village, providing relief to the victims of *tarantism* by playing special "tarantula" music (Bynum 2001).

* * * * *

In 2009, Tian Lihua, a worker at a textile mill in China, felt sick to her stomach. Then she felt her arms go numb. She then felt dizzy. Other workers had difficulty breathing. Some vomited and went into convulsions. Others went into spasms and were temporarily paralyzed (Jacobs 2009).

Ambulances rushed the victims to hospitals, but blood tests showed nothing abnormal. "Mass hysteria," said the doctors.

The police say the creature is 4'6", wears only a dark coat of hair
Eyewitness says it is 5'6", wears black and sports a helmet, with shining red eyes
ABHIMANYU

The "Monkey Man" is one of the cases of mass hysteria reported here.

In the year 2001, in New Delhi, India, a "monkey-man" stalked people who were sleeping on rooftops during the blistering summer heat. He clawed and bit a hundred victims. People would wake up screaming that the monkey-man was after them. During one of the monkey-man's attacks, a man jumped off the roof of his house. He was killed ("'Monkey'" 2001).

There was no apelike killer.

* * * * *

In 2000, in McMinnville, Tennessee, a teacher smelled a "funny odor." Students and teachers began complaining of headaches, nausea, and shortness of breath. The school was evacuated, and doctors treated more than 100 people at the local hospital. Authorities found nothing.

A few days later, a second wave of illness struck. The Tennessee Department of Health shut the high school down. For two weeks, workers dug holes in the foundation and walls and ran snake cameras through the ventilation and heating ducts. They even tested the victims' blood (Adams 2000).

The found nothing unusual.

* * * * *

In 2012, at a school in New York, twelve female students started to have body tics and seizures and to shout uncontrollably. The girls were put under medical care. Authorities tried to find out how Tourette's Syndrome could hit so many so quickly. They ran tests for air quality and mold, for carbon dioxide and drugs (Murray 2012).

Nothing.

* * * * *

"It's all in their heads," we might say. In one sense, we would be right. There was no external, objective cause of the illnesses from *tarantism*. There was no "monkey-man," no contagious illness, nor contaminants at the schools.

In another sense, however, we would be wrong to say that it is "all in their heads." The symptoms that these people experienced were real. They had real headaches and stomach aches. They did vomit and faint. They did have uncontrollable tics and seizures. And they did experience unusual sexual urges and the desire to dance until they could no longer stand.

There is no explanation for mass hysteria except suggestibility. Experts might use fancy words like "social transmission" to try to explain it, but once you cut through their terms, you find that they are really saying, "It happens." As you can see from these examples, mass hysteria occurs in many cultures. This indicates that it follows basic principles of human behavior. Someday, we will understand these principles.

For Your Consideration

➜ What do you think causes mass hysteria? Have you ever been part of mass hysteria?

Moral panics occur when large numbers of people become fearful of what they consider deteriorating morals and the fear is out of proportion to the danger. There are plenty of events to feed moral panics, such as the kidnapping of Gina DeJesus in Cleveland, Ohio. She was held as a sex slave for ten years. Two other victims were also held by the same man.

images prevailed—helpless little children, naked, tied up, and sexually assaulted. The ghoulish child care workers were sent to prison. To say anything in their defense was to defend child molesters from hell.

Moral panics occur when large numbers of people become concerned, even fearful, that something is threatening morality, and when the fear and response are out of proportion to any actual danger (Bandes 2007; Kramer 2010). With the threat perceived as enormous, hostility builds toward those thought to be responsible, erupting in overreaction.

The media feed moral panics. Each new revelation sells papers and brings viewers to their TVs. In this instance, the "revelations" made suspects of day care workers across the country. Only fearfully did parents leave their children in child care centers. Intensive investigations followed, but the stories of children supposedly subjected to bizarre sexual rituals were never substantiated.

Rumors also feed moral panics. In the 1990s, a rumor swept the country that Satanists were snatching children who were playing in their yards or walking to school. In bizarre rituals, the Satanists would sexually abuse the children and then kill them. Supposed eyewitnesses to these events told pitiful stories to horrified audiences about satanic sacrifices of children.

These fantastic stories filled in missing information: who was abducting and doing what to the nation's thousands of missing children. The police investigated, but, like the sexploitation of the nursery school children, no evidence substantiated the reports. The number of stranger kidnappings in the United States at that time was between 64 and 300 a year (Bromley 1991; Simons and Willie 2000). Currently, it is about 500 (Quinet 2012).

Like rumors, moral panics thrive on uncertainty, fear, and anxiety. With so many mothers working outside the home, concerns can grow that children are receiving inadequate care. Linked with fears about declining morality and stoked by the publicity given to high-profile cases of child kidnappings and abuse, these concerns can give birth to the idea that pedophiles and child killers are lurking almost everywhere. After all, they could be, couldn't they? When you are filled with concerns, is it, then, such a stretch from *could* to *are*?

Fads and Fashions

A **fad** is a novel form of behavior that briefly catches people's attention. The new behavior appears suddenly and spreads rapidly. After a short life, the fad fades away. Some reappear from time to time.

Fads come in many forms. Very short, intense fads are called *crazes*. They appear suddenly and are gone almost as quickly. "Tickle Me Elmo" dolls, Beanie Babies, and silly bandz were *object crazes*. There also are *behavior crazes*, such as streaking in the 1970s: As a joke, an individual or a group would run nude in some public place. "Flash mobs" was a behavior craze in the early 2000s. Alerted by e-mail, individuals would gather at a specified time, do something such as point toward the ceiling of a mall, and then, without a word, disperse. As fads do, this one has reappeared (Yee 2013).

There are also food fads: tofu, power drinks, herbal supplements, and organics. Fads in dieting also come and go. "Perfect" diets appear, with practically everyone leaving the fad diet disillusioned. There are also fads in child rearing—permissive versus directive, spanking versus non-spanking. Even children's names go through fads.

Fads can involve millions of people. In the 1950s, the hula hoop was so popular that stores couldn't keep them in stock. Children cried and pleaded for these brightly colored

moral panic a fear gripping a large number of people that some evil threatens the wellbeing of society; followed by hostility, sometimes violence, toward those thought responsible

fad a temporary pattern of behavior that catches people's attention plastic hoops. Across the nation, children—and even adults—held contests to see who could keep the hoops up the longest or who could rotate the most hoops at one time. In a matter of months, the fad was over. Hula hoops can be found in toy stores, but now they are just another toy.

Fads can go global. Minecraft appears to be headed this way. Some gamers love Minecraft because they can choose a level that allows them to battle digital opponents and slaughter enemies. Others are fascinated with Minecraft because they are able to build digital structures. Their challenge is not to dodge enemies but to follow the laws of physics. Even the United Nations is becoming involved, using Minecraft to digitally imagine the improvement of rundown public spaces (McCracken 2013).

When a fad lasts, it is called a **fashion**. Some fashions, as with clothing and furniture, are the result of a coordinated marketing system of designers, manufacturers, advertisers, and retailers. By manipulating the public's taste, they sell billions of dollars of products. Fashion also refers to hairstyles, which last for at least a few years. Sociologist John Lofland (1985) pointed out how fashion applies to common expressions. Look at these roughly comparable terms: "Neat!" in the 1950s, "Right on!" in the 1960s, "Really!" in the 1970s, "Awesome!" in the 1980s, "Bad!" in the 1990s, "Sweet" and "Tight" in the early 2000s, "Hot" in the middle 2000s, "Sick" in the late 2000s, and, recurringly, "Cool."

Fashion brings a form of peer pressure. To attain status within fashion, some people are willing to sacrifice their health, as with this woman in 1899.

Urban Legends

Did you hear about Jessica and Paul? They were parked at Bluewater Bay, listening to the radio, when the music was interrupted by an announcement that a rapist—killer had escaped from prison. Instead of a right hand, he had a hook. Jessie said they should leave, but Paul laughed and said there wasn't any reason to go. When they heard a strange noise and Jessie screamed, Paul took her home. When Jessie opened the door, she heard something clink. It was a hook hanging on the door handle!

For decades, some version of "The Hook" has circulated among Americans. It has appeared as a "genuine" letter in "Dear Abby," and some of my students heard it in grade school. **Urban legends** are stories with an ironic twist that sound realistic but are false. Although untrue, they usually are told by people who believe that they happened.

Here is another one:

A horrible thing happened. This girl in St. Louis kept smelling something bad. The smell wouldn't leave even when she took showers. She finally went to the doctor, and it turned out that her insides were rotting. She had gone to the tanning salon too many times, and her insides were cooked.

Folklorist Jan Brunvand (1981, 1984, 2004) reports that urban legends are passed on by people who often think that the event happened just one or two people down the line of transmission, sometimes to a "friend of a friend." These stories have strong appeal and gain their credibility by naming specific people or citing particular events. Note the details of where Jessica and Paul were. Brunvand views urban legends as "modern morality stories": Each one teaches a moral lesson about life.

If we apply Brunvand's analysis to these two urban legends, three principles emerge. First, these stories serve as warnings. "The Hook" warns young people that they should be careful about where they go and what they do when they get there. The tanning salon story warns us about the potential dangers of technology. Second, these stories are related to social change: "The Hook" to changing sexual morality, the tanning salon to changing technology. Third, each is calculated to instill fear: You should be afraid, for dangers lurk everywhere, from the dark countryside to your neighborhood tanning salon.

fashion a pattern of behavior that catches people's attention and lasts longer than a fad

urban legend a story with an ironic twist that sounds realistic but is false

social movement a large group of people who are organized to promote or resist some social change

proactive social movement a social movement that promotes some social change

reactive social movement a social movement that resists some social change

social movement organization an organization to promote the goals of a social movement

Read on **MySocLab** **Document:** The Rise and Fall of Aryan Nations: A Resource Mobilization Perspective

You can apply these principles to an urban legend that made the rounds in the late 1980s. I heard several versions of this one; each narrator swore that it had just happened to a friend of a friend.

> *Jerry (or whoever) went to a nightclub last weekend. He met a good-looking woman, and they hit it off. They spent the night in a motel. When he got up the next morning, the woman was gone. When he went into the bathroom, he saw a message scrawled on the mirror in lipstick: "Welcome to the wonderful world of AIDS."*

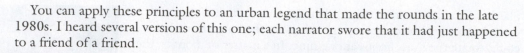

Social Movements

When the Nazis, a few malcontents in Bavaria, first appeared on the scene in the 1920s, the world found their ideas laughable. This small group believed that the Germans were a race of supermen (*Ubermenschen*) who would launch a Third Reich (reign or nation) that would control the world for a thousand years. Their race destined them for greatness; lesser races would serve them.

The Nazis started as a little band of comic characters who looked as though they had stepped out of a grade B movie (see the photo on page 325). From this inauspicious start, the Nazis gained such power that they threatened to overthrow Western civilization. How could a little man with a grotesque moustache, surrounded by a few sycophants in brown shirts, ever come to threaten the world? Such things don't happen in real life—only in novels or movies—the deranged nightmare of some author with an overactive imagination. Only this was real life. The Nazis' appearance on the human scene caused the deaths of millions of people and changed the course of world history.

Some social movements arise quickly, recruit vast numbers of people over some specific issue, and then disappear. Shown here are hundreds of thousands of Belgians protesting their lack of government.

Social movements, the second major topic of this chapter, provide the answer to Hitler's rise to power. **Social movements** consist of large numbers of people who are dissatisfied about things, who organize either to promote or to resist social change. These people hold strong ideas about what is wrong with the world—or some part of it—and how to make things right. Other examples of social movements are those centered on civil rights, women's rights, white supremacy, animal rights, and the environment.

At the heart of social movements lies a sense of injustice (Klandermans 1997). Finding a particular condition of society intolerable, people join together to promote social change. Theirs is called a **proactive social movement**. Others, in contrast, feel threatened because some condition of society is changing, and they react to resist that change. Theirs is a **reactive social movement**.

To further their goals, people establish **social movement organizations**. Those who want to promote social change develop organizations such as the National Association for the Advancement of Colored People (NAACP). In contrast, those who are trying to resist these particular changes form organizations such as the Ku Klux Klan (KKK) or Aryan Nations. To recruit followers and publicize their grievances, leaders of social movements use attention-getting devices, from marches and protest rallies to sit-ins and boycotts. These "media events" can be quite effective.

Social movements are like a rolling sea, observed sociologist Mayer Zald (1992). During one period, few social movements appear, but shortly afterward, a wave of them rolls in, each competing for the public's attention. Zald suggests that a *cultural crisis* can give birth to a wave of social movements. By this, he means that there are times when a society's institutions fail to keep up with social change. During these times, many people's needs go unfulfilled, unrest follows, and, attempting to bridge this gap, people form and become active in group campaigns.

Types and Tactics of Social Movements

21.4 Analyze the types and tactics of social movements; include the use of propaganda.

Let's look at types of social movements and then examine their tactics.

Types of Social Movements

Since social change is the goal of social movements, we can classify them according to their *target* and the *amount of change* they seek. Look at Figure 21.2, which we'll review in detail. If you read across, you will see that the first two types of social movements target *individuals*. **Alterative social movements** seek to *alter* some specific behavior. An example is the Woman's Christian Temperance Union, a powerful social movement of the early 1900s. Its goal was to get people to stop drinking alcohol. Its members were convinced that if they could shut down the saloons, such problems as poverty and wife abuse would go away. **Redemptive social movements** also target individuals, but their goal is *total* change. An example is a religious social movement that stresses conversion. In fundamentalist Christianity, for example, when someone converts to Christ, the entire person is supposed to change, not just some specific behavior. Self-centered acts are to be replaced by loving behaviors toward others as the convert becomes, in their terms, a "new creation."

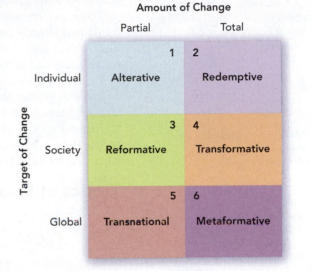

FIGURE 21.2 Types of Social Movements

Target of Change	Amount of Change: Partial	Amount of Change: Total
Individual	1 Alterative	2 Redemptive
Society	3 Reformative	4 Transformative
Global	5 Transnational	6 Metaformative

Sources: The first four types are from Aberle 1966; the last two are by the author.

The next two types of social movements target *society*. (See cells 3 and 4 of Figure 21.2.) **Reformative social movements** seek to *reform* some specific aspect of society. The animal rights movement, for example, wants to reform the ways in which society views and treats animals. **Transformative social movements**, in contrast, seek to *transform* the social order itself. Its members want to replace the social order with their vision of the good society. Revolutions, such as those in the American colonies, China, Cuba, France, and Russia, are examples.

One of the more interesting examples of transformative social movements is **millenarian social movements**, which are based on prophecies of impending calamity. Of particular interest is a type of millenarian movement called a **cargo cult** (Worsley 1957, 2009). About one hundred years ago, Europeans colonized the Melanesian Islands of the South Pacific. Ships from the home countries of the colonizers arrived one after another, each loaded with items the Melanesians had never seen. Watching the cargo being unloaded, the Melanesians expected that some of it would go to them. Instead, it all went to the Europeans. Melanesian prophets revealed the secret: Their own ancestors were manufacturing and sending the cargo to them, but the colonists were intercepting the merchandise. Since the colonists were too strong to fight and too selfish to share the cargo, there was little the Melanesians could do.

Then came a remarkable self-fulfilling prophecy. Melanesian prophets revealed that if the people would destroy their crops and food and build harbors, the ancestors would see their sincerity and send the cargo directly to them. The Melanesians destroyed their crops and then sat in the hills waiting for the cargo ships to arrive. When the island's colonial administrators informed the home government, the prospect of thousands of islanders patiently starving to death was too horrifying to allow. The British government fulfilled the prophecy by sending ships loaded with cargo earmarked for the Melanesians.

alterative social movement a social movement that seeks to alter only some specific aspects of people and institutions

redemptive social movement a social movement that seeks to change people and institutions totally, to redeem them

reformative social movement a social movement that seeks to reform some specific aspect of society

transformative social movement a social movement that seeks to change society totally, to transform it

millenarian social movement a social movement based on the prophecy of coming social upheaval

cargo cult a social movement in which South Pacific islanders destroyed their possessions in the anticipation that their ancestors would ship them new goods

transnational social movements social movements whose emphasis is on some condition around the world, instead of on a condition in a specific country; also known as *new social movements*

metaformative social movement a social movement that has the goal to change the social order not just of a country or two, but of a civilization, or even of the entire world

public in this context, a dispersed group of people relevant to a social movement; the sympathetic and hostile publics have an interest in the issues on which a social movement focuses; there is also an unaware or indifferent public

From Figure 21.2, you can see that some social movements have a global orientation. In our new global economy, many issues that concern people transcend national boundaries. Participants of **transnational social movements** (also called *new social movements*) want to change some specific condition that cuts across societies. (See cell 5 of Figure 21.2.) These social movements, which often center on improving the quality of life, are amazingly diverse, from the women's and the environmental movements to the virginity pledge and home birth movements (Walter 2001; Tilly 2004; Haenfler et al. 2012).

Cell 6 in Figure 21.2 represents a rare type of social movement. The goal of **metaformative social movements** is to change the social order itself—not just of a specific country but of an entire civilization, or even the whole world. Their objective is to change ideas and practices of race–ethnicity, class, gender, family, religion, government, and the global stratification of nations. These were the aims of the communist social movement of the early to late twentieth century and the fascist social movement of the 1920s to 1940s. (The fascists consisted of the Nazis in Germany, the Black Shirts of Italy, and other groups in Europe and the United States.)

Today, we are witnessing another metaformative social movement, that of Islamic fundamentalism. Like metaformative social movements before it, this movement is not united. Not only does it consist of many separate groups, but these groups also have different goals and tactics. Al-Qaeda, for example, would not only cleanse Islamic societies of Western influences—which they contend are demonic and degrading to men, women, and morality—but also replace Western civilization with an extremist form of Islam. This frightens both Muslims and non-Muslims, who hold sharply differing views of what constitutes quality of life. If the Islamic fundamentalists—like the communists or fascists before them—have their way, they will usher in a New World Order fashioned after their particular views of the good life.

Watch on **MySocLab** **Video:** Defining Social Movements

Watch on **MySocLab** **Video:** Organizational Structure of Social Movements

Tactics of Social Movements

The leaders of a social movement can choose from a variety of tactics. Should they boycott, stage a march, or hold an all-night candlelight vigil? Or should they bomb a building, burn down a research lab, or assassinate a politician? To understand why the leaders of social movements choose their tactics, let's examine the groups' levels of membership, the publics they address, and their relationships to authorities.

Levels of Membership. Look at Figure 21.3 below. If you begin at the center and move outward, you will see the three levels of membership of social movements. The inner core at the center is the most committed to the movement. The inner core sets the group's goals, timetables, and strategies. People at the second level are also committed to the movement, but less so than the inner core. They can be counted on to show up for demonstrations and to do the grunt work—help with mailings, pass out petitions and leaflets, make telephone calls. The third level consists of a wider circle of people who are less committed and less dependable. Their participation depends on convenience—if an activity doesn't interfere with something else they want to do, they participate.

FIGURE 21.3 The Membership and Publics of Social Movements

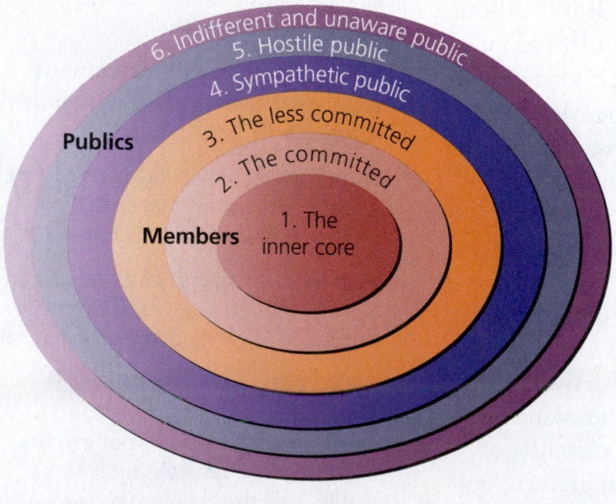

Source: By the author.

The tactics that a group uses depend largely on the backgrounds and predispositions of the inner core. Because of their differing backgrounds, some members of the inner core may prefer to demonstrate quietly. Some might even want to bypass demonstrations and just place informational ads in newspapers. For others, these tactics are far too gentle, and they seek heated, verbal confrontations. Still others may tend toward violence. Tactics also depend on the number of committed members. Different tactics are possible if the inner core can count on seven hundred—as opposed to only seven—committed members to show up.

The Publics. Outside the group's membership is the **public**, a dispersed group of people who may or may not have an interest in the issue. As you can see from Figure 21.3, there are three types of publics. Just outside the third circle of members, and blending into it, is the *sympathetic* public. These people largely agree with the movement, but they have no commitment to it. Their sympathies, however, make them prime candidates for recruitment. The second public is *hostile*. They have opposing values and want to stop the social movement. The third public consists of *disinterested* people. They are either unaware of the social movement or, if aware, are indifferent to it.

In selecting tactics, the leaders pay attention to these publics. The sympathetic public is especially significant, because it is the source of new members and support at the ballot box. Leaders avoid tactics that they think might alienate the sympathetic public and seek strategies that will elicit this group's support. To make themselves appear to be victims—people whose rights are being trampled on—leaders may even force a confrontation with the hostile public. Tactics directed toward the indifferent or unaware public are designed to neutralize their indifference and increase their awareness.

public opinion how people think about some issue

propaganda in its broad sense, the presentation of information in an attempt to influence people; in its narrow sense, one-sided information used to try to influence people

Relationship to Authorities. In determining tactics, the movement's relationship to authorities is also significant, especially when it comes to choosing between peaceful and violent actions. If a social movement is *institutionalized*—accepted by authorities—violence will not be directed toward the authorities, since they are on the movement's side. This, however, does not rule out using violence against the opposition. In contrast, authorities who are hostile to a social movement may become the object of aggression or violence. Because the goal of a transformative (revolutionary) social movement is to replace the government, activists in such a movement and the authorities are clearly on a collision course.

Multiple Realities and Social Movements

Sociology can be a liberating discipline (Berger 1963/2014). Sociology sensitizes us to *multiple realities*; that is, for any single opinion on some topic, there are competing points of view. Each point of view represents reality as people see it, their distinctive experiences leading them to different perceptions. Although the committed members of a social movement are sincere—perhaps even to the point that they make sacrifices for "the cause"—theirs is but one view of the world. With our society made up of such diverse groups—with their many contrasting and competing views and experiences—we are destined to live in an exciting society. Social movements indicate this diversity of experiences and views.

Animal rights is a global social movement. This photo, taken in Tokyo, is part of PETA's (People for the Ethical Treatment of Animals) global campaign to stop the killing of baby seals in Canada.

Propaganda and the Mass Media

The leaders of social movements try to use the mass media to influence **public opinion**, how people think about some issue. The right kind of publicity arouses sympathy and lays the groundwork for recruiting members and raising funds. PETA (People for the Ethical Treatment of Animals) is highly effective at this. Its pictures of bloody baby seals and pitiful abused dogs arouse intense emotions.

A key to understanding social movements, then, is **propaganda**. Although this word often evokes negative images, it actually is a neutral term. Propaganda is simply the presentation of information in an attempt to influence people. Its original meaning was positive. *Propaganda* referred to the name of a committee of Roman Catholic cardinals whose assignment was the care of foreign missions. (They were to *propagate*—multiply or spread—the faith.) The term has traveled a long way since then, however, and today it usually refers to one-sided information designed to distort reality.

Propaganda, in the sense of organized attempts to influence public opinion, is a part of everyday life. Our news is filled with propaganda, as various interest groups—from retailers to the government—try to manipulate our perceptions and behavior. Our movies, too, although seemingly intended as entertainment, are propaganda vehicles. The basic techniques that underlie propaganda are discussed in the Down-to-Earth Sociology box below.

Down-to-Earth Sociology

"Tricks of the Trade"—Deception and Persuasion in Propaganda

Back in the 1930s, sociologists Alfred and Elizabeth Lee (1939) found that propaganda relies on seven basic techniques. To be effective, these seven "tricks of the trade," as they called them, should be so subtle that the audience is unaware that their minds and emotions are being manipulated. Propaganda can be so effective that people will not know why they support something, but they'll fervently defend it. Becoming familiar with these techniques can help you keep your mind and emotions from being manipulated.

Name calling. This technique aims to arouse opposition to the competing product, candidate, or policy by associating it with negative images. By comparison, one's own product, candidate, or policy is attractive. Republicans who call Democrats "soft on crime" and Democrats who call Republicans "insensitive to the poor" are using this technique.

Glittering generality. Essentially the opposite of the first technique, this one surrounds the product, candidate, or policy with images that arouse positive feelings. "She's a real Democrat" has little meaning, but people feel that something substantive has been said. "This Republican stands for individual rights" is so general that it is meaningless, yet the audience thinks that it has heard a specific message about the candidate.

You probably know immediately why the photo on the left is propaganda, but do you know why the photo on the right is propaganda?

Transfer. In its positive form, this technique associates the product, candidate, or policy with something the public approves of or respects. You might not be able to get by with saying, "Samuel Adams is patriotic," but surround a beer with images of the country's flag, and beer drinkers will get the idea that it is more patriotic to drink this brand of beer than some other kind. In its negative form, this technique associates the product, candidate, or policy with something generally disapproved of by the public.

Testimonials. Famous individuals endorse a product, candidate, or policy. David Beckham lends his name to Gillette, and Beyoncé tells you that L'Oréal is a great line of cosmetics. In the negative form of this technique, a despised person is associated with the competing product. If propagandists (called "spin doctors" in politics) could get away with it, they would show the president of the Islamic Republic of Iran announcing support for a candidate they oppose.

Plain folks. Sometimes it pays to associate the product, candidate, or policy with "just plain folks." "If Mary or John Q. Public likes it, you will, too." A political candidate who kisses babies, puts on a hard hat, and has lunch at McDonald's while photographers catch him (or her) "in the act" is using the "plain folks" strategy. "I'm just a regular person" is the message of the presidential candidate who poses for photographers in jeans and work shirt—the chauffeur and Mercedes conveniently beyond the camera's lens.

Card stacking. The aim of this technique is to present only positive information about what you support and only negative information about what you oppose. The intent is to make it sound as though there is only one conclusion a rational person can draw. Falsehoods, distortions, and illogical statements are often used.

Bandwagon. "Everyone is doing it" is the idea behind this technique. Emphasizing how many other people buy the product or support the candidate or policy conveys the message that anyone who doesn't join in is on the wrong track.

The Lees (1939) added, "Once we know that a speaker or writer is using one of these propaganda devices in an attempt to convince us of an idea, we can separate the device from the idea and see what the idea amounts to on its own merits."

For Your Consideration

➤ What propaganda techniques have you seen or heard recently? Recall not just ads for products but also TV programs, political ads, movies, and newspaper articles. Explain why they were propaganda, not simply a source of information or entertainment.

Gatekeepers to Social Movements. The mass media are *the gatekeepers to social movements.* If those who control and work in the mass media—from owners to reporters—are sympathetic to some particular "cause," you can be sure that it will be given positive treatment. A social movement that goes against their views, however, will likely be ignored or receive unfavorable treatment.

If you ever get the impression that the media are trying to manipulate your opinions and attitudes—even your feelings—on some particular issue or social movement, you probably are right. Far from providing unbiased reporting, the people who control the media have an agenda. To the materials in the Down-to-Earth Sociology box on propaganda, then, add the biases of the media, its favorable and unfavorable treatment of issues and movements.

Why People Join Social Movements

21.5 To explain why people join social movements, use relative deprivation theory, declining privilege theory, and morality and ideology; include agents provocateur.

As we have seen, social movements are fed by a sense of injustice—a conviction that we can no longer tolerate some condition of society. However, not everyone who feels this way joins a social movement. Why do some join, but not others? Sociologists have found that recruitment generally follows channels of social networks. That is, people most commonly join a social movement because they have friends and acquaintances who are already in it (Snow et al. 1993; McVeigh 2009).

Let's look at three other explanations for why people join social movements.

Explore on **MySocLab** **Activity:** Where is Social Activism Taking Off in the United States or Your Community?

Relative Deprivation Theory: Improving Status and Power

One explanation of why people join social movements is *deprivation theory.* People who feel deprived—of money, justice, status, or privilege—join social movements with the hope of resolving their grievances. This theory may seem so obvious that it needs no evidence. Don't the World War I soldiers who marched on Washington after Congress refused to pay their promised bonuses provide ample evidence that the theory is true? Or the thousands of African Americans who participated in the civil rights movement of the 1950s and 1960s?

relative deprivation theory in this context, the belief that people join social movements based on their evaluations of what they think they should have compared with what others have

Relativity of Deprivation. Deprivation theory does provide a starting point, but there is more than meets the eye. About 150 years ago, Alexis de Tocqueville (1856/1955) made a telling observation. He noted that the peasants of both Germany and France had lived in oppression and poverty and that if revolution were to occur, we would expect it to take place in both countries. However, only the French peasants rebelled and overthrew their king. The reason, said de Tocqueville, was *relative* deprivation. The living conditions of the French peasants had been improving, and they anticipated even better circumstances ahead. German peasants, in contrast, had experienced only depressed conditions, giving them no comparative basis for feeling deprived.

According to relative deprivation theory, then, it is not people's actual deprivation that matters. The key is *relative* deprivation—what people *think* they should have relative to what others have, or relative to their own efforts, abilities, status, or even their perceived future. **Relative deprivation theory** provides an interesting insight into revolutions: Because improved circumstances can fuel human desire for even greater advances, *improving* conditions can spark revolutions—as happened in France. As Figure 21.4 shows, revolutions tend to occur when people's expectations outstrip the change they experience. It is likely that we can also apply this principle to at least some riots.

FIGURE 21.4 Relative Deprivation and Revolution

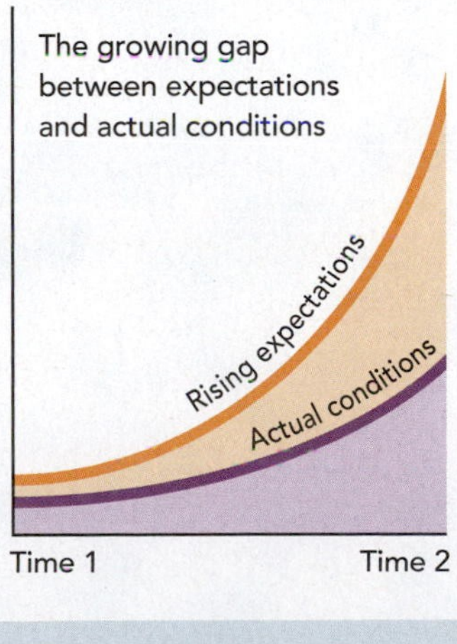

Relative Deprivation and the Civil Rights Movement. Relative deprivation also explains an interesting aspect of the civil rights movement. At the center of the sit-ins, marches, and boycotts in the South during the 1950s and 1960s were relatively well-off African Americans. These college students and church leaders went to restaurants and lunch counters that were reserved for whites. When refused service, they sat peacefully while curses and food were heaped on them (Morris 1993). You might want to review the photo on page 346. Why did they volunteer for such treatment? Remember that what is significant is not what we have or don't have, but with whom we compare ourselves. Although these African American were better off than most African Americans, they compared themselves not with them but with whites of similar status and accomplishments, and they perceived themselves as deprived.

Declining Privilege Theory: Protecting Status and Power

We just considered *improving* status and power. How about when people's status and power are *declining*? In the 1920s, skilled workers were being fired as new machinery mass-produced the items they made by hand. Other workers were losing jobs to immigrants who worked for lower wages. At the same time, many Protestants felt threatened by the growth of the Roman Catholic Church. In addition, many whites looked on with horror as black Americans achieved greater independence and mobility.

These conditions provided fertile ground for the KKK, which at that time was focused more on economic and immigration policies than on race (McVeigh 2009). The Klan offered a political solution, legislation that supported the traditional way of life for those they called "100% Americans." The appeal was so high that several million Americans paid dues to the KKK, making the Klan a national political force.

How does *declining privilege theory* differ from relative deprivation theory? Relative deprivation theory centers on people who feel they are deprived relative to others. They join a social movement to improve their position. Declining privilege theory focuses on people who have enjoyed relatively good circumstances in life. When they find their status and power declining, they join a social movement to protect their position. As you can see, with a little effort, we could merge these two theories.

Moral Issues and Ideological Commitment

Watch on **MySocLab**
Video: Sociology in Focus: Collective Behavior and Social Movements

As sociologist James Jasper (2007) points out, we will miss the *basic* reason for many people's involvement in social movements if we overlook the moral issue—people getting upset about some injustice and wanting to do something about it. For people who view a social movement in moral terms, great issues hang in the balance. They feel they must choose sides and do what they can to help right wrongs. As sociologists put it, they join because of *ideological commitment* to the movement.

Many members on *both* sides of the abortion issue, for example, perceive their involvement in such terms. Similarly, activists in the animal rights movement are convinced that there can be no justification for making animals suffer, even if they make products safer for humans. Activists in the peace and environmental movements and those who protest global capitalism view nuclear weapons, pollution, and global power in similar moral terms. To help right wrongs, they demonstrate and risk arrest and ridicule. For them, to *not* act would be inexcusable, a betrayal of future generations.

A Special Case: The Agent Provocateur

An **agent provocateur** is a unique type of participant in social movements. This person spies on a movement or tries to sabotage it. The purpose may be to get participants arrested or to provoke them to commit extreme acts. Some agents provocateurs are members of rival groups, while others are sent as spies by the government. Some are already members of the group, recruited because they are willing to betray their friends in the organization for a few Judas dollars.

When a social movement advocates social change that poses a threat to the power elite, spying by agents provocateurs is not surprising. What may be surprising, however, is that some agents convert to the social movement they infiltrate. Sociologist Gary Marx (1993) explains that to be credible, agents must share some of the class, age, gender, racial–ethnic, or religious characteristics of the group. This background makes the agents more likely to be sympathetic to the movement's goals. To be effective, agents must build trust and work their way to the center of power. This requires that

agent provocateur someone who spies on a group or tries to sabotage it they spend a lot of time with the group's committed members, which often cuts them off from their own group. The point of view they represent can start to recede in their minds, replaced with concerns about betraying and deceiving people who trust them as friends.

In Sum: There is no single reason that people join social movements. Most people join because they have friends and acquaintances in the movement. Some take part because of moral convictions, others to improve or to protect their positions and privilege, and still others because it is fun. Some even participate although they *don't want to.* The Cuban government, for example, compels people to turn out for mass demonstrations to show support of the communist regime (Aguirre 1993). As we just saw, police agents may join social movements in order to spy on their participants, some even to sabotage their activities. As in all other activities in life, people remain a complex bundle of motivations—a challenge for sociologists to unravel.

On the Success and Failure of Social Movements

21.6 Explain why most social movements fail, why some succeed, and why some continue for decades.

Some social movements have brought about extensive social change, but most are not effective. Let's look at the reasons for their success or failure.

The Rocky Road to Success

Social movements come, and social movements go—and most quietly fade away without leaving much of an impact on society. Why? To exist, a social movement must focus on a problem that concerns a large number of people. Broad problems, however, are embedded deeply in society. This means that minor tinkering with something superficial won't solve the problem. Just as the problem touches many interrelated parts of society, so the solutions must be broad. No quick fix is available for such social conditions, so the social movement must last for years. During this time, the campaign tends to lose momentum as its leaders turn inward, focusing their energies more on keeping the organization alive than on solving the problem that is the reason for the movement's existence.

Some social movements, in contrast, change society and even world history. The civil rights movement and the women's movement, for example, became powerful forces for social change, so successful that they turned society onto different paths. The fascist social movement led by Hitler in Germany and Mussolini in Italy also changed the world, but in a different direction entirely, with effects that endure to this day. Like anything else in life, the consequences of social movements can be good or bad. What they all have in common is social change, either to promote it or to resist it. With a changing society such as ours, we can anticipate that social movements will be a regular feature of our landscape.

Seeing the stages that social movements go through can help us to better understand why they succeed or fail. Let's look at these stages.

The Stages of Social Movements

Sociologists have identified five stages in social movements (Lang and Lang 1961; Mauss 1975; Spector and Kitsuse 1977; Jasper 1991; Tilly 2004):

1. *Initial unrest and agitation.* During this first stage, people are upset about some condition in society and want to change it. Leaders emerge who verbalize people's feelings and crystallize issues. Most social movements fail at this stage. Unable to gain enough support, after a brief flurry of activity, they fade away.
2. *Resource mobilization.* A crucial factor that enables social movements to make it past the first stage is **resource mobilization**. By this term, sociologists mean organizing and using resources—time, money, information, mailing lists, and people's skills,

resource mobilization a theory that social movements succeed or fail based on their ability to mobilize resources such as time, money, and people's skills even their emotions (McVeigh 2009; Jasper 2012). It also includes communications technology such as cell phones, Internet sites, blogs, and tweets—and getting the attention of the mass media. For the civil rights movement, these resources included access to churches to organize protests (Mirola 2003).

Some groups lack leadership capable of resource mobilization and turn to "guns for hire," outside specialists who sell their services. As sociologists John McCarthy and Mayer Zald (1977; Zald and McCarthy 1987) point out, even though large numbers of people may be upset over some condition of society, without resource mobilization, they are only upset people, perhaps even agitators, but they do not constitute a social movement.

3. *Organization.* A division of labor is set up. The leaders make policy decisions, and the rank and file perform the daily tasks that keep the movement going. There is still much collective excitement about the issue, the movement's focal point of concern.
4. *Institutionalization.* At this stage, the movement has developed a bureaucracy, a type of organization described in Chapter 7. Career officers control the organization. They may care more about their own positions in the organization than the cause for which the initial leaders made sacrifices. Not much collective excitement remains.
5. *Decline and death.* During this phase, managing the day-to-day affairs of the organization dominates the leadership. Sentiment may have even shifted so greatly that there no longer is a group of committed people who share a common cause. The movement withers away, although a small staff can remain for years until the last of the funds are drained.

Social movements take many forms. Organic farming and "eat local" are part of a broader environmental movement.

Resurgence

The final stage of decline and death can be postponed for decades, perhaps even for generations, if events breathe new life into a social movement and committed, fresh blood replaces faltering leaders. The outstanding example is the abortion movement, whose prochoice and prolife sides continue to energize one another. To close this chapter, let's look at this social movement.

THINKING CRITICALLY

Which Side of the Barricades? Prochoice and Prolife as a Social Movement

No issue divides Americans as much as abortion. Despite moderate views among the majority of the population, some Americans firmly believe that abortion should be permitted at all times, even during the last month of pregnancy. They are matched by individuals on the other side who are convinced that abortion should never be allowed under any circumstance, not even in the case of rape or incest or during the first month of pregnancy. This polarization constantly breathes new life into the movement.

When the U.S. Supreme Court made its 1973 decision, *Roe v. Wade,* that states could not prohibit abortion, the prochoice side relaxed. Victory was theirs, and they thought their opponents would quietly fade away. Instead, large numbers of Americans were disturbed by what they saw as the legal right to murder unborn children.

The views of the two sides could not be more incompatible. Those who favor choice view the 1.2 million abortions that are performed annually in the United States as examples of women exercising their basic reproductive rights. Those who gather under the prolife banner see these abortions as legalized murder. To the prochoice side, those who oppose abortion are blocking women's rights—they would force women to continue pregnancies they want to terminate. To the prolife side, those who advocate choice are perceived as condoning murder—they would sacrifice unborn children for the sake of school, career, or convenience.

There is no way to reconcile these contrary views. Each sees the other as unreasonable and extremist. And each uses propaganda by focusing on worst-case scenarios: prochoice images of young women ravished at gunpoint, forced to bear the children of rapists; prolife images of women who are nine months pregnant killing their babies instead of nurturing them.

With no middle ground, these views remain in perpetual conflict. As each side fights for what it considers to be basic rights, it reinvigorates the other. When in 1989 the U.S. Supreme Court decided in *Webster v. Reproductive Services* that states could restrict abortion, one side mourned it as a defeat and the other hailed it as a victory. Seeing the political battle going against them, the prochoice side regrouped for a bitter struggle. The prolife side, sensing judicial victory within its grasp, gathered forces for a push to complete the overthrow of *Roe v. Wade.*

In 1992, this goal of the prolife side almost became reality in *Casey v. Planned Parenthood.* In a 6–3 decision, the Supreme Court upheld the right of states to make women wait twenty-four hours between confirming their pregnancy and getting an abortion, to require girls under 18 to obtain the consent of one parent, and to specify that women be given materials describing the fetus as well as information about alternatives to abortion. In the same case, however, by a 5–4 decision, the Court ruled that

With sincere people on both sides of the issue—equally committed and equally convinced that their side is right—abortion is destined to remain a controversial force in U.S. life.

a wife does not have to inform her husband if she intends to have an abortion. In 2007, in another 5–4 decision, the Court ruled a certain type of abortion procedure illegal. The names given this late-term procedure represent the ongoing struggle: One side called it an "intact dilation and evacuation," while the other side termed it a "partial-birth abortion."

The struggle of the opposing sides is usually a quiet affair, but it bursts into headlines each time the Senate is asked to confirm a president's nominee to the U.S. Supreme Court. To watch these hearings is to view, in miniature, irreconcilable views of reality. This social movement also makes headlines when opposing sides confront one another in street drama, each wielding signs in the attempt to capture the attention of the mass media. On both sides, there are also rare, but powerfully headline-grabbing, events of horror. On the one side is the assassination of doctors who perform abortions. On the other side is the abortion doctor who killed babies after they were born alive.

With emotions raw and convictions firm, this social movement cannot end unless an overwhelming majority of Americans commit to one side or the other. Short of this, every legislative and judicial outcome—including the extremes of a constitutional amendment that declares abortion to be either murder or a woman's right—is a victory to one and a defeat to the other. To committed activists, no battle is ever complete. Rather, each action is only one small part of a long, hard-fought, moral struggle.

Sources: Williams 1995; Douthat 2008; Forsyth 2011; Gabriel 2013; *Statistical Abstract of the United States* 2013:Table 105.

For Your Consideration

➔ The last stage of a social movement is decline and death. Why hasn't this social movement died? Under what conditions do you think it will decline and die?

➔ The longer a pregnancy, the fewer the Americans who approve of abortion. How do you feel about abortion during the third month versus the seventh month? The first month versus the ninth month? What do you think about abortion in cases of rape and incest? Can you identify some of the social reasons that underlie your opinions? ■

MySocLab

Study and Review on MySocLab

CHAPTER 21 Summary and Review

Early Explanations: The Transformation of the Individual

21.1 Explain what early theorists meant about crowds transforming people; summarize the 5 stages of an acting crowd.

How did early theorists explain the ways that crowds affect people?

Early theorists of **collective behavior** argued that crowds transform people. Charles Mackay used the term *herd mentality* to explain why people did wild things when they were in crowds. Gustave LeBon said that a **collective mind** develops, and people are swept away by suggestions. Robert Park described a growing collective unrest, which, fed by a **circular reaction**, leads to collective impulses. Pp. 614–615.

What are the five stages of crowd behavior?

Herbert Blumer identified five stages that crowds go through before they become an **acting crowd**: social unrest, an exciting event, **milling**, a shared object of attention, and common impulses. Pp. 615–616.

The Contemporary View: The Rationality of the Crowd

21.2 Explain why sociologists today view crowds as rational and what is meant by emergent norms.

What is the current view of crowd behavior?

Sociologists view crowds as rational. Richard Berk describes a **minimax strategy**; that is, people try to minimize their costs and maximize their rewards, regardless of whether they are alone, with friends, or in crowds. In their theory of **emergent norms**, Ralph Turner and Lewis Killian suggest that new norms emerge, allowing people to do things in crowds that they otherwise would not do. Pp. 616–617.

Forms of Collective Behavior

21.3 Describe the forms of collective behavior: riots, rumors, panics, mass hysteria, moral panics, fads and fashions, and urban legends.

What forms of collective behavior are there?

Forms of **collective behavior** include lynchings, **riots**, **rumors**, **panics**, **mass hysteria, moral panics**, **fads**, **fashions**, and **urban legends**. Conditions of uncertainty and discontent provide fertile ground for collective behavior. Each form of collective behavior offers a way of dealing with these conditions. Pp. 618–626.

Types and Tactics of Social Movements

21.4 Analyze the types and tactics of social movements; include the use of propaganda.

What types of social movements are there?

Social movements consist of large numbers of people who organize to promote or resist social change. Depending on their target (individuals or society) and the amount of social change that is desired (partial or complete), social movements can be classified as **alterative**, **redemptive**, **reformative**, **transformative**, **transnational**, and **metaformative**. Pp. 626–628.

How do social movement leaders select their tactics?

Leaders choose tactics on the basis of a group's levels of membership, its **publics**, and its relationship to authorities. The three levels of membership are *the inner core*, *the committed*, and *the less committed*. The predispositions of the inner core are crucial in choosing tactics, but so is the **public** they want to address. If relationships with authorities are bad, the chances of aggressive or violent tactics increase. Pp. 628–629.

How are the mass media related to social movements?

The mass media are gatekeepers for social movements. Because the media's favorable or unfavorable coverage influences **public opinion**, leaders choose tactics with the media in mind. Leaders also use **propaganda** to further their causes. Pp. 629–631.

Why People Join Social Movements

21.5 To explain why people join social movements, use relative deprivation theory, declining privilege theory, and morality and ideology; include agents provocateur.

Why do people join social movements?

People often join social movements because they know others in the movement. According to **relative deprivation theory**, people participate in movements to protest and alleviate the deprivations they feel relative to the situations of others. A sense of justice, morality, values, and ideological commitment also motivates people to join social movements. **Agents provocateurs** illustrate that even people who oppose a cause may participate in it. Pp. 631–633.

On the Success and Failure of Social Movements

21.6 Explain why most social movements fail, why some succeed, and why some continue for decades.

Why do social movements succeed or fail?

Groups that appeal to few people cannot succeed. To appeal broadly in order to attain **resource mobilization**, the movement must focus on broad concerns. These concerns are embedded in society, which makes success difficult. Sociologists have identified five stages of social movements: initial unrest and agitation, mobilization, organization, institutionalization, and decline and death. Resurgence of a declining social movement is possible. In the social movement around abortion, opposing sides revitalize one another. Pp. 633–636.

Thinking Critically about Chapter 21

1. Describe the different forms of collective behavior, and explain why people participate in collective behavior.
2. Use sociological findings to analyze a rumor or an urban legend you have heard or a fad you've participated in.
3. Analyze a social movement of your choice according to the sociological principles and findings reviewed in this chapter.

Social Change and the Environment

22 CHAPTER

Listen to Chapter 22 on MySocLab

The job seemed to go on forever. *Two archeologists and their team spent* 25 years *mapping Caracol, perhaps the oldest and largest city in the Americas. This city in Belize, where people had lived from 600* BC *to* AD *900, when it was mysteriously abandoned, lay under thick jungle cover. The vegetation was so thick that the city had not been discovered until 1938, when some loggers stumbled onto it.*

Year after year, the archeologists slaved away. Each year, they were able to map just a small part of the city. They knew that there were roads leading to the city, also hidden by thick jungle. And what else?

At the pace they were going, maybe archeologists would know the answer in 100 years or so.

But only if more teams of archeologists joined the project.

And only if they could survive the jungle's heat, insects, animals, and disease.

This is tradition archeology. Dig and document. What else can there be? Even attempts at using radar to map the site had failed. The jungle was too thick to penetrate.

> "At the pace they were going, maybe archeologists would know the answer in 100 years or so . . . if they could survive the jungle's heat, insects, animals, and disease."

Diane and Arlen Chase, the wife-and-husband team who had been slogging away in the jungle for 25 years, searched for alternatives. "Let's try LiDAR (light detection and ranging)," they concluded. "We can try it in the dry spring, when the vegetation is somewhat lighter."

When the spring came, a little plane flew back and forth a half mile above the area. For four days, it sent laser beams onto the ground. The Chases grew anxious. Would the laser beams bounced back from the ground show anything besides the vegetation? If so, what?

The results were astounding: high-quality 3-D images of what lay beneath the jungle. And not just in the area near the excavated site. LiDAR also revealed intriguing things hidden in an 80-square-mile area. *You could see crisp images of house mounds, roadways, and agricultural terraces.*

In just four days, the new technology revealed more than the archeologists had discovered by slaving away for 25 years.

Based on Chase et al. 2010; Handwerk 2010; Wilford 2010.

Learning Objectives

After you have read this chapter, you should be able to:

22.1 Summarize how social change transforms society; include the four social revolutions, *Gemeinschaft* and *Gesellschaft*, capitalism, social movements, and global politics. (p. 639)

22.2 Summarize theories of social change: social evolution, natural cycles, conflict over power and resources, and Ogburn's theory. (p. 644)

22.3 Use the examples of the automobile and the microchip to illustrate the sociological significance of technology; include changes in ideology, norms, human relationships, education, work, business, war, and social inequality. (p. 647)

22.4 Explain how industrialization is related to environmental problems; contrast the environmental movement and environmental sociology; discuss the goal of harmony. (p. 655)

If you want a better understanding of society—and your own life—you need to understand social change, probably the main characteristic of social life today. As we will see in this chapter, technology, such as the laser imagery that reveals ancient cities hidden beneath the jungle, is the driving force behind this change.

Let's begin by reviewing how social change transforms social life.

How Social Change Transforms Social Life

22.1 Summarize how social change transforms society; include the four social revolutions, *Gemeinschaft* and *Gesellschaft*, capitalism, social movements, and global politics.

Social change, a shift in the characteristics of culture and society, is such a vital part of social life that it has been a recurring theme throughout this book. To make this theme more explicit, let's review the main points about social change that we have looked at in the preceding chapters.

social change the alteration of culture and societies over time

The Four Social Revolutions

Rapid social change is part of your everyday life. Why? To understand today's social change, we need to go back in history a bit. Let's start with forces that were set in motion thousands of years ago when humans domesticated plants and animals (pages 147–148).

The evolution of societies has been so thorough that this scene—once common for all humanity—has become strange, exotic. Our type of society, too, will be replaced by some new type yet to appear.

This first social revolution allowed hunting and gathering societies to develop into horticultural and pastoral societies. The plow brought about the second social revolution, from which agricultural societies emerged. The third social revolution, prompted by the invention of the steam engine, ushered in the Industrial Revolution. Now we are in the midst of the fourth social revolution, stimulated by the invention of the microchip. The process of change has accelerated so greatly that the mapping of the human genome system could be pushing us into yet another new type of society, one based on biotechnology.

From *Gemeinschaft* to *Gesellschaft*

Although our society has changed extensively—think of how life was for your grandparents—we have seen only the tip of the iceberg. Based on what happened in earlier social revolutions, we know that by the time this fourth—and perhaps fifth—social revolution is full-blown, little of our current way of life will remain.

Consider the change from agricultural to industrial society. This transition didn't just touch the surface. It was not simply that people changed where they lived, moving from the farm to the city (see Table 7.1 on page 172). The change was so extensive and deep that it transformed peoples' personal connections. Lives had been built around the reciprocal obligations (such as exchanging favors) that are essential to kinship, social status, and friendship. Moving to the city broke many intimate relationships, replacing them with impersonal associations built around paid work, contracts, and money. As reviewed on pages 103–105, sociologists use the terms *Gemeinschaft* and *Gesellschaft* to indicate this fundamental shift in society.

Traditional, or *Gemeinschaft*, societies are small, rural, and slow-changing. Men dominate social life, and the divisions of labor between men and women are rigid. People live in extended families, have little formal education, treat illness at home, tend to see morals in absolute terms, and consider the past the key for dealing with the present. In contrast, modern, or *Gesellschaft*, societies are large, urbanized, and fast-changing, with more fluid divisions of labor between the sexes. When a group reaches the third stage of the demographic transition, people have smaller families and low rates of infant mortality. They prize formal education, are future-oriented, have higher incomes, and enjoy vastly more material possessions.

The Protestant Reformation ushered in not only religious change but also, as Max Weber analyzed, fundamental change in economics. This painting by Johann Zoffany from about 1775 is of Sir Lawrence Dundas, a Scottish merchant. Note the wealth that he enjoyed.

The Industrial Revolution and Capitalism

As you can see, these are not just surface changes. The switch from *Gemeinschaft* to *Gesellschaft* society transformed people's social relationships and their orientations to life. In his analysis of this transition, Karl Marx stressed that when feudal society broke up, it threw people off the land, creating a surplus of labor. When these desperate masses moved to cities, they were exploited by capitalists, the owners of the means of production (factories, machinery, and tools). This set in motion antagonistic relationships between capitalists and workers that remain today.

Max Weber traced capitalism to the Protestant Reformation (see pages 173–174). He noted that the Reformation stripped Protestants of the assurance that church membership saved them. As they agonized over heaven and hell, they concluded that God did not want the elect to live in uncertainty. Surely God would give them a sign that they were predestined to heaven. That sign, they decided, was prosperity. An unexpected consequence of the Reformation, then, was to make Protestants hard-working and thrifty. This created an economic surplus, which stimulated capitalism. In this way, Protestantism laid the groundwork for the Industrial Revolution that transformed the world.

The sweeping changes ushered in by the Industrial Revolution, called **modernization**, are summarized in Table 22.1. The traits listed in this table are *ideal types* in Weber's sense of the term, since no society exemplifies all of them to the maximum degree. Actually, our new technology has created a remarkable unevenness in the characteristics of nations, making them a mixture of the traits shown in this table. For example, Uganda is a traditional society, but the elite have smaller families, emphasize formal education, and use computers. The characteristics shown in Table 22.1 should be interpreted as "more" or "less," not "either-or."

When technology changes, societies change. Consider how technology from the industrialized world transforms traditional societies. When the West exports medicine to the Least Industrialized Nations, for example, death rates drop while birth rates remain high. As a result, the population explodes, bringing hunger and uprooting masses of people who migrate to cities that have little industrialization to support them. The photo essay on pages 596–597 and the Cultural Diversity box on page 605 focus on some of these problems.

TABLE 22.1 Comparing Traditional and Industrialized (and Information) Societies

Characteristics	Traditional Societies	Industrialized (and Information) Societies
General Characteristics		
Social change	Slow	Rapid
Size of group	Small	Large
Religious orientation	More	Less
Education	Informal	Formal
Place of residence	Rural	Urban
Family size	Larger	Smaller
Infant mortality	High	Low
Life expectancy	Short	Long
Health care	Home	Hospital
Temporal orientation	Past	Future
Demographic transition	First stage	Third stage (or Fourth)
Material Relations		
Industrialized	No	Yes
Technology	Simple	Complex
Division of labor	Simple	Complex
Income	Low	High
Material possessions	Few	Many
Social Relationships		
Basic organization	*Gemeinschaft*	*Gesellschaft*
Families	Extended	Nuclear
Respect for elders	More	Less
Social stratification	Rigid	More open
Statuses	More ascribed	More achieved
Gender equality	Less	More
Norms		
View of morals	Absolute	Relativistic
Social control	Informal	Formal
Tolerance of differences	Less	More

Source: By the author.

Social Movements

Social movements often reveal the cutting edge of social change. Upset by some aspect of society, people band together to express their feelings, even their outrage. They organize to demand change, or to resist some change they don't like. Because social movements form around issues that bother large numbers of people, they indicate areas of society in which there is great pressure for change. With globalization, these issues increasingly cut across international boundaries, showing areas of discontent and sweeping change that affect many millions of people in different cultures (see pages 627–628). Although the issues can simmer for generations, a social movement can explode onto the scene, spread quickly, and, generating huge enthusiasm, topple governments. Such was the case with the Arab uprisings across North Africa in 2011.

Conflict, Power, and Global Politics

In our fast-paced world, we pay most attention to changes that directly affect our own lives or that make the headlines. But largely out of sight lies one of the most significant changes of all, the shifting arrangements of power among nations. Let's look at some of these changes.

A Brief History of Geopolitics. By the sixteenth century, global divisions of power had begun to emerge. Nations with the most advanced technology (at that time, the swiftest ships and the most powerful cannons) became wealthy through *colonialism*, conquering other nations and taking control of their resources. With the beginning of the Industrial Revolution in the eighteenth century, those nations that industrialized

modernization the transformation of traditional societies into industrial societies

Each year, the leaders of the world's eight most powerful nations meet in a secluded place to make world-controlling decisions. And each year, protesters demonstrate near the site. This photo was taken at G8's 2013 meeting in Enniskillen, Northern Ireland.

first exploited the resources of countries that had not yet industrialized. According to *world system theory*, this made the nonindustrialized nations dependent and unable to develop their own resources (see page 247). The consequences of this early domination remain with us today, including the recurring conflicts over oil in the Middle East and the Arab uprisings in North Africa, but we'll get to this shortly.

G7 Plus. Since World War II, a realignment of the world's powers has created a triadic division of the globe: a Japan-centered East (with China in the process of replacing Japan), a Germany-centered Europe, and a United States–centered western hemisphere. In an effort to align power and divide global areas of dominance, these three powers, along with four lesser ones—Canada, France, Great Britain, and Italy—formed G7, meaning the "Group of 7." Fear of Russia's nuclear arsenal prompted G7 to let Russia join this elite club, creating G8.

Dividing Up the World. At their annual meetings, these world powers set policies to guide global economic affairs. Their goal is to perpetuate their global dominance. Essential to this goal is maintaining access to abundant, cheap oil—which requires that they dominate the Middle East. For the Arab nations to become an independent power would be a direct threat to this goal. To the degree that these nations fail to implement policies and international relations that further their own interests, they undermine the New World Order they are trying to orchestrate.

Four Threats to This Coalition of Powers. The global divisions that this group is trying to work out face four major threats. The first is dissension within. Currently, Russia is at the center of intrafamilial feuding (Nichol 2011). Because Russia is still stinging after losing its empire and wants a more powerful presence on the world stage, it is quick to perceive insult and threat—and to retaliate. In the dead of winter of 2006 and again in 2009, amid a dispute with Ukraine over the price of gas, Russia turned off the pipeline that carries its gas through the Ukraine to western Europe, endangering lives in several countries (Crossland 2006; Kramer 2009).

The second threat is the resurgence of China. From a huge but sleepy, backwater nation, China is emerging as a giant on the world stage of power (Stewart 2013). As China continues to develop its economic might and flex its military muscle, this country poses a potent threat to G8's plans, especially those concerning Asia and Africa. So far, the struggle for natural resources has been limited to bidding wars and an occasional exchange of words. If this competition were to erupt into real war, all bets would be off concerning G8's success.

In a sign of changes to come, G8 is gradually—but with severe reluctance—bowing to the inevitable. Attempting to reduce the likelihood of conflict as China steps onto turf claimed by others, G8 has allowed China to become an observer at its annual summits. As mentioned in Chapter 11, if China cooperates adequately, the next step will be to add China to this exclusive club, transforming the group into G9. Unless China decides to go it alone, it will be incorporated into the coming New World Order.

The third threat is the resurgence of ethnic rivalries and conflicts. In Europe, Muslim immigrants feel unwelcome. In Africa, the Igbo in Nigeria won't let the government count them because, as they say, "We are not Nigerian." In North America, ethnic conflicts flare up in the United States and Mexico, and in Asia, they occur in China and Vietnam. We do not know how long the lid can be kept on the seemingly bottomless ethnic antagonisms or whether they will ever play themselves out. The end of these hostilities will certainly not come during our lifetimes.

For global control, G8 requires political and economic stability, both in its members' own backyards and in those countries that provide the raw materials that fuel its giant industrial machine. This explains why G8 cares little when African nations self-destruct in ethnic slaughter but refuses to tolerate interethnic warfare in its own neighborhoods. To allow warfare between different groups in Bosnia, Kosovo, or Georgia to go unchecked would be to tolerate conflict that could spread and engulf Europe. In contrast, the deaths of hundreds of thousands of Tutsis in Rwanda carried little or no political significance for these powerful countries.

The fourth threat comes from the smoldering embers of the Cold War. While relations between the United States and Russia have thawed, these countries do not have the relations one would expect between friendly nations. Each remains suspicious of the other, reading evil intentions into what the other does. The United States thinks that Russia wants to invade Europe, or at least take over the satellite nations it lost. For its part, Russia suspects that the United States may be planning a nuclear attack (Kozin 2013). When the United States announced that it was going to put a radar system and missile interceptors in Poland and Romania in what it calls a "missile-defense shield," Russia threatened to attack and destroy the system (Boudreaux 2012). Chillingly, Russia and the United States both cling stubbornly to the *right of first strike*, the right to strike the other with nuclear weapons even though the other has not launched any (Kozin 2013).

The Growing Relevance of Africa. No longer can G8 safely ignore Africa, once a remote continent but now transformed by globalization into a neighbor. As resources grow scarcer, G8 is able to see how events in Africa are related to its own well-being. These global powers are realizing that African poverty and political corruption breed political unrest that can come back to haunt them. In addition to Africa's vast natural resources, including oil reserves that could counterbalance those of the unstable Middle East, Africa is also the world's last largely untapped market. Political stability in Africa could go a long way toward transforming this continent into a giant outlet for G8's economic machinery. This combination of resources and markets helps explain why the United States has raised funds for African AIDS victims and, as in Liberia, Somalia, and Darfur, has begun to intervene in African politics.

To gain and maintain dominance over Africa and to send a not-so-subtle signal to China, its chief competitor for Africa's resources, the U.S. government has formed AFRICOM (African Command). This special command unit of the U.S. Marines was "sold" to the U.S. Congress as a "soft force." It would specialize in humanitarian missions such as bringing medical assistance to Africa (Vandiver 2013a, 2013b). The Marines found its humanitarian mission and its large civilian staff cumbersome and has succeeded in shedding its softer side. AFRICOM now proudly boasts of having changed its focus to one more to its liking: combat-ready Marines ready to strike specific targets at a moment's notice. AFRICOM has forged relationships with most African leaders and is training Africans to fight rebels in their own countries. With its rapid-reaction, crisis-response units and its new drones and Ospreys (planes that can take off and land vertically), AFRICOM is now "military ready," and is zeroing in on groups that threaten U.S. access to Africa's resources. Currently, those groups are Islamic radicals, especially those in Nigeria and Mali, not surprisingly, oil-rich countries.

To maintain global power requires the continuous development of weapons. Shown here is the Osprey. This versatile aircraft lands and takes off like a helicopter; once airborne, its wingtips go vertical, and it flies like an airplane.

22.2 Summarize theories of social change: social evolution, natural cycles, conflict over power and resources, and Ogburn's theory.

Theories and Processes of Social Change

Social change has always fascinated theorists. Earlier in the text, we reviewed the theories of Karl Marx and Max Weber, which we just summarized. Of the many other attempts to explain why societies change, we will consider just four: the evolution of societies, natural cycles, conflict and power, and the pioneering views of sociologist William Ogburn.

Evolution from Lower to Higher

Evolutionary theories of how societies change are of two types, unilinear and multilinear. *Unilinear* theories assume that all societies follow the same path: Each evolves from simpler to more complex forms. This journey takes each society through uniform sequences (Barnes 1935). Of the many versions of this theory, the one proposed by Lewis Morgan (1877) once dominated Western thought. Morgan said that all societies go through three stages: savagery, barbarism, and civilization. In Morgan's eyes, England, his own society, was the epitome of civilization. All other societies were destined to follow the same path.

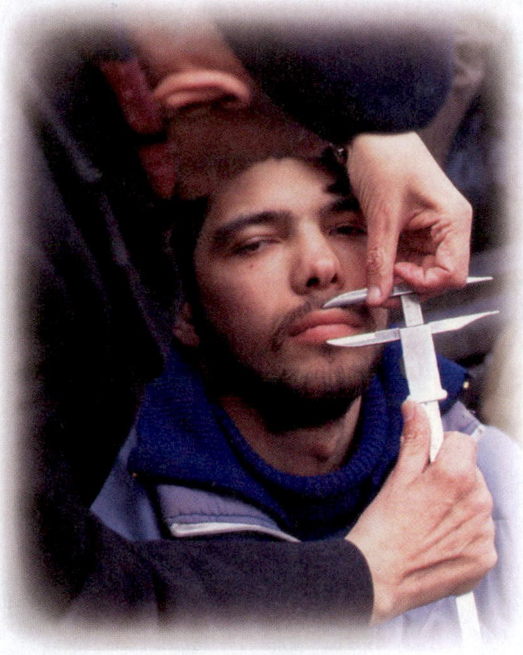

Despite the globe's vast social change, people all over the world continue to make race a fundamental distinction. Shown here is a Ukrainian being measured to see if he is really "full lipped" enough to be called a Tartar.

Multilinear views of evolution replaced unilinear theories. Instead of assuming that all societies follow the same sequence, multilinear theorists proposed that different routes lead to the same stage of development. Although the paths all lead to industrialization, societies need not pass through the same sequence of stages on their journey (Sahlins and Service 1960; Lenski and Lenski 1987).

Central to all evolutionary theories, whether unilinear or multilinear, is the assumption of *cultural progress.* Tribal societies are assumed to have a primitive form of human culture. As these societies evolve, they reach a higher state—the supposedly advanced and superior form that characterizes the Western world. Growing appreciation of the rich diversity—and complexity—of tribal cultures has discredited this idea. In addition, Western culture is now in crisis (poverty, racism, war, terrorism, sexual assaults, and unsafe streets) and no longer regarded as the apex of human civilization. Consequently, the idea of cultural progress has been cast aside, and evolutionary theories have been rejected (Eder 1990; Smart 1990).

Natural Cycles

Cyclical theories attempt to account for the rise of entire civilizations. Why, for example, did Egypt, Greece, and Rome wield such power and influence, only to crest and then decline? Cyclical theories assume that civilizations are like organisms: They are born, enjoy an exuberant youth, come to maturity, and then decline as they reach old age. Finally, they die (Hughes 1962).

The cycle does exist, but why? Historian Arnold Toynbee (1946) said that each civilization faces challenges to its existence. Groups work out solutions to these challenges, as they must if they are to continue. But these solutions are not satisfactory to all. The ruling elite manages to keep the remaining oppositional forces under control, even though they "make trouble" now and then. At a civilization's peak, however, when it has become an empire, the ruling elite loses its capacity to keep the masses in line "by charm rather than by force." Gradually, the fabric of society rips apart. Force may hold the empire together for hundreds of years, but the civilization is doomed.

In a book that provoked widespread controversy, *The Decline of the West* (1926–1928), Oswald Spengler, a high school teacher in Germany, proposed that Western civilization had passed its peak and was in decline. Although the West succeeded in overcoming the crises provoked by Hitler and Mussolini, as Toynbee noted, civilizations don't end in sudden collapse. Because the decline can last hundreds of years, perhaps the crisis in Western civilization mentioned earlier (poverty, rape, murder, and so on) indicates that Spengler was right, and we are now in decline. If so, it appears that China is waiting on the horizon to seize global power and to forge a new civilization.

Conflict over Power and Resources

Long before Toynbee, Karl Marx identified a recurring process of social change. He said that each *thesis* (a current arrangement of power) contains its own *antithesis* (contradiction or opposition). A struggle develops between the thesis and its antithesis, leading to a *synthesis* (a new arrangement of power). This new social order, in turn, becomes a thesis that will be challenged by its own antithesis, and so on. Figure 22.1 gives a visual summary of this process.

According to Marx's view (called a **dialectical process of history**), each ruling group sows the seeds of its own destruction. Consider capitalism. Marx said that capitalism (the thesis) is built on the exploitation of workers (an antithesis, or built-in opposition). With workers and owners on a collision course, the dialectical process will not stop until workers establish a classless state (the synthesis).

The analysis of G7/G8 in the previous section follows conflict theory. G8's current division of the globe's resources and markets is a thesis. Resentment on the part of have-not nations is an antithesis. The demand to redistribute power and resources will come from any Least Industrialized or Industrializing Nation that gains military power. With their nuclear weapons, China, India, and Pakistan fit this scenario. Iran and North Korea present especially threatening antitheses, as do the al-Qaedas and their desire to change the balance of power between the Middle East and the industrialized West.

Eventually, a new arrangement of power will form. Like the old, this new synthesis will contain its own antitheses, such as ethnic hostilities or leaders who feel their countries have been denied a fair share of resources. These contradictions will haunt the rearrangement of power, which at some point will be resolved into another synthesis. The process repeats, a continual cycle of thesis, antithesis, and synthesis.

FIGURE 22.1 Marx's Model of Historical Change

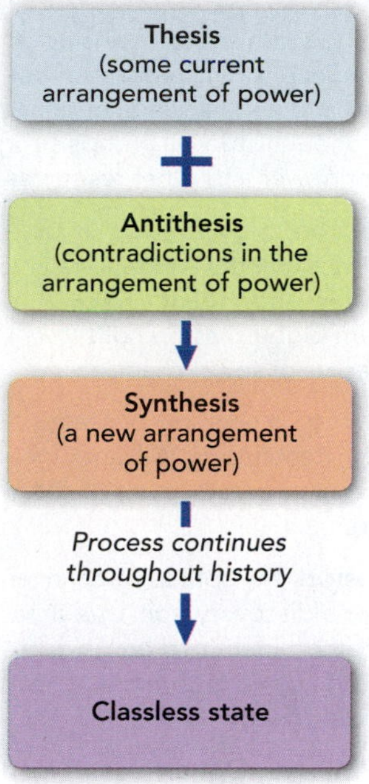

Source: By the author.

Ogburn's Theory

Sociologist William Ogburn (1922/1950, 1961, 1964) proposed a theory of social change that is based largely on technology. As you can see from Table 22.2 below, he said that technology changes society by three processes: invention, discovery, and diffusion. Let's consider each.

TABLE 22.2 Ogburn's Processes of Social Change

Process of Change	What It Is	Examples	Social Changes
Invention 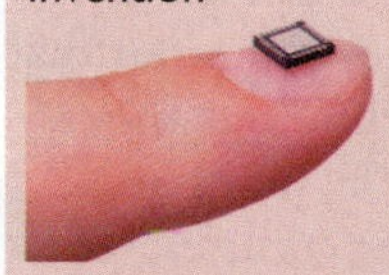	Combination of existing elements to form new ones	1. Cars 2. Microchip 3. Graphite composites	1. Urban sprawl and long commutes to work 2. Telecommuting and cyber warfare 3. New types of building construction
Discovery 	New way of seeing some aspect of the world	1. Columbus—North America 2. Gold in California 3. DNA	1. Realignment of global power 2. Westward expansion of the U.S. 3. Positive identification of criminals
Diffusion 	Spread of an invention or discovery	1. Airplanes 2. Money 3. Condom	1. Global tourism 2. Global trade 3. Smaller families

Note: For each example, there are many changes. For some of the changes ushered in by the automobile and microchip, see pages 649–655. You can also see that any particular change, such as global trade, depends not just on one item but also on several preceding changes.

Source: By the author.

dialectical process (of history) each arrangement of power (a thesis) contains contradictions (antitheses) which make the arrangement unstable and which must be resolved; the new arrangement of power (a synthesis) contains its own contradictions; this process of balancing and unbalancing continues throughout history as groups struggle for power and other resources

invention the combination of existing elements and materials to form new ones; identified by William Ogburn as one of three processes of social change

discovery a new way of seeing reality; identified by William Ogburn as one of three processes of social change

diffusion the spread of an invention or a discovery from one area to another; identified by William Ogburn as one of three processes of social change

cultural lag Ogburn's term for human behavior lagging behind technological innovations

Invention. Ogburn defined **invention** as a combining of existing elements and materials to form new ones. We usually think of inventions only as material items, such as computers, but there also are *social inventions.* We have considered many social inventions in this text, including democracy and citizenship (pages 427–428), capitalism (pages 173–174, 394–395), socialism (pages 395–396), bureaucracy (pages 175–178), the corporation (pages 185–187, 400–402), and, in Chapter 11, gender equality. We saw how these social inventions had far-reaching consequences for people's lives. Material inventions can also affect social life deeply, and in this chapter, we will examine how the automobile and the microchip have transformed society.

Discovery. Ogburn identified **discovery**, a new way of seeing reality, as a second process of change. The reality is already present, but people see it for the first time. An example is Columbus' "discovery" of North America, which had consequences so huge that they altered the course of human history. This example also illustrates another principle: A discovery brings extensive change only when it comes at the right time. Other groups, such as the Vikings, had already "discovered" North America in the sense of learning that a new land existed—obviously no discovery to the Native Americans already living there. Viking settlements disappeared into history, however, and Norse culture was untouched by the discovery.

Diffusion. Ogburn stressed how **diffusion**, the spread of an invention or discovery from one area to another, can deeply affect people's lives. Consider an object as simple as the axe. When missionaries introduced steel axes to the Aborigines of Australia, it upset their whole society. Before this, the men controlled axe-making. They used a special stone that was available only in a remote region, and fathers passed axe-making skills on to their sons. Women had to request permission to use the axe. When steel axes became common, women also possessed them, and the men lost both status and power (Sharp 1995).

Diffusion also includes the spread of social inventions and ideas. As we saw in Chapter 15, the idea of citizenship changed political structures around the world. It swept away monarchs as an unquestioned source of authority. The idea of gender equality is now circling the globe. To those who live where this concept is taken for granted, it is surprising to think that opposition to withholding rights on the basis of someone's sex can be revolutionary. Like citizenship, gender equality is destined to transform human relationships and entire societies.

Cultural Lag. Ogburn coined the term **cultural lag** to refer to how some elements of culture lag behind the changes that come from invention, discovery, and diffusion. Technology, he suggested, usually changes first, with culture lagging behind. In other words, we play catch-up with changing technology, adapting our customs and ways of life to meet its needs.

Evaluation of Ogburn's Theory. Some find Ogburn's analysis too one-directional, saying that it makes technology the cause of almost all social change. They point out that people also take control over technology, developing or adapting the technology they need, and then selectively using it. You read about the Amish on page 105, an example of people who reject technology that they perceive as threatening to their culture.

Technology and social change are certainly not one-directional. Rather, they are like a two-way street: Just as technology stimulates social change, so social change stimulates technology. The Nazi armies that marched across Europe last century and the Japanese atrocities across the Pacific stimulated the United States to build the atomic bomb. Today, the growing number of elderly is spurring the development of new medical technologies, such as treatments for Alzheimer's disease. Similarly, ideas about people with disabilities are changing—that instead of being shunted aside, they should participate in society's mainstream. This, in turn, has triggered the development of new types of wheelchairs and prosthetic devices that allow people who cannot move their legs to play basketball, participate in the Paralympics, and even compete in downhill wheelchair races. The street is so two-way that this greater visibility and participation, in turn, is changing attitudes toward people with disabilities.

Diffusion is the spread of an invention or discovery from one group or area to another. The technological revolution based on the microchip has become global, changing behaviors, relationships, and ideas. To register to vote, this Maasai woman in a remote area of Kenya is having her fingerprints taken by biometric equipment.

In fairness to Ogburn, we must note that he never said that technology is the only force for social change. Nor did he assert that people are passive pawns in the face of overwhelming technological forces. He did stress, though, that the material culture (technology) usually changes first, and the symbolic culture (people's ideas and ways of life) follows. This direction still holds. Technology underlies the rapid changes that are engulfing us today. And we are still playing catch-up with technology, with the microchip especially, which is transforming society and, with it, our way of life.

postmodern society another term for postindustrial society; a chief characteristic is the use of tools that extend human abilities to gather and analyze information, to communicate, and to travel

How Technology Is Changing Our Lives

22.3 Use the examples of the automobile and the microchip to illustrate the sociological significance of technology; include changes in ideology, norms, human relationships, education, work, business, war, and social inequality.

Extending Human Abilities

To understand what *technology* is, let's look at its three meanings. Its first meaning refers to *tools*, the items used to accomplish tasks. The tools can be as simple as a comb or as complicated as a computer. Technology's second meaning refers to the *procedures* necessary to produce tools: in this case, the ways we manufacture combs and computers. Technology's third meaning refers to the *skills* needed to use tools: in this case, the skills we need to "produce" an acceptable hairdo or to go online.

No matter what tools, procedures, or skills we are talking about, technology always refers to *artificial means of extending human abilities.* Consider our opening vignette. The essence of the story is how greatly our new technology has extended human abilities.

All human groups make and use technology. They all have tools, procedures, and skills. The chief characteristic of technology in postindustrial societies (also called **postmodern societies**) is that it greatly extends our abilities to communicate, to travel, and to retrieve and analyze information. These *new technologies*, as they are called, extend our abilities beyond anything known in human history. We can now do what

Do you know what that large object in the center of the photo is? In the 1920s, 30s, and 40s, middle-class families would gather in the living room after dinner and listen to the radio. (It was a sit-down dinner served by the wife and assisted by the daughters.) Can you see how technology is influencing this 1940s family? How about yourself?

has never been done before: transplant organs, communicate almost instantaneously anywhere on the globe, probe space, and travel vast distances quickly. And, as in our opening vignette, we can produce, store, retrieve, and analyze vast amounts of information, even if we must penetrate thick jungles to do so.

The Sociological Significance of Technology

Watch on **MySocLab**
Video: ABC Nightline: Big Brother

Our journey to the future is going to have so many twists and turns that no one knows what our lives will be like. It is intriguing, however, to try to peer over the edge of the present to catch a glimpse of that future. But because this text is about sociology, we cannot lose sight of the sociological significance of technology—*how it changes our way of life.* When a technology is introduced into a society, it forces other parts of society to give way. In fact, *new technologies can reshape society.* Let's look at four ways that technology changes social life.

Changes in Production. Technology changes how people organize themselves. In Chapter 6, we discussed how, before machine technology was developed, most people worked at home; the new power-driven machinery required them to leave their families and go to a place called a factory. In the first factories, each worker still made an entire item. Then it was discovered that production increased if each worker performed only a specific task. One worker would hammer on a single part, or turn a certain number of bolts; then someone else would go to the item and do some other repetitive task on it; a third person would then take over; and so on. Henry Ford built on this innovation by developing the assembly line: Instead of workers moving to the parts, machines moved the parts to the workers. In addition, the parts were made interchangeable and easy to attach (McKinlay and Wilson 2012).

Changes in Worker–Owner Relations. Technology also spurs ideology. Karl Marx noted that workers who performed repetitive tasks on just a small part of a product did not feel connected to the finished product. No longer did they think of the product as "theirs." As Marx put it, workers had become **alienated** from the product of their labor, an **alienation** that breeds dissatisfaction and unrest.

Marx stressed that before factories came on the scene, workers owned their tools. This made them independent. If workers didn't like something, they would pack up their hammers and saws and leave. They would build a wagon or make a table for someone else. The factory brought fundamental change: There, the capitalists owned the tools and machinery. This ownership transferred power to the capitalists, who used it to extract every ounce of sweat and blood they could. The workers had to submit, since desperate, unemployed workers were lined up, eager to take the place of anyone who left. This exploitation, Marx believed, would bring on a workers' revolution: One day, deciding that they had had enough, workers would unite, violently take over the means of production, and establish a workers' state.

Changes in Ideology. The new technology that led to factories also led to a change in ideology. As capitalists made huge profits, they developed the ideology that profits were a moral, even spiritual, endeavor. Profits benefited society—and pleased God as well. Followers of Marx, in turn, built ideologies in opposition to capitalism. In their view, profit comes from the exploitation of workers, because workers are the true owners of society's resources and it is their labor that produces the profit.

Changes in Conspicuous Consumption. Just as ideology follows technology, so does conspicuous consumption. If technology is limited to clubbing animals, then animal skins are valued. No doubt primitive men and women who wore the skins of some especially unusual or dangerous animal walked with their heads held high—while their neighbors, wearing the same old sheepskins, looked on in envy. With technological change, Americans make certain that their clothing and accessories (sunglasses, handbags, and watches) have trendy labels prominently displayed. They also proudly display their cars, boats, and second homes. In short, while envy and pride may be basic to human nature, the particular material display depends on the state of technology.

alienation Marx's term for workers' lack of connection to the product of their labor; caused by workers being assigned repetitive tasks on a small part of a product—this leads to a sense of powerlessness and normlessness; others use the term in the general sense of not feeling a part of something

Explore on **MySocLab**
Activity: How Strong is Residential Stability in the United States?

Changes in Family Relationships. Technology also changes how people relate to one another. When men left home to work in factories, they became isolated from much of the everyday lives of their families. One consequence of becoming relative strangers to their wives and children was more divorce. As more women were drawn from the home to offices and factories, there were similar consequences—greater isolation from husbands and children and even more fragile marriages. A counter-trend is now under way, as the newer technology allows millions of people to work at home. One consequence may be a strengthening of families and a reduction of divorce.

To get a better idea of how technology shapes our way of life, let's consider the changes ushered in by the automobile and the computer.

When Old Technology Was New: The Impact of the Automobile

About 100 years ago, the automobile was a new technology. You might be surprised at some of the ways in which this invention shaped U.S. society. Let's look at them.

Displacement of Existing Technology. In a process that began in earnest when Henry Ford began to mass-produce the Model T in 1908, the automobile gradually pushed aside the old technology. People found automobiles to be cleaner, more reliable, and less expensive than horses. People even thought that cars would lower their taxes, since no longer would the public have to pay to clean up the tons of horse manure that accumulated on city streets (Flink 1990). Humorous as it sounds now, they also thought that automobiles would eliminate the cities' parking problems, since an automobile took up only half as much space as a horse and buggy.

Effects on Cities. The automobile stimulated suburbanization (Kopecky and Suen 2010). By the 1920s, Americans had begun to leave the city. They found that they could live in outlying areas where housing was more affordable and commute to jobs in the city. Eventually, this exodus to the suburbs produced urban sprawl and reduced the cities' tax base. As discussed in Chapter 20, suuburbanization contributed to many of the problems that U.S. cities experience today.

Changes in Architecture. The automobile's effects on commercial architecture are easy to see—from the huge parking lots that loop around shopping malls to the drive-up windows at banks and fast-food restaurants. Not so apparent is how the automobile altered the architecture of U.S. homes (Flink 1990). Before cars came on the scene, each

In the photo on the left, Henry Ford proudly displays his 1905 car, the latest in automobile technology. As is apparent, especially from the spokes on the car's wheels, new technology builds on existing technology. At the time this photo was taken, who could have imagined that this vehicle would transform society? The photo on the right is a concept car designed in China.

home had a stable in the back where the family kept its horse and buggy. At first, people parked their cars there, as it required no change in architecture.

Then, in three steps, home architecture changed. First, new homes were built with a detached garage. It was located, like the stable, at the back of the home. As the automobile became more essential to the U.S. family, the garage was incorporated into the home. It was moved from the backyard to the side of the house, where it was connected by a breezeway. In the final step, the breezeway was removed, and the garage was integrated into the home, letting people enter their automobiles without going outside.

Changed Courtship Customs and Sexual Norms. By the 1920s, the automobile was used extensively for dating. This removed young people from the watchful eye of parents and undermined parental authority. The police began to receive complaints about "night riders" who parked their cars along country lanes, "doused their lights, and indulged in orgies" (Brilliant 1964). Automobiles became so popular for courtship that by the 1960s, about 40 percent of marriage proposals took place in them (Flink 1990).

In 1925, Jewett introduced cars with a foldout bed, as did Nash in 1937. The Nash version became known as "the young man's model" (Flink 1990). Mobile lovemaking has declined since the 1970s, not because there is less premarital sex but because the change in sexual norms has made bedrooms easily accessible to the unmarried.

Effects on Women's Roles. The automobile also lies at the heart of the change in women's roles. To see how, we first need to get a picture of what a woman's life was like before the automobile. Historian James Flink (1990) described it this way:

> *Until the automobile revolution, in upper-middle-class households groceries were either ordered by phone and delivered to the door or picked up by domestic servants or the husband on his way home from work. Iceboxes provided only very limited space for the storage of perishable foods, so shopping at markets within walking distance of the home was a daily chore. The garden provided vegetables and fruits in season, which were home-canned for winter consumption. Bread, cakes, cookies, and pies were home-baked. Wardrobes contained many home-sewn garments.*
>
> *Mother supervised the household help and worked alongside them preparing meals, washing and ironing, and housecleaning. In her spare time she mended clothes, did decorative needlework, puttered in her flower garden, and pampered a brood of children. Generally, she made few family decisions and few forays alone outside the yard. She had little knowledge of family finances and the family budget. The role of the lower-middle-class housewife differed primarily in that far less of the household work was done by hired help, so that she was less a manager of other people's work, more herself a maid-of-all-work around the house.*

Because automobiles required skill to operate rather than strength, women were able to drive as well as men. This new mobility freed women physically from the narrow confines of the home. As Flink (1990) observed, the automobile changed women "from producers of food and clothing into consumers of national-brand canned goods, prepared foods, and ready-made clothes. The automobile permitted shopping at self-serve supermarkets outside the neighborhood and in combination with the electric refrigerator made buying food a weekly rather than a daily activity." When women began to do the shopping, they gained greater control over the family budget, and as their horizons extended beyond the confines of the home, they also learned different views of life.

In Sum: The automobile helped transform society, including views of courtship and sexuality. It had a special impact on a woman's role at home, including the relationship with her husband. It altered women's attitudes as it transformed their opportunities and stimulated them to participate in areas of social life not connected with the home.

No one attributes such fundamental changes in relationships and values solely to the automobile, of course. Many historical events and other technological changes occurred during this same period, each making its own contribution to social change. Even this brief overview of the social effects of the automobile, however, illustrates that technology is much more than just a tool: It exerts profound influence on social life.

From this 1946 photo, you can see how computers have changed. This is the ENIAC, the world's first computer, which weighed 30 tons, was eight feet high, three feet deep, and 100 feet long. Most cell phones have more computing power than this monstrosity.

The New Technology: The Microchip and Social Life

With technology changing so rapidly, our way of life often meets unexpected twists and turns. Although we don't yet know where those twists and turns will lead us, it is intriguing to try to peer over the edge of the present to at least catch a glimpse of that future.

Let's do this by focusing on the computer. We will begin with its effects on social interaction, education, business, and the waging of war. We'll then consider the computer's impact on social inequalities and war.

Changes in Social Interaction. I have stressed that technology changes our lives in fundamental ways, including the ways we interact with one another. Consider this little example.

> *As I work on this edition of your text, my wife and I sit at the same large dining room table that serves as our desk, each absorbed in our computers as we go about individual tasks. Although we can easily talk to one another, and we do, we also send e-mails back and forth throughout the day, even though we are within arms' reach of one another. One of us finds something interesting, the latest news on Latvia or the global economic crisis, some sociological analysis, news from a friend or one of the kids, or even something humorous. By sending the message, instead of talking, we don't break the other's concentration. We attend to the message when it fits into our breaks, when we then chat with one another.*

This is just one example of how technology is altering my interactions. If we were to talk to one another, you could tell me about the many ways that technology is changing your social patterns. When new technology comes, we must adapt to it, but we make it fit our particular life situation. The process of change is a two-way street.

Computers in Education. Because of computers, students can take courses in Russian, German, and Spanish—even when their schools have no teachers who speak these languages. If their school also lacks sociology instructors, they can still study the sociology of gender, race, social class, or even sex, and sports. (The comma is important. It isn't sex and sports. That course isn't offered—yet.)

We've barely begun to harness the power of computers, but I imagine that the day will come when you will be able to key in the terms *social interaction* and *gender*, select your preference of historical period, geographical site, age, and ethnic group—and the computer will spew out text, maps, moving images, and sounds. You will be able to compare sexual discrimination in the military in 1985 and today, or the price of marijuana in Los Angeles and New Orleans. If you wish, the computer will give you a test—geared to the level of difficulty you choose—so that you can check your mastery of the material.

Distance learning, courses taught to students who are not physically present with their instructor, will integrate students around the world. Using apps and their laptop cameras, everyone in the class will be able to see everyone else, even though the students live in different countries. Imagine this—and likely it soon will be a reality: Your fellow students in a course on human culture will be living in Thailand, South Africa, Latvia, Egypt, China, and Australia. With zero-cost conference calls and e-mail and file

The microchip is transforming our lives—the way we shop, spend our leisure, relate to one another, and, as shown here, the way we learn. With a computer projecting a three dmensional image of the inside of a frog, students don't have to dissect real frogs.

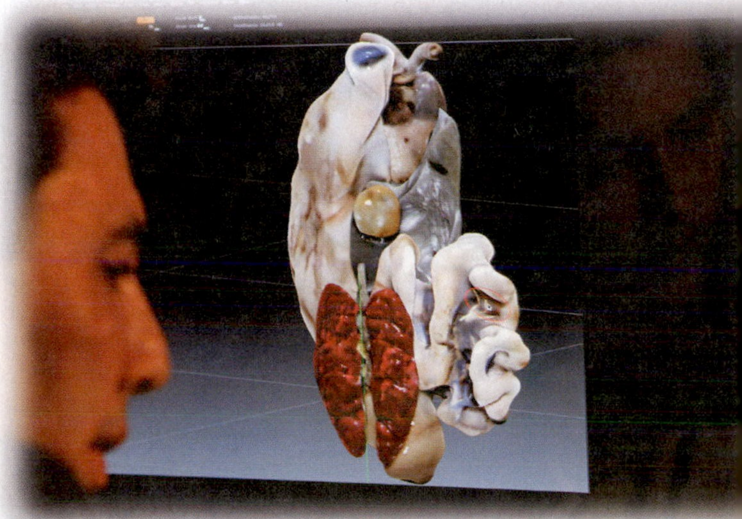

This bike actually flies—thanks to six horizontal propellers and a battery-powered motor. Changing technology changes not only the way we do things, such as travel, but also the way we think about life and the self and the way we relate to others.

sharing, you will compare your countries' customs on eating, dating, marriage, family, or burial—whatever is of interest to you. You will then write a term paper in which you apply the theories in the text to what you have learned from your fellow students. With a flourish and a smile, you then e-mail the paper to your instructor. (Okay, forget the flourish and smile, but from this, you can catch a glimpse of the future.)

Computers in Business and Finance. The advanced technology of businesses used to consist of cash registers and adding machines. Connections to the outside world were managed by telephone. Today, businesses are electronically "wired" to suppliers, salespeople, and clients around the country—and around the world. Computers track sales of items, tabulate inventory, and set in motion the process of reordering and restocking. Sales reports alert managers to changes in their customers' tastes or preferences. For retail giants like Wal-Mart, the computer reports regional changes in preferences of products.

National borders are rendered meaningless as computers instantaneously transfer billions of dollars from one country to another. No "cash" changes hands in these transactions. The money consists of digits in computer memory banks. In the same day, digitized money can be transferred from the United States to Switzerland, from there to the Grand Cayman Islands, and then to the Isle of Man. Its zigzag, encrypted path around the globe leaves few traces for sleuths to follow. "Where's my share?" governments around the world are grumbling, as they consider how to control—and tax—this new technology.

Computers in International Conflict. Computers are also having a major impact on war. Many of the changes, fortunately for us, are still theoretical. When the application arrives, the loss of lives will be horrendous. In the following Thinking Critically section we'll look at cyber war. After that, we'll consider drones and warfare in space.

THINKING CRITICALLY

Cyberwar and Cyber Defense

Iran's nuclear enrichment program had progressed quite well. But as five thousand centrifuges were whirring away, Iranian scientists stared in disbelief. Although their computers reported that everything was fine, the centrifuges suddenly sped up and slowed down, ripping their delicate parts into shreds.

Iran had been hit by the Stuxnet worm, a malware that the United States and Israel had surreptitiously entered into Iran's computer codes. Iran's goal of producing material for a nuclear bomb had been set back by months, perhaps by years. (Sanger 2012)

Every country in conflict with another looks for an edge. The computer's marvelous strength—its capacity to store and retrieve information and to execute commands—can be turned into a weakness, an Achilles heel that can bring down the powerful.

To turn strength into weakness brings both delight and fear to generals around the world. Their delight comes from the mouthwatering anticipation that they might use this capacity against their enemies. Their fear? That their enemies might turn this capacity against them.

Cyber weapons offer intriguing potential for warfare. They can make missiles that have been ordered airborne to strike enemy targets sit in their silos like wounded birds taking refuge in their nests. If an enemy were to disrupt vital communications, they could transform computer screens into windows of darkness. Or they could fill military files with false information. Easy attack could follow. This fear pervades the military—on both sides, wherever those fluid sides line up today.

This is not some far-off future. As the Iranians discovered, cyber war has begun. The United States, too, is a victim, with thousands of attacks launched against its military computers. The attacker? Just round up the usual suspect, China (Mozur 2013). The purpose of the attacks seems to be to find chinks in the armor, the spots where malicious code can be installed unawares—like Stuxnet to be unleashed at some designated moment. The targets extend beyond the military: a nation's electrical grid, its banking system, stock exchange, oil and gas pipelines, air traffic control system, and Internet and cell phone communications.

This military command post is in South Korea, with both U.S. and South Korean personnel. South Korea and North Korea accuse one another of attacking the other's communication systems. Each accusation is likely true.

The United States is spending billions of dollars preparing for cyber war. The U.S. Air Force runs an Office for Cyberspace Operations, while the Navy operates an aptly named Center for Information Dominance. An overarching group, the U.S. Cyber Command, has the assignment to integrate the cyber warfare capacities of the military with those of the National Security Agency (Barnes 2012; Sanger and Shanker 2013).

China has attempted to turn the tables, accusing the United States of tens of thousands of cyber attacks against its military Web sites (Mozur 2013). It is likely that this accusation is correct. Like China, the United States is breaking into the computers of other nations with the goal of "destroying, disrupting, degrading, deceiving, and corrupting" the ability of potential enemies (Gjelten 2013).

The games have begun. The outcome, unfortunately, might not resemble a game.

For Your Consideration

➔ Do you think the United States should insert dormant malicious codes in Russia's and China's military and central civilian computers—so it can unleash them during some future conflict? If such a code were discovered, what do you think the consequences might be? ■

At this point, the skirmishes are digital and bloodless, but this can change in a moment. In the Sociology and the New Technology box on the next page, we will look at how the microchip is bringing space weapons, destined as an essential pat of future war.

The offspring of the microchip—from computers to cell phones—offer access to vast information and efficiency of communication, manufacturing, and transportation. Will this fundamental change bring greater equality to the world's nations? This photo was taken in Cambodia.

Cyberspace and Social Inequality

We've already stepped into the future. The Net gives us access to digitized libraries. We utilize software that sifts, sorts, and transmits text, photos, sound, and video. We zap messages, images, and digital money to people on the other side of the globe—or even in our own

Sociology and the New Technology

The Coming Star Wars

Star Wars is on its way.

The Predator is an unmanned plane that flies thousands of feet above the ground. Operators at a base search its streaming video. When they identify what they call "the kill shot," they press a button. At this signal, the Predator beams a laser onto the target and launches guided bombs. The enemy sees neither the Predator nor the laser. Perhaps, however, an instant before they are blown to bits, they do hear the sound of the incoming bomb (Barry 2001).

The Pentagon's plans to "weaponize" space go far beyond the Predator. The Pentagon has built a "space plane," the X-37B, which has an airplane's agility and a spacecraft's capacity to travel 5 miles per second in space (Cooper 2010). The Pentagon is also building its own Internet, the Global Information Grid (GIG). The goal of GIG is to encircle the globe and give the Pentagon a "God's eye view" of every enemy everywhere (Weiner 2004). An arsenal of space weapons is ready: microsatellites the size of a suitcase that can pull alongside enemy satellites and, using microwave guns, fry their electronics; a laser whose beam will bounce off a mirror in space, making the night battlefield visible to ground soldiers who are wearing special goggles; pyrotechnic electromagnetic pulsers; holographic decoys; oxygen suckers—and whatever else the feverish imaginations of military planners can devise.

The Air Force has nicknamed one of its space programs "Rods from God," tungsten cylinders to be hurled from space at targets on the ground. Striking at speeds of 7,000 miles an hour, the rods would have the force of a small nuclear weapon. In another program, radio waves would be directed to targets on Earth. As the Air Force explains it, the power of the radio waves could be "just a tap on the shoulder—or they could turn you into toast" (Weiner 2005).

But what happens if enemy, or even rival, nations develop similar capacities—or even greater ones? We are beginning to see an ominous transition in international technological expertise. Already there is the Pterodactyl, China's answer to the Predator. China has advanced its technology to the point that its unmanned aerial vehicles (UAVs) have begun to rival those of the United States (Page 2010; Wall 2010). China has even begun to flaunt its space weapons in the face of the Pentagon, a not too subtle warning not to mess with China as its leaders expand their territorial ambitions.

The MQ-1 Predator.

Weapons are made to be used—despite the constant polite rhetoric about their defensive purposes. On both sides are itchy trigger fingers, and now that China is becoming an ominous threat to U.S. space superiority, the Pentagon faces a new challenge. How will it be able to contain China's political ambitions if Star Wars looms?

For Your Consideration

➜ Do you think we should militarize space? What do you think of this comment, made to Congress by the head of the U.S. Air Force Space Command? "We must establish and maintain space superiority. It's the American way of fighting" (Weiner 2005). Is it rational for the United States to think that it can always maintain technological superiority? What happens if it cannot?

homes, dorm, or office. Our world has become linked by almost instantaneous communications, with information readily accessible around the globe. Few places can still be called "remote."

Listen on **MySocLab**
Audio: NPR: Internet in Africa

This new technology carries severe implications for national and global stratification. On the national level, computer technology could perpetuate present inequalities: We could end up with information have-nots, people cut off from the flow of information on which prosperity depends. Or this technology could provide an opportunity to break out of the inner city and the rural centers of poverty. On the global level, the question is similar, but on a grander scale, taking us to one of the more profound issues of this century: Will unequal access to advanced technology destine the Least Industrialized Nations to a perpetual pauper status? Or will access to this new technology be their passport to affluence?

In Sum: As technology wraps itself around us, transforming society, culture, and our everyday lives, we confront four primary issues: What type of future will technology lead us to? Will technology liberate us or make us slaves of Big Brother? Will the new technology perpetuate or alleviate social inequalities on both national and global levels? Finally, and perhaps most ominously, will the technology that is transforming the face of war and now being used "over there" come back to haunt us in our own land?

The Growth Machine versus the Earth

22.4 Explain how industrialization is related to environmental problems; contrast the environmental movement and environmental sociology; discuss the goal of harmony.

After a frustrating struggle of twenty years, Russian environmentalists finally won a court order to stop Baikalsk Paper Mill from dumping its wastes into Lake Baikal. When the mill filed for bankruptcy, Vladimir Putin, the prime minister of Russia, boarded a minisub and said, "I'll see if the lake has been damaged." At the bottom of Lake Baikal, Putin said, "It's clean. I can see the bottom." He then told Oleg Deripaska, the major owner of the paper mill, "You can dump your wastes in the lake." (Boudreaux 2010)

Politicians are usually more subtle than this, but, befitting his power and position, Putin doesn't have to be. He can crown himself an environmental expert and give personal permission to pollute. Although the specifics differ, in country after country, similar battles are being waged. While environmentalists struggle for a clean Earth, politicians fight for jobs and votes—and while doing so, some line the pockets of their friends, and their own as well.

sustainable environment a world system that takes into account the limits of the environment, produces enough material goods for everyone's needs, and leaves a heritage of a sound environment for the next generation

The Globalization of Capitalism and the Race for Economic Growth. Like drivers and cars spinning around a NASCAR racetrack, we are in the midst of a global economic race that threatens to destroy the Earth. The racetrack is the Earth, and the cars and drivers are the Earth's nations. At the head of the pack are the Most Industrialized Nations. To maintain their lead—and cheered on by their sponsors, the multinational corporations—they continue to push for economic growth. Without an annual increase in production, the economic engines of the Most Industrialized Nations falter, sputtering into recession or depression. Behind them, furiously trying to catch up, are the Industrializing Nations. To develop their economies, China and the others strive for even larger percentage growth. Meanwhile, the Least Industrialized Nations, lagging farther behind and envious of the others, do their best to rev up their economic engines.

Sumatran Tiger
Fewer than 400, Indonesia

Texas Ocelot
Fewer than 250, southern United States, northern Mexico

Mountain Bongo
About 50, Kenya

Gaur
About 36,000, Southeast Asia

A Sustainable Environment. Many people are convinced that the Earth cannot withstand such an onslaught. Global economic production creates global pollution; faster-paced production, which feeds the globalization of capitalism, means faster-paced destruction of our environment. In this relentless pursuit of economic development, many animal species have been destroyed. Others, hanging by a claw or a wounded wing, are on the verge of extinction. If the goal is a **sustainable environment**, a world system in which we use our physical environment to meet our needs without destroying humanity's future, we cannot continue to trash the Earth. In short, the ecological message is incompatible with an economic message that implies it is okay to rape the Earth if it makes someone rich.

Watch on **MySocLab**
Video: Looking Ahead: Toward a Sustainable Society and World

Before looking at the social movement that has emerged around this issue, let's examine some major environmental problems.

Environmental Problems and Industrialization

Although even tribal groups produced pollution, the frontal assault on the natural environment did not begin in earnest until nations industrialized. Industrialization was equated with progress and prosperity. For the Most Industrialized Nations, the slogan has been "Growth at any cost."

Watch on **MySocLab**
Video: ABC Nightline: BioTown U.S.A.

Toxic Wastes. Industrial growth did come, but at a high cost. Despite their harm to the environment and the dangers they pose to people's health, much toxic waste has simply been dumped onto the land, into the oceans, and, with the occasional permission of Putin and other politicians, into our lakes. Formerly pristine streams have been turned into polluted sewers. The disease-ridden water supply of some cities is unfit to drink. The Social Map below shows the locations of the worst hazardous waste sites in the United States. Keep in mind that these are just the worst. There are thousands of others.

Pollution in the Industrializing Nations has become a major problem. The air in Beijing is hazardous to health.

Nuclear power plants are a special problem. They produce wastes that remain lethal for thousands of years. We simply don't know what to do with these piles of deadly garbage. In addition, these nuclear factories, supposedly built with redundant safety features, are vulnerable in unexpected ways. Certainly the nuclear catastrophe at Fukushima, Japan, which continues to spew radiation, is mute testimony to nuclear folly.

We certainly can't lay the cause of our polluted Earth solely at the feet of the Most Industrialized Nations. The Industrializing Nations also do their share, with China the most striking

FIGURE 22.2 The Worst Hazardous Waste Sites

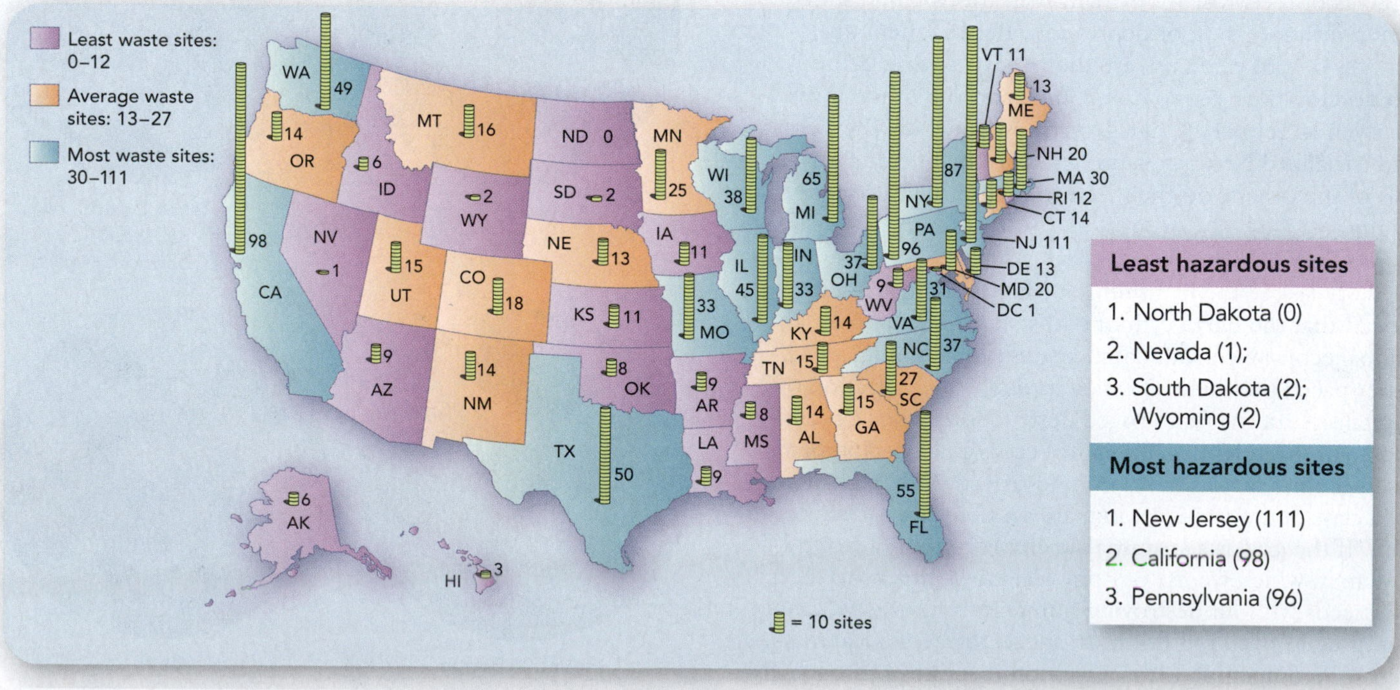

Source: By the author. Based on Environmental Protection Agency 2013.

offender. This country now emits more carbon dioxide than does the United States (Rogers and Evans 2011). Of the world's forty most polluted cities, *thirty-six* are in China (World Bank 2007:Figure 5). *Nine thousand* chemical plants line the banks of China's Yangtze River, turning this major waterway into a snaking industrial sewer (Zakaria 2008). Like the Russians before them, Chinese authorities imprison those who dare to speak out about pollution (Larson 2011; Wong 2011). As China secures its place in the industrialized world, its leaders will inevitably place more emphasis on controlling pollution. However, the harm done to our planet in the meantime is incalculable.

With limited space to address this issue, let's focus on fossil fuels, the energy shortage, and the rain forests.

Fossil Fuels and Global Warming. Burning fossil fuels to run motorized vehicles, factories, and power plants has been especially harmful to our Earth. Figure 22.3 illustrates how burning fossil fuels produces **acid rain**, which kills animal and plant life. The harm is so extensive that fish can no longer survive in some lakes in Canada and the northeastern United States.

acid rain rain containing sulfuric and nitric acids (burning fossil fuels release sulfur dioxide and nitrogen oxide that become sulfuric and nitric acids when they react with moisture in the air)

Global warming is producing many problems for Earth's inhabitants, but with the limited space we have, in the following *Thinking Critically* section, we will consider just one of them.

FIGURE 22.3 Acid Rain

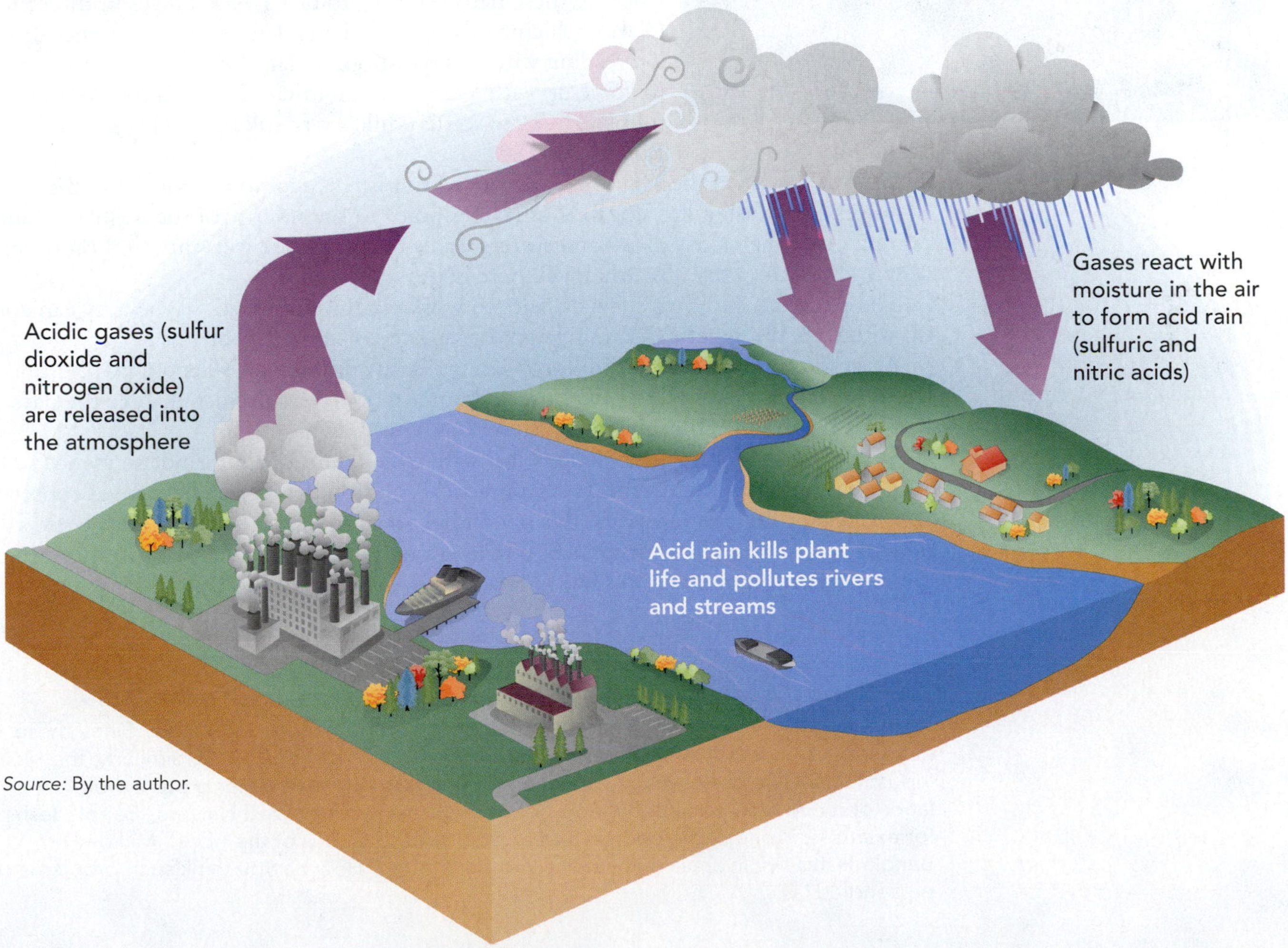
Acidic gases (sulfur dioxide and nitrogen oxide) are released into the atmosphere
Gases react with moisture in the air to form acid rain (sulfuric and nitric acids)
Acid rain kills plant life and pollutes rivers and streams

Source: By the author.

THINKING CRITICALLY

The Island Nations: "Come See Us While We Are Still Here"

The world's glaciers and the ice caps at the North and South Poles store such incredible amounts of water that if they melt, the level of the world's oceans will rise by several feet. This will devastate the world's shores and beaches. Low-lying areas, such as the bayous around New Orleans and Mississippi, will be under water. Many barrier islands off the coast of the United States will disappear. The oceans will reclaim Florida's Everglades.

Maldives

As the glaciers and ice caps melt, entire nations may find that *all* of their landmass lies below water. These are the world's low-lying little island nations. The highest point on some of them is just six feet higher than the level of the ocean.

The few residents of the Everglades will move, and its alligators will migrate a little northward. So will the alligators and humans who populate the southern bayous. New Orleans probably should be abandoned, but it is likely that once again, a broke federal government will pour billions of dollars more into saving the city, which will increasingly lie below sea level.

And the island nations? Unless their inhabitants, including their babies and elderly, learn how to live wearing wet suits, what are these nations going to do? The Maldives in the Indian Ocean, which has been an independent nation only since 1965, is wrestling with this question. So far, they have only managed to come up with a cute tongue-in-cheek slogan to promote tourism: "Come see us while we're still here" (Dickey and Rogers 2002).

No one has taken the Maldives' ministry of tourism suggestion seriously, so the Maldives aren't using this slogan. But it does point to the severity of the problem. Since no one other than a few divers and surfers wants to wear those wet suits, and then for only a few hours a day, just what will these island nations do?

These nations still have a few decades to work out a solution, so maybe they can come up with something better than slogans to promote last-minute tourism.

At least, everyone thought this problem was a few decades off (Gerken 2012). The ice, however, is melting faster than the computer models had predicted. Like the days before a big exam, this problem is rushing ominously on us.

One of these South Pacific nations, Kiribati, which didn't gain its independence until 1979, has hit upon what seems to be a practical solution. Its leaders have been conservative, and over the past few years, this nation has saved money. They have used these savings to buy land in Fiji, which is 1,500 miles away. They are making plans to move their entire population of 106,000 there (Perry 2012).

For Your Consideration

→ In the face of rising seas, what do you think the island nations should do? Since these nations have so few people, it seems that their problems can be solved. Similarly, the Most Industrialized Nations have the capital and the infrastructure to either protect their lowlands or move their people. But how about the Least Industrialized Nations? Bangladesh, for example, is one of the poorest and most crowded nations of the world. Millions of Bangladeshis live in areas that are likely to be flooded. How do you think such problems can be handled? ■

The Energy Shortage and Internal Combustion Engines. If you ever read about an energy shortage, you can be sure that what you read is false. There is no energy shortage, nor can there ever be. We have access to unlimited low-cost power, which can help to raise the living standards of humans across the globe. The Sun, for example, produces more energy than humanity could ever use. Boundless energy is also available from the tides and the winds. In some cases, we need better technology to harness these sources of energy; in others, we need only apply the technology we already have.

Explore on **MySocLab**
Activity: Riding a Bicycle to Work

Burning fossil fuels in internal combustion engines is the main source of pollution in the Most Industrialized Nations. Car and truck engines that burn natural gas, a cleaner and lower-priced fossil fuel, will become common. Of the technologies being developed to use alternative sources of energy in vehicles, the most prominent is the gas-electric hybrid. Some of these cars are expected to eventually get several hundred miles per gallon of gasoline. The hybrid, however, is simply a bridge until vehicles powered by fuel cells become practical. With fuel cells converting hydrogen into electricity, it will be water, not carbon monoxide, coming out of a car's exhaust pipe.

The Rain Forests. Of special concern are the world's rain forests. Although these forests cover just 6 percent of the Earth's land area, they are home to *one-half* of all the Earth's plant and animal species (Frommer 2007). Despite knowing the rain forests' essential role for humanity's welfare, we seem bent on destroying them for the sake of timber and farms. In the process, we extinguish plant and animal species, perhaps thousands a year. As biologists remind us, once a species is lost, it is gone forever.

Listen on **MySocLab**
Audio: NPR: Amazon Rainforest Update

As the rain forests disappear, so do the Indian tribes who live in them. With their extinction goes their knowledge of the environment, the topic of the Cultural Diversity box on the next page. Like Esau who traded his birthright for a bowl of porridge, we are exchanging our future for lumber, farms, and pastures.

The Environmental Movement

Concern about environmental problems has touched such a nerve that it has produced a worldwide social movement. In Europe, *green parties*, political groups whose central concern is the environment, have become a force for change. Germany's green party, for example, has won seats in the national legislature. In the United States, in contrast, green parties have had little success.

One concern of the environmental movement in the United States is **environmental injustice**, minorities and the poor being the ones who suffer the most from the effects of pollution (Lerner 2010). Industries locate where land is cheaper, which, as you know, is *not* where the wealthy live. Nor will the rich allow factories to spew pollution near their homes. As a result, pollution is more common in low-income communities. Sociologists have studied, formed, and joined *environmental justice* groups that fight to close polluting plants and block construction of polluting industries. Like the defeat at Lake Baikal, just mentioned, this often pits environmentalists against politicians and the wealthy.

Like the members of last century's civil rights movement, environmentalists are certain that they stand for what is right and just. Most activists seek quiet solutions in politics, education, and legislation. Despairing that pollution continues, that the rain forests are still being cleared, and that species continue to become extinct, others are convinced that the planet is doomed unless we take immediate action. This conviction motivates some to choose a more radical course, to use extreme tactics to try to arouse indignation among the public and to force the government to act. Such activists are featured in the following *Thinking Critically* section.

environmental injustice refers to how minorities and the poor are harmed the most by environmental pollution

Cultural Diversity around the World

The Rain Forests: Lost Tribes, Lost Knowledge

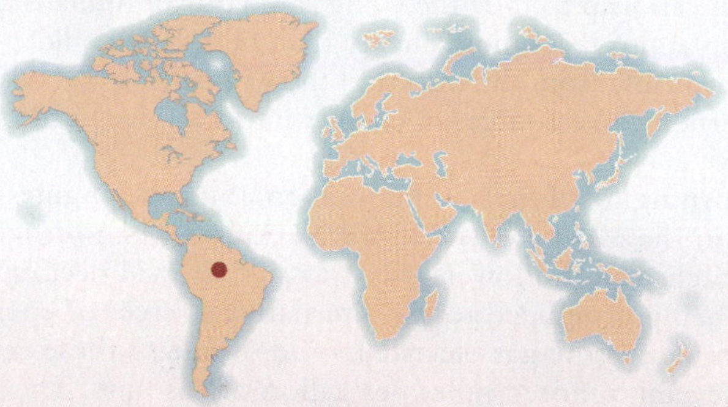

In the past hundred years, 90 of Brazil's 270 Indian tribes have disappeared. Other tribes have moved to villages as ranchers and gold miners have taken over their lands. Tribal knowledge is lost as a tribe's members adapt to village life.

Contrary to some stereotypes, tribal groups are not ignorant people who barely survive. On the contrary, these groups have developed intricate forms of social organization and possess knowledge that has accumulated over thousands of years (Briand 2013). The Kayapo Indians, for example, who belong to one of the Amazon's endangered tribes, use 250 types of wild fruit and hundreds of nut and tuber species. They cultivate thirteen types of bananas, eleven kinds of manioc (cassava), sixteen strains of sweet potato, and seventeen kinds of yams. Many of these varieties are unknown to non-Indians. The Kayapo also use thousands of plants as medicine, one of which contains a drug that is effective against intestinal parasites.

Western scientists used to dismiss tribal knowledge as superstitious and worthless. Some still do, but others have come to realize that to lose tribes is to lose valuable knowledge.

In the Central African Republic, a man whose chest was being eaten away by an amoeboid infection lay dying because the microbes did not respond to drugs. Out of desperation, the Roman Catholic nuns who were treating him sought the advice of a native doctor. He applied crushed termites to the open wounds. To the amazement of the nuns, the man made a remarkable recovery.

A member of the Uru-Eu-Wau-Wau tribe in Brazil. The way of life of the world's few remaining rain forest tribes is threatened.

The disappearance of the rain forests means the destruction of plant species that may have healing properties. I don't mean to imply that these tribes have medicine superior to ours, just that we can learn from their experience with nature.

Some of the discoveries from the rain forests have been astounding. The needles from a Himalayan tree in India contain taxol, a drug that is effective against ovarian and breast cancer. A flower from Madagascar is used in the treatment of leukemia. A frog in Peru produces a painkiller that is more powerful, but less addictive, than morphine (Wolfensohn and Fuller 1998). And do you recall the drug-resistant bacteria we discussed in Chapter 19? A researcher noticed that the Mapuche people in the rain forests of Chile were using an avocado plant to heal wounds. Tests showed that this plant overcomes the bacteria's resistance, allowing antibiotics to work (Holler et al. 2012).

On average, one tribe of Amazonian Indians has been lost each year for the past century—because of violence, greed for their lands, and exposure to infectious diseases against which these people have little resistance. Ethnocentrism underlies some of this assault. Perhaps the extreme is represented by the cattle ranchers in Colombia who killed eighteen Cueva Indians. The cattle ranchers were perplexed when they were put on trial for murder. They asked why they should be charged with a crime, since everyone knew that the Cuevas were animals, not people. They pointed out that there was even a verb in Colombian Spanish, *cuevar*, which means "to hunt Cueva Indians." So what was their crime, they asked? The jury found them not guilty because of "cultural ignorance."

Sources: Durning 1990; Gorman 1991; Linden 1991; Stipp 1992; Nabhan 1998; Simons 2006; "Last Remaining Amazon Tribes" 2011.

For Your Consideration

➔ What do you think we can do to stop the destruction of the rain forests?

THINKING CRITICALLY
Eco-sabotage

Chaining oneself to a giant Douglas fir that is slated for cutting, tearing down power lines and ripping up survey stakes, driving spikes into redwood trees, sinking whaling vessels, and torching SUVs and Hummers—are these the acts of dangerous punks who have little understanding of the needs of modern society? Or are they the efforts of brave men and women who are willing to put their freedom, and even their lives, on the line on behalf of Earth itself?

These tree-sitters are being forcibly removed. They were protesting the environmental damage that the construction of a stadium on the University of California-Berkeley campus would cause.

To understand why **ecosabotage**—actions taken to sabotage the efforts of people who are thought to be legally harming the environment—is taking place, consider the Medicine Tree, a 3,000-year-old redwood in the Sally Bell Grove near the northern California coast. Georgia Pacific, a lumber company, was going to cut down the Medicine Tree, the oldest and largest of the region's redwoods, which grows in a sacred site of the Sinkyone Indians. Members of Earth First! chained themselves to the tree. After they were arrested, the sawing began. Other protesters jumped over the police-lined barricade and stood defiantly in the path of men wielding axes and chain saws. A logger swung an axe and barely missed a demonstrator. At that moment, the sheriff radioed a restraining order, and the cutting stopped.

How many 3,000-year-old trees remain on our planet? Does our desire for fences and picnic tables for backyard barbecues justify cutting them down? Issues like these—as well as the slaughter of seals and whales, the destruction of the rain forests, and the drowning of dolphins in mile-long drift nets—spawned Earth First! and other organizations devoted to preserving the environment, such as Greenpeace, the Rainforest Action Network, the Ruckus Society, and the Sea Shepherds.

"We feel like there are insane people who are consciously destroying our environment, and we are compelled to fight back," explains a member of one of the militant groups. "No compromise in defense of Mother Earth!" says another. "With famine and death approaching, we're in the early stages of World War III," adds another.

We can't paint all radical environmentalists with the same brush. They are united neither on tactics nor on goals. Most envision a simpler lifestyle that will consume less energy and reduce pressure on Earth's resources. Some try to stop specific activities, such as the killing of whales. For others, the goal is to destroy all nuclear weapons and dismantle nuclear power plants. Some would like to see everyone become a vegetarian. Still others want Earth's population to drop to one billion, roughly what it was in 1800.

eco-sabotage actions taken to sabotage the efforts of people who are thought to be legally harming the environment

Some even want humans to return to hunting and gathering societies. These groups are so splintered that Dave Foreman—the founder of Earth First!—quit his own organization when it became too confrontational for his taste.

Radical groups have had some successes. They have brought a halt to the killing of dolphins off Japan's Iki Island, achieved a ban on whaling, established trash/recycling programs, and saved hundreds of thousands of acres of trees, including the Medicine Tree.

Sources: Carpenter 1990; Eder 1990; Foote 1990; Parfit 1990; Reed and Benet 1990; Knickerbocker 2003; Gunther 2004; Fattig 2007; Grigoriadis 2011.

For Your Consideration

→ Should we applaud eco-saboteurs or jail them? As symbolic interactionists stress, it all depends on how you view their actions. And as conflict theorists emphasize, your view depends on your social location. That is, if you own a lumber company, you will see eco-saboteurs differently than a camping enthusiast will. How does your own view of eco-saboteurs depend on your life situation? What effective alternatives to eco-sabotage are there for people who are convinced that we are destroying the very life support system of our planet? ■

environmental sociology a specialty within sociology whose focus is how humans affect the environment and how the environment affects humans

Environmental Sociology

A specialization within sociology, **environmental sociology** focuses on the relationship between human societies and the environment (Dunlap and Catton 1979, 1983; Bell 2009). Environmental sociology is built around these key ideas:

1. The physical environment should be a significant variable in sociological research.
2. Human beings are but one species among many that depend on the natural environment.
3. Human actions have unintended consequences, many of which have an impact on nature.
4. The world is finite, so there are physical limits to economic growth.
5. Economic expansion requires increased extraction of resources from the environment.
6. Increased extraction of resources leads to ecological problems.
7. These ecological problems place limits on economic expansion.
8. Governments create environmental problems by encouraging the accumulation of capital.
9. For the welfare of humanity, environmental problems must be solved.

Pollution in the Least Industrialized Nations has become a major problem. These children in the Philippines are scavenging floating waste in Manila Bay.

The goal of environmental sociology is not to stop pollution or nuclear power but, rather, to study how humans (their cultures, values, and behavior) affect the physical environment and how the physical environment affects human activities. Not surprisingly, environmental sociology attracts activists, and the Section on Environment and Technology of the American Sociological Association tries to influence governmental policies (American Sociological Association n.d.).

Technology and the Environment: The Goal of Harmony

It is inevitable that humans will develop new technologies. But the abuse of our environment by those technologies is not inevitable. To understate the matter, the destruction of our planet is an unwise choice.

If we are to live in a world worth passing on to coming generations, we must seek harmony between technology and the natural environment. This will not be easy. At one extreme are people who claim that to protect the environment, we must eliminate industrialization and go back to a tribal way of life. At the other extreme are people who are blind to the harm being done to the natural environment, who want the entire world to industrialize at full speed. Somewhere, there must be a middle ground, one that recognizes not only that industrialization is here to stay but also that we *can* control it. After all, it is our creation. Controlled, industrialization can enhance our quality of life; uncontrolled, it will destroy us.

It is essential, then, that we develop ways to reduce or eliminate the harm that technology does to the environment. This includes mechanisms to monitor the production and use of technology and the disposal of its wastes. The question, of course, is whether we have the resolve to take the steps necessary to preserve the environment for future generations. What is at stake is nothing less than the welfare of planet Earth. Surely this should be enough to motivate us to make wise choices.

The social movement that centers on the environment has become global. In all nations, people are concerned about the destruction of the earth's resources. This photo is a sign of changing times. Instead of jumping on this beached whale and carving it into pieces, these Brazilians are doing their best to save its life.

MySocLab

Study and Review on MySocLab

CHAPTER 22 Summary and Review

How Social Change Transforms Social Life

22.1 Summarize how social change transforms society; include the four social revolutions, *Gemeinschaft* and *Gesellschaft*, capitalism, social movements, and global politics.

What major trends have transformed the course of human history?

The primary changes in human history are the four social revolutions (domestication, agriculture, industrialization, and information); the change from *Gemeinschaft* to *Gesellschaft* societies; capitalism and industrialization; and global stratification. Social movements indicate cutting edges of social change. Ethnic conflicts and power rivalries threaten the global divisions that the Most Industrialized Nations have worked out. We may also be on the cutting edge of a new biotech society. Pp. 639–643.

Theories and Processes of Social Change

22.2 Summarize theories of social change: social evolution, natural cycles, conflict over power and resources, and Ogburn's theory.

What are the main theories of social change?

Evolutionary theories hold that societies move from the same starting point to some similar ending point. *Unilinear* theories assume that every society follows the same evolutionary path, while *multilinear* theories conclude that different paths lead to the same stage of development. *Cyclical* theories view civilizations as going through a process of birth, youth, maturity, decline, and death. Conflict theorists see social change as inevitable, because each *thesis* (basically an arrangement of power) contains *antitheses* (contradictions). A new *synthesis* develops to resolve these contradictions, but it, too, contains contradictions that must be resolved, and so on. This is called a **dialectical process**. Pp. 644–645.

What is Ogburn's theory of social change?

William Ogburn identified technology as the basic cause of social change, which comes through three processes: **invention**, **discovery**, and **diffusion**. The term **cultural lag** refers to symbolic culture lagging behind changes in technology. Pp. 645–647.

How Technology Is Changing Society

22.3 Use the examples of the automobile and the microchip to illustrate the sociological significance of technology; include changes in ideology, norms, human relationships, education, work, business, war, and social inequality.

How does new technology affect society?

Because technology is an organizing force of social life, changes in technology can bring profound effects. The automobile and the microchip were used as extended examples. The computer is changing the ways we interact with one another, learn, work, do business, and fight wars. We don't yet know whether information technologies will help to perpetuate or to reduce social inequalities on national and global levels. Pp. 647–655.

The Growth Machine versus the Earth

22.4 Explain how industrialization is related to environmental problems; contrast the environmental movement and environmental sociology; discuss the goal of harmony.

What are the environmental problems of the Most Industrialized Nations?

Among the most serious of the environmental problems of the most industrialized nations is **global warming**, which is likely to have severe consequences for the world. Burning fossil fuels in internal combustion engines lies at the root of many environmental problems. The location of factories and hazardous waste sites creates **environmental injustice**, environmental problems having a greater impact on minorities and the poor. Pp. 655–659.

Do the Industrializing and Least Industrialized Nations have environmental problems?

The rush of the Least Industrialized Nations to industrialize is adding to the planet's environmental decay. The pollution in China is so severe that China now emits more carbon dioxide than the United States does. Environmental activists in China are arrested and imprisoned. The world is facing a basic conflict between the lust for profits through the exploitation of Earth's resources and the need to establish a **sustainable environment**. Pp. 656–657.

What is the environmental movement?

The environmental movement is an attempt to restore a healthy environment for the world's people. This global social movement takes many forms, from peaceful attempts to influence the political process to **eco-sabotage**.Pp. 659–662.

What is environmental sociology?

Environmental sociology is not an attempt to change the environment but, rather, a study of the relationship between humans and the environment. Environmental sociologists are generally also environmental activists. P. 662.

What is the goal of harmony between technology and the environment?

The goal of harmony is to control industrialization so it doesn't harm the environment, resulting in a world worth passing on to the next generation. P. 663.

Thinking Critically about Chapter 22

1. How has social change affected your life? Be specific—what changes, how? Does Ogburn's theory help to explain your experiences? Why or why not?
2. In what ways does technology change society?
3. Do you think that a sustainable environment should be a goal of the world's societies? Why or why not? If so, what practical steps do you think we can take to produce a sustainable environment?

Epilogue: Why Major in Sociology?

As you explored social life in this textbook, I hope that you found yourself thinking along with me. If so, you should have gained a greater understanding of why people think, feel, and act as they do—as well as insights into why *you* view life the way you do. Developing your sociological imagination was my intention in writing this book. I have sincerely wanted to make sociology come alive for you.

Majoring in Sociology

If you feel a passion for peering beneath the surface—for seeking out the social influences in people's lives, and for seeing these influences in your own life—this is the best reason to major in sociology. As you take more courses in sociology, you will continue this enlightening process of social discovery. Your sociological perspective will grow, and you will become increasingly aware of how social factors underlie human behavior.

In addition to people who have a strong desire to continue this fascinating process of social discovery, there is a second type of person whom I also urge to major in sociology. Let's suppose that you have a strong, almost unbridled sense of wanting to explore many aspects of life. Let's also assume that because you have so many interests, you can't make up your mind about what you want to do with your life. You can think of so many things you'd like to try, but for each one there are other possibilities that you find equally as compelling. Let me share what one student wrote me:

> I'd love to say what my current major is—if only I truly knew. I know that the major you choose to study in college isn't necessarily the field of work you'll be going into. I've heard enough stories of grads who get jobs in fields that are not even related to their majors to believe it to a certain extent. My only problem is that I'm not even sure what it is I want to study, or what I truly want to be in the future for that matter.
>
> The variety of choices I have left open for myself are very wide, which creates a big problem, because I know I have to narrow it down to just one, which isn't something easy at all for me. It's like I want to be the best and do the best (medical doctor), yet I also wanna do other things (such as being a paramedic, or a cop, or firefighter, or a pilot), but I also realize I've only got one life to live. So the big question is: What's it gonna be?

This note reminded me of myself. In my reply, I said:

> You sound so much like myself when I was in college. In my senior year, I was plagued with uncertainty about what would be the right course for my life. I went to a counselor and took a vocational aptitude test. I still remember the day when I went in for the test results. I expected my future to be laid out for me, and I hung on every word. But then I heard the counselor say, "Your tests show that mortician should be one of your vocational choices."
>
> Mortician! I almost fell off my chair. That choice was so far removed from anything that I wanted that I immediately gave up on such tests.
>
> I like your list of possibilities: physician, cop, firefighter, and paramedic. In addition to these, mine included cowboy, hobo, and beach bum. One day, I was at the dry cleaners (end of my sophomore year in college), and the guy standing next to me was a cop. We talked about his job, and when I left the dry cleaners, I immediately went to the police station to get an application. I found out that I had to be 21, and I was just 20. I went back to college.
>
> I'm very happy with my choice. As a sociologist, I am able to follow my interests. I was able to become a hobo (or at least a traveler and able to experience different cultural settings). As far as being a cop, I developed and taught a course in the sociology of law.
>
> One of the many things I always wanted to be was an author. I almost skipped graduate school to move to Greenwich Village and become a novelist. The problem was that I was too timid, too scared of the unknown—and I had no support at all—to give it a try. My ultimate choice of sociologist has allowed me to fulfill this early dream.

It is sociology's breadth that is so satisfying to those of us who can't seem to find the limit to our interests, who can't pin ourselves down to just one thing in life. Sociology covers *all* of social life. Anything and everything that people do is part of sociology. For those of us who feel such broad, and perhaps changing interests, sociology is a perfect major.

But what if you already have a major picked out, yet you really like thinking sociologically? You can *minor* in sociology. Take sociology courses that continue to pique your sociological imagination. Then after college, continue to stimulate your sociological interests through your reading, including novels. This ongoing development of your sociological imagination will serve you well as you go through life.

But What Can You Do with a Sociology Major?

I can just hear someone say: "That's fine for you, since you became a sociologist. I don't want to go to graduate school, though. I just want to get my bachelor's degree and get out of college and get on with life. So, how can a bachelor's in sociology help me?"

This is a fair question. Just what can you do with a bachelor's degree in sociology?

A few years ago, in my sociology department we began to develop a concentration in applied sociology. At that time, since this would be a bachelor's degree, I explored this very question. I was surprised at the answer: The short answer is: *Almost anything!*

Most employers don't care what you major in. (Exceptions are some highly specialized fields such as nursing, computers, and engineering.) *Most* employers just want to make certain that you have completed college, and for most of them one degree is the same as another. *College provides the base on which the employer builds.*

Because you have your bachelor's degree—no matter what it is in—employers assume that you are a responsible person. This credential implies that you have proven yourself: You were able to stick with a four-year course, you showed up for classes, listened to lectures, took notes, passed tests, and carried out whatever assignments you were given. On top of this base of presumed responsibility, employers add the specifics necessary for you to perform their particular work, whether that be in sales or service, in insurance, banking, retailing, marketing, product development, or whatever.

If you major in sociology, you don't have to look for a job as a sociologist. If you ever decide to go on for an advanced degree, that's fine. But such plans are not necessary. The bachelor's in sociology can be your passport to most types of work in society.

Final Note

I want to conclude by stressing the reason to major in sociology that goes far beyond how you are going to make a living. It is the sociological perspective itself, the way of thinking and understanding that sociology provides. Wherever your path in life may lead, the sociological perspective will accompany you.

You are going to live in a fast-paced, rapidly changing society that, with all its conflicting crosscurrents, is going to be in turmoil. The sociological perspective will cast a different light on life's events, allowing you to perceive them in more insightful ways. As you watch television, attend a concert, converse with a friend, listen to a boss or co-worker—you will be more aware of the social contexts that underlie such behavior. The sociological perspective that you develop as you major in sociology will equip you to view what happens in life differently from someone who does not have your sociological background. Even events in the news will look different to you.

There is one more benefit of majoring in sociology. Much of the insight and understanding that I have just described can be applied in your work setting to advance your career.

The final question that I want to leave you with, then, is, "If you enjoy sociology, why not major in it?"

With my best wishes for your success in life,

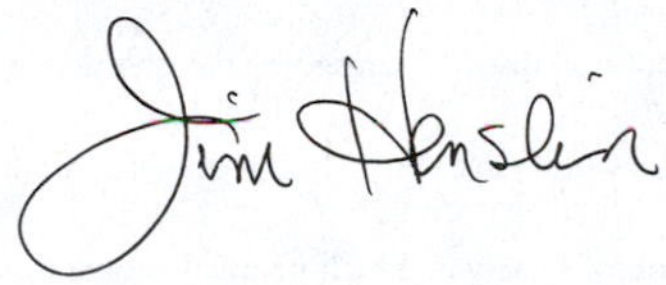

Glossary

achieved statuses positions that are earned, accomplished, or involve at least some effort or activity on the individual's part

acid rain rain containing sulfuric and nitric acids (burning fossil fuels release sulfur dioxide and nitrogen oxide that become sulfuric and nitric acids when they react with moisture in the air)

acting crowd an excited group of people who move toward a goal

activity theory the view that satisfaction during old age is related to a person's amount and quality of activity

age cohort people born at roughly the same time who pass through the life course together

ageism prejudice and discrimination directed against people because of their age; can be directed against any age group, including youth

agent provocateur someone who spies on a group or tries to sabotage it

agents of socialization people or groups that affect our self concept, attitudes, behaviors, or other orientations toward life

aggregate individuals who temporarily share the same physical space but who do not see themselves as belonging together

agricultural revolution the second social revolution, based on the invention of the plow, which led to agricultural societies

agricultural society a society based on large-scale agriculture

alienation Marx's term for workers' lack of connection to the product of their labor; caused by workers being assigned repetitive tasks on a small part of a product—this leads to a sense of powerlessness and normlessness; others use the term in the general sense of not feeling a part of something

alienation Marx's term for workers' lack of connection to the product of their labor; caused by workers being assigned repetitive tasks on a small part of a product—this leads to a sense of powerlessness and normlessness; others use the term in the general sense of not feeling a part of something

alterative social movement a social movement that seeks to alter only some specific aspects of people and institutions

alternative medicine medical treatment other than that of standard Western medicine; often refers to practices that originate in Asia, but may also refer to taking vitamins not prescribed by a doctor

anarchy a condition of lawlessness or political disorder caused by the absence or collapse of governmental authority

animism the belief that all objects in the world have spirits, some of which are dangerous and must be outwitted

anomie Durkheim's term for a condition of society in which people become detached from the usual norms that guide their behavior

anticipatory socialization the process of learning in advance an anticipated future role or status

anti-Semitism prejudice, discrimination, and persecution directed against Jews

apartheid the separation of racial–ethnic groups as was practiced in South Africa

applied sociology the use of sociology to solve problems—from the micro level of classroom interaction and family relationships to the macro level of crime and pollution

ascribed status a position an individual either inherits at birth or receives involuntarily later in life

assimilation the process of being absorbed into the mainstream culture

authoritarian leader an individual who leads by giving orders

authoritarian personality Theodor Adorno's term for people who are prejudiced and rank high on scales of conformity, intolerance, insecurity, respect for authority, and submissiveness to superiors

authority power that people consider legitimate, as rightly exercised over them; also called *legitimate power*

back stages places where people rest from their performances in everyday life, discuss their presentations, and plan future performances

background assumption a deeply embedded, common understanding of how the world operates and of how people ought to act

barter the direct exchange of one item for another

basic (or **pure) sociology** sociology in everyday life logical research for the purpose of making discoveries about life in human groups, not for making changes in those groups

basic demographic equation the growth rate equals births minus deaths plus net migration

bilineal system (of descent) a system of reckoning descent that counts both the mother's and the father's side

biotech society a society whose economy increasingly centers on modifying genetics to produce food, medicine, and materials

blended family a family whose members were once part of other families

body language the ways in which people use their bodies to give messages to others

bonded labor (indentured service) a contractual system in which someone sells his or her body (services) for a specified period of time in an arrangement very close to slavery, except that it is entered into voluntarily

born again a term describing Christians who have undergone a religious experience so life-transforming that they feel they have become new persons

bourgeoisie Marx's term for capitalists, those who own the means of production

bureaucracy a formal organization with a hierarchy of authority and a clear division of labor; emphasis on impersonality of positions and written rules, communications, and records

capital punishment the death penalty

capitalism an economic system built around the private ownership of the means of production, the pursuit of profit, and market competition

cargo cult a social movement in which South Pacific islanders destroyed their possessions in the anticipation that their ancestors would ship them new goods

case study an intensive analysis of a single event, situation, or individual

caste system a form of social stratification in which people's statuses are lifelong conditions determined by birth

category people, objects, and events that have similar characteristics and are classified together

centrist party a political party that represents the center of political opinion

charisma literally, an extraordinary gift from God; more commonly, an outstanding, "magnetic" personality

charismatic authority authority based on an individual's outstanding traits, which attract followers

charismatic leader literally, someone to whom God has given a gift; in its extended sense, someone who exudes extraordinary appeal to a group of followers

checks and balances the separation of powers among the three branches of U.S. government—legislative, executive, and judicial—so that each is able to nullify the actions of the other two, thus preventing any single branch from dominating the government

church according to Durkheim, one of the three essential elements of religion—a moral community of believers; also refers to a large, highly organized religious group that has formal, sedate worship services with little emphasis on evangelism, intense religious experience, or personal conversion

circular reaction Robert Park's term for back-and-forth communications among the members of a crowd whereby a "collective impulse" is transmitted

citizenship the concept that birth (and residence or naturalization) in a country imparts basic rights

city a place in which a large number of people are permanently based and do not produce their own food

city-state an independent city whose power radiates outward, bringing the adjacent area under its rule

civil religion Robert Bellah's term for religion that is such an established feature of a country's life that its history and social institutions become sanctified by being associated with God

class conflict Marx's term for the struggle between capitalists and workers

class consciousness Marx's term for awareness of a common identity based on one's position in the means of production

class system a form of social stratification based primarily on the possession of money or material possessions

clique (cleek) a cluster of people within a larger group who choose to interact with one another

closed-ended questions questions that are followed by a list of possible answers to be selected by the respondent

coalition the alignment of some members of a group against others

coalition government a government in which a country's largest party does not have enough votes to rule, and to do so aligns itself with one or more smaller parties

coercion power that people do not accept as rightly exercised over them; also called *illegitimate power*

cohabitation unmarried couples living together in a sexual relationship

collective behavior extraordinary activities carried out by groups of people; includes lynchings, rumors, panics, urban legends, fads, and fashions

collective mind Gustave LeBon's term for the tendency of people in a crowd to feel, think, and act in extraordinary ways

colonialism the process by which one nation takes over another nation, usually for the purpose of exploiting its labor and natural resources

common sense those things that "everyone knows" are true

compartmentalize to separate acts from feelings or attitudes

conflict theory a theoretical framework in which society is viewed as composed of groups that are competing for scarce resources

conspicuous consumption Thorstein Veblen's term for a change from the thrift, saving, and investing of the Protestant ethic to showing off wealth through spending and the display of possessions

contact theory the idea that prejudice and negative stereotypes decrease and racial-ethnic relations improve when people from different racial-ethnic backgrounds, who are of equal status, interact frequently

continuity theory a theory focusing on how people adjust to retirement by continuing aspects of their earlier lives

contradictory class locations Erik Wright's term for a position in the class structure that generates contradictory interests

control group the subjects in an experiment who are not exposed to the independent variable

control theory the idea that two control systems—inner controls and outer controls—work against our tendencies to deviate

convergence theory the view that as capitalist and socialist economic systems each adopt features of the other, a hybrid (or mixed) economic system will emerge

core values the values that are central to a group, those around which people build a common identity

corporate capitalism the domination of an economic system by giant corporations

corporate crime crimes committed by executives in order to benefit their corporation

corporate culture the values, norms, and other orientations that characterize corporate work settings

corporation a business enterprise whose assets, liabilities, and obligations are separate from those of its owners; as a legal entity, it can enter into contracts, assume debt, and sue and be sued

correspondence principle the sociological principle that schools correspond to (or reflect) the social structure of their society

cosmology teachings or ideas that provide a unified picture of the world

counterculture a group whose values, beliefs, norms, and related behaviors place its members in opposition to the broader culture

credential society the use of diplomas and degrees to determine who is eligible for jobs, even though the diploma or degree may be irrelevant to the actual work

credit card a device that allows its owner to purchase goods and to be billed later

crime the violation of norms written into law

criminal justice system the system of police, courts, and prisons set up to deal with people who are accused of having committed a crime

crude birth rate the annual number of live births per 1,000 population

crude death rate the annual number of deaths per 1,000 population

cult a new religion with few followers, whose teachings and practices put it at odds with the dominant culture and religion

cultural capital privileges accompanying a social location that help someone in life; included are more highly educated parents, from grade school through high school being pushed to bring home high grades, and enjoying cultural experiences that translate into higher test scores, better jobs, and higher earnings

cultural diffusion the spread of cultural traits from one group to another; includes both material and nonmaterial cultural traits

cultural goals the objectives held out as legitimate or desirable for the members of a society to achieve

cultural lag Ogburn's term for human behavior lagging behind technological innovations

cultural leveling the process by which cultures become similar to one another; refers especially to the process by which Western culture is being exported and diffused into other nations

cultural relativism not judging a culture but trying to understand it on its own terms

cultural transmission of values the process of transmitting values from one group to another; often refers to how cultural traits are transmitted across generations; in education, the ways in which schools transmit a society's culture, especially its core values

cultural universal a value, norm, or other cultural trait that is found in every group

culture the language, beliefs, values, norms, behaviors, and even material objects that characterize a group and are passed from one generation to the next

culture of poverty the assumption that the values and behaviors of the poor make them fundamentally different from other people, that these factors are largely responsible for their poverty, and that parents perpetuate poverty across generations by passing these characteristics to their children

culture shock the disorientation that people experience when they come in contact with a fundamentally different culture and can no longer depend on their taken-for-granted assumptions about life

currency paper money

debit card a device that electronically withdraws the cost of an item from the cardholder's bank account

defensive medicine medical practices done not for the patient's benefit but in order to protect physicians from malpractice suits

deferred gratification going without something in the present in the hope of achieving greater gains in the future

degradation ceremony a term coined by Harold Garfinkel to refer to a ritual whose goal is to remake someone's self by stripping away that individual's self-identity and stamping a new identity in its place

dehumanization the act or process of reducing people to objects that do not deserve the respect or other treatment ordinarily given humans; enables and encourages abuse and klling

deindustrialization the process of industries moving out of a country or region

democracy a government whose authority comes from the people; the term, based on two Greek words, translates literally as "power to the people"

democratic leader an individual who leads by trying to reach a consensus

democratic socialism a hybrid economic system in which the individual ownership of businesses is mixed with the state ownership of industries thought essential to the public welfare, such as the postal service, natural resources, the medical delivery system, and mass transportation

demographic transition a three-stage historical process of change in the size of populations: first, high birth rates and high death rates; second, high birth rates and low death rates; and third, low birth rates and low death rates; a fourth stage of population shrinkage in which deaths outnumber births has made its appearance in the Most Industrialized Nations

demographic variables the three factors that change the size of a population: fertility, mortality, and net migration

demography the study of the size, composition, (growth or shrinkage), and distribution of human populations

denomination a "brand name" within a major religion; for example, Methodist or Baptist

dependency ratio the number of workers who are required to support each dependent person—those 65 and older and those 15 and under

dependent variable a factor in an experiment that is changed by an independent variable

depersonalization dealing with people as though they were objects; in the case of medical care, as though patients were merely cases and diseases, not people

deposit receipt a receipt stating that a certain amount of goods are on deposit in a warehouse or bank; the receipt is used as a form of money

deviance the violation of norms (or rules or expectations)

dialectical process (of history) each arrangement of power (a thesis) contains contradictions (antitheses) which make the arrangement unstable and which must be resolved; the new arrangement of power (a synthesis) contains its own contradictions; this process of balancing and unbalancing continues throughout history as groups struggle for power and other resources

dictatorship a form of government in which an individual has seized power

differential association Edwin Sutherland's term to indicate that people who associate with some groups learn an "excess of definitions" of deviance, increasing the likelihood that they will become deviant

diffusion the spread of an invention or a discovery from one area to another; identified by William Ogburn as one of three processes of social change

direct democracy a form of democracy in which the eligible voters meet together to discuss issues and make their decisions

disabling environment an environment that is harmful to health

discovery a new way of seeing reality; identified by William Ogburn as one of three processes of social change

discrimination an act of unfair treatment directed against an individual or a group

disengagement theory the view that society is stabilized by having the elderly retire (disengage from) their positions of responsibility so the younger generation can step into their shoes

disinvestment the withdrawal of investments by financial institutions, which seals the fate of an urban area

divine right of kings the idea that the king's authority comes from God; in an interesting gender bender, also applies to queens

division of labor the splitting of a group's or a society's tasks into specialties

documents in its narrow sense, written sources that provide data; in its extended sense, archival material of any sort, including photographs, movies, CDs, DVDs, and so on

domestication revolution the first social revolution, based on the domestication of plants and animals, which led to pastoral and horticultural societies

dominant group the group with the most power, greatest privileges, and highest social status

downward social mobility movement down the social class ladder

dramaturgy an approach, pioneered by Erving Goffman, in which social life is analyzed in terms of drama or the stage; also called *dramaturgical analysis*

dumping private hospitals sending unprofitable patients to public hospitals or any hospital discharging unprofitable patients before they are well

dyad the smallest possible group, consisting of two persons

e-cash digital money that is stored on computers

ecclesia a religious group so integrated into the dominant culture that it is difficult to tell where the one begins and the other leaves off; also called a *state religion*

economy a system of producing and distributing goods and services

ecosabotage actions taken to sabotage the efforts of people who are thought to be legally harming the environment

edge city a large clustering of service facilities and residential areas near highway intersections that provides a sense of place to people who live, shop, and work there

education a formal system of teaching knowledge, values, and skills

egalitarian authority more or less equally divided between people or groups (in heterosexual marriage, for example, between husband and wife

ego Freud's term for a balancing force between the id and the demands of society

emergent norms Ralph Turner and Lewis Killian's term for the idea that people develop new norms to cope with a new situation; used to explain crowd behavior

endogamy the practice of marrying within one's own group

enterprise zone the use of economic incentives in a designated area to encourage investment

environmental injustice refers to how minorities and the poor are harmed the most by environmental pollution

environmental sociology a specialty within sociology whose focus is how humans affect the environment and how the environment affects humans

epidemiology the study of patterns of disease and disability in a population

estate stratification system the stratification system of medieval Europe, consisting of three groups or estates: the nobility, clergy, and commoners

ethnic cleansing a policy of eliminating a population; includes forcible expulsion and genocide

ethnic work activities designed to discover, enhance, maintain, or transmit an ethnic or racial identity

ethnicity (and ethnic) having distinctive cultural characteristics

ethnocentrism the use of one's own culture as a yardstick for judging the ways of other individuals or societies, generally leading to a negative evaluation of their values, norms, and behaviors

ethnomethodology the study of how people use background assumptions to make sense out of life

euthanasia mercy killing

evangelism an attempt to win converts

exchange mobility a large number of people moving up the social class ladder, while a large number move down; it is as though they have *exchanged* places, and the social class system shows little change

exogamy the practice of marrying outside of one's group

experiment the use of control and experimental groups and dependent and independent variables to test causation

experimental group the group of subjects in an experiment who are exposed to the independent variable

exponential growth curve a pattern of growth in which numbers double during approximately equal intervals, showing a steep acceleration in the later stages

expressive leader an individual who increases harmony and minimizes conflict in a group; also known as a *socioemotional leader*

extended family a family in which relatives, such as the "older generation" or unmarried aunts and uncles, live with the partents and their children

face-saving behavior techniques used to salvage a performance (interaction) that is going sour

fad a temporary pattern of behavior that catches people's attention

false class consciousness Marx's term to refer to workers identifying with the interests of capitalists

family two or more people who consider themselves related by blood, marriage, or adoption

family of orientation the family in which a person grows up

family of procreation the family formed when a couple's first child is born

fashion a pattern of behavior that catches people's attention and lasts longer than a fad

fecundity the number of children that women are capable of bearing

fee-for-service payment to a physician to diagnose and treat a patient's medical problems

feminism the philosophy that men and women should be politically, economically, and socially equal; organized activities on behalf of this principle

feminization of poverty a condition of U.S. poverty in which most poor families are headed by women

feral children children assumed to have been raised by animals, in the wilderness, isolated from humans

fertility rate the number of children that the average woman bears

fiat money currency issued by a government that is not backed by stored value

folkways norms that are not strictly enforced

formal organization a secondary group designed to achieve explicit objectives

front stage a place where people give their performances in everyday life

functional analysis a theoretical framework in which society is viewed as composed of various parts, each with a function that, when fulfilled, contributes to society's equilibrium; also *known as functionalism* and *structural functionalism*

functional equivalent a substitute that serves the same functions (or meets the same needs) as something else; for religion, an example is psychotherapy

functional illiterate a high school graduate who has difficulty with basic reading and math

gatekeeping the process by which education opens and closes doors of opportunity; another term for the *social placement* function of education

Gemeinschaft a type of society in which life is intimate; a community in which everyone knows everyone else and people share a sense of togetherness

gender the behaviors and attitudes that a society considers proper for its males and females; masculinity or femininity

gender the behaviors and attitudes that a society considers proper for its males and females; masculinity or femininity

gender age the relative value placed on men's and women's ages

gender socialization learning society's "gender map," the paths in life set out for us because we are male or female

gender stratification males' and females' unequal access to property, power, and prestige

generalizability the extent to which the findings from one group (or sample) can be generalized or applied to other groups (or populations)

generalization a statement that goes beyond the individual case and is applied to a broader group or situation

generalized other the norms, values, attitudes, and expectations of people "in general"; the child's ability to take the role of the generalized other is a significant step in the development of a self

genetic predisposition inborn tendencies (for example, a tendency to commit deviant acts)

genocide the annihilation or attempted annihilation of a people because of their presumed race or ethnicity

gentrification middle-class people moving into a rundown area of a city, displacing the poor as they buy and restore homes

Gesellschaft a type of society that is dominated by short-term impersonal relationships, individual accomplishments, and self-interest

gestures the ways in which people use their bodies to communicate with one another

glass ceiling the mostly invisible barrier that keeps women from advancing to the top levels at work

global superclass the top members of the capitalist class, who, through their worldwide interconnections, make the major decisions that affect the world

globalization the growing interconnections among nations due to the expansion of capitalism

globalization of capitalism capitalism (investing to make profits within a rational system) becoming the globe's dominant economic system

globalization of capitalism capitalism (investing to make profits within a rational system) becoming the globe's dominant economic system

goal displacement an organization replacing old goals with new ones; also known as *goal replacement*

gold standard paper money backed by gold

grade inflation higher grades given for the same work; a general rise in student grades without a corresponding increase in learning

graying of America the growing percentage of older people in the U.S. population

gross domestic product (GDP) the amount of goods and services produced by a nation

group people who have something in common and who believe that what they have in common is significant; also called a *social group*

group dynamics the ways in which individuals affect groups and the ways in which groups influence individuals

groupthink a narrowing of thought by a group of people, leading to the perception that there is only one correct answer and that to even suggest alternatives is a sign of disloyalty

growth rate the net change in a population after adding births, subtracting deaths, and either adding or subtracting net migration; can result in a negative number

health a human condition measured by four components: physical, mental, social, and spiritual

hidden corporate culture stereotypes of the traits that make for high-performing and underperforming workers

hidden curriculum the unwritten goals of schools, such as teaching obedience to authority and conformity to cultural norms

homogamy the tendency of people with similar characteristics to marry one another

Horatio Alger myth the belief that due to limitless possibilities anyone can get ahead if he or she tries hard enough

horticultural society a society based on cultivating plants by the use of hand tools

hospice a place (or services brought to someone's home) for the purpose of giving comfort and dignity to a dying person

household people who occupy the same housing unit

human ecology Robert Park's term for the relationship between people and their environment (such as land and structures); also known as *urban ecology*

humanizing the work setting organizing a workplace in such a way that it develops rather than impedes human potential

hunting and gathering society a human group that depends on hunting and gathering for its survival

hypothesis a statement of how variables are expected to be related to one another, often according to predictions from a theory

id Freud's term for our inborn basic drives

ideal culture a people's ideal values and norms; the goals held out for them

ideology beliefs about the way things ought to be that justify social arrangements

illegitimate opportunity structure opportunities for crimes that are woven into the texture of life

impression management people's efforts to control the impressions that others receive of them

incest sexual relations between specified relatives, such as brothers and sisters or parents and children

incest taboo the rule that prohibits sex and marriage among designated relatives

inclusion helping people to become part of the mainstream of society; also called *mainstreaming*

income money received, usually from a job, business, or assets

independent variable a factor that causes a change in another variable, called the *dependent variable*

individual discrimination person-to-person or face-to-face discrimination; the negative treatment of people by other individuals

Industrial Revolution the third social revolution, occurring when machines powered by fuels replaced most animal and human power

industrial society a society based on the harnessing of machines powered by fuels

inflation an increase in prices; technically, an increase in the amount of money in circulation, which leads to an increase in prices

in-group a group toward which one feels loyalty

institutional discrimination negative treatment of a minority group that is built into a society's institutions; also called *systemic discrimination*

institutionalized means approved ways of reaching cultural goals

instrumental leader an individual who tries to keep the group moving toward its goals; also known as a *task-oriented leader*

intergenerational mobility the change that family members make in social class from one generation to the next

interlocking directorates the same people serving on the boards of directors of several companies

internal colonialism the policy of exploiting minority groups for economic gain

interview direct questioning of respondents

interviewer bias effects of interviewers on respondents that lead to biased answers

invasion–succession cycle the process of one group of people displacing a group whose racial–ethnic or social class characteristics differ from their own

invention the combination of existing elements and materials to form new ones; identified by William Ogburn as one of three processes of social change

iron law of oligarchy Robert Michels' term for the tendency of formal organizations to be dominated by a small, self perpetuating elite

labeling theory the view that the labels people are given affect their own and others' perceptions of them, thus channeling their behavior into either deviance or conformity

laissez-faire capitalism literally "hands off" capitalism, meaning that the government doesn't interfere in the market

laissez-faire leader an individual who leads by being highly permissive

language a system of symbols that can be combined in an infinite number of ways and can represent not only objects but also abstract thought

latent functions unintended beneficial consequences of people's actions

leader someone who influences other people

leadership styles ways in which people express their leadership

life course the stages of our life as we go from birth to death

life expectancy the number of years that an average person at any age, including newborns, can expect to live

life span the maximum length of life of a species; for humans, the longest that a human has lived

lobbyists people who influence legislation on behalf of their clients

looking-glass self a term coined by Charles Horton Cooley to refer to the process by which our self develops through internalizing others' reactions to us

machismo an emphasis on male strength and dominance

macro-level analysis an examination of large-scale patterns of society; such as how Wall Street and the political establishment are interrelated

macropolitics the exercise of large-scale power, the government being the most common example

macrosociology analysis of social life that focuses on broad features of society, such as social class and the relationships of groups to one another; usually used by functionalists and conflict theorists

Malthus theorem an observation by Thomas Malthus that although the food supply increases arithmetically (from 1 to 2 to 3 to 4 and so on), population grows geometrically (from 2 to 4 to 8 to 16 and so forth)

mandatory education laws laws that require all children to attend school until a specified age or until they complete a minimum grade in school

manifest functions the intended beneficial consequences of people's actions

market forces the law of supply and demand

marriage a group's approved mating arrangements, usually marked by a ritual of some sort

mass hysteria an imagined threat that causes physical symptoms among a large number of people

mass media forms of communication, such as radio, newspapers, and television that are directed to mass audiences

master status a status that cuts across the other statuses that an individual occupies

material culture the material objects that distinguish a group of people, such as their art, buildings, weapons, utensils, machines, hairstyles, clothing, and jewelry

matriarchy a society in which women-as-a-group dominate men-as-a-group; authority is vested in females

matrilineal system (of descent) a system of reckoning descent that counts only the mother's side

McDonaldization of society the process by which ordinary aspects of life are rationalized and efficiency comes to rule them, including such things as food preparation

means of production the tools, factories, land, and investment capital used to produce wealth

mechanical solidarity Durkheim's term for the unity (a shared consciousness) that people feel as a result of performing the same or similar tasks

medicalization the transformation of a human condition into a medical matter to be treated by physicians

medicalization of deviance to make deviance a medical matter, a symptom of some underlying illness that needs to be treated by physicians

medicine one of the social institutions that sociologists study; a society's organized ways of dealing with sickness and injury

medium of exchange the means by which people place a value on goods and services in order to make an exchange—for example, currency, gold, and silver

megacity a city of 10 million or more residents

megalopolis an urban area consisting of at least two metropolises and their many suburbs

meritocracy a form of social stratification in which all positions are awarded on the basis of merit

metaformative social movement a social movement that has the goal to change the social order not just of a country or two, but of a civilization, or even of the entire world

metropolis a central city surrounded by smaller cities and their suburbs

metropolitan statistical area (MSA) a central city and the urbanized counties adjacent to it

micro-level analysis an examination of small-scale patterns of society; such as how the members of a group interact

micropolitics the exercise of power in everyday life, such as deciding who is going to do the housework or use the remote control

microsociology analysis of social life that focuses on social interaction; typically used by symbolic interactionists

millenarian social movement a social movement based on the prophecy of coming social upheaval

milling a crowd standing or walking around as they talk excitedly about some event

minimax strategy Richard Berk's term for the efforts people make to minimize their costs and maximize their rewards

minority group people who are singled out for unequal treatment and who regard themselves as objects of collective discrimination

modernization the transformation of traditional societies into industrial societies

monarchy a form of government headed by a king or queen

money any item (from sea shells to gold) that serves as a medium of exchange

monopoly the control of an entire industry by a single company

monotheism the belief that there is only one God

moral panic a fear gripping a large number of people that some evil threatens the wellbeing of society; followed by hostility, sometimes violence, toward those thought responsible

mores norms that are strictly enforced because they are thought essential to core values or the well-being of the group

multiculturalism (or **pluralism)** a policy that permits or encourages ethnic differences

multinational corporations companies that operate across national boundaries; also called *transnational corporations*

nationalism strongly identifying with a nation (a people) accompanied by desiring that nation to be dominant

natural sciences the intellectual and academic disciplines designed to understand, explain, and predict events in our natural environments

negative sanction an expression of disapproval for breaking a norm, ranging from a mild, informal reaction such as a frown to a formal reaction such as a prize or a prison sentence

neocolonialism the economic and political dominance of the Most Industrialized Nations over the Least Industrialized Nations

net migration rate the difference between the number of immigrants and emigrants per 1,000 population

new technology the emerging technologies of an era that have a significant impact on social life

noncentrist party a political party that represents less popular ideas

nonmaterial culture a group's ways of thinking (including its beliefs, values, and other assumptions about the world) and doing (its common patterns of behavior, including language and other forms of interaction); also called *symbolic culture*

nonverbal interaction communication without words through gestures, use of space, silence, and so on

norms expectations of "right" behavior

nuclear family a family consisting of a husband, wife, and child(ren)

objectivity value neutrality in research

oligarchy a form of government in which a small group of individuals holds power; the rule of the many by the few

open-ended questions questions that respondents answer in their own words

operational definition the way in which a researcher measures a variable

organic solidarity Durkheim's term for the interdependence that results from the division of labor; as part of the same unit, we all depend on others to fulfill their jobs

out-group a group toward which one feels antagonism

panic the condition of being so fearful that one cannot function normally and may even flee

pan-Indianism an attempt to develop an identity that goes beyond the tribe by emphasizing the common elements that run through Native American cultures

participant observation (or **fieldwork)** research in which the researcher participates in a research setting while observing what is happening in that setting

pastoral society a society based on the pasturing of animals

patriarchy men-as-a-group dominating women-as-a-group; authority is vested in males

patrilineal system (of **descent)** a system of reckoning descent that counts only the father's side

patterns of behavior recurring behaviors or events

peer group a group of individuals, often of roughly the same age, who are linked by common interests and orientations

personality disorders the view that a personality disturbance of some sort causes an individual to violate social norms

Peter Principle a tongue in-cheek observation that the members of an organization are promoted for their accomplishments until they reach their level of incompetence; there they cease to be promoted, remaining at the level at which they can no longer do good work

pluralism the diffusion of power among many interest groups that prevents any single group from gaining control of the government

pluralistic society a society made up of many different groups

police discretion the practice of the police, in the normal course of their duties, to either arrest or ticket someone for an offense or to overlook the matter

political action committee (PAC) an organization formed by one or more special-interest groups to solicit and spend funds for the purpose of influencing legislation

politics the exercise of power and attempts to maintain or to change power relations

polyandry a form of marriage in which women have more than one husband

polygyny a form of marriage in which men have more than one wife

polytheism the belief that there are many gods

population a target group to be studied

population pyramid a graph that represents the age and sex of a population (see Figure 20.7)

population shrinkage the process by which a country's population becomes smaller because its birth rate and immigration are too low to replace those who die and emigrate

population transfer the forced transfer of a minority group

positive sanction an expression of approval for following a norm, ranging from a smile or a good grade in a class to a material reward such as a prize

positivism the application of the scientific approach to the social world

postindustrial (information) society a society based on information, services, and high technology, rather than on raw materials and manufacturing

postmodern society another term for postindustrial society

poverty line the official measure of poverty; calculated to include incomes that are less than three times a low-cost food budget

power the ability to carry out one's will, even over the resistance of others

power elite C. Wright Mills' term for the top people in U.S. corporations, military, and politics who make the nation's major decisions

prejudice an attitude or prejudging, usually in a negative way

prestige respect or regard

primary group a small group characterized by cooperative intimate, longterm, face-to-face associations

proactive social movement a social movement that promotes some social change

profane Durkheim's term for common elements of everyday life

professionalization of medicine the development of medicine into a specialty that requires physicians to (1) obtain a rigorous education, (2) regulate themselves, (3) take authority over clients, (4) claim a theoretical understanding of illness, and (5) present themselves as doing a service to society (rather than just following self-interest)

proletariat Marx's term for the exploited class, the mass of workers who do not own the means of production

propaganda in its broad sense, the presentation of information in an attempt to influence people; in its narrow sense, one-sided information used to try to influence people

property material possessions: animals, bank accounts, bonds, buildings, businesses, cars, cash, commodities, copyrights, furniture, jewelry, land, and stocks

proportional representation an electoral system in which seats in a legislature are divided according to the proportion of votes that each political party receives

Protestant ethic Weber's term to describe the ideal of a self–denying, highly moral life accompanied by thrift and hard work

public in this context, a dispersed group of people relevant to a social movement; the sympathetic and hostile publics have an interest in the issues on which a social movement focuses; there is also an unaware or indifferent public

public opinion how people think about some issue

public sociology applying sociology for the public good; especially the use of the sociological perspective (how things are related to one another) to guide politicians and policy makers

questionnaires a list of questions to be asked of respondents

quiet revolution the fundamental changes in society that follow when vast numbers of women enter the workforce

race a group whose inherited physical characteristics distinguish it from other groups

racism prejudice and discrimination on the basis of race

random sample a sample in which everyone in the target population has the same chance of being included in the study

rapport (ruh-POUR) a feeling of trust between researchers and the people they are studying

rationality using rules, efficiency, and practical results to determine human affairs

rationalization of society a widespread acceptance of rationality and social organizations that are built largely around this idea

rational–legal authority authority based on law or written rules and regulations; also called *bureaucratic authority*

reactive social movement a social movement that resists some social change

real culture the norms and values that people actually follow; as opposed to *ideal culture*

recidivism rate the percentage of released convicts who are rearrested

redemptive social movement a social movement that seeks to change people and institutions totally, to redeem them

redlining a decision by the officers of a financial institution not to make loans in a particular area

reference group a group whose standards we refer to as we evaluate ourselves

reformative social movement a social movement that seeks to reform some specific aspect of society

reincarnation in Hinduism and Buddhism, the return of the soul (or self) after death in a different form

relative deprivation theory in this context, the belief that people join social movements based on their evaluations of what they think they should have compared with what others have

reliability the extent to which research produces consistent or dependable results

religion according to Durkheim, beliefs and practices that separate the profane from the sacred and unite its adherents into a moral community

religious experience a sudden awareness of the supernatural or a feeling of coming in contact with God

replication the repetition of a study in order to test its findings

representative democracy a form of democracy in which voters elect representatives to meet together to discuss issues and make decisions on their behalf

research method (or **research design**) one of seven procedures that sociologists use to collect data: surveys, participant observation, case studies, secondary analysis, documents, experiments, and unobtrusive measures

reserve labor force the unemployed; unemployed workers are thought of as being "in reserve"—capitalists take them "out of reserve" (put them back to work) during times of high production and then put them "back in reserve" (lay them off) when they are no longer needed

resocialization the process of learning new norms, values, attitudes, and behaviors

resource mobilization a theory that social movements succeed or fail based on their ability to mobilize resources such as time, money, and people's skills

respondents people who respond to a survey, either in interviews or by self-administered questionnaires

revolution armed resistance designed to overthrow and replace a government

riot violent crowd behavior directed at people and property

rising expectations the sense that better conditions are soon to follow, which, if unfulfilled, increases frustration

rituals ceremonies or repetitive practices; in religion, observances or rites often intended to evoke a sense of awe of the sacred

role the behaviors, obligations, and privileges attached to a status

role conflict conflicts that someone feels *between* roles because the expectations are at odds with one another

role extension a role being stretched to include activities that were not originally part of that role

role performance the ways in which someone performs a role; showing a particular "style" or "personality"

role strain conflicts that someone feels within a role

romantic love feelings of erotic attraction accompanied by an idealization of the other

routinization of charisma the transfer of authority from a charismatic figure to either a traditional or a rational–legal form of authority

ruling class another term for the power elite

rumor unfounded information spread among people

sacred Durkheim's term for things set apart or forbidden that inspire fear, awe, reverence, or deep respect

sample the individuals intended to represent the population to be studied

sanctions either expressions of approval given to people for upholding norms or expressions of disapproval for violating them

Sapir-Whorf hypothesis Edward Sapir and Benjamin Whorf's hypothesis that language creates ways of thinking and perceiving

scapegoat an individual or group unfairly blamed for someone else's troubles

science the application of systematic methods to obtain knowledge and the knowledge obtained by those methods

scientific method the use of objective, systematic observations to test theories

secondary analysis the analysis of data that have been collected by other researchers

secondary group compared with a primary group, a larger, relatively temporary, more anonymous, formal, and impersonal group based on some interest or activity

sect a religious group larger than a cult that still feels substantial hostility from and toward society

secular belonging to the world and its affairs

secularization of culture the process by which a culture becomes less influenced by religion

secularization of religion the replacement of a religion's spiritual or "other worldly" concerns with concerns about "this world"

segregation the policy of keeping racial–ethnic groups apart

selective perception seeing certain features of an object or situation, but remaining blind to others

self the unique human capacity of being able to see ourselves "from the outside"; the views we internalize of how others see us

self-administered questionnaires questionnaires that respondents fill out

self-fulfilling prophecy Robert Merton's term for an originally false assertion that becomes true simply because it was predicted

self-fulfilling stereotype preconceived ideas of what someone is like that lead to the person's behaving in ways that match the stereotype

serial murder the killing of several victims in three or more separate events

sex biological characteristics that distinguish females and males, consisting of primary and secondary sex characteristics

sexual harassment the abuse of one's position of authority to force unwanted sexual demands on someone

shaman the healing specialist of a tribe who attempts to control the spirits thought to cause a disease or injury; often called a witch doctor

significant other an individual who significantly influences someone else

sign-vehicle the term used by Goffman to refer to how people use social setting, appearance, and manner to communicate information about the self

slavery a form of social stratification in which some people own other people

small group a group small enough for everyone to interact directly with all the other members

social change the alteration of culture and societies over time

social class according to Weber, a large group of people who rank close to one another in property, power, and prestige; according to Marx, one of two groups: capitalists who own the means of production or workers who sell their labor

social class large numbers of people who have similar amounts of income and education and who work at jobs that are roughly comparable in prestige

social construction of reality the use of background assumptions and life experiences to define what is real

social control a group's formal and informal means of enforcing its norms

social environment the entire human environment, including interaction with others

social facts Durkheim's term for a group's patterns of behavior

social inequality a social condition in which privileges and obligations are given to some but denied to others

social institution the organized, usual, or standard ways by which society meets its basic needs

social integration the degree to which members of a group or a society are united by shared values and other social bonds; also known as *social cohesion*

social interaction one person's actions influencing someone else; usually refers to what people do when they are in one another's presence, but also includes communications at a distance

social location the group memberships that people have because of their location in history and society

social mobility movement up or down the social class ladder

social movement a large group of people who are organized to promote or resist some social change

social movement organization an organization to promote the goals of a social movement

social network the social ties radiating outward from the self that link people together

social order a group's usual and customary social arrangements, on which its members depend and on which they base their lives

social placement a function of education—funneling people into a society's various positions

social promotion passing students on to the next level even though they have not mastered basic materials

social sciences the intellectual and academic disciplines designed to understand the social world objectively by means of controlled and repeated observations

social stratification the division of large numbers of people into layers according to their relative property, power, and prestige; applies to both nations and to people within a nation, society, or other group

social structure the framework of society that surrounds us; consists of the ways that people and groups are related to one another; this framework gives direction to and sets limits on our behavior

socialism an economic system built around the public ownership of the means of production, central planning, and the distribution of goods without a profit motive

socialization the process by which people learn the characteristics of their group—the knowledge, skills, attitudes, values, norms, and actions thought appropriate for them

society people who share a culture and a territory

sociobiology a framework of thought in which human behavior is considered to be the result of natural selection and biological factors

sociological perspective understanding human behavior by placing it within its broader social context

sociology the scientific study of society and human behavior

special-interest group a group of people who support a particular issue and who can be mobilized for political action

spirit of capitalism Weber's term for the desire to accumulate capital—not to spend it, but as an end in itself—and to constantly reinvest it

split labor market workers split along racial–ethnic, gender, age, or any other lines; this split is exploited by owners to weaken the bargaining power of workers

state a political entity that claims monopoly on the use of violence in some particular territory; commonly known as a country

state religion a government–ponsored religion; also called *ecclesia*

status the position that someone occupies in a social group; also called *social status*

status consistency ranking high or low on all three dimensions of social class

status inconsistency ranking high on some dimensions of social class and low on others; also called *status discrepancy*

status set all the statuses or positions that an individual occupies

status symbols indicators of a status, especially items in that display prestige

stereotype assumptions of what people are like, whether true or false

stigma "blemishes" that discredit a person's claim to a "normal" identity

stockholders' revolt refusal by stockholders at their annual meetings to approve management's recommendations

stored value the goods that are stored and held in reserve that back up (or provide the value for) a deposit receipt or a currency

strain theory Robert Merton's term for the strain engendered when a society socializes large numbers of people to desire a cultural goal (such as success), but withholds from some the approved means of reaching that goal; one adaptation to the strain is crime, the choice of an innovative means (one outside the approved system) to attain the cultural goal

stratified random sample a sample from selected subgroups of the target population in which everyone in those subgroups has an equal chance of being included in the research

street crime crimes such as mugging, rape, and burglary

structural mobility movement up or down the social class ladder that is due more to changes in the *structure* of society than to the actions of individuals

structured interviews interviews that use closed-ended questions

subculture the values and related behaviors of a group that distinguish its members from the larger culture; a world within a world

subjective meanings the meanings that people give their own behavior

subsistence economy a type of economy in which human groups live off the land and have little or no surplus

suburb a community adjacent to a city

suburbanization the migration of people from the city to the suburbs

superego Freud's term for the conscience; the internalized norms and values of our social groups

survey the collection of data by having people answer a series of questions

sustainable environment a world system that takes into account the limits of the environment, produces enough material goods for everyone's needs, and leaves a heritage of a sound environment for the next generation

symbol something to which people attach meaning and then use to communicate with one another

symbolic culture another term for *nonmaterial culture*

symbolic interactionism a theoretical perspective in which society is viewed as composed of symbols that people use to establish meaning, develop their views of the world, and communicate with one another

system of descent how kinship is traced over the generations

taboo a norm so strong that it brings extreme sanctions, even revulsion, if violated

taking the role of the other putting yourself in someone else's shoes; understanding how someone else feels and thinks, so you anticipate how that person will act

teamwork the collaboration of two or more people to manage impressions jointly

techniques of neutralization ways of thinking or rationalizing that help people deflect (or neutralize) society's norms

technology in its narrow sense, tools; its broader sense includes the skills or procedures necessary to make and use those tools

terrorism the use of violence or the threat of violence to produce fear in order to attain political objectives

theory a general statement about how some parts of the world fit together and how they work; an explanation of how two or more facts are related to one another

Thomas theorem William I. and Dorothy S. Thomas' classic formulation of the definition of the situation: "If people define situations as real, they are real in their consequences"

total institution a place that is almost totally controlled by those who run it, in which people are cut off from the rest of society and the society is mostly cut off from them

totalitarianism a form of government that exerts almost total control over people

tracking the sorting of students into different programs on the basis of real or perceived abilities

traditional authority authority based on custom

traditional society a society in which the past is thought to be the best guide for the present; tribal, peasant, and feudal societies

transformative social movement a social movement that seeks to change society totally, to transform it

transitional adulthood a period following high school during which young adults have not yet taken on the responsibilities ordinarily associated with adulthood; also called *adultolescence*

transitional older years an emerging stage of the life course between retirement and when people are considered old; about age 63 to 74

transnational social movements social movements whose emphasis is on some condition around the world, instead of on a condition in a specific country; also known as *new social movements*

triad a group of three people

two-tier system of medical care a system of medical care in which the wealthy receive superior medical care and the poor inferior medical care

underclass a group of people for whom poverty persists year after year and across generations

underground economy exchanges of goods and services that escape taxes because they are not reported to the government

universal citizenship the idea that everyone has the same basic rights by virtue of being born in a country (or by immigrating and becoming a naturalized citizen)

unobtrusive measures ways of observing people so they do not know they are being studied

unstructured interviews interviews that use open-ended questions

upward social mobility movement up the social class ladder

urban legend a story with an ironic twist that sounds realistic but is false

urban renewal the rehabilitation of a rundown area, which usually results in the displacement of the poor who are living in that area

urbanization the process by which an increasing proportion of a population lives in cities and has a growing influence on the culture

validity the extent to which an operational definition measures what it is intended to measure

value cluster values that together form a larger whole

value contradiction values that contradict one another; to follow the one means to come into conflict with the other

value free the view that a sociologist's personal values or beliefs should not influence social research

values the standards by which people define what is desirable or undesirable, good or bad, beautiful or ugly

variable a factor thought to be significant for human behavior, which can vary (or change) from one case to another

Verstehen a German word used by Weber that is perhaps best understood as "to have insight into someone's situation"

voluntary associations groups made up of people who voluntarily organize on the basis of some mutual interest; also known as *voluntary memberships* and *voluntary organizations*

voter apathy indifference and inaction on the part of individuals or groups with respect to the political process

war armed conflict between nations or politically distinct groups

WASP white anglo saxon protestant

wealth the total value of everything someone owns, minus the debts

white ethnics white immigrants to the United States whose cultures differ from WASP culture

white-collar crime Edwin Sutherland's term for crimes committed by people of respectable and high social status in the course of their occupations; for example, bribery of public officials, securities violations, embezzlement, false advertising, and price fixing

world system theory how economic and political connections developed and now tie the world's countries together

zero population growth women bearing only enough children to reproduce the population

References

All new references are printed in cyan.

"'You Can Die Anytime.' Death Squad Killings in Mindanao." New York: Human Rights Watch, 2009.

"111 Health-Care Professionals Charged in $225 Million Medicare Scam." Associated Press, February 17, 2011.

Aaron, Henry J., William B. Schwartz, and Melissa Cox. *Can We Say No? The Challenge of Rationing Health Care.* Washington, D.C.: Brookings Institution Press, 2005.

AAUP (American Association of University Professors). "Annual Report on the Economic Status of the Profession, 2012–2013." Washington, D.C.: American Association of University Professors, April 2013.

AAUP (American Association of University Professors). "Report of the Committee on the Economic Status of the Profession." Washington, D.C.: Author, April 2010.

Abelson, Reed, and Patricia Leigh Brown. "Alternative Medicine Is Finding Its Niche in Nation's Hospitals." *New York Times,* April 14, 2002.

Aberg, Yvonne. *Social Interactions: Studies of Contextual Effects and Endogenous Processes.* Doctoral dissertation, Department of Sociology, Stockholm University, 2003.

Aberle, David F., A. K. Cohen, A. K. David, M. J. Leng, Jr., and F. N. Sutton. "The Functional Prerequisites of a Society." *Ethics, 60,* January 1950:100–111.

Aberle, David F. *The Peyote Religion among the Navaho.* Chicago: Aldine, 1966.

Ackernecht, Erwin H. "The Role of Medical History in Medical Education." *Bulletin of the History of Medicine, 21,* 1947:135–145.

ACLU. "ACLU and Asian Law Caucus Seek Records on FBI Surveillance of Mosques and Use of Informants in Northern California." ACLU Press Release, March 9, 2010.

Adam, David. "Climate: The Hottest Year." *Nature, 468,* November 15, 2010:362–364.

Adams, Noah. "All Things Considered." *New England Journal of Medicine* report, January 12, 2000.

Addams, Jane. *Twenty Years at Hull-House.* New York: Signet, 1981. Originally published 1910.

Adler, Patricia A., and Peter Adler. *Peer Power: Preadolescent Culture and Identity.* New Brunswick, N.J.: Rutgers University Press, 1998.

Adorno, Theodor W., Else Frenkel-Brunswick, D. J. Levinson, and R. N. Sanford. *The Authoritarian Personality.* New York: Harper & Row, 1950.

Aeppel, Timothy. "More Amish Women Are Tending to Business." *Wall Street Journal,* February 8, 1996:B1, B2.

Agins, Teri. "When to Carry a Purse to a Meeting." *Wall Street Journal,* October 1, 2009.

Agnew, Robert. "Reflections on 'A Revised Strain Theory of Delinquency.'" *Social Forces, 91,* 1, September 2012:33–38.

Agno, John, and Barb McEwen. *Decoding the Executive Woman's Dress Code.* Seattle, Wash: Signature e-Books, 2011.

Agranovich, Maria. "Should Russian Universities Pay Much Attention to Rankings?" *Rossiyskaya Gazeta,* July 9, 2012.

Aguirre, Benigno E. "The Conventionalization of Collective Behavior in Cuba." In *Collective Behavior and Social Movements,* Russell L. Curtis, Jr., and Benigno E. Aquirre, eds. Boston: Allyn and Bacon, 1993:413–428.

Alba, Richard, and Victor Nee. *Remaking the American Mainstream: Assimilation and Contemporary Immigration.* Cambridge, Mass.: Harvard University Press, 2003.

Albanese, Jennifer. Personal research for the author. 2010.

Albert, Ethel M. "Women of Burundi: A Study of Social Values." In *Women of Tropical Africa,* Denise Paulme, ed. Berkeley: University of California Press, 1963:179–215.

"Alcohol: Balancing Risks and Benefits." Harvard School of Public Health. Unpublished paper. January 9, 2009.

Aldrich, Nelson W., Jr. *Old Money: The Mythology of America's Upper Class.* New York: Vintage Books, 1989.

Alimahomed-Wilson, Jake. "Black Longshoremen and the Fight for Equality in an 'Anti-Racist' Union." *Race and Class, 53,* 4, 2012:39–53.

Allen, Nick. "Lottery Winner Murderer Jailed for Life." *Telegraph,* December 11, 2012.

Allhoff, Fritz. "Torture Warrants, Self-Defense, and Necessity." *Public Affairs Quarterly, 25,* 3, July 2011:217–240.

Allport, Floyd. *Social Psychology.* Boston: Houghton Mifflin, 1954.

Alter, Alexandra. "Is This Man Cheating on His Wife?" *Wall Street Journal,* August 10, 2007.

"Alternative Investment Market Letter," November 1991.

Alvarez, Lizette. "For Young Jews, a Service Says, 'Please, Do Text.'" *New York Times,* September 17, 2012.

Amato, Paul. "Research on Divorce: Continuing Trends and New Developments." *Journal of Marriage and Family, 72,* 3, June 2010: 650–666.

Amato, Paul R. "The Well-Being of Children with Gay and Lesbian Parents." *Social Science Research, 41,* 2012:771–774.

Amato, Paul R., and Jacob Cheadle. "The Long Reach of Divorce: Divorce and Child Well-Being across Three Generations." *Journal of Marriage and Family, 67,* February 2005:191–206.

Amato, Paul R., and Juliana M. Sobolewski. "The Effects of Divorce and Marital Discord on Adult Children's Psychological Well-Being." *American Sociological Review, 66,* 6, December 2001:900–921.

Amenta, Edwin. "The Social Security Debate, Now, and Then." *Contexts, 5,* 3, Summer 2006.

"America's Children in Brief: Key National Indicators of Well-Being, 2010." www.childstats.gov, July 2010.

"American Community Survey 2003." Washington, D.C.: U.S. Census Bureau, 2004.

American Society for Aesthetic Plastic Surgery. "15th Annual Cosmetic Surgery National Data Bank Statistics." New York: American Society for Aesthetic Plastic Surgery, 2012.

American Sociological Association. "An Invitation to Public Sociology." 2004.

American Sociological Association. *Code of Ethics and Policies and Procedures of the ASA Committee on Professional Ethics.* Washington, D.C.: American Sociological Association, 1999.

American Sociological Association. "Section on Environment and Technology." Pamphlet, no date.

Ananat, Elizabeth O., and Guy Michaels. "The Effect of Marital Breakup on the Income Distribution of Women with Children." Centre for Economic Performance, CEP Discussion Paper dp0787, April 2007.

Anand, Geeta, and Betsy McKay. "How Fight to Tame TB Made It Stronger." *Wall Street Journal,* November 23, 2012.

Andersen, Margaret L. *Thinking about Women: Sociological Perspectives on Sex and Gender.* New York: Macmillan, 1988.

Anderson, Cameron, and Jessica A. Kennedy. "Micropolitics: A New Model of Status Hierarchies in Teams." *Research on Managing Groups and Teams, 15,* 2012:49–80.

Anderson, Chris. "NORC Study Describes Homeless." *Chronicle,* 1986:5, 9.

Anderson, Elijah. *A Place on the Corner.* Chicago: University of Chicago Press, 1978.

Anderson, Elijah. "Streetwise." In *Exploring Social Life: Readings to Accompany Essentials of Sociology, Sixth Edition,* 2nd ed., James M. Henslin, ed. Boston: Allyn and Bacon, 2006:147–156. Originally published 1990.

Anderson, Elijah. *Streetwise: Race, Class, and Change in an Urban Community.* Chicago: University of Chicago Press, 1990.

Anderson, Elizabeth. "Recent Thinking about Sexual Harassment: A Review Essay." *Philosophy & Public Affairs, 34,* 3, 2006:284–312.

Anderson, Eric. *Inclusive Masculinity: The Changing Nature of Masculinities.* New York: Routledge, 2009.

Anderson, Jenny. "She's Warm, Easy to Talk to, and a Source of Terror for Private-School Parents." *New York Times,* December 18, 2011.

Anderson, Nels. *Desert Saints: The Mormon Frontier in Utah.* Chicago: University of Chicago Press, 1966. Originally published 1942.

Anderson, Philip. "God and the Swedish Immigrants." *Sweden and America,* Autumn 1995:17–20.

Andreev, A. L. "On the Modernization of Education in Russia: A Historical Sociological Analysis." *Russian Education and Society, 54,* 10, October 2012:53–70.

Angler, Natalie. "Do Races Differ? Not Really, DNA Shows." *New York Times,* August 22, 2000.

Aptheker, Herbert. "W. E. B. Du Bois: Struggle Not Despair." *Clinical Sociology Review, 8,* 1990:58–68.

Arías, Jesús. "La Junta rehabilita en Grenada casas que deberá tirar por ruina." *El Pais,* January 2, 1993:1.

Archibold, Randal C. "Despite Violence, U.S. Firms Expand in Mexico." *New York Times,* July 10, 2011.

Archibold, Randal C. "Mexico Holds 4 High-Ranking Army Officers." *New York Times,* May 18, 2012.

Areddy, James T. "Chinese Concern on Inequality Rises." *Wall Street Journal,* October 17, 2012.

Ariès, Philippe. *Centuries of Childhood,* R. Baldick, trans. New York: Vintage Books, 1965.

Arlacchi, P. *Peasants and Great Estates: Society in Traditional Calabria.* Cambridge, England: Cambridge University Press, 1980.

Armstrong, David. "Hard Case: When Academics Double as Expert Witnesses." *Wall Street Journal,* June 22, 2007.

Arndt, William F., and F. Wilbur Gingrich. *A Greek-English Lexicon of the New Testament and Other Early Christian Literature.* Chicago: University of Chicago Press, 1957.

Arrison, Sonia. "Living to 100 and Beyond." *Wall Street Journal,* August 29, 2011.

Asch, Solomon. "Effects of Group Pressure upon the Modification and Distortion of Judgments." In *Readings in Social Psychology,* Guy Swanson, Theodore M. Newcomb, and Eugene L. Hartley, eds. New York: Holt, Rinehart and Winston, 1952.

Ashley, Richard. *Cocaine: Its History, Uses, and Effects.* New York: St. Martin's, 1975.

Associated Press. "Sarasota Doctor Loses License for Terminating Wrong Fetus." *Palm Beach Post,* April 13, 2010.

Audi, Tamara. "A Canyon Separates Foes in Grand Battle." *Wall Street Journal,* March 22, 2012.

Aughey, Arthur. "Englishness as Class: A Re-examination." *Ethnicities, 12,* 4, 2012:394–408.

Augoustinos, Martha, Ameilia Russin, and Amanda LeCouteur. "Representations of the Stem-Cell Cloning Fraud: From Scientific Breakthrough to Managing the Stake and Interest of Science." *Public Understanding of Science, 18,* 6, 2009:687–703.

Austin, S. Byrn, Jess Haines, and Paul J. Veuglers. "Body Satisfaction and Body Weight: Gender Differences and Sociodemographic Determinants." *BMC Public Health,* 9, August 2009.

Auyero, Javier, and Augustin Burbano de Lara. "In Harm's Way at the Urban Margins." *Ethnography, 13,* 4, 2012:531–557.

Aydemir, Abdurrahman, and George J. Borjas. "Attenuation Bias in Measuring the Wage Impact of Immigration." *Journal of Labor Economics, 29,* 1, 2011:69–112.

Ayittey, George B. N. "Black Africans Are Enraged at Arabs." *Wall Street Journal,* interactive edition, September 4, 1998.

Baars, Madeline. "Marriage in Black and White: Women's Support for Law Against Interracial Marriage, 1972–2000." *Intersections, 10,* 1, 2009:219–238.

Babcock, Linda, and Sara Laschever. *Ask For It: How Women Can Use the Power of Negotiation to Get What They Really Want.* New York: Bantam Dell, 2008.

Bailey, Martha J., and Susan M. Dynarski. "Gains and Gaps: Changing Inequality in U.S. College Entry and Completion." In *Whither Opportunity?: Rising Inequality, Schools, and Children's Life Chances,* Greg J. Duncan and Richard J. Murnane, eds. Russell Sage, September 2011.

Bainbridge, William Sims. "Collective Behavior and Social Movements." In *Sociology,* Rodney Stark, ed. Belmont, Calif.: Wadsworth, 1989:608–640.

Baker, Al, and Joseph Goldstein. "Police Tactic: Keeping Crime Reports off the Books." *New York Times,* December 30, 2011.

Baker, Julie. "EMU: Dismissal Email Sent to Students by Mistake Caused 'Undue Alarm.'" www.annarbor.com, May 5, 2012.

Bales, Robert F. *Interaction Process Analysis.* Reading, Mass.: Addison-Wesley, 1950.

Bales, Robert F. "The Equilibrium Problem in Small Groups." In *Working Papers in the Theory of Action,* Talcott Parsons et al., eds. New York: Free Press, 1953:111–115.

Baltzell, E. Digby. *Puritan Boston and Quaker Philadelphia.* New York: Free Press, 1979.

Baltzell, E. Digby, and Howard G. Schneiderman. "Social Class in the Oval Office." *Society, 25,* September/October 1988:42–49.

Bandes, Susan. "The Lessons of Capturing the Friedmans: Moral Panic, Institutional Denial and Due Process." *Law, Culture and the Humanities, 3,* 2007:293–319.

Banjo, Shelly. "Prepping for the Playdate Test." *Wall Street Journal,* August 19, 2010.

Bannon, Lisa. "How a Rumor Spread about Subliminal Sex in Disney's 'Aladdin.'" *Wall Street Journal,* October 24, 1995:A1, A6.

Bardocz, Susan, Stanley Ewen, Michael Hansen, et al. "Seralini and Science: An Open Letter." *Independent Science News,* October 2, 2012.

Barnard, Anne. "Mormon Church's Plans for Land Upset Harlem." *New York Times,* January 9, 2012.

Barnes, Fred. "How to Rig a Poll." *Wall Street Journal,* June 14, 1995:A14.

Barnes, Harry Elmer. *The History of Western Civilization,* Vol. 1. New York: Harcourt, Brace, 1935.

Barnes, Helen. "A Comment on Stroud and Pritchard: Child Homicide, Psychiatric Disorder and Dangerousness." *British Journal of Social Work, 31,* 3, June 2001.

Barnes, J. C., and Bruce A. Jacobs. "Genetic Risk for Violent Behavior and Environmental Exposure to Disadvantage and Violent Crime: The Case for Gene-Environment Interaction." *Journal of Interpersonal Violence, 18,* 1, 2013:92–120.

Barnes, Julian A. "Pentagon Digs In on Cyberwar Front." *Wall Street Journal,* July 6, 2012.

Barrett, Devlin, and Michael Howard Saul. "Weiner Now Says He Sent Photos." *Wall Street Journal,* June 7, 2011.

Barry, John. "A New Breed of Soldier." *Newsweek,* December 10, 2001:24–31.

Barstow, David, and Lowell Bergman. "Death on the Job, Slaps on the Wrist." *Wall Street Journal,* January 10, 2003.

Barta, Patrick. "The Rise of the Underground." *New York Times,* March 14, 2009.

Bartlett, Donald L., and James B. Steele. "Wheel of Misfortune." *Time,* December 16, 2002:44–58.

Basten, Christoph, and Frank Betz. *Marx vs. Weber: Does Religion Affect Politics and the Economy?* Florence, Italy: European University Institute, 2011.

Bates, Marston. *Gluttons and Libertines: Human Problems of Being Natural.* New York: Vintage Books, 1967. Quoted in Crapo, Richley H. *Cultural Anthropology: Understanding Ourselves and Others,* 5th ed. Boston: McGraw Hill, 2002.

Batson, Andrew. "China Stimulus Tweaks Don't Redress Imbalances." *Wall Street Journal,* March 9, 2009.

Baum, Stephanie. "Teledocs Telemedicine Service Has Gained a Wide Following." *MedCity News,* May 31, 2013.

Baumer, Eric P., and Kevin T. Wolff. "Evaluating the Contemporary Crime Drop(s) in America, New York City, and Many Other Places." *Justice Quarterly,* 2013. (in press)

Baylis, Francoise. "Human Cloning: Three Mistakes and an Alternative." *Journal of Medicine and Philosophy, 27,* 3, 2002:319–337.

Beah, Ishmael. *A Long Way Gone: Memoirs of a Boy Soldier.* New York: Farrar, Straus and Giroux, 2007.

Beals, Ralph L., and Harry Hoijer. *An Introduction to Anthropology,* 3rd ed. New York: Macmillan, 1965.

Beaman, Jean. "New York to Belarus: Sociology in International Distance-Learning." *Footnotes,* February 2003:7.

Bean, Frank D., Jennifer Lee, Jeanne Batalova, and Mark Leach. *Immigration and Fading Color Lines in America.* Washington, D.C.: Population Reference Bureau, 2004.

Bearak, Barry. "Dead Join the Living in a Family Celebration." *New York Times,* September 5, 2010a.

Bearak, Barry. "For Some Bushmen, a Homeland Worth a Fight." *New York Times,* November 5, 2010b.

Bearak, Barry. "In Crisis, Zimbabwe Asks: Could Mugabe Lose?" *New York Times,* March 7, 2008.

Beck, Scott H., and Joe W. Page. "Involvement in Activities and the Psychological Well-Being of Retired Men." *Activities, Adaptation, & Aging, 11,* 1, 1988:31–47.

Becker, George. "The Continuing Path of Distortion: The Protestant Ethic and Max Weber's School Enrollment Statistics." *Acta Sociologica, 52,* 3, September 2009:195–212.

Becker, Howard S. *Outsiders: Studies in the Sociology of Deviance.* New York: Free Press, 1966.

Becker, Jo, and Scott Shane. "Secret 'Kill List' Proves a Test of Obama's Principles and Will." *New York Times,* May 29, 2012.

Beckman, Nils, Magda Waerm, Deborah Gustafson, and Ingmar Skoog. "Secular Trends in Self Reported Sexual Activity and Satisfaction in Swedish 70 Year Olds: Cross Sectional Survey of Four Populations, 1971–2001." *British Medical Journal,* 2008:1–7.

Beeghley, Leonard. *The Structure of Social Stratification in the United States,* 5th ed. Boston: Allyn & Bacon, 2008.

Begley, Sharon. "Twins: Nazi and Jew." *Newsweek, 94,* December 3, 1979:139.

Belkin, Douglas. "Chicago Hunts for Answers to Gang Killings." *Wall Street Journal,* July 13, 2012.

Bell, Daniel. *The Coming of Post-Industrial Society: A Venture in Social Forecasting.* New York: Basic Books, 1973.

Bell, David A. "An American Success Story: The Triumph of Asian-Americans." In *Sociological Footprints: Introductory Readings in Sociology,* 5th ed., Leonard Cargan and Jeanne H. Ballantine, eds. Belmont, Calif.: Wadsworth, 1991:308–316.

Bell, Michael Mayerfeld. *An Invitation to Environmental Sociology.* Los Angeles: Pine Forge Press, 2009.

Bellah, Robert N. *Beyond Belief.* New York: Harper & Row, 1970.

Bello, Marisol. "Poverty Affects 46 Million Americans." *USA Today,* September 30, 2011.

Belluck, Pam. "Prosecutors Say Greed Drove Pharmacist to Dilute Drugs." *New York Times,* August 18, 2001.

Belsky, Jay, Deborah Lowe Vandell, Margaret Burchinall, K. Alison Clarke-Stewart, Kathleen McCartney, and Margaret Tresch Owen. "Are There Long-Term Effects of Early Child Care?" *Child Development, 78,* 2, March/April 2007:681–701.

Belsky, Jay. "Early Child Care and Early Child Development: Major Findings of the NICHD Study of Early Child Care." *European Journal of Developmental Psychology, 3,* 1, 2006:95–110.

Belsky, Jay. "Effects of Child Care on Child Development: Give Parents Real Choice." Unpublished paper, March 2009.

Ben-Ami, Naomi, and Amy J. L. Baker. "The Long-Term Correlates of Childhood Exposure to Parental Alienation on Adult Self-Sufficiency and Well-Being." *American Journal of Family Therapy, 40,* 2012:169–183.

Benet, Sula. "Why They Live to Be 100, or Even Older, in Abkhasia." *New York Times Magazine, 26,* December 1971.

Benford, Robert D. "The College Sports Reform Movement: Reframing the 'Educational' Industry." *The Sociological Quarterly, 48,* 2007:1–28.

Bennett, Brian, and Michael Weisskopf. "The Sum of Two Evils." *Time,* May 25, 2003.

Bennett, Drake. "Who's Still Biased?" *Boston Globe,* March 7, 2010.

Bennett, Jeff. "Strong Demand Revs Up Ford Profit." *Wall Street Journal,* April 26, 2011.

Bennett, Jessica. "How to Attack the Gender Wage Gap? Speak Up." *New York Times,* December 15, 2012.

Bennett-Smith, Meredith. "Taro Aso, Japanese Finance Minster, Says Country Should Let Old People 'Hurry Up and Die.'" *Huffington Post,* January 23, 2013.

Bentley, Arthur Fisher. *The Process of Government: A Study of Social Pressures.* Chicago: University of Chicago Press, 1908.

Berger, Jeffrey T., Fred Rasner, and Eric J. Cassell. "Ethics of Practicing Medical Procedures on Newly Dead and Nearly Dead Patients." *Journal of General Internal Medicine, 17,* 2002:774–778.

Berger, Lawrence M., Maria Cancian, and Daniel R. Meyer. "Maternal Re-partnering and New-partner Fertility: Associations with Nonresident Father Investments in Children." *Children and Youth Services Review, 34,* 2012:426–436.

Berger, Peter L. *Invitation to Sociology: A Humanistic Perspective.* New York: Doubleday, 1963.

Berger, Peter. "Invitation to Sociology." In *Down to Earth Sociology: Introductory Readings,* 15th ed., James M. Henslin, ed. New York: Free Press, 2014. Originally published 1963.

Bergmann, Barbara R. "The Future of Child Care." Paper presented at the annual meetings of the American Sociological Association, 1995.

Berk, Richard A. *Collective Behavior.* Dubuque, Iowa: Brown, 1974.

Berle, Adolf, Jr., and Gardiner C. Means. *The Modern Corporation and Private Property.* New York: Harcourt, Brace and World, 1932. (As cited in Useem 1980:44.)

Berman, Marc G., John Jonides, and Stephen Kaplan. "The Cognitive Benefits of Interacting with Nature." *Psychological Science, 19,* 12, 2008:1207–1212.

Bernard, Tara Siegel. "The Key to Wedded Bliss? Money Matters." *New York Times,* September 10, 2008.

Bernard, Viola W., Perry Ottenberg, and Fritz Redl. "Dehumanization: A Composite Psychological Defense in Relation to Modern War." In *The Triple Revolution Emerging: Social Problems in Depth,* Robert Perucci and Marc Pilisuk, eds. Boston: Little, Brown, 1971:17–34.

Bernstein, David. "The $18-Million Dollar Headache." *Chicago Magazine,* April 2007.

Bernstein, Elizabeth. "More Prayer, Less Hassle." *Wall Street Journal,* June 27, 2003:W3, W4.

Bertrand, Marianne, and Sendhil Mullainathan. "Are Emily and Brendan More Employable than Lakish and Jamal? A Field Experiment on Labor Market Discrimination." Unpublished paper, November 18, 2002.

Best, Deborah L. "The Contribution of the Whitings to the Study of the Socialization of Gender." *Journal of Cross-Cultural Psychology, 41,* 2010:534–545.

Bettelheim, Bruno. "The Commitment Required of a Woman Entering a Scientific Profession in Present-Day American Society." In *Women and the Scientific Professions,* Jacquelyn A. Mattfield and Carol G. Van Aken, eds. Cambridge, Mass.: MIT Press, 1965.

Bezrukova, Katerinma, Karen A. Jehn, and Chester S. Spell. "Reviewing Diversity Training: Where We Have Been and Where We Should Go." *Academy of Management Learning and Education, 11,* 2, 2012:207–227.

Bianchi, Suzanne M. "Family Change and Time Allocation in American Families." Washington, D.C.: Alfred P. Sloan Foundation, November 29–30, 2010.

Bianchi, Suzanne M., John P. Robinson, and Melissa A. Milkie. *Changing Rhythms of American Family Life.* New York: Russell Sage Foundation, 2006.

Bilefsky, Dan. "5-Year Term for Woman Who Killed Her Husband." *New York Times,* November 10, 2011d.

Bilefsky, Dan. "Albanian Custom Fades: Woman as Family Man." *New York Times,* June 25, 2008.

Bilefsky, Dan. "An Abused Wife? Or an Executioner?" *New York Times,* September 25, 2011a.

Bilefsky, Dan. "For New Life, Blacks in City Head South." *New York Times,* June 21, 2011b.

Bilefsky, Dan. "In Mother's Trial, Man Tells of His Father's Rage." *New York Times,* September 21, 2011c.

Bilefsky, Dan. "Wife Who Fired 11 Shots Is Acquitted of Murder." *New York Times,* October 6, 2011d.

Billeaud, Jacques. "Arizona Sheriff Defends Illegal-Immigrant Sweeps." *Seattle Times,* April 26, 2008.

Bishop, Jerry E. "Study Finds Doctors Tend to Postpone Heart Surgery for Women, Raising Risk." *Wall Street Journal,* April 16, 1990:B4.

Blair, Irene V., John F. Steiner, D. L. Fairclough, et al. "Clinicians' Implicit Ethnic/Racial Bias and Perceptions of Care among Black and Latino Patients." *Annals of Family Medicine, 11,* 2013:43–52.

Blankstein, Andrew, and Richard Winton. "Paraplegic Allegedly 'Dumped' on Skid Row." *Los Angeles Times,* February 9, 2007.

Blau, David M. "The Production of Quality in Child-Care Centers: Another Look." *Applied Developmental Science, 4,* 3, 2000:136–148.

Blau, Peter M., and Otis Dudley Duncan. *The American Occupational Structure.* New York: John Wiley, 1967.

Blee, Kathleen M. "Inside Organized Racism." In *Life in Society: Readings to Accompany Sociology: A Down-to-Earth Approach, Seventh Edition,* James M. Henslin, ed. Boston: Allyn and Bacon, 2005:46–57.

Blee, Kathleen M. "Trajectories of Ideologies and Action in US Organized Racism." In *Identity and Participation in Culturally Diverse Societies: A Multidisciplinary Perspective.* Assaad E. Azzi, Xenia Chryssochoou, Bert Klandermans, and Bernd Simon, eds. Oxford, UK: Blackwell Publishing, 2011.

Bloom, Paul. "The Moral Life of Babies." *New York Times Magazine,* May 3, 2010.

Bloomfield, Ruth. "Where Did the Time Go?" *Wall Street Journal,* November 23, 2012.

Blumenthal, Ralph. "52 Girls Are Taken from Polygamist Sect's Ranch in Texas." *New York Times,* April 5, 2008a.

Blumenthal, Ralph. "Court Says Texas Illegally Seized Sect's Children." *New York Times,* May 23, 2008b.

Blumer, Herbert George. "Collective Behavior." In *Principles of Sociology,* Robert E. Park, ed. New York: Barnes and Noble, 1939:219–288.

Blumer, Herbert George. *Industrialization as an Agent of Social Change: A Critical Analysis,* David R. Maines and Thomas J. Morrione, eds. Hawthorne, N.Y.: Aldine de Gruyter, 1990.

Blumstein, Philip, and Pepper Schwartz. *American Couples: Money, Work, Sex.* New York: Pocket Books, 1985.

Bodovski, Katerina, and George Farkas. "'Concerted Cultivation' and Unequal Achievement in Elementary School." *Social Science Research, 37,* 2008:903–919.

Booth, Alan, and James M. Dabbs, Jr. "Testosterone and Men's Marriages." *Social Forces, 72,* 2, December 1993:463–477.

Borchard, Annegret, David L. B. Schwappach, Aline Barbir, et al. "A Systematic Review of the Effectiveness, Compliance, and Critical Factors for Implementation of Safety Checklists in Surgery." *Annals of Surgery, 256,* 6, December 2012:925–933.

Borger, Julian, Ian Traynor, and Ewen MacAskill. "Gaddafi Family Deaths Reinforce Doubts About NATO's UN Mandate." *Guardian,* May 1, 2011.

Boroditsky, Lera. "Lost in Translation." *Wall Street Journal,* July 24, 2010.

Borsch-Supan, Axel, Ismail Duzgun, and Matthias Weiss. "Productivity and the Age Composition of Work Teams. Evidence from the Assembly Line." Harvard School of Public Health, working paper, April 17, 2007.

Bosker, Bianca. "Fortune 500 List Boasts More Female CEOs Than Ever Before." *Huffington Post,* May 7, 2012.

Bosman, Julie. "New York Schools for Pregnant Girls Will Close." *New York Times,* May 24, 2007.

Boudreaux, Richard. "Moscow Raises Alarm Over Missile-Defense Plan for Europe." *Wall Street Journal,* May 3, 2012.

Boudreaux, Richard. "Putin Move Stirs Russian Environmentalist Row." *New York Times,* January 20, 2010.

Boulding, Elise. *The Underside of History.* Boulder, Colo.: Westview Press, 1976.

Bowles, Hannah Riley. "Claiming Authority: How Women Explain Their Ascent to Top Business Leadership Positions." Harvard Kennedy School Faculty Research Working Paper Series RWP12-047, Cambridge, Mass.: Harvard University, October 2012.

Bowles, Samuel. "Unequal Education and the Reproduction of the Social Division of Labor." In *Power and Ideology in Education,* J. Karabel and A. H. Halsely, eds. New York: Oxford University Press, 1977.

Bowles, Samuel, and Herbert Gintis. *Schooling in Capitalist America.* New York: Basic Books, 1976.

Bowles, Samuel, and Herbert Gintis. "*Schooling in Capitalist America* Revisited." *Sociology of Education, 75,* 2002:1–18.

Bradford, Phillips Verner, and Harvey Blume. *Ota Benga: The Pygmy in the Zoo.* New York: Delta, 1992.

Bradsher, Keith. "China Toughens Its Restrictions on Use of the Internet." *New York Times,* December 28, 2012.

Braig, Stefanie, Richard Peter, Gabriele Nagel, et al. "The Impact of Social Status Inconsistency on Cardiovascular Risk Factors, Myocardial Infarction and Stroke in the EPIC-Heidelberg Cohort." *BMC Public Health, 11,* 2011:104.

Brajuha, Mario, and Lyle Hallowell. "Legal Intrusion and the Politics of Fieldwork: The Impact of the Brajuha Case." *Urban Life, 14,* 4, January 1986:454–478.

Bray, Rosemary L. "Rosa Parks: A Legendary Moment, a Lifetime of Activism." *Ms., 6,* 3, November–December 1995:45–47.

Brayne, Sarah. "Explaining the United States' Penal Exceptionalism: Political, Economic, and Social Factors." *Sociology Compass, 7,* 2, 2013:75–86.

Brecher, Edward M., and the Editors of Consumer Reports. *Licit and Illicit Drugs.* Boston: Little, Brown, 1972.

Bremmer, Ian. "The Secret to China's Boom: State Capitalism." Thomson-Reuters, 2011.

Briand, Frederic. "Silent Plains . . . The Fading Sounds of Native Languages." *National Geographic News Watch,* February 28, 2013.

Bridgwater, William, ed. *The Columbia Viking Desk Encyclopedia.* New York: Viking Press, 1953.

Brilliant, Ashleigh E. *Social Effects of the Automobile in Southern California during the 1920s.* Unpublished doctoral disertation, University of California at Berkeley, 1964.

Brinkley, Christina. "Women in Power: Finding Balance in the Wardrobe." *Wall Street Journal,* January 24, 2008.

Brinton, Crane. *The Anatomy of Revolution.* New York: Vintage Books, 1965.

British Council. "Education: Skills around the World, Egypt." Manchester, England: British Council, 2013.

Britt, Jonathan P., and Daniel S. McGehee. "Presynaptic Opioid and Nicotine Receptor Modulation of Dopamine Overflow in the Nucleus Accumbens." *Journal of Neuroscience, 28,* 7, February 2008:1672–1681.

Broad, William J., and David E. Sanger. "With Eye on Iran, Rivals Also Want Nuclear Power." *New York Times,* April 15, 2007.

Brockerhoff, Martin P. "An Urbanizing World." *Population Bulletin, 55,* 3, September 2000:1–44.

Bromley, David G. "The Satanic Cult Scare." *Culture and Society,* May–June 1991:55–56.

Bronfenbrenner, Urie. "Principles for the Healthy Growth and Development of Children." In *Marriage and Family in a Changing Society,* 4th ed., James M. Henslin, ed. New York: Free Press, 1992:243–249.

Broughton, Philip Delves. "When Two People Click." *Wall Street Journal,* January 29, 2013.

Brown, Alan S. "Mexico Redux." *Mechanical Engineering,* January 2008.

Brown, Fred. "Maverick Doctor's Revolution: Services-for-Fee Clinic." *Knoxville News Sentinel,* August 20, 2007.

Brown, Patricia Leigh. "At New Rentals, the Aim Is to Age with Creativity." *Wall Street Journal,* September 10, 2006.

Browning, Christopher R. *Ordinary Men: Reserve Police Battalion 101 and the Final Solution in Poland.* New York: HarperPerennial, 1993.

Brunvand, Jan Harold. *Be Afraid, Be Very Afraid: The Book of Scary Urban Legends.* New York: W.W. Norton, 2004.

Brunvand, Jan Harold. *The Choking Doberman and Other "New" Urban Legends.* New York: Norton, 1984.

Brunvand, Jan Harold. *The Vanishing Hitchhiker: American Urban Legends and Their Meanings.* New York: Norton, 1981.

Bryant, Chalandra M., Rand D. Conger, and Jennifer M. Meehan. "The Influence of In-Laws on Changes in Marital Success." *Journal of Marriage and the Family, 63, 3,* August 2001:614–626.

Buchanan, Kim Shayo. "Our Prisons, Ourselves: Race, Gender and the Rule of Law." *Yale Law Review, 29,* 1, 2010:1–82.

Buckley, Cara. "Among Victims, an Amish Farmer Quick to Adapt." *New York Times,* July 21, 2011.

"Builder Stephen Ross Buys Half of Dolphins from Huizenga." *International Herald Tribune,* February 22, 2008.

Bumiller, Elisabeth. "First Comes Marriage—Then, Maybe, Love." In *Marriage and Family in a Changing Society,* 4th ed., James M. Henslin, ed. New York: Free Press, 1992:120–125.

Burawoy, Michael. "The Field of Sociology: Its Power and Its Promise." In *Public Sociology: Fifteen Eminent Sociologists Debate Politics and the Profession in the Twenty-First Century.* Berkeley: University of California Press, 2007:241–258.

Burger, Jerry M. "Replicating Milgram: Would People Still Obey Today?" *American Psychologist, 64,* 1, January 2009:1–11.

Burgess, Ernest W. "The Growth of the City: An Introduction to a Research Project." In *The City,* Robert E. Park et al., eds. Chicago: University of Chicago Press, 1925:47–62.

Burgess, Ernest W., and Harvey J. Locke. *The Family: From Institution to Companionship.* New York: American Book, 1945.

Burman, Jeremy Trevelyan. "Updating the Baldwin Effect: The Biological Levels Behind Piaget's New Theory." *New Ideas in Psychology,* 2013. (in press)

Burnham, Walter Dean. *Democracy in the Making: American Government and Politics.* Englewood Cliffs, N.J.: Prentice Hall, 1983.

Bush, Diane Mitsch, and Robert G. Simmons. "Socialization Processes over the Life Course." In *Social Psychology: Sociological Perspectives,* Morris Rosenberger and Ralph H. Turner, eds. New Brunswick, N.J.:Transaction, 1990:133–164.

Butler, Declan. "Hyped GM Maize Study Faces Growing Scrutiny." *Nature, 490,* 7419, October 10, 2012:158.

Butler, Robert N. "Ageism: Another Form of Bigotry." *Gerontologist, 9,* Winter 1980:243–246.

Butler, Robert N. *Why Survive? Being Old in America.* New York: Harper & Row, 1975.

Byers, Michele, and Diane Crocker. "Feminist Cohorts and Waves: Attitudes of Junior Female Academics." *Women's Studies International Forum, 35,* 2012:1–11.

Bynum, Bill. "Discarded Diagnoses." *Lancet, 358,* 9294, November 17, 2001:1736.

Byrnes, Hilary F., and Breda A. Miller. "The Relationship between Neighborhood Characteristics and Effective Parenting Behaviors: The Role of Social Support." *Journal of Family Issues, 33,* 12, 2012:1658–1687.

Cabrera, Natasha J., and Robert H. Bradley. "Latino Fathers and Their Children." *Child Development Perspectives, 6,* 3, 2012:232–238.

Caforio, Giuseppe, ed. *Handbook of the Sociology of the Military.* New York: Springer, 2006.

"Camel Racing in Dubai: Child Slavery." *Asian Times,* September 28, 2011.

Campbell, James D., Dong Phil Yoon, and Brick Johnstone. "Determining Relationships between Physical Health and Spiritual Experience, Religious Practices, and Congregational Support in a Heterogeneous Medical Sample." *Journal of Religion and Health, 49,* 2010:3–17.

Campbell, Karen E., and Holly J. McCammon. "Elizabeth Blackwell's Heirs: Women as Physicians in the U.S., 1880–1920." Unpublished paper, 2005.

Canedy, Dana. "Critics of Graduation Exam Threaten Boycott in Florida." *New York Times,* May 13, 2003.

Cannon, Lou. *Official Negligence: How Rodney King and the Riots Changed Los Angeles and the LAPD.* New York: Times Books, 1998.

Cantril, Hadley. *The Psychology of Social Movements.* New York: Wiley, 1941.

Caproni, Paula J. "Work/Life Balance: You Can't Get There from Here." *Journal of Applied Behavioral Science, 40,* 2, June 2004:208–218.

Carey, Benedict. "In the Hospital, a Degrading Shift from Person to Patient." *New York Times,* August 16, 2005.

Carlson, Lewis H., and George A. Colburn. *In Their Place: White America Defines Her Minorities, 1850–1950.* New York: Wiley, 1972.

Carnevale, Anthony P., and Stephen J. Rose. "Socioeconomic Status, Race/Ethnicity, and Selective College Admissions." New York: The Century Foundation, March 2003.

Carney, Scott. *The Red Market: On the Trail of the World's Organ Brokers, Bone Thieves, Blood Farmers and Child Traffickers.* New York: HarperCollins, 2011.

Carpenito, Lynda Juall. "The Myths of Acquaintance Rape." *Nursing Forum, 34,* 4, October–December 1999:3.

Carpenter, Betsy. "Redwood Radicals." *U.S. News & World Report, 109,* 11, September 17, 1990:50–51.

Carper, James C. "Pluralism to Establishment to Dissent: The Religious and Educational Context of Home Schooling." *Peabody Journal of Education, 75,* 1–2, 2000:8–19.

Carr, Deborah, Carol D. Ryff, Burton Singer, and William J. Magee. "Bringing the 'Life' Back into Life Course Research: A 'Person-Centered' Approach to Studying the Life Course." Paper presented at the annual meetings of the American Sociological Association, 1995.

Carr, Deborah. "Death and Dying in the Contemporary United States: What Are the Psychological Implications of Anticipated Death?" *Social and Personality Psychology Compass, 6,* 2, 2012:184–195.

Carreyrou, John, and Tom McGinty. "Top Spine Surgeons Reap Royalties, Medicare Bounty." *Wall Street Journal,* December 20, 2010.

Carrington, Tim. "Developed Nations Want Poor Countries to Succeed on Trade, but Not Too Much." *Wall Street Journal,* September 20, 1993:A10.

Carson, E. Ann, and William J. Sabol. "Prisoners in 2011." *Bureau of Justice Statistics Bulletin,* December 2012.

Carter, Nancy M. "Pipeline's Broken Promise." New York: Catalyst, 2010.

Cartwright, Dorwin, and Alvin Zander, eds. *Group Dynamics,* 3rd ed. Evanston, Ill.: Peterson, 1968.

Casey, Nicholas. "Mexico's Masked Vigilantes Defy Drug Gangs—And the Law." *Wall Street Journal,* February 2–3, 2013.

Casper, Lynne M., and Loretta E. Bass. "Voting and Registration in the Election of November 1996." Washington, D.D.: U.S. Census Bureau, 1998.

Casper, Monica J. *The Making of the Unborn Patient: A Social Anatomy of Fetal Surgery.* New Brunswick, N.J.: Rutgers University Press, 1998.

Cassel, Russell N. "Examining the Basic Principles for Effective Leadership." *College Student Journal, 33,* 2, June 1999:288–301.

"Casualties in Iraq." *Wall Street Journal,* June 27, 2011.

Catan, Thomas. "Spain's Showy Debt Collectors Wear a Tux, Collect the Bucks." *Wall Street Journal,* October 11, 2008.

Cauce, Ana Mari, and Melanie Domenech-Rodriguez. "Latino Families: Myths and Realities." In *Latino Children and Families in the United States: Current Research and Future Directions,* Josefina M. Contreras, Kathryn A. Kerns, and Angela M. Neal-Barnett, eds. Westport, Conn.: Praeger, 2002:3–25.

Cellini, Stephanie R., Signe-Mary McKernan, and Caroline Ratcliffe. "The Dynamics of Poverty in the United States: A Review of Data, Methods, and Findings." *Journal of Policy Analysis and Management, 27,* 2008:577–605.

Center for American Women in Politics. "Women in Elective Office 2013." New Brunswick, N.J.: Rutgers University, 2013.

Centers for Disease Control and Prevention. "Diagnoses of HIV Infection in the United States and Dependent Areas, 2011." *HIV Surveillance Report, 23,* April 2013.

Centers for Disease Control and Prevention. "Health Effects of Secondhand Smoke." Hyattsville, Md.: Department of Health and Human Services, 2010a.

Centers for Disease Control and Prevention. "HIV among African Americans." Hyattsville, Md.: Department of Health and Human Services, 2010b.

Centers for Disease Control and Prevention. "HIV/AIDS: Statistics Overview." Atlanta, Ga.: Centers for Disease Control and Prevention, April 2013b.

Centers for Disease Control and Prevention. "HIV/AIDS Surveillance Report," Divisions of HIV/AIDS Prevention, 1997.

Centers for Disease Control and Prevention. "National Vital Statistics System: Historical Data 1900–1998: Leading Causes of Death." Atlanta, Ga.: Centers for Disease Control and Prevention, 2009.

Centers for Disease Control and Prevention. "Smoking and Tobacco Use." Hyattsville, Md.: Department of Health and Human Services, 2010a.

Centers for Disease Control and Prevention. "Summary Health Statistics for U.S. Adults: National Health Interview Survey, 2011." *Vital Health Statistics, 10,* 256, December 2012.

Centers for Disease Control and Prevention. "Tobacco Related Mortality." Hyattsville, Maryland: Department of Health and Human Services, 2011.

Centers for Disease Control and Prevention. "2001 Surveillance Report." Divisions of HIV/AIDS Prevention, 2003.

Cerulo, Karen A., and Janet M. Ruane. "Death Comes Alive: Technology and the Re-Conception of Death." *Science as Culture, 6,* 28, 1996:444–466.

Chafetz, Janet Saltzman. *Gender Equity: An Integrated Theory of Stability and Change.* Newbury Park, Calif.: Sage, 1990.

Chafetz, Janet Saltzman, and Anthony Gary Dworkin. *Female Revolt: Women's Movements in World and Historical Perspective.* Totowa, N.J.: Rowman & Allanheld, 1986.

Chagnon, Napoleon A. *Yanomamo: The Fierce People,* 2nd ed. New York: Holt, Rinehart and Winston, 1977.

Chalfant, H. Paul. "Stepping to Redemption: Twelve-Step Groups as Implicit Religion." *Free Inquiry in Creative Sociology, 20,* 2, November 1992:115–120.

Chalkley, Kate. "Female Genital Mutilation: New Laws, Programs Try to End Practice." *Population Today, 25,* 10, October 1997:4–5.

Chambliss, William J. "The Saints and the Roughnecks." In *Down to Earth Sociology: Introductory Readings,* 15th ed., James M. Henslin, ed. New York: Free Press, 2014.

Chambliss, William J. *Power, Politics, and Crime.* Boulder: Westview Press, 2000.

Chandler, Tertius, and Gerald Fox. *3000 Years of Urban Growth.* New York: Academic Press, 1974.

Chandra, Vibha P. "Fragmented Identities: The Social Construction of Ethnicity, 1885–1947." Unpublished paper, 1993.

Chandra, Vibha P. "The Present Moment of the Past: The Metamorphosis." Unpublished paper, 1993.

Chang, Iris. *The Rape of Nanking.* New York: Basic Books, 1997.

Chang, Leslie T. "Why the One-Child Policy Has Become Irrelevant." *Atlantic,* March 20, 2013.

Chase, Arlen F., Diane Z. Chase, and John F. Weishampel. "Lasers in the Jungle." *Archeology, 63,* 4, July/August 2010.

Cheadle, Jacob, Paul R. Amato, and Valarie King. "Patterns of Nonresident Father Involvement." *Demography, 47,* 2010:205–226.

Cheang, Sopheng. "Hundreds Killed in Stampede in Cambodia." Associated Press, November 22, 2010.

Chen, Edwin. "Twins Reared Apart: A Living Lab." *New York Times Magazine.* December 9, 1979:112.

Chen, Kathy. "China's Growth Places Strains on a Family's Ties." *Wall Street Journal,* April 13, 2005.

Cherlin, J. Andrew. "Remarriage as an Incomplete Institution." In *Marriage and Family in a Changing Society,* 3rd ed., James M. Henslin, ed. New York: Free Press, 1989:492–501.

Cheyney, Melissa. "Reinscribing the Birthing Body: Homebirth as Ritual Performance." *Medical Anthropology Quarterly, 25,* 4, December 2011:519–542.

"Child Care Workers." In *2012–13 Occupational Outlook Handbook.* Washington, D.C.: Bureau of Labor Statistics, 2013.

Chin, Nancy P., Alicia Monroe, and Kevin Fiscella. "Social Determinants of (Un) Healthy Behaviors." *Education for Health: Change in Learning and Practice, 13,* 3, November 2000:317–328.

Chishti, Muzaffar, and Claire Bergeron. "Increasing Evidence That Recession Has Caused Number of Unauthorized Immigrants in US to Drop." Washington, D.C.: Migration Policy Institute, March 15, 2010.

Chivers, C. J. "Officer Resigns before Hearing in D.W.I. Case." *New York Times,* August 29, 2001.

Chodorow, Nancy J. "What Is the Relation between Psychoanalytic Feminism and the Psychoanalytic Psychology of Women?" In *Theoretical Perspectives on Sexual Difference,* Deborah L. Rhode, ed. New Haven, Conn.: Yale University Press, 1990:114–130.

Choudhary, Ekta, Jeffrey Coben, and Robert M. Bossarte. "Adverse Health Outcomes, Perpetrator Characteristics, and Sexual Violence Victimization among U.S Adult Males." *Journal of Interpersonal Violence, 25,* 8, 2010: 1523–1541.

Chumley, Cheryl K. "Suspected Witch Bound, Tortured, Burned Alive in Papua New Guinea." *Washington Times,* February 8, 2013.

Church, Wesley T., II, Tracy Wharton, and Julie K. Taylor. "An Examination of Differential Association and Social Control Theory: Family Systems and Delinquency." *Youth Violence and Juvenile Justice, 7,* 1, January 2009:3–15.

CIA (Central Intelligence Agency). "Report of Questionable Activity in Connection with Project PBSuccess." Washington, D.C.: Central Intelligence Agency, 2003.

CIA (Central Intelligence Agency). "The World Factbook." Washington, D.C: U.S. Government Printing Office, 2013. Published annually.

Clair, Jeffrey Michael, David A. Karp, and William C. Yoels. *Experiencing the Life Cycle: A Social Psychology of Aging,* 2nd ed. Springfield, Ill.: Thomas, 1993.

Clark, Candace. *Misery and Company: Sympathy in Everyday Life.* Chicago: University of Chicago Press, 1997.

Clarke, Lee. "Panic: Myth or Reality?" *Contexts,* Fall 2002:21–26.

Clarke, Philippa, Jeffrey Morenoff, Michelle Debbink, et al. "Cumulative Exposure to Neighborhood Context: Consequences for Health Transitions Over the Adult Life Course." *Research on Aging,* January 2, 2013. (in press)

Clausewitz, Carl von. *On War,* J. J. Graham, trans. London: Kegan Paul, Trench, Trubner & Co., 1918.

Clearfield, Melissa W., and Naree M. Nelson. "Sex Differences in Mothers' Speech and Play Behavior with 6-, 9-, and 14-Month-Old Infants." *Sex Roles, 54,* 1–2, January 2006:127–137.

Cleeland, Nancy. "Slowdown's Silent Victims." *Los Angeles Times,* October 21, 2001.

Cloud, John. "For Better or Worse." *Time,* October 26, 1998:43–44.

Cloward, Richard A., and Lloyd E. Ohlin. *Delinquency and Opportunity: A Theory of Delinquent Gangs.* New York: Free Press, 1960.

Cohen, Patricia. "'Culture of Poverty' Makes a Comeback." *New York Times,* October 17, 2010.

Cohen, Patricia. "Forget Lonely. Life Is Healthy at the Top." *New York Times,* May 15, 2004.

Cohn, Jonathan. "The Robot Will See You Now." *Atlantic,* March 2013.

Colapinto, John. *As Nature Made Him: The Boy Who Was Raised as a Girl.* New York: HarperCollins, 2001.

Colarco, Jessica McCrory. "'I Need Help!' Social Class and Children's Help-Seeking in Elementary School." *American Sociological Review, 76,* 6, December 2011:862–882.

Cole, Diane. "When Romance Is a Click Away." *Wall Street Journal,* July 11, 2012.

Coleman, James S., and Thomas Hoffer. *Public and Private Schools: The Impact of Communities.* New York: Basic Books, 1987.

Coleman, James William. "Politics and the Abuse of Power." In *Down to Earth Sociology: Introductory Readings,* 8th ed., James M. Henslin, ed. New York: Free Press, 1995:442–450.

Coleman, Marilyn, Lawrence Ganong, and Mark Fine. "Reinvestigating Remarriage: Another Decade of Progress." *Journal of Marriage and the Family, 62,* 4, November 2000:1288–1307.

College Board. "2012 College-Bound Seniors: Total Group Profile Report." New York: College Board, September 24, 2012.

Collins, Randall. *The Credential Society: An Historical Sociology of Education.* New York: Academic Press, 1979.

Collins, Randall. "Socially Unrecognized Cumulation." *American Sociologist, 30,* 2, Summer 1999:41–61.

Collins, Randall, Janet Saltzman Chafetz, Rae Lesser Blumberg, Scott Coltrane, and Jonathan H. Turner. "Toward an Integrated Theory of Gender Stratification." *Sociological Perspectives, 36,* 3, 1993:185–216.

Compton, Allie. "Is the U.S. Government Planning to Implement Secret Scanners That Can Detect Anything?" *Huffington Post,* July 10, 2012.

Conahan, Frank C. "Human Experimentation: An Overview on Cold War Era Programs." Washington, D.C.: U.S. General Accounting Office, September 28, 1994:1–11.

Confessore, Nicholas. "Lines Blur between Candidates and PACs with Unlimited Cash." *New York Times,* August 27, 2011.

Conlin, Michelle. "Get Healthy—Or Else." *Business Week,* February 26, 2007.

Connors, L. "Gender of Infant Differences in Attachment: Associations with Temperament and Caregiving Experiences." Paper presented at the Annual Conference of the British Psychological Society, Oxford, England, 1996.

Cooley, Charles Horton. *Human Nature and the Social Order.* New York: Scribner's, 1902.

Cooley, Charles Horton. *Social Organization.* New York: Schocken Books, 1962. Originally published by Scribner's, 1909.

Cooper, Charles. "Unmanned Space Plane Opening Door to Space Weaponization?" *CBS News,* April 22, 2010.

Copen, Casey E., Kimberly Daniels, and William D. Mosher. "First Premarital Cohabitation in the United States: Data from the 2006-2010 National Survey of Family Growth." *National Health Statistics Reports, 64,* Washington, D.C.: National Center for Health Statistics, April 4, 2013.

Copen, Casey E., Kimberly Daniels, Jonathan Vespa, et al. "First Marriages in the United States: Data from the 2006-2010 National Survey of Family Growth." *National Health Statistics Reports, 49,* March 22, 2012.

Cornwell, Christopher, David B. Mustard, and Jessica Van Parys. "Noncognitive Skills and the Gender Disparities in Test Scores and Teacher Assessments: Evidence from Primary School." *Journal of Human Resources, 48,* 1, 2013:236–264.

Cose, Ellis. "What's White Anyway?" *Newsweek,* September 18, 2000: 64–65.

Coser, Lewis A. *Masters of Sociological Thought: Ideas in Historical and Social Context,* 2nd ed. New York: Harcourt Brace Jovanovich, 1977.

Costa, Stephanie. "Where's the Outrage?" *Ms Magazine Blog.* September 12, 2011.

Costantini, Cristina. "Spanish in Miami: Diciendo 'Hola' Or Saying 'Hello.'" *Huffpost Miami,* November 29, 2011.

Costello, Daniel. "Online House Calls Click with Doctors." *Los Angeles Times,* February 4, 2008.

Cottin, Lou. *Elders in Rebellion: A Guide to Senior Activism.* Garden City, N.Y.: Anchor Doubleday, 1979.

Council of Economic Advisers. "Immigration's Economic Impact." Washington, D.C. June 20, 2007.

Cousins, Albert N., and Hans Nagpaul. *Urban Man and Society: A Reader in Urban Sociology.* New York: McGraw-Hill, 1970.

Cowan, Tadlock. "Biotechnology in Animal Agriculture: Status and Current Issues." *Congressional Research Service Reports, 32,* Washington, D. C.: Congressional Research Service, September 10, 2010.

Cowen, Emory L., Judah Landes, and Donald E. Schaet. "The Effects of Mild Frustration on the Expression of Prejudiced Attitudes." *Journal of Abnormal and Social Psychology.* January 1959:33–38.

Cowgill, Donald. "The Aging of Populations and Societies." *Annals of the American Academy of Political and Social Science, 415,* 1974:1–18.

Cowley, Joyce. *Pioneers of Women's Liberation.* New York: Merit, 1969.

Crane, Andrew. "Modern Slavery as a Management Practice: Exploring the Conditions and Capabilities for Human Exploitation." *Academy of Management Review, 38,* 1, 2012:49–69.

Crawford, Duane W., Renate M. Houts, Ted L. Huston, and Laura J. George. "Compatibility, Leisure, and Satisfaction in Marital Relationships." *Journal of Marriage and Family, 64,* May 2002: 433–449.

Crosby, Alex E., LaVonne Ortega, and Mark R. Stevens. "Suicide: United States, 1999–2007." *Morbidity and Mortality Weekly Report, 60,* 1, Supplements, January 4, 2011:56–59.

Crosnoe, Robert, Catherine Riegle-Crumb, Sam Field, Kenneth Frank, and Chandra Muller. "Peer Group Contexts of Girls' and Boys' Academic Experiences." *Child Development, 79,* 1, February 2008:139–155.

Crossen, Cynthia. "Before Social Security, Most Americans Faced Very Bleak Retirement." *Wall Street Journal,* September 15, 2004.

Crossen, Cynthia. "Déjà Vu." *New York Times,* February 25, 2004.

Crossen, Cynthia. "Deja Vu." *Wall Street Journal,* March 5, 2003.

Crossen, Cynthia. "Margin of Error: Studies Galore Support Products and Positions, but Are They Reliable?" *Wall Street Journal,* November 14, 1991:A1.

Crossen, Cynthia. "How Pygmy Ota Benga Ended Up in Bronx Zoo as Darwinism Dawned." *Wall Street Journal,* February 6, 2006.

Crossland, David. "Gas Dispute Has Europe Trembling." *Spiegel Online,* January 2, 2006.

Croydon, Helen. "Is Sex for the Disabled the Last Taboo?" *Times,* November 12, 2009.

Crumley, Bruce. "The Game of Death: France's Shocking TV Experiment." *Time,* March 17, 2010.

Cui, Ming, and Frank D. Fincham. "The Differential Effects of Parental Divorce and Marital Conflict on Young Adult Romantic Relationships." *Personal Relationships, 17,* 3, September 2010:331–343.

Cumming, Elaine. "Further Thoughts on the Theory of Disengagement." In *Aging in America: Readings in Social Gerontology,* Cary S. Kart and Barbara B. Manard, eds. Sherman Oaks, Calif.: Alfred Publishing, 1976:19–41.

Cumming, Elaine, and William E. Henry. *Growing Old: The Process of Disengagement.* New York: Basic Books, 1961.

Cussins, Jessica. "'World's First GM Babies Born': 12-Year-Old Article Continues to Cause Confusion." *Biopolitical Times,* April 25, 2013.

Dabbs, James M., Jr., and Robin Morris. "Testosterone, Social Class, and Antisocial Behavior in a Sample of 4,462 Men." *Psychological Science, 1,* 3, May 1990:209–211.

Dabbs, James M., Jr., Marian F. Hargrove, and Colleen Heusel. "Testosterone Differences among College Fraternities: Well-Behaved vs. Rambunctious." *Personality and Individual Differences, 20,* 1996:157–161.

Dabbs, James M., Jr., Timothy S. Carr, Robert L. Frady, and Jasmin K. Riad. "Testosterone, Crime, and Misbehavior among 692 Male Prison Inmates." *Personality and Individual Differences, 18,* 1995:627–633.

Daggett, Stephen. "Costs of Major U.S. Wars." Washington, D.C.: Congressional Research Service, June 29, 2010.

Dahl, Gordon B., and Enrico Moretti. "The Demand for Sons." *Review of Economic Studies, 75,* 2008:1085–1120.

Dahl, Robert A. *Dilemmas of Pluralist Democracy: Autonomy vs. Control.* New Haven, Conn.: Yale University Press, 1982.

Dahl, Robert A. *Who Governs?* New Haven, Conn.: Yale University Press, 1961.

Dao, James. "Instant Millions Can't Halt Winners' Grim Side." *New York Times,* December 5, 2005.

Darley, John M., and Bibb Latané. "Bystander Intervention in Emergencies: Diffusion of Responsibility." *Journal of Personality and Social Psychology, 8,* 4, 1968:377–383.

Darwin, Charles. *The Origin of Species.* Chicago: Conley, 1859.

Dasgupta, Nilanjana, Debbie E. McGhee, Anthony G. Greenwald, and Mahzarin R. Banaji. "Automatic Preference for White Americans: Eliminating the Familiarity Explanation." *Journal of Experimental Social Psychology, 36,* 3, May 2000:316–328.

Davis, Ann, Joseph Pereira, and William M. Bulkeley. "Security Concerns Bring Focus on Translating Body Language." *Wall Street Journal,* August 15, 2002.

Davis, Donald R., and David E. Weinstein. "Technological Superiority and the Losses from Migration." National Bureau of Economic Research, working paper, June 2002.

Davis, Kingsley, and Wilbert E. Moore. "Reply to Tumin." *American Sociological Review, 18,* 1953:394–396.

Davis, Kingsley, and Wilbert E. Moore. "Some Principles of Stratification." *American Sociological Review, 10,* 1945:242–249.

Davis, Nancy J., and Robert V. Robinson. "Class Identification of Men and Women in the 1970s and 1980s." *American Sociological Review, 53,* February 1988:103–112.

Davis, R. E., M. P. Couper, N. K. Janz, C. H. Caldwell, and K. Resnicow. "Interviewer Effects in Public Health Surveys." *Health Education Research, 25,* 1, 2010:14–28.

Davis, Stan. *Lessons From the Future: Making Sense of a Blurred World.* New York: Capstone Publishers, 2001.

Day, Jennifer Chesseman. "Population Profile of the United States: National Population Projections." Washington, D.C.: U.S. Census Bureau, 2010.

de Munck, Victor C., Audrey Korotayev, Janina de Munck, and Darya Khaltourina. "Cross-Cultural Analysis of Models of Romantic Love among U.S. Residents, Russians, and Lithuanians." *Cross-Cultural Research, 45,* 2, 2011:128–154.

Deaver, Michael V. "Democratizing Russian Higher Education." *Demokratizatsiya, 9,* 3, Summer 2001:350–366.

DeCrow, Karen. Foreword to *Why Men Earn More* by Warren Farrell. New York: AMACOM, 2005:xi–xii.

Deegan, Mary Jo. "W. E. B. Du Bois and the Women of Hull-House, 1895–1899." *American Sociologist,* Winter 1988:301–311.

Deflem, Mathieu, ed. *Sociological Theory and Criminological Research: Views from Europe and the United States.* San Diego: JAI Press, 2006.

Delaney, Arthur. "Revolving Door: 1447 Former Government Workers Lobby for Wall Street." *Huffington Post,* June 3, 2010.

Deliege, Robert. *The Untouchables of India.* New York: Berg Publishers, 2001.

Delmar-Morgan, Alex. "Qatari Poet Sentenced to Life in Prison." *Wall Street Journal,* November 30, 2012.

DeLuca, Stephanie, and Elizabeth Dayton. "Switching Social Contexts: The Effects of Housing Mobility and School Choice Programs on Youth Outcomes." *Annual Review of Sociology, 35,* 2009:457–491.

DeMartini, Joseph R. "Basic and Applied Sociological Work: Divergence, Convergence, or Peaceful Co-existence?" *The Journal of Applied Behavioral Science, 18,* 2, 1982:203–215.

DeMause, Lloyd. "Our Forebears Made Childhood a Nightmare." *Psychology Today 8,* 11, April 1975:85–88.

Demidov, Vadim. "Ten Years of Rolling the Minicircles: RCA Assays in DNA Diagnostics." *Expert Review of Molecular Diagnostics, 5,* 4, July 2005:477–478.

DeNavas-Walt, Carmen, Bernadette D. Proctor, and Jessica C. Smith. "Income, Poverty, and Health Insurance Coverage in the United States: 2009." *Current Population Reports P60-238,* Washington, D.C.: U.S. Census Bureau, September 2010.

Densley, James A. "Street Gang Recruitment: Signaling, Screening, and Selection." *Social Problems, 59,* 3, August 2012:301–321.

Denzin, Norman K. "The Suicide Machine." *Society,* July–August, 1992:7–10.

Denzin, Norman K. *Symbolic Interactionism and Cultural Studies: The Politics of Interpretation.* Cambridge, Mass.: Blackwell 2007.

DeParle, Jason. "Two Classes Divided by 'I Do.'" *New York Times,* July 14, 2012.

Dershowitz, Alan M. "Tortured Reasoning." In *Torture: A Collection,* Sanford Levinson, ed. Oxford, England: Oxford University Press, 2004:258–280.

Deutscher, Irwin. *Accommodating Diversity: National Policies that Prevent Ethnic Conflict.* Lanham, Md.: Lexington Books, 2002.

Dew, Jeffrey, and W. Bradford Wilcox. "If Momma Ain't Happy: Explaining Declines in Marital Satisfaction among New Mothers." *Journal of Marriage and Family, 73,* February 2011:1–12.

Diamond, Jeff. "Distance Learning Forever Alters the Process of Teaching and Learning." *Community College Week,* March 4, 2013.

Diamond, Milton, and Keith Sigmundson. "Sex Reassignment at Birth: Long-term Review and Clinical Implications." *Archives of Pediatric and Adolescent Medicine, 151,* March 1997:298–304.

Dickey, Christopher, and Adam Rogers. "Smoke and Mirrors." *Newsweek,* February 25, 2002.

Dickey, Christopher, and John Barry. "Iran: A Rummy Guide." *Newsweek,* May 8, 2006.

DiFonzo, Nicholas, Martin J. Bourgeois, Jerry Suls, et al. "Rumor Clustering, Consensus, and Polarization: Dynamic Social Impact and Self-Organization of Hearsay." *Journal of Experimental Social Psychology, 49,* 3, 2013:378–399.

Digest of Education Statistics. Washington, D.C.: National Center for Education Statistics, 2007.

Dillon, Sam. "States' Data Obscure How Few Finish High School." *New York Times,* March 20, 2008.

Dingwall, Robert. *Essays on Professions.* Farnham, United Kingdom: Ashgate Publishing, 2008.

DiSilvestro, Roger L. *In the Shadow of Wounded Knee: The Untold Final Chapter of the Indian Wars.* New York: Walker & Co., 2006.

Doane, Ashley W., Jr. "Dominant Group Ethnic Identity in the United States: The Role of 'Hidden' Ethnicity in Intergroup Relations." *The Sociological Quarterly, 38,* 3, Summer 1997:375–397.

Dobriner, William M. *Social Structures and Systems.* Pacific Palisades, California: Goodyear, 1969b.

Dobyns, Henry F. *Their Numbers Became Thinned: Native American Population Dynamics in Eastern North America.* Knoxville: University of Tennessee Press, 1983.

Dodds, Peter Sheridan, Roby Muhamad, and Duncan J. Watts. "An Experimental Study of Search in Global Social Networks." *Science, 301,* August 8, 2003:827–830.

Dogan, Mattei. "Status Incongruence in Advanced Societies." *Societamutamentopolitica, 2,* 3, 2011:285–294.

Dollard, John, Leonard William Doob, Neal Elgar Miller, Orval Hobart Mowrer, and Robert Richardson Sears. *Frustration and Aggression.* New Haven, Conn.: Yale University Press, 1939.

Dolnick, Sam. "The Obesity-Hunger Paradox." *New York Times,* March 12, 2010.

Domhoff, G. William. "C. Wright Mills, Power Structure Research, and the Failures of Mainstream Political Science." *New Political Science, 29,* 2007:97–114.

Domhoff, G. William. "State and Ruling Class in Corporate America (1974): Reflections, Corrections, and New Directions." *Critical Sociology, 25,* 2–3, July 1999a:260–265.

Domhoff, G. William. "The Bohemian Grove and Other Retreats." In *Down to Earth Sociology: Introductory Readings,* 10th ed., James M. Henslin, ed. New York: Free Press, 1999a:391–403.

Domhoff, G. William. "Wealth, Income, and Power." Website: Who Rules America, http://sociology.ucsc.edu/whorulesamerica/

Domhoff, G. William. *Who Rules America? Challenges to Corporate and Class Dominance,* 6th ed. New York: McGraw Hill, 2009.

Domhoff, G. William. *Who Rules America? Power, Politics, and Social Change,* 5th ed. New York: McGraw-Hill, 2006.

Domingo, Santiago, and Antonio Pellicer. "Overview of Current Trends in Hysterectomy." *Expert Review of Obstetrics and Gynecology, 4,* 6, 2009:673–685.

Donaldson, Stephen. "A Million Jockers, Punks, and Queens: Sex among American Male Prisoners and Its Implications for Concepts of Sexual Orientation." February 4, 1993. Online.

Donlon, Margie M., Ori Ash, and Becca R. Levy. "Re-Vision of Older Television Characters: A Stereotype-Awareness Intervention." *Journal of Social Issues, 61,* 2, June 2005.

Doorenspleet, Renske, and Huib Pellikaan. "Which Type of Democracy Performs Best?" *Acta Politica,* 2013. (in press)

Dougherty, Conor. "The New American Gentry." *Wall Street Journal,* January 19, 2008.

Douthat, Ross. "Abortion Politics Didn't Doom the G.O.P." *New York Times,* December 7, 2008.

Dove, Adrian. "Soul Folk 'Chitling' Test or the Dove Counterbalance Intelligence Test." Mimeo, no date.

Drakulich, Kevin M. "Strangers, Neighbors, and Race: A Contact Model of Stereotypes and Racal Anxieties about Crime." *Race and Justice, 2,* 4, 2012:322–355.

Drape, Joe. "Growing Cheers for the Home-Schooled Team." *New York Times,* March 16, 2008.

Drew, Christopher. "Military Contractor Agrees to Pay $325 Million to Settle Whistle-Blower Lawsuit." *New York Times,* April 2, 2009.

Drucker, Peter F. "There's More Than One Kind of Team." *Wall Street Journal,* February 11, 1992:A16.

Drum, Kevin. "America's Real Criminal Element: Lead." *Mother Jones,* January/February 2013.

Du Bois, W. E. B. *Black Reconstruction in America: An Essay toward a History of the Part Which Black Folk Played in the Attempt to Reconstruct Democracy in America, 1860–1880.* New York: Atheneum, 1992. Originally published 1935.

Du Bois, W. E. B. *The Autobiography of W. E. B. Du Bois: A Soliloquy on Viewing My Life from the Last Decade of Its First Century.* New York: International, 1968.

Du Bois, W. E. B. *The Philadelphia Negro: A Social Study.* New York: Schocken Books, 1967. Originally published 1899.

Du Bois, W. E. B. *The Souls of Black Folk: Essays and Sketches.* Chicago: McClurg, 1903.

Duck, W. O., and Anne W. Rawls, "Interaction Orders of Drug Dealing Spaces: Local Orders of Sensemaking in a Poor Black American Place." *Crime, Law and Social Change,* 2011.

Duff, Christina. "Superrich's Share of After-Tax Income Stopped Rising in Early '90s, Data Show." *Wall Street Journal,* November 22, 1995:A2.

Dugger, Celia W. "Abortion in India Is Tipping Scales Sharply against Girls." *New York Times,* April 22, 2001.

Dugger, Celia W. "Wedding Vows Bind Old World and New." *New York Times,* July 20, 1998.

Dunaway, Wilma A. *Women, Work, and Family in the Antebellum Mountain South.* New York: Cambridge University Press, 2008.

Duneier, Mitchell. *Sidewalk.* New York: Farrar, Straus and Giroux, 1999.

Dunlap, Riley E., and William R. Catton, Jr. "Environmental Sociology." *Annual Review of Sociology, 5,* 1979:243–273.

Dunlap, Riley E., and William R. Catton, Jr. "What Environmental Sociologists Have in Common Whether Concerned with 'Built' or 'Natural' Environments." *Sociological Inquiry, 53,* 2–3, 1983:113–135.

Dunn, Hank. "Time to Hold Students Accountable for Their Own Success." *Community College Week,* March 18, 2013.

Durkheim, Emile. *Suicide: A Study in Sociology,* John A. Spaulding and George Simpson, trans. New York: Free Press, 1966. Originally published 1897.

Durkheim, Emile. *The Division of Labor in Society,* George Simpson, trans. New York: Free Press, 1933. Originally published 1893.

Durkheim, Emile. *The Elementary Forms of the Religious Life.* New York: Free Press, 1965. Originally published 1912.

Durkheim, Emile. *The Rules of Sociological Method,* Sarah A. Solovay and John H. Mueller, trans. New York: Free Press, 1938, 1958, 1964. Originally published 1895.

Durning, Alan. "Cradles of Life." In *Social Problems 90/91,* LeRoy W. Barnes, ed. Guilford, Conn.: Dushkin, 1990:231–241.

Dwyer, Jim. "A Court Battle Over a Husband's Rage and a Wife Who'd Had Enough." *New York Times,* April 26, 2011.

Dychtwald, Ken. "Remembering Maggie Kuhn: Gray Panther Founder on the 5 Myths of Aging." *Huffington Post,* May 31, 2012.

Dye, Jane Lawler. "Fertility of American Women, June 2004." U.S. Census Bureau. *Current Population Reports,* December 2005.

Dyer, Gwynne. "Anybody's Son Will Do." In *Down to Earth Sociology: Introductory Readings,* 14th ed., James M. Henslin, ed. New York: Free Press, 2007.

Eagly, Alice H., Asia Eaton, Suzanna M. Rose, et al. "Feminism and Psychology: Analysis of a Half-Century of Research on Women and Gender." *American Psychologist, 67,* 3, 2012:211–230.

Ebaugh, Helen Rose Fuchs. *Becoming an Ex: The Process of Role Exit.* Chicago: University of Chicago Press, 1988.

"Ebola Virus Outbreak in Congo Kills 31." *Guardian,* September 14, 2012.

Eder, Donna. "On Becoming Female: Lessons Learned in School." In *Down to Earth Sociology: Introductory Readings,* 14th ed., James M. Henslin, ed. New York: Free Press, 2007.

Eder, Donna. *School Talk: Gender and Adolescent Culture.* New Brunswick, N.J.: Rutgers University Press, 1995.

Eder, Donna. "Sitting in on Adolescent Conversations." In *Social Problems: A Down-to-Earth Approach,* 11th ed., James M. Henslin, ed. Boston: Pearson, 2014.

Eder, Klaus. "The Rise of Counter-Culture Movements against Modernity: Nature as a New Field of Class Struggle." *Theory, Culture & Society, 7,* 1990:21–47.

Edgerton, Robert B. *Deviance: A Cross-Cultural Perspective.* Menlo Park, Calif.: Benjamin/Cummings, 1976.

Edgerton, Robert B. *Sick Societies: Challenging the Myth of Primitive Harmony.* New York: Free Press, 1992.

Ehrenreich, Barbara, and Deidre English. *Witches, Midwives, and Nurses: A History of Women Healers.* Old Westbury, N.Y.: Feminist Press, 1973.

Ehrlich, Paul R., and Anne H. Ehrlich. "Humanity at the Crossroads." *Stanford Magazine,* Spring–Summer 1978:20–23.

Ehrlich, Paul R., and Anne H. Ehrlich. *Population, Resources, and Environment: Issues in Human Ecology,* 2nd ed. San Francisco: Freeman, 1972.

Eibl-Eibesfeldt, Irrenäus. *Ethology: The Biology of Behavior.* New York: Holt, Rinehart, and Winston, 1970.

Eisenegger, Christoph, Johannes Haushofer, and Ernst Fehr. "The Role of Testosterone in Social Interaction." *Trends in Cognitive Sciences, 15,* 6, 2011:263–271.

Eisenhart, R. Wayne. "You Can't Hack It, Little Girl: A Discussion of the Covert Psychological Agenda of Modern Combat Training." *Journal of Social Issues, 31,* Fall 1975:13–23.

Ekman, Paul. *Faces of Man: Universal Expression in a New Guinea Village.* New York: Garland Press, 1980.

Ekman, Paul, Wallace V. Friesen, and John Bear. "The International Language of Gestures." *Psychology Today,* May 1984:64.

Elder, Glen H., Jr. "Age Differentiation and Life Course." *Annual Review of Sociology, 1,* 1975:165–190.

Elder, Glen H., Jr. *Children of the Great Depression: Social Change in Life Experience.* Boulder: Westview Press, 1999.

Elder, Miriam. "Russian Mafia Boss Shot Dead by Sniper." *Guardian,* January 16, 2013.

Elliott, Diana B., and Jamie M. Lewis. "Embracing the Institution of Marriage: The Characteristics of Remarried Americans." Paper presented at the annual meetings of Population Association of America, April 17, 2010.

Elliott, Diana B., Kristy Krivickas, Matthew W. Brault, et al. "Historical Marriage Trends from 1890–2010. A Focus on Race Differences." Paper presented at the annual meeting of the Population Association of America, San Francisco, Calif., May 3–5, 2012.

Elliott, Joel. "Birth Control Allowed for Maine Middle Schoolers." *New York Times,* October 18, 2007.

Emery, Cécile, Thomas S. Calvard, and Meghan E. Pierce. "Leadership as an Emergent Group Process: A Social Network Study of Personality and Leadership." *Group Processes and Intergroup Relations, 16,* 1, 2013:28–45.

Emsden, Christopher, and Matthew Dalton. "Europe Loosens Reins on National Budgets." *Wall Street Journal,* May 30, 2013.

England, Paula. "The Impact of Feminist Thought on Sociology." *Contemporary Sociology: A Journal of Reviews,* 2000:263–267.

Ensign, Rachel Louise. "It's Now a Grind for 2-Year-Olds." *New York Times,* March 12, 2012.

Environmental Protection Agency. "Final National Priorities List." Washington, D.C.: Environmental Protection Agency, March 29, 2013.

Epstein, Cynthia Fuchs. *Deceptive Distinctions: Sex, Gender, and the Social Order.* New Haven, Conn.: Yale University Press, 1988.

Erikson, Kai T. *Everything in Its Path: Destruction of Community in the Buffalo Creek Flood.* New York: Simon and Schuster, 1978.

Ernst, Eldon G. "The Baptists." In *Encyclopedia of the American Religious Experience: Studies of Traditions and Movements,* Vol. 1, Charles H. Lippy and Peter W. Williams, eds. New York: Scribners, 1988:555–577.

Ertel, Karen A., M. Maria Glymour, and Lisa F. Berkman. "Effects of Social Integration on Preserving Memory Function in a Nationally Representative US Elderly Population." *American Journal of Public Health, 98,* 7, July 2008:1215–1220.

Espenshade, Thomas J. "A Short History of U.S. Policy toward Illegal Immigration." *Population Today, 18,* 2, February 1990:6–9.

Espenshade, Thomas J., and Alexandria Walton Radford. *No Longer Separate, Not Yet Equal: Race and Class in Elite College Admission and Campus Life.* Princeton, N.J.: Princeton University Press, 2009.

Estes, Larissa J., Linda E. Lloyd, Michelle Teti, et al. "Perceptions of Audio Computer-Assisted Self-Interviewing (ACASI) among Women in an HIV-Positive Prevention Program." *PLoS ONE, 5,* 2, February 10, 2010:e9149.

Estruch, Ramón, Emilio Ros, Jordi Salas-Salvadó, et al. "Primary Prevention of Cardiovascular Disease with a Mediterranean Diet." *New England Journal of Medicine, 368,* 2013:1279–1290.

Ezekiel, Raphael S. *The Racist Mind: Portraits of American Neo-Nazis and Klansmen.* New York: Viking, 1995.

Fabio, Anthony, Li-Chuan Tu, Rolf Loeber, and Jacqueline Cohen. "Neighborhood Socioeconomic Disadvantage and the Shape of the Age-Crime Curve." *American Journal of Public Health, 101,* S1, 2011:S325–S331.

Fabrikant, Geraldine. "Old Nantucket Warily Meets the New." *New York Times,* June 5, 2005.

Falicov, Celia Jaes. "Changing Constructions of Machismo for Latino Men in Therapy: 'The Devil Never Sleeps.'" *Family Process, 49,* 3, 2010:309–329.

Falkenberg, Katie. "Pakistani Women Victims of 'Honor.'" *Washington Times,* July 23, 2008.

Fan, Maureen. "After Quake, China's Elderly Long for Family." *Washington Post,* June 3, 2008.

Faris, Robert E. L., and Warren Dunham. *Mental Disorders in Urban Areas.* Chicago: University of Chicago Press, 1939.

Farkas, George. *Human Capital or Cultural Capital?: Ethnicity and Poverty Groups in an Urban School District.* New York: Walter DeGruyter, 1996.

Farkas, George, Daniel Sheehan, and Robert P. Grobe. "Coursework Mastery and School Success: Gender, Ethnicity, and Poverty Groups within an Urban School District." *American Educational Research Journal, 27,* 4, Winter 1990b:807–827.

Farkas, George, Robert P. Grobe, Daniel Sheehan, and Yuan Shuan. "Cultural Resources and School Success: Gender, Ethnicity, and Poverty Groups within an Urban School District." *American Sociological Review, 55,* February 1990a:127–142.

Farr, Rachel H., Stephen L. Forssell, and Charlotte J. Patterson. "Parenting and Child Development in Adoptive Families: Does Parental Sexual Orientation Matter?" *Applied Developmental Science, 14,* 3, 2010:164–178.

Fathi, Nazila. "Starting at Home, Iran's Women Fight for Rights." *New York Times,* February 12, 2009.

Fattig, Paul. "Good Intentions Gone Bad." *Mail Tribune,* June 6, 2007.

Faunce, William A. *Problems of an Industrial Society,* 2nd ed. New York: McGraw-Hill, 1981.

Feagin, Joe R. "The Continuing Significance of Race: Antiblack Discrimination in Public Places." In *Majority and Minority: The Dynamics of Race and Ethnicity in American Life,* 6th ed., Norman R. Yetman, ed. Boston: Allyn and Bacon, 1999:384–399.

Featherman, David L. "Opportunities Are Expanding." *Society, 13,* 1979:4–11.

Feder, Barnaby J. "Services at the First Church of Cyberspace." *New York Times,* May 15, 2004.

Feiler, Bruce. "Family Inc." *Wall Street Journal,* February 9–10, 2013.

Felsenthal, Edward. "Justices' Ruling Further Defines Sex Harassment." *Wall Street Journal,* March 5, 1998:B1, B2.

Feuer, Alan. "Accommodations for the Discreetly Superrich." *New York Times,* October 6, 2008.

Fialka, John J. "Pentagon Outlines Plans to Use Troops to Join Border 'War' against Drugs." *Wall Street Journal,* February 23, 1988.

Filatova, Liudmila, Irina Abankina, Tatiana Abankina, and Elena Nikolayenko. "Education Development Trends in Russia." *Journal of US-China Public Administration, 9,* 10, October 2012:1198–1214.

File, Thom, and Sarah Crissey. "Voting and Registration in the Election of November 2008." *Current Population Reports,* May 2010.

Fine, Gary Alan, and Bill Ellis. *The Global Grapevine: Why Rumors of Terrorism, Immigration, and Trade Matter.* New York: Oxford University Press, 2010.

Finke, Roger, and Rodney Stark. *The Churching of America, 1776–1990: Winners and Losers in Our Religious Economy.* New Brunswick, N.J.: Rutgers University Press, 1992.

Finkelhor, David, and Kersti Yllo. *License to Rape: Sexual Abuse of Wives.* New York: Henry Holt, 1985.

Finkelhor, David, and Kersti Yllo. "Marital Rape: The Myth versus the Reality." In *Marriage and Family in a Changing Society,* 3rd ed., James M. Henslin, ed. New York: Free Press, 1989:382–391.

Fischer, Claude S. *The Urban Experience.* New York: Harcourt, 1976.

Fish, Jefferson M. "Mixed Blood." *Psychology Today, 28,* 6, November–December 1995:55–58, 60, 61, 76, 80.

Fisher, Bonnie S., Francis T. Cullen, and Michael G. Turner. *The Sexual Victimization of College Women.* Washington, D.C.: U.S. Department of Justice, 2000.

Fisher, Bonnie S., Leah E. Daigle, Francis T. Cullen, and Michael G. Turner. "Reporting Sexual Victimization to the Police and Others: Results from a National-Level Study of College Women." *Criminal Justice and Behavior, 30,* 1, February 2003:6–38.

Fisher, Helen E., Lucy L. Brown, Arthur Aron, Greg Strong, and Deborah Masek. "Reward, Addiction, and Emotion Regulation Systems Associated with Rejection in Love." *Journal of Neurophysiology, 104,* 2010:51–60.

Fisher, Ian, and Elisabetta Provoledo. "Surprising Few, Italy's Government Collapses." *New York Times,* January 25, 2008.

Fisher, Sue. *In the Patient's Best Interest: Women and the Politics of Medical Decisions.* New Brunswick, N.J.: Rutgers University Press, 1986.

Flanagan, William G. *Urban Sociology: Images and Structure.* Boston: Allyn and Bacon, 1990.

Flavel, John H., et al. *The Development of Role-Taking and Communication Skills in Children.* New York: Wiley, 1968.

Flavel, John, Patricia H. Miller, and Scott A. Miller. *Cognitive Development,* 4th ed. Upper Saddle River, N.J.: Prentice Hall, 2002.

Flegal, Katherine M., and Karen Hunter. "Higher Levels of Obesity Associated with Increased Risk of Death; Being Overweight Associated with Lower Risk of Death." *Journal of American Medical Association, 309,* 1, 2013:87–88.

Fleming, Kevin C., Jonathan M. Evans, and Darryl S. Chutka. "A Cultural and Economic History of Old Age in America." *Mayo Clinic Proceedings, 78,* July 2003:914–921.

Flexner, Abraham. *Medical Education in the United States and Canada: A Report to the Carnegie Foundation for the Advancement of Teaching.* Bulletin No. 4. Boston: Merrymount Press, 1910.

Flexner, E. *Century of Struggle.* Cambridge, Mass.: Belknap, 1971. In Claire M. Renzetti and Daniel J. Curran, *Women, Men, and Society,* 4th ed. Boston: Allyn and Bacon, 1999.

Flink, James J., *The Automobile Age.* Cambridge, Mass.: MIT Press, 1990.

Flippen, Annette R. "Understanding Groupthink from a Self-Regulatory Perspective." *Small Group Research, 30,* 2, April 1999:139–165.

"Focus on Health Reform: Summary of New Health Reform Law." Menlo Park, Calif.: Henry J. Kaiser Family Foundation, April 8, 2010.

Foley, Douglas E. "The Great American Football Ritual." In *Society: Readings to Accompany Sociology: A Down-to-Earth Approach, Core Concepts,* James M. Henslin, ed. Boston: Allyn and Bacon, 2006:64–76. Originally published 1990.

Food and Agriculture Organization of the United Nations. "World and Regional Review: Facts and Figures." Rome: Food and Agriculture Organization of the United Nations, 2006.

Food and Agriculture Organization of the United Nations. "FAO Statistical Yearbook: World Food and Agriculture," Rome: Food and Agriculture Organization of the United Nations, January 2013.

Foote, Jennifer. "Trying to Take Back the Planet." *Newsweek, 115,* 6, February 5, 1990:24–25.

Fordham, Brigham A. "Disability and Designer Babies." *Valparaiso University Law Review, 45,* 4, 2011:1473–1528.

Form, William. "Comparative Industrial Sociology and the Convergence Hypothesis." *Annual Review of Sociology, 5,* 1, 1979.

Forsyth, Jim. "Proabortion Group Asks Judge to Block Texas Sonogram Law." *Reuters,* July 6, 2011.

Fountain, Henry. "Archaeological Site in Peru Is Called Oldest City in Americas." *New York Times,* April 27, 2001.

Fowler, Geoffrey A., and Amy Chozick. "Cartoon Characters Get Big Makeover for Overseas Fans." *Wall Street Journal,* October 16, 2007.

Fox, Elaine, and George E. Arquitt. "The VFW and the 'Iron Law of Oligarchy.'" In *Down to Earth Sociology,* 4th ed., James M. Henslin, ed. New York: Free Press, 1985:147–155.

Frank, Reanne. "What to Make of It? The (Re)emergence of a Biological Conceptualization of Race in Health Disparities Research." *Social Science & Medicine, 64,* 2007:1977–1983.

Franklin, John Hope, and John Whittington Franklin. *My Life and an Era: The Autobiography of Buck Colbert Franklin.* Baton Rouge: Louisiana State University, 1997.

Franzosi, Roberto, Gianluca De Fazio, and Stefania Vicari. "Ways of Measuring Agency: An Application of Quantitative Analysis to Lynchings in Georgia (1875–1930). *Sociological Methodology, 42,* 1, 2012:1–42.

Fraser, Graham. "Fox Denies Free Trade Exploiting the Poor in Mexico." *Toronto Star,* April 20, 2001.

Frayer, Lauren. "Police: Baby Starved as Couple Nurtured Virtual Kid." *AOL News,* March 5, 2010.

Freedman, Jane. *Feminism.* Philadelphia: Open University Press, 2001.

Freeland, Chrystia. "The Rise of the New Global Elite." *Atlantic,* January/February 2011.

Freidson, Eliot. *Professionalism: The Third Logic.* Chicago: University of Chicago Press, 2001.

Fremson, Ruth. "Dead Bachelors in Remote China Still Find Wives." *New York Times,* October 5, 2006.

Freudenheim, Milt. "The Doctor Will See You Now. Please Log On." *New York Times,* May 29, 2010.

Friedl, Ernestine. "Society and Sex Roles." In *Conformity and Conflict: Readings in Cultural Anthropology,* James P. Spradley and David W. McCurdy, eds. Glenview, Ill.: Scott, Foresman, 1990:229–238.

Friedman, John N., and Richard T. Holden. "The Rising Incumbent Reelection Rate: What's Gerrymandering Got to Do with It?" *The Journal of Politics, 71,* 2, April 2009:93–611.

Frommer, Arthur. *Peru.* New York: Wiley, 2007.

Frosch, Dan. "Its Native Tongue Facing Extinction, Arapaho Tribe Teaches the Young." *New York Times,* October 17, 2008.

Frumkin, Robert M. "Early English and American Sex Customs." In *Encyclopedia of Sexual Behavior,* Vol. 1. New York: Hawthorne Books, 1967.

Funk, Cary, and Greg Smith. *'Nones' on the Rise: One-in-Five Adults Have No Religious Affiliation.* Washington, D.C.: PEW Research Center, October 9, 2012.

Furstenberg, Frank F., Jr., Sheela Kennedy, Vonnie C. McLoyd, Ruben G. Rumbaut, and Richard A. Settersten, Jr. "Growing Up Is Harder to Do." *Contexts, 3,* 3, Summer 2004:33–41.

Gabriel, Trip. "Doctor Avoids Death Penalty in Murders at His Clinic." *New York Times,* May 14, 2013.

Gabriel, Trip. "Under Pressure, Teachers Tamper with Test Scores." *New York Times,* June 10, 2010.

Gaither, Milton. "Homeschooling in the USA: Past, Present, and Future." *Theory and Research in Education, 7,* 2009:331–346.

Galbraith, John Kenneth. *The Nature of Mass Poverty.* Cambridge Mass.: Harvard University Press, 1979.

Gallagher, Ryan. "The Threat of Silence." *Future Tense,* February 4, 2013.

Galliher, John F. *Deviant Behavior and Human Rights.* Englewood Cliffs, N.J.: Prentice Hall, 1991.

Gallmeier, Charles P. "Methodological Issues in Qualitative Sport Research: Participant Observation among Hockey Players." *Sociological Spectrum, 8,* 1988:213–235.

Gallup Poll. "America's Preference for Smaller Families Edge Higher." Princeton, N. J. Gallup Organization, June 30, 2011a.

Gallup Poll. "Americans More Likely to Believe in God Than the Devil, Heaven More Than Hell." June 13, 2007.

Gallup Poll. "Americans See Religion Loosing Influence." Princeton, NJ: Gallup Organization, January 26, 2011.

Gallup Poll. "Election Polls—Vote by Groups, 2008." Princeton, N.J.: Gallup Organization, 2008.

Gallup Poll. "Prefer Boys to Girls Just as They Did in 1941." Princeton, N.J.: The Gallup Organization, June 23, 2011b.

Gallup Poll. "Very Religious Americans Lead Healthier Lives." Princeton, N.J.: Gallup Organization, December 23, 2010.

Gallup, George, Jr. *The Gallup Poll: Public Opinion 1989.* Wilmington, Dela.: Scholarly Resources, 1990.

Gampbell, Jennifer. "In Northeast Thailand, a Cuisine Based on Bugs." *New York Times,* June 22, 2006.

Gans, Herbert J. *People and Plans: Essays on Urban Problems and Solutions.* New York: Basic Books, 1968.

Gans, Herbert J. *People, Plans, and Policies: Essays on Poverty, Racism, and Other National Urban Problems.* New York: Columbia University Press, 1991.

Gans, Herbert J. *The Urban Villagers.* New York: Free Press, 1962.

Gardiner, Sean, and Alison Fox. "Glance May Have Led to Murder." *New York Times,* December 6, 2010.

Garfinkel, Harold. "Conditions of Successful Degradation Ceremonies." *American Journal of Sociology, 61,* 2, March 1956:420–424.

Garfinkel, Harold. *Ethnomethodology's Program: Working Out Durkheim's Aphorism.* Lanham, Md.: Rowman & Littlefield, 2002.

Garfinkel, Harold. *Studies in Ethnomethodology.* Englewood Cliffs, N.J.: Prentice Hall, 1967.

Garfinkel, Irwin, Lee Rainwater, and Timothy Smeeding. *Wealth and Welfare States: Is America a Laggard or a Leader?* New York: Oxford University Press, 2010.

Gartrell, Nanette, Henny Bos, Heidi Peyser, Amalia Deck, and Carla Rodas. "Family Characteristics, Custody Arrangements, and Adolescent Psychological Well-being after Lesbian Mothers Break Up." *Family Relations, 60,* December 2011:572–585.

Gates, Eddie Faye. "The Oklahoma Commission to Study the Tulsa Race Riot of 1921." *Harvard Black Letter Law Journal, 20,* 2004:83–89.

Gatewood, Willard B. *Aristocrats of Color: The Black Elite, 1880–1920.* Bloomington, Ind.: Indiana University Press, 1990.

Gauch, Sarah. "In Egyptian Schools, a Push for Critical Thinking." *Christian Science Monitor,* February 9, 2006.

Gautham, S. "Coming Next: The Monsoon Divorce." *New Statesman, 131,* 4574, February 18, 2002:32–33.

Geis, Gilbert, Robert F. Meier, and Lawrence M. Salinger. *White-Collar Crime: Classic and Contemporary Views,* 3rd ed. New York: Free Press, 1995.

Gelderen, Loes, Henny M. W. Bos, Nanette Gartrell, Jo Hermanns, and Ellen C. Perrin. "Quality of Life of Adolescents Raised from Birth by Lesbian Mothers: The U.S. National Longitudinal Family Study." *Journal of Developmental and Behavioral Pediatrics, 33,* 1, January 2012.

Genetski, Robert. "Privatize Social Security." *Wall Street Journal,* May 21, 1993.

Gerhard, Jane. "Revisiting 'The Myth of the Vaginal Orgasm': The Female Orgasm in American Sexual Thought and Second Wave Feminism." *Feminist Studies, 26,* 2, Fall 2000:449–477.

Gerken, James. "Arctic Ice Melt, Sea Level Rise May Pose Imminent Threat to Island Nations, Climate Scientist Says." *Huffington Post,* October 5, 2012.

Geronimus, Arline T., Margaret T. Hicken, Jay A. Pearson, Sarah J. Seashols, Kelly L. Brown, and Tracy Dawson Cruz. "Do US Black Women Experience Stress-Related Accelerated Biological Aging?" *Human Nature, 21,* 2010:19–38.

Gerth, H. H., and C. Wright Mills. *From Max Weber: Essays in Sociology.* New York: Galaxy, 1958.

Gettleman, Jeffrey. "Starvation and Strife Menace Torn Kenya." *New York Times,* February 28, 2009.

Gettleman, Jeffrey, and Josh Kron, "U.N. Report on Congo Massacres Draws Anger." *New York Times,* October 1, 2010.

Gibbs, Nancy. "Affirmative Action for Boys." *Time,* April 3, 2008.

Gibson-Davis, Christina. "Mothers but Not Wives: The Increasing Lag between Nonmarital Births and Marriage." *Journal of Marriage and Family, 73,* 1, February 2011:264–278.

Gilbert, Dennis L. *The American Class Structure in an Age of Growing Inequality,* 6th ed. Belmont, Calif.: Wadsworth Publishing, 2003.

Gilbert, Dennis L. *The American Class Structure in an Age of Growing Inequality,* 8th ed. New York: Sage, 2011.

Gillum, R. F. "Frequency of Attendance at Religious Services and Smoking: The Third National Health and Nutrition Examination Survey." *Preventive Medicine, 41,* 2005:607–613.

Gilman, Charlotte Perkins. *The Man-Made World or, Our Androcentric Culture.* New York: 1971. Originally published 1911.

Girshick, Lori B. *Woman-to-Woman Sexual Violence: Does She Call It Rape?* Boston: Northeastern University Press, 2002.

Gitlin, Todd. *The Twilight of Common Dreams: Why America Is Wracked by Culture Wars.* New York: Metropolitan Books, 1997.

Gjelten, Tom. "First Strike: US Cyber Warriors Seize the Offensive." *World Affairs Journal,* January/February 2013.

Glanton, Dahleen. "Hispanic Influx Causes Tensions with Blacks." *Daily Press* (Virginia), May 23, 2013.

Glaze, Lauren E., and Laura M. Maruschak. "Parents in Prison and Their Minor Children." Bureau of Justice Statistics Special Report, August 2008:1–25.

"Global 2000: The World's Biggest Public Companies." *Forbes,* April 17, 2013.

Gloeckner, Gene W., and Paul Jones. "Reflections on a Decade of Changes in Homeschooling and the Homeschooled into Higher Education." *Peabody Journal of Education, 88,* 3, 2–13:309–323.

Goetting, Ann. *Getting Out: Life Stories of Women Who Left Abusive Men.* New York: Columbia University Press, 2001.

Goffman, Erving. *Asylums: Essays on the Social Situation of Mental Patients and Other Inmates.* Chicago: Aldine, 1961.

Goffman, Erving. *Stigma: Notes on the Management of Spoiled Identity.* Englewood Cliffs, N.J.: Prentice Hall, 1963.

Goffman, Erving. *The Presentation of Self in Everyday Life.* New York: Peter Smith, 1999. Originally published 1959.

Gold, Ray. "Janitors versus Tenants: A Status-Income Dilemma." *American Journal of Sociology, 58,* 1952:486–493.

Goldberg, Abbie E., Deborah A. Kashy, and JuliAnna Z. Smith. "Gender-Typed Play Behavior in Early Childhood: Adopted Children with Lesbian, Gay, and Heterosexual Parents." *Sex Roles, 67,* 2012:503–515.

Goldberg, Susan, and Michael Lewis. "Play Behavior in the Year-Old Infant: Early Sex Differences." *Child Development, 40,* March 1969:21–31.

Goldstein, Jacob. "A Simple Surgical Checklist Saves Lives." *Wall Street Journal,* January 15, 2009.

Goldstein, Jacob. "In Plain Sight, A Woman Dies Unassisted on Hospital Floor." *Wall Street Journal,* July 1, 2008.

Goleman, Daniel. "Pollsters Enlist Psychologists in Quest for Unbiased Results." *New York Times,* September 7, 1993:C1, C11.

Goll, Sven. "Archaeologists Fin 'Mini-Pompeii.' "*View and News from Norway,* October 1, 2010.

Gorman, James. "High-Tech Daydreamers Investing in Immortality." *Wall Street Journal,* November 1, 2003.

Gorman, Peter. "A People at Risk: Vanishing Tribes of South America." *The World & I,* December 1991:678–689.

Gottfredson, Michael R., and Travis Hirschi. *A General Theory of Crime.* Stanford, Calif.: Stanford University Press, 1990.

Gottschalk, Peter, Sara McLanahan, and Gary Sandefur, "The Dynamics and Intergenerational Transmission of Poverty and Welfare Participation." In *Confronting Poverty: Prescriptions for Change,* Sheldon H. Danziger, Gary D. Sandefur, and Daniel H. Weinberg, eds. Cambridge, Mass.: Harvard University Press, 1994.

Grabe, Shelly, L. Monique Ward, and Janet Shibley Hyde. "The Role of the Media in Body Image Concerns among Women: A Meta-Analysis of Experimental and Correlational Studies." *Psychological Bulletin, 134,* 3:2008:460–476.

Grammich, Clifford, Kirk Hadaway, Richard Houseal, et al. *U.S. Religion Census: Religious Congregations and Membership Study, 2010.* Lenexa, Kansas: Association of Statisticians of American Religious Bodies, 2012.

Gray Panthers. "Age and Youth in Action." No date.

Greeley, Andrew M. "The Protestant Ethic: Time for a Moratorium." *Sociological Analysis, 25,* Spring 1964:20–33.

Greenhalgh, Susan. "The Chinese Biopolitical: Facing the Twenty-First Century." *New Genetics and Society, 28,* 3, September 2009:205–222.

Greenwald, Anthony G., and Linda Hamilton Krieger. "Implicit Bias: Scientific Foundations." *California Law Review,* July 2006.

Grigoriadis, Vanessa. "The Rise and Fall of the Eco-Radical Underground." *Rolling Stone,* June 21, 2011.

Grimmett, Richard E., and Paul K. Kerr. "Conventional Arms Transfers to Developing Nations 2004–2011." Washington, D.C.: Congressional Research Service, August 24, 2012.

Gross, Jan T. *Neighbors.* New Haven: Yale University Press, 2001.

Gross, Jane. "In the Quest for the Perfect Look, More Girls Choose the Scalpel." *New York Times,* November 29, 1998.

Guensburg, Carol. "Bully Factories." *American Journalism Review, 23,* 6, 2001:51–59.

"Guilds." *Columbia Encyclopedia,* 6th ed. New York: Columbia University Press, 2008.

Gunther, Marc. "The Mosquito in the Tent." *Fortune, 149,* 11, May 31, 2004:158.

Guo, Guang, Yuying Tong, and Tianji Cai. "Gene by Social Context Interactions for Number of Sexual Partners among White Male Youths: Genetics-Informed Sociology." *American Journal of Sociology, 114,* Supplement, 2008:S36–S66.

Gupta, Giri Raj. "Love, Arranged Marriage, and the Indian Social Structure." In *Cross-Cultural Perspectives of Mate Selection and Marriage,* George Kurian, ed. Westport, Conn.: Greenwood Press, 1979.

Guru, Gopal, and Shiraz Sidhva. "India's 'Hidden Apartheid.'" *UNESCO Courier,* September 2001:27.

Guthrie, Doug. "The Great Helmsman's Cultural Death." *Contexts, 7,* 3, Summer 2008:26–31.

Guthrie, Doug, and David Slocum. "Inefficient Deregulation and the Global Economic Crisis: The United States and China Compared." *Research in the Sociology of Organizations,* 2010:283–312.

Haas, Jack, and William Shaffir. "The Cloak of Competence." In *Down-to-Earth Sociology: Introductory Readings,* 7th ed. New York: Free Press, 1993:432–441.

Hacker, Helen Mayer. "Women as a Minority Group." *Social Forces, 30,* October 1951:60–69.

Haenfler, Ross, Brett Johnson, and Ellis Jones. "Lifestyle Movements: Exploring the Intersection of Lifestyle and Social Movements." *Social Movement Studies,* iFirst, 2012:1–20.

Hafner, Katie. "In Ill Doctor, a Surprise Reflection of Who Picks Assisted Suicide." *New York Times,* August 11, 2012.

Hafner, Katie. "Welding Kitchen Knives and Honing Office Skills." *New York Times,* January 13, 2007.

Hagerty, James R. "As America Ages, Shortage of Help Hits Nursing Homes." *Wall Street Journal,* April 15, 2013.

Hakim, Catherine. "Erotic Capital." *European Sociological Review,* 2010:499–518.

Hall, Edward T. *The Silent Language.* New York: Doubleday, 1959.

Hall, Edward T., and Mildred R. Hall. "The Sounds of Silence." In *Down to Earth Sociology: Introductory Readings,* 15th ed., James M. Henslin, ed. New York: Free Press, 2014.

Hall, G. Stanley. *Adolescence: Its Psychology and Its Relations to Physiology, Anthropology, Sociology, Sex, Crime, Religion, and Education.* New York: Appleton, 1904.

Hall, J. Camille. "The Impact of Kin and Fictive Kin Relationships on the Mental Health of Black Adult Children of Alcoholics." *Health and Social Work, 33,* 4, November 2008:259–266.

Hall, Richard H. "The Concept of Bureaucracy: An Empirical Assessment." *American Journal of Sociology, 69,* July 1963:32–40.

Hall, Ronald E. "The Tiger Woods Phenomenon: A Note on Biracial Identity." *The Social Science Journal, 38,* 2, April 2001:333–337.

Hallin, Daniel C. *The Uncensored War: The Media and Vietnam.* New York: Oxford University Press, 1986.

Halpern, Jack. "Iceland's Big Thaw." *New York Times,* May 13, 2011.

Hamermesh, Daniel. *Beauty Pays: Why Attractive People Are More Successful.* Princeton, N.J. Princeton University Press, 2011.

Hamid, Shadi. "Between Orientalism and Postmodernism: The Changing Nature of Western Feminist Thought towards the Middle East." *HAWWA, 4,* 1, 2006:76–92.

Hamlin, J. Kiley, and Karen Wynn. "Young Infants Prefer Prosocial to Antisocial Others." *Cognitive Development, 26,* 1, 2011:30–39.

Handel, Stephen J. "Recurring Trends and Persistent Themes: A Brief History of Transfer." New York: College Board Advocacy and Policy Center, March 2013.

Handwerk, Brian. "Maya City in 3-D." *National Geographic Daily News,* May 20, 2010.

Hansen, Casper Worm, Peter S. Jensen, and Christian Skovsgaard. "Modern Gender Roles and Agricultural History: The Neolithic Inheritance." *Social Science Research Network,* November 4, 2012.

Hanson, Chad. *The Community College and the Good Society.* New Brunswick, N.J.: Transaction Publishers, 2010.

Hardy, Dorcas. *Social Insecurity: The Crisis in America's Social Security and How to Plan Now for Your Own Financial Survival.* New York: Villard Books, 1991.

Harford, Tim. "Why Divorce Is Good for Women." *The Undercover Economist, Slate,* January 16, 2008.

Harlow, Harry F., and Margaret K. Harlow. "Social Deprivation in Monkeys." *Scientific American, 207,* 1962:137–147.

Harlow, Harry F., and Margaret K. Harlow. "The Affectional Systems." In *Behavior of Nonhuman Primates: Modern Research Trends,* Vol. 2, Allan M. Schrier, Harry F. Harlow, and Fred Stollnitz, eds. New York: Academic Press, 1965:287–334.

Harney, Alexandra. "The Plight of China's Favored Sons." *New York Times,* December 19, 2011.

Harper, Charles L., and Kevin T. Leicht. *Exploring Social Change: America and the World.* Upper Saddle River, N.J.: Prentice Hall, 2002.

Harrington, Charlene, Helen Carrillo, Megan Dowdell, et al. *Nursing Facilities, Staffing, Residents and Facility Deficiencies, 2005 Through 2010.* San Francisco, Calif.: University of California, October 2011.

Harrington, Michael. *The Vast Majority: A Journey to the World's Poor.* New York: Simon & Schuster, 1977.

Harris, Anthony R., Gene A. Fisher, and Stephen H. Thomas. "Homicide as a Medical Outcome: Racial Disparity in Deaths from Assault in US Level I and II Trauma Centers." *Journal of Trauma: Injury, Infection, and Critical Care, 20,* 20, 2011:1–10.

Harris, Chauncey D. "The Nature of Cities and Urban Geography in the Last Half Century." *Urban Geography, 18,* 1997.

Harris, Chauncey D., and Edward Ullman. "The Nature of Cities." *Annals of the American Academy of Political and Social Science, 242,* 1945:7–17.

Harris, Craig. "Fallout from Ariz. Employer Sanctions Law." *Arizona Republic,* September 15, 2008.

Harris, Gardiner. "Caustic Government Report Deals Blow to Diabetes Drug." *New York Times,* July 9, 2010.

Harris, Gardiner. "Drug Makers Told Studies Would Aid It, Papers Say." *New York Times,* March 19, 2009.

Harris, Gardiner. "F.D.A. Says Bayer Failed to Reveal Drug Risk Study." *New York Times,* September 30, 2006.

Harris, Gardiner. "In India, Kisses Are on Rise, Even in Public." *New York Times,* February 13, 2013.

Harris, Jerry. "Global Monopolies and the Transnational Capitalist Class." *International Critical Thought, 2,* 1, March 2012a:1–6.

Harris, Jerry. "Outward Bound: Transnational Capitalism in China." *Race and Class, 54,* 1, 2012b:13–32.

Harris, Marvin. "Why Men Dominate Women." *New York Times Magazine,* November 13, 1977:46, 115, 117–123.

Harrison, Paul. *Inside the Third World: The Anatomy of Poverty,* 3rd ed. London: Penguin Books, 1993.

Hart, Charles W. M., and Arnold R. Pilling. *The Tiwi of North Australia,* Fieldwork Edition. New York: Holt, Rinehart and Winston, 1979.

Hart, Hornell. "Acceleration in Social Change." In *Technology and Social Change,* Francis R. Allen, Hornell Hart, Delbert C. Miller, William F. Ogburn, and Meyer F. Nimkoff, eds. New York: Appleton, 1957:27–55.

Hart, Paul. "Groupthink, Risk-Taking and Recklessness: Quality of Process and Outcome in Policy Decision Making." *Politics and the Individual, 1,* 1, 1991:67–90.

Hartley, Eugene. *Problems in Prejudice.* New York: King's Crown Press, 1946.

Hartocollis, Anemona. "Diet Plan with Hormone Has Fans and Skeptics." *New York Times,* March 7, 2011.

"Harvard Medical School: Osher Research Center." http://www.osher.hms.harvard.edu/history.asp. 2011.

Hatch, Laurie Russell. *Beyond Gender Differences: Adaptation to Aging in Life Course Perspective.* Amityville, N.Y.: Baywood Publishing Company, 2000.

Hatfield, Elaine, Lisamarie Bensman, and Richard L. Rapson "A Brief History of Social Scientists' Attempts to Measure Passionate Love." *Journal of Social and Personal Relationships, 29,* 2, 2012:143–164.

Haub, Carl, and Mary Mederlos Kent. "World Population Data Sheet." Washington, D.C.: Population Reference Bureau, 2008.

Haub, Carl, and Nancy Yinger. "The U.N. Long-Range Population Projections: What They Tell Us." Washington, D.C.: Population Reference Bureau, 1994.

Haub, Carl, and Toshiko Kaneda. "World Population Data Sheet 2012." Washington, D.C.: Population Reference Bureau, 2012.

Haughney, Christine. "Harlem's Real Estate Boom Becomes a Bust." *New York Times,* July 8, 2009.

Haughney, Christine, and Eric Konigsberg. "Despite Tough Times, Ultrarich Keep Spending." *New York Times,* April 14, 2008.

Hauser, Philip, and Leo Schnore, eds. *The Study of Urbanization.* New York: Wiley, 1965.

Hausman, Daniel M. "Health, Naturalism, and Functional Efficiency." *Philosophy of Science, 79,* 4, October 2012:519-541.

Havrilla, Karina. "A Sociological Influence in Dora the Explorer." *ASA Footnotes, 38,* 2, February 2010.

Hawkes, Nigel. "Asbestos-Related Diseases Will Rise for 20 Years." *The Times,* September 25, 2001.

Hawkins, Harry. "Care Home Inviting in Prostitutes for Residents Is Under Investigation." *Sun* (U.K.), January 28, 2013.

Hawley, Amos H. *Urban Society: An Ecological Approach.* New York: Wiley, 1981.

Hayashi, Gina M., and Bonnie R. Strickland. "Long-Term Effects of Parental Divorce on Love Relationships: Divorce as Attachment Disruption." *Journal of Social and Personal Relationships, 15,* 1, February 1998:23–38.

Helliker, Kevin. "Body and Spirit: Why Attending Religious Services May Benefit Health." *Wall Street Journal,* May 3, 2005.

Hellinger, Daniel, and Dennis R. Judd. *The Democratic Facade.* Pacific Grove, Calif.: Brooks/Cole, 1991.

Hemmings, Annette. "The 'Hidden' Corridor Curriculum." *High School Journal, 83,* December 1999:1–12.

Hendin, Herbert. "Euthanasia and Physician-Assisted Suicide in the Netherlands." *New England Journal of Medicine, 336,* 19, May 8, 1997:1385–1387.

Hendin, Herbert. "Suicide, Assisted Suicide, and Medical Illness." *Harvard Mental Health Letter, 16,* 7, January 2000:4–7.

Hendrix, Lewellyn. "What Is Sexual Inequality? On the Definition and Range of Variation." *Gender and Society, 28,* 3, August 1994:287–307.

Henley, Nancy, Mykol Hamilton, and Barrie Thorne. "Womanspeak and Manspeak." In *Beyond Sex Roles,* Alice G. Sargent, ed. St Paul, MN: West, 1985.

Henslin, James M. *Social Problems: A Down-to-Earth Approach,* 11th ed. Boston: Pearson, 2014.

Henslin, James M., and Mae A. Biggs. "Behavior in Pubic Places: The Sociology of the Vaginal Examination." In *Down to Earth Sociology: Introductory Readings,* 15th ed., James M. Henslin, ed. New York: Free Press, 2014. Originally published 1971.

Herba, Catherine M., Richard E. Tremblay, et al. "Maternal Depressive Symptoms and Children's Emotional Problems: Can Early Child Care Help Children of Depressed Mothers?" JAMA Psychiatry, 70, 8, 2013:830–838.

Herring, Cedric. "Is Job Discrimination Dead?" *Contexts,* Summer 2002: 13–18.

Herz, Rachel. "You Eat That?" *Wall Street Journal,* January 28, 2012.

Hetherington, Mavis, and John Kelly. *For Better or for Worse: Divorce Reconsidered.* New York: W. W. Norton, 2003.

Hewitt Associates. *Worklife Benefits Provided by Major U.S. Employers, 2003–2004.* Lincolnshire, Ill.: Hewitt Associates, 2004.

Higginbotham, Elizabeth, and Lynn Weber. "Moving with Kin and Community: Upward Social Mobility for Black and White Women." *Gender and Society, 6,* 3, September 1992:416–440.

Hill, Mark E. "Skin Color and the Perception of Attractiveness among African Americans: Does Gender Make a Difference?" *Social Psychology Quarterly, 65,* 1, 2002:77–91.

Hilson, Gavin. "Family Hardship and Cultural Values: Child Labor in Malian Small-Scale Gold Mining Communities." *World Development, 40,* 8, 2012:1663–1674.

Himes, Christine L. "Elderly Americans." *Population Bulletin, 56,* 1, December 2001:1–40.

Hippler, Fritz. Interview in a television documentary with Bill Moyers in *Propaganda,* in the series "Walk through the 20th Century," 1987.

Hirschi, Travis. *Causes of Delinquency.* Berkeley: University of California Press, 1969.

"Historical Statistics of the United States: From Colonial Times to the Present." New York: Basic Books, 1976.

Hnatkovska, Viktoria, Amartya Lahiri, and Sourabh Paul. "Castes and Labor Mobility." *American Economic Journal: Applied Economics, 4,* 2 2012:274–307.

Hochschild, Arlie. "Feelings around the World." *Contexts, 7,* 2, Spring 2008:80.

Hoffman, Bert. "The International Dimensions of Authoritarian Legitimation: The Impact of Regime Evolution." Leibnitz: German Institute of Global and Area Studies. Working Paper No. 182, December 2011.

Holder, Kelly. "Voting and Registration in the Election of November 2004." *Current Population Reports,* March 2006.

Holland, Jesse J. "Prison Rape: Department of Justice Orders Increase in Anti-Rape Efforts." Associated Press, May 12, 2012.

Holler, J. G., S. B. Chrstensen, H. C. Slotved, et al. "Novel Inhibitory Activity of the Staphylococcus Aureus NorA Efflux Pump by a Kaempferol Rhamnoside Isolated from Persea Lingue Nees." *Journal of Antimicrobial Chemotherapy, 67,* 5, 2012:1138–1144.

Holtzman, Abraham. *The Townsend Movement: A Political Study.* New York: Bookman, 1963.

Homblin, Dora Jane. *The First Cities.* Boston: Little, Brown, Time-Life Books, 1973.

Honeycutt, Karen. "Disgusting, Pathetic, Bizarrely Beautiful: Representations of Weight in Popular Culture." Paper presented at the 1995 meetings of the American Sociological Association.

Hong, Lawrence. "Marriage in China." In *Til Death Do Us Part: A Multicultural Anthology on Marriage,* Sandra Lee Browning and R. Robin Miller, eds. Stamford, Conn.: JAI Press, 1999.

Hooks, bell. *Where We Stand: Class Matters.* New York: Routledge, 2000.

Hookway, James. "In Thailand Today, Teen Monks Express the Spirit to a Rock Beat." *Wall Street Journal,* August 15, 2012.

Horn, James P. *Land As God Made It: Jamestown and the Birth of America.* New York: Basic Books, 2006.

Horowitz, Ruth. *Honor and the American Dream: Culture and Identity in a Chicano Community.* New Brunswick, N.J.: Rutgers University Press, 1983.

Horowitz, Ruth. "Studying Violence among the 'Lions.'" In *Social Problems,* James M. Henslin, ed. Upper Saddle River, N.J.: Prentice Hall, 2005:135.

Horwitz, Allan V., and Jerome C. Wakefield. *The Loss of Sadness: How Psychiatry Transformed Normal Sorrow into Depressive Disorder.* New York: Oxford University Press, 2007.

Hostetler, John A. *Amish Society,* 3rd ed. Baltimore: Johns Hopkins University Press, 1980.

Hostetler, John A. *The Amish,* rev. ed. Harrisonburg, Va.: Herald Press, 2013.

Hout, Michael. "How Class Works: Objective and Subjective Aspects of Class Since the 1970s." In *Social Class: How Does It Work?* Annette Lareau and Dalton Conley, eds. New York: Russell Sage, 2008:52–64.

Houtman, Dick. "What Exactly Is a 'Social Class'?: On the Economic Liberalism and Cultural Conservatism of the 'Working Class.'" Paper presented at the annual meetings of the American Sociological Association, 1995.

Howells, Lloyd T., and Selwyn W. Becker. "Seating Arrangement and Leadership Emergence." *Journal of Abnormal and Social Psychology, 64,* February 1962:148–150.

Hoyt, Homer. "Recent Distortions of the Classical Models of Urban Structure." In *Internal Structure of the City: Readings on Space and Environment,* Larry S. Bourne, ed. New York: Oxford University Press, 1971:84–96.

Hoyt, Homer. *The Structure and Growth of Residential Neighborhoods in American Cities.* Washington, D.C.: Federal Housing Administration, 1939.

Hsu, Francis L. K. *The Challenge of the American Dream: The Chinese in the United States.* Belmont, Calif.: Wadsworth, 1971.

Huang, Penelope M., Pamela J. Smock, Wendy D. Manning, and Cara A. Bergstrom-Lynch. "He Says, She Says: Gender and Cohabitation." *Journal of Family Issues, 32,* February 2011.

Huber, Joan. "Micro-Macro Links in Gender Stratification." *American Sociological Review, 55,* February 1990:1–10.

HUD (U.S. Department of Housing and Urban Development). "The 2009 Annual Homeless Assessment Report to Congress." June 2010.

Huggins, Martha K., and Sandra Rodrigues. "Kids Working on Paulista Avenue." *Childhood, 11,* 2004:495–514.

Huggins, Martha K., Mika Haritos-Fatouros, and Philip G. Zimbardo. *Violence Workers: Police Torturers and Murderers Reconstruct Brazilian Atrocities.* Berkeley: University of California Press, 2002.

Hughes, Everett C. "Good People and Dirty Work." In *Life in Society: Readings to Accompany Sociology: A Down-to-Earth Approach,* 7th ed. James M. Henslin, ed. Boston: Allyn and Bacon, 2005:125–134. Article originally published 1962.

Hughes, H. Stuart. *Oswald Spengler: A Critical Estimate,* rev. ed. New York: Scribner's, 1962.

Hughes, John. "Bush Had Good Reason to Believe There Were WMDs in Iraq." *Christian Science Monitor,* April 12, 2006.

Hughes, Kathleen A. "Even Tiki Torches Don't Guarantee a Perfect Wedding." *Wall Street Journal,* February 20, 1990:A1, A16.

Hummer, Robert A., Richard G. Rogers, Charles B. Nam, and Chrsitopher G. Ellison. "Religious Involvement and U. S. Adult Mortality." *Demography 36,* 1999:273:285.

Humphreys, Laud. *Tearoom Trade: Impersonal Sex in Public Places,* enlarged ed. Chicago: Aldine, 1975. Originally published 1970.

Hummer, Robert A., Christopher G. Ellison, Richard G. Rogers, Benjamin E. Moulton, and Ron R. Romero. "Religious Involvement and Adult Mortality in the United States: Review and Perspective." *Southern Medical Journal, 97,* 2004:1223–1230.

Hundley, Greg. "Why Women Earn Less Than Men in Self-Employment." *Journal of Labor Research, 22,* 4, Fall 2001:817–827.

Hunt, Darnell. "American Toxicity: Twenty Years After the 1992 Los Angeles 'Riots.'" *Amerasia Journal, 38,* 1, 2012:ix–xviii.

Hurdley, Rachel. "In the Picture or Off the Wall? Ethical Regulation, Research Habitus, and Unpeopled Ethnography." *Qualitative Inquiry,* 16, 2010:517–528.

Hurtado, Aída, David E. Hayes-Bautista, R. Burciaga Valdez, and Anthony C. R. Hernández. *Redefining California: Latino Social Engagement in a Multicultural Society.* Los Angeles: UCLA Chicano Studies Research Center, 1992.

Huttenbach, Henry R. "The Roman *Porajmos:* The Nazi Genocide of Europe's Gypsies." *Nationalities Papers, 19,* 3, Winter 1991:373–394.

Hylton, Hillary. "Turning up the Heat on Polygamists." *Time,* July 24, 2008.

Hymowitz, Carol. "Raising Women to Be Leaders." *Wall Street Journal,* February 12, 2007.

Hymowitz, Carol. "Through the Glass Ceiling." *Wall Street Journal,* November 8, 2004.

Hyra, Derek S. "Racial Uplift? Intra-Racial Class Conflict and the Economic Revitalization of Harlem and Bronzeville." *City and Community, 5,* 1, March 2006:71–92.

Hyse, Karin, and Lars Tornstam. "Recognizing Aspects of Oneself in the Theory of Gerotranscendence." Uppsala, Sweden: The Social Gerontology Group, 2009.

IES (Institute of Education Sciences). *Digest of Education Statistics.* Washington, D.C.: U.S. Department of Education, 2010.

Innes, Judith E., David E. Booher, and Sarah Di Vittorio. "Strategies for Megaregion Governance—Collaborative Dialogue, Networks, and Self-Organization." *Journal of the American Planning Association. 77,* 1, 2011:55–67.

Inter-Parliamentary Union. "Women in National Parliaments." Geneva, Switzerland: Inter-Parliamentary Union, February 1, 2013.

Interlandi, Jeneen. "Not Just Urban Legend." *Newsweek,* January 10, 2009.

Iori, Ron. "The Good, the Bad and the Useless." *Wall Street Journal,* June 10, 1988:18R.

Isaac, Carol A., Anna Kaatz, and Molly Carnes. "Deconstructing the Glass Ceiling." *Sociology Mind, 2,* 1, 2012:80–86.

"It's So Much Nicer on K Street." *New York Times,* June 8, 2008.

Itard, Jean Marc Gospard. *The Wild Boy of Aveyron,* George and Muriel Humphrey, trans. New York: Appleton-Century-Crofts, 1962.

Jackson, Dimitra Lynette, Michael J. Stebleton, and Frankie Santos Laanan. "The Experience of Community College Faculty Involved in a Learning Community Program." *Community College Review, 41,* 2013:3–19.

Jackson, Elizabeth A., Mauro Moscucci, Dean E. Smith, et al. "The Association of Sex with Outcomes among Patients Undergoing Primary Percutaneous Coronary Intervention for ST Elevation Myocardial Infarction in the Contemporary Era." *American Heart Journal, 161,* 2011:106–112.

Jacobs, Andrew. "Chinese Workers Say Illness Is Real, Not Hysteria." *New York Times,* July 29, 2009.

Jacobs, Jerry A. "Detours on the Road to Equality: Women, Work and Higher Education." *Contexts,* Winter 2003:32–41.

Jacobs, Margaret A. "'New Girl' Network Is Boon for Women Lawyers." *Wall Street Journal,* March 4, 1997:B1, B7.

Jaggar, Alison M. "Sexual Difference and Sexual Equality." In *Theoretical Perspectives on Sexual Difference,* Deborah L. Rhode, ed. New Haven, Conn.: Yale University Press, 1990:239–254.

Jakab, Spencer. "An Offal Tale: For This Club, Everything Is on the Menu." *Wall Street Journal,* June 25, 2012.

Jamieson, Amie, Hyon B. Shin, and Jennifer Day. "Voting and Registration in the Election of November 2000." *Current Population Reports,* February 2002.

Janis, Irving L. *Victims of Groupthink.* Boston, Mass.: Houghton Mifflin, 1972.

Janis, Irving. L. *Groupthink: Psychological Studies of Policy Decisions and Fiascoes.* Boston: Houghton Mifflin, 1982.

Jankowiak, William R., and Edward F. Fischer. "A Cross-Cultural Perspective on Romantic Love." *Journal of Ethnology, 31,* 2, April 1992:149–155.

Jasper, James M. "Emotions and Social Movements: Twenty Years of Theory and Research." Unpublished paper, 2012.

Jasper, James M. "Moral Dimensions of Social Movements." Paper presented at the annual meetings of the American Sociological Association, 1991.

Jasper, James M. "Social Movements." *Blackwell Encyclopedia of Sociology,* January 2007:4443–4451.

Jenkins, Philip. "The Next Christianity." *Atlantic Monthly,* October 2002:53–68.

Jensen, Lene Arnett. "Through Two Lenses: A Cultural-Developmental Approach to Moral Psychology." *Developmental Review, 28,* 2009:289–315.

Jeong, Yu-Jin, and Hyun-Kyung You. "Different Historical Trajectories and Family Diversity among Chinese, Japanese, and Koreans in the United States." *Journal of Family History, 33,* 3, July 2008:346–356.

Jessop, Bob, "The Return of the National State in the Current Crisis of the World Market." *Capital and Class, 34,* 1, 2010:38–43.

Jewkes, Rachel. "Rape Perpetration: A Review." *Pretoria, South Africa: Sexual Violence Research Initiative,* July 2012:1–45.

Jneid, Hani, Gregg C. Fonarow, Christopher P. Cannon, et al. "Sex Differences in Medical Care and Early Death after Acute Myocardial Infarction." *Circulation,* December 8, 2008.

John-Henderson, Neha, Emily G. Jacobs, Rodolfo Mendoza-Denton, and Darlene D. Francis. "Wealth, Health, and the Moderating Role of Implicit Social Class Bias." *Annals of Behavioral Medicine, 45,* 2013:173–179.

Johnson, Benton. "On Church and Sect." *American Sociological Review, 28,* 1963:539–549.

Johnson, Norris R. "Panic at 'The Who Concert Stampede': An Empirical Assessment." In *Collective Behavior and Social Movements,* Russell L. Curtis, Jr., and Benigno E. Aguirre, eds. Boston: Allyn and Bacon, 1993:113–122.

Johnson, Wendy, Eric Turkheimer, Irving I. Gottesman, and Thomas J. Bouchard, Jr. "Beyond Heritability: Twin Studies in Behavioral Research." *Current Directions in Psychological Science, 18,* 4, 2009:217–220.

Johnson-Weiner, Karen. *Train Up a Child: Old Order Amish and Mennonite Schools.* Baltimore: Johns Hopkins University Press, 2007.

Johnston, Drue M., and Norris R. Johnson. "Role Extension in Disaster: Employee Behavior at the Beverly Hills Supper Club Fire." *Sociological Focus, 22,* 1, February 1989:39–51.

Johnston, Lloyd D., Patrick M. O'Malley, Jerald G. Bachman, and John E. Schulenberg. *Monitoring the Future, National Results on Adolescent Drug Use: 2012 Overview Key Findings on Adolescent Drug Use.* Ann Arbor, Mich.: Institute for Social Research, 2013.

Johnston, Lloyd D., Patrick M. O'Malley, Jerald G. Bachman, and John E. Schulenberg. *Monitoring the Future, National Survey Results on Drug Use, 1975–2011. Volume II: College Students and Adults Ages 19–50.* Ann Arbor, Mich.: Institute for Social Research, 2012.

Jones, Allen. "Let Nonviolent Prisoners Out." *Los Angeles Times,* June 12, 2008.

Jones, James H. *Bad Blood: The Tuskegee Syphilis Experiment,* 2nd ed. New York: Free Press, 1993.

Jones, Jeffrey Owen, and Peter Meyer. *The Pledge: A History of the Pledge of Allegiance.* New York: St. Martin's Press, 2010.

Jones, Nikki. *Between Good and Ghetto: African American Girls and Inner-City Violence.* New Brunswick, N.J. Rutgers University Press, 2010.

Jordan, Miriam. "Among Poor Villagers, Female Infanticide Still Flourishes in India." *Wall Street Journal,* May 9, 2000:A1, A12.

Jordan, Miriam. "Asians Top Immigration Class." *Wall Street Journal,* June 19, 2012.

Josephson, Matthew. "The Robber Barons." In *John D. Rockefeller: Robber Baron or Industrial Statesman?* Earl Latham, ed. Boston: Heath, 1949:34–48.

Joungtrakul, Jamnean, and Bobbie McGhie Allen. "Research Ethics: A Comparative Study of Qualitative Doctoral Dissertations Submitted to Universities in Thailand and the USA." *Science Journal of Business Management, 2012,* 2012:1–11.

Judge, Timothy A., and Daniel M. Cable. "The Effect of Physical Height on Workplace Success and Income: Preliminary Test of a Theoretical Model." *Journal of Applied Psychology, 89,* 3, 2004:428–441.

Judge, Timothy A., Charlice Hurst, and Lauren S. Simon. "Does It Pay to Be Smart, Attractive, or Confident (or All Three)? Relationships among General Mental Ability, Physical Attractiveness, Core Self-Evaluations, and Income." *Journal of Applied Psychology, 94,* 3, 2009:742–755.

Juergensmeyer, Mark. *Terror in the Mind of God: The Global Rise of Religious Violence.* Berkeley: University of California Press, 2000.

Kacen, Jacqueline J. "Advertising Effectiveness." New York: Wiley International Encyclopedia of Marketing, 2011.

Kaestle, C. E. "Selling and Buying Sex: A Longitudinal Study of Risk and Protective Factors in Adolescence." *Preventive Science, 13,* 2012:314–322.

Kagan, Jerome. "The Idea of Emotions in Human Development." In *Emotions, Cognition, and Behavior,* Carroll E. Izard, Jerome Kagan, and Robert B. Zajonc, eds. New York: Cambridge University Press, 1984:38–72.

Kageyama, Yuri. "Mazda Profit up on Sold Vehicle Sales Growth." Associated Press, July 31, 2008.

Kahlenberg, Susan G., and Michelle M. Hein, "Progression on Nickelodeon? Gender-Role Stereotypes in Toy Commercials." *Sex Roles, 62,* 2010:830–847.

Kahn, Joseph. "China's Elite Learn to Flaunt It While the New Landless Weep." *New York Times,* December 25, 2004.

Kahn, Joseph. "Thousands Reportedly Riot in China." *International Herald-Tribune,* March 13, 2007.

Kalb, Claudia. "Faith and Healing." *Newsweek,* November 10, 2003:44–56.

Kalberg, Stephen. "Introduction to *The Protestant Ethic.*" In *The Protestant Ethic and the Spirit of Capitalism,* rev. 1920 ed., Max Weber, Stephen Kalberg, trans. New York: Oxford University Press, 2011:8–63.

Kalinovsky, Artemy. "Soviet War in Afghanistan (1979–1992)." In *The Encyclopedia of War,* 1st ed., Gordon Martel, ed. London: Blackwell Publishing, 2012.

Kamber, Michael. "In Afghan Kilns, a Cycle of Debt and Servitude." *New York Times,* March 15, 2011.

Kanazawa, Satoshi, and Jody L. Kovar. "Why Beautiful People Are More Intelligent." *Intelligence, 32,* 2004:227–243.

Kane, Yukariitwatani, and Phred Dvorak. "Howard Stringer, Japanese CEO." *Wall Street Journal,* March 3, 2007.

Kanter, Rosabeth Moss. *Men and Women of the Corporation.* New York: Basic Books, 1977.

Kanter, Rosabeth Moss. *Supercorp: How Vanguard Companies Create Innovation, Profits, Growth, and Social Good.* New York: Random House, 2009.

Kanter, Rosabeth Moss. *The Change Masters: Innovation and Entrepreneurship in the American Corporation.* New York: Simon & Schuster, 1983.

Kantor, Jodi. "A Titan's How-To on Breaking the Glass Ceiling." *New York Times,* February 21, 2013.

Kantor, Jodi. "In First Family, a Nation's Many Faces." *New York Times,* January 16, 2009.

Kantor, Jodi. "On the Job, Nursing Mothers Find a 2-Class System." *New York Times,* September 1, 2006.

Kapner, Suzanne. "Citi to Settle Suit for $590 Million." *Wall Street Journal,* August 30, 2012.

Karon, Tony. "Why China Does Capitalism Better Than the U.S." *Time,* January 20, 2011.

Karp, David A., Gregory P. Stone, and William C. Yoels. *Being Urban: A Sociology of City Life,* 2nd ed. New York: Praeger, 1991.

Katz, Bruce, and Jennifer Bradley. "The Suburban Challenge." *Newsweek,* January 26, 2009.

Katz, Richard S. "Electoral Reform in Italy: Expectations and Results." *Acta Politica, 41,* 2006:285–299.

Kaufman, Joanne. "Married Maidens and Dilatory Domiciles." *Wall Street Journal,* May 7, 1996:A16.

Keith, Jennie. *Old People, New Lives: Community Creation in a Retirement Residence,* 2nd ed. Chicago: University of Chicago Press, 1982.

Kelley, Tina. "In an Era of School Shootings, a New Drill." *New York Times,* March 25, 2008.

Kelly, Benjamin, and Khostrow Farahbakhsh. "Public Sociology and the Democratization of Technology: Drawing on User-Led Research to Achieve Mutual Education." *American Sociologist, 44,* 1, 2013:42–53.

Kelly, Joan B. "How Adults React to Divorce." In *Marriage and Family in a Changing Society,* 4th ed., James M. Henslin, ed. New York: Free Press, 1992:410–423.

Kempner, Joanna. "The Chilling Effect: How Do Researchers React to Controversy?" *PLoS Medicine, 5,* 11, November, 2008:1571–1578.

Keniston, Kenneth. *Youth and Dissent: The Rise of a New Opposition*. New York: Harcourt, Brace, Jovanovich, 1971.

Kent, Mary, and Robert Lalasz. "In the News: Speaking English in the United States." Washington, D.C.: Population Reference Bureau, January 18, 2007.

Kephart, William M., and William W. Zellner. *Extraordinary Groups: An Examination of Unconventional Life-Styles,* 7th ed. New York: Worth Publishing, 2001.

Kerr, Clark. *The Future of Industrialized Societies.* Cambridge, Mass.: Harvard University Press, 1983.

Kifner, John. "Building Modernity on Desert Mirages." *New York Times,* February 7, 1999.

Kille, Kent J., and Ryan C. Hendrickson. "NATO and the United Nations: Debates and Trends in Institutional Coordination." *Journal of International Organizations Studies, 2,* 1, 2011:28–49.

Kim, Richard. "The L Word." *The Nation,* October 19, 2004.

Kimmel, Michael. "Racism as Adolescent Male Rite of Passage." *Journal of Contemporary Ethnography, 36,* 2, April 2007:202–218.

King, Eden B., Jennifer L. Knight, and Michelle R. Hebl. "The Influence of Economic Conditions on Aspects of Stigmatization." *Journal of Social Issues, 66,* 3, September 2010:446–460.

Kingsbury, Alex, "Many Colleges Reject Women at Higher Rates Than for Men." *U.S. News & World Report,* June 17, 2007.

Kingston, Maxine Hong. *The Woman Warrior*. New York: Vintage Books, 1975:108. Quoted in Frank J. Zulke and Jacqueline P. Kirley. *Through the Eyes of Social Science,* 6th ed. Prospect Heights, Ill.: Waveland Press, 2002.

Kissinger, Henry A. "Avoiding a US.–China Cold War." *Washington Post,* January 14, 2011.

Klandermans, Bert. *The Social Psychology of Protest.* Cambridge, Mass.: Blackwell, 1997.

Kleinfeld, Judith S. "Gender and Myth: Data about Student Performance." In *Through the Eyes of Social Science,* 6th ed., Frank J. Zulke and Jacqueline P. Kirley, eds. Prospect Heights, Ill.: Waveland Press, 2002a:380–393.

Kleinfeld, Judith S. "The Small World Problem." *Society,* January–February, 2002b:61–66.

Kluegel, James R., and Eliot R. Smith. *Beliefs about Inequality: America's Views of What Is and What Ought to Be.* Hawthorne, N.Y.: Aldine de Gruyter, 1986.

Knapp, Daniel. "What Happened When I Took My Sociological Imagination to the Dump." *Footnotes,* May–June, 2005:4.

Kneebone, Elizabeth, and Emily Garr. "The Suburbanization of Poverty: Trends in Metropolitan America, 2000 to 2008." Washington, D.C.: Brookings, January 2010.

Knickerbocker, Brad. "Firebrands of 'Ecoterrorism' Set Sights on Urban Sprawl." *Christian Science Monitor,* August 6, 2003.

Kochbar, Rakesh, and Ana Gonzalez-Barrera. "Through Boom and Bust: Minorities, Immigrants and Homeownership." Washington, D.C.: Pew Hispanic Center, May 12, 2009.

Kohlberg, Lawrence. "A Current Statement on Some Theoretical Issues." In *Lawrence Kohlberg: Consensus and Controversy,* Sohan Modgil and Celia Modgil, eds. Philadelphia: Falmer Press, 1986:485–546.

Kohlberg, Lawrence. "Moral Education for a Society in Moral Transition." *Educational Leadership, 33,* 1975:46–54.

Kohlberg, Lawrence. *The Psychology of Moral Development: Moral Stages and the Life Cycle.* San Francisco: Harper and Row, 1984.

Kohlberg, Lawrence, and Carol Gilligan. "The Adolescent as a Philosopher: The Discovery of the Self in a Postconventional World." *Daedalus, 100,* 1971:1051–1086.

Kohn, Alfie. "Make Love, Not War." *Psychology Today,* June 1988:35–38.

Kohn, Melvin L. *Change and Stability: A Cross-National Analysis of Social Structure and Personality.* Boulder, CO.: Paradigm, 2006.

Kohn, Melvin L. *Class and Conformity: A Study in Values,* 2nd ed. Homewood, Ill.: Dorsey Press, 1977.

Kohn, Melvin L. "Social Class and Parental Values." *American Journal of Sociology, 64,* 1959:337–351.

Kohn, Melvin L. "Social Class and Parent–Child Relationships: An Interpretation." *American Journal of Sociology, 68,* 1963:471–480.

Kohn, Melvin L., and Carmi Schooler. "Class, Occupation, and Orientation." *American Sociological Review, 34,* 1969:659–678.

Kolata, Gina. "The Genesis of an Epidemic: Humans, Chimps and a Virus." *New York Times,* September 4, 2001.

Kontos, Louis, David Brotherton, and Luis Barrios, eds. *Gangs and Society: Alternative Perspectives.* New York: Columbia University Press, 2003.

Kopecky, Karen A., and Richard M. H. Suen. "A Quantitative Analysis of Suburbanization and the Diffusion of the Automobile." *International Economic Review, 51,* 4, 2010:1003–1037.

Korgen, Kathleen Odell, ed. *Multiracial Americans and Social Class: The Influence of Social Class on Racial Identity.* New York: Routledge, 2010.

Koropeckyj-Cox, Tanya. "Attitudes about Childlessness in the United States." *Journal of Family Issues, 28,* 8, August 2007:1054–1082.

Kozin, Vladimir. "U.S.-NATO Missile System: First-Strike Potential Aimed at Russia." *Global Research,* March 2, 2013.

Kraft, Dina. "African AIDS Fight Uses Israeli Circumcision Skills." *The Jewish Journal,* November 26, 2008.

Kramer, Andrew E. "Putin's Grasp of Energy Drives Russian Agenda." *New York Times,* January 29, 2009.

Kramer, Ronald. "Moral Panics and Urban Growth Machines: Official Reactions to Graffiti in New York City, 1990–2005." *Qualitative Sociology, 33,* 2010:297–311.

Krause, Neal, and Christopher G. Ellison. "Forgiveness by God, Forgiveness of Others, and Psychological Well-Being in Late Life." *Journal for the Scientific Study of Religion, 42,* 1, 2003:77–93.

Kraybill, Donald B. *The Riddle of Amish Culture,* rev. ed. Baltimore, Md.: Johns Hopkins University Press, 2002.

Krienert, Jessie L., and Jeffrey A. Walsh. "Characteristics and Perceptions of Child Sexual Abuse." *Journal of Child Sexual Abuse, 20,* 2011:353–372.

Kristof, Gregory. "FCAT Scores Lower for Third Graders, State Drops Standards for More Students to Pass." *Huffington Post,* May 24, 2012.

Kristoff, Nicholas D. "Interview with a Humanoid." *New York Times,* July 23, 2002.

Kroeger, Brooke. "When a Dissertation Makes a Difference." *New York Times,* March 20, 2004.

Krueger, Alan B. "The Apple Falls Close to the Tree, Even in the Land of Opportunity." *New York Times,* November 14, 2002.

Krugman, Paul. "White Man's Burden." *New York Times,* September 24, 2002.

Krumer-Nevo, Michal, and Orly Benjamin. "Critical Poverty Knowledge: Contesting Othering and Social Distancing." *Current Sociology, 58,* 2010:693–714.

Kübler-Ross, Elisabeth. *On Death and Dying.* New York: Macmillan, 1969. 40th anniversary edition published by Routledge in 2008.

Kubrin, Charis E., and Ronald Weitzer. "Retaliatory Homicide: Concentrated Disadvantage and Neighborhood Culture." *Social Problems, 50,* 2, May 2003:157–180.

Kulish, Nicholas. "German Court Rules against Circumcising Boys." *New York Times,* June 27, 2012.

Kurian, George Thomas. *Encyclopedia of the First World,* Vols. 1, 2. New York: Facts on File, 1990.

Kurian, George Thomas. *Encyclopedia of the Second World.* New York: Facts on File, 1991.

Kurian, George Thomas. *Encyclopedia of the Third World,* Vols. 1, 2, 3. New York: Facts on File, 1992.

López, Adalberto, ed. *The Puerto Ricans: Their History, Culture, and Society.* Cambridge, Mass.: Schenkman, 1980.

La Barre, Weston. *The Human Animal.* Chicago: University of Chicago Press, 1954.

Lacey, Marc. "Tijuana Journal: Cities Mesh across Blurry Border, Despite Physical Barrier." *New York Times,* March 5, 2007.

Lacy, Karyn R. *Blue-Chip Black: Class and Status in the New Black Middle Class.* Berkeley: University of California Press, 2007.

Lacy, Karyn R., and Angel L. Harris. "Breaking the Class Monolith: Understanding Class Differences in Black Adolescents' Attachment to Racial Identity." In *Social Class: How Does It Work?* Annette Lareau and Dalton Conley, eds. New York: Russell Sage, 2008:152–178.

LaFraniere, Sharon. "As China Ages, Birthrate Policy May Prove Difficult to Reverse." *New York Times,* April 6, 2011.

LaFraniere, Sharon. "Views of North Korea Show How a Policy Spread Misery." *New York Times,* June 9, 2010.

Landry, Bart, and Kris Marsh. "The Evolution of the New Black Middle Class." *Annual Review of Sociology, 37,* 2011:373–394.

Landtman, Gunnar. *The Origin of the Inequality of the Social Classes.* New York: Greenwood Press, 1968. Originally published 1938.

Lang, Kurt, and Gladys E. Lang. *Collective Dynamics.* New York: Crowell, 1961.

Lapsley, Michael. *Redeeming the Past: My Journey from Freedom Fighter to Healer.* Maryknoll, N.Y.: Orbis Books, 2012.

Lareau, Annette. "Invisible Inequality: Social Class and Childrearing in Black Families and White Families." *American Sociological Review, 67,* October 2002:747–776.

Lareau, Annette, and Elliot B. Weininger. "Class and Transition to Adulthood." In *Social Class: How Does It Work?* Annette Lareau and Dalton Conley, eds. New York: Russell Sage, 2008:118–151.

Larson, Christina. "Green Activists Feel Sting of Chinese Government Crackdown." *Yale, e360,* June 30, 2011.

"Last Remaining Amazon Tribes Nearing Extinction." *International Business Times,* June 26, 2011.

Last, Jonathan V. "The War Against Girls." *Wall Street Journal,* June 24, 2011.

Latimer, Melissa, and Rachael A. Woldoff. "Good Country Living? Exploring Four Housing Outcomes among Poor Appalachians." *Sociological Forum, 25,* 2, June 2010:315–333.

Lauer, Jeanette, and Robert Lauer. "Marriages Made to Last." In *Marriage and Family in a Changing Society,* 4th ed., James M. Henslin, ed. New York: Free Press, 1992:481–486.

Laumann, E. O., S. A. Leitsch, and L. J. Waite. "Elder Mistreatment in the United States: Prevalence Estimates from a Nationally Representative Study." *The Journals of Gerontology, 63,* 4, July 2008:S248–S254.

Lawler, Steph. "'Getting Out and Getting Away': Women's Narratives of Class Mobility." *Feminist Review, 63,* Autumn 1999:3–24.

Lazaro, Fred de Sam. "In Senegal, a Movement to Reject Circumcision." *PBS Hour,* August 12, 2011.

Lazarsfeld, Paul F., and Jeffrey G. Reitz. "History of Applied Sociology." *Sociological Practice, 7,* 1989:43–52.

Leacock, Eleanor. *Myths of Male Dominance.* New York: Monthly Review Press, 1981.

LeBon, Gustave. *Psychologie des Foules (The Psychology of the Crowd).* Paris: Alcan, 1895. Various editions in English.

Ledger, Kate. "Sociology and the Gene." *Contexts, 8,* 3, 2009:16–20.

LeDuff, Charlie. "Handling the Meltdowns of the Nuclear Family." *New York Times,* May 28, 2003.

Lee, Alfred McClung, and Elizabeth Briant Lee. *The Fine Art of Propaganda: A Study of Father Coughlin's Speeches.* New York: Harcourt Brace, 1939.

Lee, Chulhee, "Technological Changes and Employment of Older Manufacturing Workers in Early Twentieth Century America." Working Paper 14746, Cambridge, Mass.: National Bureau of Economic Research, February 2009.

Lee, Raymond M. *Unobtrusive Methods in Social Research.* Philadelphia: Open University Press, 2000.

Lee, Sharon M. "Asian Americans: Diverse and Growing." *Population Bulletin, 53,* 2, June 1998:1–39.

Lehnert, Thomas, Diana Sonntag, Alesander Konnopka, et al. "Economic Costs of Overweight and Obesity." *Best Practice & Research Clinical Endocrinology & Metabolism, 27,* 2013:105–115.

Leland, John. "A New Harlem Gentry in Search of Its Latte." *New York Times,* August 7, 2003.

Leland, John, and Gregory Beals. "In Living Colors." *Newsweek,* May 5, 1997:58–60.

Lengermann, Madoo, and Gillian Niebrugge. *The Women Founders: Sociology and Social Theory, 1830–1930.* Prospect Heights, Ill.: Waveland Press, 2007.

Lenski, Gerhard. *Power and Privilege: A Theory of Social Stratification.* New York: McGraw-Hill, 1966.

Lenski, Gerhard. "Status Crystallization: A Nonvertical Dimension of Social Status." *American Sociological Review, 19,* 1954:405–413.

Lenski, Gerhard, and Jean Lenski. *Human Societies: An Introduction to Macrosociology,* 5th ed. New York: McGraw-Hill, 1987.

Leo, Jen. "Google's Space Explorer Sergey Brin." *Los Angeles Times,* June 12, 2008.

Leopold, Evelyn. "Female Circumcision—90 Percent of Childbearing Women in Egypt?" *Huffington Post,* January 9, 2012.

Lerner, Gerda. *Black Women in White America: A Documentary History.* New York: Pantheon Books, 1972.

Lerner, Gerda. *The Creation of Patriarchy.* New York: Oxford, 1986.

Lerner, Steve. *Sacrifice Zones: The Front Lines of Toxic Chemical Exposure in the United States.* Cambridge, Mass.: MIT Press, 2010.

"Less Rote, More Variety: Reforming Japan's Schools." *The Economist,* December 16, 2000:8.

Lesser, Alexander. "War and the State." In *War: The Anthropology of Armed Conflict and Aggression,* Morton Fried, Marvin Harris, and Robert Murphy, eds. Garden City, N.Y.: Natural History, 1968:92–96.

Letherby, Gayle. "Childless and Bereft? Stereotypes and Realities in Relation to 'Voluntary' and 'Involuntary' Childlessness and Womanhood." *Sociological Inquiry, 72,* 1, Winter 2002:7–20.

Levanthal, Tama, and Jeanne Brooks-Gunn. "The Neighborhood They Live in: Effects of Neighborhood Residence on Child and Adolescent Outcomes." *Psychological Bulletin, 126,* 2000:309–337.

Levi, Ken. "Becoming a Hit Man." In *Exploring Social Life: Readings to Accompany Essentials of Sociology: A Down-to-Earth Approach, Eighth Edition,* 4th ed, James M. Henslin, ed. Boston: Allyn and Bacon, 2009. Originally published 1981.

Levine, Alan, and Sidney Wolfe. "Hospitals Drop the Ball on Physician Oversight." *PublicCitizen,* May 27, 2009.

Levine, Robert. "Planned Guns N' Roses Deal Underscores Power of Video to Sell Songs." *Wall Street Journal,* July 14, 2008.

Levinson, D. J. *The Seasons of a Man's Life.* New York: Knopf, 1978.

Levitz, Jennifer. "Divorced but Still Living Together." *Wall Street Journal,* July 13, 2009.

Levy, Becca R., Pil H. Chung, T. Bedford, et al. "Facebook as a Site for Negative Age Stereotypes." *Gerontologist,* 2013.

Levy, Clifford J. "Doctor Admits He Did Needless Surgery on the Mentally Ill." *New York Times,* May 20, 2003.

Levy, Clifford J., and Michael Luo. "New York Medicaid Fraud May Reach into Billions." *New York Times,* July 18, 2005.

Lewin, Ellen. *Gay Fatherhood: Narratives of Family and Citizenship in America.* Chicago: University of Chicago Press, 2009.

Lewin, Tamar. "After Home Schooling, Pomp and Traditional Circumstances." *New York Times,* June 18, 2011.

Lewin, Tamar. "College of Future Could Be Come One, Come All." *New York Times,* November 19, 2012.

Lewis, Neil A. "Justice Dept. Toughens Rules on Torture." *New York Times,* January 1, 2005.

Lewis, Oscar. "The Culture of Poverty." *Scientific American, 115,* October 1966:19–25.

Lewis, Oscar. *La Vida.* New York: Random House, 1966b.

Li, Zheng. "China Faces Elderly Dilemma." *China Daily,* August 21, 2004.

Lichter, Daniel T., and Martha L. Crowley. "Poverty in America: Beyond Welfare Reform." *Population Bulletin, 57,* 2, June 2002:1–36.

Lichter, Daniel T., and Zhenchao Qian. "Serial Cohabitation and the Marital Life Course." *Journal of Marriage and Family, 70,* November 2008:861–878.

Liebow, Elliott. *Tally's Corner: A Study of Negro Streetcorner Men.* Boston: Little, Brown, 1999. Originally published 1967.

Lightfoot-Klein, A. "Rites of Purification and Their Effects: Some Psychological Aspects of Female Genital Circumcision and Infibulation (Pharaonic Circumcision) in an Afro-Arab Society (Sudan)." *Journal of Psychological Human Sexuality, 2,* 1989:61–78.

Lind, Michael. *The Next American Nation: The New Nationalism and the Fourth American Revolution.* New York: Free Press, 1995.

Lindau, Stacy Tessler, L. Philip Schumm, Edward O. Laumann, Wendy Levinson, Colm A. O'Muircheartaigh, and Linda J. Waite. "A Study of Sexuality and Health among Older Adults in the United States." *New England Journal of Medicine, 357,* 8, August 23, 2007:762–774.

Linden, Eugene. "Lost Tribes, Lost Knowledge." *Time,* September 23, 1991:46, 48, 50, 52, 54, 56.

Lindley, Joanne, and Stephen Machin. "The Postgraduate Premium: Revisiting Trends in Social Mobility and Educational Inequalities in Britain and America." London: Sutton Trust, February 2013.

Lindner, Eileen, ed. *Yearbook of American & Canadian Churches 2002.* Nashville, Tenn.: Abingdon Press, 2002.

Lines, Patricia M. "Homeschooling Comes of Age." *Public Interest,* Summer 2000:74–85.

Linton, Ralph. *The Study of Man.* New York: Appleton-Century-Crofts, 1936.

Linz, Daniel, Bryant Paul, Kenneth C. Land, Jay R. Williams, and Michael E. Ezell. "An Examination of the Assumption That Adult Businesses Are Associated with Crime in Surrounding Areas: A Secondary Effects Study in Charlotte, North Carolina." *Law & Society, 38,* 1, March 2004:69–104.

Lippitt, Ronald, and Ralph K. White. "An Experimental Study of Leadership and Group Life." In *Readings in Social Psychology,* 3rd ed., Eleanor E. Maccoby, Theodore M. Newcomb, and Eugene L. Hartley, eds. New York: Holt, Rinehart and Winston, 1958:340–365. (As summarized in Olmsted and Hare 1978:28–31.)

Lipset, Seymour Martin. "The Social Requisites of Democracy Revisited." Presidential address to the American Sociological Association, Boston, Massachusetts, 1993.

Liptak, Adam. "Blocking Parts of Arizona Law, Justices Allow Its Centerpiece." *New York Times,* June 25, 2012.

Liptak, Adam. "Justices, 5–4, Reject Corporate Spending Limit." *New York Times,* January 21, 2010.

Littleton, Heather, Carmen Radecki Breitkopf, and Abbey Berenson. "Women Beyond the Campus: Unacknowledged Rape among Low-Income Women." *Violence against Women, 14,* 3, March 2008:269–286.

Liu, Hui, and Corinne Reczek. "Cohabitation and U.S. Adult Mortality: An Examination by Gender and Race." *Journal of Marriage and Family, 74,* August 2012:794–811.

Livingston, Gretchen, and D'Vera Cohn. "Childlessness Up among All Women; Down among Women with Advanced Degrees." Washington, D.C.: PEW Research Center, June 25, 2010.

Lofland, John F. *Protest: Studies of Collective Behavior and Social Movements.* New Brunswick, N.J.: Transaction Books, 1985.

Logan, John R., Jennifer Darrah, and Sookhee Oh. "The Impact of Race and Ethnicity, Immigration and Political Context on Participation in American Electoral Politics." *Social Forces, 90,* 3, 2012:993–1022.

Lohr, Steve, and John Markoff. "Computers Learn to Listen, and Some Talk Back." *New York Times,* June 24, 2010.

Lombroso, Cesare. *Crime: Its Causes and Remedies,* H. P. Horton, trans. Boston: Little, Brown, 1911.

Longman, Jeré. "Home Schoolers Are Hoping to Don Varsity Jackets in Virginia." *New York Times,* February 8, 2012.

Lopes, Giza, Marvin D. Krohn, Alan J. Lizotte, Nicole M. Schmidt, Bob Edward Vásquez, and Jón Gunnar Bernburg. "Labeling and Cumulative Disadvantage: The Impact of Formal Police Intervention on Life Chances and Crime during Emerging Adulthood." *Crime and Delinquency, 58,* 3, 2012:456–488.

Lopoo, Leonard, and Thomas DeLeire. "Pursuing the American Dream: Economic Mobility Across Generations." Washington, D.C.: PEW Charitable Trust, 2012.

Loveless, Tom. "How Well Are American Students Learning?" *The 2013 Brown Center Report on American Education, 3,* 2, March 2013.

Loveluck, Louisa. "Education in Egypt: Key Challenges." London: Chatham House, March 2012.

Lublin, Joann S. "CEO Pay in 2010 Jumped 11%." *Wall Street Journal,* May 9, 2011.

Lublin, Joann S. "Living Well." *Wall Street Journal,* April 8, 1999.

Lublin, Joann S. "Trying to Increase Worker Productivity, More Employers Alter Management Style." *Wall Street Journal,* February 13, 1991:B1, B7.

Luke, Timothy W. *Ideology and Soviet Industrialization.* Westport, Conn.: Greenwood Press, 1985.

Lurie, Nicole, Jonathan Slater, Paul McGovern, Jacqueline Ekstrum, Lois Quam, and Karen Margolis. "Preventive Care for Women: Does the Sex of the Physician Matter?" *New England Journal of Medicine, 329,* August 12, 1993:478–482.

Lyall, Sarah. "Here's the Pub, Church and Field for Public Sex." *New York Times,* October 7, 2010.

Lynn, Michael, Michael Sturman, Christie Ganley, Elizabeth Adams, Mathew Douglas, and Jessica McNeil. "Consumer Racial Discrimination in Tipping: A Replication and Extension." *Journal of Applied Social Psychology, 38,* 4, 2008:1045–1060.

MacDonald, William L., and Alfred DeMaris. "Remarriage, Stepchildren, and Marital Conflict: Challenges to the Incomplete Institutionalization Hypothesis." *Journal of Marriage and the Family, 57,* May 1995:387–398.

MacFarquhar, Neil. "Many Muslims Turn to Home Schooling" *New York Times,* March 26, 2008.

Mack, Raymond W., and Calvin P. Bradford. *Transforming America: Patterns of Social Change,* 2nd ed. New York: Random House, 1979.

Mackay, Charles. *Memories* of *Extraordinary Popular Delusions and the Madness of Crowds.* London: Office of the National Illustrated Library, 1852.

MacLennan, Michael. "Locating the Policy Space for Inclusive Green Growth within the SADC Extractive Sector." *International Policy Centre for Inclusive Growth, 38,* December 2012:1–7.

Mahoney, Patricia. "High Rape Chronicity and Low Rates of Help-Seeking among Wife Rape Survivors in a Nonclinical Sample: Implications for Research and Practice." *Violence against Women, 5,* 9, September 1999:993–1016.

Main, Jackson Turner. *The Social Structure of Revolutionary America.* Princeton, N.J.: Princeton University Press, 1965.

Makary, Marty. "How to Stop Hospitals from Killing Us." *Wall Street Journal,* September 21, 2012.

Malinowski, Bronislaw. *Sex and Repression in Savage Society.* Cleveland, Ohio: World, 1927.

Malkin, Elisabeth. "Mexican Officials Say Prisoners Acted as Hit Men." *New York Times,* July 25, 2010.

Malthus, Thomas Robert. *First Essay on Population 1798.* London: Macmillan, 1926. Originally published 1798.

Mamdani, Mahmood. "The Myth of Population Control: Family, Caste, and Class in an Urban Village." New York: Monthly Review Press, 1973.

Mander, Jerry. *In the Absence of the Sacred: The Failure of Technology and the Survival of the Indian Nations.* San Francisco, Calif.: Sierra Club Books, 1992.

Manheimer, Ronald J. "The Older Learner's Journey to an Ageless Society." *Journal of Transformative Education, 3,* 3, 2005.

Manning, Wendy D., and Jessica A. Cohen. "Premarital Cohabitation and Marital Dissolution: An Examination of Recent Marriages." Center for Family and Demographic Research Working Paper Series 2010–11, Bowling Green, Ohio: Bowling Green State University, 2011.

"Manpower Report to the President." Washington, D.C.: U.S. Department of Labor, Manpower Administration, April 1971.

Manza, Jeff, and Michael A. McCarthy. "The Neo-Marxist Legacy in American Sociology." *Annual Review of Sociology, 37,* 2011:155–183.

Manzano, Sylvia, and Gabriel R. Sanchez. "Take One for the Team? Limits of Shared Ethnicity and Candidate Preferences." *Political Research Quarterly, 63,* 3, 2010:568–580.

Mardell, Mark. "Europe in Khaki." *BBC News,* June 14, 2007.

Marino, David. "Border Watch Group 'Techno Patriots' Still Growing." Tucson, Arizona: KVOA News 4, February 14, 2008.

Marino, Sylvia. "Debunking the Myths of the Telecommute." *New York Times,* April 16, 2010.

"Marital History for People 15 Years Old and Over by Age, Sex, Race and Ethnicity: 2001." Annual Demographic Survey, Bureau of Labor Statistics and U.S. Census Bureau, 2004.

Markoff, John, and Somini Sengupta. "Separating You and Me? 4.74 Degrees." *New York Times,* November 21, 2011.

Marolla, Joseph, and Diana Scully. "Attitudes toward Women, Violence, and Rape: A Comparison of Convicted Rapists and Other Felons." *Deviant Behavior, 7,* 4, 1986:337–355.

Marshall, Samantha. "It's So Simple: Just Lather Up, Watch the Fat Go Down the Drain." *Wall Street Journal,* November 2, 1995:B1.

Martin, Andrew W., John D. McCarthy, and Clark McPhail. "Why Targets Matter: Toward a More Inclusive Model of Collective Violence." *American Sociological Review, 74,* 2009:821–841.

Martin, Joyce A., Brady E. Hamilton, Paul D. Sutton, et al. "Births: Final Data for 2005." *National Vital Statistics Reports, 56,* 6, December 5, 2007.

Martin, Joyce A., Brady E. Hamilton, Stephanie J. Ventura, et al. "Births: Final Data for 2009." *National Vital Statistics Reports. 60,* 1, November 3, 2011.

Martineau, Harriet. *Society in America.* Garden City, N.Y.: Doubleday 1962. Originally published 1837.

Martinez, Barbara. "Cash before Chemo: Hospitals Get Tough." *Wall Street Journal,* April 28, 2008.

Marx, Gary T. "Thoughts on a Neglected Category of Social Movement Participant: The Agent Provocateur and the Informant." In *Collective Behavior and Social Movements,* Russell L. Curtis, Jr., and Benigno E. Aguirre, eds. Boston: Allyn and Bacon, 1993:242–258.

Marx, Karl. *Capital: A Critique of Political Economy,* E. Aveling, trans. Chicago: Charles Kerr, 1906.

Marx, Karl. "Contribution to the Critique of Hegel's Philosophy of Right." In *Karl Marx: Early Writings,* T. B. Bottomore, ed. New York: McGraw-Hill, 1964:45. Originally published 1844.

Marx, Karl, and Friedrich Engels. *Communist Manifesto.* New York: Pantheon, 1967. Originally published 1848.

Masheter, Carol. "Postdivorce Relationships between Ex-Spouses: The Role of Attachment and Interpersonal Conflict." *Journal of Marriage and the Family, 53,* February 1991:103–110.

Massoglia, Michael, Glenn Firebaugh, and Cody Warner. "Racial Variation in the Effect of Incarceration on Neighborhood Attainment." *American Sociological Review,* 78, 1, February 2013:142–165.

Masters, Ryan K., Robert A. Hummer, and Daniel A. Powers. "Educational Differences in U.S. Adult Mortality: A Cohort Perspective." *American Sociological Review, 77,* 4 2012:548–572.

Mathews, Anna Wilde. "Finding the Best Doctor for You." *Wall Street Journal,* September 24, 2012a.

Mathews, Anna Wilde. "Doctors Move to Webcams." *Wall Street Journal,* December 21, 2012b.

Mathews, T. J., and Brady E. Hamilton. "Delayed Childbearing: More Women Are Having Their First Child Later in Life." *NCHS Data Brief, 21,* Hyattsville, Md.: National Center for Health Statistics, August 2009:1–7.

Matsumoto, D., and B. Willingham. "Spontaneous Facial Expressions of Emotion of Congenitally and Noncongenitally Blind Individuals." *Journal of Personality and Social Psychology, 96,* 2009:1–10.

Mauss, Armand. *Social Problems as Social Movements.* Philadelphia, Pa.: Lippincott, 1975.

Mayer, Anita P., Julia A. Files, Marcia G. Ko, and Janis E. Blair. "Academic Advancement of Women in Medicine: Do Socialized Gender Differences Have a Role in Mentoring?" *Mayo Clinic Proceedings, 83,* 2, February 2008:204–207.

Mayer, John D. *Personality: A Systems Approach.* Boston: Allyn and Bacon, 2007.

McCabe, J. Terrence, and James E. Ellis. "Pastoralism: Beating the Odds in Arid Africa." In *Conformity and Conflict: Readings in Cultural Anthropology,* James P. Spradley and David W. McCurdy, eds. Glenview, Ill.: Scott, Foresman, 1990:150–156.

McCarthy, Bill. "The Attitudes and Actions of Others: Tutelage and Sutherland's Theory of Differential Association." *British Journal of Criminology 36,* 1, 2011:135–147.

McCarthy, John D., and Mayer N. Zald. "Resource Mobilization and Social Movements: A Partial Theory." *American Journal of Sociology, 82,* 6, 1977:1212–1241.

McCarthy, Michael J. "Granbury, Texas, Isn't a Rural Town: It's a 'Micropolis.'" *Wall Street Journal,* June 3, 2004.

McCaughey, Betsy. "When Hospitals Become Killers." *Wall Street Journal,* January 31, 2013.

McCormick, John. "The Sorry Side of Sears." *Newsweek,* February 22, 1999:36–39.

McCracken, Harry. "The Mystery of Minecraft." *Time,* June 3, 2013.

McDowell, Bart. "Mexico City: An Alarming Giant." *National Geographic, 166,* 1984:139–174.

McFalls, Joseph A., Jr. "Population: A Lively Introduction, 5th ed." *Population Bulletin, 62,* 1, March 2007:1–30.

McIntosh, Peggy. "White Privilege and Male Privilege: A Personal Account of Coming to See Correspondences through Work in Women's Studies." Wellesley College Center for Research on Women, Working Paper 189, 1988.

McKay, Amy. "Buying Policy? The Effect of Lobbyists' Resources on Their Policy Success." *Political Research Quarterly, 65,* 4, 2012:908–923.

McKeown, Thomas. *The Modern Rise of Population.* New York: Academic Press, 1977.

McKinlay, Alan, and James Wilson. "'All They Lose Is the Scream': Foucault, Ford and Mass Production." *Management & Organizational History, 7,* 1, 2012:45–60.

McKinnish, Terra G. "Sexually Integrated Workplaces and Divorce: Another Form of On-the-Job Search." *Journal of Human Resources, 42,* 2, 2007:331–352.

McKinnish, Terra, Randall Walsh, and Kirk White. "Who Gentrifies Low-Income Neighborhoods?" National Bureau of Economic Research, Working Paper 14036, May 2008.

McKown, Clark, and Rhona S. Weinstein. "Modeling the Role of Child Ethnicity and Gender in Children's Differential Response to Teacher Expectations." *Journal of Applied Social Psychology, 32,* 1, 2002:159–184.

McKown, Clark, and Rhona S. Weinstein. "Teacher Expectations, Classroom Context, and the Achievement Gap." *Journal of School Psychology, 46,* 2008:235–261.

McLanahan, Sara, and Christine Percheski. "Family Structure and the Reproduction of Inequalities." *Annual Review of Sociology, 34,* 2008:257–276.

McLanahan, Sara, and Dona Schwartz. "Life without Father: What Happens to the Children?" *Contexts, 1,* 1, Spring 2002:35–44.

McLanahan, Sara, and Gary Sandefur. *Growing Up with a Single Parent: What Hurts, What Helps.* Cambridge, Mass.: Harvard University Press, 1994.

McLaughlin, Heather, Christopher Uggen, and Amy Blackstone. "Sexual Harassment, Workplace Authority, and the Paradox of Power." *American Sociological Review, 77,* 4, 2012:625–647.

McLemore, S. Dale. *Racial and Ethnic Relations in America.* Boston: Allyn and Bacon, 1994.

McNeil, Donald G., Jr. "Precursor to H.I.V. Was in Monkeys for Millennia." *New York Times,* September 16, 2010a.

McNeil, Donald G., Jr. "U.S. Apologizes for Syphilis Tests in Guatemala." *New York Times,* October 1, 2010b.

McNeill, William H. "How the Potato Changed the World's History." *Social Research, 66,* 1, Spring 1999:67–83.

McPhail, Clark. "Blumer's Theory of Collective Behavior: The Development of a Non-Symbolic Interaction Explanation." *Sociological Quarterly, 30,* 3, 1989:401–423.

McPhail, Clark. *The Myth of the Madding Crowd.* Hawthorne, N.Y.: Aldine de Gruyter, 1991.

McShane, Larry. "Abraham Shakespeare, $31M Florida Lottery Winner, Found Dead 9 Months after Disappearing." *Daily News,* January 30, 2010.

McShane, Marilyn, and Frank P. Williams, III., eds. *Criminological Theory.* Upper Saddle River, N.J.: Prentice Hall, 2007.

McVeigh, Rory. *The Rise of the Ku Klux Klan: Right-Wing Movements and National Politics.* Minneapolis: University of Minnesota Press, 2009.

Mead, George Herbert. *Mind, Self and Society.* Chicago: University of Chicago Press, 1934.

Mead, Margaret. *Sex and Temperament in Three Primitive Societies.* New York: New American Library, 1950. Originally published 1935.

Meara, Ellen R., Seth Richards, and David M. Cutler. "The Gap Gets Bigger: Changes in Mortality and Life Expectancy, by Education, 1981–2000." *Health Affairs, 27,* 2, March/April 2008:350–360.

Meese, Ruth Lyn. "A Few New Children: Postinstitutionalized Children of Intercountry Adoption." *Journal of Special Education, 39,* 3, 2005:157–167.

Meier, Barry. "Defective Heart Devices Force Some Scary Medical Decisions." *New York Times,* June 20, 2005.

Meier, Barry. "Guidant Debated Device Peril." *New York Times,* January 20, 2006.

Meier, Barry. "Health Studies Suggest Asbestos Substitutes Also Pose Cancer Risk." *Wall Street Journal,* May 12, 1987:1, 21.

"Melee Breaks Out at Retirement Home." *The Daily News,* March 5, 2004.

Meltzer, Scott A. "Gender, Work, and Intimate Violence: Men's Occupational Spillover and Compensatory Violence." *Journal of Marriage and the Family, 64,* 2, November 2002:820–832.

Menaghan, Elizabeth G., Lori Kowaleski-Jones, and Frank L. Mott. "The Intergenerational Costs of Parental Social Stressors: Academic and Social Difficulties in Early Adolescence for Children of Young Mothers." *Journal of Health and Social Behavior, 38,* March 1997:72–86.

Menzel, Peter. *Material World: A Global Family Portrait.* San Francisco: Sierra Club, 1994.

Mermin, Jonathan. "In Wake of Latest Trial Results, CDC Stresses That Consistent Use Is Imperative When Using Pre-Exposure Prophylaxis to Prevent HIV Infection." Atlanta, Ga.: CDC Division of HIV/AIDS Prevention, March 4, 2013.

Merton, Robert K. *Social Theory and Social Structure.* Glencoe, Ill.: Free Press, 1949. Enlarged ed., 1968.

Merton, Robert K. "The Social-Cultural Environment and *Anomie.*" In *New Perspectives for Research on Juvenile Delinquency,* Helen L. Witmer and Ruth Kotinsky, eds. Washington, D.C.: U.S. Department of Health, Education, and Welfare, 1956:24–50.

Merwine, Maynard H. "How Africa Understands Female Circumcision." *New York Times,* November 24, 1993.

Meyers, Laurie. "Asian-American Mental Health." *APA Online,* February 2006.

Michels, Robert. *Political Parties.* Glencoe, Ill.: Free Press, 1949. Originally published 1911.

Milbank, Dana. "Guarded by Greenbelts, Europe's Town Centers Thrive." *Wall Street Journal,* May 3, 1995:B1, B4.

Milgram, Stanley. "Behavioral Study of Obedience." *Journal of Abnormal and Social Psychology, 67,* 4, 1963:371–378.

Milgram, Stanley. "Some Conditions of Obedience and Disobedience to Authority." *Human Relations, 18,* February 1965:57–76.

Milgram, Stanley. "The Small World Problem." *Psychology Today, 1,* 1967:61–67.

Milkie, Melissa A. "Social World Approach to Cultural Studies." *Journal of Contemporary Ethnography, 23,* 3, October 1994:354–380.

Miller, Laura L. "Women in the Military." In *Down to Earth Sociology: Introductory Readings,* 14th ed., James M. Henslin, ed. New York: Free Press, 2007. Originally published 1997.

Miller, Stephen. "Ensure Compliance with Reform Law's Lactation Room Requirements." Alexandria, Va.: Society for Human Resource Management, March 8, 2012.

Miller, Walter B. "Lower Class Culture as a Generating Milieu of Gang Delinquency." *Journal of Social Issues, 14,* 3, 1958:5–19.

Miller-Loessi, Karen. "Toward Gender Integration in the Workplace: Issues at Multiple Levels." *Sociological Perspectives, 35,* 1, 1992:1–15.

Mills, C. Wright. *The Power Elite.* New York: Oxford University Press, 1956.

Mills, C. Wright. *The Sociological Imagination.* New York: Oxford University Press, 1959.

Mills, Karen M., and Thomas J. Palumbo. *A Statistical Portrait of Women in the United States: 1978. Current Population Reports,* Series P-23, Number 100, U.S. Census Bureau, 1980.

Miner, Horace. "Body Ritual among the Nacirema." In *Down to Earth Sociology: Introductory Readings,* 14th ed., James M. Henslin, ed. New York: Free Press, 2007. Originally published 1956.

Mirola, William A. "Asking for Bread, Receiving a Stone: The Rise and Fall of Religious Ideologies in Chicago's Eight-Hour Movement." *Social Problems, 50,* 2, May 2003:273–293.

Mishin, Stanislav. "American Capitalism Gone with a Whimper." *Pravda,* April 27, 2009.

Mohajer, Shaya Tayefe. "FBI Mosque Spying Case: Judge Dismisses Part of Lawsuit Against the FBI." Associated Press, August 14, 2012.

Mohawk, John C. "Indian Economic Development: An Evolving Concept of Sovereignty." *Buffalo Law Review, 39,* 2, Spring 1991:495–503.

Moloney, Liam. "Pope to Spread the Faith through Twitter." *Wall Street Journal,* December 3, 2012.

Monahan, Brian A., Joseph A. Marolla, and David G. Bromley. "Constructing Coercion: The Organization of Sexual Assault." *Journal of Contemporary Ethnography, 34,* 3, June 2005:284–316.

Money, John, and Anke A. Ehrhardt. *Man and Woman, Boy and Girl.* Baltimore: Johns Hopkins University Press, 1972.

'Monkey' Gives Delhi Claws for Alarm." *The Australian,* May 17, 2001.

Montagu, M. F. Ashley. *Introduction to Physical Anthropology,* 3rd ed. Springfield, Ill.: Thomas, 1960.

Montagu, M. F. Ashley, ed. *Race and IQ: Expanded Edition.* New York: Oxford University Press, 1999.

Montagu, M. F. Ashley. *The Concept of Race.* New York: Free Press, 1964.

Moreno, Eduardo Lopez, Oyebanji Oyeyinka, and Gora Mboup. *State of the World's Cities 2010/2011: Bridging the Urban Divide.* London: UN Habitat, 2012.

Morgan, Lewis Henry. *Ancient Society.* New York: Holt, 1877.

Morin, Monte. "$1.7 Million Awarded in Retirement Home Death." *Los Angeles Times,* October 17, 2001.

Morin, Rich, and D'Vera Cohn. "Women Call the Shots at Home; Public Mixed on Gender Roles in Jobs." Pew Research Center Publications: September 25, 2008.

Morl, Kazuo, and Miho Aral. "No Need to Fake It: Reproduction of the Ash Experiment without Confederates." *International Journal of Psychology, 45,* 5, 2010:390–397.

Morris, Aldon. "Black Southern Student Sit-In Movement: An Analysis of Internal Organization." In *Collective Behavior and Social Movements,* Russell L. Curtis, Jr., and Benigno E. Aguirre, eds. Boston: Allyn and Bacon, 1993:361–380.

Morris, Joan M., and Michael D. Grimes. "Moving Up from the Working Class." In *Down to Earth Sociology: Introductory Readings,* 13th ed., James M. Henslin, ed. New York: Free Press, 2005:365–376.

Morrow, Betty Hearn. "Urban Families as Support after Disaster: The Case of Hurricane Andrew." Paper presented at the annual meetings of the American Sociological Association, 1995.

Mosca, Gaetano. *The Ruling Class.* New York: McGraw-Hill, 1939. Originally published 1896.

Mosher, Steven W. "China's One-Child Policy: Twenty-Five Years Later." *Human Life Review,* Winter 2006:76–101.

Mosher, Steven W. "Too Many People? Not by a Long Shot." *Wall Street Journal,* February 10, 1997:A18.

Mosher, Steven W. "Why Are Baby Girls Being Killed in China?" *Wall Street Journal,* July 25, 1983:9.

Mouawad, Jad. "Saudi Officials Seek to Temper the Price of Oil." *Bloomberg News,* January 27, 2007.

Mouawad, Jad. "Shell to Pay $15.5 Million to Settle Nigerian Case." *New York Times,* June 8, 2009.

Moulton, Benjamin E., and Darren E. Sherkat. "Specifying the Effects of Religious Participation and Educational Attainment on Mortality Risk for U.S. Adults." *Sociological Spectrum, 32,* 2012:1–19.

Mozur, Paul. "China Alleges Cyberattacks Originated in U.S." *Wall Street Journal,* March 1, 2013.

Mozur, Paul. "Qihoo 360's Zhou Hongyi: Taking Aim at China's Internet." *Wall Street Journal,* November 30, 2012.

Muñoz Martinez, Hepzibah. "The Double Burden on Maquila Workers: Violence and Crisis in Northern Mexico." El Colegio de la Frontera Norte, Matamoros, June 15, 2010.

Muhamad, Roby. "Search in Social Networks." Ph.D. dissertation, Columbia University, 2010.

"Mujer con cabeza humana alega religion en defensa." AOL Online News, February 14, 2006.

"Mujer 'resucite blye' en España." *BBC Mundo,* February 17, 2006.

Muntaner, Charles, Edwin Ng, Christophe Vanroelen, et al. "Social Stratification, Social Closure, and Social Class as Determinants of Mental Health Disparities." In *Handbook of the Sociology of Mental Health,* 2nd ed., C. S. Aneshensel et al., eds. New York: Springer, 2013:205–227.

Murabito, Joanne M., Rong Yuan, and Kathryn L. Lunetta. "The Search for Longevity and Healthy Aging Genes: Insights from Epidemiological Studies and Samples of Long-Lived Individuals." *Journal of Gerontology Series A: Biological Sciences and Medical Sciences, 67,* 5, May 2012:470–479.

Murdock, George Peter. "Comparative Data on the Division of Labor by Sex." *Social Forces, 15,* 4, May 1937:551–553.

Murdock, George Peter. *Social Structure.* New York: Macmillan, 1949.

Murdock, George Peter. "The Common Denominator of Cultures." In *The Science of Man and the World Crisis,* Ralph Linton, ed. New York: Columbia University Press, 1945.

Murphy, John, and Miho Inada. "Japan's Recession Hits 'Temps.'" *Wall Street Journal,* December 5, 2008.

Murray, Christopher J. L., Sandeep C. Kulkarni, Catherine Michard, Niels Tomijima, Maria T. Bulzaccheili, Terrell J. Landiorio, and Majid Ezzati. "Eight Americas: Investigating Mortality Disparities across Races, Counties, and Race-Counties in the United States." *PLoS Medicine, 3,* 9, September 2006:1513–1524.

Murray, G. W. *Sons of Ishmael.* London: Routledge, 1935.

Murray, Rheana. "Girls Who Mysteriously Developed Tourette's-like Symptoms Are Suffering from Mass Hysteria: Doctor." *New York Daily News,* January 18, 2012.

Mwiti, Neva. "Hadijatou Mani: A Slave to Freedom." *Afritorial,* January 8, 2013.

Nabhan, Gary Paul. *Cultures in Habitat: On Nature, Culture, and Story.* New York: Counterpoint, 1998.

Naik, Gautam. "A Baby, Please. Blond, Freckles—Hold the Colic." *Wall Street Journal,* February 12, 2009.

Nakamura, Akemi. "Abe to Play Hardball with Soft Education System." *The Japan Times,* October 27, 2006.

Nakao, Keiko, and Judith Treas. "Occupational Prestige in the United States Revisited: Twenty-Five Years of Stability and Change." Paper presented at the annual meetings of the American Sociological Association, 1990. (As cited in Kerbo, Harold R. *Social Stratification and Inequality: Class Conflict in Historical and Comparative Perspective,* 2nd ed. New York: McGraw-Hill, 1991:181.)

Nakao, Keiko, and Judith Treas. "Updating Occupational Prestige and Socioeconomic Scores: How the New Measures Measure Up." *Sociological Methodology, 24,* 1994:1–72.

Nash, Gary B. *Red, White, and Black.* Englewood Cliffs, N.J.: Prentice Hall, 1974.

National Center for Education Statistics. *Digest of Education Statistics.* Washington, D.C.: U.S. Government Printing Office, 1991.

National Coalition for the Homeless. NCH Fact Sheet #2, June 2008.

National Institute of Child Health and Human Development. "Child Care and Mother–Child Interaction in the First 3 Years of Life." *Developmental Psychology, 35,* 6, November 1999:1399–1413.

National School Safety Center. "School Associated Violent Deaths." Westlake Village, Calif.: National School Safety Center, 2013.

National Women's Political Caucus. "Factsheet on Women's Political Progress." Washington, D.C., June 1998.

National Women's Political Caucus. "Women in Congress," 2011.

Needham, Sarah E. "Grooming Women for the Top: Tips from Executive Coaches." *Wall Street Journal,* October 31, 2006.

Neil, Andrew. "Does a Narrow Social Elite Run the Country?" *BBC,* January 26, 2011.

Neil, Martha. "New 'Big Brother' Software Will Monitor Workers' Facial Expressions." *ABA Journal,* January 16, 2008.

Nelson, Dean. "Former Camel Jockeys Compensated by UAE." *Telegraph,* May 5, 2009.

Nelson, Margaret K. "Whither Fictive Kin? Or, What's in a Name?" *Journal of Family Issues,* 2013.

Neugarten, Bernice L. "Middle Age and Aging." In *Growing Old in America,* Beth B. Hess, ed. New Brunswick, N.J.: Transaction, 1976:180–197.

Newman, Benjamin J., Todd K. Hartman, and Charles S. Taber. "Foreign Language Exposure, Cultural Threat, and Opposition to Immigration." *Political Psychology, 33,* 5, 2012:635–657.

Newport, Frank, Dan Witters, and Sangeeta Agrawal. "Religious Americans Enjoy Higher Wellbeing." Princeton, N.J.: Gallup Poll, February 16, 2012.

Newport, Frank, Sangeeta Agrawal, and Dan Witters. "Very Religious Americans Report Less Depression, Worry." Gallup Poll, December 1, 2010.

Newport, Frank. "In U.S., Increasing Numbers Have No Religious Identity." Gallup Poll, May 21, 2010.

Newport, Frank. "U.S. Catholic Population Less Religious, Shrinking." Princeton, N.J.: Gallup Poll, February 25, 2013.

Nichol, Jim. "Russian Political, Economic, and Security Issues and U.S. Interests." Washington, D.C.: Congressional Research Service, November 4, 2011.

Nicholson, Ian. "'Torture at Yale': Experimental Subjects, Laboratory Torment and the 'Rehabilitation' of Milgram's 'Obedience to Authority.'" *Theory Psychology, 21,* 737, October 26, 2011.

Niebuhr, H. Richard. *The Social Sources of Denominationalism.* New York: Holt, 1929.

Nieuwenhuis-Mark, Ruth Elaine. "Healthy Aging as Disease?" *Frontiers in Aging Neuroscience, 3,* 3, February 22, 2011.

Noah, Timothy. "White House Forms Panel to Investigate Cold War Radiation Tests on Humans." *Wall Street Journal,* January 4, 1994:A12.

Nordberg, Jenny. "In Afghanistan, Boys Are Prized and Girls Live the Part." *New York Times,* September 20, 2010.

Nordland, Rod. "That Joke Is a Killer." *Newsweek,* May 19, 2003:10.

Norton, Michael I., and Samuel R. Sommers. "Whites See Racism as a Zero-Sum Game That They Are Now Losing." *Perspectives on Psychological Sciences, 6,* 2011:215–218.

Nuland, Sherwin B. "The Debate over Dying." *USA Weekend,* February 3–5, 1995:4–6.

O'Brien, John E. "Violence in Divorce-Prone Families." In *Violence in the Family,* Suzanne K. Steinmetz and Murray A. Straus, eds. New York: Dodd, Mead, 1975:65–75.

O'Brien, Timothy L. "Fed Assesses Citigroup Unit $70 Million in Loan Abuse." *New York Times,* May 28, 2004.

O'Hanlon, Michael E., and Ian Livingston. "Iraq Index: Tracking Variables of Reconstruction & Security in Post-Saddam Iraq." Washington, D.C.: Brookings Institute, May 25, 2010.

O'Hare, William P. "A New Look at Poverty in America." *Population Bulletin, 51,* 2, September 1996a:1–47.

O'Hare, William P. "U.S. Poverty Myths Explored: Many Poor Work Year-Round, Few Still Poor after Five Years." *Population Today: News, Numbers, and Analysis, 24,* 10, October 1996b:1–2.

Ocobock, Abigail. "The Power and Limits of Marriage: Married Gay Men's Family Relationships." *Journal of Marriage and Family, 75,* February 2013:191–205.

OECD (Organisation for Economic Co-operation and Development). "Average Annual Hours Actually Worked per Worker." Paris: Organisation for Economic Co-operation and Development, 2013.

Ogburn, William F. *On Culture and Social Change: Selected Papers,* Otis Dudley Duncan, ed. Chicago: University of Chicago Press, 1964.

Ogburn, William F. *Recent Social Trends in the United States.* New York: McGraw-Hill, 1933.

Ogburn, William F. *Social Change with Respect to Culture and Human Nature.* New York: W. B. Huebsch, 1922. (Other editions by Viking in 1927, 1938, and 1950.)

Ogburn, William F. "The Hypothesis of Cultural Lag." In *Theories of Society: Foundations of Modern Sociological Theory,* Vol. 2, Talcott Parsons, Edward Shils, Kaspar D. Naegele, and Jesse R. Pitts, eds. New York: Free Press, 1961:1270–1273.

Okada, Akito. "Education Reform and Equal Opportunity in Japan." *Journal of International and Comparative Education, 1,* 2, 2012:116–129.

Olmsted, Michael S., and A. Paul Hare. *The Small Group,* 2nd ed. New York: Random House, 1978.

Olneck, Michael R., and David B. Bills. "What Makes Sammy Run? An Empirical Assessment of the Bowles-Gintis Correspondence Theory." *American Journal of Education, 89,* 1980:27–61.

"On History and Heritage: John K. Castle." *Penn Law Journal,* Fall 1999.

Onishi, Norimitsu. "Lucrative Gambling Pits Tribe against Tribe." *New York Times,* August 4, 2012.

Orme, Nicholas. *Medieval Children.* New Haven: Yale University Press, 2002.

Orwell, George. *1984.* New York: Harcourt Brace, 1949.

Osborne, Cynthia, Wendy D. Manning, and Pamela J. Smock. "Married and Cohabiting Parents' Relationship Stability: A Focus on Race and Ethnicity." *Marriage and Family, 69,* December 2007:1345–1366.

Osborne, Lawrence. "Got Silk." *New York Times Magazine,* June 15, 2002.

Osterman, Paul. "Community Colleges: Promise, Performance, and Policy." MIT Sloan School, June 2010.

Ouchi, William. "Decision-Making in Japanese Organizations." In *Down to Earth Sociology: Introductory Readings,* 7th ed., James M. Henslin, ed. New York: Free Press, 1993:503–507.

Page, Jeremy. "China's New Drones Raise Eyebrows." *Wall Street Journal,* November 18, 2010.

Pager, Devah. "The Mark of a Criminal Record." *American Journal of Sociology, 108,* 5, March 2003:937–975.

Pager, Devah, Bruce Western, and Bart Bonikowski. "Discrimination in a Low-Wage Labor Market: A Field Experiment." *American Sociological Review, 74,* 5, October 2009:777–799.

Palen, J. John. *The Urban World,* 9th ed. Boulder: Paradigm Publishers, 2012.

Park, Alice. "Why Circumcision Lowers Risk of HIV." *Time,* April 17, 2013.

Parfit, Michael, "Earth First!ers Wield a Mean Monkey Wrench." *Smithsonian, 21,* 1, April 1990:184–204.

Park, Robert Ezra, and Ernest W. Burgess. *Human Ecology.* Chicago: University of Chicago Press, 1921.

Park, Robert. *Masse und Publikum.* Berlin: Lack and Grunau, 1904.

Parker, Chris. "Medicare Fraud Is Sweetest Crime in South Florida." Broward-Palm Beach New Times, May 2, 2013.

Parker, Kim, and Eileen Patten. "The Sandwich Generation: Rising Financial Burdens for Middle-Aged Americans." Washington D.C.: PEW Research Center, January 30, 2013.

Parker, Laura. "It's Hard to Believe in the New Lara Croft." *Gamespot,* December 5, 2012.

Parsons, Talcott. "An Analytic Approach to the Theory of Social Stratification." *American Journal of Sociology, 45,* 1940:841–862.

Partington, Donald H. "The Incidence of the Death Penalty for Rape in Virginia." *Washington and Lee Law Review, 22,* 1965:43–75.

"Past Imperfect: Geronimo's Appeal to Theodore Roosevelt." *Smithsonian,* November 9, 2012.

Pearlin, L. I., and Melvin L. Kohn. "Social Class, Occupation, and Parental Values: A Cross-National Study." *American Sociological Review, 31,* 1966:466–479.

Peck, Grant. "Australian Convicted of Insulting Thai Monarchy." Associated Press, January 19, 2009.

Pedersen, R. P. "How We Got Here: It's Not How You Think." *Community College Week, 13,* 15, March 15, 2001:4–5.

Pennar, Karen, and Christopher Farrell. "Notes from the Underground Economy." *Business Week,* February 15, 1993:98–101.

Pérez-Peña, Richard. "To Enroll More Minority Students, Colleges Work Around the Courts." *New York Times,* April 1, 2012.

Perrow, Charles. "A Society of Organizations." *Theory and Society, 20,* 6, December 1991:725–762.

Perry, Nick. "Kiribati Global Warming Fears: Entire Nation May Move to Fiji." *Huffington Post,* March 9, 2012.

Perry, William J., Ashton B. Carter, and Michael M. May. "After the Bomb." *New York Times,* June 12, 2007.

Pescosolido, Bernice. "Theories and the Rise and Fall of the Medical Profession." In *Medical Sociology on the Move,* William C. Cockerham, ed. New York: Springer, 2013:173–194.

Peter, Laurence J., and Raymond Hull. *The Peter Principle: Why Things Always Go Wrong.* New York: HarperBusiness, 2011.

Petersen, Andrea. "Checking In? Hidden Ways Hotels Court Guests Faster." *Wall Street Journal,* April 11, 2012.

Petty, Gregory C., Doo Hun Lim, Seung Won Yoon, and Johnny Fontan. "The Effect of Self-Directed Work Teams on Work Ethic." *Performance Improvement Quarterly, 21,* 2, 2008:49–63.

Pflanz, Mike. "Rwanda's Women Lead the Miraculous Recovery." *Telegraph,* October 17, 2008.

Phillips, Barbara D. "America's Forgotten Plague." *Wall Street Journal,* February 9, 1998:A15.

Phillips, Erica E. "'Three-Strikes' Prisoners Drawing a Walk." *Wall Street Journal,* April 1, 2013.

Phillips, Linda, Guifang Guo, and Haesook Kim. "Elder Mistreatment in U.S. Residential Care Facilities: The Scope of the Problem." *Journal of Elder Abuse and Neglect, 25,* 1, 2013:19–39.

Phillips, Mary. "Midwives versus Medics: A 17th-Century Professional Turf War." *Management and Organizational History, 2,* 1, 2007:27–44.

Phillips, Peter, and Kimberly Soeiro. "The Global 1%: Exposing the Transnational Ruling Class." *Project Censored,* August 22, 2012.

Piaget, Jean. *The Construction of Reality in the Child.* New York: Basic Books, 1954.

Piaget, Jean. *The Psychology of Intelligence.* London: Routledge & Kegan Paul, 1950.

"Piden en Holanda Aplicar la Eutanasia Infantil." *BBC Mundo.*

Pillemer, Karl, and J. Jill Suitor. "Violence and Violent Feelings: What Causes Them among Family Caregivers?" *Journal of Gerontology, 47,* 4, 1992:165–172.

Pines, Maya. "The Civilizing of Genie." *Psychology Today, 15,* September 1981:28–34.

Piotrow, Phylis Tilson. *World Population Crisis: The United States' Response.* New York: Praeger, 1973. *Population Today 4,* 5, September 1998.

Piven, Frances Fox. "Can Power from Below Change the World?" *American Sociological Review, 73,* 1, February 2008:1–14.

Polgreen, Lydia. "Scaling Caste Walls with Capitalism's Ladders in India." *New York Times,* December 21, 2011.

Pollack, Andrew. "Looking for a Superbug Killer." *New York Times,* November 5, 2010.

Ponzo, Michela, and Vincenzo Scoppa. "The Good, the Bad, and the Ugly: Teaching Evaluations, Beauty, and Abilities." Working Paper, Arcavata di Rende, Italy: Università della Calabria, March 2012.

Poole, Steven. "Programmer Bob Who Outsourced His Job Was a Model Modern Employee." *Guardian,* January 17, 2013.

Pope, Liston. *Millhands and Preachers: A Study of Gastonia.* New Haven, Conn.: Yale University Press, 1942.

Popescu, Ioana, Mary S. Vaughan-Sarrazin, and Gary E. Rosenthal. "Differences in Mortality and Use of Revascularization in Black and White Patients With Acute MI Admitted to Hospitals With and Without Revascularization Services." *Journal of the American Medical Association, 297,* 22, June 13, 2007:2489–2495.

Portes, Alejandro, and Rubén G. Rumbaut. *Immigrant America.* Berkeley: University of California Press, 1990.

Post, Charles. "Agrarian Class Structure and Economic Development in Colonial British North America: The Place of the American Revolution in the Origins of US Capitalism." *Journal of Agrarian Change, 9,* 4, October 2009:453–483.

Powell, Lynda H., Leila Shahabi, and Carl E. Thoresen. "Religion and Spirituality: Linkages to Physical Health." *American Psychologist, 58,* 1, January 2003:36–52.

Pratt, Timothy. "Nevada's Gambling Revenue Rises After Two Year Slump." Reuters, February 10, 2011.

Presser, Stanley, and Linda Stinson. "Data Collection Mode and Social Desirability Bias in Self-Reported Religious Attendance." *American Sociological Review, 63,* February 1998:137–145.

Preston, Julia. "Homeland Security Cancels 'Virtual Fence' after Billion Is Spent." *New York Times,* January 14, 2011.

Preston, Julia, and John H. Cushman, Jr. "Obama to Permit Young Migrants to Remain in U.S." *New York Times,* June 16, 2012.

Proctor, Robert N. *The Nazi War on Cancer.* Princeton, N.J.: Princeton University Press, 1999.

Qian, Zhenchao, and Daniel T. Lichter. "Social Boundaries and Marital Assimilation: Interpreting Trends in Racial and Ethnic Intermarriage." *American Sociological Review, 72,* February 2007:68–94.

Quadagno, Jill. *Aging and the Life Course: An Introduction to Gerontology,* 4th ed. New York: McGraw-Hill, 2007.

Quammen, David. *Spillover: Animal Infections and the Next Human Pandemic.* New York: Norton, 2012.

Quinet, Kenna. "The Problem of Missing Persons." *Guide 66,* Washington, D.C.: Center for Problem-Oriented Policing, 2012.

Rabin, Roni Caryn. "Questions about Robotic Hysterectomy." *New York Times,* February 25, 2013.

Radelet, Michael L., and Glenn L. Pierce. "Race and Death Sentencing in North Carolina, 1980–2007." *North Carolina Law Review, 89,* 2011:2119–2159.

Raice, Shayndi, and Nick Timiraos. "U.S. Sues Wells Fargo for Faulty Mortgages." *Wall Street Journal,* October 10, 2012.

Ramakrishnan, Kavita B. "Inconsistent Legal Treatment of Unwanted Sexual Advances." *Berkeley Journal of Gender, Law, and Justice, 26,* 2, 2011:291–355.

Rampell, Catherine. "In Law Schools, Grades Go Up, Just Like That." *New York Times,* June 21, 2010.

Ramstad, Evan. "Big Brother, Now at the Mall." *Wall Street Journal,* October 9, 2012.

Rapoport, Anatoli. "Patriotic Education in Russia: Stylistic Move or a Sign of Substantive Counter-Reform." *Educational Forum, 73,* 2009:141–152.

Rassbach, Eric. "Why I Defend Goat Sacrifice." *Wall Street Journal,* August 7, 2009.

Ratcliffe, Caroline, and Signe-Mary McKernan. "Childhood Poverty Persistence: Facts and Consequences." The Urban Institute, Brief 14, June 2010:1–10.

Ray, Brian. "Academic Achievement and Demographic Traits of Homeschool Students: A Nationwide Study." *Academic Leadership, 8,* 1, Winter 2010.

Ray, J. J. "Authoritarianism Is a Dodo: Comment on Scheepers, Felling and Peters." *European Sociological Review, 7,* 1, May 1991:73–75.

Read, Madlen. "Citi Pays $18M for Questioned Credit Card Practice." Associated Press, August 26, 2008.

Reat, Noble Ross. *Buddhism: A History.* Berkeley, Calif: Asian Humanities Press, 1994.

Reckless, Walter C. *The Crime Problem,* 5th ed. New York: Appleton, 1973.

Reed, Don Collins. "A Model of Moral Stages." *Journal of Moral Education, 37,* 3, September 2008:357–376.

Reed, Susan, and Lorenzo Benet. "Ecowarrior Dave Foreman Will Do Whatever It Takes in His Fight to Save Mother Earth." *People Weekly, 33,* 15, April 16, 1990:113–116.

Regalado, Antonio. "Seoul Team Creates Custom Stem Cells from Cloned Embryos." *Wall Street Journal,* May 20, 2005.

Reiman, Jeffrey, and Paul Leighton. *The Rich Get Richer and the Poor Get Prison: Ideology, Class, and Criminal Justice,* 9th ed. Boston: Allyn and Bacon, 2010.

Reiser, Christa. *Reflections on Anger: Women and Men in a Changing Society.* Westport, Conn.: Praeger Publishers, 1999.

Reskin, Barbara F. *The Realities of Affirmative Action in Employment.* Washington, D.C.: American Sociological Association, 1998.

Resnik, David B. "Financial Interests and Research Bias." *Perspectives on Science, 8,* 3, Fall 2000:255–283.

Reuters. "Fake Tiger Woods Gets 200-Years-to-Life in Prison." April 28, 2001.

Rhoads, Christopher. "Web Site to Holy Site: Israeli Firm Broadcasts Prayers for a Fee." *Wall Street Journal,* January 25, 2007.

Rhone, Nedra. "Widespread Violations Found at Care Homes." *Los Angeles Times,* April 18, 2001.

Richardson, Stacey, and Marita P. McCabe. "Parental Divorce during Adolescence and Adjustment in Early Adulthood." *Adolescence, 36,* Fall 2001:467–489.

Richman, Joe. "From the Belgian Congo to the Bronx Zoo." *National Public Radio,* September 8, 2006.

Ricks, Thomas E. "'New' Marines Illustrate Growing Gap between Military and Society." *Wall Street Journal,* July 27, 1995:A1, A4.

Rieker, Patricia P., Chloe E. Bird, Susan Bell, Jenny Ruducha, Rima E. Rudd, and S. M. Miller. "Violence and Women's Health: Toward a Society and Health Perspective." Unpublished paper, 1997.

Riessman, Catherine Kohler. "Women and Medicalization: A New Perspective." In *Dominant Issues in Medical Sociology,* 3rd ed., Howard D. Schwartz, ed. New York: McGraw-Hill, 1994:190–211.

Riley, Nancy E. "China's Population: New Trends and Challenges." *Population Bulletin, 59,* 2, June 2004:3–36.

Riley, Naomi Schaefer. "Not Your Grandfather's Southern Baptist." *Wall Street Journal,* March 2, 2012.

Riley, Naomi Schaefer. "The Real Path to Racial Harmony." *Wall Street Journal,* August 14, 2009.

Rios, Victor M. *Punished: Policing the Lives of Black and Latino Boys.* New York: New York University Press, 2011.

Rist, Ray. "Student Social Class and Teacher Expectations: The Self-Fulfilling Prophecy in Ghetto Education." *Harvard Educational Review,* reprinted in *Opportunity Gap: Achievement and Inequality in Education,* Carol DeShano, James Philip Huguley, Zenub Kakli, Radhika Rao, and Ronald F. Ferguson, eds. Cambridge, MA.: Harvard Education Publishing Group, 2007:187–225.

Ritzer, George. *The McDonaldization of Society,* 7th ed. Thousand Oaks, Calif.: Sage, 2012.

Ritzer, George. "The McDonaldization of Society." In *Down to Earth Sociology: Introductory Readings,* 11th ed., James M. Henslin, ed. New York: Free Press, 2001:459–471.

Ritzer, George. *The McDonaldization of Society: An Investigation into the Changing Character of Contemporary Life.* Thousand Oaks, Calif.: Pine Forge Press, 1993.

Ritzer, George. *The McDonaldization Thesis: Explorations and Extensions.* Thousand Oaks, Calif.: Sage Publications, 1998.

Rivera, Lauren A. "Hiring as Cultural Matching: The Case of Elite Professional Service Firms." *American Sociological Review, 77,* 6, 2012:999–1022.

Rivlin, Gary. "Beyond the Reservation." *New York Times,* September 22, 2007.

Robbins, John. *Healthy at 100.* New York: Random House, 2006.

Roberts, Andrew. "Bionic Mannequins Spy on Shoppers to Boost Luxury Sales." *Bloomberg News,* November 21, 2012.

Robertson, Christopher, Susannah Rose, and Aaron S. Kesselheim. "Effect of Financial Relationships on the Behaviors of Health Care Professionals: A Review of the Evidence." *Journal of Law, Medicine, and Ethics, 452,* 2012:452–466.

Robertson, Ian. *Sociology,* 3rd ed. New York: Worth, 1987.

Robinson, Gail, and Barbara Mullins Nelson. "Pursuing Upward Mobility: African American Professional Women Reflect on Their Journey." *Journal of Black Studies, 40,* 6, 2010:1168–1188.

Robinson, William I. "Global Capitalism and the Emergence of Transnational Elites." *Critical Sociology, 38,* 3, 2012:349–363.

Rodríguez, Victor M. "Los Angeles, U.S.A. 1992: 'A House Divided against Itself …' ?" *SSSP Newsletter,* Spring 1994:5–12.

Rodriguez, Richard. *Hunger of Memory: The Education of Richard Rodriguez.* Boston: Godine, 1982.

Rodriguez, Richard. "Mixed Blood." *Harper's Magazine, 283,* November 1991:47–56.

Rodriguez, Richard. "Searching for Roots in a Changing Society." In *Down to Earth Sociology: Introductory Readings,* 8th ed., James M. Henslin, ed. New York: Free Press, 1995:486–491.

Rodriguez, Richard. "The Education of Richard Rodriguez." *Saturday Review,* February 8, 1975:147–149.

Rodriguez, Richard. "The Late Victorians: San Francisco, AIDS, and the Homosexual Stereotype." *Harper's Magazine,* October 1990:57–66.

Rogers, Simon, and Lisa Evans. "World Carbon Dioxide Emissions Data by Country: China Speeds Ahead of the Rest." *Guardian,* January 31, 2011.

Rohter, Larry. "For Chilean Coup, Kissinger Is Numbered among the Hunted." *New York Times,* March 28, 2002.

Rohter, Larry. "Tracking the Sale of a Kidney on a Path of Poverty and Hope." *New York Times,* May 23, 2004.

Roper Center. "U.S. Elections: How Groups Voted in 2012." Storrs, Conn.: Roper Center, 2013.

Ropiequet, John L, Christopher S. Naveja, and L. Jean Noonan. "Fair Lending Developments: Testing the Limits of Statistical Evidence." *Business Lawyer, 67,* February 2012:575–584.

Rosaldo, Michelle Zimbalist. "Women, Culture and Society: A Theoretical Overview." In *Women, Culture, and Society,* Michelle Zimbalist Rosaldo and Louise Lamphere, eds. Stanford: Stanford University Press, 1974.

Rose, Frederick. "Los Angeles Tallies Losses; Curfew Is Lifted." *Wall Street Journal,* May 5, 1992:A3, A18.

Rosenberg, Charles E. *The Care of Strangers: The Rise of America's Hospital System.* New York: Basic Books, 1987.

Rosenbloom, Stephanie. "Love, Lies and What They Learned." *New York Times,* November 12, 2011.

Rosenfeld, Michael J., and Reuben J. Thomas. "Searching for a Mate: The Rise of the Internet as a Social Intermediary." *American Sociological Review, 77,* 2012:523–547.

Rosenthal, Robert. "Covert Communication in Classrooms, Clinics, and Courtrooms." *Eye on Psi Chi, 3,* 1, Fall 1998:18–22.

Rosenthal, Robert, and Lenore Jacobson. *Pygmalion in the Classroom: Teacher Expectation and Pupils' Intellectual Development.* New York: Holt, Rinehart, and Winston, 1968.

Rosin, Hanna. "The End of Men." *Atlantic,* July/August 2010.

Rossi, Alice S. "A Biosocial Perspective on Parenting." *Daedalus, 106,* 1977:1–31.

Rossi, Alice S. "Gender and Parenthood." *American Sociological Review, 49,* 1984:1–18.

Rossi, Peter H. *Down and Out in America: The Origins of Homelessness.* Chicago: University of Chicago Press, 1989.

Rossi, Peter H. "Going Along or Getting It Right?" *Journal of Applied Sociology, 8,* 1991:77–81.

Rossi, Peter H. "Half Truths with Real Consequences: Journalism, Research, and Public Policy." *Contemporary Sociology,* 1999:1–5.

Rossiter, Caleb. "How Washington, D.C., Schools Cheat Their Students Twice." *Wall Street Journal,* December 1, 2012.

Roth, Louise Marie. "Selling Women Short: A Research Note on Gender Differences in Compensation on Wall Street." *Social Forces, 82,* 2, December 2003:783–802.

Rothkopf, David. *Superclass: The Global Power Elite and the World They Are Making.* New York: Farrar, Straus and Giroux, 2008.

Rothman, Barbara Katz. "Midwives in Transition: The Structure of a Clinical Revolution." In *Dominant Issues in Medical Sociology,* 3rd ed., Howard D. Schwartz, ed. New York: McGraw-Hill, 1994:104–112.

Rothschild, Joyce, and J. Allen Whitt. *The Cooperative Workplace: Potentials and Dilemmas of Organizational Democracy and Participation.* Cambridge, England: Cambridge University Press, 1986.

Rowthorn, Robert, Ricardo Andres Guzman, and Carolos Rodriguez-Sickert. "The Economies of Social Stratification in Premodern Societies." MPRA Paper 35567, Munich, Germany: Munich Personal RePEc Archive, November 28, 2011.

Roy, Avik. "Congressmen Rejoice: Govt. to subsidize Their Health Insurance through Obamacare's Exchanges." Forbes, August 2, 2013.

Rubin, Zick. "The Love Research." In *Marriage and Family in a Changing Society,* 2nd ed., James M. Henslin, ed. New York: Free Press, 1985.

Rudner, Lawrence M. "The Scholastic Achievement of Home School Students." *ERIC/AE Digest,* September 1, 1999.

Ruggles, Patricia. "Short and Long Term Poverty in the United States: Measuring the American 'Underclass.'" Washington, D.C.: Urban Institute, June 1989.

Russell, Diana E. H. "Preliminary Report on Some Findings Relating to the Trauma and Long-Term Effects of Intrafamily Childhood Sexual Abuse." Unpublished paper, no date.

Russell, Diana E. H. *Rape in Marriage.* Bloomington: Indiana University Press, 1990.

Russell, Nestar John Charles. "Milgram's Obedience to Authority Experiments: Origins and Early Evolution." *British Journal of Social Psychology,* 2010:1–23.

"Russians Given Day Off Work to Make Babies." *Guardian,* September 12, 2007.

Sánchez-Jankowski, Martín. "Gangs and Social Change." *Theoretical Criminology, 7,* 2, 2003:191–216.

Sacirbey, Omar. "Religion is Key in Combating Female Genital Mutilation According to Activists." *Religion News Service,* October 28, 2012.

Sageman, Marc. "Explaining Terror Networks in the 21st Century." *Footnotes,* May–June 2008a:7.

Sageman, Marc. *Leaderless Jihad: Terror Networks in the Twenty-First Century.* Philadelphia: University of Pennsylvania Press, 2008b.

Sahlins, Marshall D. *Stone Age Economics.* Chicago: Aldine, 1972.

Sahlins, Marshall D., and Elman R. Service. *Evolution and Culture.* Ann Arbor: University of Michigan Press, 1960.

Saidak, Tom. "GMO Tobacco Plants Produce Antibodies to Treat Rabies." *BioBased Digest,* February 5, 2013.

Salomon, Gisela, "In Miami, Spanish Is Becoming the Primary Language." Associated Press, May 29, 2008.

Salyer, Kirsten. "In Russia, Valentine Day Is for Making Babies." *Bloomberg News,* February 4, 2013.

Samor, Geraldo, Cecilie Rohwedder, and Ann Zimmerman. "Innocents Abroad?" *Wall Street Journal,* May 5, 2006.

Samuelson, Paul Anthony, and William D. Nordhaus. *Economics,* 18th ed. New York: McGraw Hill, 2005.

Sanger, David E. "Obama Order Sped Up Waves of Cyberattacks against Iran." *New York Times,* June 1, 2012.

Sanger, David E., and Thom Shanker. "Broad Powers Seen for Obama in Cyberstrikes." *New York Times,* February 3, 2013.

Santos, Fernanda. "Are New Yorkers Satisfied? That Depends." *New York Times,* March 7, 2009.

Sapir, Edward. *Selected Writings of Edward Sapir in Language, Culture, and Personality,* David G. Mandelbaum, ed. Berkeley: University of California Press, 1949.

Saranow, Jennifer. "The Snoop Next Door." *Wall Street Journal,* January 12, 2007.

Sareen, Jitender, Tracie O. Afifi, Katherine A. McMillan, and G. J. Asmundson. "Relationship between Household Income and Mental Disorders." *Archives of General Psychiatry, 68,* 4, 2011:419–427.

"Saudis Sign Huge Airplane Order." Associated Press, October 27, 1995.

Saulny, Susan. "Black? White? Asian? More Young Americans Choose All of the Above." *New York Times,* January 29, 2011.

Savage, Charlie. "Countrywide Will Settle a Bias Suit." *New York Times,* December 21, 2011.

Savage, Charlie. "U.S. Law May Allow Killings, Holder Says." *New York Times,* March 5, 2012.

Scarf, Damian, Kana Imuta, Michael Colombo, and Harlene Hayne. "Social Evaluation or Simple Association? Simple Associations May Explain Moral Reasoning in Infants." *Plos One, 7,* 8, e42698, 2012.

Schaefer, Richard T. *Racial and Ethnic Groups,* 9th ed. Upper Saddle River, N.J.: Prentice Hall, 2004.

Schaefer, Richard T. *Racial and Ethnic Groups,* 13th ed. Boston: Pearson, 2012.

Schaefer, Richard T. *Sociology,* 3rd ed. New York: McGraw-Hill, 1989.

Schaefer, Richard T., and William W. Zellner. *Extraordinary Groups: An Examination of Unconventional Life-Styles,* 9th ed. New York: Worth, 2011.

Scheff, Thomas J. *Being Mentally Ill: A Sociological Theory,* 3rd ed. New York: Aldine de Gruyter, 1999.

Schemo, Diana Jean. "Education Dept. Says States Have Lax Standard for Teachers." *New York Times,* June 13, 2002.

Schmeer, Kammi K. "The Child Health Disadvantage of Parental Cohabitation." *Journal of Marriage and Family, 73,* February 2011:181–193.

Schmiddle Nicholas. "Getting Bin Laden." *The New Yorker,* August 8, 2011.

Schmidle, Nicholas. "Bring Up the Bodies." *New Yorker,* May 6, 2013.

Schneider, Daniel. "Gender, Deviance and Household Work: The Role of Occupation." *American Journal of Sociology, 117,* 4, January 2012:1029–1072.

Schoofs, Mark. "Scientists See Breakthrough in the Global AIDS Battle." *Wall Street Journal,* May 12, 2011.

Schottland, Charles I. *The Social Security Plan in the U.S.* New York: Appleton, 1963.

"Schwab Study Finds Four Generations of American Adults Fundamentally Rethinking Planning for Retirement." *Reuters,* July 15, 2008.

Scolforo, Mark. "Amish Population Nearly Doubles in 16 Years." *Chicago Tribune,* August 20, 2008.

Scott, Monster Cody. *Monster: The Autobiography of an L. A. Gang Member.* New York: Penguin Books, 1994.

Scott, Susie. "The Medicalization of Shyness: From Social Misfits to Social Fitness." *Sociology of Health and Illness, 28,* 2, 2006:133–153.

Scully, Diana. "Negotiating to Do Surgery." In *Dominant Issues in Medical Sociology,* 3rd ed., Howard D. Schwartz, ed. New York: McGraw-Hill, 1994:146–152.

Scully, Diana. *Understanding Sexual Violence: A Study of Convicted Rapists.* Boston: Unwin Hyman, 1990.

Scully, Diana, and Joseph Marolla. "Convicted Rapists' Vocabulary of Motive: Excuses and Justifications." *Social Problems, 31,* 5, June 1984:530–544.

Scully, Diana, and Joseph Marolla. "'Riding the Bull at Gilley's': Convicted Rapists Describe the Rewards of Rape." In *Down to Earth Sociology: Introductory Readings,* 15th ed., James M. Henslin, ed. New York: Free Press, 2014.

"Second Life Grid Survey, Region Database." January 1, 2012." http://gridsurvey.com/

Segal, Nancy L., and Scott L. Hershberger. "Virtual Twins and Intelligence." *Personality and Individual Differences, 39,* 6, 2005:1061–1073.

Seetharaman, Deepa. "Ford Quarterly Profit Beats, But Growth Push Adds Costs." *Reuters,* April 24, 2013.

Seiden, Samuel C., and Paul Barach. "Wrong-Side/Wrong-Site, Wrong Procedure, and Wrong-Patient Adverse Events." *Archives of Surgery, 141,* 2006:931–939.

Sellers, Patricia. "New Yahoo CEO Mayer Is Pregnant." *Fortune,* July 16, 2012.

Semple, Kirk. "Idea of Afghan Women's Rights Starts Taking Hold." *New York Times,* March 2, 2009.

Senders, John W., and Regine Kanzki. "The Egocentric Surgeon or the Roots of Wrong Side Surgery." *Quality and* Safety *in Health Care 17,* 2008:396–400.

Sengupta, Somini. "In the Ancient Streets of Najaf, Pledges of Martyrdom for Cleric." *New York Times,* July 10, 2004.

Senior, Jennifer. "All Joy and No Fun." *New York,* July 4, 2010.

Sennett, Richard, and Jonathan Cobb. "Some Hidden Injuries of Class." In *Down to Earth Sociology: Introductory Readings,* 5th ed., James M. Henslin ed. New York: Free Press, 1988:278–288. Excerpts from Richard Sennett and Jonathan Cobb. *The Hidden Injuries of Class.* New York: Knopf, 1972.

Séralini, Gilles-Eric, Emile Clair, Robin Mesnage, et al. "Long Term Toxicity of a Roundup Herbicide and a Roundup-Tolerant Genetically Modified Maize." *Food and Chemical Toxicology, 50,* 11, November 2012:4221–4231.

Shane, Scott. "Report Outlines Medical Workers' Role in Torture." *New York Times,* April 6, 2009.

Shane, Scott, and Charlie Savage. "Bin Laden Raid Revives Debate on Value of Torture." *New York Times,* May 3, 2011.

Shanker, Thom. "U.S. Troops Were Subjected to a Wider Toxic Testing." *New York Times,* October 8, 2002.

Shapiro, Joseph P. "Euthanasia's Home." *U.S. News and World Report, 122,* 1, January 13, 1997:24–27.

Shapiro, Robert J., and Jiwon Vellucci. "The Impact of Immigration and Immigration Reform on the Wages of American Workers." Washington, D.C.: New Policy Institute, May 2010.

Sharma, Amol, Biman Mukherji, and Rupa Subramanya. "On India's Streets, Women Run Gauntlet of Harassment." *Wall Street Journal,* February 28, 2013.

Sharp, Lauriston. "Steel Axes for Stone-Age Australians." In *Down to Earth Sociology: Introductory Readings,* 8th ed., James M. Henslin, ed. New York: Free Press, 1995:453–462.

Shaw, Emily J., Jennifer L. Kobrin, Brian F. Patterson, and Krista D. Mattern. "The Validity of the SAT for Predicting Cumulative Grade Point Average by College Major." New York: College Board, 2012.

Shefner, Jon. "The New Left in Latin America and the Opportunity for a New U.S. Foreign Policy." In *Agenda for Social Justice: Solutions 2008,* Robert Perrucci, Kathleen Ferraro, JoAnn Miller, and Glenn Muschert, eds. Knoxville, Tenn.: Society for the Study of Social Problems, 2008:16–22.

Shellenbarger, Sue. "What's a Reasonable Break?" *Wall Street Journal,* June 13, 2011.

Sheridan, Mary Beth. "Salinas Warns Mexico Against Drug Probe." *Los Angeles Times,* September 22, 1998.

Sherif, Muzafer, and Carolyn Sherif. *Groups in Harmony and Tension.* New York: Harper & Row, 1953.

Sherman, Jennifer, and Elizabeth Harris. "Social Class and Parenting: Classic Debates and New Understandings." *Sociology Compass, 6,* 1, 2012:60–71.

Shor, Eran, David J. Roelfs, Misty Currell, L. Clemow, M. M. Burg, and J. E. Schwartz. "Widowhood and Mortality: A Meta-Analysis and Meta-Regression." *Demography, 49,* 2012:575–606.

Short, Kathleen. "The Research Supplemental Poverty Measure: 2011." *Current Population Reports P60-244,* Washington, D.C.: U.S. Census Bureau, November 2012.

Siebens, Julie, and Tiffany Julian. "Native North American Languages Spoken at Home in the United States and Puerto Rico: 2006–2010." Washington, D.C.: U.S. Census Bureau, December 2011.

Siegler, Ilene C., Beverly H. Brummett, Peter Martin, and M. J. Helms. "Consistency and Timing of Marital Transitions and Survival During Midlife: The Role of Personality and Health Risk Behaviors." *Annals of Behavioral Medicine, 45,* 3, 2013:338–347.

Sifferlin, Alexandra. "Can New Circumcision Devices Help Fight AIDS in Africa?" *Time,* February 1, 2012.

Sills, David L. *The Volunteers.* Glencoe, Ill.: Free Press, 1957.

Sills, David L. "Voluntary Associations: Sociological Aspects." In *International Encyclopedia of the Social Sciences,* Vol 16, David L. Sills, ed. New York: Macmillan, 1968:362–379.

Silverman, Rachel Emma, and Quentin Fottrell. "The Home Office in the Spotlight." *Wall Street Journal,* February 27, 2013.

Simmel, Georg. *The Sociology of Georg Simmel,* Kurt H. Wolff, ed. and trans. Glencoe, Ill.: Free Press, 1950. Originally published between 1902 and 1917.

Simon, Stephanie. "Naked Pumpkin Run." *Wall Street Journal,* October 31, 2009.

Simonds, Wendy. "Presidential Address: The Art of Activism." *Social Problems, 60,* 1, 2013:1–26.

Simons, Andre B., and Jeannine Willie. "Runaway or Abduction. Assessment Tools for the First Responder." *FBI Law Enforcement Bulletin,* November 2000:1–7.

Simons, Marlise. "Social Change and Amazon Indians." In *Exploring Social Life: Readings to Accompany Essentials of Sociology: A Down-to-Earth Approach, Sixth Edition,* 2nd edition, James M. Henslin, ed. Boston: Allyn and Bacon, 2006:157–165.

Simpson, George Eaton, and J. Milton Yinger. *Racial and Cultural Minorities: An Analysis of Prejudice and Discrimination,* 4th ed. New York: Harper & Row, 1972.

Singer, Natasha. "Lawmakers Seek to Curb Drug Commercials." *New York Times,* July 28, 2009.

Singer, Natasha. "Shoppers Who Can't Have Secrets." *New York Times,* April 30, 2010.

Skeels, H. M. "Adult Status of Children with Contrasting Early Life Experiences: A Follow-up Study." *Monograph of the Society for Research in Child Development, 31,* 3, 1966.

Skeels, H. M., and H. B. Dye. "A Study of the Effects of Differential Stimulation on Mentally Retarded Children." *Proceedings and Addresses of the American Association on Mental Deficiency, 44,* 1939:114–136.

Skinner, Jonathan, James N. Weinstein, Scott M. Sporer, and John E. Wennberg. "Racial, Ethnic, and Geographic Disparities in Rates of Knee Arthroplasty among Medicare Patients." *New England Journal of Medicine, 349,* 14, October 2, 2003:1350–1359.

Sklair, Leslie. *Globalization: Capitalism and Its Alternatives,* 3rd ed. New York: Oxford: University Press, 2001.

Slackman, Michael. "Voices Rise in Egypt to Shield Girls from an Old Tradition." *New York Times,* September 20, 2007.

Sledzik, Paul S., and Nicholas Bellantoni. "Bioarcheological and Biocultural Evidence for the New England Vampire Folk Belief." *American Journal of Physical Anthropology, 94,* 1994.

Sloan, Allan. "A Lot of Trust, But No Funds." *Newsweek,* July 30, 2001:34.

Smart, Barry. "On the Disorder of Things: Sociology, Postmodernity and the 'End of the Social.'" *Sociology, 24,* 3, August 1990:397–416.

Smedley, Audrey, and Brian D. Smedley. "Race as Biology Is Fiction, Racism as a Social Problem Is Real: Anthropological and Historical Perspectives on the Social Construction of Race." *American Psychologist, 60,* 1, January 2005:16–26.

Smith, Beverly A. "An Incest Case in an Early 20th-Century Rural Community." *Deviant Behavior, 13,* 1992:127–153.

Smith, Christian, and Robert Faris. "Socioeconomic Inequality in the American Religious System: An Update and Assessment." *Journal for the Scientific Study of Religion, 44,* 1, 2005:95–104.

Smith, Clark. "Oral History as 'Therapy': Combatants' Account of the Vietnam War." In *Strangers at Home: Vietnam Veterans Since the War,* Charles R. Figley and Seymore Leventman, eds. New York: Praeger, 1980:9–34.

Smith, Harold. "A Colossal Cover-Up." *Christianity Today,* December 12, 1986:16–17.

Smith, Kevin R., Sarah Chan, and John Harris. "Human Germline Genetic Modification: Scientific and Bioethical Perspectives." *Archives of Medical Research, 43,* 2012a:491–513.

Smith, Ryan A. "A Test of the Glass Ceiling and Glass Escalator Hypotheses." *Annals of the American Academy of Social Sciences, 639,* January 2012:149–172.

Smith, Simon C. "The Making of a Neo-Colony? Anglo-Kuwaiti Relations in the Era of Decolonization." *Middle Eastern Studies, 37,* 1, January 2001:159–173.

Smith, Stacy L., Marc Choueiti, Ashley Prescott, Katherine Pieper, and Annenberg School for Communication & Journalism. "Gender Roles and Occupations" A Look at Character Attributes and Job-Related Aspirations in Film and Television." Marina Del Rey, Calif.: Geena Davis Institute on Gender in Media, 2012b.

Smith, Wesley J. "Dependency or Death? Oregonians Make a Chilling Choice." *Wall Street Journal*, February 25, 1999.

Smith-Bynum, Mia A., "African American Families: Research Progress and Potential in the Age of Obama." In *Handbook of Marriage and the Family*, G. W. Peterson and K. R. Bush, eds. New York: Springer, 2013:683–704.

Snow, David A., Louis A. Zurcher, Jr., and Sheldon Ekland-Olson. "Social Networks and Social Movements: A Microstructural Approach to Differential Recruitment." In *Collective Behavior and Social Movements*, Russell L. Curtis, Jr., and Benigno E. Aguirre, eds. Boston: Allyn and Bacon, 1993:323–334.

Snyder, Mark. "Self-Fulfilling Stereotypes." In *Down to Earth Sociology: Introductory Readings*, 7th ed., James M. Henslin, ed. New York: Free Press, 1993:153–160.

Solt, Frederick. "The Social Origins of Authoritarianism." *Political Research Quarterly, 65*, 4, 2012:703–713.

Sorokin, Pitirim A. *Social and Cultural Dynamics*, 4 vols. New York: American Book Company, 1937–1941.

Sosinsky, Laura Stout, and Se-Kang Kim. "A Profile Approach to Child Care Quality, Quantity, and Type of Setting: Parent Selection of Infant Child Care Arrangements." *Applied Development Science, 17*, 1, 2013:39–56.

Sosnaud, Benjamin, David Brady, and Steven M. Frenk. "Class in Name Only: Subjective Class Identity, Objective Class Position, and Vote Choice in American Presidential Elections." *Social Problems, 60*, 1, 2013:81–99.

"Sourcebook of Criminal Justice Statistics." Washington, D.C.: U.S. Government Printing Office, published annually.

South African Police Service. *Crime Statistics 2011/2012*. Pretoria, South Africa: South African Police Service, 2013.

Spector, Malcolm, and John Kitsuse. *Constructing Social Problems*. Menlo Park, Calif.: Cummings, 1977.

Spence, David B., and Robert Prentice. "The Transformation of American Energy Markets and the Problem of Market Power." *Boston College Law Review, 53*, 1, 2012:131–202.

Spengler, Oswald. *The Decline of the West*, 2 vols., Charles F. Atkinson, trans. New York: Knopf, 1926–1928. Originally published 1919–1922.

Spitzer, Steven. "Toward a Marxian Theory of Deviance." *Social Problems, 22*, June 1975:608–619.

Spivak, Gayatri Chakravorty. "Feminism 2000: One Step Beyond." *Feminist Review, 64*, Spring 2000:113.

Sprague, Jeb. "Transnational State." *Wiley-Blackwell Encyclopedia of Globalization*, George Ritzer, ed. Hoboken, N.J.: Blackwell Publishing, 2012.

Sprecher, Susan, and Rachita Chandak. "Attitudes about Arranged Marriages and Dating among Men and Women from India." *Free Inquiry in Creative Sociology, 20*, 1, May 1992:59–69.

Srole, Leo, and Anita K. Fisher. *Mental Health in the Metropolis: The Midtown Manhattan Study*. Albany, N.Y.: New York University Press, 1978.

Stack, Carol B. *All Our Kin: Strategies for Survival in a Black Community*. New York: Harper, 1974.

Stampp, Kenneth M. *The Peculiar Institution: Slavery in the Ante-Bellum South*. New York: Vintage Books, 1956.

Stansberry, Porter. "Correspondence" *S&A Digest Premium*, December 19, 2012.

Staples, Brent. "Loving v. Virginia and the Secret History of Race." *New York Times*, May 14, 2008.

Stark, Rodney. *Sociology*, 3rd ed. Belmont, Calif.: Wadsworth, 1989.

Starr, Paul. *The Social Transformation of American Medicine*. New York: Basic Books, 1982.

"State of Recidivism: The Revolving Door of America's Prisons." Washington, D.C.: Pew Center on the States, 2011.

Statham, Anne, Eleanor M. Miller, and Hans O. Mauksch. "The Integration of Work: Second-Order Analysis of Qualitative Research." In *The Worth of Women's Work: A Qualitative Synthesis*, Anne Statham, Eleanor M. Miller, and Hans O. Mauksch, eds. Albany, N.Y.: State University of New York Press, 1988:11–35.

"Statistical Abstract of the United States." Washington D.C.: U.S. Census Bureau, published annually.

Stayner, Leslie, Laura S. Welch, and Richard Lemen. "The Worldwide Pandemic of Asbestos-Related Diseases." *Annual Review of Public Health, 34*, 2013:205–216.

Steinhauer, Jennifer, and Ford Fessenden. "Medical Retreads: Doctor Punished by State but Prized at the Hospitals." *New York Times*, March 27, 2001.

Stets, Jan E. "Current Emotion Research in Sociology: Advances in the Discipline." *Emotion Review, 4*, 3, July 2012:326–334.

Stets, Jan E., and Michael J. Carter. "A Theory of the Self for the Sociology of Morality." *American Sociological Review, 77*, 1, 2012:120–140.

Stevens, Amy, and Sarah Lubman. "Deciding Moment of the Trial May Have Been Five Months Ago." *Wall Street Journal*, May 1, 1992:A6.

Stevens, Mitchell. *Creating a Class: College Admissions and the Education of Elites*. Cambridge, Mass.: Harvard University Press, 2009.

Stevens, Mitchell L. *Kingdom of Children: Culture and Controversy in the Homeschooling Movement*. Princeton: N.J.: Princeton University Press, 2001.

Stevenson, Richard W. "U.S. Debates Investing in Stock for Social Security." *New York Times*, July 27, 1998.

Stewart, Phil. "U.S. Can Intercept North Korean Missiles but May Opt Not To, Says Admiral Samuel Locklear." *Reuters*, April 9, 2013.

"Sticky Ticket: A New Jersey Mother Sues Her Son over a Lottery Jackpot She Claims Belongs to Them Both." *People Weekly*, February 9, 1998:68.

Stiles, Daniel. "The Hunters Are the Hunted." *Geographical, 75*, June 2003:28–32.

Stinnett, Nicholas. "Strong Families." In *Marriage and Family in a Changing Society*, 4th ed., James M. Henslin, ed. New York: Free Press, 1992:496–507.

Stipp, David. "Himalayan Tree Could Serve as Source of Anti-Cancer Drug Taxol, Team Says." *Wall Street Journal*, April 20, 1992:B4.

Stockard, Jean, and Miriam M. Johnson. *Sex Roles: Sex Inequality and Sex Role Development*. Englewood Cliffs, N.J.: Prentice Hall, 1980.

Stockwell, John. "The Dark Side of U.S. Foreign Policy." *Zeta Magazine*, February 1989:36–48.

Stodgill, Ralph M. *Handbook of Leadership: A Survey of Theory and Research*. New York: Free Press, 1974.

Stokes, Myron, and David Zeman. "The Shame of the City." *Newsweek*, September 4, 1995.

Stokes, Randall. "Over 60 Years of Sociology at UMass–Amherst." *ASA Footnotes*, May–June 2009:6.

Stolberg, Sheryl Gay. "Blacks Found on Short End of Heart Attack Procedure." *New York Times*, May 10, 2001.

Stouffer, Samuel A., Arthur A. Lumsdaine, Marion Harper Lumsdaine, Robin M. Williams, Jr., M. Brewster Smith, Irving L. Janis, Shirley A. Star, and Leonard S. Cottrell, Jr. *The American Soldier: Combat and Its Aftermath*, Vol. 2. New York: Wiley, 1949.

Strang, David, and Michael W. Macy. "In Search of Excellence: Fads, Success Stories, and Adaptive Emulation." *American Journal of Sociology, 197*, 1, July 2001:147–182.

Strategic Energy Policy: Challenges for the 21st Century. New York: Council on Foreign Relations, 2001.

"Strategic Maneuvers: The Revolving Door from the Pentagon to the Private Sector." Washington, D.C.: Citizens for Responsibility and Ethics in Washington, November 16, 2012.

Straus, Murray A. "Gender Symmetry and Mutuality in Perpetration of Clinical-level Partner Violence: Empirical Evidence and Implications for Prevention and Treatment." *Aggression and Violent Behavior, 16*, 2011:279–288.

Suddath, Claire, and Alex Altman. "How Does Kidney-Trafficking Work?" *Time*, July 27, 2009.

Suizzo, Marie-Anne. "The Social-Emotional and Cultural Contexts of Cognitive Development: Neo-Piagetian Perspectives." *Child Development, 71*, 4, August 2000:846–849.

Sullivan, Andrew. "What We Look Up to Now." *New York Times Magazine*, November 15, 1998.

Sullivan, Andrew. "What's So Bad about Hate?" *New York Times Magazine*, September 26, 1999.

Sullivan, Kevin. "India Embraces Online Worship." *Washington Post*, March 15, 2007.

Sulzberger, A. G. "As Survivors Dwindle, Tulsa Confronts Past." *New York Times*, June 19, 2011.

Sumner, William Graham. *Folkways: A Study in the Sociological Importance of Usages, Manners, Customs, Mores, and Morals.* New York: Ginn, 1906.

Sun, Lena H. "China Seeks Ways to Protect Elderly." *Washington Post,* October 23, 1990:A1.

Surgeon General of the United States. "The Health Consequences of Involuntary Exposure to Tobacco Smoke." Washington, D.C.: Centers for Disease Control and Prevention, 2006.

Surgeon General of the United States. "The Surgeon General's Annual Report: Health Consequences of Smoking." Washington, D.C.: Centers for Disease Control, 2005.

Surowiecki, James. *The Wisdom of Crowds.* New York: Anchor Books, 2005.

Susman, Tina. "Lottery Winner Who Drew Outrage for Getting Welfare Is Found Dead." *Los Angeles Times,* October 2, 2012.

Sutherland, Edwin H. *Criminology.* Philadelphia: Lippincott, 1924.

Sutherland, Edwin H. *Principles of Criminology,* 4th ed. Philadelphia: Lippincott, 1947.

Sutherland, Edwin H. *White Collar Crime.* New York: Dryden Press, 1949.

Suzuki, Bob H. "Asian-American Families." In *Marriage and Family in a Changing Society,* 2nd ed., James M. Henslin, ed. New York: Free Press, 1985:104–119.

Swati, Pandey. "Do You Take This Stranger?" *Los Angeles Times,* June 26, 2008.

Sweeney, Megan M. "Remarriage and the Nature of Divorce: Does It Matter Which Spouse Chose to Leave?" *Journal of Family Issues, 23,* 3, April 2002:410–440.

Swigonski, Mary E., and Salome Raheim. "Feminist Contributions to Understanding Women's Lives and the Social Environment." *Affilia: Journal of Women and Social Work, 26,* 1, 2011:10–21.

Sykes, Gresham M., and David Matza. "Techniques of Neutralization." In *Down to Earth Sociology: Introductory Readings,* 5th ed., James M. Henslin, ed. New York: Free Press, 1988:225–231. Originally published 1957.

Szasz, Thomas S. *Cruel Compassion: Psychiatric Control of Society's Unwanted.* Syracuse, N.Y.: Syracuse University Press, 1998.

Szasz, Thomas. "Fifty Years After *The Myth of Mental Illness.*" In *The Myth of Mental Illness: Foundations of a Theory of Personal Conduct, 50th Anniversary Edition.* New York: Harper Perennial, 2010.

Szasz, Thomas S. "Mental Illness Is Still a Myth." In *Deviant Behavior 96/97,* Lawrence M. Salinger, ed. Guilford, Conn.: Dushkin, 1996:200–205.

Tabenkin, H., C. B. Eaton, M. B. Roberts, D. R. Parker, J. H. McMurray, and J. Borkan. "Differences in Cardiovascular Disease Risk Factor Management in Primary Care by Sex of Physician and Patient." *Annals of Family Medicine, 8,* 1, January-February 2010:25–32.

Tadic, Maja, Wido G. M. Oerlemans, Arnold B. Bakker, and Ruut Veenhoven. "Daily Activities and Happiness in Later Life: The Role of Work Status." *Journal of Happiness Studies,* September 28, 2012.

Tafoya, Sonya M., Hans Johnson, and Laura E. Hill. "Who Chooses to Choose Two?" Washington, D.C.: Population Reference Bureau, 2005.

"Tales of Saddam's Brutality." Washington, D.C.: White House, September 29, 2003.

Taneja, V., S. Sriram, R. S. Beri, V. Sreenivas, R. Aggarwal, R. Kaur, and J. M. Puliyel. "'Not by Bread Alone': Impact of a Structured 90-Minute Play Session on Development of Children in an Orphanage." *Child Care, Health & Development, 28,* 1, 2002:95–100.

Tasker, Fiona. "Same-Sex Parenting and Child Development: Reviewing the Contribution of Parental Gender." *Journal of Marriage and Family, 72,* 1, February 2010:35–40.

Tatlow, Didi Kirsten. "Visit Your Parents—In China, It Could Soon Be the Law." *International Herald Tribune,* June 29, 2012.

Tavernise, Sabrina. "Day Care Centers Adapt to Round-the-Clock Demand." *New York Times,* January 15, 2012.

Taylor, Chris. "The Man behind Lara Croft." *Time,* December 6, 1999:78.

Taylor, Howard F. "The Structure of a National Black Leadership Network: Preliminary Findings." Unpublished manuscript, 1992. (As cited in Margaret L. Andersen and Howard F. Taylor, *Sociology: Understanding a Diverse Society.* Belmont, Calif.: Wadsworth, 2000.)

Tejada, Carlos. "Beijing Moves to Enforce Care for Older Parents." *Wall Street Journal,* December 31, 2012.

Terhune, Chad. "Pepsi, Vowing Diversity Isn't Just Image Polish, Seeks Inclusive Culture." *Wall Street Journal,* April 19, 2005.

"Testing Times." *The Economist,* December 31, 2011.

Tewary, Amarnath. "At a Sperm Bank in Bihar, Caste Divisions Start Before Birth." *New York Times,* July 12, 2012.

"The Global Religious Landscape," Washington, D.C.: Pew Research Center, December 18, 2012.

"The Interaction of Genes, Behavior, and Social Environment." *Today's Research on Aging, 27,* December 2012:1-6.

"The World of the Child 6 Billion." Washington, D.C.: Population Reference Bureau, 2000.

Thomas, Patricia A. "Trajectories of Social Engagement and Mortality in Late Life." *Journal of Aging and Health, 24,* 4, 2012:547–568.

Thomas, Paulette. "Boston Fed Finds Racial Discrimination in Mortgage Lending Is Still Widespread." *Wall Street Journal,* October 9, 1992:A3.

Thomas, Paulette. "U.S. Examiners Will Scrutinize Banks with Poor Minority-Lending Histories." *Wall Street Journal,* October 22, 1991:A2.

Thomas, W. I., and Dorothy Swaine Thomas. *The Child in America: Behavior Problems and Programs.* New York: Alfred A. Knopf, 1928.

Thompson, Ginger. "Chasing Mexico's Dream into Squalor." *New York Times,* February 11, 2001.

Thompson, Ginger. "Where Education and Assimilation Collide." *New York Times,* March 14, 2009.

Thompson, Paul. "Pentagon Buys and Destroys 9,500 Copies of Soldier's Afghanistan Book 'to Protect Military Secrets.'" *Mail Online,* September 27, 2010.

Thornton, Russell. *American Indian Holocaust and Survival: A Population History Since 1492.* Norman: University of Oklahoma Press, 1987.

Thurm, Scott. "What's a CEO Worth? More Firms Say $10 Million." *Wall Street Journal,* May 15, 2013.

Thurow, Roger. "Farms Destroyed, Stricken Sudan Faces Food Crisis." *Wall Street Journal,* February 7, 2005.

Tierney, John. "For Lesser Crimes, Rethinking Life Behind Bars." *New York Times,* December 11, 2012.

Tilly, Charles. *Social Movements, 1768–2004.* Boulder, Colo.: Paradigm Publishers, 2004.

Timasheff, Nicholas S. *War and Revolution.* Joseph F. Scheuer, ed. New York: Sheed & Ward, 1965.

Tocqueville, Alexis de. *Democracy in America,* J. P. Mayer and Max Lerner, eds. New York: Harper & Row, 1966. Originally published 1835.

Tocqueville, Alexis de. *The Old Regime and the French Revolution.* Stuart Gilbert, trans. Garden City, N.Y.: Doubleday Anchor, 1955. First published in 1856.

Tokc-Wilde, Iwona. "Workforce Surveillance: Is Your Boss Keeping a Private Eye on You?" *The Guardian,* May 7, 2011.

Tokoro, Masabumi. "The Shift towards American-Style Human Resource Management Systems and the Transformation of Workers' Attitudes at Japanese Firms." *Asian Business and Management, 4,* 2005:23–44.

Tomsho, Robert, and Daniel Golden. "Educating Eric." *Wall Street Journal,* May 12, 2007.

Tönnies, Ferdinand. *Community and Society (Gemeinschaft und Gesellschaft),* with a new introduction by John Samples. New Brunswick, N.J.: Transaction, 1988. Originally published 1887.

Torres, Blanca. "Employers Bring Childcare Onsite to Keep Workers' Lives Balanced." *San Francisco Business Times,* August 9, 2012.

Torres, Jose B., V. Scott H. Solberg, and Aaron H. Carlstrom. "The Myth of Sameness among Latino Men and Their Machismo." *American Journal of Orthopsychiatry, 72,* 2, 2002:163–181.

Toshkov, Veselin. "Europe's 'Oldest Town' Identified Near Provadia in Eastern Bulgaria." *Huffington Post,* November 1, 2012.

Toynbee, Arnold. *A Study of History,* D. C. Somervell, abridger and ed. New York: Oxford University Press, 1946.

"Trafficking in Persons" *Report.* Washington, D.C.: U.S. Department of State, June 2012.

Treiman, Donald J. *Occupational Prestige in Comparative Perspective.* New York: Academic Press, 1977.

Tresniowski, Alex. "Payday or Mayday?" *People Weekly,* May 17, 1999:128–131.

Trice, Harrison M., and Janice M. Beyer. "Cultural Leadership in Organization." *Organization Science, 2,* 2, May 1991:149–169.

Troeltsch, Ernst. *The Social Teachings of the Christian Churches.* New York: Macmillan, 1931.

Troianovski, Anton. "New Wi-Fi Pitch: Tracker." *Wall Street Journal,* June 19, 2012.

Tuhus-Dubrow, Rebecca. "Rites and Wrongs." *Boston Globe,* February 11, 2007.

Tumin, Melvin M. "Some Principles of Social Stratification: A Critical Analysis." *American Sociological Review, 18,* August 1953:394.

Turner, Darrell J. "Religion: Year in Review 2010." *Encyclopedia Britannica,* 2011.

Turner, Jonathan H. *The Structure of Sociological Theory.* Homewood, Ill.: Dorsey, 1978.

Turner, Ralph H., and Lewis M. Killian. *Collective Behavior,* 2nd ed. Englewood Cliffs, N.J.: Prentice Hall, 1987.

Twenge, J. M., W. K. Campbell, and C. A. Foster. "Parenthood and Marital Satisfaction: A Meta-analytic Review." *Journal of Marriage and Family, 65,* 2003:574–583.

Tyler, Patrick E. "A New Life for NATO? But It's Sidelined for Now." *New York Times,* November 20, 2002.

U.S. Census Bureau. "50 Million Children Lived with Married Parents in 2007." Washington, D.C.: U.S. Government Printing Office, 2007.

U.S. Census Bureau. "America's Families and Living Arrangements: 2012." Washington, D.C.: U.S. Census Bureau, 2013b.

U.S. Census Bureau. "Annual Social and Economic Supplement to Current Population Survey." Washington, D.C.: U.S. Government Printing Office, 2010.

U.S. Census Bureau. "U.S. Census Bureau International Database." Washington, D.C.: U.S. Census Bureau, 2013a.

U.S. Census Bureau. "Current Population Survey, 2012 Annual Social and Economic (ASEC) Supplement," Washington, D.C.: U.S. Census Bureau, November 2012.

U.S. Census Bureau, Population Division. "Percent of the Projected Population by Race and Hispanic Origin for the United States: 2010 to 2050." Constant Net International Migration Series (NP2009-T6-C):Table 6-C, December 16, 2009.

U.S. Department of Defense. "Casualty Releases." Washington, D.C.: U.S. Department of Defense, March 30, 2013.

U.S. Department of Energy, Advisory Committee on Human Radiation Experiments. Final Report, 1995. Washington, D.C.: U.S. Government Printing Office, 1995.

U.S. Department of State. "2010 Human Rights Report: Iran." 2010 Country Reports on Human Rights Practices, April 8, 2011.

Uchitelle, Louis. "How to Define Poverty? Let Us Count the Ways." *New York Times,* May 28, 2001.

Udry, J. Richard. "Biological Limits of Gender Construction." *American Sociological Review, 65,* June 2000:443–457.

Udy, Stanley H., Jr. "Bureaucracy and Rationality in Weber's Organizational Theory: An Empirical Study." *American Sociological Review, 24,* December 1959:791–795.

Ullman, Edward, and Chauncey Harris. "The Nature of Cities." In *Urban Man and Society: A Reader in Urban Ecology,* Albert N. Cousins and Hans Nagpaul, eds. New York: Knopf, 1970:91–100.

UNAIDS. "World AIDS Day Report." Geneva, Switzerland: UNAIDS, 2012.

UNAIDS. Report on the Global AIDS Epidemic, 2010.

UNESCO. "Adult and Youth Literacy." Paris: UNESCO, September 2012.

UNIFEM. "Progress of the World's Women 2008/2009." United Nations Development Fund for Women, 2008.

United Nations. "An Overview of Urbanization, Internal Migration, Population Distribution and Development in the World." United Nations Population Division, January 14, 2008.

United Nations. "World Urbanizing Prospects: The 2009 Revision." U.N. Department of Economic and Social Affairs, Population Division, 2010.

UPI. "Experts: Cleveland Killer a Sexual Sadist." November 9, 2009.

Ur, Jason A. "Cycles of Civilization in Northern Mesopotamia, 4400–2000 BC." *Journal of Archaeological Research, 18,* 4, 2010:387–431.

Urbina, Ian. "As School Exit Tests Prove Tough, States Ease Standards." *New York Times,* January 11, 2010.

Useem, Michael. *The Inner Circle: Large Corporations and the Rise of Business Political Activity in the U.S. and U.K.* New York: Oxford University Press, 1984.

Utar, Hale, and Luis Bernardo Torres Ruiz. "International Competition and Industrial Evolution: Evidence from the Impact of Chinese Competition on Mexican Maquiladoras." University of Colorado at Boulder and Banco de Mexico, July 2010.

"VA Testing Drugs on War Veterans." *Washington Post,* June 17, 2008.

Vandell, Deborah Lowe, Jay Belsky, Margaret Burchinal, Laurence Steinberg, and Nathan Vandergrift. "No Effects of Early Child Care Extend to Age 15 Years? Results from the NICHD Study of Early Child Care and Youth Development." *Child Development, 81,* 3, May/June 2010:737–756.

Vandiver, John. "550 Marines Head to Spain in Support of AFRICOM." *Stars and Stripes,* April 25, 2013b.

Vandiver, John. "New Combat Focus for U.S. Africa Command." *Stars and Stripes,* April 5, 2013a.

Varese, Federico. *The Russian Mafia: Private Protection in a New Market Economy.* Oxford: Oxford University Press, 2005.

Vartabedian, Ralph, and Scott Gold. "New Questions on Shuttle Tile Safety Raised." *Los Angeles Times,* February 27, 2003.

Vaughan, Diane. "Uncoupling: The Social Construction of Divorce." In *Marriage and Family in a Changing Society,* 2nd ed., James M. Henslin, ed. New York: Free Press, 1985:429–439.

Veblen, Thorstein. *The Theory of the Leisure Class.* New York: Macmillan, 1912.

Venkatesh, Sudhir. *Gang Leader for a Day: A Rogue Sociologist Takes to the Streets.* New York: Penguin, 2008.

Vergakis, Brock. "Utah High Court: Polygamist Leader Can Go to Texas." Associated Press, November 23, 2010.

Vidal, David. "Bilingual Education Is Thriving but Criticized." *New York Times,* January 30, 1977.

Vidal, Jordi Blanes, Mirko Draca, and Christian Fons-Rosen. "Revolving Door Lobbyists." Center for Economic Performance, Discussion Paper 993, August 2010.

Vigil, Tammy. "Boulder Police: No Full Frontal Nudity." Fox 31, Denver Colorado, June 11, 2009.

Volti, Rudi. *Society and Technological Change,* 3rd ed. New York: St. Martin's Press, 1995.

Von Hoffman, Nicholas. "Sociological Snoopers." *Transaction 7,* May 1970:4, 6.

Wagley, Charles, and Marvin Harris. *Minorities in the New World.* New York: Columbia University Press, 1958.

Wald, Matthew L., and John Schwartz. "Alerts Were Lacking, NASA Shuttle Manager Says." *New York Times,* July 23, 2003.

Waldfogel, Jane, Terry-Ann Craigie, and Jeanne Brooks-Gunn. "Fragile Families and Child Wellbeing." In *Fragile Families, 20,* 2, Fall 2010:87–112.

Walker, Alice, and Pratibha Parmar. *Warrior Marks: Female Genital Mutilation and the Sexual Blinding of Women.* New York: Harcourt Brace, 1993.

Walker, Marcus, and Andrew Higgins. "Zimbabwe Can't Paper over Its Million Percent Inflation Anymore." *Wall Street Journal,* July 2, 2008.

Wall, Robert. "China's Armed Predator." *Aviation Week,* November 17, 2010.

Wallace, John M., Ryoko Yamaguchi, Jerald G. Bachman, Patrick M. O'Malley, John E. Schulenberg, and Lloyd D. Johnston. "Religiosity and Adolescent Substance Use: The Role of Individual and Contextual Influences." *Social Problems, 54,* 2, 2007:308–327.

Wallerstein, Immanuel. "Culture as the Ideological Battleground of the Modern World-System." In *Global Culture: Nationalism, Globalization, and Modernity,* Mike Featherstone, ed. London: Sage, 1990:31–55.

Wallerstein, Immanuel. *Modern World System I: Capitalist Agriculture and the Origins of the European World-Economy in the Sixteenth Century.* Berkeley, Calif.: University of California Press, 2011.

Wallerstein, Immanuel. *The Capitalist World-Economy.* New York: Cambridge University Press, 1979.

Wallerstein, Immanuel. *The Modern World System: Capitalist Agriculture and the Origins of the European World-Economy in the Sixteenth Century.* New York: Academic Press, 1974.

Wallerstein, Judith S., Sandra Blakeslee, and Julia M. Lewis. *The Unexpected Legacy of Divorce: A 25-Year Landmark Study.* Concord, N.H.: Hyperion Press, 2001.

Walsh, Anthony, and Kevin M. Beaver. "Biosocial Criminology." In *Handbook on Crime and Deviance,* M. D. Krohn et al., eds. Dordrecht, New York: Springer, 2009:79–101.

Walter, Lynn. *Women's Rights: A Global View.* Westport, Conn.: Greenwood Press, 2001.

Wang, Hongyu, and Paul R. Amato. "Predictors of Divorce Adjustment: Stressors, Resources, and Definitions." *Journal of Marriage and the Family, 62,* 3, August 2000:655–668.

Wang, Mo, and Kenneth S. Shultz. "Employee Retirment: A Review and Recommendations for Future Investigation." *Journal of Management, 36,* January 2010:172–206.

Wang, Stephanie. "Colleges Divided Over Value of Free Online Classes." *Community College Week,* April 1, 2013.

Wang, Wendy. "The Rise of Intermarriage: Rates, Characteristics Vary by Race and Gender." Washington, D.C.: PEW Research Center, February 16, 2012.

Wanzer, Sidney. "'Dr. Death' Served Us All with Time in Prison." *USA Today,* June 6, 2007.

Ward, Rose Marie, Halle C. Popson, and Donald G. DiPaolo. "Defining the Alpha Female: A Female Leadership Measure." *Journal of Leadership and Organizational Studies 17,* 3, 2010:309–320.

Wark, Gillian R., and Dennis L. Krebs. "Gender and Dilemma Differences in Real-Life Moral Judgment." *Developmental Psychology, 32,* 1996:220–230.

Warren, Jennifer, Adam Gelb, Jake Horowitz, and Jessica Riordan. "One in 100: Behind Bars in America 2008." Washington, D.C.: Pew Charitable Trust, February 2008.

Watson, J. Mark. "Outlaw Motorcyclists." In *Society: Readings to Accompany Sociology: A Down-to-Earth Approach, Core Concepts,* James M. Henslin ed. Boston: Allyn and Bacon, 2006:105–114. Originally published 1980 in *Deviant Behavior, 2,* 1.

Webb, Amy. *Data, A Love Story: How I Gamed Online Dating to Meet My Match.* New York: Dutton, 2013.

Weber, Max. *Economy and Society,* G. Roth and C. Wittich, eds. Berkeley: University of California Press, 1978. Originally published 1922.

Weber, Max. *From Max Weber: Essays in Sociology,* Hans Gerth and C. Wright Mills, trans. and ed. New York: Oxford University Press, 1946.

Weber, Max. *The Protestant Ethic and the Spirit of Capitalism.* New York: Scribner's, 1958. Originally published 1904–1905.

Weber, Max. *The Protestant Ethic and the Spirit of Capitalism,* rev. 1920 ed. Stephen Kalberg, trans. New York: Oxford University Press, 2011.

Weber, Max. *The Theory of Social and Economic Organization,* A. M. Henderson and Talcott Parsons, trans., Talcott Parsons, ed. Glencoe, Ill.: Free Press, 1947. Originally published 1913.

Weinberger, Catherine. "In Search of the Glass Ceiling: Gender and Earnings Growth among U.S. College Graduates in the What is this?" *Industrial and Labor Relations Review, 64,* 5, October 2011.

Weiner, Jill Caryl. "The Home-Schooled Don't Just Stay at Home." *New York Times,* March 14, 2012.

Weiner, Tim. "Air Force Seeks Bush's Approval for Space Weapons Programs." *New York Times,* May 18, 2005.

Weiner, Tim. "Pentagon Envisioning a Costly Internet for War." *New York Times,* November 13, 2004.

Weiss, Karen G. "'Boys Will Be Boys' and Other Gendered Accounts: An Exploration of Victims' Excuses and Justifications for Unwanted Sexual Contact and Coercion." *Violence against Women, 15,* 2009:810–834.

Weiss, Rick. "Mature Human Embryos Cloned." *Washington Post,* February 12, 2004:A1.

Weitoft, Gunilla Ringback, Anders Hjern, Bengt Haglund, and Mans Rosen. "Mortality, Severe Morbidity, and Injury in Children Living with Single Parents in Sweden: A Population-Based Study." *Lancet, 361,* January 25, 2003:289–295.

Welker, Marina, Damani J. Partridge, and Rebecca Hardin. "Corporate Lives: New Perspectives on the Social Life of the Corporate Form." *Current Anthropology, 52,* 3, April 2011:S3–S16.

Wells, Tom. *The War Within: America's Battle over Vietnam.* Bloomington, Indiana: iUniverse, 2005.

Wen, Ming. "Family Structure and Children's Health and Behavior." *Journal of Family Issues, 29,* 11, November 2008:1492–1519.

Wertz, Richard W., and Dorothy C. Wertz. "Notes on the Decline of Midwives and the Rise of Medical Obstetricians." In *The Sociology of Health and Illness: Critical Perspectives,* Peter Conrad and Rochelle Kern, eds. New York: St. Martin's Press, 1981:165–183.

Western, Bruce, Deirdre Bloome, Benjamin Sosnaud, and Laura Tach. "Economic Insecurity and Social Stratification." *Annual Review of Sociology, 38,* 2012:341–359.

"What Scares Doctors? Being the Patient." *Time,* May 1, 2006.

Wheaton, Blair, and Philippa Clarke. "Space Meets Time: Integrating Temporal and Contextual Influences on Mental Health in Early Adulthood." *American Sociological Review, 68,* 2003:680–706.

Whipple, Tom. "Nursing Home Defends Prostitutes' Visits." *Times,* January 29, 2013.

White, Jack E. "Forgive Us Our Sins." *Time,* July 3, 1995:29.

White, Joseph B., Stephen Power, and Timothy Aeppel. "Death Count Linked to Failures of Firestone Tires Rises to 203." *Wall Street Journal,* June 19, 2001:A4.

Whitehead, Barbara Dafoe, and David Popenoe. "The Marrying Kind: Which Men Marry and Why." Rutgers University: The State of Our Unions: The Social Health of Marriage in America, 2004.

Whiteley, Paul, Thomas Sy, and Stefanie K. Johnson. "Leaders' Conceptions of Followers: Implications for Naturally Occurring Pygmalion Effects." *Leadership Quarterly, 23,* 2012:822–834.

Whorf, Benjamin. *Language, Thought, and Reality,* J. B. Carroll, ed. Cambridge, MA: MIT Press, 1956.

Whyte, William Foote. "Street Corner Society." In *Down to Earth Sociology: Introductory Readings,* 11th ed., James M. Henslin, ed. New York: Free Press, 2001:61–69.

Whyte, William H. *The City: Rediscovering the Center.* New York: Doubleday, 1989.

Wiebe, Richard P. "Integrating Criminology through Adaptive Strategy and Life History Theory." *Journal of Contemporary Justice, 28,* 3, 2012:346–365.

Wienberg, Christian. "Call Girls at Nursing Home Fuel Debate in Denmark." *Bloomberg News,* April 15, 2008.

Wilde, Elizabeth Ty, Lily Batchelder, and David T. Ellwood. "The Mommy Track Divides: The Impact of Childbearing on Wages of Women of Differing Skill Levels." NBER Working Paper N. 16582. December 2010.

Wilford, John Noble. "In Maya Ruins, Scholars See Evidence of Urban Sprawl." *New York Times,* December 19, 2000.

Wilford, John Noble. "Mapping Ancient Civilization, in a Matter of Days." *New York Times,* May 10, 2010.

Wilkinson, Steven L. "Riots." *Annual Review of Political Science, 12,* 2009:329–343.

Williams, Dmitri, Nicole Martins, Mia Consalvo, and James D. Ivory. "The Virtual Census: Representations of Gender, Race, and Age in Video Games." *New Media & Society, 11,* 5, 2009:815–834.

Williams, Jasmin K. "Utah—The Beehive State." *New York Post,* June 12, 2007.

Williams, Rhys H. "Constructing the Public Good: Social Movements and Cultural Resources." *Social Problems, 42,* 1, February 1995:124–144.

Williams, Robin M., Jr. *American Society: A Sociological Interpretation,* 2nd ed. New York: Knopf, 1965.

Williams, Timothy. "Old Sound in Harlem Draws New Neighbors' Ire." *New York Times,* July 6, 2008.

Willie, Charles Vert. "Caste, Class, and Family Life Experiences." *Research in Race and Ethnic Relations, 6,* 1991:65–84.

Willie, Charles Vert, and Richard J. Reddick. *A New Look at Black Families,* 5th ed. Walnut Creek, Calif.: AltaMira Press, 2003.

Wilson, Duff. "Cigarette Giants in a Global Fight on Tighter Rules." *New York Times,* November 13, 2010.

Wilson, Duff. "Harvard Medical School in Ethics Quandary." *New York Times,* March 2, 2009.

Wilson, Edward O. *Sociobiology: The New Synthesis.* Cambridge, Mass.: Harvard University Press, 1975.

Wilson, James Q., and Richard J. Herrnstein. *Crime and Human Nature.* New York: Simon & Schuster, 1985.

Wilson, William Julius. "Jobless Poverty: A New Form of Social Dislocation in the Inner-City Ghetto." In *The Inequality Reader: Contemporary and Foundational Readings in Race, Class and Gender,* David B. Grusky and Szonja Szelenyi, eds. Boulder: Westview Press, 2007:142–152.

Wilson, William Julius. *More Than Just Race: Being Black and Poor in the Inner City*. New York: W.W. Norton, 2009.

Wilson, William Julius. *The Bridge over the Racial Divide: Rising Inequality and Coalition Politics*. Berkeley: University of California Press, 2000.

Wilson, William Julius. *The Declining Significance of Race: Blacks and Changing American Institutions*. Chicago: University of Chicago Press, 1978.

Wilson, William Julius. *When Work Disappears: The World of the New Urban Poor*. Chicago: University of Chicago Press, 1996.

Wimmer, Andreas, and Kevin Lewis. "Beyond and Below Racial Homophily: ERG Models of a Friendship Network Documented on Facebook." *American Journal of Sociology, 116*, 2, 2010: 583–642.

Winerip, Michael. "Ex-Schools Chief in Atlanta Is Indicted in Testing Scandal." *New York Times,* March 29, 2013.

Wines, Michael. "Africa Adds to Miserable Ranks of Child Workers." *New York Times,* August 24, 2006a.

Wines, Michael. "How Bad Is Inflation in Zimbabwe?" *Wall Street Journal,* May 2, 2006b.

"Winner, Dumbest Moment, Marketing." CNN, February 1, 2006.

Wirth, Louis. "The Problem of Minority Groups." In *The Science of Man in the World Crisis,* Ralph Linton, ed. New York: Columbia University Press, 1945.

Wirth, Louis. "Urbanism as a Way of Life." *American Journal of Sociology, 44,* July 1938:1–24.

Wolfensohn, James D., and Kathryn S. Fuller. "Making Common Cause: Seeing the Forest for the Trees." *International Herald Tribune,* May 27, 1998:11.

Wolfinger, Nicholas H. "Family Structure Homogamy: The Effects of Parental Divorce on Partner Selection and Marital Stability." *Social Science Research, 32,* 2003:80–97.

Wolinsky, Frederic D., Timothy E. Stump, and Christopher M. Callahan. "Does Being Placed in a Nursing Home Make You Sicker and More Likely to Die?" In *Societal Mechanisms for Maintaining Competence in Old Age,* Sherry L. Willis, K. Warner Schaie, and Mark Hayward, eds. New York: Springer Publishing Company, 1997:94–130.

"Woman Ordered to Hold 'Idiot' Sign and 6 Other Cases of Court-Ordered Shaming." Associated Press, November 13, 2012.

Women's Bureau of the United States, Department of Labor. *Handbook on Women Workers.* Washington, D.C.: U.S. Government Printing Office, 1969.

Wong, Gillian. "Wife Visits Jailed China Activist Ahead of Release." Associated Press, June 20, 2011.

Wood, Daniel B., "Latinos Redefine What It Means to Be Manly." *Christian Science Monitor, 93,* 161, July 16, 2001.

World Bank. "Cost of Pollution in China: Economic Estimates of Physical Damages." Washington, D.C: World Bank, February 2007.

World Health Organization. *Constitution of the World Health Organization.* New York: World Health Organization. Washington, D.C.: Interim Commission, 1946.

World Population Prospects: The 2011 Revision. New York,: United Nations, 2012.

Worsley, Peter M. "50 Years Ago: Cargo Cults of Melanesia." *Scientific American,* April 24, 2009. A reprint of an article that appeared in *Scientific American,* May 1959.

Worsley, Peter. *The Trumpet Shall Sound.* London: MacGibbon and Kee, 1957.

Wright, Erik Olin. *Class.* London: Verso, 1985.

Wright, Lawrence. "Double Mystery." *New Yorker,* August 7, 1995:45–62.

Wright, Lawrence. "One Drop of Blood." *New Yorker,* July 25, 1994:46–50, 52–55.

www.amnestyusa.org, 2005.

www.cnn.com, November 15, 2008.

www.fiveoclockclub.com, 2001.

Xie, Min, Karen Heimer, and Janet L. Lauritsen. "Violence against Women in U.S. Metropolitan Areas: Change in Women's Status and Risk, 1980–2004." *Criminology,* 2011:1–38.

Yager, Mark, Beret Strong, Linda Roan, Davd Matsumoto, and Kimberly A. Metcalf. "Nonverbal Communication in the Contemporary Operating Environment." United States Army Research Institute for the Behavioral and Social Sciences, Technical Report 1238, January 2009.

Yakaboski, Tamara, and Leah Reinert. "Review of Women in Academic Leadership: Professional Strategies, Personal Choices." *Women in Higher Education, 4,* 1, 2011.

Yamamoto, Yoko, and Mary C. Brinton. "Cultural Capital in East Asian Educational Systems: The Case of Japan." *Sociology of Education, 83,* 1, 2010:67–83.

Yardley, Jim. "As Wealth and Literacy Rise in India, Report Says, So Do Sex-Selective Abortions." *New York Times,* May 24, 2011.

Yardley, Jim. "Faces of Abortion in China: A Young, Single Woman." *New York Times,* May 13, 2007.

Yardley, Jim. "In India, Castes, Honor and Killings Intertwine." *New York Times,* July 9, 2010.

Yardley, Jim. "India Tries Using Cash Bonuses to Slow Birthrates." *New York Times,* August 21, 2010.

Yardley, Jim. "Soaring above India's Poverty, a 27-Story Home." *New York Times,* October 28, 2010.

Yardley, Jim, and Keith Bradsher. "China, an Engine of Growth, Faces a Global Slump." *New York Times,* October 22, 2008.

Yarris, Lynn. "New Synthetic Biology Technique Boosts Microbial Production of Diesel Fuel." Berkeley, Calif.: Berkeley Lab News Center, March 26, 2012.

Yee, Vivian. "Flash Mob in Times Square Honors Victims of Newtown." *New York Times,* February 24, 2013.

Yenfang, Qian. "Fast Growth of Economy, Fast Rise of Wealthiest." *China Daily,* March 4, 2011.

Yinger, J. Milton. *The Scientific Study of Religion.* New York: Macmillan, 1970.

Yinger, J. Milton. *Toward a Field Theory of Behavior: Personality and Social Structure.* New York: McGraw-Hill, 1965.

"'You Can Die Anytime.' Death Squad Killings in Mindanao." New York: Human Rights Watch, 2009.

Young, Antonia, and Larenda Twigg. "'Sworn Virgins' as Enhancers of Albanian Patriarchal Society in Contrast to Emerging Roles for Albanian Women." *Emoloska Tribuna, 39,* 2009:117–134.

Young, Robert D., Bertrand Desjardins, Kirsten McCaughlin, Michel Poulain, and Thomas T. Perls. "Typologies of Extreme Longevity Myths." *Current Gerontology and Geriatrics Research,* 2010:1–12.

Yu, Rongqin, John R. Geddes, and Seena Fazel. "Personality Disorders, Violence, and Antisocial Behavior: A Systematic Review and Meta-Regression Analysis." *Journal of Personality Disorders, 26,* 5, 2012:775–792.

Zachary, G. Pascal. "Behind Stocks' Surge Is an Economy in Which Big U.S. Firms Thrive." *Wall Street Journal,* November 22, 1995:A1, A5.

Zakaria, Fareed. *The Post-American World.* New York: W. W. Norton, 2008.

Zald, Mayer N. "Looking Backward to Look Forward: Reflections on the Past and the Future of the Resource Mobilization Research Program." In *Frontiers in Social Movement Theory,* Aldon D. Morris and Carol McClurg Mueller, eds. New Haven, Conn.: Yale University Press, 1992:326–348.

Zald, Mayer N., and John D. McCarthy, eds. *Social Movements in an Organizational Society.* New Brunswick, N.J.: Transaction, 1987.

Zamiska, Nicholas. "Pressed to Do Well on Admissions Tests, Students Take Drugs." *Wall Street Journal,* November 8, 2004.

Zaslow, Jeffrey. "Thinness, Women, and School Girls: Body Image." *Wall Street Journal,* September 2, 2009.

Zaslow, Jeffrey. "Will You Still Need Me When I'm … 84? More Couples Divorce after Decades." *Wall Street Journal,* June 17, 2003:D1.

Zellner, William W. *Countercultures: A Sociological Analysis.* New York: St. Martin's, 1995.

Zerubavel, Eviatar. *The Fine Line: Making Distinctions in Everyday Life.* New York: Free Press, 1991.

Zhang, Yuanting, and Franklin W. Goza. "Who Will Care for the Elderly in China?" Bowling Green, OH: Center for Family and Demographic Research, May 2007.

Zoepf, Katherine. "A Dishonorable Affair." *New York Times,* September 23, 2007.

Zuboff. Shoshanna. "New Worlds of Computer-Mediated Work." In *Down to Earth Sociology: Introductory Readings,* 6th edition, James M. Henslin, ed. New York: Free Press, 1991:476–485.

Zumbrun, Joshua. "The Sacrifices of Albania's 'Sworn Virgins.'" *Washington Post,* August 11, 2007.

Name Index

N

O

P

Q

R

S

Subject Index

D

E

F

G

H

N

Credits

Photo Credits

Chapter 1: p. 1: imago stock&people/Newscom; **p. 6:** Ian Cumming/Axiom/ZUMAPRESS.com/Newscom; **p. 8:** The Gallery Collection/Corbis; **p. 9:** Roger-Viollet/The Image Works; **p. 9:** Huton-Deutsch Collection/Corbis; **p. 10:** Bettmann/Corbis; **p. 10:** Bettmann/Corbis; **p. 11:** CHINATOPIX/AP Images; **p. 11:** Tuul/Robert Harding World Imagery/Corbis; **p. 12:** The Granger Collection, New York; **p. 14:** picture alliance/Robert Geiss/Newscom; **p. 16:** The Granger Collection, NYC—All rights reserved.; **p. 16:** The Granger Collection, NYC—All rights reserved.; **p. 16:** The Granger Collection, NYC—All rights reserved.; **p. 16:** Bettmann/Corbis; **p. 16:** Mary Evans Picture Library/The Image Works; **p. 16:** Wellesley College Archives; **p. 16:** Bettmann/Corbis; **p. 16:** The University of Chicago Library Special Collections Research Center; **p. 16:** The University of Chicago Library Special Collections Research Center; **p. 16:** Bettmann/Corbis; **p. 17:** The New York Public Library/Art Resource, NY; **p. 17:** The Granger Collection, NYC—All rights reserved.; **p. 18:** The Granger Collection, New York; **p. 19:** George Barker/Corbis; **p. 20:** Fritz Goro/Time Life Pictures/Getty Images; **p. 21:** Nickelodeon/Courtesy Everett Collection; **p. 23:** University of Chicago; **p. 25:** Pictorial Parade/Getty Images; **p. 26:** TopFoto/The Image Works;

Chapter 2: p. 33: Martin Harvey/Alamy; **p. 35:** Karim Sahib/AFP Photo/Newscom; **p. 36:** Melanie Stetson Freeman/The Christian Science Monitor/Getty Images; **p. 37:** Domenech Castello/EPA/Landov; **p. 38:** Kim Ludbrook/EPA/Newscom; **p. 39:** Pornchai Kittiwongsakul/AFP/Getty Images; **p. 40:** GlowImages/Alamy; **p. 40:** ONOKY - Photononstop/Alamy; **p. 40:** Jean-Pierre Lescourret/Corbis; **p. 40:** Panorama/The Image Works; **p. 40:** Piers Cavendish/Impact/HIP/The Image Works; **p. 40:** Tom Cockrem/Lonely Planet Images/Getty Images; **p. 40:** Picture Finders Ltd./eStock Photo; **p. 40:** Peter Skinner/Danita Delimont/Alamy; **p. 42:** C.M. Holmgren; **p. 42:** C.M. Holmgren; **p. 42:** C.M. Holmgren; **p. 42:** Steve Hamblin/Alamy; **p. 42:** C.M. Holmgren; **p. 42:** Lena Leal-Floyd; **p. 42:** James M. Henslin; **p. 44:** Jeff Greenberg/PhotoEdit, Inc.; **p. 45:** Andre Camara/I-Images/ZUMA Press/Newscom; **p. 46:** David Grossman/Alamy; **p. 47:** Frank Fife/AFP/Getty Images/Newscom; **p. 48:** Kyodo/AP Images; **p. 48:** Dan Riedlhuber/Reuters/Landov; **p. 49:** James X Nova; **p. 49:** Nicky Loh/Reuters/Landov; **p. 49:** Don Mason/Alamy; **p. 49:** David Pu'u/Corbis; **p. 49:** Jarrett Robertson/Demotix/Corbis; **p. 49:** Timothy A. Clary/AFP/Getty Images/Newscom; **p. 50:** Muen/Newscom; **p. 53:** Dragan Trifunovic/La Nacion de Costa Rica/Newscom; **p. 54:** Clarke Memorial Museum, Eureka, California; **p. 55:** Stuart Wilson/Photo Researchers/Getty Images; **p. 56:** Bill Bachmann/The Image Works; **p. 57:** Dave Carpenter/www.CartoonStock.com; **p. 58:** Paulo Santos/Reuters/Corbis;

Chapter 3: p. 61: Kymri Wilt/DanitaDelimont.com "Danita Delimont Photography"/Newscom; **p. 63:** Ridarz'9/Digital Vision/Getty Images; **p. 64:** James M. Henslin; **p. 65:** Cai Yang/Xinhua/Landov; **p. 66:** Nina Leen/Time Life Pictures/Getty Images; **p. 68:** BE&W/SuperStock; **p. 69:** Ariel Skelley/Corbis; **p. 69:** Tappe/ullstein bild/The Image Works; **p. 70:** AP Images; **p. 72:** Gary Hershorn/Reuters/Corbis; **p. 72:** Kristin Callahan/Everett Collection; **p. 72:** Dee Cercone/Everett Collection/Newscom; **p. 72:** Pool/Tim Graham Picture Library/Getty Images; **p. 72:** Jonathan Alcorn/ZUMAPRESS/Newscom; **p. 74:** Sidney Bahrt/Photo Researchers/Getty Images; **p. 75:** Frank and Ernest used with the permission of the Thaves and the Cartoonist Group. All rights reserved.; **p. 76:** Ben Speck/Getty Images; **p. 78:** Joerg Carstensen/dpa/picture-alliance/Newscom; **p. 79:** Lannis Waters/The Palm Beach Post; **p. 81:** Colorblind/Cardinal/Corbis; **p. 82:** Katrina Wittkamp/Digital Vision/Getty Images; **p. 83:** Stefanie Grewel/cultura/Corbis; **p. 85:** Scott Olson/Photonica World/Getty Images; **p. 86:** Photos 12/Alamy; **p. 86:** Bob Adelman/Corbis; **p. 87:** Michael MacIntyre/The Hutchison Library; **p. 89:** AP Images;

Chapter 4: p. 93: Fred Dufour/AFP/Getty Images; **p. 95:** Vince Mannino/Bettmann/Corbis; **p. 96:** Chris Helgren/Reuters/Landov; **p. 99:** Yang Chen/ZUMA Press/Newscom; **p. 102:** John Bazemore/AP Images; **p. 103:** Visions of America/UIG/Getty Images; **p. 104:** Dorothy Alexander/Alamy; **p. 104:** Lee Snider/The Image Works; **p. 105:** Bill Bachmann/The Image Works; **pp. 106–107:** James M. Henslin; **p. 108:** Ng Han Guan/AP Images; **p. 108:** Solent News/Splash News/Newscom; **p. 109:** i love images/Alamy; **p. 109:** Image Source/AP Images; **p. 110:** Hill Street Studios/Blend Images/Corbis; **p. 111:** Monty Brinton/CBS/Landov; **p. 114:** face to face/ZUMAPRESS/Newscom; **p. 114:** Michael Germana/Everett Collection/Newscom; **p. 115:** McPherson © 2008. Reprinted with permission of UNIVERSAL UCLICK. All rights reserved.; **p. 116:** Carlos Avila Gonzalez/San Francisco Chronicle/Corbis; **pp. 119–120:** James M. Henslin;

Chapter 5: p. 124: Abd Raouf/AP Images; **p. 127:** Richard Ellis/Getty Images; **p. 129:** Robert Weber/The New Yorker Collection/www.cartoonbank.com; **p. 130:** Hemis/Alamy; **p. 130:** DOONESBURY © 1989 G. B. Trudeau. Reprinted with permission of UNIVERSALUCLICK. All rights reserved.; **p. 131:** C.M. Holmgren; **p. 133:** Dinodia/The Image Works; **p. 134:** Stephen Lovekin/WireImage/Getty Images; **p. 135:** Gaston Brito/Reuters/Landov; **p. 137:** St Petersburg Times/Daniel Wallace/The Image Works; **p. 138:** Dan D''Errico/Photoshot/Newscom; **p. 140:** Zoriah/EyePress EyePress/Newscom;

Chapter 6: p. 144: Andy Clark/Reuters/Landov; **p. 146:** imago sportfotodienst/Newscom; **p. 147:** Nigel Pavitt/JAI/Corbis; **p. 151:** Jennifer Szymaszek/AP Images; **p. 152:** George Doyle/Stockbyte/Getty Images; **p. 153:** John Birdsall/The Image Works; **p. 153:** Konstantin Sutyagin/Shutterstock; **p. 153:** Michael N. Paras/Veer Royalty Free; **p. 153:** Stan Carroll/The Commercial Appeal/Landov; **p. 153:** Andre Jenny Stock Connection Worldwide/Newscom; **p. 153:** Oli Scarff/Getty Images; **p. 154:** Robert Weber/The New Yorker Collection/www.cartoonbank.com; **p. 155:** David J. Phillip/AP Images; **p. 156:** PhotoInc/E+/Getty Images; **p. 156:** David M. Grossman/The Image Works; **p. 157:** Barbara Davidson,pool/AP Images; **p. 158:** Lee Frost/Robert Harding/Newscom; **p. 159:** Digital Vision/Getty Images; **p. 160:** Ocean/Corbis; **p. 162:** James M. Henslin; **p. 163:** Pictorial Press Ltd/Alamy; **p. 166:** Courtesy of Alexandra Milgram. Copyright 1968 by Stanley Milgram. Copyright renewed 1993 by Alexandra Milgram. From the film OBEDIENCE, distributed by Penn State Media Sales;

Chapter 7: p. 170: Lauren Salkin/ZUMA/Corbis; **p. 173:** Pavel Rahman/AP Images; **p. 174:** AFP/Getty Images; **p. 175:** North Wind Picture Archives/Alamy; **p. 177:** Ronen Zvulun/Reuters/Corbis; **p. 178:** Keystone/Corbis; **p. 179:** Bettmann/Corbis; **p. 179:** March of Dimes; **p. 180:** Tom Cheney/The New Yorker Collection/www.cartoonbank.com; **p. 181:** ColorBlind Images/Blend Boost/AGE Fotostock; **p. 182:** PRNewsFoto/AKQA/AP Images; **p. 184:** Paul Rodriguez/ZUMA Press/Corbis; **p. 185:** Maya Alleruzzo/The Washington Times/Landov; **p. 186:** Chris Wildt/www.CartoonStock.com; **p. 187:** Hero Images/Corbis; **p. 189:** Charlie Varley/Sipa USA/Newscom; **p. 190:** Zhao Bing/Xinhua/Landov;

Chapter 8: p. 193: Mario Azunioni/EPA/Landov; **p. 195:** James M. Henslin; **p. 196:** Nigel Pavitt/JAI/Corbis; **p. 197:** Babu/Reuters/Landov; **p. 199:** Maxim Konyayev/Reuters/Landov; **p. 199:** Charles Mcquillan/EPA/Landov; **p. 201:** Eau Claire Leader-Telegram, Dan Reiland/AP Images; **p. 202:** Booking Photo/Supplied by PacificCoastNews/Newscom; **p. 202:** Ronaldo Schemidt/AFP/Getty Images/Newscom; **p. 203:** Scott Olson/Getty Images; **p. 204:** AP Images; **p. 205:** Michael Democker/The Times-Picayune /Landov; **p. 207:** Pam Francis/Hulton Archive/Getty Images; **p. 208:** A. Ramey/PhotoEdit, Inc.; **p. 210:** Underwood Photo Archives/SuperStock; **p. 211:** Leo Cullum/The New Yorker Collection/www.cartoonbank.com; **p. 218:** AP Images; **p. 219:** Henry Romero/Reuters/Landov; **p. 221:** AP Images; **p. 222:** George Rose/Getty Images;

Chapter 9: p. 225: Jack Kurtz/The Image Works; **p. 227:** Shawn G. Henry; **p. 228:** Album/Oronoz/Newscom; **p. 229:** James M. Henslin; **p. 230:** James M. Henslin; **p. 232:** Partha Sarkar/Xinhua Press/Corbis; **p. 232:** Doug Murray/Icon SMI/Newscom; **p. 233:** Bettmann/Corbis; **p. 234:** Lewis W. Hine/Buyenlarge/Getty Images; **p. 234:** Bettmann/Corbis; **p. 236:** John Angelillo/UPI /Landov; **p. 237:** Chen Jianli/Xinhua/Landov; **p. 239:** Art Media/Heritage-Images/The Image Works; **p. 245:** Ric Francis/AP Images; **p. 247:** James M. Henslin; **p. 248:** Steve Mann/Shutterstock; **pp. 248–249:** James M. Henslin; **p. 250:** Keith Dannemiller/ZUMAPRESS/Newscom; **p. 251:** David Bacon/The Image Works;

Chapter 10: p. 256: Mark Evans/the Agency Collection/Getty Images; **p. 258:** Heather Wines/CBS/Landov; **p. 261:** Massimo Cebrelli/Getty Images; **p. 264:** Karim Sahib/AFP/Getty Images/Newscom; **p. 265:** Skip O''Rourke/ZUMAPRESS/Newscom; **p. 267:** Jim Watson/AFP/Getty Images/Newscom; **p. 268:** Landov; **p. 268:** Junko Kimura/ZUMA Press/Corbis; **p. 268:** Panoramic/ZUMAPRESS/Newscom; **p. 268:** Kristin Callahan/Everett Collection/Newscom; **p. 269:** Boris Drucker/The New Yorker Collection/www.cartoonbank.com; **p. 270:** James M. Henslin; **p. 271:** Tim Chapman/Getty Images; **p. 271:** David Bacon/The Image Works; **p. 272:** Bob Daemmrich/The Image Works; **p. 273:** Bettmann/Corbis; **p. 274:** Marmaduke St. John/Alamy; **p. 275:** Corey Hochachka/Design Pics/Newscom; **p. 276:** Corbis/SuperStock; **p. 277:** Library of Congress Prints and Photographs Division [Dorothea Lange/LC-USF34-T01-009095-C]; **p. 279:** James M. Henslin; **p. 285:** Photo by James M. Henslin;

Chapter 11: p. 287: Ilyas Dean/Newscom; **p. 289:** Monika Graff/UPI/Landov; **p. 290:** Monica Rodriguez/Lifesize/Getty Images; **p. 290:** Nevada Wier/Stockbyte/Getty Images; **p. 290:** Jake Warga/Corbis; **p. 290:** Bill Bachmann/The Image Works; **p. 290:** Reuters/Corbis; **p. 290:** © Deco/Alamy; **p. 290:** Doug Pearson/JAI/Corbis; **p. 290:** Torrione Stefano/Hemis/ZUMAPRESS.com/Newscom; **p. 291:** Thomas Dallal/SIPA Press; **p. 292:** Martin Stuart-Fox/Bettmann/Corbis; **p. 293:** Darrin Klimek/The Image Bank/Getty Images; **p. 293:** Yakima Herald-Republic, Gordon King/AP Images; **p. 294:** Jeremy Horner/Corbis; **p. 295:** Abedin Taherkenareh/EPA/Newscom; **p. 296:** Chandan Robert Rebeiro/Drik/

Majority World/The Image Works; **p. 297:** Bartosz Hadyniak/Vetta/Getty Images; **p. 298:** Blue Moon/Fotolia; **pp. 298–299:** James M. Henslin; **p. 300:** Francoise Sylvie/SIPA/Newscom; **p. 301:** Sala Lewis/PA Photos/Landov; **p. 302:** Hulton-Deutsch Collection/Corbis; **p. 303:** From Dick and Jane: Fun with Our Family, Illustrations © copyright 1951, 1979, and Dick and Jane: We Play Outside, copyright © 196. Pearson Education, Inc., published by Scott Foresman and Company. Used with permission.; **p. 306:** Frank and Helena/cultura/Corbis; **p. 308:** Tom Grill/Corbis; **p. 313:** Larry Williams Associates/Corbis; **p. 314:** Mario Tama/Getty Images; **p. 314:** Kes. Reproduction rights available from www.cartoonstock.com; **p. 316:** Image Source/Corbis; **p. 317:** Ali Haider/EPA/Landov;

Chapter 12: p. 320: Steve bly/Alamy; **p. 322:** John Stillwell/PA Photos/Landov; **p. 323:** Doug Murray/Icon SMI/Newscom; **p. 324:** Didi/Alamy; **p. 325:** Time & Life Pictures/Getty Images; **p. 325:** akg-images/Newscom; **p. 326:** Jenny Vaughan/AFP/Getty Images; **p. 327:** James M. Henslin; **p. 327:** Lisa Dejong/The Plain Dealer/Landov; **p. 327:** LIncoln Journal Star, Ken Blackbird/AP Images; **p. 327:** Rick Wilking/Reuters/Landov; **p. 327:** Robert Galbraith/Reuters/Corbis; **p. 328:** Charles Moore/Black Star/Alamy; **p. 329:** Bill Hogan/KRT/Newscom; **p. 336:** Missouri History Museum, St. Louis.; **p. 338:** AP Images; **p. 339:** momentimages/Tetra Images/Corbis; **p. 340:** Jim West Image Broker/Newscom; **p. 341:** Arianne Starnes/UPI/Landov; **p. 343:** David McNew/Getty Images; **p. 345:** U.S. Coast Guard/HO/Landov; **p. 346:** Photo by Fred Blackwell; **p. 347:** Brooks Kraft/Corbis; **p. 348:** Ted Thai/Time Life Pictures/Getty Images; **p. 349:** Kyodo/Newscom; **p. 350:** SuperStock; **p. 352:** Antonio Ribeiro/Gamma-Rapho/Getty Images; **p. 355:** momentimages/Tetra Images/Newscom;

Chapter 13: p. 358: Picavet/Workbook Stock/Getty Images; **p. 360:** Song Wen/Xinhua/Landov; **p. 362:** Benjamin Benschneider KRT/Newscom; **p. 365:** Kyodo/Landov; **p. 366:** James M. Henslin; **p. 366:** PEANUTS ® Charles M. Schulz; **p. 367:** TopPhoto/AP Images; **p. 368:** AJM/PA Photos/Landov; **p. 369:** Eric Risberg/AP Images; **p. 375:** Michael Dwyer/AP Images; **p. 377:** Peter & Georgina Bowater Stock Connection Worldwide/Newscom; **p. 378:** Chandler Chou/Flickr Open/Getty Images; **p. 379:** Alison Wright/Corbis; **p. 379:** Digital Vision/Getty Images; **p. 381:** Quad-City Times/ZUMA Press/Corbis; **p. 383:** s70/ZUMA Press/Newscom;

Chapter 14: p. 387: Porter Gifford/Corbis; **p. 389:** Michele Falzone/AWL Images/Getty Images; **p. 390:** Lewis W. Hine/Buyenlarge/Getty Images; **p. 390:** Kevin Schafer/Danita Delimont Stock Photography; **p. 392:** andriig-orulko/Fotolia; **p. 393:** James M. Henslin; **p. 395:** Buyenlarge/Getty Images; **p. 396:** Frank Trapper/Corbis; **p. 397:** TKG Private Collection/Lebrecht Music & Arts/Corbis; **p. 397:** Galerie Bilderwelt/Getty Images; **p. 399:** Chen Yehua/Xinhua/Landov; **p. 401:** Demashita! Powerpuff Girls Z © 2009 Cartoon Network, Toei Animation & Aniplex. All Rights Reserved. THE POWERPUFF GIRLS and all related characters and elements are trademarks of and ©Cartoon Network; **p. 404:** James M. Henslin; **p. 407:** Michael Szönyi Image Broker/Newscom; **p. 412:** Martin Barraud/OJO Images Ltd/Alamy; **p. 415:** Romeo Ranoco/Reuters /Landov; **p. 416:** Andrew Holbrooke/Corbis;

Chapter 15: p. 420: Amy Peterson/MCT/Landov; **p. 422:** Eddie Adams/AP Images; **p. 423:** dominic dibbs/Alamy; **p. 424:** Arthur C.Michael/The Stapleton Collection/Bridgeman Art Library; **p. 425:** AKG London; **p. 426:** Art Media - Gallerie des Batailles/HIP/The Image Works; **p. 427:** STR/AFP/Getty Images/Newscom; **p. 429:** Daniel Wallace/ZUMA Press, Inc./Alamy; **p. 430:** The Wall Street Journal, permission Cartoon Features Syndicate.; **p. 433:** ©'06 Wiley Ink, Inc. Dist. By Universal Press Syndicate 9-22. Wileyink@earthlin.net Gocomics.com; **p. 434:** Bettmann/Corbis; **p. 437:** Lockheed Martin/UPI/Newscom; **p. 438:** James M. Henslin; **p. 440:** Lynne Fernandes/The Image Works; **p. 440:** Francis Miller/Time Life Pictures/Getty Images; **p. 441:** Charles Dharapak/AP Images; **p. 443:** Handout/Reuters/Landov; **p. 444:** Getty Images; **p. 445:** Nic Bothma/EPA/Newscom; **p. 447:** Anton Hammerl/Africa Media Online/The Image Works; **p. 447:** Corbis; **p. 447:** TopFoto/The Image Works;

Chapter 16: p. 450: WPA Rota/Press Association/The Image Works; **p. 452:** Courtesy of the Center for Talent Innovation, N.Y. copyright 1994.; **p. 454:** Jason Love/www.CartoonStock.com; **p. 456:** James M. Henslin; **p. 459:** James M. Henslin; **p. 460:** Diane Bondareff/AP Images; **p. 461:** St Petersburg Times/Lara Cerri/The Image Works; **p. 463:** Shironina/Shutterstock; **p. 466:** StockbrokerXtra/Alamy; **p. 467:** Bill Varie/Somos Images/Corbis; **p. 468:** Anastasia Walsh KRT/Newscom; **p. 470:** Burger/Phanie/The Image Works; **p. 471:** Monika Graff/UPI/Newscom; **p. 475:** Sidney Harris, ScienceCartoonsPlus.com; **p. 477:** HO/AFP/Getty Images/Newscom; **p. 478:** Courtesy of the Center for Talent Innovation, N.Y. copyright 1994.; **p. 480:** Image Source/Alamy; **p. 481:** Europics/Newscom; **p. 483:** Novastock/Alamy;

Chapter 17: p. 486: Mustafiz Mamun/Drik/Majority World/The Image Works; **p. 488:** Prisma/SuperStock; **p. 489:** Lewis Wickes Hine/Everett Collection/Newscom; **p. 490:** Marty Heitner/The Image Works; **p. 491:** Fujifotos/The Image Works; **p. 493:** David Snyder/ZUMA Press/Newscom; **p. 494:** Robert Mankoff/The New Yorker Collection/www.cartoonbank.com; **p. 495:** Jim West/The Image Works; **p. 497:** Erin Moroney LaBelle/The Image Works; **p. 498:** GoGo Images Corporation/Alamy; **p. 499:** Jim Cummins/Taxi/Getty Images; **p. 505:** Kathleen Flynn/ZUMApress/Newscom; **p. 508:** HO/AP Images; **p. 509:** Travis Long/MCT/Landov;

Chapter 18: p. 512: Zurab Kurtsikidze/EPA/Newscom; **p. 514:** Munish Sharma/Reuters/Landov; **p. 515:** The Star-Ledger/The Image Works; **p. 516:** dbimages/Alamy; **p. 517:** Bob Henriques/Magnum Photos; **p. 518:** Scala/Art Resource, NY; **p. 519:** Soe Zeya Tun/Reuters/Landov; **p. 522:** Zvonimir Atletic/Shutterstock; **pp. 522–523:** James M. Henslin; **p. 524:** Robert Weber/The New Yorker Collection/www.cartoonbank.com; **p. 526:** Joe Kohen/AP Images; **p. 528:** Mohammad Kheirkhah/UPI /Landov; **p. 529:** James M. Henslin; **p. 531:** Mohsin Raza/Reuters/Landov; **p. 532:** James M. Henslin; **p. 537:** Ethel Wolvovitz/The Image Works; **p. 540:** PEANUTS® Charles M. Schulz; **p. 542:**Reuters/shipoffools.com/HO/Landov; **p. 542:** The Star-Ledger/John O'Boyle/The Image Works;

Chapter 19: p. 545: Kevin Steele/Aurora Photos/Alamy; **p. 547:** James M. Henslin; **p. 549:** Farah Abdi Warsameh/AP Images; **p. 550:** David Chang/epa/Corbis; **p. 551:** Buyenlarge/Getty Images; **p. 552:** SHOUT/Alamy; **p. 554:** Bettmann/Corbis; **p. 554:** James M. Henslin; **p. 557:** Grant Turner/AFP/Getty Images/Newscom; **p. 560:** Richard Ellis/Alamy; **p. 562:** Frank and Ernest used with the permission of the Thaves and the Cartoonist Group. All rights reserved.; **p. 563:** Seth Wenig/AP Images; **p. 564:** Friedrich Stark/Alamy; **p. 567:** Carl Court/AFP/Getty Images; **p. 569:** Ezio Petersen/UPI Photo Service/Newscom; **p. 570:** National Archives; **p. 572:** Agnes Montanari/Gamma-Rapho/Getty Images; **p. 574:** Denis Sinyakov/Reuters/Landov; **p. 575:** ZSB/WENN.com/Newscom;

Chapter 20: p. 578: STR/AFP/Getty Images/Newscom; **p. 580:** Karl Opsata/Bettmann/Corbis; **p. 584:** Reprinted from Food and Chemical Toxicology, Volume 50, Gilles-Eric Séralini, Page No 4226, Copyright (2012), with permission from Elsevier; **p. 585:** Mustafa Abdi/AFP/Getty Images/Newscom; **p. 585:** James M. Henslin; **p. 590:** Monika Graff/The Image Works; **p. 591:** Ulyanovsk press service/HO/AP Images; **p. 592:** Julia Waterlow/Eye Ubiquitous/Alamy; **p. 593:** Rafiq Maqbool/AP Images; **p. 594:** age fotostock/SuperStock; **p. 596:** IgorGolovniov/Shutterstock; **pp. 596–597:** James M. Henslin; **p. 601:** Julie Jacobson/AP Images; **p. 605:** Tang Chhin SothyAFP/Getty Images; **p. 606:** Paula Solloway/Alamy; **p. 608:** nagelestock.com/Alamy; **p. 610:** Glow Images/Newscom;

Chapter 21: p. 613: Liang Sen/ZUMAPRESS/Newscom; **p. 615:** Brazil/Reuters/Landov; **p. 618:** Bob Galbraith/AP Images; **p. 620:** Hulton Archive/Getty Images; **p. 621:** Alberto Galdona/AFP/Getty Images; **p. 623:** Hindustan Times/AP Images; **p. 624:** Tony Dejak/AP Images; **p. 625:** bilwissedition Ltd. & Co. KG/Alamy; **p. 626:** Francois Lenoir/REUTERS/Landov; **p. 629:** Mark Eite/Aflo Co. Ltd./Alamy; **p. 630:** LHB Photo/Alamy; **p. 630:** Brian Kersey/UPI/Landov; **p. 634:** UK City Images/Alamy; **p. 635:** Shawn Thew/EPA/Landov;

Chapter 22: p. 638: Mark Conlin/V&W/The Image Works; **p. 640:** Jim Zuckerman/Alamy; **p. 640:** The Zetland Collection; **p. 642:** Mark Pearce/EPA/Newscom; **p. 643:** JO1 Mike Jones/AFP/Getty Images/Newscom; **p. 644:** Transit Leipzig/Sovfoto; **p. 645:** LeoSad/Fotolia; **p. 645:** aquatic creature/Shutterstock; **p. 645:** Rob Wilson/Shutterstock; **p. 646:** Carl De Souza/AFP/Getty Images; **p. 647:** H. Armstrong Roberts/ClassicStock/The Image Works; **p. 649:** Corbis; **p. 649:** Yuan Hongwei/Xinhua/Landov; **p. 651:** Bettmann/Corbis; **p. 651:** Tampa Bay Times/Jim Damaske/The Image Works; **p. 652:** Michal Cizek/AFP/Getty Images; **p. 653:** Kim Jae-Hwan/AFP/Getty Images; **p. 653:** Sean Sprague/The Image Works; **p. 654:** Leslie Pratt/SIPA/Newscom; **p. 655:** byrdyak/Fotolia; **p. 655:** mlorenz/Shutterstock; **p. 655:** Gabriela/Fotolia; **p. 655:** wildlywise/Shutterstock; **p. 656:** Mark Ralston/AFP/Getty Images/Newscom; **p. 658:** TopFoto/Scott-Taggart/The Image Works; **p. 660:** Loren McIntyre Stock Connection Worldwide/Newscom; **p. 661:** Marcio José Sanchez/AP Images; **p. 662:** Hartmut Schwarzbach -UNEP/Still Pictures/The Image Works; **p. 663:** Bruno Domingos/Reuters/Landov;

Text Credits

Chapter 1: p. 3 excerpt: Excerpt from Mills, C. Wright. The Sociological Imagination. New York: Oxford University Press, 1959; **p. 10 excerpt:** Excerpt from Dobriner, William M. Social Structures and Systems. Pacific Palisades, California: Goodyear, 1969b; Gitlin, Todd. The Twilight of Common Dreams: Why America Is Wracked by Culture Wars. New York: Metropolitan Books, 1997; **p. 11 excerpt:** Excerpt from Durkheim, Emile. Suicide: A Study in Sociology, John A. Spaulding and George Simpson, trans. New York: Free Press, 1966. Originally published 1897; **Fig** 1.1: Based on Centers for Disease Control and Prevention 2012 and earlier years; **p. 13 excerpt:** Excerpt from Galliher, John F. Deviant Behavior and Human Rights. Englewood Cliffs, N.J.: Prentice Hall, 1991; **Fig 1.2:** SOURCE: James M. Henslin, Copyrighted Pearson Education, Upper Saddle River, NJ; **p. 14 excerpt:** Excerpt from Durkheim, Emile. Suicide: A Study in Sociology, John A. Spaulding and George Simpson, trans. New York: Free Press, 1966. Originally published 1897; **p. 17 excerpt:** Excerpt from SOURCE: Harriet Martineau, Society in America, 1837; **p. 17 excerpt:** Excerpt from SOURCE: Harriet Martineau, Society in America, 1837; **p. 17 excerpt:** Excerpt from SOURCE: Harriet Martineau, Society in America, 1837; **p. 19 box:** SOURCE: W. E. B. Du Bois, The Souls of Black Folk (1903); **Fig** 1.4: Based on DeMartini 1982, plus events since then; **Fig** 1.5: SOURCE: Pager, Devah. "The Mark of a Criminal Record." American Journal of Sociology, 108, 5, March 2003:937–975. (c) 2003 by University of Chicago Press. Reproduced by permission; **Fig** 1.6: Based on Statistical Abstract of the United States 1998:Table 92 and 2013:Tables 81, 134; earlier editions for earlier years. The broken lines indicate the author's estimates; Table 1.1: SOURCE: James M. Henslin, Copyrighted Pearson Education, Upper Saddle River, NJ;

Chapter 2: p. 35 excerpt: Excerpt from Linton, Ralph. The Study of Man. New York: Appleton-Century-Crofts, 1936; **p. 36 excerpt:** Excerpt from SOURCE: William Sumner (1906); **p. 38 box:** Based on Bearak 2010; Consulate General of Madagascar in Cape Town 2012; **p. 39 excerpt:** Excerpt from Bates, Marston. Gluttons and Libertines: Human Problems of Being Natural. New York: Vintage Books, 1967. Quoted in Crapo, Richley H. Cultural Anthropology: Understanding Ourselves and Others, 5th ed. Boston: McGraw Hill, 2002; **p. 39 excerpt:** Excerpt from SOURCE: Dusty Friedman; **p. 39 excerpt:** Excerpt from Kingston, Maxine Hong. The Woman Warrior. New York: Vintage Books, 1975:108. Quoted in Frank J. Zulke and Jacqueline P. Kirley. Through the Eyes of Social Science, 6th ed. Prospect Heights, Ill.: Waveland Press, 2002; **Fig** 2.1: SOURCE: James M. Henslin, Copyrighted Pearson Education, Upper Saddle River, NJ; **p. 44 box:** Based on Kent and Lalasz 2007; Salomon 2008; Costantini 2011; Nelson 2011; **p. 47 excerpt:** Excerpt from Robertson, Ian. Sociology, 3rd ed. New York: Worth, 1987; **p. 47 excerpt:** Excerpt from Dickey, Christopher, and John Barry. "Iran: A Rummy Guide." Newsweek, May 8, 2006; **p. 50 excerpt:** Excerpt from SOURCE: Krumer-Nevo, Michal, and Orly Benjamin. "Critical Poverty Knowledge: Contesting Othering and Social Distancing. Current Sociology September 2010 vol. 58 no. 5 **pp.** 693–714; **p. 50 excerpt:** Excerpt from Zellner, William W. Countercultures: A Sociological Analysis. New York: St. Martin's, 1995; **p. 57 excerpt:** Excerpt from Ogburn, William F. Social Change with Respect to Culture and Human Nature. New York: W. B. Huebsch, 1922. (Other editions by Viking in 1927, 1938, and 1950.);

Chapter 3: p. 62 excerpt: Excerpt from Davis, Kingsley. "Extreme Isolation." In Down to Earth Sociology: Introductory Readings, 15th ed., James M. Henslin, ed. New York: Free Press, 2012. Originally published as "Extreme Social Isolation of a Child." American Journal of Sociology, 45, January 4, 1940:554–565; **p. 63 box:** Based on Begley 1979; Chen 1979; Wright 1995; Segal and Hershberger 2005; Ledger 2009; Johnson et al. 2009; Segal 2011; **p. 64 excerpt:** Excerpt from Davis, Kingsley. "Extreme Isolation." In Down to Earth Sociology: Introductory Readings, 15th ed., James M. Henslin, ed. New York: Free Press, 2012. Originally published as "Extreme Social Isolation of a Child." American Journal of Sociology, 45, January 4, 1940:554–565; **p. 64 excerpt:** Excerpt from Skeels, H. M. Adult Status of Children with Contrasting Early Life Experiences: A Follow-up Study. Monograph of the Society for Research in Child Development, 31, 3, 1966; **p. 66 excerpt:** Excerpt from Skeels, H. M. Adult Status of Children with Contrasting Early Life Experiences: A Follow-up Study. Monograph of the Society for Research in Child Development, 31, 3, 1966; **p. 67 excerpt:** Excerpt from SOURCE: Cooley, Charles Horton. Human Nature and the Social Order. New York: Scribner's, 1902; **Fig** 3.1: SOURCE: James M. Henslin, Copyrighted Pearson Education, Upper Saddle River, NJ; **p. 72 excerpt:** Excerpt from Horwitz, Allan V., and Jerome C. Wakefield. The Loss of Sadness: How Psychiatry Transformed Normal Sorrow into Depressive Disorder. New York: Oxford University Press, 2007; **p. 74 excerpt:** Excerpt from Connors 1996; Clearfield and Nelson 2006; Best 2010; **p. 76 box:** Based on Zumbrun 2007; Bilefsky 2008; Young and Twigg 2009; **p. 77 excerpt:** Excerpt from Smith and Cook 2008; Smith et al. 2012; **p. 78 excerpt:** Excerpt from SOURCE: Laura Parker. It's Hard to Believe in the New Lara Croft. GameSpot, 2012; **p. 82 box:** Based on Richard Rodriguez 1975, 1982, 1990, 1991, 1995; **p. 83 box:** SOURCE: James M. Henslin, Copyrighted Pearson Education, Upper Saddle River, NJ; **p. 85 box:** Based on Garfinkel 1956; Goffman 1961; Ricks 1995; Dyer 2007. **p. 87 excerpt:** Excerpt from DeMause, Lloyd. "Our Forebears Made Childhood a Nightmare." Psychology Today 8, 11, April 1975:85–88; **Fig** 3.2: SOURCE: Furstenberg, Frank F., Jr., Sheela Kennedy, Vonnie C. McLoyd, Ruben G. Rumbaut, and Richard A. Settersten, Jr. "Growing Up Is Harder to Do." Contexts, 3, 3, Summer 2004:33–41; **p. 88 excerpt:** Excerpt from Keniston, Kenneth. Youth and Dissent: The Rise of a New Opposition. New York: Harcourt, Brace, Jovanovich, 1971.**p. 88 excerpt:** Excerpt from Neugarten, Bernice L. "Middle Age and Aging." In Growing Old in America, Beth B. Hess, ed. New Brunswick, N.J.:Transaction, 1976:180–197;

Chapter 4: Fig 4.1: SOURCE: James M. Henslin, Copyrighted Pearson Education, Upper Saddle River, NJ; **p. 99 excerpt:** Excerpt from SOURCE: William Shakespeare, As You Like It, Act II, Scene 7; **p. 99 excerpt:** Excerpt from SOURCE: William Shakespeare; **Fig 4.2:** SOURCE: James M. Henslin, Copyrighted Pearson Education, Upper Saddle River, NJ; **p. 105 box:** Aeppel 1996; Kephart and Zellner 2001; Kraybill 2002; Johnson-Weiner 2007; Scolforo 2008; Buckley 2011; **Fig 4.3:** SOURCE: James M. Henslin, Copyrighted Pearson Education, Upper Saddle River, NJ; **p. 108, 110 excerpt:** Excerpt from Hall, Edward T. The Silent Language. New York: Doubleday, 1959 (Hall and Hall 2014); **p. 111 excerpt:** Excerpt from Hughes, Kathleen A. "Even Tiki Torches Don't Guarantee a Perfect Wedding." Wall Street Journal, February 20, 1990:A1, A16; **Fig 4.4**: SOURCE: James M. Henslin, Copyrighted Pearson Education, Upper Saddle River, NJ; **p. 114 excerpt:** Excerpt from Marshall, Samantha. "It's So Simple: Just Lather Up, Watch the Fat Go Down the Drain." Wall Street Journal, November 2, 1995:B1; **p. 116 excerpt:** Excerpt from Garfinkel, Harold. Studies in Ethnomethodology. Englewood Cliffs, N.J.: Prentice Hall, 1967; **p. 117 excerpt:** Excerpt from Thomas, W. I., and Dorothy Swaine Thomas. The Child in America: Behavior Problems and Programs. New York: Alfred A. Knopf, 1928; **p. 117 excerpt:** Excerpt from Henslin, James M., and Mae A. Biggs. "Behavior in Pubic Places: The Sociology of the Vaginal Examination." In Down to Earth Sociology: Introductory Readings, 15th ed., James M. Henslin, ed. New York: Free Press, 2012. Originally published 1971;

Chapter 5: Fig 5.1: Adapted from Table 5.1 Modification of Table 1 in O'Brien, John E. "Violence in Divorce-Prone Families." In Violence in the Family, Suzanne K. Steinmetz and Murray A. Straus, eds. New York: Dodd, Mead, 1975:65–75; **p. 131 box:** Based on Crossen 1991; Goleman 1993; Barnes 1995; Resnik 2000; Augoustinos et al. 2009; **p. 134 box:** Based on Venkatesh, Sudhir. Gang Leader for a Day: A Rogue Sociologist Takes to the Streets. New York: Penguin, 2008; **Fig 5.2:** SOURCE: James M. Henslin, Copyrighted Pearson Education, Upper Saddle River, NJ; **p. 138 box:** Based on Anderson 1986; Rossi 1989, 1991, 1999; National Coalition for the Homeless 2008; HUD 2010; **p. 141 box:** Marolla and Scully 1986; Scully 1986; Scully and Marolla 1984, 2007, 2013;

Chapter 6: p. 145 excerpt: Excerpts from Scott, Monster Cody. Monster: The Autobiography of an L. A. Gang Member. New York: Penguin Books, 1994:8–13, 103; **Fig 6.1:** SOURCE: James M. Henslin, Copyrighted Pearson Education, Upper Saddle River, NJ; **Fig 6.2:** SOURCE: James M. Henslin, Copyrighted Pearson Education, Upper Saddle River, NJ; **p. 148 excerpt:** Excerpt from Boulding, Elise. The Underside of History. Boulder, Colo.: Westview Press, 1976; **p. 151 box:** Based on Davis 2001; Weiss 2004; Regalado 2005; Smith et al. 2012; Baylis 2013; **p. 154 excerpt:** Excerpt from SOURCE: Cooley, Charles Horton. Social Organization. New York: Schocken Books, 1962. Originally published by Scribner's, 1909; **p. 155 excerpt:** Excerpt from Merton, Robert K. Social Theory and Social Structure. Glencoe, Ill.: Free Press, 1949. Enlarged ed., 1968; **p. 155 excerpt:** Excerpt from Dershowitz 2004; Allhoff 2011; **p. 157 excerpt:** Excerpt from Milgram, Stanley. "The Small World Problem." Psychology Today, 1, 1967:61–67; **p. 158 excerpt:** Excerpt from Kleinfeld, Judith S. "The Small World Problem." Society, January–February, 2002b:61–66; **p. 159 excerpt:** Excerpt from Kantor, Jodi. "In First Family, a Nation's Many Faces." New York Times, January 16, 2009; **Fig 6.4:** SOURCE: Asch 1952:452–453; **p. 165 excerpt:** Excerpt from Milgram, Stanley. "Behavioral Study of Obedience." Journal of Abnormal and Social Psychology, 67, 4, 1963:371–378; Milgram, Stanley. "Some Conditions of Obedience and Disobedience to Authority." Human Relations, 18, February 1965:57–76; **p. 165 excerpt:** Excerpt from Milgram, Stanley. "Behavioral Study of Obedience." Journal of Abnormal and Social Psychology, 67, 4, 1963:371–378; Milgram, Stanley. "Some Conditions of Obedience and Disobedience to authority." Human Relations, 18, February 1965:57–76; **p. 166 excerpt:** Excerpt from Milgram, Stanley. "Behavioral Study of Obedience." Journal of Abnormal and Social Psychology, 67, 4, 1963:371–378; Milgram, Stanley. "Some Conditions of Obedience and Disobedience to Authority." Human Relations, 18, February 1965:57–76; **p. 166 excerpt:** Excerpt from Milgram, Stanley. "Behavioral Study of Obedience." Journal of Abnormal and Social Psychology, 67, 4, 1963:371–378; Milgram, Stanley. "Some Conditions of Obedience and Disobedience to Authority." Human Relations, 18, February 1965:57–76; **p. 166 excerpt:** Excerpt from Milgram, Stanley. "Behavioral Study of Obedience." Journal of Abnormal and Social Psychology, 67, 4, 1963:371–378; Milgram, Stanley. "Some Conditions of Obedience and Disobedience to Authority." Human Relations, 18, February 1965:57–76; **p. 166 excerpt:** Excerpt from Milgram, Stanley. "Behavioral Study of Obedience." Journal of Abnormal and Social Psychology, 67, 4, 1963:371–378; Milgram, Stanley. "Some Conditions of Obedience and Disobedience to Authority." Human Relations, 18, February 1965:57–76; **p. 168 excerpt:** Excerpt from Shane, Scott. "Report Outlines Medical Workers' Role in Torture." New York Times, April 6, 2009;

Chapter 7: Table 7.1: SOURCE: James M. Henslin, Copyrighted Pearson Education, Upper Saddle River, NJ; **p. 173 excerpt:** Excerpt from SOURCE: Max Weber (1864–1920); **p. 173 excerpt:** Excerpt from SOURCE: Max Weber (1864–1920); **p. 174 excerpt:** Excerpt from SOURCE: Max Weber (1864–1920); **Fig 7.1:** SOURCE: James M. Henslin, Copyrighted Pearson Education, Upper Saddle River, NJ; **p. 179 excerpt:** Excerpt from Tyler, Patrick E. "A New Life for NATO? But It's Sidelined for Now." New York Times, November 20, 2002; **p. 179 excerpt:** Excerpt from SOURCE: Kille, Kent J., and Ryan C. Hendrickson. "NATO and the United Nations: Debates and Trends in Institutional Coordination." Journal of International Organizations Studies, 3, 1, 2012:28-49; **p. 186 excerpt:** Excerpt from Kanter, Rosabeth Moss. Supercorp: How Vanguard Companies Create Innovation, Profits, Growth, and Social Good. New York: Random House, 2009;

Chapter 8: **p. 194 excerpt:** Excerpt from Chagnon, Napoleon A. Yanomamo: The Fierce People, 2nd ed. New York: Holt, Rinehart and Winston, 1977; **p. 194 excerpt:** Excerpt from Becker, Howard S. Outsiders: Studies in the Sociology of Deviance. New York: Free Press, 1966; **p. 198 excerpt:** Excerpt from Kubrin, Charis E., and Ronald Weitzer. "Retaliatory Homicide: Concentrated Disadvantage and Neighborhood Culture." Social Problems, 50, 2, May 2003:157–180; **p. 199 excerpt:** Excerpt from Arlacchi, P. Peasants and Great Estates: Society in Traditional Calabria. Cambridge, England: Cambridge University Press, 1980; **p. 201 excerpt:** Excerpt from Chivers, C. J. "Officer Resigns before Hearing in D.W.I. Case." New York Times, August 29, 2001; Table 8.1: Based on Merton, Robert K. Social Theory and Social Structure. Glencoe, Ill.: Free Press, 1949. Enlarged ed., 1968; **p. 207 excerpt:** Excerpt from McCormick, John. "The Sorry Side of Sears." Newsweek, February 22, 1999b:36–39; **Fig 8.1:** Based on Statistical Abstract of the United States 2013:Table 314; Table 8.2: Based on Statistical Abstract of the United States 2013:Table 338 and earlier years; **p. 210 excerpt:** Excerpt from Drew, Christopher. "Military Contractor Agrees to Pay $325 Million to Settle Whistle-Blower Lawsuit." New York Times, April 2, 2009; **p. 212 box:** Based on Lyall, Sarah. "Here's the Pub, Church and Field for Public Sex." New York Times, October 7, 2010; **Fig 8.2:** Based on Carson and Sabol 2012; Statistical Abstract of the United States 1995:Table 349; 2013:Tables 2, 6, 354. The broken line is the author's estimate; Table 8.3: Based on Sourcebook of Criminal Justice Statistics 2004:Table 6.45.2003; 2011:Table 6.33.2010; Statistical Abstract of the United States 2013:Tables 11, 56, 236, 358; **p. 215 excerpt:** Excerpt from Cloud, John. "For Better or Worse." Time, October 26, 1998:43–44; **Fig 8.3:** Based on Sourcebook of Criminal Justice Statistics 2003:Table 6.50, the latest data available; **Fig 8.4:** Based on Statistical Abstract of the United States 2013:Table 360; **Fig 8.5:** Based on Statistical Abstract of the United States 2013:Table 359; Table 8.4: Based on Sourcebook of Criminal Justice Statistics 2013:Table 6.80.2012; Statistical Abstract of the United Sates 2013:Table11; **p. 219 box:** Based on Sheridan 1998; Malkin 2010; Archibald 2012; Casey 2013; **p. 221 excerpt:** Excerpt from Thomas Szasz (1986, 1998, 2012); **p. 221 excerpt:** Excerpt from Thomas Szasz (1986, 1998, 2012); **p. 222 excerpt:** Excerpt from SOURCE: Durkheim (1895/1964:68);

Chapter 9: **p. 229 excerpt:** Excerpt from Du Bois, W. E. B. Black Reconstruction in America: An Essay toward a History of the Part Which Black Folk Played in the Attempt to Reconstruct Democracy in America, 1860–1880. New York: Atheneum, 1992. Originally published 1935; **p. 230 excerpt:** Excerpt from Guru, Gopal, and Shiraz Sidhva. "India's 'Hidden Apartheid.'" UNESCO Courier, September 2001:27; **p. 231 excerpt:** Excerpt from SOURCE: Lapsley, Michael. Redeeming the Past: My Journey from Freedom Fighter to Healer. Maryknoll, N.Y.: Orbis Books, 2012; **p. 232 excerpt:** Excerpt from Yardley, Jim. "A Village Rape Shatters a Family, and India's Traditional Silence." New York Times, October 27, 2012; **p. 233 excerpt:** Excerpt from Rothkopf, David. Superclass: The Global Power Elite and the World They Are Making. New York: Farrar, Straus and Giroux, 2008; **Fig 9.1:** Based on Rothkopf, David. Superclass: The Global Power Elite and the World They Are Making. New York: Farrar, Straus and Giroux, 2008:37; **Fig 9.2:** SOURCE: James M. Henslin, Copyrighted Pearson Education, Upper Saddle River, NJ; Table 9.2: SOURCE: James M. Henslin, Copyrighted Pearson Education, Upper Saddle River, NJ; **p. 240 excerpt:** Excerpt from SOURCE: Morgan 2012; **p. 241 excerpt:** Excerpt from Robertson, Ian. Sociology, 3rd ed. New York: Worth, 1987; Table 9.3: Computed from Kurian 1990, 1991, 1992; **p. 247 excerpt:** Excerpt from Krugman, Paul. "White Man's Burden." New York Times, September 24, 2002; **p. 251 excerpt:** Excerpt from Fraser, Graham. "Fox Denies Free Trade Exploiting the Poor in Mexico." Toronto Star, April 20, 2001; **Fig 9.3:** Based on CIA World Factbook 2013; Table 9.4: SOURCE: James M. Henslin, Copyrighted Pearson Education, Upper Saddle River, NJ;

Chapter 10: **Fig 10.1:** Based on Beeghley 2008; **p. 259 excerpt:** Excerpt from Samuelson, Paul Anthony, and William D. Nordhaus. Economics, 18th ed. New York: McGraw Hill, 2005; **Fig 10.2:** Based on Statistical Abstract of the United States 2013:Tables 693, 711; **Fig 10.3:** Based on Statistical Abstract of the United States 1960:Table 417; 1970:Table 489; 2013:Table 708; Table 10.1: Lublin, Joann S. "CEO Pay in 2010 Jumped 11%." Wall Street Journal, May 9, 2011; **p. 261 excerpt:** Excerpt from SOURCE: John Castle; Table 10.2: Treiman 1977:Appendices A and D; Nakao and Treas 1990, 1994:Appendix D; **p. 265 excerpt:** Excerpt from Tresniowski, Alex. "Payday or Mayday?" People Weekly, May 17, 1999:128–131; **p. 265 excerpt:** Excerpt from Tresniowski, Alex. "Payday or Mayday?" People Weekly, May 17, 1999:128–131; **p. 265 excerpt:** Excerpt from "Sticky Ticket: A New Jersey Mother Sues Her Son over a Lottery Jackpot She Claims Belongs to Them Both." People Weekly, February 9, 1998:68; **p. 265 excerpt:** Excerpt from Dao, James. "Instant Millions Can't Halt Winners' Grim Side." New York Times, December 5, 2005; **p. 265 excerpt:** Excerpt from McShane, Larry. "Abraham Shakespeare, $31M Florida Lottery Winner, Found Dead 9 Months after Disappearing." Daily News, January 30, 2010; **p. 265 excerpt:** Excerpt from SOURCE: Allen 2012; **Fig 10.4:** SOURCE: James M. Henslin, Copyrighted Pearson Education, Upper Saddle River, NJ; Table 10.3: SOURCE: James M. Henslin, Copyrighted Pearson Education, Upper Saddle River, NJ; **Fig 10.5:** Based on Gilbert and Kahl 1998 and Gilbert 2011; income estimates are inflation-adjusted and modified from Duff 1995; **p. 266 excerpt:** Excerpt from Beeghley, Leonard. The Structure of Social Stratification in the United States, 5th ed. Boston: Allyn & Bacon, 2008; **p. 267 excerpt:** Excerpt from SOURCE: Gilbert Dennis and Joseph Kahl, The American Class Structure: A New Synthesis (Belmont, CA: Wadsworth, 1998); **p. 269 excerpt:** Excerpt from Cohen, Patricia. "Forget Lonely. Life Is Healthy at the Top." New York Times, May 15, 2004; **Fig 10.6:** Lopoo, Leonard, and Thomas DeLeire. "Pursuing the American Dream: Economic Mobility Across Generations." Figure 3, p. 6. Copyright (c) 2012 by PEW Charitable Trust. Reproduced by permission; **p. 275 excerpt:** Excerpt from Blau, Peter M., and Otis Dudley Duncan. The American Occupational Structure. New York: John Wiley, 1967; Featherman, David L. "Opportunities Are Expanding." Society, 13, 1979:4–11; **p. 275 excerpt:** Excerpt from Davis, Nancy J., and Robert V. Robinson. "Class Identification of Men and Women in the 1970s and 1980s." American Sociological Review, 53, February 1988:103–112; Western et al. 2012; **Fig 10.7:** Based on Statistical Abstract of the United States 2013:Table 721; **Fig 10.8:** Based on Statistical Abstract of the United States 2013:Tables 36, 722, and 724; **Fig 10.9:** Based on Statistical Abstract of the United States 2007:Table 694. Table dropped in later editions; **p. 281 excerpt:** Excerpt from Garfinkel, Irwin, Lee Rainwater, and Timothy Smeeding. Wealth and Welfare States: Is America a Laggard or a Leader? New York: Oxford University Press, 2010; **Fig 10.10:** Dye, Jane Lawler. "Fertility of American Women, June 2004." U.S. Census Bureau. Current Population Reports, December 2005; **p. 281 excerpt:** Excerpt from Ruggles, Patricia. "Short and Long Term Poverty in the United States: Measuring the American 'Underclass.'" Washington, D.C.: Urban Institute, June 1989.:7; **Fig 10.11:** Gottschalk, Peter, Sara McLanahan, and Gary Sandefur, "The Dynamics and Intergenerational Transmission of Poverty and Welfare Participation." In Confronting Poverty: Prescriptions for Change, Sheldon H. Danziger, Gary D. Sandefur, and Daniel H. Weinberg, eds. Cambridge, Mass.: Harvard University Press, 1994.:89;

Chapter 11: **p. 291 excerpt:** Excerpt from SOURCE: Money, John, and Anke A. Ehrhardt. Man and Woman, Boy and Girl. Baltimore: Johns Hopkins University Press, 1972; **p. 292 excerpt:** Excerpt from SOURCE: Anderson, Eric. Inclusive Masculinity: The Changing Nature of Masculinities. New York: Routledge, 2009:43; **p. 294 excerpt:** Excerpt from SOURCE: Lerner, Gerda. The Creation of Patriarchy. New York: Oxford, 1986; **p. 295 box:** SOURCE: Based on Fathi, Nazila. "Starting at Home, Iran's Women Fight for Rights." New York Times, February 12, 2009; Semple, Kirk. "Idea of Afghan Women's Rights Starts Taking Hold." New York Times, March 2, 2009. U.S. Department of State 2011; **p. 301 box:** SOURCE: As cited, and Lightfoot-Klein, A. "Rites of Purification and Their Effects: Some Psychological Aspects of Female Genital Circumcision and Infibulation (Pharaonic Circumcision) in an Afro-Arab Society (Sudan)." Journal of Psychological Human Sexuality, 2, 1989:61–78; Merwine, Maynard H. "How Africa Understands Female Circumcision." New York Times, November 24, 1993; Chalkley, Kate. "Female Genital Mutilation: New Laws, Programs Try to End Practice." Population Today, 25, 10, October 1997:4–5; Tuhus-Dubrow, Rebecca. "Rites and Wrongs." Boston Globe, February 11, 2007; UNIFEM. Progress of the World's Women 2008/2009. United Nations Development Fund for Women, 2008; Lazaro 2011; Sacirbey 2012; **p. 301 excerpt:** Excerpt from Source: Walker, Alice, and Pratibha Parmar. Warrior Marks: Female Genital Mutilation and the Sexual Blinding of Women. New York: Harcourt Brace, 1993:107–108; **p. 302 excerpt:** Excerpt from SOURCE: Crossen, Cynthia. "Deja Vu." Wall Street Journal, March 5, 2003; **p. 302 excerpt:** Excerpt from SOURCE: Cowley, Joyce. Pioneers of Women's Liberation. New York: Merit, 1969; **p. 303 excerpt:** Excerpt from Source: Bettleheim, Bruno. "The Commitment Required of a Woman Entering a Scientific Profession in Present-Day American Society." In Women and the Scientific Professions, U. S. Mattfield and C. G. Van Aken, eds. Cambridge, MA: MIT Press, 1965, **pp. 3–19**; **p. 304 excerpt:** Excerpt from SOURCE: Miller, Laura L. "Women in the Military." In Down to Earth Sociology: Introductory Readings, 14th ed., James M. Henslin, ed. New York: Free Press, 2007. Originally published 1997; **p. 304 excerpt:** Excerpt from SOURCE: Jones, Nikki. Between Good and Ghetto: African American Girls and Inner-City Violence. New Brunswick, N.J. Rutgers University Press, 2010; **p. 304 excerpt:** Excerpt from SOURCE: Stockard, Jean, and Miriam M. Johnson. Sex Roles: Sex Inequality and Sex Role Development. Englewood Cliffs, N.J.: Prentice Hall, 1980:12); **p. 306 excerpt:** Excerpt from SOURCE: Scully, Diana. "Negotiating to Do Surgery." In Dominant Issues in Medical Sociology, 3rd ed., Howard D. Schwartz, ed. New York: McGraw-Hill, 1994:146–152; **p. 305 excerpt:** Excerpt from SOURCE: Flexner, E. Century of Struggle. Cambridge, Mass.: Belknap, 1971. In Claire M. Renzetti and Daniel J. Curran, Women, Men, and Society, 4th ed. Boston: Allyn and Bacon, 1999; **p. 305 excerpt:** Excerpt from SOURCE: Andersen, Margaret L. Thinking about

Women: Sociological Perspectives on Sex and Gender. New York: Macmillan, 1988; **Fig 11.2:** SOURCE: Based on Statistical Abstract of the United States 1938:Table 114; 1959:Table 158; 1991:Table 261; 2011:Table 273; 2013:Table 278; **Fig 11.3:** SOURCE: Based on Statistical Abstract of the United States 2013:Table 279; **Fig 11.4:** SOURCE: Based on Digest of Education Statistics 2007:Table 269; Statistical Abstract of the United States 2013:Table 304; **p. 307 excerpt:** Excerpt from SOURCE: Statistical Abstract 2013:Table 302; Table 11.1: Based on statistical abstract of the united states 2013:tables 821, 825; **Fig 11.5:** SOURCE: Based on Women's Bureau of the United States 1969: 10; Manpower Report to the President, 1971: 203, 205; Mills and Palumbo 1980: 6, 45; Statistical Abstract of the United States 2013:Table 597; **Fig 11.6:** SOURCE: Based on Statistical Abstract of the United States 2013:Table 604; **Fig 11.7:** SOURCE: Based on Statistical Abstract of the United States 2013:Table 717; **Fig 11.8:** SOURCE: Based on Statistical Abstract of the United States 1995:Table 739; 2002:Table 666; 2013:Table 717, and earlier years. Broken lines indicate the author's estimate; **p. 313 excerpt:** Excerpt from SOURCE: Carter, Nancy M. "Pipeline's Broken Promise." New York: Catalyst, 2010. Table 11.2: SOURCE: A ten-year average, based on Statistical Abstract of the United States 2003:Table 295; 2004:Table 322; 2005:Table 306; 2006:Table 308; 2007:Table 311; 2008:Table 313; 2009:Table 305; 2010:Table 305; 2011:Table 312; 2012:Table 316; 2013:Table 322; Table 11.3: SOURCE: A ten-year average, based on Statistical Abstract of the United States 2003:Table 323; 2004:Table 323; 2005:Table 307; 2006:Table 311; 2007: Table 315; 2008:Table 316; 2009:Table 306; 2010:Table 306; 2011:Table 313; 2012:Table 317; 2013:Table 323; **p. 316 excerpt:** Excerpt from SOURCE: Carpenito, Lynda Juall. "The Myths of Acquaintance Rape." Nursing Forum, 34, 4, October–December 1999:3;**Fig 11.9:** SOURCE: Based on Statistical Abstract of the United States 2013:Tables 317, 338; Table 11.4: SOURCE: Center for American Women and Politics 2013;

Chapter 12: p. 323 excerpt: Excerpt from SOURCE: Wright, Lawrence. "One Drop of Blood." New Yorker, July 25, 1994:46–50, 52–55; **p. 322 excerpt:** Excerpt from SOURCE: Thomas, W. I., and Dorothy Swaine Thomas. The Child in America: Behavior Problems and Programs. New York: Alfred A. Knopf, 1928; **Fig 12.1:** SOURCE: Based on Doane 1997; **p. 329 box:** Excerpt from SOURCE: Based on Riley, Naomi Schaefer. "The Real Path to Racial Harmony." Wall Street Journal, August 14, 2009; **p. 330 box:** SOURCE: Raphael Ezekiel, The Racist Mind (1995); **Fig 12.2:** SOURCE: Based on Kochbar and Gonzalez-Barrera 2009; Table 12.1: SOURCE: Based on Statistical Abstract of the United States 2013:Tables 110, 118. **p. 336 box:** SOURCE: Based on Bradford, Phillips Verner, and Harvey Blume. Ota Benga: The Pygmy in the Zoo. New York: Delta, 1992; Crossen, Cynthia. "How Pygmy Ota Benga Ended Up in Bronx Zoo as Darwinism Dawned." Wall Street Journal, February 6, 2006; Richman, Joe. "From the Belgian Congo to the Bronx Zoo." National Public Radio, September 8, 2006; **Fig 12.3:** SOURCE: James M. Henslin, Copyrighted Pearson Education, Upper Saddle River, NJ; **p. 335 excerpt:** Excerpt from SOURCE: Schaefer, Richard T. Racial and Ethnic Groups, 9th ed. Upper Saddle River, N.J.: Prentice Hall, 2004; **p. 337 excerpt:** Excerpt from SOURCE: Huttenbach, Henry R. "The Roman Porajmos: The Nazi Genocide of Europe's Gypsies." Nationalities Papers, 19, 3, Winter 1991:373–394; Browning, Christopher R. Ordinary Men: Reserve Police Battalion 101 and the Final Solution in Poland. New York: HarperPerennial, 1993; Gross, Jan T. Neighbors. New Haven: Yale University Press, 2001; **Fig 12.4:** SOURCE: James M. Henslin, Copyrighted Pearson Education, Upper Saddle River, NJ; **Fig 12.5:** SOURCE: Based on Statistical Abstract of the United States 2013:Tables 10, 52; **Fig 12.6:** SOURCE: Based on Statistical Abstract of the United States 2013:Table 18; **p. 340 excerpt:** Excerpt from SOURCE: in Alba, Richard, and Victor Nee. Remaking the American Mainstream: Assimilation and Contemporary Immigration. Cambridge, Mass.: Harvard University Press, 2003:17; **Fig 12.7:** SOURCE: Based on Statistical Abstract of the United States 2013:Table 37; **Fig 12.8:** SOURCE: Based on Statistical Abstract of the United States 2013:Table 18; Table 12.2: SOURCE: Based on Statistical Abstract of the United States 2013:Table 36; **Table 12.3:** SOURCE: Based on Statistical Abstract of the United States 2013:Tables 36, 37, 300, and Table 12.4: SOURCE: Based on Statistical Abstract of the United States 2013:Table 710; **p. 348 excerpt:** Excerpt from SOURCE: Bertrand, Marianne, and Sendhil Mullainathan. "Are Emily and Brendan More Employable than Lakish and Jamal? A Field Experiment on Labor Market Discrimination." Unpublished paper, November 18, 2002; **p. 348 excerpt:** Excerpt from SOURCE: Feagin, Joe R. "The Continuing Significance of Race: Antiblack Discrimination in Public Places." In Majority and Minority: The Dynamics of Race and Ethnicity in American Life, 6th ed., Norman R. Yetman, ed. Boston: Allyn and Bacon, 1999:384–399:398; **Fig 12.9:** SOURCE: Based on U.S. Census Bureau 2010; **p. 349 excerpt:** Excerpt from SOURCE: Hsu, Francis L. K. The Challenge of the American Dream: The Chinese in the United States. Belmont, Calif.: Wadsworth, 1971; **p. 350 excerpt:** Excerpt from SOURCE: Teddy Roosevelt, 1886; **p. 350 excerpt:** Excerpt from SOURCE: Nash, Gary B. Red, White, and Black. Englewood Cliffs, N.J.: Prentice Hall, 1974; in McLemore, S. Dale. Racial and Ethnic Relations in America. Boston: Allyn and Bacon, 1994; **p. 352 excerpt:** Excerpt from SOURCE: Mander, Jerry. In the Absence of the Sacred: The Failure of Technology and the Survival of the Indian Nations. San Francisco, Calif.: Sierra Club Books, 1992; **p. 352 excerpt:** Excerpt from SOURCE: W. E. B. Du Bois, 1903; **Fig 12.10:** SOURCE: Based on U.S. Census Bureau 2009; Statistical Abstract of the United States 2013:Tables 5, 12. I modified the projections based on the new census category of membership in two or more groups and trends in interethnic marriage; **p. 353 excerpt:** Excerpt from SOURCE: Portes, Alejandro, and Rubén G. Rumbaut. Immigrant America. Berkeley: University of California Press, 1990; **p. 353 excerpt:** Excerpt from SOURCE: Portes, Alejandro, and Rubén G. Rumbaut. Immigrant America. Berkeley: University of California Press, 1990;

Chapter 13: p. 359 excerpt: Excerpt from SOURCE: Hart, Charles W. M., and Arnold R. Pilling. The Tiwi of North Australia, Fieldwork Edition. New York: Holt, Rinehart and Winston, 1979:125–126; **Fig 13.1:** SOURCE: Based on Statistical Abstract of the United States; 2013:Table 1350; **p. 360 excerpt:** Excerpt from SOURCE: Zaslow, Jeffrey. "Will You Still Need Me When I'm . . . 84? More Couples Divorce after Decades." Wall Street Journal, June 17, 2003:D1; **Fig 13.2:** SOURCE: Based on Historical Statistics of the United States, Colonial Times to 1970, Bicentennial Edition, Part I, Series B, 107–115; Statistical Abstract of the United States 2013:Table 108; **Fig 13.3:** SOURCE: Based on Statistical Abstract of the United States 2013:Table 9, and earlier years; **Fig 13.4:** SOURCE: Based on Statistical Abstract of the United States 2000:Table 14; 2013:Table 9, and earlier years; **Fig 13.5:** SOURCE: Based on Statistical Abstract of the United States 2013:Table 1355; **Fig 13.6:** SOURCE: Based on Statistical Abstract of the United States 2013:Table 16. **p. 367 excerpt:** Excerpt from SOURCE: Zhao; **p. 367 excerpt:** Excerpt from SOURCE: Sun, Lena H. "China Seeks Ways to Protect Elderly." Washington Post, October 23, 1990:A1; **Fig 13.7:** SOURCE: Based on Social Security Administration; Statistical Abstract of the United States 2013:Tables 554, 555; **p. 371 excerpt:** Excerpt from Source: Sloan, Allan. "A Lot of Trust, But No Funds." Newsweek, July 30, 2001:34; **p. 371 box:** Smith, Harold. "A Colossal Cover-Up." Christianity Today, December 12, 1986:16–17; Hardy, Dorcas. Social Insecurity: The Crisis in America's Social Security and How to Plan Now for Your Own Financial Survival. New York: Villard Books, 1991; Genetski, Robert. "Privatize Social Security." Wall Street Journal, May 21, 1993; Stevenson, Richard W. "U.S. Debates Investing in Stock for Social Security." New York Times, July 27, 1998; Statistical Abstract 2013. Government publications that list Social Security receipts as deficits can be found in Monthly Treasury Statement of Receipts and Outlays, the Winter Treasury Bulletin, and the Statement of Liabilities and Other Financial Commitments of the United States Government; **Fig 13.8:** SOURCE: Based on Statistical Abstract of the United States 1997:Table 518; 2013:Table 481. Broken line indicates the author's projections. **Fig 13.9:** SOURCE: Based on Statistical Abstract of the United States various years, and 2013:Tables 147, 154. Broken lines indicate the author's projections; **Fig 13.10:** SOURCE: Based on Statistical Abstract of the United States, various years, and 2013:Table 725. Broken lines indicate the author's projections; **Fig 13.11:** SOURCE: Based on Statistical Abstract of the United States 2013:Table 34; **Fig 13.12:** SOURCE: Based on Statistical Abstract of the United States 2013:Table 34; **p. 376 excerpt:** Excerpt from SOURCE: Morin, Monte. "$1.7 Million Awarded in Retirement Home Death." Los Angeles Times, October 17, 2001; **p. 378 box:** SOURCE: Based on Wienberg 2008; Croydon 2009; Hawkins 2013; Whipple 2013; **p. 378 excerpt:** Excerpt from SOURCE: Pillemer, Karl, and J. Jill Suitor. "Violence and Violent Feelings: What Causes Them among Family Caregivers?" Journal of Gerontology, 47, 4, 1992:165–172; **Fig 13.13:** SOURCE: Only the groups are listed in the source. Based on Statistical Abstract of the United States 2013:Table 725; **Fig 13.14:** SOURCE: Based on Statistical Abstract of the United States 2013:Table 34;

Chapter 14: p. 390 excerpt: Excerpt from SOURCE: Anonymous; **p. 390 excerpt:** Excerpt from SOURCE: Wines, Michael. "Africa Adds to Miserable Ranks of Child Workers." New York Times, August 24, 2006a. Wines, Michael. "How Bad Is Inflation in Zimbabwe?" Wall Street Journal, May 2, 2006b; **Fig 14.1:** Source: James M. Henslin, Copyrighted Pearson Education, Upper Saddle River, NJ; **Fig 14.2:** SOURCE: Based on "Alternative Investment Market Letter," November 1991; Table 14.1: SOURCE: James M. Henslin, Copyrighted Pearson Education, Upper Saddle River, NJ; **p. 399 excerpt:** Excerpt from SOURCE: Yardley, Jim, and Keith Bradsher. "China, an Engine of Growth, Faces a Global Slump." New York Times, October 22, 2008; **p. 400 excerpt:** Excerpt from SOURCE: Zachary, G. Pascal. "Behind Stocks' Surge Is an Economy in Which Big U.S. Firms Thrive." Wall Street Journal, November 22, 1995:A1, A5; **p. 401 excerpt:** Excerpt from SOURCE: Parker Pen; **p. 401 excerpt:** Excerpt from SOURCE: Frank Perdue; **p. 00 excerpt:** Excerpt from SOURCE: Berle, Adolf, Jr., and Gardiner C. Means. The Modern Corporation and Private Property. New York: Harcourt, Brace and World, 1932. (As cited in Useem 1980:44.); Table 14.2: SOURCE: "Global 2000: The World's Biggest Public Companies." Forbes, April 20, 2011; **p. 402 excerpt:** Excerpt from SOURCE: Rothkopf, David. Superclass: The Global Power Elite and the World They Are Making. New York: Farrar, Straus and Giroux, 2008:xix; Exhibit 14.1: SOURCE: Associated Press (October 29, 1995); **p. 400 excerpt:** Excerpt from SOURCE: Useem, Michael. The Inner Circle: Large Corporations and the Rise of Business Political Activity in the U.S. and U.K. New York: Oxford University Press, 1984; Exhibit 14.2: SOURCE: Rothkopf, David. Superclass: The Global Power Elite and the World They Are Making. New York: Farrar, Straus and Giroux, 2008:129–130; **Fig 14.3:** SOURCE: Based on Statistical Abstract of the United States 2013:Table 1311; **Fig 14.4:** SOURCE: Based on Statistical Abstract of the United States 2013:Table 1308; Exhibit 14.3: SOURCE: Freeland, Chrystia. "The Rise of the New Global Elite." Atlantic, January/February 2011; **Fig 14.5:** SOURCE: Based on Statistical Abstract of the United

States, various years, and 2013:Tables 626, 631; **Fig** 14.6: SOURCE: Based on Statistical Abstract of the United States 2013:Table 1383; **Fig** 14.7: SOURCE: Based on Statistical Abstract of the United States 1989:Tables 638, 639, 640; 1990:Tables 625, 627, 637; 2001:Table 578; 2013:Tables 597, 603, 607, 610; **p. 412 box:** SOURCE: Anonymous; Exhibit 14.4: SOURCE: Pennar, Karen, and Christopher Farrell. "Notes from the Underground Economy." Business Week, February 15, 1993:98–101;**Fig** 14.8: SOURCE: Based on Statistical Abstract of the United States 1992:Table 650; 1999:Table 698; 2013:Table 656; Exhibit 14.5: SOURCE: Zuboff. Shoshanna. "New Worlds of Computer-Mediated Work." In Down to Earth Sociology: Introductory Readings, 6th edition, James M. Henslin, ed. New York: Free Press, 1991:476–485; **Fig** 14.9: SOURCE: James M. Henslin, Copyrighted Pearson Education, Upper Saddle River, NJ. **p. 414 excerpt:** Excerpt from SOURCE: Stansberry 2012; **Fig** 14.10: SOURCE: Based on Statistical Abstract of the United States 2013:Table 708;

Chapter 15: p. 422 excerpt: Excerpt from SOURCE: Berger, Peter L. Invitation to Sociology: A Humanistic Perspective. New York: Doubleday, 1963; **p. 423 excerpt:** Excerpt from SOURCE: Berger, Peter L. Invitation to Sociology: A Humanistic Perspective. New York: Doubleday, 1963; **p. 424 excerpt:** Excerpt from SOURCE: Bridgwater, William, ed. The Columbia Viking Desk Encyclopedia. New York: Viking Press, 1953; **p. 425 excerpt:** Excerpt from SOURCE: John F. Kennedy; **p. 426 excerpt:** Excerpt from SOURCE: James M. Henslin, Copyrighted Pearson Education, Upper Saddle River, NJ; **p. 428 excerpt:** Excerpt from SOURCE: In Hellinger, Daniel, and Dennis R. Judd. The Democratic Facade. Pacific Grove, Calif.: Brooks/Cole, 1991; **Fig** 15.1: SOURCE: Based on Statistical Abstract of the United States 2013:Table 427; Table 15.1: SOURCE: Based on Casper and Bass 1998; Jamieson et al. 2002; Holder 2006; File and Crissey 2010:Table 1; Statistical Abstract of the United States 1991:Table 450; 1997:Table 462; 2011:Table 416; **p. 434 excerpt:** Excerpt from SOURCE: Portes, Alejandro, and Rubén G. Rumbaut. Immigrant America. Berkeley: University of California Press, 1990; Table 15.2: SOURCE: Based on Gallup Poll 2008; Statistical Abstract of the United States 1999:Table 464; 2002:Table 372; 2013:Table 412; Roper 2013; **Fig** 15.2: SOURCE: Based on Mills 1956; **p. 438 excerpt:** Excerpt from SOURCE: Carl von Clausewitz; Table 15.3: SOURCE: Daggett, Stephen. "Costs of Major U.S. Wars." Washington, D.C.: Congressional Research Service, June 29, 2010:Table 1; Statistical Abstract of the United States 2013:Table 480; **p. 441 excerpt:** Excerpt from SOURCE: Stockwell, John. "The Dark Side of U.S. Foreign Policy." Zeta Magazine, February 1989:36–48; **p. 442 box:** SOURCE: Iris Chang. The Rape of Nanking. New York: Basic Books, 1997; **p. 441 excerpt:** Excerpt from SOURCE: Smith, Clark. "Oral History as 'Therapy': Combatants' Account of the Vietnam War." In Strangers at Home: Vietnam Veterans Since the War, Charles R. Figley and Seymore Leventman, eds. New York: Praeger, 1980:9–34; **p. 443 excerpt:** Excerpt from SOURCE: Sengupta, Somini. "In the Ancient Streets of Najaf, Pledges of Martyrdom for Cleric." New York Times, July 10, 2004; **p. 445 box:** SOURCE: Based on Beah, Ishmael. A Long Way Gone: Memoirs of a Boy Soldier. New York: Farrar, Straus and Giroux, 2007; quotations are summaries; **p. 446 excerpt:** Excerpt from SOURCE: Based on Savage 2011; Becker and Shane 2012; Savage 2012; Table 15.4: SOURCE: Based on Grimmett and Kerr 2012:Tables 20, 23;

Chapter 16: Table 16.1: SOURCE: James M. Henslin, Copyrighted Pearson Education, Upper Saddle River, NJ; **p. 454 excerpt:** Excerpt from Source: Broughton 2013; **p. 454 excerpt:** Excerpt from Source: Cole 2012; Webb 2013; **Fig** 16.1: Source: Based on Morin, Rich, and D'Vera Cohn. "Women Call the Shots at Home; Public Mixed on Gender Roles in Jobs." Pew Research Center Publications: September 25, 2008; **Fig** 16.2: Source: Based on Bianchi 2010:Tables 1, 2; **p. 458 excerpt:** Excerpt from Source: Rubin, Zick. "The Love Research." In Marriage and Family in a Changing Society, 2nd ed., James M. Henslin, ed. New York: Free Press, 1985; **p. 459 box:** Source: Based on Gupta, Giri Raj. "Love, Arranged Marriage, and the Indian Social Structure." In Cross-Cultural Perspectives of Mate Selection and Marriage, George Kurian, ed. Westport, Conn.: Greenwood Press, 1979; Bumiller, Elisabeth. "First Comes Marriage—Then, Maybe, Love." In Marriage and Family in a Changing Society, 4th ed., James M. Henslin, ed. New York: Free Press, 1992:120–125; Sprecher, Susan, and Rachita Chandak. "Attitudes about Arranged Marriages and Dating among Men and Women from India." Free Inquiry in Creative Sociology, 20, 1, May 1992:59–69; Dugger, Celia W. "Wedding Vows Bind Old World and New." New York Times, July 20, 1998; Gautham, S. "Coming Next: The Monsoon Divorce." New Statesman, 131, 4574, February 18, 2002:32–33; Swati, Pandey. "Do You Take This Stranger?" Los Angeles Times, June 26, 2008; Harris 2013; Berger, Peter L. Invitation to Sociology: A Humanistic Perspective. New York: Doubleday, 1963; **Fig** 16.3: Source: Based on Statistical Abstract of the United States 1990:Table 53; 2013:Table 60; **Fig** 16.4: Source: Based on Siegler, Ilene C., Beverly H. Brummett, Peter Martin, and Michael J. Helms. "Consistency and Timing of Marital Transitions and Survival During Midlife: The Role of Personality and Health Risk Behaviors." Annals of Behavioral Medicine, January 9, 2013; **Fig** 16.5: Copyright (c) 2011 Gallup, Inc. All rights reserved. The content is used with permission; however, Gallup retains all rights of republication; **Fig** 16.6: Source: Adapted from Naik 2009. Reproduced with permission; **Fig** 16.7: Source: Based on America's Children in Brief: Key National Indicators of Well-Being, 2010. www.childstats.gov, July 2010:Table FAM3A; **Fig** 16.8: Source: Based on For Native Americans, Kreider and Elliott 2009:Table 1. For other groups, Statistical Abstract of the United States 2013:Table 69; **Fig** 16.9: Source: Based on Statistical Abstract of the United States 1995:Table 79; 2013:Table 69; **p. 470 excerpt:** Excerpt from Source: based on DeParle 2012; **Fig** 16.11: Sources: Based on U.S. Census Bureau 2010; Elliott et al. 2012; **Fig** 16.12: Source: Based on Statistical Abstract of the United States 1993:Table 60; 2002:Table 48; 2012:Table 57; 2013:Table 57; **Fig** 16.13: Source: Based on U.S. Census Bureau 2007 and Statistical Abstract of the United States 1995:Table 60; 2013:Table 63; **Fig** 16.14: Source: Based on Statistical Abstract of the United States 1995:Table 149; 2002:Table 111; 2013:Table 134; **Fig** 16.15: Source: Based on Statistical Abstract of the United States 1995:Table 58; 2013:Table 56; **Table 16.3:** Source: Based on Cheadle et al. 2010. **Fig** 16.16: Source: Based on Statistical Abstract of the United States 2000:Table 145. Table dropped in later editions; **p. 481 excerpt:** Excerpt from Source: LeDuff, Charlie. "Handling the Meltdowns of the Nuclear Family." New York Times, May 28, 2003. Table 16.2: Source: Whitehead, Barbara Dafoe, and David Popenoe. "The Marrying Kind: Which Men Marry and Why." Rutgers University: The State of Our Unions: The Social Health of Marriage in America, 2004; Copen et al. 2012;

Chapter 17: Fig 17.1: Source: Based on National Center for Education Statistics 1991:Table 8; Statistical Abstract of the United States 2013:Table 236; **Fig** 17.2: Source: Based on Statistical Abstract of the United States 2013:Table 238; **p. 491 excerpt:** Excerpt from Source: "Testing Times" 2011; **p. 494 excerpt:** Excerpt from Source: Nakamura, Akemi. "Abe to Play Hardball with Soft Education System." The Japan Times, October 27, 2006;**Fig** 17.3: Source: Based on Statistical Abstract of the United States 2013:Table 275; **Fig** 17.4: -----; **Fig** 17.5: Source: Based on Statistical Abstract of the United States 2013:Table 272; Table 17.1: Source: Based on Statistical Abstract of the United States 2013:Table 279; **Fig** 17.6: Source: Based on College Board 2012; Statistical Abstract of the United States 2013:Table 266; **Fig** 17.7: Source: Based on Teacher Average Starting Salaries by State, National Education Association, 2011; Statistical Abstract of the United States 2013:Table 298; **p. 506 excerpt:** Excerpt from Source: Gabriel, Trip. "Under Pressure, Teachers Tamper with Test Scores." New York Times, June 10, 2010b; **p. 507 excerpt:** Excerpt from Source: Based on Winerip, Michael. "Ex-Schools Chief in Atlanta Is Indicted in Testing Scandal." New York Times, March 29, 2013; **p. 507 excerpt:** Excerpt from Source: Dillon, Sam. "States' Data Obscure How Few Finish High School." New York Times, March 20, 2008; **p. 507 excerpt:** Excerpt from Source: Kelley, Tina. "In an Era of School Shootings, a New Drill." New York Times, March 25, 2008. Table 17.2: Source: Based on National School Safety Center 2012. The CDC (Centers for Disease Control also reports data on school deaths, but they, too, go only to 2010 and do not include a breakdown by sex. The killings at Sandy Hook will change the totals, but likely not the long-term trend of fewer school deaths;

Chapter 18: p. 527 excerpt: Excerpt from Source: Durkheim, Emile. The Elementary Forms of the Religious Life. New York: Free Press, 1965. Originally published 1912; **p. 516 excerpt:** Excerpt from Source: Powell, Lynda H., Leila Shahabi, and Carl E. Thoresen. "Religion and Spirituality: Linkages to Physical Health." American Psychologist, 58, 1, January 2003:36–52; **p. 521 excerpt:** Excerpt from Source: (Marx 1844/1964). **Fig** 18.1: -------; **Fig** 18.2: Reprinted with permission from Grammich et al. 2010 U.S. Religious Census: Religious Congregations & Membership Study. Fairfield, Ohio: Glenmary Research Center, 2012. © Glenmary Research Center. All rights reserved. Fig : Source: Based on Troeltsch 1931; Pope. 1942; and Johnson 1963; **Fig** 18.5: Source: Based on Smith and Faris 2005; Table 18.1: Sources: Pew Research Center, The Global Religious Landscape. 2012:Table 12; Yearbook of American & Canadian Churches 2012.**Fig** 18.6: Source: Based on Yearbook of American & Canadian Churches 2002 and 2012; Table 18.2: Sources: Finke, Roger, and Rodney Stark. The Churching of America, 1776–1990: Winners and Losers in Our Religious Economy. New Brunswick, N.J.: Rutgers University Press, 1992; Statistical Abstract of the United States 2002:Table 64; Gallup Poll. "Americans More Likely to Believe in God Than the Devil, Heaven More Than Hell." June 13, 2007a and Gallup Poll. "Americans See Religion Loosing Influence." Princeton, NJ: Gallup Organization, January 26, 2011; **p. 542 excerpt:** Excerpt from Source: Based on Hookway, James. "In Thailand Today, Teen Monks Express the Spirit to a Rock Beat." Wall Street Journal, August 15, 2012; **p. 542 excerpt:** Excerpt from Source: Rhoads, Christopher. "Web Site to Holy Site: Israeli Firm Broadcasts Prayers for a Fee." Wall Street Journal, January 25, 2007; **p. 542 excerpt:** Excerpt from Source: Sullivan, Kevin. "India Embraces Online Worship." Washington Post, March 15, 2007; **p. 542 excerpt:** Excerpt from Source: Based on Moloney, Liam. "Mass Set to Flock to Pope's Tweets." Wall Street Journal, December 4, 2012; **p. 542 excerpt:** Excerpt from Source: Bernstein, Elizabeth. "More Prayer, Less Hassle." Wall Street Journal, June 27, 2003:W3, W4;

Chapter 19: Fig 19.2: Source: Based on Statistical Abstract of the United States 2013:Table 1355; **p. 550 excerpt:** Excerpt from Source: Rohter, Larry. "Tracking the Sale of a Kidney on a Path of Poverty and Hope." New York Times, May 23, 2004; Wilson 2011; **p. 552 box:** Wertz, Richard W., and Dorothy C. Wertz. "Notes on the Decline of Midwives and the Rise of Medical Obstetricians." In The Sociology of Health and Illness: Critical Perspectives, Peter Conrad and Rochelle Kern, eds. New York: St. Martin's Press, 1981:165–183; Rothman, Barbara Katz. "Midwives in Transition: The Structure of a Clinical Revolution." In Dominant Issues in Medical Sociology,

3rd ed., Howard D. Schwartz, ed. New York: McGraw-Hill, 1994:104–112; Phillips, Mary. "Midwives versus Medics: A 17th-Century Professional Turf War." Management and Organizational History, 2, 1, 2007:27–44; Cheyney 2011; **Fig 19.3:** Source: 1900 data from CDC 2009. Current data from Statistical Abstract of the United States 2013:Table 125; **p. 554 excerpt:** Excerpt from Source: Martinez, Barbara. "Cash before Chemo: Hospitals Get Tough." Wall Street Journal, April 28, 2008; **Fig 19.4:** Source: Based on Statistical Abstract of the United States 2013:Table 137, and earlier years; **Fig 19.5:** Source: Based on Centers for Disease Control and Prevention 2010b:Table 17. **p. 557 excerpt:** Excerpt from Source: Statistical Abstract 2013:Table 125; **p. 00 excerpt:** Excerpt from Source: Carey, Benedict. "In the Hospital, a Degrading Shift from Person to Patient." New York Times, August 16, 2005; **p. 559 excerpt:** Excerpt from Source: Levy, Clifford J., and Michael Luo. "New York Medicaid Fraud May Reach into Billions." New York Times, July 18, 2005; **p. 559 excerpt:** Excerpt from Source: "111 Health-Care Professionals Charged in $225 Million Medicare Scam." Associated Press, February 17, 2011; **p. 560 excerpt:** Excerpt from Source: Nuland, Sherwin B. "The Debate over Dying." USA Weekend, February 3–5, 1995:4–6; **p. 560 excerpt:** Excerpt from Source: Hendin, Herbert. "Euthanasia and Physician-Assisted Suicide in the Netherlands." New England Journal of Medicine, 336, 19, May 8, 1997:1385–1387; Hendin, Herbert. "Suicide, Assisted Suicide, and Medical Illness." Harvard Mental Health Letter, 16, 7, January 2000:4–7; **p. 561 excerpt:** Excerpt from Source: Denzin, Norman K. "The Suicide Machine." Society, July–August, 1992:7–10; **p. 561 excerpt:** Excerpt from Source: Hafner, Katie. "An Ill Doctor, a Surprise Reflection of Who Picks Assisted Suicide." New York Times, August 11, 2012; **p. 562 excerpt:** Excerpt from Source: Blankstein, Andrew, and Richard Winton. "Paraplegic Allegedly 'Dumped' on Skid Row." Los Angeles Times, February 9, 2007; **Fig 19.6:** Source: Based on Centers for Disease Control and Prevention 2003:Table 21; 2013 a, 2013 b; **Fig 19.7:** Source: Based on UNAIDS 2012; Haub and Kaneda 2012; **Fig 19.8:** Source: Centers for Disease Control and Prevention 2013b; **Fig 19.9:** Source: Based on Figure 12.4 of this text and Centers for Disease; Table 19.1: Source: Based on Johnston et al 2013:Tables 2, 17; Table 19.2: Source: Based on Johnston et al. 2012:Tables 8-2, 8-3; **Fig 19.10:** Source: Based on Statistical Abstract of the United States 1996:Table 222; 2013:Table 206; **p. 569 excerpt:** Excerpt from Source: Brecher, Edward M., and the Editors of Consumer Reports. Licit and Illicit Drugs. Boston: Little, Brown, 1972; **p. 570 excerpt:** Excerpt from Source: U.S. Department of Energy 1995; **p. 571 excerpt:** Excerpt from Source: Phillips, Barbara D. "America's Forgotten Plague." Wall Street Journal, February 9, 1998:A15; **p. 557 excerpt:** Excerpt from Source: Statistical Abstract 2013:Table 126; **p. 563 excerpt:** Excerpt from Source: Lohr, Steve, and John Markoff. "Computers Learn to Listen, and Some Talk Back." New York Times, June 24, 2010;

Chapter 20: **Fig 20.1:** Source: Based on Haub and Kaneda 2012; **p. 580 excerpt:** Excerpt from Source: Faunce, William A. Problems of an Industrial Society, 2nd ed. New York: McGraw-Hill, 1981; **Fig 20.2:** Sources: Modified from Piotrow, Phylis Tilson. World Population Crisis: The United States' Response. New York: Praeger, 1973; McFalls, Joseph A., Jr. "Population: A Lively Introduction, 5th ed." Population Bulletin, 62, 1, March 2007:1–30; based on projections from Haub and Kaneda 2012; **Fig 20.5:** Source: Data only from Haub, Carl, and Toshiko Kaneda. "Population Data Sheet." Washington, D.C.: Population Reference Bureau, 2012; **Fig 20.6:** Source: Data only from U.N. Fund for Population Activities; **p. 587 excerpt:** Excerpt from Source: Mamdani, Mahmood. The Myth of Population Control: Family, Caste, and Class in an Urban Village. New York: Monthly Review Press, 1973; **Fig 20.7:** Source: Based on Population Today, 26, 9, September 1998:4, 5; Table 20.1: Source: Based on Haub, Carl, and Toshiko Kaneda. "Population Data Sheet." Washington, D.C.: Population Reference Bureau, 2012; Table 20.2: Source: Based on Statistical Abstract of the United States 2013:Table 50; **Fig 20.8:** Source: Statistical Abstract of the United States 2013:Table 45; **p. 591 excerpt:** Excerpt from Source: Vladimir Zhirinovsky, Russian politician, January 2010; **p. 00 excerpt:** Excerpt from Source: Another politician in Russia; **p. 591 box:** Sources: Jordan, Miriam. "Among Poor Villagers, Female Infanticide Still Flourishes in India." Wall Street Journal, May 9, 2000:A1, A12; Dugger, Celia W. "Abortion in India Is Tipping Scales Sharply against Girls." New York Times, April 22, 2001; Riley, Nancy E. "China's Population: New Trends and Challenges." Population Bulletin, 59, 2, June 2004:3–36; Yardley, Jim. "Faces of Abortion in China: A Young, Single Woman." New York Times, May 13, 2007; Harney 2011; Sharma 2013; **Fig 20.9:** Source: Based on Day 2010; **Fig 20.10:** Source: Based on Chandler and Fox 1974; Brockerhoff 2000; United Nations 2008; **Fig 20.13:** Source: Based on Statistical Abstract of the United States 2013:Table 29; Table 20.3: Source: Based on Statistical Abstract of the United States 2013:Table 20; **p. 601 box:** Sources: Based on Leland, John. "A New Harlem Gentry in Search of Its Latte." New York Times, August 7, 2003; Hyra, Derek S. "Racial Uplift? Intra-Racial Class Conflict and the Economic Revitalization of Harlem and Bronzeville." City and Community, 5, 1, March 2006:71–92; Williams, Timothy. "Old Sound in Harlem Draws New Neighbors' Ire." New York Times, July 6, 2008; Haughney, Christine. "Harlem's Real Estate Boom Becomes a Bust." New York Times, July 8, 2009; Barnard 2012; **p. 602 excerpt:** Excerpt from SOURCE: James M. Henslin, Copyrighted Pearson Education, Upper Saddle River, NJ; **Fig 20.14:** Source: Cousins, Albert N., and Hans Nagpaul. Urban Man and Society: A Reader in Urban Sociology. New York: McGraw-Hill, 1970; Harris, Chauncey D. "The Nature of Cities and Urban Geography in the Last Half Century." Urban Geography, 18, 1997; **p. 605 excerpt:** Excerpt from Source: McDowell, Bart. "Mexico City: An Alarming Giant." National Geographic, 166, 1984:139–174:172; **p. 605 excerpt:** Excerpt from Source: Stokes, Myron, and David Zeman. "The Shame of the City." Newsweek, September 4, 1995; **p. 606 excerpt:** Excerpt from Source: Herbert Gans,The Urban Villagers (1962); **p. 607 excerpt:** Excerpt from Source: Karp, David A., Gregory P. Stone, and William C. Yoels. Being Urban: A Sociology of City Life, 2nd ed. New York: Praeger, 1991; **p. 608 excerpt:** Excerpt from Source: Karp, David A., Gregory P. Stone, and William C. Yoels. Being Urban: A Sociology of City Life, 2nd ed. New York: Praeger, 1991; **p. 609 excerpt:** Excerpt from Source: David Allen Karp, Gregory Prentice Stone, William C. Yoels, Being urban: a sociology of city life, 1991, p. 238-239;

Chapter 21: **p. 615 excerpt:** Excerpt from Source: Park and Burgess 1921; **Fig 21.1:** Source: Based on McPhail, Clark. The Myth of the Madding Crowd. Hawthorne, N.Y.: Aldine de Gruyter, 1991:11; **p. 618 excerpt:** Excerpt from Source: Rose, Frederick. "Los Angeles Tallies Losses; Curfew Is Lifted." Wall Street Journal, May 5, 1992:A3, A18; Stevens, Amy, and Sarah Lubman. "Deciding Moment of the Trial May Have Been Five Months Ago." Wall Street Journal, May 1, 1992:A6; Cannon, Lou. Official Negligence: How Rodney King and the Riots Changed Los Angeles and the LAPD. New York: Times Books, 1998; Hunt 2012; **p. 619 excerpt:** Excerpt from Source: Anna Runge in article by Lisa Bannon, Subliminal Messages, Gainesville Sun, October 30, 1995; **p. 619 excerpt:** Excerpt from Source: Sledzik, Paul S., and Nicholas Bellantoni. "Bioarcheological and Biocultural Evidence for the New England Vampire Folk Belief." American Journal of Physical Anthropology, 94, 1994. Copyright (c) 1994 by John Wiley & Sons. Reproduced with permission of Wiley Inc; **p. 620 excerpt:** Excerpt from Source: Franklin, John Hope, and John Whittington Franklin. My Life and an Era: The Autobiography of Buck Colbert Franklin. Baton Rouge: Louisiana State University, 1997; **p. 621 excerpt:** Excerpt from Source: Cheang, Sopheng. "Hundreds Killed in Stampede in Cambodia." Associated Press, November 22, 2010; Table 21.1: Source: Based on Johnston, Drue M., and Norris R. Johnson. "Role Extension in Disaster: Employee Behavior at the Beverly Hills Supper Club Fire." Sociological Focus, 22, 1, February 1989:39–51; **Fig 21.2:** Sources: The first four types are from Aberle, David. The Peyote Religion among the Navaho. Chicago: Aldine, 1966; the last two are by the author. **Fig 21.3:** SOURCE: James M. Henslin, Copyrighted Pearson Education, Upper Saddle River, NJ; **p. 630 excerpt:** Excerpt from Source: Lee, Alfred McClung, and Elizabeth Briant Lee. The Fine Art of Propaganda: A Study of Father Coughlin's Speeches. New York: Harcourt Brace, 1939; **p. 635 box:** Sources: Williams, Rhys H. "Constructing the Public Good: Social Movements and Cultural Resources." Social Problems, 42, 1, February 1995:124–144; Douthat, Ross. "Abortion Politics Didn't Doom the G.O.P." New York Times, December 7, 2008; Forsyth, Jim. "Proabortion Group Asks Judge to Block Texas Sonogram Law." Reuters, July 6, 2011; Gabriel 2013; Statistical Abstract of the United States 2013:Table 105;

Chapter 22: Table 22.1: SOURCE: James M. Henslin, Copyrighted Pearson Education, Upper Saddle River, NJ; **Fig 22.1:** SOURCE: James M. Henslin, Copyrighted Pearson Education, Upper Saddle River, NJ; Table 22.2: SOURCE: James M. Henslin, Copyrighted Pearson Education, Upper Saddle River, NJ; **p. 650 excerpt:** Excerpt from Source: Flink, James J., The Automobile Age. Cambridge, Mass.: MIT Press, 1990; **p. 650 excerpt:** Excerpt from Source: Flink, James J., The Automobile Age. Cambridge, Mass.: MIT Press, 1990; **p. 652 excerpt:** Excerpt from Source: Sanger, David E. "Obama Order Sped Up Waves of Cyberattacks Against Iran." New York Times, June 1, 2012; **p. 655 excerpt:** Excerpt from Source: Boudreaux, Richard. "Putin Move Stirs Russian Environmentalist Row." New York Times, January 20, 2010;**Fig 22.2:** Source: Based on Environmental Protection Agency 2013; **Fig 22.3:** SOURCE: James M. Henslin, Copyrighted Pearson Education, Upper Saddle River, NJ; **p. 660 box:** Sources: Durning, Alan. "Cradles of Life." In Social Problems 90/91, LeRoy W. Barnes, ed. Guilford, Conn.: Dushkin, 1990:231–241; Gorman, Peter. "A People at Risk: Vanishing Tribes of South America." The World & I, December 1991:678–689; Linden, Eugene. "Lost Tribes, Lost Knowledge." Time, September 23, 1991:46, 48, 50, 52, 54, 56; Stipp, David. "Himalayan Tree Could Serve as Source of Anti-Cancer Drug Taxol, Team Says." Wall Street Journal, April 20, 1992:B4; Nabhan, Gary Paul. Cultures in Habitat: On Nature, Culture, and Story. New York: Counterpoint, 1998; Simons, Marlise. "Social Change and Amazon Indians." In Exploring Social Life: Readings to Accompany Essentials of Sociology: A Down-to-Earth Approach, Sixth Edition, 2nd edition, James M. Henslin, ed. Boston: Allyn and Bacon, 2006:157–165; "Last Remaining Amazon Tribes Nearing Extinction." International Business Times, June 26, 2011; **p. 658 excerpt:** Excerpt from Source: Based on Dickey and Rogers 2002; **p. 661 box:** Sources: Carpenter, Betsy. "Redwood Radicals." U.S. News & World Report, 109, 11, September 17, 1990:50–51; Eder, Klaus. "The Rise of Counter-Culture Movements against Modernity: Nature as a New Field of Class Struggle." Theory, Culture & Society, 7, 1990:21–47; Foote, Jennifer. "Trying to Take Back the Planet." Newsweek, 115, 6, February 5, 1990:24–25; Parfit, Michael, "Earth First!ers Wield a Mean Monkey Wrench." Smithsonian, 21, 1, April 1990:184–204; Reed, Susan, and Lorenzo Benet. "Ecowarrior Dave Foreman Will Do Whatever It Takes in His Fight to Save Mother Earth." People Weekly, 33, 15, April 16, 1990:113–116; Knickerbocker, Brad. "Firebrands of 'Ecoterrorism' Set Sights on Urban Sprawl." Christian Science Monitor, August 6, 2003; Gunther 2004; Gunther 2007; Grigoriadis, Vanessa. "The Rise and Fall of the Eco-Radical Underground." Rolling Stone, June 21, 2011; **p. 654 excerpt:** Excerpt from Source: Weiner, Tim. "Air Force Seeks Bush's Approval for Space Weapons Programs." New York Times, May 18, 2005.